New England
2007

Connecticut

Maine

Massachusetts

New Hampshire

Rhode Island

Vermont

ExonMobil
Travel Publications

Acknowledgements

We gratefully acknowledge the help of our representatives for their efficient and perceptive inspections of the lodging and dining establishments listed; the establishments' proprietors for their cooperation in showing their facilities and providing information about them; and the many users of previous editions who have taken the time to share their experiences. Mobil Travel Guide is also grateful to all the talented writers who contributed entries to this book.

www.mobiltravelguide.com

Front cover photo: Bass Harbor Lighthouse, Fall country scene, and the skyline of Boston by Shutterstock

ISBN: 0-7627-4258-5 or 978-0-7627-4258-5

ISSN: 1550-1930

Manufactured in the United States of America.

10 9 8 7 6 5 4 3 2 1

Contents

MAP SYMBOLS

TRANSPORTATION

CONTROLLED ACCESS HIGHWAYS

Freeway
Tollway
Under Construction
Interchange and Exit Number

OTHER HIGHWAYS

Primary Highway
Secondary Highway
Divided Highway
Other Paved Road
Unpaved Road
Check conditions locally

HIGHWAY MARKERS

Interstate Route
U.S. Route
State or Provincial Route
County or Other Route
Trans-Canada Highway
Canadian Provincial Autoroute
Mexican Federal Route

OTHER SYMBOLS

Distances along Major Highways
Miles in U.S.; kilometers in Canada and Mexico
Tunnel; Pass
Auto Ferry; Passenger Ferry

OTHER MAP FEATURES

Time Zone Boundary
Mt. Olympus Mountain Peak; Elevation
7,965 In Feet
Perennial; Intermittent River

RECREATION

National Park
National Forest; National Grassland
Other Large Park or Recreation Area
Small State Park
with and without Camping
Military Lands
Indian Reservation
Trail
Ski Area
Point of Interest

CITIES AND TOWNS

National Capital
State or Provincial Capital
Cities, Towns, and Populated Places
Type size indicates relative importance
Urban Area
State and province maps only
Large Incorporated Cities
City maps only

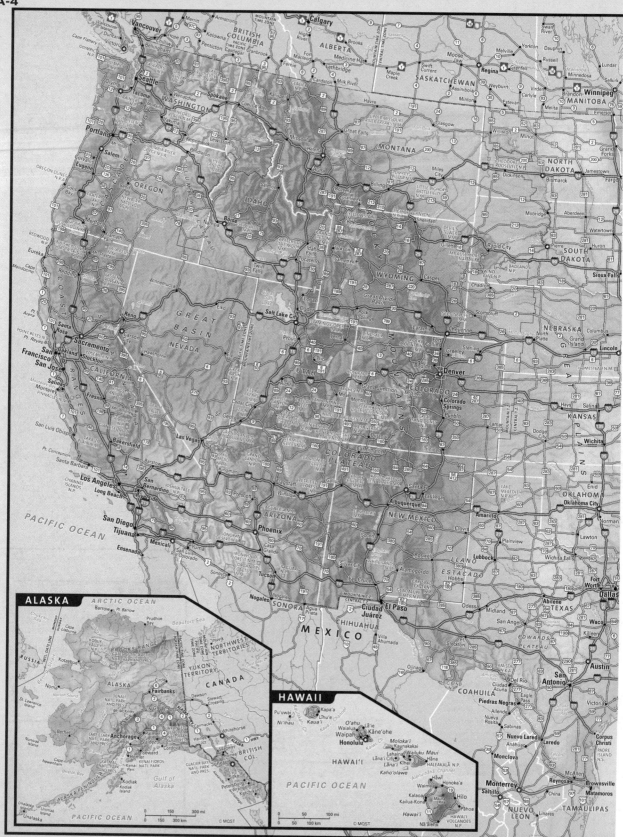

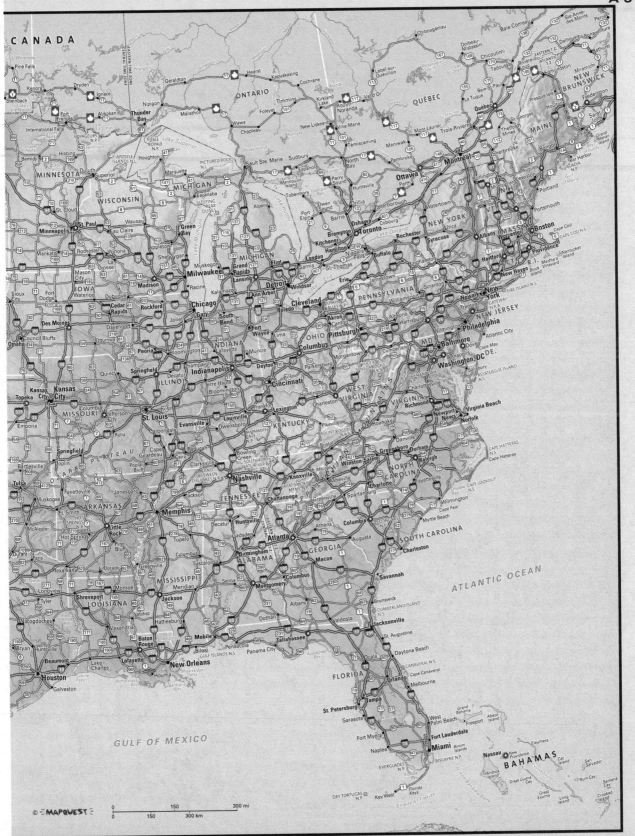

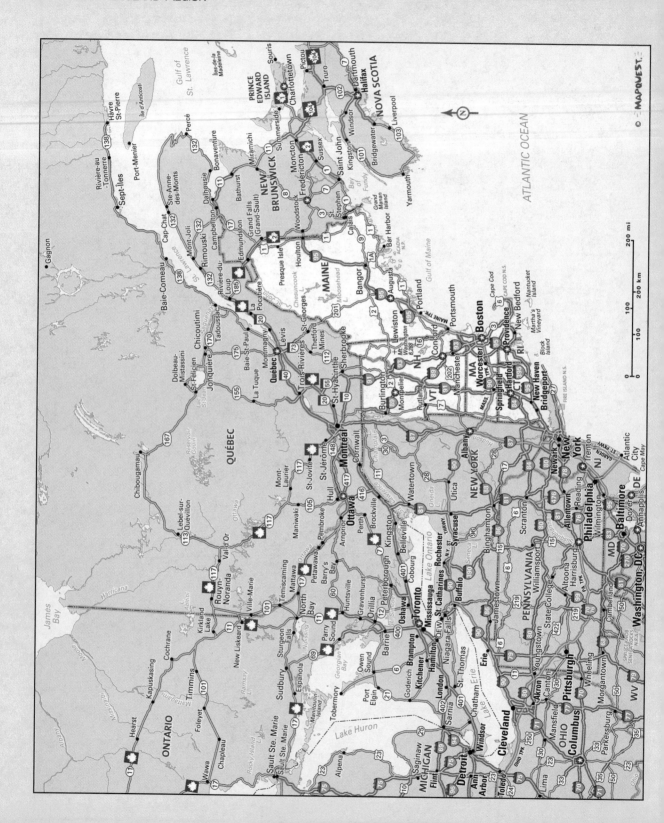

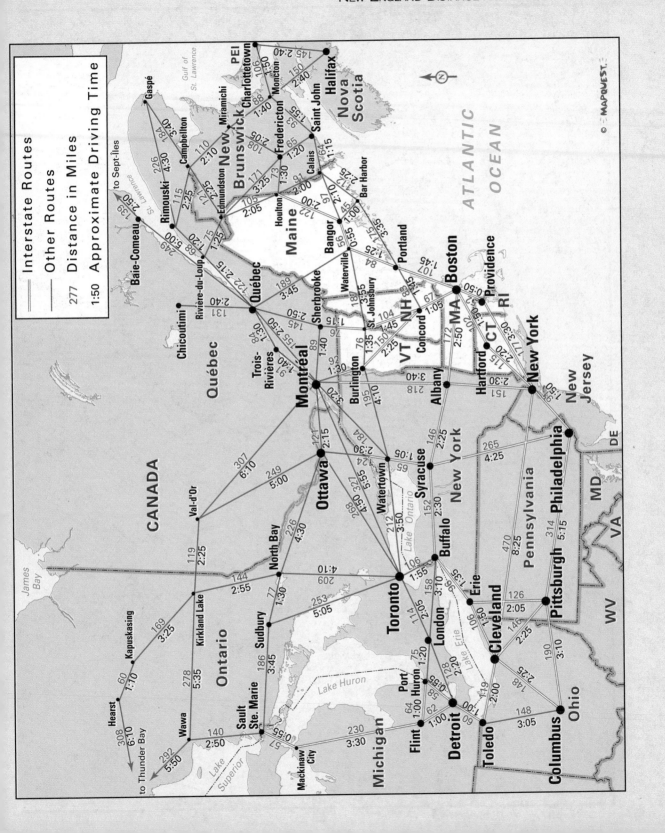

Conn., Mass. & Rhode Island

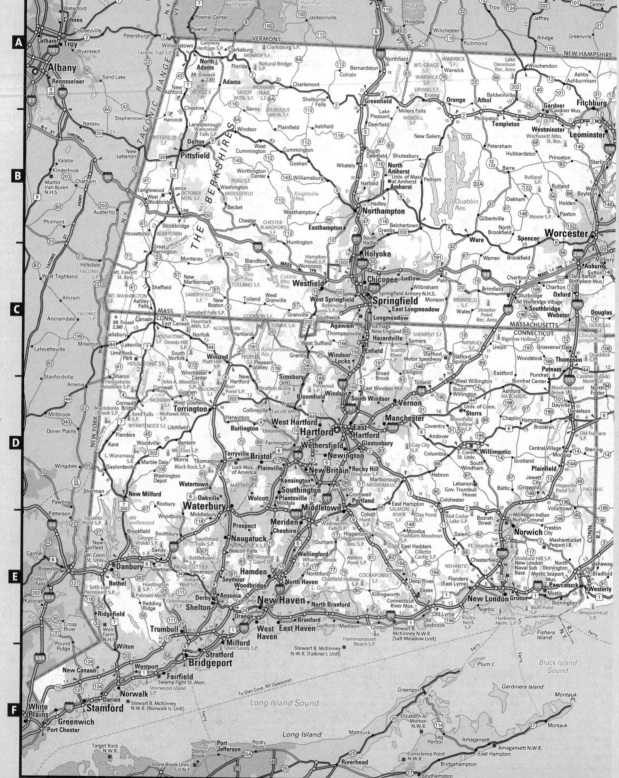

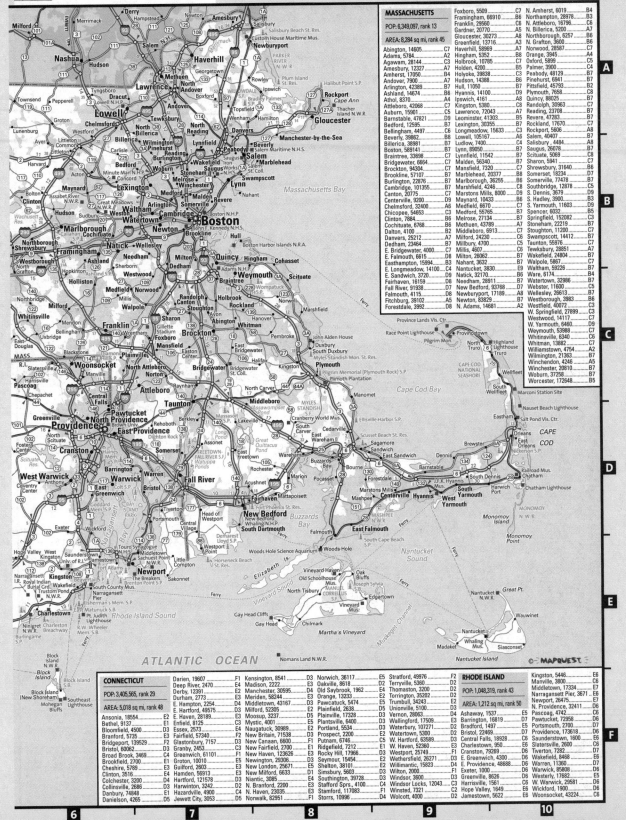

MASSACHUSETTS

POP: 6,349,097, rank 13

AREA: 8,284 sq mi, rank 45

City	Grid	City	Grid	City	Grid
Abington, 14605	C7	Foxboro, 5509	C7	N. Amherst, 6019	B4
Adams, 5784	A2	Framingham, 66910	B6	Northampton, 29978	B3
Agawam, 28144	C3	Franklin, 29560	C6	N. Attleboro, 16796	C6
Amesbury, 12327	A7	Gardner, 20770	A5	N. Billerica, 5200	A7
Amherst, 17050	B4	Gloucester, 30273	A8	Northborough, 6257	B6
Andover, 7900	A7	Greenfield, 13716	A3	N. Grafton, 3600	B6
Arlington, 42389	B7	Haverhill, 58969	A7	Norwood, 28587	C7
Ashland, 14674	B6	Hingham, 5352	B8	Orange, 3945	A4
Athol, 8370	A4	Holbrook, 10785	C7	Oxford, 5899	C5
Attleboro, 42068	C7	Holden, 4200	B5	Palmer, 3900	C4
Auburn, 15901	C5	Holyoke, 39838	C3	Peabody, 48129	B7
Barnstable, 47821	D9	Hudson, 14388	B6	Pinehurst, 6941	B7
Bedford, 12595	B7	Hull, 11050	B8	Pittsfield, 45793	B2
Bellingham, 4497	C6	Hyannis, 14100	D9	Plymouth, 7658	C8
Beverly, 39862	B8	Ipswich, 4161	A8	Quincy, 88025	B7
Billerica, 38981	A7	Kingston, 5380	C8	Randolph, 30963	C7
Boston, 589141	B7	Lawrence, 72043	A7	Reading, 23708	B7
Braintree, 33698	C7	Leominster, 41303	A5	Revere, 47283	B7
Bridgewater, 6664	C7	Lexington, 30355	B7	Rockland, 17670	C7
Brockton, 94304	C7	Longmeadow, 15633	C3	Rockport, 5606	A8
Brookline, 57107	B7	Lowell, 105167	A6	Salem, 40407	B7
Burlington, 22876	B7	Ludlow, 7400	C4	Salisbury, 4484	A8
Cambridge, 101355	B7	Lynn, 89050	B7	Saugus, 26078	B7
Canton, 20775	C7	Lynnfield, 11542	B7	Scituate, 5069	C8
Centerville, 9200	D9	Malden, 56340	B7	Sharon, 5941	C7
Chelmsford, 32400	A6	Mansfield, 7320	C7	Shrewsbury, 31640	B6
Chicopee, 54653	C3	Marblehead, 20377	B8	Somerset, 18234	D7
Clinton, 7884	B6	Marlborough, 36255	B6	Somerville, 77478	B7
Cochituate, 6768	B6	Marshfield, 4246	C8	Southbridge, 12878	C5
Dalton, 4100	B2	Marstons Mills, 8000	D9	S. Dennis, 3679	D9
Danvers, 25212	A7	Maynard, 10433	B6	S. Hadley, 3900	B3
Dedham, 4100	C7	Medfield, 6670	C7	S. Yarmouth, 11603	D9
E. Bridgewater, 4000	C7	Medford, 55765	B7	Spencer, 6032	B5
E. Falmouth, 6615	D8	Melrose, 27134	B7	Springfield, 152082	C3
Easthampton, 15994	B3	Methuen, 43789	A7	Stoneham, 22219	B7
E. Longmeadow, 14100	C4	Middleboro, 6913	C7	Stoughton, 11200	C7
E. Sandwich, 3720	D9	Milford, 24230	C6	Swampscott, 14412	B7
Fairhaven, 16159	D8	Millbury, 4700	C5	Taunton, 55976	C7
Fall River, 91938	D7	Millis, 4607	C6	Tewksbury, 28851	A7
Falmouth, 4115	D8	Milton, 26062	C7	Wakefield, 24804	B7
Fitchburg, 39102	A5	Nantucket, 3830	E9	Walpole, 5867	C7
Forestdale, 3992	D9	Natick, 32631	B6	Waltham, 59226	B7
		Needham, 28911	B7	Ware, 6174	B4
		New Bedford, 93768	D7	Watertown, 32986	B7
		Newburyport, 17189	A8	Webster, 11600	C5
		Newton, 83829	B7	Wellesley, 26613	B7
		N. Adams, 14681	A2	Westborough, 3983	B6
				Westfield, 40072	C3
				W. Springfield, 27899	C3
				Westwood, 14117	C7
				W. Yarmouth, 6460	D9
				Weymouth, 53988	C7
				Whitinsville, 6340	C6
				Whitman, 13882	C7
				Williamstown, 4754	A2
				Wilmington, 21363	B7
				Winchendon, 4246	A5
				Winchester, 20810	B7
				Woburn, 37258	B7
				Worcester, 172648	B5

CONNECTICUT

POP: 3,405,565, rank 29

AREA: 5,018 sq mi, rank 48

City	Grid	City	Grid	City	Grid	City	Grid	City	Grid
Ansonia, 18554	E2	Darien, 19607	F1	Kensington, 8541	D3	Norwich, 36117	E5	Stratford, 49976	F2
Bethel, 9137	E1	Deep River, 2470	E4	Madison, 2222	E3	Oakville, 8618	D2	Terryville, 5360	D2
Bloomfield, 4500	D3	Derby, 12391	E2	Manchester, 30595	D4	Old Saybrook, 1962	E4	Thomaston, 3200	D2
Branford, 5735	E3	Durham, 2773	E3	Meriden, 58244	D3	Orange, 13233	E2	Torrington, 35202	D2
Bridgeport, 139529	F2	E. Hampton, 2254	D4	Middletown, 43167	D3	Pawcatuck, 5474	E5	Trumbull, 34243	E2
Bristol, 60062	D3	E. Hartford, 49575	D3	Milford, 52305	E2	Plainfield, 2638	D5	Unionville, 5100	D3
Broad Brook, 3469	C4	E. Haven, 28189	E3	Moosup, 3237	D5	Plainville, 17328	D3	Vernon, 28063	D4
Brookfield, 2700	E1	Enfield, 8125	C3	Mystic, 4001	E5	Plantsville, 6400	D3	Wallingford, 17509	D3
Cheshire, 5789	E3	Essex, 2573	E4	Naugatuck, 30989	E2	Portland, 5534	D3	Waterbury, 107271	D2
Clinton, 3516	E3	Fairfield, 57340	F2	New Britain, 71538	D3	Prospect, 2200	E2	Watertown, 5300	D2
Colchester, 2686	D4	Glastonbury, 7157	D3	New Canaan, 6600	F1	Putnam, 6746	C5	W. Hartford, 63589	D3
Collinsville, 2966	D2	Greenwich, 61101	F1	New Haven, 123626	E3	Ridgefield, 7212	E1	W. Haven, 52360	E3
Danbury, 74848	E1	Groton, 10010	E5	New London, 25671	E5	Rocky Hill, 17966	D3	Westport, 25749	F1
Danielson, 4265	D5	Guilford, 2603	E3	New Milford, 6633	D1	Seymour, 15454	E2	Wethersfield, 26271	D3
		Hamden, 56913	E3	Niantic, 3085	E4	Shelton, 38101	E2	Willimantic, 15823	D4
		Hartford, 121578	D3	N. Branford, 2200	E3	Simsbury, 5603	D3	Wilton, 2000	F1
		Harwinton, 3242	D2	N. Haven, 23035	E3	Southington, 39728	D3	Windsor, 3600	D3
		Hazardville, 4900	C4	Norwalk, 82951	F1	Stafford Sprs., 4100	C4	Windsor Locks, 12043	C3
		Jewett City, 3053	D5			Stamford, 117083	F1	Winsted, 7321	C2
						Storrs, 10996	D4	Wolcott, 4000	D2

RHODE ISLAND

POP: 1,048,319, rank 43

AREA: 1,212 sq mi, rank 50

City	Grid	City	Grid
Ashaway, 1537	F6	Kingston, 5446	E6
Barrington, 16819	D7	Manville, 3800	C6
Bradford, 1497	F6	Middletown, 17334	E7
Bristol, 22469	D7	Narragansett Pier, 3671	E6
Central Falls, 18928	C6	Newport, 26475	E7
Charlestown, 950	F6	N. Providence, 32411	C6
Cranston, 79299	D6	Pascoag, 4742	C6
E. Greenwich, 4300	D6	Pawtucket, 72958	C6
E. Providence, 48688	D6	Portsmouth, 2700	D7
Exeter, 1000	E6	Providence, 173618	C6
Greenville, 8626	C6	Saunderstown, 1600	E6
Harrisville, 1561	C6	Slatersville, 2600	C6
Hope Valley, 1669	E6	Tiverton, 7282	D7
Jamestown, 5622	E6	Wakefield, 8468	E6
		Warren, 11360	D7
		Warwick, 85808	D6
		Westerly, 17682	F6
		W. Warwick, 29581	D6
		Wickford, 3900	E6
		Woonsocket, 43224	C6

© MAPQUEST

Maine

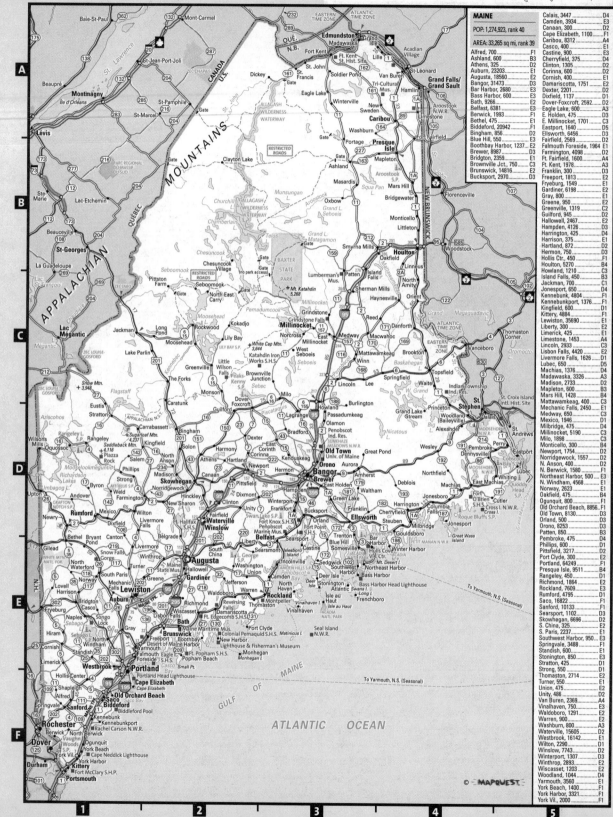

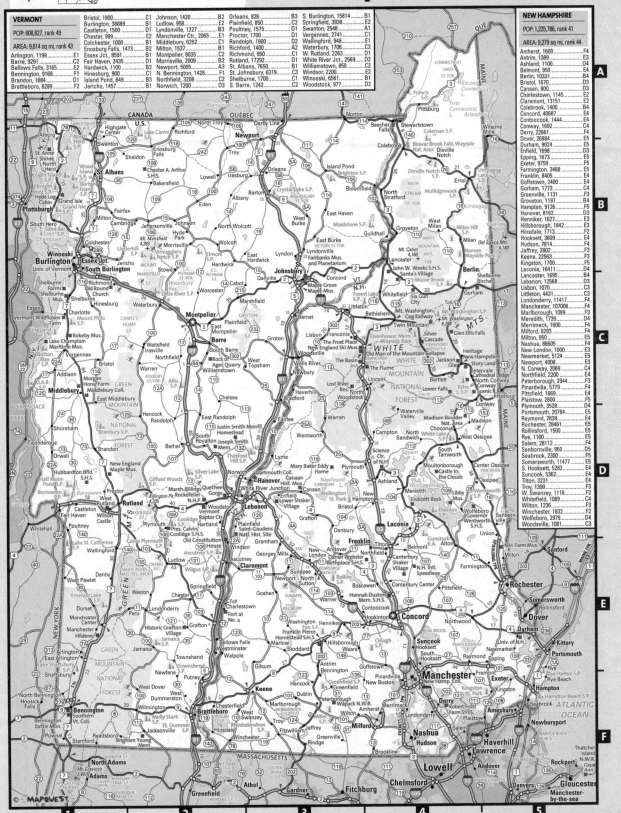

Rio Vista • Nutting Lake • Wilmington • Lynnfield • Peabody • **Beverly**
Beverly Harbor

Pinehurst • Reading • Northshore Mall (114)

Burlington • Wakefield • Salem • **Marblehead**
Witch House • Salem Witch Museum

Bedford Springs • Woburn • Stoneham • Lynn • Swampscott

Bedford • Winchester • Melrose • Saugus • E. Saugus

West Bedford • HANSCOM A.F.B. • North Lexington • Winchester Highlands

Lexington • Arlington Heights • Medford • **Malden** • **Revere**

Lincoln • De Cordova Mus. & Sculpture Park • East Lexington • **Arlington** • Everett • Chelsea

South Lincoln • Waltham • Belmont • **Somerville** • Winthrop

Weston • Watertown • **Cambridge** • Logan International Airport

ATLANTIC OCEAN

Massachusetts Bay

Newton • Brookline • **Boston** • Boston Harbor • Deer Island

Wellesley • Needham • Dedham • Milton • **Quincy** • Boston Light

Quincy Bay • Hull • Hingham Bay • Kenberma

Needham • Oakdale • Blue Hills • **Milton** • Wollaston Beach • Merrymount Park

Islington • Ponkapoag • North Randolph • **Weymouth** • **Hingham**

Randolph • **Braintree** • South Weymouth • East Weymouth

Holbrook • North Abington

Stoughton • Avon • North Hanover • **Rockland** • West Hanover

Abington • Hanover Center

Brockton • **Whitman** • **Hanson**

North Easton

Inset map (Boston downtown):

CHARLESTOWN • Bunker Hill Pavilion • U.S.S. Constitution • Boston Inner Harbor

NORTH END • Old North Church • WEST END • Union Wharf

Museum of Science • Science Park • Charles St. Jail • North Station

BEACON HILL • State House • FINANCIAL DISTRICT • Faneuil Hall • New England Aquarium

Boston Common • Public Garden • Downtown Crossing • Long Wharf • Rowe's Wharf

CHINATOWN • Boston Massacre Monument • Children's Museum • Boston Tea Party Ship

SOUTH BOSTON

© MQST 0 0.1 0.2 mi / 0 0.1 0.2 0.3 km

© MQST 0 1 2 mi / 0 1 2 3 km

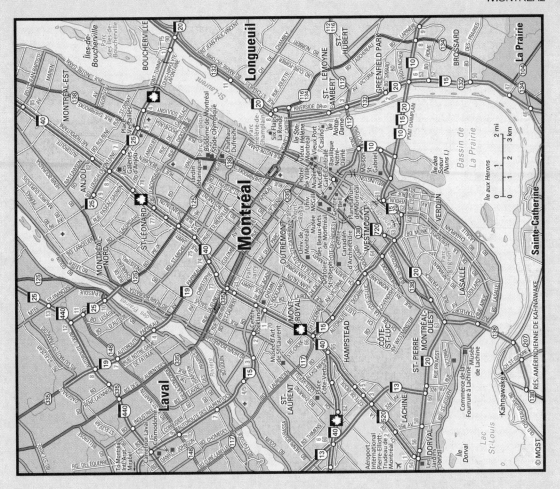

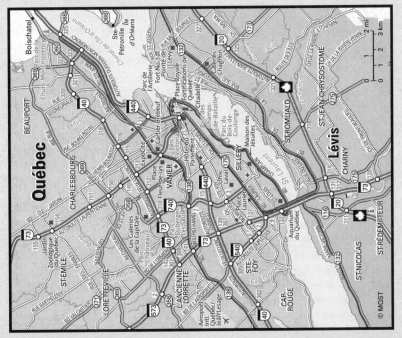

Distances in chart are in miles. To convert miles to kilometers, multiply the distance in miles by 1.609

Example:
New York, NY to Boston, MA = 215 miles or 346 kilometers (215 x 1.609)

	ALBUQUERQUE, NM	ATLANTA, GA	BALTIMORE, MD	BILLINGS, MT	BIRMINGHAM, AL	BISMARCK, ND	BOISE, ID	BOSTON, MA	BUFFALO, NY	BURLINGTON, VT	CHARLESTON, SC	CHARLESTON, WV	CHARLOTTE, NC	CHEYENNE, WY	CHICAGO, IL	CINCINNATI, OH	CLEVELAND, OH	DALLAS, TX	DENVER, CO	DES MOINES, IA	DETROIT, MI	EL PASO, TX	HOUSTON, TX	INDIANAPOLIS, IN	JACKSON, MS	KANSAS CITY, MO	LAS VEGAS, NV	LITTLE ROCK, AR	LOS ANGELES, CA	LOUISVILLE, KY	MEMPHIS, TN	MIAMI, FL	MILWAUKEE, WI	MINNEAPOLIS, MN	MONTRÉAL, QC	NASHVILLE, TN	NEW ORLEANS, LA	NEW YORK, NY	OKLAHOMA CITY, OK	OMAHA, NE	ORLANDO, FL	PHILADELPHIA, PA	PHOENIX, AZ	PITTSBURGH, PA	PORTLAND, ME	PORTLAND, OR	RAPID CITY, SD	RENO, NV	RICHMOND, VA	ST. LOUIS, MO	SALT LAKE CITY, UT	SAN ANTONIO, TX	SAN DIEGO, CA	SAN FRANCISCO, CA	SEATTLE, WA	TAMPA, FL	TORONTO, ON	VANCOUVER, BC	WASHINGTON, DC	WICHITA, KS
ALBUQUERQUE, NM		1490	1902	991	1274	1333	966	2240	1808	2178	1793	1568	1649	538	1352	1409	1619	754	438	1091	1608	263	994	1298	1157	894	578	900	806	1320	1033	2155	1426	1339	2172	1248	1276	2015	546	973	1934	1954	466	1670	2338	1395	841	1020	1876	1051	624	818	825	1111	1463	1949	1841	1597	1896	707
ATLANTA, GA	1490		679	1889	150	1559	2218	1100	910	1158	317	503	238	1482	717	476	726	792	1403	967	735	1437	800	531	386	801	2067	528	2237	419	389	661	813	1129	1241	242	473	869	944	989	440	782	1868	676	1197	2647	1511	2440	527	549	1916	1000	2166	2618	2705	455	958	2838	636	989
BALTIMORE, MD	1902	679		1959	795	1551	2401	422	370	481	583	352	441	1665	708	521	377	1399	1690	1031	532	2045	1470	600	1032	1087	2445	1072	2705	602	933	1109	805	1121	564	716	1142	192	1354	1168	904	104	2366	246	520	2830	1626	2623	152	841	2100	1671	2724	2840	2775	960	565	2908	38	1276
BILLINGS, MT	991	1889	1959		1839	413	626	2254	1796	2181	2157	1755	2012	455	1246	1552	1597	1433	554	1007	1534	1255	1673	1432	1836	1088	965	1530	1239	1547	1625	2554	1175	839	2093	1648	1955	2049	1227	904	2333	2019	1199	1719	2352	889	379	960	2053	1341	548	1500	1302	1176	816	2348	1762	949	1953	1067
BIRMINGHAM, AL	1274	150	795	1839		1509	2170	1215	909	1241	466	578	389	1434	667	475	725	647	1356	919	734	1292	678	481	241	753	1852	381	2092	369	241	812	763	1079	1289	194	351	985	729	941	591	897	1723	763	1313	2599	1463	2392	678	501	1868	878	2021	2472	2657	606	958	2791	758	838
BISMARCK, ND	1333	1559	1551	413	1509		1039	1846	1388	1773	1749	1347	1604	594	838	1144	1189	1342	693	675	1126	1597	1582	1024	1548	801	1378	1183	1702	1139	1337	2224	767	431	1685	1315	1734	1641	1136	616	2003	1611	1662	1311	1944	1301	320	1372	1645	1053	960	1599	1765	1749	1229	2018	1354	1362	1545	934
BOISE, ID	966	2218	2401	626	2170	1039		2697	2239	2624	2520	2182	2375	737	1708	1969	2040	1711	833	1369	1977	1206	1952	1852	2115	1376	760	1808	1033	1933	1954	2883	1748	1465	2535	1976	2234	2491	1506	1234	2662	2462	993	2161	2795	432	930	430	2496	1628	342	1761	1096	646	500	2677	2204	633	2395	1346
BOSTON, MA	2240	1100	422	2254	1215	1846	2697		462	214	1003	741	861	1961	1003	862	654	1819	2004	1326	741	2465	1890	940	1453	1427	2757	1493	3046	964	1353	1529	1100	1417	313	1136	1563	215	1694	1463	1324	321	2706	592	107	3126	1921	2919	572	1181	2395	2092	3065	3135	3070	1380	570	3204	458	1616
BUFFALO, NY	1808	910	370	1796	909	1388	2239	462		375	899	431	695	1502	545	442	197	1393	1546	868	277	2039	1513	508	1134	995	2299	1066	2572	545	927	1425	642	958	397	716	1254	400	1262	1005	1221	414	2274	217	560	2667	1463	2460	485	749	1936	1665	2632	2677	2612	1276	106	2745	384	1184
BURLINGTON, VT	2178	1158	481	2181	1241	1773	2624	214	375		1061	782	919	1887	930	817	567	1763	1931	1253	652	2409	1916	878	1479	1366	2684	1437	2957	915	1297	1587	1027	1343	92	1086	1588	299	1632	1390	1383	371	2644	587	233	3052	1848	2845	630	1119	2322	2036	3020	3062	2997	1438	419	3130	517	1554
CHARLESTON, SC	1793	317	583	2157	466	1749	2520	1003	899	1061		468	204	1783	907	622	724	1109	1705	1204	879	1754	1110	721	703	1102	2371	900	2554	610	760	583	1003	1319	1145	543	783	773	1248	1290	379	685	2184	642	1101	2948	1824	2741	428	850	2218	1310	2483	2934	2973	434	1006	3106	539	1291
CHARLESTON, WV	1568	503	352	1755	578	1347	2182	741	431	782	468		265	1445	506	209	255	1072	1367	802	410	1718	1192	320	816	764	2122	745	2374	251	606	994	601	918	822	395	926	515	1022	952	790	454	2035	217	839	2610	1422	2403	322	512	1880	1344	2393	2620	2571	845	537	2705	346	953
CHARLOTTE, NC	1649	238	441	2012	389	1604	2375	861	695	919	204	265		1637	761	476	520	1031	1559	1057	675	1677	1041	575	625	956	2225	754	2453	464	614	730	857	1173	1003	397	713	631	1102	1144	525	543	2107	438	959	2802	1678	2595	289	704	2072	1241	2405	2759	2827	581	802	2960	397	1145
CHEYENNE, WY	538	1482	1665	455	1434	594	737	1961	1502	1887	1783	1445	1637		972	1233	1304	979	100	633	1241	801	1220	1115	1382	640	843	1076	1116	1197	1217	2147	1012	881	1799	1240	1502	1755	773	497	1926	1725	1004	1425	2059	1166	305	959	1760	892	436	1046	1179	1176	1234	1941	1468	1368	1659	613
CHICAGO, IL	1352	717	708	1246	667	838	1708	1003	545	930	907	506	761	972		302	346	936	1015	337	283	1543	1108	184	750	532	1768	662	2042	299	539	1382	89	409	841	474	935	797	807	474	1161	768	1819	467	1101	2137	913	1930	802	294	1406	1270	2105	2146	2062	1176	510	2196	701	728
CINCINNATI, OH	1409	476	521	1552	475	1144	1969	862	442	817	622	209	476	1233	302		253	958	1200	599	261	1605	1079	116	700	597	1955	632	2215	106	493	1141	398	714	815	281	820	636	863	736	920	576	1876	292	960	2398	1219	2191	530	350	1667	1231	2234	2407	2368	935	484	2501	517	785
CLEVELAND, OH	1619	726	377	1597	725	1189	2040	654	197	567	724	255	520	1304	346	253		1208	1347	669	171	1854	1328	319	950	806	2100	882	2374	356	742	1250	443	760	588	531	1070	466	1073	806	1045	437	2085	136	751	2469	1264	2262	471	560	1738	1481	2437	2478	2413	1101	303	2547	370	995
DALLAS, TX	754	792	1399	1433	647	1342	1711	1819	1393	1763	1109	1072	1031	979	936	958	1208		887	752	1218	647	241	913	406	554	1331	327	1446	852	466	1367	1010	999	1772	681	525	1589	209	669	1146	1501	1077	1246	1917	2140	1077	1933	1309	635	1410	271	1375	1827	2208	1161	1441	2342	1362	367
DENVER, CO	438	1403	1690	554	1356	693	833	2004	1546	1931	1705	1367	1559	100	1015	1200	1347	887		676	1284	701	1127	1088	1290	603	756	984	1029	1118	1116	2069	1055	924	1843	1162	1409	1799	681	541	1847	1744	904	1460	2102	1261	404	1054	1688	855	531	946	1092	1271	1329	1862	1512	1463	1686	521
DES MOINES, IA	1091	967	1031	1007	919	675	1369	1326	868	1253	1204	802	1057	633	337	599	669	752	676		606	1283	992	481	931	194	1429	567	1703	595	720	1632	378	246	1165	725	1117	1121	546	136	1411	1091	1558	791	1424	1798	629	1591	1126	436	1067	1009	1766	1807	1822	1426	834	1956	1025	390
DETROIT, MI	1608	735	532	1534	734	1126	1977	741	277	652	879	410	675	1241	283	261	171	1218	1284	606		1799	1338	318	960	795	2037	891	2310	366	752	1401	380	697	564	541	1079	622	1062	743	1180	592	2074	292	838	2405	1201	2198	627	549	1675	1490	2373	2415	2350	1194	233	2483	526	984
EL PASO, TX	263	1437	2045	1255	1292	1597	1206	2465	2039	2409	1754	1718	1677	801	1543	1605	1854	647	701	1283	1799		758	1489	1051	1085	717	974	801	1499	1112	1959	1617	1530	2363	1328	1118	2235	737	1236	1738	2147	432	1893	2563	1767	1105	1315	1955	1242	864	556	730	1181	1944	1753	2032	2087	2008	898
HOUSTON, TX	994	800	1470	1673	678	1582	1952	1890	1513	1916	1110	1192	1041	1220	1108	1079	1328	241	1127	992	1338	758		1033	445	795	1474	447	1558	972	586	1201	1193	1240	1892	801	360	1660	449	910	980	1572	1188	1366	1988	2381	1318	2072	1330	863	1650	200	1487	1938	2449	995	1561	2583	1433	608
INDIANAPOLIS, IN	1298	531	600	1432	481	1024	1852	940	508	878	721	320	575	1115	184	116	319	913	1088	481	318	1489	1033		675	485	1843	587	2104	112	464	1196	279	596	872	287	826	715	752	618	975	655	1764	370	1038	2280	1101	2073	641	239	1549	1186	2122	2290	2249	990	541	2383	596	674
JACKSON, MS	1157	386	1032	1836	241	1548	2115	1453	1134	1479	703	816	625	1382	750	700	950	406	1290	931	960	1051	445	675		747	1735	269	1851	594	211	915	835	1151	1514	423	185	1223	612	935	694	1135	1482	988	1550	2544	1458	2337	914	505	1813	644	1780	2232	2612	709	1183	2746	996	771
KANSAS CITY, MO	894	801	1087	1088	753	801	1376	1427	995	1366	1102	764	956	640	532	597	806	554	603	194	795	1085	795	485	747		1358	382	1632	516	536	1466	573	441	1359	559	932	1202	348	188	1245	1141	1360	857	1525	1805	710	1598	1085	252	1074	812	1695	1814	1872	1259	1028	2007	1083	192
LAS VEGAS, NV	578	2067	2445	965	1852	1378	760	2757	2299	2684	2371	2122	2225	843	1768	1955	2100	1331	756	1429	2037	717	1474	1843	1735	1358		1478	274	1874	1611	2733	1808	1677	2596	1826	1854	2552	1124	1294	2512	2500	285	2215	2855	1188	1035	442	2444	1610	417	1272	337	575	1256	2526	2265	1390	2441	1276
LITTLE ROCK, AR	900	528	1072	1530	381	1183	1808	1493	1066	1437	900	745	754	1076	662	632	882	327	984	567	891	974	447	587	269	382	1478		1706	526	140	1190	747	814	1446	355	455	1262	355	570	969	1175	1367	920	1590	2237	1093	2030	983	416	1507	600	1703	2012	2305	984	1115	2439	1036	464
LOS ANGELES, CA	806	2237	2705	1239	2092	1702	1033	3046	2572	2957	2554	2374	2453	1116	2042	2215	2374	1446	1029	1703	2310	801	1558	2104	1851	1632	274	1706		2126	1839	2759	2082	1951	2869	2054	1917	2820	1352	1567	2538	2760	369	2476	3144	971	1309	519	2682	1856	691	1356	124	385	1148	2553	2538	1291	2702	1513
LOUISVILLE, KY	1320	419	602	1547	369	1139	1933	964	545	915	610	251	464	1197	299	106	356	852	1118	595	366	1499	972	112	594	516	1874	526	2126		386	1084	394	711	920	175	714	739	774	704	863	678	1786	394	1062	2362	1215	2155	572	264	1631	1125	2144	2372	2364	878	589	2497	596	705
MEMPHIS, TN	1033	389	933	1625	241	1337	1954	1353	927	1297	760	606	614	1217	539	493	742	466	1116	720	752	1112	586	464	211	536	1611	140	1839	386		1051	624	940	1306	215	396	1123	487	724	830	1035	1500	780	1451	2382	1247	2175	843	294	1652	739	1841	2144	2440	845	975	2574	896	597
MIAMI, FL	2155	661	1109	2554	812	2224	2883	1529	1425	1587	583	994	730	2147	1382	1141	1250	1367	2069	1632	1401	1959	1201	1196	915	1466	2733	1190	2759	1084	1051		1478	1794	1671	907	874	1299	1609	1654	232	1211	2390	1167	1627	3312	2176	3105	954	1214	2581	1401	2688	3140	3370	274	1532	3504	1065	1655
MILWAUKEE, WI	1426	813	805	1175	763	767	1748	1100	642	1027	1003	601	857	1012	89	398	443	1010	1055	378	380	1617	1193	279	835	573	1808	747	2082	394	624	1478		337	939	569	1020	894	880	514	1257	865	1892	564	1198	2063	842	1970	899	367	1446	1343	2145	2186	1991	1272	607	2124	799	769
MINNEAPOLIS, MN	1339	1129	1121	839	1079	431	1465	1417	958	1343	1319	918	1173	881	409	714	760	999	924	246	697	1530	1240	596	1151	441	1677	814	1951	711	940	1794	337		1255	886	1337	1211	793	383	1573	1181	1805	881	1515	1727	606	1839	1216	621	1315	1257	2014	2055	1654	1588	924	1788	1115	637
MONTRÉAL, QC	2172	1241	564	2093	1289	1685	2535	313	397	92	1145	822	1003	1799	841	815	588	1772	1843	1165	564	2363	1892	872	1514	1359	2596	1446	2869	920	1306	1671	939	1255		1094	1632	383	1625	1300	1466	454	2637	607	282	2963	1758	2756	714	1112	2232	2043	2931	2972	2907	1522	330	3041	600	1547
NASHVILLE, TN	1248	242	716	1648	194	1315	1976	1136	716	1086	543	395	397	1240	474	281	531	681	1162	725	541	1328	801	287	423	559	1826	355	2054	175	215	907	569	886	1094		539	906	703	747	686	818	1715	569	1234	2405	1269	2198	626	307	1675	954	2056	2360	2463	701	764	2597	679	748
NEW ORLEANS, LA	1276	473	1142	1955	351	1734	2234	1563	1254	1588	783	926	713	1502	935	820	1070	525	1409	1117	1079	1118	360	826	185	932	1854	455	1917	714	396	874	1020	1337	1632	539		1332	731	1121	653	1245	1548	1108	1660	2663	1643	2431	1002	690	1932	560	1846	2298	2731	668	1302	2865	1106	890
NEW YORK, NY	2015	869	192	2049	985	1641	2491	215	400	299	773	515	631	1755	797	636	466	1589	1799	1121	622	2235	1660	715	1223	1202	2552	1262	2820	739	1123	1299	894	1211	383	906	1332		1469	1258	1094	91	2481	367	313	2920	1716	2713	342	956	2189	1861	2839	2929	2864	1150	507	2998	228	1391
OKLAHOMA CITY, OK	546	944	1354	1227	729	1136	1506	1694	1262	1632	1248	1022	1102	773	807	863	1073	209	681	546	1062	737	449	752	612	348	1124	355	1352	774	487	1609	880	793	1625	703	731	1469		463	1388	1408	1012	1124	1792	1934	871	1727	1331	505	1204	466	1370	1657	2002	1403	1295	2136	1350	161
OMAHA, NE	973	989	1168	904	941	616	1234	1463	1005	1390	1290	952	1144	497	474	736	806	669	541	136	743	1236	910	618	935	188	1294	570	1567	704	724	1654	514	383	1300	747	1121	1258	463		1433	1228	1440	928	1561	1662	525	1455	1263	440	932	927	1630	1672	1719	1448	971	1853	1162	307
ORLANDO, FL	1934	440	904	2333	591	2003	2662	1324	1221	1383	379	790	525	1926	1161	920	1045	1146	1847	1411	1180	1738	980	975	694	1245	2512	969	2538	863	830	232	1257	1573	1466	686	653	1094	1388	1433		1006	2169	963	1422	3091	1955	2884	750	993	2360	1180	2467	2918	3149	82	1327	3283	860	1434
PHILADELPHIA, PA	1954	782	104	2019	897	1611	2462	321	414	371	685	454	543	1725	768	576	437	1501	1744	1091	592	2147	1572	655	1135	1141	2500	1175	2760	678	1035	1211	865	1181	454	818	1245	91	1408	1228	1006		2420	306	419	2890	1686	2683	254	895	2160	1774	2779	2900	2835	1062	522	2968	140	1330
PHOENIX, AZ	466	1868	2366	1199	1723	1662	993	2706	2274	2644	2184	2035	2107	1004	1819	1876	2085	1077	904	1558	2074	432	1188	1764	1482	1360	285	1367	369	1786	1500	2390	1892	1805	2637	1715	1548	2481	1012	1440	2169	2420		2136	2804	1335	1308	883	2343	1517	651	987	358	750	1513	2184	2307	1655	2362	1173
PITTSBURGH, PA	1670	676	246	1719	763	1311	2161	592	217	587	642	217	438	1425	467	292	136	1246	1460	791	292	1893	1366	370	988	857	2215	920	2476	394	780	1167	564	881	607	569	1108	367	1124	928	963	306	2136		690	2590	1386	2383	341	611	1859	1519	2494	2599	2534	1019	321	2668	240	1046
PORTLAND, ME	2338	1197	520	2352	1313	1944	2795	107	560	233	1101	839	959	2059	1101	960	751	1917	2102	1424	838	2563	1988	1038	1550	1525	2855	1590	3144	1062	1451	1627	1198	1515	282	1234	1660	313	1792	1561	1422	419	2804	690		3223	2019	3016	670	1279	2493	2189	3162	3233	3168	1478	668	3301	556	1714
PORTLAND, OR	1395	2647	2830	889	2599	1301	432	3126	2667	3052	2948	2610	2802	1166	2137	2398	2469	2140	1261	1798	2405	1767	2381	2280	2544	1805	1188	2237	971	2362	2382	3312	2063	1727	2963	2405	2663	2920	1934	1662	3091	2890	1335	2590	3223		1268	578	2925	2057	771	2322	1093	638	170	3106	2633	313	2824	1775
RAPID CITY, SD	841	1511	1626	379	1463	320	930	1921	1463	1848	1824	1422	1678	305	913	1219	1264	1077	404	629	1201	1105	1318	1101	1458	710	1035	1093	1309	1215	1247	2176	842	606	1758	1269	1643	1716	871	525	1955	1686	1308	1386	2019	1268		1151	1720	963	628	1335	1372	1368	1195	1970	1429	1328	1620	712
RENO, NV	1020	2440	2623	960	2392	1372	430	2919	2460	2845	2741	2403	2595	959	1930	2191	2262	1933	1054	1591	2198	1315	2072	2073	2337	1598	442	2030	519	2155	2175	3105	1970	1839	2756	2198	2431	2713	1727	1455	2884	2683	883	2383	3016	578	1151		2718	1850	524	1870	642	217	755	2899	2426	898	2617	1568
RICHMOND, VA	1876	527	152	2053	678	1645	2496	572	485	630	428	322	289	1760	802	530	471	1309	1688	1126	627	1955	1330	641	914	1085	2444	983	2682	572	843	954	899	1216	714	626	1002	342	1331	1263	750	254	2343	341	670	2925	1720	2718		834	2194	1530	2684	2934	2869	805	660	3003	108	1274
ST. LOUIS, MO	1051	549	841	1341	501	1053	1628	1181	749	1119	850	512	704	892	294	350	560	635	855	436	549	1242	863	239	505	252	1610	416	1856	264	294	1214	367	621	1112	307	690	956	505	440	993	895	1517	611	1279	2057	963	1850	834		1326	968	1875	2066	2125	1008	782	2259	837	441
SALT LAKE CITY, UT	624	1916	2100	548	1868	960	342	2395	1936	2322	2218	1880	2072	436	1406	1667	1738	1410	531	1067	1675	864	1650	1549	1813	1074	417	1507	691	1631	1652	2581	1446	1315	2232	1675	1932	2189	1204	932	2360	2160	651	1859	2493	771	628	524	2194	1326		1419	754	740	839	2375	1902	973	2094	1044
SAN ANTONIO, TX	818	1000	1671	1500	878	1599	1761	2092	1665	2036	1310	1344	1241	1046	1270	1231	1481	271	946	1009	1490	556	200	1186	644	812	1272	600	1356	1125	739	1401	1343	1257	2043	954	560	1861	466	927	1180	1774	987	1519	2189	2322	1335	1870	1530	968	1419		1285	1737	2275	1195	1714	2410	1635	624
SAN DIEGO, CA	825	2166	2724	1302	2021	1765	1096	3065	2632	3020	2483	2393	2405	1179	2105	2234	2437	1375	1092	1766	2373	730	1487	2122	1780	1695	337	1703	124	2144	1841	2688	2145	2014	2931	2056	1846	2839	1370	1630	2467	2779	358	2494	3162	1093	1372	642	2684	1875	754	1285		508	1271	2481	2601	1414	2720	1531
SAN FRANCISCO, CA	1111	2618	2840	1176	2472	1749	646	3135	2677	3062	2934	2620	2759	1176	2146	2407	2478	1827	1271	1807	2415	1181	1938	2290	2232	1814	575	2012	385	2372	2144	3140	2186	2055	2972	2360	2298	2929	1657	1672	2918	2900	750	2599	3233	638	1368	217	2934	2066	740	1737	508		816	2933	2643	958	2834	1784
SEATTLE, WA	1463	2705	2775	816	2657	1229	500	3070	2612	2997	2973	2571	2827	1234	2062	2368	2413	2208	1329	1822	2350	1944	2449	2249	2612	1872	1256	2305	1148	2364	2440	3370	1991	1654	2907	2463	2731	2864	2002	1719	3149	2835	1513	2534	3168	170	1195	755	2869	2125	839	2275	1271	816		3164	2577	140	2769	1843
TAMPA, FL	1949	455	960	2348	606	2018	2677	1380	1276	1438	434	845	581	1941	1176	935	1101	1161	1862	1426	1194	1753	995	990	709	1259	2526	984	2553	878	845	274	1272	1588	1522	701	668	1150	1403	1448	82	1062	2184	1019	1478	3106	1970	2899	805	1008	2375	1195	2481	2933	3164		1383	3297	916	1448
TORONTO, ON	1841	958	565	1762	958	1354	2204	570	106	419	1006	537	802	1468	510	484	303	1441	1512	834	233	2032	1561	541	1183	1028	2265	1115	2538	589	975	1532	607	924	330	764	1302	507	1295	971	1327	522	2307	321	668	2633	1429	2426	660	782	1902	1714	2601	2643	2577	1383		2711	563	1217
VANCOUVER, BC	1597	2838	2908	949	2791	1362	633	3204	2745	3130	3106	2705	2960	1368	2196	2501	2547	2342	1463	1956	2483	2087	2583	2383	2746	2007	1390	2439	1291	2497	2574	3504	2124	1788	3041	2597	2865	2998	2136	1853	3283	2968	1655	2668	3301	313	1328	898	3003	2259	973	2410	1414	958	140	3297	2711		2902	1977
WASHINGTON, DC	1896	636	38	1953	758	1545	2395	458	384	517	539	346	397	1659	701	517	370	1362	1686	1025	526	2008	1433	596	996	1083	2441	1036	2702	596	896	1065	799	1115	600	679	1106	228	1350	1162	860	140	2362	240	556	2824	1620	2617	108	837	2094	1635	2720	2834	2769	916	563	2902		1272
WICHITA, KS	707	989	1276	1067	838	934	1346	1616	1184	1554	1291	953	1145	613	728	785	995	367	521	390	984	898	608	674	771	192	1276	464	1513	705	597	1655	769	637	1547	748	890	1391	161	307	1434	1330	1173	1046	1714	1775	712	1568	1274	441	1044	624	1531	1784	1843	1448	1217	1977	1272	

© MapQuest.com, Inc.

A Word to Our Readers

Travelers are on the roads in great numbers these days. They're exploring the country on day trips, weekend getaways, business trips, and extended family vacations, visiting major cities and small towns along the way. Because time is precious and the travel industry is ever-changing, having accurate, reliable travel information at your fingertips is critical. Mobil Travel Guide has been providing invaluable insight to travelers for more than 45 years, and we are committed to continuing this service well into the future.

The Mobil Corporation (known as Exxon Mobil Corporation since a 1999 merger) began producing the Mobil Travel Guide books in 1958, following the introduction of the US interstate highway system in 1956. The first edition covered only five Southwestern states. Since then, our books have become the premier travel guides in North America, covering all 50 states and Canada.

Since its founding, Mobil Travel Guide has served as an advocate for travelers seeking knowledge about hotels, restaurants, and places to visit. Based on an objective process, we make recommendations to our customers that we believe will enhance the quality and value of their travel experiences. Our trusted Mobil One- to Five-Star rating system is the oldest and most respected lodging and restaurant inspection and rating program in North America. Most hoteliers, restaurateurs, and industry observers favorably regard the rigor of our inspection program and understand the prestige and benefits that come with receiving a Mobil Star rating.

The Mobil Travel Guide process of rating each establishment includes:

- Unannounced facility inspections
- Incognito service evaluations for Mobil Four-Star and Mobil Five-Star properties
- A review of unsolicited comments from the general public
- Senior management oversight

For each property, more than 450 attributes, including cleanliness, physical facilities, and employee attitude and courtesy, are measured and evaluated to produce a mathematically derived score, which is then blended with the other elements to form an overall score. These quantifiable scores allow comparative analysis among properties and form the basis that we use to assign our Mobil One- to Five-Star ratings.

This process focuses largely on guest expectations, guest experience, and consistency of service, not just physical facilities and amenities. It is fundamentally a relative rating system that rewards those properties that continually strive for and achieve excellence each year. Indeed, the very best properties are consistently raising the bar for those that wish to compete with them. These properties proactively respond to consumers' needs even in today's uncertain times.

Only facilities that meet Mobil Travel Guide's standards earn the privilege of being listed in the guide. Deteriorating, poorly managed establishments are deleted. A Mobil Travel Guide listing constitutes a positive quality recommendation; every listing is an accolade, a recognition of achievement. Our Mobil One- to Five-Star rating system highlights its level of service. Extensive in-house research is constantly underway to determine new additions to our lists.

- The Mobil Five-Star Award indicates that a property is one of the very best in the country and consistently provides gracious and courteous service, superlative quality in its facility, and a unique ambience. The lodgings and restaurants at the Mobil Five-Star level consistently and proactively respond to consumers' needs and continue their commitment to excellence, doing so with grace and perseverance.

- Also highly regarded is the Mobil Four-Star Award, which honors properties for outstanding achievement in overall facility and for providing very strong service levels in all areas. These award winners provide a distinctive experience for the ever-demanding and sophisticated consumer.

- The Mobil Three-Star Award recognizes an excellent property that provides full services and amenities. This category ranges from exceptional hotels with limited services to elegant restaurants with a less-formal atmosphere.

- A Mobil Two-Star property is a clean and comfortable establishment that has expanded amenities or a distinctive environment. A Mobil Two-Star property is an excellent place to stay or dine.

- A Mobil One-Star property is limited in its amenities and services but focuses on providing a value experience while meeting travelers' expectations. The property can be expected to be clean, comfortable, and convenient.

Allow us to emphasize that we do not charge establishments for inclusion in our guides. We have no relationship with any of the businesses and attractions we list and act only as a consumer advocate. In essence, we do the investigative legwork so that you won't have to.

Keep in mind, too, that the hospitality business is ever-changing. Restaurants and lodgings—particularly small chains and stand-alone establishments—change management or even go out of business with surprising quickness. Although we make every effort to double-check information during our annual updates, we nevertheless recommend that you call ahead to make sure the place you've selected is still open and offers all the amenities you're looking for. We've provided phone numbers; when available, we also list fax numbers and Web site addresses.

We hope that your travels are enjoyable and relaxing and that our books help you get the most out of every trip you take. If any aspect of your accommodation, dining, or sightseeing experience motivates you to comment, please drop us a line. We depend a great deal on our readers' remarks, so you can be assured that we will read your comments and assimilate them into our research. General comments about our books are also welcome. You can write to us at Mobil Travel Guide, 7373 N Cicero Ave, Lincolnwood, IL 60712, or send an e-mail to info@ mobiltravelguide.com.

Take your Mobil Travel Guide books along on every trip you take. We're confident that you'll be pleased with their convenience, ease of use, and breadth of dependable coverage.

Happy travels!

How to Use This Book

The Mobil Travel Guide Regional Travel Planners are designed for ease of use. Each state has its own chapter, beginning with a general introduction that provides a geographical and historical orientation to the state and gives basic statewide tourist information, from climate to calendar highlights to seatbelt laws. The remainder of each chapter is devoted to travel destinations within the state—mainly cities and towns, but also national parks and tourist areas—which, like the states, are arranged in alphabetical order.

The following sections explain the wealth of information you'll find about those travel destinations: information about the area, things to see and do there, and where to stay and eat.

Maps and Map Coordinates

At the front of this book in the full-color section, we have provided state maps as well as maps of selected larger cities to help you find your way around once you leave the highway. You'll find a key to the map symbols on the Contents page at the beginning of the map section.

Next to most cities and towns throughout the book, you'll find a set of map coordinates, such as C-2. These coordinates reference the maps at the front of this book and help you find the location you're looking for quickly and easily.

Destination Information

Because many travel destinations are close to other cities and towns where travelers might find additional attractions, accommodations, and restaurants, we've included cross-references to those cities and towns when it makes sense to do so. We also list addresses, phone numbers, and Web sites for travel information resources—usually the local chamber of commerce or office of tourism—as well as pertinent statistics and, in many cases, a brief introduction to the area.

Information about airports, ground transportation, and suburbs is included for large cities.

Driving Tours and Walking Tours

The driving tours that we include for many states are usually day trips that make for interesting side excursions, although they can be longer. They offer you a way to get off the beaten path and visit an area that travelers often overlook. These trips frequently cover areas of natural beauty or historical significance.

Each walking tour focuses on a particularly interesting area of a city or town. Again, these tours can provide a break from everyday tourist attractions. The tours often include places to stop for meals or snacks.

What to See and Do

Mobil Travel Guide offers information about nearly 20,000 museums, art galleries, amusement parks, historic sites, national and state parks, ski areas, and many other types of attractions. A white star on a black background ★ signals that the attraction is a must-see—one of the best in the area. Because municipal parks, public tennis courts, swimming pools, and small educational institutions are common to most towns, they generally are not mentioned.

Following an attraction's description, you'll find the months, days, and, in some cases, hours of operation; the address/directions, telephone number, and Web site (if there is one); and the admission price category. The following are the ranges we use for admission fees, based on one adult:

- ✪ **FREE**
- ✪ **$** = Up to $5
- ✪ **$$** = $5.01-$10
- ✪ **$$$** = $10.01-$15
- ✪ **$$$$** = Over $15

Special Events

Special events are either annual events that last only a short time, such as festivals and fairs, or longer, seasonal events such as horse racing, theater, and summer concerts. Our Special Events listings also include infrequently occurring occasions that mark certain dates or events, such as a centennial or other commemorative celebration.

Listings

Lodgings, spas, and restaurants are usually listed under the city or town in which they're located. Make sure to check the related cities and towns that appear right beneath a city's heading for additional options, especially if you're traveling to a major metropolitan area that includes many suburbs. If a property is located in a town that doesn't have its own heading, the listing appears under the town nearest it, with the address and town given immediately after the establishment's name. In large cities, lodgings located within 5 miles of major commercial airports may be listed under a separate "Airport Area" heading that follows the city section.

LODGINGS

Travelers have different wants and needs when it comes to accommodations. To help you pinpoint properties that meet your particular needs, Mobil Travel Guide classifies each lodging by type according to the following characteristics.

Mobil Rated Lodgings

- **Limited-Service Hotel.** A limited-service hotel is traditionally a Mobil One-Star or Mobil Two-Star property. At a Mobil One-Star hotel, guests can expect to find a clean, comfortable property that commonly serves a complimentary continental breakfast. A Mobil Two-Star hotel is also clean and comfortable but has expanded amenities, such as a full-service restaurant, business center, and fitness center. These services may have limited staffing and/or restricted hours of use.

- **Full-Service Hotel.** A full-service hotel traditionally enjoys a Mobil Three-Star, Mobil Four-Star, or Mobil Five-Star rating. Guests can expect these hotels to offer at least one full-service restaurant in addition to amenities such as valet parking, luggage assistance, 24-hour room service, concierge service, laundry and/or dry-cleaning services, and turndown service.

- **Full-Service Resort.** A resort is traditionally a full-service hotel that is geared toward recreation and represents a vacation and holiday destination. A resort's guest rooms are typically furnished to accommodate longer stays. The property may offer a full-service spa, golf, tennis, and fitness facilities or other leisure activities. Resorts are expected to offer a full-service restaurant and expanded amenities, such as luggage assistance, room service, meal plans, concierge service, and turndown service.

- **Full-Service Inn.** An inn is traditionally a Mobil Three-Star, Mobil Four-Star, or Mobil Five-Star property. Inns are similar to bed-and-breakfasts (see below) but offer a wider range of services, most significantly a full-service restaurant that serves at least breakfast and dinner.

Specialty Lodgings

Mobil Travel Guide recognizes the unique and individualized nature of many different types of lodging establishments, including bed-and-breakfasts, limited-service inns, and guest ranches. For that reason, we have chosen to place our stamp of approval on the properties that fall into these two categories in lieu of applying our traditional Mobil Star ratings.

- **B&B/Limited-Service Inn.** A bed-and-breakfast (B&B) or limited-service inn is traditionally an owner-occupied home or residence found in a residential area or vacation destination. It may be a structure of historic significance. Rooms are often individually decorated, but telephones, televisions, and private bathrooms may not be available in every room. A B&B typically serves only breakfast to its overnight guests, which is included in the room rate. Cocktails and refreshments may be served in the late afternoon or evening.

- **Guest Ranch.** A guest ranch is traditionally a rustic, Western-themed property that specializes in stays of three or more days. Horseback riding is often a feature, with stables and trails found on the property. Facilities can range from clean, comfortable establishments to more luxurious facilities.

Mobil Star Rating Definitions for Lodgings

- ★ ★ ★ ★ ★ : A Mobil Five-Star lodging provides consistently superlative service in an exceptionally distinctive luxury environment, with expanded services. Attention to detail is evident throughout the hotel, resort, or inn, from bed linens to staff uniforms.

○ ★ ★ ★ ★ : A Mobil Four-Star lodging provides a luxury experience with expanded amenities in a distinctive environment. Services may include, but are not limited to, automatic turndown service, 24-hour room service, and valet parking.

○ ★ ★ ★ : A Mobil Three-Star lodging is well appointed, with a full-service restaurant and expanded amenities, such as a fitness center, golf course, tennis courts, 24-hour room service, and optional turndown service.

○ ★ ★ : A Mobil Two-Star lodging is considered a clean, comfortable, and reliable establishment that has expanded amenities, such as a full-service restaurant on the premises.

○ ★ : A Mobil One-Star lodging is a limited-service hotel, motel, or inn that is considered a clean, comfortable, and reliable establishment.

Information Found in the Lodging Listings

Each lodging listing gives the name, address/location (when no street address is available), neighborhood and/or directions from downtown (in major cities), phone number(s), fax number, total number of guest rooms, and seasons open (if not year-round). Also included are details on business, luxury, recreational, and dining facilities at the property or nearby. A key to the symbols at the end of each listing can be found on the page following the "A Word to Our Readers" section.

For every property, we also provide pricing information. Because lodging rates change frequently, we list a pricing category rather than specific prices. The pricing categories break down as follows:

○ **$** = Up to $150

○ **$$** = $151-$250

○ **$$$** = $251-$350

○ **$$$$** = $351 and up

All prices quoted are in effect at the time of publication; however, prices cannot be guaranteed. In some locations, short-term price variations may exist because of special events, holidays, or seasonality. Certain resorts have complicated rate structures that vary with the time of year; always confirm rates when making your plans.

Because most lodgings offer the following features and services, information about them does not appear in the listings:

○ Year-round operation

○ Bathroom with tub and/or shower in each room

○ Cable television in each room

○ In-room telephones

○ Cots and cribs available

○ Daily maid service

○ Elevators

○ Major credit cards accepted

SPAS

Mobil Travel Guide is pleased to announce its newest category: hotel and resort spas. Until now, hotel and resort spas have not been formally rated or inspected by any organization. Every spa selected for inclusion in this book underwent a rigorous inspection process similar to the one Mobil Travel Guide has been applying to lodgings and restaurants for more than four decades. After spending a year and a half researching more than 300 spas and performing exhaustive incognito inspections of more than 200 properties, we narrowed our list to the 48 best spas in the United States and Canada.

Mobil Travel Guide's spa ratings are based on objective evaluations of more than 450 attributes. Approximately half of these criteria assess basic expectations, such as staff courtesy, the technical proficiency and skill of the employees, and whether the facility is maintained properly and hygienically. Several standards address issues that impact a guest's physical comfort and convenience, as well as the staff's ability to impart a sense of personalized service and anticipate clients' needs. Additional criteria measure the spa's ability to create a completely calming ambience.

The Mobil Star ratings focus on much more than the facilities available at a spa and the treatments it offers. Each Mobil Star rating is a cumulative score achieved from multiple inspections that reflects the spa management's attention to detail and commitment to consumers' needs.

Mobil Star Rating Definitions for Spas

⚙ ★ ★ ★ ★ ★ : A Mobil Five-Star spa provides consistently superlative service in an exceptionally distinctive luxury environment with extensive amenities. The staff at a Mobil Five-Star spa provides extraordinary service above and beyond the traditional spa experience, allowing guests to achieve the highest level of relaxation and pampering. A Mobil Five-Star spa offers an extensive array of treatments, often incorporating international themes and products. Attention to detail is evident throughout the spa, from arrival to departure.

⚙ ★ ★ ★ ★ : A Mobil Four-Star spa provides a luxurious experience with expanded amenities in an elegant and serene environment. Throughout the spa facility, guests experience personalized service. Amenities might include, but are not limited to, single-sex relaxation rooms where guests wait for their treatments, plunge pools and whirlpools in both men's and women's locker rooms, and an array of treatments, including at a minimum a selection of massages, body therapies, facials, and a variety of salon services.

⚙ ★ ★ ★ : A Mobil Three-Star spa is physically well appointed and has a full complement of staff to ensure that guests' needs are met. It has some expanded amenities, such as, but not limited to, a well-equipped fitness center, separate men's and women's locker rooms, a sauna or steam room, and a designated relaxation area. It also offers a menu of services that at a minimum includes massages, facial treatments, and at least one other type of body treatment, such as scrubs or wraps.

RESTAURANTS

All Mobil Star rated dining establishments listed in this book have a full kitchen and offer seating at tables; most offer table service.

Mobil Star Rating Definitions for Restaurants

⚙ ★ ★ ★ ★ ★ : A Mobil Five-Star restaurant offers one of few flawless dining experiences in the country. These establishments consistently provide their guests with exceptional food, superlative service, elegant décor, and exquisite presentations of each detail surrounding a meal.

⚙ ★ ★ ★ ★ : A Mobil Four-Star restaurant provides professional service, distinctive presentations, and wonderful food.

⚙ ★ ★ ★ : A Mobil Three-Star restaurant has good food, warm and skillful service, and enjoyable décor.

⚙ ★ ★ : A Mobil Two-Star restaurant serves fresh food in a clean setting with efficient service. Value is considered in this category, as is family friendliness.

⚙ ★ : A Mobil One-Star restaurant provides a distinctive experience through culinary specialty, local flair, or individual atmosphere.

Information Found in the Restaurant Listings

Each restaurant listing gives the cuisine type, street address (or directions if no address is available), phone and fax numbers, Web site (if available), meals served, days of operation (if not open daily year-round), and pricing category. Information about appropriate attire is provided, although it's always a good idea to call ahead and ask if you're unsure; the meaning of "casual" or "business casual" varies widely in different parts of the country. We also indicate whether the restaurant has a bar, whether a children's menu is offered, and whether outdoor seating is available. If reservations are recommended, we note that fact in the listing. When valet parking is available, it is noted in the description. In many cases, self-parking is available at the restaurant or nearby.

Because menu prices can fluctuate, we list a pricing category rather than specific prices. The pricing categories are defined as follows, per diner, and assume that you order an appetizer or dessert, an entrée, and one drink:

⚙ **$** = $15 and under

⚙ **$$** = $16-$35

⚙ **$$$** = $36-$85

⚙ **$$$$** = $86 and up

Again, all prices quoted are in effect at the time of publication, but prices cannot be guaranteed.

SPECIAL INFORMATION FOR TRAVELERS WITH DISABILITIES

The Mobil Travel Guide 🄳 symbol indicates that an establishment is not at least partially accessible to people with mobility problems. When the 🄳 symbol follows a listing, the establishment is not equipped with facilities to accommodate people using wheelchairs or crutches or otherwise needing easy access to doorways and rest rooms. Travelers with severe mobility problems or with hearing or visual impairments may or may not find the facilities they need. Always phone ahead to make sure hat an establishment can meet your needs.

Understanding the Symbols

What to See and Do

⭐	=	One of the top attractions in the area
$	=	Up to $5
$$	=	$5.01 to $10
$$$	=	$10.01 to $15
$$$$	=	Over $15

Lodgings

$	=	Up to $150
$$	=	$151 to $250
$$$	=	$251 to $350
$$$$	=	Over $350

Restaurants

$	=	Up to $15
$$	=	$16 to $35
$$$	=	$36 to $85
$$$$	=	Over $85

Lodging Star Definitions

★★★★★ A Mobil Five-Star lodging establishment provides consistently superlative service in an exception-ally distinctive luxury environment with expanded services. Attention to detail is evident through-out the hotel/resort/inn from the bed linens to the staff uniforms.

★★★★ A Mobil Four-Star lodging establishment is a hotel/resort/inn that provides a luxury experience with expanded amenities in a distinctive environment. Services may include, but are not limited to, automatic turndown service, 24-hour room service, and valet parking.

★★★ A Mobil Three-Star lodging establishment is a hotel/resort/inn that is well appointed, with a full-service restaurant and expanded amenities, such as, but not limited to, a fitness center, golf course, tennis courts, 24-hour room service, and optional turndown service.

★★ A Mobil Two-Star lodging establishment is a hotel/resort/inn that is considered a clean, comfortable, and reliable establishment, but also has expanded amenities, such as a full-service restaurant on the premises.

★ A Mobil One-Star lodging establishment is a limited-service hotel or inn that is considered a clean, comfortable, and reliable establishment.

Restaurant Star Definitions

★★★★★ A Mobil Five-Star restaurant is one of few flawless dining experiences in the country. These res-taurants consistently provide their guests with exceptional food, superlative service, elegant décor, and exquisite presentations of each detail surrounding the meal.

★★★★ A Mobil Four-Star restaurant provides professional service, distinctive presentations, and wonder-ful food.

★★★ A Mobil Three-Star restaurant has good food, warm and skillful service, and enjoyable décor.

★★ A Mobil Two-Star restaurant serves fresh food in a clean setting with efficient service. Value is considered in this category, as is family friendliness.

★ A Mobil One-Star restaurant provides a distinctive experience through culinary specialty, local flair, or individual atmosphere.

Symbols at End of Listings

Ⓓ Facilities for people with disabilities not available

🐾 Pets allowed

🎿 Ski in/ski out access

⛳ Golf on premises

🎾 Tennis court(s) on premises

🏊 Indoor or outdoor pool

🏋 Fitness room

✈ Major commercial airport within 5 miles

🏃 Business center

Making the Most of Your Trip

A few hardy souls might look back with fondness on a trip during which the car broke down, leaving them stranded for three days, or a vacation that cost twice what it was supposed to. For most travelers, though, the best trips are those that are safe, smooth, and within budget. To help you make your trip the best it can be, we've assembled a few tips and resources.

Saving Money

ON LODGING

Many hotels and motels offer discounts—for senior citizens, business travelers, families, you name it. It never hurts to ask—politely, that is. Sometimes, especially in the late afternoon, desk clerks are instructed to fill beds, and you might be offered a lower rate or a nicer room to entice you to stay. Simply ask the reservation agent for the best rate available. Also, make sure to try both the toll-free number and the local number. You may be able to get a lower rate from one than from the other.

Timing your trip right can cut your lodging costs as well. Look for bargains on stays over multiple nights, in the off-season, and on weekdays or weekends, depending on the location. Many hotels in major metropolitan areas, for example, have special weekend packages that offer leisure travelers considerable savings on rooms; they may include breakfast, cocktails, and/or dinner discounts.

Another way to save money is to choose accommodations that give you more than just a standard room. Rooms with kitchen facilities enable you to cook some meals yourself, reducing your restaurant costs. A suite might save money for two couples traveling together. Even hotel luxury levels can provide good value, as many include breakfast or cocktails in the price of a room.

State and city taxes, as well as special room taxes, can increase your room rate by as much as 25 percent per day. We are unable to include information about taxes in our listings, but we strongly urge you to ask about taxes when making reservations so that you understand the total cost of your lodgings before you book them.

Watch out for telephone-usage charges that hotels frequently impose on long-distance, credit-card, and other calls. Before phoning from your room, read the information given to you at check-in, and then be sure to review your bill carefully when checking out. You won't be expected to pay for charges that the hotel didn't spell out. Consider using your cell phone if you have one; or, if public telephones are available in the hotel lobby, your cost savings may outweigh the inconvenience of using them.

Here are some additional ways to save on lodgings:

- Stay in B&B accommodations. They're generally less expensive than standard hotel rooms, and the complimentary breakfast cuts down on food costs.

- If you're traveling with children, find lodgings at which kids stay free.

- When visiting a major city, stay just outside the city limits; these rooms are usually less expensive than those in downtown locations.

- Consider visiting national parks during the low season, when prices of lodgings near the parks drop by 25 percent or more.

- When calling a hotel, ask whether it is running any special promotions or if any discounts are available; many times reservationists are told not to volunteer these deals unless they're specifically asked about them.

- Check for hotel packages; some offer nightly rates that include a rental car or discounts on major attractions.

ON DINING

There are several ways to get a less expensive meal at an expensive restaurant. Early-bird dinners are popular in many parts of the country and offer considerable savings. If you're interested in visiting a Mobil Four- or Five-Star establishment, consider going at lunchtime. Although the prices are probably still relatively high at midday, they may be half of those at dinner, and you'll experience the same ambience, service, and cuisine.

ON ENTERTAINMENT

Although many national parks, monuments, seashores, historic sites, and recreation areas may be visited free of charge, others charge an entrance fee and/or a usage fee for special services and facilities. If you plan to make several visits to national recreation areas, consider one of the following money-saving programs offered by the National Park Service:

○ **National Parks Pass.** This annual pass is good for entrance to any national park that charges an entrance fee. If the park charges a per-vehicle fee, the pass holder and any accompanying passengers in a private noncommercial vehicle may enter. If the park charges a per-person fee, the pass applies to the holder's spouse, children, and parents as well as the holder. It is valid for entrance fees only; it does not cover parking, camping, or other fees. You can purchase a National Parks Pass in person at any national park where an entrance fee is charged; by mail from the National Park Foundation, PO Box 34108, Washington, DC 20043-4108; by calling toll-free 888/467-2757; or at www.nationalparks .org. The cost is $50.

○ **Golden Eagle Sticker.** When affixed to a National Parks Pass, this hologram sticker, available to people who are between 17 and 61 years of age, extends coverage to sites managed by the US Fish and Wildlife Service, the US Forest Service, and the Bureau of Land Management. It is good until the National Parks Pass to which it is affixed expires and does not cover usage fees. You can purchase one at the National Park Service, the Fish and Wildlife Service, or the Bureau of Land Management fee stations. The cost is $15.

○ **Golden Age Passport.** Available to citizens and permanent US residents 62 and older, this passport is a lifetime entrance permit to fee-charging national recreation areas. The fee exemption extends to those accompanying the permit holder in a private noncommercial vehicle or, in the case of walk-in facilities, to the holder's spouse and children. The passport also entitles the holder to a 50 percent discount on federal usage fees charged in park areas, but not on con-

cessions. Golden Age Passports must be obtained in person and are available at most National Park Service units that charge an entrance fee. The applicant must show proof of age, such as a driver's license or birth certificate (Medicare cards are not acceptable proof). The cost is $10.

○ **Golden Access Passport.** Issued to citizens and permanent US residents who are physically disabled or visually impaired, this passport is a free lifetime entrance permit to fee-charging national recreation areas. The fee exemption extends to those accompanying the permit holder in a private noncommercial vehicle or, in the case of walk-in facilities, to the holder's spouse and children. The passport also entitles the holder to a 50 percent discount on usage fees charged in park areas, but not on concessions. Golden Access Passports must be obtained in person and are available at most National Park Service units that charge an entrance fee. Proof of eligibility to receive federal benefits (under programs such as Disability Retirement, Compensation for Military Service-Connected Disability, and the Coal Mine Safety and Health Act) is required, or an affidavit must be signed attesting to eligibility.

A money-saving move in several large cities is to purchase a **CityPass.** If you plan to visit several museums and other major attractions, CityPass is a terrific option because it gets you into several sites for one substantially reduced price. Currently, CityPass is available in Boston, Chicago, Hollywood, New York, Philadelphia, San Francisco, Seattle, southern California (which includes Disneyland, SeaWorld, and the San Diego Zoo), and Toronto. For more information or to buy one, call toll-free 888/330-5008 or visit www. citypass.net. You can also buy a CityPass from any participating CityPass attraction.

Here are some additional ways to save on entertainment and shopping:

○ Check with your hotel's concierge for various coupons and special offers; they often have two-for-one tickets for area attractions and coupons for discounts at area stores and restaurants.

○ Purchase same-day concert or theater tickets for half-price through the local cheap-tickets outlet, such as TKTS in New York or Hot Tix in Chicago.

⊙ Visit museums on their free or "by donation" days, when you can pay what you wish rather than a specific admission fee.

⊙ Save receipts from purchases in Canada; visitors to Canada can get a rebate on federal taxes and some provincial sales taxes.

ON TRANSPORTATION

Transportation is a big part of any vacation budget. Here are some ways to reduce your costs:

⊙ If you're renting a car, shop early over the Internet; you can book a car during the low season for less, even if you'll be using it in the high season.

⊙ Rental car discounts are often available if you rent for one week or longer and reserve in advance.

⊙ Get the best gas mileage out of your vehicle by making sure that it's properly tuned up and keeping your tires properly inflated.

⊙ Travel at moderate speeds on the open road; higher speeds require more gasoline.

⊙ Fill the tank before you return your rental car; rental companies charge to refill the tank and do so at prices of up to 50 percent more than at local gas stations.

⊙ Make a checklist of travel essentials and purchase them before you leave; don't get stuck buying expensive sunscreen at your hotel or overpriced film at the airport.

FOR SENIOR CITIZENS

Always call ahead to ask if a discount is being offered, and be sure to carry proof of age. Additional information for mature travelers is available from the American Association of Retired Persons (AARP), 601 E St NW, Washington, DC 20049; phone 202/434-2277; www.aarp.org.

Tipping

Tips are expressions of appreciation for good service. However, you are never obligated to tip if you receive poor service.

IN HOTELS

⊙ Door attendants usually get $1 for hailing a cab.

⊙ Bell staff expect $2 per bag.

⊙ Concierges are tipped according to the service they perform. Tipping is not mandatory when you've asked for suggestions on sightseeing or restaurants or for help in making dining reservations. However, a tip of $5 is appropriate when a concierge books you a table at a restaurant known to be difficult to get into. For obtaining theater or sporting event tickets, $5 to $10 is expected.

⊙ Maids should be tipped $1 to $2 per day. Hand your tip directly to the maid, or leave it with a note saying that the money has been left expressly for the maid.

IN RESTAURANTS

Before tipping, carefully review your check for any gratuity or service charge that is already included in your bill. If you're in doubt, ask your server.

⊙ Coffee shop and counter service waitstaff usually receive 15 percent of the bill, before sales tax.

⊙ In full-service restaurants, tip 18 percent of the bill, before sales tax.

⊙ In fine restaurants, where gratuities are shared among a larger staff, 18 to 20 percent is appropriate.

⊙ In most cases, the maitre d' is tipped only if the service has been extraordinary, and only on the way out. At upscale properties in major metropolitan areas, $20 is the minimum.

⊙ If there is a wine steward, tip $20 for exemplary service and beyond, or more if the wine was decanted or the bottle was very expensive.

⊙ Tip $1 to $2 per coat at the coat check.

AT AIRPORTS

Curbside luggage handlers expect $1 per bag. Car-rental shuttle drivers who help with your luggage appreciate a $1 or $2 tip.

Staying Safe

The best way to deal with emergencies is to avoid them in the first place. However, unforeseen situations do happen, so you should be prepared for them.

IN YOUR CAR

Before you head out on a road trip, make sure that your car has been serviced and is in good working order. Change the oil, check the battery and belts, make sure that your windshield washer fluid is full and your tires are properly inflated (which can also improve your gas mileage). Other inspections recommended by the vehicle's manufacturer should also be made.

Next, be sure you have the tools and equipment needed to deal with a routine breakdown:

- Jack
- Spare tire
- Lug wrench
- Repair kit
- Emergency tools
- Jumper cables
- Spare fan belt
- Fuses
- Flares and/or reflectors
- Flashlight
- First-aid kit
- In winter, a windshield scraper and snow shovel

Many emergency supplies are sold in special packages that include the essentials you need to stay safe in the event of a breakdown.

Also bring all appropriate and up-to-date documentation—licenses, registration, and insurance cards—and know what your insurance covers. Bring an extra set of keys, too, just in case.

En route, always buckle up! In most states, wearing a seatbelt is required by law.

If your car does break down, do the following:

- Get out of traffic as soon as possible—pull well off the road.
- Raise the hood and turn on your emergency flashers or tie a white cloth to the roadside door handle or antenna.
- Stay in your car.
- Use flares or reflectors to keep your vehicle from being hit.

IN YOUR HOTEL

Chances are slim that you will encounter a hotel or motel fire, but you can protect yourself by doing the following:

- Once you've checked in, make sure that the smoke detector in your room is working properly.
- Find the property's fire safety instructions, usually posted on the inside of the room door.
- Locate the fire extinguishers and at least two fire exits.
- Never use an elevator in a fire.

For personal security, use the peephole in your room door and make sure that anyone claiming to be a hotel employee can show proper identification. Call the front desk if you feel threatened at any time.

PROTECTING AGAINST THEFT

To guard against theft wherever you go:

- Don't bring anything of more value than you need.
- If you do bring valuables, leave them at your hotel rather than in your car.
- If you bring something very expensive, lock it in a safe. Many hotels put one in each room; others will store your valuables in the hotel's safe.
- Don't carry more money than you need. Use traveler's checks and credit cards or visit cash machines to withdraw more cash when you run out.

For Travelers with Disabilities

To get the kind of service you need and have a right to expect, don't hesitate when making a reservation to question the management about the availability of accessible rooms, parking, entrances, restaurants, lounges, or any other facilities that are important to you, and confirm what is meant by "accessible."

The Mobil Travel Guide ▣ symbol indicates establishments that are not at least partially accessible to people with special mobility needs (people using wheelchairs or crutches or otherwise needing easy access to buildings and rooms). Further information about these criteria can be found in the earlier section "How to Use This Book."

A thorough listing of published material for travelers with disabilities is available from the Disability Bookshop, Twin Peaks Press, Box 129, Vancouver, WA 98666; phone 360/694-2462; disabilitybookshop.virtualave.net. Another reliable organization is the Society for Accessible Travel & Hospitality (SATH), 347 Fifth Ave, Suite 610, New York, NY 10016; phone 212/447-7284; www.sath.org.

Important Toll-Free Numbers and Online Information

Hotels

Adams Mark..............................800/444-2326
www.adamsmark.com
America's Best Value Inn..................888/315-2378
www.americasbestvalueinn.com
AmericInn 800/634-3444
www.americinn.com
AmeriHost Inn 800/434-5800
www.amerihostinn.com
Amerisuites..............................800/833-1516
www.amerisuites.com
Baymont Inns.............................800/621-1429
www.baymontinns.com
Best Inns & Suites 800/237-8466
www.bestinn.com
Best Western 800/780-7234
www.bestwestern.com
Budget Host Inn 800/283-4678
www.budgethost.com
Candlewood Suites 888/226-3539
www.candlewoodsuites.com
Clarion Hotels 800/252-7466
www.choicehotels.com
Comfort Inns and Suites 800/252-7466
www.comfortinn.com
Country Hearth Inns 800/848-5767
www.countryhearth.com
Country Inns & Suites....................800/456-4000
www.countryinns.com
Courtyard by Marriott 800/321-2211
www.courtyard.com
Crowne Plaza Hotels and Resorts...........800/227-6963
www.crowneplaza.com
Days Inn.................................800/544-8313
www.daysinn.com
Delta Hotels 800/268-1133
www.deltahotels.com
Destination Hotels & Resorts................800/434-7347
www.destinationhotels.com
Doubletree Hotels.......................800/222-8733
www.doubletree.com
Drury Inn 800/378-7946
www.druryhotels.com
Econolodge 800/553-2666
www.econolodge.com

Embassy Suites..........................800/362-2779
www.embassysuites.com
ExelInns of America.....................800/367-3935
www.exelinns.com
Extended StayAmerica 800/398-7829
www.extendedstayhotels.com
Fairfield Inn by Marriott 800/228-2800
www.fairfieldinn.com
Fairmont Hotels.........................800/441-1414
www.fairmont.com
Four Points by Sheraton............... 888/625-5144
www.fourpoints.com
Four Seasons 800/819-5053
www.fourseasons.com
Hampton Inn.............................800/426-7866
www.hamptoninn.com
Hard Rock Hotels, Resorts, and Casinos 800/473-7625
www.hardrockhotel.com
Harrah's Entertainment 800/427-7247
www.harrahs.com
Hawthorn Suites 800/527-1133
www.hawthorn.com
Hilton Hotels and Resorts (US) 800/774-1500
www.hilton.com
Holiday Inn Express.....................800/465-4329
www.hiexpress.com
Holiday Inn Hotels and Resorts.............800/465-4329
www.holiday-inn.com
Homestead Studio Suites............... 888/782-9473
www.extendedstayhotels.com
Homewood Suites........................800/225-5466
www.homewoodsuites.com
Howard Johnson 800/406-1411
www.hojo.com
Hyatt 800/633-7313
www.hyatt.com
Inns of America.........................800/826-0778
www.innsofamerica.com
InterContinental...................... 888/424-6835
www.intercontinental.com
Joie de Vivre...........................800/738-7477
www.jdvhospitality.com
Kimpton Hotels 888/546-7866
www.kimptonhotels.com
Knights Inn.............................800/843-5644
www.knightsinn.com
La Quinta...............................800/531-5900
www.lq.com

Le Meridien................................800/543-4300
www.lemeridien.com

Leading Hotels of the World................800/223-6800
www.lhw.com

Loews Hotels 800/235-6397
www.loewshotels.com

MainStay Suites 800/660-6246
www.mainstaysuites.com

Mandarin Oriental 800/526-6566
www.mandarinoriental.com

Marriott Hotels, Resorts, and Suites 800/228-9290
www.marriott.com

Microtel Inns & Suites 800/771-7171
www.microtelinn.com

Millennium & Copthorne Hotels 866/866-8086
www.millenniumhotels.com

Motel 6...................................800/466-8356
www.motel6.com

Omni Hotels 800/843-6664
www.omnihotels.com

Pan Pacific Hotels and Resorts.............800/327-8585
www.panpacific.com

Park Inn & Park Plaza 888/201-1801
www.parkinn.com

The Peninsula Group .... Contact individual hotel
www.peninsula.com

Preferred Hotels & Resorts Worldwide.......800/323-7500
www.preferredhotels.com

Quality Inn...............................800/228-5151
www.qualityinn.com

Radisson Hotels 800/333-3333
www.radisson.com

Raffles International Hotels and Resorts.....800/637-9477
www.raffles.com

Ramada Plazas, Limiteds, and Inns..........800/272-6232
www.ramada.com

Red Lion Inns.............................800/733-5466
www.redlion.com

Red Roof Inns.............................800/733-7663
www.redroof.com

Regent International 800/545-4000
www.regenthotels.com

Relais & Chateaux 800/735-2478
www.relaischateaux.com

Renaissance Hotels 888/236-2427
www.renaissancehotels.com

Residence Inn 800/331-3131
www.residenceinn.com

Ritz-Carlton...............................800/241-3333
www.ritzcarlton.com

RockResorts............................. 888/367-7625
www.rockresorts.com

Rodeway Inn..............................800/228-2000
www.rodeway.com

Rosewood Hotels & Resorts............. 888/767-3966
www.rosewoodhotels.com

Select Inn 800/641-1000
www.selectinn.com

Sheraton 888/625-5144
www.sheraton.com

Shilo Inns 800/222-2244
www.shiloinns.com

Shoney's Inn..............................800/552-4667
www.shoneysinn.com

Signature/Jameson Inns....................800/822-5252
www.jamesoninns.com

Sleep Inn 877/424-6423
www.sleepinn.com

Small Luxury Hotels of the World...........800/525-4800
www.slh.com

Sofitel...................................800/763-4835
www.sofitel.com

SpringHill Suites 888/236-2427
www.springhillsuites.com

St. Regis Luxury Collection............. 888/625-5144
www.stregis.com

Staybridge Suites.........................800/238-8000
www.staybridge.com

Summit International 800/457-4000
www.summithotelsandresorts.com

Super 8 Motels 800/800-8000
www.super8.com

The Sutton Place Hotels................ 866/378-8866
www.suttonplace.com

Swissôtel.................................800/637-9477
www.swissotels.com

TownePlace Suites...................... 888/236-2427
www.towneplace.com

Travelodge 800/578-7878
www.travelodge.com

Vagabond Inns.............................800/522-1555
www.vagabondinn.com

W Hotels 888/625-5144
www.whotels.com

Wellesley Inn and Suites...................800/444-8888
www.wellesleyinnandsuites.com

WestCoast Hotels 800/325-4000
www.westcoasthotels.com
Westin Hotels & Resorts 800/937-8461
www.westinhotels.com
Wingate Inns 800/228-1000
www.thewingateinns.com
Woodfin Suite Hotels 800/966-3346
www.woodfinsuitehotels.com
WorldHotels 800/223-5652
www.worldhotels.com
Wyndham Hotels & Resorts 800/996-3426
www.wyndham.com

Airlines

Air Canada 888/247-2262
www.aircanada.com
AirTran 800/247-8726
www.airtran.com
Alaska Airlines 800/252-7522
www.alaskaair.com
American Airlines 800/433-7300
www.aa.com
ATA 800/435-9282
www.ata.com
Continental Airlines 800/523-3273
www.continental.com
Delta Air Lines 800/221-1212
www.delta.com
Frontier Airlines 800/432-1359
www.frontierairlines.com
Hawaiian Airlines 800/367-5320
www.hawaiianairlines.com
Jet Blue Airlines 800/538-2583
www.jetblue.com

Midwest Airlines 800/452-2022
www.midwestairlines.com
Northwest Airlines 800/225-2525
www.nwa.com
Southwest Airlines 800/435-9792
www.southwest.com
Spirit Airlines 800/772-7117
www.spiritair.com
United Airlines 800/241-6522
www.united.com
US Airways 800/428-4322
www.usairways.com

Car Rentals

Advantage 800/777-5500
www.arac.com
Alamo 800/327-9633
www.alamo.com
Avis 800/831-2847
www.avis.com
Budget 800/527-0700
www.budget.com
Dollar 800/800-4000
www.dollar.com
Enterprise 800/325-8007
www.enterprise.com
Hertz 800/654-3131
www.hertz.com
National 800/227-7368
www.nationalcar.com
Payless 800/729-5377
www.paylesscarrental.com
Rent-A-Wreck.com 800/535-1391
www.rentawreck.com
Thrifty 800/847-4389
www.thrifty.com

Meet The Stars

Mobil Travel Guide 2007 *Five-Star* Award Winners

CALIFORNIA
Lodgings
The Beverly Hills Hotel, *Beverly Hills*
Chateau du Sureau, *Oakhurst*
Four Seasons Hotel San Francisco, *San Francisco*
Hotel Bel-Air, *Los Angeles*
The Peninsula Beverly Hills, *Beverly Hills*
Raffles L'Ermitage Beverly Hills, *Beverly Hills*
St. Regis Monarch Beach Resort & Spa, *Dana Point*
St. Regis San Francisco, *San Francisco*
The Ritz-Carlton, San Francisco, *San Francisco*

Restaurants
The Dining Room, *San Francisco*
The French Laundry, *Yountville*

COLORADO
Lodgings
The Broadmoor, *Colorado Springs*
The Little Nell, *Aspen*

CONNECTICUT
Lodging
The Mayflower Inn, *Washington*

DISTRICT OF COLUMBIA
Lodging
Four Seasons Hotel Washington, DC *Washington*

FLORIDA
Lodgings
Four Seasons Resort Palm Beach, *Palm Beach*
The Ritz-Carlton Naples, *Naples*
The Ritz-Carlton, Palm Beach, *Manalapan*

GEORGIA
Lodgings
Four Seasons Hotel Atlanta, *Atlanta*

The Lodge at Sea Island Golf Club, *St. Simons Island*

Restaurants
The Dining Room, *Atlanta*
Seeger's, *Atlanta*

HAWAII
Lodging
Four Seasons Resort Maui, *Wailea, Maui*

ILLINOIS
Lodgings
Four Seasons Hotel Chicago, *Chicago*
The Peninsula Chicago, *Chicago*
The Ritz-Carlton, A Four Seasons Hotel, *Chicago*

Restaurants
Alinea, *Chicago*
Charlie Trotter's, *Chicago*

MAINE
Restaurant
The White Barn Inn, *Kennebunkport*

MASSACHUSETTS
Lodgings
Blantyre, *Lenox*
Four Seasons Hotel Boston, *Boston*

NEVADA
Lodging
Tower Suites at Wynn, *Las Vegas*

Restaurants
Alex, *Las Vegas*
Joel Robuchon at the Mansion, *Las Vegas*

NEW YORK
Lodgings
Four Seasons, Hotel New York, *New York*
Mandarin Oriental, *New York*
The Point, *Saranac Lake*

The Ritz-Carlton New York, Central Park, *New York*
The St. Regis, *New York*

Restaurants
Alain Ducasse, *New York*
Jean Georges, *New York*
Masa, *New York*
per se, *New York*

NORTH CAROLINA
Lodging
The Fearrington House Country Inn, *Pittsboro*

PENNSYLVANIA
Restaurant
Le Bec-Fin, *Philadelphia*

SOUTH CAROLINA
Lodging
Woodlands Resort & Inn, *Summerville*

Restaurant
Dining Room at the Woodlands, *Summerville*

TENNESSEE
Lodging
The Hermitage, *Nashville*

TEXAS
Lodging
The Mansion on Turtle Creek, *Dallas*

VERMONT
Lodging
Twin Farms, *Barnard*

VIRGINIA
Lodgings
The Inn at Little Washington, *Washington*
The Jefferson Hotel, *Richmond*

Restaurant
The Inn at Little Washington, *Washington*

Mobil Travel Guide has been rating establishments with its Mobil One- to Five-Star system since 1958. Each establishment awarded the Mobil Five-Star rating is one of the best in the country. Detailed information on each award winner can be found in the corresponding regional edition listed on the back cover of this book.

Four- and Five-Star Establishments in New England

Connecticut

★★★★★ Lodging
The Mayflower Inn, *Washington*

Maine

★★★★ Lodging
The White Barn Inn, *Kennebunkport*

★★★★★ Restaurant
The White Barn Inn Restaurant, *Kennebunkport*

Massachusetts

★★★★★ Lodgings
Blantyre, *Lenox*
Four Seasons Hotel Boston, *Boston*

★★★★ Lodgings
Boston Harbor Hotel, *Boston*
Charlotte Inn, *Martha's Vineyard*
The Ritz-Carlton, Boston, *Boston*
The Ritz-Carlton, Boston Common, *Boston*
The Wauwinet, *Nantucket Island*
XV Beacon, *Boston*

★★★★ Restaurants
Aujourd'hui, *Boston*
Clio, *Boston*
Hamersley's Bistro, *Boston*
L'Espalier, *Boston*
Meritage, *Boston*
No. 9 Park, *Boston*
Twenty-Eight Atlantic, *Chatham*

Rhode Island

★★★★ Restaurant
Mill's Tavern, *Providence*

Vermont

★★★★★ Lodging
Twin Farms, *Barnard*

Connecticut

Connecticut is a state of beautiful hills and lakes and lovely old towns with white church steeples rising above green commons. It is also a state with a tradition of high technical achievement and fine machining. Old houses and buildings enchant the visitor; a re-creation of the life of the old sailing ship days at Mystic Seaport leads the traveler back to times long gone.

Adriaen Block sailed into the Connecticut River in 1614. This great river splits Massachusetts and Connecticut and separates Vermont from New Hampshire. It was the river by which Connecticut's first settlers, coming from Massachusetts in 1633, settled in Hartford, Windsor, and Wethersfield. These three towns created a practical constitution called the Fundamental Orders, through which a powerful "General Court" exercised both judicial and legislative duties. The Royal Charter of 1662 was so liberal that Sir Edmund Andros, governor of New England, tried to seize it (1687). To save it, citizens hid the charter in the Charter Oak, which once stood in Hartford.

Poultry, dairy products, and tobacco are the state's most important agricultural products; forest products, nursery stock, and fruit and vegetable produce follow in importance. Aircraft engines, helicopters, hardware, tools, nuclear submarines, and machinery are the principal manufactured products. The home offices of more than 40 insurance companies are located in the state.

When to Go/Climate

Connecticut's climate is the mildest of all the New England states. Coastal breezes help keep the humidity manageable, and mud season (between winter and spring, when topsoil thaws and lower earth remains frozen) is shorter here than in other New England states.

Population: 3,405,565

Area: 4,872 square miles

Elevation: 0-2,380 feet

Peak: Mount Frissel (Litchfield County)

Entered Union: Fifth of original 13 states (January 9, 1788)

Capital: Hartford

Motto: He Who Transplanted, Still Sustains

Nickname: Constitution State

Flower: Mountain Laurel

Bird: American Robin

Tree: White Oak

Time Zone: Eastern

Web Site: www.tourism.state.ct.us

Fun Facts:

- Connecticut is home to the oldest US newspaper still being published: *The Hartford Courant*, established in 1764.
- The world's first written constitution, the Fundamental Orders, was created in 1639 by English settlements that united to form the Connecticut Colony. That is why Connecticut is often referred to as the "Constitution State."

AVERAGE HIGH/LOW TEMPERATURES (°F)

Bridgeport

Jan 29/22	May 59/50	Sept 66/58
Feb 31/23	June 68/59	Oct 56/47
Mar 39/31	July 74/66	Nov 46/38
Apr 49/40	Aug 73/65	Dec 35/28

Hartford

Jan 25/16	May 60/48	Sept 64/52
Feb 28/19	June 69/57	Oct 53/41
Mar 38/28	July 74/62	Nov 42/33
Apr 49/38	Aug 72/60	Dec 30/21

Calendar Highlights

APRIL

Connecticut Storytelling Festival *(New London). Connecticut College. Phone 860/439-2764.* Nationally acclaimed artists; workshops, concerts.

MAY

Garlicfest *(Fairfield). Notre Dame Catholic High School. Phone 203/372-6521.* Vendors prepare international array of garlic-seasoned cuisine. Sales, entertainment.

International Festival of Arts and Ideas *(New Haven). Phone toll-free 888/278-4332.* Celebration of the arts and humanities.

Lobsterfest *(Mystic). Seaport. Phone 860/57-0711. www.visitmysticseaport.com.* Outdoor food festival.

JUNE

Barnum Festival *(Bridgeport). Phone toll-free 866/867-8495.* Commemorates the life of P. T. Barnum.

Taste of Hartford *(Hartford). Constitution Plz. Phone 860/920-5337. www.tasteofhartford.com.* Four-day event features specialties of more than 50 area restaurants; continuous entertainment.

JULY

Mark Twain Days *(Hartford). Phone 860/247-0998.* Celebration of Twain's legacy and Hartford's cultural heritage with more than 100 events. Concerts, riverboat rides, medieval jousting, tours of Twain House, entertainment.

Riverfest *(Hartford). Charter Oak Landing and Constitution Plz. Phone 860/713-3131.* Celebration of America's independence and the Connecticut River. Family entertainment, concerts, food, fireworks display over river.

AUGUST

Pilot Pen International Tennis Tournament *(New Haven). Phone toll-free 888/997-4568.* Connecticut Tennis Center, near Yale Bowl. Championship Series on the ATP Tour.

SEPTEMBER

Durham Fair *(Middletown). Fairgrounds, in Durham on Hwy 17. Phone 860/349-9495.* State's largest agricultural fair.

OCTOBER

Apple Harvest Festival *(Meriden). 3 miles S on Hwy 120, in Southington, on Town Green. Phone 860/628-8036.* Street festival celebrating local apple harvest. Carnival, arts and crafts, parade, road race, food booths, entertainment.

DECEMBER

Christmas Torchlight Parade *(Old Saybrook). Phone 860/388-3266.* More than 40 fife and drum corps march down Main Street.

Parks and Recreation

Water-related activities, hiking, riding, various other sports, picnicking and visitor centers, as well as camping, are available in designated areas. There are 32 state forests and 92 state parks inland and on the shore. A parking fee ($4-$12) is charged at many of these. Camping, mid-April-September; shore parks $15/site/night; inland parks with swimming $13/site/night; inland parks without swimming $11/site/night; additional charge per person for groups larger than four persons. Two- to three-week limit, mid-April-September; three-day limit, October-December. No camping January-mid-April; selected parks allow camping October-December. Forms for reservations for stays of more than two days may be obtained after January 15 by writing to the address in Hartford; these reservations should then be mailed to the park itself; no reservations by phone. Parks and forests are open all year, 8 am-sunset. Most shore parks allow all-night fishing (with permit). Inland swimming areas are open 8 am-sunset. No pets are allowed in state park campgrounds. For further information, reservations, and regulations contact the Department of Environmental Protection, Bureau of Outdoor Recreation, 79 Elm St, Hartford 06106; phone 860/424-3200.

A CLASSIC NEW ENGLAND ROAD TRIP

The town of Mystic (roughly halfway between New York and Boston on I-95) represents the states top coastal lodgings/attractions hub. Mystic Seaport Museum, Mystic Aquarium, and a shopping mall in the shape of a New England village are popular attractions. Foxwoods Resort Casino, in nearby Ledyard, is the worlds largest gambling casino; its complex includes lodging and a museum devoted to the Mashantucket Pequot, the tribe that owns the casino. From Mystic, take I-95 to Old Lyme, home of the Florence Griswold Art Museum and Rocky Neck State Park beach. Cross the bridge into Old Saybrook, and follow Highway 9 to Essex, a picturesque village with shops and restaurants. The Connecticut River Museum is located here, as is the departure point for the Valley Railroad, which runs along the river. (Railroad passengers can connect with a riverboat for a one-hour Connecticut River cruise.) Follow scenic Highway 154 to Chester, and take the countrys oldest continuous ferry (it also carries cars) across to Gillette Castle in East Haddam. Or continue over the bridge to East Haddam for a great view of the Victorian Goodspeed Opera House, which stages American musicals and is a destination in its own right. You can return via Highway 9 (limited-access highway) or take the scenic way (country roads), Highway 82 to Highway 156 to I-95, back along the eastern side of the river. Continue west on I-95 to Hammonasset Beach State Park in Madison (the big beach in this area). Then head down Highway 1, past the towns classic historic homes, to Guilford (classic green), site of the Henry Whitfield State Museum. Get back on I-95 and follow it into New Haven. Another trip option from Mystic is to head east on I-95 to Stonington, a picturesque fishing village, and then to Watch Hill, a resort town with good beaches. From Stonington, its a scenic 40-mile coastal drive along Highway 1, which passes the Rhode Island fishing resort towns of Charlestown and Narragansett (departure point for ferries to Block Island) and crosses to Jamestown Island in Newport, Rhode Island. **(Approximately 112 miles round-trip; approximately 124 miles round-trip from Mystic to Jamestown Island)**

FISHING AND HUNTING

Hunting license: nonresident, $42 (firearms). Archery permit (including big and small game): nonresident, $44. Deer permit: nonresident, $30 (firearms). Fishing license: nonresident, season, $25; three-day, $8. Combination firearm hunting, fishing license: nonresident, $55. Further information, including the latest regulations, can be obtained from Department of Environmental Protection, Licensing and Revenue, 79 Elm St, Hartford 06106; phone 860/424-3105. www.dep.state.ct.us

Driving Information

Safety belts are mandatory for all persons in front seat of vehicle. Children under 4 years must be in approved passenger restraints anywhere in a vehicle: ages 1-3 may use regulation safety belts; under age 1 must use approved safety seats.

INTERSTATE HIGHWAY SYSTEM

The following alphabetical listing of Connecticut towns in this book shows that these cities are within 10 miles of the indicated interstate highways. A highway map, however, should be checked for the nearest exit.

Highway Number	Cities/Towns within 10 Miles
Interstate 84	Danbury, Farmington, Hartford, Manchester, Southbury, Stafford Springs, Vernon, Waterbury.
Interstate 91	Enfield, Hartford, Meriden, Middleton, New Haven, New London, Norwalk, Old Saybrook, Stamford, Stonington, Stratford, Westport.
Interstate 395	Groton, New London, Norwich, Plainfield, Putnam.

Additional Visitor Information

Pamphlets, maps, and booklets, including the *Connecticut Vacation Guide*, are available to tourists by contacting the State of Connecticut, Department of Economic and Community Development, 505 Hudson St, Hartford 06106; phone toll-free 800/282-6863. In addition, *Connecticut*—a monthly magazine published by Communications International, 789 Reservoir Ave, Bridgeport 06606—gives a listing of activities around the state; available by subscription or at newsstands.

Connecticut tourism information centers also provide useful information: on I-95 southbound at North Stonington, northbound at Darien, northbound at Westbrook (seasonal); on I-84 eastbound at Danbury, eastbound at Southington (seasonal), westbound at Willington; on I-91 northbound at Middletown, southbound at Wallingford; on Merritt Parkway (Hwy 15) northbound at Greenwich (seasonal). Also, several privately operated tourism centers are located throughout the state.

Avon (D-3)

See also Bristol, Farmington, Hartford, Simsbury, Wethersfield

Population 13,937
Elevation 202 ft
Area Code 860
Zip 06001
Information Greater Hartford Tourism District, 31 Prat St, Hartford 06103; phone 860/244-8181 or toll-free 800/793-4480
Web Site www.visitctriver.com

What to See and Do

Farmington Valley Arts Center. *25 Arts Center Ln, Avon (06001). Off Hwy 44. Phone 860/678-1867. www.fvac. net.* Twenty studios, located in a historic stone explosives plant, occupied by artists and artisans and open to the public at artist's discretion. Fisher Gallery and Shop featuring guest-curated exhibitions and a juried collection of handmade crafts, gifts, and artwork. (Jan-Oct: Wed-Sat, Sun afternoons; Nov-Dec: daily; closed holidays) **FREE**

Roaring Brook Nature Center. *70 Gracey Rd, Canton (06019). 1 1/2 miles N of Hwy 44. Phone 860/693-0263. www.roaringbrook.org.* This 112-acre wildlife refuge has an interpretive building with seasonal natural history exhibits, wildlife observation area; 6 miles of marked trails. Gift shop. (Sept-June: Tues-Sun; rest of year: daily; closed holidays) **$**

Ski Sundown. *126 Ratlum Rd, New Hartford (06057). 6 miles W via Hwy 44, then 1 1/2 miles NE on Hwy 219.* *Phone 860/379-9851. www.skisundown.com.* Three triple, double chairlift; Pomalift; snowmaking; school, patrol, rentals, half-day rate; bar, snack bar. Fifteen trails. Longest run 1 mile; vertical drop 625 feet. (Dec-Mar, daily) **$$$$**

Full-Service Hotel

★ ★ ★ **AVON OLD FARMS HOTEL.** *279 Avon Mountain Rd, Avon (06001). Phone 860/677-1651; toll-free 800/836-4000; fax 860/677-0364. www.avonoldfarmshotel.com.* Guests can enjoy nature with walks to nearby parks and trails, or simply kick back and take in the hometown feel. 160 rooms, 3 story. Complimentary continental breakfast. Check-in 3 pm, check-out noon. Restaurant. Fitness room. Outdoor pool. **$**

Restaurants

★ ★ ★ **AVON OLD FARMS INN.** *1 Nod Rd, Avon (06001). Phone 860/677-2818; fax 860/676-0280. www. avonoldfarmsinn.com.* Serving classic entrée favorites from the past, with a seasonally changing menu, this restaurant (a 1757 stagecoach stop) draws a local and tourist clientele. American menu. Lunch, dinner, Sun brunch. Bar. Children's menu. **$$**

★ ★ **DAKOTA.** *225 W Main St, Avon (06001). Phone 860/677-4311; fax 860/677-2872. www.dakotarestaurant.com.* Seafood, steak menu. Dinner. Bar. Children's menu. **$$**

Branford (E-3)

See also Guilford, Madison, Meriden, Milford, New Haven

Settled 1644
Population 27,603
Elevation 49 ft
Area Code 203, 860
Zip 06405
Information Connecticut River Valley & Shoreline Visitors Council, 393 Main St, Middletown 06457; phone 860/347-0028 or toll-free 800/486-3346
Web Site www.cttourism.org

Once a busy shipping center, Branford has become a residential and industrial suburb of New Haven. The community's bays and beaches attract many summertime vacationers. Branford's large green, dating from colonial days, is surrounded by public buildings.

What to See and Do

Harrison House. *124 Main St, Branford (06405). Phone 203/488-4828.* (Circa 1725) Classic colonial saltbox restored by J. Frederick Kelly, an early 20th-century architect; stone chimney, herb garden, period furnishings, and farm implements. (June-Sept, Fri-Sat mid-late afternoon; also by appointment) **FREE**

Thimble Islands Cruise. *Thimble Island and Prospect Hill rds, Branford (06405). Departs from Stony Creek Dock. Phone 203/481-3345. www.thimbleislands.com.* Legends of treasures hidden by Captain Kidd, along with picturesque shores and vegetation, have for more than 250 years lured people to these 20 to 30 rocky islets in Long Island Sound. Narrated tours (30-45 minutes) leave hourly aboard the *Volsunga III.* (May-Oct, Tues-Sun) Reservations required. **$$**

Bridgeport (F-2)

See also Fairfield, Milford, Norwalk, Stratford, Westport

Settled 1639
Population 141,686
Elevation 20 ft
Area Code 203
Information Chamber of Commerce, 10 Middle St, 14th floor, 06604; phone 203/335-3800
Web Site www.brbc.org

An important manufacturing city, Bridgeport is home to dozens of well-known companies that produce a highly diversified array of manufactured products. The University of Bridgeport (1927) is also located in the city.

Bridgeport's most famous resident was probably P. T. Barnum. The city's most famous son was 28-inch Charles S. Stratton, who was promoted by Barnum as General Tom Thumb. There was a time when train passengers in and out of Bridgeport occasionally saw elephants hitched to plows; the elephants, of course, were from Barnum's winter quarters. As well as running the "Greatest Show on Earth," Barnum was for a time the mayor of Bridgeport.

What to See and Do

⭐ **Barnum Museum.** *820 Main St, Bridgeport (06604). Phone 203/331-1104. www.barnum-museum.org.* Houses memorabilia from P. T. Barnum's life and circus career, including artifacts relating to Barnum's legendary discoveries, General Tom Thumb and Jenny Lind; scale model of three-ring circus; displays of Victorian Bridgeport; changing exhibits; art gallery. (Tues-Sun; closed holidays) **$**

Beardsley Zoological Gardens. *Beardsley Park, 1875 Noble Ave, Bridgeport (06604). Off I-95 exit 27A. Phone 203/394-6565. www.beardsleyzoo.org.* This 30-acre zoo, the state's only, houses more than 200 animals; Siberian tiger exhibit; farmyard; concession; gift shop. (Daily; closed Jan 1, Thanksgiving, Dec 25) **$$**

Captain's Cove Seaport. *1 Bostwick Ave, Bridgeport (06605). I-95 exit 26. Phone 203/335-1433. www.captainscoveseaport.com.* Replica of the HMS *Rose*, the British warship that triggered the founding of the American Navy during the Revolutionary War. Marina; shops, restaurant, fish market. (Schedule varies)

Discovery Museum. *4450 Park Ave, Bridgeport (06604). Off Merritt Pkwy, exit 47. Phone 203/372-3521. www.discoverymuseum.org.* Planetarium; films; approximately 120 hands-on science and art exhibits; children's museum; Challenger Learning Center; changing art exhibits; lectures, demonstrations, and workshops. (Tues-Sun; closed Labor Day, Thanksgiving, Dec 25) **$$**

Ferry to Port Jefferson, Long Island. *Bridgeport. Phone 203/335-2040.* Car and passenger service across Long Island Sound (1 hour, 20 minutes). (Daily)

Statue of Tom Thumb. *Mountain Grove Cemetery, North Ave and Dewey St, Bridgeport (06604).* Life-size statue on 10-foot base.

Special Event

Barnum Festival. *Main St and Fairfield, Bridgeport (06604). Phone 203/367-8495; toll-free 866/867-8495. www.barnumfestival.com.* Commemorates the life of P. T. Barnum. Mar-Sept

Limited-Service Hotel

⭐ ⭐ **HOLIDAY INN.** *1070 Main St, Bridgeport (06604). Phone 203/334-1234; toll-free 800/465-4329; fax 203/367-1985. www.holiday-inn.com.* 234 rooms, 9 story. Pets accepted, some restrictions; fee. Check-in 3 pm, check-out noon. High-speed Internet access. Restaurant, bar. Fitness room. Indoor pool, outdoor pool. Airport transportation available. Business center. **$**

Full-Service Hotel

★ ★ ★ **MARRIOTT TRUMBULL MERRITT PARKWAY.** *180 Hawley Ln, Trumbull (06611). Phone 203/378-1400; toll-free 800/682-4095; fax 203/375-0632. www.marriott.com.* 320 rooms, 5 story. Check-in 4 pm, check-out noon. High-speed Internet access. Restaurant, bar. Fitness room. Indoor pool, outdoor pool, whirlpool. Business center. **$$**
🏃 🛌 🏊

Restaurant

★ **BLACK ROCK CASTLE.** *2895 Fairfield Ave, Bridgeport (06605). Phone 203/336-3990; fax 203/331-9325. www.blackrockcastle.com.* Irish menu. Dinner. Closed Jan 1, Dec 25. Children's menu. Valet parking. **$$**

Bristol (D-3)

See also Avon, Farmington, Litchfield, Meriden, New Britain, Waterbury, Woodbury

Settled 1727
Population 60,640
Elevation 289 ft
Area Code 860
Zip 06010
Information Greater Bristol Chamber of Commerce, 200 Main St; phone 860/584-4718. Litchfield Hills Visitors Bureau, PO Box 968, Litchfield 06759; phone 860/567-4506
Web Site www.bristol-chamber.org

Gideon Roberts began making and selling clocks here in 1790. Bristol has since been famous for clocks--particularly for Sessions and Ingraham. Today, Bristol is also the home of the Associated Spring Corporation; Dana Corporation/Warner Electric; Theis Precision Steel; and ESPN, the nation's first all-sports cable television network.

What to See and Do

American Clock and Watch Museum. *100 Maple St, Bristol (06010). Phone 860/583-6070. www.clockmuseum.org.* More than 3,000 timepieces; exhibits and video show on history of clock and watch manufacturing located in historic house built 1801. Also award-winning sundial garden; bookshop. (Apr-Nov, daily; closed Easter, Thanksgiving) **$**

Burlington Trout Hatchery. *34 Belden Rd, Burlington (06013). 10 miles N via Hwy 69, then approximately 1 mile E on Hwy 4 to Belden Rd. Phone 860/673-2340.* Hatchery building houses incubators and tanks; development of trout from egg to fish. (Daily) **FREE**

H. C. Barnes Memorial Nature Center. *175 Shrub Rd, Bristol (06010). 3 miles N on Hwy 69. Phone 860/589-6082. www.elcct.org.* Self-guiding trails through 70-acre preserve. Interpretive building features ecological and animal displays. (Sat) Trails (daily; closed holidays). **$**

Lake Compounce Theme Park. *822 Lake Ave, Bristol (06010). Phone 860/583-3631. www.lakecompounce.com.* One of the oldest continuously operating amusement parks in the nation. Over 25 wet and dry attractions include roller coasters, whitewater raft ride, vintage trolley, bumper cars, and 1911 carousel. Special events. (June-Aug) **$$$$**

Lock Museum of America. *230 Main St, Terryville (06786). 3 1/2 miles NW on Hwy 72, then W 3/4 mile on Hwy 6 to 130 Main St. Phone 860/589-6359. www.lockmuseum.com.* Antique locks, displays on lock history and design. (May-Oct, Tues-Sun 1:30-4:30 pm) **$** Two blocks west is

   Eli Terry Jr. Waterwheel. *160 Main St, Terryville (06786).* Built in the early 1840s, this 20-foot diameter, rack-and-pinion, breast-type wheel is an excellent example of the type of waterwheel used to supply power to industrial buildings during this period.

New England Carousel Museum. *95 Riverside Ave, Bristol (06010). Phone 860/585-5411. www.thecarouselmuseum.org.* Displays more than 300 carved, wooden antique carousel figures, including two chariots. Restoration workshop on view. (Apr-Oct, daily; rest of year, Thurs-Sat, also Sun afternoons; closed holidays) **$**

Special Event

Chrysanthemum Festival. *130 Main St, Bristol (06010). Phone 860/584-4718. bristolmumfestival.org/mumfestival.* Music, art, theater, hayrides, picking pumpkins, parades, and dances, Historical Society tours. Late Sept.

Specialty Lodging

CHIMNEY CREST MANOR. *5 Founders Dr, Bristol (06010). Phone 860/582-4219; fax 860/584-5903.* This historic (1930) Tudor-style bed-and-breakfast is located in the beautiful Federal Hill district of Bristol. The

home features framed artwork and beamed ceilings. 6 rooms, 3 story. Closed Dec 24-25. Complimentary full breakfast. Check-in 3 pm, check-out 11 am. **$**
🅳

Clinton (E-4)

See also Essex, Guilford, Madison, New Haven, Old Saybrook

Settled 1663
Population 12,767
Elevation 25 ft
Area Code 860
Zip 06413
Information Chamber of Commerce, 50 E Main St, PO Box 334; phone 860/669-3889
Web Site www.clintonct.com

What to See and Do

Chamard Vineyards. *115 Cow Hill Rd, Clinton (06413). Phone 860/664-0299; toll-free 800/371-1609. www. chamard.com.* A 15-acre vineyard and winery offering chardonnay, pinot noir, merlot, and other varieties. Tours and tastings (Tues-Sun). **FREE**

Chatfield Hollow State Park. *381 Hwy 80, Killing-worth (06419). 7 miles NW via Hwys 80 and 81, on N Branford Rd. Phone 860/663-2030.* Approximately 550 acres situated in a heavily wooded hollow with fine fall scenery and natural caves that once provided shelter for Native Americans. Pond swimming, fishing; hiking, ice skating, picnicking. **$$$**

Stanton House. *63 E Main St, Clinton (06413). Phone 860/669-2132.* (1789) Thirteen-room house connected to general store; original site of the first classroom of Yale University. Period furnishings; antique American and Staffordshire dinnerware; weapon collection; bed used by Marquis de Lafayette during 1824 visit. (June-Sept, by appointment) **FREE**

Limited-Service Hotel

★ **CLINTON MOTEL.** *163 E Main St, Clinton (06413). Phone 860/669-8850; fax 860/669-3849.* 15 rooms. Check-in, check-out 11 am. Outdoor pool. **$**
🅳 🏊

Restaurant

★ **LOG CABIN RESTAURANT AND LOUNGE.** *232 Boston Post Rd, Clinton (06413). Phone 860/669-*

6253. Italian menu. Lunch, dinner. Closed Dec 25. Bar. Children's menu. **$$**

Cornwall Bridge (D-1)

See also Kent, Lakeville, Litchfield, New Preston

Population 450
Elevation 445 ft
Area Code 860
Zip 06754
Information Litchfield Hills Visitors Bureau, PO Box 968, Litchfield 06759; phone 860/567-4506
Web Site www.litchfieldhills.com

The small central valley containing the villages of Cornwall, West Cornwall, and Cornwall Bridge was avoided by early settlers because its heavy stand of pine made the clearing of land difficult.

What to See and Do

Covered bridge. *Hwy 7 atf Hwy 128, West Cornwall.* 4 miles N via Hwy 7 to Hwy 128 near West Cornwall, at Housatonic River. Phone 860/571-7130. Designed by Ithiel Town, in continuous service since 1837. **FREE**

Housatonic Meadows State Park. *Hwys 7 and 4, Cornwall Bridge (06754). 1 mile N on Hwy 7. Phone 860/927-3238.* A 452-acre park bordering the Housatonic River. Fishing, boating, canoeing; picnicking, camping (dump station). No pets. **FREE**

Mohawk Mountain Ski Area. *Cornwall Bridge. 4 miles NE on Hwy 4, S on Hwy 128, on Great Hollow Rd in Mohawk Mountain State Park. Phone 860/672-6100. www.mohawkmtn.com.* More than 20 trails and slopes, most with snowmaking; triple, four double chairlifts; patrol, school, rentals; cafeteria. Longest run 1 1/4 mile; vertical drop 650 feet. More than 40 miles of cross-country trails. Night skiing Mon-Sat. (Late Nov-early Apr, daily; closed holidays) **$$$$**

Sharon Audubon Center. *325 Cornwall Bridge Rd, Sharon (06069). Approximately 8 miles NW on Hwy 4. Phone 860/364-0520. www.sharon.audubon.org.* National Audubon Society wildlife sanctuary (684 acres) including nature center, 11 miles of walking trails, self-guided tours, herb and wildflower garden, gift/bookstore. Grounds (daily). Nature center, store (Tues-Sat 9 am-5 pm, Sun 1-5 pm; closed holidays). **$**

Restaurant

★ ★ **CORNWALL INN.** *270 Kent Rd (Hwy 7), Cornwall Bridge (06754). Phone 860/672-6884. www. cornwallinn.com.* American menu. Dinner. Bar. Casual attire. Outdoor seating. **$$**
🅳

Danbury (E-1)

See also Brewster, Ridgefield, Southbury, Woodbury

Settled 1685
Population 65,585
Elevation 378 ft
Area Code 203
Information Housatonic Valley Tourism District, 39 West St, PO Box 406, 06810; phone 203/743-5565
Web Site www.danburychamber.com

Danbury, originally settled by eight Norwalk families seeking fertile land, played an important role during the American Revolution as a supply depot and site of a military hospital for the Continental Army. After the war and until the 1950s, the community was the center of the hat industry. Zadoc Benedict is credited with the first factory in 1790, which made three hats a day.

What to See and Do

Candlewood Lake. *35 E Hayestown Rd, Danbury (06811). 2 miles NW on Hwy 37, then E on Hayestown Ave to E Hayestown Rd.* Connecticut's largest lake, more than 14 miles long and with more than 60 miles of shoreline, extends one finger into Danbury. Swimming, fishing, boating; picnicking, concession. Fees for some activities. On the west shore are Pootatuck State Forest and

> **Squantz Pond State Park.** *178 Shortwoods Rd, New Fairfield (06812). 10 miles N on Hwys 37 and 39. Phone 203/797-4165.* More than 170 acres. Freshwater swimming, scuba diving, fishing, boating (7 1/2 hp limit), canoeing; hiking, biking, picnicking, concessions. No pets. **$$$**

Scott-Fanton Museum. *43 Main St, Danbury (06810). Phone 203/743-5200. www.danburyhistorical.org.* Includes Rider House (1785), period furnishings, New England memorabilia; Dodd Shop (circa 1790), historical display of hat industry; Huntington Hall, changing exhibits and research library. (by appointment) **DONATION**

Special Event

Charles Ives Center for the Arts. *Mill Plain Rd, Danbury (06810). Phone 203/837-9226. www.ivesconcertpark.com.* At Westside campus, Western Connecticut State University. Outdoor classical, country, folk, jazz, and pop concerts. Fri-Sun, July-early Sept.

Taste of Greater Danbury. *Danbury Green, Green Ives and White sts, Danbury (06810). Phone 203/792-1711. www.citycenterdanbury.com.* Food vendors, live music, and children's games draw crowds together year after year. Sept.

Limited-Service Hotels

★ ★ **ETHAN ALLEN HOTEL.** *21 Lake Ave, Danbury (06811). Phone 203/744-1776; toll-free 800/742-1776; fax 203/791-9673. www.ethanalleninn.com.* 195 rooms, 6 story. Check-out noon. Restaurant, bar. Fitness room. Outdoor pool. Airport transportation available. Business center. **$**
🕴 ➰ 🕴

★ ★ **HOLIDAY INN.** *80 Newtown Rd, Danbury (06810). Phone 203/792-4000; toll-free 800/465-4329; fax 203/797-0810. www.holiday-inn.com.* 114 rooms, 4 story. Pets accepted; fee. Check-in 2 pm, check-out noon. High-speed Internet access. Restaurant, bar. Outdoor pool. Airport transportation available. **$**
🐾 ➰

Full-Service Hotel

★ ★ ★ **SHERATON DANBURY HOTEL.** *18 Old Ridgebury Rd, Danbury (06810). Phone 203/794-0600; toll-free 800/325-3535; fax 203/830-5188. www. sheraton.com.* Conveniently located just 3 miles from Danbury Airport. 242 rooms, 10 story. Pets accepted, some restrictions. Check-in 3 pm, check-out noon. Restaurant, bar. Fitness room. Indoor pool, whirlpool. Tennis. Business center. **$**
🐾 🕴 ➰ 🎾 🕴

Specialty Lodging

THE HOMESTEAD INN. *5 Elm St, New Milford (06776). Phone 860/354-4080; fax 860/354-7046. www.homesteadct.com.* Inn built in 1853; many of the rooms are furnished with country antiques. 14 rooms, 2 story. Complimentary continental breakfast. Check-in 2 pm, check-out 11 am. **$**

Restaurant

★ ★ **CIAO CAFE AND WINE BAR.** *2B Ives St, Danbury (06810). Phone 203/791-0404; fax 203/730-1962.* Italian menu. Lunch, dinner. Closed Labor Day, Dec 25. Bar. Reservations recommended. Outdoor seating. **$$**

★ ★ **TWO STEPS DOWNTOWN GRILLE.** *5 Ives St, Danbury (06810). Phone 203/794-0032; fax 203/730-1962.* American, Southwestern menu. Lunch, dinner, Sun brunch. Closed Labor Day, Dec 25. Bar. Children's menu. Outdoor seating. **$$**

East Haddam (E-4)

See also Essex, Middletown

Population 6,676
Elevation 35 ft
Area Code 860
Zip 06423
Information Connecticut River Valley & Shoreline Visitors Council, 393 Main St, Middletown 06457; phone 860/347-0028 or toll-free 800/486-3346
Web Site www.visitctriver.com

The longest remaining swinging bridge in New England crosses the Connecticut River to Haddam.

What to See and Do

Amasa Day House. *Rtes 149 and 151, Moodus (06469). 4 miles N on Hwy 149 at junction Hwy 15. Phone 860/873-8144.* (1816) Period furnishings include some pieces owned by three generations of the Day family; stenciled floors and stairs. (June-Labor Day, Sun) **$**

Eagle Aviation. *Goodspeed Airport and Seaplane Base, Lumberyard Rd, East Haddam (06423). Phone 860/873-8568.* Scenic airplane rides over the Connecticut River Valley. (Daily; closed Dec 25-early Jan) **$$$$**

Gillette Castle State Park. *67 River Rd, East Haddam. 4 miles SE via local roads. Phone 860/526-2336.* The 184-acre park surrounds a 24-room castle built by turn-of-the-century actor and playwright William Gillette; medieval German design with dramatically decorated rooms. (Late May-mid-Oct: daily; mid-Oct-mid-Dec: Sat-Sun) You'll find picnicking and hiking trails in the surrounding park. **$$**

Goodspeed Opera House. *6 Main St, East Haddam (06423). On Hwy 82 at East Haddam Bridge. Phone 860/873-8668. www.goodspeed.org.* Home of the American Musical Theatre (1876). Performances of American musicals. Guided tours (June-late Oct, Sat; $). **$**

Nathan Hale Schoolhouse. *33 Main St, East Haddam (06423). Main St (Hwy 149) at rear of St. Stephen's Church. Phone 860/873-3399.* One-room school where the American Revolutionary patriot taught during the winter of 1773; period furnishings, memorabilia. Church has bell said to have been cast in Spain in AD 815. (Memorial Day-Labor Day, Sat-Sun, and holidays, limited hours) **FREE**

Specialty Lodging

BISHOPSGATE INN. *7 Norwich Rd, East Haddam (06423). Phone 860/873-1677; fax 860/873-3898. www.bishopsgate.com.* Near Connecticut River. 6 rooms, 2 story. Children over 5 years only. Complimentary full breakfast. Check-in 2 pm, check-out 11 am. **$**

Enfield (C-3)

See also Holyoke, Springfield, Stafford Springs, Windsor, Windsor Locks

Settled 1680
Population 45,532
Elevation 150 ft
Area Code 860
Zip 06082
Information Connecticut's Heritage Valley North Central Tourism Bureau, 111 Hazard Ave; phone 860/763-2578 or toll-free 800/248-8283
Web Site www.cnctb.org

Located on the Connecticut River, Enfield was an important embarking point for flat-bottom boats transporting wares to Springfield, Massachusetts, in the 18th century. The Enfield Society for the Detection of Horse Thieves and Robbers was founded here over a century ago. Jonathan Edwards, a famous theologian, delivered his fire and brimstone sermon "Sinners in the Hands of an Angry God" here in 1741.

What to See and Do

Martha A. Parsons House. *1387 Enfield St, Enfield (06082). Phone 860/745-6064.* (1782) Constructed on land put aside for use by parsons or ministers, this house holds 180 years' worth of antiques collected by the Parsons family; tables brought from West Indies, George Washington memorial wallpaper. (May-Oct, Sun afternoons or by appointment) **FREE**

Old Town Hall (Purple Heart Museum). *1294 Enfield St, Enfield (06082). Phone 860/745-1729.* Includes inventions of the Shakers, a religious sect that observed a doctrine of celibacy, common property, and community living; medals and service memorabilia, 46-star flag; local historical displays and artifacts. (May-Oct, Sun afternoons or by appointment) **FREE**

Full-Service Hotel

★ ★ ★ **CROWNE PLAZA HOTEL.** *1 Bright Meadow Blvd, Enfield (06082). Phone 860/741-2211; fax 860/741-6917.* The 11-acre, country setting attracts a business clientele to this property. Outdoor recreation includes landscaped walking trails. 176 rooms, 6 story. Check-in 3 pm, check-out 11 am. High-speed Internet access, wireless Internet access. Restaurant, bar. Fitness room. Indoor pool, outdoor pool, whirlpool. Tennis. Airport transportation available. Business center. **$$**

Restaurant

★ ★ **RESTAURANT DOLCE.** *1 Bright Meadow Blvd, Enfield (06082). Phone 860/741-2211; fax 860/741-6917. www.crowneplaza.com.* Italian, American menu. Breakfast, lunch, dinner. Bar. Children's menu. Casual attire. **$$**

Essex (E-3)

See also Clinton, East Haddam, Middletown, Old Lyme, Old Saybrook

Population 5,904
Elevation 100 ft
Area Code 860
Zip 06426
Information Connecticut River Valley & Shoreline Visitors Council, 393 Main St, Middletown 06457; phone 860/347-0028 or toll-free 800/486-3346
Web Site www.visitctriver.com

What to See and Do

Connecticut River Museum. *67 Main St, Essex (06426). At the foot of Main St at the river. Phone 860/767-8269. www.ctrivermuseum.org.* Housed in the last remaining steamboat dock building on the Connecticut River. Presents exhibits celebrating the rich cultural heritage and natural resources of the river valley. Includes the only full-size, operating replica of the *Turtle*, America's

first successful submarine, built along the Connecticut River during the Revolutionary War. (Tues-Sun; closed holidays) **$$**

Valley Railroad. *1 Railroad Ave, Essex (06426). Phone 860/767-0103. www.essexsteamtrain.com.* Scenic 12-mile steam train excursion along Connecticut River to Chester; can opt to connect with a riverboat for one-hour Connecticut River cruise (additional fare). Cruise passengers are returned to Essex via later connecting trains. Turn-of-the-century equipment. (Early May-late Oct, days vary; also Christmas trips) **$$$$**

Special Event

Deep River Ancient Muster and Parade. *Devitt's Field, Main St, Deep River. 2 1/2 miles N via Hwy 9. Phone 860/388-7575.* Approximately 60 fife and drum corps recall the revolutionary War period; displays. Third Sat in July.

Full-Service Inn

★ ★ ★ **THE COPPER BEECH INN.** *46 Main St, Ivoryton (06442). Phone 860/767-0330; toll-free 888/809-2056. www.copperbeechinn.com.* Travelers looking for a romantic New England getaway will not want to miss this charming 1889 Victorian inn (once the residence of a prominent ivory importer) with sprawling wooded surroundings. This quaint country retreat will relax the mind and soul. 13 rooms, 2 story. Closed Dec 24-25; also first week in Jan. Children over 12 years only. Complimentary full breakfast. Check-in 4 pm, check-out noon. Two restaurants. **$$**

★ ★ ★ **GRISWOLD INN.** *36 Main St, Essex (06426). Phone 860/767-1776; fax 860/767-0481. www.griswoldinn.com.* Located near the Connecticut River, this inn has been in operation since 1776. 31 rooms, 3 story. Complimentary continental breakfast. Check-in 2 pm, check-out 11 am. Restaurant. **$$**

Restaurants

★ ★ ★ **COPPER BEECH INN.** *46 Main St, Ivoryton (06442). Phone 860/767-0330. www.copperbeechinn.com.* Dine in hearty, French country style with fresh flowers, sparkling silver, and soft candlelight. The atmosphere is pure romance and warm elegance. French menu. Dinner, Sun brunch. Closed Mon-Tues (Jan-Mar); Jan 1, Dec 24-25. Bar. Jacket required. **$$$**

★ ★ ★ **GRISWOLD INN.** *36 Main St, Essex (06426). Phone 860/767-1776; fax 860/767-0481. www.*

The Best Small Town in America

The lower reaches of the Connecticut River are so unspoiled by development that about ten years ago, the Nature Conservancy named the area to its list of Last Great Places in the Western Hemisphere. Then in 1996, the riverfront town of Essex won honors as The Best Small Town in America in a much-publicized book by Norman Crampton. The village part of the town is ideal for walking and sightseeing; a loop that takes in the whole peninsula is just about a mile in length. Start at the top of Main Street at Essex Square (street parking is free and easy to find), then walk south along Main. You'll pass dozens of appealing shops selling everything from clothing to antiques. The towns brick post office is next to Essex Park, a lovely swath of grass and trees overlooking Middle Cove. St. Johns Episcopal Church is across the street in an imposing brownstone. Built in the late 1800s in the style of H. H. Richardson, the church is decades younger than many of the white clapboard houses that line

Main Street. The older houses date to the mid-1700s, when Essex was a major shipbuilding center. Ships' captains and merchants built their houses close to what is now the Town Dock at the foot of Main. Today, some of these houses have been converted to delis, coffeehouses, and shops, but others are still private homes, decked with window boxes and encircled with blooming gardens. The Griswold Inn (locally known as The Griz) is a landmark that has been offering travelers hospitality since 1776. Its famous for its Sunday morning English-style Hunt Breakfast. The Connecticut River Museum is housed in a former steamboat warehouse next to the Town Dock; it showcases the history of the river with memorabilia and ship models. Reversing direction, head north on Main, then turn right onto Ferry Street to the Dauntless Shipyard and Essex Island Marina. Turn left onto Pratt Street to return to the starting point at Essex Square.

griswoldinn.com. This historic inn has been serving typical country fare since 1776. The continental specialties are sure to satisfy. American menu. Lunch, dinner, Sun brunch. Closed Dec 24-25. Bar. Children's menu. **$$**

★ ★ **SAGE AMERICAN BAR & GRILL.** *129 W Main St, Chester (06412). Phone 860/526-9898; fax 860/526-2201. www.sageamerican.com.* In converted 19th-century mill with wheels and belts overhead. Seafood, steak menu. Dinner. Children's menu. Outdoor seating. **$$**

Fairfield (F-4)

See also Bridgeport, Milford, Norwalk, Stamford, Stratford, Westport

Settled 1639
Population 53,418
Elevation 15 ft
Area Code 203
Information Chamber of Commerce, 1597 Post Rd, 06430; phone 203/255-1011
Web Site www.fairfieldctchamber.com

A small band of colonists led by Roger Ludlowe settled Fairfield two years after the Pequot were subdued in the Great Swamp Fight. In 1779, British troops under General Tyron marched into the area and requested that the people submit to royal authority. When this was refused, the village was put to the torch.

What to See and Do

Connecticut Audubon Society Birdcraft Museum and Sanctuary. *314 Unquowa Rd, Fairfield (06824). Phone 203/259-0416. www.ctaudubon.org.* Established in 1914, this vest-pocket, 6-acre sanctuary houses a natural history museum with wildlife displays, dinosaur footprints, trails, ponds. (Tues-Sun) **$**

Connecticut Audubon Society Fairfield Nature Center and Larsen Sanctuary. *2325 Burr St, Fairfield (06824). Phone 203/259-6305. www.ctaudubon.org.* Center features Connecticut wildlife and flora, solar greenhouse, natural history library, nature store. (Tues-Sat; also Sun in spring, fall; closed holidays; donation). Adjacent is 160-acre sanctuary with 6 miles of trails through woodlands, meadows, ponds, streams. (Daily) Trail for the disabled. **$**

Fairfield Historical Society. *636 Old Post Rd, Fairfield (06824). Phone 203/259-1598.* Museum with permanent displays of furniture, paintings, maritime memorabilia, dolls, toys, farm implements, clocks; changing exhibits of history, costumes, decorative arts; genealogical and research library. (Tues-Sun; closed holidays) **$$**

Ogden House. *1520 Bronson Rd, Fairfield (06824). Phone 203/259-1598.* (Circa 1750) Maintained by the Fairfield Historical Society, this 18th-century saltbox farmhouse, with authentic furnishings, has been restored to the time of its building by David and Jane Ogden; mid-18th-century kitchen garden. (June-Sept, Sun afternoon; other times by appointment) **$**

Special Event

Chamber Arts & Crafts Festival. *Fairfield. Phone 203/255-1011.* On Sherman Green. Mid-June.

Dogwood Festival. *Greenfield Hill Congregational Church, 1045 Old Academy Rd, Fairfield (06824). Phone 203/259-5596.* Herbs, plants; arts and crafts; walking tours, music programs; food. Early or mid-May.

Limited-Service Hotel

★ ★ **FAIRFIELD INN.** *417 Post Rd, Fairfield (06430). Phone 203/255-0491; toll-free 800/347-0414; fax 203/255-2073.* 80 rooms, 2 story. Check-out 11 am. Restaurant, bar. Outdoor pool. **$**

Farmington (D-3)

See also Avon, Bristol, Hartford, New Britain, Simsbury, Wethersfield

Settled 1640
Population 20,608
Elevation 245 ft
Area Code 860
Zip 06032
Information Greater Hartford Tourism District, 31 Pratt St, Hartford 06114; phone 860/244-8181 or toll-free 800/793-4480
Web Site www.visitctriver.com

In 1802 and 1803, 15,000 yards of linen cloth were loomed in Farmington, and 2,500 hats were made in a shop on Hatter's Lane. There were silversmiths,

tinsmiths, cabinetmakers, clockmakers, and carriage builders. Today, Farmington is a beautiful community—one of New England's museum pieces. It is also the home of Miss Porter's School (1844), a well-known private preparatory school for girls.

What to See and Do

Hill-Stead Museum. *35 Mountain Rd, Farmington (06032). Phone 860/677-9064. www.hillstead.org.* (1901) Colonial Revival-style country house designed by Theodate Pope in collaboration with McKim, Mead, and White for industrialist A. A. Pope; contains Pope's collection of French impressionist paintings and decorative arts. Set on 152 acres, which include a sunken garden. One-hour tours. (Tues-Sun) **$$**

Stanley-Whitman House. *37 High St, Farmington (06032). Phone 860/677-9222. www.stanleywhitman.org.* (Circa 1720) This is one of the finest early 18th-century houses in the United States; period furniture, local artifacts; changing displays; living history presentations; 18th-century herb and flower gardens. (May-Oct, Wed-Sun afternoons; Nov-Apr, Sat-Sun afternoons, also by appointment) **$**

Special Event

Farmington Antiques Weekend. *Farmington (06032). Polo Grounds. Phone 860/677-7862. www.farmington-antiques.com.* One of the largest antique events in Connecticut; approximately 600 dealers. Mid-June and early Sept.

Limited-Service Hotel

★ ★ **CENTENNIAL INN SUITES.** *5 Spring Lake, Farmington (06032). Phone 860/677-4647; toll-free 800/852-2052; fax 860/676-0685. www.centennialinn.com.* 112 rooms, 2 story, all suites. Pets accepted; fee. Complimentary continental breakfast. Check-in 3 pm, check-out 11 am. Outdoor pool. **$$**

Full-Service Hotel

★ ★ ★ **MARRIOTT HARTFORD FARMING-TON.** *15 Farm Springs Rd, Farmington (06032). Phone 860/678-1000; toll-free 800/228-9190; fax 860/677-8849. www.marriott.com.* Tucked away in suburban Farmington, guests will enjoy a relaxed atmosphere at this modern hotel that's just minutes from downtown Hartford. 380 rooms, 4 story. Check-in 4 pm, check-out 11 am. High-speed Internet access. Restaurant, bar. Fitness room, fitness classes available. Indoor pool, outdoor pool, whirlpool. Tennis. Business center. **$$**

Full-Service Inn

★ ★ ★ **THE FARMINGTON INN OF GREAT-ER HARTFORD.** *827 Farmington Ave, Farmington (06032). Phone 860/677-2821; toll-free 800/648-9804; fax 860/677-8332. www.farmingtoninn.com.* 72 rooms, 2 story. Pets accepted, some restrictions; fee. Complimentary continental breakfast. Check-in 3 pm, check-out noon. Wireless Internet access. Restaurant, bar. **$**

Restaurants

★ ★ **APRICOT'S.** *1593 Farmington Ave, Farmington (06032). Phone 860/673-5405; fax 860/673-7138.* Situated by a gently rolling stream and surrounded by wildflowers, this converted trolley house has both an impressive location and menu. American menu. Lunch, dinner, brunch. Bar. Casual attire. Reservations recommended. Outdoor seating. **$$**

★ **STONEWELL.** *354 Colt Hwy, Farmington (06032). Phone 860/677-8855; fax 860/674-9789. www.thestonewell.com.* In addition to its menu of American favorites, this relaxed restaurant offers karaoke on Friday and Saturday nights. American menu. Lunch, dinner. Bar. Children's menu. Casual attire. **$$**

Greenwich (F-1)

See also Norwalk, Stamford

Settled 1640
Population 58,441
Elevation 71 ft
Area Code 203
Information Chamber of Commerce, 45 E Putnam Ave, 06830; phone 203/869-3500
Web Site www.greenwichchamber.com

Greenwich (GREN-itch) is on the New York state line just 28 miles from Times Square. Behind the city's old New England façade, community leaders continue searching for ways to preserve 18th-century charm in the face of present-day economic, political, and social problems.

What to See and Do

Audubon Center in Greenwich. *613 Riversville Rd, Greenwich (06830). Phone 203/869-5272.* This 522-acre sanctuary includes a self-guided nature trail; interpretive building with exhibits. (Daily) **$**

Bruce Museum. *1 Museum Dr, Greenwich (06830). Phone 203/869-0376.* Arts and sciences museum features exhibits, lectures, concerts, and educational programs. (Tues-Sun) **$$**

Bush-Holley House. *39 Strickland Rd, Cos Cob (06807). S off Hwy 1. Phone 203/869-6899.* (1732) Headquarters of the Historical Society of the Town of Greenwich. Residence of a successful 18th-century farmer, it became the site of the Cos Cob art colony at the turn of the century. Exhibits include late 18th-century Connecticut furniture; paintings by Childe Hassam, Elmer Livingston MacRae, John Henry Twachtman; sculptures by John Rogers; pottery by Leon Volkmar. (Tues-Sun afternoons; closed holidays) **$$**

Putnam Cottage/Knapp Tavern. *243 E Putnam Ave, Greenwich (06830). Phone 203/869-9697. www.putnamcottage.org.* (Circa 1690) Near this tavern, Revolutionary General Israel Putnam made a daring escape from the Redcoats in 1779; museum exhibits; rare scalloped shingles; herb garden, restored barn on grounds. (Apr-Dec, Sun afternoon; also by appointment) **$**

Full-Service Hotels

★ ★ ★ **DE LA MAR.** *500 Steamboat Rd, Greenwich (06830). Phone 203/661-9800; fax 203/661-2513. www.thedelamar.com.* Overlooking the Greenwich Marina, this elegant property has French accents. The impressive lobby features beautiful artwork, lots of marble, chandeliers, and sconces. Both business and leisure travelers will appreciate the well-appointed guest rooms which feature flat-screen televisions, CD and DVD players, luxurious Italian linens, and down pillows and duvets. The large bathrooms have marble vanities and cast-iron tubs. Guests can experience a delicious French meal at the in-house L'Escale restaurant and then head to the bar for a nightcap. Feel free to bring Fido along—dogs are also treated well here. The Sophisticated Pet program offers a doggie bed, personalized ID tag, food and water bowls, a welcome note from the hotel General Manager, and a Pet Services Menu. 82 rooms. Pets accepted, some restrictions; fee. Children over 12 years only. Check-in 3 pm, check-out 11 am. Restaurant, bar. Fitness room. **$$$**

★ ★ ★ **HYATT REGENCY GREENWICH.** *1800 E Putnam Ave, Old Greenwich (06870). Phone 203/637-1234; toll-free 800/633-7313; fax 203/637-2940. www.hyatt.com.* 374 rooms, 4 story. Check-in 3 pm, check-out noon. High-speed Internet access. Restaurant, bar. Fitness room. Indoor pool, whirlpool. Business center. **$$$**

Full-Service Inn

★ ★ ★ **HOMESTEAD INN.** *420 Field Point Rd, Greenwich (06830). Phone 203/869-7500; fax 203/869-7502. www.homesteadinn.com.* Secluded and romantic, elegant and sumptuous, this 1799 inn is just a short walk from the center of Greenwich. Purchased in 1997 by Thomas and Theresa Henkelmann, renovations were completed in 2001, and the historic New England Inn now stands as a tribute to Theresa's interior decorating skills and Thomas's magnificent cooking (the Thomas Henkelmann restaurant is off the lobby). Outside, the Homestead looks for all intents and purposes like a traditional New England country inn. But step inside and you'll find an eclectic mix of antique furniture, imported pieces, and one-of-a-kind touches. The ground floor of the main house includes a backgammon room with fireplace, a cocktail lounge, and the restaurant Thomas Henkelmann (see); suites and rooms (or chambers) are on the second and third floors. They are decorated with a mix of imported pieces from India, China, Bali, and Morocco combined with solid cherry bespoke furniture, Frette linens, and original artwork. And although there is a 24-hour concierge, there's no need to ring if you've forgotten your bedroom slippers. The bathroom floors are heated, of course. 18 rooms. Closed two weeks in Mar. Children over 14 years only. Check-in 3 pm, check-out noon. Wireless Internet access. Restaurant, bar. **$$$**

Specialty Lodgings

HARBOR HOUSE INN. *165 Shore Rd, Old Greenwich (06870). Phone 203/637-0145; fax 203/698-0943. www.hhinn.com.* 22 rooms, 3 story. Complimentary continental breakfast. Check-in 3 pm, check-out 11 am. **$**

STANTON HOUSE INN. *76 Maple Ave, Greenwich (06830). Phone 203/869-2110; fax 203/629-2116. www.shinngreenwich.com.* Built in 1900; antiques. 24 rooms, 3 story. Complimentary continental breakfast. Check-in 2:30 pm, check-out 11 am. Outdoor pool. **$$**

Restaurant

★ ★ ★ **JEAN-LOUIS.** *61 Lewis St, Greenwich (06830). Phone 203/622-8450; fax 203/622-5845. www.restaurantjeanlouis.com.* Sophisticated and elegant with professional service to match, this cozy restaurant in a small home has a menu grounded in the precision of French classicism. French menu. Lunch, dinner. Closed Sun. Bar. Business casual attire. Reservations recommended. **$$$**

★ ★ ★ **L'ESCALE.** *500 Steamboat Rd, Greenwich (06830). Phone 203/661-4600; fax 203/661-4601. www.lescalerestaurant.com.* Provence goes Yankee at L'Escale in tony Greenwich. The fine French restaurant earns its props for re-creating the Mediterranean on the North Atlantic shore, importing a stone fireplace and terra-cotta floors to warm the dining room and affixing light-filtering thatched bamboo to shade the patio. The solidly traditional menu from French expat Frederic Kieffer keeps pace with a salad of caramelized leeks and chanterelles; apple- and prune-paired foie gras; bouillabaisse; and crispy duck breast. Because it serves lunch, as well as a substantial menu at the pewter-topped oak bar, L'Escale is gathering place for both locals and passers-through staying at the neighboring Delamar Hotel. French for the port of call, L'Escale allows guests to yacht to dinner, tying up at its waterfront dock. French, seafood menu. Breakfast, lunch, dinner. Bar. Business casual attire. Reservations recommended. Valet parking. Outdoor seating. **$$$**

★ ★ **TERRA RISTORANTE ITALIANO.** *156 Greenwich Ave, Greenwich (06830). Phone 203/629-5222; fax 203/629-4354. www.terraofgreenwich.com.* Stop in for a taste of Tuscany at this popular Italian eatery. American, Italian menu. Lunch, dinner, brunch. Bar. Casual attire. Reservations recommended. Outdoor seating. **$$$**

★ ★ **THAT LITTLE ITALIAN RESTAURANT.** *228-230 Mill St (Henry St), Greenwich (06830). Phone 203/531-7500; fax 203/531-7546. www.tlirgreenwich.com.* Murals depicting scenes of Italy are found throughout this restaurant that serves favorites like eggplant parmigiana and linguine with clam sauce. Italian, Spanish menu. Lunch, dinner. Closed Mon. Bar. Children's menu. Casual attire. Outdoor seating. **$$**

★ ★ ★ **THOMAS HENKELMANN.** *420 Field Point Rd, Greenwich (06830). Phone 203/869-7500; fax*

203/869-7502. *www.homesteadinn.com.* You'll find the luxury-laden restaurant known as Thomas Henkelmann tucked inside the charming Homestead Inn (see), a 1799 Victorian manor house in Greenwich. Named for the gifted German-born, French-trained chef (and pastry chef) who founded the enchanted inn in 1997 with his wife, Theresa, Thomas Henkelmann epitomizes stylish French dining. The menu offers clever, but careful, modern takes on traditional French dishes, playing with delicate herbs and spices and the flawless ingredients of the season. The service is correct and formal, as you would expect in the company of such stunning fare and breathtaking surroundings. The heavenly wine list is delivered by the restaurant's wonderful sommelier; it is as impressive as the cuisine. Dining here is like watching *Casablanca.* It is a classic. You won't want it to end. And you'll probably cry (tears of joy, not regret) when it does. French menu. Dinner. Closed two weeks in Mar. Bar. Reservations recommended. **$$$**

Groton (E-5)

See also Mystic, New London, Norwich, Stonington

Settled 1705
Population 9,837
Elevation 90 ft
Area Code 860
Zip 06340
Information Connecticut's Mystic & More, 32 Huntington St, PO Box 89, New London 06320; phone 860/444-2206 or toll-free 800/863-6569 (outside CT)
Web Site www.mysticcountry.com

Groton is the home of a huge US naval submarine base. It is also the place where the Electric Boat Division of the General Dynamics Corporation, the world's largest private builder of submarines, built the first diesel-powered submarine (1912) and the first nuclear-powered submarine, *Nautilus* (1955). Pfizer Incorporated operates one of the largest antibiotic plants in the world and maintains a research laboratory here.

What to See and Do

Charter fishing trips. *Groton. Phone toll-free 800/863-6569.* Several companies offer full- and 1/2-day saltwater fishing trips both for small and large groups.

Fort Griswold Battlefield State Park. *57 Fort St, Groton (06340). 1 1/2 miles S of Hwy 1. Phone 860/449-6877.* Includes a 135-foot monument to 88 Revolutionary soldiers slain here in 1781 by British troops under the command of Benedict Arnold. Park (daily). Monument and museum (Memorial Day-Labor Day: Wed-Sun).

Historic Ship *Nautilus* and Submarine *Force* Museum. *Naval Submarine Base New London, 1 Crystal Lake Rd, Groton (06349). 2 miles N on Hwy 12. Phone 860/694-3174; toll-free 800/343-0079.* Permanent home for *Nautilus,* the world's first nuclear-powered submarine. Self-guided, audio tour; museum exhibits depicting history of the US Submarine *Force*; working periscopes; authentic submarine control room; four mini-subs; mini-theaters. Picnicking. (Spring-fall, daily; winter, Mon, Wed-Sun; closed Jan 1, Thanksgiving, Dec 25, the first two weeks in May and the last two weeks in Oct) **FREE**

Oceanographic cruise. *Avery Point, 1084 Shennecossett Rd, Groton (06340). Phone 860/445-9007; toll-free 800/364-8472. www.oceanology.org.* A 2 1/2-hour educational cruise on Long Island Sound aboard marine research vessels *Enviro-lab II* and *Enviro-lab III* (summer). Also board a Harbor Seal Watch on Long Island Sound (winter), or visit Ledge Lighthouse. Opportunity to use nets and scientific instruments to explore marine environment firsthand. (June-Aug) **$$$$**

Full-Service Hotel

★ ★ ★ **MARRIOTT MYSTIC HOTEL AND SPA.** *625 North Rd, Groton (06340). Phone 860/446-2600; toll-free 800/228-9290; fax 860/446-2601. www.marriott.com.* The Marriott Mystic Hotel and Spa is a perfect home-away-from-home for business or leisure travelers. Located just outside the historic seafaring town of Mystic, this full-service hotel is a perfect base for exploring the charming village, checking out the creatures at the renowned Mystic Aquarium, or gaming at nearby Foxwoods and Mohegan Sun casinos. A complete business center and accommodations fitted with business amenities put a smile on corporate visitors' faces. The guest rooms and suites are sophisticated and show off a continental flair. The centerpiece of the hotel is its Elizabeth Arden Red Door Spa, favored for its superior treatments and fine service. From aged steaks at Octagon and freshly brewed coffee at Starbucks to light cuisine at the Red Door Spa Café, this hotel has dining covered as well. 285 rooms, 6 story. Check-in 4 pm, check-out 11 am. High-speed Internet access. Two restaurants, bar. Fitness room, spa. Indoor pool. Airport transportation available. **$$**

Restaurants

★ ★ ★ **OCTAGON.** *625 North Rd, Groton (06340). Phone 860/326-0360. www.octagonsteakhouse.com.* Steak menu. Breakfast, dinner. Bar. Children's menu. Business casual attire. Reservations recommended. Valet parking. **$$$**

★ ★ **VINES.** *625 North Rd (Rte 117), Groton (06340). Phone 860/446-2600.* This American bistro-style café and lounge is located off the lovely lobby of the Mystic Marriott Hotel. American menu. Dinner. Bar. Children's menu. Casual attire. Valet parking. **$$**

Guilford (E-3)

See also Branford, Clinton, Madison, New Haven

Founded 1639
Population 19,848
Elevation 20 ft
Area Code 203
Zip 06437
Information Chamber of Commerce, 63 Whitfield St; phone 203/453-9677
Web Site www.guilfordct.com

Guilford was settled by a group of Puritans who followed Reverend Henry Whitfield here from England. One of the residents, Samuel Hill, gave rise to the expression "run like Sam Hill" when he repeatedly ran for political office.

What to See and Do

Henry Whitfield State Museum. *248 Old Whitfield St, Guilford (06437). 1/2 mile S. Phone 203/453-2457.* (1639) The oldest house in the state and among the oldest of stone houses in New England. Restored with 17th- and 18th-century furnishings; exhibits. Gift shop. (Apr-mid-Dec, Wed-Sun; closed holidays) **$**

Hyland House. *84 Boston St, Guilford (06437). Phone 203/453-9477.* (1660) Restored and furnished in 17th-century period, herb garden; guided tours. (Early June-Oct, Tues-Sun) A map of historic houses in Guilford is available. **FREE**

Thomas Griswold House Museum. *171 Boston St, Guilford (06437). Phone 203/453-3176.* (Circa 1775) Fine example of a saltbox house; costumes of 1800s, changing historical exhibits, period gardens, restored working blacksmith shop. (Early June-Oct, Tues-Sun; winter by appointment) **$**

Limited-Service Hotel

★ **TOWER SUITES MOTEL.** *320 Boston Post Rd, Guilford (06437). Phone 203/453-9069; fax 203/458-2727.* 14 rooms, all suites. Check-out 11 am. **$**
🅓

Restaurant

★ ★ **SACHEM COUNTRY HOUSE.** *111 Goose Ln, Guilford (06437). Phone 203/453-5261; fax 203/453-4111.* In 18th-century house; fireplace. Seafood menu. Dinner, Sun brunch. Children's menu. Reservations recommended. **$$**

Hartford (D-3)

See also Avon, Farmington, Manchester, Meriden, Middletown, New Britain, Riverton, Simsbury, Storrs, Vernon, Wethersfield, Windsor, Windsor Locks

Settled 1633
Population 139,739
Elevation 50 ft
Area Code 860
Information Greater Hartford Convention & Visitors Bureau, 31 Pratt St, 06103; phone 860/728-6789 or toll-free 800/446-7811 (outside CT)
Web Site www.enjoyhartford.com

The capital of Connecticut and a major industrial and cultural center on the Connecticut River, Hartford is headquarters for many of the nation's insurance companies.

Roots of American democracy are deep in Hartford's history. The city was made virtually independent in 1662 by Charles II, but an attempt was made by Sir Edmund Andros, governor of New England, to seize its charter. The document was hidden by Joseph Wadsworth in a hollow tree, since known as the Charter Oak. The tree was blown down in 1856; a plaque on Charter Oak Avenue marks the spot.

Hartford has what is said to be the oldest continuously published newspaper in the United States, the *Hartford Courant.* Founded in 1764, it became a daily in 1837. Trinity College (1823), the American School for the Deaf, the Connecticut Institute for the Blind, and the Institute of Living (for mental disabilities) are located in the city.

Public Transportation

Buses (Connecticut Transit), phone 860/525-9181.

Airport Hartford-Bradley International Airport. Cash machines, Terminal B, Concourse A.

Information Phone 860/627-3000

Lost and Found Phone 860/627-3340

What to See and Do

Bushnell Park. *Elm and Trinity sts, Hartford (06103). Downtown, between Jewell, Elm, and Trinity sts. Phone 860/246-7739. www.bushnellpark.org.* The 41-acre park contains 150 varieties of trees and a restored 1914 carousel (schedule varies; fee); concerts and special events (spring-fall). **FREE**

Butler-McCook Homestead and Main Street History Center. *396 Main St, Hartford (06103). Phone 860/522-1806.* (1782) Preserved house, occupied by four generations of one family (1782-1971), has possessions dating back 200 years; collection of Victorian toys; Japanese armor; Victorian garden. (Wed-Sun; closed holidays) **$**

Center Church and Ancient Burying Ground. *675 Main St, Hartford (06103). Phone 860/247-4080.* Church (1807) is patterned after London's St. Martin-in-the-Fields, with Tiffany stained-glass windows. Cemetery contains markers dating back to 1640.

Children's Museum. *950 Trout Brook Dr, West Hartford (06119). Phone 860/231-2824. www.thechildrens-museumct.org.* Computer lab; UTC Wildlife Sanctuary; physical sciences discovery room; walk-in replica of sperm whale; "KaleidoSight," a giant walk-in kaleidoscope; planetarium shows; changing exhibits. (Tues-Sat, also Sun afternoons, Mon during summer; closed holidays) **$$**

Connecticut Audubon Society Holland Brook Nature Center. *1361 Main St, Hartford (06103). Phone 860/633-8402.* On 48 acres adjacent to the Connecticut River, the center features a variety of natural history exhibits and includes a discovery room. Many activities. (Tues-Sun; closed holidays) **$**

Connecticut Historical Society. *1 Elizabeth St, Hartford (06105). Phone 860/236-5621. www.chs.org.* The library contains more than 3 million books and manuscripts. (Tues-Sat; closed holidays). The museum has nine galleries featuring permanent and changing exhibits on state history (Tues-Sun). **$$**

Connecticut River Cruise. *152 River St, Deep River (06108). Departs from Charter Oaks Landing. Phone 860/526-4954.* The *Silver Star*, a reproduction of an 1850s steam yacht, makes 1- to 2 1/2-hour trips on the Connecticut River. (Memorial Day-Labor Day, daily; after Labor Day-Oct, Sat-Sun). **$$$**

Elizabeth Park. *Prospect and Asylum aves, Hartford (06101). Phone 860/231-9443.* Public gardens feature 900 varieties of roses and more than 14,000 other plants; first municipal rose garden in country; greenhouses (all year). Outdoor concerts in summer; ice skating in winter. (Daily) **FREE**

Harriet Beecher Stowe Center. *77 Forest St, Hartford (06105). Phone 860/522-9258. www.harrietbeecher-stowecenter.org.* (1871) The restored Victorian cottage of the author of *Uncle Tom's Cabin* contains original furniture and memorabilia. Tours. (Mon-Sat 9:30 am-4:30 pm, Sun noon-4:30 pm; also Mon from Memorial Day-Columbus Day and Dec) **$$**

Heritage Trails Sightseeing. *Departs from Hartford hotels, Hartford. Phone 860/677-8867. www.charteroak-tree.com.* Guided and narrated tours of Hartford and Farmington. (Daily) **$$$$**

Mark Twain House. *351 Farmington Ave, Hartford (06105). Phone 860/247-0998.* (1874) *Tom Sawyer, Huckleberry Finn,* and other books were published while Samuel Clemens (Mark Twain) lived in this three-story Victorian mansion featuring the decorative work of Charles Comfort Tiffany and the Associated Artists; Tiffany-glass light fixtures, windows, and Tiffany-designed stencilwork in gold and silver leaf. Tours. (May-Dec: daily; rest of year: Mon, Wed-Sun; closed holidays) **$$$**

Museum of Connecticut History. *Connecticut State Library, 231 Capitol Ave, Hartford (06106). Opposite the Capitol. Phone 860/757-6535.* Exhibits include the Colt Collection of Firearms; Connecticut artifacts, including the original 1662 Royal Charter; portraits of Connecticut's governors. Library features law, social sciences, history, genealogy collections, and official state archives. (Mon-Sat; closed holidays) **FREE**

Noah Webster Foundation and Historical Society. *227 S Main St, West Hartford (06107). Phone 860/521-5362. www.noahwebsterhouse.org.* This 18th-century homestead was the birthplace of America's first lexicographer, writer of the *Blue-Backed Speller* (1783) and the *American Dictionary* (1828). Period furnishings, memorabilia; costumed guides; period gardens. (Thurs-Mon 1-4 pm; closed holidays) **$$**

Old State House. *800 Main St, Hartford (06103). Phone 860/522-6766. www.ctosh.org.* (1796) Oldest state house in the nation, designed by Charles Bulfinch; restored Senate chamber with Gilbert Stuart portrait of Washington; displays and rotating exhibitions. Tourist information center; museum shop. Guided tours by appointment. (Tues-Sat; closed holidays) **FREE**

State Capitol. *210 Capitol Ave, Hartford (06106). Capitol Ave, at Trinity St. Phone 860/240-0222.* (1879) Guided tours (one hour) of the restored, gold-domed capitol building and the contemporary legislative office building (Mon-Fri; closed holidays, also Dec 25-Jan 1); includes historical displays. **FREE**

Talcott Mountain State Park. *Simsbury. 8 miles NW via Hwy 44, off Hwy 185. Phone 860/677-0662.* This 557-acre park features the 165-foot Heublein Tower, on a mountaintop 1,000 feet above the Farmington River, considered the best view in the state. Picnicking, shelters. (Late May-late Aug: Thurs-Sun 10 am-5 pm; Labor Day weekend-Oct: daily 10 am-5 pm)

University of Hartford. *200 Bloomfield Ave, West Hartford (06117). 4 miles W. Phone 860/768-4100. www.hartford.edu.* (1877) (6,844 students) Independent institution on 320-acre campus. Many free concerts, operas, lectures, and art exhibits. Located here is

> **Museum of American Political Life.** *Harry Jack Gray Center, 200 Bloomfield Ave, West Hartford (06117). Phone 860/768-4262.* Exhibits include life-size mannequins re-creating political marches from the 1830s to the 1960s; 70-foot wall of historical pictures and images; political television commercials since 1952. (Mon-Fri 8:30 am-4:30 pm; closed holidays) **FREE**

⭐ **Wadsworth Atheneum Museum of Art.** *600 Main St, Hartford (06103). Phone 860/278-2670. www.wadsworthatheneum.org.* One of the nation's oldest continuously operating public art museums with more than 40,000 works of art, spanning 5,000 years; 15th- to 20th-century paintings, American furniture, sculpture, porcelains, English and American silver, the Amistad Collection of African-American art; changing contemporary exhibits. (Wed-Sun; closed holidays)

Special Events

Christmas Crafts Expo I & II. *Connecticut Expo Center, Jennings Rd, Hartford (06103). Phone 860/653-6671.* Exhibits and demonstrations of traditional and contemporary craft media. First and second weekends in Dec.

Mark Twain Days. *351 Farmington Ave, Hartford (06105). Phone 860/247-0998.* Celebration of Twain's legacy and Hartford's cultural heritage with more than 100 events. Concerts, riverboat rides, medieval jousting, tours of Twain House, entertainment. Mid-July.

Riverfest. *Charter Oak Landing and Constitution Plz, Hartford (06103). Phone 860/713-3131.* Celebration of America's independence and the Connecticut River. Family entertainment, concerts, food, fireworks display over river. Early July.

Taste of Hartford. *East Hartford Town Green, Constitution Plz, Hartford (06103). Phone 860/920-5337.www.tasteofhartford.com.* Four-day event features specialties of more than 50 area restaurants; continuous entertainment. Mid-June.

Limited-Service Hotels

★ ★ **CROWNE PLAZA.** *50 Morgan St, Hartford (06120). Phone 860/549-2400; toll-free 800/227-6963; fax 860/549-7844. www.crowneplaza.com.* 350 rooms, 18 story. Pets accepted, some restrictions; fee. Check-in 3 pm, check-out noon. Restaurant, bar. Fitness room. Outdoor pool. Airport transportation available. Business center. **$**
🔳 👤 🛏 🏃

★ ★ **HOLIDAY INN.** *363 Roberts St, East Hartford (06108). Phone 860/528-9611; toll-free 800/465-4329; fax 860/289-0270. www.holiday-inn.com.* 130 rooms, 5 story. Pets accepted; fee. Check-in 3 pm, check-out 11 am. High-speed Internet access, wireless Internet access. Restaurant, bar. Fitness room. Indoor pool. **$**
🔳 🔳 👤 🛏

Full-Service Hotels

★ ★ ★ **GOODWIN HOTEL.** *225 Asylum St, Hartford (06013). Phone 860/246-7500; toll-free 800/922-5006; fax 860/247-4576. www.goodwinhotel.com.* Visitors in the know stay at the sophisticated Goodwin Hotel. This luxury hotel is among Hartford's best, and its downtown location across from the Civic Center makes it a popular choice with business travelers. Built in 1881 for business tycoon J. P. Morgan, the red brick building was fashioned in the Queen Anne style. The rooms and suites have a masculine, clubby décor with mahogany furnishings, ruby red and hunter green colors, and striped patterns. The clubby appeal extends to the two restaurants, where patrons enjoy breakfast in the wood-paneled Pierpont's Restaurant and lunch and dinner in the casually elegant America's

Cup Bar & Lounge. 124 rooms, 6 story. Pets accepted; fee. Check-in 3 pm, check-out noon. Restaurant, bar. Fitness room. **$$**

★ ★ ★ **SHERATON HARTFORD HOTEL.** *100 E River Dr, East Hartford (06108). Phone 860/528-9703; toll-free 888/530-9703; fax 860/289-4728. www. sheraton.com.*199 rooms, 8 story. Pets accepted, some restrictions. Check-in 3 pm, check-out noon. Restaurant, bar. Indoor pool. **$$**

Restaurants

★ ★ **BUTTERFLY.** *831 Farmington Ave, West Hartford (06119). Phone 860/236-2816; fax 860/231-7911.* Chinese menu. Lunch, dinner, Sun brunch. Closed Thanksgiving. Bar. **$$**

★ ★ ★ **CARBONE'S.** *588 Franklin Ave, Hartford (06114). Phone 860/296-9646; fax 860/296-9145. www. carbonesct.com.* Hearty Italian dishes and friendly service have kept Carbone's a longtime Hartford favorite, as evidenced by the many autographed pictures of politicians, sports figures, and other satisfied customers that adorn the entrance. Italian menu. Lunch, dinner. Closed Sun. Bar. Casual attire. Reservations recommended. **$$$**

★ **HOT TOMATOES.** *1 Union Pl, Hartford (06103). Phone 860/249-5100; fax 860/524-8120.* A fun and eclectic restaurant with tomato-based pop art throughout the room, Hot Tomatoes is a great place to kick back with a group of friends. American menu. Lunch, dinner, late-night. Bar. Casual attire. Outdoor seating. **$$**

★ ★ ★ **MAX DOWNTOWN.** *185 Asylum St, Hartford (06103). Phone 860/522-2530; fax 860/246-5279. www.maxrestaurantgroup.com.* Hartford's busy downtown area is the setting for this sophisticated restaurant. Although popular with professionals from surrounding businesses and the nearby Capital Building, Max Downtown's extensive wine list, inventive New American menu, and upscale atmosphere is a perfect spot for a night out on the town. American menu. Lunch, dinner, late-night. Bar. Business casual attire. Reservations recommended. Valet parking. **$$$**

★ ★ **PASTIS.** *201 Ann St, Hartford (06103). Phone 860/278-8852; fax 860/278-8854.* Guests can enjoy intimate dining at this authentic French-style bistro, which offers spacious dining. Lace curtains, Toulouse-Lautrec reproductions, and tiled floors add to the Pa-

risian feel. French bistro menu. Lunch, dinner. Closed Sun. Bar. Casual attire. Reservations recommended. Valet parking. **$$**

★ ★ **PEPPERCORN'S GRILL.** *357 Main St, Hartford (06106). Phone 860/547-1714; fax 860/724-7612. www.peppercornsrestaurant.com.* This contemporary trattoria serves a menu of Italian favorites in a colorful and lively setting. Italian menu. Lunch, dinner, late-night. Closed Sun; also one week in summer. Bar. Business casual attire. Reservations recommended. Valet parking. Outdoor seating. **$$$**

★ **RESTAURANT BRICCO.** *78 LaSalle Rd, West Hartford (06903). Phone 860/233-0220; fax 860/233-7503. www.restaurantbricco.com.* Italian, Mediterranean menu. Lunch, dinner. Children's menu. Outdoor seating. **$$**

Kent (D-1)

See also Cornwall Bridge, New Preston

Population 2,918
Elevation 395 ft
Area Code 860
Zip 06757
Information Litchfield Hills Visitors Bureau, PO Box 968, Litchfield 06759; phone 860/567-4506
Web Site www.kentct.com

Kent, a small community near the western border of Connecticut, has become an art and antique center. Home to a large art colony, the surrounding area is characterized by massive hills that overlook the plain of the Housatonic River. The village of Kent was incorporated in 1738, after the tract of land was sold in a public auction. Although early development was based on agriculture, by the middle of the 19th century Kent was a booming industrial village with three iron furnaces operating in the area.

What to See and Do

Kent Falls State Park. *Hwy 7, Kent (06757). 5 miles N on Hwy 7. Phone 860/927-4100.* This 295-acre park is beautiful in spring when the stream is high and in fall when leaves are changing; 200-foot cascading waterfall. Stream fishing; hiking, picnicking. (Daily)

Macedonia Brook State Park. *159 Macedonia Brook Rd, Kent (06757). 2 miles E on Hwy 341, N on Macedonia Brook Rd. Phone 860/927-4100.* These 2,300 acres provide one of the state's finest nature study areas, as well as views of the Catskills and Taconic mountains. Trout-stocked stream fishing; hiking, picnicking, camping (late Apr-Sept) on 84 sites in open and wooded settings. (Daily) **FREE**

Sloane-Stanley Museum and Kent Furnace. *Rt 7, Kent (06757). 1 mile N on Hwy 7. Phone 860/927-3849.* New England barn houses Eric Sloane's collection of Early American tools, re-creation of his studio, artifacts, works; on site of old Kent furnace (1826); video presentation. (Mid-May-Oct, Wed-Sun) **$**

Special Event

Fall Festival. *Connecticut Antique Machinery Museum, Rte 7, Kent (06757). 1 mile N on Hwy 7. Phone 860/927-0050.* Exhibits include steam and traction engines, road roller (circa 1910), windmill; threshers; broom making, shingle sawing; antique cars, steamboats, tractors, and trucks. Late Sept.

Full-Service Inn

★ ★ ★ **FIFE 'N DRUM RESTAURANT & INN.** *53 N Main St, Kent (06757). Phone 860/927-3509; fax 860/927-4595. www.fifendrum.com.* 8 rooms. Check-in 2 pm, check-out 11 am. Restaurant, bar. **$$**

Restaurant

★ ★ ★ **FIFE 'N DRUM.** *53 N Main St, Kent (06757). Phone 860/927-3509; fax 860/927-4595. www. fifendrum.com.* Signed prints by the late, renowned artist Eric Sloane adorn the walls. International menu. Lunch, dinner, Sun brunch. Closed Tues; Dec 25. Bar. Children's menu. **$$**

Lakeville (C-1)

See also Cornwall Bridge, Norfolk

Settled 1740
Population 1,800
Elevation 764 ft
Area Code 860
Zip 06039
Information Litchfield Hills Visitors Bureau, PO Box 968, Litchfield 06759; phone 860/567-4506
Web Site www.litchfieldhills.com

Lakeville, located on Lake Wononscopomuc in the Litchfield Hills area, developed around a major blast furnace once owned by Ethan Allen. The furnace and nearby metals foundry cast many of the weapons used in the American Revolution as well as the guns for the USS *Constellation*. When the furnace was torn down in 1843, the first knife manufacturing factory was erected there. Nearby is the famous Hotchkiss School, a coed prep school.

What to See and Do

Holley House. *15 Millerton Rd, Lakeville (06039). Phone 860/435-2878.* Museums of 18th- and 19th-century history including 1768 iron-master's home with 1808 Classical Revival wing; Holley Manufacturing Company pocketknife exhibit from 1876; hands-on 1870s kitchen exhibit illustrating the debate over women's roles. 1876 Living History Tours (four tours daily). (Mid-June-Labor Day, Fri-Sat, and holiday afternoons; also by appointment) Also here is

> **Salisbury Cannon Museum.** *15 Millerton Rd, Lakeville (06039). Phone 860/435-2878.* Hands-on exhibits illustrate contributions of local iron industry to American Revolution. Includes ice house, cutting tools, outhouse, 19th-century heritage gardens, and Nature's Medicine Cabinet exhibit. (June-Labor Day, Sat-Sun; also by appointment) **FREE**

Special Events

Music Mountain Summer Music Festival. *Music Mountain Rd, Falls Village (06039). On Music Mountain, 5 miles NE via Hwy 44, 3 miles S on Hwy 126 to Falls Village, then 2 1/2 miles E on Hwy 126 to top of Music Mountain Rd. Phone 860/824-7126. www.musicmountain.org.* Performances by known ensembles and guest artists; also jazz series. Sat-Sun. Mid-June-early Sept.

Road Racing Classic. *497 Lime Rock Rd, Lakeville (06039). 2 miles S on Hwy 41, then 4 miles E on Hwy 112, at junction Hwy 7. Phone toll-free 800/722-3577. www.limerock.com.* The Mohegan Sun Grand Prix and NASCAR Busch North 200 events are held the same weekend racing fans should try to make time for this action-packed weekend of racing. Memorial Day weekend.

Limited-Service Hotel

★ ★ **INN AT IRON MASTERS.** *229 N Main St, Lakeville (06039). Phone 860/435-9844; fax 860/435-2254. www.innatironmasters.com.* 28 rooms. Pets accepted, some restrictions. Check-out 11 am. Restaurant, bar. Outdoor pool. **$**

Full-Service Resort

★ ★ ★ **INTERLAKEN INN.** *74 Interlaken Rd, Lakeville (06039). Phone 860/435-9878; toll-free 800/222-2909; fax 860/435-2980. www.interlakeninn. com.* 80 rooms, 2 story. Pets accepted, some restrictions; fee. Check-in 3 pm, check-out noon. Restaurant. Outdoor pool. Golf. Tennis. **$**

Specialty Lodging

WAKE ROBIN INN. *106 Sharon Rd, Lakeville (06039). Phone 860/435-2515; fax 860/435-2000. www. wakerobininn.com.* 39 rooms, 2 story. Pets accepted, some restrictions; fee. Check-in 3 pm, check-out noon. **$$**

Litchfield (D-2)

See also Bristol, Cornwall Bridge

Settled 1720
Population 8,365
Elevation 1,085 ft
Area Code 860
Zip 06759
Information Litchfield Hills Visitors Bureau, PO Box 968; phone 860/567-4506
Web Site www.litchfieldhills.com

Litchfield, on a plateau above the Naugatuck Valley, has preserved a semblance of the 18th century through both its many early homes and its air of peace and quiet. Because the railroads laid their main lines below in the valley, industry largely bypassed Litchfield. The Reverend Henry Ward Beecher and his sister, Harriet Beecher Stowe, author of *Uncle Tom's Cabin,* grew up in Litchfield. Tapping Reeve established the first law school in the country here in the late 18th century.

What to See and Do

Haight Vineyard and Winery. *29 Chestnut Hill Rd, Litchfield (06759). Phone 860/567-4045.* First Connecticut winery; one of the few to grow vinifera grapes in New England. Tours, tastings; vineyard walk, picnic tables; gift shop. (Daily; closed holidays) **FREE**

Litchfield History Museum. *7 South St, Litchfield (06759).* On the Green, at the junction of East and South sts. *Phone 860/567-4501. www.litchfieldhistoricalsociety.org.* Houses an outstanding collection of American art and artifacts from the 18th-21st centuries; research library, changing exhibits, video presentation. (Mid-Apr-Nov, Tues-Sun; closed holidays) **$**

Tapping Reeve House. *82 South St, Litchfield (06759). Phone 860/567-4501. www.litchfieldhistoricalsociety.org.* (1773) **And Law School** (1784). Introducing visitors to 19th-century Litchfield through the lives of the students who attended the Litchfield Law School and the Litchfield Female Academy; graduates include Aaron Burr and John C. Calhoun; garden. (Mid-Apr-Nov, Tues-Sun; closed July 4, Labor Day) **$**

Topsmead State Forest. *46 Chase Rd, Litchfield (06759). Phone 860/567-5694.* This 511-acre forest includes an English Tudor mansion overlooking a 40-acre wildlife preserve. Tours of the mansion (second and fourth weekends of June-Oct). **FREE**

White Memorial Foundation, Inc. *Hwy 202, Litchfield (06759).* 2 1/2 miles W on Hwy 202. *Phone 860/567-0857.* The 4,000-acre conservation area is contiguous with part of Bantam Lake shoreline (largest natural lake in the state), the Bantam River, and several small streams and ponds. Rolling woodland has wide variety of trees, flowers, ferns, mosses, 35 miles of trails; woodland birds, both nesting and in migration; and other woodland animals. The Conservation Center has displays and exhibits, extensive nature library with children's room (daily; fee). Swimming, fishing, boating; hiking trails, including a "trail of the senses," cross-country skiing, camping.

Special Event

Open House Tour. *39 Goshen Rd # B, Litchfield (06759). Phone 860/567-9423.* Tour of Litchfield's historic homes, special exhibits, tea, and luncheon. Early July. **$$$$**

Full-Service Inn

★ ★ ★ **LITCHFIELD INN.** *432 Bantam Rd, Litchfield (06759). Phone 860/567-4503; toll-free 800/499-3444; fax 860/567-5358. www.litchfieldinnct.com.* 32 rooms, 2 story. Complimentary continental breakfast. Check-in 3 pm, check-out 11 am. Restaurant, bar. **$**

Restaurants

★ **SEÑOR PANCHOS.** *7 Village Green Dr, Litchfield (06759). Phone 860/567-3663. www.senor-panchos.com.* Mexican menu. Lunch, dinner. Casual attire. **$$**

★ ★ **VILLAGE RESTAURANT.** *25 West St, Litchfield (06759). Phone 860/567-8307; fax 860/567-8450.* American menu. Lunch, dinner, Sun brunch. Closed Dec 25. Bar. Children's menu. **$$**

★ ★ ★ **WEST STREET GRILL.** *43 West St, Litchfield (06759). Phone 860/567-3885; fax 860/567-1374.* Owner James O'Shea has created the improbable: a trendy hot spot that appeals to both second-home New Yorkers as well as local residents. American menu. Lunch, dinner. Closed Dec 25. Bar. Children's menu. Reservations recommended. **$$$**

Madison (E-3)

See also Branford, Clinton, Guilford, New Haven

Settled 1649
Population 15,485
Elevation 22 ft
Area Code 203
Zip 06443
Information Chamber of Commerce, 22 Scotland Ave, PO Box 706; phone 203/245-7394; Tourism Office, 22 School St; phone 203/245-5659
Web Site www.madisonct.com

What to See and Do

Allis-Bushnell House and Museum. *853 Boston Post Rd, Madison (06443). Phone 203/245-4567.* (Circa 1785) Period rooms with four-corner fireplaces; doctor's office and equipment; exhibits of costumes, dolls, household implements, farming, fishing and shipbuilding tools; original paneling; herb garden. (May-Oct, Wed, Fri-Sat, limited hours; other times by appointment)**DONATION**

Deacon John Grave House. *571 Boston Post Rd, Madison (06443). Phone 203/245-4798.* Frame garrison colonial house (1685). (Memorial Day-Labor Day, Fri-Sun; spring and fall, weekends only) **$**

Hammonasset Beach State Park. *1288 Boston Post Rd, Madison (06443). 1 mile S of I-95, exit 62. Phone 203/245-2785.* More than 900 acres with a 2-mile long beach on Long Island Sound. Saltwater swimming, scuba diving, fishing, boating; hiking, picnicking (shelters), camping. Nature center.

Limited-Service Hotel

★ ★ **MADISON BEACH HOTEL.** *94 W Wharf Rd, Madison (06443-0546). Phone 203/245-1404; fax 203/245-0410. www.madisonbeachhotel.com.* 35 rooms, 4 story. Closed Jan-Feb. Pets accepted, some restrictions; fee. Complimentary continental breakfast. Check-in 2pm. Check-out 11 am. Restaurant, bar. **$**

Restaurants

★ ★ ★ **CAFE ALLEGRE.** *725 Boston Post Rd, Madison (06443). Phone 203/245-7773; fax 203/245-6256. www.allegrecafe.com.* Italian menu. Lunch, dinner. Closed Mon; Jan 1, Dec 25. Bar. Children's menu. **$$**

★ ★ **FRIENDS AND COMPANY.** *11 Boston Post Rd, Madison (06443). Phone 203/245-0462; fax 203/245-4396.* Seafood, steak menu. Dinner, Sun brunch. Closed Thanksgiving, Dec 25; last Mon in June. Bar. Children's menu. **$$**

Manchester (D-4)

See also Hartford, Storrs, Vernon, Windsor

Settled 1672
Population 51,618
Elevation 272 ft
Area Code 860
Zip 06040
Information Greater Manchester Chamber of Commerce, 20 Hartford Rd; phone 860/646-2223
Web Site www.manchesterchamber.com

The "city of village charm" has the peaceful air of another era, with great trees and 18th-century houses. Manchester, once the silk capital of the Western world, is still a major manufacturing center with more than 100 industries—many, more than a century old.

What to See and Do

Cheney Homestead. *106 Hartford Rd, Manchester (06040). Phone 860/643-5588.* (Circa 1780) Birthplace of the brothers that launched the state's once-promising silk industry; built by Timothy Cheney, clockmaker. Paintings and etchings, early 19th-century furniture; replica of schoolhouse. (Fri-Sun) **$**

Connecticut Firemen's Historical Society Fire Museum. *230 Pine St, Manchester (06040). Phone 860/649-9436.* Located in a 1901 firehouse, this museum exhibits antique firefighting equipment and memorabilia; leather fire buckets, hoses, and helmets, hand-pulled engines, horse-drawn hose wagon, old prints and lithographs. (Mid-Apr-mid-Nov, Fri-Sun) **DONATION**

Lutz Children's Museum. *247 S Main St, Manchester (06040). Phone 860/643-0949. www.lutzmuseum.org.* Houses participatory exhibits on natural and physical science, art, ethnology, and history; live animal exhibit. (Tues-Sun; closed holidays) **$**

Oak Grove Nature Center. *Oak Grove St, Manchester (06040). Phone 860/647-3321.* More than 50 acres of woods, fields, stream, pond; trails. (Daily) **FREE**

Wickham Park. *1329 W Middle Tpke, Manchester (06040). Entrance on Hwy 44, off I-84 exit 60.Phone 860/528-0856.* More than 200 acres with gardens, including ornamental, woods, ponds; log cabin (refreshments weekends); playgrounds, picnic areas; nature center; aviary and small zoo; tennis courts, softball fields (Apr-Oct, daily). **$**

Limited-Service Hotels

★ **BEST VALUE INN-MANCHESTER.** *400 Tolland Tpke, Manchester (06040). Phone 860/643-1555; toll-free 888/315-2378; fax 860/643-1881. www.bestvalueinn.com.* 31 rooms. Check-out 11 am. **$**
🅱

★ **CLARION HOTEL.** *191 Spencer St, Manchester (06040). Phone 860/643-5811; toll-free 800/992-4004; fax 860/646-3341. www.clarionsuites.com.* 104 rooms, 2 story, all suites. Pets accepted; fee. Complimentary full breakfast. Check-out noon. Fitness room. Outdoor pool, whirlpool. **$**
🅱 ➘ 🧍 ✈ 🌊

Restaurants

★ ★ ★ **CAVEY'S FRENCH RESTAURANT.** *45 E Center St, Manchester (06040). Phone 860/643-2751; fax 860/649-0344.* French menu. Dinner. Closed Sun-Mon; holidays. Bar. **$$$**
🅱

★ ★ ★ **CAVEY'S ITALIAN RESTAURANT.** *45 E Center St, Manchester (06040). Phone 860/643-2751; fax 860/649-0344.* Italian menu. Dinner. Closed Sun-Mon; holidays. Bar. **$$**

Meriden (E-3)

See also Branford, Bristol, Hartford, Middletown, New Britain, New Haven, Waterbury

Settled 1661
Population 59,479
Elevation 144 ft
Area Code 203
Zip 06450
Information Greater Meriden Chamber of Commerce, 3 Colony St, 06451; phone 203/235-7901
Web Site www.meridenchamber.com

Located in the heart of the central Connecticut Valley, Meriden was named after Meriden Farm in Warwickshire, England. Once called the "silver city of the world" because its principal business was the manufacture of silver products, Meriden now has a broad industrial base.

What to See and Do

Castle Craig Tower. *Hubbard Park, W Main St, Meriden. 2 miles W on I-691/Hwy 66.* Road leads to tower atop East Peak, site of Easter sunrise services. (May-Oct)

Mount Southington Ski Area. *396 Mount Vernon Rd, Southington (06479). Approximately 10 miles W, 1/2 mile W of I-84 exit 30, at Mount Vernon Rd. Phone 860/628-0954; fax 860/621-1833. www.mountsouthington.com.* Triple, double chairlifts, two T-bars, two handle tows, J-bar; snowmaking, patrol, school, rentals; cafeteria, lounge. Fourteen trails; longest run approximately 1 mile; vertical drop 425 feet. Night skiing. (Dec-Mar, daily) **$$$$**

Solomon Goffe House. *667 N Colony St, Meriden (06489). Phone 203/237-6629.* (1711) Gambrel-roofed house features period furnishings, artifacts. Costumed guides. (Apr-Nov: first Sun of month) **$**

Special Events

Apple Harvest Festival. *51 N Main St, Southington (06489). 3 miles S on Hwy 120, on Town Green. Phone 860/276-8461. www.appleharvestfestival.com.* Street festival celebrating local apple harvest. Carnival, arts and crafts, parade, road race, food booths, entertainment. Two weekends in Sept-Oct.

Daffodil Festival. *Hubbard Park, W Main St, Meriden (06450). Phone 203/630-4259.* Approximately 500,000 daffodils in bloom; various events. Mid-Apr.

Limited-Service Hotels

★ **HAMPTON INN.** *10 Bee St, Meriden (06450). Phone 203/235-5154; toll-free 800/426-4329; fax 203/235-7139. www.hamptoninn.com.* 125 rooms, 4 story. Complimentary continental breakfast. Check-in 3 pm, check-out noon. High-speed Internet access. **$**

★ **HOLIDAY INN EXPRESS.** *120 Laning St, Southington (06489). Phone 860/276-0736; toll-free 800/465-4329; fax 860/276-9405. www.holiday-inn. com.* 122 rooms, 3 story. Complimentary continental breakfast. Check-in 3 pm, check-out 11 am. High-speed Internet access. Fitness room. Outdoor pool. **$**

★ ★ **RAMADA PLAZA HOTEL AND CONFER-ENCE CENTER.** *275 Research Pkwy, Meriden (06450). Phone 203/238-2380; fax 203/238-3172. www.ramada. com.* 150 rooms, 6 story. Check-in 3 pm, check-out noon. High-speed Internet access. Restaurant, bar. Fitness room. Indoor pool. Business center. **$**

Middletown (D-3)

See also East Haddam, Essex, Hartford, Meriden

Settled 1650
Population 42,762
Elevation 51 ft
Area Code 860
Zip 06457
Information Connecticut River Valley & Shoreline Visitors Council, 393 Main St; phone 860/347-0028 or toll-free 800/486-3346
Web Site www.visitctriver.com

On the Connecticut River between Hartford and New Haven, Middletown was once an important shipping point for trade with the West Indies. The first official pistol-maker to the US Government, Simeon North, had his factory here in 1799. Today, Middletown boasts diversified industry and one of the longest and widest main streets in New England.

What to See and Do

Powder Ridge Ski Area. *99 Powder Hill Rd, Middlefield (06457). 5 miles SW off Hwy 147. Phone 860/349-3454. www.powderridgect.com.* Quad, three double chairlifts, handletow; patrol, school, rentals; snowmaking; bar, restaurant, cafeteria; nursery. Fourteen trails; vertical drop 500 feet. (Nov-Apr, daily) **$$$$**

Wadsworth Falls State Park. *721 Wadsworth St, Middletown (06457). 3 miles SW off Hwy 66, on Hwy 157. Phone 860/424-3200.* These 285 acres surround Wadsworth Falls and lookout. Pond swimming, stream fishing; hiking along wooded area with mountain laurel display, picnicking. Beautiful waterfall with overlook.

Special Event

Durham Fair. *Fairgrounds, Jct of Hwys 68, 17 and 79, Durham (06422). Phone 860/349-9495. www.durham-fair.com.* State's largest agricultural fair. Last weekend in Sept.

Limited-Service Hotel

★ ★ **CROWNE PLAZA HOTEL HARTFORD-CROMWELL.** *100 Berlin Rd, Cromwell (06416). Phone 860/635-2000; fax 860/635-3970.* Located in the greater Hartford area, this is the area's premier hotel. 211 rooms, 4 story. Check-out noon. Restaurant, bar. Fitness room. Indoor pool, whirlpool. **$**

Milford (E-2)

See also Branford, Bridgeport, Fairfield, New Haven, Stratford

Settled 1639
Population 49,938
Elevation 89 ft
Area Code 203
Zip 06460
Information Milford Chamber of Commerce, 5 Broad St; phone 203/878-0681
Web Site www.milfordct.com

What to See and Do

Milford Historical Society Wharf Lane Complex. *34 High St, Milford (06460). Phone 203/874-2664.* Three historical houses include Eells-Stow House (circa 1700), believed to be oldest house in Milford and featuring unusual "dog sled" stairway; Stockade House (circa 1780), first house built outside the city's early stockade; and Bryan-Downs House (circa 1785), two-story Early American structure housing more than 400 Native American artifacts spanning more than 10,000 years. (Memorial Day-Columbus Day, Sat-Sun; also by appointment)

Special Event

Oyster Festival. *Milford (06460). Milford town green. Phone 203/878-5363.* Arts and crafts exhibits, races, boat tours; games, food; entertainment. Mid-Aug.

Limited-Service Hotel

★ **HAMPTON INN.** *129 Plains Rd, Milford (06460). Phone 203/874-4400; toll-free 800/426-7866; fax 203/874-5348. www.hamptoninn.com.* 148 rooms, 3 story. Check-in 3 pm, check-out noon. High-speed Internet access. **$**

Restaurants

★ **ALDARIO'S.** *240 Naugatuck Ave, Milford (06460). Phone 203/874-6096; fax 203/874-5579. www.aldarios. com.* Italian menu. Lunch, dinner. Closed Mon; holidays. Bar. Children's menu. **$$**

★ ★ **SCRIBNER'S.** *31 Village Rd, Milford (06460). Phone 203/878-7019; fax 203/878-2238. www.scrib-nersrestaurant.com.* Seafood, steak menu. Dinner. Closed holidays. Bar. Children's menu. **$$**

Mystic (E-5)

See also Groton, New London, Norwich, Stonington

Settled 1654
Population 2,618
Elevation 16 ft
Area Code 860
Zip 06355
Information Tourist Information Center, Building 1D, Olde Mistick Village; phone 860/536-1641; or Connecticut's Mystic & More!, 32 Huntington St, PO Box 89, New London 06320; phone 860/444-2206 or toll-free 800/863-6569 (outside CT)
Web Site www.mysticcountry.com

The community of Mystic, divided by the Mystic River, was a shipbuilding and whaling center from the 17th to the 19th centuries. It derives its name from the Pequot, "Mistuket."

What to See and Do

Denison Homestead. *120 Pequotsepos Rd, Mystic (06355). 2 miles E of I-95 exit 90, on Pequotsepos Rd. Phone 860/536-9248.* (1717) Restored in the style of five eras (18th to mid-20th centuries); furnished with the heirlooms of 11 generations of a single family. Guided tour (mid-May-mid-Oct, Thurs-Mon afternoons; rest of year, by appointment). **$**

Denison Pequotsepos Nature Center. *109 Pequotsepos Rd, Mystic (06355). 2 miles NE of I-95 exit 90. Phone 860/536-1216. www.dpnc.org.* An environmental education center and natural history museum active in wildlife rehabilitation. The 125-acre sanctuary has more than 7 miles of trails; family nature walks, films, lectures. (Daily; closed holidays) **$$**

Mystic Aquarium. *55 Coogan Blvd, Mystic (06355). Phone 860/572-5955. www.mysticaquarium.org.* The exhibits here feature more than 6,000 live specimens from all the world's waters. Demonstrations with dolphins, sea lions, and the only whales in New England delight young and old alike, as do Seal Island, an outdoor exhibit of seals and sea lions in natural settings, and the penguin pavilion. The facility also includes Dr. Robert Ballards Institute for Exploration, which is dedicated to searching the deep seas for lost ships. The museums Challenge of the Deep exhibit allows patrons to use state-of-the-art technology to re-create the search for the *Titanic* or explore the biology of undersea ocean vents. (Daily; hours vary by season; closed Jan 1, Thanksgiving, Dec 25) **$$$$**

⭐ **Mystic Seaport.** *75 Greenmanville Ave (Hwy 27), Mystic (06355). 1 mile S of I-95 exit 90. Phone 860/572-5315. www.visitmysticseaport.com.* This 17-acre complex is the nation's largest maritime museum, dedicated to preservation of 19th-century maritime history. Visitors may board the 1841 wooden whaleship *Charles W. Morgan*, square-rigged ship *Joseph Conrad*, or fishing schooner *L.A. Dunton.* Collection also includes some 400 smaller vessels; representative seaport community with historic homes and waterfront industries, some staff in 19th-century costume; exhibits, demonstrations, working shipyard; children's museum, planetarium (fee), 1908 steamboat cruises (May-Oct, daily; fee); restaurants; shopping; special events throughout the year. (Daily; closed Dec 25) **$$$$**

Olde Mistick Village. *Coogan Blvd and Hwy 27, Mystic (06355). Phone 860/536-4941. www.oldemistickvillage. com.* More than 60 shops and restaurants in 1720s-style New England village, on 22 acres; duck pond, millwheel, waterfalls; entertainment, carillon (May-Oct, Sat-Sun). Village (daily). **FREE**

Special Event

Lobsterfest. *Mystic Seaport, 75 Greenmanville Ave, Mystic (06355). Phone 860/572-5315. www.visitmystic-seaport.com.* Outdoor food festival. Late May.

Limited-Service Hotel

★ **COMFORT INN.** *48 Whitehall Ave, Mystic (06355). Phone 860/572-8531; toll-free 800/572-9339; fax 860/572-9358. www.comfortinn.com.* This no-frills and convenient property is perfect for an overnight stay. Guest rooms have Internet access, and a complimentary continental breakfast is offered. The pool is shared with the Days Inn next door. 120 rooms, 2 story. Complimentary continental breakfast. Check-in 3 pm, check-out 11 am. High-speed Internet access, wireless Internet access. Fitness room. **$$**

Full-Service Hotel

★★★ **HILTON MYSTIC.** *20 Coogan Blvd, Mystic (06355). Phone 860/572-0731; toll-free 800/774-1500; fax 860/572-0328. www.hilton.com.* Conveniently located on a side road close to Olde Mystic Village, just a block from I-95, this business-oriented hotel has a vaguely nautical theme. Several popular attractions, including the Mystic Seaport Museum, outlet shopping, and the Mystic Aquarium, are nearby. 183 rooms, 4 story. Check-in 3 pm, check-out 11 am. High-speed Internet access, wireless Internet access. Restaurant, bar. Children's activity center. Fitness room. Indoor pool. **$$**

Full-Service Inns

★★★ **INN AT MYSTIC.** *Hwys 1 and 27, Mystic (06355). Phone 860/536-9604; toll-free 800/237-2415; fax 860/572-1635. www.innatmystic.com.* A variety of accommodations are available at this five-building property, the only inn in Connecticut that overlooks both Mystic Harbor and Long Island Sound. The Gatehouse, East Wing, and two modern hotels (collectively called the Main House) are spread over the inn's 15 acres, but sitting like a jewel at the crest of the hill is the 1904 Classical Revival mansion that is known not just for its elegance, but also as the place where Lauren Bacall and Humphrey Bogart honeymooned.

Mansion rooms are decorated with period furnishings and designer fabrics, have whirlpools, overlook the orchard and grounds, and are for adults only. The East Wing and Gatehouse, also for adults only, are similarly decorated, while the Main House, beautifully appointed with antiques or antique reproductions, has accommodations for couples and families. 68 rooms, 2 story. Pets accepted. Check-in 3 pm, check-out 11 am. Restaurant, bar. Outdoor pool. Tennis. **$$**

★★★ **WHALER'S INN.** *20 E Main St, Mystic (06355). Phone 860/536-1506; toll-free 800/243-2588; fax 860/572-1250.www.whalersinnmystic.com.*Homey, comfortable, and located in the heart of historic Mystic, the Whaler's Inn is designed for guests who want New England ambience with a bed-and-breakfast feel. You can almost see the sea captain rising from his rocking chair on the front porch of the 1865 colonial clapboard mansion as you approach, ready to greet you; inside, modern-day innkeepers take you to your guest room, where Waverly fabrics and wall coverings, a four-poster bed, wing-back chair, and large bathroom with pedestal sinks and whirlpool tub makes your stay cozy and comfortable. Each of the inns eight guest rooms has a breathtaking view of the scenic Mystic River and bascule drawbridge. And that makes a decision about whether to leave that comfy chair on your veranda (most rooms have them) and go down to a bountiful breakfast or take a five-minute walk into town rather difficult. 49 rooms, 2 story. Complimentary continental breakfast. Check-in 3 pm, check-out 11 am. Restaurant, bar. **$$**

Specialty Lodging

THE OLD MYSTIC INN. *52 Main St, Old Mystic (06372). Phone 860/572-9422; fax 860/572-9954. www.oldmysticinn.com.* Built in 1784, the main house is Colonial architecture and is set in a serene neighborhood a few miles from downtown Mystic. The main house has guest rooms on both floors which feature Early American décor, antiques, private baths, and fireplaces. The carriage house (built in 1988), sits behind the main house. Its four guest rooms all have private entrances, private baths, fireplaces, and are equipped with Internet access. A complimentary gourmet breakfast is offered each morning to start the day off right. 8 rooms, 2 story. Children over 15 years only. Complimentary full breakfast. Check-in 2 pm, check-out 11 am. **$$**

Restaurants

★ ★ ★ **BRAVO BRAVO.** *20 E Main St, Mystic (06355). Phone 860/536-3228. www.whalersinnmystic. com.* This local favorite, located on the premises of the Whaler's Inn (see) and close to the water, serves creative gourmet dishes. The dining room is fresh and bright with floor-to-ceiling windows. Italian menu. Lunch, dinner. Bar. Casual attire. Reservations recommended. **$$**

★ ★ ★ **FLOOD TIDE.** *Jct Hwy 1 and Hwy 27, Mystic (06355). Phone 860/536-8140; toll-free 800/237-2415; fax 860/572-1635. www.mysticinns.com.* Complimentary hors d'oeuvres are served in the piano lounge at this waterfront restaurant. The gourmet dishes, Sunday brunch, and harbor views are all impressive. American, Continental menu. Lunch, dinner, Sun brunch. Bar. Children's menu. Casual attire. Reservations recommended. Outdoor seating. **$$$**

★ ★ **GO FISH.** *Olde Mystic Village, Mystic (06355). Phone 860/536-2662; fax 860/536-4619.* Olde Mystic Village is home to this comfortable restaurant, where fish lovers can find everything from clam chowder to sushi. Seafood menu. Lunch, dinner. Bar. Casual attire. Reservations recommended. **$$**

★ **MYSTIC PIZZA.** *56 W Main St, Mystic (06355). Phone 860/536-3700. www.mysticpizza.com.* This is the popular pizza parlor immortalized in the Julia Roberts film of the same name. Many photos of the scenes shot from the movie are here. Pizza. Lunch, dinner. Casual attire. **$**

★ ★ **SEAMEN'S INNE.** *105 Greenmanville Ave, Mystic (06355). Phone 860/572-5303; fax 860/572-5304. www.seamensinne.com.* This nautical, historic restaurant is conveniently located next to the Mystic Aquarium and overlooking the Mystic River. American, seafood menu. Lunch, dinner. Bar. Children's menu. Casual attire. Reservations recommended. Outdoor seating. **$$**

New Britain (D-3)

See also Bristol, Farmington, Hartford, Meriden, Waterbury, Wethersfield

Settled 1686
Population 75,491
Elevation 179 ft
Area Code 860
Information Chamber of Commerce, 1 Court St, 06051; phone 860/229-1665; or the River Valley Central Regional Tourism District 860/244-8181
Web Site www.visitctriver.com

This is the "hardware city." Production of sleigh bells and farm tools began about 1800, followed by locks and saddlery hardware. Many tool, hardware, and machinery manufacturers, including The Stanley Works, organized in 1843, are headquartered in New Britain.

What to See and Do

Central Connecticut State University. *1615 Stanley St, New Britain (06050). Phone 860/832-2278; toll-free 888/733-2278. www.ccsu.edu.* (1849) (14,000 students) On campus is Copernican Planetarium and Observatory, featuring one of the largest public telescopes in the United States; planetarium shows (Fri-Sat; children's shows Sat) **$$**

New Britain Museum of American Art. *56 Lexington St, New Britain (06052). Phone 860/229-0257.* Works by outstanding American artists from 1740 to the present; works by Whistler, Church, Sargent, Wyeth; Thomas Hart Benton murals; Sanford Low Collection of American illustrations; Charles and Elizabeth Buchanan Collection of American impressionists. (Tues-Sun afternoons; closed holidays) **$$**

New Britain Youth Museum. *30 High St, New Britain (06051). Phone 860/225-3020.* Exhibits of Americana, cultures of other nations, circus miniatures, dolls, hands-on displays. (June-Aug: Mon-Fri; rest of year: Tues-Sat) **$**

Special Event

Baseball. *New Britain Stadium, 230 John Karbonic Way, New Britain (06051). Phone 860/224-8383. www. rockcats.com.* New Britain Rock Cats (AA team). Mid-Apr-Sept.

Dozynki Polish Harvest Festival. *8437 Valley Pike, New Britain (06053). Phone 860/826-9020.* Street dancing; polka bands; cultural displays; beer, singing, ethnic food; pony and hayrides; Polish arts and crafts. Third weekend in Aug.

Restaurant

★ **EAST SIDE.** *131 Dwight St, New Britain (06051). Phone 860/223-1188; fax 860/827-0327. www.eastsiderestaurant.com.* American, German menu. Lunch, dinner. Closed Mon; July 4, Dec 25. Bar. Children's menu. **$$**

New Canaan (F-1)

See also Norwalk, Ridgefield, Stamford

Founded 1801
Population 17,864
Elevation 300 ft
Area Code 203
Zip 06840
Information Chamber of Commerce, 111 Elm St; phone 203/966-2004
Web Site www.newcanaanchamber.com

New Canaan was settled in 1731 as Canaan Parish, a church society encompassing parts of Norwalk and Stamford. A quiet residential community situated on high ridges, New Canaan has retained its rural character despite its proximity to industrial areas.

What to See and Do

New Canaan Historical Society. *13 Oenoke Ridge Rd, New Canaan (06840). Phone 203/966-1776.* The First Town House (original town hall) has costume museum, library, and Cody Drugstore (1845), a restoration of the town's first pharmacy; on grounds of Hanford-Silliman House Museum (circa 1765) are a tool museum, hand press, one-room schoolhouse, and sculptor John Roger's studio and museum. Town House (Tues-Sat). Other buildings (by appointment).

New Canaan Nature Center. *144 Oenoke Ridge Rd, New Canaan (06840). Phone 203/966-9577.* More than 40 acres of woodland, ponds, and meadows; discovery center with hands-on exhibits; suburban ecology exhibits; solar greenhouse; cider house, and maple sugar shed; herb and wildflower gardens; trails, marsh boardwalk; animals. Grounds (daily). Buildings (Mon-Sat; closed holidays). **FREE**

Silvermine Guild Arts Center. *1037 Silvermine Rd, New Canaan (06840). Phone 203/966-5618.* Art center in rustic 6-acre setting has a school of the arts and three galleries with changing exhibits by member artists and artisans; invitational and juried exhibitions; many educational events and programs. (Tues-Sun; closed Jan 1, Thanksgiving, Dec 25)

Full-Service Inn

★ ★ ★ **ROGER SHERMAN INN.** *195 Oenoke Ridge, New Canaan (06840). Phone 203/966-4541; fax 203/966-0503. www.rogershermaninn.com.* Built in 1740, this colonial landmark is top notch when it comes to attentive service. The guest rooms are romantic and the dining is superb. 18 rooms, 2 story. Pets accepted, some restrictions. Complimentary continental breakfast. Check-in 2 pm, check-out 11 am. Restaurant. **$**

New Haven (E-3)

See also Branford, Clinton, Guilford, Madison, Meriden, Milford

Settled 1638
Population 130,474
Elevation 25 ft
Area Code 203
Information Greater New Haven Convention & Visitors Bureau, 169 Orange St, first floor, 06510; phone 203/777-8550 or toll-free 800/332-7829
Web Site www.newhavencvb.org

New Haven is only 75 miles from New York City, but it is typical New England. Its colorful history is built into the stones and timbers of the area. Here, Eli Whitney worked out the principle of interchangeable parts for mass production. Around the corner, Nathan Hale roomed as a student, not far from where Noah Webster compiled the first dictionary. In addition to all this, Yale University puts New Haven on any list of the world's cultural centers.

Northwest of New Haven is a 400-foot red sandstone cliff called West Rock. In 1661 three Cromwellian judges, who had ordered Charles I beheaded, took refuge here from the soldiers of Charles II.

What to See and Do

Amistad Memorial. *165 Church St, New Haven (06510). In front of City Hall.* This 14-foot bronze relief sculpture is a unique three-sided form. Each side depicts a significant episode of the life of Joseph Cinque, one of 50 Africans kidnapped from Sierra Leone and slated for sale in Cuba in 1839. After secretly rerouting the slave ship to Long Island Sound, the battle for the would-be slaves' freedom ensued in New Haven. Two years later, their victory was complete. Ed Hamilton sculpted this important piece.

East Rock Park. *Orange and Cold Spring sts, New Haven (06511). 1 mile NE at foot of Orange St, on E Rock Rd. Phone 203/946-6086.* City's largest park includes

Pardee Rose Gardens, bird sanctuary, hiking trails, athletic fields, tennis courts, picnic grounds. Excellent view of harbor and Long Island Sound. (Daily) **FREE**

Fort Nathan Hale Park and Black Rock Fort. *36 Woodward Ave, New Haven (06510).* Here, Federal guns kept British warships out of the harbor in 1812. Old Black Rock Fort, from Revolutionary War days, has been restored, and archaeological excavations are in progress. Fort Nathan Hale, from the Civil War era, also has been reconstructed. Both offer spectacular views of the harbor. Picnicking. Group guided tours (Memorial Day-Labor Day, daily).

The Green. *Church and Elm sts, New Haven (06510).* In 1638, these 16 acres were laid out, making New Haven the first planned city in America. On the town common are three churches--United (1813), Trinity Episcopal (1814), and Center Congregational (1813), which is one of the masterpieces of American Georgian architecture. **FREE**

Grove Street Cemetery. *227 Grove St, New Haven (06510).* First cemetery in the United States divided into family plots. Buried here are Noah Webster, Charles Goodyear, Eli Whitney, and many early settlers of the area. **FREE**

Lighthouse Point Park. *2 Lighthouse Rd, New Haven (06510). End of Lighthouse Rd, 5 miles SE off I-95, exit 50. Phone 203/946-8005.* This 82-acre park on Long Island Sound has a lighthouse built in 1840; restored antique carousel (fee); bird sanctuary. Beach, bathhouse, playfield, picnic facilities, boat ramp. (Daily) Parking fee (Memorial Day-Labor Day). **$$**

New Haven Colony Historical Society Museum. *114 Whitney Ave, New Haven (06510). Phone 203/562-4183.* Museum of local history; special exhibits; also research library (fee). (Tues-Sat; closed holidays) **$**

Shore Line Trolley Museum. *17 River St, East Haven (06512). 5 miles E via I-95 exit 51 or 52. Phone 203/467-6927. www.bera.org.* Collection of trolley, interurban, and rapid-transit cars from 15 states and Canada. A National Historic Site. Cars on display include pre-1900 trolleys (1893, 1899), the first commercially produced electric locomotive (1888), and a trolley parlor car. Exhibits on electric railways. Scenic trolley ride in authentic, restored cars; operator narrates on tour of display buildings and restoration shop; trolleys depart every 30 minutes (inquire for schedule). Picnic grove (May-Oct); gift shop; special events. (Memorial Day-Labor Day: daily; May, Sept-

Oct, Dec: weekends and holidays; Apr and Nov: Sun only) **$$**

Shubert Performing Arts Center. *247 College St, New Haven (06510). Phone 203/562-5666; toll-free 888/736-2663.* Full-service performing arts venue opened in 1914. Known as the "Birthplace of the Nation's Greatest Hits." Home to dance, musical, comedy, and dramatic performances. (Sept-June)

West Rock Nature Center. *1020 Wintergreen Ave, Hamden (06514). 1 mile N of Southern Connecticut State University. Phone 203/946-8016.* Nature center features native Connecticut wildlife in outdoor bird and mammal sections; indoor nature house with reptiles and other displays. Hiking trails; picnic areas. (Mon-Fri; closed holidays) **FREE**

★ **Yale University.** *149 Elm St, New Haven (06511). On N side of New Haven Green. Phone 203/432-2300. www.yale.edu.* (1701) (10,000 students) Founded by ten Connecticut ministers and named for Elihu Yale, an early donor to the school. In September, 1969, the undergraduate school became coeducational. Walking tours conducted daily by undergraduate students. Hear about Yale's rich 300-year history. See the school's distinctive architecture and visit both Sterling Memorial Library and the Beinecke Rare Book Library. Tours leave from Yale Visitor Center. Weekdays 10:30 am, 2 pm; Sat-Sun 1:30 pm (free). Of special interest are

Beinecke Rare Book and Manuscript Library. *121 Wall St, New Haven (06511). Best approach is from College St via Cross Campus Walk, on High St. Phone 203/432-2977.* Exhibits of famous collections, Gutenberg Bible. (Sept-July: Mon-Sat; Aug: Mon-Fri; closed holidays) **FREE**

Collection of Musical Instruments. *15 Hillhouse Ave, New Haven (06511). Phone 203/432-0822.* Total holdings of 850 musical instruments; permanent displays and changing exhibits; lectures, concerts, special events. (Sept-June, Tues-Thurs afternoons; closed school holidays) Under 14 only with adult. **$**

Old Campus. *149 Elm St, New Haven (06511). Phone 203/432-2300.* Where Nathan Hale (class of 1773) roomed. One-hour guided walking tours (Mon-Fri, one tour morning, one tour afternoon; Sat-Sun, one tour afternoon). Inquire at Visitor Information Office. **FREE**

Peabody Museum of Natural History. *170 Whitney Ave, New Haven (06511). Whitney Ave at Sachem St.Phone 203/432-5050.* Exhibits on mammals, invertebrate life, Plains and Connecticut Native Americans, meteorites, minerals and rocks, birds of Connecticut; several life-size dinosaur exhibits include a brontosaurus (60-feet long) reconstructed from original fossil material; dioramas of North American flora and fauna; weekend films (free). (Daily; closed holidays) **$$**

Yale Art Gallery. *1111 Chapel St, New Haven (06511). Chapel St at York St. Phone 203/432-0600.* Collections include Italian Renaissance paintings, American paintings and decorative arts, ancient art, African sculpture, Near and Far Eastern art, and European paintings from the 13th-20th centuries. (Tues-Sat, also Sun afternoons; closed holidays) **FREE**

Yale Bowl. *Central Ave, New Haven (06511). 2 miles W on Chapel St.Phone 203/432-4747.* An Ivy League football mecca.

Yale Center for British Art. *1080 Chapel St, New Haven (06511). Phone 203/432-2800.* British paintings, prints, drawings, sculpture, and rare books from Elizabethan period to present. Reference library and photo archive. Lectures, tours, films, concerts. (Tues-Sun; closed holidays) **FREE**

Special Events

International Festival of Arts and Ideas. *195 Church St, New Haven (06511). Phone 203/498-1212; toll-free 888/278-4332. www.artidea.org.* Celebration of the arts and humanities. Late June.

Long Wharf Theatre. *222 Sargent Dr, New Haven (06511). I-95 exit 46. Phone 203/787-4282.* Features new plays as well as classics. Sept-June.

New Haven Symphony Orchestra. *Woolsey Hall, College and Grove sts, New Haven (06511). Phone 203/776-1444.* Series of concerts by leading artists. Oct-May.

Pilot Pen International Tennis Tournament. *Connecticut Tennis Center, Central Ave, New Haven (06511). Near Yale Bowl. Phone toll-free 888/997-4568.* Championship Series on the ATP tour. Mid-Aug.

Yale Repertory Theater. *1120 Chapel St, New Haven (06511). Phone 203/432-1234; toll-free 800/833-8134. www.yale.edu/yalerep.* The Yale Repertory Theater prides itself on creating bold and passionate theatri-

cal productions. The troupe successfully trains artistic leaders, proven by the fact that four of their productions have won the Pulitzer Prize. Early Oct-mid-May.

Limited-Service Hotels

★ ★ **THE COLONY.** *1157 Chapel St, New Haven (06511). Phone 203/776-1234; toll-free 800/458-8810; fax 203/772-3929. www.colonyatyale.com.*86 rooms, 4 story. Check-in 3 pm, check-out noon. Restaurant. Airport transportation available. **$**

★ ★ **COURTYARD BY MARRIOTT.** *30 Whalley Ave, New Haven (06511). Phone 203/777-6221; toll-free 800/228-9290; fax 203/772-1089. www.courtyard.com.*160 rooms, 8 story. Check-out noon. Restaurant, bar. Outdoor pool. **$**🅳 🏊

Full-Service Hotel

★ ★ ★ **OMNI NEW HAVEN HOTEL.** *155 Temple St, New Haven (06510). Phone 203/772-6664; toll-free 800/843-6664; fax 203/974-6777. www.omnihotels.com.* 306 rooms, 25 story. Pets accepted, some restrictions; fee. Check-in 3 pm, check-out noon. Restaurant, bar. Fitness room. Indoor pool, whirlpool. Business center. **$$**
🔊 🏋 🏊 🚶

Specialty Lodging

THREE CHIMNEYS. *1201 Chapel St, New Haven (06511). Phone 203/789-1201; toll-free 800/443-1554; fax 203/776-7363. www.threechimneysinn.com.* This lovely historic inn, built in the 1870s, is one block from Yale University. Guest rooms provide luxurious comfort featuring canopy beds with Edwardian bed drapes. 11 rooms, 3 story. Complimentary full breakfast. Check-in 3 pm, check-out 11 am. **$$**

Restaurant

★ **INDOCHINE PAVILLION.** *1180 Chapel St, New Haven (06511). Phone 203/865-5033; fax 203/865-6495.* Vietnamese menu. Lunch, dinner. Closed holidays. Bar. **$$**

New London (E-5)

See also Groton, Mystic, Norwich, Old Lyme, Old Saybrook, Stonington

Settled 1646
Population 28,540
Elevation 33 ft
Area Code 860
Zip 06320
Information Connecticut's Mystic & More!, 32 Huntington St, PO Box 89; phone 860/444-2206 or toll-free 800/863-6569
Web Site www.mysticcountry.com

New London is a seagoing community and always has been; it has one of the finest deep-water ports on the Atlantic coast. From the first days of the republic into the 20th century, whalers brought fortunes home to New London. Townspeople still welcome all ships—submarines, cutters, yachts, cruisers. Today, the city's manufacturing industries include turbines, steel fabrication, high-tech products, medicines, electronics, and other products.

What to See and Do

Eugene O'Neill Theater Center. *305 Great Neck Rd, Waterford (06385). W via Hwy 1.* Phone 860/443-5378; fax 860/443-9653. *www.oneilltheatercenter.org.* Complex includes O'Neill Playwrights Conference, O'Neill Critics Institute, O'Neill Music Theater Conference, O'Neill Puppetry Conference, National Theater Institute. Staged readings of new plays and musicals during summer at Barn Theater, Amphitheater, and Instant Theater (June-Aug).
Ferries.

New London-Block Island, RI. *2 Ferry St, New London (06320).* Phone 860/442-9553. Auto ferry makes two-hour crossing; one round-trip (mid-June-Labor Day). **$$$$**

New London-Fishers Point, NY. *New London Pier, New London (06320).* Phone 860/443-6851. Auto ferries *Race Point* and *Munnatawket* make crossing to Fishers Island; several departures daily. Departs from New London Pier, foot of State Street. **$$$$**

New London-Orient Point, NY. *2 Ferry St, New London (06320).* Phone 860/443-7394. Five auto ferries make 90-minute trips across Long Island Sound. High-speed passenger ferry makes a 40-minute trip daily. (Daily; no trip Dec 25) Advance reservations required for vehicles. **$$$$**

Joshua Hempsted House. *11 Hempstead Ct, New London (06320).* Phone 860/443-7949. (1678) The oldest house in the city; restored, 17th- and 18th-century furnishings; Hempsted family diary detailing life in the house during colonial times. (Mid-May-mid-Oct, Thurs-Sun afternoons) **$$** Admission includes

Nathaniel Hempsted House. *11 Hempstead Ct, New London (06320).* Phone 860/443-7949. (1759) One of two surviving examples of mid-18th-century cut-stone architecture in state. Stone exterior bake oven, seven rooms with period furnishings. (Mid-May-mid-Oct, Thurs-Sun afternoons)

Lyman Allyn Art Museum. *625 Williams St, New London (06320).* Phone 860/443-2545. *www.lymanallyn. org.* Over 15,000 works of art. The collection includes Contemporary, Modern, and Early American fine arts; collection of dolls, doll houses; American and European paintings; Asian and primitive art. (Tues-Sat 10 am-5 pm, Sun 1-5 pm; closed holidays) **$**

Monte Cristo Cottage. *325 Pequot Ave, New London (06320).* Phone 860/443-0051. Restored boyhood home of playwright and Nobel prize winner Eugene O'Neill; houses research library and memorabilia. Multimedia presentation. Literary readings. (Mid-June-Labor Day, Tues-Sat) **$**

Ocean Beach Park. *1225 Ocean Ave, New London (06320). 3 miles S on Ocean Ave, on Long Island Sound.* Phone toll-free 800/510-7263. Swimming in the ocean, Olympic-size pool (fee), water slide; sheltered pavilion, boardwalk, picnic area, concessions, miniature golf (fee), novelty shop, amusement arcade, entertainment. (Sat before Memorial Day-Labor Day, daily) **$$$**

Shaw Perkins Mansion. *11 Blinman St, New London (06320).* Phone 860/443-1209. (1756) Naval headquarters for state during Revolution; genealogical and historical library. Unique paneled cement fireplace walls. (Wed-Sat) **$**

Sunbeam Fleet Nature Cruises. *15 1st St, Waterford (06385). Departs from dock near Niantic River bridge, W via I-95 exit 74, S on Hwy 161, left on Hwy 156 to first dock on left past bridge.* Phone 860/443-7259; fax 860/437-3699. *www.sunbeamfleet.com.* Cruises to view bald eagles (Feb-Mar) and seals (Apr-May). Reservations suggested. **$$$$**

US Coast Guard Academy. *15 Mohegan Ave, New London (06320). 1 mile N on I-95 exit 83. Phone 860/444-8270.* (1876) 800 cadets. Visitors' Pavilion with multimedia show (May-Oct, daily). US Coast Guard Museum (daily; closed holidays). Cadet parade-reviews (fall, spring, usually Fri). Barque *Eagle,* 295 feet, open to visitors (Fri-Sun, when in port; limited hours); photography permitted. **FREE**

Ye Antientiest Burial Ground. *Huntington St, New London (06320).* (1653) **FREE**

Ye Olde Towne Mill. *8 Mill St, New London (06320). Under Gold Star Bridge. Phone 860/443-6375. www.mysticmore.com.* (1650) Built for John Winthrop Jr, the founder of New London and Connecticut's sixth governor. The mill was restored in 1981; overshot waterwheel (closed to the public).

Special Events

Connecticut Storytelling Festival. *Connecticut College, 270 Mohegan Ave, New London (06320). Phone 860/439-2764; fax 860/439-2895. www.connstorycenter.org/festival.html.* Nationally acclaimed artists; workshops, concerts. Weekend in late Apr.

Sailfest. *New London City Pier, Bank St, New London (06320). Phone 860/443-3786.www.sailfest.org.* Arts and crafts and food vendors line the streets downtown while people of all ages browse, eat, and enjoy the three stages of entertainment. The largest fireworks show on the East Coast takes place on Saturday night. One weekend in early July. **FREE**

Limited-Service Hotel

★ ★ **RADISSON HOTEL NEW LONDON.** *35 Governor Winthrop Blvd, New London (06320). Phone 860/443-7000; toll-free 800/333-3333; fax 860/443-1239. www.radisson.com.* Midway between Boston and New York, this hotel is convenient to nearby casinos and other area attractions. 120 rooms, 5 story. Check-out noon. Restaurant, bar. Indoor pool, whirlpool. Tennis. Airport transportation available. Business center. **$**

New Preston (D-1)

See also Cornwall Bridge, Kent

Population 1,217
Elevation 700 ft
Area Code 860
Zip 06777
Information Litchfield Hills Visitors Bureau, PO Box 968, Litchfield 06759; phone 860/567-4506
Web Site www.litchfieldhills.com

What to See and Do

Historical Museum of Gunn Memorial Library. *5 Wykeham Rd, Washington (06793). 4 miles SW via Hwy 47 at junction Wykeham Rd, on the green. Phone 860/868-7756; fax 860/868-7247. www.gunnlibrary.org.* House built in 1781; contains collections and exhibits on area history; paintings, furnishings, gowns, dolls, dollhouses, and tools. (Thurs-Sat 10 am-4 pm; otherwise by appointment) **FREE**

★ **Institute for American Indian Studies.** *38 Curtis Rd, Washington (06793). 4 miles SW via CT 47 to CT 199 S, then 1 1/2 miles to Curtis Rd. Phone 860/868-0518; fax 860/868-1649. www.birdstone.org.* A museum of Northeastern Woodland Indian artifacts with permanent exhibit hall. Exhibits include changing Native American art displays; also a replicated indoor longhouse, outdoor replicated Algonkian village, simulated archaeological site, and nature trail. Special programs. (Mon-Sat 10 am-5 pm, Sun noon-5 pm; closed holidays) **$**

Lake Waramaug State Park. *30 Lake Waramaug Rd (Hwy 478), Kent (06777). 5 miles N. Phone 860/868-2592.* Swimming, fishing, scuba diving; field sports, hiking, ice skating, camping, picnicking.

Full-Service Inn

★ ★ ★ **BOULDERS INN.** *E Shore Rd (Hwy 45), New Preston (06777). Phone 860/868-0541; toll-free 800/455-1565; fax 860/868-1925.www.bouldersinn.com.*Enjoy country comforts in this quiet lakeside bed-and-breakfast. Guest rooms are homey and have canopy beds.5 rooms, 2 story. Check-in 3 pm, check-out noon. Restaurant, bar. Beach. **$$$$**

Specialty Lodging

HOPKINS INN. *22 Hopkins Rd, New Preston (06777). Phone 860/868-7295; fax 860/868-7464. www. thehopkinsinn.com.* Established in 1847. Lake Waramaug opposite. 11 rooms, 3 story. Closed Jan-Mar. Check-in 1 pm, check-out 11 am. Restaurant, bar. Beach. **$**

Restaurant

★ ★ ★ **BOULDERS.** *387 E Shore Rd (Hwy 45), New Preston (06777). Phone 860/868-0541; fax 860/868-1925. www.bouldersinn.com.* Fine dining in a turn-of-the-century summer home overlooking crystalline Lake Waramaug. American menu. Dinner. Closed Mon-Tues; Dec 25. Reservations recommended. Outdoor seating. **$$**

Norfolk (C-2)

See also Lakeville, Riverton

Founded 1758
Population 2,060
Elevation 1,230 ft
Area Code 860
Zip 06058
Information Litchfield Hills Visitors Bureau, PO Box 968, Litchfield 06759; phone 860/567-4506
Web Site www.litchfieldhills.com

What to See and Do

Campbell Falls. *Burr Pond State Park, 384 Burr Mountain Rd, Winsted (06098). 6 miles N on Hwy 272. Phone 860/482-1817.* Winding trails through woodland composed of many splashing cascades; focal point is Campbell Falls. Fishing; hiking, picnicking. **FREE**

Dennis Hill. *Burr Pond State Park, 384 Burr Mountain Rd, Winsted (06098). 2 miles S on Hwy 272. Phone 860/482-1817.* A unique summit pavilion (formerly a summer residence) is located at an elevation of 1,627 feet, providing a panoramic view of the Litchfield Hills and beyond. Picnicking, hiking, cross-country skiing. **FREE**

Haystack Mountain State Park. *Hwy 272, Norfolk. 1 mile N on Hwy 272. Phone 860/482-1817; toll-free 866/287-2757; fax 860/424-4070. www.dep.state.ct.us/stateparks/parks/haystack.htm.* A 34-foot-high stone tower at the summit, 1,716 feet above sea level, provides an excellent view of Long Island Sound, the Berkshires, and peaks in New York. A 1/2-mile trail leads from parking lot to tower. Picnicking; hiking. **FREE**

Historical Museum. *13 Village Green, Norfolk (06058). On the green. Phone 860/542-5761. www.norfolkhistoricalsociety.com.* Located in former Norfolk Academy (1840). Exhibits on the history of Norfolk include displays of a country store and post office as well as a children's room with an 1879 doll house. (Memorial Day-Columbus Day: Sat-Sun noon-4 pm; Nov-Apr: first Thurs of month 1-5 pm; otherwise by appointment) **FREE**

Special Event

Norfolk Chamber Music Festival. *E. B. Stoeckel Estate, Jct Hwy 44 and Hwy 272, Norfolk (06058). Phone 860/542-3000; fax 860/542-3004. www.yale.edu/norfolk.* Musical performances Friday-Saturday evenings in acoustically superb 1906 Music Shed located on grounds of 19th-century estate; also picnicking, indoor performances, and art gallery before concerts; informal chamber music recitals Thurs and Sat. Mid-June-mid-Aug. **$$$$**

Norwalk (F-1)

See also Bridgeport, Fairfield, Greenwich, New Canaan, Pound Ridge, Ridgefield, Stamford, Stratford, Westport

Founded 1651
Population 78,331
Elevation 42 ft
Area Code 203
Information Coastal Fairfield County Convention & Visitors Bureau, 297 West Ave, 06850; phone 203/853-7770 or toll-free 800/866-7925
Web Site www.coastalct.com

Norwalk's growth was heavily influenced by Long Island Sound. The city evolved rapidly from an agriculturally based community to a major seaport, then to a manufacturing center known for high-fashion hats, corsets, and clocks. The sound still plays an important part in Norwalk's development, providing beauty, recreation and, of course, oysters.

What to See and Do

Charter fishing trips. *Norwalk. Phone 203/854-7825; toll-free 800/866-7925. www.ctbound.org.* Several companies offer full- and 1/2-day saltwater fishing excursions. Contact the Coastal Fairfield County Tourism District for details.

Ferry to Sheffield Island Lighthouse. *132 Water St, 3rd Floor, South Norwalk (06854). Departs from Hope Dock, junction Washington and N Water Street. Phone 203/838-9444. www.seaport.org.* Ferry through Norwalk Harbor to historic Sheffield lighthouse (1868) on 3-acre island. Tour. Picnicking. (Memorial Day-June, weekends; July-Labor Day, daily) **$$$$**

Historic South Norwalk (SoNo). *Washington and Water sts, South Norwalk (06854). 1 mile SE via I-95, exit 14 N/15 S. Phone toll-free 800/866-7925. www.southnorwalk.com.* Nineteenth-century waterfront neighborhood on National Register featuring historical buildings, unique shops, art galleries, and restaurants.

Lockwood-Mathews Mansion Museum. *295 West Ave, Norwalk (06850). Phone 203/838-9799; fax 203/838-1434. www.lockwoodmathewsmansion.org.* (1864-1868) Sixty-room Victorian mansion built by financier Le-Grand Lockwood; 42-foot skylit rotunda, ornamented doors, and carved marble, inlaid woodwork throughout, period furnishings, musical boxes, and mechanical music exhibit; one-hour guided tour. Victorian Ice-Cream Social (mid-July) and Antiques Show (late Oct). Tours on the hour. (Mid-Mar-Dec: Wed-Sun noon-4 pm; rest of year: by appointment only; closed holidays) **$$**

Maritime Aquarium at Norwalk. *10 N Water St, Norwalk (06854). 2 miles S via I-95, exit 14 N or 15 S. Phone 203/852-0700; fax 203/838-5416. www.maritimeaquarium.org.* Hands-on maritime museum featuring shark touch tank and harbor seal pool; 125 species, touch tanks, films on IMAX screen; boat building exhibit. Guided harbor study tours. (Daily; closed Thanksgiving, Dec 25) **$$$**

Mill Hill Historic Park. *2 E Wall St, Norwalk (06852). Phone 203/846-0525. www.geocities.com/Heartland/Trail/8030.* Complex of historic Early American buildings includes the Town House Museum (circa 1835), Fitch House Law Office (circa 1740), and schoolhouse (circa 1826); also old cemetery. (Memorial Day-Labor Day, Sun 1-4 pm) **FREE**

St. Paul's-on-the-Green. *60 East Ave, Norwalk (06851). Phone 203/847-2806. www.stpaulsnorwalk.org.* This Gothic-style stone church contains the Seabury Altar; medieval stained glass; exquisite needlepoint. Antique organ. Also here is a colonial cemetery. **FREE**

WPA Murals. *125 East Ave, Norwalk (06851). City Hall (parking entrance, Sunset Hill Ave). Phone 203/852-0000. www.norwalktransit.com.* America's largest collection of Works Progress Administration murals, found throughout Norwalk, depict life in southeastern Fairfield County in the 1930s. (Mon-Fri; closed holidays) **FREE**

Special Events

International In-Water Boat Show. *Norwalk Cove Marina, 48 Calf Pasture Beach Rd, Norwalk (06855). Phone 212/984-7007. www.boatshownorwalk.com.* In addition to featuring more than 750 of the newest and most innovative crafts including performance boats, sailboats, and sailing yachts, guests at this waterside boat show can also try scuba diving, view a restored classic boat, or grab a drink at the Sand Bar. Third weekend in Sept. **$$$**

Norwalk Harbor Splash. *90 Washington St, South Norwalk (06854). Phone 203/853-7770; toll-free 800/866-7925. www.norwalkharborsplash.com.* Regatta, harbor tours, music, chowder cook-off (fee). Late May or early June. **FREE**

Oyster Festival. *Veteran's Park, Seaview Ave, East Norwalk (06855). Phone toll-free 800/866-7925. www.seaport.org.* Featuring appearances from tall ships and vintage oyster boats, this festival has regularly drawn 60,000 visitors a year since it began in 1978. More than 3,000 volunteers make the festival possible each year, and many local nonprofit groups benefit. Norwalk is less than a two-hour drive from many of New Englands larger cities, making it easy to attend the festival during a trip to New York or Hartford. Weekend after Labor Day. **$$**

Round Hill Highland Games. *Cranbury Park, Kensett Rd, Norwalk (06851). www.roundhill.org.* Heritage celebration with Highland dancing, pipe bands, caber tossing, clan tents, Scottish and American food. Late June or early July. **$$**

SoNo Arts Celebration. *Washington St & S Main St, South Norwalk (06854). Phone 203/866-7916. www.sonoarts.org.* Juried crafts, kinetic sculpture race, entertainment, concessions, block party. In Historic South Norwalk. First weekend in Aug.

Limited-Service Hotels

★ ★ **DOUBLETREE CLUB HOTEL NORWALK.** *789 Connecticut Ave, Norwalk (06854). Phone 203/853-3477 toll-free 800/222-8733; fax 203/855-9404. www.doubletree.com.* Business travelers will appreciate this hotel located in the heart of Norwalk. Guests can enjoy the on-site bowling. 268 rooms, 8 story. Check-in

3 pm, check-out 11 am. High-speed Internet access, wireless Internet access. Restaurant, bar. Fitness room. Indoor pool. Business center. **$**

★ ★ **FOUR POINTS BY SHERATON.** *426 Main Ave, Norwalk (06851). Phone 203/849-9828; toll-free 800/329-7466; fax 203/846-6925. www.fourpoints.com.* 127 rooms, 4 story. Check-in 3 pm, check-out noon. Restaurant, bar. Fitness room. **$$**

Full-Service Inn

★ ★ ★ **THE SILVERMINE TAVERN.** *194 Perry Ave, Norwalk (06850). Phone 203/847-4558; fax 203/847-9171. www.silverminetavern.com.* 10 rooms, 2 story. Closed Dec 25; Tues (Sept-May). Complimentary continental breakfast. Check-in 3 pm, check-out 11 am. Restaurant, bar. **$$**

Restaurants

★ ★ **PASTA NOSTRA.** *116 Washington St, South Norwalk (06854). Phone 203/854-9700. www.pastanostra.com.* This former pasta retail store cooks with only the highest quality of ingredients. Italian menu. Dinner. Reservations recommended. **$$**

★ ★ **SILVERMINE TAVERN.** *194 Perry Ave, Norwalk (06850). Phone 203/847-4558; fax 203/847-9171. www.silverminetavern.com.* This 18th-century colonial tavern overlooking a mill pond serves Old New England cuisine and features many antiques. A country store is opposite. American menu. Lunch, dinner, Sun brunch. Closed Tues. Bar. Casual attire. Reservations recommended. Outdoor seating. **$$**

Norwich (E-5)

See also Groton, Mystic, New London, Plainfield, Stonington

Settled 1659
Population 37,391
Elevation 52 ft
Area Code 860
Zip 06360
Information Connecticut's Mystic and More!, 32 Huntington St, PO Box 89, New London 06320; phone 860/444-2206 or toll-free 800/863-6569 (outside CT)
Web Site www.mysticcountry.com

Norwich was one of the first cities chartered in Connecticut. Since the end of the 18th century, it has been a leader in the industrial development of the state. Here, the colony's first paper mill was opened in 1766, and the first cut nails in America were made in 1772. Cotton spinning began about 1790.

There are three distinct sections: Norwichtown to the northwest, a living museum of the past; the business section near the Thames docks; and a central residential section with many 19th-century homes.

What to See and Do

Indian Leap. *Yantic and Sachem sts, Norwich (06360). Yantic Falls off Yantic St. Phone 860/886-4683.* The falls was a favorite resort and outpost of the Mohegan. Legend has it that a band of Narragansetts, during the Battle of Great Plains in 1643, fled from pursuing Mohegans. As they came upon the falls, many were forced to jump off the cliffs and into the chasm below, hence the name. Can be viewed from the Monroe Street footbridge. **FREE**

Leffingwell Inn. *348 Washington St, Norwich (06360). Phone 860/889-9440. www.leffingwellhousemuseum.com.* (1675) Scene of Revolutionary War councils. Museum; period rooms. (Mid-May-Labor Day, Sat 1-4 pm; otherwise by appointment) **$$**

Mohegan Park and Memorial Rose Garden. *20 Park Center Rd, Norwich (06360). Entrances on Judd Rd and Rockwell St. Phone 860/823-3759.* Picnic and play area; swimming area (June-Labor Day, daily). Rose garden; best time to visit, June-Sept. (Daily) **FREE**

Old Burying Ground. *Cemetery Ln and E Town St, Norwich (06360). Entrance from E Town St; brochure available at Cemetery Ln entrance. Phone 860/886-4683. www.norwichct.org.* Burial place of many Revolutionary War soldiers, including French soldiers; also Samuel Huntington, signer of the Declaration of Independence.

Royal Mohegan Burial Grounds. *Sachem and Washington sts, Norwich (06360). Phone 860/862-6390. www.mohegan.nsn.us.* The resting place of Uncas, chief of the Mohegans (more popularly known as the Mohicans), who gave the original land for the settlement of Norwich. **FREE**

Slater Memorial Museum & Converse Art Gallery. *108 Crescent St, Norwich (06360). Approximately 1 mile N via I-395, exit 81 E, on campus of Norwich Free Academy. Phone 860/887-2506; fax 860/885-0379. www.*

norwichfreeacademy.com/slater_museum. Roman and Greek casts; Vanderpoel Collection of Oriental Art; 17th to 20th-century American art and furnishings; changing exhibits. (Tues-Fri 9 am-4 pm; Sat 1-4 pm; closed holidays) **$**

Tantaquidgeon Indian Museum. *1819 Norwich-New London Tpke, Uncasville (06382). 5 miles S on Hwy 32. Phone 860/842-6100.* Works of Mohegan and other New England tribes, past and present; also displays of Southeast, Southwest, and Northern Plains Native Americans. (May-Nov Mon-Fri 10 am-3 pm) **DONATION**

Special Events

Blue Grass Festival. *Strawberry Park, 42 Pierce Rd, Preston (06365). Phone 860/886-1944; toll-free 888/794-7944. www.strawberrypark.net/bluegrass.html.* You can either come for the day or make reservations for a campsite and enjoy four full days of bluegrass music. Past performers have included Rhonda Vincent, The Tim O'Brien Band, and The Waybacks. Late May-early June. **$$$$**

Rail & Sail Festival. *Brown Park, Norwich (06360). Brown Memorial Park, at waterfront. Phone 860/887-3289. www.norwichct.org.* Raft race; boat rides; dunking booth; arts and crafts; entertainment. Late July. **$$$**

Rose-Arts Festival. *Rose City Senior Center, 8 Mahan Dr, Norwich (06360). Phone 860/887-9113. www.norwichct.org.* Look at the roses grown in the city known as the "Rose of New England." Mid-June. **FREE**

Full-Service Resort

★ ★ ★ **THE SPA AT NORWICH INN.** *607 W Thames St, Norwich (06360). Phone 860/886-2401; toll-free 800/275-4772; fax 860/886-9483. www. thespaatnorwichinn.com.* The Spa at Norwich Inn offers visitors the best of both worlds. Its historic country inn on 42 acres allows guests to take a step back in time, while its award-winning spa employs cutting-edge techniques and treatments to enhance relaxation and renewal. This is the place to come to truly unwind, with 32 treatment rooms dedicated to relieving stress and soothing tired souls. This spa's menu goes beyond the traditional facials and massages to include hydrotherapy, astrology, and energy work. From physical fitness and mind/body awareness to beautifying and pampering treatments, this spa offers the complete package. Dining is far from Spartan, although guests wishing to enjoy lighter spa cuisine

appreciate the weight- and health-conscious menu. 65 rooms, 3 story. Check-in 4 pm, check-out noon. Restaurant, bar. Fitness room. Indoor pool, outdoor pool, whirlpool. Tennis. Business center. **$**

Spa

★ ★ ★ **ELEMIS SPA.** *1 Mohegan Sun Blvd, Uncasville (06382). Phone 860/862-8000; fax 860/862-4822.* With 1,200 guest rooms; 300,000 square feet of gaming space; more than 40 restaurants and retail shops; and a 10,000-seat arena, tranquil may be the last word that comes to mind to describe the Mohegan Sun. But on the third floor of this glistening 34-story crystal tower, Elemis Spa epitomizes the word. Taking its inspiration from the Mohegan Native American Indian tribe, the 22,300-square-foot Elemis Spa features 15 private spa therapy rooms (all named after a specific moon); a relaxation lounge with refreshment bar; hair and nail salon; and fitness center. All rooms honor the Mohegan creation story with a suspended ceiling frame that represents the Grandfather Turtle, the keeper of time upon whose back the world was formed, while the salon features an 8-foot-tall maple tree that represents the Fair Tree, a sacred gathering place for Mohegan Indians. Warm earth tones and a soothing stillness permeate Elemis Spa, offering the perfect atmosphere for exotic facials, massages, and body treatments that will make you forget your cares. Renew and detoxify with the Cellutox Aroma Spa Ocean Wrap or Float. Here, a warm seaweed body mask containing essential oils of lemon and juniper is applied to the body before it is enveloped in either a comforting foil wrap or The Spa's unique sensory dry float bed, which cocoons the body in warmth while simulating weightlessness. Skin care includes the Active Deep-Cleaning Facial, a treatment that incorporates strawberry and kiwi fruit extracts for a radiant complexion, and the Repairing Herbal Lavender Facial, which combines absolutes and essential oils to balance and oxygenate the skin. Exotic Rituals & Ceremonies such as the Ceremony of Whirling River and the Purification Ritual combine a package of therapies with ancient rituals to achieve balance, harmony, and wellness. After such a peaceful experience at Elemis Spa, you'll be ready for the fast-paced action of the Mohegan Suns casino. And if you win big, there will be no question about where to spend it another trip to Elemis Spa, of course.

Restaurant

★ ★ **KENSINGTON.** *607 W Thames St, Norwich (06360). Phone 860/886-2401.* American menu. Breakfast, lunch, dinner, Sun brunch. Bar. Outdoor seating. **$$$**

Old Lyme (E-4)

See also Essex, New London, Old Saybrook, Stonington

Settled 1665
Population 6,535
Elevation 17 ft
Area Code 860
Zip 06371
Information Connecticut's Mystic and More!, 32 Huntington St, PO Box 89, New London 06320; phone 860/444-2206 or toll-free 800/863-6569
Web Site www.mysticcountry.com

Once, long ago, they say a sea captain lived in every house in Old Lyme. Fortunately, a good many of the houses are still standing on the tree-lined streets of this sleepy old village. Named for Lyme Regis, England, it is a summer resort and an artists' colony, one of the first on the coast.

What to See and Do

Florence Griswold Museum. *96 Lyme St, Old Lyme (06371). 1 block W off CT Tpke exit 70. Phone 860/434-5542; fax 860/434-9778. www.florencegriswoldmuseum. org.* (1817) Stately late Georgian mansion that housed America's most celebrated art colony at the turn of the century. Paintings by Willard Metcalf, Childe Hassam, and other artists of the colony; exhibits of 18th- and 19th-century New England furnishings and decorative arts. (Krieble Gallery: Tues-Sat 10 am-5 pm, Sun 1-5 pm; Chadwick Studio: mid-May-Oct; closed holidays) **$$**

Rocky Neck State Park. *244 W Main St, East Lyme (06371). 6 miles E via I-95, exit 72, on Hwy 156. Phone 860/739-5471.* Approximately 560 acres with 1/2-mile frontage on Long Island Sound. Saltwater swimming, scuba diving, fishing; hiking, picnicking (shelters, concessions). Camping.

Full-Service Inns

★ ★ ★ **BEE AND THISTLE INN.** *100 Lyme St, Old Lyme (06371). Phone 860/434-1667; toll-free 800/622-4946; fax 860/434-3402. www.beeandthistleinn.com.* This

1756 inn has been rated as one of Connecticut's most romantic getaways. 11 rooms, 3 story. Closed two weeks in Jan. Children over 12 years only. Check-in 2 pm, check-out 11 am. Restaurant, bar. **$**

★ ★ ★ **OLD LYME INN.** *85 Lyme St, Old Lyme (06371). Phone 860/434-2600; toll-free 800/434-5352; fax 860/434-5352. www.oldlymeinn.com.* Located in the historic district of Old Lyme, this bed-and-breakfast (built in 1850) is close to Essex, Mystic Seaport, Mystic Aquarium, and art galleries. Guests can also enjoy outlet shopping and visiting the local museums. 13 rooms, 2 story. Pets accepted, some restrictions; fee. Complimentary continental breakfast. Check-in 3 pm, check-out 11 am. Restaurant, bar. **$$**

Restaurants

★ ★ ★ **BEE AND THISTLE INN.** *100 Lyme St, Old Lyme (06371). Phone 860/434-1667; toll-free 800/622-4046; fax 860/434-3402. www.beeandthistleinn.com.* Romance and service are in full force here. Innovative American cuisine is prepared fresh by the staff. American menu. Lunch, dinner, Sun brunch. Closed Dec 24 evening-Dec 25; two weeks in Jan. Bar. **$$$**

★ ★ ★ **OLD LYME INN.** *85 Lyme St, Old Lyme (06371). Phone 860/434-2600; toll-free 800/434-5352; fax 860/434-5352. www.oldlymeinn.com.* Located in the historic district, this restored 1850 home features three fireplaces, many antiques, and murals by a local artist. Superb desserts are made daily from scratch. American menu. Lunch, dinner. Closed Mon. Bar. **$$$**

Old Saybrook (E-4)

See also Clinton, Essex, New London, Old Lyme, Stonington

Settled 1635
Population 9,552
Elevation 31 ft
Area Code 860
Zip 06475
Information Chamber of Commerce, 665 Boston Post Rd; phone 860/388-3266.
Web Site www.oldsaybrookct.com

Old Saybrook, at the mouth of the Connecticut River, is popular with summer vacationers. It is the third-oldest named community in Connecticut and is the oldest officially chartered town in the state. It was also the original site of Yale College until 1716.

What to See and Do

Fort Saybrook Monument Park. *Hwy 154, Saybrook Point, Old Saybrook (06475). On College St, at Saybrook Point.* Phone 860/395-3152. Nearly 18-acre park with remains of Fort Saybrook, first military fortification in the state; picnicking. (Daily) **FREE**

General William Hart House. *350 Main St, Old Saybrook (06475).* Phone 860/388-2622. (1767) Provincial Georgian-style, colonial residence of well-to-do New England merchant and politician; features include eight corner fireplaces, one of which is decorated with Sadler and Green transfer-print tiles illustrating *Aesop's Fables*; original wainscotting; Federal-style pieces, several of which are Hart family items; antique furniture, costumes, artifacts; on grounds are re-created colonial gardens, including award-winning herb garden. (mid-June-Labor Day, Fri-Sun 1-4 pm). **DONATION**

Special Events

Arts and Crafts Show. *Town Green, Main St, Old Saybrook (06475).* Phone 860/388-3266. www.oldsaybrookct.com. More than 200 artists and craftspersons exhibiting. Last full weekend in July.

Christmas Torchlight Parade. *Main St, Old Saybrook (06475).* Phone 860/388-3266. www.connecticutblues.com. More than 40 fife and drum corps march down Main Street. Second Sat in Dec.

Full-Service Resorts

★ ★ ★ **SAYBROOK POINT INN AND SPA.** *2 Bridge St, Old Saybrook (06475).* Phone 860/395-2000; toll-free 800/243-0212; fax 860/388-1504. The charming coastal village of Old Saybrook is home to the exceptional Saybrook Point Inn and Spa. Warm interiors and courteous service define this seaside getaway, while views of Long Island Sound and the Connecticut River make for a scenic backdrop. The guest rooms and suites are classically styled with 18th-century period-style furnishings and accessories. Guests work out with a view of the sound in the comprehensive fitness center and luxuriate at the spa, where a complete menu of treatments tempts clients. The hotel's restaurant, Terra Mar Grille, wins rave reviews for its sophisticated cuisine matched only by

the water views. The chef dazzles with contemporary American dishes, and spa cuisine is available for those guests watching their waistlines. 62 rooms, 3 story. Pets accepted, some restrictions; fee. Check-in 4 pm, check-out noon. Restaurant, bar. Fitness room. Indoor pool, outdoor pool, whirlpool. **$$**

★ ★ ★ **WATER'S EDGE RESORT AND CONFERENCE CENTER.** *1525 Boston Post Rd, Westbrook (06498).* Phone 860/399-5901; toll-free 800/222-5901; fax 860/399-8644. www.watersedge-resort.com. This resort has a stunning view of Connecticut's Long Island Sound. Guests can enjoy such activities as softball, face painting, scavenger hunts, kite flying, football, horseshoes, and volleyball. 32 rooms, 3 story. Check-in 3 pm, check-out noon. Restaurant, bar. Children's activity center. Fitness room. Beach. Indoor pool, outdoor pool, whirlpool. Tennis. **$$**

Restaurant

★ ★ **DOCK AND DINE.** *College St, Old Saybrook (06475).* Phone 860/388-4665; fax 860/536-0695. Seafood, steak menu. Lunch, dinner. Closed Mon-Tues (mid-Oct-mid-Apr); Thanksgiving, Dec 24-25. Bar. Children's menu. **$$**

Plainfield (D-5)

See also Norwich, Putnam

Settled 1689
Population 14,363
Elevation 203 ft
Area Code 860
Zip 06374
Information Northeast Connecticut Visitors District, 13 Cantebury Rd, Suite 3, PO Box 145, Putnam 06260; phone 860/779-6383 or toll-free 888/628-1228
Web Site www.ctquietcorner.org

What to See and Do

Plainfield Greyhound Park. *137 Lathrop Rd, Plainfield (06374).* Phone 860/564-3391. www.trackinfo/pl. Parimutuel betting. Concessions, bar. No minors. Races daily. (Daily) **$$**

Prudence Crandall House. *Hwys 14 and 169, Canterbury (06331). W on Hwy 14A at junction Hwy 169.* Phone 860/546-9916. Site of New England's first academy for African-American girls (1833-1834). Restored two-story frame building with changing exhibits, period furnishings; research library. Gift shop. (Apr-mid-Dec, Wed-Sun; closed Thanksgiving) **$**

Quinebaug Valley Trout Hatchery. *151 Trout Hatchery Rd, Plainfield (06374). Phone 860/564-7542.* A 1,200-acre hatchery for brook, brown, and rainbow trout. Exhibits and displays (daily). Fishing by permit only (Mar-May, weekends and holidays). **FREE**

Limited-Service Hotel

★ **BEST WESTERN PLAINFIELD YANKEE INN.** *55 Lathorp Rd, Plainfield (06374). Phone 860/564-4021; fax 860/564-4021.* 48 rooms, 2 story. Check-in 2 pm, check-out 11 am. **$**

Putnam (C-5)

See also Norwich, Putnam

Population 9,031
Elevation 290 ft
Area Code 860
Zip 06260
Information Northeast Connecticut Visitors District, 13 Canterbury Rd, Suite 3, PO Box 145; phone 860/779-6383 or toll-free 888/628-1228
Web Site www.ctquietcorner.org

Named for Revolutionary War hero Israel Putnam, this town is situated on four small hills. Because it was located at Cargill Falls on the Quinebaug River and a railroad station served as a connecting point between New York and Boston, Putnam at one time ranked eighth in New England in the volume of freight handled.

What to See and Do

⭐ **Roseland Cottage.** *556 Hwy 169, Woodstock (06281). 7 miles NW via Hwys 171 and 169. Phone 860/928-4074.* (1846) Influential abolitionist publisher Henry C. Bowen's summer home. One of the most important surviving examples of a Gothic Revival "cottage," complete with period furnishings. Located on Woodstock Hill with its bright pink exterior and picturesque profile, it stands in contrast to the otherwise colonial character of this New England village. Surrounded by original outbuildings, includes one of the oldest indoor bowling alleys in the country; aviary. Boasts one of the oldest parterre gardens in New England, edged by 1,800 feet of dwarf boxwood. Presidents Grant, Hayes, Harrison, and McKinley attended Bowen's celebrated Fourth of July parties here. (June-mid-Oct, Fri-Sun; closed holidays) **$$**

Limited-Service Hotel

★ **KINGS INN.** *5 Heritage Rd, Putnam (06260). Phone 860/928-7961; toll-free 800/541-7304; fax 860/963-2463.* 4 rooms, 2 story. Pets accepted. Complimentary continental breakfast. Check-out 11 am. Bar. Outdoor pool. **$**

Full-Service Inn

★ ★ ★ **INN AT WOODSTOCK HILL.** *94 Plaine Hill Rd, South Woodstock (06267). Phone 860/928-0528; fax 860/928-3236. www.woodstockhill.com.* Located on 14 acres, this inn (1815) is listed on the National Register of Historic Places. Guests can enjoy a stroll through the well-manicured lawns that adorn this property. 22 rooms, 3 story. Complimentary continental breakfast. Check-in 2 pm, check-out 11 am. Restaurant, bar. **$**

Ridgefield (E-1)

See also Danbury, New Canaan, Norwalk, Stamford

Settled 1709
Population 20,919
Elevation 749 ft
Area Code 203
Zip 06877
Information Chamber of Commerce, 9 Bailey Ave; phone 203/438-5992 or toll-free 800/386-1708; or Housatonic Valley Tourism Commission, Box 406, 30 Main St, Danbury 06810; phone 203/743-0546 or toll-free 800/841-4488 (outside CT)
Web Site www.ridgefieldchamber.org

Ridgefield is unusual among communities settled in the 19th century because it has a main street of boulevard width--99 feet lined with tree-shaded houses. On this street in 1777, Benedict Arnold (still a revolutionary) set up barricades and fought the Battle of Ridgefield against General Tyron.

What to See and Do

Aldrich Museum of Contemporary Art. *258 Main St, Ridgefield (06877). Phone 203/438-4519; fax 203/438-*

0198. www.aldrichart.org. Changing exhibits; sculpture garden (daily; free). Museum (Tues-Sun noon-5 pm; closed on holidays). **$$**

Keeler Tavern. *132 Main St, Ridgefield (06877). Phone 203/438-5485; fax 203/438-9953. www.keelertavern-museum.org.* Restored 18th-century tavern, stagecoach stop, home. Once Revolutionary patriot headquarters; British cannonball still embedded in wall. Summer home of architect Cass Gilbert. Period furnishings; gardens; tours; museum shop. (Wed, Sat-Sun 1-4 pm; closed Jan, holidays) **$**

Full-Service Inns

★ ★ ★ **THE ELMS INN.** *500 Main St, Ridgefield (06877).Phone 203/438-2541. www.elmsinn.com.* Open since 1799, this inn (built in the 1760s) is located in Ridgefield, which boasts much of the original architecture. Guests can visit the Community Center, which is the site of the Governor's Mansion (built in 1896), or stop by the town library. 23 rooms, 3 story. Complimentary continental breakfast. Check-in 3 pm, check-out 11 am. Restaurant, bar. **$$$**

★ ★ ★ **STONEHENGE INN.** *35 Stonehenge Rd, Ridgefield (6877). Phone 203/438-6511; fax 203/438-2478. www.stonehengeinn-ct.com.* This property is a lakeside colonial-style inn. The inn's elegant restaurant specializes in French cuisine. 16 rooms, 2 story. Pets accepted, some restrictions; fee. Complimentary continental breakfast. Check-in 3 pm, check-out 11 am. Restaurant, bar. **$$**

★ ★ ★ **WEST LANE INN.** *22 West Ln, Ridgefield (06877). Phone 203/438-7323; fax 203/438-7325. www. westlaneinn.com.*18 rooms, 3 story. Complimentary continental breakfast. Check-in 2 pm, check-out 11 am. Restaurant. **$$**

Restaurants

★ ★ ★ **THE ELMS.** *500 Main St, Ridgefield (06877). Phone 203/438-9206. www.elmsinn.com.* Established in 1799, this is the oldest continuously run inn in Ridgefield. American menu. Lunch, dinner. Closed Mon-Tues; Easter, Dec 25. Bar. Reservations recommended. Outdoor seating. **$$**

★ ★ ★ **STONEHENGE.** *35 Stonehenge Rd, Ridgefield (06877). Phone 203/438-6511; fax 203/438-2478. www. stonehengeinn-ct.com.* This restored home (circa 1853) is located near a pond. Tranquil scenery and attentive service make it a popular place. French menu. Dinner. Reservations recommended. Valet parking. **$$$**

★ **VENICE RESTAURANT.** *3 Cops Hill Rd, Ridgefield (06877). Phone 203/438-3333.* Italian menu. Lunch, dinner. Bar. Children's menu. Casual attire. Outdoor seating. **$$**

Riverton (C-2)

See also Hartford, Norfolk

Population 500
Elevation 505 ft
Area Code 860
Zip 06065
Information Litchfield Hills Visitors Bureau, PO Box 968, Litchfield 06759; phone 860/567-4506
Web Site www.northwestct.com

Lambert Hitchcock, one of America's greatest chairmakers, built his original chair factory here in 1826. His famous stenciled chairs and cabinet furniture are now prized pieces. The old factory is still in operation, and some antiques are on display. Today, the grand colonial houses and tree-lined streets of this New England village are filled with emporiums and shops.

What to See and Do

Solomon Rockwell House. *225 Prospect St, Winsted (06098). 3 miles SW on Hwy 20, 2 miles S on Hwy 8. Phone 860/379-8433.* (1813) Antebellum house built by early industrialist; Hitchcock chairs, antique clocks, Revolutionary and Civil War memorabilia, wedding gown collection, melodeon. (June-Oct, by appointment) **$**

Special Event

Riverton Fair. *Hwy 20, Riverton (06065). Phone 860/738-4227.* 1800s country village fair, held since 1909; chopping, sawing, and pie-eating competitions; displays, art and crafts, entertainment. Second weekend in Oct. **$**

Simsbury (D-3)

See also Avon, Farmington, Hartford

Settled 1660
Population 22,023
Elevation 181 ft
Area Code 860
Zip 06070
Information Simsbury Chamber of Commerce, 749 Hopmeadow St, PO Box 224; phone 860/651-7307
Web Site www.simsburycoc.org

Hopmeadow Street, in this characteristic New England village, is so named because hops were grown in the area to supply early distillers. Simsbury's handsome Congregational Church was built in 1830.

After it was founded, Simsbury developed steadily until 1676, when the settlers fled in terror during King Philip's War. Scouts returning three days later and found the settlement in ashes. Soon the village was reconstructed and activity was again stimulated by the discovery of copper at East Granby (then part of Simsbury).

What to See and Do

Phelps Tavern Museum. *Simsbury Historical Society, 800 Hopmeadow St, Simsbury (06070). Phone 860/658-2500. www.simsburyhistory.org/phelps-tav.-mus.html.* Period rooms and interactive exhibition galleries interpret the use of the historic Captain Elisha Phelps house as an inn from 1786 to 1849. Three successive generations of the Phelps tavernkeepers are chronicled along with the social history of taverns in New England. Part of a 2-acre complex, which includes a museum store, research library, and award-winning period gardens. Group tours available. (Tues-Sat noon-4 pm) **$$**

Simsbury Farms. *100 Old Farms Rd, Simsbury (06070). Phone 860/658-3836. www.simsburyfarms.com.* Recreational facility covering 300 acres; swimming; picnicking, ice skating, tennis, golf, cross-country skiing, nature and family fitness trails, volleyball, paddle tennis. (Daily; some activities seasonal) Fees for most activities.

Limited-Service Hotel

★ **IRON HORSE INN.** *969 Hopmeadow St, Simsbury (06070). Phone 860/658-2216; toll-free 800/245-9938; fax 860/651-0822. www.ironhorseofsimsbury.com.*

27 rooms, 2 story. Pets accepted, some restrictions; fee. Complimentary continental breakfast. Check-out 11 am. Outdoor pool. **$**

Full-Service Hotel

★ ★ ★ **SIMSBURY INN.** *397 Hopmeadow St, Simsbury (06070). Phone 860/651-5700; toll-free 800/634-2719; fax 860/651-8024. www.simsburyinn.com.* This inn offers a true escape for the active traveler. 98 rooms, 4 story. Complimentary continental breakfast. Check-in 3 pm, check-out 11 am. Restaurant, bar. Indoor pool, whirlpool. Tennis. Airport transportation available. **$$**

Specialty Lodging

SIMSBURY 1820 HOUSE. *731 Hopmeadow St, Simsbury (06070). Phone 860/658-7658; toll-free 800/879-1820; fax 860/651-0724. www.simsbury-1820house.com.* Built in 1820; antiques. 32 rooms, 3 story. Complimentary continental breakfast. Check-in 3 pm, check-out 11 am. Restaurant. **$**

Restaurant

★ **ONE-WAY FARE.** *4 Railroad St, Simsbury (06070). Phone 860/658-4477; fax 860/651-9087. www.onewayfare.org.* Old brick train station (1874); train memorabilia. American menu. Lunch, dinner, Sun brunch. Closed Labor Day, Thanksgiving, Dec 25. Bar. Outdoor seating. **$$**

Southbury (E-2)

See also Danbury, Waterbury, Woodbury

Settled 1673
Population 15,818
Elevation 257 ft
Area Code 203
Zip 06488
Information Litchfield Hills Visitors Bureau, PO Box 968, Litchfield 06759; phone 860/567-4506
Web Site www.northwestct.com

What to See and Do

Bullet Hill Schoolhouse. *215 Main St S, Southbury (06488). 1/2 mile E of I-84, exit 15, on Hwy 6. Phone 203/264-8781.* One of the oldest school buildings in the country, estimated to have been built in 1789, in use until 1942; some experts believe that it pre-dates the Revolutionary War. Early schooling exhibits. (By appointment)**DONATION**

Kettletown. *1400 George's Hill Rd, Southbury (06488). 5 miles S via I-84, exit 15. Phone 203/264-5678; toll-free 866/287-2757. www.dep.state.ct.us/stateparks/parks/kettletown.htm.* The name of this park is derived from the time when settlers first arrived and purchased this tract of land from the Native Americans for one brass kettle. Swimming, fishing; hiking, sports field, picnicking, camping (fee). Nature trail for the disabled. **$$**

Southford Falls. *175 Quaker Farms Rd, Southbury (06488). 4 miles SE via Hwys 67 and 188.Phone 203/264-5169; toll-free 866/287-2757. www.dep.state.ct.us/stateparks/parks/southford.htm.* Approximately 120 acres. Former site of Diamond Match Company. Stream and pond fishing; ice skating, bridle trail nearby, scenic hiking along Eight Mile River; picnicking. (Daily) **FREE**

Full-Service Hotel

★ ★ ★ **CROWNE PLAZA SOUTHBURY.** *1284 Strongtown Rd, Southbury (06488). Phone 203/598-7600; fax 203/598-7541. www.crowneplaza.com.* Located in the Litchfield Hills area between Boston and New York, this property is sprawled in a country setting near numerous local antique centers and shops. The Quassy Amusement Park and several ski areas are also nearby. 198 rooms, 3 story. Pets accepted, some restrictions. Check-in 3 pm, check-out noon. Restaurant, bar. Fitness room. Indoor pool, whirlpool. **$**

Southington (D-3)

See also Waterbury, Woodbury

Special Event

Apple Harvest Festival. *51 N Main St, Southington (06489). 3 miles S on Hwy 120, on Town Green. Phone 860/276-8461. www.appleharvestfestival.com.* Street festival celebrating local apple harvest. Carnival, arts and crafts, parade, road race, food booths, entertainment. Two weekends in Sept-Oct.

Restaurant

★ ★ **BRANNIGAN'S.** *176 Laning St, Southington (06489). Phone 860/621-9311; fax 860/628-0803.*

American menu. Lunch, dinner. Closed Memorial Day, Dec 25. Bar. Children's menu. **$$**

Stafford Springs (E-3)

See also Enfield, Storrs, Windsor

Settled 1719
Population 4,100
Elevation 591 ft
Area Code 860
Zip 06076
Information Connecticut North Central Tourism & Visitors Bureau, 73 Hazard Ave, Enfield 06082; phone 860/763-2578 or toll-free 800/793-4480
Web Site www.cnctb.org

Stafford Springs is known for its production of woolen fabrics, printed circuits, and industrial filters.

What to See and Do

Civilian Conservation Corps Museum. *166 Chestnut Hill Rd (Hwy 190), Stafford Springs (06076). Phone 860/684-3013.* New Deal program devoted to state and national parks is commemorated. Video and photograph exhibits; equipment and uniforms; camp memorabilia. (Memorial Day-Labor Day,Thurs-Sun) **DONATION**

Mineral Springs. *Hwy 190 and Spring St, Stafford Springs (06076). Spring St, between Grace Episcopal Church and the library. Phone 860/684-1777. www.staffordct.org.* Located here are the springs that gave the town its name. In 1771, John Adams, future president of the United States, came to bathe in the springs after hearing of their healing effects. **FREE**

Special Event

Stafford Motor Speedway. *55 West St, Stafford Springs (06076). Hwy 140 W. Phone 860/684-2783; fax 860/684-6236. www.staffordmotorspeedway.com.* A 1/2-mile paved oval track for stock car racing. Apr-Sept.

Stamford (F-1)

See also Fairfield, Greenwich, New Canaan, Norwalk, Ridgefield, Westport

Settled 1641
Population 108,056
Elevation 10 ft
Area Code 203
Information Chamber of Commerce, 733 Summer St, 06901; phone 203/359-4761
Web Site www.stamfordchamber.com

Stamford is a corporate headquarters, manufacturing, and research center, as well as a residential suburb of New York City. More than 20 *Fortune* 500 corporations are located in this area. An assortment of marinas and beaches provide recreation on Long Island Sound.

What to See and Do

Bartlett Arboretum and Gardens. *151 Brookdale Rd, Stamford (06903). Off High Ridge Rd, 1 mile N of Merritt Pkwy (Hwy 15) exit 35. Phone 203/322-6971; fax 203/595-9168. www.bartlett.arboretum.uconn.edu.* Collections of dwarf conifers, rhododendrons, azaleas, wildflowers, perennials, and witches brooms; ecology trails and swamp walk are within the natural woodlands surrounding the gardens. (Gardens daily, 8:30 am-sunset; visitors center Mon-Fri 8:30 am-4:30 pm, closed holidays; greenhouse Mon-Fri 9:30 am-11 am, closed holidays)

First Presbyterian Church. *1101 Bedford St, Stamford (06905). Phone 203/324-9522. www.fishchurch.org.* (1958) Contemporary building shaped like a fish, designed by Wallace Harrison; glass by Gabriel Loire of Chartres, France; 56-bell carillon tower (1968), summer concerts (July, Thurs night). **FREE**

Special Event

Art in Public Places. *Stamford (06901). Phone 203/348-5285. www.stamford-downtown.com.* Throughout downtown Stamford. Various exhibits of sculpture and photography. June-Aug.

Limited-Service Hotel

★ ★ **HOLIDAY INN.** *700 Main St, Stamford (06901). Phone 203/358-8400; toll-free 800/465-4329; fax 203/358-8872. www.holiday-inn.com.* 383 rooms, 10 story. Check-in 3 pm, check-out noon. High-speed Internet access, wireless Internet access. Restaurant, bar. Indoor pool. Business center. **$**

Full-Service Hotels

★ ★ ★ **MARRIOTT STAMFORD.** *243 Tresser Blvd, Stamford (06901). Phone 203/357-9555; toll-free 800/732-9689; fax 203/324-6897. www.marriott.com.* Located across the street from the Stamford Town Center Mall, guests have access to over 130 stores. For those who don't enjoy shopping, there are other places to explore such as the Palace Theater, Playland Amusement Park, or the Whitney Museum. 507 rooms, 16 story. Pets accepted; fee. Check-in 3 pm, check-out noon. Two restaurants, bar. Fitness room. Indoor/outdoor pool, whirlpool. Business center. **$$**

★ ★ ★ **SHERATON STAMFORD HOTEL.** *2701 Summer St, Stamford (06905). Phone 203/359-1300; toll-free 888/627-8315; fax 203/348-7937. www.sheraton.com.* This property is located 45 minutes from Manhattan and within the bustling corporate center of Connecticut's Gold Coast. 448 rooms, 5 story. Check-in 3 pm, check-out 11 am. Two restaurants, bar. Fitness room. Indoor pool, whirlpool. Business center. **$$**

★ ★ ★ **THE WESTIN STAMFORD.** *1 Stamford Pl, Stamford (06901). Phone 203/967-2222; toll-free 800/228-3000; fax 203/967-3475. www.westin.com.* 480 rooms, 10 story. Pets accepted, some restrictions; fee. Check-in 3 pm, check-out noon. Restaurant, bar. Fitness room. Indoor pool, whirlpool. Tennis. Business center. **$$**

Restaurants

★ **CRAB SHELL.** *46 Southfield Ave, Stamford (06902). Phone 203/967-7229; fax 203/967-7223. www.crabshell.com.* American, seafood menu. Lunch, dinner. Bar. Casual attire. Outdoor seating. **$$**

★ ★ **FIO'S RISTORANTE & PIZZERIA.** *299 Long Ridge Rd, Stamford (06902). Phone 203/964-9802; fax 203/964-9806. www.fiosristorante.com.* Dine around the stone fireplace in the open, airy dining room or outside on the lovely patio, where live music is featured in summer. American, International menu. Lunch, dinner. Bar. Casual attire. Reservations recommended. Outdoor seating. **$$**

★ ★ **IL FALCO.** *59 Broad St, Stamford (06902).* *Phone 203/327-0002; fax 203/967-8315. www.ilfalco. com.* Italian menu. Lunch, dinner. Closed Sun. Bar. Casual attire. Valet parking. **$$$**

★ ★ **LA BRETAGNE.** *2010 W Main St (Hwy 1), Stamford (06902). Phone 203/324-9539; fax 203/961-9468.* Continental, French menu. Lunch, dinner. Closed Sun. Bar. Business casual attire. Reservations recommended. **$$$**

★ ★ **LA HACIENDA.** *222 Summer St, Stamford (06901). Phone 203/324-0577; fax 203/324-0177.* Mexican menu. Lunch, dinner. Bar. Children's menu. Casual attire. Reservations recommended. Outdoor seating. **$$**

Stonington (E-5)

See also Groton, Mystic, New London, Norwich, Old Lyme, Old Saybrook

Settled 1649
Population 16,919
Elevation 7 ft
Area Code 860
Zip 06378
Information Connecticut's Mystic and More!, 32 Huntington St, PO Box 89, New London 06320; phone 860/444-2206 or toll-free 800/863-6569 (outside CT)
Web Site www.mysticcountry.com

Until their defeat at Mystic Fort in 1637, the Pequot dominated the area around Stonington. In 1649, the first European settlers came here from Rehoboth, Massachusetts. Connecticut and Massachusetts both claimed ownership of the territory. In 1662, permanent control was granted to Connecticut by charter from King Charles II. Three years later the area was officially called Mystic, and in 1666 the name was changed to Stonington (which includes Stonington Borough).

The conclusion of the King Philip War in 1676 effectively ended the Native American threat in southern New England. The local economy, based on farming, shipping, and manufacturing, thrived. Prior to the Civil War, whaling and sealing expeditions left Stonington's port at regular intervals. After the war, maritime interests flourished as Stonington served as the connecting point for rail and steamer service to New York City. Today this maritime heritage is represented by a commercial fishing fleet and recreational boating.

What to See and Do

Old Lighthouse Museum. *7 Water St, Stonington (06378). Phone 860/535-1440. www.stoningtonhistory. org/light.htm.* First government-operated lighthouse in Connecticut (1823); exhibits include Stonington-made firearms, stoneware; ship models, whaling gear; China trade objects; folk art; local artifacts. Children's gallery. Visitors can climb the tower for a panoramic view of Long Island Sound. (May-Oct: daily 10 am-5 pm) **$**

Storrs (D-4)

See also Hartford, Manchester, Stafford Springs

Population 12,198
Elevation 600 ft
Area Code 860
Zip 06268
Information Northeast Connecticut Visitors District, 13 Cantebury Rd, Suite 3, PO Box 145, Brooklyn 06234; phone 860/928-1228 or toll-free 888/628-1228
Web Site www.ctquietcorner.org

What to See and Do

Ballard Institute and Museum of Puppetry. *University of Connecticut, 6 Boum Pl, Storrs (06269). Phone 860/468-4605. www.bimp.uconn.edu.* Features changing exhibits from collection of more than 2,000 puppets. Gives visitors appreciation of puppetry as art form. (Mid-Apr-mid-Nov, Fri-Sun noon-5 pm) **FREE**

Caprilands Herb Farm. *534 Silver St, Coventry (06238). 8 miles SW via Hwy 44. Phone 860/742-7244. www. caprilands.com.* More than 30 different theme gardens using herbs, spices, and wild grasses; 18th-century farm building; lunchtime lectures (Sat; $$$$). Tea program (Sun; $$$). Basket and bookshops. (Daily) **FREE**

Nathan Hale Homestead. *2299 South St, Coventry (06238). 8 miles SW via Hwy 44. Phone 860/742-6917.* (1776) Country-Georgian-style structure built by Nathan's father, Richard. Restored; many original furnishings. (Mid-May-mid-Oct, Wed-Sun afternoons) **$**

University of Connecticut. *115 N Eagleville Rd, Storrs (06269). SE on I-84, exit 68, then S on Hwy 195. Phone 860/486-2000. www.uconn.edu.* (1881) (26,200 students) On campus are the state's largest public research library, art galleries, museums, animal barns, biological and floricultural greenhouses (daily tours; free, reservations required). Also here are

Connecticut State Museum of Natural History. *University of Connecticut, 2019 Hillside Rd, Storrs (06269). Phone 860/486-4460; fax 860/486-0827.* Exhibits on Native Americans, mounted birds of prey, honey bees, sharks, minerals. (Mon-Fri 9 am-4 pm, Sun 1-4 pm) **FREE**

William Benton Museum of Art. *University of Connecticut, 245 Glenbrook Rd, Storrs (06269). Phone 860/486-4520; fax 860/486-0234.* Permanent collection includes American and European paintings, sculpture, prints, and drawings; changing exhibits. (Tues-Fri 10 am-4:30 pm, Sat-Sun 1-4:30 pm) **FREE**

Special Event

Connecticut Repertory Theatre. *University of Connecticut, Studio Theatre, 802 Bolton Rd, Storrs (06269). Phone 860/486-4226. www.crt.uconn.edu.* Musicals, comedies, and dramas. Nightly. Feb-May, July, Sept-Dec.

Stratford (F-2)

See also Bridgeport, Fairfield, Milford, Norwalk

Settled 1639
Population 49,389
Elevation 25 ft
Area Code 203
Information Chamber of Commerce, 10 Middle St, PO Box 999, Bridgeport, 06601-0999; phone 203/335-3800
Web Site www.townofstratford.com

A fine port on the Housatonic River, Stratford has been a hub of shipbuilding and industry for more than three centuries.

What to See and Do

Boothe Memorial Park. *134 Main St, Stratford (06614). Phone 203/381-2068.* Former Boothe homestead (1663-1949) on 30 acres; unusual, historical buildings; Boothe home and carriage house (mid-May-late Oct, Tues-Sun), Americana Museum, blacksmith shop, architecturally eccentric "technocratic cathedral"; flower gardens, rose garden, picnicking, playgrounds. Park (daily). Other buildings (Memorial Day-late Oct, daily). **FREE**

Captain David Judson House. *967 Academy Hill, Stratford (06615). Phone 203/378-0630. www.stratfor-*

dhistoricalsociety.com. (Circa 1750) Restored and furnished colonial house; period furnishings and crafts, slave quarters, tool display; local history exhibits. (June-Oct, Wed, Sun 11 am-3 pm; closed Memorial Day, July 4) **$** Admission includes

Catharine B. Mitchell Museum. *967 Academy Hill, Stratford (06615). Connected to the Judson House. Phone 203/378-0630.* Changing and permanent exhibits depict the history of the Stratford area 1639-1830; local memorabilia. (Same hours as Judson House)

Limited-Service Hotels

★ **HONEYSPOT LODGE.** *360 Honeyspot Rd, Stratford (06497). Phone 203/375-5666; fax 203/378-1509.* 90 rooms, 2 story. Check-out noon. **$**

★ ★ **RAMADA INN.** *225 Lordship Blvd, Stratford (06615). Phone 203/375-8866; toll-free 800/272-6232; fax 203/375-2482. www.ramada.com.* 145 rooms, 6 story. Check-in 3 pm, check-out noon. Restaurant, bar. Indoor pool. Airport transportation available. **$**

Restaurant

★ ★ ★ **PLOUF!** *14 Beach Dr, Stratford (06615). Phone 203/386-1477.* French bistro menu. Lunch, dinner. Bar. Casual attire. **$$**

Vernon (D-4)

See also Hartford, Manchester, Windsor

Population 29,841
Elevation 350 ft
Area Code 860
Zip 06066
Information Greater Hartford Tourism District, 234 Murphy Rd, Hartford 06114; phone 860/244-8181 or toll-free 800/793-4480
Web Site www.visitctriver.com

Limited-Service Hotel

★ ★ **QUALITY INN.** *51 Hartford Tpke, Vernon (06066). Phone 860/646-5700; toll-free 800/235-4667; fax 860/646-0202. www.qualityinn.com.* 127 rooms, 2 story. Check-in 3 pm, check-out 11 am. Restaurant, bar. Outdoor pool. **$**

Specialty Lodging

TOLLAND INN. *63 Tolland Green, Tolland (06084). Phone 860/872-0800; toll-free 877/465-0800; fax 860/870-7958. www.tollandinn.com.* New England inn built in 1800; handcrafted furniture. 7 rooms, 2 story. Children over 10 years only. Complimentary full breakfast. Check-in 4 pm, check-out 11 am. **$**

Restaurant

★ **REIN'S NEW YORK-STYLE DELI.** *435 Hartford Tpke, Vernon (06066). Phone 860/875-1344.* Deli menu. Breakfast, lunch, dinner. Bar. Children's menu. **$**

Washington)

Area Code 860

Full-Service Inn

★ ★ ★ ★ **THE MAYFLOWER INN.** *118 Woodbury Rd, Washington (06793). Phone 860/868-9466; fax 860/868-1497. www.mayflowerinn.com.* Just under two hours from New York City in Connecticut's verdant countryside, The Mayflower Inn is a pastoral paradise. Dating from the early 1900s, The Mayflower revives the great tradition of splendid country house hotels. The hotel is set within 28 acres of rolling hills, gurgling streams, stone walls, and lush gardens. Spread among three buildings, the guest rooms and suites bring to mind the English countryside. Four-poster, canopied beds and fireplaces enhance the romantic feel of The Mayflower Inn, perfect for a romantic getaway or a restorative retreat. The hotel's lovely grounds inspire poetry and instill serenity in visitors. The fitness center, pool, and tennis court provide diversions for active-minded guests, while others head straight for the area's well-known main streets lined with antique shops. Completing the heavenly experience is the restaurant, where fresh local ingredients inspire the creative menu. 25 rooms, 3 story. Children over 12 years old only. Check-in 3 pm, check-out 1 pm. Restaurant, bar. Fitness room, spa. Outdoor pool Tennis. **$$$$**

Waterbury (D-2)

See also Bristol, Meriden, New Britain, Southbury, Woodbury

Settled 1674
Population 108,961
Elevation 290 ft
Area Code 203
Information Waterbury Region Convention & Visitors Bureau, 21 Church St, 06702-2106; phone 203/597-9527 or toll-free 888/588-7880 (outside CT)
Web Site www.waterburyregion.com

Waterbury, the fourth-largest city in Connecticut, was once an important manufacturing center for brass-related products. Today, high-technology manufacturing and the banking industry dominate the economy. Waterbury's location near major highways provides quick and direct access to all Eastern cities.

What to See and Do

Brass Mill Center. *495 Union St, Waterbury (06706). I-84, exit 22 or 23. Phone 203/755-5000. www.brassmill-center.com.* More than 1 million-square-foot indoor mall with many shops, food court, and 12-screen movie theater. (Mon-Sat 10 am-9:30 pm, Sun 11 am-6 pm)

Mattatuck Museum. *144 W Main St, Waterbury (06702). Phone 203/753-0381; fax 203/756-6283. www.mattatuckmuseum.org.* Industrial history exhibit, decorative arts, period rooms, paintings and prints by Connecticut artists. (Tues-Sat 10 am-5 pm, Sun noon-5 pm; closed holidays) **$**

Quassy Amusement Park. *2132 Middlebury Rd, Middlebury (06762). 5 miles W on I-84, exit 17, on Hwy 64. Phone 203/758-2913. www.quassy.com.* More than 30 different rides and activities set against Lake Quassapaug; beach, swimming, boating; picnicking, concession. (Late May-Labor Day, daily; after Labor Day-Oct, weekends) **$$$$**

Full-Service Hotel

★ ★ ★ **CONNECTICUT GRAND HOTEL.** *3580 E Main St, Waterbury (06705). Phone 203/706-1000; toll-free 800/541-0469; fax 203/755-1555. www.sheraton.com.* 279 rooms, 4 story. Check-in 3 pm, check-out 11 am. Restaurant, bar. Fitness room. Indoor pool, whirlpool. **$**

Specialty Lodging

HOUSE ON THE HILL BED & BREAKFAST. *92 Woodlawn Terr, Waterbury (06710). Phone 203/757-9901. www.houseonthehill.biz.* This historic mansion, built in 1888, features a library, gardens, and many fireplaces. 4 rooms, 3 story. Complimentary full breakfast. Check-in 3 pm, check-out 11 am. **$$**

Westport (F-1)

See also Bridgeport, Fairfield, Norwalk, Stamford

Settled 1648
Population 24,410
Elevation 78 ft
Area Code 203
Information Westport/Weston Chamber of Commerce, 60 Church Ln, PO Box 30; phone 203/227-9234
Web Site www.westportchamber.com

Westport is a fashionable community on Long Island Sound 45 miles from New York City. Well-known writers and many successful actors, illustrators, and corporate and advertising executives make their homes here. Westport is surrounded by wooded hills and has three municipal beaches and a state park on the sound.

Special Events

Levitt Pavilion for the Performing Arts. *Jesup Green, 260 Compo Rd S, Westport (06880). On the Saugatuck River. Phone 203/226-7600; fax 203/226-2330. www.levittpavilion.com.* Nightly free outdoor performances of classical, jazz, pop, rock; dance, children's series. Late June-early Aug. **FREE**

Westport Country Playhouse. *25 Powers Ct, Westport (06880). Phone 203/227-4177.* Broadway and pre-Broadway presentations by professional companies. Nightly Mon-Sat; matinees Wed and Sat; children's shows Fri. Apr-Nov.

Westport Handcrafts Fair. *Staples High School Field House, 70 North Ave, Westport (06880). Phone 203/227-7844.* Features 100 crafts artisans. Memorial Day weekend.

Limited-Service Hotel

★ ★ **WESTPORT INN.** *1595 Post Rd E, Westport (06880). Phone 203/259-5236; toll-free 800/446-8997; fax 203/254-8439. www.westportinn.com.* 116 rooms, 2 story. Pets accepted, some restrictions. Check-in 3 pm, check-out noon. Restaurant, bar. Fitness room. Indoor pool, whirlpool. **$**

Full-Service Hotel

★ ★ ★ **INN AT NATIONAL HALL.** *2 Post Rd W, Westport (06880). Phone 203/221-1351; toll-free 800/628-4255; fax 203/221-0276. www.innatnationalhall.com.* Nestled along the banks of the Saugatuck River in Westport, within walking distance to shops, galleries, and the beach, The Inn at National Hall is perhaps one of the most distinctive properties in New England. Slightly quirky with an *Alice in Wonderland* quality to it, this 1873 Italianate inn has just 15 individually designed rooms gloriously decorated in vibrant colors. Each room lives up to its name, with themes such as the watermelon room and the equestrian suite. River views add an enchanting touch to many of the accommodations, and several chambers boast soaring two-story ceilings and crystal chandeliers. Rather like the house of a very well traveled but slightly eccentric relative, this inn surprises guests at each turn with whimsical accessories from around the world. Imaginations could truly run wild here, and even a ride in the elevator inspires creativity with its library-like murals and mysterious happenings. 15 rooms, 3 story. Complimentary continental breakfast. Check-in 3 pm, check-out 11:30 am. **$$$**

Specialty Lodging

THE INN AT LONGSHORE. *260 Compo Rd S, Westport (06880). Phone 203/226-3316; fax 203/227-5344. www.innatlongshore.com.* Overlooking Long Island Sound, this inn was built as a private estate in 1890. 12 rooms, 3 story. Complimentary continental breakfast. Check-in 3 pm, check-out noon. Restaurant. Outdoor pool. Golf. Tennis. **$**

Restaurants

★ ★ ★ **COBB'S MILL INN.** *12 Old Mill Rd, Westton (06880). Phone 203/227-7221; fax 203/226-1599. www.cobbsmillinn.com.* Excellent service with an elegant, historic ambience. Cuisine is beautifully presented. Seafood, steak menu. Lunch, dinner. Bar. Valet parking. **$$$**

★ ★ **NISTICO'S RED BARN.** *292 Wilton Rd, Westport (06880). Phone 203/222-9549; fax 203/222-8935. www.redbarnrestaurant.com.* American menu. Lunch, dinner, brunch. Closed Dec 24-25. Children's menu. Valet parking. Outdoor seating. **$$$**

Wethersfield (D-3)

See also Avon, Farmington, Hartford, New Britain, Windsor

Settled 1634
Population 25,651
Elevation 45 ft
Area Code 860
Zip 06109
Information Wethersfield Historical Society, 150 Main St; phone 860/529-7656
Web Site www.wethhist.org

Wethersfield, "the most ancient towne in Connecticut," has a rich heritage. Settled by a group of Massachusetts colonists, it became the commercial center of the Connecticut River communities and an important post in the trade between the American colonies and the West Indies. Agriculture, especially corn, rye, and, later, the famous red onion, was the source of Wethersfield's trade. During the Revolutionary War years, notable figures, such as George Washington and Count de Rochambeau, came to Wethersfield and decided upon plans that became part of US history. Many existing buildings date from the Revolutionary War.

With the birth and development of the railroad and the shift of trade to the coastal villages, Wethersfield's importance as an industrial and commercial center declined.

What to See and Do

Buttolph-Williams House. *249 Broad St, Wethersfield (06109). Phone 860/529-0460.* (Circa 1700) Restored building contains fine collection of pewter, delft, fabrics, period furniture. (May-Oct, Wed-Mon, limited hours) **$**

Dinosaur State Park. *400 West St, Rocky Hill (06067). 3 miles S via I-91, exit 23, off West St. Phone 860/529-8423. www.dinosaurstatepark.org.* While excavating the site of a new building, a stone slab bearing the three-toed tracks of dinosaurs, which roamed the area 200 million years ago, was discovered. Construction was halted, and a 65-acre area was designated a state park. Eventually more than 2,000 prints were unearthed. A geodesic dome was set up over parts of the trackway to protect the find. Visitors are able to examine the crisscrossing tracks and view a skeletal cast and life-size models of the area's prehistoric inhabitants. Nature trails; picnicking. Exhibit center (Tues-Sun; closed Jan 1, Thanksgiving, Dec 25). Park (daily). **$**

First Church of Christ, Congregational United Church of Christ. *250 Main St, Wethersfield (06109). Phone 860/529-1575.* The church was established in 1635; the Meetinghouse (1761; restored 1973) is the third one to stand on or near this site. (Mon-Fri; also by appointment) **FREE**

Hurlburt-Dunham House. *200 Main St, Wethersfield (06109). Phone 860/529-7656.* Georgian house updated in Italianate style. Rich in decoration, includes original Rococo Revival wallpapers, painted ceilings, and a varied collection of furniture. (Mid-Mar-mid-May and mid-Oct-Dec 25, Sat-Sun) **$**

Webb-Deane-Stevens Museum. *211 Main St, Wethersfield (06109). Phone 860/529-0612.* Consists of three 18th-century houses that stand at the center of old Wethersfield: the Joseph Webb house (1752), the Silas Deane house (1766), and the Isaac Stevens house (1789). The houses have been restored and are furnished with objects to reflect the different ways of life of their owners--a merchant, a diplomat, and a tradesman; also Colonial Revival garden. (May-Nov, Wed-Mon; rest of year, Sat-Sun) **$$**

Wethersfield Museum. *Keeney Memorial Cultural Center, 200 Main St, Wethersfield (06109). Phone 860/529-7161.* Changing exhibit galleries; permanent Wethersfield exhibit. (Daily) **$**

Limited-Service Hotel

★ **BEST WESTERN CAMELOT INN.** *1330 Silas Deane Hwy, Wethersfield (06109). Phone 860/563-2311; toll-free 888/563-3930; fax 860/529-2974. www.bestwestern.com.* 112 rooms, 4 story. Pets accepted, some restrictions; fee. Complimentary continental breakfast. Check-out 11 am. Bar. **$**

Windsor (E-3)

See also Enfield, Hartford, Manchester, Stafford Springs, Vernon, Wethersfield, Windsor Locks

Settled 1633
Population 27,817
Elevation 57 ft
Area Code 860
Zip 06095
Information Chamber of Commerce, 261 Broad St, PO Box 9, 06095-0009; phone 860/688-5165; or the Heritage Valley North Central Tourism Bureau, 111 Hazard Ave, Enfield 06082; phone 860/763-2578
Web Site www.windsorcc.org

Windsor was first settled by members of an expeditionary group from the original Plymouth Colony. A farming center since the 17th century, it is only 9 miles north of Hartford. The village is divided by the Farmington River; there is a green and many colonial houses on each side of the river.

What to See and Do

Connecticut Trolley Museum. *58 North Rd, Windsor Locks. In East Windsor at 58 North Rd (Hwy 140); from Windsor Locks proceed NE on I-91 to exit 45, then 3/4 mile E on Hwy 140 (for clarification of directions, phone ahead). Phone 860/627-6540.* Exhibits include more than 50 antique trolley cars from 1894-1949; operating trolleys take visitors on 3-mile ride through countryside; electric passenger trains also operate some weekends. (Memorial Day-Labor Day, Wed-Mon; rest of year, Sat, Sun, and holidays; closed Thanksgiving, Dec 25) **$$** On grounds is

Connecticut Fire Museum. *58 North Rd, East Windsor (06088). Phone 860/627-6540.* Collection of fire engines and antique motorcoaches from 1856-1954. (June-Aug: Wed-Mon; Apr-May and Sept-Nov: Sat-Sun) **$$**

First Church in Windsor. *107 Palisado Ave, Windsor (06095). Phone 860/688-7229.* (1630) United Church of Christ Congregational. Classic Georgian-style architecture (1794); cemetery (1633) adjacent. Request key at church office, 107 Palisado Avenue. (Daily) **FREE**

Oliver Ellsworth Homestead. *778 Palisado Ave, Windsor (06095). Phone 860/688-8717.* (1781) Home of one of five men who drafted the Constitution; third

Chief Justice of the United States and one of the first senators from Connecticut; Washington and Adams visited the house. Restored to period; many original Ellsworth furnishings. (May-Oct: Wed, Thurs, Sat) **$$**

Windsor Historical Society. *96 Palisado Ave, Windsor (06095). Phone 860/688-3813.* Walking tours of the John and Sarah Strong House (1758) and the Dr. Hezekiah Chaffee House (1765); period costumes and furnishings; Puritan cemetery. (Tues-Sat) **$**

Limited-Service Hotel

★ ★ **COURTYARD BY MARRIOTT.** *1 Day Hill Rd, Windsor (06095). Phone 860/683-0022; toll-free 800/321-2211; fax 860/683-1072. www.courtyard.com.* 149 rooms, 2 story. Check-in 3 pm, check-out noon. High-speed Internet access. Restaurant. Indoor pool, whirlpool. **$**

Windsor Locks (C-3)

See also Enfield, Hartford, Windsor, Springfield

Population 12,358
Elevation 80 ft
Area Code 860
Zip 06096
Information Chamber of Commerce, PO Box 257; phone 860/623-9319
Web Site www.wmch.com

What to See and Do

New England Air Museum. *36 Perimeter Rd, Windsor Locks (06096). Adjacent to Bradley International Airport, 3 miles SW via I-91, exit 40, W on Hwy 20 to Hwy 75, follow signs. Phone 860/623-3305. www.neam. org.* One of the largest and most comprehensive collections of aircraft and aeronautical memorabilia in the world. More than 80 aircraft on display including bombers, fighters, helicopters, and gliders dating from 1909-present era; movies; jet fighter cockpit simulator. (Daily; closed Jan 1, Thanksgiving, Dec 25) **$$**

Noden-Reed House & Barn. *58 West St, Windsor Locks (06096). Phone 860/627-9212.* Housed in a 1840 house and a 1825 barn are an antique sleigh bed, 1871 taffeta evening dress, 1884 wedding dress, antique quilts, kitchen utensils, 1880s newspapers and periodicals. (May-Oct, Sun afternoons)

Old Newgate Prison. *115 Newgate Rd, East Granby (06026). 8 miles W on I-91 to exit 40; at junction Newgate Rd and Hwy 120. Phone 860/653-3563.* Site of a copper mine (1707) converted to Revolutionary prison for Tories (1775-1782) and a state prison (until 1827); self-guided tour of underground caverns where prisoners lived. (Mid-May-Oct, Wed-Sun) **$**

Limited-Service Hotels

★ ★ **DOUBLETREE HOTEL.** *16 Ella Grasso Tpke, Windsor Locks (06096). Phone 860/627-5171; toll-free 800/222-8733; fax 860/627-7029. www.doubletree.com.* This hotel is located just 1 mile from Bradley International and minutes from Old Newgate Prison and Six Flags. 200 rooms, 5 story. Check-in 3 pm, check-out noon. Restaurant, bar. Fitness room. Indoor pool, whirlpool. Airport transportation available. **$**

★ **HOMEWOOD SUITES.** *65 Ella Grasso Tpke, Windsor Locks (06096). Phone 860/627-8463; toll-free 800/225-5466; fax 860/627-9313. www.homewood-suites.com.* 132 rooms, 3 story, all suites. Pets accepted, some restrictions; fee. Complimentary continental breakfast. Check-in 3 pm, check-out noon. Fitness room. Outdoor pool. Airport transportation available. Business center. **$**

Full-Service Hotel

★ ★ ★ **SHERATON BRADLEY AIRPORT HO-TEL.** *1 Bradley International Airport, Windsor Locks (06096). Phone 860/627-5311; toll-free 877/422-5311; fax 860/627-9348. www.sheraton.com/bradleyairport.* 237 rooms, 8 story. Pets accepted. Check-in 3 pm, check-out noon. Restaurant, bar. Fitness room. Indoor pool. **$**

Woodbury (E-2)

See also Bristol, Danbury, Southbury, Waterbury

Population 1,290
Elevation 264 ft
Area Code 203
Zip 06798
Information Litchfield Hills Visitors Bureau, PO Box 968, Litchfield 06759; phone 860/567-4506
Web Site www.northwestct.com

What to See and Do

Flanders Nature Center. *5 Church Hill Rd, Woodbury (06798). Phone 203-263-3711. www.flandersnaturecenter.org.* Large conservation area with woodland hiking trails, wildlife marshes; wildflower trails. Self-guided tour; special events include maple syrup demonstration (Mar). (Daily) **FREE**

Glebe House and Gertrude Jekyll Garden. *Hollow Rd, Woodbury (06798). Off Hwy 6. Phone 203/263-2855. www.theglebehouse.org.* (Circa 1770) Minister's farmhouse or *glebe*, where Samuel Seabury was elected America's first Episcopal bishop in 1783; restored with 18th-century furnishings, original paneling; garden designed by Gertrude Jekyll. (Apr-Nov: Wed-Sun afternoons; rest of year: by appointment) **$**

Restaurants

★ ★ **CAROLE PECK'S GOOD NEWS CAFE.** *694 Main St S, Woodbury (06798). Phone 203/266-4663.* American menu. Lunch, dinner. Closed Tues; holidays. Bar. Outdoor seating. **$$**

★ **CURTIS HOUSE.** *506 Main St S, Woodbury (06798). Phone 203/263-2101; fax 203/263-6265.* American menu. Lunch, dinner. Closed holidays. Bar. Children's menu. **$$**

Maine

Here are the highest tides (28 feet in Passamaquoddy Bay), the tastiest potatoes, and the tartest conversation in the country. Flat Yankee twang and the patois of French Canadians make Maine's speech as salty as its sea. Hunters, anglers, canoeists, and campers appreciate its 6,000 lakes and ponds, and summer vacationers enjoy its 3,500 miles of seacoast even though the water is a bit chilly.

Downeasters brag about the state's temperature range from -46° F to 105° F, as well as its famous lobsters. Paper and allied products are the chief manufactured products; machine tools, electronic components, and other metal products are important. Food canning and freezing are major industries. Potatoes, blueberries, poultry, eggs, dairy products, and apples are leading farm crops.

Maine's first settlement (1604) was on St. Croix Island; it lasted one winter. Another early settlement was established near Pemaquid Point. The short-lived Popham Colony, at the mouth of the Kennebec River, built America's first transatlantic trader, the *Virginia,* in 1607. Until 1819, Maine was a part of Massachusetts. It was admitted to the Union in 1820.

Most of Maine's 17.6 million acres of forestland is open to public recreational use including more than 580,000 acres owned by the state. For more information about recreational use of public and private forestland, contact the Maine Bureau of Public Lands, phone 207/287-3061, or the Maine Forest Service at 207/287-2791.

When to Go/Climate

Maine is a large state affected by several different weather patterns. Coastal temperatures are more moderate than inland temperatures, and fog is common in spring and fall. In general, winters are cold and snowy. Summers are filled with warm, sunny days and cool, clear nights. Fall's famous "nor'easters" can bring high tides, gale-force winds, and huge amounts of rain to the coastal areas.

Population: 1,227,928
Area: 30,995 square miles
Elevation: 0-5,268 feet
Peak: Mount Katahdin (Piscataquis County)
Entered Union: March 15, 1820 (23rd state)
Capital: Augusta
Motto: I Lead
Nickname: Pine Tree State
Flower: Pine Cone and Tassel
Bird: Chickadee
Tree: Eastern White Pine
Fair: August in Skowhegan
Time Zone: Eastern
Web Site: www.visitmaine.com
Fun Facts:
- Nearly 90 percent of the nation's lobster supply is caught off the coast of Maine.
- Maine has over 5,000 miles of coastline, more than California.

AVERAGE HIGH/LOW TEMPERATURES (°F)

Caribou

Jan 19/-2	May 62/40	Sept 64/43
Feb 23/7	June 72/49	Oct 52/34
Mar 34/15	July 77/55	Nov 38/24
Apr 47/29	Aug 74/52	Dec 42/6

Portland

Jan 45/34	May 67/47	Sept 75/52
Feb 51/36	June 74/53	Oct 64/45
Mar 56/39	July 80/57	Nov 53/40
Apr 61/41	Aug 80/57	Dec 46/35

Calendar Highlights

FEBRUARY

Kennebunk Winter Carnival *(Kennebunk). Phone 207/985-6890.* Snow sculpture contests, snow palace moonwalk, magic show, ice-skating party, chili and chowder contests, children's events.

MAY

Maine State Parade *(Lewiston and Auburn). Downtown Lewiston and Auburn. Phone Androscoggin County Chamber of Commerce, 207/783-2249.* Maine's largest parade; more than 30,000 people represent 60 communities.

JUNE

Great Whatever Family Festival Week *(Augusta). Kennebec Valley Chamber of Commerce. Phone 207/623-4559.* More than 60 events include tournaments, carnival, barbecue, parade, and fireworks. Festivities culminate with the canoe and kayak regatta on the Kennebec River between Augusta and Gardiner. There are also canoe and kayak races.

Windjammer Days *(Boothbay Harbor). Phone 207/633-2353.* Old schooners that formerly sailed the trade routes and now cruise the Maine coast sail en masse into the harbor. Waterfront food court, entertainment, street parade, children's activities.

JULY

Bangor State Fair *(Bangor). Phone 207/947-5555. www.bangorstatefair.com.* One of the country's oldest fairs. Horse racing, exhibits, stage shows.

Festival de Joie *(Lewiston and Auburn).* Central Maine Civic Center. Androscoggin County Chamber of Commerce. Phone 207/782-6231. www.festivaldejoie.org. A celebration of Lewiston and Auburn's Franco-American heritage. Features ethnic song, dance, cultural activities, and traditional foods.

Schooner Days & North Atlantic Blues Festival *(Rockland). Phone 207/596-0376.* A three-day festival celebrating Maine's maritime heritage; features Parade of Schooners, arts, entertainment, concessions, fireworks; blues bands and club crawl.

AUGUST

Maine Lobster Festival *(Rockland). Phone 207/596-0376 or toll-free 800/562-2529.* A five-day event centered around Maine's chief marine creature, with a huge tent cafeteria serving lobster and other seafood. Parade, harbor cruises, maritime displays, bands, entertainment.

Skowhegan State Fair *(Skowhegan). Phone 207/474-2947.* One of the oldest fairs in the country (1818). Mile-long midway, stage shows, harness racing; contests, exhibits.

DECEMBER

Christmas by the Sea *(Camden). Phone 207/236-4404.* A celebration of the holiday season with musical entertainment, horse-drawn wagon rides, Holiday House Tour, Santa's arrival by lobsterboat.

Parks and Recreation

Water-related activities, hiking, biking, various other sports, picnicking and visitor centers, as well as camping, are available in many of Maine's state parks. Most state parks and historic sites are open seasonally from 9 am-sunset; Popham Beach, John Paul Jones Memorial, and Reid are open year-round. Most areas have day-use and/or parking fees, $1.50-$3 per person; annual pass, $40/vehicle, $20/individual. Camping May-October (areas vary), nonresidents $11-$17 per site, residents $9-$13 per site; reservations fee $2 a night. Camping reservations may be made by mail to the Bureau of Parks and Lands, Station #22, Augusta 04333, Attention Reservation Clerk; in person at the office of the Bureau of Parks and Lands in Augusta; by phone, 207/287-3824 or toll-free 800/332-1501 (ME). Maine historic sites fee $2.50-$3. Pets on leash only in most parks. No dogs on beaches or at Sebago Lake campground. For more information, contact the Bureau of Parks and Lands, Maine Department of Conservation, 286 Water Street, Key Bank Plaza, Augusta 04333. Phone 207/287-3821.

THE COASTAL ROUTE

Most tourists stick to coastal Route 1 when it splits from Interstate 95 at Brunswick, home of the Bowdoin College museums, the Joshua Chamberlain Museum, and outstanding summer music and theater. Bath is worth a stop to see the Maine Maritime Museum and Shipyard. Traffic streams down a peninsula to Boothbay Harbor, a resort village with a footbridge across its harbor that is a departure point for numerous excursion boats. Rockland is the next must-see stop on Route 1. Visit the Farnsworth Art Museum and Wyeth Center or Owls Head Transportation Museum. Maine Windjammers and ferries to Vinalhaven and North Haven depart from here. Next on our route is Camden, a town backed by hills and filled with inns, restaurants, and shops. Camden Hills State Park offers spectacular views of the coast, as well as hiking, camping, and picnic facilities. Belfast, another interesting old port, is a departure point for excursion boats and for the Belfast & Moosehead Lake Railroad Company excursion train. Continue up coastal Route 1 to Ellsworth, then turn down Route 3 to Mount Desert Island, site of Acadia National

Park. The big tourist town here is Bar Harbor (the park is the big draw, also many excursion boats). Return the same way, perhaps taking the ferry to Yarmouth, Nova Scotia, for an interesting side trip. Another option is to continue north on Route 1 past Ellsworth (the turnoff for Bar Harbor). Here Route 1 changes, becoming far quieter, especially after the turnoff for Schoodic Point, which is part of Acadia National Park. The obvious next stop is in Machias, where the Burnham Tavern Museum tells the area's revolutionary history. Take a detour at the cliffside walking trails of Quoddy Head State Park (the easternmost point in the United States). Then continue on to Lubec and over the bridge to Campobello Island (New Brunswick, Canada), to see the Roosevelt Campobello International Park with Franklin D. Roosevelt's summer home as its centerpiece. The park also includes a golf course and extensive hiking trails. Return to Bar Harbor along the same route. **(Approximately 306 miles; add 128 miles if continuing on to Lubec)**

FISHING AND HUNTING

Nonresident fishing license: $51; 12-15 years, $8; 15-day license, $39; seven-day license, $35; three-day license, $22; one-day license, $10. Nonresident hunting license for birds and animals except deer, bear, turkey, moose, bobcat, and raccoon: $56; includes all legal game species: $86. These fees do not include agent fees, which range from $1-$2. Detailed information about the state's regulations is available in the brochures *Maine Hunting and Trapping Laws* and *Maine Open Water Fishing Laws* from the Maine Fish and Wildlife Department, Station 41, 284 State Street, Augusta 04333; phone 207/287-8000.

Driving Information

Every person must be in an approved passenger restraint anywhere in a vehicle; children under age 4 must use approved safety seats. For further information, phone 207/871-7771.

INTERSTATE HIGHWAY SYSTEM

The following alphabetical listing of Maine towns

in this book shows that these cities are within 10 miles of the indicated interstate highway. Check a highway map for the nearest exit.

Highway Number	Cities/Towns within 10 Miles
Interstate 95	Augusta, Bangor, Bath, Biddeford, Brunswick, Freeport, Houlton, Kennebunk, Kittery, Lincoln, Millinocket, Newport, Ogunquit, Old Orchard Beach, Orono, Portland, Saco, Scarborough, Waterville, Wells, Yarmouth, York.

Additional Visitor Information

The pulp and paper industry mills throughout Maine offer tours of their woodlands and manufacturing facilities at various times of the year. For further information, contact the Maine Pulp & Paper Association Information Office, 104 Sewall Street, PO Box 5670, Augusta 04330; phone 207/622-3166.

There are eight official information service centers in Maine. Visitors who stop by will find information and brochures helpful in planning stops to points of interest. Their locations are as follows: in Bethel, on Highway 2; at Kittery, between Interstate 95 and Highway 1; in Fryeburg (summer only), on Highway 302; in Calais, on Union Street, off Highway 1; in Hampden, on Interstate 95 N at mile marker 169; on Interstate 95 S between mile markers 171 and 172; in Houlton, on Ludlow Road; in Yarmouth, between Interstate 95, exit 17 and Highway 1.

Acadia National Park (E-3)

See also Bar Harbor, Northeast Harbor, Southwest Harbor

Web Site www.nps.gov/acad

On Mount Desert Island, south and west of Bar Harbor; entrance off Highway 3.

Waves crashing against a rocky coastline, thick woodlands abundant with wildlife, and mountains scraping the sky—Acadia National Park is the Maine of storybooks. Occupying nearly half of Mount Desert Island, with smaller areas on Isle au Haut, Little Cranberry Island (see CRANBERRY ISLES), Baker Island, Little Moose Island, and part of the mainland at Schoodic Point, Acadia amazes visitors. It is a sea-lashed granite coastal area of forested valleys, lakes, and mountains, all created by the force of the glaciers. At 40,000 acres, Acadia is small compared to other national parks; however, it is one of the most visited national parks in the United States and the only national park in the northeastern United States. A 27-mile loop road connects the park's eastern sites on

Mount Desert Island, and ferry services take travelers to some of the smaller islands. Visitors can explore 1,530-foot Cadillac Mountain, the highest point on the Atlantic Coast of the United States; watch waves crash against Thunder Hole, creating a thunderous boom; or swim in the ocean at various coastal beaches. A road to the summit of Cadillac provides views of Frenchman, Blue Hill, and Penobscot bays. Mount Desert Island was named by French explorer Samuel de Champlain in 1604. Shortly thereafter, French Jesuit missionaries settled here until driven off by an armed vessel from Virginia. This was the first act of

overt warfare between France and England for control of North America. Until 1713, the island was a part of French Acadia. It was not until after the Revolutionary War that it was settled extensively. In 1916, a portion of the area was proclaimed Sieur de Monts National Monument. It was changed to Lafayette National Park in 1919, and finally, in 1929, it was enlarged and renamed Acadia National Park.

Like all national parks, Acadia is a wildlife sanctuary. Fir, pine, spruce, many hardwoods, and hundreds of varieties of wildflowers thrive. Nature lovers will be delighted with the more than 120 miles of trails; park rangers take visitors on various walks and cruises, pointing out and explaining the natural, cultural, and historical features of the park. Forty-five miles of carriage roads offer bicyclists scenic rides through Acadia. Copies of ranger-led programs and trail maps are available at the visitor center.

There is saltwater swimming at Echo Lake. Snowmobiles are allowed in some areas, and cross-country skiing is available. Most facilities are open Memorial Day-September; however, portions of the park are open year-round, and the picnic grounds are open May-October. Limited camping is available at two park campgrounds: Blackwoods, open year-round, requires reservations from mid-June-mid-September; and Seawall, open late May-late September, is on a first-come, first-served basis. The park headquarters, 2 1/2 miles west of Bar Harbor (see) on Highway 233, provides visitor information (Nov-Apr, daily; closed Jan 1, Thanksgiving, Dec 24-25). For further information, contact the Superintendent, PO Box 177, Bar Harbor 04609; phone 207/288-3338. Golden Eagle, Golden Age and Golden Access passports are accepted (see MAKING THE MOST OF YOUR TRIP).

What to See and Do

Auto Tape Tours. *Mount Desert Island.* A scenic, 56-mile self-guided tour gives a mile-by-mile description of the points of interest, history, and geology of the park. Tapes are available May-October at the visitor center. Cassette player and tape rental, deposit required; or tape may be purchased. **$$$$**

Ferry Service. *Northeast Harbor. Phone 207/244-3575.* Connects Islesford, Great Cranberry Island, and Northeast Harbor on a regular schedule all year. **$$$**

Isle au Haut (EEL-oh-HO). *Isle au Haut.* Mountains rise more than 540 feet on this island of forested shores and cobblestone beaches; hiking trails; small primitive campground (advance mail reservations; phone 207/288-3338 for reservation form). A ferry from Stonington (see DEER ISLE) takes visitors on the 45-minute trip to the island (Mon-Sat; closed holidays; fee).

Islesford Historical Museum. *Islesford. On Little Cranberry Island; 2 miles S of Seal Harbor.* A 30-minute boat trip from Northeast Harbor. (See Cranberry Isles) **FREE**

Islesford Naturalist Sea Cruises. *Northeast Harbor. Phone 207/276-5352.* Marine life and history of the area are explained. (Daily during summer season, schedule varies; phone for fees)

Park Tours. *Main St, Bar Harbor (04609). Phone 207/288-3327.* Narrated sightseeing trips through the park. Buses leave Main Street, in Bar Harbor. (June-early Oct) For tickets and information about tour schedules and fees, contact Testa's Cafe, 53 Main Street, Bar Harbor. **$$$$**

Visitor Center. *Rte 3, Hulls Cove (04644). 3 miles NW of Bar Harbor at Hulls Cove. Phone 207/288-3338.* (May-Oct, daily)

Allagash Wilderness Waterway

See also Fort Kent

In 1970, the Allagash River was designated a national wild river. Stretching 95 miles through 200,000 acres of lakes, rivers, and timberland in Maine's northern wilderness, this waterway is a favorite of canoeists. A good put-in point is Chamberlain Thoroughfare at the junction of Chamberlain and Telos lakes. The trip ends at Allagash Village, 8 miles north of Allagash Falls, near the Canadian border, where the Allagash flows into the St. John River. Some canoe experience is necessary before attempting the entire trip as high winds can be a problem on the lakes and, depending on the level of the Allagash, the rapids can be dangerous.

Registration is required upon entering and leaving the waterway; rangers are at Allagash Lake, Chamberlain Thoroughfare, Eagle Lake, Churchill Dam, Long Lake Thoroughfare, and the Michaud Farm. Supplies and canoes must be brought in; gasoline is not available. There are restrictions regarding the size of parties using the waterway, as well as watercraft permitted. Numerous primitive campsites accessible only by water

are scattered along the waterway (mid-May-mid-Oct). Campsite fee per person, per night ($).

For further information and rules, contact the Bureau of Parks & Lands, Maine Department of Conservation, Northern Regional Office, BMHI Complex, Building H, 106 Hogan Road, Bangor, 04401; phone 207/941-4014.

Auburn (E-1)

See also Lewiston, Poland Spring

Settled 1797
Population 24,309
Elevation 188 ft
Area Code 207
Information Androscoggin County Chamber of Commerce, 179 Lisbon St, PO Box 59, Lewiston 04243-0059; phone 207/783-2249
Web Site www.androscoggincounty.com

Auburn, together with its sister city Lewiston, make up an important manufacturing center. In 1836, the first organized shoe company was started here. The Minot Shoe Company prospered, selling more than $6 million in shoes by 1900, and becoming the fifth-largest shoe company in the United States by 1920. When the Depression hit, the company suffered a severe blow. The city continued to expand, however, and today Auburn is one of the largest cities in the state.

What to See and Do

Androscoggin Historical Society Library and Museum. *County Building, 2 Turner St, Auburn (04210). Turner St at Court St. Phone 207/784-0586.* Exhibits trace local, county and state history. (Wed-Fri; closed holidays) Museum; library. **FREE**

Lost Valley Ski Area. *200 Lost Valley Rd, Auburn (04210). Follow signs off Hwy 11. Phone 207/784-1561. www.lostvalleyski.com.* Two double chairlifts, T-bar; snowmaking; patrol, school, rentals; bar, lounge, restaurant. (Dec-mid-Mar, daily) **$$$$**

Norlands Living History Center. *290 Norlands Rd, Livermore (04523). 25 miles N just off Hwy 4. Phone 207/897-4366. www.norlands.org.* Life as it was lived a century ago; clothing, customs. Year-round working farm with oxen, horses, cows, crops, and seasonal activities. Features 19th-century Victorian home of Washburn family; school, library, church, farmer's cottage, barn.

Tours (July-Labor Day, daily; rest of year, by appointment). Picnicking. (See SPECIAL EVENTS) **$$**

Special Events

Autumn Celebration. *Norlands Living History Center, 290 Norlands Rd, Livermore (04523). Phone 207/897-4366.* Cider pressing, hayrides, and building tours are some of the activities at this traditional harvest festival. Oct.

Maple Days. *Norlands Living History Center, 290 Norlands Rd, Livermore (04523). Phone 207/897-4366.* Mid-Mar.

Augusta (E-2)

See also Lewiston, Poland Spring, Waterville

Settled 1628
Population 21,325
Elevation 153 ft
Area Code 207
Information Kennebec Valley Chamber of Commerce, 21 University Dr, PO Box 676, 04332-0192; phone 207/623-4559
Web Site www.augustamaine.com

Augusta, the capital of Maine, began in 1628 when men from Plymouth established a trading post on the site of Cushnoc, a Native American village. From there, Fort Western was built in 1754 to protect settlers against Native American raids, and the settlement grew. Today, 39 miles from the sea, Augusta is at the head of navigation on the Kennebec River; some of the town's leading industries include steel and food processing and service-related industries.

What to See and Do

Old Fort Western. *City Center Plaza, 16 Cony St, Augusta (04330). Phone 207/626-2385. www.oldfortwestern. org.* Fort complex built in 1754 by Boston merchants; main house and reproduction blockhouse, watchboxes, and palisade. Costumed staff interprets 18th-century life on the Kennebec River. (Memorial Day-Labor Day: daily; after Labor Day-Columbus Day: Sat-Sun, limited hours) **$**

State House. *83 State House Station, Augusta (04330). State and Capitol sts. Phone 207/287-2301. www.maine. gov.* (1829-1832) The original design for this impressive building was by Charles Bulfinch (architect of the Massachusetts State House). Remodeled and enlarged (1909-1910), it rises majestically above Capitol Park and the Kennebec River. On its 185-foot dome is a statue, designed by W. Clark Noble, of a classically robed woman bearing a pine bough torch. (Mon-Fri; closed holidays) **FREE** Also here is

Blaine House. *State and Capitol sts, Augusta (04330). Phone 207/287-2301.* (1833) House of James G. Blaine, Speaker of the US House of Representatives and 1884 presidential candidate. Since 1919, this 28-room house has been the official residence of Maine's governors. Originally built in Federal-style, it was remodeled several times and today appears semicolonial. Tours (Tues-Thurs, limited hours; closed holidays). **FREE**

Maine State Museum. *83 State House Station, Augusta (04330). Phone 207/287-2301.* Exhibits of Maine's natural environment, prehistory, social history, and manufacturing heritage. "This Land Called Maine" features five natural history scenes as well as a presentation of 40 spectacular gems and gem minerals found in Maine. "Made in Maine" presents 19th-century products and manufacturing technologies and includes a water-powered woodworking mill, a two-story textile factory, and more than 1,000 Maine-made objects. Other exhibits examine the early economic activities of agriculture, fishing, granite quarrying, ice harvesting, lumbering, and shipbuilding. Also featured are a display of military, political, and geographical artifacts relating to the formation of the state of Maine as well as an exhibition on Maine glass. Gift shop. (Daily; closed holidays) **$**

Special Events

Great Whatever Family Festival Week. *21 University Dr, Augusta (04330). Augusta/Gardiner area. Phone 207/623-4559.* More than 60 events include tournaments, carnival, barbecue, parade, and fireworks. Festivities culminate with the canoe and kayak regatta on the Kennebec River between Augusta and Gardiner. There are also canoe and kayak races. Contact Chamber of Commerce. Ten days in late June-early July.

New England Music Camp. *8 Goldenrod Ln, Augusta (04330). 5 miles W on Hwy 137 to Oakland, then 4 miles S on Hwy 23. Phone 207/465-3025. www. nemusiccamp.com.* Student concerts, Sat-Sun; faculty concerts, Wed. Late June-late Aug.

Limited-Service Hotels

★ **BEST INN.** *65 Whitten Rd, Augusta (04330).* *Phone 207/622-3776; toll-free 800/237-8466; fax 207/622-3778. www.bestinnmaine.com.* 58 rooms, 2 story. Complimentary continental breakfast. Check-out 11 am. Outdoor pool. **$**

★ **COMFORT INN.** *281 Civic Center Dr, Augusta (04330). Phone 207/623-1000; toll-free 800/808-1188; fax 207/623-3505. www.choicehotels.com.* 99 rooms, 3 story. Pets accepted. Complimentary continental breakfast. Check-in 3 pm, check-out 11 am. Restaurant, bar. Fitness room. Indoor pool. **$**

Full-Service Resort

★ ★ ★ **BEST WESTERN SENATOR INN & SPA.** *284 Western Ave, Augusta (04330). Phone 207/622-5804; toll-free 877/772-2224; fax 207/622-8803. www.senatorinn.com.* 124 rooms, 2 story. Pets accepted, some restrictions; fee. Complimentary full breakfast. Check-in 3 pm, check-out noon. High-speed Internet access, wireless Internet access. Restaurant, bar. Children's activity center. Fitness room, fitness classes available, spa. Indoor pool, outdoor pool, whirlpool. **$$**

Specialty Lodging

WINGS HILL INN. *Rte 27 and Dry Point Dr, Belgrade Lakes (04918). Phone 207/495-2400; toll-free 866/495-2400; fax 207/495-3400. www.wingshillinn. com.* Renovated farmhouse built in 1800; antique quilts. 8 rooms, 2 story. Complimentary full breakfast. Check-in 3-9 pm. Check-out 11 am. **$**

Bailey Island (E-2)

See also Lewiston, Poland Spring

Elevation 20 ft
Area Code 207
Zip 04003
Information Chamber of Commerce of the Bath-Brunswick Region, 59 Pleasant St, Brunswick 04011; phone 207/725-8797
Web Site www.midcoastmaine.com

At the terminus of Highway 24, along the northern shore of Casco Bay, lies Bailey Island, the most popular of the 365 Calendar Islands. Together with Orr's Island, to which it is connected by a cribstone bridge, Bailey is a resort and fishing center. Originally called Newwaggin by an early trader from Kittery, Bailey Island was renamed after Deacon Timothy Bailey of Massachusetts, who claimed the land for himself and banished early settlers. Bailey Island and Orr's Island partially enclose an arm of Casco Bay called Harpswell Sound—the locale of John Whittier's poem "The Dead Ship of Harpswell" and of Harriet Beecher Stowe's "Pearl of Orr's Island."

What to See and Do

Bailey Island Cribstone Bridge. *Bailey Island. On Hwy 24 S, over Will Straits.* Unique construction of uncemented granite blocks laid honeycomb fashion, allowing the tides to flow through. **FREE**

Giant Staircase. *Washington St, Bailey Island.* Natural rock formation dropping 200 feet in steps to ocean. Scenic overlook area. **FREE**

Specialty Lodging

LOG CABIN ISLAND INN. *5 Log Cabin Ln, Bailey Island (04003). Phone 207/833-5546; fax 207/833-7858. www.logcabin-maine.com.* Log cabin; panoramic view of bay, islands. 8 rooms. Closed Nov-Mar. Complimentary full breakfast. Check-in 2 pm. Check-out 11 am. Restaurant. **$**

Restaurant

★ **COOK'S LOBSTER HOUSE.** *68 Garrison Cove Rd, Bailey Island (04003). Phone 207/833-2818; fax 207/833-5851. www.cookslobsterhouse.com.* Dockage. Seafood menu. Lunch, dinner. Bar. Children's menu. Outdoor seating. **$$$**

Bangor (D-3)

See also Bucksport

Settled 1769
Population 33,181
Elevation 61 ft
Area Code 207
Zip 04401
Information Bangor Convention and Visitors Bureau,

PO Box 1938, 04402; phone 207/947-5205
Web Site www.bangorcvb.org

In 1604, Samuel de Champlain sailed up the Penobscot River to the area that was to become Bangor and reported that the country was "most pleasant and agreeable," the hunting good, and the oak trees impressive. As the area grew, these things remained true. Begun as a harbor town, as did many of Maine's coastal areas, Bangor turned to lumber when the railroads picked up much of the shipping business. In 1842, it became the second-largest lumber port in the country.

Bangor received its name by mistake. An early settler, Reverend Seth Noble, was sent to register the new town under its chosen name of Sunbury; however, when officials asked Noble for the name, he thought they were asking him for the name of a tune he was humming, and replied "Bangor" instead. Today, the city is the third largest in Maine and a trading and distribution center.

What to See and Do

Bangor Museum & Center for History. *6 State St, Bangor (04401). Phone 207/942-1900.* Features exhibits of regional artifacts and the Quipus collection of historic clothing (Tues-Sat). **FREE**

Cole Land Transportation Museum. *405 Perry Rd, Bangor (04401). Phone 207/990-3600. www.colemuseum.org.* The Cole Museum takes great pride in depicting the history of transportation in the American Northeast. The museum houses one of the largest collections of snow removal equipment found in one place anywhere in the country, as well as a cache of military vehicles. A great place to take children, more than 20,000 visitors go through the turnstiles each year to see the museum's permanent collection including local railroad pieces and cars and trucks, uniquely designed to traverse the streets of Bangor. Historic photographs of Maine are also on display. (May-mid-Nov, daily 9 am-5 pm) **$$**

Monument to Paul Bunyan. *Bass Park, Main St, Bangor.* A 31-foot-tall statue commemorating the legendary lumberjack. **FREE**

Special Event

Bangor State Fair. *100 Dutton St, Bangor (04401). Phone 207/947-5555. www.bangorstatefair.com.* One of the country's oldest fairs. Horse racing, exhibits, stage shows. Late July-first week in Aug.

Limited-Service Hotels

★ **FAIRFIELD INN.** *300 Odlin Rd, Bangor (04401). Phone 207/990-0001; toll-free 800/228-2800; fax 207/990-0917. www.fairfieldinn.com.* 153 rooms, 3 story. Complimentary continental breakfast. Check-in 3 pm, check-out noon. Fitness room. Indoor pool, whirlpool. **$**

★ ★ **HOLIDAY INN.** *500 Main St, Bangor (04401). Phone 207/947-8651; toll-free 800/799-8651; fax 207/942-2848. www.holiday-inn.com/bangor-civic.* Opposite Civic Center. 123 rooms, 6 story. Pets accepted, some restrictions. Check-in 2 pm, check-out noon. Restaurant, bar. Outdoor pool. Airport transportation available. **$**

Specialty Lodging

THE LUCERNE INN. *Rte 1A Bar Harbor Rd, Holden (04429). Phone 207/843-5123; toll-free 800/325-5123; fax 207/843-6138. www.lucerneinn.com.* Colonial-style farmhouse and connecting stable, established as an inn in 1814. 31 rooms, 3 story. Complimentary continental breakfast. Check-in 2 pm. Check-out 11 am. Restaurant. Outdoor pool. **$$**

Restaurant

★ **CAPTAIN NICK'S SEAFOOD HOUSE.** *1165 Union St, Bangor (04401). Phone 207/942-6444; fax 207/947-8630.* Seafood menu. Lunch, dinner. Bar. Children's menu. Casual attire. **$$**

Bar Harbor (E-3)

See also Acadia National Park, Blue Hill, Cranberry Isles, Ellsworth, Northeast Harbor, Southwest Harbor

Population 2,768
Elevation 20 ft
Area Code 207
Zip 04605
Information Chamber of Commerce, 1201 Bar Harbor Rd, PO Box 158; phone 207/288-5103
Web Site www.barharbormaine.com

Bar Harbor, the largest village on Mount Desert Island, has a summer population of as many as 20,000 and is headquarters for the surrounding summer resort area. The island, which includes most of Acadia National Park, is mainly rugged granite, forested and flowered, with many bays and inlets where sailing is popular. In the mid-1800s, socially prominent figures, including publisher Joseph Pulitzer, had elaborate summer cottages built on the island. The era of elegance ebbed, however, with the Great Depression, World War II, and the "Great Fire of 1947," which destroyed many of the estates and scorched more than 17,000 acres. As a result, the forests in the area now have younger, more varied trees bearing red, yellow, and orange leaves instead of just evergreens.

What to See and Do

Abbe Museum. *26 Mount Desert St, Bar Harbor (04609). Rte 3 S to Sieur de Monts exit. Phone 207/288-3519. www.abbemuseum.org.* This museum holds an extensive collection of Native American artifacts. (Daily 9 am-5 pm; closed Thanksgiving, Dec 25; also Jan) The original location in Acadia National Park, open Memorial Day-mid-October, now houses exhibits on the archaeology of Maine and the history of the Abbe. **$$**

Bar Harbor Historical Society Museum. *33 Ledgelawn Ave, Bar Harbor (04609). Jesup Memorial Library. Phone 207/288-0000. www.barharborhistorical.org.* Collection of early photographs of hotels, summer cottages, and Green Mountain cog railroad; hotel registers from the early to late 1800s; maps, scrapbook of the 1947 fire. (Mid-June-Oct, Mon-Sat 1-4 pm; closed holidays) **FREE**

Bar Harbor Whale Watch Company. *1 West St, Bar Harbor (04609). 1 mile N on Hwy 3. Phone 207/288-2386; toll-free 888/533-9253. www.barharborwhales.com.* Offers a variety of cruises aboard catamarans *Friendship V* or *Helen H* to view whales, seal, puffin, osprey, and more. Also nature cruises and lobster and seal-watching. Cruises vary in length and destination. (May-Oct, daily) Depart from Bluenose Ferry Terminal.

Ferry service to Yarmouth, Nova Scotia. *121 Edens St, Bar Harbor (04609). Phone toll-free 888/249-7245. www.catferry.com.* Passenger and car carrier *Cat Ferry* makes three-hour trips. **$$$$**

Fishing. Fresh water in many lakes and streams (check regulations, obtain license). Salt water off coast; commercial boat operators will arrange trips.

George B. Dorr Museum of Natural History. *105 Eden St, Bar Harbor (04609). In the historic Turrets Building on the College of the Atlantic waterfront campus.*

Phone 207/288-5015. More than 50 exhibits depicting animals in their natural settings; 22-foot Minke whale skeleton. Interpretive programs; evening lectures in summer (Wed). (June-Labor Day: Mon-Sat 10 am-5 pm; rest of year: by appointment) **$**

The Jackson Laboratory. *600 Main St, Bar Harbor (04609). 2 miles S on Hwy 3. Phone 207/288-6049. www.jax.org.* An internationally known mammalian genetics laboratory conducting research relevant to cancer, diabetes, AIDS, heart disease, blood disorders, birth defects, aging, and normal growth and development. Audiovisual and lecture programs (early June-late Aug, Wed afternoons). **FREE**

Oceanarium-Bar Harbor. *Rte 3, Bar Harbor (04609). 9 miles N on Hwy 3. Phone 207/288-5005. www.the-oceanarium.earthlink.com.* An extension of the Mount Desert Oceanarium in Southwest Harbor (see); features include salt-marsh walks, viewing tower; also lobster museum with hands-on exhibits. (Mid-May-lat Oct, Mon-Sat) **$$$** Also included is the

> **Lobster Hatchery.** *Rte 3, Bar Harbor (04609). Phone 207/288-5005.* Young lobsters are hatched from eggs to 1/2 inch in length, then returned to the ocean to supplement the supply; guides narrate process. (Mid-May-late Oct, Mon-Sat)

Special Event

Art in the Park. *Village Green, Bar Harbor (04069). Phone 207/288-5103.* Third weekend in July-Sept.

Limited-Service Hotels

★ **ACADIA INN.** *98 Eden St, Bar Harbor (04609). Phone 207/288-3500; toll-free 800/638-3636; fax 207/288-8424. www.acadiainn.com.* 95 rooms, 3 story. Closed mid-Nov-Mar. Complimentary continental breakfast. Check-in 2 pm, check-out 11 am. Outdoor pool, whirlpool. **$$**
🛏

★ ★ **BAR HARBOR INN.** *Newport Dr, Bar Harbor (04609). Phone 207/288-3351; toll-free 800/248-3351; fax 207/288-5296. www.barharborinn.com.* This inn is located on 8 acres of nicely groomed gardens and lawns, directly on Frenchman Bay. There are three guest buildings featuring rooms with patios or balconies overlooking the ocean or grounds. A large selection of recreational activities are nearby. Pier; sailing cruises on 19th-century replica schooner. 153 rooms, 2 story. Pets accepted, some restrictions; fee.

Complimentary continental breakfast. Check-in 2 pm, check-out 11 am. Restaurant, bar. Fitness room. Outdoor pool. Beach. **$$**

★ **BAR HARBOR MOTEL.** *100 Eden St (Rte 3), Bar Harbor (04609). Phone 207/288-3453; toll-free 800/388-3453; fax 207/288-3598. www.barharbormotel.com.* 70 rooms. Closed mid-Oct-mid-May. Check-in 2:30 pm, check-out 11 am. Outdoor pool. **$**

★ **BEST WESTERN INN.** *452 Rte 3, Bar Harbor (04609). Phone 207/288-5823; toll-free 800/937-8376; fax 207/288-9827. www.bestwesterninn.com.* 70 rooms. Closed Nov-Apr. Pets accepted, some restrictions. Complimentary continental breakfast. Check-in 2 pm, check-out 11 am. Outdoor pool. **$$**

★ ★ **HARBORSIDE HOTEL & MARINA.** *55 West St, Bar Harbor (04609). Phone 207/288-5033; toll-free 800/328-5033; fax 207/288-3661. www.theharborside-hotel.com.* 88 rooms, 2 story. Closed Nov-Mar. Complimentary continental breakfast. Check-in 4 pm, check-out 11 am. Restaurant, bar. Whirlpool. **$$**

★ ★ **HOLIDAY INN.** *123 Eden St, Bar Harbor (04609). Phone 207/288-9723; toll-free 800/465-4329; fax 207/288-3089. www.barharborholidayinn.com.* This inn is located close to the Hancock County Airport and 50 miles from Bangor International Airport. The restaurant specializes in local seafood and features a lovely view. The Edenfield lounge serves cocktails until late evening. 221 rooms, 4 story. Closed Nov-Apr. Check-in 3 pm, check-out 11 am. Restaurant, bar. Children's activity center. Fitness room. Outdoor pool. Tennis. **$$**

★ **QUALITY INN.** *40 Kebo St, Bar Harbor (04609). Phone 207/288-5403; toll-free 800/282-5403; fax 207/288-5473. www.barharborqualityinn.com.* 77 rooms, 2 story. Closed Nov-mid-Apr. Check-in 2 pm, check-out 11 am. Outdoor pool, whirlpool. **$$**

★ ★ **WONDER VIEW INN.** *50 Eden St, Bar Harbor (04609). Phone 207/288-3358; toll-free 888/439-8439; fax 207/288-2005. www.wonderviewinn.com.* 79 rooms, 2 story. Closed Nov-Apr. Pets accepted, some restrictions; fee. Check-in 3 pm, check-out 11 am. Restaurant, bar. Outdoor pool. **$$**

Full-Service Hotel

★ ★ ★ **BAR HARBOR HOTEL - BLUENOSE INN.** *90 Eden St, Bar Harbor (04609). Phone 207/288-3348; toll-free 800/445-4077; fax 207/288-2183. www.barharborhotel.com.* From its hilltop location on Mount Desert Island, this hotel offers breathtaking views of Frenchman Bay. Rooms and suites are spread between the Mizzentop and Stenna Nordica buildings. Guests can explore nearby Acadia National Park or walk down to the dock and catch the *Cat Ferry* for a day trip to Yarmouth, Nova Scotia. Enjoy gourmet dining in the Rose Garden Restaurant. 97 rooms, 4 story. Closed Nov-Mar. Check-in 3 pm, check-out 11 am. Restaurant, bar. Fitness room. Indoor pool, whirlpool. **$$**

Full-Service Inn

★ ★ ★ **THE BAYVIEW.** *111 Eden St, Bar Harbor (04609). Phone 207/288-5861; toll-free 800/356-3585; fax 207/288-3173. www.bahabamaine.com.* This 8-acre inn is close to shopping, restaurants, the town pier, the historical district, and Acadia National Park. 33 rooms, 3 story. Closed Nov-mid-May. Complimentary full breakfast. Check-in 3 pm, check-out 11 am. Restaurant, bar. Whirlpool. Airport transportation available. **$$**

Specialty Lodgings

BALANCE ROCK INN. *21 Albert Meadow, Bar Harbor (04609). Phone 207/288-2610; toll-free 800/753-0494. www.balancerockinn.com.* 23 rooms. Closed late Oct-early May. Pets accepted; fee. Complimentary full breakfast. Check-in 3 pm, check-out 11 am. **$$**

BAR HARBOR GRAND HOTEL. *269 Main St, Bar Harbor (04609). Phone 207/288-5226; toll-free 888/766-2529; fax 207/288-8548. www.barharborgrandhotel.com.* 70 rooms. Closed Dec-Apr. Complimentary continental breakfast. Check-in 2 pm, check-out 11 am. **$$**

BLACK FRIAR INN. *10 Summer St, Bar Harbor (04609). Phone 207/288-5091; fax 207/288-4197. www.blackfriarinn.com.* Victorian décor. 7 rooms, 3 story. Children over 12 years only. Complimentary full breakfast. Check-in after 3-6 pm. Check-out 11 am. **$**

CASTLEMAINE. *39 Holland Ave, Bar Harbor (04609). Phone 207/288-4563; toll-free 800/338-4563;*

fax 207/288-4525. www.castlemaineinn.com. Tucked away on a quiet side street, this inn is a rambling, Victorian-style house (1886) located 1 mile from Acadia National Park and within walking distance of the ocean. It was once the summer residence of the Austro-Hungarian ambassador. 17 rooms, 3 story. Closed Nov-Apr. Complimentary continental breakfast. Check-in 2-6 pm, check-out 10:30 am. **$**

CLEFTSTONE MANOR. *92 Eden St, Bar Harbor (04609). Phone 207/288-8086; toll-free 888/288-4951; fax 207/288-2089. www.cleftstone.com.* This Victorian inn (1894) is set on a hill of terraced grounds and is located less than 1 mile from downtown Bar Harbor and only a few minutes from Acadia National Park. The inn was once owned by the Blair family of Washington DC. 16 rooms, 3 story. Closed Nov-Apr. Children over 10 years only. Complimentary full breakfast. Check-in 2 pm, check-out 11 am. **$**
ᴅ

INN AT BAY LEDGE. *150 Sand Point Rd, Bar Harbor (04609). Phone 207/288-4204; fax 207/288-5573. www.innatbayledge.com.* This inn (built in 1907) is located at the top of an 80-foot cliff on Mount Desert Island near Acadia National Park. It offers the mixture of luxury and rustic Maine living and is beautifully decorated with antiques. Guests can view eagles and dolphins as they enjoy the lavish breakfast on the deck overlooking Frenchman's Bay and nearby mountains. 10 rooms, 2 story. Closed late Oct-Apr. Children over 16 years only. Complimentary full breakfast. Check-in 3-6 pm, check-out 11 am. **$$$**
ᴅ

MANOR HOUSE INN. *106 West St, Bar Harbor (04609). Phone 207/288-3759; toll-free 800/437-0088; fax 207/288-2974. www.barharbormanorhouse.com.* This is a restored historic Victorian mansion (1887). 18 rooms, 3 story. Children over 12 years only. Complimentary full breakfast. Check-in 2 pm, check-out 10:30 am. **$$**
ᴅ

MIRA MONTE INN & SUITES. *69 Mount Desert St, Bar Harbor (04609). Phone 207/288-4263; toll-free 800/553-5109; fax 207/288-0930. www.miramonte. com.* This is a restored Victorian home (1864) on 2 1/2 acres; wraparound porch, period furnishings. 16 rooms, 2 story. Closed mid-Oct-Apr. Complimentary full breakfast. Check-in 3-9 pm, check-out 11 am. **$$**
ᴅ

THORNHEDGE INN. *47 Mount Desert St, Bar Harbor (04609). Phone 207/288-5398; toll-free 877/288-5398. www.thornhedgeinn.com.* This Queen Anne-style inn is located in the Historic Corridor District of Bar Harbor, close to many shops, galleries, and restaurants. It was built by the publisher of Louisa May Alcott's *Little Women* as a summer cottage (1900). 13 rooms, 3 story. Check-in noon. Check-out 11 am. **$**
ᴅ

Restaurants

★ **124 COTTAGE STREET.** *124 Cottage St, Bar Harbor (04609). Phone 207/288-4383.* This restaurant is located in a restored, turn-of-the-century cottage. American menu. Dinner. Closed Nov-May. Bar. Children's menu. Outdoor seating. **$$**
ᴅ

★ ★ **MAGGIE'S.** *6 Summer St, Bar Harbor (04609). Phone 207/288-9007. www.maggiesbarharbor.com.* For years, Maggie's has been a Bar Harbor favorite. This small, intimate restaurant is located on a short side street in downtown Bar Harbor. The chef/owner uses only regional farm produce and meats and fresh local seafood to support her seasonally changing menus. Everything is made from scratch on the premises with all breads and desserts oven baked on-site. The simple décor has a touch of country, and the ambience is somewhat romantic, with candelit tables. International menu. Dinner. Closed Sun; late Oct-mid-June. Casual attire. Reservations recommended. Outdoor seating. **$$**
ᴅ

★ ★ ★ **READING ROOM.** *Newport Dr, Bar Harbor (04609). Phone 207/288-3351; toll-free 800/248-3351; fax 207/288-5296. www.barharborinn.com.* The Reading Room is a perfect spot for that special dinner or brunch. Located in the Bar Harbor Inn (see), it overlooks Frenchman's Bay and offers picturesque views from two sides of the water and islands, which can be seen from most tables. Adding to the ambience, a pianist plays at dinner on weekends, and during Sunday brunch. The traditional décor is reminiscent of the inn's origins (originally opened in 1887), with forest green carpet and light peach walls. Lots of white woodwork surrounds the large picture windows that open the dining room to the excellent views. Tables are formally set with crisp white linens, an oil lamp and flowers, and silver-plated flatware. American menu. Breakfast, lunch, dinner, Sun brunch. Closed

Dec-Mar. Bar. Children's menu. Business casual attire. Reservations recommended. Valet parking. **$$$**

★ **ROUTE 66.** *21 Cottage St, Bar Harbor (04609). Phone 207/288-3708. www.bhroute66.com.* Route 66 is part roadhouse, part soda fountain, and part country store. The interior features faux marble formica booths, a 1954 juke box, a mezzanine with more seating and a model train, and tin and neon signs everywhere. Some of the windows are stained glass from an old church, and an old Mobil gas pump sits next to the door. Traditional New England dishes are offered along with a good selection of burgers and sandwiches. The biggest draw, though, is the incredible collection of fun stuff! American menu. Lunch, dinner. Closed Nov-mid-Apr. Bar. Children's menu. Casual attire. Outdoor seating. **$$**

★ ★ **SEASONS.** *51 Rodick St, Bar Harbor (04609). Phone 207/288-5117. www. seasonsbarharbor.com.* Chef/Owner Kyle Yarborough offers a creative menu of American favorite foods not found in the many seafood restaurants in town. Offerings include house-smoked, sugar-cured pork chop with maple barbecue sauce, served with whipped sweet potatoes; and fresh grilled wild Alaskan salmon with olive and smoked tomato pesto, served over rosemary-infused white bean puree. Seasons is a casual, contemporary restaurant located on quiet Rodick Street in a two-story light avocado and creamy yellow house with wide porches on either side of the front door; in nice weather, tables are set up on the porches for dining. American menu. Dinner. Closed mid-Nov-late Mar. Bar. Children's menu. Casual attire. Outdoor seating. **$$**

Bath (E-2)

See also Boothbay Harbor, Brunswick, Freeport, Wiscasset

Population 9,799
Elevation 13 ft
Area Code 207
Zip 04530
Information Chamber of Commerce of the Bath-Brunswick Region, 59 Pleasant St; phone 207/443-9751
Web Site www.midcoastmaine.com

For more than two centuries, Bath has been a shipbuilding center on the west bank of the Kennebec River. The Bath Iron Works, which dates to 1833, began building ships in 1889. It has produced destroyers,

cruisers, a battleship, pleasure craft, and steamers, and now also produces patrol frigates. Altogether, Bath has launched more than 4,000 ships from its shores, and launching a ship today is still a great event.

Many fine old mansions, built when Bath was a great seaport, still stand. A restored 19th-century business district, waterfront park, and public landing are also part of the city.

What to See and Do

Fort Popham Memorial. *Popham Beach. 16 miles S on Hwy 209. Phone 207/389-1335.* Construction of the fort began in 1861. Never finished, it was garrisoned in 1865-1866 and remains an impressive masonry structure with gun emplacements. Picnic tables (no garbage receptacles). (May-Nov, daily)

Maine Maritime Museum. *243 Washington St, Bath (04530). 2 miles S of Hwy 1, located on Kennebec River. Phone 207/443-1316. www.mainemaritimemuseum.org.* Maritime History Building has exhibits of maritime art and artifacts, shipmodels and paintings. Tours of original shipyard buildings, demonstrations of seafaring techniques (seasonal); waterfront picnic area and playground. Museum store. (Daily; closed Jan 1, Thanksgiving, Dec 25) **$$**

Popham Beach State Park. *10 Perkins Farm Ln, Bath (04562). 12 miles S on Hwy 209. Phone 207/389-1335.* Swimming, tidal pools (mid-Apr-Nov), surfing; fishing; picnicking. (Daily) **$**

Popham Colony. *Bath. 16 miles S on Hwy 209 on Sabino Head.* A picturesque drive. In 1607, the first American vessel, the *Virginia,* was built here by colonists who shortly thereafter returned to England, many of them in the ship they had built. On the hilltop nearby is Fort Baldwin, built during World War I. A 70-foot tower offers a panoramic view of the coast and the Kennebec River. **FREE**

Reid State Park. *Seguinland Rd, Georgetown (04548). 1 mile E on Hwy 1 to Woolwich, then 13 miles SE on Hwy 127 to Georgetown, then SE. Phone 207/371-2303. www. maine.gov/doc/parks.* Swimming, saltwater lagoon, bathhouse, fishing; picnic facilities, concession. (Daily) **$**

Limited-Service Hotel

★ ★ **HOLIDAY INN.** *139 Richardson St, Bath (04530). Phone 207/443-9741; toll-free 800/465-4329; fax 207/442-8281. www.holiday-inn.com.* 141 rooms,

4 story. Pets accepted, some restrictions. Check-in 3 pm, check-out noon. Restaurant, bar. Fitness room. Outdoor pool, whirlpool. **$**

Specialty Lodging

GALEN C. MOSES HOUSE. *1009 Washington St, Bath (04530). Phone 207/442-8771; toll-free 888/442-8771. www.galenmoses.com.* This inn, built in 1874, is a lovely plum, pink, and teal house, which is on the National Register of Historic Houses. It features a Victorian interior and stained-glass windows. All the rooms are tastefully decorated with antiques. Guests can take leisurely walks along the waterfront, visit antiques stores, and enjoy many fine restaurants in the area. 6 rooms. Children over 12 years only. Complimentary full breakfast. Check-in 4-8 pm, check-out 11 am. **$$**

Restaurants

★ **MAE'S CAFÉ AND BAKERY.** *160 Centre St, Bath (04530). Phone 207/442-8577; fax 207/443-5498. www.maescafeandbakery.com.* American menu. Breakfast, lunch, dinner. Casual attire. Outdoor seating. **$$**

★ **TASTE OF MAINE.** *Hwy 1, Woolwich (04579). Phone 207/443-4554; fax 207/443-6394. www.tasteofmaine.com.* Seafood, steak menu. Lunch, dinner. Children's menu. Outdoor seating. **$$**

Baxter State Park

See also Millinocket

18 miles NW of Millinocket via park roads.

While serving as a legislator and as governor of Maine, Percival P. Baxter urged creation of a wilderness park around Mount Katahdin—Maine's highest peak (5,267 feet). Rebuffed but not defeated, Baxter bought the land with his own money and deeded to the state of Maine a 201,018-acre park "to be forever left in its natural, wild state." The park can be reached from Greenville via paper company roads, from Millinocket via Hwy 157, or from Patten via Hwy 159.

The Park Authority operates the following campgrounds: Katahdin Stream, Abol and Nesowadnehunk, Roaring Brook (Roaring Brook Road), Chimney Pond (by trail 3.3 miles beyond Roaring Brook), Russell Pond (Wassataquoik Valley, 7 miles by trail beyond

Roaring Brook), South Branch Pond (at outlet of Lower South Branch Pond), Trout Brook Farm (Trout Brook Crossing). There are cabins ($17/person/night) at Daicey Pond off Nesowadnehunk Road and at Kidney Pond. All areas except Chimney, Kidney, and Daicey ponds have tent space, and all areas except Trout Brook Farm, Kidney, and Daicey ponds have lean-tos ($6/person/night), water (unprotected, should be purified), and primitive facilities (no indoor plumbing, no running water; some springs); bunkhouses ($7/night) at some campgrounds. Under age 7 free throughout the park.

Reservations should be made by mail (and paid in full) in advance. For detailed information, contact the Reservation Clerk, Baxter State Park, 64 Balsam Drive, Millinocket 04462. Swimming, fishing, canoes for rent at Russell Pond, South Branch Pond, Daicey Pond, Kidney Pond, and Trout Brook farm.

The park is open for camping mid-May-mid-October. No pets or motorcycles are permitted. Vehicles exceeding 7 feet wide, 9 feet high, or 22 feet long will not be admitted. For further information, contact Park Manager, 64 Balsam Drive, Millinocket 04462. Nonresident vehicle fee **$$**

Belfast (E-3)

See also Bucksport, Camden, Searsport

Settled 1770
Population 6,355
Elevation 103 ft
Area Code 207
Zip 04915
Information Chamber of Commerce, 17 Main St, PO Box 58; phone 207/338-5900
Web Site www.belfastmaine.org

Belfast, named for the city in Northern Ireland, was settled in 1770 by Irish and Scottish immigrants. An old seaport on the west shore of Penobscot Bay, Belfast, is also a hub of small boat traffic to the bay islands. It is the seat of Waldo County, with sardine canneries, potato processing, window making, and printing as its major industries.

What to See and Do

Lake St. George State Park. *Liberty. 19 miles W on Hwy 3, near Montville. Phone 207/589-4255. www.maine.gov/doc.* More than 360 acres. Swimming, bathhouse, lifeguard, fishing, boating (ramp, rentals); snowmobiling permitted, picnicking, camping. (Mid-May-mid-Oct).

Special Event

Belfast Bay Festival. *City Park, 1 Main St, Belfast (04915). Phone 207/338-5719.* Parade, concerts, carnival. July.

Limited-Service Hotel

★ **BELFAST HARBOR INN.** *91 Searsport Ave, Belfast (04915). Phone 207/338-2740; toll-free 800/545-8576; fax 207/338-5205. www.belfastharborinn.com.* Overlooks Penobscot Bay. 61 rooms, 2 story. Pets accepted, some restrictions; fee. Complimentary continental breakfast. Check-in 3 pm, check-out 11 am. Restaurant. Outdoor pool. **$**

Specialty Lodging

PENOBSCOT BAY INN. *192 Northport Ave, Belfast (04915). Phone 207/338-5715; toll-free 800/335-2370. www.penobscotbayinn.com.* This turn-of-the-century country inn overlooks the bay. 19 rooms, 3 story. Pets accepted, some restrictions; fee. Complimentary full breakfast. Check-in 2-6 pm, check-out 11 am. **$$**

Restaurants

★ ★ **DARBY'S.** *153 High St, Belfast (04915). Phone 207/338-2339; fax 207/338-5521. www.darbys.com.* International menu. Lunch, dinner. Bar. Children's menu. Casual attire. Reservations recommended. **$$**

★ **YOUNG'S LOBSTER POND.** *2 Fairview St, Belfast (04915). Phone 207/338-1160; fax 207/338-3498.* Seafood menu. Breakfast, lunch, dinner. Outdoor seating. Casual attire. Reservations recommended. **$$**

Bethel (E-1)

See also Rumford

Settled 1774
Population 2,329
Elevation 700 ft
Area Code 207

Information Chamber of Commerce, 8 Station Pl; phone 207/824-2282 or toll-free 800/442-5826
Web Site www.bethelmaine.com

Bethel, on both banks of the winding Androscoggin River, is built on the rolling Oxford Hills and is backed by the rough foothills of the White Mountains. In addition to being a year-round resort, it's an educational and wood products center. One of Maine's leading preparatory schools, Gould Academy (founded in 1836), is located here.

What to See and Do

Carter's X-Country Ski Center. *420 Main St, Bethel (04270). Phone 207/539-4848. www.cartersxcski.com.* One thousand acres with 55 kilometers of groomed cross-country trails. Rentals, lessons; lounge, shop; two lodges. (Dec-Mar) **$$$$**

Dr. Moses Mason House Museum. *14 Broad St, Bethel (04217). In the National Historic District. Phone 207/824-2908. www.bethelhistorical.org/museum.html.* (1813) Restored home of prominent congressman who served during administration of Andrew Jackson. Antique furnishings, Early American murals. (July-Labor Day: Tues-Sun afternoons; rest of year: by appointment) **$**

Grafton Notch State Park. *Bethel. Approximately 9 miles NW via Hwy 2, Hwy 26. Phone 207/824-2912. www.maine.gov/doc.* The Appalachian Trail passes through the notch; interpretive displays, scenic view, picnicking; fishing. (Mid-May-mid-Oct) **$**

Sunday River Ski Resort. *Sunday River Rd, Bethel (04217). 6 miles NE on Hwy 2. Phone 207/824-3000; toll-free 800/543-2754. www.sundayriver.com.* Nine quad, four triple, two double chairlifts (including four high-speed detachables and one surface lift); patrol, school, rentals, ski shop; snowmaking; cafeterias, restaurants; bars. 127 runs; longest run 3 miles; vertical drop 2,340 feet. (mid-Nov-mid-Apr, daily) 100 cross-country trails adjacent. Mountain biking (May-Labor Day: daily; Labor Day-late Oct: weekends). **$$$$**

Swimming, picnicking, camping, boating, fishing. *Bethel. E on Hwy 26.* Songo Lake in Bethel; Christopher Lake in Bryant Pond; North and South ponds in Locke Mills; Littlefield beaches and Stony Brook campgrounds.

White Mountain National Forest. *Bethel. Phone 603/528-8721. www.fs.fed.us/r9/white.* (See NEW HAMPSHIRE) More than 49,000 acres of this forest extend into Maine southwest of here. Birches and sugar maples turn fall into a season of breathtaking color. Fishing; hiking, rock hounding, camping (fee). For more information, contact the Supervisor, 719 Main St, PO Box 638, Laconia, NH 03247.

Limited-Service Hotel

★ **NORSEMAN INN.** *134 Mayville Rd, Bethel (04217). Phone 207/824-2002; fax 207/824-0640. www. norsemaninn.com.* 31 rooms, 2 story. Complimentary continental breakfast. Check-in 3 pm, check-out 10:30 am. **$$**

Full-Service Resort

★ ★ ★ **BETHEL INN & COUNTRY CLUB.** *On the Common, Bethel (04217). Phone 207/824-2175; toll-free 800/654-0125; fax 207/824-2233. www.bethelinn. com.* 60 rooms. Pets accepted, some restrictions; fee. Check-in 3 pm. Check-out 11 am. Restaurant, bar. Children's activity center. Fitness room. Outdoor pool, whirlpool. Golf. Tennis. **$$**

Full-Service Inn

★ ★ ★ **BRIAR LEA INN & RESTAURANT.** *150 Mayville Rd, Bethel (04217). Phone 207/824-4717; toll-free 877/311-1299; fax 207/824-7121. www.briarleainn. com.* Built in the 1850s; farmhouse atmosphere. 6 rooms. Pets accepted, some restrictions; fee. Complimentary full breakfast. Check-in 4 pm, check-out 11 am. Restaurant. **$**

Restaurant

★ **S. S. MILTON.** *43 Main St, Bethel (04217). Phone 207/824-2589.* Seafood, steak menu. Lunch (May-Oct), dinner. Closed Tues; Thanksgiving, Dec 25. Children's menu. Casual attire. Reservations recommended. Outdoor seating. **$$**

Bingham (D-2)

See also Skowhegan

Settled 1785
Population 1,071
Elevation 371 ft
Area Code 207

What to See and Do

Wilderness Expeditions. *1 Birches Dr, Rockwood (04478). Phone 207/534-7305; toll-free 800/825-9453. www.birches.com.* Guided raft trips on the Kennebec, Penobscot, and Dead rivers; also canoe outfitting, guided kayaking and ski tours. (May-Sept, daily) **$$$$**

Limited-Service Hotel

★ **BINGHAM MOTOR INN & SPORTS COMPLEX.** *Rte 201, Bingham (04920). Phone 207/672-4135; fax 207/672-4138. www.binghammotorinn.com.* 20 rooms. Pets accepted, some restrictions. Check-out 10 am. Outdoor pool. **$**

Blue Hill (E-3)

See also Bar Harbor, Ellsworth

Settled 1722
Population 1,941
Elevation 40 ft
Area Code 207
Zip 04614
Information Blue Hill Peninsula Chamber of Commerce, PO Box 520; phone 207/374-3242
Web Site www.bluehillme.com

Named for a nearby hill that gives a beautiful view of Mount Desert Island, Blue Hill changed from a thriving seaport to a summer colony known for its crafts and antiques. Mary Ellen Chase, born here in 1887, wrote about Blue Hill in *A Goodly Heritage* and *Mary Peters*.

What to See and Do

Holt House. *Water St, Blue Hill (04614). Phone 207/374-3242.* One of the oldest houses in Blue Hill; now home of the Blue Hill Historical Society. Memorabilia. (July-Sept 1, Tues, Fri-Sat afternoons; closed holidays) For further information contact the town clerk. **$**

Rackliffe Pottery. *132 Elsworth Rd, Blue Hill (04614). Phone 207/374-2297. www.rackliffepottery.com.* Family manufactures wheel-thrown dinnerware from native red-firing clay. Open workshop. (July-Aug: daily; rest of year: Mon-Sat; closed holidays) **FREE**

Rowantrees Pottery. *84 Union St, Union (04862). Phone 207/374-5535.* Manufactures functional pottery and wheel-thrown handcrafted dinnerware. (June-Sept, Mon-Sat; closed holidays) **FREE**

Wooden Boat School. *41 Wooden Boat Ln, Brooklin (04616). Naskeag Rd and Brooklyn. Phone 207/359-4651. www.thewoodenboatschool.com.* (June-Sept, Mon-Thurs)

Special Event

Blue Hill Fair. *Blue Hill. Phone 207/374-3701. www.bluehillfair.com.* Sheep dog trials, agriculture and livestock exhibits; midway, harness racing, crafts. Five days over Labor Day weekend.

Full-Service Inn

★ ★ ★ **BLUE HILL INN.** *40 Union St, Blue Hill (04614). Phone 207/374-2844; toll-free 800/826-7415; fax 207/374-2829. www.bluehillinn.com.* This Federal-style home has provided bed-and-breakfast amenities at the tip of the bay since 1840 and is on the National Register of Historic Houses. Choose one of the quaint guest rooms or the adjacent Cape House suite for a more private retreat. 12 rooms, 3 story. Check-in 2:30 pm, check-out 10:30 am. Restaurant. Airport transportation available. **$$**

Boothbay Harbor (E-2)

See also Bath, Damariscotta, Monhegan Island, Wiscasset

Population 1,267
Elevation 16 ft
Area Code 207
Zip 04538
Information Boothbay Harbor Region Chamber of Commerce, 192 Townsend Ave; phone 207/633-2353 or toll-free 800/266-8422
Web Site www.boothbayharbor.com

Native Americans were paid 20 beaver pelts for the area encompassing Boothbay Harbor. Today, its protected harbor, a haven for boatmen, is the scene of well-attended regattas several times a summer. Boothbay Harbor, on the peninsula between the Sheepscot and Damariscotta rivers, shares the peninsula and adjacent islands with a dozen other communities, including Boothbay (settled 1630), of which it was once a part.

What to See and Do

Balmy Days Boat Trips. *Pier 8, Commercial St, Boothbay Harbor (04538). Phone 207/633-2284. www.balmy-*

dayscruises.com. Makes trips to Monhegan Island (see) with four-hour stopover. (June-mid-Oct, daily)

Boothbay Railway Village. *Hwy 27, Boothbay (04537). 1 mile N of Boothbay Center on Hwy 27. Phone 207/633-4727. www.railwayvillage.org.* Historical Maine exhibits of rural life, railroads, and antique autos and trucks. Rides on a coal-fired, narrow-gauge steam train to an antique vehicle display. Also on exhibit on 8 acres are displays of early fire equipment, a general store, a one-room schoolhouse, and two restored railroad stations. (Mid-June-mid-Oct, daily) **$$**

Boothbay Region Historical Society Museum. *72 Oak St, Boothbay Harbor (04538). Phone 207/633-0820. www.boothbayhistorical.org.* Artifacts of Boothbay Region. (July-Labor Day: Wed, Fri- Sat; rest of year: Fri-Sat) **DONATION**

Cap'n Fish's Boat Trips and Deep Sea Fishing. *Pier 1, 65 Atlantic Ave, Boothbay Harbor (04538). Phone 207/633-3244.* Boats make varied excursions: 1 1/4- to 3-hour trips; puffin, seal, and whale watches; scenic, sunset, and cruises; fall foliage and Kennebec River trips; charters. (Mid-May-Oct; days vary) **$$$$**

Fishing. In inland waters, Golf Course Brook, Adams, West Harbor and Knickerbocker ponds in Boothbay; Meadow Brook in East Boothbay. Ocean fishing from harbor docks. Boat rentals, deep-sea fishing.

Novelty Boat Trips. *Commercial St, Pier 8, Boothbay Harbor (04538). Phone 207/633-2284. www.balmydayscruises.com.* One-hour harbor cruises with stop at Squirrel Island; Night Lights cruises (July-Aug, Tues-Sat). Harbor cruises (Apr-Oct, Daily). **$$$**

Picnicking. *99 Atlantic Ave, Boothbay Harbor (04538). Phone 207/633-5160.* Boothbay Region Lobstermen's Cooperative, Atlantic Avenue. Lobsterman's Wharf, East Boothbay. Robinson's Wharf, Highway 27 at bridge, Southport. Boiled lobsters and steamed clams, snacks available.

Special Events

Fall Foliage Festival. *Phone 207/633-4743.* Foliage drives, harvest suppers, boat trips, country fair. Columbus Day weekend.

Fisherman's Festival. *Phone 207/633-2353.* Celebration of the rich fishing heritage of the region includes a fish relay race, a lobster trap hauling competition, a lobster crate race, and lobster trap running. Other events include the Shrimp Princess Pageant, a pancake breakfast, arts and crafts show, old-fashioned fish fry, church suppers, dockside dancing, lighthouse tours, and tall tales as only fishermen can tell them. Late-Apr.

Harbor Lights Festival. *192 Townsend Ave, Boothbay Harbor (04538). Phone 207/633-2353.* Craft fair, lighted boat parade. First Sat in Dec.

Windjammer Days. *192 Townsend Ave, Boothbay Harbor (04538). Phone 207/633-2353.* Old schooners that formerly sailed the trade routes and now cruise the Maine coast sail en masse into harbor. Waterfront food court, entertainment, street parade, children's activities. Late June.

Limited-Service Hotels

★ ★ **BROWN'S WHARF MOTEL.** *121 Atlantic Ave, Boothbay Harbor (04538). Phone 207/633-5440; toll-free 800/334-8110. www.brownswharfinn.com.* This marina property overlooks the ocean directly on inner Boothbay Harbor and has both guest rooms and efficiencies overlooking the water. Brown's Wharf Restaurant features delicious seafood dinners, and there is a comfortable rustic bar and lounge. Visit downtown Boothbay via the footbridge from the motel. 70 rooms, 3 story. Closed Nov-Apr. Pets accepted, some restrictions. Check-in 3 pm, check-out 11 am. Restaurant, bar. **$**

★ ★ **FISHERMAN'S WHARF INN.** *22 Commercial St, Boothbay Harbor (04538). Phone 207/633-5090; toll-free 800/628-6872; fax 207/633-5092. www.fishermanswharfinn.com.* 54 rooms, 3 story. Closed Nov-mid-May. Complimentary continental breakfast. Check-in 2 pm, check-out 11 am. Restaurant, bar. **$**

★ **TUGBOAT INN.** *80 Commercial St, Boothbay Harbor (04538). Phone 207/633-4434; toll-free 800/248-2628. www.tugboatinn.com.* 64 rooms, 2 story. Closed Dec-mid-Mar. Check-in 3 pm, check-out 11 am. Restaurant, bar. **$**

Full-Service Resort

★ ★ ★ **SPRUCE POINT INN.** *88 Grandview Ave, Boothbay Harbor (04538). Phone 207/633-4152; toll-free 800/553-0289; fax 207/633-6347. www.sprucepointinn.com.* Located on 15 secluded acres of a quiet peninsula on the Atlantic ocean, this beautiful retreat is the perfect getaway. 85 rooms, 3 story. Closed mid-Oct-mid-May, pets accepted. Check-in 3 pm.

Check-out 11 am. Restaurant, bar. Fitness room. Two outdoor pools, whirlpool. Tennis. **$**

Specialty Lodgings

1830 ADMIRAL'S QUARTERS INN. *71 Commercial St, Boothbay Harbor (04538). Phone 207/633-2474; toll-free 800/644-1878; fax 207/633-5904. www.admiralsquartersinn.com.* Built in 1830. 7 rooms. Closed mid-Dec-mid-Feb. Children over 12 years only. Complimentary full breakfast. Check-in 2-6 pm. Check-out 11 am. **$$**

ANCHOR WATCH BED & BREAKFAST. *9 Eames Rd, Boothbay Harbor (04538). Phone 207/633-7565; fax 207/633-5319. www.anchorwatch.com.* 5 rooms, 3 story. Children over 9 years only. Complimentary full breakfast. Check-in 2-6 pm. Check-out 11 am. **$$**

FIVE GABLES INN. *107 Murray Hill Rd, East Boothbay (04544). Phone 207/633-4551; toll-free 800/451-5048. www.fivegablesinn.com.* This inn, built in 1890, features Victorian décor. 15 rooms, 3 story. Nov-mid-May, Children over 12 years only. Complimentary full breakfast. Check-in 2-8 pm. Check-out 11 am. **$**

HARBOUR TOWNE INN ON WATERFRONT. *71 Townsend Ave, Boothbay Harbor (04538). Phone 207/633-3934; toll-free 800/722-4240; fax 207/633-2442. www.harbourtowneinn.com.* On harbor. 12 rooms, 3 story. Complimentary continental breakfast. Check-in 3 pm, check-out 10 am. **$$**

HOWARD HOUSE LODGE. *347 Townsend Ave, Boothbay Harbor (04538). Phone 207/633-3933; toll-free 800/466-6697; fax 207/633-6244. www.howardhouselodge.com.* Country, chalet-style building in wooded area. 14 rooms, 2 story. Complimentary full breakfast. Check-in 3-9 pm, check-out 11 am. **$**

KENNISTON HILL INN. *Wiscasset Rd (Hwy 27), Boothbay (04537). Phone 207/633-2159; toll-free 800/992-2915; fax 207/633-2159. www.kennistonhillinn.com.* Restored Colonial-style farmhouse (1786); antiques. 10 rooms, 2 story. Children over 10 years only. Complimentary full breakfast. Check-in 3-6 pm, check-out 11 am. **$$**

Restaurants

★ ★ ★ **88 GRANDVIEW.** *88 Grandview, Boothbay Harbor (04538). Phone 207/633-4152; toll-free 800/553-0289; fax 207/633-7138. www.sprucepointinn. com.* This fine-dining venue of the Spruce Point Inn (see) is located at the end of a 100-acre peninsula, overlooking the Atlantic Ocean. Tables are covered with crisp white linen and set with fine china, silver flatware, and high-quality stemware. The tall windows provide views of the beautifully manicured grounds that lead all the way to the ocean. Seating is also provided on the enclosed sunporch and outdoor deck with umbrella-topped tables. Menu selections include candied duck breast and crispy confit leg, veal chop and sun-dried blueberry demi over Romano bean cassoulet, and tenderloin of beef with Bordelaise sauce and celeriac fritters. A pianist performs nightly. American menu. Dinner. Closed mid-Oct-mid-May. Bar. Children's menu. Business casual attire. Reservations recommended. Outdoor seating. **$$$**
▣

★ **ANDREWS' HARBORSIDE RESTAURANT.** *12 Bridge St, Boothbay Harbor (04538). Phone 207/633-4074.* A local favorite for seafood, Andrews' is located on the waterfront in the center of the village of Boothbay Harbor—it overlooks "The Footbridge," which connects the east side of the harbor with the village. This family-run, casual restaurant and the accompanying bar/lounge are simply furnished and decorated with a nautical theme. New England seafood is the primary fare, with crab cakes and haddock being two notable items on the menu, and the oven-fresh cinnamon buns are a breakfast favorite. Seafood menu. Breakfast, lunch, dinner. Closed Columbus Day-Memorial Day. Children's menu. Casual attire. Reservations recommended. **$$**
▣

★ **BLUE MOON CAFE.** *54 Commercial St, Boothbay Harbor (04538). Phone 207/633-2349.* Guests dining at the casual and friendly Blue Moon Cafe place their order selections at the counter. The décor is modern, light, and airy, with an upbeat feel tables and floor are blond wood, chairs are blue, dinnerware is plastic or paper, and windows overlook the water and fishing boats. The waterside deck, overlooking the inner harbor, is a great place to enjoy a casual salad or sandwich. Soups, salads, breakfast muffins, and desserts are all homemade. Box lunches to go are available for picnics or boat trips. American menu. Breakfast, lunch. Closed Nov-Mar. Casual attire. Outdoor seating. **$**
▣

★ ★ **CHINA BY THE SEA.** *96 Townsend Ave, Boothbay Harbor (04538). Phone 207/633-4449. www. chinabythesea.com.* China by the Sea is a large two-story white house with forest green shutters and an awning over the entrance. The green theme continues inside, with the walls, napkins, and carpet. Paper mats are set on glass-covered tables with a white cloth underneath. Lots of plants are set in the windows, and silk flowers are in table vases. A lobster tank is featured, along with four computers in the bar area. For a change of pace, guests can enjoy a Chinese meal in this primarily seafood town. American, Chinese menu. Lunch, dinner. Closed Dec 25. Bar. Children's menu. Casual attire. Reservations recommended. **$$**
▣

★ ★ **CHOWDER HOUSE.** *22 Granary Way, Boothbay Harbor (04538). Phone 207/633-5761.* Chowder House, a two-story forest green house with white trim, is located waterside on inner Boothbay Harbor. The inside dining room is only available for private functions; the largely popular deck is open seasonally and serves casual food lobster and crab rolls, chowders, ribs, etc. The deck is also readily accessible to those arriving by boat. For a great setting and good local seafood, this is the spot. Seafood, barbecue menu. Lunch, dinner. Closed Oct-May. Bar. Casual attire. Outdoor seating. **$**
▣

★ ★ **FISHERMAN'S WHARF INN.** *22 Commercial St, Boothbay Harbor (04538). Phone 207/633-5090; toll-free 800/628-6872; fax 207/633-5092. www. fishermanswharfinn.com.* Guests dining here will enjoy the the varied menu and the wonderful location with a view of the wharf. The décor is nautical, and there is a cozy sitting area by a fireplace. Menu specialties include baked, stuffed haddock with a roasted red pepper stuffing; hazelnut-crusted roasted rack of lamb; apple dijon chicken; and broiled herbed sea scallops. American, seafood menu. Breakfast, lunch, dinner. Closed Nov-mid-May. Bar. Children's menu. Casual attire. Reservations recommended. Valet parking. Outdoor seating. **$$**

Bridgton (E-1)

See also Poland Spring, Sebago Lake

Population 2,195
Elevation 494 ft
Area Code 207
Zip 04009
Information Bridgton Lakes Region Chamber of Commerce, PO Box 236; phone 207/647-3472
Web Site www.mainelakeschamber.com

Primarily a resort, this community between Long and Highland lakes is within easy reach of Pleasant Mountain (2,007 feet), a recreational area that offers skiing as well as a magnificent view of 50 lakes. Bridgton also has many unique craft and antiques shops located within a 2-mile radius of the town center.

What to See and Do

Gibbs Avenue Museum. *44 Gibbs Ave, Bridgton (04009). Phone 207/647-3699.* Headquarters of Bridgton Historical Society. Permanent exhibits include narrow-gauge railroad memorabilia; Civil War artifacts; Sears "horseless carriage" (1911). Special summer exhibits. Genealogy research facility includes Bridgton and Saw River railroad documents. (Sept-June: by appointment; rest of year: Mon-Fri afternoons; closed holidays)

Shawnee Peak Ski Area. *119 Mountain Rd, Bridgton (04009). 6 miles W, off Hwy 302. Phone 207/647-8444. www.shawneepeak.com.* Quad, two triple, double chairlift; snowmaking, school, rentals, patrol; nursery; restaurant, cafeteria, bar. Longest run 1 1/2 miles; vertical drop 1,350 feet. Night skiing. (Dec-Mar, daily) **$$$$**

Special Event

Quilt Show. *Town hall, Bridgton (04009). Phone 207/647-3472.* New and old quilts; demonstrations. Contact Chamber of Commerce. Mid-July.

Full-Service Inn

★ ★ ★ **THE INN AT LONG LAKE.** *Lake House Rd and Hwy 302, Naples (04055). Phone 207/693-6226; toll-free 800/437-0328. www.innatlonglake.com.* The colonial styling of this Lakes Region inn (1906) fits right in with the ambience of historic Naples Village. Amenities include country breakfasts, cozy common rooms, and a landscaped backyard. 16 rooms, 4 story.

Closed Jan-Mar. Complimentary continental breakfast. Check-in 3-8 pm. Check-out 11 am. **$$**
🐾

Restaurant

★ **BLACK HORSE TAVERN.** *8 Portland St, Bridgton (04099). Phone 207/647-5300; fax 207/647-5310.* In restored homestead. Seafood, steak menu. Lunch, dinner, Sun brunch. Closed Thanksgiving, Dec 25. Bar. Children's menu. **$$**
🐾

Brunswick (E-2)

See also Bailey Island, Bath, Freeport, Yarmouth

Settled 1628
Population 20,906
Elevation 67 ft
Area Code 207
Zip 04011
Information Chamber of Commerce of the Bath-Brunswick Region, 59 Pleasant St; phone 207/725-8797
Web Site www.midcoastmaine.com

Once a lumbering center and later a mill town, Brunswick is now mainly concerned with trade, health care, and education; it is the home of Bowdoin College and Brunswick Naval Air Station. The city lies northeast of a summer resort area on the shores and islands of Casco Bay. Magnificent Federalist mansions along Federal Street and Park Row remind visitors of Brunswick's past.

What to See and Do

Bowdoin College. *1 College St, Brunswick (04011). Phone 207/725-3000. www.bowdoin.edu.* (1794)(1,500 students) Nathaniel Hawthorne, Henry Wadsworth Longfellow, Robert Peary, Franklin Pierce, and Joan Benoit Samuelson graduated from here. Tours.

Peary-MacMillan Arctic Museum. *Hubbard Hall, Bowdoin College, 9500 College Station, Brunswick (04011). Phone 207/725-3416.* Exhibits relating to Arctic exploration, ecology, and Inuit (Eskimo) culture. (Tues-Sun; closed holidays) **FREE**

Pejepscot Historical Society Museum. *159 Park Row, Brunswick (04011). Phone 207/729-6606. www.curtislibrary.com/pejepscot.htm.* Regional historical museum housed in an 1858 sea captain's home; changing exhibits, research facilities. (Tues-Sat; closed holidays) **FREE** The Society also operates

> **Joshua L. Chamberlain Museum.** *226 Maine St, Brunswick (04011).* Former residence of Maine's greatest Civil War hero, four-term Governor of Maine, and president of Bowdoin College. Guided tours. (May-Oct, Tues-Sun; closed holidays)

> **Skolfield-Whittier House.** *161 Park Row, Brunswick (04011). Phone 207/729-6606.* An 18-room Victorian structure last occupied in 1925; furnishings and housewares of three generations. Guided tours. (Memorial Day-Columbus Day, Tues-Sat; closed holidays) **$**

> **Thomas Point Beach.** *29 Meadow Rd, Brunswick (04011). Off Hwy 24, at Cook's Corner. Phone 207/725-6009. www.thomaspointbeach.com.* Swimming, lifeguard. Picnicking, tables, fireplaces. Snack bar; gift shop, arcade, playground; camping (fee). (Memorial Day-Labor Day, daily)

Special Events

Bluegrass Festival. *Thomas Point Beach, 29 Meadow Rd, Brunswick (04011). Phone 207/725-8797.* Many bluegrass bands perform at this 85-acre park, where the music meets the sea. Labor Day weekend.

Bowdoin Summer Music Festival and School. *Brunswick High School and Bowdoin College campus, 116 Maquoit Rd, Brunswick (04011). Phone 207/373-1400.* Chamber music, concert series. Fri evenings, late June-early Aug.

Maine State Music Theater. *Pickard Theater, Bowdoin College campus, 14 Maine St, Brunswick (04011). Phone 207/725-8769. www.msmt.org.* Broadway musicals by professional cast. Tues-Sat evenings; Wed, Fri, Sun matinees. Mid-June-Aug.

Music on the Mall. *Downtown, 59 Pleasant St, Brunswick (04011). Phone 207/725-8797.* Free outdoor family concert series. Wed evenings, July and Aug.

Topsham Fair. *Phone 207/725-8797.* N via Hwy 24 in Topsham. Entertainment, arts and crafts. Seven days in early Aug.

Limited-Service Hotel

★ **COMFORT INN.** *199 Pleasant St, Brunswick (04011). Phone 207/729-1129; toll-free 877/424-6423; fax 207/725-8310. www.comfortinn.com.* 80 rooms, 2 story. Complimentary continental breakfast. Check-in 3 pm, check-out 11 am. **$**

Full-Service Inn

★ ★ ★ **CAPTAIN DANIEL STONE INN.** *10 Water St, Brunswick (04011). Phone 207/725-9898; toll-free 877/573-5151; fax 207/527-5858. www. captaindanielstoneinn.com.* This 1819 inn has been elegantly restored in an old-world charm but comes equipped with many of today's plusses. Most rooms come equipped with TVs and VCRs. Relax in classic ambience while feasting in the restaurant featuring marvelous New England flavor with an international flair. 34 rooms, 3 story. Complimentary continental breakfast. Check-in 3 pm, check-out 11 am. Restaurant, bar. **$$**
🄳

Restaurant

★ **GREAT IMPASTA.** *42 Maine St, Brunswick (04011). Phone 207/729-5858; fax 207/729-8576. www.thegreatimpasta.com.* This small, unpretentious restaurant serves up fine Italian cuisine prepared by the highly regared, hands-on chef/owner. The décor is simple, in keeping with the small-town atmosphere. An Italian mural adorns one wall, while another has large mirrors, and a third is brick. Located in downtown Brunswick, Great Impasta is just off US 1. Italian menu. Lunch, dinner. Closed Sun; Thanksgiving, Dec 25. Children's menu. Casual attire. Reservations recommended. **$$**

Bucksport (D-3)

See also Bangor, Belfast, Ellsworth, Searsport

Settled 1762
Population 4,825
Elevation 43 ft
Area Code 207
Information Bucksport Chamber of Commerce, 52 Main St; phone 207/469-6818
Web Site www.bucksportbaychamber.org

Although originally settled in 1762, the Penobscot Valley town of Bucksport was so thoroughly burned by the British in 1779 that it was not resettled until 1812. On the east bank of the Penobscot River, Bucksport is a shopping center for the area, but is primarily an industrial town with an emphasis on paper manufacturing. The Waldo Hancock Bridge crosses the Penobscot to Verona Island.

What to See and Do

Accursed Tombstone. *Buck Cemetery, Main and Hinks sts, Bucksport (04416). Near Verona Island Bridge.* Granite obelisk over grave of founder Jonathan Buck bears an indelible mark in the shape of a woman's leg—said to have been put there by a witch whom he had hanged. **FREE**

Fort Knox State Park. *S on Hwy 1 across Waldo Hancock Bridge. Phone 207/469-7719. www.maine.gov.* The park consists of 124 acres around a huge granite fort started in 1844 and used as a defense in the Aroostook War. The structure includes spiral staircases. Hiking, picnicking. Interpretive displays. Tours (Aug-Sept). (May-Oct)

Fort Point State Park. *8 miles S on Hwy 1. Phone 207/469-6818.* Ocean view. Fishing; picnicking. (Memorial Day-Labor Day)

Northeast Historic Film. *85 Main St, Bucksport (04416). Phone 207/469-0924. www.oldfilm.org.* The Alamo Theatre (1916) houses a museum, theater, store, and archives of northern New England film and video. Exhibits present 100 years of moviegoing, from nickelodeons to mall cinemas. Video and film presentations interpret regional culture. (Mon-Fri) **FREE**

Wilson Museum. *107 Perkins St, Castine (04421). 18 miles S via Hwy 175, 166. Phone 207/326-9247. www.wilsonmuseum.org.* Prehistoric, historic, geologic, and art exhibits (Late May-Sept, Tues-Sun, also holidays). On grounds are John Perkins House (1763-1783), Hearse House, Blacksmith Shop (Memorial Day-Sept, Tues-Sun afternoons). **FREE**

Specialty Lodgings

CASTINE INN. *33 Main St, Castine (04421). Phone 207/326-4365; fax 207/326-4570. www.castineinn.com.* Built in 1898. 19 rooms, 3 story. Closed Nov-Apr. Children over 8 years only. Complimentary full breakfast. Check-in 3 pm, check-out 11 am. Restaurant, bar. **$$**

PENTAGOET INN. *26 Main St, Castine (04421). Phone 207/326-8616; toll-free 800/845-1701; fax 207/326-9382. www.pentagoet.com.* Victorian main building (1894) with smaller, colonial annex (circa 1770); library/sitting room, antiques, period furnishings. 16 rooms, 3 story. Closed Nov-Apr. Pets accepted, some restrictions; fee. Complimentary full breakfast. Check-in 3 pm. Check-out 10:30 am. Restaurant, bar. **$**

Calais (D-4)

Settled 1770
Population 3,963
Elevation 19 ft
Area Code 207
Zip 04619
Information Calais Regional Chamber of Commerce, 16 Swan St, PO Box 368; phone 207/454-2308 or toll-free 888/422-3112
Web Site www.visitcalais.com

International cooperation is rarely as warm and helpful as it is between Calais (KAL-iss) and St. Stephen, New Brunswick, just across the St. Croix River in Canada. Because of an early closing law in St. Stephen, Canadians stroll over to the United States for a nightcap, and fire engines and ambulances cross the International Bridge in both directions as needed. (For Border Crossing Regulations, see MAKING THE MOST OF YOUR TRIP.) *Note:* New Brunswick is on Atlantic Time, one hour ahead of Eastern Standard Time.

Calais has a unique distinction—it is located exactly halfway between the North Pole and the equator. The 45th Parallel passes a few miles south of town; a marker on Highway 1 near Perry indicates the spot. Bass, togue, trout, and salmon fishing is available in many lakes and streams in Calais, and there is swimming at Meddybemps Lake, 13 miles north on Highway 191.

What to See and Do

Moosehorn National Wildlife Refuge. *4 miles N via Hwy 1, on Charlotte Rd. Contact Refuge Manager, PO Box 1077. Phone 207/454-7161. moosehorn.fws.gov.* Glacial terrain with forests, valleys, lakes, bogs, and marshes. Abundant wildlife. Fishing; hiking, hunting, cross-country skiing, bird-watching. (Daily) **FREE**

St. Croix Island International Historic Site. *8 miles S via Hwy 1, opposite Red Beach in St. Croix River; accessible only by boat. Phone 207/288-3338. www.nps.gov/sacr.* In 1604, French explorers Pierre Duguaf and Samuel de Champlain, leading a group of approximately 75 men, selected this as the site of the first attempted European settlement on the Atlantic Coast north of Florida. Information shelter; no facilities. (Daily)

Special Event

International Festival Week. *Phone 207/454-2308; toll-free 888/422-3112.* Celebration of friendship between Calais and St. Stephen, New Brunswick; entertainment, concessions, contests, fireworks, parade. Early Aug.

Restaurant

★ **WICKACHEE.** *282 Main St, Calais (04619). Phone 207/454-3400.* American menu. Breakfast, lunch, dinner. Closed Sun. Children's menu. Casual attire. **$**

Camden (E-3)

See also Belfast, Rockland

Population 5,060
Elevation 33 ft
Area Code 207
Zip 04843
Information Camden-Rockport-Lincolnville Chamber of Commerce, Public Landing, PO Box 919; phone 207/236-4404
Web Site www.visitcamden.com

Camden's unique setting—where the mountains meet the sea—makes it a popular four-season resort area. Recreational activities include boat cruises and boat rentals, swimming, fishing, camping, hiking, and picnicking, as well as winter activities. The poet Edna St. Vincent Millay began her career in Camden.

What to See and Do

Camden Hills State Park. *280 Belfast, Camden (04843). 2 miles NE on Hwy 1. Phone 207/236-3109.* Maine's third-largest state park, surrounding 1,380-foot Mount Megunticook. Road leads to Mount Battie (800 feet). Spectacular view of coast. Hiking, picnic facilities, camping (dump station). (Memorial Day-Columbus Day)

Camden Opera House. *29 Elm St, Camden (04843). Phone 207/236-7963. www.camdenoperahouse.com.* Elm St. Theater with musical and theatrical performances and concerts.

Camden Snow Bowl. *S on Hwy 1 to John St to Hosmer Pond Rd. Phone 207/236-3438. www.camdensnowbowl.*

com. Double chairlift, two T-bars; patrol, school, rentals; toboggan chute and rentals; snowboarding; snowmaking; snack bar, lodge. (Late Dec-mid-Mar, daily) **$$$$**

Conway Homestead-Cramer Museum. *Hwy 1 and Conway Rd, Camden (04843). Phone 207/236-2257.* Authentically restored 18th-century farmhouse. Collection of carriages, sleighs, and farm implements in old barn; blacksmith shop, privy, and herb garden. Mary Meeker Cramer Museum contains paintings, ship models, quilts; costumes, documents, and other memorabilia; changing exhibits. (July-Aug, Mon-Thurs) **$**

Maine State Ferry Service. *McKay St and Hwy 1, Lincolnville Beach (04849). 6 miles N on Hwy 1. Phone 207/789-5611.* 20-minute trip to Islesboro (Dark Harbor) on *Margaret Chase Smith.* (Mid-May-late Oct: weekdays, nine trips; Sun, eight trips; rest of year: six trips daily) **$$$**

Sailing trips. Old-time schooners leave from Camden and Rockport Harbors for half- to six-day trips along the coast of Maine. (May-Oct) For further information, rates, schedules, or reservations, contact the individual companies.

> **Angelique.** *Public Landing in Camden (04843). Phone toll-free 800/282-9989. www.sailangelique. com.*

> **Appledore.** *Hwy 1 and Bayview, Camden (04843). Phone 207/236-8353. www.appledore2.com.*

> **Maine Windjammer Cruises.** *46 John St, Camden (04843). Phone 207/236-2938. www. mainewindjammercruises.com.*

> **Schooner *Lewis R. French*.** *Public Landing, Camden (04843). Phone toll-free 800/469-4635. www. schoonerfrench.com.*

> **Schooner *Mary Day*.** *Public Landing, Camden (04843). Phone toll-free 800/992-2218. www. schoonermaryday.com.*

> **Schooner *Olad*.** *Phone 207/236-2323.*

> **Schooner *Surprise*.** *Phone 207/236-4687. www. mainesailing.com.*

> **Schooner *Roseway*.** *Hwy 1 and Bayview, Camden (04843). Phone toll-free 800/255-4449.*

Schooner *Timberwind*. *PO Box 247, Rockport (04856). Phone 207/236-0801; toll-free 800/759-9250.*

Schooner Yacht Wendameen. *PO Box 252, Rockport (04856). Phone 207/594-1751.*

Sightseeing cruises on Penobscot Bay. *Phone 207/236-4404. www.visitcamden.com.* Cruises (one to four hours) leave from public landing. Contact Chamber of Commerce.

Special Events

Bay Chamber Concerts. *Central St, Rockport (04856). Rockport Opera House. Phone 207/236-2823.www. baychamberconcerts.org.* Classical music performances by Vermeer Quartet and guest artists (July-Aug, Thurs-Fri evenings). Jazz musicians perform Sept-June (one show each month).

Camden Opera House. *29 Elm St, Camden (04843). Phone 207/236-7963.* Elm St. Theater with musical and theatrical performances and concerts. July-Aug.

Christmas by the Sea. *Phone 207/236-4404.* Celebration of the holiday season with musical entertainment, horse-drawn wagon rides, Holiday House Tour, Santa's arrival by lobster boat. First weekend in Dec.

Garden Club Open House Day. *Hwy 1 and Bayview, Camden (04843). Phone 207/230-6509.* Tour of homes and gardens (fee). Third Thurs in July.

Windjammer Weekend. *Phone 207/236-4404. www. windjammerweekend.com.* Celebration of windjammer industry; fireworks. Labor Day weekend.

Limited-Service Hotels

★ **BEST WESTERN CAMDEN RIVERHOUSE HOTEL.** *11 Tannery Ln, Camden (04843). Phone 207/236-0500; toll-free 800/757-4837; fax 207/236-4711. www.camdenmaine.com.* 35 rooms, 4 story. Pets accepted, some restrictions; fee. Complimentary continental breakfast. Check-in 3 pm, check-out 11 am. Fitness room. Indoor pool, whirlpool. **$$**

★ ★ **CEDAR CREST MOTEL.** *115 Elm St, Camden (04845). Phone 207/236-4859; toll-free 800/422-4964. www.cedarcrestmotel.com.* 37 rooms, 2 story. Closed Nov-Apr. Check-out 11 am. Restaurant. Outdoor pool. **$**

Full-Service Inns

★ ★ ★ **BLUE HARBOR HOUSE, A VILLAGE INN.** *67 Elm St, Camden (04843). Phone 207/236-3196; toll-free 800/248-3196; fax 207/236-6523. www. blueharborhouse.com.* Built in 1768 as the home of the first Camden settler, James Richards, this property now offers guest rooms filled with quilts and antiques. Enjoy a hearty breakfast before hiking Camden Hills State Park or taking a Penobscot Bay boat ride. 11 rooms, 2 story. Complimentary full breakfast. Check-in 3-6 pm, check-out 11 am. **$$**

★ ★ ★ **DARK HARBOR HOUSE.** *117 Jetty Rd, Islesboro (04848). Phone 207/734-6669; fax 207/734-6938. www.darkharborhouse.com.* Built in 1896, this island inn represents Georgian Revival architecture and is listed on the National Register of Historic Places. Visitors will be impressed by the grand double staircase in the entrance foyer and hilltop location overlooking Dark Harbor. 11 rooms, 3 story. Closed Nov-Apr. No children under 12. Complimentary full breakfast. Check-in 1:30 pm, check-out 11 am. Restaurant, bar. **$$**

Specialty Lodgings

CAMDEN WINDWARD HOUSE. *6 High St, Camden (04843). Phone 207/236-9656; toll-free 877/492-9656; fax 207/230-0433. www.windwardhouse. com.* This 1854 inn is located in the center of Camden's historic district, walking distance to many restaurants, shops, and Camden Harbor. Mount Battie and Camden Hills State Park are nearby. 8 rooms, 3 story. Children over 12 years only. Complimentary full breakfast. Check-in 3 pm. Check-out 11 am. **$$**

ELMS BED & BREAKFAST. *84 Elm St, Camden (04843). Phone 207/236-6250; toll-free 800/755-3567; fax 207/236-7330. www.elmsinn.net.* This Federal-style home, built in 1806, features a lighthouse theme. 7 rooms, 3 story. Children over 5 years only. Complimentary full breakfast. Check-in 3-6 pm, check-out 11 am. **$$**

HAWTHORN INN. *9 High St, Camden (04843). Phone 207/236-8842; toll-free 866/381-3647; fax 207/236-6181. www.camdenhawthorn.com.* This 1894 Victorian inn is conveniently located for guests to tour Camden and the surrounding area. The rooms all have private baths, and some have fireplaces, whirlpools, and

private decks with harbor views. In Camden, you can explore the many galleries, shops, restaurants, and the Camden docks. 10 rooms, 3 story. Closed Jan. Children over 12 years only. Complimentary full breakfast. Check-in 3 pm, check-out 11 am. **$$**
🅳

INN AT OCEAN'S EDGE. *24 Stone Coast Rd, Camden (04849). Phone 207/236-0945; fax 207/236-0609. www.innatoceansedge.com.* This contemporary inn (circa 1999) overlooks Penobscot Bay. Spacious contemporary rooms feature reproduction four-poster king beds. Most rooms have an ocean view. 30 rooms, 3 story. No children under 14. Complimentary full breakfast. Check-in 3 pm, check-out 11 am. Fitness room. **$$**
🏌

INN AT SUNRISE POINT. *Hwy 1, Fireroad 9, Camden (04843). Phone 207/236-7716; toll-free 800/435-6278; fax 207/236-0820. www.sunrisepoint. com.* This 4-acre oceanfront hideaway is just minutes from Camden Harbor with its old windjammers and modern yachts. Guests can choose to stay at a restored 1920s Maine-style cottage or in the main house and listen to the soothing sound of waves breaking at shore. Breakfast is served in the conservatory and hors d'oeuvres are available in the library in the afternoons.13 rooms, 2 story. Children over 12 years only. Complimentary full breakfast. Check-in 3-7 pm, check-out 11 am. Whirlpool. **$$$**

THE LODGE AND COTTAGES AT CAMDEN HILLS. *Hwy 1, Camden (04843). Phone 207/236-8478; toll-free 800/832-7058; fax 207/236-7163. www. thelodgeatcamdenhills.com.* View of bay. 14 rooms. Pets accepted, some restrictions; fee. Check-in 2 pm, check-out 11 am. **$$**
🐾

MAINE STAY BED & BREAKFAST. *22 High St, Camden (04843). Phone 207/236-9636; fax 207/236-0621. www.mainestay.com.* Farmhouse built in 1802; barn and carriage house. Antiques include a 17th-century samurai chest. 8 rooms, 3 story. Children over 10 years only. Complimentary full breakfast. Check-in 3-6 pm, check-out 11 am. **$$**
🅳

NORUMBEGA INN. *63 High St, Camden (04843). Phone 207/236-4646; fax 207/236-0824. www. norumbegainn.com.* This stone castle-by-the-sea was designed and built by the investor of duplex telegraphy and is located near Penobscot Bay with a

panoramic view of the ocean. The property has been fully restored and is furnished with modern conveniences. Close by are the windjammers and yachts, shops, restaurants, and galleries. Each room has a king bed, private bath, and evening turndown service is provided. 13 rooms, 4 story. Children over 7 years only. Complimentary full breakfast. Check-in 3-9 pm, check-out 11 am. **$$**
🅳

THE VICTORIAN BY THE SEA. *Sea View Dr, Lincolnville (04843). Phone 207/236-3785; toll-free 800/382-9817; fax 207/236-0017. www. victorianbythesea.com.* This Victorian summer cottage was built in 1881.7 rooms, 3 story. Children over 12 years only. Complimentary full breakfast. Check-in 3 pm, check-out 11 am. **$$**
🅳

WHITEHALL INN. *52 High St, Camden (04843). Phone 207/236-3391; toll-free 800/789-6565; fax 207/236-4427. www.whitehall-inn.com.* Spacious old resort inn (1834); poet Edna St. Vincent Millay gave a reading here in 1912. 50 rooms, 3 story. Closed mid-Oct-mid-May. Check-in 3 pm, check-out 11 am. Restaurant, bar. Tennis. **$$**
🏃

Restaurants

★ ★ **ATLANTICA.** *1 Bayview Landing, Camden (04843). Phone 207/236-6011. www.atlanticarestaurant. com.* Open since 2000, this local favorite offers weekly menus of the freshest local seafood plus, at least one organic chicken dish and, often, rack of lamb for those not interested in eating fish. This bright, contemporary restaurant uses color effectively cobalt water glasses, red glass candle holders, and black wood tables. A colorful mosaic tile bar is just inside the entry, and fish watercolors and oil paintings, curtains, and stylish artifacts brighten the walls. A large skylight and a special table in the turret are upstairs. Atlantica is located harborside, on Bay Wharf in a weathered gray-shingled two-story cottage. Seafood menu. Dinner. Closed Tues in winter; also month of Jan or Mar. Bar. Business casual attire. Reservations recommended. Outdoor seating. **$$$**
🅳

★ ★ **THE HELM.** *U.S. Route 1, Rockport (04856). Phone 207/236-4337.* American, French menu. Lunch, dinner. Closed mid-Dec-early Apr. Bar. Children's menu. **$$**

★★ **THE LOBSTER POUND.** *US Route 1. Lincolnville Beach (04849). Phone 207/789-5550; fax 207/789-5656. www.lobsterpoundmaine.com.* Lobster tanks. Seafood menu. Lunch, dinner. Closed Nov-Apr. Children's menu. Outdoor seating. **$$$**

★★ **PETER OTT'S.** *16 Bayview St, Camden (04843). Phone 207/236-4032; fax 207/236-3836.* This upscale family-style dining spot offers three dining areas, all with polished wood tables, striped cloth napkins, and an open kitchen. Open since 1974, Peter Ott's is housed in a dark tomato-colored, yellow-trimmed building, about one half block from the water. Special evenings include Cajun night, and wine tastings are offered occasionally. All soups, sauces, breads, desserts, and sugar-free and regular ice creams are made in house. Seafood, steak menu. Dinner. Bar. Children's menu. Casual attire. Outdoor seating. **$$**

★★★ **VINCENT'S.** *52 High St (Hwy 1), Camden (04843). Phone 207/236-3391; toll-free 800/789-6565; fax 207/236-4427. www.whitehall-inn.com.* Located in the quaint Whitehall Inn (see), the dining room attracts not only overnight guests but also local residents. The cuisine is New American, with a healthy focus on seafood. Guests can dine in the large main dining room, the glass-enclosed dining porch, the seasonal side patio, or order bar food in the adjacent lounge. American menu. Breakfast, dinner, Sun brunch. Closed late Oct-mid-May. Bar. Children's menu. Casual attire. Outdoor seating. **$$**
🅱

★★ **WATERFRONT.** *40 Bayview St, Camden (04843). Phone 207/236-3747; fax 207/236-3815. www. waterfrontcamden.com.* For more than 25 years, the Waterfront has specialized in presenting fresh regional seafood in both traditional and adventurous ways. Originally a boat shed, this restaurant is located on Camden Harbor with docking and access for boaters as well as those arriving by land. The outdoor deck is the place to be for an exceptional harbor view. The décor includes open beamed ceilings, hanging lanterns, and a double fireplace. Polished wood tables are topped with a small vase of flowers. A lobster tank is featured, and bread and desserts are homemade. Seafood menu. Lunch, dinner. Bar. Children's menu. Casual attire. Outdoor seating. **$$**
🅱

Cape Neddick

Restaurant

★★★ **CLAY HILL FARM.** *220 Clay Hill Rd, Cape Neddick (03907). Phone 207/361-2272. www. clayhillfarm.com.* This dining establishment, set in a historic farmhouse (1780), is situated on 30 acres of protected woodlands and is certified by the National Wildlife Association as a wildlife habitat and bird sanctuary. Enjoy fresh local seafood and game, or one of the vegetarian dishes of the week. Seafood menu. Dinner. Closed Mon-Wed (Nov-Apr). Bar. Valet parking. **$$$**

Caribou (A-4)

See also Presque Isle

Population 9,415
Elevation 442 ft
Area Code 207
Information Chamber of Commerce, 24 Sweden St, Suite 101; phone toll-free 800/722-7648
Web Site www.cariboumaine.net

Caribou, the nation's northeasternmost city, is primarily an agricultural area but has become diversified in manufacturing. Located here are a food processing plant, a paper bag manufacturing plant, and an electronics manufacturing plant. Swimming, fishing, boating, camping, and hunting are available in the many lakes located 20 miles northwest on Highway 161.

What to See and Do

Caribou Historical Center. *Hwy 1, Caribou (04736). 3 miles S on Hwy 1. Phone 207/498-2556.* Museum housing history of northern Maine. (June-Aug: Thurs-Sat; rest of year: by appointment) **DONATION**

Nylander Museum. *657 Main St, Caribou (04736). 1/4 mile S on Hwy 161. Phone 207/493-4209. www. nylandermuseum.org.* Fossils, rocks, minerals, butterflies, and shells collected by Olof Nylander, Swedish-born geologist and naturalist; early man artifacts; changing exhibits. Gift shop. (Memorial Day-Labor Day: Tues-Sat; rest of year: by appointment) **FREE**

Rosie O'Grady's Balloon of Peace Monument. *Main St, Caribou (04736). 2 miles S on S Main St.* Honor-

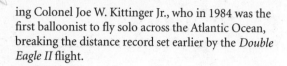

ing Colonel Joe W. Kittinger Jr., who in 1984 was the first balloonist to fly solo across the Atlantic Ocean, breaking the distance record set earlier by the *Double Eagle II* flight.

Special Event

Winter Carnival. *111 High St, Caribou (04736). Phone toll-free 800/722-7648.* Snow sculptures, ski jumping, and family fun slide are just a few of the events held at Teague Park. Feb.

Limited-Service Hotel

★ ★ **CARIBOU INN & CONVENTION CENTER.** *19 Main St, Caribou (04736). Phone 207/498-3733; toll-free 800/235-0466. www.caribouinn.com.* 73 rooms, 3 story. Check-out 11 am. Restaurant, bar. Indoor pool, whirlpool. Airport transportation available. **$**

Restaurants

★ **JADE PALACE.** *Skyway Plz, Caribou (04736). Phone 207/498-3648.* American, Chinese menu. Lunch, dinner. Closed Thanksgiving. Bar. **$$**

★ **RENO'S.** *117 Sweden St, Caribou (04736). Phone 207/496-5331; fax 207/492-1612.* American, Italian menu. Breakfast, lunch, dinner. Closed Memorial Day, Thanksgiving, Dec 25. Children's menu. **$**

Center Lovell

Population 100
Elevation 532 ft
Area Code 207
Zip 04016

This community on Kezar Lake is close to the New Hampshire border and the recreational opportunities of the White Mountain National Forest (see New Hampshire). The surrounding region is rich in gems and minerals.

Full-Service Resort

★ ★ **QUISISANA LODGE.** *Pleasant Point Rd, Center Lovell (04016). Phone 207/925-3500; fax 914/833-4140. www.quisisanaresort.com.* 16 rooms. Closed Sept-May. Check-in 2 pm, check-out 11 am. Restaurant. Private sand beaches. Tennis. **$$$**

Specialty Lodgings

ADMIRAL PEARY HOUSE. *27 Elm St, Fryeburg (04037). Phone 207/935-3365; toll-free 877/423-6779. www.admiralpearyhouse.com.* Located in the oldest village in the White Mountains of western Maine, this bed-and-breakfast named after the renowned discoverer of the North Pole, sits on 10 acres of landscaped lawns and gardens. 7 rooms, 3 story. Complimentary full breakfast. Check-in 4-7 pm, check-out 11 am. Whirlpool. Tennis. Airport transportation available. **$**

OXFORD HOUSE INN. *548 Main St, Fryeburg (04037). Phone 207/935-3442; toll-free 800/261-7206; fax 207/935-7046. www.oxfordhouseinn.com.* Historic house (1913); veranda. 4 rooms, 3 story. Complimentary full breakfast. Check-in 1-6 pm. Check-out 11 am. Restaurant. **$**

Restaurant

★ ★ **OXFORD HOUSE INN.** *548 Main St, Fryeburg (04037). Phone 207/935-3442; toll-free 800/261-7206. www.oxfordhouseinn.com.* Seafood, steak menu. Dinner. Closed Dec 24-25; also Mon-Wed in winter and spring. Bar. Children's menu. Reservations recommended. Outdoor seating. **$$**

Chebeague Islands

Population 300
Elevation 40 ft
Area Code 207
Zip 04017

Little Chebeague (sha-BEEG) and Great Chebeague islands, off the coast of Portland in Casco Bay, were at one time a favorite camping spot of various tribes. The Native Americans had a penchant for clams; the first European settlers thus found heaps of clamshells scattered across the land. Those shells were later used to pave many of the islands' roads, some of which still exist today.

Great Chebeague, 6 miles long and approximately 3 miles wide, is connected to Little Chebeague at low tide by a sandbar. There are various locations for swimming. Additionally, both islands lend themselves well to exploring on foot or bicycle. At one time, Great

Chebeague was home to a bustling fishing and ship-building community, and it was a quarrying center in the late 1700s. Today, it welcomes hundreds of visitors every summer.

What to See and Do

Casco Bay Lines. *56 Commercial St, Portland (04101). Phone 207/774-7871. www.cascobaylines.com.* From Portland, Commercial, and Franklin streets; one-hour crossing. (Daily) **$$**

Chebeague Transportation. *Phone 207/846-3700. www.chebeaguetrans.com.* From Cousins Island, near Yarmouth; 15-minute crossing. (Daily) Off-site parking with shuttle to ferry. **$$**

Cranberry Isles

See also Bar Harbor, Northeast Harbor, Southwest Harbor

Population 189
Elevation 20 ft
Area Code 207
Zip 04625

The Cranberry Isles, named because of the rich, red cranberry bogs that once covered Great Cranberry Isle, lie off the southeast coast of Mount Desert Island. There are five islands in the group: Little and Great Cranberry, Sutton, Bear, and Baker. Great Cranberry, the largest, covers about 900 acres. Baker Island is part of Acadia National Park, and Sutton is privately owned. In 1830, the islands petitioned the state to separate from Mount Desert Island. In the late 1800s, the area was a thriving fishing community.

What to See and Do

Islesford Historical Museum. *Main St and Sand Beach Rd, Cranberry Isles (04625). Islesford, on Little Cranberry Island. Phone 207/244-9224.* Exhibits on local island history from 1604. (mid-June-Sept, daily) **FREE**

Damariscotta (E-2)

See also Boothbay Harbor, Monhegan Island, Wiscasset

Settled 1730
Population 1,811
Elevation 69 ft
Area Code 207
Zip 04543

Information Chamber of Commerce, PO Box 13; phone 207/563-8340
Web Site www.damariscottaregion.com

Damariscotta, whose name is an Abenaki word meaning "river of many fishes," has a number of colonial, Greek Revival, and pre-Civil War houses. With the neighboring city of Newcastle across the Damariscotta River, this is a trading center for a seaside resort region extending to Pemaquid Point and Christmas Cove.

What to See and Do

Chapman-Hall House. *Main and Church sts, Damariscotta (04543).* (1754) Restored house with original whitewash kitchen, period furniture; local shipbuilding exhibition. (July-early Sept, Mon-Sat) **$**

Colonial Pemaquid State Park. *Colonial Pemaquid Rd, New Harbor (04554). 14 miles S via Hwy 130. Phone 207/677-2423.* Excavations have uncovered foundations of a jail, tavern, and private homes. Fishing, boat ramp; picnicking; free parking. (Memorial Day-Labor Day, daily) Also here is

> **Fort William Henry State Memorial.** *Phone 207/677-2423.* Reconstructed 1692 fort tower; museum contains relics, portraits, maps, and copies of Native American deeds. (Memorial Day-Sept, daily)

⭐ **Pemaquid Point Lighthouse Park.** *Pemaquid Lighthouse, New Harbor (04554). 15 miles S at end of Hwy 130 on Pemaquid Point. Phone 207/677-2494.* Includes a 1827 lighthouse that towers above the pounding surf (not open to public); Fishermen's Museum housed in old lightkeeper's dwelling (donation); art gallery; some recreational facilities. Fishermen's Museum (Memorial Day-Columbus Day: daily; rest of year: by appointment). **$**

St. Patrick's Church. *Academy Hill Rd, Newcastle (04543). W to Newcastle, then 2 miles N off Hwy 1. Phone 207/563-3240. www.stpatricksnewcastle.org.* (1808) Early Federal architecture; Revere bell in steeple; one of the oldest surviving Catholic churches in New England.

Swimming. *Pemaquid Beach, N of lighthouse.*

Full-Service Inns

★ ★ ★ **THE BRADLEY INN.** *3063 Bristol Rd, New Harbor (04554). Phone 207/677-2105; toll-free 800/942-5560; fax 207/677-3367. www.bradleyinn.com.*

This inn, built by a sea captian for his new bride in 1880, is located at the tip of Pemaquid Peninsula, near Johns Bay and the Pemaquid Lighthouse. It is a lovely country property with nicely appointed guest rooms. Guests can sit or walk on the well-groomed grounds and enjoy a fantastic view of the ocean. Nearby activities include golfing, fishing, boating, walks on the beach, a winery, nature area, and fine restaurants. 16 rooms, 3 story. Complimentary full breakfast. Check-in 2 pm. Check-out 11 am. Restaurant. **$$$**

★ ★ ★ **NEWCASTLE INN.** *60 River Rd, Newcastle (04553). Phone 207/563-5685; toll-free 800/832-8669; fax 207/563-6877. www.newcastleinn.com.* Overlooking lupine gardens and the Damariscotta river, this Federal-style inn (1850) provides guests with many relaxing options. Reading a book or lounging outside on an Adirondack chair are just two of them. Some of the inn's rooms and suites have four-poster or canopy beds, while others have sitting areas or fireplaces. A four-course dinner preceded by complimentary hors d'oeuvres, is served in one of the two dining rooms. 15 rooms, 3 story. Children over 12 years only. Check-in 3-9 pm, check-out 11 am. Restaurant, bar. **$$**
🅱

Specialty Lodgings

BRANNON-BUNKER INN. *349 Hwy 129, Walpole (04573). Phone 207/563-5941; toll-free 800/563-9225. www.brannonbunkerinn.com.* World War I memorabilia. On river. 8 rooms, 2 story. Pets accepted, some restrictions; fee. Complimentary continental breakfast. Check-in 2 pm, check-out 11 am. **$$**
🐾

DOWN EASTER INN. *220 Bristol Rd, Damariscotta (04543). Phone 207/563-5332; fax 207/563-1134. www.downeasterinn.com.* This Greek Revival farmhouse (1785)was built by a ship chandler whose ancestors were among the first settlers of Bristol. 22 rooms, 2 story. Closed Columbus Day-Memorial Day. Complimentary continental breakfast. Check-in 2 pm, check-out 11 am. Restaurant. **$**

Deer Isle

See also Boothbay Harbor, Monhegan Island, Wiscasset

Settled 1762
Population 1,829
Elevation 23 ft
Area Code 207

Zip 04627
Information Deer Isle/Stonington Chamber of Commerce, PO Box 490, Stonington 04627; phone 207/348-6124 (in season)
Web Site www.deerisle.com

A bridge over Eggemoggin Reach connects these islands with the mainland. There are two major villages here—Deer Isle (the older) and Stonington. Lobster fishing and tourism are the backbone of the economy, and Stonington also cans sardines. Fishing, sailing, tennis, and golf are available in the area.

What to See and Do

Isle au Haut. *Deer Isle.* (EEL-oh-HO) Reached by ferry from Stonington. Much of this island—with hills more than 500 feet tall, forested shores, and cobblestone beaches—is in Acadia National Park (see).

Isle au Haut Ferry Service. *Seabreeze Ave, Stonington (04681). Phone 207/367-5193.* Service to the island and excursion trips available.

Limited-Service Hotel

★ ★ **GOOSE COVE LODGE.** *300 Goose Cove Rd, Sunset (04683). Phone 207/348-2508; toll-free 800/728-1963; fax 207/348-2624. www.goosecovelodge.com.* 23 rooms. Closed mid-Oct-Apr. Check-in 3 pm, check-out 10:30 am. Children's activity center. **$**
🅱

Full-Service Inn

★ ★ ★ **PILGRIMS INN.** *20 Main St, Deer Isle (04627). Phone 207/348-6615; fax 207/348-6615. www.pilgrimsinn.com.* This restored, historic wood frame building was built in 1793 and has eight-foot-wide fireplaces. For families or guests with pets, there are two housekeeping units on property. Nearby are art galleries and a famous art school. The chef prepares meals from local seafood, produce, and fresh-grown ingredients from the garden. 16 rooms, 4 story. Closed Nov-mid-May, pets accepted, some restrictions; fee. Check-in 2-5 pm, check-out 11 am. Restaurant. **$$**
🅱 🐾

Eastport (D-5)

See also Lubec

Settled 1780

Population 1,965
Elevation 60 ft
Area Code 207
Zip 04631
Information Chamber of Commerce, PO Box 254; phone 207/853-4644
Web Site www.eastportme.net

At the southern end of Passamaquoddy Bay, Eastport is a community with 150-year-old houses and ancient elms. The average tide at Eastport is approximately 18 feet, but tides up to 25 feet have been recorded here. Eastport was the site of one of the country's first tide-powered electric generating projects, and though never completed, it resulted in the construction of two tidal dams. The city also boasts of being the nation's salmonid aquaculture capital, where millions of salmon and trout are raised in pens in the chilly off-shore waters.

What to See and Do

Barracks Museum. *74 Washington St, Eastport (04631).* This 1822 building once served as the officers' barracks for a nearby fort, which was held by British troops during the War of 1812. Museum. (Memorial Day-Labor Day, Wed-Sat afternoons) **FREE**

Ferry to Deer Island, New Brunswick. A 20-minute trip; camping, picnicking on Deer Island. (June-Sept, daily) For schedules, fees inquire locally. (For border crossing regulations, see MAKING THE MOST OF YOUR TRIP.) **$$**

Fishing. Pollock, cod, flounder, and others caught from wharves. Charter boats available for deep-sea fishing in sheltered waters.

Old Sow Whirlpool. *Between Dog and Deer islands. www.oldsowwhirlpool.com.* One of largest in the Western Hemisphere; most active three hours before high tide.

Passamaquoddy Indian Reservation. *Hwy 190, Perry (04667). About 5 miles N on Hwy 190 at Pleasant Point. Phone 207/853-2551.* Champlain, in 1604, was the first European to encounter members of this Algonquin tribe. Festivals and ceremonies throughout the year (see SPECIAL EVENTS). **FREE**

Whale-watching trips. Boat excursions during the summer to view whales in the bay.

Special Events

Indian Festival. *Passamaquoddy Indian Reservation,* *Hwy 190, Eastport (04631). Phone 207/853-4644.* Ceremonies, fireworks, traditional celebrations. Second weekend in Aug.

Salmon Festival. *78 Water St, Eastport (04631). Phone 207/853-4644.* Tours of aquaculture pens; music, crafts, educational displays; farm-raised Atlantic salmon dinners. Sun after Labor Day.

Specialty Lodgings

TODD HOUSE. *1 Capen Ave, Eastport (04631). Phone 207/853-2328.* This authentic New England Cape once housed soldiers during the War of 1812. It is near ocean and features views of the bay. 8 rooms, 2 story. Pets accepted; fee. Complimentary continental breakfast. Check-in 2 pm, check-out 11 am. **$**

WESTON HOUSE BED & BREAKFAST. *26 Boyton St, Eastport (04631). Phone 207/853-2907; toll-free 800/853-2907; fax 207/853-0981. www. westonhouse-maine.com.* Restored 19th-century residence; sitting room with tin ceiling. 4 rooms. No children allowed. Complimentary full breakfast. Check-in before dark, check-out 11 am. **$**

Ellsworth (D-3)

See also Bar Harbor, Blue Hill, Bucksport

Settled 1763
Population 5,975
Elevation 100 ft
Area Code 207
Zip 04605
Information Chamber of Commerce, 163 High St, PO Box 267; phone 207/667-5584
Web Site www.ellsworthchamber.org

This is the shire town and trading center for Hancock County—which includes some of the country's choicest resort territory, including Bar Harbor. In the beginning of the 19th century, Ellsworth was the second-largest lumber shipping port in the world. Its business district was destroyed by fire in 1933, but was handsomely rebuilt, contrasting with the old residential streets.

What to See and Do

Lamoine State Park. *Lamoine Rd, Lamoine (04605).* 8

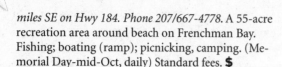

miles SE on Hwy 184. Phone 207/667-4778. A 55-acre recreation area around beach on Frenchman Bay. Fishing; boating (ramp); picnicking, camping. (Memorial Day-mid-Oct, daily) Standard fees. **$**

Stanwood Sanctuary (Birdsacre) and Homestead Museum. *289 High St, Ellsworth (04605). On Bar Harbor Rd (Hwy 3). Phone 207/667-8460.* Trails, ponds, and picnic areas on 130-acre site. Collections include mounted birds, nests, and eggs. Wildlife rehabilitation center with shelters for injured birds, including hawks and owls. Museum was home of pioneer ornithologist, photographer and writer Cordelia Stanwood (1865-1958). Sanctuary and rehabilitation center (daily; free); museum (mid-June-mid-Oct). Gift shop. **$$**

Limited-Service Hotel

★ ★ **HOLIDAY INN.** *215 High St, Ellsworth (04605). Phone 207/667-9341; toll-free 800/465-4329; fax 207/667-7294. www.holidayinnellsworth.com.* 103 rooms, 2 story. Pets accepted, some restrictions; fee. Check-in 3 pm, check-out noon. Restaurant, bar. Fitness room. Indoor pool, whirlpool. Tennis. **$**

🐾 🧍 🛏 🎿

Fort Kent (A-3)

See also Allagash Wilderness Waterway

Settled 1829
Population 4,268
Area Code 207
Zip 04743
Information Chamber of Commerce, PO Box 430; phone 207/834-5354 or toll-free 800/733-3563

Fort Kent, at the northern end of famous Highway 1 (the other end is at Key West, Florida), is the chief community of Maine's "far north." A bridge across the St. John River leads to Clair, New Brunswick. (For border crossing regulations, see MAKING THE MOST OF YOUR TRIP.) The town is a lumbering, farming, hunting, and fishing center, and canoeing, downhill and cross-country skiing, and snowmobiling are popular here. A campus of the University of Maine is located here.

What to See and Do

Canoeing. Fort Kent is the downstream terminus of the St. John-Allagash canoe trip, which starts at East Seboomook on Moosehead Lake, 156 miles and six portages away. (See ALLAGASH WILDERNESS WATERWAY)

Cross-country skiing. Fort Kent has 11 1/2 miles of scenic intermediate and advanced trails. **FREE**

Fishing. Guides, boats, and gear available for short or long expeditions up the Fish River chain of lakes for salmon or trout; St. John or Allagash rivers for trout.

Fort Kent Block House. *N edge of town. Phone 207/834-3866.* Built in 1839, during the Aroostook Bloodless War with Britain, used for training exercises and as a guard post. Restored; antique hand tools in museum; interpretive displays. Picnicking. (Memorial Day-Labor Day, daily)

Fort Kent Historical Society Museum and Gardens. *54 W Main St, Fort Kent (04743). For further information contact the Chamber of Commerce.* Former Bangor and Aroostook railroad station, built in early 1900s, now houses historical museum. (Usually last two weeks in June-Aug, Tues-Fri)

Lonesome Pine Trails. *Forest Ave, Fort Kent (04743). Phone 207/834-5202.* Thirteen trails, 2,300-foot slope with 500-foot drop; beginners slope and tow; rope tow, T-bar; school, patrol, rentals; lodge, concession. (Dec-Apr) **$$$$**

Special Event

Can Am Crown Sled Dog Races. *W Main St, Fort Kent (04743). Phone 207/834-3312; toll-free 800/733-3563. can-am.sjv.net.* Three races (30-, 60-, and 250-mile) begin on Main Street and finish at the Lonesome Pine Ski Lodge. Late Feb-early Mar.

Freeport (E-2)

See also Bath, Brunswick, Yarmouth

Population 6,905
Elevation 130 ft
Area Code 207
Zip 04032
Information Freeport Merchants Association, Hose Tower **Information** Center, 23 Depot St, PO Box 452; phone 207/865-1212 or toll-free 800/865-1994
Web Site www.freeportusa.com

It was in Freeport that legislators signed papers granting Maine independence from Massachusetts and, eventually, its statehood. The town is home to the renowned L. L. Bean clothing and sporting goods store;

its major industries include retail, tourism, crabbing, and crabmeat packing.

What to See and Do

Atlantic Seal **Cruises.** *South Freeport. Depart from Town Wharf, foot of Main St in South Freeport, 2 miles S on S Freeport Rd. Phone 207/865-6112.* Cruises aboard 40-foot, 28-passenger vessel on Casco Bay to Eagle Island and Robert E. Peary house museum; also seal- and bird-watching trips, fall foliage sightseeing cruises. (Schedules vary) Tickets must be purchased at Main Street office, South Freeport.

⭐ Factory outlet stores. *42-28 Main St, Freeport (04032). Phone toll-free 800/865-1994. www.freeportusa. com.* Freeport is home to more than 120 outlet stores and centers that offer brand-name merchandise at discounted prices, including the famous L. L. Bean clothing and sporting goods store, which stays open 24 hours a day. For a list of outlet stores, contact the Freeport Merchants Association.

Mast Landing Sanctuary. *20 Gilsland Farm Rd, Falmouth (04105). Upper Mast Landing Rd, 1 1/2 miles E. Phone 207/781-2330. www.maineaudubon.com.* A 140-acre area maintained by the Maine Audubon Society. Hiking, cross-country skiing. (Daily) **FREE**

Winslow Memorial Park. *End of Staples Point Rd, Freeport. 5 miles S off Hwy 1, I-95. Phone 207/865-4198. www.freeportmaine.com.* Campground with swimming, boating (fee), cross-country skiing; picnicking. (Schedule varies) **$**

Limited-Service Hotels

★ ★ BEST WESTERN FREEPORT INN. *31 Hwy 1, Freeport (04032). Phone 207/865-3106; toll-free 800/780-7234; fax 207/865-6364. www.bestwestern. com.* On 25 acres; river; canoe. 80 rooms, 3 story. Pets accepted, some restrictions. Check-in 3 pm, check-out 11 am. Restaurant. Two outdoor pools. **$**
🐾 ≈

★ CASCO BAY INN. *107 Hwy 1, Freeport (04032). Phone 207/865-4925; toll-free 800/570-4970; fax 207/865-0696. www.cascobayinn.com.* 45 rooms, 2 story. Closed mid-Dec-mid-Apr. Check-in 3 pm, check-out 11 am. **$**

Full-Service Inn

★ ★ ★ HARRASEEKET INN. *162 Main St, Freeport (04032). Phone 207/865-9377; toll-free 800/342-*

6423; fax 207/865-1684. www.harraseeketinn.com. This inn is located just two blocks from L. L. Bean and more than 170 stores. It features rooms filled with antiques. Each afternoon complimentary tea is served in the paneled drawing room. Guest rooms feature Colonial Revival décor and many have working fireplaces. The inn consists of three structures: Federalist house (1798), early Victorian house (1850) modern, colonial-style inn. 84 rooms, 3 story. Pets accepted, some restrictions; fee. Complimentary full breakfast. Check-in 3 pm, check-out 11 am. Restaurant, bar. Indoor pool. Airport transportation available. **$$$**
🐾 ≈

Specialty Lodgings

BREWSTER HOUSE BED & BREAKFAST. *180 Main St, Freeport (04032). Phone 207/865-4121; toll-free 800/865-0822; fax 207/865-4221. www.brewsterhouse. com.* Built in 1888. 7 rooms, 3 story. Children over 8 years only. Complimentary full breakfast. Check-in 3-6 pm, check-out 11 am. **$$$**
🅳

FREEPORT CLIPPER INN. *181 Main St, Freeport (04032). Phone 207/865-9623; toll-free 866/866-4002. www.freeportclipperinn.com.* This restored Greek Revival Cape home (circa 1840) features colonial furnishings. 7 rooms, 2 story. Children over 12 years only. Complimentary full breakfast. Check-in 3-6 pm, check-out 11 am. Outdoor pool. **$**
🅳 ≈

KENDALL TAVERN B&B. *213 Main St, Freeport (04032). Phone 207/865-1338; toll-free 800/341-9572; fax 207/865-3544. www.kendalltavern.com.* Restored New England farmhouse (circa 1850). 7 rooms, 3 story. Children over 8 only. Complimentary full breakfast. Check-in 3-7 pm, check-out 11 am. **$$**
🅳

ROYALSBOROUGH INN AT BAGLEY HOUSE. *1290 Royalsborough Rd, Durham (04222). Phone 207/865-6566; toll-free 800/765-1772; fax 207/353-5878. www.royalsboroughinn.com.* Restored country inn (1772); hand-hewn wood beams, wide pine floors, original beehive oven. 8 rooms, 2 story. Complimentary full breakfast. Check-in 3-8 pm, check-out 11 am. **$$**
🅳

WHITE CEDAR INN. *178 Main St, Freeport (04032). Phone 207/865-9099; toll-free 800/853-1269. www. whitecedarinn.com.* Former home of Arctic explorer Donald MacMillan. 7 rooms, 2 story. Pets accepted, some restrictions; fee, Children over 8 years only. Complimentary full breakfast. Check-in 3-7 pm. Check-out 11 am. **$**

Restaurants

★ **CORSICAN.** *9 Mechanic St, Freeport (04032). Phone 207/865-9421. www.corsicanrestaurant.com.* A two-story cottage in the center of Freeport, Corsican has been serving some of the best clam chowder on the coast of Maine since 1986. American, Italian menu. Lunch, dinner. Closed holidays. Children's menu. Casual attire. **$$**

★ **GRITTY MCDUFF'S.** *187 Lower Main St, Freeport (04032). Phone 207/865-4321; fax 207/865-2109. www.grittys.com.* Although this seat-yourself brewpub offers handcrafted beer that is famous throughout New England, beer lovers aren't the only ones welcome here. Many families frequent this casual spot for its great pub menu, which features items like a pan-seared tuna sandwich, Mediterranean lamb burger, and Maine fried shrimp. Seafood menu. Lunch, dinner. Closed Thanksgiving, Dec 25. Bar. Children's menu. Casual attire. Outdoor seating. **$$**

★ ★ **JAMESON TAVERN.** *115 Main St (Hwy 1), Freeport (04032). Phone 207/865-4196; fax 207/865-6769. www.jamesontavern.com.* This historic tavern opened in 1779, and it became, in essence, the birthplace of the State of Maine, when in 1820, the final papers were signed, officially separating Maine from the Commonwealth of Massachusetts. The décor is essentially colonial, and the dining rooms are simply furnished (booths and tables). Jameson Tavern offers a taste of Maine history and wholesome, tradtional American entrées. The restaurant is located in the heart of the downtown Freeport an outlet shopper's mecca. American menu. Lunch, dinner. Closed Dec 25. Bar. Children's menu. Casual attire. Reservations recommended. Outdoor seating. **$$**

★ **LOBSTER COOKER.** *39 Main St (Hwy 1), Freeport (04032). Phone 207/865-4349; fax 207/865-3883. www.lobstercooker.com.* Seafood lovers looking for a casual place to enjoy the treasures of the sea flock to this cafeteria-style eatery located in the heart of downtown Freeport. Fast, friendly service and award-winning chowders are signatures here. Seafood menu. Lunch, dinner. Closed Jan. Children's menu. Casual attire. Outdoor seating. **$$**

★ ★ ★ **THE MAINE DINING ROOM.** *162 Main St, Freeport (04032). Phone 207/865-9377; toll-free 800/342-6423. www.harraseeketinn.com.* Two light and airy rooms invite guests to dine at this charming restaurant located in the Harraskeet Inn (see). Dining areas are cozy and feature two wood-burning fireplaces; views of the inn's grounds and perennial garden; and tables that are elgantly topped with clean and crisp double white cloths, bright yellow napkins, white china, and lovely flowers. The restaurant is known for its interest in naturally grown, organic food; they employ their own lobstermen and farmers and have established connections with growers around the country who supply fresh, organic foods during the winter season. The result is a creative American menu bursting with freshness and flavor. And to complement, the restaurant offers a collection of wines that is one of the largest in Maine. American menu. Breakfast, lunch, dinner, late-night, brunch. Bar. Children's menu. Casual attire. Reservations recommended. Valet parking. Outdoor seating. **$$$**

Greenville (C-2)

See also Moosehead Lake

Settled 1824
Population 1,884
Elevation 1,038 ft
Area Code 207
Zip 04441
Information Moosehead Lake Region Chamber of Commerce, PO Box 581; phone 207/695-2702 or toll-free 888/876-2778
Web Site www.mooseheadlake.org

Greenville is a starting point for trips into the Moosehead Lake region (see). Until it was incorporated in 1836, it was known as Haskell, in honor of its founder Nathaniel Haskell.

What to See and Do

Lily Bay State Park. *8 miles N via local roads, near Beaver Cove. Phone 207/695-2700. www.campwithme.com.* A 924-acre park on Moosehead Lake. Swimming, fishing, boating (ramp); picnicking, camping (dump station). (Mid-May-mid-Oct) Snowmobiling permitted.

Moosehead Marine Museum. *12 Lily Bay Rd, Greenville (04441). In the center of town behind the Fleet Bank, across the street from Shaw Public Library. Phone 207/695-2716. www.katahdincruises.com.* On steamboat *Katahdin*, berthed in East Cove. Exhibits of the steamboat era and the Kineo Hotel; cruises available. (July-Columbus Day) **$$**

Special Event

MooseMainea. *Various locations around Greenville. Phone 207/695-2702.* Celebration honoring the moose. Canoe race, rowing regatta, fly-fishing championship, Tour de Moose bike race. Family Fun Day with parade, crafts, entertainment. Moose-sighting tours. Mid-May-mid-June.

Limited-Service Hotels

★ **CHALET MOOSEHEAD LAKEFRONT MOTEL.** *12 N Birch St, Greenville (04441). Phone 207/695-2950; toll-free 800/290-3645. www.mooseheadlodging.com.* 27 rooms, 2 story. Pets accepted, some restrictions; fee. Check-in 1 pm, check-out 10 am. **$**

★ **INDIAN HILL.** *127 Moosehead Lake Rd, Greenville (04441). Phone 207/695-2623; toll-free 800/771-4620; fax 207/695-2950. www.mooseheadlodging.com.* 15 rooms. Check-out 10:30 am. **$**

Specialty Lodgings

GREENVILLE INN. *40 Norris St, Greenville (04441). Phone 207/695-2206; toll-free 888/695-6000; fax 207/695-0335. www.greenvilleinn.com.* 13 rooms, 3 story. Complimentary continental breakfast. Check-in 3-11 pm, check-out 11 am. Restaurant (May-Oct), bar. **$$**
🅳

THE LODGE AT MOOSEHEAD LAKE. *Lily Bay Rd, Greenville (04441). Phone 207/695-4400; toll-free 800/825-6977; fax 207/695-2281. www. lodgeatmooseheadlake.com.* This romantic nature retreat offers lodge rooms and adjacent carriage house suites each with charming rustic interiors including hand-carved poster beds, twig tables, and woodsy fabrics. Most guest rooms afford dramatic sunset views over the water and Squaw Mountain. Explore nearby Lily Bay State Park or take part in the year-round recreations of the lake and surrounding wilderness. 8 rooms, 2 story. Children over 14 years only. Complimentary full breakfast. Check-in 3-6 pm, check-out 11 am. **$$$$**

Houlton (B-4)

Settled 1805

Population 6,613
Elevation 366 ft
Area Code 207
Information Greater Houlton Chamber of Commerce, 109 Main St; phone 207/532-4216
Web Site www.greaterhoulton.com

Houlton prospered first from lumber, then from the famous Maine potatoes. It is young by New England standards, but was the first town settled in Aroostook County. Industries include woodworking and wood chip and waferboard factories. It is 2 miles from the Canadian border and a major port of entry. Swimming is available at Nickerson Lake. Fishing is available in several nearby lakes. (For border crossing regulations, see MAKING THE MOST OF YOUR TRIP.)

What to See and Do

Aroostook Historical and Art Museum. *109 Main St, Houlton (04730). Phone 207/532-4216.* Pioneer exhibits, local historical items include model and artifacts from Hancock Barracks, memorabilia from the now closed Ricker College. (Memorial Day-Labor Day, Tues-Sat) **FREE**

Hancock Barracks. *Garrison Hill, Houlton (04730). 1 mile E on Hwy 2.* Second-northernmost Federal outpost in the country; manned by troops from 1828-1846. **FREE**

Market Square Historic District. *Main and Broadway sts, Houlton (04730).* These historic 1890s buildings show a high degree of design artistry. Contact the Chamber of Commerce for walking tour maps. **FREE**

Special Events

Houlton Fair. *Community Park, Randall Ave, Houlton (04730). Phone 207/532-4216.* Entertainment, concessions, rides. Early July.

Houlton Potato Feast Days. *Phone 207/532-4216.* Events held throughout the city. Late Aug-early Sept.

Meduxnekeag River Canoe Race. *7 Bird St, Houlton (04730). Phone 207/532-4216.* Late Apr.

Limited-Service Hotels

★ **IVEYS MOTOR LODGE.** *Hwy 1 and I-95, Houlton (04730). Phone 207/532-4206; toll-free 800/244-4206. www.houlton.com/iveys.htm.* 24 rooms. Check-in 2 pm, check-out 11 am. Bar. **$**

★ **SCOTTISH INN.** *239 Bangor St, Houlton (04730). Phone 207/532-2236; fax 207/532-9893.* 43 rooms. Pets accepted, some restrictions; fee. Check-in noon, check-out 11 am. **$**

★ **SHIRETOWN MOTOR INN.** *282 North St at I-95, Houlton (04730). Phone 207/532-9421; toll-free 800/441-9421; fax 207/532-3390. www.shiretownmotorairport.com.* 51 rooms. Check-in 2 pm, check-out 11 am. Restaurant, bar. Fitness room. Indoor pool. Tennis. **$**

Kennebunk (F-1)

See also Kennebunkport, Ogunquit, Old Orchard Beach, Portland, Saco, Wells

Settled 1650
Population 8,004
Elevation 50 ft
Area Code 207
Zip 04043
Information Chamber of Commerce, 17 Western Ave, Hwy 9-Lower Village, PO Box 740; phone 207/967-0857 or toll-free 800/982-4421
Web Site www.visitthekennebunks.com

The original settlement that was to become Kennebunk was at one time a part of Wells. When Maine separated from Massachusetts in 1820, Kennebunk separated from Wells. Once a shipbuilding community on the Mousam and Kennebunk rivers, Kennebunk today is the principal business center of a summer resort area that includes Kennebunkport (see) and Kennebunk Beach.

What to See and Do

Brick Store Museum. *117 Main St, Kennebunk (04043). Hwy 1, opposite library. Phone 207/985-4802. www.brickstoremuseum.org.* A block of restored 19th-century buildings including William Lord's Brick Store (1825); exhibits of fine and decorative arts, historical and maritime collections. (Tues-Sat; closed holidays)

Limited-Service Hotel

★ **THE SEASONS INN OF THE KENNEBUNK.** *55 York St, Kennebunk (04043). Phone 207/985-6100; toll-free 800/336-5634; fax 207/985-4031. www. theseasonsinnofthekennebunks.com.* 44 rooms, 2 story.

Complimentary continental breakfast. Check-out 11 am. Outdoor pool. **$**

Specialty Lodgings

ARUNDEL MEADOWS INN. *1024 Portland Rd, Kennebunk (04046). Phone 207/985-3770.* Restored farmhouse (1827); artwork, antiques, garden. 7 rooms, 2 story. Children over 12 years only. Complimentary full breakfast. Check-in 2-12 pm, check-out 11 am. **$**

THE BEACH HOUSE. *211 Beach Ave, Kennebunk Beach (04043). Phone 207/967-3850; fax 207/967-4719. www.beachhseinn.com.* This inn (circa 1890) is located on Kennebunk Beach, which is just 2 miles from Kennebunkport. The inn is a few minutes from the Port Village, where guests can visit many boutiques, shops, galleries, and restaurants. Guests may also partake in deep-sea fishing, whale-watching, or visit the Rachel Carson Wildlife Refuge. 34 rooms, 4 story. Complimentary continental breakfast. Check-in 3 pm, check-out 11 am. **$$$$**

THE KENNEBUNK INN. *45 Main St, Kennebunk (04043). Phone 207/985-3351; fax 207/985-8865. www. thekennebunkinn.com.* Built in 1799; turn-of-the-century décor. 22 rooms, 3 story. Pets accepted, some restrictions; fee. Complimentary continental breakfast. Check-in 3 pm, check-out 11 am. Restaurant. **$**

Restaurants

★ **FEDERAL JACK'S RESTAURANT AND BREW PUB.** *8 Western Ave, Kennebunk (04043). Phone 207/967-4322; fax 207/967-4903. www.federaljacks. com.* American, searfood menu. Lunch, dinner, late-night. Closed Thanksgiving, Dec 25. Bar. Children's menu. Casual attire. Outdoor seating. **$$**

★ ★ ★ **GRISSINI.** *27 Western Ave, Kennebunk (04043). Phone 207/967-2211; fax 207/967-0960. www. restaurantgrissini.com.* Grissini offers Italian/Tuscan cooking in an airy, loftlike setting. The restaurant features a large stone fireplace, an open kitchen, and an outdoor garden dining area. Italian menu. Dinner. Closed July 4, Thanksgiving, Dec 25. Bar. Casual attire. Reservations recommended. Outdoor seating. **$$**

★ ★ **THE KENNEBUNK INN.** *45 Main St, Kennebunk (04043). Phone 207/985-3351; fax 207/985-*

8865. www.thekennebunkinn.com. Located in a 1799 inn, this restaurant features an antique dining décor, stained-glass windows, and an outdoor garden eating area. Pub dining is also offered. American, seafood menu. Lunch, dinner, brunch. Closed Jan 1, Thanksgiving, Dec 25. Bar. Children's menu. Casual attire. Reservations recommended. Outdoor seating. **$$$**

★ ★ ★ **WINDOWS ON THE WATER.** *12 Chase Hill Rd, Kennebunk (04043). Phone 207/967-3313; toll-free 800/773-3313; fax 207/967-5377. www.windowsonthewater. com.* This local favorite opened in 1985 and is family owned and operated. Situated in the historic downtown area, it features large windows with views of the river and marina. American menu. Lunch, dinner. Children's menu. Casual attire. Reservations recommended. Outdoor seating. **$$$**

Kennebunkport (F-1)

See also Kennebunk, Old Orchard Beach, Portland, Saco

Settled 1629
Population 3,356
Elevation 20 ft
Area Code 207
Zip 04046
Information Chamber of Commerce, 17 Western Ave, Hwy 9-Lower Village, PO Box 740, Kennebunk 04043; phone 207/967-0857
Web Site www.kkcc.maine.org

At the mouth of the Kennebunk River, this coastal town is a summer and winter resort, as well as an art and literary colony. It was the home of author Kenneth Roberts and the scene of his novel *Arundel.* During the Bush administration, the town achieved fame as the summer residence of the 41st president.

What to See and Do

Architectural Walking Tour. *Phone 207/985-4802.* Tours of historic district (June-Sept) **$**

The Nott House. *8 Maine St, Kennebunkport (04046). Phone 207/967-2751.* (1853) Greek Revival house with original wallpaper and furnishings from the Perkins-Nott family. Tours. (June-mid-Oct, Tues-Sat) **$**

School House. *135 North St, Kennebunkport (04046). Phone 207/967-2751.* (1899) Headquarters of the Kennebunkport Historical Society. Houses collections of genealogy, photographs, maritime history, and many artifacts and documents on Kennebunkport's history. (Tues-Fri) **FREE**

Seashore Trolley Museum. *Log Cabin Rd, Kennebunkport (04046). 3 1/2 miles N on Log Cabin Rd (North St). Phone 207/967-2712. www.trolleymuseum.org.* Approximately 200 antique streetcars from the United States and abroad; special events. (Late May-mid-Oct, daily) **$$**

Swimming. *6 Community House Way, Kennebunkport (04046).* Colony Beach and Goose Rocks Beach.

Limited-Service Hotels

★ ★ **THE BREAKWATER INN AND HOTEL.** *127-131 Ocean Ave, Kennebunkport (04046). Phone 207/967-5333; fax 207/967-2040. www.thebreakwater-inn.com.* 37 rooms, 3 story. Complimentary continental breakfast. Check-in 3-7 pm, check-out 11 am. Restaurant. **$$$**

★ **RHUMB LINE MOTOR LODGE.** *41 Turbats Creek Rd., Kennebunkport (04046). Phone 207/967-5457; toll-free 800/337-4862; fax 207/967-4418. www.rhumblineresort.com.* This secluded woodland location is on the trolley route. 59 rooms, 3 story. Complimentary continental breakfast. Check-in 2 pm, check-out 11 am. Bar. Fitness room. Indoor pool, outdoor pool, whirlpool. **$**

Full-Service Hotels

★ ★ ★ **THE COLONY HOTEL.** *140 Ocean Ave, Kennebunkport (04046). Phone 207/967-3331; toll-free 800/552-2363; fax 207/967-8738. www.thecolonyhotel. com/maine.* Located on a rock promontory overlooking the Atlantic Ocean and the mouth of the Kennebunk River, this hotel provides guests with many activities. There is a heated saltwater pool, beach, and gardens on the premises, and nearby are golf, tennis, kayaking, bicycling, boating, shopping, and touring of art galleries. Maine lobster and local seafoods are the featured cuisine, and afternoon tea is served daily. 125 rooms, 4 story. Closed Nov-mid-May. Pets accepted; fee. Check-in 4 pm, check-out 11 am. Restaurant, bar. Beach. Outdoor pool. **$$**

★ ★ ★ **KENNEBUNKPORT INN.** *1 Dock Sq, Kennebunkport (04046). Phone 207/967-2621; toll-free 800/248-2621; fax 207/967-3705. www.kennebunkportinn. com.* A Victorian mansion (1899), conveniently located at the heart of the historic seaport of Kennebunkport, Maine, the inn is an easy walk to the harbor and all the shops and galleries of Dock Square. Many of the inn's rooms have antiques and four-poster beds, several have gas fireplaces, and all have private baths. This inn is also known for creative cuisine served in the dining room. The house was built by a wealthy tea and coffee merchant and was renovated to an inn in 1926. 49 rooms, 3 story. Check-in 3 pm, check-out 11 am. Restaurant, bar. Outdoor pool. **$**

Full-Service Resort

★ ★ ★ **NONANTUM RESORT.** *95 Ocean Ave, Kennebunkport (04046). Phone 207/967-4050; toll-free 800/552-5651; fax 207/967-8451. www.nonantumresort. com.* Located in the picturesque, historic town of Kennebunkport with fine shops, art galleries, and historic landmarks, the guest rooms are in two buildings and all have air-conditioning, cable, and private baths. Guests can walk to a nearby beach or to the summer home of former President Bush to view the rocky coast of Maine or take a swim or lounge by the outdoor heated pool and whirlpool. Maine seafood is featured on the cuisine side. This is one of the oldest operating inns in the state. 115 rooms, 4 story. Closed mid-Nov-Apr. Check-in 3 pm, check-out 11 am. Restaurant, bar. Outdoor pool. **$**

Full-Service Inn

★ ★ ★ ★ **THE WHITE BARN INN.** *37 Beach Ave, Kennebunkport (04043). Phone 207/967-2321; fax 207/967-1100. www.whitebarninn.com.* The White Barn Inn is a picture-perfect New England hideaway. This cluster of cottages, restored barns, and 1860s homestead offers its guests a leisurely change of pace. Maine's craggy coastline is only a short walk away, as is the quaint town of Kennebunkport, where guests wander in and out of antique and specialty stores. Period furnishings, wall coverings, and antiques capture the essence of colonial New England in the charming rooms and suites. Warm and inviting, the rooms are topped off by wood-burning fireplaces, whirlpool tubs, and stunning views of the countryside. Simple pleasures, like relaxing by the stone infinity pool or riding a bike along the coast, are the draw here. Composed of two converted barns, the Inn has one of the regions most acclaimed restaurants (see THE WHITE BARN INN RESTAURANT). The haute cuisine of the four-course dinner and the romantic, candlelit setting are perfectly suited for a tête-à-tête. 29 rooms, 3 story.

Children over 12 years only. Complimentary continental breakfast. Check-in 3 pm, check-out 11 am. Restaurant, bar. Fitness room. Outdoor pool. **$$$$**

Specialty Lodgings

BUFFLEHEAD COVE. *Bufflehead Cove Ln, Kennebunkport (04046). Phone 207/967-3879; fax 207/967-3879. www.buffleheadcove.com.* This secluded Victorian inn is hidden away in the woods, on the Kennebunk River. The inn is spacious, old-fashioned, and close to downtown Kennebunkport. Guests can leisurely explore the local beaches, or visit the numerous restaurants, art galleries, antique shops, and old bookstores. 6 rooms, 2 story. Children over 11 years only. Complimentary full breakfast. Check-in 3-8 pm, check-out 11 am. **$$$**

CAPE ARUNDEL INN. *208 Ocean Ave, Kennebunkport (04046). Phone 207/967-2125; fax 207/967-1199. www.capearundelinn.com.* This Victorian-style inn (1890) features turn-of-the-century décor and overlooks the seacoast. 14 rooms. Closed mid-Dec-mid-Apr. Complimentary continental breakfast. Check-in 3-9 pm, check-out 11 am. Restaurant. **$$**

CAPTAIN FAIRFIELD INN. *8 Pleasant St, Kennebunkport (04046). Phone 207/967-4454; toll-free 800/322-1928; fax 207/967-8537. www.captainfairfield. com.* This Federal-style historic bed-and-breakfast (1813) is in the heart of the seaport resort of Kennebunkport. It is surrounded by towering trees, gardens, and overlooks the river and harbor. It is within walking distance to shops and art galleries, as well as the ocean and a variety of restaurants. Guest rooms are decorated with antique and period furniture and each has its own private bath and sitting area. 9 rooms, 2 story. Children over 6 years only. Complimentary full breakfast. Check-in 3-7 pm, check-out 11 am. **$$**

THE CAPTAIN JEFFERDS INN. *5 Pearl St, Kennebunkport (04046). Phone 207/967-2311; toll-free 800/839-6844; fax 207/964-0721. www.captainjef-ferdsinn.com.* This historic inn, built in 1804, has been restored and is furnished with antiques and period reproductions. All rooms have private baths, fresh flowers, down-filled comforters, fireplaces, porches, CD players, and whirlpools. A three-course breakfast is included as well as afternoon refreshments. 15 rooms, 3 story. Closed last two weeks in Dec. Pets accepted, some restrictions; fee. Children over 8 years only. Complimentary full breakfast. Check-in 3 pm, check-out 11 am. **$$$**

THE CAPTAIN LORD MANSION. *6 Pleasant St, Kennebunkport (04046). Phone 207/967-3141; toll-free 800/522-3141; fax 207/967-3172. www.captainlord. com.* The Captain Lord Mansion is the kind of place that mandates repeat visits. Indeed, this bewitching bed-and-breakfast rewards its guests with an engraved stone in the delightful Memory Garden upon their tenth arrival. Set on an acre of blooming gardens, this inn wholeheartedly welcomes visitors to the charming village of Kennebunkport on the southern coast of Maine. From the gentle-mannered innkeepers to the mouthwatering morning feasts, the experience is exceptional. The interiors represent a departure from the traditional country inn style, with an opulent and worldly mix of unique touches, period furnishings, and even several items belonging to the original Lord family. Each guest room is distinguished by a different theme, yet all feel luxurious. 17 rooms, 3 story. Children over 12 years only. Complimentary full breakfast. Check-in 3-11 pm, check-out 11 am. **$$**

ENGLISH MEADOWS INN. *141 Port Rd, Kennebunkport (04043). Phone 207/967-5766; toll-free 800/272-0698; fax 207/967-3868. www. englishmeadowsinn.com.* Victorian farmhouse (1860) and attached carriage house. 12 rooms, 3 story. Closed Jan. Pets accepted, some restrictions; fee. Complimentary full breakfast. Check-in 3 pm, check-out 11 am. **$**

THE INN AT HARBOR HEAD. *41 Pier Rd, Kennebunkport (04046). Phone 207/967-5564; fax 207/967-1294. www.harborhead.com.* This 100-year-old shingled farmhouse is intimate and informal, with uniquely decorated, romantic guest rooms filled with antiques, books, chintz, and paddle fans. Stop by the ocean-view breakfast room for a morning meal, then head to nearby Goose Rocks Beach, or just sit on the dock and watch the day pass. The inn overlooks picturesque Cape Porpoise Harbor. 4 rooms, 2 story. Closed Nov-Apr. Children over 12 years only. Complimentary full breakfast. Check-in 3-7 pm, check-out 11 am. **$$$**

MAINE STAY INN & COTTAGES AT THE MELVILLE WALKER HOUSE. *34 Maine St, Kennebunkport (04046). Phone 207/967-2117; toll-free 800/950-2117; fax 207/967-8757. www.mainestayinn. com.* This 19th-century bed-and-breakfast (1860) is located in the residential area of Kennebunkport's historic district. It is near the harbor and beach. 17 rooms, 2 story. Complimentary full breakfast. Check-in 3-7 pm, check-out 11 am. **$$$**

OLD FORT INN. *8 Old Fort Ave, Kennebunkport (04046). Phone 207/967-5353; toll-free 800/828-3678; fax 207/967-4547. www.oldfortinn.com.* This inn, located just one block from the Atlantic Ocean, has guest rooms in a turn-of-the-century carriage house built of red brick and local stone. There is a tennis court and heated freshwater pool on the premises, and nearby guests can explore boutiques and art galleries or the beaches and rugged coastline. 16 rooms, 2 story. Closed mid-Dec-mid-Apr. Complimentary full breakfast. Check-in 3-8 pm, check-out 11 am. Outdoor pool. Tennis. **$$$$**

TIDES INN BY THE SEA. *252 Kings Hwy, Kennebunkport (04046). Phone 207/967-3757; fax 207/967-5183. www.tidesinnbythesea.com.* Built as an inn in 1899. Original guest book on display; signatures include Theodore Roosevelt and Arthur Conan Doyle. 22 rooms, 3 story. Closed mid-Oct-mid-May. Complimentary continental breakfast. Check-in 3 pm, check-out 10:30 am. Restaurant. **$$$**

YACHTSMAN LODGE & MARINA. *57 Ocean Ave, Kennebunkport (04046). Phone 207/967-2511; fax 207/967-5056. www.yachtsmanlodge.com.* 30 rooms. Closed Dec-Apr. Pets accepted, some restrictions; fee. Complimentary continental breakfast. Check-in 3 pm, check-out 11 am. **$**

Restaurants

★ **ALISSON'S.** *11 Dock Sq, Kennebunkport (04046). Phone 207/967-4841; fax 207/967-2532. www.alissons. com.* If you're looking for a good spot to grab a bite while wandering around town, Alisson's is conveniently located on Dock Square, in the heart of town. Two rooms with wood floors, wood tables, and wood banquettes and chairs make up the décor here. The walls are a cheery cranberry, and forest green napkins add complement to the color. Some tables are windowside, so guests can enjoy some people-watching while eating; other tables are in the larger bar and dining room. Six TVs are placed around the room and over the bar in the lounge. Seafood menu. Lunch, dinner. Bar. Children's menu. Casual attire. **$$**

★ **BARTLEY'S DOCKSIDE.** *Western Ave, Kennebunkport (04046). Phone 207/967-5050; fax 207/967-4795. www.bartleysdining.com.* This simple family restaurant has been a favorite of locals, tourists, and traveling celebrities/politicians for three generations. Two small dining rooms and outdoor tables on a front deck and side patio are offered to guests. Located at the bridge leading to Kennebunkport and its Dock Square, it fronts Route 9 and backs onto the Kennebunk River, offering views of the working port. Bartley's is well known for its seafood menu—including "jumbo" lobsters—but Mrs. B's blueberry pies have been regional favorites for years. Seafood menu. Lunch, dinner. Children's menu. Casual attire. Outdoor seating. **$$**

★ ★ **THE BELVIDERE ROOM.** *252 Kings Hwy, Kennebunkport (04046). Phone 207/967-3757; fax 207/967-5183. www.tidesinnbythesea.com.* Located in the historic Tides Inn by the Sea (1899), this dining room features great views of the ocean. Before dinner, guests can enjoy a beverage on the large front porch while admiring the scenery. American menu. Dinner. Closed Tues; also mid-Oct-mid-May. Bar. Children's menu. Casual attire. Reservations recommended. **$$**
🅳

★ ★ **THE LANDING HOTEL & RESTAURANT.** *21 Ocean Ave, Kennebunkport (04046). Phone 207/967-4221; toll-free 866/967-4221. www.thelandinghotelandrestaurant. com.* American, Seafood menu. Lunch, dinner. Closed late Oct-early May. Bar. Children's menu. Casual attire. Outdoor seating. **$$**
🅳

★ **MABEL'S LOBSTER CLAW.** *124 Ocean Ave, Kennebunkport (04046). Phone 207/967-2562.* This popular southern Maine favorite has been serving up great seafood (particularly the chowder), with excellent service, for years. The dining room is simply decorated with knotty pine tables and booths; paper mats and napkins are set at each place. Mabel's is located approximately 1 mile from the bustling downtown Dock Square of Kennebunkport, near the mouth of the river (without view). It is housed in a one-story cottage and offers front porch seating. Seafood menu. Lunch, dinner. Closed Nov-early Apr. Children's menu. Casual attire. Reservations recommended. Outdoor seating. **$$**

★ **NUNAN'S LOBSTER HUT.** *9 Mills Rd, Kennebunkport (04046). Phone 207/967-4362.* Nunan's Lobster Hut is a casual dining spot for good, fresh seafood lobsters, crab, chowders, stews, rolls, etc. The exterior of the restaurant is dark brown wood siding with bright red and yellow trim. Inside, Nunan's is loaded with nautical gear buoys, nets, markers mainly hanging from the rafters and open-beamed ceiling. Wood flooring, tables, and benches are all painted gray, befitting a New England lobster "hut." Seafood menu. Dinner. Closed mid-Oct-Apr. Children's menu. Casual attire. **$$**

★ ★ ★ **STRIPERS.** *131-133 Ocean Ave, Kennebunkport (04046). Phone 207/967-5333; fax 207/967-0675. www.thebreakwaterinn.com.* With an appealing menu, a lovely setting, and great attention to each detail, Stripers offers a gracious, relaxed fine-dining experience. Located within the Breakwater Inn and Spa (see), it is approximately 1 mile from Dock Square's shops and galleries; it is waterside, with 15 pairs of French doors, affording marvelous views of the Kennebunk River. The décor is that of a contemporary seaside cottage, with a soft green banquette along one wall, blue with green piping chair covers, steel-rimmed tabletops, and a see-through aquarium wall that divides the entry from the main dining room. The seafood cuisine includes options such as local Kennenunkport oysters, farm-raised stiped bass, halibut, and scallops. Seafood menu. Dinner, brunch. Closed late Oct-early Apr. Bar. Business casual attire. Reservations recommended. Valet parking. Outdoor seating. **$$$**
🅳

★ ★ ★ ★ ★ **THE WHITE BARN INN RESTAURANT.** *37 Beach Ave, Kennebunkport (04046). Phone 207/967-2321; fax 207/967-1100. www. whitebarninn.com.* A pair of restored barns dating to the 1860s now houses The White Barn Inn (see) and its restaurant. A New England classic, this charming candlelit space, filled with fresh flowers, white linen-topped tables, and beautiful pastoral views, is a perfect place for a relaxed but elegant dining experience. The wide floor-to-ceiling window at the rear showcases seasonally changing floral displays, which include a 600-pound pumpkin in the fall and holiday lighting with a winter scene in December. The specialty of the house is, as you might expect, contemporary New England cuisine; the chef offers delicious regional dishes expertly accented with a European flair. The four-course prix fixe menu changes weekly, highlighting seafood from Maine's icy waters as well as native game and poultry. An ant-loving picnic menu is available in summer months for dining under the sun or stars. The vast wine selection perfectly complements the cuisine, and a rolling cheese cart offers some of the best local artisans' products to savor after your meal. In addition to the cozy vibe and mouthwatering menu, The White Barn Inn Restaurant offers exemplary service. The end result is an overwhelming urge to snuggle in and never leave. American menu. Dinner. Closed three weeks in Jan. Bar. Jacket required. Reservations recommended. Valet parking. **$$$$**

Kingfield (D-2)

Population 1,114
Elevation 560 ft
Area Code 207

On a narrow intervale in the valley of the Carrabassett River, Kingfield once had several lumber mills. The town was named after William King, Maine's first governor, and was the birthplace of F. E. and F. O. Stanley, the twins who developed the Stanley Steamer. There is good canoeing, hiking, trout fishing, and hunting in nearby areas.

What to See and Do

Carrabassett Valley Ski Area. *Sugarloaf Access Rd, Kingfield (04947). 15 miles N via Hwy 16/27. Phone 207/237-2000. www.sugarloaf.com.* Approximately 50 miles of ski touring trails. Center offers lunch (daily); school, rentals; skating rink (fee), rentals; trail information area; shop. (Early Dec-late Apr, daily) Half-day rates. **$$$$** Also here is

Sugarloaf/USA Ski Area. *Sugarloaf Access Rd, Kingfield (04947). 15 miles N on Hwy 16/27. Phone 207/237-2000; toll-free 800/843-5623.* Two quad, triple, eight double chairlifts; T-bar; school, patrol, rentals; snowmaking; lodge; restaurants, coffee shop, cafeteria, bars; nursery; bank, health club, shops. Six Olympic runs, 45 miles of trails; longest run 3 1/2 miles; vertical drop 2,820 feet. 65 miles of cross-country trails. (Early Nov-May, daily). **$$$$**

Limited-Service Hotels

★ ★ **THE HERBERT GRAND HOTEL.** *Main St, Kingfield (04947). Phone 207/265-2000; toll-free 800/843-4372; fax 207/265-4597. www.herbertgrandhotel.com.* Built in 1917; elaborate fumed oak woodwork. On river. 33 rooms, 3 story. Pets accepted; fee. Complimentary continental breakfast. Check-in noon, check-out 11 am. Restaurant. **$**

★ ★ **SUGARLOAF INN.** *Hwy 27, Kingfield (04947). Phone 407/237-6814; fax 207/237-3768. www.sugarloaf.com.* 42 rooms, 4 story. Check-in 4 pm, check-out 11 am. Restaurant, bar. Indoor pool, outdoor pool, whirlpool. Golf. Tennis. Ski in/ski out. **$**

Full-Service Resort

★ ★ ★ **GRAND SUMMIT RESORT HOTEL.** *5091 Access Rd., Kingfield (04947). Phone 207/237-2222; toll-free 800/527-9879; fax 207/237-2874. www.sugarloaf.com.* Each room in this hotel has a view of the mountains and features oak furniture and brass fixtures, television with a VCR, and a coffee maker. Guests can enjoy skiing, golfing, or can just relax and enjoy the mountain scenery. The hotel is located at the base of the slopes. 120 rooms, 6 story. Check-in 4 pm, check-out 11 am. Restaurant, bar. Fitness room. Whirlpool. Golf, 18 holes. Tennis. Ski in/ski out. **$**

Restaurant

★ ★ **LONGFELLOW'S.** *Main and Kingfield sts, Kingfield (04947). Phone 207/265-4394.* One of town's oldest buildings (1860s). American, seafood menu. Lunch, dinner. Children's menu. Outdoor seating. **$**

Kittery (F-1)

See also Ogunquit, York

Settled 1623
Population 9,372
Elevation 22 ft
Area Code 207
Zip 03904
Information Greater York Region Chamber of Commerce, 1 Stonewall Ln; phone 207/363-4422
Web Site www.gatewaytomaine.org

This old sea community has built ships since its early days. Kittery men built the *Ranger*, which sailed to France under John Paul Jones with the news of Burgoyne's surrender. Across the Piscataqua River from

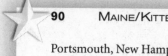

Portsmouth, New Hampshire, Kittery is the home of the Portsmouth Naval Shipyard, which sprawls over islands on the Maine side of the river.

What to See and Do

Factory Outlet Stores. *Hwy 1, Kittery (03904).* Approximately 120 outlet stores can be found throughout Kittery. For a complete listing, contact the Chamber of Commerce.

Fort Foster Park. *NE via Hwy 103 to Gerrish Island. Phone 207/439-3800. www.kittery.org.* A 92-acre park with picnicking, pavilion; beach; baseball field; fishing pier. Cross-country skiing in winter. (June-Aug: daily; May and Sept: Sat-Sun) Entrance fee per individual and per vehicle.

Fort McClary Memorial. *Kittery Point (03905). 3 1/2 miles E of Hwy 1.* Restored hexagonal blockhouse on site of 1809 fort. Interpretive displays; picnicking. For further information, contact the Chamber of Commerce.

Hamilton House. *Vaughan Ln, South Berwick (03908). N on I-95 to Hwy 236, then approximately 10 miles NW to Vaughan Ln. Phone 207/384-2454.* (Circa 1785) This Georgian house, situated overlooking the Salmon Falls River, was redecorated at the turn of the century with a mixture of antiques, painted murals, and country furnishings to create an interpretation of America's colonial past. Perennial garden, flowering trees and shrubs, and garden cottage. Tours. (June-mid-Oct, Wed-Sun afternoons) **$$**

John Paul Jones State Memorial. *River bank, E side of Hwy 1 at entrance to Kittery. Phone 207/384-5160.* Memorial to the sailors and soldiers of Maine. (Daily) **FREE**

Kittery Historical and Naval Museum. *Hwy 1 and Rogers Rd, Kittery (03904). Rogers Rd, off Rte 1 by Rotary at Hwy 236. Phone 207/439-3080.* Exhibits portray history of US Navy and Kittery—Maine's oldest incorporated town—as well as southern Maine's maritime heritage. (June-Oct, Tues-Sat) **$**

Sarah Orne Jewett House. *5 Portland St, South Berwick (03908). N on I-95 to Hwy 236, then approximately 10 miles NW. Phone 207/384-2454.* (1774) Novelist Sarah Orne Jewett spent most of her life in this fine Georgian residence. Interior restored to re-create the appearance of the house during her time (1849-1909). Contains some original 18th- and 19th-century wallpaper; fine paneling. Her own bedroom-study has been left as she arranged it. (June-mid-Oct, Fri-Sun) **$$**

Limited-Service Hotel

★ **COACHMAN INN.** *380 Hwy 1, Kittery (03904). Phone 207/439-4434; toll-free 800/824-6183; fax 207/439-6757. www.coachmaninn.net.* 43 rooms, 2 story. Complimentary continental breakfast. Check-in 3 pm, check-out 11 am. Outdoor pool. **$**

Restaurants

★ **CAP'N SIMEON'S GALLEY.** *90 Pepperell Rd (Rte 103), Kittery Point (03905). Phone 207/439-3655. www.capnsimeons.com.* Located in a 17th-century boathouse, this restaurant features nautical décor with original hand-hewn beams. There are views of the pier and lighthouses, and entertainment is offered on weekends. Seafood menu. Lunch, dinner, Sun brunch. Bar. Children's menu. Casual attire. **$$**

★ ★ **WARREN'S LOBSTER HOUSE.** *11 Water St, Kittery (03904). Phone 207/439-1630; fax 207/439-8829. www.lobsterhouse.com.* Seafood menu. Lunch, dinner. Bar. Children's menu. Casual attire. Valet parking. Outdoor seating. **$$**

Lewiston (E-1)

See also Auburn

Settled 1770
Population 39,757
Elevation 210 ft
Area Code 207
Information Androscoggin County Chamber of Commerce, 179 Lisbon St, PO Box 59, 04243-0059; phone 207/783-2249
Web Site www.androscoggincounty.com

Maine's second-largest city is 30 miles up the Androscoggin River from the sea, directly across the river from its sister city of Auburn (see). Known as the Twin Cities, both are strong manufacturing and service-oriented communities. Lewiston was the first of the two cities to harness the water power of the Androscoggin Falls; however, both cities have benefited from the river.

What to See and Do

Bates College. *56 Campus Ave, Lewiston (04240). Phone 207/786-6255. www.bates.edu.* (1855) (1,600 students) New England's oldest and the nation's second-oldest coeducational institution of higher learning; originally the Maine State Seminary, it was renamed after a prominent Boston investor. Liberal arts and sciences. On its well-landscaped campus are the Edmund S. Muskie Archives (1936 alumnus and former Senator and US Secretary of State) and a beautiful chapel containing a hand-crafted tracker-action organ. Also on campus are

> **Mount David.** A 340-foot rocky hill offering a view of Lewiston, the Androscoggin Valley, and the Presidential Range of the White Mountains to the west.

> **Olin Arts Center.** *College St and Campus Ave, Lewiston (04240). Phone 207/786-6158.* Multilevel facility overlooking campus lake houses a concert hall and a Museum of Art that contains a variety of changing and permanent exhibits (Tues-Sat; closed holidays). **FREE**

Special Events

Festival de Joie. *190 Birch St, Lewiston (04240). Phone 207/782-6231. www.festivaldejoie.org.* Celebration of Lewiston and Auburn's Franco-American heritage. Features ethnic song, dance, cultural activities, and traditional foods. Late July-early Aug.

Lewiston-Auburn Garden Tour. *215 Lisbon St, Lewiston (04240). Phone 207/782-1403.* Tour of six gardens in the area. Ticket purchase required. July.

Limited-Service Hotel

★ ★ **RAMADA INN.** *490 Pleasant St, Lewiston (04240). Phone 207/784-2331; toll-free 800/272-6232; fax 207/784-2332. www.ramadamaine.com.* 117 rooms, 2 story. Complimentary continental breakfast. Check-out 11 am. Restaurant, bar. Fitness room. Indoor pool, whirlpool. Business center. **$**

Lincoln (C-3)

Population 5,587
Elevation 180 ft
Area Code 207
Zip 04457
Information Lincoln Lakes Region Chamber of Com-

merce, 75 Main St, PO Box 164; phone 207/794-8065 or toll-free 800/794-8065
Web Site www.lincolnmechamber.org

What to See and Do

Mount Jefferson Ski Area. *Lee (04455). 12 miles NE via Hwy 6. Phone 207/738-2377.* Novice, intermediate, and expert trails; two T-bar, rope tow; patrol, school, rentals; lodge, concession. Longest run 0.7 miles, vertical drop 432 feet. (Jan-Mar: Tues-Thurs, Sat-Sun; daily during school vacations)

Limited-Service Hotel

★ **BRIARWOOD MOTOR INN.** *Outer West Broadway, Lincoln (04457). Phone 207/794-6731. www. briarwoodmotorinn.com.* 24 rooms, 2 story. Pets accepted; fee. Check-out 11 am. **$**

Lubec (D-5)

See also Eastport, Machias

Population 1,853
Elevation 20 ft
Area Code 207
Zip 04652

Quoddy Head State Park, the easternmost point in the United States, is located in Lubec. There is a lighthouse here, as well as the Franklin D. Roosevelt Memorial Bridge, which stretches over Lubec Narrows to Campobello Island. Herring smoking and sardine packing are local industries.

What to See and Do

Roosevelt Campobello International Park. *459 Hwy 774, New Brunswick. 1 1/2 miles E off Hwy 189 on Campobello Island. Phone 506/752-2922. www.nps.gov/roca.* Canadian property jointly maintained by Canada and United States. Approximately 2,800 acres includes the 11-acre estate where Franklin D. Roosevelt had his summer home and was stricken with poliomyelitis. Self-guided tours of 34-room house, interpretive guides available; films shown in visitor center; picnic sites in natural area; observation platforms and interpretive panels at Friar's Head; vistas. No Camping. (Sat before Memorial Day-Oct 31, daily) **FREE**

Specialty Lodgings

HOME PORT INN. *45 Main St, Lubec (04652). Phone 207/733-2077; toll-free 800/457-2077; fax 207/733-2950. www.homeportinn.com.* Built in 1880. 7 rooms, 2 story. Closed mid-Oct-late May. Complimentary continental breakfast. Check-in 2 pm, check-out noon. Restaurant. **$**

OWEN HOUSE. *11 Welshpool Rd, Campobello Island (E0G 3H0). Phone 506/752-2977. www.owenhouse.ca.* 9 rooms, 3 story. Closed mid-Oct-mid-May. Complimentary continental breakfast. Check-in 3 pm, check-out 11 am. Built by son of first settler of Campobello Island. **$**

Restaurant

★ ★ **HOME PORT INN.** *45 Main St, Lubec (04652). Phone 207/733-2077; fax 207/733-2950. www.homeportinn. com.* American menu. Dinner. Closed Nov-Apr. Casual attire. Reservations recommended. **$$**

Machias (D-4)

See also Eastport, Lubec

Settled 1763
Population 2,569
Elevation 70 ft
Area Code 207
Information Machias Bay Area Chamber of Commerce, PO Box 606; phone 207/255-4402
Web Site www.nemaine.com/mbacc

For almost a hundred years before 1750, Machias (muh-CHY-as) was the headquarters for a number of pirates including Samuel Bellamy, called the Robin Hood of Atlantic pirates. After pirating abated, Machias became a hotbed of Revolutionary fervor. Off Machiasport, downriver, the British schooner *Margaretta* was captured (June 1775) in the first naval engagement of the war. Today, the area is noted particularly for hunting, fishing, and nature trails. Bear, deer, puffin, salmon, and striped bass abound nearby. The University of Maine has a branch in Machias.

What to See and Do

Burnham Tavern Museum. *Main St, Machias (04654). Just off Hwy 1 on Hwy 192.Phone 207/255-4432. www.burnhamtavern.com.* (1770) Memorabilia from 1770-1830. (June-Labor Day, Mon-Fri; rest of year, by appointment) **$**

Cobscook Bay State Park. *20 miles NE on Rte 1, near Whiting. Phone 207/726-4412. www.state.me.us/doc/parksinds.* Fishing, boating (ramp); hiking, picnicking, snowmobiling permitted, camping (dump station). (Mid-May-mid-Oct, daily) **$**

Fort O'Brien State Historic Site. *5 miles E on Hwy 92. Phone 207/941-4014. www.maine.gov/doc.* The remains of a fort commanding the harbor, commissioned by George Washington in 1775. Hiking, picnicking. (Daily) **FREE**

Roque Bluffs. *145 Schoppee Point Rd, Machias (04654). 7 miles S, off Hwy 1. Phone 207/255-3475.* Oceanfront pebble beach; freshwater pond. Swimming, fishing; picnicking. (Mid-May-mid-Oct, daily) **$**

Ruggles House. *Columbia Falls (04623). 20 miles S on Hwy 1, then 1/4 mile off Hwy 1. Phone 207/483-4637.* (1820) This home exhibits Adam-style architecture and unusual "flying" staircase. Intricate wood carving; period furnishings. (June-mid-Oct, daily) **$**

Special Event

Wild Blueberry Festival. *Downtown area, Machias (04654). Phone 207/255-4402. www.machiasblueberry. com.* Located in Washington County, which produces 85 percent of the world's blueberries, this festival's activities include a children's parade, pancake breakfast, craft fair, and pie-eating contest. Third weekend in Aug.

Millinocket (C-3)

See also Baxter State Park

Population 6,956
Elevation 350 ft
Area Code 207
Zip 04462
Information Katahdin Area Chamber of Commerce, 1029 Central St; phone 207/723-4443
Web Site www.katahdinmaine.com

Limited-Service Hotels

★ ★ **BEST VALUE HERITAGE MOTOR INN-MILLINOCKET.** *935 Central St, Millinocket (04462). Phone 207/723-9777.* 49 rooms, 2 story. Pets accepted. Complimentary continental breakfast. Check-out 11 am. Restaurant, bar. Fitness room. **$**

★ ★ **KATAHDIN INN.** *740 Central St, Millinocket (04462). Phone 207/723-4555; toll-free 877/902-4555; fax 297/723-6480. www.katahdininn.com.* 82 rooms, 3 story. Pets accepted, some restrictions. Complimentary continental breakfast. Check-out noon. Bar. Fitness room. Indoor pool, children's pool, whirlpool. **$**

★ ★ **PAMOLA MOTOR LODGE.** *973 Central St, Millinocket (04462). Phone 207/723-9746; fax 207/723-9746. www.pamolamotorlodge.com.* 29 rooms, 2 story. Complimentary continental breakfast. Check-out 11 am. Restaurant, bar. Outdoor pool, whirlpool. **$**

Monhegan Island (E-3)

See also Boothbay Harbor, Damariscotta, Rockland

Settled 1720
Population 88
Elevation 50 ft
Area Code 207
Zip 04852

Monhegan Plantation, 9 miles out to sea, approximately 2 miles long and 1 mile wide, is profitably devoted to lobsters and summer visitors. Rockwell Kent and Milton Burns were among the first of many artists to summer here. Today, the warm-weather population is about 20 times the year-round number. There is more work in winter: by special law, lobsters may be trapped in Monhegan waters only from January to June. This gives them the other six months to fatten. Monhegan lobsters thus command the highest prices.

Leif Ericson may have landed on Monhegan Island in AD 1000. In its early years, Monhegan Island was a landmark for sailors, and by 1611 it was well known as a general headquarters for European fishermen, traders, and explorers. For a time, the island was a pirate den. Small compared to other Maine islands, Monhegan is a land of contrasts. On one side of the island sheer cliffs drop 150 feet to the ocean below, while on the other side, Cathedral Woods offers visitors a serene haven.

What to See and Do

Ferry from Port Clyde. *Main St, Port Clyde (04855). Foot*

The Fragile Beauty of Monhegan Island

Just 1 square mile in area, Monhegan is one of Maine's best known islands because it is spectacularly beautiful. No roads are paved, and there are 17 miles of walking trails. They lead through woods and over rocky ledges, along some of the highest ocean cliffs along the coast of Maine. Less than 20 percent of the island is inhabited.

Ideally, visitors should spend at least a night or two on Monhegan, but most come for just a few hours. The following loop offers a sense of the islands variety with time to still make the boat. (*Note:* Wear sensible shoes and appropriate weather gear. Respect the fragile beauty of the island and do not litter or pick flowers.)

The Lupine Gallery near the ferry wharf is the logical first stop because it showcases the work of the many artists who work on the island and hold open studios. Turn right on the single village street and follow it past Swim Beach and Fish Beach to the first and only intersection. Turn left here at

Monhegan House and walk up Horn Hill. Note the island's only public rest rooms (behind the hotel) and the small signs indicating open artists studios. At a Y in the path, follow the main path to the left as it climbs steeply up to Burnt Head, a cliff that rises a sheer 140 feet above the open ocean. Its the obvious spot for a picnic or at least to catch your breath and take in the beauty of the rocks, fir trees, and flowers. The narrow path continues along the cliffs, dipping between unusual rock formations at Gull Cove, and on to more cliffs at White Head and Little White Head. Turn onto the Whitehead Trail and follow it across the island to Monhegan Island Light, built in 1850, automated in 1959. The former keepers cottage is now the Monhegan Museum, with a spellbinding display on local flora and fauna, art, and history. A separate art museum offers special exhibits. One of the most memorable along the entire coast, the view of the village from the lighthouse appears in numerous art museums. Walk back down to the main road and turn left toward the dock.

of Hwy 131. Phone 207/372-8848. www.monheganboat. com. Laura B makes an 11-mile journey (1 hour, 10 minutes) from Muscongus Bay. No cars permitted; reservations required. **$$$$**

⭐ **Monhegan Lighthouse.** Historic lighthouse has been in operation since 1824; automated since 1959. Magnificient views. **FREE**

Trips from Boothbay Harbor. *5 Eames Rd, Monhegan Island (04538). Phone 207/633-2284. Balmy Days* makes trips from the mainland (see BOOTHBAY HARBOR). (June-Sept, daily) **$$$$**

Moosehead Lake (E-3)

See also Greenville, Rockwood

Web Site www.mooseheadlake.org

N of Greenville; approximately 32 miles E of Jackman.

The largest of Maine's countless lakes, Moosehead is also the center for the state's wilderness sports. The source of the Kennebec River, Moosehead Lake is 40 miles long and 20 miles wide, with many bays, islands, ponds, rivers, and brooks surrounding it. Its waters are good for ice fishing in the winter, and trout, landlocked salmon, and togue can be caught in the summer. The lake is located in the heart of Maine's North Woods. Here is the largest moose population in the continental United States. Moose can best be seen in the early morning or at dusk. Being placid creatures, the moose allow watchers plenty of time to snap pictures. It is possible to hunt moose in northern Maine in season, but only by permit granted through a lottery.

Greenville (see), at the southern tip of the lake, is the headquarters for moose-watching, hunting, fishing, camping, whitewater rafting, canoeing, hiking, snowmobiling, and cross-country and alpine skiing. The town has an airport with two runways, one 3,000 feet long. Other communities around Moosehead Lake include Rockwood, Kokadjo, and Greenville Junction.

Newport (D-2)

See also Skowhegan

Population 3,036
Elevation 202 ft
Area Code 207
Zip 04953

Specialty Lodging

BREWSTER INN. *37 Zions Hill Rd, Dexter (04930). Phone 207/924-3130; fax 207/924-9768. www.brewsterinn. com.* Built in 1935; original fixtures. 11 rooms, 2 story. Complimentary full breakfast. Check-in 3 pm, check-out 11 am. **$**

Northeast Harbor (E-3)

See also Acadia National Park, Bar Harbor, Cranberry Isles

Population 650
Elevation 80 ft
Area Code 207
Zip 04662

This coastal village is located on Mount Desert Island, a land of rocky coastlines, forests, and lakes. The island is reached from the mainland by a short bridge.

What to See and Do

Ferry Service. *33 Main St, Cranberry Isles (04679). Phone 207/244-3575.* Connects Northeast Harbor with the Cranberry Isles (see); 3-mile, 30-minute crossing. (Summer: daily; rest of year: schedule varies) **$$$**

Woodlawn Museum (The Black House). *172 Surrey Rd, Northeast Harbor (04605). Phone 207/667-8671. www.woodlawnmuseum.com.* (Circa 1820) Federal house built by a local landowner; antiques. Garden; carriage house with old carriages and sleighs. (May-OCt, Tues-Sun; rest of year, by appointment) **$$**

Full-Service Inn

★ ★ ★ **ASTICOU INN.** *15 Peabody Dr, Northeast Harbor (04662). Phone 207/276-3344; toll-free 800/258-3373; fax 207/276-3373. www.asticou.com.* Renovated country inn (1883). At head of harbor, public dock adjacent. 31 rooms. Closed mid-Sept-mid-June. Check-in 3 pm. Check-out 11 am. Restaurant, bar. Outdoor pool. Tennis. **$$$**
🅳 ⛱ 🎿

Specialty Lodging

MAISON SUISSE INN. *144 Main St, Northeast Harbor (04662). Phone 207/276-5223; toll-free 800/624-7668; fax 207/276-5223. www.maisonsuisse. com.* This restored, single-style summer cottage (1892) was once a speakeasy during Prohibition. 15 rooms,

2 story. Closed Nov-Apr. Pets accepted, some restrictions. Complimentary full breakfast. Check-in 3-7 pm, check-out 11 am. **$$$**

Restaurant

★ **DOCKSIDER.** *14 Sea St, Northeast Harbor (04662). Phone 207/276-3965.* Seafood menu. Lunch, dinner. Closed Columbus Day-mid-May. Children's menu. Casual attire. Outdoor seating. **$$**

Norway (E-1)

See also Poland Spring

Population 4,754
Elevation 383 ft
Area Code 207
Information Oxford Hills Chamber of Commerce, 213 Main St, South Paris 04281; phone 207/743-2281
Web Site www.oxfordhillsmaine.com

What to See and Do

Pennesseewassee Lake. *W of town.* This 7-mile-long lake, covering 922 acres, received its name from the Native American words meaning "sweet water." Swimming, beaches, water-skiing; fishing for brown trout, bass, and perch; boating (marina, rentals, launch). Ice skating. Contact Chamber of Commerce. **FREE**

Full-Service Inn

★ ★ ★ **WATERFORD INNE.** *258 Chadbourne Rd, Waterford (04088). Phone 207/583-4037; fax 207/583-4037. www.waterfordinn.com.* This 19th-century eight-room farmhouse (1825) is surrounded by fields and woods and is furnished with both the old and the new. A pond, an old red barn, and hundreds of birds are outside, and inside are antiques, art, barnwood, and brass as well as pewter and a library. 8 rooms, 2 story. Pets accepted; fee. Complimentary full breakfast. Check-in 2 pm, check-out 11 am. Restaurant. **$**

Restaurant

★ ★ **MAURICE RESTAURANT FRANCAIS.** *109 Main St, South Paris (04281). Phone 207/743-2532; fax 207/743-5810. www.mauricerestaurant.com.* French menu. Lunch, dinner. Closed Thanksgiving, Dec 24-25. Bar. **$$**

Ogunquit (F-1)

See also Kennebunk, Kittery, Wells, York

Population 974
Elevation 40 ft
Area Code 207
Zip 03907
Information Chamber of Commerce, PO Box 2289; phone 207/646-2939
Web Site www.ogunquit.org

Here Maine's "stern and rockbound coast" becomes a sunny strand—a great white beach stretching 3 miles, with gentle (though sometimes chilly) surf. The Ogunquit public beach is one of the finest on the Atlantic. Marine views, with the picturesque little harbor of Perkins Cove, have attracted a substantial art colony.

What to See and Do

Marginal Way. A beautiful and unusual walk along the cliffs overlooking the ocean, with tidepools at the water's edge.

Ogunquit Museum of American Art. *543 Shore Rd, Ogunquit (03907). At Narrow Cove. Phone 207/646-4909. www.ogunquitmuseum.org.* Twentieth-century American sculpture and painting. Museum overlooks the ocean and sculpture gardens. (July-mid-Oct, daily) **$**

Special Event

Ogunquit Playhouse. *10 Hwy 1, Northeast Harbor (03907). 1 mile S on Hwy 1. Phone 207/646-2402. www.ogunquitplayhouse.org.* Established in the early 1930s. Top plays and musicals with professional actors. Late June-Labor Day weekend.

Limited-Service Hotels

★ **THE BEACHMERE INN.** *62 Beachmere Pl, Ogunquit (03907). Phone 207/646-2021; toll-free 800/336-3983; fax 207/646-2231. www.beachmereinn.com.* Victorian-style inn (1889). 53 rooms, 3 story. Closed mid-Dec-Apr. Complimentary continental breakfast. Check-in 3 pm, check-out 11 am. **$$**

★ ★ **GORGES GRANT HOTEL.** *449 Main St, Ogunquit (03907). Phone 207/646-7003; toll-free 800/646-5001; fax 207/646-0660. www.ogunquit.com.* This year-round smoke-free property offers a variety of guest rooms each with full bath, refrigerator, and television. It is located in the heart of Ogunquit within easy walking distance of the shops and galleries, and guests can relax and enjoy the heated pool and lounge area either indoors or outside. 81 rooms. Closed mid-Dec-Mar. Check-in 2:30 pm, check-out 11 am. Restaurant. Fitness room. Indoor pool, outdoor pool, whirlpool. **$**

★ ★ **THE GRAND HOTEL.** *276 Shore Rd, Ogunquit (03907). Phone 207/646-1231; toll-free 800/806-1231. www.thegrandhotel.com.* 28 rooms, 3 story. Closed Sept-Mar. Complimentary continental breakfast. Check-in 2 pm, check-out 11 am. Indoor pool. **$**

★ **JUNIPER HILL INN.** *336 Main St, Ogunquit (03907). Phone 207/646-4501; toll-free 800/646-4544; fax 207/646-4595. www.ogunquit.com.* 100 rooms, 2 story. Check-in 2:30 pm, check-out 11 am. Fitness room. One indoor pool, two outdoor pools, two whirlpools. **$**

★ ★ **MEADOWMERE.** *Hwy 1, Ogunquit (03907). Phone 207/646-9661; toll-free 800/633-8718; fax 207/646-6952. www.meadowmere.com.* On trolley route. 145 rooms, 2 story. Complimentary continental breakfast. Check-in 2 pm, check-out 11 am. Restaurant. Fitness room. Indoor pool, outdoor pool, whirlpool. **$$**

★ **THE MILESTONE.** *687 Main St, Ogunquit (03907). Phone 207/646-4562; toll-free 800/646-6453; fax 207/646-1739. www.ogunquit.com.* 70 rooms. 3 story. Closed Nov-Mar. Check-in 2:30 pm, check-out 11 am. Fitness room. Outdoor pool, whirlpool. **$**

★ **RIVERSIDE.** *50 Riverside Ln, Ogunquit (03907). Phone 207/646-2741; fax 207/646-0216. www.riversidemotel.com.* Overlooks Perkins Cove. 38 rooms, 2 story. Closed Nov-mid-Apr. Complimentary continental breakfast. Check-in 3 pm, check-out 11 am. **$**

Full-Service Resorts

★ ★ ★ **ANCHORAGE BY THE SEA.** *125 Shore Rd, Ogunquit (03907). Phone 207/646-9384; fax 207/646-6256. www.anchoragebythesea.com.* This property has a sensational location directly on the ocean. The rooms are nicely decorated and appointed and have wonderful views of the ocean. A short walk will take guests to a 3-mile stretch of beach for pure relaxation or a visit to the galleries and shops located in Ogunquit Village. On trolley route. 212 rooms, 3 story. Check-in 3 pm, check-out 11 am. Restaurant. Indoor pool, outdoor pool, children's pool, whirlpool. **$**

★ **THE TERRACE BY THE SEA.** *23 Wharf Ln, Ogunquit (03907). Phone 207/646-3232. www.terracebythesea.com.* 36 rooms, 2 story. Closed Jan-Feb. Complimentary continental breakfast. Check-in 3 pm, check-out 11 am. Outdoor pool. **$**

Specialty Lodgings

HARTWELL HOUSE. *312 Shore Rd, Ogunquit (03907). Phone 207/646-7210; toll-free 800/235-8883; fax 207/646-6032. www.hartwellhouseinn.com.* Located in the countryside of Maine, this bed-and-breakfast is only minutes from a summer resort. It is open year-round, and each room is furnished with Early American and English antiques. Most of the rooms have French doors leading to terraces or balconies that overlook the gardens. A complimentary full gourmet breakfast and afternoon tea are served daily. The lily pond is home to exotic fish, flowering plants, and a small waterfall providing a great retreat. 16 rooms, 2 story. Children over 14 years only. Complimentary full breakfast. Check-in 3-9 pm, check-out 11 am. **$$**

THE PINE HILL INN. *14 Pine Hill Rd S, Ogunquit (03907). Phone 207/361-1004; fax 207/361-1815. www.pinehillinn.com.* Turn-of-the-century cottage with sun porch. 6 rooms, 2 story. Children over 12 years only. Complimentary full breakfast. Check-in 4-6 pm, check-out 11 am. **$**

Restaurants

★ ★ **98 PROVENCE.** *262 Shore Rd, Ogunquit (03907). Phone 207/646-9898; fax 207/641-8786. www.98provence.com.* This welcoming country French restaurant offers an appealing menu in a small clapboard house. The cottagelike setting provides a warm, comfortable atmosphere. French menu. Dinner. Closed Tues; mid-Dec-mid-Apr. Bar. Casual attire. **$$**

★ ★ ★ **ARROW'S.** *Berwick Rd, Ogunquit (03907). Phone 207/361-1100; fax 207/361-1183. www.arrowsrestaurant.com.* Co-owners and co-chefs, Clark Frasier and Mark Gaier, have made this idyllic restaurant in an 18th-century farmhouse a seasonsal dining destination. They bake their own breads, grow their own organic vegetables, and devise a creative, elegant menu that reflects their diverse backgrounds and passion for travel. American menu. Dinner. Closed Mon; also Dec-early Apr. Bar. Business casual attire. Reservations recommended. **$$$**

★ **BARNACLE BILLY'S.** *Perkins Cove, Ogunquit (03907). Phone 207/646-5575; toll-free 800/866-5575; fax 207/646-1219. www.barnbilly.com.* Lobster tank. Seafood menu. Lunch, dinner. Casual attire. Valet parking. Outdoor seating. **$$**

★ ★ **BILLY'S ETC.** *Oarweed Cove Rd, Ogunquit (03907). Phone 207/646-4711; fax 207/646-1219. www.barnbilly.com.* American, seafood menu. Lunch, dinner. Closed Nov-mid-Apr. Bar. Valet parking. Outdoor seating. **$$**

★ ★ **BLUE ELEPHANT.** *309 Shore Rd, Ogunquit (03907). Phone 207/641-2028.* Thai menu. Dinner. Bar. Casual attire. Reservations recommended. Outdoor seating. **$$**

★ ★ **GYPSY SWEETHEARTS.** *30 Shore Rd, Ogunquit (03907). Phone 207/646-7021. www.gypsysweethearts.com.* This converted early-1800s home features original décor, perennial gardens, and an enclosed sunporch. Live entertainment is offered. International menu. Dinner. Closed Mon; Dec-mid-Nov. Bar. Casual attire. Reservations recommended. Outdoor seating. **$$**

★ ★ ★ **JONATHAN'S.** *92 Bourne Ln, Ogunquit (03907). Phone 207/646-4777; fax 207/646-4526. www.jonathansrestaurant.com.* This is a great place to enjoy live entertainment while vacationing in Ogunquit. Don't miss the unique offerings from JJ's Oyster Bar oysters prepared in an international style, including Japanese, Greek, French, and Russian oysters on the half shell. American menu. Dinner. Closed Mon. Bar. Casual attire. **$$**

★ ★ **NO. FIVE-O.** *50 Shore Rd, Ogunquit (03907). Phone 207/646-5001. www.five-oshoreroad.com.* American menu. Dinner. Closed Dec 24-28, late Feb-late Mar. Bar. Casual attire. Reservations recommended. Outdoor seating. **$$**

★ **OARWEED COVE.** *65 Perkins Cove Rd, Ogunquit (03907). Phone 207/646-4022; fax 207/646-1525. www.oarweed.com.* American, seafood menu. Lunch, dinner. Closed mid-Oct-early May. Bar. Children's menu. Casual attire. Valet parking. Outdoor seating. **$$**

★ **OGUNQUIT LOBSTER POUND.** *504 Main St, Ogunquit (03907). Phone 207/646-2516; fax 207/646-4713.* Seafood menu. Dinner. Closed mid-Nov-mid-Feb. Bar. Children's menu. Casual attire. Outdoor seating. **$$**

★ ★ **OLD VILLAGE INN.** *250 Main St, Ogunquit (03907). Phone 207/646-7088; fax 207/646-7089. www.theoldvillageinn.net.* This cozy restaurant with Victorian décor is located in a mid-19-century inn. It is a perfect choice for a romantic meal. Guest rooms are available. American menu. Dinner. Closed Dec 25. Bar. Children's menu. **$$**

★ ★ **POOR RICHARD'S TAVERN.** *331 Shore Rd, Ogunquit (03907). Phone 207/646-4722. www.poorrichardstavern.com.* American menu. Dinner. Closed Sun; Jan-mid-Apr. Bar. Casual attire. Reservations recommended. Valet parking. **$$**

★ ★ **S. W. SWAN BISTRO.** *309 Shore Rd, Ogunquit (03907). Phone 207/646-1178. www.swanbistro.com.* American, French menu. Dinner. Bar. Casual attire. Reservations recommended. Outdoor seating. **$$$**

Old Orchard Beach (F-1)

See also Kennebunk, Kennebunkport, Portland, Saco

Settled 1630
Population 7,789
Elevation 40 ft
Area Code 207
Zip 04064
Information Chamber of Commerce, PO Box 600; phone 207/934-2500 or toll-free 800/365-9386
Web Site www.oldorchardbeachmaine.com

This popular beach resort, 12 miles south of Portland, is one of the long-time favorites on the Maine Coast. It has a crescent beach 7 miles long and about 700 feet wide—which in rocky Maine is a good deal of beach. In summer, it is the vacation destination of thousands.

What to See and Do

Palace Playland. *1 Old Orchard St, Old Orchard Beach (04064). Off Hwy 5, on beachfront. Phone 207/934-2001. www.palaceplayland.com.* Amusement park featuring restored 1906 carousel, arcade, games, rides, water slide; concessions. (Late June-Labor Day: daily; Memorial Day-mid June: weekends) Fee for individual attractions or one-price daily pass. **$$$$**

The Pier. Extends 475 feet into the harbor; features shops, boutiques, restaurant. (May-Sept, daily)

Limited-Service Hotels

★ **THE EDGEWATER.** *57 W Grand Ave, Old Orchard Beach (04064). Phone 207/934-2221; toll-free 800/203-2034; fax 207/934-3731. www.janelle.com.* 35 rooms, 2 story. Closed mid-Nov-mid-Mar. Check-out 11 am. Outdoor pool. **$**

★ **THE GULL MOTEL INN & COTTAGES.** *89 W Grand Ave, Old Orchard Beach (04064). Phone 207/934-4321; toll-free 877/662-4855; fax 207/934-1742. www.gullmotel.com.* 25 rooms, 2 story. Closed mid-Oct-Apr. Check-in 1 pm, check-out 10 am. Outdoor pool. **$**

★ **HORIZON.** *2 Atlantic Ave, Old Orchard Beach (04064). Phone 207/934-2323; toll-free 888/550-1745; fax 207/934-3215. www.horizonmotel.com.* 14 rooms, 3 story, all suites. Closed mid-Oct-Apr. Check-in 2 pm, check-out 10 am. **$**

★ **ROYAL ANCHOR RESORT.** *203 E Grand Ave, Old Orchard Beach (04064). Phone 207/934-4521; toll-free 800/934-4521. www.royalanchor.com.* 40 rooms, 3 story. Closed mid-Oct-Apr. Complimentary continental breakfast. Check-in 2 pm, check-out 10:30 am. Outdoor pool. Tennis. **$**

Specialty Lodging

ATLANTIC BIRCHES INN. *20 Portland Ave, Old Orchard Beach (04064). Phone 207/934-5295; toll-free 888/934-5295; fax 207/934-3781. www.atlanticbirches.*

com. Restored Victorian house. 10 rooms, 3 story. Complimentary continental breakfast. Check-in 3-7 pm, check-out 11 am. Outdoor pool. **$**

Restaurants

★ ★ **BELL BUOY RESTAURANT.** *24 Old Orchard St, Old Orchard Beach (04064). Phone 207/934-2745.* American, seafood menu. Breakfast, dinner. Closed major holidays. Bar. Children's menu. Casual attire. Reservations recommended. **$$**

★ ★ **CAPTAIN'S GALLEY RESTAURANT.** *168 Saco Ave (Rte 5), Old Orchard Beach (04064). Phone 207/934-1336; fax 207/934-2797.* Seafood, steak menu. Breakfast, lunch, dinner. Closed major holidays. Bar. Children's menu. Casual attire. **$$**

★ ★ ★ **JOSEPH'S BY THE SEA.** *55 W Grand Ave, Old Orchard Beach (04064). Phone 207/934-5044; fax 207/934-1862. www.josephsbythesea.* American, seafood menu. Breakfast, dinner. Closed Dec 25-Apr; hours vary in May, Nov-Dec. Bar. Casual attire. Reservations recommended. Outdoor seating. **$$**

★ ★ **OCEANSIDE GRILLE AT THE BRUNSWICK.** *39 W Grand Ave, Old Orchard Beach (04064). Phone 207/934-4873. www.thebrunswick.com.* American, seafood menu. Lunch, dinner, late-night. Bar. Casual attire. Reservations recommended. Outdoor seating. **$$**

Orono (D-3)

Settled 1774
Population 10,573
Elevation 80 ft
Area Code 207
Zip 04473
Information Bangor Region Chamber of Commerce, 519 Main St, PO Box 1443, Bangor 04401; phone 207/947-0307
Web Site www.bangorregion.com

The Penobscot River flows through this valley town, which was named for a Native American chief called Joseph Orono (OR-a-no). The "Maine Stein Song" was popularized here in the 1930s by Rudy Vallee.

What to See and Do

University of Maine-Orono. *5703 Alumni Hall, Orono (04469). Phone 207/581-1110. www.umaine.edu.* (1865) (11,500 students) This is the largest of seven campuses of the University of Maine system. On campus is Jordan Planetarium (207/581-1341). Also on campus is

> **Hudson Museum.** *5746 Maine Center for Arts, Orono (04469). Phone 207/581-1901.* Exhibits relating to history and anthropology. (Tues-Sat) **FREE**

Restaurant

★ ★ **MARGARITA'S.** *15 Mill St, Orono (04473). Phone 207/866-4863; fax 207/866-3023. www.margs. com.* American, Mexican menu. Lunch, dinner. Bar. Children's menu. Casual attire. **$$**

Poland Spring (E-1)

See also Auburn, Bridgton, Norway, Sebago Lake

Settled 1768
Population 200
Elevation 500 ft
Area Code 207
Zip 04274

The Poland Spring Inn, once New England's largest private resort (5,000 acres), stands on a rise near the mineral spring that has made it famous since 1844. Actually, the hotel had even earlier beginnings with the Mansion House, built in 1794 by the Ricker brothers. In 1974, the original inn burned and was replaced by a smaller hotel.

What to See and Do

⭐ **Shaker Museum.** *707 Shaker Rd, Poland Spring (04274). 1 mile S on Hwy 26. Phone 207/926-4597.* Shaker furniture, folk and decorative arts, textiles, tin and woodenware; Early American tools and farm implements displayed. Guided tours of buildings in this last active Shaker community includes Meetinghouse (1794), Ministry Shop (1839), Boys' Shop (1850), Sisters' Shop (1821), and Spin House (1816). Workshops, demonstrations, concerts, and other special events. Extensive research library (Tues-Thurs, by appointment only). (Memorial Day-Columbus Day, Mon-Sat) **$$**

Portland (F-1)

See also Kennebunk, Kennebunkport, Old Orchard Beach, Saco, Scarborough, Yarmouth

Settled 1632
Population 64,358
Elevation 50 ft
Area Code 207
Information Convention & Visitors Bureau of Greater Portland, 305 Commercial St, 04101; phone 207/772-5800
Web Site www.visitportland.com

Maine's largest city is on beautiful Casco Bay, dotted with islands popular with summer visitors. Not far from the North Atlantic fishing waters, it leads Maine in this industry. Shipping is also important. It is a city of fine elms, stately old homes, historic churches, and charming streets.

Portland was raided by Native Americans several times before the Revolution. In 1775, it was bombarded by the British, who afterward burned the town. Another fire, in 1866, wiped out large sections of the city. Longfellow remarked that the ruins reminded him of Pompeii.

What to See and Do

Boat trips. Cruises along Casco Bay, some with stops at individual islands or other locations; special charters also available. Most cruises (May-Oct). For further information, rates, schedules, or fees, contact the individual companies.

> **Bay View Cruises.** *Fisherman's Wharf, 184 Commercial St, Portland (04101). Phone 207/761-0496.*

> **Casco Bay Lines.** *56 Commercial St, Portland (04101). Phone 207/774-7871.*

> **Eagle Island Tours.** *19 Raybon Rd Extension, York (03909). Phone 207/774-6498.*

Children's Museum of Maine. *142 Free St, Portland (04101). Phone 207/828-1234. www.childrensmuseumofme. org.* Hands-on museum where interactive exhibits allow children to become a Maine lobsterman, storekeeper, computer expert, or astronaut. (Memorial Day-Labor Day, daily; rest of year, Tues-Sun) **$$**

Crescent Beach. *66 Two Lights Rd, Cape Elizabeth (04107). 10 miles SE on Hwy 77. Phone 207/799-5871.*

www.mainehistory.org. Swimming, sand beach, bathhouse, fishing; picnicking, playground, concession. (Memorial Day-mid-Oct)

Maine Historical Society. *489 Congress St, Portland (04101). Phone 207/774-1822.* Research library for Maine history and genealogy. (Tues-Sat; closed holidays)

Maine History Gallery. *489 Congress St, Portland (04101). Phone 207/774-1822. www.mainehistory.org.* Features Museums Collection with more than 2,000 paintings, prints, and other original works of art, and approximately 8,000 artifacts. Collection includes costume and textiles, decorative arts, Native American artifacts and archaeological material, political items, and military artifacts. Changing programs and exhibits trace the history of life in Maine. Gallery talks and hands-on workshops also offered. (Daily) **$**

Old Port Exchange. *Congress and Exchange sts, Portland (04101). Between Exchange and Pearl sts, extending five blocks from waterfront to Congress St.* A charming collection of shops and restaurants located in 19th-century brick buildings built after the fire of 1866.

Portland Head Lighthouse Museum. *1000 Shore Rd, Cape Elizabeth (04107). Phone 207/799-2661. www. portlandheadlight.com.* (1791) Said to be first lighthouse authorized by the United States and oldest lighthouse in continuous use; erected on orders from George Washington. (June-Oct, daily; Nov-Dec and Apr-May, weekends) **$**

Portland Museum of Art. *7 Congress Sq, Portland (04101). Phone 207/775-6148. www.portlandmuseum. org.* Collections of American and European painting, sculpture, prints, and decorative art; State of Maine Collection with works by artists from and associated with Maine; John Whitney Payson Collection (Renoir, Monet, Picasso, and others). Free admission Friday evenings. (May-Oct: daily; Nov-Apr: Tues-Sun; closed holidays) **$$**

Portland Observatory. *138 Congress St, Portland (04101). Phone 207/774-5561.* (1807) This octagonal, shingled landmark is the last surviving 19th-century signal tower on the Atlantic. There are 102 steps to the top. (Memorial Day-Columbus Day, daily) **$**

Research Library. *489 Congress St, Portland (04101). Phone 207/774-1822.* World's most complete collection of Maine history materials. Includes 125,000 books and newspapers, 3,500 maps, 70,000 photos, 500 pamphlets, over 2,000,000 manuscripts, and 100,000 architectural and engineering drawings. Also

Fogg collection of autographs and rare original copy of Dunlap version of the Declaration of Independence. (Tues-Sat; closed holidays) **$$$$**

Southworth Planetarium. *96 Falmouth St, Portland (04103). Phone 207/780-4249. www.usm.maine. edu/planet.* Astronomy programs, laser light concerts, children's shows. (Fri-Sat; additional shows summer months) **$**

Tate House. *1270 Westbrook St, Portland (04102). Phone 207/774-6177. www.tatehouse.org.* (1755) Georgian structure built by George Tate, mast agent for the British Navy. Furnished and decorated in the period of Tate's residence, 1755-1800; 18th-century herb gardens. (Mid-June-mid-Oct, Tues-Sun; weekends through Oct 31; closed July 4, Labor Day) **$$**

Two Lights. *66 Two Lights Rd, Cape Elizabeth (04107). 9 miles SE off Hwy 77. Phone 207/799-5871. www.state. me.us.* Approximately 40 acres along Atlantic Ocean. Fishing; picnicking. (Mid-Apr-Nov)

University of Southern Maine. *Portland campus, off I-295 exit 6; Gorham campus, junction Hwy 25 and College Ave. Phone 207/780-4141. www.usm.maine.edu.* (1878) (11,000 students) One of the seven units of the University of Maine system. Special shows are held periodically in the university planetarium and in the art gallery. Also theatrical and musical events.

Victoria Mansion. *109 Danforth St, Portland (04101). At Park St. Phone 207/772-4841. www.victoriamansion. org.* (1858) One of the finest examples of 19th-century architecture surviving in the United States. Opulent Victorian interior includes frescoes, carved woodwork, and stained and etched glass. (May-Oct, Tues-Sun; closed holidays) **$$**

Wadsworth-Longfellow House. *489 Congress St, Portland (04101). Phone 207/772-1807.* (1785) Boyhood home of Henry Wadsworth Longfellow. Built by the poet's grandfather, General Peleg Wadsworth, it is maintained by the Maine Historical Society. Contains furnishings, portraits, and personal possessions of the family. (June-mid-Oct, daily; closed July 4, Labor Day) **$$**

Special Events

New Year's Eve Portland. *582 Congress St, Portland (04101). Phone 207/772-5800.* Fifteen indoor and many outdoor locations. More than 90 performances, mid-afternoon to midnight; a citywide, nonalcoholic celebration with parade and fireworks. Dec 31.

Old Port Festival. *400 Congress St #100, Portland (04101).* Phone 207/772-6828. Celebration of Portland's restored waterfront district between Commercial Street and Congress Street, is the host of this one-day event; it features a parade, entertainment and food. Early June.

Sidewalk Art Show. *1 Congress Sq, Portland (04101).* Phone 207/772-5800. Exhibits extend along Congress Street from Congress Square to Monument Square. Third Sat in Aug.

Limited-Service Hotels

★ ★ **BEST WESTERN MERRY MANOR INN.** *700 Main St, South Portland (04106).* Phone 207/774-6151; toll-free 800/780-7234; fax 207/871-0537. *www.merrymanorinn.com.* 151 rooms, 3 story. Pets accepted. Check-in 2 pm, check-out 11 am. Restaurant. Indoor pool/ outdoor pool, children's pool. **$**

★ ★ **EASTLAND PARK HOTEL.** *157 High St, Portland (04101).* Phone 207/775-5411; toll-free 888/671-8008; fax 207/775-2872. *www.eastlandparkhotel.com.* 202 rooms, 12 story. Pets accepted; fee. Check-in 3 pm, check-out noon. Restaurant, bar. Fitness room. Airport transportation available. Business center. **$**

★ ★ **EMBASSY SUITES.** *1050 Westbrook St, Portland (04102).* Phone 207/775-2200; toll-free 800/753-8767; fax 207/775-4052. *www.embassysuitesportland.com.* This hotel is located close to the Portland jetport and has an indoor pool, sauna, whirlpool, and fitness area. In addition to complimentary transportation to and from the airport, there is free parking, a complimentary newspaper, a gift shop, and a great spot for Sunday brunch. 119 rooms, 6 story, all suites. Pets accepted; some restrictions. Complimentary full breakfast. Check-in 3 pm, check-out noon. Restaurant, bar. Fitness room. Indoor pool, whirlpool. Airport transportation available. **$$**

★ **HAMPTON INN.** *171 Philbrook Ave, South Portland (04106).* Phone 207/773-4400; toll-free 800/426-7866; fax 207/773-6786. *www.portlandhamptoninn.com.* 117 rooms, 4 story. Pets accepted; fee. Complimentary continental breakfast. Check-in 3 pm, check-out noon. High-speed Internet access. Airport transportation available. **$**

★ ★ **HOLIDAY INN.** *88 Spring St, Portland (04101).* Phone 207/775-2311; toll-free 800/345-5050; fax

207/761-8224. *www.innbythebay.com.* Some rooms overlook harbor. 239 rooms, 11 story. Check-in 4 pm, check-out noon. Restaurant, bar. Fitness room. Indoor pool. Airport transportation available. **$**

Full-Service Hotels

★ ★ ★ **MARRIOTT PORTLAND AT SABLE OAKS.** *200 Sable Oaks Dr, South Portland (04106).* Phone 207/871-8000; toll-free 800/752-8810; fax 207/871-7971. *www.marriott.com.* This hotel is located on a hill close to historic downtown Portland. Rooms are specifically designed for the business traveler with a spacious work desk, two-line phone, speaker phone, voice mail, and data ports. Nearby is golf, jogging, tennis, a spa, and the beach. 222 rooms, 6 story. Pets accepted, some restrictions; fee. Check-in 4 pm, check-out noon. Restaurant, bar. Fitness room. Indoor pool, whirlpool. **$**

★ ★ ★ **PORTLAND HARBOR HOTEL.** *468 Fore St, Portland (04101).* Phone 207/775-9090; toll-free 888/798-9090; fax 207/775-9990. *www.portlandharborhotel.com.* 97 rooms. Pets accepted, some restrictions; fee. Check-in 3 pm, check-out noon. High-speed Internet access. Restaurant, bar. Fitness room. Airport transportation available. Business center. **$$**

★ ★ ★ **PORTLAND REGENCY HOTEL.** *20 Milk St, Portland (04101).* Phone 207/774-4200; toll-free 800/727-3436; fax 207/775-2150. *www.theregency.com.* This small, European-style hotel is located in the center of Portland's historic district and is surrounded by galleries, shops, and restaurants. Attractions include Casco Bay, the Portland Museum of Art, and the symphony orchestra. Amenities include turndown service, room service, honor bar, and complimentary coffee served with wakeup notice. The health club is a complete fitness area including Cybex equipment, jacuzzi, steamroom, sauna, massage therapy, and tanning. 95 rooms, 4 story. Pets accepted. Check-in, check-out noon. Restaurant, bar. Fitness room. Airport transportation available. **$$**

Full-Service Resort

★ ★ ★ **INN BY THE SEA.** *40 Bowery Beach Rd, Cape Elizabeth (04107).* Phone 207/799-3134; toll-free 800/888-4287; fax 207/799-4779. *www.innbythesea.*

com. This all-suite resort property is located close to the historic city of Portland on the coast. Every guest room has a porch or deck with a view of the ocean. Recreational activities include an outdoor pool, tennis, shuffleboard, walking or jogging, and volleyball. Amenities for guests include terry robes and turndown service with 24-hour business and concierge service. 43 rooms, 3 story, all suites. Pets accepted, some restrictions. Check-in 4 pm, check-out noon. Restaurant. Outdoor pool. Tennis. **$$**

Full-Service Inn

★ ★ ★ **BLACK POINT INN.** *510 Black Point Rd, Scarborough (04074). Phone 207/883-2500; toll-free 800/258-0003; fax 207/883-9976. www.blackpointinn. com.* This seaside resort is located on a hill at the tip of Prouts Neck with the natural rugged beauty of the Maine coast on three sides. There are numerous rooms and many cottages which were former sea captains' homes. Each room has fine furnishings, period wallpaper, Martha Washington bedspreads, and both porcelain and crystal lamps. Terry robes and turndown service are just a few of the amenities offered guests. 65 rooms. Closed Dec-Apr. Pets accepted, some restrictions; fee. Check-in 4 pm, check-out noon. Restaurant, bar. Fitness room. Beach. Indoor pool, outdoor pool, whirlpool. Airport transportation available. **$$$**

Specialty Lodgings

INN AT SAINT JOHN. *939 Congress St, Portland (04102). Phone 207/773-6481; toll-free 800/636-9127; fax 207/756-7629. www.innatstjohn.com.* Built in 1896; European motif, antiques. 39 rooms, 4 story. Pets accepted, some restrictions. Complimentary continental breakfast. Check-in 1 pm, check-out 11 am. Airport transportation available. **$**

INN ON CARLETON. *46 Carleton St, Portland (04102). Phone 207/775-1910; toll-free 800/639-1779; fax 207/761-0956. www.innoncarleton.com.* This brick townhouse was built in 1869. 6 rooms, 3 story. Children over 9 years only. Complimentary full breakfast. Check-in 4-6 pm, check-out 10:30 am. **$$**

POMEGRANATE INN. *49 Neal St, Portland (04102). Phone 207/772-1006; toll-free 800/356-0408; fax 207/773-4426. www.pomegranateinn.com.* This inn (house built in 1884) is small yet sophisticated and located in the Western Promende historic neighborhood. There are antiques and art throughout the property, and a lovely urban garden awaits guests. It is a short walk to the midtown arts district and there are museums, art galleries, boat rides, fine restaurants, and recreational activities nearby. 8 rooms, 3 story. Children over 16 years only. Complimentary full breakfast. Check-in 4-6 pm, check-out 11 am. **$$**

Restaurants

★ ★ ★ **BACK BAY GRILL.** *65 Portland St, Portland (04101). Phone 207/772-8833; fax 207/874-0451.www. backbaygrill.com.* Located in downtown Portland in a restored pharmacy (1888), this local favorite offers innovative cuisine and a great degree of charm and ambience. The intimate dining room features a brown leather banquette under a full-length wall mural of local friends. Tables are set with double crisp white linen cloths and napkins; candles; a rose; and fine dinnerware, stemware, and flatware. The pressed-tin ceiling adds to the ambience of the cozy rooms. The daily menu features the freshest locally sourced foods the restaurant is a member of the Maine Organic Farmers Growers Association and emphasizes fresh, high-quality ingredients. Special dinners are offered with a prix fixe menu (wine tastings, wine dinners, lobster evenings, etc.). Live jazz is featured occasionally. American menu. Dinner. Closed Sun; holidays. Bar. Business casual attire. Reservations recommended. **$$$**

★ ★ **DI MILLO'S FLOATING RESTAURANT.** *25 Long Wharf, Portland (04101). Phone 207/772-2216; fax 207/772-1081. www.dimillos.com.* Enjoy a meal "at sea" at Di Millo's Floating Restaurant, located in the Old Port area of downtown Portland—it is moored at the end of Long Wharf, which juts out into Portland Harbor. The floating restaurant is quite unique while operating at sea, it was an auto ferry (during its last runs, in the mid-1960s, between Newport and Jamestown, RI). Since 1982, the former ferry has been serving as a family-run restaurant. The main dining room features nautical décor—propellers, ship wheels, ship models, binnacles, chronometers, etc. The menu is largely seafood, and meals are served on tables with white cloths, mauve-colored napkins, and table lamps. American, Italian, seafood menu. Lunch, dinner. Closed Thanksgiving, Dec 25. Bar. Children's menu. Business casual attire. Reservations recommended. Outdoor seating. **$$**

★ ★ **EGGSPECTATION.** *125 Western Ave, South Portland (04106). Phone 207/871-7000; fax 207/871-7075. www.eggspectationusa.com.* Eggspectation is a fun, interesting, and appealing eatery with an imaginative menu. As you would "eggspect," eggs are a major element in the breakfast, lunch, and dinner menus. The interior's décor is industrial: exposed ceiling piping, brick walls, and varnished concrete flooring. Modern art graces several of the walls, and funky lights hang from the ceiling. A demonstration kitchen is located along a side wall of the large dining room. This popular restaurant features a coffee bar, cheese bar, traditional drinking bar, and a menu that offers "all meals, all day." American menu. Breakfast, lunch, dinner. Closed Dec 25. Bar. Children's menu. Casual attire. Reservations recommended. Outdoor seating. **$$**
🄳

★ ★ ★ **FORE STREET.** *288 Fore St, Portland (04101). Phone 207/772-2717; fax 207/772-6778. www.forestreet.biz.* Chef Sam Hayward runs the unpretentious and acclaimed Fore Street in the Old Port district of Portland. Foodies call weeks in advance for a reservation at the destination eatery where Hayward, who strongly supports local farmers, works regional foodstuffs into recipes that aficionados claim are both honest and magical. Wood-fired ovens and rotisseries manage most of the menu highlighted by wood-grilled Vermont quail with hasty corn pudding and roast plums, oven-roasted Maine mussels, and Maine-raised rabbit with wild mushrooms. The down-to-earth restaurant dressed in salvaged wood floors and recycled metal tables displays its vegetable cooler near the front door, underscoring Fore Streets farm-fresh philosophy. Seafood, steak menu. Dinner. Closed Thanksgiving, Dec 25. Bar. Casual attire. Reservations recommended. **$$**

★ ★ ★ **NATASHA.** *82 Exchange St, Portland (04104). Phone 207/774-4004.* The trendy Natasha is located in the heart of downtown Portland on the edge of the historic waterfront district. The décor here is nicely sophisticated, with modern art displayed on an indirectly lit brick wall, plush felt chair covers, cushioned banquette seating, and interesting inlaid tabletops. The restaurant's side façade is intriguingly painted with a large trompe l'oeil mural of Palazzo di Thomasino. Beneath it, there are cafe-style tables with blue umbrellas for outdoor dining. The menu is eye-catching and pleasing to the taste. International menu. Lunch, dinner. Closed Sun. Bar. Business casual attire. Reservations recommended. Outdoor seating. **$$**
🄳

★ **NEWICK'S SEAFOOD.** *740 Broadway, South Portland (04106). Phone 207/799-3090; toll-free 877/439-0255; fax 207/799-3619. www.newicks.com.* Newick's is housed in a large red barnlike building with buoys that hang on the exterior walls. Guests walk across a wooden "bridge" with a rope railing to reach the front door. Inside, you will find gingham vinyl-covered tables, many nautical-themed objects decoys, photos, lobster traps, and fishing nets and a fish counter and small gift shop. This casual, family-friendly eatery is well known for its fresh, homemade chowder; onion rings; and sautés. Seafood menu. Lunch, dinner. Closed Mon (off-season). Bar. Children's menu. Casual attire. **$**
🄳

★ ★ ★ **PARK KITCHEN.** *422 NW 8th Ave, Portland (97209). Phone 503/223-7275; fax 503/223-7282. www.parkkitchen.com.* Wines and microbrews are recommended for each entrée chef Scott Dolich creates at this welcoming restaurant, which features a great open kitchen. Located in a historic building along the North Park blocks, it is surrounded by the Pearl District. American, Northwest menu. Lunch, dinner, brunch. Closed Mon. Bar. Children's menu. Casual attire. Reservations recommended. Outdoor seating. Credit cards accepted. **$$**

★ ★ **RIBOLITA.** *41 Middle St, Portland (04101). Phone 207/774-2972.* Ribolita is an intimate, appealing neighborhood restaurant located on the east end of downtown Portland—a few blocks from the Old Port area. The décor is reminiscent of the "old country," with pottery and paintings from "Italia" on the walls—one wall is brick, with wine racks. Italian music adds to the ambience. There are two small dining rooms inside and seasonal café-style dining on the brick front sidewalk. Tables are topped with white butcher paper over white cloths and are set with candles and plain stemware. This local favorite serves very inviting Italian cuisine. Italian menu. Dinner. Closed holidays. Children's menu. Casual attire. Reservations recommended. Outdoor seating. **$$**
🄳

★ ★ ★ **THE ROMA CAFE.** *769 Congress St, Portland (04102). Phone 207/773-9873; fax 207/756-6768. www.theromacafe.com.* Established in 1924, Roma's has been a Portland culinary institution for many decades. Housed in a historic Victorian mansion (circa 1887), this restaurant features small dining rooms with fireplaces, a beautiful carved wood staircase, and beveled glass windows in a charming atmosphere.

Menu offerings include seafood, lobster, and Italian dishes. The restaurant is located on Portland's west end, about 1/2 mile from downtown a red entry awning and neatly trimmed front hedging help serve as markers for the restaurant. Italian, seafood menu. Lunch, dinner. Closed Sun-Mon. Bar. Casual attire. Reservations recommended. **$$**

★ ★ ★ **STREET & CO.** *33 Wharf St, Portland (04101). Phone 207/775-0887.* Located in the Old Port District on a cobblestone street, this 19th-century building was formerly a fish warehouse and later a marine warehouse. The décor is upscale rustic, with exposed bricks, original plank hardwood flooring, and beamed ceilings. Tables are heavy black stone slabs with rough-hewn wood legs and are set with fine flatware, dinnerware, and stemware, along with a a vase of flowers. A fully open kitchen is opposite the center dining room, which offers large windows that open to the street. Only fish is served, along with the freshest seasonal organic produce. American, seafood menu. Dinner. Bar. Casual attire. Reservations recommended. **$$$**

★ ★ **TYPHOON! ON BROADWAY.** *410 SW Broadway, Portland (97210). Phone 503/243-7577; fax 503/243-7144. www.typhoonrestaurants.com.* Located next door to the Hotel Lucia (see), this chic, hip Thai restaurant is one of the six Typhoon! chain locations. A local favorite, it is perfect for those looking to enjoy a fun night out. The enticing menu offers a variety of Thai dishes, including chicken in green curry and stir-fry peppercorn sirloin. Thai menu. Lunch, dinner. Casual attire. Reservations recommended. Outdoor seating. Credit cards accepted. **$$**

★ ★ **VILLAGE CAFE.** *112 Newbury St, Portland (04101). Phone 207/772-5320; toll-free 800/866-5320; fax 207/772-5652. www.villagecafemaine.com.* Family owned and operated since 1936, Village Café is a longtime Portland favorite, offering several large dining rooms along with a large bar and lounge. A wine press, built by the founder, sits in the lobby, and historical photos hang in the bar and lounge. The décor is simple inside (tables and booths are wood, with a paper mat and napkins), and menu options are reasonably priced. An outside deck is available for dining in good weather. American, Italian, seafood menu. Lunch, dinner. Closed Thanksgiving, Dec 25. Bar. Children's menu. Casual attire. Outdoor seating. **$$**

★ ★ **WALTER'S CAFE.** *15 Exchange St, Portland (04101). Phone 207/871-9258; fax 207/871-1018. www.walterscafe.com.* Located on the cusp of Portland's Old Port area, Walter's Cafe is a storefront restaurant housed in an old commercial building (mid-1800s). It is a bright and inviting restaurant (California-style) with two dining rooms: the primary one is downstairs and a second one is upstairs off the lounge. The décor has an attractive, contemporary look, with blond hardwood floors, brick walls, appealing artwork, and unique hanging lamps. Beautiful handmade pottery plates adorn the upstairs dining room walls. The chef/owner offers an eclectic menu, which changes daily. International menu. Lunch, dinner. Closed Thanksgiving, Dec 24-25. Bar. Business casual attire. Reservations recommended. **$$**

Presque Isle (B-4)

See also Caribou

Settled 1820
Population 10,550
Elevation 446 ft
Area Code 207
Zip 04769
Information Presque Isle Area Chamber of Commerce, 3 Holden Rd; phone 207/764-6561 or toll-free 800/764-7420
Web Site www.pichamber.org

Commercial and industrial center of Aroostook County, this city is famous for its potatoes. A deactivated air base nearby is now a vocational school and industrial park.

What to See and Do

Aroostook Farm–Maine Agricultural Experiment Station. *59 Houlton Rd, Presque Isle (04769). 2 miles S on Hwy 1. Phone 207/762-8281.* Approximately 375 acres operated by University of Maine; experiments to improve growing and marketing of potatoes and grain. (Tours by appointment; closed holidays) **FREE**

Aroostook State Park. *87 State Park Rd, Presque Isle (04769). 4 miles S on Hwy 1, then W. Phone 207/768-8341.* 577 acres. Swimming, bathhouse, fishing, boating (rentals, ramp on Echo Lake); hiking, cross-country trails, picnicking, camping. (Mid-May-mid-Oct, daily) Snowmobiling permitted.

Double Eagle II Launch Site Monument. *Spragueville Rd, Presque Isle (04769). 4 miles S on Hwy 1, then W. Double Eagle II*, the first balloon to travel across the Atlantic Ocean, was launched from this site in 1978. **FREE**

University of Maine at Presque Isle. *181 Main St, Presque Isle (04769). Phone 207/768-9400. www.umpi. maine.edu.* (1903) (1,500 students) During the summer there is the Pioneer Playhouse and an Elderhostel program. In winter, the business breakfast program, theater productions, and a number of other cultural and educational events are open to the public.

Special Events

Northern Maine Fair. *84 Machane St, Presque Isle (04769). Phone 207/764-6561. www. northernmainefairgrounds.com.* Midway, harness racing, entertainment. Late July-early Aug.

Spudland Open Amateur Golf Tournament. *Presque Isle Country Club, 35 Parkhurst Siding Rd, Presque Isle (04769). Phone 207/769-7431. www.picountryclub.com.* Held for more than 30 years, this is one of Maine's major amateur golf tournaments. Fourth Sat in July.

Limited-Service Hotel

★ **NORTHERN LIGHTS.** *72 Houlton Rd, Presque Isle (04769). Phone 207/764-4441; fax 207/769-6931. www.northernlightsmotel.com.* 13 rooms. Pets accepted. Check-in 2 pm, check-out 11 am. **$**

Rangeley (D-1)

Settled 1825
Population 1,063
Elevation 1,545 ft
Area Code 207
Zip 04970
Information Rangeley Lakes Chamber of Commerce, 6 Park Rd; phone 207/864-5364 or toll-free 800/685-2537 (reservations)
Web Site www.rangeleymaine.com

Within 10 miles of Rangeley there are 40 lakes and ponds. The six lakes that form the Rangeley chain—Rangeley, Cupsuptic, Mooselookmeguntic, Aziscoos, Upper Richardson, and Lower Richardson—spread over a wide area and give rise to the Androscoggin River. Some of Maine's highest mountains rise beside the lakes. The development of ski and snowmobiling

areas has turned this summer vacation spot into a year-round resort.

What to See and Do

Camping. Several designated public camp and picnic sites; wilderness sites on islands.

Fishing. Boats for rent; licensed guides. The lakes are stocked with square-tailed trout and landlocked salmon.

Rangeley Lake State Park. *S Shore Dr, Rangeley (04970). 4 miles S on Hwy 4, then 5 miles W via local road. Phone 207/864-3858.* More than 690 acres on Rangeley Lake. Swimming, fishing, boating (ramp, floating docks); snowmobiling permitted, picnicking, camping (dump station). (May-Oct)

Saddleback Ski & Summer Lake Preserve. *7 miles E off Hwy 4. Phone 207/864-5671. www.saddlebackmaine. com.* Two double chairlifts, three T-bars; rentals, school, patrol; snowmaking; cafeteria, bar; nursery, lodge. Longest run 2.5 miles; vertical drop 1,830 feet. (Late Nov-mid-Apr, daily) Cross-country trails.

Swimming, boating. Several public beaches and docks on lakefront. Rangeley Lakeside Park on lakeshore has public swimming, picnicking areas.

Wilhelm Reich Museum. *19 Dodge Pond Rd, Rangeley (04970). 4 miles W off Hwy 4. Phone 207/864-3443. www.wilhelmreichmuseum.org.* Unusual stone building housing scientific equipment, paintings, and other memorabilia of this physician-scientist; slide presentation, nature trail, discovery room. (July-Aug: Wed-Sun; Sept, Sun only; rest of year: by appointment) **$$**

Special Event

Logging Museum Field Days. *123 Main St, Rangeley (04970). Phone 207/864-5595.* Logging competitions, Miss Woodchip contest, parade, logging demonstrations. Last weekend in July.

Limited-Service Hotel

★ ★ **COUNTRY CLUB INN.** *1 Country Club Dr, Rangeley (04970). Phone 207/864-3831. www. countryclubinnrangeley.com.* 19 rooms, 2 story. Closed Apr, Nov. Pets accepted, some restrictions; fee. Check-in 1 pm, check-out 10:30 am. Restaurant, bar. Outdoor pool. Airport transportation available. **$$**

Full-Service Inn

★ ★ ★ **RANGELEY INN.** *2443 Main St (Hwy 4), Rangeley (04970). Phone 207/864-3341; toll-free 800/666-3687; fax 207/864-3634. www.rangeleyinn. com.* This restored inn is located within the mountain lake wilderness of the Longfellow mountains of western Maine. This year-round resort offers skiing and snowmobiling in the winter and swimming and boating in the summer. Moose can be spotted here, and loons can be both seen and heard. 50 rooms. Pets accepted, some restrictions; fee. Check-in 3 pm, check-out 11 am. Restaurant, bar. **$**

Restaurant

★ ★ ★ **RANGELEY INN.** *2443 Main St, Rangeley (04970). Phone 207/864-3341; fax 207/864-3634. www. rangeleyinn.com.* This romantic inn has been in operation for more than ninety years, and the dining room still showcases an ornate tin ceiling and glittering chandeliers. Enjoy an elegant dinner in the main dining room and then retire to the pub that has a crackling fire in the fireplace and local microbrews on tap. American, seafood menu. Breakfast, dinner. Closed Sun-Thurs; Dec 25; also Apr-May. Bar. Children's menu. Outdoor seating. **$**

Rockland (E-3)

See also Camden, Monhegan Island

Settled 1770
Population 7,972
Elevation 35 ft
Area Code 207
Zip 04841
Information Rockland-Thomaston Area Chamber of Commerce, 1 Park Dr, PO Box 508; phone 207/596-0376 or toll-free 800/562-2529
Web Site www.therealmaine.com

This town on Penobscot Bay is the banking and commercial center of the region and seat of Knox County. It is also the birthplace of the poet Edna St. Vincent Millay. Its economy is geared to the resort trade, but there is commercial fishing and light industry. It is the railhead for the whole bay. Supplies for boats, public landing, and guest moorings are here.

What to See and Do

Coasting schooners *American Eagle* and *Heritage.* *Phone 207/594-8007; toll-free 800/648-4544. www. schoonerheritage.com.* Four- and six-day cruises (Late May-mid-Oct).

Farnsworth Art Museum and Wyeth Center. *16 Museum St, Rockland (04841). Phone 207/596-6457. www.farnsworthmuseum.org.* Cultural and educational center for the region. Collection of more than 10,000 works of 18th- to 20th-century American art. Center houses personal collection of Wyeth family art and archival material. (Memorial Day-Columbus Day: daily; rest of year: Tues-Sun) **$$** Included in admission and adjacent is

> **Farnsworth Homestead.** *356 Main St, Rockland (04841). Phone 207/596-6457.* A 19th-century Victorian mansion with period furniture. (Memorial Day-Columbus Day, daily)

Fisherman's Memorial Pier and Chamber of Commerce. *Public landing, Harbor Park.*

Maine Lighthouse Museum. *1 Park Dr, Rockland (04841). Phone 207/594-3301. www.mainelighthouse-museum.com.* A large collection of lighthouse lenses and artifacts; Civil War collection. Museum shop. (Daily) **$**

Maine State Ferry Service. *517A Main St, Rockland (04841). Phone 207/596-2202.* Ferries make a 15-mile (1 hour, 15 minute) trip to Vinalhaven and a 12 1/2-mile (1 hour, 10 minute) trip to North Haven. (All year, two to three trips daily) Also a 23-mile (2 hour, 15 minute) trip to Matinicus Island once a month.

Owls Head Transportation Museum. *Hwy 73 and Museum Dr, Owls Head (04854). 2 miles S via Hwy 73. Phone 207/594-4418. www.owlshead.com.* Working display of antique cars, airplanes, and 100-ton steam engine. (Daily) **$$**

Schooner *J. & E. Riggin.* *Phone 207/594-1875; toll-free 800/869-0604. www.mainewindjammer.com.* Three-, four-, five-, and six-day cruises (May-Oct).

Windjammers. Old-time schooners sail out for three to six days following the same basic route through Penobscot Bay, into Blue Hill and Frenchman's Bay, stopping at small villages and islands along the way. Each ship carries an average of 30 passengers. (Memorial Day-Columbus Day) For further information, rates, schedules, or reservations, contact the individual companies.

Nathaniel Bowditch. Phone toll-free 800/288-4098.

Victory Chimes. 120 Tillson Ave, Rockland (04841). Phone toll-free 800/745-5651.

Special Events

Maine Lobster Festival. *Harbor Park, or at the public landing, Rockland (04841). Phone 207/596-0376; toll-free 800/562-2529.* A five-day event centered on Maine's chief marine creature, with a huge tent cafeteria serving lobster and other seafood. Parade, harbor cruises, maritime displays, bands, entertainment. First weekend in Aug.

Schooner Days & North Atlantic Blues Festival. *Phone 207/596-0376.* Three-day festival celebrating Maine's maritime heritage, featuring Parade of Schooners, arts, entertainment, concessions, fireworks; blues bands and club crawl. Weekend after July 4.

Limited-Service Hotel

★ **GLEN COVE MOTEL.** *Hwy 1, Glen Cove (04846). Phone 207/594-4062; toll-free 800/453-6268. www.glencovemotel.com.* Overlooks Penobscot Bay. 36 rooms, 2 story. Closed Feb. Check-in 3 pm, check-out 11 am. Outdoor pool. **$**

Full-Service Resort

★ ★ ★ **SAMOSET RESORT.** *220 Warrenton St, Rockport (04856). Phone 207/594-2511; toll-free 800/341-1650; fax 207/594-0722. www.samosetresort. com.* Named for the chief of the Pemaquid Indians who greeted the Pilgrims, this inn has welcomed guests since 1889. It is a year-round resort set on 230 oceanside acres of the rugged coast of Maine. 178 rooms, 4 story. Check-in 3 pm, check-out noon. Restaurant, bar. Children's activity center. Fitness room. Indoor pool, outdoor pool, whirlpool. Tennis. **$$**

Full-Service Inn

★ ★ ★ **CAPTAIN LINDSEY HOUSE INN.** *5 Lindsey St, Rockland (04841). Phone 207/596-7950; toll-free 800/523-2145; fax 207/596-2758. www.lindseyhouse.com.* This inn (built in 1830) is located in downtown Rockland, close to galleries, shops, and the waterfront. The guest rooms have furnishings from around the world. There are four museums nearby and many shops and restaurants to explore. 10 rooms,

3 story. Children over 10 years only. Complimentary continental breakfast. Check-in 3 pm, check-out 11 am. Restaurant. **$$**

Specialty Lodgings

CRAIGNAIR INN. *5 Third St, Spruce Head (04859). Phone 207/594-7644; toll-free 800/320-9997; fax 207/596-7124. www.craignair.com.* Built in 1930; boarding house converted to an inn in 1947. 21 rooms, 3 story. Pets accepted, some restrictions; fee. Complimentary full breakfast. Check-in 3 pm, check-out 11 am. Restaurant **$**

LAKESHORE INN. *184 Lakeview Dr, Rockland (04841). Phone 207/594-4209; toll-free 866/540-8800; fax 207/596-6407. www.lakeshorebb.com.* This Colonial New England farmhouse was built in 1767. 4 rooms, 2 story. Children over 12 years only. Complimentary full breakfast. Check-in 3 pm, check-out 11 am. Whirlpool. **$$**

Restaurants

★ **HARBOR VIEW.** *Thomaston Landing, Thomaston (04861). Phone 207/354-8173; fax 207/354-0036.* Seafood, steak menu. Lunch, dinner. Closed Sun-Mon (Nov-Apr); Thanksgiving, Dec 25. Bar. Outdoor seating. **$$**

★ ★ ★ **PRIMO.** *2 S Main St, Rockland (04841). Phone 207/596-0770; fax 207/596-5938. www.primorestaurant.com.* Chef Melissa Kelly has helped moved Maine from the state known for lobster rolls onto serious foodie maps with Primo. An ardent supporter of sustainable agriculture, Kelly uses mostly local, organic produce much of it grown on the restaurant's farm and makes vegetables distinct contributors even to meat dishes. The menu, which changes weekly, draws on coastal Italy and France, resulting in asparagus soup with goat cheese, olive oil-poached salmon with bitter greens and beets, wood-roasted oysters, grilled calamari with house-made cavatelli pasta, and ham-wrapped roast monkfish. Co-owner and pastry chef Price Kushner contributes equally savory desserts. Primo's location in a restored Victorian home, with five dining rooms downstairs and a bar upstairs, contributes to the warmth seeded by the chef's passions. American menu. Dinner. Closed Tues. Bar. Casual attire. Reservations recommended. **$$$**

Rockwood (C-2)

See also Moosehead Lake

Population 190
Elevation 1,050 ft
Area Code 207
Zip 04478

What to See and Do

Northern Outdoors, Inc. *Martins Pond and Hwy 201, Rockwood (04478). Phone 207/663-4466; toll-free 800/765-7238. www.northernoutdoors.com.* Specializes in outdoor adventures including whitewater rafting on Maine's Kennebec, Penobscot, and Dead rivers (May-Oct). Also snowmobiling (rentals), hunting, and resort facilities. Rock climbing, freshwater kayak touring. **$$$$**

Wilderness Expeditions, Inc. *Phone 207/534-2242; toll-free 800/825-9453. www.birches.com.* Whitewater rafting on the Kennebec, Penobscot, and Dead rivers; also canoe trips and ski tours. (May-Sept, daily) **$$$$**

Limited-Service Hotel

★ ★ **MOOSEHEAD MOTEL.** *Hwy 15, Rockwood (04478). Phone 207/534-7787. www.maineguide.com/moosehead/motel.* 14 rooms, 2 story. Check-in 2 pm, check-out 11 am. Restaurant. **$**
🅓

Rumford (D-1)

See also Bethel

Settled 1774
Population 7,078
Elevation 505 ft
Area Code 207
Zip 04276
Information River Valley Chamber of Commerce, 34 River St; phone 207/364-3241
Web Site www.rivervalleychamber.com

This papermill town is located in the valley of the Oxford Hills, where the Ellis, Swift, and Concord rivers flow into the Androscoggin. The spectacular Penacook Falls of the Androscoggin are right in town. Rumford serves as a year-round resort area.

What to See and Do

Mount Blue State Park. *Weld (04285). 4 miles E on Hwy 2 to Dixfield, then 14 miles N on Hwy 142. Phone 207/585-2347. www.campwithme.com.* Recreation areas on Lake Webb include swimming, bathhouse, lifeguard, fishing, boating (ramp, rentals); hiking trail to Mount Blue, cross-country skiing, snowmobiling permitted, picnicking, camping (dump station). (Memorial Day-Labor Day)

Limited-Service Hotels

★ **BLUE IRIS MOTOR INN.** *Hwy 2, Rumford (04276). Phone 207/364-4495; toll-free 800/601-1515. www.blueiris.50megs.com.* On river. 13 rooms. Check-in, check-out 10 am. Outdoor pool. **$**
🅓 ⌦

★ ★ **MADISON RESORT INN.** *Hwy 2, Rumford (04276). Phone 207/364-7973; toll-free 800/258-6234; fax 207/369-0341. www.madisoninn.com.* 38 rooms, 2 story. Pets accepted. Check-in 2 pm, check-out 11 am. Restaurant, bar. Fitness room. Outdoor pool, whirlpool. **$**
🐾 🎿 ⌦

Saco (F-1)

See also Kennebunk, Kennebunkport, Old Orchard Beach, Portland

Settled 1631
Population 15,181
Elevation 60 ft
Area Code 207
Zip 04072
Information Biddeford/Saco Chamber of Commerce, 110 Main St, Suite 1202; phone 207/282-1567
Web Site www.biddefordsacochamber.org

Saco, on the east bank of the Saco River, facing its twin city Biddeford, was originally called Pepperellboro, until its name was changed in 1805. The city has diversified industry, including a machine and metal-working plant. Saco is only 4 miles from the ocean.

What to See and Do

Aquaboggan Water Park. *980 Portland Rd, Saco (04072). 4 miles N on US 1. Phone 207/282-3112. www.aquaboggan.com.* More than 40 acres of water and land attractions, including five water slides, wave pool, children's pool, "aquasaucer," games, miniature golf, bumper boats, race cars. Picnicking. (mid-June-Labor Day, daily) **$$$$**

Dyer Library & Saco Museum. *371 Main St, Saco (04072). On Hwy 1.* Phone 207/283-3861. Public library has arts and cultural programs. Museum features local history, decorative and fine art; American paintings, ceramics, glass, clocks, and furniture; changing exhibits. (Tues-Fri)

Ferry Beach State Park. *Hwy 9, Saco (04072). 3 1/2 miles N via Hwy 9.* Phone 207/283-0067. *www.maine. gov/doc/parks.* Beach, swimming, picnicking, nature and cross-country trails. (Memorial Day-Labor Day, daily)

Funtown Splashtown USA. *774 Portland Rd, Saco (04072). 2 miles NE on Hwy 1.* Phone 207/284-5139. *www.funtownsplashtownusa.com.* Theme park featuring adult and kiddie rides; log flume ride; Excalibur wooden roller coaster; Grand Prix Racers; games. Picnicking. (Mid-June-Sept: daily; early May-mid-June: weekends) **$$$$**

Restaurant

★ ★ **CASCADE INN.** *941 Portland Rd (Hwy 1), Saco (04072).* Phone 207/283-3271; fax 207/282-2371. *www.cascademaine.com.* American, seafood menu. Lunch, dinner. Bar. Children's menu. Reservations recommended. **$$**

Scarborough (F-1)

See also Old Orchard Beach, Portland

Population 12,518
Elevation 17 ft
Area Code 207
Zip 04074
Information Convention & Visitors Bureau of Greater Portland, 245 Commercial St, Portland 04101; phone 207/772-5800
Web Site www.visitportland.com

Scarborough contains some industry, but it is primarily a farming community and has been for more than 300 years. It is also a bustling tourist town during the summer months as vacationers flock to nearby beaches and resorts. The first Anglican church in Maine is here, as is painter Winslow Homer's studio, now a national landmark.

What to See and Do

Scarborough Marsh Audubon Center. Phone 207/883-5100. *www.maineaudubon.org.* Miles of nature and waterway trails through marshland area; canoe tours, special programs (fee). (Mid-June-Labor Day, daily) **FREE**

Sebago Lake State Park. *11 Park Access Rd, Scarborough (04015). 2 miles S of Naples off Hwy 11/114.* Phone 207/693-6231. *www.maine.gov/doc/parks.* A 1,300-acre area. Extensive sand beaches, bathhouse, lifeguards; fishing, boating (rentals, ramps); picnicking, concession, camping (dump station). No pets. (May-mid-Oct, daily) Standard fees.

Special Event

Harness racing. Scarborough Downs. *Hwy 1, Scarborough (04074). ME Tpke, exit 6.* Phone 207/883-4331. *www.scarboroughdowns.com.* Evenings and matinees.

Limited-Service Hotels

★ **FAIRFIELD INN.** *2 Cummings Rd, Scarborough (04074).* Phone 207/883-0300; toll-free 800/228-2800; fax 207/883-0572. *www.fairfieldinn.com.* 120 rooms, 3 story. Complimentary continental breakfast. Check-in 3 pm, check-out noon. Outdoor pool. **$**
🏊

★ **TOWNEPLACE SUITES BY MARRIOTT PORTLAND SCARBOROUGH.** *700 Roundwood Dr, Scarborough (04074).* Phone 207/883-6800; toll-free 800/491-2268; fax 207/883-6866. *www.towne-placesuites.com.* 95 rooms, 3 story. Pets accepted; fee. Check-in 3 pm, check-out noon. Fitness room. Outdoor pool. **$**
🐾 🏋 🏊

Searsport (D-3)

See also Belfast, Bucksport

Settled 1770
Population 2,603
Elevation 60 ft
Area Code 207
Zip 04974
Information Chamber of Commerce, Main St, PO Box 139; phone 207/548-6510

On the quiet upper reaches of Penobscot Bay, this is an old seafaring town. In the 1870s, at least ten percent of the captains of the US Merchant Marines lived here. Sea terminal of the Bangor and Aroostook Railway, Searsport ships potatoes and newsprint. This village abounds with antiques shops and is sometimes referred to as the "antique capital of Maine."

What to See and Do

Fishing, boating on bay. Town maintains wharf and boat landing, beachside park.

Penobscot Marine Museum. *5 Church St, Searsport (04974). Off Hwy 1.* Phone 207/548-2529. *www. penobscotmarinemuseum.org.* Old Town Hall (1845), Merithew House (circa 1860), Fowler-True-Ross House (1825), Phillips Library, and Carver Memorial Gallery. Ship models, marine paintings, American and Asian furnishings. (Memorial Day weekend-mid-Oct, daily; rest of year, Mon-Sat) **$$**

Specialty Lodging

INN BRITANNIA. *132 W Main St, Searsport (04974).* Phone 207/548-2007; toll-free 866/466-2748; fax 207/548-0304. *www.innbritannia.com.* This former captain's house was built in 1850. 8 rooms, 2 story. Pets accepted, some restrictions; fee, Children over 11 years only. Complimentary full breakfast. Check-in 4-8 pm, check-out 11 am. **$$**

Sebago Lake (E-1)

See also Bridgton, Poland Spring

Second largest of Maine's lakes, this is perhaps the most popular, partly because of its proximity to Portland. About 12 miles long and 8 miles wide, it lies among wooded hills. Boats can run a total of more than 40 miles from the south end of Sebago Lake, through the Songo River to the north end of Long Lake. Numerous resort communities are hidden in the trees along the shores. Sebago, home of the landlocked salmon (*Salmo sebago*), is also stocked with lake trout.

What to See and Do

Marrett House and Garden. *Hwy 25, Standish (04084). Approximately 2 miles S on Rte 25 to center of Standish.* Phone 207/642-3032. (1789) Built in Georgian style, but later enlarged and remodeled in the Greek Revival fashion; period furnishings; farm implements. Coin

from Portland banks was stored here during the War of 1812, when it was thought that the British would take Portland. Perennial and herb garden. Tours (June-Oct, first Sat of the month). **$**

Full-Service Resort

★ ★ ★ **MIGIS LODGE.** *Hwy 302, South Casco (04077).* Phone 207/655-4524; fax 207/655-2054. *www. migis.com.* This property is set on more than 100 acres of wooded land and on the shore of a lake. A gift shop sells crafts from Maine. Wood for the fireplace in each guest room is delivered daily and there are handmade quilts on every bed and fresh flowers in the room. Sunsets are beautiful. 58 rooms, 2 story. Closed mid-Oct-May. Check-in 3 pm, check-out noon. Restaurant, bar. Children's activity center. Fitness room. Beach. Tennis. Airport transportation available. **$$$**

Restaurant

★ ★ **BARNHOUSE TAVERN RESTAURANT.** *61 Hwy 35, Windham (04062).* Phone 207/892-2221; fax 207/892-6704. *www.barnhousetavern.com.* Authentically restored post-and-beam barn and farmhouse (1872); country atmosphere, loft dining. Seafood, steak menu. Lunch, dinner. Closed Mon; also Dec 25. Bar. Outdoor seating. **$$**

Skowhegan (D-2)

See also Bingham, Newport, Waterville

Settled 1771
Population 8,725
Elevation 175 ft
Area Code 207
Zip 04976
Information Chamber of Commerce, 23 Commercial St; phone 207/474-3621 or toll-free 888/772-4392
Web Site www.skowheganchamber.com

Skowhegan, on the Kennebec River, is surrounded by beautiful lakes. Shoes, paper pulp, and other wood products are made here. In the village's center stands a 12-ton, 62-foot-high Native American carved of native pine by Bernard Langlais. Skowhegan is the birthplace of Margaret Chase Smith, who served three terms in the US House of Representatives and four terms in the Senate.

What to See and Do

History House. *2 Coburn Ave, Skowhegan (04976). Phone 207/474-6632.* (1839) Old household furnishings; museum contains books, china, dolls, and documents. (Mid-June-mid-Sept, Tues-Fri afternoons) **$**

Special Event

Skowhegan State Fair. *Madison Ave Fairgrounds, Skowhegan (04976). Phone 207/474-2947. www. skowheganstatefair.com.* One of oldest in country (1818). One-mile-long midway, stage shows, harness racing; contests, exhibits. Aug.

Restaurant

★ ★ **HERITAGE HOUSE.** *182 Madison Ave, Skowhegan (04976). Phone 207/474-5100.*Restored home; oak staircase. Seafood, steak menu. Lunch, dinner. Bar. Casual attire. **$$**

Southwest Harbor (E-3)

See also Acadia National Park, Bar Harbor, Cranberry Isles

Population 1,952
Elevation 50 ft
Area Code 207
Zip 04679
Information Chamber of Commerce, 204 Main St; phone 207/244-9264 or toll-free 800/423-9264
Web Site www.acadiachamber.com

This is a prosperous, working seacoast village on Mount Desert Island. There are lobster wharves, where visitors can watch about 70 fishermen bring in their catch, and many shops where boats are constructed. Visitors may rent sail and power boats in Southwest Harbor to explore the coves and islands; hiking trails and quiet harbors offer relaxation.

What to See and Do

Cranberry Cove Boating Company. *Phone 207/244-5882.* Cruise to Cranberry Islands. See native wildlife and learn island history. Six departures daily. (Mid-June-mid-Sept, daily) Departs from Upper Town Dock. **$$$$**

Ferry service. *33 Main St, Southwest Harbor (04679). Phone 207/244-3575.* Ferry connects Little Cranberry and Great Cranberry with Northeast Harbor (see) on Mount Desert Island; 3-mile, 30-minute crossing. (Summer: daily; rest of year: varied schedule) **$$$**

Maine State Ferry Service. *Grandville Rd, Bass Harbor (04653). 4 miles S on Hwy 102 and Hwy 102A. Phone 207/244-3254.* Ferry makes 6-mile (40-minute) trip to Swans Island and 8 1/4-mile (50-minute) trip to Frenchboro (limited schedule). Swans Island (all-year, one to six trips daily).

Mount Desert Oceanarium. *172 Clark Point Rd., Southwest Harbor (04679). Phone 207/244-7330. www. theoceanarium.com.* More than 20 tanks with Gulf of Maine marine creatures. Touch tank permits animals to be picked up. Exhibits on tides, seawater, plankton, fishing gear, weather. Inquire for information on special events. (Mid-May-mid-Oct, Mon-Sat) **$$**

Wendell Gilley Museum. *4 Herrick Rd, Southwest Harbor (04679). Phone 207/244-7555. www. wendellgilleymuseum.org.* Art and natural history museum featuring a collection of bird carvings by local artist Wendell Gilley; changing exhibits of local and historical art; films. (June-Oct: Tues-Sun; May and Nov-Dec: Fri-Sun) **$**

Specialty Lodgings

THE CLARK POINT INN. *109 Clark Point Rd, Southwest Harbor (04679). Phone 207/244-9828; toll-free 888/775-5953; fax 207/244-9924. www.clarkpointinn. com.* Captain's house (1857); deck with harbor view. 5 rooms, 2 story. Closed mid-Oct-Apr. Children over 8 years only. Complimentary full breakfast. Check-in 2-6 pm. Check-out 11 am. **$$**
🔊

KINGSLEIGH INN. *373 Main St, Southwest Harbor (04679). Phone 207/244-5302; fax 207/244-7691. www. kingsleighinn.com.* Built in 1904, wraparound porch. 8 rooms, 3 story. Children over 10 years only. Complimentary full breakfast. Check-in 3-6 pm. Check-out 11 am. **$**
🔊

Restaurant

★ **BEAL'S LOBSTER PIER.** *Clark Point Rd, Southwest Harbor (04679). Phone 207/244-3202; fax 207/244-9479.* The lobsters at this self-service eatery are boiled to order. All seating is outdoors on a working wharf overlooking the Southwest Harbor. Seafood menu. Lunch, dinner. Casual attire. Outdoor seating. **$$**

Waterville (D-2)

See also Augusta, Skowhegan

Settled 1754
Population 17,173
Elevation 113 ft
Area Code 207
Information Mid-Maine Chamber of Commerce, One Post Office Sq, PO Box 142, 04903; phone 207/873-3315
Web Site www.mid-mainechamber.com

A large Native American village once occupied the west bank of the Kennebec River where many of Waterville's factories now stand. An important industrial town, Waterville is the center of the Belgrade and China lakes resort area. Manufactured goods include men's and women's shirts, paper and molded pulp products, and woolens.

What to See and Do

Colby College. *4601 Mayflower Hill Dr, Waterville (04901). 2 miles W, 1/2 mile E of I-95. Phone 207/872-3000. www.colby.edu.* (1813) (1,700 students) This 714-acre campus includes an art museum in the Bixler Art and Music Center (daily; closed holidays; free); a Walcker organ designed by Albert Schweitzer in Lorimer Chapel; and books, manuscripts, and letters of Maine authors Edwin Arlington Robinson and Sarah Jewett in the Miller Library (Mon-Fri; closed holidays; free).

Old Fort Halifax. *Winslow. 1 mile E on Hwy 201, on Bay St in Winslow, on E bank of Kennebec River.* (1754) Blockhouse. Bridge over Kennebec gives view of Ticonic Falls. (Memorial Day-Labor Day, daily)

Redington Museum. *62 Silver St, Waterville (04901). Phone 207/872-9439. www.redingtonmuseum.org.* (1814) Waterville Historical Society collection includes 18th- and 19th-century furnishings, manuscripts, Civil War and Native American relics; historical library; children's room; apothecary museum. (Mid-May-Labor Day, Tues-Sat) **$**

Two-Cent Footbridge. *Front St, Waterville (04901).* One of the few remaining former toll footbridges in the United States. **FREE**

Special Event

New England Music Camp. *8 Goldenrod Ln, Augusta (04330). 5 miles W on Hwy 137 to Oakland, then 4 miles S on Hwy 23. Phone 207/465-3025. www.nemusiccamp.com.* Student concerts, Sat-Sun; faculty concerts, Wed. Late June-late Aug.

Limited-Service Hotels

★★ **BEST WESTERN WATERVILLE INN.** *356 Main St, Waterville (04901). Phone 207/873-3335; toll-free 800/780-7234; fax 207/873-3335. www.bestwestern.com.* 86 rooms, 2 story. Pets accepted. Check-in 3 pm, check-out 11 am. Restaurant, bar. Outdoor pool. **$**

★★ **HOLIDAY INN.** *375 Main St, Waterville (04901). Phone 207/873-0111; fax 207/872-2310. www.holiday-inn.com.* 139 rooms, 3 story. Pets accepted, some restrictions. Check-in 3 pm, check-out noon. Restaurant, bar. Fitness room. Indoor pool, whirlpool. **$**

Restaurants

★ **BIG G'S DELI.** *581 Benton Ave, Winslow (04901). Phone 207/873-7808. www.big-g-s-deli.com.* Deli menu. Breakfast, lunch, dinner. Children's menu. **$**

★★ **JOHN MARTIN'S MANOR.** *54 College Ave, Waterville (04901). Phone 207/873-5676; fax 207/877-9158. www.johnmartinsmanor.com.* American, seafood menu. Lunch, dinner. Closed Dec 25. Bar. Children's menu. Casual attire. Reservations recommended. **$**

★ **WEATHERVANE.** *470 Kennedy Memorial Dr, Waterville (04901). Phone 207/873-4522; toll-free 800/654-4369; fax 207/859-9846. www.weathervane-seafoods.com.* Seafood menu. Lunch, dinner. Closed Thanksgiving, Dec 25. Children's menu. Casual attire. Reservations recommended. **$$**

Wells (F-1)

See also Kennebunk, Ogunquit, York

Settled 1640
Population 7,778
Elevation 70 ft
Area Code 207
Zip 04090

Information Chamber of Commerce, PO Box 356; phone 207/646-2451
Web Site www.wellschamber.org

One of the oldest English settlements in Maine, Wells includes Moody, Wells Beach, and Drake's Island. It was largely a farming center, with some commercial fishing, until the resort trade began in the 20th century. Charter boats, surfcasting, and pier fishing attract anglers; 7 miles of beaches entice swimmers.

What to See and Do

⭐ **Rachel Carson National Wildlife Refuge.** *3 miles SW on Hwy 9. Phone 207/646-9226. www.fws.gov/northeast/ rachelcarson.* Approximately 5,000 acres of salt marsh and coastal edge habitat; more than 250 species of birds may be observed during the year. Visitor center; 1-mile interpretive nature trail. (All year, sunrise-sunset)

Wells Auto Museum. *1181 Post Rd, Wells (04090). Phone 207/646-9064.* Approximately 80 antique cars dating to 1900 trace progress of the automotive industry. Also displayed is a collection of nickelodeons, picture machines, and antique arcade games to play. (June-Sept, daily) **$**

Wells Natural Estuarine Research Reserve. *342 Laudholm Farm Rd, Wells (04090). 1 1/2 miles N of Wells Corner on Hwy 1. Phone 207/646-1555. www. wellsreserve.org.* Approximately 1,600 acres of fields, forest, wetlands, and beach. Laudholm Farm serves as visitor center. Programs on coastal ecology and stewardship, exhibits, and tours. Reserve (daily). Visitor center (May-Oct: daily; rest of year: Mon-Fri). **FREE**

Limited-Service Hotels

⭐ **GARRISON SUITES.** *1099 Post Rd (Hwy 1), Wells (04090). Phone 207/646-3497; toll-free 800/646-3497. www.garrisonsuites.com.* 47 rooms. Closed mid-Oct-Apr, pets accepted, some restrictions. Check-in 2 pm, check-out 11 am. Outdoor pool, whirlpool. **$**

⭐⭐ **VILLAGE BY THE SEA.** *Hwy 1 S, Wells (04090). Phone 207/646-1100; toll-free 800/444-8862; fax 207/646-1401. www.vbts.com.* Located between Kennebunkport and Ogunquit on Maine's southern coast, this 11-acre property is near Wells Beach and the Rachel Carson Wildlife Preserve. 73 rooms, 4 story, all suites. Check-in 3 pm, check-out 10 am. Indoor pool, outdoor pool. **$$**

Restaurants

⭐⭐ **GREY GULL.** *475 Webhannet Dr, Wells (04090). Phone 207/646-7501; fax 207/646-0938. www. thegreygullinn.com.* This restaurant is located in a 19th-century inn, which looks out onto the ocean. American menu. Dinner. Bar. Children's menu. Casual attire. Reservations recommended. **$$**

⭐ **HAYLOFT.** *Hwy 1, Moody (04054). Phone 207/646-4400.* Seafood menu. Lunch, dinner. Closed week before Dec 25. Bar. Children's menu. **$$**

⭐ **LITCHFIELD'S.** *2135 Post Rd (Hwy 1), Wells (04090). Phone 207/646-5711; fax 207/646-0594. www. litchfields-restaurant.com.* American menu. Lunch, dinner. Bar. Children's menu. Casual attire. **$$**

⭐⭐ **LORD'S HARBORSIDE.** *352 Harbor Rd, Wells (04090). Phone 207/646-2651; fax 207/646-0818. www.lordsharborside.com.* Seafood menu. Lunch, dinner. Closed Tues. Bar. Children's menu. Casual attire. **$$**

⭐ **MAINE DINER.** *2265 Post Rd, Wells (04090). Phone 207/646-4441; fax 207/641-8470. www. mainediner.com.* American menu. Breakfast, lunch, dinner, brunch. Children's menu. Casual attire. **$$**

⭐⭐ **STEAKHOUSE.** *1205 Post Rd (Hwy 1), Wells (04090). Phone 207/646-4200; fax 207/646-0835. www. the-steakhouse.com.* Steak menu. Dinner. Closed Mon. Bar. Children's menu. Casual attire. Reservations recommended. **$$**

Wiscasset (E-2)

See also Bath, Boothbay Harbor, Damariscotta

Settled 1653
Population 3,339
Elevation 50 ft
Area Code 207
Zip 04578

Many artists and writers live here in beautiful old houses put up in the golden days of clipper ship barons and sea captains. Chiefly a summer resort area centered around its harbor, Wiscasset is half as populous as it was in 1850. Its pictorial charm is extraordinary even on the picturesque Maine coast. A noted sight in Wiscasset are the remains of two ancient wooden schooners, which were hauled into the harbor in 1932.

What to See and Do

Lincoln County Museum and Old Jail. *133 Federal St, Wiscasset (04578). Phone 207/882-6817. www. lincolncountyhistory.org.* First penitentiary built in the District of Maine (1809-1811). Jailer's house has changing exhibits, relics of Lincoln County. (June and Sept, Sat-Sun; July-Aug, Tues-Sun)

Maine Art Gallery. *In Old Academy Building (1807),Warren St, Wiscasset (04578). Phone 207/882-7511. www.maineartgallery.org.* Exhibits by Maine artists. (May-mid-Nov, Tues-Sun) **DONATION**

Nickels-Sortwell House. *121 Main St, Wiscasset (04578). At Federal St. Phone 207/882-6218.* (1807) Classic Federal-style elegance. Built for a shipmaster in the lumber trade, William Nickels, it was used as a hotel between 1820 and 1900. The mansion was then bought by Mayor Alvin Sortwell of Cambridge, Massachusetts, as a private home. Graceful elliptical stairway; many Sortwell family furnishings; restored garden. (June-mid-Oct, Fri-Sun) **$**

Pownalborough Courthouse. *Dresden. 8 miles N on Hwy 27, then 3 miles S on Hwy 128, bordering Kennebec River. Phone 207/882-6817. www.lincolncountyhistory. org.* (1761) Oldest pre-Revolutionary courthouse in Maine. Three-story building houses furnished courtroom, judges' chambers, spinning room, tavern, bedrooms, parlor, and kitchen. Nature trails along river; picnic areas; Revolutionary cemetery. (June and Sept, Sat-Sun; July-Aug, Tues-Sun) **$$**

Specialty Lodgings

COD COVE INN. *22 Cross Rd, Edgecomb (04556). Phone 207/882-9586; toll-free 800/882-9586; fax 207/882-9294. www.codcoveinn.com.* Located high on a hill, this New England-style inn overlooks the Sheepscott River and the harbor. Amenities for guests include a flowering garden with gazebo and outdoor swimming pool and whirlpool. Area activities include lighthouse touring, antique shopping, whale-watching or dining on lobster. 30 rooms, 2 story. Complimentary continental breakfast. Check-in 3 pm, check-out 11 am. Outdoor pool, whirlpool. **$**

SQUIRE TARBOX INN. *1181 Main Rd, Westport Island (04578). Phone 207/882-7693; toll-free 800/818-0626; fax 207/882-7107. www.squiretarboxinn.com.* Restored 18th-century farmhouse situated on working dairy goat farm. 11 rooms, 2 story. Closed Jan-Mar.

Pets accepted, some restrictions. Complimentary full breakfast. Check-in 2:30-6:30 pm. Check-out 11 am. Restaurant. **$$**

Restaurant

★ ★ **LE GARAGE.** *Water St, Wiscasset (04578). Phone 207/882-5409; fax 207/882-6370.* Seafood, steak menu. Lunch, dinner. Closed holidays; Jan. Bar. **$$**

Yarmouth (E-1)

See also Brunswick, Freeport, Portland

Settled 1636
Population 7,862
Elevation 100 ft
Area Code 207
Zip 04096
Information Chamber of Commerce, 162 Main St; phone 207/846-3984
Web Site www.yarmouthmaine.org

Yarmouth is a quaint New England village 10 miles north of Portland (see) on Highway 1. There are many well-maintained older homes and specialty shops. It is linked by a bridge to Cousins Island in the bay.

What to See and Do

Eartha. *2 DeLorme Dr, Yarmouth (04096). I-95, exit 17. Phone 207/846-7000. www.delorme.com.* World's largest globe. Three stories high, Eartha is the largest printed image of the Earth ever created and spins in the lobby of the DeLorme Map Company. (Daily) **FREE**

Yarmouth Historical Society Museum. *215 Main St, Yarmouth (04096). Third floor, Merrill Memorial Library. Phone 207/846-6259.* Two galleries with changing exhibits of local and maritime history, fine and decorative arts. Local history research room; historical lecture series. (July-Aug: Mon-Fri afternoons; rest of year: Tues-Sat) **FREE**

Old Ledge School. *215 Main St, Yarmouth (04096). Phone 207/846-6259.* (1738) Restored one-room schoolhouse. (By appointment) **FREE**

Special Event

Clam Festival. *158 Main St, Yarmouth (04096). Phone 207/846-3984. www.clamfestival.com.* Celebration of soft-shelled clams. Arts and crafts, entertainment, parade, fireworks. Third weekend in July.

Restaurant

★ ★ **ROYAL RIVER GRILLHOUSE.** *106 Lafayette St, Yarmouth (04096). Phone 207/846-1226; fax 207/846-0920. www.royalrivergrillhouse.com.* American menu. Lunch, dinner, Sun brunch. Closed Thanksgiving, Dec 25. Bar. Children's menu. Outdoor seating. **$$**

York (F-1)

See also Kittery, Ogunquit, Wells

Settled 1624
Population 9,818
Elevation 60 ft
Area Code 207
Zip 03909
Information Greater York Region Chamber of Commerce, 1 Stonewall Ln, PO Box 417; phone 207/363-4422
Web Site www.gatewaytomaine.org

Originally named Agamenticus by the Plymouth Company, which settled the area in 1624, the settlement was chartered as a city—the first in America—in 1641 and renamed Gorgeanna. Following a reorganization in 1652, the "city" in the wilderness took the name York. The present-day York area includes York Village, York Harbor, York Beach, and Cape Neddick.

What to See and Do

⭐ **Old York Historical Society.** *140 Lindsay Rd, York (03909). Phone 207/363-4974. www.oldyork.org.* Tours of seven buildings dating to the early 1700s. (Mid-June-Sept) Visitor orientation and tickets at Jefferds Tavern. Administration Office houses museum offices (Mon-Fri) and historical and research library. **$$**

Elizabeth Perkins House. Turn-of-the-century summer house on the banks of the York River, at Sewall's Bridge. Former home of a prominent York preservationist. The furnishings reflect the Colonial Revival period.

Emerson-Wilcox House. *York and Lindsey rds, York (03909).* Built in 1742, with later additions. Served at various times as a general store, tavern, and post office, as well as the home of two of the town's prominent early families. Now contains a series of period rooms dating to 1750; antique furnishings.

George Marshall Store. *Lindsay Rd, York (03909). At the York River. Phone 207/351-1083.* Mid-19th-century general store houses local art exhibits. **FREE**

Jefferds Tavern and Schoolhouse. Built by Captain Samuel Jefferds in 1750 and furnished as a tavern in coastal Maine in the late 18th century; used as an orientation center and educational facility. Schoolhouse adjacent is probably the state's oldest surviving one-room schoolhouse; contains exhibit on one-room schooling in Maine.

John Hancock Warehouse. *York and Lindsey rds, York (03909). Phone 207/363-4974.* Owned by John Hancock until 1794, this is one of the earliest surviving customs houses in Maine. Used now to interpret the maritime history of this coastal village. (mid-June-mid-Oct, Tues-Sat afternoons)

Old Gaol. *Lindsay Rd, York. On Hwy 1A at the York River.* Built in 1719 with 18th-century additions. One of the oldest English public buildings in the United States, it was used as a jail until 1860. Has dungeons and cells for felons and debtors, as well as galleries of local historical artifacts, late 1800s photography exhibit.

Sayward-Wheeler House. *9 Barrell Ln, York Harbor (03909). 2 miles S.* (1718) Home of the 18th-century merchant and civic leader Tory Jonathan Sayward. Tours. (June-Oct, first Sat of the month) **$**

Special Event

Harvest Fest. *Hwy 95, York (03909). Exit 4, last exit before the toll. Phone 207/363-4422.* Juried crafts, ox roast, colonial theme. Mid-Oct.

Limited-Service Hotel

★ ★ **ANCHORAGE MOTOR INN.** *265 Long Beach Ave, York Beach (03910). Phone 207/363-5112; fax 207/363-6753. www.anchorageinn.com.* 179 rooms, 3 story. Check-in 3 pm, check-out 11 am. Bar. Fitness room. Two indoor pools, outdoor pool, whirlpool. **$**
🧍 ⛖

Full-Service Resort

★ ★ ★ **STAGE NECK INN.** *8 Stage Neck Rd, York Harbor (03909). Phone 207/363-3850; toll-free 800/340-1130; fax 207/363-2221. www.stageneck.com.*

This inn is located on an ocean-bound peninsula in York Harbor. The resort offers a beach and is also close to the Kittery outlet malls, antiques shops, art galleries, and historic attractions of York. 58 rooms, 3 story. Check-in 3 pm, check-out 11 am. Restaurant, bar. Fitness room. Beach. Indoor pool, outdoor pool, whirlpool. Tennis. **$$**

Specialty Lodgings

DOCKSIDE GUEST QUARTERS. *Harris Island Rd, York (03909). Phone 207/363-2868; toll-free 888/860-7428; fax 207/363-1977. www.docksidegq.com.* 25 rooms. Closed weekdays late Oct-Dec, Mar-Memorial Day, completely Dec-Feb. Check-in 3-9 pm. Check-out 11 am. Restaurant. **$$**

EDWARDS HARBORSIDE INN. *Stage Neck Rd, York Harbor (03911). Phone 207/363-3037; fax 207/363-1544. www.edwardsharborside.com.* Turn-of-the-century house with period furnishings. 9 rooms, 3 story. Complimentary continental breakfast. Check-in 3 pm, check-out 11 am. **$$$**

YORK HARBOR INN. *Coastal Hwy 1A, York Harbor (03911). Phone 207/363-5119; toll-free 800/343-3869; fax 207/363-7151. www.yorkharborinn.com.* 54 rooms, 2 story. Complimentary continental breakfast. Check-in 2:30 pm, check-out 11 am. Restaurant. Whirlpool. **$$**

Restaurants

★ ★ **DOCKSIDE.** *Harris Island Rd, York (03909). Phone 207/363-2722; fax 207/363-1977. www.docksidegq. com.* Seafood, steak menu. Lunch, dinner. Closed Mon; day after Columbus Day-late May. Bar. Casual attire. Reservations recommended. Outdoor seating. **$$**

★ ★ **FAZIO'S ITALIAN.** *38 Woodbridge Rd, York (03909). Phone 207/363-7019; fax 207/363-8473. www. fazios.com.* Located in the heart of downtown York, this Italian eatery is decorated with soft gold walls, wrought iron, and upholstered chairs and booths. A pleasant staff awaits guests. Italian menu. Dinner. Closed Easter, Dec 24-25. Bar. Children's menu. Casual attire. Reservations recommended. **$$**

★ ★ ★ **YORK HARBOR INN.** *Hwy 1A, York Harbor (03911). Phone 207/363-5119; fax 207/363-7151.*

www.yorkharborinn.com. The menu at this seaside inn features local seafood, much of it caught close to the restaurant. Antique furnishings, floral wallpaper, and lace curtains add to the warm ambience of this quaint, colonial inn. Seafood menu. Dinner, Sun brunch. Closed Mon-Thurs (fall-spring). Children's menu. Casual attire. Reservations recommended. **$$**

Massachusetts

Leif Ericson—or even a French or Spanish fisherman—may have originally discovered the Cape Cod coast. However, the first recorded visit of a European to Massachusetts was that of John Cabot in 1497. Not until the Pilgrims landed at Provincetown and settled at Plymouth was there a permanent settlement north of Virginia. Ten years later, Boston was founded with the arrival of John Winthrop and his group of Puritans.

Native American wars plagued Massachusetts until the 1680s, after which the people experienced a relatively peaceful period combined with a fast-growing, mostly agricultural economy. In the 1760s, opposition to British taxation without representation exploded into the American Revolution. It began in Massachusetts, and from here, the American tradition of freedom and justice spread around the world. The Constitution of Massachusetts is the oldest written constitution still in effect. The New England town meeting, a basic democratic institution, still governs most of its towns. The state had a child labor law in 1836, a law legalizing trade unions in 1842, and the first minimum wage law for women and children.

Massachusetts proved to be fertile ground for intellectual ideas and activities. In the early 19th century, Emerson, Thoreau, and their followers expounded the Transcendentalist theory of the innate nobilty of man and the doctrine of individual expression, which exerted a major influence on American thought, then and now. Social improvement was sought through colonies of idealists, many of which hoped to prove that sharing labor and the fruits of labor were the means to a just society. Dorothea Dix crusaded on behalf of the

Population: 6,016,425

Area: 7,826 square miles

Elevation: 0-3,491 feet

Peak: Mount Greylock (Berkshire County)

Entered Union: Sixth of original 13 states (February 6, 1788)

Capital: Boston

Motto: By the Sword We Seek Peace, but Peace Only Under Liberty

Nickname: Bay State

Flower: Mayflower

Bird: Chickadee

Tree: American Elm

Time Zone: Eastern

Web Site: www.mass-vacation.com

Fun Facts:

• James Naismith invented basketball in Springfield in 1891. He taught physical education and wanted an indoor sport for his students during the winter months.

• Harvard University, the nation's oldest college, was chartered in Cambridge in 1636.

mentally disturbed, and Horace Mann promoted universal education. In 1831, William Lloyd Garrison, an ardent abolitionist, founded his weekly, *The Liberator*. Massachusetts was the heartland of the Abolitionist movement, and her soldiers fought in the Civil War because they were convinced it was a war against slavery.

Massachusetts was also an important center during the Industrial Revolution. After the Civil War, the earlier success of the textile mills, like those in Lowell, generated scores of drab, hastily built, industrial towns. Now these mills are being replaced by modern plants with landscaped grounds. Modern industry is as much a part of Massachusetts as the quiet sandy beaches of Cape Cod with their bayberry and beach plum bushes.

Calendar Highlights

APRIL

Boston Marathon *(Boston). Phone 617/236-1652.
www.bostonmarathon.org.* Famous 26-mile footrace
from Hopkinton to Boston.

Daffodil Festival *(Nantucket Island). Siasconset Village. Phone Chamber of Commerce, 508/228-1700.
www.nantucket.net.* The Daffodil festival celebrates
the budding of millions of daffodils on the main
roads of Nantucket. Parade of antique cars, open
houses, garden tours, and entertainment.

Reenactment of Battle of Lexington and Concord
*(Lexington). Phone Lexington Historical Society,
781/862-1703.* Massachusetts Ave. Reenactment of
opening battle of American Revolution; parade.

JUNE

Green River Music and Balloon Festival *(Greenfield).
Phone 413/733-9393. www.greenriverfestival.com.* Hot
air balloon launches, craft show, musical entertainment, food.

Harborfest *(Boston). Hatch Shell on the Esplande.
Phone 617/227-1528.* Concerts, chowder fest, children's activites, Boston Pops Orchestra, fireworks.

La Festa *(North Adams). Phone 413/663-3782.* Ethnic
festival, food, entertainment, events.

SEPTEMBER

The "Big E" *(Springfield). Phone 413/737-2443.
www.thebige.com.* Largest fair in the Northeast;
entertainment, exhibits, historic Avenue of States,
Storrowton Village; hores show, agricultural events,
"Better Living Center" exhibit.

OCTOBER

Haunted Happenings *(Salem). Various sites. Phone
Salem Halloween Office, 978/744-0013.* Psychic
festival, historical exhibits, haunted house, costume
parade, contests, dances.

NOVEMBER

Thanksgiving Week *(Plymouth). Phone 508/747-
7525 or toll-free 800/872-1620.* Programs for various
events may be obtained by contacting Destination
Plymouth.

DECEMBER

Stockbridge Main Street at Christmas *(Stockbridge
and West Stockbridge). Phone 413/298-5200.* Events
include a re-creation of Norman Rockwell's painting. Holiday marketplace, concerts, house tour,
silent auction, sleigh/hayrides, caroling.

Massachusetts has also been home to several generations of the politically prominent Kennedy family.
John F. Kennedy, 35th president of the United States,
was born in the Boston suburb of Brookline, as was
his younger brother, Senator Robert Kennedy.

The Bay State offers mountains, ocean swimming,
camping, summer resorts, freshwater and saltwater
fishing, and a variety of metropolitan cultural advan-
tages. No other state in the Union can claim so much
history in so small an area, for in Massachusetts each
town or city has a part in the American story.

When to Go/Climate

Massachusetts enjoys a moderate climate with four
distinct seasons. Cape Cod and the Islands offer

milder temperatures than other parts of the state
and rarely have snow, while the windchill in Boston
(the windiest city in the United States) can make
temperatures feel well below zero, and snow is not
uncommon.

AVERAGE HIGH/LOW TEMPERATURES (°F)

Boston

Jan 36/22	May 67/50	Sept 73/57
Feb 38/23	June 76/60	Oct 63/47
Mar 46/31	July 82/65	Nov 52/38
Apr 56/40	Aug 80/64	Dec 40/27

Worcester

Jan 31/15	May 66/45	Sept 70/51
Feb 33/17	June 75/54	Oct 60/41
Mar 42/25	July 80/60	Nov 47/31
Apr 54/35	Aug 77/59	Dec 35/20

Parks and Recreation

Water-related activities, hiking, riding, various other sports, picnicking and visitor centers, as well as camping, are available in many state parks. Day-use areas (approximately Memorial Day-Labor Day, some areas all year): $5/car. Camping (approximately mid-April-October, schedule may vary, phone ahead; two-week maximum, last Saturday in May-Saturday before Labor Day at many parks): campsites $10-$15/day; electricity $5/day. Pets on leash only; no pets in bathing areas. Information available from the Department of Environmental Management, Division of Forests & Parks, phone 617/727-3180.

FISHING AND HUNTING

Deep-sea and surf fishing are good; boats are available in most coastal towns. For information on saltwater fishing, contact the Division of Marine Fisheries, phone 617/626-1520. Inland fishing is excellent in more than 500 streams and 3,000 ponds. Nonresident fishing license $40.50; three-consecutive-day nonresident license $25.50. Nonresident hunting license: small game $75.50; big game $110.50. Inquire for trapping licenses. Fees subject to change. Licenses issued by town clerks, selected sporting good stores, or from the Division of Fisheries and Wildlife. Information on freshwater fishing, regulations, and a guide to stocked trout waters and best bass ponds are also available from the Division of Fisheries and Wildlife.

Driving Information

Safety belts are mandatory for all persons. Children under 13 years must be in federally approved child safety seats or safety belts anywhere in a vehicle: it is recommended that children 40 pounds and under use federally approved child safety seats and be placed in the back seat.

INTERSTATE HIGHWAY SYSTEM

The following list shows that these cities are within 10 miles of the indicated interstate highways. Check a highway map for the nearest exit.

Highway Number	Cities/Towns within 10 Miles
Interstate 90	Boston, Cambridge, Framingham, Great Barrington, Holyoke, Lee, Lenox, Natick, Newton, Pittsfield, Springfield, Stockbridge and West Stockbridge, Sturbridge, Sudbury Center, Waltham, Wellesley, Worcester.
Interstate 91	Amherst, Deerfield, Greenfield, Holyoke, Northampton, Springfield.
Interstate 93	Andover, Boston, Lawrence, Lowell.
Interstate 95	Bedford, Boston, Burlington, Concord, Danvers, Dedham, Foxboro, Framingham, Lexington, Lynn, Lynnfield, Natick, Newton, Saugus, Sudbury Center, Waltham, Wellesley.

Additional Visitor Information

The Massachusetts Office of Travel and Tourism, phone 617/727-3201, has travel information. For a free *Massachusetts Getaway Guide,* phone toll-free 800/447-6277.

Many properties of the Society for the Preservation of New England Antiquities (SPNEA) are located in Massachusetts and neighboring states. For complete information on these properties, contact SPNEA Headquarters, 141 Cambridge St, Boston 02114; phone 617/227-3956. For information regarding the 71 properties owned and managed by the Trustees of Reservations, contact 527 Essex St, Beverly, MA 01905, phone 508/921-1944.

Massachusetts has many statewide fairs, though none is considered the official state fair; contact the Massachusetts Department of Agriculture, Division of Fairs, phone 617/626-1742.

Several visitor centers are located in Massachusetts; they are located on the MA Turnpike (daily, 9 am-6 pm) at Charlton (eastbound and westbound), Lee (eastbound), and Natick (eastbound); also I-95 at Mansfield, between exits 5 and 6 (northbound); and on Highway 3 at Plymouth (southbound).

TO THE BERKSHIRES!

Two major limited-access highways link Boston with the Berkshires, traversing the width of Massachusetts. The older, slower, more scenic Route 2 runs across the state's hilly northern tier; the Massachusetts Turnpike (I-90) is the quick way home. Begin on Route 2 in Cambridge. To explore Revolutionary War battle sites, take exit 56 (Waltham Street) into the center of Lexington and turn left on Route 2A for Battle Green. Continue west on Route 2A, stopping at the Battle Road Visitors Center and moving on to Concord's Minute Man National Historical Park sights. Pick up Route 2 west again in Concord. In Harvard, take exit 38A to the hilltop Fruitlands Museums with its paintings, Shaker furnishings, and local Indian artifacts. This is the Nashoba Valley, known for its orchards, served by the Johnny Appleseed information center just west of exit 35. Wachusett Mountain in Princeton (exit 25) is a popular ski area; there is also a state reservation with a road to its summit. Templeton (exit 21), just off the highway, is a classic old village with interesting shops and a local historical museum.

For a sense of central Massachusetts' countryside, detour south on Route 32 (exit 17) to the handsome old ridge town of Petersham. South of the village, turn west on Route 122, skirting the Quabbin Fervor, said to be one of the largest reservoirs in the world. Rejoin the highway in the town of Orange. Here, Route 2 officially becomes "The Mohawk Trail" because it's said to shadow an old Indian trail through the hills. (Note the information center at the junction of Reservoir 2, I-91, and Route 5.) Take a detour to Old Deerfield and its many historic house museums, located 12 miles south on Route 5. Or continue on Route 2 as it climbs steeply from Greenfield out of the Connecticut River Valley and into the Berkshire Hills. The vintage 1930s lookout towers and Indian trading posts along this stretch are relics from when this was the state's first scenic "auto touring" route.

The village of Shelburne Falls, just off Route 2, is known for its Bridge of Flowers, shops, and restaurants. The "trail" continues through the Deerfield River Valley, threads the heavily wooded Mohawk Trail Forest (camping, swimming), and finally plunges down a series of hairpin turns into the Hoosac Valley and through the town of North Adams, site of MASS MoCA, the country's largest center for contemporary art. The Western Gateway Heritage State Park here tells the story of Hoosac Railroad Tunnel construction beneath the mountains you have just crossed.

Williamstown, 126 miles from Boston, marks the state's northwest corner. It's home to Williams College and two outstanding art museums, the Clark Art Institute and the Williams College Museum of Art. This is an obvious stop for food and lodging.

If you have more than one day, continue south on Route 7 from Williamstown. In Lanesborough, note the main access road to Mount Greylock, the highest mountain in the state. Pittsfield, site of the Berkshire Museum, is also the turnoff point for the Hancock Shaker Village (5 miles west on Route 20). Continue down Route 7 to Lenox, site of the Tanglewood summer music festival, summer Shakespeare productions, several museums, and ample lodging. Take Route 7A south to Stockbridge and through the village to the Norman Rockwell Museum. Return on Route 102 to the entrance to the Massachusetts Turnpike (Route 90) at Lee, the quick way back to Boston. Stop at Sturbridge (exit 9) to tour Old Sturbridge Village.

(Approximately 290 miles)

Amesbury (A-7)

See also Haverhill, Newburyport

Settled 1654
Population 16,450
Elevation 50 ft
Area Code 978
Zip 01913
Information Alliance for Amesbury, 5 Market Sq, 01913-2440; phone 978/388-3178

Web Site www.amesburymass.com

In 1853, Jacob R. Huntington, "the Henry Ford of carriage-making," began a low-cost, high-quality carriage industry that became the economic backbone of Amesbury.

What to See and Do

Amesbury Sports Park. *12 Hunt Rd, Amesbury (01913). Off Hwy 495, exit 54. Phone 978/388-5788;*

fax 978/388-4397. www.goslide.com. Winter snow tubing, summer go-carts, golf range, miniature golf, bumper boats, volleyball park. Restaurant; lounge. (Daily 9 am-10 pm; closed Easter, Thanksgiving, Dec 25) **$$$$**

Bartlett Museum. *270 Main St, Amesbury (01913). Phone 978/388-4528.* (1870) Houses memorabilia of Amesbury's history dating from prehistoric days to the settlement and beyond. The Native American artifact collection, consisting of relics of local tribes, is considered one of the finest collections in the state. (Memorial Day-Labor Day, Wed-Sun afternoons; Labor Day-Columbus Day, Fri-Sun 1-4 pm) **$**

John Greenleaf Whittier Home. *86 Friend St, Amesbury (01913). Phone 978/388-1337.* John Greenleaf Whittier lived here from 1836 until his death in 1892; six rooms contain books, manuscripts, pictures, and furniture; the Garden Room, where he wrote *Snow-Bound,* and many other works, remains unchanged. (May-Oct, Tues-Sat 10 am-4 pm) **$**

Limited-Service Hotel

★ **FAIRFIELD INN.** *35 Clarks Rd, Amesbury (01913). Phone 978/388-3400; toll-free 800/228-2800; fax 978/388-9850. www.fairfieldinn.com.* Convenient to I-95 and I-495 and across the street from a family restaurant, this motel gets quite a bit of traffic noise, but the guest rooms are large and comfortable. Guest laundry facilities are available. 105 rooms, 4 story. Complimentary continental breakfast. Check-in 3 pm, check-out noon. Wireless Internet access. Outdoor pool. **$**
⛱

Amherst (B-4)

See also South Hadley

Founded 1759
Population 34,874
Elevation 320 ft
Area Code 413
Zip 01002
Information Chamber of Commerce, 409 Main St; phone phone 413/253-0700
Web Site www.amherstchamber.com

Amherst College, founded in 1821 to educate "promising but needy youths who wished to enter the Ministry," has educated several of the nation's leaders, including Calvin Coolidge and Henry Ward Beecher.

Amherst is also the seat of the University of Massachusetts and of Hampshire College. This attractive, academic town was the home of three celebrated American poets: Emily Dickinson, Eugene Field, and Robert Frost; Noah Webster also lived here and apparently completed A-K of his famous dictionary in Amherst.

What to See and Do

Amherst College. *100 Boltwood Ave, Amherst (01002). Phone 413/542-2000. www.amherst.edu.* (1821) (1,550 students) On the tree-shaded green in the middle of town. The Robert Frost Library owns approximately half of Emily Dickinson's poems in manuscript and has a Robert Frost collection, as well as materials of Wordsworth, Eugene O'Neill, and others. Also on campus are

Mead Art Museum. *Phone 413/542-2335.* A notable art collection of nearly 14,000 works is housed here. (Sept-May, Tues-Sun 10 am-4:30 pm, Thurs until 9 pm) **FREE**

Amherst History Museum. *67 Amity St, Amherst (01002). Phone 413/256-0678; fax 413/256-0672. www. amhersthistory.org.* In the circa-1750 Strong House, which reflects changing tastes in local architecture and interior decoration, this museum boasts an extensive collection of 18th- and 19th-century textiles and artifacts. Gallery. (Apr-mid-May, Nov: Wed and Sat noon-4 pm; mid-May-Oct: Wed-Sat noon-4 pm) 18th-century herb and flower gardens to the east of Strong House are open to the public (spring-summer). **$**

Emily Dickinson Museum: the Homestead and the Evergreens. *280 Main St, Amherst (01002). Phone 413/542-8161; fax 413/542-2152. www. emilydickinsonmuseum.org.* (1813) The Homestead was the birthplace and home of poet Emily Dickinson; the Evergreens housed her brother and his family. Selected rooms are open for tours on a first-come, first-served basis. (Mar-May, Sept-Oct: Wed-Sat 1-5 pm; June-Aug: Wed-Sat 10 am-5 pm, Sun 1-5 pm; Nov-mid-Dec, Wed, Sat 1-5 pm) **$$**

Eric Carle Museum of Picture Book Art. *125 W Bay Rd, Amherst (01002). Phone 413/658-1100; fax 413/658-1139. www.picturebookart.org.* This 40,000-square-foot facility opened in 2002 as the first museum in the United States exclusively devoted to children's picture book art. Its founder, Eric Carle, has illustrated more than 70 picture books, including *The Very Hungry Caterpillar,* which has been published in more than 30 languages and has sold more than

18 million copies. Nestled within a 7.5-acre apple orchard adjacent to the campus of Hampshire College, the museum features three galleries and a hands-on art studio, along with an auditorium, library, and café. A past exhibit celebrated the picture book art of Maurice Sendak, author and illustrator of such classics as *Where the Wild Things Are.* (Tues-Fri 10 am-4 pm, Sat until 5 pm, Sun noon-5 pm; closed holidays) **$$**

Hadley Farm Museum. *208 Middle St, Hadley (01035). 5 miles SW at junction Hwys 9, 47. www. hadleyonline.com/farmmuseum.* A restored 1782 barn houses agricultural implements, tools, and domestic items dating from the 1700s; broom-making machines, spinning wheels, cobblers' benches, and other historic artifacts. (May-Oct, Tues-Sat 10 am-4:30 pm, Sun 1:30-4:30 pm) **FREE**

Jones Library. *43 Amity St, Amherst (01002). Phone 413/256-4090; fax 413/256-4096. www.joneslibrary. org.* Amherst's public library houses collections of the local authors, including a Robert Frost collection and an Emily Dickinson room with some of Dickinson's personal articles, manuscripts, and a model of her bedroom. Historical collection (Mon-Sat); library (Sept-May: daily; rest of year: Mon-Sat; closed holidays). **FREE**

National Yiddish Book Center. *1021 West St, Amherst (01002). Hwy 116, on the campus of Hampshire College. Phone 413/256-4900; fax 413/256-4700. yiddishbookcenter. org.* This 37,000-square-foot nonprofit facility was founded by Aaron Lansky to preserve Yiddish literature and its history and to ensure its lasting legacy. Book Repository houses a core collection of 120,000 Yiddish booksthe largest in the worldand 150,000 folios of rare Yiddish and Hebrew sheet music. The Book Processing Center, shipping and receiving area, and Bibliography Center are all open for viewing as rare books are catalogued and shipped to libraries across the country. The vistor center includes three exhibit halls, a kosher dairy kitchen, and educational story rails that introduce visitors to the books and the Center's important work. Reading Room, Yiddish Resource Center, Yiddish Writers Garden. Also galleries for print, spoken, and performing arts. Bookstore; gift shop. (Mon-Fri 10 am-3:30 pm, Sun 11 am-4 pm; closed holidays) **FREE**

University of Massachusetts. *Massachusetts Ave and N Pleasant St, Amherst (01002). N edge of town on Hwy 116. Phone 413/545-0111. www.umass.edu.* (1863) (24,000 students) The state's major facility of public higher education. More than 150 buildings on a 1,450-acre campus. Tours (daily). Also here is

Fine Arts Center and Gallery. *Phone 413/545-3670.* A variety of nationally and internationally known performances in theater, music, and dance. Art galleries (daily). Performances (Sept-May).

Special Event

Maple sugaring. *Mount Toby Sugar House, Amherst. NW via Hwy 116 to Sunderland, then 2 miles N on Hwy 47. Phone 413/253-0700.* Visitors are welcome at maple camps, daily. (Late Feb-Mar)

Limited-Service Hotel

★ **HOWARD JOHNSON.** *401 Russell St, Hwy 9, Hadley (01035). Phone 413/586-0114; fax 413/584-7163. www.hojo.com.* 100 rooms, 3 story. Pets accepted, some restrictions; fee. Complimentary full breakfast. Check-in 3 pm, check-out noon. Fitness room. Outdoor pool. **$**

Specialty Lodgings

ALLEN HOUSE VICTORIAN INN. *599 Main St, Amherst (01002). Phone 413/2 53-5000. www.allenhouse. com.* This Queen Anne-style house was built in 1886 and is decorated with many antiques. 7 rooms, 2 story. Children over 10 years only. Complimentary full breakfast. Check-in 3-9 pm, check-out 11 am. **$**

LORD JEFFERY INN. *30 Boltwood Ave, Amherst (01002). Phone 413/253-2576; toll-free 800/742-0358; fax 413/256-6152. www.lordjefferyinn.com.* 48 rooms, 4 story. Check-in 3 pm, check-out 11 am. Two restaurants, bar. **$**

Andover and North Andover (A-7)

Settled circa 1643
Population 31,247
Elevation 164 ft
Area Code 978
Zip Andover: 01810; North Andover: 01845
Information Merrimack Valley Chamber of Commerce, 264 Essex St, Lawrence 01840-1496; phone

978/686-0900
Web Site www.merrimackvalleychamber.com

An attempt was made in Andover in the 19th century to surpass Japan's silk industry by growing mulberry trees on which silkworms feed. But Andover has had to be content with making electronic parts and woolen and rubber goods instead. Its true fame rests on Phillips Academy, the oldest incorporated school in the United States, founded in 1778 by Samuel Phillips.

What to See and Do

Amos Blanchard House. *97 Main St, Andover (01810). Phone 978/475-2236; fax 978/470-2741. www.andhist. org.* (1819) **Barn Museum** (1818) Also **Research Library** (1978). House features period rooms; special local history exhibits; 17th- to 20th-century themes. Barn Museum features early farm equipment; household items; hand-pumped fire wagon. Library houses local history, genealogy, and special collections. Guided tours (by appointment). (Sept-July, Tues-Fri 1-4 pm; closed holidays) **$**

Phillips Academy. *180 Main St, Andover (01810). Hwy 28. Phone 978/749-4000; fax 978/749-4123. www. andover.edu.* (1778) (1,065 students) A coed residential school for grades 9-12. Notable alumni include photographer Walker Evans, poet Oliver Wendell Holmes, child-rearing expert Benjamin Spock, and actor Humphrey Bogart. The campus sits on 450 acres with 170 buildings, many of historical interest. The Cochran Sanctuary, a 65-acre landscaped area, has walking trails, a brook, and two ponds. (Daily) Also on the grounds are

> **Addison Gallery of American Art.** *Phone 978/749-4015; fax 978/749-4025.* More than 12,000 works, including paintings, sculpture, and photography. Changing exhibits. A ship model collection traces the history of American sailing vessels. (Sept-July, Tues-Sat 10 am-5 pm, Sun 1-5 pm; closed holidays) **FREE**

> **Peabody Museum.** *175 Main St, Andover (01810). Phone 978/749-4490; fax 978/749-4495.* This Native American archaeological museum has exhibits on the physical and cultural evolution of man and the prehistoric archaeology of New England, the Southwest, Mexico, and the Arctic. (Mon-Fri 9 am-5 pm, by appointment only) **FREE**

Stevens-Coolidge Place. *137 Andover St, North Andover (01845). Phone 978/682-3580. www.thetrustees.org/ stevens-coolidgeplace.cfm.* House and extensive gardens are maintained as they were in the early 20th century by diplomat John Gardener Coolidge and his wife, Helen Stevens Coolidge, who summered here. Collection of Chinese porcelain, Irish and English cut glass, linens, and clothing. Early American furnishings. House (late May-Oct, Sun 1-5 pm; also Wed 2-4 pm in July-Aug). Gardens (daily dawn-dusk; free). **$**

Limited-Service Hotels

★ ★ **ANDOVER WYNDHAM HOTEL.** *123 Old River Rd, Andover (01810). Phone 978/975-3600; fax 978/975-2664. www.wyndham.com.* 293 rooms, 5 story. Pets accepted; fee. Check-in 3 pm, check-out noon. Restaurant, bar. Fitness room. Indoor pool, whirlpool. Airport transportation available. **$$**

★ ★ **LA QUINTA INN & SUITES ANDOVER.** *131 River Rd, Andover (01810). Phone 978/685-6200; fax 978/794-9626.* 185 rooms, 3 story. Pets accepted. Complimentary continental breakfast. Check-in 3 pm, check-out noon. Restaurant. Fitness room. Indoor pool, whirlpool. Tennis. **$**

Full-Service Inn

★ ★ ★ **ANDOVER INN.** *4 Chapel Ave, Andover (01810). Phone 978/475-5903; toll-free 800/242-5903; fax 978/475-1053. www.andoverinn.com.* Located on the campus of Philips Andover Academy, this neo-Georgian country inn was built in 1930 to provide lodging for visiting parents and alumni. 29 rooms, 3 story. Check-in 4 pm, check-out noon. Restaurant, bar. Business center. **$**

Bedford (B-7)

Population 12,595
Elevation 135 ft
Area Code 781
Zip 01730

Limited-Service Hotel

★ ★ **BEST WESTERN SOVEREIGN HOTEL.** *340 Great Rd, Bedford (01730). Phone 781/275-6700; toll-free 800/602-9876; fax 781/275-3011. www. sovereignhotels.com.* In a busy suburban commercial area, this 99-room hotel underwent a major renovation completed in 2004. The unadorned brown stucco exterior belies a much more attractive interior, with spacious guest rooms arranged around a three-story atrium housing a large indoor pool. 99 rooms, 3 story. Complimentary full breakfast. Check-in 2 pm, check-out noon. Wireless Internet access. Restaurant, bar. Fitness room. Indoor pool. **$**

Full-Service Hotels

★ ★ ★ **RENAISSANCE BEDFORD HOTEL.**
44 Middlesex Tpke, Bedford (01730). Phone 781/275-5500; toll-free 888/236-2427; fax 781/275-8956. www. renaissancehotels.com. Nestled in a corporate office park area on 24 attractively landscaped acres, this contemporary hotel is great for business travelers and group functions. Indoor tennis courts with equipment and a pro available, as well as a glass-enclosed lap pool, sand volleyball court, and basketball court, offer lots of options for leisure travelers, too. Guests also enjoy complimentary shuttle service to public transportation, area businesses, and nearby recreational destinations, such as the Burlington Mall. 284 rooms, 3 story. Complimentary continental breakfast. Check-in 3 pm, check-out 1 pm. High-speed Internet access. Restaurant, bar. Fitness room. Indoor pool, whirlpool. Tennis. Business center. **$**

★ ★ ★ **WYNDHAM BILLERICA HOTEL.** *270 Concord Rd, Bedford (01821). Phone 978/670-7500; fax 978/670-8898. www.wyndham.com.* 210 rooms, 8 story. Check-in 4 pm, check-out noon. Restaurant, bar. Fitness room. Indoor pool, whirlpool. Business center. **$**

Berkshire Hills

Web Site www.berkshire.org

This western Massachusetts resort area is just south of Vermont's Green Mountains, but has neither the ruggedness nor the lonesomeness of the range to its north. The highest peak, Mt Greylock (elevation: 3,491 feet), is cragless and serene. Farms and villages dot the landscape. The area is famous for its variety of accommodations, culture, and recreation. There are also countless summer homes and camps for children by the lakes, ponds, and brooks.

Berkshire County is about 45 miles long from north to south, and half that from east to west. It has 90 lakes and ponds, 90,000 acres of state forest, golf courses, ski areas, ski touring centers, numerous tennis facilities, and campsites. The area first became famous when Nathaniel Hawthorne wrote *Tanglewood Tales,* and it has since become distinguished for its many summer cultural activities, including the Tanglewood Music Festival at Tanglewood (see LENOX) and the Berkshire Theatre Festival (see STOCKBRIDGE and WEST STOCKBRIDGE).

Beverly (B-8)

See also Danvers, Salem

Settled 1626
Population 39,862
Elevation 26 ft
Area Code 978
Zip 01915
Information North Shore Chamber of Commerce, 5 Cherry Hill Dr, Danvers 01923; phone 978/774-8565
Web Site www.northshorechamber.org

When George Washington commissioned the first US naval vessel, the schooner *Hannah,* on September 5, 1775, at Glover's Wharf in Beverly, the town was already well established. In 1693, the local Puritan minister's wife, Mistress Hale, was accused of witchcraft. She was so far above reproach that the charge—and the hysteria—collapsed. Today, Beverly is a popular summer resort area. Saltwater fishing, boating, and scuba diving are available near Glover's Wharf.

What to See and Do

Balch House. *448 Cabot St, Beverly (01915). Phone 978/922-1186. www.beverlyhistory.org.* (17th century) One of the two oldest wood-frame houses in America. Born in 1579, John Balch came to America in 1623 as one of the first permanent settlers of Massachusetts Bay. (Mid-May-mid-Oct, Tues-Sat noon-4 pm; closed holidays) Inquire about combination ticket (includes Hale and Cabot houses). **$$**

Cabot House. *117 Cabot St, Beverly (01915). Phone 978/922-1186. www.beverlyhistory.org.* (1781) Headquarters of the Beverly Historical Society. Brick mansion of Revolutionary War privateer John Cabot, built a year after it was written that "the Cabots of Beverly are now said to be by far the most wealthy in New

England." Changing exhibits. (Tues-Sat 10 am-4 pm) Inquire about combination ticket (includes Hale and Balch houses). **$$**

Hale House. *39 Hale St, Beverly (01915). Phone 978/922-1186. www.beverlyhistory.org.* (1694) Built by the Reverend John Hale, who was active in the witchcraft trials and whose own wife was accused of witchcraft. Rare wallpaper and furnishings show changes through the 18th and 19th centuries. (July-Aug, Sat afternoons; closed holidays) Inquire about combination ticket (includes Cabot and Balch houses). **$$**

"Le Grand David and His Own Spectacular Magic Company." *286 Cabot St, Beverly (01915). Cabot Street Cinema Theatre (1920). Phone 978/927-3677. www. legranddavid.com.* Resident stage magic company, New England's longest running theatrical attraction. This 2 1/4-hour stage magic production features magic, music, comedy, and dance. Five hundred costumes, two dozen sets and backdrops; 50 magic illusions. (Sun at 3pm) Additional performances at Larcom Theatre (1912), 13 Wallis Street. Advance tickets recommended. **$$$$**

Wenham Museum. *132 Main St, Wenham (01984). 2 1/2 miles N on Hwy 1A. Phone 978/468-2377. wenhammuseum.org.* The Wenham's doll collection, comprised of more than 5,000 dolls, represents cultures from 1500 BC to the present. The toy room houses British lead soldiers, board games and puzzles, and 20th-century mechanical toys. The Claflin-Richards House (circa 1690) contains collections of quilts, costumes, and fans, along with period furniture. The Winslow Shoe Shop has displays on the history of shoemaking, early ice-cutting tools, and a research library. Changing arts, crafts, and antique exhibits. (Tues-Sun 10 am-4 pm; closed holidays) **$**

Special Events

Band Concerts. *Lynch Park, 55 Ober St, Beverly (01915). Phone 978/774-8565.* Lynch Park Bandshell Sun evening; downtown Ellis Square, Thurs evening. (Late June-mid-Aug)

North Shore Music Theatre. *62 Dunham Rd, Beverly (01915). At Hwy 128 N exit 19. Phone 978/232-7200. www.nsmt.org.* Broadway musicals and plays; children's musicals; celebrity concerts. (Late Apr-late Dec)

Restaurant

★ **BEVERLY DEPOT.** *10 Park St, Beverly (01915). Phone 978/927-5402; fax 978/927-9897. www.*

barnsiderrestaurants.com. In 1800s train depot. Seafood, steak menu. Dinner. Bar. Children's menu. **$$**

Boston (B-7)

See also Braintree, Cambridge, Ipswich, Lynn, Marblehead, Newton, Quincy, Saugus, Sudbury Center, Waltham, Wellesley

Founded 1630
Population 589,141
Elevation 0-330 ft
Area Code 617
Information Greater Boston Convention & Visitors Bureau, 2 Copley Pl, Suite 105, 02116; phone 617/536-4100 or toll-free 888/733-2678
Web Site www.bostonusa.com
Suburbs Braintree, Burlington, Cambridge, Dedham, Framingham, Lexington, Lynn, Newton, Quincy, Saugus, Waltham, Wellesley. (See individual alphabetical listings.)

Greater Boston is a fascinating combination of old and new. It consists of 83 cities and towns in an area of 1,057 square miles with a total population of more than 3 million people. Boston proper is the hub of this busy complex, which many Bostonians still believe is the hub of the universe.

Boston is a haven for walkers; in fact, strolling along its streets is advised to get a true sense of this most European of all American cities. If you drive, a map is invaluable. Traffic is heavy. The streets (many of them narrow and one-way) run at odd angles and expressway traffic speeds.

Boston's wealth of historic sights makes it a must for all who are interested in America's past. John Winthrop and 800 colonists first settled in Charlestown, just north of the Charles River, and moved to Boston in 1630. Arriving too late to plant crops, 200 colonists died during the first winter, mostly of starvation. In the spring, a ship arrived with provisions, and the new Puritan commonwealth began to thrive and grow. Fisheries, fur trapping, lumbering, and trading with Native Americans were the foundation of Boston's commerce. The port is still viable, with 250 wharves along 30 miles of berthing space.

The Revolutionary War began here in 1770. British troops fired on an angry mob, killing five in what has

BOSTON CHEFS

The Boston area's most famous chef never had her own restaurant, but **Julia Child** helped establish a taste for French cooking in Boston as well as the rest of the country. Two current restaurateurs who share the cooking doyennes ability to juggle television appearances, cookbook writing, and cooking are the master of East-West fusion, **Ming Tsai** of Blue Ginger in Wellesley, and the omnipresent **Todd English,** who owns Olives in Charlestown, Bonfire and Kingfish Hall in Boston, and several Figs locations in the Boston area. Known for his lusty, Italian-inspired food, English has diversified across the country, with additional restaurants in New York, Connecticut, Washington, DC, and Las Vegas.

Other disciples and friends of Julia Child (a category that includes most of Boston's chefs) with recent cookbooks to bolster the fame of their already accomplished and much-lauded restaurants include **Jody Adams** of Rialto and blu (*In the Hands of Chef*) and the chef for whom she was sous chef, **Gordon Hamersley** of Hamersleys Bistro (*Bistro Cooking at Home*). **Chris Schlesinger** of East Coast Grill is now author or co-author of seven cookbooks, most of them devoted to the pleasures of grilling (such as *Let the Flames Begin*). Schlesinger is also a contributing editor to *Saveur* magazine. Pho République serves top-notch southeast Asian fusion cooking, but chef/owner **Didi Emmons** is best known to her reading public as a champion of meatless dining (*Vegetarian Planet* and *Entertaining for a Vegetarian Planet*). The father figure of Boston dining, **Jasper White,** is credited with helping to launch nouvelle cuisine in Boston in the early 1980s but has since simplified his outlook. The author of *Lobster at Home* operates Jasper Whites Summer Shack, one of the most casual fine-dining establishments around.

White's collaborator in Boston's culinary revolution was **Lydia Shire,** now the widely hailed owner of two of the citys most upscale and formal restaurants, the venerable Locke-Ober (established in the 1870s) and the newer Excelsior (established in 2003). **Ken Oringer** of Clio is already legendary for the sheer complexity of his tasting menus, which sometimes run to 11 courses. **Michael Schlow** of Radius and Via Matta exercises the same kind of exacting control as Oringer, but with pared-down gestures that read as simple luxury.

Several of the city's most dynamic chefs represent unusual, if not unique, approaches to fusion cuisine. **Thomas John** of Mantra brings a French-Italian touch to the flavors of the Indian subcontinent, while **Paul OConnell** of Chez Henri explores the intersection of French bistro cooking and Cuban traditions in his re-creation of pre-Castro haute Havana dining.

BOSTON WINE EXPO

Just as winter turns nasty at the end of January and the beginning of February, Bostonians ignore the weather and turn out by the hundreds for the citys biggest gastronomic blowouts of the year: the Friday night Anthony Spinazzola Gala, followed immediately by the two-day Boston Wine Expo.

The Spinazzola Gala, named in honor of the late *Boston Globe* food and wine critic, raises about $600,000 each year for hunger-relief agencies, programs for the homeless, and scholarships for students at eight area culinary schools. The black-tie evening at the World Trade Center features 120 stations where some of Boston's leading chefs prepare signature dishes from their restaurants while winemakers pour some of their best bottles. Boston foodies take advantage of the gala to keep current with the local dining scene.

For wine-lovers, the gala is just a warm-up for two days of seminars, lectures, and tastings. The Trade Center is transformed overnight into the citys most extensive wine bar. Already the largest consumer wine event in the country, the Boston Wine Expo gets more ambitious every year, attracting more than 440 wineries from a dozen countries. In the most recent edition, winemakers and their marketing representatives poured more than 1,800 different wines for consumer tastings. The Grand Tasting, which takes place for four hours on each of the event's two days (with two extra hours daily for the wine trade), is considered one of the top American showcases for wine producers. Consumers not only get the chance to sample a range of wines, but also garner advice on serving, pricing, and choosing the right vintage.

During the tasting hours, Boston-area chefs, food journalists, and cookbook authors provide cooking demonstrations on three stages, while the seminar rooms fill with groups discussing such subjects as Washington State's red wines and the differences between single-quinta (farm) ports and simple vintage ports. (Most seminars include extensive tastings.) Seminars vary from year to year, often highlighting a specific spectacular vintage from a classic region. (One recent seminar featured tastings of ten Grand Cru Classé wines from Bordeaux producers, paired with their second-tier wines of the same outstanding vintage.) Each seminar has a fee in addition to the general admission ticket. A vintner's dinner is served each night for a select 150 ticket holders, who dine on five to seven courses, each paired with a wine from the sponsoring vintner.

Tickets to the Spinazzola Gala and the Boston Wine Expo go on sale in the fall preceding the events. For information, visit www.wine-expos.com/boston or www.spinazzola.org.

CHOWDERFEST

Chowder competitions come and chowder competitions go, but Boston's civic celebration of clam chowder during the annual Fourth of July-week Harborfest tops them all. Its a bad day for quahogs, littlenecks, and steamers when restaurants from all over the metropolitan area gather on City Hall Plaza to ladle out more than 1,000 gallons (in 2-ounce servings) of New Englands signature clam chowder to more than 11,000 self-anointed experts. The prize consists of bragging rights to the title of Boston's Best Chowder for at least a year —rights prominently exercised on a number of menus in the city. To keep the same recipe from leading the field year after year, an establishment that has won three times (Mass Bay Company, Turner Fisheries at the Westin Hotel, and the Chart House) accepts induction into the Chowderfest Hall of Fame and retires from competition.

New Englanders have an almost mystical relationship with clam chowder, considering the inclusion of tomatoes (or worse, tomato juice) a form of regional sacrilege that only a New Yorker would commit. More than a century and a half ago, Herman Melville devoted a long passage in *Moby-Dick* to the pleasures of chowder. Faced with the grim grub of a whaling voyage, his protagonist Ishmael recalled the perfect chowder in a reverie: Oh sweet friends! Hearken to me. It was made of small juicy clams, scarcely bigger than hazelnuts, mixed with pounded ship biscuit, and salted pork cut up into little flakes; the whole enriched with butter, and plentifully seasoned with pepper and salt.

The whaling ships are gone, but clam chowder remains. Nowadays, the winners include milk or cream, some sautéed onions, and slices or chunks of potato. Ships biscuit has (fortunately) given way to flour for thickening. The Chowderfest usually takes place in the days immediately following July 4 as one of the crowning events of Harborfest.

GOOD FOOD, GOOD CAUSES

Splashy social events like the Spinazzola Gala give chefs and their restaurants a lot of exposure while also raising funds for charity. But many Boston chefs and restaurateurs work behind the scenes throughout the year on causes that range from nutritional education to feeding patients living with AIDS to building commercial networks that help regional family farmers stay in business.

You can spot the members of the Greater Boston chapter of Chefs Collaborative by their menus, which almost always credit local farmers, fishermen, herbalists, foragers, and distributors for the ingredients used in their kitchens. Its all part of the sustainable agriculture focus of the organization. By dealing directly with small producers, the restaurants get the pick of the harvest and the artisanal producers get to stay in business. Some of the names that signal the finest in their respective fields are Woodburys clams (aka Pat's

Clams), produce from Verrill Farms, and cheeses from around the world aged at and distributed by Formaggio Kitchen. One of the more prominent fund-raising events of Chefs Collaborative is the outdoor grilling festival in early July at the Seaport Hotel, where a dozen or more chefs from exclusive restaurants don their barbecue garb for Chefs in Shorts. For information, visit www.seaport.hotel.

Many restaurant staffers quietly donate time to such organizations as Share Our Strength, teaching nutrition classes and the like. They and their establishments are more visible in raising funds for direct hunger-relief programs such as the Greater Boston Food Bank, which gives away the equivalent of 16 million meals per year in eastern Massachusetts. The annual Taste of Boston extravaganza, held on Boston Common each September, offers dishes from more than 50 Boston-area restaurants for tickets costing $1-$3 each. Each $10 raised provides meals for five needy people. For the Super Hunger Brunch, usually held the weekend before Valentine's Day, about 50 restaurants donate the food and their employees donate their time for an extravagant brunch. All proceeds go to the Food Bank. For information see www.gbfb.org.

Another key charity supported by the Boston restaurant community is Community Servings, a program that delivers nutritionally tailored meals to men, women, and children either infected with or affected by AIDS. About 3,500 lunches and dinners are delivered weekly. Many restaurant professionals donate their time and sometimes their kitchens for food preparation. During late October and November, nearly 150 restaurants bake and sell pies for the Pie in the Sky fundraiser for Community Servings. For details, visit www.servings.org.

The annual Scooper Bowl relies on the region's largest ice cream producers rather than the city's chefs. The three-day event on Boston Common during the second weekend in June dishes out more than 10 tons of ice cream to about 50,000 ice cream lovers. Considered the unofficial start of summer by Bostonians, the Scooper Bowl raises money for the cancer cure and research work of the Jimmy Fund and the Dana-Farber Cancer Institute. For information, see www.jimmyfund.org.

since been called the "Boston Massacre." In 1773, the Boston Tea Party dumped East Indian tea into the bay in a dramatic protest against restriction of colonial trade by British governors. Great Britain closed the port in retaliation. The course of history was set.

In April 1775, British General Thomas Gage decided to march on Concord to capture military supplies and overwhelm the countryside. During the night of April 18-19, Paul Revere, William Dawes, and Samuel Prescott spread the news to Lexington and Concord in a ride immortalized, somewhat inaccurately, by Henry Wadsworth Longfellow. The Revolutionary War had begun in earnest; the Battle of Bunker Hill followed the battles of Lexington and Concord. On March 17, 1776, General William Howe, commander of the British forces, evacuated the city.

Boston's list of distinguished native sons includes John Hancock, Samuel Adams, Paul Revere, Henry Ward Beecher, Edward Everett Hale, Ralph Waldo Emerson, William Lloyd Garrison, Oliver Wendell Holmes (father and son), and hundreds of others.

Mention Boston, and many people automatically think of the gentry of Beacon Hill, with their elegant homes and rigid social code. However, the Irish have long had a powerful influence in Boston's politics and personality, while a stroll through an Italian neighborhood in the North End will be like stepping back to the old country.

Boston today manages to retain its heritage and charm while thriving in the modern age. Urban renewal and increased construction have reversed an almost 40-year slump that plagued Boston earlier in the 20th century. With more than 100 universities, colleges, and trade and vocational schools in the area, Boston is a city as full of vigor and promise for the future as it is rich with the past.

Public Transportation

Buses, subway, and elevated trains (Massachusetts Bay Transportation Authority), visitor pass available, phone 617/722-3200. Information phone toll-free 800/235-6426

Airport Logan International Airport; weather 617/936-1234; cash machines in Terminals A, B, C

Information Phone 617/561-1800 or toll-free 800/235-6426.

Lost and found Phone 617/561-1714

Airlines Aer Lingus, Air Canada/Air Canada Jazz, Air France, Air Jamaica, AirTran, Alaska Airlines, Alitalia, America West, American, American Eagle, ATA, British Airways, Cape Air, Continental, Delta Air Lines, Delta Connection/Atlantic Coast, Delta Connection/Com Air, Delta Shuttle (LaGuardia.), Delta Shuttle/Comair (Washington, DC), Icelandair KLM, Lufthansa, Midwest, Northwest, Qantas, SATA, Song, Swiss, TACA, United, United Express/Atlantic Coast, US Airways Shuttle (LaGuardia & DC), US Airways, US Airways Express, Virgin Atlantic

---

Boston Fun Facts

- Boston boasts the nation's first subway, built in 1897.
- The Boston University Bridge (on Commonwealth Avenue) is the only place in the world where a boat can sail under a train driving under a car driving under an airplane.
- Boston Common became the first public park in 1634.
- The first post office, free public school, and public library were all founded in Boston.

What to See and Do

Bay State Cruise Company. *Commonwealth Pier, World Trade Center, 184 High St, Boston (02110).* *Phone 617/748-1428. www.boston-ptown.com.* All-day sail to Provincetown and Cape Cod from Commonwealth Pier. The 2 1/2- and 3 1/2-hour harbor and island cruises aboard *Spirit of Boston* highlight adventure and history. (May-Columbus Day, daily) Contact Bay State Cruise Company. **$$$$**

Bean Pot Hockey. *Fleet Center, Boston.* The Bean Pot refers to games between four Boston-based teams: Boston College, Boston University, Harvard University, and Northeastern University. Attending a hockey game between any two of the four is sure to be an intense experience, because all four teams compete vigorously for the Bean Pot each year. If you like to see body checking up close, get the lowest seats you can afford at any of the four corners of the rink. (Oct-Apr) **$$$$**

Berklee Performing Center at Berklee College of Music. *136 Massachusetts Ave, Boston (02115). Take the Green Line ("T") to the Hynes Convention Center/ICA stop. Exit left onto Massachusetts Ave and cross Boylston St. The Berklee Performance Center is about 30 yards from the corner. Phone 617/747-2261. www.berkleebpc. com.* The Berklee Performance Center is the performing arm of the Berklee College of Music, a prestigious Boston institution. Housed in a 1,200-seat renovated theater, this state-of-the-art venue hosts both student performances and national concerts, most notably featuring jazz and pop musicians. Ticket prices for nationally known performers are higher than admission fees for student performances. **$$**

Bernard Toale Gallery. *450 Harrison Ave, Boston (02118). Phone 617/482-2477. www.bernardtoalegallery. com.* The Bernard Toale Gallery offers you an opportunity to view (and buy, if you're so inclined) paintings, drawings, photographs, and sculptures from some of todays hottest artists. Both established artists and select up-and-comers display works at the gallery, so you get a chance to take in cutting-edge works that have not yet made their way into contemporary art museums. Look for occasional readings, videos, and fashion shows, too. Allow one or two hours. (Tues-Sat; Aug by appointment only; closed Sat in July) **FREE**

Bible Exhibit. *Belvidere St, Boston (02115). Opposite the Prudential Center.* Nondenominational exhibit; audiovisual activities; rare Biblical treasures; historical timeline; large Plexiglas wall-map with lighted journeys of six Biblical figures; historic editions; children's story corner; exploring center for reference; film and slide program on the hour. (Wed-Sun; closed Jan 1, Thanksgiving, Dec 25)

Blue Hills Reservation. *695 Hillside St, Milton (02186). Phone 617/698-1802. www.mass.gov/mdc/blue.htm.* Blue Hills offers more than 200 miles of trails in the 6,500-acre reservation, about a third of which are set aside for mountain biking, making the other two-thirds ideal for hiking, bird-watching, and sightseeing. Climb Summit Road (which is paved) 635 feet to get to Great Blue Hill and the stunning view that rewards you there. In winter, the reservation opens for downhill skiing. (Wed-Sun) **FREE** On reservation is the

Blue Hills Trailside Museum. *Phone 617/333-0690.* Visitor center for the 7,000-acre Blue Hills Reservation. Deer, turkeys, otters, snakes, owls, and honeybees. Exhibit hall with natural science/history displays, including a Native American wigwam; viewing tower. Activities include hikes, films, and animal programs. Special events include maple sugaring (March), Hawks Weekend (September), and Honey Harvest (October). Visitor center and buildings (Wed-Sun 10 am-5 pm) **$**

Blue Man Group. *74 Warrenton St, Boston (02116). Phone 617/931-2787. www.blueman.com.* Blue Man Group is a percussion (drums) band and performance group that's literally blueall three members cover themselves in blue body paint. The group performs by thumping on drums, banging on barrels, and pounding on pipes. The heart-pounding, entertaining, dramatic performance includes audience members (although no one is forced to participate against his will); if you so choose, you may even get painted, too! Performances last just over two hours. (Closed Mon-Tues) **$$$$**

Boston African American National Historic Site. *8 Smith Court, Boston (02114). Smith Ct, off Joy St on Beacon Hill. Phone 617/742-5415. www.nps.gov/boaf.* Includes **African Meeting House.** Part of the Museum of Afro-American History. Built by free black Bostonians in 1806, the building was an educational and religious center and site of the founding of the New England Anti-Slavery Society in 1832. (May-Sept, daily; rest of year, Mon-Sat) Thirty-minute tour (Memorial Day-Labor Day: Mon-Sat; rest of year: by appointment) of Meeting House by museum staff. **FREE** Meeting house is the starting point for

Black Heritage Trail. *14 Beacon St, Boston (02114). Phone 617/742-5415.* Marked walking tour conducted by the National Park Service, past sites in the Beacon Hill section that relate the history of 19th-century black Boston. Brochure and maps are at National Park Visitor Center. Two-hour guided tours by National Park Service (by appointment). **FREE**

Boston Ballet. *270 Tremont St, Boston (02116). Phone 617/695-6955. www.bostonballet.com.* A delight for children and adults, the Boston Ballet offers classic and more contemporary performances by a company of some of the finest dancers in the world. If you're visit-

ing Boston in late November or December, don't miss *The Nutcracker,* performed annually before more than 140,000 people, the largest audience for a ballet production in the world. (Performances held Oct-May) **$$$$**

Boston Beer Museum. *30 Germania St, Jamaica Plain (02130). Take the Orange Line ("T") to the Stony Brook stop. Phone 617/522-9080.* Take a tour of the Boston Beer Museum (formerly the Haffenreffer Brewery) and discover the critical details of the brewing process. And check out all the museum's artifacts, which span two centuries of brewing. At the end of the tour, you're offered a sampling of Samuel Adams beers, the host company of the museum. (Tours Thurs-Sat) **$**

Boston Breakers. *200 Highland Ave, 4th Floor, Needham (02494). Harry Agganis Way at Commonwealth Ave. Take the Green Line B to the Pleasant St stop. Phone 617/931-2000. www.bostonbreakers.com.* The professional women's soccer team in the Boston area plays at Nickerson Field at Boston University. Unlike some professional sports that pay extraordinary base salaries that can lead to isolation among players, Breakers players are extremely accessible, offering autographs, appearing at youth soccer clinics and camps, and spending time in the community to promote the sport. (Closed Apr-Sept)

Boston Bruins (NHL). *TD Bank North Garden, 100 Legends Way, Boston (02114). Take the Green/Orange Line (the T) to North Station. Phone 617/624-1000. www.bostonbruins.com.* The Bruins are one of the great hockey traditions in the NHL; in fact, the team was one of the original six teams in the league. In the early 1940s, the Bruins won back-to-back Stanley Cup championships, and the team won the Cup again 30 years later, when Bobby Orr scored a game-winning goal in overtime. Today, you can spend an exciting evening of Bruins hockey with family or friends; if you like to see a lot of body checking, try to get a seat as close to the ice as you can afford on one of the four corners of the rink. If you can manage the high price tag, pick up a Bobby Orr game sweater at the Bruins gift shop. **$$$$**

Boston by Little Feet. *1 Faneuil Hall Sq, Boston (02114). Phone 617/367-2345. www.bostonbyfoot.com.* Designed especially for 6- to 12-year-olds (accompanied by an adult), Boston by Little Feet is a 60-minute walking tour that follows the Freedom Trail and explores local architecture and history. You can take the tour regardless of the weather, but be sure to bring rain boots and an umbrella during inclement weather.

Every young walker gets a free Explorers Map and Guide. (May-Oct, Sat-Mon; closed Nov-Apr) **$$**

Boston Celtics (NBA). *TD Bank North Garden, 100 Legends Way, Boston (02114). Take the Green/Orange Line (the T) to North Station. Phone 617/624-1000. www.nba.com/celtics.* The Celtics were more of a must-see tourist attraction when they played in Boston Garden. Today, playing at TD Banknorth Garden (formerly the Fleet Center), the Celts seem less impressive. Still, with 16 NBA championships notched in its belt, the team boasts more NBA titles than any other franchise. (Oct-June). **$$$$**

Boston College. *140 Commonwealth Ave, Chestnut Hill (02467). Phone 617/552-8000. www.bc.edu.* (1863) (14,500 students) On campus is

> **Bapst Library.** *140 Commonwealth Ave, Chestnut Hill (02467). Phone 617/552-3200; fax 617/552-0510.* English Collegiate Gothic building with fine stained glass. Rare books display; changing exhibits. (Summer, Mon-Fri 9 am-5 pm; rest of year, daily)
>
> **Boston College Football.** *At Alumni Stadium. Phone 617/552-3000.* Although Boston College hasnt won a national championship since 1940, as the only Division I-A football team in the area, BC football remains a fall tradition in Boston. Tickets can be difficult to obtain as game day nears, so plan to buy your tickets online ahead of time. Keep yourself entertained before the game by spotting the BC superfans—students and alums who paint their bodies, wear multicolored wigs, and carry in-your-face signs meant for TV cameras. (Weekends in fall) **$$$$**

⭐ **Boston Common.** *Beacon and Tremont sts, Boston (02108). Take the Red or Green Line (T) to Park St.* As the oldest public park in the United States, Boston Common is steeped in history. Established in 1640, Bostonians used the Common as a pasture for grazing their cattle; later, the colonial militia used it to train soldiers, and it even served as a British military camp. Colonists gathered to hear speeches, witness public hangings, and watch spirited fencing duels. Today, the Common's 45 acres are still a vibrant center of the city—a perfect place to stroll, in-line skate, play Frisbee, catch a free concert, or enjoy a picnic (watch out for dog droppings, however). The park is a perfect place to begin walking the Freedom Trail; the park itself is loaded with signs, plaques, and monuments, most notably that of Robert Gould Shaw, who led the Union Armys 54th Massachusetts Colored Regiment, the first all-black army unit in the United States. (Daily) **FREE** Also here are

Boston Common Frog Pond Rink. *Phone 617/635-2120.* Ice skating abounds each winter in Boston, with outdoor rinks spread throughout the city. Frog Pond, the largest of these rinks, is a natural mud pond on Boston Common during spring, summer, and fall. From November to March, however, the city transforms the wading pool into an enormous outdoor skating rink and maintains it all winter, regardless of the weather. At the rink, you can rent skates ($), get the feeling back in your toes by standing in the warming room, and use the public rest room. Other skating rinks in the area—all of which are free—include Bajko Memorial Rink (Boston), Turtle Pond Parkway, phone 617/364-9188; Devine Memorial Rink (Boston), Morrissey Blvd, phone 617/436-4356; Porazzo Memorial Rink (Boston), Constitution Beach, phone 617/567-9571; and Simoni Memorial Rink (Cambridge), Gore St, phone 617/354-9523. (Mid-Nov-mid-Mar daily; closed in spring, summer, and fall) **$**

Central Burying Ground. *Boylston and Tremont sts, Boston (02116).* The grave of Gilbert Stuart, the painter, is here; technically not a part of the Common, although it's in it.

Swan Boats/Boston Public Garden. *Arlington, Boylston, Charles, and Beacon sts, Boston (02108). Take the Green Line to Arlington Station. Phone 617/522-1966.* The launching point for the swan boats is the Boston Public Garden (daily), the first botanical garden in the United States, with 24 acres featuring a splendid variety of flowers and ornamental shrubs that bloom from early April until mid-October. Entry to the Public Garden is free. Each swan boat, so named because its decorated with a larger-than-life swan, operates by pedal power (the drivers, not yours) for a 15-minute ride around the Public Garden Lagoon. (Daily) **$**

⭐ **Boston Harbor Islands National Recreation Area.** *Building 45, 349 Lincoln St, Hingham (02043). 45 minutes from downtown Boston via ferry. Phone 781/740-1605. bostonharborislands.areaparks.com.* The Boston Harbor Islands national park area encompasses several islands in Boston Harbor. Take the ferry to Georges Island (phone 617/227-4321); from there, a free water taxi sails you to Lovells, Peddocks, Gallops, Grape, and Bumpkin islands. The islands boast sand dunes, a freshwater pond, and unique wildlife habitats. Camp on Lovells Island (the only island that allows swimming) and Peddocks Island (the largest at 134 acres) by petitioning in writing for a permit from the Metropolitan District Commission; write to MDC Reservations and Historic Sites, 98 Taylor St, Dorchester, MA 02122. Note that sites don't have electricity; you must carry in your own fresh water; and you're responsible for carrying out your trash when you leave. (May-mid-Oct) **$$**

Boston Massacre Monument. *206 Washington St, Boston (02109).* Commemorates this 1770 event, which has been called the origin of the Revolution.

Boston Public Library. *700 Boylston St, Boston (02116). Phone 617/536-5400. www.bpl.org.* (1895) This Italian Renaissance building by Charles McKim includes a central courtyard and fountain. Mural decorations, bronze doors, sculpture. Contemporary addition (1972), by Philip Johnson, houses large circulating library, recordings, and films. Film and author programs; exhibits. Central Library (Mon-Thurs 9 am-9 pm; Fri-Sat 9 am-5 pm)

⭐ **Boston Red Sox (MLB).** *Fenway Park, 4 Yawkey Way, Boston (02215). Near Brookline Ave; take the Green Line (the T or subway) to Kenmore or Fenway. Phone 617/482-4769. www.redsox.mlb.com.* Going to Fenway isn't just about watching men play baseball; its about steeping yourself in the tradition of one of the finest ball clubs in history. Fenway, built in 1901, is home of the Green Monster, the 37-foot, left-field wall where balls disappear in blazing green reflections. Cy Young pitched a perfect game at Fenway in 1904, and in 1914, young Babe Ruth came to play for the Sox. Since the Red Sox first began wearing numbers on their uniforms in 1931, the team has retired the uniforms of five players: Joe Cronin, Ted Williams, Bobby Doerr, Carl Yastremski, and Carlton Fisk. (Mar-Oct) **$$$$**

Boston Symphony Orchestra/Boston Pops. *301 Massachusetts Ave, Boston (02115). Phone 617/266-1492. www.bso.org.* Symphony Hall, with its perfect acoustics, is home to both the Boston Symphony Orchestra (BSO) and the Boston Pops (a livelier version of the symphony), both of which are world-class orchestras. If the pricey tickets (up to $120) are an obstacle, stop by the box office at 9 am Friday or 5 pm Tuesday or Thursday—you may be able to pick up a special ticket for just $8, although it certainly won't be the best seat in the house. The Boston Pops also give free outdoor concerts in the Hatch Shell Amphitheater on the Esplanade during Harborfest on the Fourth

of July. If you're not in town while either orchestra is playing, find out which musical act is playing at Symphony Hall so that you can appreciate its terrific design. (BSO performances Oct-Apr; Pops performances May-early July, mid- to late Dec) **$$$$**

Boston Tours from Suburban Hotels. *3 Copley Pl, Waltham (02453). Phone 781/899-1454. www.bostontours.com.* Escorted bus tours departing from suburban hotels and motels along I-95/Hwy 128. Also departures from metrowest suburban hotels in Natick/Framingham area. Tours follow the Freedom Trail and include stops at Old North Church, "Old Ironsides," Faneuil Hall Marketplace, and Cambridge. Six-hour tour (daily). **$$$$**

Boston University. *595 Commonwealth Ave, Boston (02115). Phone 617/353-2300. www.bu.edu.* (1839) (28,000 students) The information center is located at 771 Commonwealth Avenue in the George Sherman Union. Also located here is the George Sherman Union Gallery. Mugar Memorial Library houses papers of Dr. Martin Luther King Jr., as well as those of Robert Frost, Isaac Asimov, and other writers and artists. Boston University Art Gallery exhibits at the School for the Arts, 855 Commonwealth Avenue. Campus tours from the Admissions Office, 121 Bay State Road.

Boston Women's Heritage Trail. *22 Holbrook St, Boston (02130). Phone 617/522-2872. www.bwht.org.* Women played an essential role in Boston's rich history, yet their contributions were often overlooked. The Boston Womens Heritage Trail (BWHT) leads you through Boston's historical, cultural, religious, and scientific sites, highlighting the critical part that women played in each. To walk the entire trail may take several days, but you can walk a portion of the trail and visit only the sites that interest you in just an hour or two. **FREE**

BostonWalks. *Phone 617/489-5020. bostonwalks.tripod. com.* Although several groups offer guided tours of Boston, those arranged by BostonWalks are among the most unique. Nearly every guided-tour company, including BostonWalks, offers historical tours, but where else can you find walking and biking tours of churches and synagogues, unique ethnic areas, universities, medical areas, high-tech areas, and Boston's delightful neighborhoods? Groups must include 15 to 55 participants, and tours last two to three hours. **$$$$**

Brush Hill Tours. *14 Charles St S, Boston (02116). Phone 781/986-6100; toll-free 800/343-1328. www. brushhilltours.com.* Fully lectured three-hour bus tours of Boston/Cambridge (late Mar-mid-Nov); 1/2-day tours of Lexington/Concord, Salem/Marblehead (mid-June-Oct), and Plymouth (May-Oct); full-day tours of Cape Cod (includes Provincetown) and Newport, Rhode Island (June-Sept). Also 1 1/2-hour tours along Freedom Trail aboard the Beantown Trolleys. Departures from major downtown hotels, Copley Square, and Boston Common (daily). **$$$$**

⭐ **Charles River Pathway (the Esplanade).** *Take the Red Line (T) to the Charles/MGHT stop.* The Charles River Pathway, a flat, smooth asphalt surface, extends 18 miles along the Charles River, connecting Boston and Cambridge and ending in Watertown. The view of the Charles River is stunning, and at certain times of the year you may see university crew teams training. Use the trail to run or walk, joining the hundreds of Bostonians who train there daily. To bike the path, rent a bike at Back Bay Bikes & Boards (Boston), 336 Commonwealth Ave, phone 617/247-2336, www.backbaybicycles.com; Community Bicycle Supply (Boston), 496 Tremont St, phone 617/542-8623, www.communitybicycle.com; Cambridge Bicycle (Cambridge), 259 Massachusetts Ave, phone 617/876-6555; or Ata Cycle (Cambridge), 1773 Massachusetts Ave, phone 617/354-0907, www.atabike.com. The trail is also perfect for in-line skating, even if you're a novice. Rent blades at Beacon Hill Skate Shop (Boston), 135 Charles St, phone 617/482-7400; or Blades Board & Skate, with locations in Boston and Cambridge, phone 617/437-6300, www.blades.com. (Always open) **FREE**

⭐ **Children's Museum of Boston.** *300 Congress St, Boston (02110). Phone 617/426-8855. www.bostonkids.org.* Advertised as "Boston's best place for kids 0-10," the Children's Museum lives up to its billing with interactive exhibits that highlight science, technology, art, and culture. Exhibitions range from re-creations of favorite kids' stories, a kid-size construction site, and a messy artist studio to performances on KidStage, a Latin American supermarket, a real loom and weaving area, a full-size wigwam, and a rock climbing area. Offerings change periodically, and three or four are always housed outdoors in the Science Playground. Each Friday from 3 to 5 pm and Saturday and Sunday from 2 to 4 pm, take the ZOOMSci challenge at the ZOOM Zone within the museum: you solve puzzles and work through a variety of math challenges. Note that admission is just $1 on Fridays from 5 to 9 pm. Plan on at least half a day. (Sat-Thurs 10 am-5 pm, Fri 10 am-9 pm; closed Thanksgiving, Dec 25) **$$**

Community Boating, Inc. *21 David Mugar Way, Boston (02114). Embankment Rd on the Charles River Esplanade between the Hatch Shell and the Longfellow Bridge. Phone 617/523-7406. www.community-boating.org.* Whether you're an experienced sailor or have always wanted to learn, you can spend a day or two sailing while in Boston. Community Boating runs the largest and oldest public sailing program in the country. Purchasing a two-day membership allows you unlimited use of boats and sailing instruction, along with windsurfing and kayaking. Also check out Boston Sailing Center, Lewis Wharf, phone 617/227-4198, www.bostonsailingcenter.com, which is more expensive but is open year-round, even in the chilliest weather. (Apr-Nov, daily; closed Dec-Mar) **$$$$**

Copley Place. *100 Huntington Ave, Boston (02116). Phone 617/369-5000. www.shopcopleyplace.com.* With more than 100 stores and a glass atrium in a beautiful setting, Copley Place is all about upscale, including names like Neiman Marcus, Louis Vuitton, Christian Dior, and Gucci. If you're looking for dinner and a movie, Copley Place fills that bill, too, with ten restaurants and an 11-screen theater. (Daily)

Duck Tours. *3 Copley Pl, Boston (02199). Phone toll-free 800/226-7442. www.bostonducktours.com.* Boston Duck Tours take you from land to sea in a World War II half-boat, half-truck vehicle known as a Duck. Your conDUCKtor starts the 80-minute tour on land, leading you past Boston Common, the golden-domed State House, Public Gardens, the Big Dig, Faneuil Hall Marketplace, Boston's North End, Government Center, Copley Square, Prudential Tower, Newbury Street, Bunker Hill, and the Fleet Center. The Duck then transforms into an amphibious vehicle and dives into the Charles River for more sightseeing. (Apr-Nov; on the hour from 9 am to one hour before sunset) **$$$$**

Fenway Park Tours. *Fenway Park, 4 Yawkey Way, Boston (02215). Phone 617/236-6666. boston.redsox.mlb.com.* Take a tour of Fenway Park, not only the oldest park in Major League Baseball but also the most charming. Soak in over 100 years of Red Sox history and tradition as you stroll next to the famous Green Monster (Fenway's 37-foot left-field wall that obscures even the easiest pop-ups), take a tour of the press box, and stand on the warning track. The brick stadium is aging by today's standards—views are obstructed, seats are small, and plush boxes are rare—so it, too, will likely be torn down to make way for a new one. Take a tour while you still can. (Daily 9 am-4 pm) **$$$**

Filene's Basement. *426 Washington St, Boston (02108). Take the Red or Orange Line (T) to the Downtown Crossing stop. Phone 617/348-7974. www.filenesbasement.com.* Located directly beneath Filene's Department Store, the Basement is famous for its automatic markdowns: after two weeks at full price, merchandise falls by percentages until, five weeks later, its 75 percent off. (Any unsold merchandise is then given to charity.) Filene's Basement is also the site of an annual wedding gown sale—brides-to-be race each other to racks in the hopes of finding the right dress for a fraction of its retail price. (Mon-Fri 9:30 am-8 pm, Sat 9 am-8 pm, Sun 11 am-7 pm; closed Easter, Thanksgiving, Dec 25)

Franklin Park Golf Course (William J. Devine Golf Course). *1 Circuit Dr, Dorchester (02121). Take the Orange Line (T) to Forest Hills Station and board the #16 bus, which has a stop right along the parking lot. Phone 617/265-4084. www.sterlinggolf.com.* This 6,009-yard, par-70 golf course lies within Boston's city limits and is the second-oldest public golf course in the US. Rates are reasonable, especially for kids under 18, and club rentals are just $10. The course is wide open but demanding, with some steep hills. Gram Slam winner Bobby Jones practiced at Franklin Park when he was a student at Harvard. (Daily dawn-dusk; closed for snow and inclement weather) **$$$$$**

Franklin Park Zoo. *1 Franklin Park Rd, Dorchester (02121). S on Jamaicaway, E on Hwy 203. Phone 617/541-5466. www.zoonewengland.org.* "Bird's World" indoor/outdoor aviary complex with natural habitats; African tropical forest; hilltop range with camels, antelopes, zebras, mouflon; children's zoo. (Daily; closed Jan 1, Thanksgiving, Dec 25) **$$**

Frederick Law Olmsted National Historic Site. *99 Warren St, Brookline (02445). Phone 617/566-1689. www.nps.gov/frla.* Former home and office of the founder of landscape architecture in America. Site archives contain documentation of the firm's work. Also here are landscaped grounds designed by Olmsted. Guided tours of historic offices. (Fri-Sun)

⭐ **Freedom Trail.** *Phone 617/242-5642. www.thefreedomtrail.org.* This two- or three-hour walking tour takes you past Boston's most famous historical sites while also meandering through the city's vibrant neighborhoods. The Freedom Trail begins at Boston Common (see) and ends at the Bunker Hill Monument, with more than a dozen sites in between. Red bricks or red paint mark the trail, which you can follow on your own (free brochures are available) or with guided assistance. Purchase the official Freedom

Trail Guidebook ($$) as your step-by-step guide, travel with earphones and take an audio tour ($$$), or take a guided tour that's led by historic characters in costume ($$$). Dress appropriately—the weather in Boston can change rapidly. **FREE**

State House. *24 Beacon St, Boston (02114). Phone 617/727-3676.* The Massachusetts State House (which replaced the Old State House, next to the site of the Boston Massacre) is an architectural marvel. As you travel around Boston, you can't miss the golden dome (sheathed in 23-carat gold leaf) of the state house that replaced the original copper. Designed by Charles Bulfinch and built on land owned by John Hancock, patriot Paul Revere, and Governor Samuel Adams laid the cornerstone on July 4, 1795. Tours are free. (Mon-Fri 10 am-3:30 pm; closed state holidays) **FREE**

Park Street Church. *1 Park St, Boston (02108). Phone 617/523-3383.* (1809) Often called "Brimstone Corner" because brimstone for gunpowder was stored here during the War of 1812. William Lloyd Garrison delivered his first antislavery address here in 1829. (mid-June-Aug, limited hours; Sun services all year)

Granary Burying Ground. *Tremont and Bromfield sts, Boston (02108). Take the T to Park St, walk 1 block on Tremont St. Phone 617/635-4505.* Although Granary is Boston's third-oldest cemetery, it is, perhaps, its most famous. Revolutionary War patriots Paul Revere, John Hancock, Samuel Adams, and Peter Faneuil (whose headstone is marked Peter Funal) all lie here. The name stems from a grain storage building (called a granary) that used to sit nearby. (Daily 9 am-7 pm) **FREE**

King's Chapel and Burying Ground. *58 Tremont St, Boston (02108). Phone 617/227-2155.* King's Chapel, started by the Massachusetts Royal Governor who had no desire to worship in a Puritan church, has held church services at its location longer than any other church in the United States. When the congregation outgrew the church in 1754, a new building was erected around the old, which was then dismantled. The Burying Ground next door is the oldest cemetery in Boston. Stop in for concerts on Tuesdays at 12:15 pm and Sundays at 5 pm. (Daily; closed Sun-Fri in winter) **FREE**

Site of the first US free public school. *School St at City Hall Ave, Boston (02108). Blue or Orange Line.* A mosaic in the sidewalk marks the site of the first free US public school. The original building was demolished to make room for the expansion of King's Chapel. The school, now known as the Boston Latin School, was moved across the street.

Statue of Benjamin Franklin. *School St at City Hall Ave, Boston (02108).* This, Boston's first portrait statue, was created by Richard S. Greenough in 1856.

Old South Meeting House. *310 Washington St, Boston (02108). Corner of Washington and Milk sts. Phone 617/482-6439.* Built as a Puritan meeting house (or church), colonists congregated at the Old South Meeting House each year from 1771 to 1775 to mark the death of those killed in the Boston Massacre and listen to speeches by prominent colonists. The most important date in Old South's history, however, is December 16, 1773, when 5,000 colonists gathered at the church to protest the British tax on tea and decide on a course of action. From there, men dressed as Native Americans, snuck onto three ships laden with tea on Griffin's Wharf, and dumped all the tea overboard. Restored in 1997, the church no longer has an active congregation but is still a gathering place for political debate. An interactive exhibit called Voices of Protest recalls the Old South Meeting House's historic legacy. (Daily; closed Jan 1, Thanksgiving, Dec 24-25) **$**

Old State House/Site of Boston Massacre. *206 Washington St, Boston (02108). Phone 617/720-1713.* The Old State House (not to be confused with the golden-dome new State House) was originally built as the headquarters of the British government in Boston and is Boston's oldest surviving public building. Inside, the Bostonian Society operates a museum that reflects the prominent role the Old State House played in the American Revolution. The Massachusetts Assembly met there and debated political issues in front of all citizens who wanted to observe. After these issues were decided, politicians read summaries—including the Declaration of Independence on July 18, 1776—from the House's balcony. The balcony hovers above the spot where the Boston Massacre occurred in 1770, when British troops shot into a crowd that had gathered to hear a proclamation. There, in a small triangle surrounded by dense city traffic, the site of the massacre is marked with a circle of paving stones. Plan on one hour for a tour. (Daily 9 am-6 pm; closed Jan 1, Thanksgiving, Dec 25) **$**

Faneuil Hall Marketplace. *4 S Market Bldg, 5th Fl, Boston (02109). Take the Blue or Green Line ("T") to Government Center, then walk across the plaza, down the long set of stairs, and across busy Congress St. Phone 617/523-1300.* Faneuil Hall Marketplace offers the best variety of shops and kiosks in Boston, housed in five buildings and several plazas. The central building, Quincy Market, is filled with dining options, from coffee to seafood and everything in between; many are open earlier and later than the shops. Look for delightful street performers even in winter months, and especially the rest of the year. Faneuil Hall (pronounced FAN-yal or FAN-yoo-ul) is more than just a shopping center: it has operated as a local marketplace since 1742, when wealthy merchant Peter Faneuil built and donated the marketplace to the city. The Hall is remembered as the site of town meetings that produced the policy of "no taxation without representation." Listen to a historical talk every half hour from 9:30 am to 4:30 pm in the second-floor auditorium. (Daily; closed Thanksgiving, Dec 25)

Paul Revere House. *19 North Sq, Boston (02113). Phone 617/523-2338.* Built in 1680 and well preserved today, the Paul Revere House is Boston's oldest building and includes authentic furnishings from the Revere family. This historical landmark offers a rare glimpse at colonial life, because few other houses from the period survived remodeling, fire damage, and demolition. At his house, Paul Revere plied his silversmith trade and sold his wares, often in exchange for food or livestock when case-strapped colonists couldnt pay. Although a staunch patriot, Revere was largely undistinguished among Sam Adams, John Hancock, and Ben Franklin. However, Revere's successful ride to Lexington and Concord on April 18, 1775, to warn of the approaching British army—a feat immortalized in Henry Wadsworth Longfellow's poem, "The Midnight Ride of Paul Revere"—made him one of the best-known American historic figures. (Mid-Apr-late Oct, daily 9:30 am-5:15 pm; early Nov-mid-Apr, daily 9:30 am-4:15 pm; closed Jan 1, Thanksgiving, Dec 25, Mon in Jan-Mar) **$**

Old North Church. *193 Salem St, Boston (02113). Phone 617/523-6676.* Old North Church is the oldest church in Boston and continues today as Christ Church, with an Episcopal congregation of 150 members. On April 18, 1775, in the steeple of Old North Church, church sexton Robert

Newman hung two lanterns to signal that the British Army was heading up the Charles River to Cambridge in order to march to Lexington and take possession of weapons stored there. When Paul Revere saw the signal, he jumped on his horse and rode to Lexington to warn the militia. The next day, the "shot heard 'round the world" was fired on Lexington Green, officially beginning the Revolutionary War. Sit in one of the box pews and listen to the ten-minute talk about the history of the church; its free, although donations are gladly accepted. Behind-the-scenes tours and other presentations are available by appointment for a fee. (Daily; closed holidays) **FREE**

Copp's Hill Burying Ground. *Hull and Snow Hill sts, Boston (02113). Take Causeway St to North Washington St. When North Washington becomes Commercial St, walk 2 more blocks, turn right, and climb the hill. Phone 617/635-4505.* Copp's Hill Burying Ground, named after William Copp, who owned the land, is the second-oldest burying ground in Boston. Robert Newman, who hung the lanterns in the steeple of Old North Church, is buried at Copp's Hill, as are the Mather family of Puritan ministers and a host of African Americans from the nearby New Guinea Community, who lie in unmarked graves. (Daily) **FREE**

Bunker Hill Monument. *Monument Sq, Charlestown (02129). Phone 617/242-5641.* Standing 221 feet high (that's 294 steps, with no elevator), the Bunker Hill Monument marks the site of the first major battle of the Revolutionary War on June 17, 1775. It was here that American Colonel William Prescott ordered his troops "not to fire until you see the whites of their eyes," so that no bullets would be wasted. The British won the battle but suffered heavy casualties, and that limited success encouraged the colonists to continue the fight. (Daily) **FREE**

USS *Constitution*. *Charlestown Navy Yard, Boston National Historical Park, Constitution Rd, Boston (02129). I-93 northbound exit 25 and follow signs across Charlestown bridge; southbound, exit 28 to Sullivan Sq and follow signs. Phone 617/426-1812.* The USS *Constitution*, the oldest commissioned warship in the world, got the nickname "Old Ironsides" during the War of 1812. Some 600 miles off the coast of Boston, it engaged the British HMS *Guerriere* in battle; while the *Guerriere* was so badly damaged that it had to be sunk and its

crew rescued, cannonballs merely bounced off the *Constitution's* sides, as if they were "made of iron," although they were actually made of three layers of oak. In 1830, the ship was saved from the scrap heap because of public response to Oliver Wendell Holmes's poem "Old Ironsides." It was restored in 1925 and today is available for daily tours. The museum next door offers hands-on exhibits, historic displays, and reenactments. (May-September: daily 9 am-6 pm, Oct-Apr: daily 10 am-5 pm)

Gibson House Museum. *137 Beacon St, Boston (02116). Phone 617/267-6338. www.thegibsonhouse.org.* Victorian townhouse with period furnishings. Tours (Wed-Sun afternoons; closed holidays). **$$**

Guided Walking Tours. Boston by Foot. *77 N Washington St, Boston (02113). Hull and Snow Hill sts. Phone 617/367-2345.* Ninety-minute architectural walking tours includes the heart of the Freedom Trail (daily); Beacon Hill (daily, departures vary); Victorian Back Bay Tour (Fri-Sun); North End (Fri-Sat); children's tour (daily); downtown Boston (Sun). All tours (May-Oct). Tour of the month each fourth Sun; custom tours. **$$$**

Guild of Boston Artists. *162 Newbury St, Boston (02116). Phone 617/536-7660.* Changing exhibits of paintings, graphics, and sculpture by New England artists. (Sun-Mon, by appointment only; closed Jan 1, Thanksgiving, Dec 25) **FREE**

Harborwalk. *www.bostonharborwalk.com.* A blue line guides visitors from the Old State House to the New England Aquarium, ending at the Boston Tea Party Ship and Museum, forming a walking tour with many stops in between.

Harrison Gray Otis House. *141 Cambridge St, Boston (02114). Enter from Lynde St. Phone 617/227-3956.* (1796) Otis, a lawyer and statesman, built this first of three houses designed for him by Charles Bulfinch. A later move to Beacon Hill left this house as a rooming house for 100 years. Restored to reflect Boston taste and decoration of 1796-1820. Some family furnishings are present. The house reflects the proportion and delicate detail Bulfinch introduced to Boston, strongly influencing the Federal style in New England. Museum. The headquarters for the Society for the Preservation of New England Antiquities is located here. Tours (Wed-Sun 11 am-4:30 pm). **$$**

Harvard Medical Area. *180 Longwood Ave, Cambridge (02115). Phone 617/432-1000.* One of the world's great centers of medicine.

Haymarket. *Blackstone St, Boston (02109). Around the corner from Faneuil Hall Marketplace; take the Orange or Green line to the Haymarket stop.* Rain or shine, winter or summer, Bostonians flock to Haymarket for the freshest fruits, vegetables, and seafood you've ever seen. If you do your shopping in a grocery store back home, you won't believe the differences in price (far lower) and quality (much higher) here. The market is bustling with lively scents and sounds, including languages from around the world. Haggling is the norm and remains friendly—you'll want three yellow peppers for $1, and the vendor will want to sell you six for $2. Start your day at Haymarket, buying a few pieces of fruit to snack on, and then meander through the city or walk the Freedom Trail. (Fri-Sat) **FREE**

Institute of Contemporary Art. *100 Northern Ave, Boston (02115). Opposite Prudential Center. Phone 617/266-5152. www.icaboston.org.* The Institute of Contemporary Art offers some of the world's finest modern art exhibits. Because no collection is permanent, every trip to the Institute is likely to be different from the last. Note that museum admission is free every Thursday after 5 pm, as is the *Viewpoints* series, held at 6:30 pm on certain Thursdays, in which artists, staff members, and others speak to visitors about particular works of art. Allow two to four hours for a visit. (Tues-Sun; closed Mon, Thanksgiving, Dec 25, Jan 1, between exhibitions) **$$**

Isaac Royall House. *15 George St, Medford (02155). 3/4 mile S off I-93. Phone 781/396-9032. www.royallhouse. org.* (1637) Originally built as a four-room farmhouse by John Winthrop, first governor of the Bay State Colony; enlarged in 1732 by Isaac Royall. Example of early Georgian architecture; examples of Queen Anne, Chippendale, and Hepplewhite furnishings. (May-Sept, Wed-Sun 2-5 pm) **$$**

Isabella Stewart Gardner Museum. *280 The Fenway, Boston (02115). Take the Green Line E ("T") to the Museum stop; walk 2 blocks straight ahead. Phone 617/566-1401. www.gardnermuseum.com.* The Gardner Museum is housed in the 19th-century home of Isabella Stewart Gardner that itself is a work of art. The collections include masterpieces from around the world—both paintings and sculptures—that are displayed year-round, and special exhibits are installed from time to time. You can spend from two hours to half a day at the museum. On weekends in fall, winter, and spring, look for free afternoon concerts. (Tues-Sun; concerts late Sept-May; closed Thanksgiving, Dec 25) **$$$**

Kitchen Arts. *161 Newbury St, Boston (02116). Phone 617/266-8701. www.kitchenartz.biz.* Dubbed a hardware store for cooks, Kitchen Arts isn't just any cooking store: its the best-stocked cooking store you'll likely ever find—an absolute foodies paradise. You'll find everything you see in ordinary culinary stores—pots and pans, mixing bowls, appliances, kitchen tools, knives, measuring cups, cutting boards, spatulas—but a greater variety and a much wider selection than anywhere else. (Mon-Sat 10 am-6 pm, Sun noon-5 pm; closed holidays)

L'Arte Di Cucinare. *6 Charter St, Boston (02113). Take the Green Line (T) to Haymarket Station and walk beneath the Expressway to Salem St. Phone 617/523-6032; fax 617/367-2185. www.cucinare.com.* Michele Topor, a 30-year resident of the North End and a passionate gourmet chef herself, takes you on a 3 1/2-hour tour of the North End markets, where you taste a delicious variety of local foods in a historic setting (the North End is Boston's oldest neighborhood). You're introduced to shopkeepers and chefs throughout your tour and hear fascinating recipes and ideas for food selection. You can also arrange for special tours: 2 hours instead of 3 1/2, a morning tour with cappuccino and pastries, an olive-oil and balsamic-vinegar-tasting tour, an Italian regional dinner tour at North End restaurants, or anything else you can dream up. Reservations are required, and each tour is limited to 13 people. (Wed, Fri-Sat) **$$$$**

Louis Boston. *234 Berkeley St, Boston (02116). Phone 617/262-6100; toll-free 800/225-5135. www.louisboston. com.* Louis Boston is about as upscale as upscale gets; in fact, this men's and women's clothing store is considered among the finest in the world. The 140-year-old building is an architectural delight: it once housed the New England Museum of Natural History. Although Louis Boston has been at the location only since 1989, the company dates back to the late 1800s. The building also houses a café and a salon. (Mon-Wed 10 am-6 pm, Thurs-Sat 10 am-7 pm; closed Thanksgiving, Dec 25)

Louisburg Square. *Beacon Hill, Boston.* This lovely little residential square with its central park is the ultimate in traditional Boston charm. Louisa May Alcott, William Dean Howells, and other famous Bostonians have lived here. It is one of the most treasured spots in Boston. Christmas caroling is traditional here.

Make Way for Ducklings Tour. *99 Bedford St, Boston (02111). Phone 617/266-5669. www. historic-neighborhoods.org.* When Robert McCloskey wrote *Make Way for Ducklings* in 1940, he described two duck parents, Mr. and Mrs. Mallard, trying to find the perfect spot in which to raise their family. After the fictional duck family toured Boston's well-known sites, they settled in Boston's Public Garden, and Bostonians have been in love with this Caldecott-winning children's book ever since. Now you can re-create the duck's route via the Make Way for Ducklings tour, although you must make reservations in advance. Take advantage of other duckling events, such as the fancy and expensive Ducklings Day Tea held in April (reservations required) and the Ducklings Day Parade that begins at 1 pm on Mothers Day at Boston Common—children come to the parade dressed as their favorite characters from the story. **$$**

MDC Memorial Hatch Shell. *On the Charles River, between Storrow Dr and the water. www.mass.gov/dcr/ hatch_events.htm.* Packing as much as possible into the three months of the summer tourist season, the MDC Memorial Hatch Shell offers free entertainment nearly every night of the week. Offerings range from dance performances to rock concerts by big-name bands to a Boston Pops concerts sometime around the Fourth of July. Enjoy Free Friday Flicks throughout the summer; although the offerings are those that you'd find on DVD (either recent releases or classics), the movies somehow look better on the big screen. Bring a blanket to sit on, a picnic dinner to munch on, and a sweater to ward off cool river breezes. (Early June-early Sept) **FREE**

Minuteman Commuter Bikeway. *Begins near Alewife (T) station, goes through Lexington and Arlington, and ends at Bedford (note that you can't bring a bike on the T during rush hour) www.minutemanbikeway.org.* This 11-mile bike path looks like a miniature highway (but without the cars, of course), complete with on- and off-ramps, a center line, and traffic signs. The trail mimics portions of Paul Reveres famous ride, so you can stop off for a break from riding at the battleground at Battle Green and historic park at Lexington Center. The path mingles with the Great Meadows Wildlife Refuge for a time. In winter, the bikeway opens for cross-country skiing. (Daily) **FREE**

Mother Church, the First Church of Christ, Scientist. *Christian Science Center, Huntington and Massachusetts aves, Boston (02115). Phone 617/450-3793. www. tfccs.com.* (Daily; closed holidays) Adjacent is

> **Christian Science Publishing Society.** *175 Huntington Ave, Boston (02115). Phone 617/450-3793. (The Christian Science Monitor)* Mapparium, a walk-through stained-glass globe, is here. Call ahead.

Museum at the John Fitzgerald Kennedy Library. *5 miles SE on I-93, off exit 15, at University of Massachusetts Columbia Point campus (02125). Phone 617/514-1600; toll-free 866/535-1960. www.jfklibrary.org.* Designed by I. M. Pei, the library is considered one of the most beautiful contemporary works of architecture in the country. The library tower houses a collection of documents from the Kennedy administration as well as audiovisual programs designed to re-create the era. (Daily 9 am-5 pm; closed Jan 1, Thanksgiving, Dec 25) Picnic facilities on oceanfront. **$$**

⭐ **Museum of Afro American History/Black Heritage Trail.** *46 Joy St, Boston (02108). The self-guided trail begins at the Robert Gould Shaw/45th Massachusetts Regiment Memorial on Beacon Hill. Phone 617/725-0022. www.afroammuseum.org.* The Museum of Afro American History (MAAH) preserves and exhibits the contributions of African-American Bostonians and New Englanders during colonial settlement and the Revolutionary War. The museum also features workshops for kids and adults, a public lecture series, storytelling for children, and poet and author visits. The Black Heritage Trail explores stops on the Underground Railroad; Phillip's School, one of Boston's first integrated public schools; African-American churches, in which, unlike other churches in the area, members could sit on the main level during services and participate in church business; and historic homes of prominent African-American leaders. Guided walking tours are offered daily throughout the summer and at other times by request. (Mon-Sat 10 am-4 pm; closed Jan 1, Thanksgiving, Dec 25) **FREE**

Museum of Fine Arts. *465 Huntington Ave, Boston (02115). Take the Green Line E. Phone 617/267-9300. www.mfa.org.* The Museum of Fine Arts (MFA) is a rare treasure, even if art museums have never been your favorite tourist spots. The vast number of collections are unique, combining classic and contemporary art with ancient artifacts. To see everything the museum has to offer takes from a half to a full day. If the museum seems intimidating, try taking a free guided tour before heading off to see what interests you. If you're hoping to see a particular exhibit, check the Web site before leaving on your trip. Note that from 4 pm to closing on Wednesdays, admission is free, although a $14 contribution is suggested. Also on Wednesday evenings throughout the summer, the MFA hosts courtyard concerts. (Mon-Tues and Sat-Sun 10 am-4:45 pm, Wed-Fri to 9:45 pm) **$$$**

Museum of Science. *Science Park, Charles River Dam and Storrow Dr, Boston (02114). Take the Lechmere Green Line to the Science Park stop. Phone 617/723-2500. www.mos.org.* The Museum of Science blends science with entertainment that the whole family can enjoy. Exhibitions range from a T. Rex model (complete with 58 teeth), presentations with live animals at the Wright Theater, a chick hatchery, and a beautiful lighthouse that explains light, optics, and color. One exhibit, called "Where in the world are you?" allows visitors to enter clue-filled geographic areas and make educated guesses about where they are. Another exhibit, Cahners ComputerPlace, features a gallery of the most effective software for kids. While visiting Boston, the city of Ben Franklin's youth, visit the museum's Theater of Electricity for presentations about lightning and electrical currents. The museum also sponsors a Community Solar System, a scale-model solar system that includes a model of Mercury in the museum and one of Pluto all the way across Boston at the Riverside T stop. You can easily spend half a day at this museum. (Sat-Thurs 9 am-5 pm, Fri to 9 pm; closed Thanksgiving, Dec 25) **$$$** Also here is

> **Charles Hayden Planetarium.** *Phone 617/723-2500.* Shows are approximately 50 minutes. (Same hours as museum) Children under 4 years not admitted. **$$$**

New England Aquarium. *Central Wharf, Boston (02110). Near Faneuil Hall Marketplace. Phone 617/973-5200. www.neaq.org.* Boston's Central Wharf houses the New England Aquarium, which boasts a colorful array of dolphins, sea lions, penguins, turtles, sharks, eels, harbor seals, and fish from around the world. You can't miss the bright-red Echo of the Waves sculpture that rotates high above the expansive Aquarium plaza, or the 187,000-gallon Giant Ocean Tank inside. The Aquarium has an educational and research bent, so ecological and medical exhibits abound, but all the aquatic sights will captivate your entire family. Every 90 minutes, sea lions perform. Kids and adults alike will marvel at aquatic films offered at the Simons IMAX Theater ($$). To get a hands-on look at marine life in Boston Harbor—including taking water samples and hauling in lobster traps—take the Science at Sea harbor tour ($$$), which operates daily except in winter. Plan to spend from a few hours to a full day. (Mon-Fri 9 am-5 pm, Sat-Sun, holidays to 6 pm; closed Thanksgiving, Dec 25) **$$$**

New England Aquarium Whale Watches. *Central Wharf, Boston (02110). Phone 617/973-5206. www.neaq.org/ visit/ww.tickets.html.* Stellwagen Bank, 25 miles from Boston, is a terrific area for whale-watching. From Boston, the New England Aquarium's tour takes you out to see to the feeding grounds of a variety of whales, many of which are endangered, and you may see dolphins as well. The tour emphasizes education—it puts naturalists on board to teach about whale behavior, allows kids and adults to experiment with hands-on exhibits, and shows films about whale history. Allow four to five hours round-trip. Purchase tickets in advance. Boston Harbor Cruises (phone 617/227-4321; www.bostonharborcruises.com) and Beantown Whale Watch (phone 617/542-8000; www.beantownwhalewatch.com) also operate whale cruises in Boston. (mid-April-late Oct; closed Thanksgiving, Dec 25) **$$$$**

Newbury Street. *1-361 Newbury St, Boston (02116). www.newbury-st.com.* If you're a shop-a-holic, Newbury Street's eight blocks between Arlington Street and Massachusetts Avenue are a must-stop during your Boston vacation. Shops and galleries—from clothing to antiques to art galleries—tend to be pricey, so you may want to plan to window-shop only. Special finds include the Society of Arts and Crafts (glassware, jewelry), Simeon Pearce (glassware), Kitchen Arts (gourmet kitchen supplies), and the Avenue Victor Hugo Bookshop. In fair weather, get a bite to eat at a café with outdoor seating and people-watch for an afternoon. Also consider visiting at Christmas, when the street lights up with decorations, music, and food.

Nichols House Museum. *55 Mt. Vernon St, Boston (02108). Phone 617/227-6993. www.nicholshousemuseum. org.* (1804) Typical domestic architecture of Beacon Hill from its era; one of two homes on Beacon Hill open to the public. Attributed to Charles Bulfinch; antique furnishings and art from America, Europe, and the Orient from the 17th to early 19th centuries. Collection of Rose Standish Nichols, landscape designer and writer. (May-October, Tues-Sat noon-4 pm; Nov-April, Thurs-Sat noon-4 pm). **$$**

Old South Church. *645 Boylston St, Boston (02116). Phone 617/536-1970. www.oldsouth.org.* Operating continuously as a church community since 1669, Old South Church began when colonists objected to Massachusetts's requirement that religious dissenters join the First Church of Boston and formed Third Church of Boston (later Old South Church) in protest. The current building—sometimes referred to as New Old South Church—was completed in 1875 in a medieval architectural style that boasts impressive mosaics, stained glass, and cherry woodwork. (Worship held Sun)

Peter L. Stern. *55 Temple Pl, Boston (02111). Phone 617/542-2376. www.abebooks.com/home/plsabe.* Peter L. Stern stocks rare and antique books, including many first editions of 19th- and 20th-century literature, and a full offering of mystery books. If you've never stepped foot inside a rare bookstore before, Stern is a great place to start. Seeing books that have remained intact for nearly 200 years makes a terrific connection with the past, especially in this historic city. (Mon-Fri 9 am-5 pm, Sat 10 am-4 pm; closed holidays)

Reel Pursuit Fishing Charters. *Constitution Marina, 28 Constitution Rd, Charlestown (02129). On the Freedom Trail near the Bunker Hill Monument. Phone 617/922-3474. www.bostonfishing.com.* Jump aboard the *Reel Pursuit*, a 34-foot fishing boat that comfortably seats six passengers for a memorable day of fishing striped bass, bluefish, cod, and tuna. You can charter the *Reel Pursuit* for four hours, six hours, an entire day, or a nighttime excursion. The captain and his first mate are seasoned veterans who'll even bait your hook for you, if fishing is new to you, and are more than willing to clean and fillet your catch. Wear boat shoes or other white-soled shoes so as not to scuff the deck, and pack a bag with warm clothes, rain gear, sunscreen, sunglasses, and a hat. **$$$$**

Samuel Adams Brewery. *30 Germania St, Boston (02130). Take the Orange Line (T) to the Stony Brook stop. Phone 617/522-9080.* Take a tour of the Boston Beer Museum (formerly the Haffenreffer Brewery) and discover the critical details of the brewing process. And check out all the museums artifacts, which span two centuries of brewing. At the end of the tour, you're offered a sampling of Samuel Adams beers, the host company of the museum. (Tours Thurs-Sat) **$**

Shirley-Eustis House. *33 Shirley St, Boston (02119). Phone 617/442-2275. www.shirleyeustishouse.org.* (1747) This Georgian-style home, one of only four remaining in the country, was built for British Royal Governor William Shirley and restored to the style of the period when Governor William Eustis lived here from 1818 to 1825. Tours (June-Sept, Tues-Sun; also by appointment)

The Shops at the Pru. *800 Boylston St, Boston (02199). Take the Green Line E (T) to the Prudential stop. Phone toll-free 800/746-7778. www.prudentialcenter.com.* The presence of Saks Fifth Avenue as the mall's anchor may lead you to believe that The Shops at the Pru are expensive, but they're actually midpriced and very much like those in your local mall at home. The mall connects to Copley Place (see), which is far more upscale. The Prudential Center also boasts the Skywalk ($$), which offers you a panoramic view of the city from the 50th floor. (Daily; closed Jan 1, Easter, Thanksgiving, Dec 25)

Shreve, Crump & Low. *440 Boylston St, Boston (02116). Phone 617/267-9100; toll-free 800/324-0222. www.shrevecrumpandlow.com.* Any store that's more than 200 years old is worth a visit, and Shreves is no exception. For two centuries, this jewelry store has been selling engagement rings, watches, silver gifts, and estate jewelry. Now the oldest jeweler in the United States, the store also includes the country's oldest antique shop and oldest bridal registry. (Mon-Sat 10 am-6 pm, Thurs until 7 pm, Sun noon-5 pm; holidays)

Suffolk Downs. *111 Waldemar Ave, East Boston (02128). Take the Blue Line (the T or subway) to Suffolk Downs station, and then take a shuttle bus or walk for ten minutes. Phone 617/567-3900. www.suffolkdowns.com.* Suffolk Downs, which opened its doors in 1935, is steeped in horse racing history; in fact, Seabiscuit once won at Suffolk. The track offers pari-mutuel betting, which, unlike casino gambling, doesn't involve betting against the house, only against other spectators. The minimum wager per race is $2, and you can place as many bets as you'd like. Even if your horse doesn't come in first, you can still win: simply bet to win (first), place (second), show (third), and so on. Check out the Suffolk Downs Web site (www.suffolkdowns.com) to perfect your horse betting jargon before you go. (Daily; closed Dec 25) **$**

Symphony Hall. *301 Massachusetts Ave, Boston (02115). Huntington and Massachusetts aves. Phone 617/266-1492.* Home of Boston Symphony (late Sept-early May) and Boston Pops (May-mid-July, Tues-Sun).

Tealuxe. *108 Newbury St, Boston (02116). Phone 617/927-0400. www.tealuxe.com.* Tealuxe, a tea lover's utopia, offers more than 100 varieties of tea in its café. The interior architecture is reminiscent of a British estate, and jazz music plays in the background. You can also purchase teas to take home, along with teapots, teacups and mugs, and other tea paraphernalia. Don't let the historical significance of a tea shop in Boston escape you. Also check out a second location at Zero Brattle Street in Cambridge. (Daily; closed Thanksgiving, Dec 25)

Trinity Church. *206 Clarendon St, Boston (02116). Phone 617/536-0944. www.trinitychurchboston.org.*

This Henry Hobson Richardson building is the noblest work of the architect. It was inspired by Phillips Brooks, the ninth rector of Trinity Church, and author of the Christmas carol, "O Little Town of Bethlehem." The church combines Romanesque design with beautiful frescos, Craftsman-style stained glass, and ornate carvings. Trinity still serves as an Episcopal church today, with services at 8 am, 9 am, 11 am, and 6 pm. On Fridays at 12:15 pm, stop in for a free organ recital and take a guided or unguided tour. (Daily) **$**

Wang Theater/The Shubert Theater. *265 and 270 Tremont St, Boston (02116). Phone 617/482-9393. www.wangcenter.org.* Broadway shows, theater productions, dance and opera companies, and musical performers appear at the 3,600-seat Wang Theater, which is a world-class venue for the performing arts. Formerly called the Metropolitan Theater, The Wang Theater was designed to look like a French palace and has been completely restored to its original grandeur and beauty. The Shubert Theater across the street hosts an impressive array of quality local theater, dance, and opera productions, many of which appeal to children. **$$$$**

"Whites of Their Eyes" *Bunker Hill Pavilion, 55 Constitution Rd, Charlestown (02129). Just W of the USS Constitution. Phone 617/241-7575.* This specially designed pavilion houses a multimedia reenactment of the Battle of Bunker Hill using life-size figures and eyewitness narratives. Audience "viewpoint" from atop Breed's Hill. Continuous 30-minute shows. (Apr-Nov, daily 9 am-5 pm; closed Thanksgiving)

Wonderland Greyhound Park. *190 VFW Pkwy, Revere (02151). 5 miles north of historic downtown Boston on Hwy 1A N. Phone 781/284-1300. www.wonderlandgreyhound.com.* Open since 1935, Wonderland offers greyhound racing and pari-mutuel betting, which means that you're betting against other people at the track, not against the house. The minimum wager per race is $2, you can place at many bets as you'd like, and your dog doesn't have to come in first for you to win. (See the list of betting terms on Wonderlands Web site.) Wonderland hosts two annual premier events: the Grady Memorial Sprint and the Wonderland Derby. Note that Massachusetts voters frequently put dog-racing referendums on the ballot; before planning to attend Wonderland, check its Web site (www.wonderlandgreyhound.com) to ensure that voters haven't approved a greyhound-racing ban. (Daily; closed Thanksgiving, Dec 25) **$**

Special Events

Boston Kite Festival. *Franklin Park, Bluehill Ave and Circuit Dr, Dorchester (02121). Phone 617/635-4505. www.cityofboston.gov.* Bring your kite when you visit Boston in mid-May and visit the annual Boston Kite Festival. If you don't have a kite, don't let that stop you—festivities include kite-making clinics, face painting, live music, and kite-flying competitions. See thousands of kites, from beautiful and elaborate to simple, homemade varieties. Mid-May. **FREE**

Boston Marathon. *Starts in Hopkington, MA, and finishes at Copley Square, in front of the Boston Public Library. The Copley Square T stop is closed on Marathon day; take the Green Line C to any stop on Beacon St to see the finish. Phone 617/236-1652. www.bostonmarathon.org.* What separates the Boston Marathon from other marathons around the United States is that every person running the race has run another marathon in a fast enough time to qualify for this one. Qualifying standards, which are based on a combination of a previous marathon finish time, sex, and age, are tough—some people train for a lifetime to make the standard and run in this race. Because the course is notoriously hilly and difficult, few elite runners are able to run record times, and because the fast and flat London Marathon is held at about the same time of year as Boston, elite runners as a whole aren't as prevalent here as they once were. Still, Boston is one of the world's best marathons, so you won't find a single spot along the course where you're not in a crowd. Try to find a shady area in which to cheer on the runners. Third Mon in Apr. **FREE**

Bunker Hill Day. *Charlestown. Phone 617/536-4100.* Mid-June.

Charles River Regatta. *Harvard and Mass Ave bridges, Boston (02115). Phone 617/868-6200; toll-free 888/733-2678. www.hocr.org.* Third weekend in Oct.

Chowderfest. *1 City Hall Plz, Boston (02201). Phone 617/227-1528. www.bostonharborfest.com/chowderfest.* During Harborfest, an event that begins a few days before July 4 and ends a few days after, Boston's finest restaurants compete to have their *chowda* called "Boston's Best Chowder." More than 2,000 gallons of New England clam chowder (you won't find that tomatoey Manhattan variety here) are yours to sample and judge in this enjoyable annual event. Early July.

Esplanade Concerts. *Hatch Shell, Charles River Esplanade, Boston (02114). Phone 617/536-4100; toll-free 888/733-2678.* Musical program by the Boston

Pops in the Hatch Shell on the Esplanade on the Fourth of July.

First Night Boston. *Phone 617/542-1399. www. firstnight.org.* First Night is Boston's alternative to traditional New Year's Eve celebrations. This alcohol-free celebration begins with a Mardi Gras—style Grand Procession and features more than 250 performances in both indoor and outdoor venues. You'll be entertained with concerts, films (on seven screens), tango dancing, stand-up comedy, orchestral music, Boston Rock Opera, a magic show, puppets, and ice sculptures. The evening literally ends with a bang: a fireworks display at midnight. A badge gives you entrance to every event, and badges are for sale at retail outlets throughout the city. If you hang onto your badge after the event, it gets you discounts throughout the city later in the spring. After 8 pm on First Night, MTBA offers free transportation service. Keep in mind that Boylston Street and adjoining streets close in the afternoon for the Grand Procession; Atlantic Avenue and adjoining streets close later in the evening for the fireworks displays. Dec 31. **$$$**

Harborfest. *Hatch Shell, Charles River Esplanade, Boston (02114). Phone 617/227-1528. www.bostonharborfest. com.* Boston Pops Orchestra, fireworks. Six days over July 4.

Patriot's Day Celebration. *City Center, Boston (02108). Phone 617/536-4100.* Third Mon in Apr.

Limited-Service Hotels

★ **BEST WESTERN ROUNDHOUSE SUITES.** *891 Massachusetts Ave, Boston (02118). Phone 617/989-1000; toll-free 888/468-3562; fax 617/541-9588. www. bestwestern.com.* A decent lodging at a good price if you have your own wheels, this new-construction hotel inside the shell of a former railroad roundhouse is convenient to the Southeast Expressway, the Massachusetts Turnpike, and Boston City Hospital. But its far from downtown and nearly a mile from the nearest subway stop (there is frequent bus service, however). Guest rooms are large for the price and the mini-fridges are handy, especially since you're not going to run out at night for a snack. 92 rooms. Pets accepted. Complimentary continental breakfast. Check-in 3 pm, check-out 11 am. Fitness room. Airport transportation available. Business center. **$**
🐾 🏋 🏃

★ ★ **DOUBLETREE GUEST SUITES.** *400 Soldiers Field Rd, Boston (02134). Phone 617/783-*

0090; toll-free 800/222-8733; fax 617/783-0897. www. doubletree.com. Alternately described as being in Boston or in Cambridge, this highway-side high-rise sits at the Allston-Cambridge exit from the Massachusetts Turnpike. Regular shuttles to Harvard Square ameliorate the awkward location, and you get a lot of room in a bright and spacious open-atrium hotel. Besides the suite design—a bedroom separate from the office/living area—the best reason to stay here might be Scullers Jazz Club, one of the top venues in the Northeast for touring jazz headliners. The Doubletree Guest Suites is also a good bet for drivers leery of coping with urban traffic. 308 rooms, 15 story, all suites. Pets accepted; fee. Check-in 3 pm, check-out noon. Restaurant, bar. Fitness room. Indoor pool, whirlpool. Business center. **$**
🐾 🏋 ≈ 🏃

★ **HARBORSIDE INN OF BOSTON.** *185 State St, Boston (02109). Phone 617/723-7500; toll-free 888/723-7565; fax 617/670-6015. www.harborsideinnboston. com.* This 1858 brick and granite spice warehouse building has an enviable location next to Faneuil Hall Marketplace and is literally steps from the waterfront. The modestly priced boutique hotel features exposed-brick walls, hardwood floors, Turkish rugs, Federal-style cherry furniture, and reproductions of paintings from the Museum of Fine Arts. Limited off-site parking is available for a fee; make sure to arrange for this when reserving your room. 54 rooms, 8 story. Closed one week in late Dec. Check-in 3 pm, check-out noon. Wireless Internet access. **$$**

★ **RAMADA INN.** *800 Morrissey Blvd, Boston (02122). Phone 617/287-9100; fax 617/265-9287. www. bostonhotel.com.* 177 rooms, 5 story. Pets accepted, some restrictions. Check-in 3 pm, check-out noon. Outdoor pool. **$**
🐾 ≈

Full-Service Hotels

★ ★ ★ ★ **BOSTON HARBOR HOTEL.** *70 Rowes Wharf, Boston (02110). Phone 617/439-7000; toll-free 800/752-7077; fax 617/330-9450. www.bhh.com.* Privileged guests rest their weary heads at the Boston Harbor Hotel. Boston's rich heritage comes alive here at Rowes Wharf, once home to revolutionaries and traders. Occupying an idyllic waterfront location, the hotel is across the street from the financial district and three blocks from the Freedom Trail and Faneuil Hall Marketplace. Guests enjoy an especially civilized lifestyle here. They need not worry about the snarls of traffic, thanks to the hotels fantastic airport ferry service. This full-service hotel takes care of every possible amenity, ensuring satisfaction and comfort. Rooms and suites are beautifully appointed in rich colors; to pay a few dollars more for one with a view is well worth it. The views of the harbor are sensational, whether enjoyed in the privacy of a guest room or in one of the public spaces. Meritage presents diners with an inventive menu and an extensive wine list in striking contemporary surroundings. In the summer, the hotel hosts live music and dancing, along with an outdoor movie night. 230 rooms, 8 story. Pets accepted. Check-in 3 pm, check-out 1 pm. High-speed Internet access. Two restaurants, two bars. Fitness room, fitness classes available, spa. Indoor pool, whirlpool. Airport transportation available. Business center. **$$$$**

★ ★ ★ **THE COLONNADE HOTEL.** *120 Huntington Ave, Boston (02116). Phone 617/424-7000; toll-free 800/962-3030; fax 617/424-1717. www.colonnadehotel.com.* One of Back Bay's more family-friendly hotels, the Colonnade boasts the city's only outdoor rooftop swimming pool. The pool is an attraction for Bostonians as well as hotel guests, and there's often a lively singles scene at the poolside bar. A subway stop of the Green Line's E branch is just outside the door, making the Colonnade convenient for getting downtown or out to the major museums. The hotel often hosts meetings and small conferences. The street-level restaurant, Brasserie Jo (see), is a popular after-work watering hole for Back Bay professionals. 285 rooms, 1 story. Pets accepted. Check-in 3 pm, check-out noon. High-speed Internet access, wireless Internet access. Restaurant, bar. Fitness room. Outdoor pool. Business center. **$$$**

★ ★ **COPLEY SQUARE HOTEL.** *47 Huntington Ave, Boston (02116). Phone 617/536-9000; toll-free 800/225-7062; fax 617/267-3547. www.copleysquarehotel.com.* Location, location, location—this older hotel stands across Huntington Avenue from the Copley Place shopping center and the complex of conference meeting rooms associated with the nearby Westin, Marriott, Sheraton, and Hilton hotels. It's typically cheaper than those conference hotels, with smaller guest rooms and less posh furniture, but it does have a "home away from home" feel. It's very popular with European budget travelers, so you might meet some interesting people in the elevator. Amenities are limited here, but guests receive complimentary access to the fitness center at the nearby Lenox Hotel. 143 rooms, 7 story.

Pets accepted. Check-in 3 pm, check-out noon. Two restaurants, two bars. Business center. **$$**

★ ★ ★ **THE ELIOT HOTEL.** *370 Commonwealth Ave, Boston (02215). Phone 617/267-1607; toll-free 800/443-5468; fax 617/536-9114. www.eliothotel.com.* This 95-room European-style hotel is located just off the Mass Turnpike in the Back Bay area, convenient to the Hynes Convention Center and various shopping, entertainment, and cultural sites. A quiet elegance pervades the lobby, which is richly furnished; a superb faux finish on the walls mimics the look of stone. Most of the accommodations are spacious suites, which feature pull-out sofas, French doors to the bedrooms, Italian marble baths, and down comforters. Surrounded by lush greenery, the hotel has no fitness room of its own, but guests have complimentary use of the health club around the corner. The Eliot is also home to the critically acclaimed Clio restaurant (see), serving contemporary French-American cuisine. 95 rooms, 9 story. Pets accepted. Check-in 3 pm, check-out noon. High-speed Internet access, wireless Internet access. Restaurant, bar. Business center. **$$$**

★ ★ ★ **THE FAIRMONT COPLEY PLAZA BOSTON.** *138 St. James Ave, Boston (02116). Phone 617/267-5300; toll-free 800/441-1414; fax 617/375-9648. www.fairmont.com.* Ideally situated in the heart of the theater district, this landmark hotel was built in 1925 and is considered by many as the grande dame of Boston. Named after the great American painter John Singleton Copley, this traditional lodging offers elegant surroundings. The lobby flaunts an exquisite high-domed ceiling with beautiful ornate furnishings, as well as dramatic marble pillars and remarkable imported rugs. Guest rooms are furnished with top-quality materials and sport crown moldings. Lending a personal touch is Catie Copley, the resident black Lab, who's happy to be petted or even taken for walks by hotel guests. 384 rooms, 7 story. Pets accepted; fee. Check-in 3 pm, check-out 1 pm. High-speed Internet access. Restaurant, bar. Fitness room. Business center. **$$$**

★ ★ ★ ★ **FOUR SEASONS HOTEL BOSTON.** *200 Boylston St, Boston (02116). Phone 617/338-4400; toll-free 800/330-3442; fax 617/423-0154. www.fourseasons.com.* The Four Seasons Hotel would make any Boston Brahmin proud. Discriminating travelers are drawn to this refined hotel where the finer things in life may be enjoyed. The Four

Seasons offers its guests a prime location overlooking Beacon Hills Public Garden and the State Capitol. All of Boston is easily explored from here, and the hotel makes it carefree with courtesy town car service. The contemporary lobby, complete with a dramatic yellow marble and black granite floor in a startling geometric pattern, absolutely gleams. Antiques, fine art, sumptuous fabrics, and period furniture create a magnificent setting in the guest rooms and suites, while impeccable and attentive service heightens the luxurious experience. Aquatic workouts with a view are available at the indoor pool with floor-to-ceiling windows overlooking the city, and the fitness center keeps guests in tip-top shape. Aujourd'hui (see) is an epicurean's delight with its sensational New American cuisine and distinguished dining room. The Bristol presents diners with a casually elegant alternative. 273 rooms, 15 story. Pets accepted, some restrictions. Complimentary continental breakfast. Check-in 4 pm, check-out noon. High-speed Internet access. Two restaurants, bar. Fitness room. Indoor pool, whirlpool. Business center. **$$$$**

★ ★ ★ **HILTON BOSTON BACK BAY.** *40 Dalton St, Boston (02115). Phone 617/236-1100; toll-free 800/445-8667; fax 617/867-6104. www.hilton.com.* Built in the age of glass-box towers, the Hilton Back Bay is a premium conference and convention hotel across the street from the Hynes Convention Center at the western edge of Back Bay. A recent update reconfigured the hotel to make the guest rooms larger and furnish them with the kind of dark wood, plush-fabric ambience that visitors expect in Back Bay. Business travelers make up the bulk of the clientele, so you can count on excellent desks, a top-notch fitness center, and a business center that's open around the clock. The location is also ideal for sightseeing. Newbury Street boutiques are a block away, and the Hynes/ Auditorium subway stop is just outside. It's even a convenient stroll to Symphony Hall. 385 rooms, 26 story. Check-in 3 pm, check-out noon. Wireless Internet access. Restaurant, two bars. Fitness room. Indoor pool. Business center. **$$**

★ ★ ★ **HILTON BOSTON LOGAN AIRPORT.** *1 Hotel Dr, Boston (02128). Phone 617/568-6700; toll-free 800/445-8667; fax 617/568-6800. www.hilton. com.* The 599-room Hilton is the most convenient and plushest lodging at Boston's airport. A skybridge provides pedestrian access to and from the terminals, and the hotel runs free shuttles to the airport subway stop and water taxi dock for quick transport to downtown. There's something comfortingly familiar for road warriors about the ruddy wood of Hiltons furnishings and its attention to the needs of business travelers who might have to crank out a report overnight, make conference calls, or just kick back with in-room entertainment while waiting for tomorrows flight home. 599 rooms, 8 story. Pets accepted, some restrictions. Check-in 3 pm, check-out noon. Wireless Internet access. Two restaurants, bar. Fitness room. Indoor pool, whirlpool. Airport transportation available. Business center. **$$**

★ ★ **HOLIDAY INN SELECT-GOVERNMENT CENTER.** *5 Blossom St, Boston (02114). Phone 617/742-7630; toll-free 800/465-4329; fax 617/742-4192. www.holiday-inn.com.* The institutional décor and floral-print fabrics don't exactly scream chic, but this urban renewal-era tower near Massachusetts General Hospital and the Government Center is a road warrior's dream, with large work spaces and Executive Edition floors where rooms are equipped almost as offices. Frequent specials make the hotel a good deal, and although the immediate surroundings are unattractive, Beacon Hill is literally just across the street. 303 rooms, 14 story. Check-in 4 pm, check-out noon. Wireless Internet access. Restaurant, bar. Fitness room. Outdoor pool. **$**

★ ★ ★ **HOTEL COMMONWEALTH.** *500 Commonwealth Ave, Boston (02215). Phone 617/933-5000; toll-free 866/784-4000; fax 617/266-6888. www. hotelcommonwealth.com.* The Commonwealth functions as Boston University's elegant lodging to host visiting scholars, trustees, and parents who can afford full tuition. Constructed in the heart of once-funky Kenmore Square, its architecture suggests the mansard-roofed Victorian structures it replaced, but the Victoriana is really a conservative skin on a thoroughly contemporary deluxe hotel. Gestures of grace and stateliness abound—oversized writing desks with French Empire lines, heavy draperies that slide back to reveal large windows, a plethora of dark wood, and earth- and forest-tone carpets, wall coverings, and upholstery. Fenway Park is around the corner, and the Boston University campus begins a few yards up the street. Great Bay, one of the hotel's restaurants, has made a name for itself with upscale and innovative seafood. 148 rooms. Pets accepted, some restrictions; fee. Check-in 3 pm, check-out noon. High-speed Internet access, wireless Internet access. Two restaurants, three bars. Fitness room. Business center. **$$$**

★ ★ ★ **HYATT HARBORSIDE.** *101 Harborside Dr, Boston (02128). Phone 617/568-1234; toll-free 800/233-1234; fax 617/567-8856. www.hyatt.com.* Located adjacent to Logan Airport, this elegant hotel has a friendly staff, spacious guest rooms, and a meeting facility designed with the business traveler in mind. For leisure activities, guests can enjoy the indoor lap pool or the premier health and fitness center, both with views of the scenic waterfront and Boston skyline. 270 rooms, 15 story. Check-in 3 pm, check-out noon. High-speed Internet access, wireless Internet access. Restaurant, bar. Fitness room. Indoor pool, whirlpool. Airport transportation available. Business center. **$$**

★ ★ ★ **HYATT REGENCY BOSTON FINANCIAL DISTRICT.** *1 Ave de Lafayette, Boston (02111). Phone 617/912- 1234; toll-free 800/233-1234; fax 617/451-2198. www.hyatt.com.* Hyatt took over this former Swissôtel and wisely kept much of the elegant décor as well as the policy of running frequent discount packages on weekends. Principally a business hotel, it sits a block off Boston Common at the intersection of the financial and theater districts. Public areas suggest old-world refinement with antique furniture, marble floors, and Waterford crystal chandeliers. Many upper-level corner suites have breathtaking views of either Boston Common or downtown architecture. The hotel's pedestrian entrance from Avenue de Lafayette subjects everyone coming or going to the close scrutiny of the staff—a reminder that the hotel was a pioneer in the city's now nearly vanished red-light district. Today, the trendy restaurants and nightclubs of the Ladder District are just a few steps away. 498 rooms, 22 story. Pet accepted, some restrictions. Check-in 4 pm, check-out noon. High-speed Internet access, wireless Internet access. Restaurant, bar. Fitness room. Indoor pool. Business center. **$$$**

★ ★ ★ **THE LANGHAM BOSTON.** *250 Franklin St, Boston (02110). Phone 617/451-1900; toll-free 800/791-7781; fax 617/423-2844. www.langhamhotels. com.* Just a stone's throw from Faneuil Hall, the Freedom Trail, and other historic sites, the elegant Langham Hotel (formerly Le Meridien) is a perfect base for retracing the steps of famous patriots. A sense of old-world Europe is felt throughout the Langham, from the discreet façade with its signature red awnings to the magnificent lobby done in jewel tones. The guest rooms are equally delightful, and many offer wonderful views of the gardens of Post Office Square.

Extra touches are provided to ensure exceedingly comfortable visits. The remarkable French cuisine at Julien is only the beginning, where sparkling chandeliers and glittering gold leaf details will make any guest feel like royalty. Once the Governor's Reception Room of Boston's Federal Reserve Bank, the Julien Bar is a sensational place, while the Mediterranean dishes of Café Fleuri have universal appeal. 325 rooms, 9 story. Pets accepted, some restrictions; fee. Check-in 3 pm, check-out 1 pm. High-speed Internet access. Restaurants, bar. Fitness room. Indoor pool, whirlpool. Business center. **$$$**

★ ★ ★ **LENOX HOTEL.** *61 Exeter St, Boston (02116). Phone 617/536-5300; toll-free 800/225-7676; fax 617/267-1237. www.lenoxhotel.com.* This replica of a classic European hotel is centrally located in the heart of Boston. Although it isn't much to look at on the outside, this Boston landmark welcomes guests with a beautiful lobby and mezzanine—notice the lovely ceilings with ornate gridworks of gilded mouldings. Charmingly appointed guest rooms exude a level of elegance and style that stand up to even the most discriminating travelers' expectations. 214 rooms, 11 story. Check-in 3 pm, check-out noon. Wireless Internet access. Two restaurants, two bars. Fitness room. Business center. **$$$**

★ ★ ★ **MARRIOTT BOSTON COPLEY PLACE.** *110 Huntington Ave, Boston (02116). Phone 617/236-5800; toll-free 877/901-2079; fax 617/236-5885. www. copleymarriott.com.* With a prime location in the heart of Back Bay, the 1,147-room Marriott is a family-friendly hotel offering lots of amenities. An enclosed walkway connects the hotel to a large mall with many shops and restaurants, as well as to the Hynes Convention Center. Just minutes from the Museum of Fine Arts and Newbury Street shops, the hotel boasts one of the largest ballrooms in New England and offers a variety of dining options, including a sushi bar. 1,147 rooms, 38 story. Check-in 4 pm, check-out noon. High-speed Internet access. Three restaurants, two bars. Fitness room. Indoor pool, whirlpool. Business center. **$$**

★ ★ ★ **MARRIOTT BOSTON LONG WHARF.** *296 State St, Boston (02109). Phone 617/227-0800; toll-free 800/228-9290; fax 617/227-2867. www.marriott.com.* Adjacent to Faneuil Hall and near the Fleet Center, this mid-20th-century hotel was a generation ahead of its time in anticipating the cleanup of Boston's downtown shores. Most rooms have stunning harbor or city skyline views, and you need only walk out the door to catch the ferry to the harbor islands park, a whale-watching boat, or a water taxi to anywhere on the harbor. The hotel's public spaces capitalize on the nautical theme as well, featuring enormous murals of fishermen at work on Long Wharf and a railing system that mimics the levels on a cruise ship. Summertime nirvana is a bucket of steamed clams and a bottle of cold beer on the outdoor patio of the hotel's casual restaurant, Tias on the Waterfront. 402 rooms, 7 story. Check-in 4 pm, check-out noon. High-speed Internet access. Restaurant, bar. Fitness room. Indoor pool, whirlpool. Airport transportation available. Business center. **$$**

★ ★ ★ **MARRIOTT COURTYARD BOSTON TREMONT HOTEL.** *275 Tremont St, Boston (02116). Phone 617/426-1400; toll-free 800/321-2211; fax 617/482-6730. www.marriott.com.* This sophisticated 322-room hotel is located in the Western Promenade historic neighborhood, across the street from the Wang Center for the Performing Arts and not far from the Boston Garden. The midtown Arts District is a short walk away, and museums, art galleries, boat rides, fine restaurants, and recreational activities are nearby. Antiques and artwork are found throughout the hotel, and the lobby is punctuated with abundant marble and rich hanging tapestries. 322 rooms, 15 story. Check-in 3 pm, check-out noon. High-speed Internet access, wireless Internet access. Restaurant, bar. Fitness room. Business center. **$$**

★ ★ ★ **MARRIOTT PEABODY.** *8A Centennial Dr, Peabody (01960). Phone 978/977-9700; toll-free 800/228-9290; fax 978/977-0297. www.marriott.com.* 260 rooms, 6 story. Check-in 4 pm, check-out noon. Restaurant, bar. Fitness room. Indoor pool, whirlpool. Business center. **$**

★ ★ ★ **MILLENNIUM BOSTONIAN HOTEL.** *26 North St, Boston (02109). Phone 617/523-3600; toll-free 800/343-0922; fax 617/523-2454. www.millenniumhotels.com.* It's hard to believe that this spacious and modern luxury hotel was able to squeeze into one of the oldest neighborhoods in Boston without disturbing the ambience. Good soundproofing provides a serene sanctuary from the bustle of Faneuil Hall Marketplace next door—a location that makes the Millennium ideal for tourists (although the hotel caters mainly to business travelers given its proximity to the Government Center). Because the hotel was constructed around some older buildings, guest rooms vary from tiny to palatial; be sure to inquire carefully when booking. The hotel's restaurant (see SEASONS) was a pioneer in introducing contemporary upscale cuisine to Boston years ago and remains one of the poshest dining spots in town. City Hall is nearby, so plenty of local business gets accomplished in the lobby bar. 201 rooms, 8 story. Check-in 3 pm, check-out noon. High-speed Internet access. Restaurant, bar. Fitness room. Business center. **$$**

★ ★ ★ **NINE ZERO HOTEL.** *90 Tremont St, Boston (02108). Phone 617/772-5800; toll-free 866/646-3937; fax 617/772-5810. www.ninezero.com.* This midtown hotel is located on the famed Boston Freedom Trail, a short walk from the financial district and top attractions such as Faneuil Hall, Back Bay, and Beacon Hill. A red brick and limestone façade contrasts with the inner décor—a contemporary mix of nickel, chrome, stainless steel, and glass with accents of color and wood finishes. Rooms marry comfort and technology for business and leisure travelers. Luxe trappings include Frette linens, goose-down comforters and pillows, CD stereo sound systems, and Mario Russo bath products. In-room personal offices feature task lighting, high-performance desk chairs, printers, complimentary high-speed Internet access, and dual-in cordless telephones with speaker capabilities. 189 rooms, 19 story. Pets accepted. Check-in 3 pm, check-out noon. High-speed Internet access, wireless Internet access. Restaurant, bar. Fitness room. Business center. **$$$**

★ ★ ★ **OMNI PARKER HOUSE.** *60 School St, Boston (02108). Phone 617/227-8600; toll-free 800/843-6664; fax 617/227-9607. www.omnihotels.com.* The Parker House, which gave the world its eponymous dinner rolls and the Boston cream pie, is the oldest hotel in the United States in continuous operation (part of the building dates from 1856). The plush lobby and dining room, which date from just before World War I, are breathtaking examples of Edwardian excess. The guest rooms are up to modern standard, although some are quite compact. The location, just beneath the peak of Beacon Hill and in the midst of downtown shopping, is marvelously convenient. Great history is attached to the hotel—from the literary dinners with Emerson and Longfellow playing host to

Dickens to the stories about JFK, who made this his political headquarters. 551 rooms, 15 story. Pets accepted, some restrictions; fee. Check-in 3 pm, check-out noon. High-speed Internet access. Restaurant, two bars. Fitness room. **$$$**

★ ★ ★ ★ THE RITZ-CARLTON, BOSTON.

15 Arlington St, Boston (02117). Phone 617/536-5700; toll-free 800/241-3333; fax 617/536-9340. www.ritzcarlton. com. Distinguished and refined, The Ritz-Carlton is unquestionably the grande dame of Boston. This lovely hotel, faithfully restored to its 1920s splendor, has been a cherished city landmark for many years. Located across from the Public Garden, this aristocratic hotel opens its doors to a rarefied world of genteel manners and distinguished surroundings. With its intricate "wedding cake" ceiling detail, elaborate mouldings, lavish carpets and upholstery, and graceful marble staircases, the lobby is a truly elegant space. The guest rooms are a celebration of traditional style; luxurious marble bathrooms encourage soothing soaks. Suites include wood-burning fireplaces, and the hotel even offers a considerate fireplace butler service. The sun-filled Café is an ideal place for shoppers to take a break from the boutiques of Newbury Street, while a proper afternoon tea can be enjoyed in the Lounge. The Bar has a fascinating history, having survived Prohibition, and its wood-paneled walls and roaring fireplace exude a clubby feel. Even pets are pampered here; a special treat bag is presented on a silver tray, and food and water bowls are provided, along with a dog tag engraved with the hotel's name on one side and the dog's name on the other. 273 rooms, 17 story. Pets accepted; fee. Check-in 3 pm, check-out noon. High-speed Internet access. Restaurant, two bars. Fitness room. Business center. **$$$$**

★ ★ ★ ★ THE RITZ-CARLTON, BOSTON

COMMON. *10 Avery St, Boston (02111). Phone 617/574-7100; toll-free 888/709-2027; fax 617/574-7200. www.ritzcarlton.com.* While only a short skip across the park from its sister property, The Ritz-Carlton, Boston Common is a world apart from its traditional counterpart with its modern sensibility of clean lines, neutral tones, and hip atmosphere. This contemporary construction attracts the fashionable set seeking the high levels of service synonymous with Ritz-Carlton properties. Flanked by the financial and theater districts, The Ritz-Carlton, Boston Common is convenient for business and leisure travelers alike. In the inviting lobby, a dramatic arched ceiling is lit for effect, while leather seating beside a black marble fireplace encourages conversation. The guest rooms and suites have a distinctly serene feel with muted tones of taupe, cream, and celadon and polished woods. JER-NE Restaurant is a feast for the tongue and the eyes with its inventive creations and sensational décor. An open kitchen enables guests to watch the talented chefs in action, while the bar has a vibrant scene. After a night of indulgence, Ritz-Carlton guests often head to the massive Sports Club/LA, a veritable temple of fitness. Dogs are welcomed in style with the Pampered Pet Package, consisting of bowls, biscuits, and a personalized dog tag. 193 rooms, 4 story. Pets accepted, some restrictions; fee. Check-in 3 pm, check-out noon. High-speed Internet access. Restaurant, bar. Fitness room, fitness classes available, spa. Indoor pool. Business center. **$$$$**

★ ★ ★ SEAPORT HOTEL.

1 Seaport Ln, Boston (02210). Phone 617/385-4000; toll-free 877/732-7678; fax 617/385-4001. www.seaportboston.com. Looking a bit like a beached ocean liner, the Seaport is joined to the World Trade Center by an overhead walkway and serves as a base hotel for many conferences, conventions, and sales events. The ship metaphor only goes so far: the soothing, modern-styled rooms are much larger and better appointed than most staterooms. The surrounding area will be a bustling part of the city by 2010, or so developers promise, but the Seaport is currently a bit removed from the downtown action. Frequent shuttles to South Station and the financial district help ease the sense of isolation, as will a soon-to-be-completed train line. The health club is large and well equipped, and the restaurant is one of Boston's best for upscale seafood dining. The Seaport is also convenient to many casual fish restaurants near Fish Pier and to the summertime concert pavilion on the harbor. Canine guests are registered just like humans, and the lucky ones munch on dog treats from guest-room minibars. 426 rooms, 18 story. Pets accepted, some restrictions. Check-in 3 pm, check-out 1 pm. High-speed Internet access. Restaurant, bar. Fitness room, fitness classes available, spa. Indoor pool. Airport transportation available. Business center. **$$$**

★ ★ ★ SHERATON BOSTON HOTEL.

39 Dalton St, Boston (02199). Phone 617/236-2000; toll-free 800/325-3535; fax 617/236-1702. www.sheraton.com/ boston. Ideally located in the historic Back Bay and adjacent to the Hynes Convention Center, this hotel offers guests attentive service along with an elegant atmosphere. 1,216 rooms, 29 story. Pets accepted, some restrictions. Check-in 3 pm, check-out noon. High-speed Internet access. Two restaurants, bar. Fitness room, fitness classes available. Indoor pool, outdoor pool, whirlpool. Business center. **$$$**

★ ★ ★ **WESTIN COPLEY PLACE.** *10 Huntington Ave, Boston (02116). Phone 617/262-9600; toll-free 800/937-8461; fax 617/424-7483. www.westin.com/copleyplace.* This grand, contemporary hotel is located in the heart of historic Back Bay and boasts some of the largest guest rooms in Boston, along with panoramic views of the city. Conveniently connected by skybridge to the Hynes Convention Center and elite shopping at Copley Place, the hotel is frequented by business travelers but also welcomes vacationing families with its Westin Kids Club. Pets, too, are greeted warmly here, and are given their own Heavenly Beds and snack menu. An immaculate fitness facility and spa and salon tempt guests to enjoy a rigorous workout and then to treat themselves to some pampering. 803 rooms, 36 story. Pets accepted. Check-in 3 pm, check-out noon. High-speed Internet access. Three restaurants, two bars. Fitness room, spa. Indoor pool, whirlpool. Business center. **$$$**

★ ★ ★ ★ **XV BEACON.** *15 Beacon St, Boston (02108). Phone 617/670-1500; toll-free 877/982-3226; fax 617/670-2525. www.xvbeacon.com.* Dazzling and daring, XV Beacon is the hipster's answer to the luxury hotel. This turn-of-the-century Beaux Arts building in Beacon Hill belies the sleek décor found within. This highly stylized, seductive hotel flaunts a refreshing change of pace in traditional Boston. Decidedly contemporary, XV Beacon employs whimsical touches, like the plaster busts found at reception, to wink at the city's past. (Sam Adams is buried next door, and Thomas Jefferson lived around the corner.) Original artwork commissioned specifically for the hotel by well-known artists decorates the walls of both public and private spaces. The guest rooms and suites are furnished in an eclectic style in a palette of rich chocolate browns, blacks, and creams. Rooms feature canopy beds with luxurious Italian linens and gas fireplaces covered in cool stainless steel. Completed in crisp white with simple fixtures, the bathrooms are a modernist's dream. The nouvelle cuisine at The Federalist (see) is delicious and fresh, thanks to the chef's rooftop garden and in-kitchen fish tanks. 60 rooms, 10 story. Pets accepted, some restrictions. Check-in 3 pm,

check-out noon. High-speed Internet access. Restaurant, bar. Fitness room. Whirlpool. **$$$$**

Specialty Lodgings

CHARLES STREET INN. *94 Charles St, Boston (02114). Phone 617/314-8900; toll-free 877/772-8900; fax 617/371-0009. www.charlesstreetinn.com.* Step into the past without sacrificing modern conveniences at this utterly charming inn, which occupies a building constructed as a showcase of architectural styles of the 1880s. Guest rooms are large and regal enough to qualify as decadent, although the street-level reception and staircases are rather tight. Expect to find working fireplaces, massive antique armoires, and heavily draped canopy beds, along with period artwork. The location is perfect for exploring Beacon Hill, downtown, or Back Bay on foot—a good thing, since parking is limited. There's no dining room, so a bounteous continental breakfast is delivered to your door. Guest rooms are themed to artists and writers associated with Boston, such as Louisa May Alcott. What would Henry James have made of the sub-zero refrigerator and high-speed Internet access? 9 rooms, 5 story. Pets accepted, some restrictions. Complimentary full breakfast. Check-in 3 pm, check-out noon. High-speed Internet access, wireless Internet access. **$$$**

GRYPHON HOUSE. *9 Bay State Rd, Boston (02215). Phone 617/375-9003; toll-free 877/375-9003; fax 617/425-0716. www.gryphonhouseboston.com.* More a luxury bed-and-breakfast than a hotel, this circa-1895 brownstone townhouse stands at the juncture of Back Bay and Fenway. Its one of the more architecturally distinctive residential neighborhoods in Boston, and the Gryphon House stands up nicely to its neighbors. The rooms are huge—each about the size of a studio apartment and individually decorated in an array of Victorian styles. Each room has a working gas fireplace and wet bar as well as remote-controlled air conditioning. The Kenmore subway stop and Fenway Park are just a brief saunter away, and Boston University begins just a few doors down on Bay State Road. 8 rooms. Complimentary continental breakfast. Check-in 3 pm, check-out 11 am. High-speed Internet access, wireless Internet access. **$$**

NEWBURY GUEST HOUSE. *261 Newbury St, Boston (02116). Phone 617/437-7666; toll-free 800/437-7668; fax 617/670-6100. www.newburyguesthouse.com.* A string of residences along upper Newbury Street was linked with indoor staircases and hallways to create this pioneer among Back Bay bed-and-breakfasts. Rooms tend to be on the small side, in part because bathrooms stole space from bedrooms when the conversions were made. The décor is eclectic, with a bias toward the kind of furniture that Granny jettisoned when she bought her recliner. The bed-and-breakfast offers good value for the location, but ask for a room on the back side to escape weekend street noise. 32 rooms, 4 story. Complimentary full breakfast. Check-in 3 pm, check-out noon. Wireless Internet access. **$$**

Restaurants

★ ★ **ABE & LOUIE'S.** *793 Boylston St, Boston (02116). Phone 617/536-6300; fax 617/437-6291. www.abeandlouies.com.* Fittingly situated at the Convention Center end of Back Bay, this New York-style steakhouse satisfies by fulfilling expectations. The clubby décor of dark wooden booths and a flickering fireplace is a perfect match for the high-protein menu of charred steaks and grilled fish. The dessert trolley even features New York cheesecake. Atkins dieters can pass on the extra carbs, like the side of mashed potatoes. Steak menu. Lunch, dinner, brunch. Closed Dec 25. Bar. Casual attire. Reservations recommended. Valet parking. Outdoor seating. **$$$**

★ ★ ★ **AQUITAINE.** *569 Tremont St, Boston (02118). Phone 617/424-8577; fax 617/424-0249. www.aquitaineboston.com.* An offshoot of fellow South End restaurant Metropolis (both are owned by Seth Woods), this French bistro wavers between classical and nouveau. Regulars rave about the steak frites; there's also an intriguing wine list as well as a helpful staff. French bistro menu. Dinner, brunch. Closed Jan 1, Thanksgiving, Dec 25. Bar. Casual attire. Reservations recommended. Valet parking. **$$**

★ ★ ★ ★ **AUJOURD'HUI.** *200 Boylston St, Boston (02116). Phone 617/338-4400; fax 617/423-0154. www.fourseasons.com.* With floor-to-ceiling windows overlooking Boston's famed Public Garden, Aujourd'hui is a beautiful spot for a business lunch or an intimate dinner. Brimming with old-world charm, this spacious and elegant dining room, located in the Four Seasons, is lined with rich oak paneling and decorated with tall potted palms and oil paintings. The tables are set with Italian damask linens and decorated with antique plates and lovely fresh flowers. The kitchen aims to please here, and it succeeds with an innovative selection of seasonal modern French fare prepared with regional ingredients and global flavors. The predominantly American wine list complements the kitchen's talent. A lighter menu of more, shall we say, nutritionally responsible dishes (read: low salt, low fat, low cholesterol) is also available. The service at Aujourd'hui enhances the dining experience. Like the restaurant, it is formal yet charming. American menu. Dinner, Sun brunch. Bar. Children's menu. Jacket required. Reservations recommended. Valet parking. **$$$**

★ ★ ★ **AURA.** *1 Seaport Ln, Boston (02210). Phone 617/385-4000. www.seaporthotel.com.* Seafood menu. Breakfast, lunch, dinner, late-night, brunch. Bar. Children's menu. Business casual attire. Valet parking. **$$$**
🅳

★ ★ **B & G OYSTERS LTD.** *550 Tremont St, Boston (02116). Phone 617/423-0550. www.bandgoysters.com.* The Maine lobster roll at B & G Oysters costs over $20, fried Ipswich clams are close behind, and raw oysters are $2 each, but customers line up day and night to spend barrels of cash at James Beard award-winning chef Barbara Lynch's latest enterprise. Why? Lynch and business partner Garrett Hasker are using ingredients fresh enough to remind you of summers spent by the sea. The quality is so superior that dishes can be presented simply. Flavors are pure: raw items are briny and fried dishes crisp. The atmosphere is urban chic—in a cellar, a noisy, well-informed crowd dines casually on food that is the antithesis of casual. Lynch and Hasker have used the old-fashioned concept of a New England seafood and fish shack to create a restaurant that's closer to what you find on coastal France than on the coast of Maine. Nostalgia has a price. Seafood menu. Lunch, dinner. Closed holidays. Casual attire. Valet parking. Outdoor seating. **$$$**

★ ★ ★ **BLACKFIN CHOP HOUSE & RAW BAR.** *116 Huntington Ave, Boston (02116). Phone 617/247-2400. www.blackfinchophouse.com.* Seafood, steak menu. Dinner. Bar. Business casual attire. Reservations recommended. Valet parking. **$$$**
🅳

★ ★ ★ **BLU.** *4 Avery St, Boston (02111). Phone 617/375-8550; fax 617/375-8551. www.blurestaurant.com.* Located in the ladder district, Blu is a sleek, sharp American restaurant owned by the folks who created Rialto in Cambridge (see). With two-story-high glass walls, chrome accents, and a hip crowd to match, Blu is an edgy addition to this neighborhood. If you feel like a taste of the briny waters, start with the Out of the Blu raw bar sampler—an easy fix for anyone with a sushi, sashimi, or shellfish fetish. The kitchen turns out a whimsical and delicious menu of upscale comfort food-ish dishes like seared foie gras on cornbread and stylish, seasonal American plates like roasted chicken with autumn vegetable hash. For a business lunch, a hot date, or just a night out with friends, Blu is a sure thing. American menu. Lunch, dinner. Closed Sun. Bar. Business casual attire. Reservations recommended. Valet parking. Outdoor seating. Credit cards accepted. **$$$**

★ ★ **BOB THE CHEF'S.** *604 Columbus Ave, Boston (02118). Phone 617/536-6204; fax 617/536-0907. www.bobthechefs.com.* Owner Daryl Settles serves a lightened version of American soul food—cornbread, collard greens, ribs, chicken, barbecue, and fried corn—with a healthy side of live jazz, often played by students from nearby Berklee College of Music. The Sunday jazz brunch is an institution in the South End. Don't let the cuisine fool you into dressing down—Bob the Chef's is a stylish joint. American menu. Dinner, brunch. Closed holidays. Bar. Casual attire. Reservations recommended. **$$**

★ ★ ★ **BONFIRE.** *50 Park Plz, Boston (02116). Phone 617/262-3473; fax 617/457-2403. www. bonfiresteakhouse.com.* Steak menu. Bar. Business casual attire. Reservations recommended. Valet parking. **$$$**
🅳

★ ★ **BRASSERIE JO.** *120 Huntington Ave, Boston (02116). Phone 617/425-3240; fax 617/424-1717. www. brasseriejoboston.com.* Like its sister French brasserie in Chicago, this restaurant serves authentic French, or more specifically Alsatian, cuisine with the usual flair of the Lettuce Entertain You group. Shoppers and theater attendees will delight in its location: the Colonnade Hotel (see) next to Copley Place. French bistro menu. Breakfast, lunch, dinner. Bar. Children's menu. Casual attire. Reservations recommended. Valet parking. Outdoor seating. **$$**

★ ★ **BROWN SUGAR CAFE.** *129 Jersey St, Boston (02215). Phone 617/266-2928; fax 617/266-2928. www. brownsugarcafe.com.* A steady crowd of Thai-hungry folks fills the Brown Sugar Cafe, a cramped spot for terrific traditional and contemporary dishes of this lemongrass-tinged Southeast Asian land. The airy room is filled to capacity most of the time, yet there is an easiness to the service and the pace of the place; every table is set with a pot of brown sugar, an ode to the restaurant's sweet name. The menu offers a lengthy list of reasonably priced rice and noodle dishes, prepared to your preferred level of scorch. A selection of fresh

fish and meats balances out the voluminous number of vegetarian plates. Thai menu. Lunch, dinner. Closed holidays. Casual attire. Outdoor seating. **$$**

★ ★ **THE BUTCHER SHOP.** *552 Tremont St, Boston (02118). Phone 617/423-4800; fax 617/423-4820. www.thebutchershopboston.com.* The Butcher Shop is a lot like the wine bars in Paris, Madrid, and Venice. At the front, a long bar offers a variety of terrific wines by the glass from small growers around the globe. Chef Barbara Lynch pairs the wines with flavorful, French-inspired dishes like marrow with toast, sea salt, and haricots verts; pork rillettes; a torchon of duck foie gras; or a selection of house-cured meats. The wine and small plates of upscale bar food have a calming effect on the palate. What's also fun about this informal restaurant is the ease with which guests are induced to slow down and savor life. In that sense, it has captured what travelers to Europe enjoy: a rhythm that eschews a race to the finish line. When it's time to leave this oasis, you can buy products from its retail section. International menu. Lunch, dinner, brunch. Closed holidays. Children's menu. Casual attire. Valet parking. **$$$**

★ **CAFE MARLIAVE.** *10 Bosworth St, Boston (02108). Phone 617/423-6340; fax 617/542-1133.* Tucked into a nook near the downtown section of the Freedom Trail, Cafe Marliave has a long history of its own. Established in 1875, it was one of Boston's first red-sauce Italian-American restaurants, and the tin walls and minuscule booths supply a romantic atmosphere. Portions are generous, as if a nonna were peering out from the kitchen, exhorting Mangia! Mangia! Italian menu. Lunch, dinner. Closed Sun; holidays. Bar. Casual attire. Reservations recommended. **$$**

★ ★ **CAFFE UMBRA.** *1395 Washington St, Boston (02118). Phone 617/867-0707. www.caffeumbra.com.* Located in Boston's South End neighborhood, Caffe Umbra treats diners to inventive Italian and French country cooking. The creative dishes are best enjoyed with a selection from the restaurant's extensive wine list, featuring vintages from some of the lesser-known regions of Italy and France. A warm atmosphere pervades the restaurant, where exposed-brick walls, a large cherry bar, and windows framing views of the Cathedral of the Holy Cross make this a particularly inviting spot for urban sophisticates. French, Italian menu. Dinner. Closed Mon. Bar. Casual attire. Valet parking. **$$**

★ ★ ★ **THE CAPITAL GRILLE.** *359 Newbury St, Boston (02115). Phone 617/262-8900; fax 617/262-9449. www.thecapitalgrille.com.* The Capital Grille is a man's man sort of restaurant. Sporting dark wainscoted walls and an extensive single-malt Scotch list, this high-roller steakhouse is heavy with testosterone, beef, and a bold dash of big-time expense account. Indeed, The Capital Grille has all the bells and whistles you'd expect from a steakhouse, including a stunning raw bar and generous portions of well-marbled steak, served any and every way you want it. The house specialty is the gargantuan dry-aged porterhouse. Weighing in at 24 juicy, bold ounces, it should come with its own defibrillator. If you're feeling gluttonous, finish off dinner with a slice of cheesecake. Steak menu. Dinner. Closed July 4, Thanksgiving, Dec 25. Bar. Business casual attire. Reservations recommended. Valet parking. **$$$**

★ ★ **CARMEN.** *33 North Sq, Boston (02113). Phone 617/742-6421.* The handful of tables and exposed-brick walls of the narrow room make Carmen about as intimate and romantic a trattoria as you'll find in the North End, yet it's easy to locate because the Freedom Trail stripe runs past the door. (The Paul Revere House is a neighbor.) For tapas-style snacking, sit at the bar, sip a nebbiola d'Alba, and enjoy olives marinated with cherry peppers and orange or a plate of grilled squid. Among the full dinner entrées, seared scallops fit the bill for light eaters, while hearty crespelle stuffed with wild mushrooms and topped with a meaty Bolognese sauce can stave off the strongest hunger pangs. Mediterranean menu. Lunch, dinner. Closed Mon. Bar. Casual attire. **$$**
🅳

★ ★ **CASA ROMERO.** *30 Gloucester St, Boston (02115). Phone 617/536-4341; fax 617/536-6191. www. casaromero.com.* For more than three decades, chef/owner Leo Romero has been serving a taste of traditional Mexican cooking to Back Bay residents and visitors. Decorated with exposed brick and colorful Talavera tiles from Puebla, Casa Romero is a hidden gem, secreted in an alleyway between Newbury Street and Commonwealth Avenue. You will be hard-pressed to find a burrito on the menu, but you will find lots of authentic regional Mexican dishes, like huitlacoche folded into spinach tortillas, pork tenderloin marinated in oranges and smoked chipotle peppers, and mole poblano, accompanied by potent and tart margaritas. In the balmy weather, have dinner in the charming courtyard garden. Mexican menu. Dinner, Sun brunch. Closed Jan 1, July 4, Dec 25. Bar. Outdoor seating. **$$$**

★ ★ **CHAU CHOW CITY.** *83 Essex St, Boston (02111). Phone 617/338-8158; fax 617/338-8258.* The top floor of this three-level Chinatown institution is

Boston's most adventurous dim sum venue. Even on weekday mornings, the rolling carts proffer a range of dishes worthy of a Hong Kong dim sum emporium. For a full meal on the other levels, stick to the kitchen's seafood specialties, including such delicacies as clams in black bean sauce or crab with ginger and scallion. Chinese menu. Lunch, dinner, late-night. Bar. Children's menu. Casual attire. Reservations recommended. **$$**

★ **CHEERS.** *84 Beacon St, Boston (02108). Phone 617/227-9605; fax 617/723-1898. www.cheersboston. com.* Life imitates art imitating life. Well, if not art, then television. Born as The Bull & Finch, this neighborhood watering hole was the model for TV's *Cheers.* The fame of its progeny eclipsed the charm of the original, but even if nobody knows your name, you can get a decent burger and a draft—once you get in the door. American menu. Lunch, dinner. Closed Dec 25. Bar. Children's menu. Casual attire. **$$**

★ ★ **CIAO BELLA.** *240A Newbury St, Boston (02116). Phone 617/536-2626; fax 617/437-7585. www. ciaobella.com.* In the summer, the sidewalk tables at this townhouse restaurant on the corner of Fairfield and Newbury are some of the most coveted people-watching and flirting seats in town. The menu is a curious blend of steakhouse (robust veal chops, planks of swordfish) and Italian-American (specials like eggplant ravioli). Many professional athletes hang here with their best buddies. Italian menu. Lunch, dinner. Closed Thanksgiving, Dec 25. Bar. Casual attire. Reservations recommended. Valet parking. Outdoor seating. **$$$**
🅳

★ ★ **CLARKE'S TURN OF THE CENTURY.** *21 Merchants Row, Boston (02109). Phone 617/227-7800.* American menu. Lunch, dinner, late-night. Bar. Casual attire. **$$**

★ ★ ★ ★ **CLIO.** *370 Commonwealth Ave, Boston (02215). Phone 617/536-7200; fax 617/578-0394. www. cliorestaurant.com.* Once you dine at Clio, you may want to write to chef/owner Ken Oringer and ask him to clone his modern restaurant and open one in your neighborhood. Picture-perfect plates arrive and practically glisten with attention to detail. The presentations are so intricate that you may want to photograph rather than eat. Ingredients are treated like notes in a melody; each one complements the next, and the result is a culinary symphony. Fresh fish plays a big role on the menu, and for those who prefer their seafood raw, Clio has a separate sashimi bar that features a pricey selection of rare fish that Oringer has flown in from around the world. With food this global and attentive service to match, the room is jammed nightly with a who's who of Boston's media and financial elite. The energy of the room gives Clio a steady buzz of Bostonian social electricity, and the food coming out of the kitchen gives you reason to return. French, Pan-Asian menu. Breakfast, dinner. Closed Mon; Jan 1, July 4, Dec 25. Bar. Business casual attire. Reservations recommended. Valet parking. **$$$**

★ ★ **DAVIDE.** *326 Commercial St, Boston (02109). Phone 617/227-5745; fax 617/227-8976. www. davideristorante.com.* Named for Michelangelo's *David,* this North End Italian restaurant has been a standard favorite for handmade pastas, prime meats and seafood, and a terrific list of grappas for over two decades. The intimate subterranean dining room is set in a restored 18th-century church, and it has the worn, but warm, feel of a treasure from long ago and far away. Lovers of veal scaloppine can take comfort in knowing that chef/owner Franco Caritano's is one of the best in the city, while fans of Caesar salad, mixed tableside, will applaud this rich and creamy version. Pastas are wonderful as well, so be sure to come with an appetite. In short, dinner at Davide is delicious and uncomplicated, and sometimes that is all you need. Italian menu. Dinner. Bar. Valet parking. **$$**

★ ★ ★ **DAVIO'S.** *75 Arlington St, Boston (02116). Phone 617/357-4810; fax 617/357-1997. www.davios. com.* This established northern Italian steakhouse has been a Boston institution for more than 20 years. It's located in Back Bay in the former Paine Furniture building in Park Square and is convenient to the theater district and Boston Common. The large dining room features dramatic high ceilings, contemporary décor, imposing columns, and a display kitchen where you could watch chef Steve DiFillippo at work whipping up favorite dishes including grilled porterhouse veal chops, hand-rolled potato gnocchi, and chocolate cake. The popular restaurant also houses a bakery and a wine room with more than 300 wines. A Davio's to Go Shop, serving delicious takeout foods such as pizza, sandwiches, and desserts, is located in the adjacent 10 St. James building. Northern Italian menu. Lunch, dinner, late night. Closed Thanksgiving, Dec 25. Bar. Children's menu. Business casual attire. Reservations recommended. Valet parking. **$$$**

★ **DURGIN PARK.** *340 Faneuil Hall Marketplace, Boston (02109). Phone 617/227-2038; fax 617/720-1542. www.durgin-park.com.* While the menu runs the gamut from fish chowder to chicken pot pie, prime rib is the specialty at Durgin Park (established in 1826), a loud, fun, kitschy, red-and-white-checked-tablecloth spot in Faneuil Hall that's packed with good cheer nightly. Like the crowds, the food is unpretentious. The theme here is simple, honest home cookin'. Durgin Park is on two levels. Go upstairs if you feel like sitting elbow-to-elbow at communal-style tables and sharing a wilder time, and downstairs if you need privacy and a table of your own. American menu. Lunch, dinner. Closed Dec 25. Bar. Children's menu. Casual attire. Outdoor seating. **$$**

★ ★ ★ **THE FEDERALIST.** *15 Beacon St, Boston (02108). Phone 617/670-2515; toll-free 877/982-3226; fax 617/670-2525. www.xvbeacon.com.* This much-acclaimed-before-it-opened restaurant is becoming one of Boston's "to be seen" places. Its clubby, tongue-in-cheek salute to old Boston, with faux crumbling columns and plaster busts of colonial luminaries, continues on to the menu, where you can find updated versions of Yankee classics. American menu. Breakfast, lunch, dinner, brunch. Bar. Business casual attire. Reservations recommended. **$$$**

★ ★ **EXCELSIOR.** *272 Boylston St, Boston (02116). Phone 617/426-7878. www.excelsiorrestaurant.com/ home.* Executive chef Eric Brennan designs contemporary American cuisine at one of Boston's famed locations. This dramatic restaurant pleases both the palate and the eye, even if its price comes as a bit of a shock. A "see and be seen" ambience defines this modern and sophisticated setting crafted by the darling of the design world, Adam Tihany, and its location in one of the city's landmarks overlooking Beacon Hills Public Garden makes it a natural choice for celebrating special occasions. Everything is over the top here, from the 7,000-bottle wine cellar to the decadent meals. American menu. Dinner, late-night. Bar. Casual attire. **$$$**

★ ★ **FILIPPO.** *283 Causeway St, Boston (02114). Phone 617/742-4143; fax 617/742-4245. www.filipporistorante.com.* The movie *Big Night* comes to mind at Filippo, a full-throttle Italian eatery with all the bells and whistles—mirrors, marble, and murals. Located in the North End, Filippo is known for its gargantuan portions and matching larger-than-life prices, but the cuisine is far more subtle and tasteful than the room might suggest. Although it's a far cry from haute cuisine, you'll find nicely done grilled meats and fish along with a delicious selection of pastas. Italian menu. Lunch, dinner. Closed Mon-Tues, Thanksgiving, Dec 25. Bar. Children's menu. Valet parking. **$$$**

★ ★ **FRANKLIN CAFE.** *278 Shawmut Ave, Boston (02118). Phone 617/350-0010. www.franklincafe.com.* The Franklin stands on an ungentrified street, and the neo-Beatnik, all-black décor can scare off casual browsers. But there's usually a wait for tables as South End twentysomethings on a budget and smart foodies with a yen for Dave Du Boiss no-nonsense cooking fill the place. Each simple dish has an original twist, such as a grilled double-thick pork chop served on apple-sage bread pudding with bourbon gravy. The whole menu is available until 1 am. American menu. Dinner, late-night. Bar. Casual attire. **$$**

★ ★ **GINZA.** *16 Hudson St, Boston (02111). Phone 617/338-2261; fax 617/426-3563. www.bostonginza. com.* Packed with Japanese patrons, Chinatown's first Japanese restaurant, Ginza, feels like a scene out of To-kyo. Waitresses are decked out in beautiful kimonos, and Japanese pop music fills the room as sushi chefs focus on their intricate craft, constructing maki at the speed of sound, their sushi knives flying in a blur of steel. The menu offers several house maki that tend to be gigantic, like an overstuffed roll filled with fried soft-shell crab, cucumber, avocado, flying fish roe, and spicy mayo; but it also includes more traditional Japanese (that is, normal-sized) sushi rolls and authentic barbecue and hot pot meals. Japanese menu. Lunch, dinner, late-night. Closed Thanksgiving. Casual attire. Credit cards accepted. **$$**

★ **GRAND CHAU-CHOW.** *45 Beach St, Boston (02111). Phone 617/292-5166; fax 617/292-4646.* Authentic Cantonese cuisine is the star of the show at Grand Chau-Chow, a fast-paced restaurant featuring fresh fish brought straight from the tank to the flame to your plate, as well as traditional fare like spicy, fried, salted squid; steamed flounder; and clams in black bean sauce. The only issue with Grand Chau-Chow may be the fact that it seems to have a beat-the-clock mentality when it comes to serving you your meal. Expect to feel rushed, but good food has its price. Chinese menu. Lunch, dinner, late-night. Casual attire. **$$**

★ ★ **GRILL 23 & BAR.** *161 Berkeley St, Boston (02116). Phone 617/542-2255; fax 617/542-5114. www. grill23.com.* The restaurant market is filled with for-mulaic steakhouse concepts: lots of beef paired with lots of testosterone, served up in a dark wood-paneled boys' club of a room. Grill 23 may serve lots of beef (seven juicy cuts are available, and each is dry-aged USDA Prime sirloin) and indeed houses its share of testosterone (hoards of handsome men in suits line the buzzing bar), but this high-energy beefeat-ers heaven is formulaic in no other way. Set in the historic Salada Tea Building in Boston's Back Bay, Grill 23 & Bar is a vast and stunning space, with original sculptured ceilings, massive Corinthian columns, mahogany paneling, and hardwood and marble floors that give the space a sense of history and warmth. In addition to the terrific selection of USDA Prime sirloin prepared in the restaurant's grand exhibi-tion kitchen, the menu offers exciting and decidedly nonsteakhouse dishes as well. The "Fruits of the Sea" section includes tastings from the shimmering raw bar—lobster, shrimp, and clams—as well as caviar, sashimi, and assorted fish tartare, while entrées offer inventive American fare: roasted and grilled fish, poultry, lamb shanks, and the like. In colder months, the upstairs lounge is the place to be with its blazing fire and cozy seating. Seafood, steak menu. Dinner. Closed holidays. Bar. Business casual attire. Reserva-tions recommended. Valet parking. **$$$**

★ ★ ★ **HAMERSLEY'S BISTRO.** *553 Tremont St, Boston (02116). Phone 617/423-2700; fax 617/423-7710. www.hamersleysbistro.com.* Buttercup walls, mile-deep plush banquettes, authentic farmhouse wood-beamed ceilings, and a warm amber glow give Hamersley's Bistro the air of home. The food coming out of chef/owner Gordon Hamersley's lively open kitchen (Hamersley is usually on the line, cooking in a baseball hat) makes you realize that you are, in fact, not at home. If the food were this good at your home, it is doubtful that you would ever bother leaving. The house specialty, chicken roasted with garlic, lemon, and parsley, is the perfect example of how simple food can shine. The bird has a crisp, taut, golden skin, and its flesh is moist, succulent, and saturated with flavor. While the menu centers on hearty American bistro fare, do not take this to mean that the food here is boring, dull, or tired. Standards are expertly prepared with care and skill, and the kitchen is not afraid to bring in eclec-tic global flavors to create inventive dishes for guests who have been dining here for more than a decade. The kitchen also offers a weekly vegan special that could turn on the most ardent of carnivores. Hamersley's eclectic wine list changes with the seasons, as does the menu, and the restaurant's warm staff is more than happy (and very able) to help guide you to the right selection for your meal. French bistro menu. Dinner. Closed July 4, Thanksgiving, Dec 24-25. Bar. Casual attire. Reservations recommended. Valet parking. Out-door seating. **$$$**

★ ★ **THE HUNGRY I.** *71 1/2 Charles St, Boston (02114). Phone 617/227-3524; fax 617/227-0237.*

Romantic, but drafty in the winter (perhaps better for snuggling up next to that special someone), The Hungry I specializes in intimate, cozy, candlelit dining in a historic 1840s house. If you are planning an evening of gazing across the table, this is a good choice. The menu is old-school French, so expect dishes like frogs' legs, rabbit, venison, and pheasant, dressed in classic sauces thickened with decadent amounts of butter. The specials are always a treat, especially the tomato and garlic soup. French bistro menu. Lunch, dinner, Sun brunch. Closed July 4, Dec 25. Bar. Business casual attire. Reservations recommended. Valet parking. Outdoor seating. **$$$**

★ ★ ★ **ICARUS.** *3 Appleton St, Boston (02116). Phone 617/426-1790; fax 617/426-2150. www.icarusrestaurant. com.* Located in the South End in a converted 1860s building, Icarus is one of those rare restaurants where the evening is over way too soon. The intimate bar serves tasty cocktails and delicious homemade rosemary breadsticks, while the lovely, serene dining room (there's live jazz every Friday evening) is an easy place to relax and enjoy chef/owner Chris Douglas's flavorful seasonal New American menu, with whimsical dishes like slow-roasted tomato soup with Timson cheese panini, polenta with braised exotic mushrooms, and duck in a show-stopping cider and bourbon sauce. It's tough to fit dessert in, but its worth loosening the belt—the chocolate molten cake with homemade vanilla bean ice cream and raspberry sauce is a necessary evil. American menu. Dinner. Closed holidays. Bar. Valet parking. **$$$$**

★ **JASPER WHITE'S SUMMER SHACK.** *50 Dalton St, Boston (02115). Phone 617/867-9955. www.summershackrestaurant.com.* Celebrate the fun-loving spirit of summer year-round at Jasper White's Summer Shack. This casual and lively joint, styled after the classic clam shacks of the New England coast, brings the best of the beach to the heart of the city. Armed with large appetites, diners come in groups to strap on bibs and dig into heaping portions of fresh and delicious seafood served broiled, boiled, grilled, fried, or raw. Live music and a bustling bar add to the Summer Shack's inimitable gregarious atmosphere. Seafood menu. Lunch, dinner. Bar. Children's menu. Casual attire. **$$**

★ ★ **KASHMIR.** *279 Newbury St, Boston (02116). Phone 617/536-1695; fax 617/536-1598. www.kashmir-spices.com.* Kashmir is a sophisticated local spot for extra-special Indian cuisine. Located in the Back Bay, Kashmir is not your typical Indian all-you-can-eat restaurant. While it does offer an extensive daily buffet (a culinary paradise for lovers of this savory, spiced cuisine), Kashmir is a soothing, cozy space, swathed in off-white and turquoise, with lovely, deep banquettes. If the buffet is too overwhelming, stick to the dinner menu, where you'll find wonderful standards like mulligatawny, samosas, and a tandoori mixed grill. Indian menu. Lunch, dinner. Casual attire. Reservations recommended. Valet parking. Outdoor seating. **$$**

★ ★ ★ **L'ESPALIER.** *30 Gloucester St, Boston (02115). Phone 617/262-3023; fax 617/375-9297. www.lespalier.com.* Housed in a charming 19th-century townhouse, L'Espalier makes it easy to slip into another era. The restaurant feels like a Merchant-Ivory film come to life. Luxuriously appointed with vintage drapes framing tall bay windows, fresh flowers, fine linens, and antique china adorning each table, L'Espalier is a decidedly sophisticated venue for a decadent and delicious dining experience. The menu is prepared with impeccable French technique and a nod to New England's regional ingredients and comfortable style. The chef prepares prix fixe and tasting menus as well as a Degustation of Caviar—each of five courses is prepared with caviar—for those feeling very indulgent. At L'Espalier, you'll find that your first bite tastes as good as your last. The kitchen consistently wows, sending out one extraordinary dish after another. A glorious monster of a wine list offers an amazing variety of wines and vintages, with a wide enough price range to allow for great choices under $50. French menu. Dinner, Sat tea. Closed Sun in Jan-Apr and July-Oct; holidays. Bar. Business casual attire. Reservations recommended. Valet parking. **$$$$**

★ ★ **LALA ROKH.** *97 Mt. Vernon St, Boston (02108). Phone 617/720-5511. www.lalarokh.com.* If you've never tasted Persian cuisine, you simply must, and Lala Rokh is the perfect place to experiment with the authentic, home-style dishes of this exotic region of the Middle East. Fragrant pots of silky rice make up the base of almost every meal, topped with a variety of stews made with slow-cooked, fork-tender beef or with lamb, stewed with aromatics like saffron or dill and intense traditional flavors like sumaq and preserved lemon. The restaurant prides itself on its hospitality, which it delivers with grace, ensuring that every diner leaves feeling pampered and with a happy, full belly. Persian menu. Lunch, dinner. Closed holidays. Business casual attire. **$$**

★ ★ **LES ZYGOMATES.** *129 South St, Boston (02111). Phone 617/542-5108; fax 617/482-8806. www.winebar.com.* Mixing French cuisine with select Mexican and Italian dishes, Les Zygomates is a comfortable Paris bistro that's right at home in Boston's old leather district. An extensive wine list is featured, with 66 wines by the glass offered each night. Six nights per week, enjoy live jazz performed by local and national musicians while you top off your meal with a decadent chocolate dessert. French menu. Lunch, dinner. Closed Sun; major holidays. Bar. Casual attire. Reservations recommended. Valet parking. Credit cards accepted. **$$$**

★ ★ ★ **LOCKE-OBER.** *3 Winter Pl, Boston (02108). Phone 617/542-1340; fax 617/542-6452. www.lockeober.com.* Established in 1875, Boston's famed Locke-Ober restaurant is a classic's classic. This glitzy, turn-of-the-(previous)-century dining landmark buzzes with electricity as the room fills to the seams with assorted foodies, superstars, financiers, and celebrity political types. Under the skilled leadership of chef/co-owner Lydia Shire, traditional American fare feels fresh and exciting and makes a persuasive case for eating nothing that flirts with fusion ever again. The menu speaks in simple yet spectacular terms, featuring classic plates from America's past, like beef Stroganoff with hand-cut egg noodles, as well as old French standards like duck l'orange and onion soup gratine. The Indian pudding is a signature dessert, as is the fresh strawberry shortcake, when in season. American menu. Lunch, dinner. Closed Sun; holidays. Bar. Business casual attire. Reservations recommended. Valet parking. **$$$**

★ ★ **LUCIA.** *415 Hanover St, Boston (02113). Phone 617/367-2353; fax 617/367-8952. www.luciaboston.com.* Lucia, a North End favorite since 1977, remains a steady choice for regional Italian fare. Owned by the Frattaroli family, the restaurant is marked by over-the-top and very large floor-to-ceiling murals of Italian country scenes, while the menu is most noted for the robust dishes of Italy's Abruzzi region, like Granasso d'Italia (a light dish of veal, peas, artichokes, prosciutto, pine nuts, eggplant, and mozzarella), and Gnocchi d'Abruzzo (with pesto), as well as a bold selection of country-style meat dishes. There's also a second location in Winchester. Italian menu. Lunch, dinner. Closed Thanksgiving, Dec 25. Bar. Casual attire. Reservations recommended. Valet parking. Credit cards accepted. **$$**

★ ★ ★ **MAMMA MARIA.** *3 North Sq, Boston (02113). Phone 617/523-0077; fax 617/523-4348. www.mammamaria.com.* Located in North Square, Mamma Maria is one of Boston's most beloved Italian restaurants. Filled nightly with celebrities and savvy locals, this romantic spot, set in an early 19th-century brick townhouse, serves an elegant New American and contemporary Italian menu that features seasonal ingredients and steers clear of heavy, cheesy, red-sauced pastas. This is the sort of restaurant that easily impresses diners, from its impeccable service to its delicious menu, so if you're out to, say, meet the parents for the first time, this would be a good choice. Italian menu. Dinner. Closed holidays. Bar. Casual attire. Valet parking. **$$$**

★ ★ ★ **MANTRA.** *52 Temple Pl, Boston (02111). Phone 617/542-8111; fax 617/542-8666. www.mantrarestaurant.com.* Chef/owner Thomas John has created a jewel of a restaurant with Mantra, a low-lit, sexy restaurant set in a stunning turn-of-the-century former bank in Boston's über-hip ladder district. Decked out in raw silk upholstery, with chainmail drapery and red crushed suede banquettes, Mantra is an exotic space that makes you feel wildly beautiful. The menu is a perfect blend of French technique and Indian accents like saffron, cumin, tamarind, and cloves, and the kitchen delivers aromatic dishes marked by exciting, deliciously bold flavor pairings. Desserts are wonderful and include such delights as vanilla bean kulfi, an Indian ice cream that has a delicate, dreamy creaminess. Indian, French menu. Lunch, dinner, late-night. Closed Sun; also Jan 1, Labor Day, Thanksgiving. Bar. Business casual attire. Reservations recommended. Valet parking. **$$$**

★ ★ ★ **MASA.** *439 Tremont St, Boston (02116). Phone 617/338-8884; fax 617/338-6019. www.masarestaurant.com.* This lively Southwestern restaurant is located on the edge of the South End, near the Chinatown and theater districts. Its stunning bar area overlooks the romantic chandelier-lit dining room which features exposed brick walls, large mirrors, black-and-white checkered floors, highback booths, and flowing drapes. The flavorful cuisine is offered in tapas, dinner, and brunch menus. There are also separate menus for wines, tequilas, and other cocktails. Southwestern menu. Dinner. Closed Thanksgiving, Dec 25. Bar. Casual attire. Reservations recommended. Valet parking. Outdoor seating. Credit cards accepted. **$$**

★ ★ ★ ★ **MERITAGE.** *70 Rowes Wharf, Boston (02110). Phone 617/439-3995. www.*

meritagetherestaurant.com. As longtime chef of the Boston Harbor Hotel's annual Boston Wine Festival, Daniel Bruce certainly knows his wine. That's why it was only natural that he teamed up with the hotel to open its signature restaurant, Meritage, in 2002. Fulfilling Chef Bruce's passion for pairing wine and food, Meritage offers more than 900 selections of wine and a unique concept that is Bruce's own: eclectic, seasonal dishes that are paired with wine flavors rather than varietals. Chef Bruce offers a menu of French-influenced New American cuisine that is categorized by styles of wine, progressing from light to heavy; the "Sparklers" section features dishes such as fennel-cured smoked salmon, while herb- and mustard-marinated grilled filet mignon with horseradish shallot cream and cabernet syrup is featured under "Robust Reds." All menu items are available as large or small plates, allowing diners the flexibility to sample several different dishes. And as if all this weren't enough of a draw, Meritage's setting is one of the most spectacular in the city. Overlooking Rowes Wharf, the long, rectangular dining room is contemporary but elegant and features comfortably spaced black marble tables, colorful abstract photographs, tones of orange, cream, and black; and unique stainless steel track lighting that illuminates the room with countless tiny white lights. Without a doubt, Meritage offers one of the most unique dining experiences in Boston, and after a visit, you'll find that it's one of the best. American menu. Dinner, Sun brunch. Closed Mon. Bar. Business casual attire. Reservations recommended. Valet parking. **$$$**

★ **MIKE'S CITY DINER.** *1714 Washington St, Boston (02118). Phone 617/267-9393.* Mike's serves breakfast and lunch only, but its worth getting up early for the corned-beef hash or the fat Belgian waffles. A survivor from the era of real diners, it has a patina that no imitation can match. Customers range from construction workers to artsy loft dwellers, but watch out when politicians are in town—they love the place for photo ops. American menu. Breakfast, lunch. Casual attire. **$**

★ ★ ★ **MISTRAL.** *223 Columbus Ave, Boston (02116). Phone 617/867-9300; fax 617/351-2601. www.mistralbistro.com.* Although the vaulted ceilings and sophisticated décor may scream glam central, chef/owner Jamie Mammanno's creative yet uncomplicated cuisine departs from those kinds of expectations. Menu items such as tuna tartare, grilled thin-crust pizzas, and skillet-roasted Cornish game hen are complemented by a superb wine list. French, Mediter-ranean menu. Dinner. Closed holidays. Bar. Casual attire. Reservations recommended. Valet parking. **$$$**

★ ★ **NIGHTINGALE.** *578 Tremont St, Boston (02109). Phone 617/236-5658.* French menu. Lunch, dinner, brunch. Bar. Casual attire. Reservations recommended. Valet parking. **$$**

★ ★ ★ ★ **NO. 9 PARK.** *9 Park St, Boston (02108). Phone 617/742-9991; fax 617/742-9993. www.no9park.com.* In the shadow of the Massachusetts State House in historic Beacon Hill, you will find No. 9 Park, a 19th-century mansion turned elegant dining salon. Inside, you'll find a kitchen that serves some of the most wonderful European country-style cuisine in the region. Many of the ingredients on the seasonal menu are identified by farm; chef/owner Barbara Lynch makes an effort to support top-of-the-line small producers of sustainable agriculture. Perfectly prepared with a healthy dose of flavor and style, Lynch's sophisticated, tempting menu of modern European fare runs the gamut from beef to fish to venison and pheasant, depending on the season. After dinner, stop at the beautifully appointed bar for a cognac or port, and give yourself some more time to relax before you go back to the real world. No. 9 Park is a magical sort of place that you just won't want to leave. French, Mediterranean menu. Lunch, dinner. Closed Sun; holidays. Bar. Business casual attire. Reservations recommended. Valet parking. **$$$**

★ ★ ★ **THE OAK ROOM.** *138 St. James Ave, Boston (02116). Phone 617/267-5300; fax 617/247-6681. www.fairmont.com.* This old-world steakhouse, located in the Fairmont Copley Plaza Boston Hotel (see), is steeped in Edwardian charm, with a restored carved-plaster ceiling, baroque woodwork, and garnet-red draperies. Drawing a boisterous crowd of twenty- and thirtysomethings and more sophisticated, mature audiences alike, The Oak Room's mass appeal is attributed to its stunning slabs of grilled fish and beef tenderloin, and classics like chateaubriand (for two), oysters Rockefeller, and clams casino. American menu. Breakfast, lunch, dinner, Sun brunch. Bar. Children's menu. Business casual attire. Reservations recommended. Valet parking. **$$$**

★ ★ ★ **OLIVES.** *10 City Sq, Charlestown (02129). Phone 617/242-1999; fax 617/242-1333. toddenglish.com.* Some celebrity chefs rest on their laurels while their restaurants unravel at the culinary seams. Not so for Todd English. Olives, his first restaurant, has remained a destination for wildly good, boldly flavored Mediterranean fare. While the food is a big reason to dine here, the atmosphere may not be for every-one. The rustic European décor and large windows overlooking the square add appeal, but tables tend to be full nightly, which can make the dining room a bit crampedthis may not be the best choice for quiet conversation. But who really needs to talk when mouths are filled with such good food? Mediterranean menu. Dinner. Closed holidays. Bar. Valet parking. **$$$**

★ ★ ★ **THE PALM.** *200 Dartmouth St, Boston (02116). Phone 617/867-9292; fax 617/867-0789. www. thepalm.com.* "Let them eat meat!" might be an apt phrase to hang on a wall at The Palm, a boys' club of a steakhouse located in the Westin Copley Place (see). This branch of the New York City favorite attracts local celebrities, financial moguls, and out-of-town dealmakers looking to talk shop over copious amounts of perfectly seared prime beef. The service is efficient and knowledgeable, and the kitchen is expert at making sure that your beef is cooked to specification every time. In addition to the carnivorous menu items, you'll find fat, fillerless crab cakes, lobsters the size of small pets, and Italian fare like veal marsala. Of course, no steakhouse would be complete without sides, and the creamed spinach here, laced with Parmesan, is an absolute pinup. Steak menu. Lunch, dinner. Closed Jan 1, Thanksgiving, Dec 25. Bar. Casual attire. Reservations recommended. Valet parking. **$$$**

★ ★ ★ **PARKER'S.** *60 School St, Boston (02108). Phone 617/227-8600; fax 617/227-2120. www.omnihotels.com.* JFK's grandfather made Parker's the de facto headquarters of Massachusetts pols, Ho Chi Minh worked in the kitchen, and Charles Dickens ate here with Ralph Waldo Emerson whenever he was in town. Its the birthplace of Parker House rolls and Boston cream pie, and one of the oldest dining rooms in the nation—though lovingly updated. Parker's is Boston's first choice for pomp and history—and the roast beef's not bad either. American menu. Breakfast, lunch, dinner. Bar. Children's menu. Business casual attire. Reservations recommended. Valet parking. **$$$**

★ **PEKING TOM'S.** *25 Kingston St, Boston (02111). Phone 617/482-6282. www.pekingtom.com.* Peking Tom's resurrects the whole package of 1950s Chinese glamour dining: food with glazes, electric-colored drinks, and hostesses in shiny silk dresses. The sushi bar is the culinary star, as the regular menu is filled with the retro likes of crab rangoon (made with cream cheese) and tamarind-glazed spareribs. The bar is a hot singles spot. Chinese menu. Lunch, dinner. Bar. Casual attire. **$$**

★ ★ **PERDIX.** *560 Tremont St, Boston (02118). Phone 617/338-8070; fax 617/338-2201. www. perdixrestaurant.com.* After a successful run with just ten tables in Boston's Jamaica Plain neighborhood, chef/owner Tim Partridge has moved into a South End space big enough for lots of people to enjoy. His family bistro cooking produces food with visual and sensual punch—a nori roll of tuna, scallions, and flash-fried radishes, or monkfish with roasted fresh tomatoes. The entrée list is short, but specials abound. For romance, ask for a greenhouse table. American menu. Lunch, dinner. Closed Mon; Thanksgiving, Dec 25. Casual attire. Reservations recommended. Valet parking. **$$**

★ ★ **PHO REPUBLIQUE.** *1415 Washington St, Boston (02118). Phone 617/262-0005.* While an old-country version of pho (the noodle soup that's the national dish of Vietnam) reigns supreme here, chef Didi Emmons also conjures up French-Vietnamese food for hipsters with great taste but modest budgets. The crowd tends to be young and multiethnic; the food, such as shrimp and sweet potato nests, tends to be bright and sassy. Several vegetarian and vegan options are available. Vietnamese menu. Dinner, late-night. Bar. Casual attire. **$$**

★ ★ ★ **RADIUS.** *8 High St, Boston (02110). Phone 617/426-1234; fax 617/426-2526. www.radiusrestaurant. com.* Chef/partner Michael Schlow is a man who understands what people are looking for in a dining experience. First, there's atmosphere. Radius is a stunningly chic, slick, modern space decked out in silver and garnet red. Crowded with some of Boston's most stylish residents, you will step inside and instantly feel like you're on the set of *Sex and the City*. Second, there's the food. Schlow offers diners a chance to taste some truly inspired modern French cooking. There is an emphasis on the seasons here, so the menu changes often, but what doesn't change is the quality of the ingredients and the care with which the kitchen assembles each magnificent dish. Schlow doesn't like to overload the plate (or the belly) with heavy sauces. This is refined, light-handed cooking using infused oils, emulsions, juices, vegetable pures, and reductions to heighten flavors and add texture and balance to every dish. Dining here is a wonderful feast for all the senses. French menu. Lunch, dinner. Closed Sun; holidays. Bar. Business casual attire. Reservations recommended. Valet parking. **$$$**

★ ★ **THE RED FEZ.** *1222 Washington St, Boston (02118). Phone 617/338-6060; fax 617/338-6666. www. theredfez.com.* First opened in 1940, The Red Fez celebrates the foods of the Middle East and the Mediterranean. The menu is heavy on salads and hot and cold mezze but also offers a variety of grilled meats and skewers. Small, tasty plates of marinated olives, grape leaves, and savory lamb and tomato pie are great for sharing. You'll also find a nice selection of international beers and wines. The lively dining room features tall windows, exposed-brick walls, and cheerful blue glassware. Middle Eastern menu. Dinner, late-night, Sun brunch. Bar. Casual attire. Outdoor seating. **$$**

★ ★ **RISTORANTE TOSCANO.** *47 Charles St, Boston (02114). Phone 617/723-4090; fax 617/720-4280. www.ristorantetoscanoboston.com.* Toscano is one of Beacon Hill's hottest destinations for rustic Italian fare. The exposed-brick dining room is just a few blocks from the State House, so it's often filled with political movers and shakers, but it's also home to many locals who come in several times a week for their fix of chef/owner Vinicio Paolis country-style dishes, like braised lamb, roast pork, grilled beef, and homemade pasta. The heavenly ricotta pie is a must for dessert. Italian menu. Lunch, dinner. Closed Sun; Dec 25. Bar. Business casual attire. Reservations recommended. Valet parking. **$$**

★ ★ ★ **SAGE.** *69 Prince St, Boston (02113). Phone 617/248-8814; fax 617/248-1879. www.sageboston.com.* Great things do indeed come in small packages, and Boston's Sage is one such small but precious thing. Located in the North End, the 35-seat bistro (reserve ahead), has a warm, rustic charm. Sage is a petite but perfect stage for chef/owner Anthony Susi's beautiful modern Italian fare, including a stunning selection of handmade pastas like gnocchi and ravioli that are as light as air, but rich in flavor. If you can't decide, the pasta sampler is a wonderful way to try a few. Italian menu. Dinner. Closed Sun; major holidays. Casual attire. Reservations recommended. Credit cards accepted. **$$$**

★ ★ ★ **SEASONS.** *26 North St, Boston (02109). Phone 617/523-4119; fax 617/523-2593. www. millenniumhotels.com.* Set in the Millennium Bostonian Hotel (see), with views of Faneuil Hall, Seasons is a sophisticated destination for romantic, charming dining. While the delicious, if pricey, fusion menu features a global mix of dishes from Asia, Italy, France, and America, the wine list is 100 percent American, a nice tribute to our domestic wineries. Seasons is a lovely place to spend an evening, especially if you believe that conversation should be heard without the need to yell, that service should be gracious, and that dinner should never be rushed. American menu. Breakfast, lunch, dinner. Closed holidays. Bar. Children's menu. Valet parking. **$$$**

★ ★ **SISTER SOREL.** *647 Tremont St, Boston (02118). Phone 617/266-4600. www.tremont647.com.* Snuggled up to the lauded Tremont 647, Sister Sorel is a trendy wine bar and café that is most often used as a holding pen for those looking to dig into the full, bold flavors of Tremont's chef/owner Andy Husbands. Also the chef/owner of Sister Sorel, he turns out the same arrestingly robust cuisine at this café, only in smaller portions and at smaller prices. The modest menu includes spit-roasted chicken; salt-and-pepper fried skirt steak; and the Burger Daddy, a gorgeous pup infused with smoke and topped with chipotle mustard. American menu. Dinner, Sat-Sun brunch. Bar. Casual attire. Outdoor seating. **$$**

★ ★ **SONSIE.** *327 Newbury St, Boston (02115). Phone 617/351-2500; fax 617/351-2565. www.sonsieboston.com.* Chic shoppers in need of sustenance head for Newbury Street's favorite sidewalk café, Sonsie. A stylish clientele flocks to this delightful restaurant, where open-air tables and French doors create a Parisian feel. The fusion menu is matched only by the superior people-watching. Since it can be a bit of a scene, those in the know arrive early to avoid the long lines and snag a table in the front for better viewing. Sunday brunch is a best bet, offering consistently good meals and value. International menu. Breakfast, lunch, dinner, late-night, brunch. Bar. Casual attire. Reservations recommended. Valet parking. Outdoor seating. **$$**

★ ★ **TAPEO.** *266 Newbury St, Boston (02116). Phone 617/267-4799; fax 617/267-1602. www.tapeo. com.* Tapeo is a Back Bay charmer with a singular Spanish vision. Serving all things from this Iberian land, expect a long menu of hot and cold authentic tapas, including shrimp sizzling in garlic and classic tortilla d'Espana, and an all-Spanish wine and sherry list. The restaurant is low-lit, romantic, and extremely popular with locals for people-watching, tasty fare, and pitchers of fruity sangria with a good kick. Spanish, tapas menu. Dinner. Closed Thanksgiving, Dec 25. Bar. Casual attire. Reservations recommended. Outdoor seating. **$$**

★ ★ **TARANTA.** *210 Hanover St, Boston. Phone 617/720-0052; fax 617/507-0492. www.tarantarist. com.* Chef/owner Jose Duarte hails from Peru, got started cooking among Italian immigrants in

Venezuela, and has had a steady hit on his hands since opening the North End's only Peruvian-Italian fusion restaurant. His signature shrimp ravioli in a pesto of pine nuts and Peruvian black mint demonstrates the easy cohibitation of the two cuisines, as does his substitution of quinoa for rice in the saffron "risotto" accompanying braised veal shanks. The piquant lift to many of Duarte's sauces comes from his careful use of the rocoto pepper, another Peruvian native, but the new-world fillips never overwhelm what is essentially old-world comfort food prepared with flair and served with style. Peruvian, Italian menu. Dinner. Closed July 4, Thanksgiving. Casual attire. **$$$**

★ ★ **TERRAMIA.** *98 Salem St, Boston (02113). Phone 617/523-3112. www.terramiaristorante.com.* Located in the North End, Terramia is a lovely Italian restaurant with a warm and charming atmosphere that makes you feel at home in an instant. The menu is of the modern trattoria genre—a great selection of meats, pastas, and salads that may sound straightforward in style, but in substance rise above and beyond. Dishes that could be run-of-the-mill are freshened up by quality seasonal ingredients and by the skill of co-owner and chef Mario Nocera. The restaurant's culinary reputation is well known around town, so be sure and reserve in advance if possible. Italian menu. Dinner. Closed holidays. Reservations recommended. **$$$**

★ ★ ★ **TOP OF THE HUB.** *800 Boylston St, Boston (02199). Phone 617/536-1775; fax 617/859-8298. www.topofthehub.net.* If sweeping, awesome views are your thing, Top of the Hub should make it onto your short list while you're in Boston. Located in the trendy Back Bay area, this special-occasion spot specializes in elegant and romantic, yet decidedly comfortable, dining. The New American menu takes some chances but for the most part stays true to the seasons, featuring a wide selection of fish, game, pork, and beef. Main courses are ample, like the slow-roasted pork tenderloin (enough to feed a family of four) and a plate of supple slices of seared yellowfin tuna with fragrant coconut-jasmine rice. American menu. Lunch, dinner. Bar. Business casual attire. Reservations recommended. **$$$**

★ ★ ★ **TROQUET.** *140 Boylston St, Boston (02116). Phone 617/695-9463. www.troquetboston.com.* The marriage of food and wine is the focus of this authentic Back Bay bistro. Troquet pairs wine with food, with wine running the show. For instance, a flight of Sauvignon Blanc would require you to start with a

fresh, tangy goat cheese coated in nuts and deep-fried over an arugula salad. If you are craving a jammy Merlot, you'll have to deal with a leg of lamb. (It's a nice problem to have.) The couplings work well for the most part and will teach you a thing or two about relationships that are worth continuing and those that really aren't worth it. American, French menu. Dinner. Closed Sun-Mon; Thanksgiving, Dec 24-25. Bar. Business casual attire. Reservations recommended. Valet parking. Credit cards accepted. **$$$**

★ ★ ★ **UNION BAR AND GRILLE.** *1357 Washington St, Boston (02118). Phone 617/423-0555. www.unionrestaurant.com.* With sleek leather banquettes and blazingly white tablecloths, Union Bar and Grille caps the gentrification process of Washington Street. Stephen Sherman, the Culinary Institute of America-trained chef, produces a seasonally shifting menu that nods to trendy dishes (tuna with grilled fennel) but leans heavily on updated New England classics, such as lobster meat tossed with corn and chanterelle mushrooms and a succulent rack of lamb drizzled with fig sauce. The wine list is as aggressively new world as the menu, pulling in a lot of Californian meritage bottles along with New Zealand whites. Pastry chef Joshua Steinberg's dessert menu seems to have a spot of chocolate on almost every plate. American menu. Dinner, Sun brunch. Bar. Casual attire. Valet parking. **$$$**

★ ★ **UNION OYSTER HOUSE.** *41 Union St, Boston (02108). Phone 617/227-2750; fax 617/227-2306. www.unionoysterhouse.com.* This popular 1826 oyster bar and tavern, decorated in old-fashioned Federalist style, has served such dignitaries as John F. Kennedy and Bill Clinton. But not to worry—they'll serve you too. This crowded hotspot attracts hordes of businessmen, ties tucked behind white shirts, slurping down hearty bowls of chowder and slipping chilled oysters out of their shells. The menu also caters to lovers of fresh fish, prepared perfectly every time. Seafood menu. Lunch, dinner, late-night. Closed Thanksgiving, Dec 25. Bar. Children's menu. Casual attire. Reservations recommended. Valet parking. **$$**

★ ★ ★ **VIA MATTA.** *79 Park Plz, Boston (02116). Phone 617/422-0008; fax 617/422-0014. www.viamattarestaurant.com.* Michael Schlow, Christopher Myers, and Esti Benson, the savvy team behind Radius (see), are the folks you can thank for opening Via Matta, a trendy spot for authentic Italian fare located across the street from the Park Plaza Hotel. You have several choices of where to dine here—the bustling, stylish dining room; the cozy, softly lit bar; or the casual café—but fret not about your decision. Regardless of where you decide to sit, you will feast happily on chef Schlow's gorgeous traditional Italian dishes. Plates are alive with flavor and fitted with the highest-quality ingredients. Hearty appetites should be required here, as the menu lists close to a dozen antipasti, followed by several pasta selections, and a half-dozen entrées. But empty stomachs will be rewarded, as the food here is truly an inspiration. From the simple spaghetti aglio e olio to pan-roasted chicken, dishes are simple and perfectly executed. To get from course to course without being parched, check out the all-Italian wine list that showcases rare winemakers. Italian menu. Lunch, dinner. Closed Sun; holidays. Bar. Casual attire. Reservations recommended. Valet parking. Outdoor seating. **$$$**

Bourne (Cape Cod) (D-8)

See also Cape Cod, Sandwich

Settled 1627
Population 18,721
Elevation 19 ft
Area Code 508
Zip 02532
Information Cape Cod Chamber of Commerce, Hwys 6 and 132, PO Box 790, Hyannis 02601-0790; phone 508/362-3225 or toll-free 888/332-2732
Web Site www.capecodchamber.org

Named for Jonathan Bourne, a successful whaling merchant, this town has had a variety of industries since its founding. Originally a center for herring fishing, the town turned to manufacturing stoves, kettles, and later, freight cars. Bourne's current prosperity is derived from cranberries and tourism.

What to See and Do

Aptucxet Trading Post. *24 Aptucxet Rd, Bourne (02532). Off Shore Rd, 1/2 mile W of Bourne Bridge. Phone 508/759-8167. www.bournehistoricalsoc.org.* A replica of a 1627 trading post that may have been the first of its kind in America. Native American artifacts; rune stone believed to be proof of visits to the area by the Phoenicians in 400 BC; artifacts in two rooms. On grounds are herb garden, site of original spring, saltworks; railroad station built for President Grover Cleveland for use at his Gray Gables home, his summer White House; Dutch-style windmill; picnic area adjacent to Cape Cod Canal. (June-mid-Oct, Mon-Sat 10 am-4 pm, Sun 2 pm-5 pm) **$**

Bourne Scenic Park. *370 Scenic Hwy, Bourne (02532). North bank of Cape Cod Canal. Phone 508/759-7873. www.bournescenicpark.com.* Playground, picnicking; bike trails; swimming pool, bathhouse; recreation building; camping (fee); store. (Apr-May: weekends; June-Oct: daily)

Pairpoint Crystal Company. *851 Sandwich Rd (Hwy 6), Sagamore (02561). Phone 508/888-2344. www.pairpoint.com.* (Established in 1837) Handmade lead crystal ware, glassblowing demonstrations. Viewing (Mon-Fri). Store (daily). **FREE**

Braintree (C-7)

See also Boston

Settled 1634
Population 33,828
Elevation 90 ft
Area Code 781
Zip 02184
Information South Shore Chamber of Commerce, 36 Miller Stile Rd, Quincy 02169; phone 617/479-1111
Web Site www.southshorechamber.org

What to See and Do

Abigail Adams House. *180 Norton St, Weymouth (02188). 2 miles E. Phone 781/335-4205.* Birthplace of Abigail Smith Adams (1744), daughter of a local clerygyman, wife of President John Adams, mother of President John Quincy Adams. Period furnishings. (July-Labor Day, Tues-Sun) **$**

Gilbert Bean Museum. *786 Washington St, Braintree (02184). Phone 781/848-1640.* (1720) Thayer, a soldier and educator, served as fifth Superintendent of West Point, 1817-1833. House contains 17th- and 18th-century furnishings, military exhibits, and local historical displays. (Tues-Wed, Sat-Sun 10 am-4:30 pm) **$$** Adjacent is a

Reconstructed 18th-Century Barn. Houses farm equipment, ice-cutting and wood tools; costumes; research library and genealogical records. (Tues-Wed, Sat-Sun)**$**

Limited-Service Hotels

★ ★ **HOLIDAY INN.** *1374 N Main St, Randolph (02368). Phone 781/961-1000; toll-free 800/465-4329; fax 781/963-0089. www.holiday-inn.com.* 158 rooms, 4 story. Pets accepted. Check-in 3 pm, check-out noon. Restaurant, bar. Outdoor pool. **$**

★ **HOLIDAY INN EXPRESS.** *909 Hingham St, Rockland (02370). Phone 781/871-5660; fax 781/871-7255.* 76 rooms, 2 story. Complimentary continental breakfast. Check-in 3 pm, check-out 11 am. **$**

Full-Service Hotel

★ ★ ★ **SHERATON BRAINTREE HOTEL.** *37 Forbes Rd, Braintree (02184). Phone 781/848-0600; toll-free 800/325-3535; fax 781/843-9492. www.sheraton.com/braintree.* The Sheraton is located 12 miles from the Logan International Airport and near the JFK library and Bayside Exposition Center. Rooms were designed and furnished with a guest's needs in mind. Relax in the indoor or outdoor pool, sauna and steamrooms, or enjoy an invigorating workout at the extensive health club with racquetball, aerobics, and Nautilus machines. 396 rooms, 6 story. Check-in 3 pm, check-out noon. Restaurant, bar. Fitness room. Indoor pool, outdoor pool. **$**

Restaurant

★ ★ **CAFFE BELLA.** *19 Warren St, Randolph (02368). Phone 781/961-7729; fax 781/961-3681.* Italian menu. Dinner. Closed Sun; holidays. Bar. **$$$**

Brewster (Cape Cod) (D-9)

See also Cape Cod, Sandwich

Settled 1656
Population 10,094
Elevation 39 ft
Area Code 508
Zip 02631
Information Cape Cod Chamber of Commerce, Hwys 6 and 132, PO Box 790, Hyannis 02601-0790; phone 508/362-3225 or toll-free 888/332-2732
Web Site www.capecodchamber.org

This quiet community on Cape Cod Bay is dominated by its miles of beautiful saltwater beaches, where the tides have caused the water to recede by more than a mile, creating an expanse of sand and tidepools. The New England Fire and History Museum is located here, as are plentiful opportunities to shop for crafts and antiques. The outstanding Chillingsworth is a standout among both lodgings and restaurants here.

What to See and Do

Cape Cod Museum of Natural History. *869 Rte 6A, Brewster (02631). Phone 508/896-3867; fax 508/896-8844. www.ccmnh.org.* Exhibits on wildlife and ecology of the area; art exhibits; library; lectures; nature trails; field walks; trips to Monomoy Island. Gift shop. (Daily 9:30 am-4 pm; closed holidays) **$$**

Cape Cod Repertory Theater Company. *3379 Hwy 6A, Brewster (02631). Phone 508/896-1888. www.caperep.org.* Boasting both an indoor and outdoor theater, the Cape Cod Repertory Theater offers a children's theater two mornings per week (Tues and Fri) in July and August. In addition, you'll find productions for the whole family in the outdoor theater, which sits back in the beautiful woods near Nickerson State Park and is open in fair weather. The indoor theater offers plays and musicals year-round. **$$$$**

⭐ **New England Fire & History Museum.** *1439 Main St, Brewster (02631). 1/2 mile W of Hwy 137 on Hwy 6A. Phone 508/896-5711.* This six-building complex houses an extensive collection of fire-fighting equipment and includes the Arthur Fiedler Memorial Fire Collection; diorama of Chicago fire of 1871; engines dating from the Revolution to the 1930s; world's only 1929 Mercedes Benz fire engine; life-size reproduction of Ben Franklin's firehouse; 19th-century blacksmith shop; largest apothecary shop in the country contains 664 gold-leaf bottles of medicine; medicinal herb gardens; library; films; theater performances. Guided tours. Picnic area. (Memorial Day weekend-Labor Day: Mon-Sat 10 am-4 pm, Sun from noon; mid-Sept-Columbus Day: weekends) **$$**

Nickerson State Park. *3488 Rte 6A, Brewster (02631). Phone 508/896-3491. www.state.ma.us/dem/parks/nick.htm.* Nickerson State Park offers an unusual experience on Cape Cod: densely wooded areas that show no signs of the marshy areas that abound on the Cape. Nickerson offers camping, challenging hiking trails, an 8-mile bike path that connects to the Cape Cod Rail Trail (a 25-mile paved bike trail), fishing, swimming, canoeing, and bird-watching. Also consider areas on the Cape that offer similar activities: Green Briar Nature Center in Sandwich, Lowell Holly Reservation in Mashpee, Ashumet Holly and Wildlife Sanctuary in East Falmouth, Great Island Trail in Wellfleet, Coatue-Coksata-Great Point on Nantucket. (Daily) **FREE**

Ocean Edge Golf Course. *2660 Hwy 6A, Brewster (02631). Phone 508/896-9000. www.oceanedge.com.* This beautiful golf course, just a stones throw from the ocean, offers 6,665 yards of manicured green, plus five ponds for challenging play. Play during the week in the off-season, and you'll pay extremely reasonable greens fees. Lessons from PGA pros are available. The course is part of a resort that offers accommodations, tennis courts and lessons, a private beach, and 26 miles of paved bike trails (bike rentals are available). (Daily; closed for snow and inclement weather) **$$$$**

Stoney Brook Mill. *830 Stoney Brook Rd, Brewster (02631). Old Gristmill in West Brewster, on site of one of first gristmills in America. Phone 508/896-1734.* Museum upstairs includes historical exhibits, weaving. Corn grinding (Thurs-Sat afternoons). **FREE**

Full-Service Resort

★ ★ ★ **OCEAN EDGE RESORT.** *2907 Main St, Brewster (02631). Phone 508/896-9000; toll-free 800/343-6074; fax 508/896-27. www.oceanedge.com.* Ideally situated on the charming Cape Cod Bay and surrounded by lush gardens, this charming English country manor offers guests an oasis of comfort and privacy while being surrounded by understated elegance and superb service. Discover the charm and character of this 19th-century mansion and carriage house. From the quiet elegance of their luxurious guest rooms to the championship 18-hole golf course, 11 tennis courts, and premiere health and fitness center, this resort offers timeless tranquility and complete relaxation for a romantic weekend or a quiet business retreat. 406 rooms, 2 story. Check-in 3 pm, check-out 10 am. Restaurant, bar. Children's activity center. Fitness room. Two indoor pools, four outdoor pools, whirlpool. Golf. Tennis. Airport transportation available. Business center. **$$**

Specialty Lodgings

BRAMBLE INN. *2019 Main St, Brewster (02631). Phone 508/896-7644; fax 508/896-9332. www.brambleinn. com.* Family owned and operated, this attractive inn,

with its pine floors, lovely antiques, and charmingly appointed guest rooms, offers guests a truly delightful stay. 8 rooms, 2 story. Closed Jan-Apr. Children over 8 years only. Complimentary full breakfast. Check-in 2-9 pm. Check-out 11 am. Restaurant. **$**

BREWSTER BY THE SEA. *716 Main St, Brewster (02631). Phone 508/896-3910; toll-free 800/892-3910; fax 508/896-4232. www.brewsterbythesea.com.* Get away from it all, rejuvenate, and relax at this charming and elegant inn. Built in 1846 and set amidst a country like setting, this inn has been charmingly restored and offers guests a delightful stay. 8 rooms, 2 story. Children over 10 years only. Complimentary full breakfast. Check-in 3 pm, check-out 11 am. Outdoor pool, whirlpool. **$**

CAPTAIN FREEMAN INN. *15 Breakwater Rd, Brewster (02631). Phone 508/896-7481; toll-free 800/843-4664; fax 508/896-5618. www.captainfreemaninn. com.* 12 rooms, 3 story. Children over 10 years only. Complimentary full breakfast. Check-in 2-7 pm, check-out 11 am. Outdoor pool. **$**

ISAIAH CLARK HOUSE. *1187 Main St, Brewster (02631). Phone 508/896-2223; toll-free 800/822-4001; fax 508/896-2138. www.isaiahclark.com.* Former sea captain's house (1780). 7 rooms, 2 story. Children over 10 years only. Complimentary full breakfast. Check-in 2-5 pm, check-out 11 am. **$**

THE OLD MANSE INN. *1861 Main St, Brewster (02631). Phone 508/896-3149; toll-free 866/896-3149. www.oldmanseinn.com.* 9 rooms. Complimentary full breakfast. Check-in 2 pm, check-out 11 am. **$$**

OLD SEA PINES INN. *2553 Main St, Brewster (02631). Phone 508/896-6114; fax 508/632-0084. www. oldseapinesinn.com.* Founded in 1907 as School of Charm and Personality for Young Women. 24 rooms, 3 story. Children over 8 years only (except in family suites). Complimentary full breakfast. Check-in 2 pm, check-out 11 am. **$**

Restaurants

★ ★ **BRAMBLE INN.** *2019 Main St, Brewster (02631). Phone 508/896-7644; fax 508/896-*

9332. *www.brambleinn.com*. This restaurant is located in the charming Bramble Inn (built in 1861), in the heart of Brewster's historic district. Chef/owner Ruth Manchester delights guests with creative cuisine and heartwarming hospitality. The four quaint dining rooms, including an enclosed porch, make the Bramble Inn a perfect choice for a romantic dinner. American menu. Dinner. Closed Jan-Apr. Bar. Business casual attire. Reservations recommended. **$$$**

★ ★ **BREWSTER FISH HOUSE.** *2208 Main St, Brewster (02631). Phone 508/896-7867.* Those with sophisticated palates who enjoy a good meal in an unstuffy atmosphere rave about the Brewster Fish House. Seafood is prepared in a variety of innovative ways here, with meat and vegetarian options rounding out the menu. Consistently crowded, this restaurant often sees long lines—and for good reason. American, seafood menu. Lunch, dinner. Closed Dec-Apr. **$$$**

★ **BREWSTER INN AND CHOWDER HOUSE.** *1993 Main St, Brewster (02631). Phone 508/896-7771.* The Brewster Inn and Chowder House is a Cape Cod institution, feeding hungry souls for over a century. Diners are attracted by the promise of deliciously prepared, unfussy seafood in an unpretentious setting. As the name suggests, clam chowder is a signature dish here, and the thick, tasty soup is not to be skipped. American menu. Lunch, dinner. Closed Labor Day, Thanksgiving, Dec 25. Bar. Casual attire. Outdoor seating. **$$**

★ ★ ★ **CHILLINGSWORTH.** *2449 Main St, Brewster (02631). Phone 508/896-3640; toll-free 800/430-3640; fax 508/896-7540. www.chillingsworth. com.* The grand 300-year-old Chillingsworth Foster estate sprawls along the edge of the King's Highway. For the last 30 years, Chillingsworth has been synonymous with epicurean dining on Cape Cod. The formal main dining rooms, furnished in fine antiques, are spread through the central house, while the more casual bistro occupies a glassed-in porch and greenhouse. The seven-course table d'hôte dinner offers a contemporary interpretation of classic French cuisine—seared veal steak with truffle risotto, for example, or lobster with sautéed spinach and fennel. Its a dressy, ceremonial meal that takes all evening. Quicker, lighter fare is available à la carte in the bistro. French menu. Lunch, dinner. Closed Mon; also Dec-mid-May. Bar. Reservations recommended. Outdoor seating. **$$$**

★ ★ **SPARK FISH.** *2671 Main St, Brewster (02631). Phone 508/896-1067; fax 508/896-1075. www. sparkfish.com.* Simple, uncomplicated food takes center stage at Spark Fish. This mellow spot serves dinner to a casual crowd who come here for the wood-fired grill specialties. The menu focuses on seafood, but there are plenty of meat and chicken selections for non-fish eaters. Seating on the outdoor deck is highly coveted during the summer months. American menu. Dinner. Closed Thanksgiving, Dec 24-25. Bar. Children's menu. Casual attire. Reservations recommended. Outdoor seating. **$$**

Brockton (C-7)

Settled 1700
Population 94,304
Elevation 112 ft
Area Code 508
Information Metro South Chamber of Commerce, 60 School St, 02301; phone 508/586-0500
Web Site www.metrosouthchamber.com

Half of the Union Army in the Civil War marched in Brockton-made shoes. Known as the nation's shoe capital until the 20th century, diverse manufacturing and service industries contribute to the city's economic base today. Brockton was home of boxing champions Rocky Marciano and "Marvelous" Marvin Hagler.

What to See and Do

Brockton Historical Society Museums. *216 N Pearl St, Brockton (02301). Phone 508/583-1039. www.brocktonma. com.* The Heritage Center, the main building of the complex, consists of the Shoe Museum, Fire Museum, and "The Homestead," an early Brockton shoemaker's home. "The Homestead" features exhibits on Thomas Edison, who electrified the first shoe factory in the world in Brockton in 1883, and former local shoemaker and undefeated world champion boxer, Rocky Marciano. (First and third Sun afternoon of each month or by appointment) **$**

Fuller Museum of Art. *455 Oak St, Brockton (02301). On Porter's Pond. Phone 508/588-6000; fax 508/587-6191. www.fullermuseum.org.* Permanent exhibits of 19th- and 20th-century American art; children's gallery; changing exhibits; lectures, gallery talks, and tours. Museum (Daily 10 am-5 pm; closed holidays). **$**

Special Event

Brockton Fair. *Fairgrounds on Belmont St, Brockton (02301). Phone 508/586-8000; fax 508/821-3239. www.*

brocktonfair.com. Midway, agricultural exhibits, entertainment. (Early July)

Limited-Service Hotels

★ ★ BEST WESTERN CARLTON HOUSE.
1005 Belmont St, Brockton (02301). Phone 508/588-3333; toll-free 800/780-7234; fax 508/588-3333. www.bestwestern.com. 69 rooms, 2 story. Check-in 3 pm, check-out 11 am. Restaurant, bar. Outdoor pool. **$**

★ ★ HOLIDAY INN BROCKTON.
195 Westgate Dr, Brockton (02301). Phone 508/588-6300; fax 508/580-4384. www.holidayinn.com. 186 rooms, 3 story. Check-in 3 pm, check-out noon. Restaurant, bar. Fitness room. Indoor pool, whirlpool. **$**

Restaurant

★ CHRISTOS.
782 Crescent St, Brockton (02402). Phone 508/588-4200; fax 508/583-6946. www.nedine.com/Christos.htm. Greek menu, steak menu. Lunch, dinner. Closed Thanksgiving, Dec 25. Bar. **$$**

Brookline (B-7)

Population 57,107
Area Code 617
Zip 02445, 02446
Web Site www.townofbrooklinemass.com

This booming commuter suburb to the east of Boston has a history dating to the 1630s. Having started out as a rural community, it developed into a residential area in the 1800s, when wealthy merchants and politicians began purchasing farms and turning them into summer estates. Landscape architect Frederick Law Olmstead was among its 19th-century residents and served on its planning board; a National Historic Site remembers his achievements today. Its major attraction for travelers is the John F. Kennedy National Historic Site, the president's birthplace and boyhood home. Foodies will enjoy the Brookline Farmers Market in the Center Street parking lot, where area growers come to sell their fresh fruits, vegetables, herbs, cut flowers, and more.

What to See and Do

John F. Kennedy National Historic Site. *83 Beals St, Brookline (02446). Phone 617/566-7937; fax 617/730-9884. www.nps.gov/jofi.* The birthplace and early childhood home of the nation's 35th president is restored in appearance to 1917, the year of his birth. Ranger-guided tours. (May-Oct, Wed-Sun 10 am-4:30 pm; closed holidays) Golden Eagle Passport accepted (see MAKING THE MOST OF YOUR TRIP). **$**

Restaurants

★ ★ ★ THE FIREPLACE.
1634 Beacon St, Brookline (02446). Phone 617/975-1900; fax 617/975-1600. www.fireplacerest.com. Situated in a section of Brookline heavily populated with young professionals, The Fireplace can seem like a cross between *Friends* and *Cheers,* where everyone knows everyone and half the diners are just stopping off for a glass of Sancerre and a small plate of duck sausage and mashed turnips. But the wood-fired oven, the rotisserie, and the kitchen's own smoke box make Jim Solomon's neighborhood bistro a fine destination for a hearty meal of braised brisket or grilled halibut. Desserts (such as gingerbread pudding with burnt lemon sauce) are rich, dark, and treacly. The eponymous hearth provides the welcome tang of woodsmoke in cold weather. American, seafood menu. Lunch, dinner, brunch. Children's menu. Casual attire. **$$**

★ ★ ★ FUGAKYU.
1280 Beacon St, Brookline (02446). Phone 617/734-1268; fax 617/739-1368. www.fugakyujapanese.com. Snappy sushi bars abound in Boston, but only this elegant restaurant outside of Coolidge Corner offers the full Japanese dining experience, with soups, broiled dishes, tempuras, stir-fries, noodles, pickle plates, and tableside braises. Like other great Japanese restaurants, Fugakyu exudes formality and serenity in its discreet tatami rooms divided by rice paper walls. The sashimi deluxe platter is a triumph of the sushi chef's craft: each individual slice of fish is a carefully wrought piece of art. Japanese and Western diners alike rave over the dessert of tempura-fried green tea ice cream topped with just a dab of red-bean paste. Reserve far ahead; Fugakyu fills up quickly even on weekday evenings in bad weather. Japanese, sushi menu. Lunch, dinner, late-night. Closed Sun. Reservations recommended.

★ RUBIN'S KOSHER DELICATESSEN.
500 Harvard St, Brookline (02446). Phone 617/731-8787; fax 617/566-3354. www.rubinskosher.com. Since 1927, central and eastern European immigrants have made Rubin's their kitchen away from home. The full-service deli sells all the classics, from chopped liver

(chicken or beef) to lean pastrami, pickled herring, countless varieties of latkes, and both potato and sweet potato kugel. Most customers stop in to stock the larder at home, but for those too hungry to wait, the staff behind the counter will make sandwiches or heat up cooked dishes to eat at the few small tables. Kosher deli menu. Breakfast, lunch, dinner Sun-Thurs. Closed Sat; Jewish holidays. **$**

★ ★ WASHINGTON SQUARE TAVERN.

714 Washington St, Brookline (02446). Phone 617/232-8989; fax 617/232-8201. washingtonsquaretavern.com. Chef/owner Paul Hathaway accommodates late and early diners alike at his classic neighborhood tavern by offering a choice between inexpensive hearty sandwich plates (grilled chicken with Gruyre cheese and onion jam, for example) and more refined New American entrées, such as pan-roasted cod with sautéed potatoes. The single large room gets boisterous as the night progresses, in part a tribute to the smartly chosen and reasonably priced wine list. Unfortunately, there are no desserts on the menu. American menu. Dinner, Sun brunch. Bar. Casual attire. **$$**

Burlington (B-7)

Settled 1641
Population 22,876
Elevation 218 ft
Area Code 781
Zip 01803

Limited-Service Hotel

★ HAMPTON INN. *315 Mishawum Rd, Woburn (01801). Phone 781/935-7666; fax 781/933-6899. www.hamptoninn.com.* 99 rooms, 5 story. Complimentary continental breakfast. Check-in 3 pm, check-out noon. **$**

Full-Service Hotel

★ ★ ★ MARRIOTT BOSTON BURLINGTON.

1 Mall Rd, Burlington (01803). Phone 781/229-6565; toll-free 800/371-3625; fax 781/229-7973. www.marriott.com. 423 rooms, 9 story. Check-in 4 pm, check-out noon. Restaurant, bar. Fitness room. Indoor, outdoor pool; whirlpool. **$**

Restaurant

★ DANDELION GREEN RESTAURANT. *90 Burlington Mall Rd, Burlington (01803). Phone 781/273-1616; fax 781/273-5426. www.barnsiderrestaurants.com.* Seafood, steak menu. Lunch, dinner. Closed holidays. Bar. Children's menu. **$$$**

Cambridge (B-7)

See also Boston

Settled 1630
Population 101,355
Elevation 40 ft
Area Code 617
Information Chamber of Commerce, 859 Massachusetts Ave, 02139; phone 617/876-4100
Web Site www.cambcc.org

The city of Cambridge—academically inclined, historically rich, internationally flavored—occupies an enviable geographic position alongside the northern banks of the Charles River. It is home to two of the nation's most prestigious institutions of higher learning, Harvard University and the Massachusetts Institute of Technology (MIT). The Radcliffe Institute for Advanced Study and Lesley University can also be found here. It should come as no surprise that one-fourth of Cambridges 95,000 residents are students and that one-sixth of the city's jobs are in higher education.

A group of approximately 700 Puritans set sail from England in 1630, making their way across the Atlantic Ocean to the Massachusetts Bay Colony, where they settled in the area now known as Cambridge. The nations oldest university, Harvard, was founded six years later. At the time of the American Revolution, Cambridge existed as a quiet farming village, its population comprised mainly of descendants of the original Puritans. Over the course of the 18th century, an increasing number of immigrants, mostly Irish, arrived. The immigration trend continued into the 20th century, with Italians, Portuguese, and Russians seeking a better life in this hamlet to the immediate northwest of Boston. Today, Cambridge is well known for its diversity and multiculturalism, a reputation underscored by the fact that 80 different nations are represented by the children attending the citys public schools.

Cambridge offers a vibrant nightlife, with numerous restaurants, theaters, and clubs surrounding the city's squares: Central Square, Harvard Square, and Inman Square. Some of the best entertainment can be enjoyed on the city's sidewalks, where street performers—ranging from illusionists to musicians to puppeteers—often draw large crowds. Like most college towns, Cambridge has plenty of bookshops. One of the most popular is Curious George Goes to WordsWorth, a two-story bookshop housing more than 20,000 children's titles.

What to See and Do

Cambridge Antique Mall. *201 Msgr O'Brien Hwy, Cambridge (02140). Take the Green Line (T) to the Lechmere stop. Phone 617/868-9655; fax 617/876-0515. www.marketantique.com.* Stroll through five floors of antique furniture, books, artwork, toys, clothing, and more. More than 150 dealers offer up antiques here, which seems most appropriate in this historic town. Although no ones making any promises, you can't help but wonder whether a dresser or rocking chair once sat prominently in John Hancocks house or Paul Reveres workshop. (Tues-Sun 11 am-6 pm; closed holidays)

Christ Church. *Zero Garden St, Cambridge (02138). At the Common. Phone 617/876-0200; fax 617/876-0201. www.cccambridge.org.* (1759) Episcopal. The oldest church building in Cambridge. A fine Georgian colonial building designed by Peter Harrison that was used as a colonial barracks during the Revolution. (Daily) **FREE**

Dance Complex. *536 Massachusetts Ave, Cambridge (02139). Take the Red Line to the Central Square MBTA station, exit toward Pearl St/Main St. Phone 617/547-9363. www.dancecomplex.org.* Ready to dance the night away but need to first brush up on your skills? Sashay into The Dance Complex, a not-for-profit dance studio that offers drop-in classes in everything from salsa to hip-hop. With more than 60 teachers on staff, you're sure to find a class to fit your needs. After you're ready to rumba, check out www.havetodance.com for links to some of the best dancing venues in Boston. (Daily) **$$$**

Formaggio Kitchen. *244 Huron Ave, Cambridge (02138). Phone 617/354-4750. www.formaggiokitchen. com.* Whether you consider yourself a *gourmet* or a *gourmand*, you'll easily lose yourself in this culinary playground. With a selection of 200 artisanal cheeses, the finest pastas, chocolates from Italy, France, and the United States, as well as a variety of exotic spices, mouthwatering snacks, and Italian coffees, the famed Formaggio Kitchen is a food-lovers dream. While you're here, pick up some professional-quality cutlery or select one of the many gift baskets for a foodie friend back home. A second location has opened in South Boston at 268 Shawmut Avenue.

Fresh Pond Golf Course. *691 Huron Ave, Cambridge (02138). Phone 617/349-6282. www.freshpondgolf.com.* This nine-hole, par-35 course lies next to the Fresh Pond Reservoir, creating a few challenging water hazards. However, this course plays gently and is a perfect starting point for beginners. More experienced players will appreciate Fresh Ponds quick play, which means that you'll have time to get back to more sightseeing around Boston. (Daily dawn-dusk; closed for snow and inclement weather) **$$$$**

Grolier Poetry Book Shop. *6 Plympton St, Cambridge (02138). Take the Red Line (T) to Harvard Square. Phone 617/547-4648; toll-free 800/234-7636; fax 617/547-4230. www.grolierpoetrybookshop.com.* With more than 15,000 volumes of poetry, Grolier's is a gathering place for poets and those who delight in poetry books and readings. The shop holds weekly readings on Tuesdays, Fridays, or Sundays. Founded in 1927, it is the oldest continuously operating poetry bookshop in the United States. (Mon-Sat 1 pm-6:30 pm; closed Sun, holidays)

★ **Harvard University.** *24 Quincy St, Cambridge (02138). Harvard Square. www.harvard.edu.* (18,179 students) This magnificent university, America's oldest, was founded in 1636. Two years later, when a minister named John Harvard died and left half his estate and his considerable personal library, it was named for him. Includes Harvard and Radcliffe colleges as well as ten graduate and professional schools. Harvard Yard, as the original campus is called, is tree-shaded and occupied by stately red-brick buildings. In and around the yard are

Harvard Museum of Natural History. *26 Oxford St, Cambridge (02138). Phone 617/495-3045.* The Harvard Museum of Natural History (HMNH) combines three museums in one: a botanical museum that examines the study of plants, the museum of zoology that examines the study of animals, and a geological museum that examines the study of rocks and minerals. All three explore the evolution of science and nature throughout time. A collection of glass models of plants— more than 3,000 plant lookalikes rendered carefully in glass—is the only exhibit of its kind in the world. (Daily 9 am-5 pm; closed holidays) **$$**

Harvard University Art Museums. *32 Quincy St, Cambridge (02138). Phone 617/495-9400.* Three museums make up the Harvard Art Museums: the Fogg Art Museum (including wide-ranging collections of paintings and sculpture), the Busch-Reisinger Museum (which features mostly German art), and the Arthur M. Sackler Museum (offering ancient art, plus Asian and Islamic collections). Admission to one museum covers all three; allow a half day for all. Entry to the museums is free on Wednesdays and Saturdays until noon. (Daily; closed holidays) **$$**

Houses of Harvard-Radcliffe. Between Harvard Square and the Charles River, and northeast of Harvard Yard between Shepard and Linnaean streets.

Information Center. *1350 Massachusetts Ave, Cambridge (02138). Phone 617/495-1573.* Provides maps, brochures. (June-Aug, daily; rest of year, Mon-Sat) Student-guided tours begin here.

John F. Kennedy School of Government. *79 John F. Kennedy St, Cambridge (02138). On the banks of the Charles River. Phone 617/495-1100.* (1978) Contains a library, classrooms, and a public affairs forum for lectures.

Massachusetts Hall. *24 Quincy St, Cambridge (02138).* Oldest building (1720) and architectural inspiration for the campus. **FREE**

Peabody Museum of Archaeology and Ethnology. *11 Divinity Ave, Cambridge (02138). Phone 617/496-1027.* Anthropology and ethnology are sciences that record how humans develop culturally. The Peabody Museum, one of the oldest anthropology museums in the world, traces human cultural history in the Western Hemisphere with four major exhibits. In addition, the museum sponsors interactive programs for kids, public lectures, and summer science camps. (Daily; closed holidays) **$$**

University Hall. *Harvard Yard, Cambridge (02138). Phone 617/495-0450.* (1813-1815) Designed by Charles Bulfinch, made of Chelmsford granite in contrast to the surrounding brick, and one of the Yard's most handsome buildings. **FREE**

Widener Library. *1329 Massachusetts Ave, Cambridge (02138). S side of Harvard Yard. Phone* *617/495-4166.* (1915) Has an enormous Corinthian portico; more than 3 million books. Near it are Houghton, with a fine collection of rare books, and Lamont, the first undergraduate library in America. **FREE**

Longfellow National Historic Site. *105 Brattle St, Cambridge (02138). 1/2 mile from Harvard. Phone 617/876-4491; fax 617/497-8718. www.nps.gov/long.* This Georgian-style house, built in 1759, was Washington's headquarters during the 1775-1776 siege of Boston, and Henry Wadsworth Longfellow's home from 1837 until his death in 1882. Longfellow taught at Harvard, and his books are located here. (Wed-Sun 10 am-4:30 pm; closed Jan 1, Thanksgiving, Dec 25) **$**

Massachusetts Institute of Technology. *77 Massachusetts Ave, Cambridge (02139). Phone 617/253-1000. www.mit.edu.* (1861) (9,500 students) One of the greatest science and engineering schools in the world. On the Charles River, the campus includes 135 acres of impressive neoclassic and modern buildings. Information center in the lobby of the main building; guided tours, two departures (Mon-Fri). On campus are

Hart Nautical Galleries. *55 Massachusetts Ave, Cambridge (02139). Phone 617/253-5942; fax 617/258-9107.* Shows ship and marine engineering development through displays of rigged merchant and naval ship models; changing exhibits. (Daily 9 am-8 pm) **FREE**

List Visual Arts Center at MIT. *Wiesner Building, 20 Ames St, Cambridge (02139).* Changing exhibits of contemporary art. (Oct-June, daily; closed holidays; free) The MIT campus also has an outstanding permanent collection of outdoor sculpture, including works by Calder, Moore, and Picasso, and significant architecture, including buildings by Aalto, Pei, and Saarinen. Walking tour map at information center.

MIT Museum. *265 Massachusetts Ave, Cambridge (02139). Phone 617/253-4444.* Collections and exhibits that interpret the Institute's social and educational history, developments in science and technology, and the interplay of technology and art. (Tues-Fri 10am-5pm, Sat-Sun from noon; closed Mon, holidays) **$**

Radcliffe College's Schlesinger Library Culinary Collection. *10 Garden St, Cambridge (02138). Take the Red Line ("T") to the Harvard Square station. Walk through Harvard Square, down Brattle St; Radcliffe*

Yard is 3 blocks away, at the corner of Brattle and James sts. Phone 617/495-8647. www.radcliffe.edu/schles. Through Radcliffe's culinary collection, you'll have access to more than 9,000 cookbooks and other culinary texts. Although you can't borrow from the library, you can conduct culinary research by tapping into the books of some of the world's greatest chefs, including Samuel Narcisse Chamberlain, Julia Child, and Sophie Coe. (Mon-Fri; closed holidays, Dec 25-Jan 1) **FREE**

The Radcliffe Institute for Advanced Study. *10 Garden St, Cambridge (02138). Admissions office. Phone 617/495-8601; fax 617/496-4640. www.radcliffe.edu.* (1879) (2,700 women) Coordinate institution with Harvard. Unique women's educational and scholarly resources including the Arthur and Elizabeth Schlesinger Library on the History of Women in America (at 3 James St). More than 850 major collections of history of women from 1800 to present.

Special Event

Head of the Charles Regatta. *2 Gerry's Landing Rd, Cambridge (02138). The race starts on the Charles, near Boston University. Take the Green Line B to Boston University and walk to the BU Bridge. Phone 617/868-6200; fax 617/868-6072. www.hocr.org.* The Head of the Charles Regatta is a 3-mile rowing race that involves 7,000 athletes, 1,470 rowing shells, and 300,000 spectators. Oarspeople, including Olympic and World champions, Olympic medalists, and national champions from around the world, race the Charles River, from Boston to Cambridge and under the Charles Eliot Bridge to the finish line. In addition, after the close of the Head of the Charles Regatta, you can watch the Charles Schwab Championship sprint at 5 pm Sunday, when the top three rowers from the preceding days Championship Single take to their shells for a 550-meter dead sprint along the Charles, from River Street Bridge to the Weeks Footbridge. Late Oct. **FREE**

Limited-Service Hotels

★ ★ **BEST WESTERN HOTEL TRIA.** *220 Alewife Brook Pkwy, Cambridge (02138). Phone 617/491-8000; toll-free 866/333-8742; fax 617/491-4932. www.bestwestern.com.* Boutique room design has filtered down to value-priced lodging at this completely overhauled (as of 2004) property 2 miles outside Harvard Square on a busy traffic circle. The interior belies its strip setting, with luxurious mattresses, hip but soothing design, snappy contemporary furniture (including ergonomic desk chairs), and free high-speed Internet access (both wired and wireless) throughout. The walk to the Alewife subway stop is short but crosses a busy highway. If the TV show *Divine Design* took on a circa-1963 roadside hotel, this might be the result. 69 rooms, 4 story. Pets accepted; fee. Complimentary continental breakfast. Check-in 3 pm, check-out noon. High-speed Internet access. Restaurant, bar. Indoor pool, whirlpool. **$**

★ ★ **HOLIDAY INN.** *30 Washington St, Somerville (02143). Phone 617/628-1000; toll-free 800/465-4329; fax 617/628-0143. www.holiday-inn.com.* 184 rooms, 9 story. Check-in 3 pm, check-out noon. Restaurant, bar. Fitness room. Indoor pool, whirlpool. **$$**

Full-Service Hotels

★ ★ ★ **CHARLES HOTEL.** *1 Bennett St, Cambridge (02138). Phone 617/864-1200; toll-free 800/882-1818; fax 617/864-5715. www.charleshotel. com.* This upscale hotel just off Harvard Square on the Charles River defines luxury lodging in Cambridge. For that reason, it attracts celebrities and other high-profile guests, as well as the wealthy parents of Harvard students. Its guest rooms mix Shaker-inspired design with a multitude of modern amenities—duvets, three two-line phones, Bose Wave radios, televisions in the bathrooms, and more. Dine in either of its two restaurants, and be sure to tune into the sweet sounds of jazz at the Regattabar, where swingin' national bands hit the stage. The hotel also has an on-site athletic center with indoor pool, a day spa, and indoor parking. 294 rooms, 10 story. Pets accepted. Check-in 3 pm, check-out 1 pm. High-speed Internet access, wireless Internet access. Two restaurants, three bars. Fitness room, fitness classes available, spa. Indoor pool, whirlpool. Business center. **$$$**

★ ★ ★ **HOTEL @ MIT.** *20 Sidney St, Cambridge (02139). Phone 617/577-0200; toll-free 800/774-1500; fax 617/551-0444. www.hotelatmit.com.* This high-tech-themed hotel identifies closely with the Massachusetts Institute of Technology, even incorporating printed circuit boards as a design motif in the bedroom furniture. Predictably, the hotel is wired every which way, with Internet access about ten times faster than so-called broadband and Sony PlayStations in all guest rooms. The hotel functions as a conference and meeting center for cutting-edge companies in media, biotech, robotics, and computing as well as a venue for purely academic meetings. Sidney's Grill continues the spirit of innovation with a contemporary Mediterranean menu. Central Square, with a Red Line subway stop, is a ten-minute walk away. This hotel is part of the Doubletree Hotel chain. 210 rooms. Pets accepted. Check-in 3 pm, check-out noon. High-speed Internet access, wireless Internet access. Restaurant, bar. Fitness room. Business center. **$$**

★ ★ ★ **HOTEL MARLOWE.** *25 Edwin H Land Blvd, Cambridge (02141). Phone 617/868-8000; toll-free 800/825-7140; fax 617/868-8001. www.hotelmarlowe. com.* It's rare to find a luxury hotel with a sense of whimsy in its design, but the Marlowe sets itself apart from the other East Cambridge lodgings with a bold palette of crimson red, deep blue, and bright gold and a variety of subtle nautical references, such as carpets with a compass rose and painted nautical banners. It shares the once-industrial Lechmere canal with luxury condos and an upscale shopping mall—all less than a block from the Museum of Science and its subway stop. Some hotels tolerate pets; the Marlowe caters to them (the concierge can even order Rover a birthday cake from the Polka Dog Bakery). Amenities are top of the line (Frette linens, Aveda bath products), and the Sony PlayStation in every room wins youngsters over. 236 rooms. Pets accepted. Check-in 3 pm, check-out noon. High-speed Internet access. Restaurant, bar. Fitness room. Business center. **$$$**

★ ★ ★ **HYATT REGENCY CAMBRIDGE.** *575 Memorial Dr, Cambridge (02139). Phone 617/492-1234; toll-free 800/633-7313; fax 617/491-6906. www. hyatt.com.* Ideally situated along the picturesque Charles River and with views of the alluring Boston skyline, guests are offered a level of style and comfort that's expected from Hyatt. From the lavishly appointed lobby and spacious guest rooms, as well as the charming gazebo nestled in the well-maintained courtyard, guests will immediately feel relaxed and welcomed. 469 rooms, 16 story. Pets accepted; fee. Check-in 3 pm, check-out noon. High-speed Internet access, wireless Internet access. Restaurant, bar. Fitness room. Indoor pool, whirlpool. Business center. **$$$**

★ ★ ★ **THE INN AT HARVARD.** *1201 Massachusetts Ave, Cambridge (02138). Phone 617/491-2222; toll-free 800/458-5886; fax 617/520-3711. www. theinnatharvard.com.* Apart from private clubs, there's hardly a lodging in greater Boston quite like The Inn

at Harvard. Acclaimed postmodernist Cambridge architect Graham Gund showed great restraint in creating this neoclassical structure at the edge of Harvard Square and within a block of Harvard University's art museums. Guest rooms have a casual, homey feel, but the most important feature is the four-story atrium that turns the reception area into a soaring library and lounge that works equally well for relaxing with a good book, sipping afternoon tea, or dining in the evening. Harvard frequently books many of the rooms for visiting scholars and dignitaries. It's especially hard to find a vacancy during commencement, homecoming, or alumni weekend. 112 rooms, 4 story. Check-in 3 pm, check-out noon. High-speed Internet access, wireless Internet access. Restaurant, bar. **$$**

★ ★ ★ **MARRIOTT BOSTON CAMBRIDGE.** *2 Cambridge Ctr, Cambridge (02142). Phone 617/494-6600; toll-free 800/228-9290; fax 617/494-0036. www. marriott.com.* Nestled in the heart of the Cambridge Business Community and only a few short miles from Logan International Airport, this hotel offers guests all the comforts of home. Rooms are spacious and have been equipped with guests' needs in mind. Guests can relax in the indoor pool or enjoy a invigorating workout in the well-maintained health club. Nearby attractions include downtown Boston, Harvard Square, and the Museum of Science. 431 rooms, 26 story. Check-in 4 pm, check-out noon. High-speed Internet access. Two restaurants, two bars. Fitness room. Indoor pool, whirlpool. Business center. **$$**

★ ★ ★ **ROYAL SONESTA HOTEL BOSTON.** *5 Cambridge Pkwy, Cambridge (02142). Phone 617/806-4200; toll-free 800/766-3782; fax 617/806-4232. www.sonesta.com/boston.* Perched along the Charles River, this magnificent hotel offers guests panaromic Boston views, handsomely appointed and spacious guest rooms, as well as a state-of-the-art health spa featuring massage therapists, reflexology, and an indoor and outdoor pool with a retractable roof and sun deck. This luxury hotel is ideally situated across from the waterfront shopping area and next door to the Museum of Science. 400 rooms, 10 story. Pets accepted, some restrictions. Check-in 3 pm, check-out noon. High-speed Internet access, wireless Internet access. Two restaurants, two bars. Fitness room, spa. Indoor pool, whirlpool. Business center. **$$$**

Specialty Lodging

A CAMBRIDGE HOUSE BED AND BREAKFAST INN. *2218 Massachusetts Ave, Cambridge (02140). Phone 617/491-6300; toll-free 800/232-9989; fax 617/868-2848. www.acambridgehouse. com.* Despite its location in metro Boston, about 1 1/2 miles from Harvard Square, this cozy inn offers couples the perfect setting for a romantic getaway. Many of the guest rooms in this turn-of-the-century, three-story frame house have heavenly four-poster beds lavishly dressed with fine linens and pillows, and most have gas-log fireplaces. In warm weather, the lovely backyard garden adds even more charm. The nightly rate includes a hearty breakfast buffet and hors d'oeuvres and pasta in the evening. 15 rooms. Complimentary continental breakfast. Check-in 3 pm, check-out 11 am. High-speed Internet access, wireless Internet access. **$$**

Restaurants

★ ★ **BARAKA CAFE.** *80 1/2 Pearl St, Cambridge (02139). Phone 617/868-3951. www.barakacafe.com.* Menu descriptions only hint at the subtlety of the North African dishes in this tiny, cash-only neighborhood restaurant outside Central Square. The warm and bright cuisine laced with saffron, star anise, and cinnamon is perhaps best exemplified in the vegetarian couscous (often with luscious bites of melon). Reserve your dessert before the kitchen runs out: one of the co-owners worked for many years as a classic French pastry chef. Call ahead for groups of more than five. Tunisian. Lunch, dinner. Closed Mon. Casual attire. No credit cards accepted. **$$**

★ ★ **BLUE ROOM.** *One Kendall Sq, Cambridge (02139). Phone 617/494-9034. www.theblueroom. net.* The Blue Room's Sunday buffet brunch, which features live entertainment, is one of the most popular in Cambridge, a veritable United Nations of flavors can range from Moroccan chicken thighs to quesadillas with avocado and pepper jack cheese. The equally cosmopolitan dinner menu, drawing extensively from Latin American and Mediterranean inspirations, relies heavily on a huge wood grill. Part of the fun is watching the ballet of the cooks in the open kitchen. Mediterranean menu. Dinner, Sun brunch. Closed major holidays. Bar. Casual attire. Reservations recommended. Outdoor seating. Credit cards accepted. **$$$**

★ ★ **CASABLANCA.** *40 Brattle St, Cambridge (02138). Phone 617/876-0999; fax 617/661-1373. www. casablanca-restaurant.com.* You can always count on a great burger in the bar of this landmark Harvard Square hangout. Befitting its name, the front dining room also explores the North African side of Mediterranean bistro cooking, jumping between Moroccan and French dishes. The cassoulet, redolent of duck confit, rarely seems to go off the menu, and almost anything with preserved lemon is a great bet. Murals from the classic Bogart movie provide the atmosphere. Mediterranean menu. Lunch, dinner. Closed major holidays. Bar. Casual attire. Reservations recommended. Credit cards accepted. **$$$**

★ ★ **CHEZ HENRI.** *1 Shepard St, Cambridge (02138). Phone 617/354-8980; fax 617/441-8784. www. chezhenri.com.* Brassy as a trumpet solo, Chez Henri puts a Cuban shake on French bistro cooking. Chef/owner Paul O'Connell maintains a lively bar scene (the only place to get his acclaimed Cubano sandwiches) while simultaneously offering a warm but more formal dining room that's a favorite with Harvard professors and graduate students looking for a big night out. Such upscale dishes as grilled marlin in a macadamia nut crust and steak frites with hot pepper-dusted fries could make you think you're in South Beach. Even the bistro classic of roast chicken makes a pass through the Caribbean, arriving at the table with yucca fries. Chez Henri's wine list is commendably French and features many obscure finds; the restaurant is also celebrated for its mojitos and caipirinhas. Cuban menu, French menu. Dinner. Closed Memorial Day, July 4. **$$$**

★ ★ **CRAIGIE STREET BISTROT.** *5 Craigie Cir, Cambridge (02138). Phone 617/497-5511. www. craigiestreetbistrot.com.* This tiny, very French bistro in the basement of an apartment building a couple of blocks outside Harvard Square is something of a local secret. Chef/owner Tony Maws trained with the best in the United States, but his heart belongs to Lyon. His French bistro cooking is lovingly old-fashioned: he grinds and blends his own mustard, makes terrines and pates for appetizers and garnishes, and puts up his own duck confit. The menu is in constant flux, truly depending on what the market yields. Trust his delicate way with whatever fish looked best at the morning market. Vegetarian entrées, such as wild mushrooms on cheese-enriched polenta, are feasts rather than afterthoughts. French bistro, International menu. Dinner. Closed Mon-Tues; also late June-early July. Casual attire. Reservations recommended. **$$**

★ ★ **EAST COAST GRILL & RAW BAR.** *1271 Cambridge St, Cambridge (02139). Phone 617/491-6568; fax 617/868-4278. www.eastcoastgrill.net.* Guests should plan to wait during peak hours at this local favorite—strong margaritas, fresh dishes, and friendly staff keep guests coming back. Although the menu focuses on seafood, vegetarians will delight in the "All Vegetable Experience of the Day." American, Caribbean, seafood menu. Dinner, Sun brunch. Closed Dec 25. **$$**

★ ★ **THE ELEPHANT WALK.** *2067 Mass Ave, Cambridge (02140). Phone 617/492-6900. www.elephantwalk.com/cambridge.* Two distinct menus tempt diners at The Elephant Walk. Rather than offering fusion cuisine, this sophisticated establishment entices guests to mix and match from its authentic and delicious French and Cambodian menus—diners may choose a French appetizer and a Cambodian entrée. Tradition blends with creativity here, where classic favorites are offered in addition to inventive dishes. Stylish interiors with a tropical-meets-Asian urban feel and an award-winning wine list prove that ethnic dining need not be basic and uninspiring. Pacific-Rim/Pan-Asian menu. Dinner. Closed Mon. Bar. Children's menu. Casual attire. **$$**

★ ★ **FLORA.** *190 Massachusetts Ave, Arlington (02474). Phone 781/641-1664. www.florarestaurant.com.* American menu. Dinner. Closed Mon. Bar. Casual attire. **$$**
🄳

★ ★ ★ **HARVEST.** *44 Brattle St, Cambridge (02138). Phone 617/868-2255; fax 617/868-5422. www.harvestcambridge.com.* Although this restaurant is located in a modern building, the interior creates a rustic, traditional mood—dark wood, lots of dried flowers, pewter tableware, and harvest scenes in the artwork. It is owned by the same three partners who own Grill 23 & Bar (see BOSTON), and offers American dishes enhanced by classic techniques. Guests will enjoy the open kitchen, great bread, and large number of seafood choices, as well as the nightly risotto special. American menu. Lunch, dinner, Sun brunch. Closed July 4, Dec 24-25. Bar. Children's menu. Casual attire. Reservations recommended. Valet parking (Fri-Sat). Outdoor seating. Credit cards accepted. **$$$**

★ ★ **HELMAND.** *143 1st St, Cambridge (02142). Phone 617/492-4646; fax 617/497-6507. www.helmandrestaurantcambridge.com.* The East Cambridge location can be a little hard for out-of-towners to find, but this first and finest of the region's Afghan restaurants makes the search worthwhile. The cuisine comes from the historic overland spice trade route between South Asia and Europe, and Helmand's dishes are rich with the characteristic cardamom, coriander, cinnamon, and turmeric. Lamb dishes are among the menus stars. Middle Eastern menu. Dinner. Closed Jan 1, Thanksgiving, Dec 25. **$$**

★ ★ ★ **OLEANA.** *134 Hampshire St, Cambridge (02139). Phone 617/661-0505; fax 617/661-3336. www.oleanarestaurant.com.* Menus that roam the perimeter of the Mediterranean are nothing new in the Boston area, but few chefs coax out the Arabic influences on Mediterranean bistro fare as well as Oleana's chef/owner Ana Sortun. To create a luscious, complex style, Sortun gleefully matches Arabic almonds to the herbs of Provence in a chicken dish. The food is always comforting, yet often as surprising as a Basque-influenced venison with caramelized turnip or a rabbit and mushroom paella salad. Regulars would revolt if she removed the scallops with basmati-pistachio pilaf from the menu. The fireplace offers cozy comfort in the winter, while an outdoor patio beckons in the summertime. Mediterranean, Middle Eastern menu. Dinner. Bar. Casual attire. Outdoor seating. **$$**

★ ★ ★ **RIALTO.** *1 Bennett St, Cambridge (02138). Phone 617/661-5050; fax 617/234-8093. www.rialto-restaurant.com.* Located in the Charles Hotel (see), Rialto is home to chef/owner Jody Adams's distinctive brand of boldly flavored Mediterranean-inspired fare. Adams's approach to food is honest and straightforward, paying homage to the seasons and to fresh, locally grown fruits and vegetables. This approach allows her to create stellar up-to-the-minute dishes from the varying culinary regions of France, Italy, and Spain. If you'd like to actually enjoy your dinner, try not to fill up on the basket of incredible home-baked breads beforehand. A complementary wine list features more than 100 bottles from Spain, Italy, France, and the United States. The sunny room is filled with deep, dramatic, high-backed banquettes; flower-topped tables; and richly colored hardwood floors and is lined with soaring floor-to-ceiling windows equipped with vintage wooden shutters. The effect is a sophisticated yet immensely comfortable urban space—a room that seduces you into lingering over dessert, cheese, and after-dinner drinks. Mediterranean menu. Dinner. Closed holidays. Bar. Business casual attire. Reservations recommended. Valet parking. **$$$**

★ ★ **ROKA.** *1001 Massachusetts Ave, Cambridge (02138). Phone 617/661-0344. www.2nite.com/roka/*

home.htm. The panache of this Osaka-style Japanese restaurant midway between Harvard and Central squares belies its below-street-level digs in a district of furniture stores. Sushi is the main attraction, and many patrons gravitate to the temaki combination plate, which includes sheets of nori and all the fixings to roll your own crab stick, shrimp, tuna, and squid rolls. The tempura is especially light, and Roka boasts an extensive selection of Japanese beers and sakes. Japanese menu. Lunch, dinner. Casual attire. **$$**

★ ★ ★ **SALTS.** *798 Main St, Cambridge (02139). Phone 617/876-8444; fax 617/876-8569. www. saltsrestaurant.com.* Located in Central Square, this tiny neighborhood place, with warm colors and dark wood floors, has a quiet and elegant atmosphere. The menu changes seasonally and has a strong French influence, with local—often organic—produce. Mainly French and American wines are offered, with around 200 selections to choose from. American menu. Dinner. Closed Sun-Mon; major holidays. Business casual attire. Reservations recommended. Credit cards accepted. **$$$**

★ ★ ★ **SANDRINE'S.** *8 Holyoke St, Cambridge (02138). Phone 617/497-5300; fax 617/497-8504. www.sandrines.com.* Chef/owner Raymond Ost has created a little oasis of his native Alsace in the heart of Harvard Square. The bar around the restaurant's hearth oven is a favorite gathering spot to snack on Ost's signature flammekuechea flatbread topped with fromage blanc, smoked bacon, and caramelized onions. The dinner menu features such hearty dishes as a classic choucroute of homemade sauerkraut studded with sausages, grilled smoked pork, and bacon. French bistro menu. Lunch, dinner. Closed Dec 25. Bar. Business casual attire. Reservations recommended. Credit cards accepted. **$$$**

Cape Cod

See also Bourne, Brewster, Cape Cod National Seashore, Chatham, Dennis, Eastham, Falmouth, Harwich, Hyannis and Barnstable, Orleans, Provincetown, Sandwich, Truro and North Truro, Wellfleet, Yarmouth

The popularity of the automobile changed Cape Cod from a group of isolated fishing villages, large estates, and cranberry bogs into one of the world's prime resort areas. The Cape's permanent population of about 201,000 witnesses this change each year with the arrival of nearly 500,000 summer visitors.

A great many hotels and motels have sprung up since World War II, and cottages line the beaches in some areas. Yet the villages have remained virtually unchanged. The long main streets of villages like Yarmouthport and Brewster are still lined with old houses, some dating from the 17th century. The sea wind still blows across the moors below Truro and the woods of the Sandwich Hills.

The Cape is about 70 miles long and bent like an arm with its fist upraised. Buzzards Bay and the Cape Cod Canal are at the shoulder, Chatham and Nauset beach are at the elbow, and Provincetown is the fist. Because the Cape extends so far out toward the warm Gulf Stream (about 30 miles), its climate is notably gentler than that of the mainland; summers are cooler and winters are milder. It has almost 560 miles of coastline, most of which is gleaming beach—the Cape being composed of sand rather than bedrock. As if to please every taste, many towns on the Cape have two coasts—the Nantucket Sound beaches with warm, calm waters; the Atlantic Ocean beaches with colder water and high breakers; or Cape Cod Bay with cool, calm waters. Inland woods are dotted with 365 clear freshwater ponds known as kettle ponds.

Surf casting (day and night) and small-boat and deep-sea fishing are major sports along the entire Cape coastline. At least a dozen varieties of game fish are found, including giant tuna.

The current summer gaiety belies the Cape's hardy pioneer history. It was in Provincetown harbor that the *Mayflower* first set anchor for the winter and the first party of Pilgrims went ashore. Eighteen years earlier, in 1602, Cape Cod was named by the English explorer Bartholomew Gosnold after the great schools of fish he saw in the bay.

The following towns, villages, and special areas on Cape Cod are included in the *Mobil Travel Guide.* For information about any of them, see the individual alphabetical listing: Barnstable, Bourne, Brewster, Buzzards Bay, Cape Cod National Seashore, Centerville, Chatham, Dennis, Eastham, Falmouth, Harwich, Hyannis, Orleans, Provincetown, Sandwich, Truro & North Truro, Wellfleet, and Yarmouth.

Cape Cod National Seashore

This recreation area consists of 44,600 acres, including submerged lands located offshore along the eastern part of Barnstable County. Headquarters are at South Wellfleet. Exhibits, interpretive programs at the Salt Pond Visitor Center in Eastham (mid-Feb-Dec, daily; Jan-mid-Feb weekends only), phone 508/255-3421; Province Lands Visitor Center on Race Point Rd in Provincetown (mid-Apr-Nov, daily), phone 508/487-1256. Numerous private homes are within park boundaries. Swimming, lifeguards at designated areas (late June-Labor Day), fishing; hunting, bicycle trails, self-guided nature trails, guided walks, and evening programs in summer. Parking at beaches (fee); free after Labor Day. Buttonbush Trail has Braille trail markers. For further information, contact the Superintendent, 99 Marconi Site, Wellfleet 02667.

Chatham (Cape Cod) (D-10)

Settled 1656
Population 6,625
Elevation 46 ft
Area Code 508
Zip 02633
Information Chamber of Commerce, PO Box 793; phone toll-free 800/715-5567; or the Cape Cod Chamber of Commerce, Hwys 6 and 132, PO Box 790, Hyannis 02601-0790; phone 508/362-3225 or toll-free 888/227-3263
Web Site www.capecodchamber.org

Chatham is among the Cape's fashionable shopping centers. Comfortable estates in the hilly country nearby look out on Pleasant Bay and Nantucket Sound. Monomoy Island, an unattached sand bar, stretches 10 miles south into the sea. It was once a haunt of "moon-cussers"—beach pirates who lured vessels aground with false lights and then looted the wrecks.

What to See and Do

Chatham Light. *Bridge and Main sts, Chatham (02633). Phone 508/430-0628.* Chatham Light is a quintessential Cape Cod lighthouse: gleaming white, with a charming keepers house attached. Originally built with two towers to distinguish the signal from a single lighthouse farther north, the first pair—built of wood—decayed three decades later. A second pair, made of brick, fell to the beach far below when bad weather eroded the cliff on which they were built. A third pair was built inland, and one was moved to Nauset Beach and forever disconnected from her Chatham sister. Today, the lighthouse offers a superb view of the Atlantic and seals on the beach below, and the Coast Guard uses the keepers house as its station. (Daily) **FREE**

Gristmill. *Shattuck Pl, off Cross St, Chatham (02633). W shore of Mill Pond in Chase Park. Phone 508/945-5158.* (1797) (Daily 10 am-3 pm) **FREE**

Monomoy National Wildlife Refuge. *Monomoy Island, Chatham (02633). Take Hwy 6 E to Hwy 137 S to Hwy 28 E to the Coast Guard Station. Take the first left after the Chatham Lighthouse, and then take the first right. Follow signs for the refuge, which is on your left off Morris Island Rd. Phone 508/945-0594; fax 508/945-9559. monomoy.fws.gov.* The Monomoy National Wildlife Refuge is 2,750 acres of birdlovers paradise. You'll spot a wealth of shorebirds all year round, although the spectacle is greatest in spring, when birds exhibit bright plumage while breeding. Also visit Sandy Neck Recreation Area in Barnstable, Wellfleet Bay/Audubon Sanctuary in Brewster, Crane Reservation in Mashpee, and Beech Forest in Provincetown. **FREE**

Old Atwood House. *347 Stage Harbor Rd, Chatham (02633). 1/2 mile off Hwy 28. Phone 508/945-2493. www.chathamhistoricalsociety.org.* (1752) Chatham Historical Society. Memorabilia of Joseph C. Lincoln, Cape Cod novelist. Shell collection, murals by Alice Stallknecht, "Portrait of a New England Town." China trade collection. Maritime collection. (Mid-June-Sept, Tues-Sat 1 pm-4 pm; schedule may vary) **$**

Railroad Museum. *153 Depot Rd, Chatham (02633). Phone 508/945-5199.* Restored "country railroad depot" houses scale models, photographs, railroad memorabilia, and relics; restored 1910 New York Central caboose. (Mid-June-mid-Sept, Tues-Sat 10 am-4 pm) **DONATION**

Top Rod and Cape Cod Charters. *1082 Orleans Rd, Chatham (02650). Next to Ryders Cove. Phone 508/945-2256; toll-free 800/316-5484. www.*

CAPE COD HARVEST FESTIVALS

Most people think of Cape Cod and its associated islands as a summer playground, but the area is still dotted with working farms and the docks are as full of commercial fishermen as day-sailors. During the summer and fall, roadside farm stands all along Routes 6 and 28 spill over with asparagus, corn, lettuce, and tomatoes from the small farms of Cape Cod, and a handful of festivals celebrate the harvest and local flavor.

The harvest festival season begins on the last weekend in June in Provincetown. Known for its artists and counterculture, P'town is also the base of a traditional Portuguese-American fishing community. Some of the most colorful events of the **Provincetown Portuguese Festival** involve the Saturday parade and the Blessing of the Fleet on Sunday, but the tastiest portions continue all weekend long at the food booths, where it's possible to feast on linguia and chourio sausages, bowls of caldo verde (green soup), and sweet malasadas (puffy fried dough). For information, see www.capecodaccess.com/portuguese_festival.

Traditional agriculture takes center stage for two country fairs: the **Barnstable County Fair** in late July and the **Martha's Vineyard Agricultural Livestock Show & Fair** in mid-August. Both events have roots in the mid-19th century, and offer a chance to admire prize fruits and vegetables, sample home-baked goods, and purchase preserves. The Barnstable County Fair in East Falmouth also raises scholarship funds for college-bound students studying agriculture, ecology, food and nutrition, and related fields. The Vineyard Fair, held in the farming community of West Tisbury, is one of the most old-fashioned farm-life fairs in the country. For information, see www.barnstablecountyfair.org and mvas.vineyard.net.

Although musical performances and a crafts show are the featured highlights of the **Bourne Scallop Festival,** held in the village of Buzzards Bay on the Cape Cod Canal in early September, inexpensive scallop dinners are just as big a draw. For information, see www.capecodcanalchamber.org.

One of Cape Cod's chief agricultural products is the cranberry, subject of sporadic local celebrations and the dependable annual **Harwich Cranberry Festival** in mid-September. Food vendors prove that sauce and juice only touch the surface of what can be done with the humble cranberry. For information, see www.harwichcranberryfestival.com.

The combination of currents, tides, and vigilant protection of the marshes and shores have made Wellfleet one of the Northeasts leading producers of Atlantic bluepoint oysters, some of the finest cold-water oysters in the country. Restaurateurs show off their oyster dishes and champion shuckers compete against each other to separate the bivalves from their shells during the mid-October **Wellfleet Oysterfest.** Hard core oyster lovers can purchase a town license and harvest their own. For information, see www.wellfleetoysterfest.org.

capefishingcharters.com. Captain Joe Fitzback takes you to Cape Cod's prime saltwater fishing areas, providing tackle, bait, and anything else you need to bring in the big one. Although a days adventure will cost you a bundle, each additional person adds little to the cost, so plan on bringing a group and splitting the fee. (May-Oct by reservation; closed Nov-Apr) **$$$$**

Special Events

Band Concerts. *Kate Gould Park, Main St, Chatham (02633). Phone 800/715-5567.* Fri evenings. Late June-early Sept.

Monomoy Theatre. *776 Main St, Chatham (02633). Phone 508/945-1589.* Ohio University Players in comedies, musicals, dramas, classics. Late June-late Aug.

Limited-Service Hotels

★ **THE CHATHAM MOTEL.** *1487 Main St, Chatham (02633). Phone 508/945-2630; toll-free 800/770-5545. www.chathammotel.com.* 32 rooms. Closed Nov-Apr. Check-in 3 pm, check-out 11 am. Outdoor pool. **$**
🏊

★ **CHATHAM SEAFARER.** *2079 Main St, Chatham (02633). Phone 508/432-1739; toll-free 800/786-2772;*

SEAFOOD SHACKS

The best way to enjoy seafood on Cape Cod and even in Boston, where many fishermen come to unload their catch, is at the small restaurants and takeout stands attached to fresh fish markets. On Martha's Vineyard, drive out to the tiny fishing village of Menemsha, where **Larsens' Fish Market,** (Menemsha Harbor, phone 508/645-2680) not only sells a full range of fin fish and shellfish but also prepares crab cakes, lobster, steamed clams, and mussels (as well as raw oysters and clams) to eat on the spot. Not all the vessels on Nantucket are yachts—the village is still home port to a number of fishermen. The best seafood shack in the town of Nantucket is **Straight Wharf Fish Store** (Straight Wharf, phone 508/228-1095), which sells swordfish and tuna steak sandwiches, lobster rolls, seafood gumbo, and its own tangy bluefish pâté from early morning until late afternoon.

On the Cape Cod mainland, finding a seafood shack is a matter of knowing which cove holds the fishing fleet. In Falmouth, that means heading to the fingerlike peninsulas of East Falmouth to **Green Pond Seafood** (366 Menauhant Rd, phone 508/540-1901), locally famous for its stuffed quahogs. (Quahog is the local name for the same hardshell clam known as a cherrystone when young and a littleneck when a year older. The stuffing usually includes bread crumbs, butter, herbs, and minced clams.) The prime source for steamed lobster and the highly prized raw Atlantic bluepoint oysters in Wellfleet is **Hatch's Fish Market** (310 Main St, phone 508/349-2810), located in the parking lot behind Town Hall, while in Orleans, **Sir Cricket Fish & Chips** (38 Route 6A, phone 508/255-4453) functions as the quick-cook outlet of the Nauset Fish Market and Lobster Pool.

Perhaps the best-kept secret on the Cape is Barnstable's **Mill Way Fish & Lobster Market** (275 Mill Way, phone 508/362-2760), where CIA-trained chef Ralph Binder not only serves to-die-for fish and chips, but also makes perfect onion rings and a signature seafood sausage of shrimp, scallops, and lobster meat.

In Boston, the only bona fide waterfront seafood shack is **Barking Crab** (88 Sleeper St, phone 617/426-2722) on Fort Point Channel between the Seaport and the Financial District. Open all year, Barking Crab flourishes in the summer, when diners take their lobster to outdoor picnic tables. Large rocks on each table do more than keep the napkins from blowing—they're heavy enough to crack open a lobster claw. There are fewer places to sit but no less atmosphere nearby at **J. Hook** (15 Northern Ave, phone 617/423-5500), which is principally a wholesale fish broker but has steamed lobster, clam chowder, and fish sandwiches available inside the shop.

fax 508/432-8969. www.chathamseafarer.com. 20 rooms. Check-in 2-10 pm, check-out 11 am. **$**

Full-Service Resorts

★ ★ ★ **CHATHAM BARS INN.** *297 Shore Rd, Chatham (02633). Phone 508/945-0096; toll-free 800/527-4884; fax 508/945-5491. www.chathambarsinn. com.* Built in 1814, this grand and elegant Cape Cod landmark has managed to maintain all of the historic charm of a bygone era. Beauty and allure are reflected in the charmingly appointed guest rooms, some of which offer private decks along with breathtaking views of Pleasant Bay. With well-maintained gardens and a private beach just steps away, guests can not help but find serenity and peace of mind amidst the luxurious setting. 205 rooms, 3 story. Check-in 4 pm, check-out 11 am. Wireless Internet access. Four restaurants, two bars. Children's activity center. Fitness room, spa. Beach. Outdoor pool, children's pool, whirlpool. Tennis. Airport transportation available. Business center. **$$$$**

★ ★ ★ **PLEASANT BAY VILLAGE RESORT.** *1191 Orleans Rd, Chatham (02633). Phone 508/945-1133; toll-free 800/547-1011; fax 508/945-9701. www.pleasantbayvillage.com.* From the exquisitely arranged rock garden, where a waterfall bravely cascades its way down into a stone-edged pool and offers guests a delighted view of colorful and flashing koi, to the lavishly appointed gardens, this 6-acre woodland retreat welcomes guests to a place of timeless tranquility. The individually decorated rooms have private patios, most with grills, some with screened-in porches. 58 rooms. Closed late Oct-Apr. Pets accepted, some restrictions. Check-in 3 pm, check-out 11 am. Wireless Internet access. Restaurant. Outdoor pool, whirlpool. Credit cards accepted. **$$**

★ ★ ★ **WEQUASSETT INN.** *On Pleasant Bay, Chatham (02633). Phone 508/432-5400; toll-free 800/225-7125; fax 508/430-3131. www.wequassett.com.* The Wequassett Inn is the perfect place for those who like the charm of a country inn with the amenities of a resort. Situated on 22 acres overlooking Pleasant Bay and the Atlantic Ocean in the picturesque seafaring village of Chatham, this full-service resort is the last word in country chic. The rooms and suites are decorator showpieces with a cosmopolitan slant on country décor. From golf privileges at the prestigious Cape Cod National Golf Club to onsite tennis and water sports at the private beach, this resort entitles its guests to a world of recreational opportunities. Sophisticated palates seek refuge at the sensational twenty-eight atlantic, while more casual fare is served at Thoreau's tavern and the poolside cafés. 104 rooms, 2 story. Closed Dec-Mar. Check-in 3 pm, check-out 11 am. Wireless Internet access. Two restaurants, bar. Children's activity center. Fitness room. Beach. Outdoor pool. Tennis. Airport transportation available. Business center. **$$$$**

Full-Service Inns

★ ★ ★ **THE BRADFORD OF CHATHAM.** *26 Cross St, Chatham (02633). Phone 508/945-1030; toll-free 888/242-8426; fax 508/945-9652. www.bradfordinn.com.* 38 rooms. Children over 12 only. Complimentary full breakfast. Check-in 4 pm, check-out 11 am. Outdoor pool, whirlpool. **$$**

★ ★ ★ **CHATHAM WAYSIDE INN.** *512 Main St, Chatham (02633). Phone 508/945-5550; toll-free 800/242-8426; fax 508/945-1884. www.waysideinn.com.* This classic village inn's house dates to the 1860s, and its lobby still has the original knotty pine flooring. The lobby sets the tone for the rest of the informal and cozy property. The rooms are large, clean, and comfortable—some have private balconies and jetted tubs. The grounds are within walking distance to the water and the town center. 56 rooms. Check-in 4 pm, check-out 11 am. Restaurant, bar. Outdoor pool. Credit cards accepted. **$$$**

★ ★ ★ **CRANBERRY INN.** *359 Main St, Chatham (02633). Phone 508/945-9232; toll-free 800/332-4667; fax 508/945-3769. www.cranberryinn.com.* Built in 1830, and nestled in the heart of the historic district, this elegant inn offers guests all the comforts of home. Relax in one of the charming guest rooms, or enjoy the picturesque view of a windmill while lazying away in one of the Kennedy rocking chairs set along the expansive front porch.18 rooms, 2 story. Children over 12 years only. Complimentary full breakfast. Check-in 3 pm, check-out 11 am. **$**

★ ★ ★ **QUEEN ANNE INN.** *70 Queen Anne Rd, Chatham (02633). Phone 508/945-0394; toll-free 800/545-4667; fax 508/945-0113. www.queenanneinn. com.* The rooms in this 1840 inn feature antique furniture. 34 rooms, 3 story. Closed Jan. Complimentary continental breakfast. Check-in 3 pm. Check-out 11 am. Restaurant. Outdoor pool, whirlpool. Tennis. **$**

Specialty Lodgings

CAPTAIN'S HOUSE INN. *369-377 Old Harbor Rd, Chatham (02633). Phone 508/945-0127; toll-free 800/315-0728; fax 508/945-0866. www.captainshouseinn. com.* Once a sea captain's estate, this charming inn was built in 1839 and features exquisite period wallpapers, Williamsburg antiques, and elegantly refined Queen Anne chairs. Some of the charming guest rooms are named after the ships the captain skippered. 16 rooms, 2 story. Children over 12 only. Complimentary full breakfast. Check-in 3 pm, check-out 11 am. Outdoor pool. **$$**

MOSES NICKERSON HOUSE INN. *364 Old Harbor Rd, Chatham (02633). Phone 508/945-5859; toll-free 800/628-6972; fax 508/945-7087. www.mosesnickersonhouse.com.* Built in 1839. 7 rooms, 2 story. Children over 10 years only. Complimentary full breakfast. Check-in 2:30-7:30 pm. Check-out 10:30 am. **$**

OLD HARBOR INN. *22 Old Harbor Rd, Chatham (02633). Phone 508/945-4434; toll-free 800/942-4434; fax 508/945-7665. www.chathamoldharborinn.com.* Built in 1933, this former residence of a prominent doctor has been renovated and is furnished with a blend of antiques and modern conveniences. 8 rooms, 2 story. Children over 14 years only. Complimentary full breakfast. Check-in 3-7 pm, check-out 11 am. **$**

Restaurants

★ ★ **CHATHAM SQUIRE.** *487 Main St, Chatham (02633). Phone 508/945-0945; fax 508/945-4708. www. thesquire.com.* The Squire represents the salty side of Chatham, where its possible to belly up to the bar with the fishermen for a bowl of Monomoy mussels or a rack of barbecued ribs, or sit down with the police chief or the mayor over scallops meunière. The Squire also does a bustling lunch business with hearty sandwiches and fried fish. Seafood menu. Lunch, dinner. Bar. Children's menu. Casual attire. **$$**

★ ★ **CHRISTIAN'S.** *443 Main St, Chatham (02633). Phone 508/945-3362; fax 508/945-9058. www. christiansrestaurant.com.* Tucked inside a former sea captain's home (built in 1819) in the center of town, Christians is a Chatham favorite. Floral wallpaper and Shaker-style furnishings define the traditional New England décor in the dining room, where an extensive menu caters to the tastes of all diners. Lighter fare is served in the mahogany-paneled bar and in the upstairs sunroom. American menu. Dinner. Closed winter. Bar. Casual attire. Reservations recommended. **$$$**

★ ★ **IMPUDENT OYSTER.** *15 Chatham Bars Ave, Chatham (02633). Phone 508/945-3545; fax 508/945-9319.* One of Chatham's liveliest casual bars for much of the day, the Oyster becomes a serious restaurant at mealtimes, specializing in the catch that comes ashore daily at this busy fishing port. Some of the zestiest dishes, such as cataplana (pork and clams) are, like the fishermen, Portuguese by background. During off-peak hours, the lower-level bar in back serves a limited tavern menu that includes good calamari and clam chowder. Seafood menu. Lunch, dinner. Bar. Children's menu. Casual attire. Reservations recommended. **$$$**

★ ★ **PATE'S.** *1260 Main St, Chatham (02633). Phone 508/945-9777. www.patesrestaurant.com.* Pate's ignites diners' thrill for the grill with its wide variety of tasty steaks, chops, and seafood. Sear marks are a sign of good things to come at this clubby restaurant, where even first-time visitors feel like regulars. The relaxed atmosphere and friendly service also make Pate's a favorite of families. American menu. Dinner. Closed Feb-Mar. Bar. Children's menu. Casual attire. **$$**

★ ★ ★ **TWENTY-EIGHT ATLANTIC.** *Pleasant Bay Rd, Chatham (02633). Phone 508/432-5400; toll-free 800/225-7125. www.wequassett.com.* Black truffle risotto, truffled salmon tartare, and the petite clambake are among the enticing entrées offered at this waterfront restaurant located in the Wequassett Resort (see). The large, open dining room features floor-to-ceiling windows, which present a wide view of Pleasant Bay. Guests may also dine in the beautiful outdoor dining area or the smaller library room. Live jazz and a pianist are featured most nights during the high season (July-Aug). American menu. Breakfast, lunch, dinner. Closed Dec-Mar. Bar. Children's menu. Business casual attire. Reservations recommended. Outdoor seating. Credit cards accepted. **$$$**
🅳

★ ★ **VINING'S BISTRO.** *595 Main St, Chatham (02633). Phone 508/945-5033. www.viningsbistro.com.* This mom-and-pop bistro with attitude occupies the upstairs rooms of a small shopping center. Even marooned in the heart of town, it exudes the carefree ambience of a beachside establishment for sailors whove been around the world and just want to kick back with a good meal. The menu borrows wildly from spicy cuisines from around the globe, such as jerk chicken tossed with fettucine ("rasta pasta") and braised lamb shanks rubbed with hot-pepper harissa. International menu. Dinner. Closed in winter. Casual attire. **$$**

Concord (B-6)

See also Lexington, Sudbury Center

Settled 1635
Population 16,993
Elevation 141 ft
Area Code 978
Zip 01742
Information Concord Chamber of Commerce, 105 Everett St, phone 978/369-3120
Web Site www.ultranet.com/~conchamb/

This town shares with Lexington the title of Birthplace of the Republic. But it was Ralph Waldo Emerson who saw to it that the shot fired "by the rude bridge" was indeed heard 'round the world.

The town's name arose because of the "peace and concord" between the settlers and the Native Americans in the 17th century. The famous Concord grape was developed here in 1849 by Ephraim Bull.

The town of Lincoln, adjoining Concord on the east, was the scene of a running battle with the Redcoats on their withdrawal toward Boston. Here the harassing fire of the Minutemen was perhaps most effective.

What to See and Do

Codman House. *Codman Rd, Lincoln (01773). 5 miles S of Hwy 2 via Bedford Rd. Phone 781/259-8843.* (Circa 1740) Originally a two-story, L-shaped Georgian mansion. In 1797-1798, it was more than doubled in size by Federal merchant John Codman to imitate an English country residence. Family furnishings. Grounds have many unusual trees and plants; formal Italian garden. (June-mid-Oct, 1st Sat of each month, tours hourly 11 am-4 pm) **$**

Concord Free Public Library. *129 Main St, Concord (01742). Main St at Sudbury Rd. Phone 978/318-3300.* Modern public library, historical collections of famous Concord authors. On display is a mantelpiece from the US Capitol (circa 1815). Also statues of Emerson and others by Daniel Chester French. (Nov-May: daily, limited hours Sun; rest of year: Mon-Sat) **FREE**

Concord Museum. *200 Lexington Rd, Concord (01742). Phone 978/369-9763. www.concordmuseum.org.* Period rooms and galleries of domestic artifacts and decorative arts chronicling history of Concord from Native American habitation to present. Exhibits include Ralph Waldo Emerson's study, Henry David Thoreau's belongings used at Walden Pond, and Revolutionary War relics, including Paul Revere's signal lantern. Self-guided tours. (Daily; closed Easter, Thanksgiving, Dec 25) **$$**

DeCordova Museum & Sculpture Park. *51 Sandy Pond Rd, Lincoln (01773). SE on Sandy Pond Rd. Phone 781/259-8355. www.decordova.org.* The DeCordova Museum exhibits an eclectic and delightful collection of paintings, posters, photography, sculpture, and media. The Sculpture Park, which is free, displays large contemporary sculptures throughout its 35 wooded acres. In early June—rain or shine—the museum sponsors the Annual Art in the Park Festival and Art Sale ($$), featuring musical performers, terrific food, and extraordinary art exhibitions, many of which are for sale. You can easily make the DeCordova an all-day event. (Tues-Sun 11 am-5 pm) **$$**

Drumlin Farm Education Center. *208 S Great Rd, Lincoln (01773). 2 1/2 miles S on Hwy 126, then E on Hwy 117 (S Great Rd). Phone 781/259-2200.* Demonstration farm with domestic and native wild animals and birds; gardens; hayrides; special events. (Tues-Sun and Mon holidays; closed Jan 1, Thanksgiving, Dec 24-25) **$$**

Fruitlands Museums. *102 Prospect Hill Rd, Harvard (01451). 15 miles W via Hwy 2, exit 38A. Phone 978/456-3924. www.fruitlands.org.* Four museums, including the Fruitlands Farmhouse, the scene of Bronson Alcott's experiment in community life, which contains furniture, books, and memorabilia of the Alcott family and the Transcendentalists; Shaker Museum, formerly in the Harvard Shaker Village, with furniture and handicrafts; Picture Gallery, with American primitive portraits and paintings by Hudson River School artists; American Indian Museum, with prehistoric artifacts and Native American art. Hiking trails with views west to Mount Wachusett and north to Mount Monadnock. Tearoom; gift shop. (Mid-May-Oct, Mon-Fri 11 am-4 pm, Sat-Sun until 5 pm) **$$**

Great Meadows National Wildlife Refuge. *Lincoln St and Weir Hill Rd, Sudbury Center (01776). Office and visitor center off Lincoln Rd, 20 miles W of Boston. Phone 978/443-4661. www.fws.gov/greatmeadows.* Great Meadows combines terrific dirt trails with a wildlife refuge that attracts more than 200 species of birds, including the magnificent great blue heron and other heron species. As you hike near the marsh, you'll see nesting boxes for wood ducks and lodges built by muskrats, who will come out to take a peek at you near nightfall. (Daily dawn-dusk) **FREE**

Gropius House. *68 Baker Bridge Rd, Lincoln (01773). SE in Lincoln. Phone 781/259-8098.* (1937-1938) Family home of architect Walter Gropius. First building he designed upon arrival in the United States in 1937; blends New England traditions and Bauhaus principles of function and simplicity with New England's building materials and environment. Original furniture, artwork. (June-Oct: first Sat of the month, tours every hour 11 am-4 pm) **$**

Minute Man National Historical Park. *174 Liberty St, Concord (01742). From I-95, take Hwy 2A W. The park is 1 mile west off the ramp. Phone 978/369-6993; fax 978/318-7800. www.nps.gov/mima.* The Minute Man National Historical Park consists of 900 acres along the Battle Road between Lexington and Concord. Walk the 5 1/2-mile Battle Road Trail, stop at Hartwell Tavern to see reenactments of colonial life, and continue to North Bridge, site of the first battle of the Revolutionary War (the "shot heard 'round the world"). Your visit can last from a couple hours to all day, depending on how much you hike and how many sites you visit within the park. Note that some of the attractions are open only seasonally. While at the park, take advantage of multimedia programs, a lecture series, and workshops. (Spring, summer, fall: daily; winter: Sat-Sun) **FREE**

Old Manse. *269 Monument St, Concord (01742). Monument St at the North Bridge. Phone 978/369-3909.*(1770) Parsonage of Concord's early ministers, including Reverend William Emerson, Ralph Waldo Emerson's grandfather. Nathaniel Hawthorne lived here for a time and made it the setting for *Mosses from an Old Manse.* Original furnishings. (Mid-Apr-Oct, Mon-Sat 10 am-5 pm) **$$**

Orchard House. *399 Lexington Rd, Concord (01742). Phone 978/369-4118.* Here Louisa May Alcott wrote *Little Women.* Alcott memorabilia. Guided tours. (Open year-round, hours vary seasonally) **$$**

Ralph Waldo Emerson House. *28 Cambridge Tpke, Concord (01742). At Lexington Rd (Hwy 2A). Phone 978/369-2236.* Ralph Waldo Emerson's home from 1835 to 1882. Original furnishings and family memorabilia; 30-minute guided tours. (Mid-Apr-late Oct, Thurs-Sat 10 am-4:30 pm, Sun from 1 pm) **$$$**

Sleepy Hollow Cemetery. *Bedford St, NE of square.*The Alcotts, Ralph Waldo Emerson, Nathaniel Hawthorne, Margaret Sidney, Daniel Chester French, and Henry David Thoreau are buried here.

⭐ **Walden Pond State Reservation.** *915 Walden St, Concord (01742). 1/2 mile S of Hwy 2 on Hwy 126. Phone 978/369-3254.* Henry David Thoreau, the American writer and naturalist you probably studied in tenth grade, made Walden Pond famous when he lived near the pond in a rustic cabin for two quiet years (minus a few evenings here and there, when he went to Ralph Waldo Emersons place for dinner). The cabin still stands and is part of the park's collection. A 1 1/2-mile trail circles the pond—perfect for hiking, running, or a guided tour from the park staff. You can also fish or swim in Walden Pond; a bathhouse by the beach offers rest rooms. Visitors are limited to 1,000 or 350 cars, whichever comes first; in the summer, you'll need to arrive before 11 am to gain entry. (Daily) **FREE**

Wayside. *455 Lexington Rd (MA 2A), Concord (01742).* Well-known 19th-century authors Nathaniel Hawthorne, the Alcotts, and Margaret Sidney, author of the *Five Little Peppers* books, lived here. Orientation program; 45-minute tours (May-Oct)

Special Event

Patriots Day Parade. *Phone 617/635-3911; toll-free 888/733-2678.* Patriots Day commemorates the Battle of Lexington and Concord, which marked the beginning of the Revolutionary War on April 18 and 19, 1775. Schools and many businesses close, and the entire city celebrates. Watch parades and reenactments of the night of Paul Revere's famous ride (including one actor hanging two lanterns in Old North Church and two others riding to Lexington before meeting up with a third riding actor who finishes in Concord). At noon, the famous Boston Marathon begins in Hopkington and ends on Boylston Street. Because the historical significance of the day centers around Lexington and Concord, those two cities begin festivities the weekend preceding Patriot's Day. (Third Mon in Apr, one-day-only event) **FREE**

Limited-Service Hotels

★ **BEST WESTERN AT HISTORIC CONCORD.** *740 Elm St, Concord (01742). Phone 978/369-6100; toll-free 800/780-7234; fax 978/371-1656. www.bestwestern.com.* 106 rooms, 2 story. Pets accepted; fee. Complimentary continental breakfast. Check-in 2 pm, check-out noon. Fitness room. Outdoor pool, whirlpool. **$**

★★ **HOLIDAY INN.** *242 Adams Pl, Boxborough (01719). Phone 978/263-8701; fax 978/263-0518. www.holiday-inn.com.* 143 rooms, 3 story. Pets accepted. Check-in 3 pm, check-out noon. Restaurant, bar. Fitness room. Indoor pool. **$**

Full-Service Inn

★★★ **COLONIAL INN.** *48 Monument Sq, Concord (01742). Phone 978/369-9200; toll-free 800/370-9200; fax 978/371-1533. www.concordscolonialinn.com.* Historically prominent guests noted have stayed at this inn. Walden Pond is 2 miles away. 56 rooms. Check-in 3 pm, check-out 11 am. Wireless Internet access. Restaurant, bar. **$$**

Specialty Lodging

HAWTHORNE INN. *462 Lexington Rd, Concord (01742). Phone 978/369-5610; fax 978/287-4949. www.concordmass.com.* 7 rooms, 2 story. Complimentary continental breakfast. Check-in 3-9 pm, check-out 11 am. **$$**

Restaurant

★ ★ **COLONIAL INN.** *48 Monument Sq, Concord (01742). Phone 978/369-2373; toll-free 800/370-9200; fax 978/371-1533. www.concordscolonialinn.com.* Henry David Thoreau's house. Built in 1716. American menu. Breakfast, lunch, dinner, Sun brunch. Bar. Children's menu. Casual attire. Reservations recommended. Outdoor seating. **$$**

Danvers (A-7)

See also Beverly, Salem

Settled 1636
Population 25,212
Elevation 48 ft
Area Code 978
Zip 01923
Information North Shore Chamber of Commerce, 5 Cherry Hill Dr; phone 978/774-8565
Web Site www.northshorechamber.org

This small industrial town was once Salem Village—a community started by settlers from Salem looking for more farmland. In 1692, Danvers was the scene of some of the most severe witchcraft hysteria; 20 persons were put to death.

What to See and Do

Glen Magna Farms. *Ingersoll St, Danvers. 2 miles N on Hwy 1, then 1/4 mile E via Centre St to Ingersoll St. Phone 978/774-9165. www.glenmagnafarms.org.* A 20-room mansion; 1790-1890 furnishings; Chamberlain gardens. Derby summer house was built by Samuel McIntire (1794); on the roof are two life-size carvings (reaper and milkmaid) by the Skillin brothers; reproduction of 1844 gazebo. Various special events and programs. (May-July, by appointment only; closed holidays) **$$$**

Rebecca Nurse Homestead. *149 Pine St, Danvers (01923). Phone 978/774-8799. www.rebeccanurse.org.* The house (circa 1680), an excellent example of the New England saltbox, was the homestead of Rebecca Nurse, a saintly woman accused of and executed for witchcraft during the hysteria of 1692. House includes restored rooms with furnishings from 17th and 18th centuries; outbuildings, a reproduction of the 1672 Salem Village Meetinghouse and exhibit areas. (Mid-June-mid-Sept: Tues-Sun; mid-Sept-Oct: weekends; rest of year: by appointment; closed holidays) **$**

Witchcraft Victims Memorial. *176 Hobart St, Danvers (01923).* Memorial includes names of those who died, as well as quotes from eight victims.

Special Event

Danvers Family Festival. *Phone 978/777-0001.* Exhibits, fireworks, races, music. Late June-early July.

Limited-Service Hotels

★ ★ **COURTYARD BY MARRIOTT.** *275 Independence Way, Danvers (01923). Phone 978/777-8630; toll-free 800/321-2211; fax 978/777-7341. www.courtyard.com.* 120 rooms, 3 story. Check-in 3 pm, check-out noon. High-speed Internet access. Restaurant, bar. Fitness room. Outdoor pool. **$**
⎈ ⌨

★ **DAYS INN.** *152 Endicott St, Danvers (01923). Phone 978/777-1030; toll-free 800/329-7466; fax 978/777-0264. www.daysinn.com.* 129 rooms, 2 story. Complimentary continental breakfast. Check-in 2 pm, check-out 11 am. Outdoor pool. **$**
⌨

Full-Service Hotel

★ ★ ★ **SHERATON FERNCROFT RESORT.** *50 Ferncroft Rd, Danvers (01923). Phone 978/777-2500; toll-free 800/325-3535; fax 978/750-7959. www.sheraton.com.* This hotel boasts luxurious guest rooms, world class dining, and a distinctive, state-of-the-art, and fully staffed business center. For the leisure traveler, guests can pamper themselves at the salon and day spa, enjoy a game of golf on the 18-hole Robert Trent Jones-designed golf course, or luxuriate in the indoor pool. 367 rooms, 8 story. Check-in 3 pm, check-out 11 am. High-speed Internet access. Restaurant, bar. Fitness room. Indoor pool, whirlpool. Golf. Tennis. Airport transportation available. Business center. **$$**
⎈ ⌨ ⛷ ⚐ ⛹

Restaurant

★ ★ **THE HARDCOVER.** *15-A Newbury St, Danvers (01923). Phone 978/774-1223; fax 978/777-5038. www.barnsiderrestaurants.com.* Seafood, steak menu. Dinner. Bar. Children's menu. **$$$**

Dedham (B-7)

See also Beverly, Salem

Settled 1635
Population 23,464
Elevation 120 ft
Area Code 781
Zip 02026
Information Neponset Valley Chamber of Commerce, 190 Vanderbilt Ave, Suite 1, Norwood 02062-5047; phone 781/769-1126
Web Site www.nvcc.com

What to See and Do

Dedham Historical Society. *612 High St, Dedham (02027). Phone 781/326-1385. www.dedhamhistorical. org.* Small but important collection of 16th- to 19th-century furniture; collection of work by silversmith Katharine Pratt; world's largest public collection of Dedham and Chelsea pottery; changing exhibits. Also 10,000-volume historical and genealogical library. (Tues-Fri, some Sat; closed holidays) **$**

Fairbanks House. *511 East St, Dedham (02026). At Eastern Ave, off Hwy 1. Phone 781/326-1170. www. fairbankshouse.org.* (1636) One of the oldest frame houses still standing in the United States. Fine example of 17th-century architecture, furnished with Fairbanks family heirlooms; guided tours. (May-Oct, Tues-Sat 10 am-4 pm, Sun 1 pm-5 pm) **$**

Limited-Service Hotel

★ ★ **HOLIDAY INN.** *55 Ariadne Rd, Dedham (02026). Phone 781/329-1000; toll-free 800/465-4329; fax 781/329-0903. www.holiday-inn.com.* 203 rooms, 8 story. Pets accepted; fee. Check-in 3 pm, check-out noon. High-speed Internet access. Restaurant. Fitness room. Indoor pool. **$**
🐾 ⚕ ☝

Full-Service Hotel

★ ★ ★ **HILTON BOSTON/DEDHAM.** *25 Allied Dr, Dedham (02026). Phone 781/329-7900; toll-free 800/345-6565; fax 781/329-5552. www.bostondedham. hilton.com.* Located just 20 minutes from downtown Boston, this hotel's focus is to ensure that guests are offered all of the services and facilities needed to make their trip pleasurable. Make sure to take time and enjoy the outdoor jogging trail or state-of-the-art fitness center. 254 rooms, 4 story. Check-in 3 pm, check-out noon. Restaurant, bar. Fitness room. Indoor pool, whirlpool. Tennis. Business center. **$**
⚕ ☝ ⚓ ☝

Deerfield (B-3)

See also Beverly, Salem

Settled 1669
Population 4,750
Elevation 150 ft
Area Code 413
Information Historic Deerfield, Inc, PO Box 321; phone 413/774-5581
Web Site www.historic-deerfield.org

Twice destroyed by French and Native American attacks when it was the northwest frontier of New England, and almost forgotten by industry, Deerfield is noted for its unspoiled meadowland, beautiful houses, and nationally famous boarding schools (Deerfield Academy, 1797, a coeducational preparatory school; the Bement School, a coeducational school; and Eaglebrook School for boys).

In 1675, the Bloody Brook Massacre (King Philip's War) crippled the settlement, which was then a struggling frontier outpost. In 1704 (Queen Anne's War), half of the resettled town was burned. Forty-nine inhabitants were killed and more than 100 were captured and taken to Canada.

The village boasts that it has one of the most beautiful streets in America, known just as "The Street," a mile-long stretch of 80 houses, many dating from the 18th and early 19th centuries.

What to See and Do

⭐ **Historic Deerfield.** *Hwys 5 and 10, Deerfield (01342). Phone 413/774-5581. www.historic-deerfield. org.* Maintains 14 historic house museums (fee) furnished with collections of antique furniture, silver, ceramics, textiles. A 28,000-square-foot Collections Study Center features changing exhibits and study-storage displays of portions of the museum's collections. Daily walking tours, meadow walk, antique forums and workshops, special events weekends. Information Center is located at Hall Tavern, The Street. (Daily 9:30 am-4:30 pm; closed Thanksgiving, Dec 24-25) **$$$$**

Memorial Hall Museum. *10 Memorial St, Deerfield (01342). Phone 413/774-3768.deerfield-ma.org/ museum.htm.* (1798) The first building of Deerfield Academy; contains colonial furnishings, Native American relics. (May-Oct, daily 11 am-5 pm) **$$**

Full-Service Inn

★ ★ ★ **DEERFIELD INN.** *81 Old Main St, Deerfield (01342). Phone 413/774-5587; toll-free 800/926-3865; fax 413/775-7221. www.deerfieldinn. com.* There is a tavern in this historic 1884 inn, and elegant sitting parlors with authentic period wallpaper and antiques, and it is filled with nooks and alcoves where you can sink in and relax. This is a classic New England inn, one of the few originals still in operation, where its first guests arrived by stagecoach and then trolleys. Today, the main building has ten rooms, and the new wing, built to resemble a barn, has 13. While the accommodations have modern bathrooms, they also have four-poster beds and period furniture, each room unique and named after a historical figure with a local connection. But beware: it is said there are a couple of ghosts wandering the premises—clearly figures who can't bring themselves to leave the inn's warmth and charm. 23 rooms, 2 story. Closed Dec 24-Dec 26, Pets accepted, some restrictions; fee. Complimentary full breakfast. Check-in 2 pm, check-out 11 am. Two restaurants, bar. **$$**

Restaurants

★ ★ ★ **DEERFIELD INN.** *81 Old Main St, Deerfield (01342). Phone 413/774-5587; toll-free 800/926-3865; fax 413/775-7221. www.deerfieldinn. com.* This warm and elegant dining room is located in a quintessential New England country inn that is nestled among a street full of historic houses. The menu features New England cuisine and changes seasonally. American menu. Breakfast, dinner. Closed Tues-Wed; Dec 24-26. Bar. Children's menu. Business casual attire. Reservations recommended. **$$**

★ ★ ★ **SIENNA.** *6B Elm St, Deerfield (01373). Phone 413/665-0215; fax 413/665-6644. www.siennarestaurant. com.* Chef Richard Labonte changes the menu to take advantage of seasonal ingredients. His creative American cuisine is enhanced by flavors from many other cuisines. American menu. Dinner. Closed Tues. **$$**

Dennis (Cape Cod) (D-9)

Settled 1639
Population 15,973
Elevation 24 ft
Area Code 508
Zip 02638
Information Chamber of Commerce, 242 Swan River Rd, phone 508/398-3568
Web Site www.dennischamber.com

Dennis heads a group, often called "the Dennises," that includes Dennisport, East Dennis, South Dennis, West Dennis, and Dennis. It was here, in 1816, that Henry Hall developed the commercial cultivation of cranberries. Swimming beaches are located throughout the area.

What to See and Do

Jericho House and Historical Center. *Old Main St and Trotting Park Rd, West Dennis (02670). Phone 508/385-2232.* (1801) Period furniture. Barn museum contains old tools, household articles, model of salt works, photographs. (July-Aug, Wed and Fri) **DONATION**

Josiah Dennis Manse. *77 Nobscusset Rd, Dennis (02638). Phone 508/385-3528.* (1736) and **Old West School House** (1770). Restored home of minister for whom town was named; antiques, Pilgrim chest, children's room, spinning and weaving exhibit, maritime wing. (July-Aug, Tues and Thurs) **DONATION**

Sand Bar Club and Lounge. *35 Lighthouse Rd, West Dennis (02670). Phone 508/398-7586. www. lighthousesandbar.com.* Local talent Philo Rockwell King, better known as Rock King, has been performing musical and comedy acts at the Sand Bar for nearly 40 years and is still going strong—catch his act Wednesdays through Saturdays. Other acts include jazz musicians, singers, comedians, and more. Check the Web site for performance schedules. The Sand Bar is on the grounds of The Lighthouse Inn, a country inn that offers outstanding entertainment for children.

Special Events

Cape Playhouse. *820 Main St, Dennis (02638). Phone 508/385-3911; toll-free 877/385-3911. www.capeplayhouse. com.* The Cape Playhouse offers opportunities to watch both established Broadway stars and up-and-coming actors for two-week runs of musicals, comedies, and other plays. Putting on performances since 1927, the Playhouse is the oldest professional summer theater in the United States—you can sometimes take a backstage tour of this historic facility. On Friday mornings during summer, attend the special children's performance that includes puppetry, storytelling, and musicals. The Playhouse complex also houses the Cape Museum of Fine Arts, the Playhouse Bistro, and the Cape Cinema. (Late June-Labor Day) **$$$$**

Festival Week. *Phone 508/398-3568.* Canoe and road races, antique car parade, craft fair, antique show. (Late Aug)

Limited-Service Hotels

★ **HUNTSMAN MOTOR LODGE.** *829 Main St (Hwy 28), West Dennis (02670). Phone 508/394-5415; toll-free 800/628-0498. www.thehuntsman.com.* 25 rooms, 2 story. Check-in, check-out 11 am. Outdoor pool. **$**

★ **SESUIT HARBOR.** *1421 Main St, East Dennis (02641). Phone 508/385-3326; toll-free 800/359-0097; fax 508/385-3326. www.sesuitharbormotel.com.* 20 rooms, 2 story. Check-in 1-8 pm, check-out 10:30 am. Outdoor pool. **$**

★ ★ **SOUNDINGS SEASIDE RESORT.** *79 Chase Ave, Dennisport (02639). Phone 508/394-6561; fax 508/394-7537. www.thesoundings.com.* When location, not luxury, is important, you can't beat the Soundings Seaside Resort. Set on the beach facing Nantucket Sound, this family-friendly inn is near many restaurants, shops, and tennis courts. The well-manicured grounds are spacious, and many rooms feature magnificent ocean views and private patios. 102 rooms, 2 story. Closed mid-Oct-mid-May. Check-in 3 pm, check-out 11 am. Restaurant. Beach. Indoor pool, outdoor pool, whirlpool. **$$**

★ ★ **THREE SEASONS MOTOR LODGE.** *421 Old Wharf Rd, Dennisport (02639). Phone 508/398-6091; fax 508/398-3762. www.threeseasonsmotel.com.* Located on a private beach facing Nantucket Sound, Three Seasons offers many rooms with ocean views and private patios. 61 rooms, 2 story. Closed Nov-Apr. Check-in 2 pm, check-out 11 am. Wireless Internet access. Restaurant. Beach. **$$**

Full-Service Resort

★ ★ **LIGHTHOUSE INN.** *1 Lighthouse Inn Rd, West Dennis (02670). Phone 508/398-2244; fax 508/398-5658. www.lighthouseinn.com.* 63 rooms. Closed mid-Oct-late May. Check-in 3 pm, check-out 11 am. Restaurant, bar. Children's activity center. Beach. Outdoor pool. Tennis. Business center. **$$**

Specialty Lodgings

BY THE SEA GUESTS. *57 Chase Ave, Dennisport (02639). Phone 508/398-8685; toll-free 800/447-9202; fax 508/398-0334. www.bytheseaguests.com.* Located on a beachfront road facing beautiful Nantucket Sound, By The Sea Guests offers a soothing and quaint environment for your Cape Cod getaway. Rooms are clean and bright and feature genteel, elegant décor that includes chenille bed spreads and fine art prints, while the large veranda provides exquisite scenery for your morning meal. For those chilly nights, take a seat in one of the comfy chairs in the living room and enjoy the cozy, crackling fire.12 rooms, 3 story. Complimentary full breakfast. Check-in 2 pm, check-out 11 am. Beach. **$$**

CORSAIR AND CROSSRIP OCEANFRONT. *41 Chase Ave, Dennisport (02639). Phone 508/398-6600; fax 508/760-6681. www.corsaircrossrip.com.* 46 rooms. Closed late Oct-mid-Apr. Complimentary continental breakfast. Check-in 3 pm, check-out 11 am. Wireless Internet access. Children's activity center. Beach. Indoor pool, two outdoor pools, children's pool, whirlpool. **$$**

ISAIAH HALL BED AND BREAKFAST INN. *152 Whig St, Dennis (02638). Phone 508/385-9928; toll-free 800/736-0160; fax 508/385-5879. www. isaiahhallinn.com.* This former farmhouse was built in 1857. 10 rooms, 2 story. Closed Nov-mid-Apr. Children over 7 years only. Complimentary continental breakfast. Check-in 2-9:30 pm, check-out 11 am. **$**

Restaurants

★ **BOB'S BEST SANDWICHES.** *613 Main St (Hwy 28), Dennisport (02639). Phone 508/394-8450.* The owner wakes early to bake his own bread at Bob's Best Sandwiches, and the crusty, delicious result is worth the wake-up call. Roast turkey and roast beef are this sandwich shop's two most requested selections, and the breakfasts of savory French toast and fluffy omelets are noteworthy. Deli menu. Lunch. Children's menu. Casual attire. Outdoor seating. No credit cards accepted. **$**

★ ★ **CLANCY'S.** *8 Upper County Rd, Dennisport (02639). Phone 508/394-6661; fax 508/394-6074. www. clancysrestaurant.com.* Lunch, brunch, and dinner come with a view at the country clublike setting of Clancy's. This likable restaurant enjoys one of the most scenic locations in the area, nestled alongside the Swan River. From chicken and steak to pasta and fish, the menu truly has something for everyone, and Sunday brunch here is outstanding. American, seafood menu. Lunch, dinner, Sun brunch. Closed Thanksgiving, Dec 25. Bar. Children's menu. Casual attire. Valet parking. Outdoor seating. **$$**

★ ★ **GINA'S BY THE SEA.** *134 Taunton Ave, Dennis (02638). Phone 508/385-3213.* Gina's by the Sea whips up Italian food just like your grandmother used to make—if your grandmother happened to be Italian. Located in Dennis's Little Italy neighborhood right near the beach, this casual restaurant has been a culinary landmark since 1938. Bring a hearty appetite along with a bit of patience, since Gina's doesn't take reservations. Italian menu. Dinner. Closed Dec-Mar. Casual attire. **$$**

★ ★ **LA SCALA.** *106 Depot St, Dennisport (02639). Phone 508/398-3910.* Diners sing praises for the food at La Scala. This recently transformed restaurant once known as the Captain William's House features American and Italian cuisine. Generous portions of tasty meals that are easy on the wallet make this a popular choice for families. Takeout is also available here. Italian, American menu. Dinner. Closed Jan-Mar. Bar. Children's menu. **$$**

★ **MARSHSIDE.** *28 Bridge St, East Dennis (02641). Phone 508/385-4010.* Good home cooking and a waterside location make Marshside a true find. This East Dennis diner earns a loyal following among locals and visitors alike for its reliable, reasonably priced meals and freshly baked desserts. Its location at Sesuit Creek with views extending to the harbor makes this restaurant a visitor's dream come true. Seafood menu. Breakfast, lunch, dinner. Closed Thanksgiving, Dec 25. Children's menu. **$**

★ ★ ★ **RED PHEASANT INN.** *905 Main St, Dennis (02638). Phone 508/385-2133; toll-free 800/480-2133; fax 508/385-2112. www.redpheasantinn.com.*

The Red Pheasant Inn is the very essence of country charm. Housed within a 200-year-old barn, this gourmet restaurant delights romantics and gourmands alike with its quaint surroundings and fine food. The American menu consists of fish and meat specialties, with lamb and game offerings changing nightly. A 300-bottle wine list is sure to please the most demanding connoisseurs. The dining room is lovely during the winter months with two blazing fireplaces, while the gardens provide an enchanting setting in summer. American menu. Dinner. Bar. Reservations recommended. Valet parking. **$$$**

★ ★ **SCARGO CAFE.** *799 Main St, Dennis (02638). Phone 508/385-8200; toll-free 888/355-0112; fax 508/385-6977. www.scargocafe.com.* Located across from the Cape Playhouse (the nation's oldest stock company theater) and the Cape Cinema, Scargo serves a hearty menu of grilled steaks and chops and a full range of Cape Cod seafood. The house special is an inventive "seafood strudel," a pot pie of crab, shrimp, and scallops in Newburg sauce with a flaky pastry crust. For a romantic tête-à-tête, ask for the table for two beneath the stairs. International menu. Lunch, dinner. Closed Thanksgiving, Dec 25. Bar. Children's menu. Casual attire. Outdoor seating. **$$**

★ **SWAN RIVER SEAFOOD.** *5 Lower County Rd, Dennisport (02639). Phone 508/394-4466; fax 508/398-3201. www.swanriverseafoods.com.* Fish doesn't get any fresher. Local fishermen unload their catch here at the restaurant and fish market that sits at the marshy mouth of the Swan River. While deep-fried treatments make up a good part of the menu, the kitchen also knows how to grill, broil, and sauté, resulting in such treats as fresh fillets poached in garlic broth and grilled swordfish and shark encrusted in black pepper. Seafood menu. Lunch, dinner. Closed mid-Sept-late May. Bar. Children's menu. **$$**

Eastham (Cape Cod) (D-10)

See also Orleans

Settled 1644
Population 5,453
Elevation 48 ft
Area Code 508
Zip 02642
Information Chamber of Commerce, PO Box 1329;

phone 508/240-7211 or 508/255-3444 (summer only); or visit the Information Booth at Hwy 6 and Fort Hill **Web Site** www.easthamchamber.com

On the bay side of the Cape, in what is now Eastham town, the *Mayflower* shore party met their first Native Americans. Also in the town is a magnificent stretch of Nauset Beach, which was once a graveyard of ships. Nauset Light is an old friend of mariners.

What to See and Do

Eastham Historical Society. *190 Samoset Rd, Eastham (02642). Just off Hwy 6. Phone 508/240-0871. www.easthamhistorical.org.* 1869 schoolhouse museum; Native American artifacts; farming and nautical implements. (July-Aug, Mon-Fri afternoons) **DONATION** The society also maintains the

> **Swift-Daley House.** *Phone 508/240-1247.* (1741) Cape Cod house contains period furniture, clothing, original hardware. (July-Aug, Mon-Fri 10 am-1 pm; Sept, Sat only)

Eastham Windmill. *Windmill Green, Eastham (02642). In town center. Phone 508/240-7211.* Oldest windmill on the Cape (1680); restored in 1936. (Late June-Labor Day, daily) **DONATION**

Limited-Service Hotels

★ **CAPTAIN'S QUARTERS.** *Hwy 6, North Eastham (2651). Phone 508/255-5686; toll-free 800/327-7769; fax 508/240-0280. www.captains-quarters.com.* 75 rooms. Closed mid-Nov-mid-Apr. Complimentary continental breakfast. Check-in 2 pm, check-out 11 am. Outdoor pool. Tennis. **$**

★ ★ **FOUR POINTS BY SHERATON.** *3800 Hwy 6, Eastham (02642). Phone 508/255-5000; toll-free 800/533-3986; fax 508/240-1870. www.fourpoints.com.* 107 rooms, 2 story. Check-in 3 pm, check-out 11 am. Restaurant, bar. Fitness room. Indoor pool, outdoor pool, whirlpool. Tennis. **$$**

Specialty Lodgings

OVERLOOK INN OF CAPE COD. *3085 County Rd (Hwy 6), Eastham (02642). Phone 508/255-1886; toll-free 877/255-1886; fax 508/240-0345. www.overlookinn. com.* 10 rooms, 3 story. Pets accepted; restrictions.

Complimentary full breakfast. Check-in 2-7 pm, check-out 11 am. **$$**

THE PENNY HOUSE INN. *4885 County Rd, Eastham (02642). Phone 508/255-6632; toll-free 800/554-1751; fax 508/255-4893. www.pennyhouseinn. com.* 12 rooms, 2 story. Children over 8 years only. Complimentary full breakfast. Check-in 2 pm, check-out 11 am. **$$**

THE WHALEWALK INN. *220 Bridge Rd, Eastham (02642). Phone 508/255-0617; toll-free 800/440-1281; fax 508/240-0017. www.whalewalkinn.com.* 16 rooms. Children over 12 only. Complimentary full breakfast. Check-in 2 pm, check-out 11 am. **$$$**

Fall River (D-7)

See also New Bedford; also see Providence, RI

Settled 1656
Population 91,938
Elevation 200 ft
Area Code 508
Information Fall River Area Chamber of Commerce, 200 Pocasset St, 02721; phone 508/676-8226
Web Site www.fallriverchamber.com

The city's name, adopted in 1834, was translated from the Native American "quequechan." In 1892, Fall River was the scene of one of the most famous murder trials in American history—that of Lizzie Borden, who was acquitted of the ax murders of her father and stepmother. Water power and cotton textiles built Fall River into one of the largest cotton manufacturers in the world, but its industry is now greatly diversified.

What to See and Do

Battleship Cove. *5 Water St, Fall River (02721). At jct Hwy 138, I-195. Phone 508/678-1100. www.battleshipcove.org.* Five historic naval ships of the World War II period. The submarine *Lionfish*, a World War II attack sub with all her equipment intact, and the battleship USS *Massachusetts* are open to visitors. The *Massachusetts*, commissioned in 1942, was active in the European and Pacific theaters of operation in the Second World War and now houses the state's official World War II and Gulf War Memorial; on board is a full-scale model of a Patriot missile. Also here are *PT Boat 796, PT Boat 617*, and the destroyer USS *Joseph P.*

Kennedy Jr., which saw action in both the Korean and Vietnam conflicts and the Cuban missile blockade. The PT boats may be viewed from walkways. A landing craft (LCM) exhibit is located on the grounds. Gift shop; snack bar. (Daily 9 am-5:30 pm; closed Jan 1, Thanksgiving, Dec 25) **$$$**

Factory Outlet District. *638 Quequechan St, Fall River (02721). Phone 508/677-4949.* Fall River is an extensive factory outlet area.

Fall River Heritage State Park. *100 Davol St, Fall River (02720). Phone 508/675-5759.* Nine acres on the riverfront; sailing. Visitor center (daily) has multimedia presentation on how Fall River developed into the greatest textile producer in the country; tourist information. (Daily; closed Jan 1, Dec 25) **FREE**

Fall River Historical Society. *451 Rock St, Fall River (02720). Phone 508/679-1071. www.lizzieborden.org.* Historical displays in 16-room Victorian mansion. Exhibits of Fall River Steamship Line, dolls, fine art, glassware, costumes; artifacts relating to the Lizzie Borden trial. Gift shop. (Apr-May, Oct-Nov, Tues-Fri; June-Sept, Tues-Sun; Dec, Mon) **$$**

Marine Museum. *70 Water St, Fall River (02720). Phone 508/674-3533.* More than 100 ship models on display, including a 28-foot, 1-ton model of the *Titanic,* trace the growth of maritime steam power from the early 1800s to 1937; paintings, photographs, artifacts. (Daily; closed Jan 1, Thanksgiving, Dec 25) **$$**

St. Anne's Church and Shrine. *818 Middle St, Fall River (02721). S Main St, facing Kennedy Park. Phone 508/674-5651. www.stanneshrine.com.* (1906) Designed by Canadian architect Napoleon Bourassa, the upper church is constructed of Vermont blue marble; the lower church is of solid granite. In the upper church are stained-glass windows produced by E. Rault in Rennes, France, a "Casavant Freres" organ, and exceptional oak wood ornamentation in the vault of the ceiling. The shrine is in the lower church.

Limited-Service Hotels

★ **HAMPTON INN.** *53 Old Bedford Rd, Westport (02790). Phone 508/675-8500; toll-free 800/426-7866; fax 508/675-0075. www.hamptoninn.com.* 133 rooms, 4 story. Complimentary continental breakfast. Check-in 3 pm, check-out noon. Fitness room. Whirlpool. Tennis. **$**

★ **QUALITY INN.** *1878 Wilbur Ave, Somerset (02725). Phone 508/678-4545; toll-free 800/228-5151;* fax 508/678-9352. www.qualityinn.com. 107 rooms, 2 story. Pets accepted, some restrictions. Complimentary continental breakfast. Check-in 3 pm, check-out noon. Fitness room. Indoor pool. **$**

Restaurants

★ ★ **THE BACK EDDY.** *1 Bridge Rd, Westport (02790). Phone 508/636-6500. www.thebackeddy.com.* American, seafood menu. Dinner. Closed Jan-Mar. Casual attire. **$$$**

★ ★ **WHITE'S OF WESTPORT.** *66 State Rd, Westport (02790). Phone 508/675-7185; fax 508/679-9324. www.lafrancehospitality.com.* Seafood, steak menu. Lunch, dinner. Closed Dec 25. Bar. Children's menu. **$$**

Falmouth (Cape Cod) (D-8)

See also Martha's Vineyard

Settled circa 1660
Population 32,660
Elevation 10 ft
Area Code 508
Information Cape Cod Chamber of Commerce, Hwys 6 and 132, PO Box 790, Hyannis 02601-0790; phone 508/362-3225 or toll-free 888/227-3263
Web Site www.capecodchamber.org

Falmouth, at the southwest corner of the Cape, boasts a whopping 68 miles of coastline, with 12 public beaches. Its pride and joy is the Woods Hole Oceanographic Institution, a research facility dedicated to marine science—the largest independent oceanographic institution in the world. In East Falmouth is the Cape Cod Winery, which grows six varieties of grapes.

What to See and Do

Ashumet Holly & Wildlife Sanctuary. *Ashumet and Currier rds, Falmouth (02540). Just N of Hwy 151. Phone 508/362-1426.* (Massachusetts Audubon Society) A 45-acre wildlife preserve with holly trail; herb garden; observation beehive. Trails open dawn to dusk. (Daily, dawn to dusk) **$**

Bradley House Museum. *579 Woods Hole Rd, Woods Hole (02543). Phone 508/548-7270. www.woodsholemuseum.org.* Model of Woods Hole Village (circa 1895); audiovisual show of local history; restored spritsail sailboat; model ships. Walking tour of village. (July-Aug: Tues-Sat; June and Sept: Wed, Sat; schedule may vary) **FREE**

Cape Cod Canal Cruises. *Onset Pier, Onset (02558). 3 miles W via Hwys 6 and 28. Phone 508/295-3883.* Cruises with historical narration. Also evening cocktail and entertainment cruises. (June-Oct, daily; May, Sat-Sun) **$$$$**

⭐ **Cape Cod Kayak.** *1270 Rte 28A, Cataumet (02556). Phone 508/563-9377. www.capecodkayak.com.* Guided kayak tours on area lakes, rivers, harbors, and coves last from three hours to a full day. Guides are happy to teach you kayaking basics before you set out, so even if you've never kayaked before, you'll enjoy this unique way to see Cape Cod. If you're an experienced kayaker and know the area, rent a kayak for a day, weekend, or entire week. (Mar-Nov; closed Dec-Feb) **$$$$$**

Car/Passenger Boat Trips. *509 Falmouth Rd, Woods Hole (02649). Phone 508/477-8600. www.steamshipauthority.com.* Woods Hole, Martha's Vineyard Steamship Authority conducts trips to Martha's Vineyard (all year). Schedule may vary. **$$$$**

Falmouth Historical Society Museums. Julia Wood House. *55 Palmer Ave, Falmouth (02540). Phone 508/548-4857. www.falmouthhistoricalsociety.org.* (1790) and **Conant House** (circa 1740). Whaling collection; period furniture; 19th-century paintings; glassware; silver; tools; costumes; widow's walk; memorial park; colonial garden. (Mid-June-mid-Sept: Tues-Sat; rest of year: by appointment) Katharine Lee Bates exhibit in Conant House honors author of "America the Beautiful." (Mid-June-mid-Sept, Tues-Sat) On village green. **$**

Island Queen. *Falmouth Harbor, Falmouth. Phone 508/548-4800. www.islandqueen.com.* Passenger boat trips to Martha's Vineyard; 600-passenger vessel. (Late May-mid-Oct) **$$$**

Porter's Thermometer Museum. *49 Zarahemla Rd, Onset (02532). Just E of the junction of I-495 and I-195. Phone 508/295-5504.* Heralded as the only museum of its kind in the world, the Porter Thermometer Museum in tiny Onset houses some 2,600 distinct specimens. Varieties include those used by astronauts, ones that can be worn as earrings, and temperature-telling instruments from around the world. One thermometer from Alaska can accurately record temperatures all the way down to -100 degrees! Run by former high school science teacher Richard Porter out of his house, the museum is free, as long as you call ahead. Make sure to admire the world's largest thermometer out front, which can be read from as far as a mile. **FREE**

Special Events

Arts & Crafts Street Fair. *Main St, Falmouth (02540). Phone 508/548-8500.* On a midsummer Wednesday each year in Falmouth, more than 200 painters, weavers, glassworkers, woodworkers, potters, and others artisans set up booths along Main Street. The Arts & Crafts Street Fair is a classic summer festival, with food and entertainment for the entire family. The Falmouth Artists Guild also hosts a fundraising art auction during the fair. Mid-July. **FREE**

Barnstable County Fair. *Barnstable County Fairgrounds, 1220 Nathan Ellis Hwy, Falmouth (02536). 8 miles N on Hwy 151. Phone 508/563-3200. www.barnstablecountyfair.org.* Horse and dog shows, horse-pulling contest; exhibits. Last week in July.

College Light Opera Company at Highfield Theatre. *Highfield Dr, Falmouth (02540). Phone 508/548-2211.* Nine-week season of musicals and operettas with full orchestra. Mon-Sat. Late June-Aug.

Falmouth Road Race. *661 E Main St (race headquarters), Falmouth (02540). Phone 508/540-7000. www.falmouthroadrace.com.* Starting in scenic Woods Hole and winding back into Falmouth Heights, this hilly and hot course takes you past some of the best scenery in the country. This 7.1-mile race has been called the Best USA Road Race by *Runners World* magazine. The entry is a lottery, which means that far more people try to enter than are allowed in. Your best bet is to join the over 70,000 spectators who line the course. If you want to race and don't get in, check the Internet for at least a dozen other summer road races on Cape Cod. Third Sun in Aug. **$$$**

Music on the Green. *Peg Noonan Park, Main St, Falmouth (02540). Phone 508/362-0066. www.artsfoundationcapecod.org.* Professional musicians from the Cape Cod area take part in the Music on the Green series, held on the town green in Falmouth. You'll enjoy rock, swing, marches, and folk music, all performed in the breezy park, and you're encouraged to bring a picnic and beach chair or blanket. The town of Hyannis also offers a Jazz by the Sea concert in early August on its town green. Early July-late Aug. **FREE**

Limited-Service Hotels

★ **NAUTILUS MOTOR INN.** *539 Woods Hole Rd, Woods Hole (02543). Phone 508/548-1525; toll-free 800/654-2333; fax 508/457-9674. www.nautilusinn. com.* 54 rooms, 2 story. Closed late Oct-mid-Apr. Check-in 2 pm, check-out 11 am. Outdoor pool. Tennis. **$**

★ ★ **RAMADA INN.** *40 N Main St, Falmouth (02540). Phone 508/457-0606; toll-free 888/744-5394; fax 508/457-9694. www.innonthesquare.com.* 72 rooms, 2 story. Check-in 3 pm, check-out 11 am. Restaurant, bar. Indoor pool. **$**

★ **RED HORSE INN.** *28 Falmouth Hts Rd, Falmouth (02540). Phone 508/548-0053; toll-free 800/628-3811; fax 508/540-6563. www.redhorseinn. com.* 22 rooms, 2 story. Check-in 3 pm, check-out 11 am. Outdoor pool. **$**

Full-Service Resorts

★ ★ ★ **NEW SEABURY RESORT AND CONFERENCE CENTER.** *Rock Landing Rd, New Seabury (02649). Phone 508/477-9111; toll-free 800/999-9033; fax 508/477-9790. www.newseabury. com.* This resort, conference center, and residential community sits on 2,300 recreation-filled acres and offers rentals from early March to early January. The resort's villa development began in 1962 and consists of two golf courses, 16 tennis courts, and private beaches. 160 rooms. Check-in 4 pm, check-out 10 am. Restaurant, bar. Children's activity center. Fitness room. Outdoor pool, children's pool. Golf. Tennis. Business center. **$**

★ ★ **SEA CREST RESORT.** *350 Quaker Rd, North Falmouth (02556). Phone 508/540-9400; toll-free 800/225-3110; fax 508/540-7602. www.seacrest-resort. com.* 266 rooms, 3 story. Check-in 3 pm, check-out 11 am. Restaurant, bar. Children's activity center. Fitness room. Beach. Indoor pool, outdoor pool, whirlpool. Tennis. Business center. **$$**

Full-Service Inn

★ ★ ★ **COONAMESSETT INN.** *311 Gifford St, Falmouth (02540). Phone 508/548-2300. www.*

capecodrestaurants.org. 28 rooms. Check-in 3 pm, check-out 11 am. High-speed Internet access. Restaurant, bar. **$**

Specialty Lodgings

CAPT. TOM LAWRENCE HOUSE. *75 Locust St, Falmouth (02540). Phone 508/540-1445; toll-free 800/266-8139; fax 508/457-1790. www. captaintomlawrence.com.* Vaulted ceilings, hardwood floors, and a spiral staircase add to the romantic, old-world charm of this intimate inn located within walking distance of the town's historic main street. Built in 1861, it is a former whaling captain's home. 7 rooms, 2 story. Closed Jan. Complimentary full breakfast. Check-in 3-6 pm. Check-out 11 am. **$$**

ELM ARCH INN. *26 Elm Arch Way, Falmouth (02540). Phone 508/548-0133. www.elmarchinn.com.* This former private residence of a whaling captain was built in 1810. It was attacked by the British in 1814, and the hole where the cannonball hit can still be seen in the dining area. 24 rooms, 2 story. Check-in 2 pm, varies, check-out 11 am. Outdoor pool. **$**

GRAFTON INN. *261 Grand Ave S, Falmouth (02540). Phone 203/531-5065. www.graftoninn.com.* This former home of a sea captain was built in 1850 and is located on Nantucket Sound. 10 rooms, 3 story. Children over 16 years only. Complimentary full breakfast. Check-in 3-6 pm, check-out 10 am. **$$**

INN ON THE SOUND. *313 Grand Ave, Falmouth (02540). Phone 508/457-9666; toll-free 800/564-9668; fax 508/457-9631. www.innonthesound.com.* Overlooking Vineyard Sound. Built in 1880. 10 rooms, 2 story. Children over 18 years only. Complimentary full breakfast. Check-in 3-6 pm. Check-out 11 am. **$$**

MOSTLY HALL. *27 Main St, Falmouth (02540). Phone 508/548-3786; toll-free 800/682-0565; fax 508/548-5778. www.mostlyhall.com.* This 1849 plantation-style house, which is the only one of its kind on Cape Cod, offers a secluded location in the heart of the town's historic district. 6 rooms, 3 story. Children over 16 years only. Complimentary full breakfast. Check-in 3-6 pm, check-out 11 am. **$**

THE PALMER HOUSE INN. *81 Palmer Ave, Falmouth (02540). Phone 508/548-1230; toll-free 800/472-2632; fax 508/540-1878. www.palmerhouse-inn.com.* Perched at the upper end of Cape Cod, this 1901 Queen Anne-style inn and guesthouse welcomes visitors year-round. Beaches, the Shining Sea Bikeway, and ferries to the islands are all nearby. 16 rooms, 3 story. Children over 10 only. Complimentary full breakfast. Check-in 3-8 pm, check-out 11 am. **$$**

WILDFLOWER INN. *167 Palmer Ave, Falmouth (02540). Phone 508/548-9524; toll-free 800/294-5459; fax 508/548-9524. www.wildflower-inn.com.* Conveniently located near Martha's Vineyard, guests will enjoy the relaxing and peaceful atmosphere offered at this bed-and-breakfast. Built in 1898. 6 rooms, 3 story. Complimentary full breakfast. Check-in 3-6 pm, check-out 11 am. **$$**
🅱

Restaurants

★ **BETSY'S DINER.** *457 Main St, Falmouth (02540). Phone 508/540-0060.* Save a few coins for the jukebox when visiting Betsy's Diner. Reminiscent of the diners of the 1950s, this place knows how to satisfy a hungry appetite with all-day breakfast and good old American comfort food, including meat loaf and turkey dinners. Always bustling, Betsy's high-spirited atmosphere is part of its charm. American menu. Breakfast, lunch, dinner. Children's menu. Casual attire. **$**

★ **THE FLYING BRIDGE.** *220 Scranton Ave, Falmouth (02540). Phone 508/548-2700; fax 508/457-7675. www.capecodrestaurants.org.* Bring the whole family to The Flying Bridge. Fronting Falmouth Harbor with views of Martha's Vineyard, this restaurant's location is superb. A nautical feel permeates the place, from the three hopping bars to the dockside seating. A seafood-centric menu also includes steaks and lighter bar food. Seafood menu. Lunch, dinner. Closed late Oct-Mar. Bar. Children's menu. Casual attire. Valet parking. Outdoor seating. **$$**

★ ★ **LANDFALL.** *2 Luscombe Ave, Woods Hole (02543). Phone 508/548-1758. www.woodshole.com/landfall.* Like many restaurants on Cape Cod, Landfall exists to serve fresh seafood in a lovely setting. Perched directly over Woods Hole Harbor, this 60-year-old restaurant (regulars know that it's been in the same family since it opened) was constructed of wood from wrecked ships and old buildings, giving it a gently weathered look and a deep sense of the area's history.

Articles inside the dining room, like the Grecian urn that hangs from the rafters, were rescued from the sea. American, seafood menu. Lunch, dinner, Sun brunch. Closed Dec-Mar. Bar. Children's menu. Outdoor seating. **$$**

★ **THE NIMROD.** *100 Dillingham Ave, Falmouth (02540). Phone 508/540-4132. www.thenimrod.com.* The Nimrod offers delicious lunch and dinner fare at great prices, but the entertainment and atmosphere are what draw people there. Musical choices range from live jazz performances to singalongs at the piano bar to big band dancing. American menu. Lunch, dinner, Sun brunch. Bar. Children's menu. Casual attire. Outdoor seating. **$$**

Foxborough (C-7)

Settled 1704
Population 16,246
Elevation 280 ft
Area Code 508
Zip 02035
Information Neponset Valley Chamber of Commerce, 190 Vanderbilt Ave, Suite 1, Norwood 02062; phone 781/769-1126
Web Site www.nvcc.com

What to See and Do

New England Patriots (NFL). *60 Washington St, Foxboro (02035). Take I-93 S (SE Expressway) to I-95 S; take I-95 S to exit 9 (Wrentham) onto Hwy 1 S. Follow Hwy 1 S approximately 3 miles to Gillette Stadium (on the left). Phone toll-free 800/543-1776. www.patriots.com.* The 2002 and 2004 Super Bowl Champion Patriots are exciting to watch, but games at the new Gillette Stadium are more expensive to view. If you go, enjoy the Patriot tailgating experience; if you don't want to hang out with your hibachi in the parking lot, head over the End Zone (or Picnic Zone) Plaza, which features picnic tables. (Closed Feb-July) **$$$$**

New England Revolution (MLS). *60 Washington St, Foxboro (02035). 45 miles S of Boston (halfway between Boston and Providence, RI). Phone toll-free 877/438-7387. www.revolutionsoccer.net.* The New England Revolution is the men's soccer team in the Northeast. To make a game even more memorable, consider renting the Revolution Netside Terrace, a special café and seating area located in the South End of Gillette field, directly behind the net. The $300 price tag includes free parking and a meal and beverage for four people. At the gift shop, the teams unique logo is well worth the price of a T-shirt. (Closed Oct-Mar) **$$$$**

Limited-Service Hotels

★ ★ **COURTYARD BY MARRIOTT.** *35 Foxborough Blvd, Foxborough (02035). Phone 508/543-5222; toll-free 800/321-2211; fax 508/543-0445. www.courtyard.com.* 161 rooms, 3 story. Check-in 3 pm, check-out noon. High-speed Internet access. Restaurant, bar. Fitness room. Indoor pool, whirlpool. **$**

★ ★ **HOLIDAY INN.** *31 Hampshire St, Mansfield (02048). Phone 508/339-2200; toll-free 800/465-4329; fax 508/339-1040. www.holiday-inn.com/bos-mansfield.* 202 rooms, 3 story. Pets accepted. Check-in 3 pm, check-out 11 am. Restaurant, bar. Fitness room. Indoor pool. Tennis. **$**

Framingham (B-6)

Settled 1650
Population 66,910
Elevation 165 ft
Area Code 508
Zip 01701

Framingham is an industrial, commercial, and residential community. Framingham Centre, the original town, was bypassed by the railroad in the 19th century and is 2 miles north of downtown.

What to See and Do

Danforth Museum of Art. *123 Union Ave, Framingham (01702). Phone 508/620-0050. www.danforthmuseum.org.* Six galleries, including a children's gallery; changing exhibits, special events; art reference library. (Closed holidays) **$**

Garden in the Woods. *180 Hemenway Rd, Framingham (01701). Phone 508/877-7630. www.newfs.org/garden.htm.* A 45-acre botanical garden and sanctuary. Largest landscaped collection of wild flowers in northeast. Exceptional collection of wildflowers and other native plants; variety of gardens and habitats. Headquarters of New England Wildflower Society. (daily 9 am-5 pm) Guided walks (daily). Visitor center; museum shop. **$$$**

Full-Service Hotels

★ ★ ★ **DOUBLETREE HOTEL BOSTON/ WESTBOROUGH.** *5400 Computer Dr, Westborough (01581). Phone 508/366-5511; fax 508/870-5965. doubletree.hilton.com.* 223 rooms, 4 story. Check-in 3 pm. Check-out noon. Restaurant, bar. Fitness room. Indoor pool, whirlpool. Business center. **$$**

★ ★ ★ **SHERATON FRAMINGHAM HOTEL.** *1657 Worcester Rd, Framingham (01701). Phone 508/879-7200; toll-free 800/277-1150; fax 508/875-7593. www.sheraton.com.* The brick façade of this property in Metrowest Boston is styled after a 17th-century Irish castle. 373 rooms, 6 story. Check-in 3 pm, check-out noon. Restaurant, bar. Fitness room. Indoor pool, outdoor pool, whirlpool. Business center. **$**

Restaurant

★ ★ **LAFAYETTE HOUSE.** *109 Washington St (Hwy 1), Foxborough (02035). Phone 508/543-5344; fax 508/543-0773. www.lafayettehouse.com.* Historic colonial tavern built in 1784. Seafood menu. Lunch, dinner. Bar. Children's menu. **$$**

Gloucester (A-8)

Settled 1623
Population 30,273
Elevation 50 ft
Area Code 978
Information Cape Ann Chamber of Commerce, 33 Commercial St; phone 978/283-1601 or toll-free 800/321-0133
Web Site www.capeannvacations.com

It is said that more than 10,000 Gloucester men have been lost at sea in the last three centuries, which emphasizes how closely the community has been linked with seafaring. Today, it is still a leading fishing port—although the fast schooners made famous in *Captains Courageous* and countless romances have been replaced by diesel trawlers. Gloucester is also the center of an extensive summer resort area that includes the famous artists' colony of Rocky Neck.

What to See and Do

Beauport, the Sleeper-McCann House. *75 Eastern Point Blvd, Gloucester (01930). Phone 978/283-0800. www. historicnewengland.org.* (1907-1934) Henry Davis Sleeper, early 20th-century interior designer, began by building a 26-room house, continually adding rooms with the help of Halfdan Hanson, a Gloucester architect, until there were 40 rooms; 25 are now on view, containing extraordinary collections of antique furniture, rugs, wallpaper, ceramics, and glass; American and European decorative arts. Many artists, statesmen, and businessmen were entertained here. (Mid-May-mid-Sept: Mon-Fri; mid-Sept-mid-Oct: daily) **$$**

Cape Ann Historical Museum. *27 Pleasant St, Gloucester (01930). Phone 978/283-0455. www. capeannhistoricalmuseum.org.* Paintings by Fitz Hugh Lane; decorative arts and furnishings; Federal-style house (circa 1805). Emphasis on Gloucester's fishing industry; fisheries/maritime galleries and changing exhibitions depict various aspects of Cape Ann's history. (Tues-Sat 10 am-5 pm, Sun 1 pm-4 pm; closed holidays, also Feb) **$$**

Gloucester Fisherman. *On Stacy Blvd on the harbor.* Bronze statue by Leonard Craske, a memorial to anglers lost at sea.

Hammond Castle Museum. *80 Hesperus Ave, Gloucester (01930). Off Hwy 127. Phone 978/283-2080. www.hammondcastle.org.* (1926-1929) Built like a medieval castle by inventor Dr. John Hays Hammond, Jr., the museum contains a rare collection of art objects. The great Hall contains a pipe organ with 8,200 pipes; concerts (selected days throughout the year). (Memorial Day-Labor Day: daily; after Labor Day-Columbus Day: Thurs-Sun; rest of year: Sat-Sun; closed Jan 1, Thanksgiving, Dec 25). Schedule may vary. **$$**

Sargent House Museum. *49 Middle St, Gloucester (01930). Phone 978/281-2432.* Late 18th-century Georgian residence, built for Judith Sargent, an early feminist writer and sister of Governor Winthrop Sargent; also the home of her second husband, John Murray, leader of Universalism. Period furniture, china, glass, silver, needlework, Early American portraits, and paintings by John Singer Sargent. (Memorial Day-Columbus Day, Fri-Mon noon-4 pm; closed holidays) **$**

Special Events

Schooner Festival. *33 Commercial St, Gloucester (01930). Phone 978/283-1601.* Races and a parade of sail and maritime activities. Labor Day weekend.

St. Peter's Fiesta. *Phone 978/283-1601.* A four-day celebration with sports events, fireworks; procession; Blessing of the Fleet. Last weekend in June.

Waterfront Festival. *33 Commercial St, Gloucester (01930). Phone 978/283-1601.* Arts and crafts show, entertainment, food. Third weekend in Aug.

Whale-watching. *33 Commercial St, Gloucester (01930). Phone 978/283-1601.* Half-day trips, mornings and afternoons. May-Oct.

Limited-Service Hotels

★ **BEST WESTERN BASS ROCKS OCEAN INN.** *107 Atlantic Rd, Gloucester (01930). Phone 978/283-7600; toll-free 800/780-7234; fax 978/281-6489. www.bestwestern.com/bassrocksoceaninn.* 48 rooms, 2 story. Closed Dec-Mar. Complimentary full breakfast. Check-in 3 pm, check-out noon. Outdoor pool. **$$**
🔖 ⛱

★ **THE MANOR INN.** *141 Essex Ave, Gloucester (01930). Phone 978/283-0614; fax 978/283-3154. www. themanorinnofgloucester.com.* Victorian manor house. 10 rooms. Closed Nov-Apr, Pets accepted, some restrictions; fee. Complimentary continental breakfast. Check-in 2 pm, check-out 11 am. **$**
🔖 🐾

Full-Service Resort

★ ★ **OCEAN VIEW INN AND RESORT.**
171 Atlantic Rd, Gloucester (01930). Phone 978/283-6200; toll-free 800/315-7557; fax 978/283-1852. www. oceanviewinnandresort.com. Several buildings have accommodations, including a turn-of-the-century English manor house. 62 rooms, 3 story. Pets accepted, some restrictions. Check-in 3 pm, check-out 11 am. Restaurant. Two outdoor pools. **$**
🔖 🐾 ⛱

Restaurant

★ ★ **GLOUCESTER HOUSE RESTAURANT.**
7 Seas Wharf, Gloucester (01930). Phone 978/283-1812; toll-free 888/283-1812; fax 978/281-0369. www. lobster-express.com. Seafood menu. Lunch, dinner. Closed Thanksgiving, Dec 25. Bar. Children's menu. Outdoor seating. **$$**

Great Barrington

Settled 1726
Population 7,527
Elevation 721 ft
Area Code 413
Zip 01230
Information Southern Berkshire Chamber of Commerce, 362 Main St; phone 413/528-1510 or 413/528-4006
Web Site www.greatbarrington.org

As early as 1774, the people of Great Barrington rose up against the King, seizing the courthouse. Today, Great Barrington is the shopping center of the southern Berkshire resort country. Writer, professor, and lawyer James Weldon Johnson, cofounder of the NAACP, and W. E. B. du Bois, black author and editor, lived here. Another resident, the poet William Cullen Bryant, was the town clerk for 13 years.

What to See and Do

Beartown State Forest. *Blue Hill Rd, Monterey (01245). Approximately 5 miles E on Hwy 23. Phone 413/528-0904.* Swimming, fishing; hunting; boating, bridle and hiking trails, snowmobiling, picnicking, camping.

Catamount Ski Area. *7 miles W on Hwy 23.* Four double chairlifts, tow, J-bar; patrol, school, rentals; snowmaking; cafeteria, bar; nursery. Longest run 2 miles; vertical drop 1,000 feet. Night skiing. (Dec-Mar, daily) Half-day rates.

Colonel Ashley House. *117 Cooper Hill Rd, Sheffield (01257). 9 miles S via Hwys 7 and 7A to Ashley Falls, then 1/2 mile on Rannapo Rd to Cooper Hill Rd. Phone 413/229-8600.* (1735) Elegance of the home reflects Colonel Ashley's prominent place in his society. One political meeting he held here produced the Sheffield Declaration, forerunner to the Declaration of Independence. Period furnishings. Adjacent to Bartholowmew's Cobble. (July-Aug: Wed-Sun; Memorial Day-June and Sept-Columbus Day: weekends; open Mon holidays) **$**

Otis Ridge. *159 Monterey Rd, Otis (01253). 16 miles E on Hwy 23. Phone 413/269-4444. www.otisridge.com.* Double chairlift, T-bar, J-bar, three rope tows; patrol, school, rentals; snowmaking; cafeteria. Night skiing

(Tues-Sun). Longest run 1 mile; vertical drop 400 feet. (Dec-Mar, daily) **$$$$**

Ski Butternut. *380 State Rd, Great Barrington (01230). 1 1/2 miles E on Hwy 23. Phone 413/528-2000; toll-free 800/438-7669. www.butternutbasin.com.* Quad, triple, four double chairlifts; Pomalift; rope tow; patrol, school, rentals, snowmaking; nursery (weekends and holidays after Dec 26); cafeterias; wine room; electronically timed slalom race course. Longest run approximately 1 1/2 miles; vertical drop 1,000 feet. Also 7 miles of cross-country trails; rentals. (Dec-Mar, daily) **$$$$**

Special Event

Berkshire Craft Fair. *Monument Mountain Regional High School, 600 Stockbridge Rd, Great Barrington (01230). Phone 413/528-3346. www.berkshirecraftsfair. org.* Juried fair with more than 100 artisans. Mid Aug.

Limited-Service Hotel

★ **MONUMENT MOUNTAIN MOTEL.** *249 Stockbridge Rd, Great Barrington (01230). Phone 413/528-3272; fax 413/528-3132. www.monumentmountainmotel. com.* 18 rooms. Check-out 11 am. Outdoor pool. Tennis. **$**

Specialty Lodgings

THE EGREMONT INN. *10 Old Sheffield Rd, South Egremont (01258). Phone 413/528-2111; toll-free 800/859-1780; fax 413/528-3284. www.egremontinn. com.* 20 rooms, 4 story. Complimentary continental breakfast. Check-in 3 pm, check-out 11 am. Restaurant. Outdoor pool. Tennis. **$**

RACE BROOK LODGE. *864 S Undermountain Rd, Sheffield (01257). Phone 413/229-2916; toll-free 888/725-6343; fax 413/229-6629. www.rblodge.com.* 32 rooms, 3 story. Pets accepted, some restrictions; fee. Complimentary full breakfast. Check-in 2 pm, check-out 11 am. Bar. **$$**

THORNEWOOD INN & RESTAURANT. *453 Stockbridge Rd, Great Barrington (01230). Phone 413/528-3828; toll-free 800/458-1008; fax 413/528-3307. www.thornewood.com.* 15 rooms, 2 story. Children over 12 years only. Complimentary full breakfast. Check-in 3-7 pm, check-out 11:30 am. Restaurant. Outdoor pool. **$$**

WINDFLOWER INN. *684 S Egremont Rd, Great Barrington (01230). Phone 413/528-2720; toll-free 800/992-1993; fax 413/528-5147. www.windflowerinn.com.* On 10 acres of Berkshire hillside, this white clapboard, country inn is classically New England with its screened porch and 13 antique-filled rooms. The estate dates back to the 1850s and is near year-round recreation including Tanglewood music center. 13 rooms. Complimentary full breakfast. Check-in 2 pm, check-out 11 am. Outdoor pool. **$$**

Restaurants

★ ★ ★ **CASTLE STREET CAFE.** *10 Castle St, Great Barrington (01230). Phone 413/528-5244. www.castlestreetcafe.com.* Chef/owner Michael Ballon delights guests of the Berkshires with his creative cooking and hospitable service. Enjoy live entertainment several nights of the week and relax in the comfortable Celestial Bar. American menu. Dinner. Closed Tues; Thanksgiving, Dec 25. Bar. **$$**

★ ★ **JOHN ANDREW'S RESTAURANT.** *Hwy 23, South Egremont (01258). Phone 413/528-3469; fax 413/528-2535.* American menu. Dinner. Closed Wed in Sept-June. Bar. Children's menu. Outdoor seating. **$$**

★ ★ **THE OLD MILL.** *53 Main St (Hwy 23), South Egremont (01258). Phone 413/528-1421; fax 413/528-0007.* Built in 1978. In gristmill. American menu. Dinner. Closed Mon; Thanksgiving, Dec 25. Bar. Children's menu. **$$**

★ ★ ★ **SPENCER'S.** *453 Stockbridge Rd, Great Barrington (01230). Phone 413/528-3828; toll-free 800/854-1008; fax 413/528-3307. www.thornewood.com.* This restaurant is located in the turn-of-the-century Thornewood Inn (see). The fresh produce is provided by the inn's gardens. Guests will feel like family at this cozy establishment, especially when they learn the restaurant is named after the owners' grandson. American menu. Dinner Thurs-Sat. Closed Jan 1. Bar. Outdoor seating. **$$**

Greenfield (A-3)

See also Brattleboro, VT

Settled 1686
Population 18,168
Elevation 250 ft
Area Code 413
Zip 01301
Information Franklin County Chamber of Commerce, 395 Main St, PO Box 898; phone 413/773-5463
Web Site www.co.franklin.ma.us

The center of a prosperous agricultural area, Greenfield is also the home of many factories and a center for winter and summer sports, hunting, and fishing. The first cutlery factory in America was established in Greenfield in the early 19th century.

What to See and Do

Northfield Mountain Recreation and Environmental Center. *99 Miller's Falls Rd, Northfield (01360). Hwy 63. Phone 413/659-3714.* On the site of Northeast Utilities Hydro Electric Pump storage plant. Hiking, camping, riverboat ride, and picnicking. (Dec-Mar: Mon-Fri; May-Oct: Wed-Sun) Fee for some activities.

Special Events

Franklin County Fair. *89 Wisdom Way, Greenfield (01301). Phone 413/774-4282. www.fcas.com.* Four days starting first Thurs after Labor Day.

Green River Music & Balloon Festival. *Colrain Rd, Greenfield (01301). Phone 413/773-9393. www.greenriverfestival.com.* Hot air balloon launches, craft show, musical entertainment, food. July. **$$$$**

Specialty Lodging

BRANDT HOUSE. *29 Highland Ave, Greenfield (01301). Phone 413/774-3329; toll-free 800/235-3329; fax 413/772-2908. www.brandthouse.com.* This turn-of-the-century Colonial Revival mansion offers contemporary creature comforts. The owner is an interior decorator and has given each room its own personality. Antiques, fresh flowers, and feather beds allow guests to bask in comfort. 8 rooms, 3 story. Pets accepted, some restrictions; fee. Complimentary full breakfast. Check-in 2 pm. Check-out 11 am. Golf. Tennis. **$$**

Restaurants

★ ★ **BELLA-NOTTE.** *199 Huckle Hill Rd, Bernardston (01337). Phone 413/648-9107; fax 413/648-0217.* Italian menu. Dinner. Closed Dec 24-25. Bar. **$$**

★ ★ **FAMOUS BILL'S.** *30 Federal St, Greenfield (01301). Phone 413/773-9230; fax 413/774-3671. www. billsrestaurant.com.* American menu. Dinner, Sun brunch. Bar. Children's menu. Casual attire. **$$**

Harwich (Cape Cod)

Settled circa 1670
Population 12,386
Elevation 55 ft
Area Code 508
Zip 02646
Information Harwich Chamber of Commerce, PO Box 34; phone 508/432-1600; or the Cape Cod Chamber of Commerce, Hwys 6 and 132, PO Box 790, Hyannis 02601-0790, phone 508/362-3225 or toll-free 888/227-3263
Web Site www.capecodchamber.org

Harwich, whose namesake in England was dubbed "Happy-Go-Lucky Harwich" by Queen Elizabeth, is one of those towns made famous in New England literature. It is "Harniss" in the Joseph C. Lincoln novels of Cape Cod. A local citizen, Jonathan Walker, was immortalized as "the man with the branded hand" in Whittier's poem about helping escaped slaves; Enoch Crosby of Harwich was the Harvey Birch of James Fenimore Cooper's novel *The Spy*. Today, summer residents own three-quarters of the land.

What to See and Do

Brooks Free Library. *Harwich Center, 739 Main St, Harwich (02646). Phone 508/430-7562.* Houses 24 John Rogers's figurines. (Tues-Thurs 11 am-7 pm; Fri-Sat until 5 pm; closed holidays) **FREE**

⭐ **Cape Cod Baseball League.** *11 North Rd, Harwich (02645). Phone 508/432-6909. www.capecodbaseball. org.* The Cape Cod Baseball League is baseball as you remember it: local, passionate, affordable, and played only with wooden bats. The ten teams are all drawn from college players from around the country, who live with host families for the summer, visit schools to interact with kids, and host a summer baseball clinic. Spectators sit on wooden benches, pack a picnic lunch or dinner, and cheer for their favorite players during each of the 44 games played each season at venues throughout Cape Cod. (Mid-June-mid-Aug) **FREE**

Harwich Historical Society. *80 Parallel St, Harwich (02645). At Sisson Rd, in Harwich Center. Phone 508/432-8089.* Includes Brooks Academy Building and Revolutionary War Powder House. Native American artifacts, marine exhibit, cranberry industry articles, early newspapers and photographs. Site of one of the first schools of navigation in the United States. (Usually mid-June-mid-Oct, Wed-Fri; schedule may vary) **DONATION**

Red River Beach. *Deep Hole and Uncle Venies rds, South Harwich (02646). Off Hwy 28, S on Uncle Venies Rd.* A fine Nantucket Sound swimming beach (water 68 F to 72 F in summer). Sticker fee per weekday.

Saquatucket Municipal Marina. *715 Main St, Harwich (02646). Off Hwy 28. Phone 508/432-2562.* Boat ramp for launching small craft. (May-mid-Nov) **$$$**

Special Events

Cranberry Harvest Festival. *Hwy 58 N and Rochester Rd, Harwich (02645).* Family Day, antique car show, music, arts and crafts, fireworks, carnival, parade. One weekend in mid-Sept.

Harwich Junior Theatre. *105 Division St, West Harwich (02671). Phone 508/432-2002. www.hjtcapecod.org.* Plays for the family and children through high school age. Reservations required. (July-Aug, daily; Sept-June, monthly)

Limited-Service Hotels

★ ★ **THE COMMODORE INN.** *30 Earle Rd, West Harwich (02671). Phone 508/432-1180; toll-free 800/368-1180; fax 508/432-3263. www.commodoreinn. com.* 27 rooms. Closed Nov-Apr. Complimentary continental breakfast. Check-in 2 pm, check-out 11 am. Restaurant, bar. Outdoor pool. **$**
🏊

★ **THE SANDPIPER BEACH INN.** *16 Bank St, Harwich Port (02646). Phone 508/432-0485; toll-free 800/433-2234. www.sandpiperbeachinn.com.* 20 rooms. Check-in 3 pm, check-out 11 am. Beach. **$**

★ **SEADAR INN.** *Braddock Ln @ Bank St Beach, Harwich Port (02646). Phone 508/432-0264; toll-free 800/888-5250; fax 508/430-1916. www.seadarinn.com.* Main building is an old colonial house (1789). Early American décor; some rooms with bay windows. Near beach. 20 rooms, 2 story. Closed mid-Oct-late May. Complimentary continental breakfast. Check-in 1 pm, check-out 11 am. **$**

Specialty Lodgings

CIRCADIA BISTRO. *86 Sisson Rd, Harwich Port (02646). Phone 508/432-2769; fax 508/430-1455. www.circadiabistro.com.* 6 rooms, 2 story. Complimentary continental breakfast. Check-in 2 pm. Check-out noon. Restaurant. Beach. Outdoor pool. **$**

DUNSCROFT BY THE SEA. *24 Pilgrim Rd, Harwich Port (02646). Phone 508/432-0810; toll-free 800/432-4345; fax 508/432-5134. www.dunscroftbythesea.com.* Guests will enjoy the white-sand beach, just steps away, as well as such nearby activities as shopping, miniature golf, fishing, water sports, clambakes, and whale-watching. 8 rooms, 2 story. Children over 12 years only. Complimentary full breakfast. Check-in 2 pm. Check-out 11 am. Whirlpool. **$$**

FIDDLERS GREEN INN. *79 Main St, West Harwich (02671). Phone 508/430-2440; fax 508/432-6039.* Former Baptist parsonage (circa 1900). 9 rooms, 3 story. Closed Jan-Mar. Pets accepted, some restrictions. Complimentary full breakfast. Check-in 2 pm, check-out 11 am. Restaurant. Outdoor pool. **$**

Restaurants

★ **400 EAST.** *1421 Orleans Rd, Harwich (02645). Phone 508/432-1800; fax 508/432-3615. www.the400east.com.* Large crowds waiting for tables pack 400 East. This popular restaurant is recognized for its good food and good fun. A thriving bar scene makes this nouveau tavern a great place to kick back with a beer. Sandwiches, burgers, pasta, and pizzas round out the comprehensive menu, and the daily specials are a source of pride. American menu. Lunch, dinner, late-night. Bar. Children's menu. Casual attire. **$**

★ ★ **AY! CARAMBA CAFE.** *703 Main St, Harwich (02645). Phone 508/432-9800; fax 508/432-9977. www.aycarambacafe.com.* The authentic flavors of Mexico shine at Ay! Caramba Café. This standout packs a punch with its tasty dishes and festive, easygoing atmosphere. The kitchen takes great pride in using original recipes and top-quality ingredients. Brightly colored walls decorated with scenes of the Mexican seaside add a kitschy charm. Mexican menu. Lunch, dinner. Bar. Children's menu. Casual attire. Outdoor seating. **$**

★ ★ **L'ALOUETTE.** *787 Main St, Harwich Port (02646). Phone 508/430-0405; fax 508/430-0975. www.capecodmenu.com.* The romance of the French countryside comes alive at L'Alouette. Owners Danielle and Jean-Louis Bastres, a husband-and-wife team, originally from France, show off their hometown pride with a series of well-executed, classic dishes, such as chateaubriand and rack of lamb. The dining room, with its Provençal furnishings, is especially cozy. French menu. Dinner. Closed Mon; Dec 25; also Feb. Reservations recommended. **$$$**

Haverhill (A-7)

See also Amesbury

Settled 1640
Population 58,969
Elevation 27 ft
Area Code 978
Information Chamber of Commerce, 87 Winter St, 01830; phone 978/373-5663
Web Site www.haverhillchamber.com

Haverhill is a thriving manufacturing and commercial center located along the Merrimack River. Long known for its role in the manufacturing of women's shoes, Haverhill now boasts a highly diversified high-tech industrial base. The city features fine neighborhoods of early 19th-century homes. The Quaker poet John Greenleaf Whittier was born here.

A statue at Winter and Main Streets commemorates the remarkable Hannah Dustin, who, according to legend, was kidnapped by Native Americans in March 1697, and escaped with the scalps of ten of her captors.

What to See and Do

Haverhill Historical Society. *240 Water St, Haverhill (01830). Hwy 97. Phone 978/374-4626.* Located in The Buttonwoods, an early 19th-century house. Period furnishings, china, glass, Hannah Dustin relics, memorabilia from turn-of-the-century theaters, Civil

War artifacts, and archaeological collection. Also on grounds is the John Ward House (1641), furnished with colonial items; and an 1850s shoe factory with displays. Guided tours. (Tues-Sun 10 am-5 pm) **$$**

John Greenleaf Whittier Birthplace. *305 Whittier Rd, Haverhill (01830). I-495 exit 52, 1 mile E on Hwy 110. Phone 978/373-3979. www.johngreenleafwhittier.com.* Whittier family homestead since the 17th century, this is the setting of his best-known poems, including "Snow-Bound," and "Barefoot Boy." His writing desk and mother's bedroom, built over a rock too large to move, are here. The house is furnished with original pieces and arranged as it would have appeared in his childhood. Grounds (69 acres) still actively farmed. (Wed-Sun; closed Jan 1, Thanksgiving, Dec 25; limited hours in winter) **$**

Limited-Service Hotels

★ **BEST WESTERN MERRIMACK VALLEY.** *401 Lowell Ave, Haverhill (01832). Phone 978/373-1511; toll-free 888/645-2025; fax 978/373-1517. www.bestwestern.com.* 127 rooms, 3 story. Pets accepted, some restrictions; fee. Complimentary continental breakfast. Check-in 3 pm, check-out noon. High-speed Internet access. Indoor pool, whirlpool. Airport transportation available. Business center. **$**

★ **COMFORT SUITES.** *106 Bank Rd, Haverhill (01832). Phone 978/374-7755; toll-free 800/517-4000; fax 978/521-1894. www.comfortsuites.com.* 131 rooms, 4 story. Complimentary continental breakfast. Check-in 3 pm, check-out noon. Fitness room. Whirlpool. **$**

Holyoke (C-3)

See also South Hadley, Springfield; also see Enfield, CT

Settled 1745
Population 39,838
Elevation 270 ft
Area Code 413
Zip 01040
Information Greater Holyoke Chamber of Commerce, 177 High St; phone 413/534-3376
Web Site www.holycham.com

Captain Elizur Holyoke explored the Connecticut Valley as early as 1633. His name is preserved in the industrial city made possible with the development of the great river by an unusual set of power canals.

What to See and Do

Holyoke Heritage State Park. *221 Appleton St, Holyoke (01040). Phone 413/534-1723. www.state.ma.us/dem/parks/hhsp.htm.* At this canalside park, the visitor center features cultural, environmental, and recreational programs; a slide show; and exhibits on the region and on Holyoke's history as a planned city, its canals, industries, and people. The restored antique Holyoke Merry-Go-Round is also here (Sat-Sun afternoons; expanded summer hours). (Wed-Sun afternoons; schedule may vary) **FREE** Also on the site and adjacent is

Children's Museum. *444 Dwight St, Holyoke (01040). Phone 413/536-7048. www.childrensmuseumholyoke.org.* Participatory museum. Exhibits include papermaking, sand pendulum, bubble making, TV studio, two-story climbing structure, tot lot, "Cityscape," and other changing exhibits. (Tues-Sat 9:30 am-4:30 pm, Sun noon-5 pm) **$$**

Wistariahurst Museum. *238 Cabot St, Holyoke (01040). Phone 413/322-5660. www.wistariahurst.org.* Victorian mansion, family home of noted silk manufacturer William Skinner. House highlights include interior architectural detail unique to late 19th and early 20th centuries, including a leather-paneled room, conservatory and music hall; period furniture, decorative arts. Textile and archival collections available for research scholars. Changing exhibits. (Mon, Sat-Sun noon-4 pm; schedule may vary) **DONATION**

Limited-Service Hotel

★ ★ **HOLIDAY INN.** *245 Whiting Farms Rd, Holyoke (01040). Phone 413/534-3311; toll-free 800/465-4329; fax 413/533-8443. www.holiday-inn.com.* At a busy commercial intersection off I-91, this 216-room hotel is a Holidome property, which means that it has lots to offer active families. A large atrium at the back of the hotel houses a pool, whirlpool, sauna, video arcade, and shuffleboard court, along with foosball, air hocky, and pool tables. A New England tradition for ice cream and tuna melts, Friendly's serves as the hotel's restaurant. If the kids tire of all this, the large and upscale Holyoke Mall is just down the street, and Six Flags New England is 12 miles away. For adults, the hotel also has a huge sports bar and a ballroom for group functions. 216 rooms, 4 story. Pets accepted. Check-in 3 pm, check-out noon. High-speed

Internet access. Restaurant, bar. Fitness room. Indoor pool, whirlpool. Business center. **$**

Restaurants

★ ★ ★ **DELANY HOUSE.** *Hwy 5 at Smith's Ferry, Holyoke (01040). Phone 413/532-1800; fax 413/533-7137. www.delaneyhouse.com.* This charming restaurant is located in picturesque Smith's Ferry. The American menu features the freshest of ingredients and the atmosphere is casually elegant. International menu. Dinner. Closed Jan 1, Dec 25. Bar. Casual attire. Reservations recommended. Valet parking. Outdoor seating. **$$$**

★ ★ **YANKEE PEDLAR.** *1866 Northhamptons St, Holyoke (01040). Phone 413/532-9494; fax 413/536-8877. www.yankeepedlarinn.com.* American menu. Lunch, dinner, Sun brunch. Closed Mon; Dec 25. Bar. Outdoor seating. **$$**

Hyannis and Barnstable (Cape Cod) (D-9)

See also Martha's Vineyard, Nantucket, Yarmouth

Settled 1639
Population 14,120
Elevation 19 ft
Area Code 508
Zip 02601
Information Chamber of Commerce, 1481 Hwy 132; phone 508/362-5230 or toll-free 877/492-6647
Web Site www.hyannis.com

Hyannis is the main vacation and transportation center of Cape Cod. Recreational facilities and specialty areas abound, including tennis courts, golf courses, arts and crafts galleries, theaters, and antique shops. There are libraries, museums, and the Kennedy Memorial and Compound. Candle-making tours are available. Scheduled airliners and Amtrak stop here, and it is also a port for boat trips to Nantucket Island and Martha's Vineyard. More than 6 million people visit the village every year, and it is within an hour's drive of the many attractions on the Cape.

What to See and Do

Auto Ferry/Steamship Authority. *Ocean St, Hyannis (02601). Phone 508/477-8600. www.steamshipauthority. com.* Woods Hole, Martha's Vineyard, and Nantucket Steamship Authority conduct trips to Nantucket from Hyannis (year-round); depart from South Street dock.

Beaches. *Phone 508/790-6345.* **Craigville Beach.** Basset Ln. SW of town center. **Sea St Beach.** Sea St. Overlooking Hyannis Port harbor, bathhouse. **Kalmus Park.** Ocean St, bathhouse. **Veteran's Park.** Ocean St. Picnicking at Kalmus and Veteran's parks. There is a parking fee at all beaches.

Cape Cod Art Association Gallery. *3480 Hwy 6A, Barnstable (02630). Phone 508/362-2909. www. capecodartassoc.org.* Changing exhibits, exhibitions by New England artists; demonstrations, lectures, classes. (Apr-Nov: Mon-Sat 9 am-4 pm, Sun from noon; rest of year: inquire for schedule) **FREE**

Cape Cod Crusaders. *112 State Rd, Buzzards Bay (02532). Games are played at Dennis-Yarmouth High School. Take Hwy 6 to exit 8, turn right off the ramp, and the stadium is about 2 miles down on your left. Phone 508/888-0865. www.capecodcrusaders.com.* If you want to see a professional sports team on Cape Cod, the Crusaders are the only team to watch. As members of the USISL (United States Independent Soccer League), the Crusaders play about 12 home games throughout late spring and summer. The Crusaders are the farm team for the New England Revolution, which means that Crusaders players are often recruited from around the world and start out in Cape Cod. **$$**

Cape Cod Melody Tent. *21 W Main St, Hyannis (02601). Phone 508/775-5630. www.melodytent.org.* Looking for top-notch musical acts? The Cape Cod Melody Tent draws top musicians from around the country—mostly easy listening and country music—plus comedians. The venue is a huge white tent that's been hosting concerts on Cape Cod for over 50 years. Wednesday mornings in July and August bring theater and musical productions for kids. Call, or visit the Web site for all concert dates and times, and if you want to be sure you get tickets, purchase them the day they go on sale. You may be able to pick up tickets left behind by no-shows just before performances begin. (Late May-mid-Sept)

Cape Cod Pathways. *3225 Main St, Barnstable (02630). Phone 508/362-3828. www. capecodcommission.org/pathways.* This network of walking and hiking trails is composed of a perfect mix of dirt, sand, and gravel, and when completed will link all the towns in Cape Cod. The Cape Cod Commission oversees the trails and produces a detailed map, yours for the asking by calling or writing. Don't miss the Cape Walk in early June, in which hearty souls hike from one end of the cape to another, or the Walking Weekend in late October, when trail guides lead walks and hikes of varying lengths. (Daily) **FREE**

⭐ **Cape Cod Potato Chip Company.** *100 Breed's Hill Rd, Hyannis (02601). Phone 508/775-3358. www. capecodchips.com.* Cape Cod Potato Chips, which are now sold all over the world, may be Cape Cod's most recognizable food product (although Nantucket Nectars, a local brand of juices available on the island and around the world, may take issue with that assessment). Perhaps the best part about taking the ten-minute self-guided tour of the facility is tasting the free samples, although seeing the unique kettles in which these crunchy chips are cooked is a close second. (Mon-Fri 9 am-5 pm; closed holidays) **FREE**

Centerville Historical Society Museum. *513 Main St, Centerville (02632). Phone 508/775-0331. www. centervillehistoricalmuseum.org.* Houses 14 exhibition rooms interpreting Cape Cod's history, art, industry, and domestic life. Displays include Early American furniture, housewares, quilts; dolls, costumes; Crowell carved birds, Sandwich glass collection, marine room, tool room, research library. (June-Oct, Wed-Sun noon-5 pm) **$**

Donald G. Trayser Memorial Museum. *Old Custom House and Post Office, 3353 Main St, Barnstable (02630). In Old Custom House and Post Office, Main St on Cobb's Hill, Rte 6A (02630). Phone 508/362-2092.* Marine exhibits, scrimshaw, Barnstable silver, historic documents. (July-mid-Oct, Tues-Sat afternoons)

Hyannis *Whale Watcher* Cruises. *Barnstable Harbor, 269 Mill Way, Barnstable (02630). Phone 508/362-6088. www.whales.net.* View whales aboard the *Whale Watcher*, a 297-passenger super-cruiser, custom designed and built specifically for whale-watching. Naturalist on board will narrate. Café on board. (Apr-Oct, daily) Reservations necessary. **$$$$**

Hyannis-Nantucket or Martha's Vineyard Day Round-Trip. *Hy-Line, Pier #1, Ocean St Dock, Hyannis (02601). Phone 508/778-2600. www.hylinecruises.com.* (May-Oct) Also hourly sightseeing trips to Hyannis

Port (late Apr-Oct, daily); all-day or half-day deep-sea fishing excursions (late Apr-mid-Oct, daily).

John F. Kennedy Hyannis Museum. *397 Main St, Hyannis (02601). In Old Town Hall. Phone 508/790-3077.* Photographic exhibits and a seven-minute video narrated by Walter Cronkite focus on President Kennedy's relationship with Cape Cod. (Mid-Apr-Oct: Mon-Sat 9 am-5 pm, Sun and holidays noon-5 pm; rest of year: Thurs-Sat 10 am-4 pm, Sun and holidays noon-4 pm) **$**

John F. Kennedy Memorial. *Ocean St, Hyannis (02601).* This 12-foot-high circular fieldstone wall memorial with presidential seal, fountain, and small pool honors the late president, who grew up nearby.

Osterville Historical Society Museum. *155 W Bay Rd, Osterville (02655). 3 miles SW, at junction West Bay and Parker rds. Phone 508/428-5861.* Sea captain's house with 18th- and 19th-century furnishings; Sandwich glass, Chinese porcelain, majolica and Staffordshire pottery; doll collection. Special events throughout the summer. Boat-building museum, ship models; catboat *Cayugha* is on display. Restored Cammett House (circa 1730) is on grounds. (Mid-June-Sept, Thurs-Sun 1:30 pm-4:30 pm; other times by appointment) **$$**

Pufferbellies Entertainment Complex. *183 Rear Iyanough Rd, Hyannis (02601). Phone 508/790-4300; toll-free 800/233-4301. www.pufferbellies.com.* Pufferbellies is a unique collection of nightclubs and places to eat and drink. On four separate dance floors, you'll dance the night away to swing, disco, country, and Top 40 music. If you have two left feet, be sure to take an on-site dance lesson. The sports bar entertains you with three big-screen TVs, dart boards, pool tables, and basketball machines, and a beach volleyball court in the Jimmy Buffet Parrothead Bar extends the fun outdoors in the summer months. (Fri-Sun; hours and activities vary by season) **$$**

Sturgis Library. *3090 Main St, Barnstable (02630). Phone 508/362-6636; fax 508/362-5467. www.sturgislibrary.org.* Oldest library building (1644) in the United States has material on the Cape, including maritime history; genealogical records of Cape Cod families. Research fee for nonresidents. (Mon-Sat; closed holidays) **FREE**

West Parish Meetinghouse. *2049 Meetinghouse Way, West Barnstable (02668). Jct Hwys 6, 149. Phone 508/362-4445. www.westparish.org.* (1717) Said to be the oldest Congregational church in the country;

restored. Congregation established in London, 1616. Regular Sunday services are held here all year. **FREE**

Special Events

Cape Cod Oyster Festival. *20 Independence Dr, Hyannis (02601). Phone 508/775-4746. www. capecodoysterfestival.com.* What you get at the Cape Cod Oyster Festival is oysters—as many as you care to eat—accompanied by wine from local vineyards. Sample raw, baked, and roasted oysters, and also taste oyster stew. Held at the Naked Oyster restaurant under a big tent, the Oyster Festival draws locals and tourists alike. Early Oct. **$$$$$**

Figawi Sailboat Race and Charity Ball. *70 Jobys Ln, Osterville (02655). Phone 508/420-5981. www.figawi. com.* The Figawi Sailboat Race (the East Coasts largest) features 200 sailboats racing from Hyannis to Nantucket on Saturday—and back again in a fun Return Race on Monday. Don't miss the Clam Bake on Nantucket Sunday afternoon and numerous cocktails parties, too. The annual Charity Ball (black-tie optional) precedes the event by one week. Held in Hyannis and featuring live bands, dancing, and a feast prepared by local restaurants, the Charity Ball is a major social event on Cape Cod. Memorial Day weekend. **FREE**

Fleet Pops by the Sea. *Town Green, Hyannis (02601). Phone 508/362-0066. www.artsfoundationcapecod.org.* In early August, the Boston Pops makes its way from Boston to Cape Cod for a once-a-year concert on the Hyannis Town Green. You'll enjoy classics, pops, and Sousa marches. Each year brings a new celebrity guest conductor, from actors to poets to famous chefs. The performance serves as a fundraiser that supports the Arts Foundation of Cape Cod. **$$$$**

Hyannis Harbor Festival. *On the waterfront at Bismore Park. Phone 508/362-5230.* Coast Guard cutter tours, sailboat races, marine displays, food, entertainment. Weekend in early June.

Limited-Service Hotels

★ **ANCHOR-IN.** *1 South St, Hyannis (02601). Phone 508/775-0357; fax 508/775-1313. www.anchorin.com.* 43 rooms. Complimentary continental breakfast. Check-in 3 pm, check-out noon. Beach. Outdoor pool, whirlpool. **$**

★ ★ **CAPE CODDER RESORT & SPA.** *1225 Iyanough Rd, Hyannis (02601). Phone 508/771-3000; toll-free 888/297-2200; fax 508/771-6564. www. capecodderresort.com.* 258 rooms, 2 story. Check-in 3 pm, check-out 11 am. High-speed Internet access. Restaurant, bar. Fitness room, spa. Indoor pool, whirlpool. Tennis. Business center. **$**

★ **CENTERVILLE CORNERS MOTOR LODGE.** *369 S Main St, Centerville (02632). Phone 508/775-7223; toll-free 800/242-1137; fax 508/775-4147. www. centervillecorners.com.* 48 rooms, 2 story. Closed Nov-Apr. Pets accepted, some restrictions; fee. Complimentary continental breakfast. Check-in 2 pm, check-out 11 am. Indoor pool. **$**

★ ★ **COURTYARD BY MARRIOTT.** *707 Hwy 132, Hyannis (02601). Phone 508/775-6600; toll-free 800/321-2211; fax 508/790-0119. www.marriott.com.* 120 rooms. Check-in 3 pm, check-out noon. High-speed Internet access. Indoor pool. Business center. **$**

★ ★ **HERITAGE HOUSE HOTEL.** *259 Main St, Hyannis (02601). Phone 508/775-7000; toll-free 800/352-7189; fax 508/778-5687. www.heritagehousehotel.com.* 143 rooms, 3 story. Check-out 11 am. Restaurant. Indoor, outdoor pool; whirlpool. **$**

★ ★ **INTERNATIONAL INN.** *662 Main St, Hyannis (02601). Phone 508/775-5600; toll-free 877/588-3353; fax 508/775-3933. www.cuddles.com.* With a trademark like "cuddle and bubble," it's obvious romance is the distinguishing feature of this Cape Cod hotel conveniently located within walking distance of town and ferries. Geared toward couples, each room or suite has a Jacuzzi built for two. 141 rooms, 2 story. Check-in 3 pm, check-out 11 am. Restaurant, bar. Indoor pool, outdoor pool. **$**

Specialty Lodgings

ACWORTH INN. *4352 Old King's Hwy, Hwy 6A, Cummaquid (02637). Phone 508/362-3330; toll-free 800/362-6363; fax 508/375-0304. www.acworthinn. com.* Whether guests come here to relax and unwind or for a romantic getaway, this bed-and-breakfast has everything one needs for both. Guests can enjoy a day of sightseeing, mountain biking, or golf and then return to enjoy a nice cozy evening in the gathering room. 5 rooms, 2 story. Children over 12 years only. Complimentary full breakfast. Check-in 3-5 pm, check-out 11 am. **$**

ASHLEY MANOR. *3660 Olde King?s Hwy, Barnstable (02630). Phone 508/362-8044; toll-free 888/535-2246; fax 508/362-9927. www.ashleymanor. net.* A lovely garden and gazebo adorn this beautiful inn. Guests can unwind with a book in the library or with afternoon tea in front of the fire. Some activities available to guests include whale-watching, biking, and even off-Cape excursions. 6 rooms, 2 story. Children over 14 years only. Complimentary full breakfast. Check-in 2-8 pm, check-out 11 am. Tennis. **$**

BEECHWOOD INN. *2839 Main St, Barnstable (02630). Phone 508/362-6618; toll-free 800/609-6618; fax 508/362-0298. www.beechwoodinn.com.* Situated near Barnstable Village, guests can enjoy biking, whale-watching, and golf. The guest who prefers a relaxing vacation may sit on the porch and enjoy an iced tea or lemonade while rocking on the gliders. 6 rooms, 3 story. Children over 12 only. Complimentary full breakfast. Check-in 2 pm, check-out 11 am. **$**

CAPTAIN DAVID KELLEY HOUSE. *539 Main St, Centerville (02632). Phone 508/775-4707; toll-free 888/815-5700. www.captaindavidkelleyhouse.com.* 5 rooms, 2 story. Complimentary full breakfast. Check-in 3 pm, check-out 11 am. **$**

HONEYSUCKLE HILL B&B. *591 Old King's Hwy, Hwy 6A, West Barnstable (02668). Phone 508/362-8418; toll-free 866/444-5522; fax 508/362-8386. www. honeysucklehill.com.* Built in 1810. 5 rooms, 2 story. Children over 12 years only. Complimentary full breakfast. Check-in 3-9 pm. Check-out 11 am. Restored Victorian décor. **$**

SEA BREEZE INN. *270 Ocean Ave, Hyannis (02601). Phone 508/771-7213; fax 508/534-1050. www. seabreezeinn.com.* Near beach; some rooms with ocean view. 14 rooms, 2 story. Complimentary continental breakfast. Check-in 2-11 pm, check-out 11 am. **$**

SIMMONS HOMESTEAD INN. *288 Scudder Ave, Hyannis Port (02647). Phone 508/778-4999; toll-free 800/637-1649; fax 508/790-1342. www.simmonshome*

steadinn.com. Restored sea captain's home built in 1820; some canopied beds. 14 rooms, 2 story. Pets accepted, some restrictions; fee. Complimentary full breakfast. Check-in 1 pm, check-out 11 am. **$$**

Restaurants

★ ★ **BARNSTABLE TAVERN AND GRILLE.** *3176 Main St, Barnstable (02630). Phone 508/362-2355; fax 508/362-9012.* The Barnstable has been an inn and tavern since 1799. Seafood menu. Lunch, dinner. Closed Dec 24-25. Bar. Children's menu. Outdoor seating. **$$**

★ ★ **DOLPHIN RESTAURANT.** *3250 Main St, Barnstable (02630). Phone 508/362-6610. www.the dolphinrestaurant.com.* From the pale gray clapboards outside to the maple captain's chairs and ship's wheel inside, the Dolphin is the quintessential Cape Cod townie restaurant, where folks stop off for burgers, lobster rolls, and club sandwiches at lunch and return in the evening for pan-fried sole. Some modern twists enliven the plate as well, like an orange-scallion sauce to dress up broiled codfish. American, seafood menu. Lunch, dinner. Bar. Children's menu. Casual attire. Reservations recommended. **$$**

★ **EGG & I.** *521 Main St, Hyannis (02601). Phone 508/771-1596; fax 508/778-6385.* Breakfast lovers rejoice at the Egg & I restaurant. This delightful place celebrates the first meal of the day like no other, and diners enjoy the friendly service and unfussy atmosphere. Diner. American menu. Breakfast. Closed Dec-Feb; weekends only in Mar, Nov. Children's menu. **$**

★ ★ **FIVE BAYS BISTRO.** *825 Main St, Osterville (02655). Phone 508/420-5559. www.fivebaysbistro. com.* This polished storefront bistro offers some nice twists on traditional Cape fare. Rare tuna is paired with lo mein noodles and wasabi soy, while from-the-land options like veal medallions and grilled chicken risotto please those in the mood for something other than fish and shellfish. The bar serves up a selection of martinis and wines by the glass, including grappa and port, and homemade desserts satisfy a sweet tooth. American menu. Dinner. Bar. Casual attire. **$$$**

★ **HARRY'S.** *700 Main St, Hyannis (02601). Phone 508/778-4188.* Harry's lets the good times roll. Belly-busting tastes from the Bayou are the inspiration behind this rollicking joint. From crawdaddies and shrimp Creole to jambalaya, the fiery flavors of the South come alive here. This place rocks year-round, with some of the area's best R&B and blues music performed here nightly. Cajun/Creole menu. Lunch, dinner. Bar. Casual attire. Outdoor seating. **$$**

★ **MARKETPLACE RAW BAR.** *Popponesset Marketplace, Mashpee (02649). Phone 508/539-4858.* Seafood menu. Lunch, dinner. Closed late Oct-Apr. Casual attire. **$$**

★ **MILL WAY FISH AND LOBSTER.** *275 Mill Way, Barnstable (02630). Phone 508/362-2760.* Mill Way may look like a simple harborside fish shack with a few picnic tables sitting on the deck by the order window, but looks are deceiving. Chef/owner Ralph Binder runs the Upper Cape's top gourmet-to-go shop with takeout treats that range from homemade seafood sausage to tubs of bouillabaisse and clam chowder. The mostly fried quick food (too good to be called fast food) features giant portions of the local catch. Seafood menu. Lunch, dinner. Closed Oct-Mar. Casual attire. Outdoor seating. **$$**

★ ★ **NAKED OYSTER.** *20 Independence Dr, Hyannis (02601). Phone 508/778-6500. www.naked oyster.com.* Raw-seafood cravings meet their match at Naked Oyster, a bistro and raw bar near the Cape Cod Mall. The Chilled Seafood Tower—a selection of clams, oysters, shrimp, lobster, and tuna sashimi— makes for a fun cocktail hour; add a bottle of Veuve Cliquot for an extra-special celebration. On the menu, you'll also find a variety of dressed oysters and seafood and steak entrées, along with a nice selection of wines by the glass. Seafood menu. Lunch, dinner. Closed Sun. Bar. Casual attire. **$$**

★ **ORIGINAL GOURMET BRUNCH.** *517 Main St, Hyannis (02601). Phone 508/771-2558; fax 508/778-6052. www.theoriginalgourmetbrunch.com.* Hungry diners come armed with large appetites to Hyannis's beloved Original Gourmet Brunch. This country-casual restaurant does breakfast like none other, with more than 100 different omelet choices available. Eggs are a large part of the menu here, but those with a sweet tooth dig into fluffy Belgian waffles and savory French toast. American menu. Breakfast, lunch. Closed Thanksgiving, Dec 25. Casual attire. **$**
🅓

★ ★ **THE PADDOCK.** *W Main St Rotary, Hyannis (02601). Phone 508/775-7677; fax 508/771-9517. www.paddockcapecod.com.* Elegant Victorian surroundings, fine wine, and exceptional food make for a winning combination at The Paddock restaurant. Pressed linens and abundant flowers add to the

sophistication, yet children are welcomed here. The menu pays tribute to the region with a variety of seafood dishes, although poultry, steak, and pasta also present enticing choices. The wine list is award winning for its well-priced selections. American menu. Lunch, dinner. Closed Nov-Apr. Bar. Children's menu. Casual attire. Valet parking. **$$**

★ ★ ★ **THE REGATTA OF COTUIT.** *4631 Falmouth Rd, Cotuit (02635). Phone 508/428-5715; fax 508/428-5742. www.regattaofcotuit.com.* Refined piano music provides the background for diners in eight intimate, candlelit rooms in this circa-1790 stagecoach inn. Chef Heather Allen makes culinary music of her own with variations on French, American, and Asian themes. Her lacquered duck is a neatly Americanized version of Peking duck, and the tempura dish of Vietnamese-style fish and chips with vegetable slaw varies daily, depending on what the local fishermen catch and what's harvested from local gardens. Owners Wendy and Branz Bryan have accrued a nearly legendary wine list over the last three decades, making The Regatta a must-stop for oenophiles visiting Cape Cod. From October to May, The Regatta offers an alluring early-bird special of three courses for the price of an entrée. American menu. Dinner, Sun brunch (in the off-season). Bar. Business casual attire. Reservations recommended. **$$**

★ ★ **ROADHOUSE CAFE.** *488 South St, Hyannis (02601). Phone 508/775-2386; fax 508/778-1025. www.roadhousecafe.com.* The Roadhouse Cafe jazzes up the American standards. This tasteful restaurant, located in a 1903 house, is cherished by locals for its consistent food, elegant surroundings, and fabulous entertainment. The menu is well rounded, with a large variety of Italian-influenced seafood, poultry, and meat dishes. The vintage piano bar is among the best in town for enjoying live entertainment on the weekends. International/Fusion menu. Dinner. Closed Dec 24-25. Bar. Valet parking. **$$**

★ **SAM DIEGO'S.** *950 Hyannis Rd (Hwy 132), Hyannis (02601). Phone 508/771-8816. www.cape restaurantassociation.com.* Sam Diego's is fun for the entire family. This Tex-Mex spot shares a playful attitude with guests. From its whimsical décor to its Texas iced teas served in boot-shaped glasses, this restaurant puts a smile on everyone's face. Standard Mexican fare includes burritos and tacos, while baby back ribs show off the Texan influence. Mexican menu. Lunch, dinner. Closed Easter, Thanksgiving, Dec 25. Bar. Children's menu. Outdoor seating. **$**

★ **STARBUCKS.** *668 Hwy 132, Hyannis (02601). Phone 508/778-6767; fax 508/790-0036. www.starbucks capecod.com.* Mexican menu. Dinner. Closed Dec 25. Bar. Children's menu. Outdoor seating. **$$**

★ **YING'S.** *59 Center St, Hyannis (02601). Phone 508/790-2432.* Asian menu. Lunch, dinner. Casual attire. Reservations recommended. Outdoor seating. **$$**

Ipswich (A-8)

See also Boston, Gloucester

Settled 1633
Population 12,987
Elevation 50 ft
Area Code 978
Zip 01938
Information Ipswich Visitors Center-Hall Haskell House, 36 S Main St, next to Town Hall; phone 978/356-8540

Ipswich is a summer resort town and home of the Ipswich clam; it has beaches nearby and a countryside of rolling woodland. Historically, Ipswich claims to have been the nation's first lacemaking town, the birthplace of the US hosiery industry, and of the American independence movement. In 1687, the Reverend John Wise rose in a meeting and denounced taxation without representation. His target was the hated Sir Edmund Andros, the British Colonial governor.

Andros and the lace are gone, but Ipswich retains the aura of its past. Besides a fine green, it has nearly 50 houses built before 1725, many from the 17th century.

What to See and Do

Crane Beach. *290 Argilla Rd, Ipswich (01938). End of Argilla Rd, on Ipswich Bay. Phone 978/356-4354.* Among the best on the Atlantic coast; 5 miles of beach; lifeguards, bathhouses, refreshment stand, trail. (Daily 8 am-sunset) **$$$**

The John Whipple House. *1 S Village Green, Ipswich (01938). On Hwy 1A. Phone 978/356-2811. www.ipswichmuseum.net.* (1640) Contains 17th- and 18th-century furniture; garden. (May-mid-Oct, Wed-Sat 10 am-4 pm, Sun from 1 pm; closed holidays) **$$** Opposite is

John Heard House. *54 S Main St, Ipswich (01938). Phone 978/356-2811.* (1795) Bought as memorial to Thomas F. Waters, house has Chinese furnish-

ings from the China sea trade. (Schedule same as Whipple House) **$$**

Special Event

Old Ipswich Days. *Phone 978/356-8540.* Arts and crafts exhibits, games, clambakes, entertainment. Late July.

Limited-Service Hotel

★ **COUNTRY GARDEN INN AND MOTEL.** *101 Main St, Rowley (01969). Phone 978/948-7773; toll-free 800/287-7773; fax 978/948-7947. www.countrygarden motel.com.* 24 rooms, 3 story. Check-in 3 pm, check-out 10 am. Fitness room. Outdoor pool, whirlpool. **$**

Restaurant

★ ★ ★ **1640 HART HOUSE.** *51 Linebrook Rd, Ipswich (01938). Phone 978/356-1640; fax 978/356-8847. www.1640harthouse.com.* This restored property was built 20 years after the Pilgrims landed in the town of Ipswich. The original room has since been sold to the Metropolitan Museum of Art. American menu. Lunch, dinner. Closed Mon; Dec 25. Bar. Children's menu. Reservations recommended. **$$**

Lawrence (A-7)

Founded 1847
Population 72,043
Elevation 50 ft
Area Code 978
Information Chamber of Commerce, 264 Essex St, 01840; phone 978/686-0900
Web Site www.merrimackvalleychamber.com

Lawrence was founded by a group of Boston financiers to tap the water power of the Merrimack River for the textile industry. As textiles moved out, diversified industries have been attracted to the community.

What to See and Do

Lawrence Heritage State Park. *1 Jackson St, Lawrence (01840). Canal St. Phone 978/794-1655. www.massparks.org.* Twenty-three acres in the city center includes the restored Campagnone Common, canal and riverside esplanades. The visitor center in a restored workers' boardinghouse has participatory exhibits on the workers' experiences with industry in Lawrence and their contribution to the city's vitality. (Daily; closed Jan 1, Thanksgiving, Dec 25) **FREE**

Lee (B-2)

Founded 1777
Population 5,985
Elevation 1,000 ft
Area Code 413

Lee's major industry has been papermaking since the first years of the 19th century. Today, it is also a summer and ski resort area.

What to See and Do

October Mountain State Forest. *317 Woodland Rd, Lee (01238). I-90 exit 2, Hwy 20 W. Phone 413/243-1778. www.massparks.org.* Fine mountain scenery overlooking 16,000 acres. Hiking, hunting; snowmobiling. Camping on west side of forest.

Santarella. *75 Main Rd, Tyringham (01238). 4 miles SE. Phone 413/243-2819. www.santarella.us.* Former studio of sculptor Sir Henry Kitson, creator of the *Minuteman* statue in Lexington. Built in the early 1920s, the house's major element is the roof, which was designed to look like thatching and to represent the rolling hills of the Berkshires in autumn; the fronting rock pillars and the grottoes between them are fashioned after similar edifices in Europe; Santarella Sculpture garden. **$**

Special Event

Jacob's Pillow Dance Festival. *358 George Carter Rd, Becket (01223). 8 miles E via Hwy 20. Phone 413/243-0745; fax 413/243-0749. Ted Shawn Theatre and Doris Duke Theatre.* America's oldest and most prestigious dance festival includes performances by international dance companies. Performances Tues-Sat, some Sun. Late June-Aug.

Limited-Service Hotel

★ ★ **BEST WESTERN BLACK SWAN INN.** *435 Laurel St; Hwy 20 W, Lee (01238). Phone 413/243-2700; toll-free 800/876-7926; fax 413/637-0798. www.bestwestern.com.* 52 rooms, 2 story. Check-in 3 pm, check-out 11 am. Restaurant, bar. Outdoor pool. Business center. **$**

Specialty Lodgings

APPLEGATE. *279 W Park St, Lee (01238). Phone 413/243-4451; toll-free 800/691-9012; fax 413/243-9832. www.applegateinn.com.* Built in the 1920s, this Georgian Colonial is a charming bed-and-breakfast. Each guest room is individually decorated, and guests can enjoy strolls through the 6 acres of rose gardens, perennial beds, and apple trees. 11 rooms, 2 story. Children over 12 years only. Complimentary full breakfast. Check-in 2-6 pm. Check-out 11 am. Outdoor pool. **$**

CHAMBERY INN. *199 Main St (Hwy 20 W), Lee (01238). Phone 413/243-2221; toll-free 800/537-4321; fax 413/243-0039. www.chamberyinn.com.* This property was originally built as the county's first parochial school. The owners saved the building from destruction and restored it, keeping the unique structure and even the original blackboards. Guests enjoy the "menu selected" breakfasts, delivered to the guest room door in a charming country basket. 9 rooms, 3 story. Children over 16 years only. Check-in 2 pm, check-out 11 am. **$$**

DEVONFIELD INN. *85 Stockbridge Rd, Lee (01238). Phone 413/243-3298; toll-free 800/664-0880; fax 413/243-1360. www.devonfield.com.* Located in the heart of the Berkshires, this Federal-era manor house offers a comfortable and fun experience. 10 rooms, 3 story. Children over 10 years only. Complimentary full breakfast. Check-in 3 pm, check-out 11 am. Outdoor pool. Tennis. **$$**

FEDERAL HOUSE INN. *1560 Pleasant St (Hwy 102), South Lee (01260). Phone 413/243-1824; toll-free 800/243-1824; fax 413/243-1828. www.federalhouseinn. com.* Originally built in 1824, this inn is nestled beside the Housatonic River and at the base of Beartown State Forest. The guest rooms have a casual, country-style décor and all include golf and tennis privileges at nearby Stockbridge Country Club. 10 rooms, 2 story. Children over 12 years only. Complimentary full breakfast. Check-in 3 pm. Check-out 11 am. Bar. **$$**

HISTORIC MERRELL INN. *1565 Pleasant St (Hwy 102), South Lee (01260). Phone 413/243-1794; toll-free 800/243-1794; fax 413/243-2669. www.merrell-inn.com.* Listed on the National Register of Historic Places, this old-stagecoach inn sits on 2 acres of picturesque, Housatonic River-front property. All rooms have private baths, include a country breakfast, and offer a

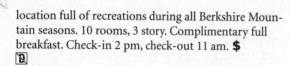

location full of recreations during all Berkshire Mountain seasons. 10 rooms, 3 story. Complimentary full breakfast. Check-in 2 pm, check-out 11 am. **$**

MORGAN HOUSE. *33 Main St, Lee (02563). Phone 413/243-3661; toll-free 877/571-0837; fax 413/243-3103. www.morganhouseinn.com.* Built in 1817. Stagecoach inn (1853); antiques; country-style décor. 11 rooms, 3 story. Complimentary full breakfast. Check-in 2 pm, check-out 11 am. Restaurant, bar. **$**

Restaurants

★ ★ **CORK N' HEARTH.** *635 Lowell St, Lee (01238). Phone 413/243-0535; fax 413/637-1945.* Three dining rooms. Seafood, steak menu. Dinner. Closed Mon; Thanksgiving, Dec 24-25. Bar. Children's menu. **$$**

★ ★ **SULLIVAN STATION RESTAURANT.** *109 Railroad St, Lee (01238). Phone 413/243-2082. www.sullivanstationrestaurant.com.* American menu. Lunch, dinner. Closed Thanksgiving, Dec 25; also two weeks in late Feb-early Mar. Bar. Outdoor seating. **$$**

Lenox (B-2)

See also Pittsfield, Stockbridge and West Stockbridge

Settled circa 1750
Population 5,985
Elevation 1,200 ft
Area Code 413
Zip 01240
Information Chamber of Commerce, 65 Main St, PO Box 646; phone 413/637-3646
Web Site www.lenox.org

This summer resort became world-famous for music when the Boston Symphony began its Berkshire Festival here in 1939. Nearby is Stockbridge Bowl, one of the prettiest lakes in the Berkshires.

What to See and Do

⭐ **Edith Wharton Restoration (The Mount).** *2 Plunkett St, Lenox (01240). Plunkett St at S junction of Hwys 7 and 7A. Phone 413/637-1899. www.edithwharton.org.* Edith Wharton's summer estate; was planned from a book she coauthored in 1897, *The Decoration of Houses,* and built in 1902. This Classical Revival house is architecturally significant; ongoing restoration. On 49 acres, with gardens. Tour of house and gardens

(May-Oct, daily 9 am-5 pm). (See SPECIAL EVENTS) **$$$$**

Pleasant Valley Wildlife Sanctuary. *472 W Mountain Rd, Lenox (01240). On West Mountain Rd, 1 1/2 miles W of Hwy 7/20. Phone 413/637-0320. www.massaudubon.org.* Sanctuary of the Massachusetts Audubon Society. 1,500 acres with 7 miles of trails; beaver colony; office. No dogs. (Mid-June-Columbus Day) **$**

⭐ **Tanglewood.** *297 West St, Lenox (02140). On West St, 1 1/2 miles SW on Hwy 183. Phone 413/637-1600. www.tanglewood.org.* Where Nathaniel Hawthorne lived and wrote. Here he planned *Tanglewood Tales.* Many of the 526 acres, developed into a gentleman's estate by William Aspinwall Tappan, are in formal gardens. Well known today as the summer home of the Boston Symphony Orchestra and the Tanglewood Music Center, the symphony's training academy for young musicians. (See SPECIAL EVENTS) Grounds (daily; free except during concerts).

Chamber Music Hall. *197 West St, Lenox (02140).* Small chamber music ensembles, lectures, seminars, and large classes held here. Designed by Eliel Saarinen, who also designed the

Formal Gardens. *197 West St, Lenox (02140).* Manicured hemlock hedges and lawn, tall pine. Picnicking.

Hawthorne Cottage. *197 West St, Lenox (02140).* Replica of the "Little Red House" where Hawthorne lived 1850-1851, now contains music studios, Hawthorne memorabilia. (Open before each festival concert.)

Koussevitzky Music Shed. *197 West St, Lenox (02140).* (1938) The so-called "Shed," where Boston Symphony Orchestra concerts take place; holds 5,121.

Main Gate Area. *197 West St, Lenox (01240).* Friends of Tanglewood, box office, music and bookstore; cafeteria; gift shop.

Maron House. *197 West St, Lenox (02140).* Original mansion, now the Boston Symphony Orchestra Visitors Center and the Community Relations Office. Excellent view of Lake Mahkeenac, Monument Mountain.

Seiji Ozawa Concert Hall. *197 West St, Lenox (02140).* (1941) Festival chamber music programs, Tanglewood Music Center activities; seats 1,200.

Special Events

Apple Squeeze Festival. *65 Main St, Lenox (01240). Phone 413/637-3646. www.lenox.org.* Celebration of apple harvest; entertainment, food, music. Usually the third weekend in Sept.

Shakespeare & Company. *70 Kemble St (box office), Lenox (01240). Phone 413/637-3353.* Professional theater company performs plays by Shakespeare and Edith Wharton, as well as other events. Four stages, one outdoor. Main season runs from late June-early Sept, Tues-Sun.

Tanglewood Music Festival. *1277 Main St, Springfield (02115). Phone 617/266-1200.* Tanglewood Boston Symphony Orchestra. Concerts performed on Friday and Saturday evenings and Sunday afternoons. Inquire for other musical events. July-Aug.

Limited-Service Hotel

APPLE TREE INN. *10 Richmond Mountain Rd, Lenox (01240). Phone 413/637-1477; fax 413/637-2528. www.appletree-inn.com.* Just outside the center of town, the Apple Tree Inn sits majestically on 22 hilltop acres, affording beautiful views of the Berkshires and a tranquil getaway. 34 rooms, 3 story. Complimentary full breakfast (off-season). Check-in 2 pm, check-out 11:30 am. Restaurant, bar. Outdoor pool. Tennis. **$$**

Full-Service Hotels

★ ★ ★ ★ ★ **BLANTYRE.** *16 Blantyre Rd, Lenox (01240). Phone 413/637-3556; fax 413/637-4282. www.blantyre.com.* Listen closely and you can still hear the laughter of Gilded Age garden parties at Blantyre. A private home in the early 1900s, this Tudor-style mansion set on 100 acres in the Berkshire Mountains now welcomes guests seeking to live out a splendid pastoral fantasy. Blantyre's rooms maintain a decidedly British country style of floral fabrics and overstuffed furniture. Fireplaces are available in many rooms to warm the often-chilly evenings. Country pursuits like croquet, tennis, and swimming entice many, while the cultural festivals of Tanglewood and Jacob's Pillow attract others. Dining at Blantyre is a special occasion, whether you're lingering over breakfast in the conservatory or enjoying the romantic ambience of a candlelit dinner. The chef even packs gourmet picnics for lazy summer afternoons that guests spend lounging within Blantyre's grounds or exploring the beautiful countryside. 25 rooms, 2 story. Children over 12 years

only. Complimentary continental breakfast. Check-in 3 pm, check-out noon. High-speed Internet access. Restaurant, bar. Fitness room, spa. Outdoor pool, whirlpool. Tennis. **$$$$**

★ ★ ★ **WHEATLEIGH.** *Hawthorne Rd, Lenox (01240). Phone 413/637-0610; fax 413/637-4507. www.wheatleigh.com.* Wheatleigh is a country house hotel of the finest order. This 19th-century Italianate palazzo is gloriously set on 22 acres of rolling hills and lush gardens in the Berkshire Mountains. The magical estate shares in the grand Gilded Age heritage of this celebrated region. This bucolic retreat, with a Frederick Law Olmstead-designed private park as its backyard, maintains an urbane spirit. The interiors present a crisp, contemporary approach to classic sensibilities. Lacking the formality of the past and avoiding the starkness of modern style, the guest rooms are comfortably elegant. Details make the difference here, from the dazzling Tiffany windows to the ornate fireplace in the Great Hall. The restaurant is a great source of pride, and its updated French dishes draw gourmets. 19 rooms, 2 story. Children over 8 years only. Check-in 3 pm, check-out 11 am. High-speed Internet access. Restaurant, bar. Fitness room. Outdoor pool. Tennis. **$$$$**

Full-Service Resort

★ ★ ★ **CRANWELL RESORT SPA AND GOLF CLUB.** *55 Lee Rd, Lenox (01240). Phone 413/637-1364; toll-free 800/272-6935; fax 413/637-0571. www.cranwell.com.* This historic 100-year-old country hotel is set on a hill and has a 60-mile view of the southern Berkshires. Situated on 380 acres, the property has a fantastic 18-hole championship golf course that is host to Beecher's golf school. 108 rooms, 3 story. Pets accepted, some restrictions; fee. Check-in 3:30 pm, check-out 11 am. Three restaurants, three bars. Children's activity center. Fitness room, fitness classes available, spa. Indoor pool, outdoor pool, whirlpool. Golf, 18 holes. Business center. **$$$**

Full-Service Inns

★ ★ ★ **GATEWAYS INN.** *51 Walker St, Lenox (01240). Phone 413/637-2532; toll-free 888/492-9466; fax 413/637-1432. www.gatewaysinn.com.* The gorgeous country rooms in this restored 1912 mansion will make your trip to Lenox one to remember. 11

rooms, 2 story. Complimentary full breakfast. Check-in 2 pm, check-out 11 am. Restaurant, bar. **$$**

THE VILLAGE INN. *16 Church St, Lenox (01240). Phone 413/637-0020; toll-free 800/253-0917; fax 413/637-9756. www.villageinn-lenox.com.* Surrounded by shopping, restaurants, art galleries, and ski resorts, and located near historic Tanglewood, this charming country inn features clean and comfortable accommodations. 32 rooms, 3 story. Complimentary full breakfast. Check-in 2 pm, check-out 11 am. Restaurant, bar. **$$**

★ **YANKEE INN.** *461 Pittsfield Rd, Lenox (01240). Phone 413/499-3700; toll-free 800/835-2364; fax 413/499-3634. www.yankeeinn.com.* Clean and comfortable rooms with fireplaces are found at this family-friendly inn. 96 rooms, 2 story. Complimentary continental breakfast. Check-in 2 pm, check-out 11 am. Bar. Fitness room. Indoor pool, outdoor pool, whirlpool. **$$**

Specialty Lodgings

BIRCHWOOD INN. *7 Hubbard St, Lenox (01240). Phone 413/637-2600; toll-free 800/524-1646; fax 413/637-4604. www.birchwood-inn.com.* This historic bed-and-breakfast is decorated with beautiful antiques and collectables and features meticulously kept rooms and gardens. 11 rooms, 3 story. Pets accepted, some restrictions; fee. Complimentary full breakfast. Check-in 3 pm, check-out 11 am. Wireless Internet access. **$$**

BROOK FARM INN. *15 Hawthorne St, Lenox (01240). Phone 413/637-3013; toll-free 800/285-7638; fax 413/637-4751. www.brookfarm.com.* The interior of this Victorian inn has a very literary feel perfectly suited to its historic location. Visit nearby cultural venues, including Tanglewood Music Center, or curl up with a treasure from the impressive library of poetry, fiction, and history. 15 rooms, 3 story. Children over 15 years only. Complimentary full breakfast. Check-in 3 pm, check-out 11 am. Wireless Internet access. Outdoor pool. **$$**

HARRISON HOUSE. *174 Main St, Lenox (01240). Phone 413/637-1746; fax 413/637-9957. www.harrison-house.com.* The circular drive and immaculate porch of this country inn are directly across from Kennedy Park and overlook Tanglewood. Rooms vary in size and décor. 6 rooms, 2 story. No children al-

lowed. Complimentary full breakfast. Check-in 3 pm, check-out 11 am. **$$**

KEMBLE INN. *2 Kemble St, Lenox (01240). Phone 413/637-4113; toll-free 800/353-4113. www.kembleinn.com.* Located on 3 acres in the center of historic Lenox, this inn features magnificent views of the Berkshire Mountains. The guest rooms are named after American authors. 14 rooms, 3 story. Children over 12 years only. Complimentary continental breakfast. Check-in 3 pm, check-out 11 am. **$$**

ROOKWOOD INN. *11 Old Stockbridge Rd, Lenox (01240). Phone 413/637-9750; toll-free 800/223-9750; fax 413/637-1532. www.rookwoodinn.com.* This 1885 Victorian inn is furnished with English antiques and is located in the center of Lenox, close to the art, music, and theater of Tanglewood. 21 rooms, 3 story. Complimentary full breakfast. Check-in 3 pm, check-out 11 am. **$$**

THE SUMMER WHITE HOUSE. *17 Main St, Lenox (01240). Phone 413/637-4489; toll-free 800/382-9401. www.thesummerwhitehouse.com.* Located in the heart of historic Lenox, only 1 mile from Tanglewood, summer home of the Boston Symphony, this inn is an original Berkshire cottage built in 1885. Guest rooms feature private baths and air conditioning. 6 rooms. Children over 12 years only. Complimentary full breakfast. Check-in 3 pm, check-out 11 am. Indoor pool. Tennis. **$$**

WHISTLER'S INN. *5 Greenwood St, Lenox (01240). Phone 413/637-0975; toll-free 866/637-0975; fax 419/637-2190. www.whistlersinnlenox.com.* This historic inn was once the home of Ross Whistler, a railroad tycoon and nephew of legendary American painter, James Abbott McNeil Whistler. Original artwork and furniture inside this English Tudor mansion add to the inn's old-world charm. 12 rooms, 2 story. Closed Nov-May. Children over 10 years only. Complimentary full breakfast. Check-in 3 pm, check-out noon. **$$**

Restaurants

★ ★ ★ **BISTRO ZINC.** *56 Church St, Lenox (01240). Phone 413/637-8800. www.bistrozinc.com.* This lively, edgy hotspot is located in town and not too far from Tanglewood which makes it a good choice for a pre-concert meal. The contemporary décor features a black-and-white herringbone tile floor in one room, hardwood floors, tin ceilings, pale yellow walls, burgundy banquettes, wood chairs, and a large bar area. Ginger Encrusted Salmon and Entrecote aux Oignons are just two of the delicious items offered on the dinner menu. And don't feel like you need to leave after dinner—the bar is open until 1 am. French bistro menu. Lunch, dinner, late-night. Bar. Casual attire. Reservations recommended. **$$$**

★ ★ ★ **BLANTYRE.** *16 Blantyre Rd, Lenox (01240). Phone 413/637-3556. www.blantyre.com.* Dining at this 1902 mansion is a special experience. The luxurious dining room is located in the Main House of the award-winning Blantyre inn. Upon arrival, head to the Main Hall or the terrace to enjoy a pre-dinner glass of champagne and canaps, or head to the Music Room for a glass of red wine. Then continue on to the dining room where your delectable meal prepared by Chef Christopher Brooks will be served. Antique glassware and place settings, sterling silver, crystal, soft candlelight, fresh flowers, and harp music all combine for a romantic atmosphere. This is truly an experience you will never forget. French menu. Breakfast, lunch, dinner. Jacket required. Reservations recommended. Valet parking. **$$$**

★ ★ **CAFE LUCIA.** *80 Church St, Lenox (01240). Phone 413/637-2640.* This family-owned northern Italian restaurant located in the heart of the Berkshires features a seasonally changing menu. The décor is contemporary with a display kitchen, track lighting, and family photographs. There is a bar and outdoor seating for weather-permitting alfresco dining. Weekend reservations are essential during Tanglewood—call about a month ahead. Italian, seafood menu. Dinner. Closed Mon in July-Aug, Sun-Mon in Sept-June. Bar. Casual attire. Outdoor seating. **$$$**

★ **CAROL'S.** *8 Franklin St, Lenox (01240). Phone 413/637-8948.* You'll feel like one of the town folk when you step into this favorite all-day breakfast spot—brunch and lunch are also served. Since it's located in the center of town, it's just a short walk from most hotels. American menu. Breakfast, lunch, brunch. Casual attire. No credit cards accepted. **$**

★ ★ **CHURCH STREET CAFE.** *65 Church St, Lenox (01240). Phone 413/637-2745; fax 413/637-2050. www.churchstreetcafe.biz.* This cozy American bistro offers three dining rooms and a beautiful outdoor patio surrounded by greenery and flowers. The restaurant is nicely decorated with the works of local artists and features lunch and dinner menus which change with the seasons. Church Street has been open for business since 1981 (starting with just nine tables),

and has grown into a 90-seat facility. The restaurant is open seven days a week during tourist season. American, International menu. Lunch, dinner. Closed Mar-Apr; also Sun-Mon in May-June and Sept-Feb. Bar. Children's menu. Casual attire. Reservations recommended. Outdoor seating. **$$$**

★ ★ ★ **GATEWAYS INN.** *51 Walker St, Lenox (01240). Phone 413/637-2532; toll-free 888/492-9466; fax 413/637-1432. www.gatewaysinn.com.* Located in the Town Center near Tanglewood Park, the elegant restaurant at this charming inn features American cuisine with international influences. The chefs use locally grown produce and dairy products, and the menu changes seasonally. Choose to sit in the main room that has French doors and terra cotta painted walls, or, for a more private experience, dine in the Rockwell Room. American menu. Breakfast, lunch, dinner. Closed Mon in Sept-June. Bar. Casual attire. Reservations recommended. **$$$**

★ ★ ★ **LENOX 218 RESTAURANT.** *218 Main St, Lenox (01240). Phone 413/637-4218. www.lenox218. com.* A convenient place to dine when visiting Tanglewood, this contemporary restaurant specializes in northern Italian dishes and can handle banquets for up to 100 people. Italian menu. Lunch, dinner. Bar. Casual attire. Reservations recommended. **$$$**

★ **PANDA HOUSE CHINESE RESTAURANT.** *506 Pittsfield Rd, Lenox (01240). Phone 413/499-0660; fax 413/499-0786.* This casual Chinese restaurant is close to hotels and is a great place for kids and groups. The décor is relaxed with muted colors and contemporary artwork. Chinese menu. Lunch, dinner. Bar. Children's menu. Casual attire. **$$**
🅳

★ ★ ★ **WHEATLEIGH.** *Hawthorne Rd, Lenox (01240). Phone 413/637-0610; fax 413/637-4507. www. wheatleigh.com.* Polished mahogany doors lead to this historic hotel's elegant restaurant. The dining room's design is just as regal as the building itself, which was modeled in 1893 after a 16th-century Florentine palazzo. Guests dine on contemporary French cuisine in a beautiful sun-drenched room filled with oil paintings, hand-carved Chippendale chairs, and sparkling crystal chandeliers. French menu. Breakfast, lunch, dinner. Bar. Business casual attire. Reservations recommended. Valet parking. **$$$**

★ ★ ★ **THE WYNDHURST RESTAURANT.** *55 Lee Rd, Lenox (01240). Phone 413/637-1364; fax 413/637-4364. www.cranwell.com.* The elegant dining room of the Cranwell Resort is situated on the main floor of the 100-year-old Tudor mansion. Large windows offer vistas of the Berkshire Hills, and the fireplace keeps diners warm on cold New England nights. The French and American cuisine highlights local produce, including game and cheeses. American, French menu. Lunch, dinner. Business casual attire. Reservations recommended. Valet parking. **$$$**

Leominster (B-5)

Settled 1653
Population 41,303
Area Code 978
Zip 01453
Information Johnny Appleseed Visitor Center, 110 Erdman Way; phone 978/840-4300
Web Site www.leominster-ma.gov

Leominster (LEMMINst'r) has retained the pronunciation of the English town for which it was named. Known at one time as "Comb City," in 1845 Leominster housed 24 factories manufacturing horn combs. It is the birthplace of "Johnny Appleseed"—John Chapman (1774-1845)—a devout Swedenborgian missionary who traveled throughout America on foot, planting apple orchards and the seeds of his faith. The National Plastics Center and Museum is located here.

Limited-Service Hotels

★ ★ **FOUR POINTS BY SHERATON.** *99 Erdman Way, Leominster (01453). Phone 978/534-9000; fax 978/534-0891. www.fourpoints.com.* 187 rooms, 7 story. Complimentary continental breakfast. Check-in 3 pm, check-out noon. Restaurant, bar. Indoor pool, whirlpool. Business center. **$**

★ ★ **WACHUSETT VILLAGE INN.** *9 Village Inn Rd, Westminster (01473). Phone 978/874-2000; toll-free 800/342-1905; fax 978/874-1753. www.wachusett villageinn.com.* Situated on 100 acres near the Wachusett Mountain ski area, this inn's 3,000 square feet of meeting space and retreat-like setting attract group clientele. Take a wintertime sleigh ride then retreat to the casual, American restaurant for a bite to eat. 74 rooms, 2 story. Check-out 11 am. Restaurant. Fitness room. Indoor pool, outdoor pool. Tennis. **$**

Lexington (B-7)

See also Concord

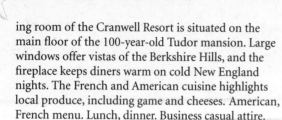

Settled circa 1640
Population 30,355
Elevation 210 ft
Area Code 781
Zip 02173
Information Chamber of Commerce Visitors Center, 1875 Massachusetts Ave; phone 781/862-1450. The center, open daily, offers a diorama depicting the Battle of Lexington and has a walking tour map.
Web Site www.lexingtonchamber.org

Lexington is called the birthplace of American liberty. On its Green, April 19, 1775, eight Minutemen were killed in what is traditionally considered the first organized fight of the War for Independence. However, in 1908, the US Senate recognized the counterclaim of Point Pleasant, West Virginia, as the first battle site. It is still possible to visualize the Battle of Lexington. Down the street came the British, 700 strong. To the right of the Green is the tavern the militia used as headquarters. It was here that 77 Minutemen lined up near the west end of the Green, facing down the Charlestown road. Nearby is a boulder with a plaque bearing the words of Captain John Parker, spoken just before the Redcoats opened fire: "Stand your ground. Don't fire unless fired upon. But if they mean to have a war, let it begin here!" It did—the fight then moved on to Concord.

What to See and Do

Battle Green. *At the center of town.* The Old Monument, the *Minuteman* statue, and the Boulder mark the line of the Minutemen, seven of whom are buried under the monument.

Lexington Historical Society. *1332 Massachusetts Ave, Lexington (02421). Phone 781/862-1703. www. lexingtonhistory.org.* Revolutionary period houses. Guided tours. **$**

Buckman Tavern. *1 Bedford St, Lexington (02420). Facing the Battle Green. Phone 781/862-1703.* (1709) Minutemen assembled here before the battle. Period furnishings, portraits. (Mid-Apr-May, weekends only; June-Oct, daily 10 am-4 pm) **$**

Hancock-Clarke House. *36 Hancock St, Lexington (02420). Phone 781/862-1703.* (1698) Here John Hancock and Samuel Adams were awakened by Paul

Revere's alarm on April 18, 1775. Furniture, portraits, utensils; small museum. Fire engine exhibit in barn (by appointment). (Mid-Apr-May, weekends only; June-Oct, daily; tours hourly 11 am-2 pm) **$**

Munroe Tavern. *1332 Massachusetts Ave, Lexington (02420). Phone 781/862-1703.* (1695) British hospital after the battle. George Washington dined here in 1789. Period furnishings, artifacts. (Mid-Apr-Oct, tour at 3 pm daily)

National Heritage Museum. *33 Marrett Rd (Hwy 2A), Lexington (02421). At junction Massachusetts Ave. Phone 781/861-6559. www.monh.org.* Museum features exhibits on American history and culture, from its founding to the present; also history of Lexington and the Revolutionary War. (Mon-Sat 10 am-5 pm, Sun from noon) **FREE**

Special Event

Reenactment of the Battle of Lexington and Concord. *Lexington Green, Lexington (02173). Phone 781/862-1450.* Reenactment of the opening battle of the Revolutionary War; parade. Patriots Day. Mon nearest Apr 19.

Limited-Service Hotels

★ **QUALITY INN AND SUITES.** *440 Bedford St, Lexington (02420). Phone 781/861-0850; fax 781/861-0821. www.qualityinnlexington.com.* 204 rooms, 2 story. Pets accepted; restrictions, fee. Complimentary continental breakfast. Check-in 3 pm, check-out 11 am. Outdoor pool, whirlpool. **$**

★ ★ ★ **SHERATON LEXINGTON INN.** *727 Marrett Rd, Lexington (02421). Phone 781/862-8700; fax 781/863-0404. www.sheraton.com.* Centrally located in a historical town 15 miles from Boston, this inn has 5,000 square feet of meeting space and an outdoor pool. Cracker Barrel Restaurant and Tavern is on-site for traditional, New-England-style dining. 121 rooms, 2 story. Check-in 3 pm, check-out noon. Restaurant, bar. Fitness room. Outdoor pool. **$**

Lowell (A-6)

Settled 1655
Population 105,167
Elevation 102 ft
Area Code 978

Information Greater Lowell Chamber of Commerce, 77 Merrimack St, 01852; phone 978/459-8154
Web Site www.greaterlowellchamber.org

In the 19th century, the powerful Merrimack River and its canals transformed Lowell from a handicraft center to a textile industrial center. The Francis Floodgate, near Broadway and Clare Streets, was called "Francis's Folly" when it was built in 1848, but it saved the city from flood in 1936. Restoration of the historic canal system is currently in progress.

What to See and Do

American Textile History Museum. *491 Dutton St, Lowell (01854). Phone 978/441-0400. www.athm.org.* Permanent exhibit, "Textiles in America," features 18th- to 20th-century textiles, artifacts, and machinery in operation, showing the impact of the Industrial Revolution on labor. Collections of cloth samples, books, prints, photographs, and preindustrial tools may be seen by appointment. Tours; activities. Library; education center. Restaurant; museum store. (Tues-Sun; closed Jan 1, Thanksgiving, Dec 25) **$$**

Lowell Heritage State Park. *246 Market St, Lowell (01852). Phone 978/369-6312.* Six miles of canals and associated linear parks and 2 miles of park on the bank of Merrimack River offer boating, boathouse; concert pavilion, interpretive programs. (Schedule varies) **FREE**

Lowell National Historical Park. *67 Kirk St, Lowell (01852). Phone 978/970-5000. www.nps.gov/lowe.* Established to commemorate Lowell's unique legacy as the most important planned industrial city in America. The nation's first large-scale center for the mechanized production of cotton cloth, Lowell became a model for 19th-century industrial development. Park includes mill buildings and a 5 1/2-mile canal system. Visitor center at Market Mills includes audiovisual show and exhibits (daily; closed Jan 1, Thanksgiving, Dec 25). Free walking and trolley tours (Mar-Nov). Tours by barge and trolley (May-Columbus Day weekend; fee), reservations suggested. Located here are

Boott Cotton Mills Museum. *115 John St, Lowell (01852). Phone 978/970-5000.* Industrial history museum with operating looms (ear plugs supplied). Interactive exhibits, video presentations. (Late May-early Oct: daily 9:30 am-5 pm; closed Jan 1, Thanksgiving, Dec 24-25) **$**

Patrick J. Mogan Cultural Center. *40 French St, Lowell (01852). Phone 978/970-5000.* Restored

1836 boarding house of the Boott Cotton Mills including a re-created kitchen, keeper's room, parlor, and mill girls' bedroom; exhibits on working people, immigrants, and labor history; also local history. (Daily 9 am-5 pm)

New England Quilt Museum. *18 Shattuck St, Lowell (01852). Phone 978/452-4207. www.nequiltmuseum. org.* Changing exhibits feature antique, traditional, and contemporary quilts. Museum shop. (Tues-Sat 10 am-4 pm, Sun from noon; closed holidays) **$**

University of MA-Lowell. *1 University Ave, Lowell (01854). Phone 978/934-4000. www.uml.edu.* (15,500 students) State-operated university formed by the 1975 merger of Lowell Technological Institute (1895) and Lowell State College (1894). Music ensembles at Durgin Hall Performing Arts Center.

Whistler House Museum of Art. *243 Worthen St, Lowell (01852). Phone 978/452-7641. www.whistlerhouse.org.* Birthplace of the painter James Abbott McNeill Whistler. Exhibits include several of his etchings. Collection of 19th- and early 20th-century American art. (Wed-Sat 11 am-4 pm; closed holidays) **$**

Special Events

Lowell Celebrates Kerouac Festival. *PO Box 1111, Lowell (01852). Phone toll-free 877/537-6822. lckorg. tripod.com.* Tours, music, poetry competition, book signings, and panel discussions. First weekend in Oct.

Lowell Folk Festival. *246 Market St, Lowell (01852). Phone 978/970-5000. www.lowellfolkfestival.org.* Concerts, crafts, and demonstrations, ethnic food, street parade. Last full weekend in July.

Limited-Service Hotels

★ **BEST WESTERN CHELMSFORD INN.** *187 Chelmsford St, Chelmsford (01824). Phone 978/256-7511; toll-free 888/770-9992; fax 978/250-1401. www. bestwestern.com/chelmsfordinn.* 120 rooms, 5 story. Check-in 3 pm, check-out noon. High-speed Internet access. Fitness room. Outdoor pool, whirlpool. **$**

★ ★ **COURTYARD BY MARRIOTT.** *30 Industrial Ave E, Lowell (01852). Phone 978/458-7575; toll-free 888/236-2427; fax 978/458-1302. www.courtyard.com.* Large rooms with free, high-speed Internet access, two phone lines, a TV with cable, and an all-news channel are in each room. Fax, copying, and printing services are available, and a rental car desk is on-site.

While there is no doubt that this hotel is designed for business travelers, there are also conveniences for those who are here for pleasure. There is, for instance, shuttle service into Lowell for those who want to stroll the streets of this historic little town at the confluence of the Concord and Merrimack rivers, while others stroll the hallways of the myriad of businesses and corporations within a 5-mile radius. In addition to an on-site fitness room and outdoor pool for working out after-hours kinks, guests have privileges at a nearby health club. But you can't miss the relaxation element of this contemporary brick hotel. Part of its common area is designed as a library, filled with bookcases and a sitting area nestled around a large fireplace and flat-screen TV. A small, casual dining area sits at the opposite end of the room. 120 rooms, 3 story. Check-in 3 pm, check-out 1 pm. High-speed Internet access. Restaurant. Fitness room. Outdoor pool. **$**

★ ★ **DOUBLETREE HOTEL.** *50 Warren St, Lowell (01852). Phone 978/452-1200; toll-free 800/876-4586; fax 978/453-4674. www.doubletree.com.* It's hard to find a more ideal location. This is the closest hotel to the UMass Lowell campus, and it's just across the canal from Middlesex Community College. This modern, nine-story hotel is also in the heart of downtown, where old brick mill structures have been turned into multiuse buildings of shops and restaurants. Many of the Doubletrees 252 rooms, as well as its Rivers Edge restaurant, overlook the city's scenic canals, and guests have easy access to the popular and historic Canal Walk. Brass sconces, marble bathroom floors, and contemporary décor with natural touches of copper and wood make this a soothing place to come home to at the end of a day of work or play. 252 rooms, 9 story. Check-in 3 pm, check-out noon. High-speed Internet access, wireless Internet access. Restaurant, bar. Fitness room. Indoor pool, outdoor pool, whirlpool. **$**

Full-Service Hotels

★ ★ **RADISSON HOTEL AND SUITES CHELMSFORD.** *10 Independence Dr, Chelmsford (01824). Phone 978/256-0800; toll-free 800/333-3333; fax 978/256-0750. www.radisson.com.* 194 rooms, 5 story. Check-in 3 pm, check-out noon. Restaurant, bar. Fitness room. Indoor pool. **$**

★ ★ **WESTFORD REGENCY INN AND CONFERENCE CENTER.** *219 Littleton Rd,*

Westford (01886). Phone 978/692-8200; toll-free 800/543-7801; fax 978/692-7403. www.westfordregency. com. Take in the joys of New England at this inn and conference center with 20,000 square feet of meeting space. Every Thursday from June through August, there's a classic lobster boil and clambake hosted outdoors under a 6,000-square-foot tent. 193 rooms, 4 story. Pets accepted, some restrictions; fee. Check-in 2 pm, check-out noon. Restaurant, bar. Fitness room. Indoor pool, whirlpool. **$$**

Full-Service Inn

★ ★ ★ **STONEHEDGE INN.** *160 Pawtucket Blvd, Tyngsboro (01879). Phone 978/649-4400; fax 978/649-9256. www.stonehedgeinn.com.* This contemporary inn is an American imitation of an English country manor. It has an intimate feel, and the staff is eager to meet guests' needs. Large, comfortable guest rooms feature spacious bathrooms and heated towel racks. Set on the grounds of a horse farm, this out-of-the-way inn is perfect for a romantic rendezvous or a corporate retreat. 30 rooms, 2 story. Check-in 3 pm, check-out noon. Restaurant, bar. Fitness room. Indoor pool, outdoor pool, whirlpool. Golf. Tennis. **$$**

Restaurants

★ ★ **COBBLESTONES.** *91 Dutton St, Lowell (01852). Phone 978/970-2282; fax 978/970-0266. www. cobblestonesoflowell.com.* For guests who appreciate the wilderness, this restaurant is sure to please. Seasonal game dishes include ostrich, antelope, and kangaroo, and the property is set within the Lowell National Historic Park. For dessert, be sure to try the bananas flambé. American menu. Lunch, dinner, late-night. Closed Sun; one week in Aug. Bar. Children's menu. Casual attire. **$$**

★ ★ ★ **LA BONICHE.** *143 Merrimack St, Lowell (01852). Phone 978/458-9473.* Though the food is upscale, the dress is casual at this fine restaurant. International menu. Lunch, dinner. Closed Sun-Mon; first week of July. Bar. Casual attire. **$$**

★ ★ ★ **SILKS.** *160 Pawtucket Blvd, Tyngsboro (01879). Phone 978/649-4400; fax 978/649-9256. www. stonehedgeinn.com.* If you are searching for a little hideaway in the country for dinner and are hoping to find a place that happens to have one of the world's most impressive wine caves, schedule a visit to Silks. Secreted away in 36 acres of New England horse country, Silks is located in the Stonehedge Inn (see), a charming old English-style manor house. This enchanted spot has not only an incredible international wine collection (there are over 90,000 bottles in the cave, with about 2,000 wines offered daily), but also a talented team of chefs in the kitchen cooking up a spectacular selection of very French, very haute cuisine. Although the food plays second fiddle to the wine, the menu offers exciting, modern riffs on classic French dishes. Herbs and spices are borrowed from around the globe, successfully bringing flavor, style, and flair to the extensive selection of cold and hot appetizers, fish, and meats. The green and burgundy room is warm, comfortable, and romantic. Considering the size of the wine list, several toasts should be made; this is a great spot for a special occasion. While the service is impeccable and European in style, it is free from pretension. French menu. Breakfast, lunch, dinner, Sun brunch. Closed Mon. Outdoor seating. **$$$**

Lynn (B-7)

See also Boston, Salem

Settled 1629
Population 89,050
Elevation 30 ft
Area Code 781
Information Chamber of Commerce, 100 Oxford St, Suite 416, 01901; phone 781/592-2900
Web Site www.lynnareachamber.com

Shoe manufacturing began as a home craft in Lynn as early as 1635. Today, Lynn's industry is widely diversified. Founded here in 1883, General Electric is the biggest single enterprise. Lynn also has more than 3 miles of sandy beaches.

What to See and Do

Grand Army of the Republic Museum. *58 Andrew St, Lynn (01901). Phone 781/477-7085.* Features Revolutionary War, Civil War, Spanish-American War, and World War I weapons, artifacts, and exhibits. (Mon-Fri 7 am-3 pm by appointment; closed holidays) **DONATION**

Horizon's Edge Casino Cruises. *76 Marine Blvd, Lynn (01905). Take Hwy 1A N to the Lynnway. Proceed 1 mile past the General Edwards Bridge, and see Horizons Edge* entrance on right onto Marine Blvd. Phone 781/581-7733; toll-free 800/582-5932. www.horizonsedge.com. Horizons Edge takes its 500-passenger cruise ship 3 miles into international waters, where casino-style gambling is legal. On board, you'll find blackjack, Caribbean stud poker, three-card poker, let it ride, roulette, craps, slot machines, and bingo. (Note that you must be 21 to board.) Your admission fee includes a buffet in the ships nonsmoking restaurant, and Horizons Edge provides live musical entertainment. (Daily; closed Dec-mid-Apr) **$$$$**

Lynn Heritage State Park. *590 Washington St, Lynn (01901). Phone 781/598-1974.* Five-acre waterfront park and marina. (Daily; closed Jan 1, Dec 25) The visitor center (590 Washington St) has museum-quality exhibits from past to present, from hand-crafted shoes to high-tech items; inquire for hours. **FREE**

Lynn Woods Reservation. *106 Pennybrook Rd, Lynn (01905). 10 miles N of Boston. Phone 781/477-7096.* Situated on 2,200 acres, Lynn Park is a mountain bikers paradise and also offers excellent cross-country ski trails. The park boasts single tracks of gravel and dirt, many with steep hills, sheer ledges, and large boulders. Head up the hills to look down on Walden Pond or the Boston city skyline. Hardwood forests offer protection to a variety of bird species, making this site a good spot for bird-watching as well. (Daily dawn-dusk) **FREE**

Specialty Lodging

DIAMOND DISTRICT BREAKFAST INN. *142 Ocean St, Lynn (01902). Phone 781/599-4470; toll-free 800/666-3076; fax 781/599-5122. www. diamonddistrictinn.com.* Located just minutes away from Boston and only steps away from the water, this Georgian-style inn (built in 1911) offers a great location on a quiet block of town. Guest rooms are named for types of shoes or shoe parts. 11 rooms, 3 story. Pets accepted, some restrictions. Children over 12 only. Complimentary full breakfast. Check-in 3 pm, check-out 11 am. **$$**

Lynnfield (B-7)

Settled 1639
Population 11,542
Elevation 98 ft
Area Code 781
Zip 01940

Full-Service Hotel

★ ★ ★ **SHERATON COLONIAL HOTEL AND GOLF CLUB BOSTON NORTH.** *1 Audubon Rd, Wakefield (01880). Phone 781/245-9300; toll-free 800/325-3535; fax 781/245-0842. www.sheraton.com.* Fifteen miles from downtown Boston, this 220-acre golf resort offers an 18-hole PGA course. For more outdoor recreation, Lake Quannapowitt is nearby. 280 rooms, 11 story. Check-in 3 pm, check-out noon. High-speed Internet access. Restaurant. Fitness room. Indoor pool, whirlpool. Golf. Tennis. **$**

Restaurant

★ ★ **KERNWOOD.** *55 Salem St, Lynnfield (01940). Phone 781/245-4011; fax 781/255-3530.* New England menu. Lunch, dinner. Closed July 4, Dec 25. Bar. Children's menu. **$$**

Marblehead (B-8)

See also Boston, Salem

Settled 1629
Population 20,377
Elevation 65 ft
Area Code 781
Zip 01945
Information Chamber of Commerce, 62 Pleasant St, PO Box 76; phone 781/631-2868
Web Site www.visitmarblehead.com

A unique blend of old and new, Marblehead is situated on a peninsula 17 miles north of Boston. Named Marble Harbor for a short time, the town was settled in 1629 by hardy fishermen from England's West counties. It now boasts a beautiful harbor and a number of busy boatyards. Pleasure craft anchor in this picturesque port each summer, and a record number of modern racing yachts participate in the annual Race Week. Beaches, boating, fishing, art exhibits, antique and curio shops—all combine to offer a choice of quiet relaxation or active recreation.

What to See and Do

Abbot Hall. *188 Washington St, Marblehead (01945). Abbot Hall, Washington Sq. Phone 781/631-0000.* Displays the original "Spirit of '76" painting and deed to town (1684) from the Nanepashemet. Museum,

Marine Room. Gift shop. (Last weekend in May-last weekend in Oct: daily; rest of year: Mon-Fri; closed winter holidays) **DONATION**

Jeremiah Lee Mansion. *170 Washington St, Marblehead (01945). Phone 781/631-1069.* (1768) Marblehead Historical Society. Where Generals Glover, Lafayette, and Washington were entertained. Opulent Georgian architecture and interiors; Marblehead history; antiques of the period, rare original hand-painted wallpaper. (June-Oct, Tues-Sat 10 am-4 pm; closed holidays) **$**

King Hooper Mansion. *8 Hooper St, Marblehead (01945). Phone 781/631-2608. www.marbleheadarts.org.* (1728) Restored house with garden. Art exhibits. (Tues-Sat 10 am-4 pm, Sun 1-5 pm ; closed Jan 1, Dec 25) **FREE**

Special Event

Sailing races. *Boston Yacht Club, 1 Front St, Marblehead (01945). Phone 781/631-3100.* May-Oct, Wed evening and weekends. Race week third week in July.

Specialty Lodgings

HARBOR LIGHT INN. *58 Washington St, Marblehead (01945). Phone 781/631-2186; fax 781/631-2216. www.harborlightinn.com.* Plenty of shops, galleries, and restaurants are near this bed-and-breakfast in the historic harbor district. All rooms have fireplaces, romantic canopied beds, and Jacuzzi baths. Continental breakfast and afternoon, fresh-baked cookies are served in the colonial dining room. 21 rooms. Children over 8 only. Complimentary continental breakfast. Check-in 1 pm, check-out 11 am. Outdoor pool. **$**

MARBLEHEAD INN. *264 Pleasant St, Marblehead (01945). Phone 781/639-9999; toll-free 800/399-5843; fax 781/639-9996. www.marbleheadinn.com.* Victorian inn (1872) near beach. 10 rooms, 3 story. Children over 10 only. Complimentary continental breakfast. Check-in 3 pm, check-out 11 am. **$$**

SEAGULL INN. *106 Harbor Ave, Marblehead (01945). Phone 781/631-1893; fax 781/631-3535. www.seagullinn.com.* Built in 1880; turn-of-the-century atmosphere. 6 rooms, 2 story. Pets accepted; fee. Complimentary continental breakfast. Check-in 2 pm, check-out 11 am. **$$**

Restaurants

★ ★ **MARBLEHEAD LANDING.** *81 Front St, Marblehead (01945). Phone 781/639-1266; fax 781/631-8439. www.thelandingrestaurant.com.* Seafood menu. Lunch, dinner, Sun brunch. Closed Thanksgiving, Dec 25. Bar. Children's menu. Outdoor seating. **$$**

★ ★ **PELLINO'S.** *261 Washington St, Marblehead (01945). Phone 781/631-3344; fax 978/777-5920. www.pellinos.com.* Italian menu. Dinner. Closed Tues, Jan 1; Easter, Dec 25. Bar. Reservations recommended. **$$**

Martha's Vineyard (E-8)

See also Falmouth, Hyannis and Barnstable, Nantucket

Settled 1642
Population 12,690
Elevation 0-311 ft
Area Code 508
Information Chamber of Commerce, Beach Rd, PO Box 1698, Vineyard Haven 02568; phone 508/693-0085
Web Site www.mvy.com

This triangular island below the arm of Cape Cod combines moors, dunes, multicolored cliffs, flower-filled ravines, farmland, and forest. It is less than 20 miles from west to east and 10 miles from north to south.

There was once a whaling fleet at the island, but Martha's Vineyard now devotes itself almost entirely to being a vacation playground, with summer houses that range from small cottages to elaborate mansions. The colonial atmosphere still survives in Vineyard Haven, the chief port; Oak Bluffs; Edgartown; West Tisbury; Gay Head; and Chilmark.

Gay Head is one of the few Massachusetts towns in which many inhabitants are of Native American descent.

What to See and Do

Aquinnah Cliffs. *State Rd, Aquinnah (02535).* These cliffs—a national landmark—are the most popular and most photographed tourist attraction on Martha's Vineyard because of the stunning view they offer. The 150-foot, brilliantly colored cliffs were formed over millions of years by glaciers; today, the cliffs are owned by the Wampanoag Indians, who hold them sacred. (Previous names of the cliffs include Dover Cliffs, so named by settlers in 1602, and Gay Head Cliffs, a name that originated from British sailors. Gay Head was the official name of this part of Martha's Vineyard until 1998.) On top of the Cliffs stands Aquinnah Light lighthouse, which was commissioned by President John Adams in 1798 and rebuilt in 1844 to protect ships from the treacherous stretch of sea below and built with clay from the cliffs. (Apr-Nov)

Black Dog Bakery. *11 Water St, Vineyard Haven (02568). Near Steamship Authority parking lot. Phone 508/693-4786. www.theblackdog.com.* The Black Dog is more than just a bakery: its a cultural phenomenon. Everywhere you look, you see the Black Dog logo (a black Labrador retriever) on T-shirts, hats, mugs, and so on. The Black Dog General Store (with four locations on Martha's Vineyard) sells these souvenirs, along with special treats for your dog. The bakery, which sits just in front of one of the stores, is a great place to start your day, serving coffee, pastries, torts, truffles, and other human treats. Also visit the Black Dog Tavern (see) for tasty seafood and other dishes in an ideal location right on the harbor. (Daily 5:30 am-5 pm, to 8 pm in summer; closed Dec 25)

Chicama Vineyards. *Stoney Hill Rd, West Tisbury (02575). Phone 508/693-0309; toll-free 888/244-2262. www.chicamavineyards.com.* Martha's Vineyard was once awash in winemaking; today Chicama Vineyards is reviving the practice. The European grapes are used to produce a variety of wines, including merlot, chardonnay, and cabernet. You'll also find other food-stuffs for sale, including vinegars and salad dressings, mustards and chutneys, and jams and jellies. Tours and wine tastings are available, but hours vary with the day and season. (Hours vary; call ahead) **FREE**

East Beach. *Chappaquiddick Rd, Chappaquiddick Island (02539). Take your four-wheel drive car on the On Time ferry from Martha's Vineyard to Chappaquiddick Island. From the ferry dock, take Chappaquiddick Road until a sharp right turn, where the road becomes Dike Bridge Road. Park near the bridge or obtain an oversand vehicle permit to drive on the beach. Phone 508/627-7689.* East Beach is the popular name for two adjoining beaches: Wasque Reservation and Cape Pogue Wildlife Refuge. You'll go to a lot of trouble to get to this rustic beach that has no restrooms or concessions, but the quiet, beautiful stretch of shoreline makes the preparation and trip

worthwhile. Chances are you'll have this stunning beach all to yourself. (Daily) **$$**

Featherstone Meeting House For the Arts. *Barnes Rd, Oak Bluffs (02568). Phone 508/693-1850. www.feather-stonearts.org.* This unique arts center offers tourists the hourly use of artists' studios and also features classes in photography, woodworking, pottery, weaving, and stained glass. Nestled on a former horse farm on 18 acres, the Meeting House also includes a gallery of works from local artists. Call for details about a summer art camp for kids. (Daily; call for studio availability)

Felix Neck Sanctuary. *Edgartown-Vineyard Haven Rd, Vineyard Haven (02539). 3 miles from Edgartown off Edgartown-Vineyard Haven Rd. Phone 508/627-4850. www.massaudubon.org/nature_connection/sancturaries/felix_neck.* This 350-acre wildlife preserve is a haven for kids and bird lovers alike. Six miles of trails (guided or self-guided) meander through the sanctuarys meadows, woods, salt marshes, and beaches. The visitors center offers unique exhibits along with a more traditional gift shop. In the summer, consider enrolling the kids in Fern & Feather Day Camp at the Sanctuary. Park (daily dawn-7 pm). Visitor Center (daily 8 am-4 pm; closed Mon in Sept-May). **$**

Flying Horse Carousel. *33 Oak Bluffs Ave, Oak Bluffs (02557). Circuit and Lake aves. Phone 508/693-9481.* Whether you're traveling with a youngster who loves horses (but is too young to ride them for real) or want to hop on for yourself, Flying Horse Carousel is a treat not to be missed. This carousel, the oldest in the country and a national historic landmark, looks nothing like modern carousels you may have seen in malls or shopping centers. Instead, Flying Horse features gorgeous, hand-carved, lifelike horses that glide to festive music. Try to grasp the brass ring in the center to earn your next ride free.

Hyannis-Martha's Vineyard Day Round-Trip. *Ocean St Dock, Hyannis (02601). Phone 508/778-2600. www.hy-linecruises.com.* Passenger service from Hyannis (year-round). **$$$$$**

Menemsha Fishing Village. *North St, Menemsha (02552). Take a shuttle bus or bike ferry from Aquinnah.* Menemsha is a picturesque fishing village, which means you'll see plenty of cedar-sided fishing shacks, fishermen in waterproof gear, and lobster traps strewn about. The movie *Jaws* was filmed here, and if you saw it, you may have haunting flashbacks while you're here! You'll find quaint shopping areas in the village, as well.

Mytoi. *Dike Rd, Chappaquiddick (02539). Phone 508/693-7662.* Although Martha's Vineyard may not be a logical location for a Japanese garden, Mytoi has won praises for its breathtaking mix of azaleas, irises, dogwood, daffodils, rhododendron, and Japanese maple for nearly 50 years. You'll spy goldfish and koi swimming in a pond that's the centerpiece of the garden; you can visit the small island at the ponds center via the ornamental bridge. Take an easy 1-mile hike that weaves through the gardens and into forested area and salt marshes. Allow from an hour to a half day. (Daily) **FREE**

Oak Bluffs. In 1835, this Methodist community served as the site of annual summer camp meetings for church groups. As thousands attended these meetings, the communal tents gave way to family tents, which in turn became wooden cottages designed to look like tents. Today, visitors to the community may see these "Gingerbread Cottages of the Campground."

Recreation. Swimming. Many sheltered beaches, among them public beaches at Menemsha, Oak Bluffs, Edgartown, and Vineyard Haven. Surf swimming on south shore. **Tennis.** Public courts in Edgartown, Oak Bluffs, West Tisbury, and Vineyard Haven. **Boat rentals** at Vineyard Haven, Oak Bluffs, and Gay Head. **Fishing.** Good for striped bass, bonito, bluefish, weakfish. **Golf** at Farm Neck Club.

Steamship Authority. *509 Salmouth Rd, Mashpee (02744). Phone 508/477-8600. www.steamshipauthority. com.* New Bedford-Martha's Vineyard Ferry. Daily passenger service (mid-May-mid-Sept) to New Bedford. Same-day round-trips available. Also bus tours of the island. Schedule may vary. **$$$$**

★ **Vincent House.** *Pease's Point Way, Edgartown (02539). Phone 508/627-4440.* The oldest known house on the island, built in 1672, has been carefully restored to allow visitors to see how buildings were constructed 300 years ago. Original brickwork, hardware, and woodwork. (June-early Oct, Mon-Fri 11 am-3 pm; rest of year, by appointment) **$** Also on Main Street is

> **Old Whaling Church.** *89 Main St, Edgartown (02539). Phone 508/627-4442.* Built in 1843, this is a fine example of Greek Revival architecture. Now a performing arts center with seating for 500.

Vineyard Haven and Edgartown Shopping. *Phone 508/693-0085. www.mvy.com.* Vineyard Haven is where most of Martha's Vineyards year-round residents live, so its shops are a bit less upscale than those in ritzy Edgartown, where you could spend an afternoon or even an entire day. In both areas, you'll find clothing (both casual and upscale), books, jewelry, home-decorating items, and goodies to eat (fudge, candy, and jams). Vineyard Haven is perhaps best known as the location of the Black Dog General Store (along with the Black Dog Bakery and Black Dog Tavern) that sell T-shirts and other goods bearing the logo of its now-famous black Lab. Edgartown is home to an astounding number of art galleries.

Vineyard Museum. *59 School St, Edgartown (02539). Phone 508/627-4441. www.marthasvineyardhistory.org.* Four buildings dating back to pre-Revolutionary times join together to form the Vineyard Museum. Thomas Cooke House, a historic colonial home, specializes in antiques and folk art; Foster Gallery displays exhibits from the whaling industry; Pease Galleries specializes in Native American exhibits, and Gale Huntington Library is a useful tool for genealogy. A Cape Cod museum wouldnt be complete without displaying a huge Fresnel (lighthouse) lens—view it just outside the front doors. (Tues-Sat 10 am-5 pm) **$$**

Woods Hole, Martha's Vineyard & Nantucket Steamship Authority. *Phone 508/477-8600. www. steamshipauthority.com.* Conducts round-trip service to Martha's Vineyard (all year, weather permitting).

The Yard. *Middle Rd, Chilmark (02535). Phone 508/645-9662; fax 508/645-3176. www.dancetheyard.org.* For 30 years, The Yard has hosted dance performances throughout the summer. The theater is intimate, with just 100 seats available, and makes its home in a renovated barn nestled in the Chilmark woods. The Yard also offers community dance classes, and free performances for children and senior citizens. (June-Sept) **$$$**

Special Events

Martha's Vineyard Windsurfing Challenge. *Joseph Sylvia State Beach, Beach Rd, Oak Bluffs (02557). On Beach Rd between Oak Bluffs and Edgartown. Phone 508/693-7900. www.mvchallenge.com.* Windsurfing (sometimes called sailboarding) is a combination of sailing and surfing: You stand up on a surfboard and guide a sail that's attached to the board. The Martha's Vineyard Windsurf Challenge is an awesome display of some of the best athletes in this sport, which is largely amateur but no less intense than many pro sports. On windy days, the race is especially fun to watch, as windsurfers zoom along the 30 mile-per-hour winds. Mid- to late Sept. **FREE**

Striped Bass & Bluefish Derby. *1A Dock St, Edgartown (02539). Phone 508/693-0085. www.mvderby.com.* Just after midnight on the first day of the Derby, fishing enthusiasts seek out their favorite fishing holes and cast off, hoping to land the big one during the following month. Whenever contestants haul in striped bass, bluefish, bonito, or false albacore, the catch is weighed and measured at Edgartown Harbor. Prizes are awarded daily for the largest fish; a grand prize awaits the contestant who nets the largest fish caught during the tournament. Watching the weighing in at the Harbor is a unique Cape Cod treat. Mid-Sept-mid-Oct.

Limited-Service Hotels

★ ★ **MANSION HOUSE HOTEL & HEALTH CLUB.** *9 Main St, Vineyard Haven (02568). Phone 508/693-2200; toll-free 800/332-4112. www. mvmansionhouse.com.* 32 rooms. Check-in 3 pm, check-out noon. High-speed Internet access. Restaurant. Fitness room. Indoor pool. Business center. **$$**

★ **THE NASHUA HOUSE HOTEL.** *30 Kennebec Ave, Oak Bluffs (02557). Phone 508/693-0043. www.nashuahouse.com.* 16 rooms. Check-in 2 pm, check-out 11 am. **$**

Full-Service Hotels

★ ★ ★ **HARBOR VIEW HOTEL.** *131 N Water St, Edgartown (02539). Phone 508/627-7000; toll-free 800/225-6005; fax 617/742-1042. www.harbor-view. com.* Built in 1891, this resort is a prime example of the heritage of Martha's Vineyard. Overlooking Egartown Harbor, guests can relax in a rocking chair on one of the verandas, stroll among the beautifully maintained gardens, enjoy a swim in the heated outdoor pool, or practice their backhand at a game of tennis. 124 rooms, 4 story. Check-in 3 pm, check-out 11 am. Restaurant, bar. Outdoor pool. Tennis. **$**

★ ★ ★ **KELLEY HOUSE.** *23 Kelley St, Edgartown (02539). Phone 508/627-7900; toll-free 800/225-6005; fax 508/627-8142. www.kelley-house.com.* 53 rooms, 3 story. Complimentary continental breakfast. Check-in 3 pm, check-out 11 am. Restaurant. Outdoor pool. **$$**

Full-Service Resort

★ ★ ★ **THE WINNETU INN & RESORT.** *31 Dunes Rd, Edgartown (02539). Phone 508/627-4747; fax 508/627-4749. www.winnetu.com.* 52 rooms.

Check-in 4 pm, check-out 10 am. Restaurant, bar. Children's activity center. Fitness room, fitness classes available. Outdoor pool, whirlpool. **$$**

Full-Service Inns

★ ★ ★ **BEACH PLUM INN.** *50 Beach Plum Ln, Menemsha (81432). Phone 508/645-9454; toll-free 877/645-7398; fax 508/645-2801. www.beachpluminn. com.* Built in 1890 from the salvage of a shipwreck, this Martha's Vineyard inn sits on a hilltop overlooking the ocean and boasts one of the island's most well-regarded restaurants. A stone drive and garden-like path lead to the main house, and several other cottages dot the 7-acre property. 11 rooms, 2 story. Complimentary full breakfast. Check-in 2 pm. Check-out 11 am. Restaurant. Tennis. **$$**

★ ★ ★ **CHARLOTTE INN.** *27 S Summer St, Edgartown (02539). Phone 508/627-4751; fax 508/627-4652. www.relaischateaux.com.* The Charlotte Inn extends open arms to guests seeking the quintessential New England experience. This charming inn enjoys a central location among Edgartown's quaint streets and stately sea captains' homes. Convenient to the village, the Charlotte Inn is the perfect place to enjoy the many delights of Martha's Vineyard. A wrought-iron fence stands guard over the manicured grounds of this irresistible colonial inn. Inside, a romantic English country style dominates the public and private rooms. Artwork, antiques, and other decorative objects lend a hand in creating a historical flavor in the bedrooms. Individually designed, some rooms feature luxurious canopy beds. Spread throughout the main house, carriage house, and coach house, the rooms and suites are simply delightful. Light French cuisine enhanced by American and French wine is served in the restaurant, where candlelit dinners are particularly unforgettable. 25 rooms. Children over 14 years only. Check-in 1 pm, check-out 11 am. Restaurant. **$$$**

Specialty Lodgings

THE ARBOR INN. *222 Upper Main St, Edgartown (02539). Phone 508/627-8137; toll-free 888/748-4383; fax 508/627-9104. www.arborinn.net.* 10 rooms, 2 story. Closed Nov-Apr. Children over 12 years only. Complimentary continental breakfast. Check-in 2 pm, check-out 10 am. **$$**

ASHLEY INN. *129 Main St, Edgartown (02539). Phone 508/627-9655; fax 508/627-6629. www.ashleyinn. net.* 10 rooms, 3 story. Children over 12 years only. Complimentary continental breakfast. Check-in 2 pm, check-out 11 am. **$**
▯

COLONIAL INN OF MARTHA'S VINEYARD. *38 N Water St, Edgartown (02539). Phone 508/627-4711; toll-free 800/627-4701; fax 508/627-5904. www.colonialinnmvy.com.* 43 rooms, 4 story. Closed Jan-mid-Apr. Complimentary continental breakfast. Check-in 3 pm, check-out 11 am. Restaurant. **$**

DOCKSIDE INN. *Circuit Ave Ext, Oak Bluffs (02557). Phone 508/693-2966; toll-free 800/245-5979; fax 508/696-7293. www.vineyardinns.com/dockside. html.* This gingerbread-style inn overlooks the harbor in the seaside village of Oak Bluffs and is walking distance to many attractions, miles of beaches, and shopping areas. 22 rooms, 3 story. Closed Dec-Mar. Complimentary continental breakfast. Check-in 3 pm, check-out 11 am. **$**

THE EDGARTOWN INN. *56 N Water St, Edgartown (02539). Phone 508/627-4794; fax 508/627-9420. www. edgartowninn.com.* Historic (1798) sea captain's home. Inn since 1820; colonial furnishings and antiques in rooms. 12 rooms, 3 story. Closed Nov-Mar. Check-in 2 pm, check-out 11 am. Restaurant. **$**
▯

GREENWOOD HOUSE. *40 Greenwood Ave, Vineyard Haven (02568). Phone 508/693-6150; toll-free 866/693-6150; fax 508/696-8113. www.greenwoodhouse. com.* 5 rooms, 3 story. Complimentary full breakfast. Check-in 2 pm. Check-out 10 am. **$$**
▯

THE HANOVER HOUSE. *28 Edgartown Rd, Vineyard Haven (02568). Phone 508/693-1066; toll-free 800/696-8633; fax 508/696-6099. www.hanoverhouseinn. com.* Set on a half acre of land, this cozy bed-and-breakfast is walking distance to the ferry, shopping, restaurants, and the library. Shuttles are available for travel to Edgartown and Oak Bluffs. 15 rooms, 2 story. Complimentary continental breakfast. Check-in 3 pm. Check-out 10 am. **$$**
▯

HOB KNOB INN. *128 Main St, Edgartown (02539). Phone 508/627-9510; toll-free 800/696-2723; fax 508/627-4560. www.hobknob.com.* Welcoming guests with a warm country atmosphere and personalized

service, this remarkable inn offers timeless tranquility. Charmingly furnished guest rooms, fireplaces that ensnare guests with their warmth, and fine food add to the historic ambience. 16 rooms, 3 story. Complimentary full breakfast. Check-in 2 pm. Check-out 11 am. Fitness room. **$$**
⚞

LAMBERT'S COVE COUNTRY INN. *Lambert's Cove Rd, Vineyard Haven (02568). Phone 508/693-2298; fax 508/693-7890. www.lambertscoveinn.com.* 15 rooms, 2 story. Complimentary full breakfast. Check-in 2 pm. Check-out 11 am. Restaurant (public by reservation). Tennis. **$$**
▯ ⚟

THE OAK HOUSE. *Seaview and Pequot aves, Oak Bluffs (02557). Phone 508/693-4187; fax 508/696-7385. www.vineyardinns.com/oakhouse.html.* Opposite beach. 10 rooms, 3 story. Closed mid-Oct-Apr. Children over 10 years only. Complimentary continental breakfast. Check-in 3 pm, check-out 11 am. **$$**
▯

OUTERMOST INN. *81 Lighthouse Rd, Chilmark (02535). Phone 508/645-3511; fax 508/645-3514. www. outermostinn.com.* Picture windows provide excellent views of Vineyard Sound and Elizabeth Islands. 7 rooms, 2 story. Children over 12 years only. Complimentary full breakfast. Check-in 2 pm, check-out 11 am. Restaurant. **$$**
▯

PEQUOT HOTEL. *19 Pequot Ave, Oak Bluffs (02557). Phone 508/693-5087; toll-free 800/947-8704; fax 508/696-9413. www.bnblist.com/ma/pequothotel.* 29 rooms, 3 story. Closed Nov-Apr. Complimentary continental breakfast. Check-in 3 pm, check-out 11 am. **$**
▯

SHIRETOWN INN. *44 N Water St, Edgartown (02539). Phone 508/627-3353; fax 508/627-8478. www. shiretowninn.com.* An 18th-century whaling house. 35 rooms, 3 story. Closed mid-Oct-Apr, pets accepted; restrictions, fee. Complimentary continental breakfast. Check-in 3 pm. Check-out 11 am. Restaurant, bar. **$**
▯ ⬤

THORNCROFT INN. *460 Main St, Vineyard Haven (02568). Phone 508/693-3333; fax 508/693-5419. www.thorncroft.com.* Secluded on a tree-lined, 3-acre peninsula, this charming, white-shuttered home houses romantic guest rooms, some with hot tubs and fireplaces. A full country breakfast can be enjoyed in the dining room or requested for breakfast-in-bed delivery. 14 rooms, 2 story. Complimentary full breakfast. Check-in 3-9 pm. Check-out 11 am. **$$$**

Restaurants

★ ★ ★ **ALCHEMY.** *71 Main St, Edgartown (02539). Phone 508/627-9999.* A smart, casual crowd frequents Edgartown's popular Alchemy. This American bistro offers upscale dining in a relaxed setting. The New American menu leans heavily toward seafood, and the dishes are artfully prepared. The happening bar and stylish dining room make this restaurant one of the best places to see and be seen. American menu. Lunch, dinner. Closed Jan. Bar. Casual attire. Outdoor seating. **$$$**
🅳

★ ★ ★ **COACH HOUSE.** *131 N Water St, Edgartown (02539). Phone 508/627-3761; toll-free 800/225-6005; fax 508/627-8417. www.harbor-view. com.* Casual refinement is the calling card of the Coach House. This breezily elegant restaurant situated right on Edgartown Harbor is the picture of contemporary coastal living. Large windows let the magnificent ocean views inside, where an updated take on the classics defines the tasteful space. An upscale crowd comes here for modern twists on old standbys at breakfast and lunch, while fresh seafood and shellfish dominate the dinner menu. The wine list is comprehensive, providing the perfect complement to an exceptional meal, and desserts are not to be missed. American menu. Breakfast, lunch, dinner, Sun brunch. Closed Sun-Mon evenings. Bar. Children's menu. Casual attire. Reservations recommended. Valet parking. **$$$**
🅳

★ **ESPRESSO LOVE CAFE.** *17 Church St, Edgartown (02539). Phone 508/627-9211.* International menu. Breakfast, lunch, dinner. Children's menu. Casual attire. Reservations recommended. Outdoor seating. **$$**
🅳

★ ★ ★ **L'ETOILE.** *22 N Water St, Edgartown (02539). Phone 508/627-5187. www.letoile.net.* The Charlotte Inn (see), one of the islands finest lodgings, is home to the much-heralded L'Etoile. This elegant restaurant speaks to special occasions with its classic French menu and stunning glass-enclosed dining room. The wine list, though pricey, features great selections from Europe and California, and the service is appropriately attentive. French menu. Dinner. Closed

Mon-Thurs (off-season). Jacket required. Reservations recommended. **$$$$**
🅳

★ **LATTANZI'S PIZZERIA.** *Old Post Office Sq, Edgartown (02539). Phone 508/627-9084. www.lattanzis. com.* Pizza takes on a whole new meaning at Lattanzi's. This Edgartown pizzeria makes an art form out of brick-oven pizzas. From the classics, such as pepperoni and mushroom, to the more exotic, including white clams, the toppings add panache to these appealing pies. The entire family can enjoy this relaxed restaurant, where pastas and gelato also tempt diners. Italian, pizza menu. Dinner. Children's menu. Casual attire. Reservations recommended. Outdoor seating. **$**
🅳

★ ★ **LURE.** *31 Dunes Rd, Edgartown (02539). Phone 508/627-3663; fax 508/627-4749. www.winnetu.com.* Executive chef Ed Gannon came to the Winnetu Inn from Aujourd'hui, the Four Seasons Hotel Boston's anchor restaurant, so he knows a thing or two about fine dining. Befitting its location, the menu at Lure focuses on simple but flavorful preparations of fresh seafood, including raw bar items. If you wish, hop on the complimentary sunset water taxi from Edgartown and take a few minutes to stroll through the historic Vineyard Art Gallery before or after your meal. Seafood menu. Dinner. Closed Labor Day-Columbus Day Mon-Tues, Columbus Day-Thanksgiving Mon-Thurs, Thanksgiving-May. **$$$**
🅳

★ ★ **SQUARE RIGGER.** *235 State Rd, Edgartown (02539). Phone 508/627-9968; fax 508/627-4837.* Tucked inside a historic whaling captains home, Square Rigger epitomizes New England charm. This traditional seafood restaurant is adored by locals and visitors alike for its tempting preparations of fresh seafood. Grilled selections and broiled specialties are well liked, and lobster is prepared in a variety of tantalizing ways. Seafood menu. Dinner. Closed Jan. Bar. Casual attire. Reservations recommended. **$$**
🅳

★ ★ **THE NAVIGATOR.** *2 Lower Main St, Edgartown (02539). Phone 508/627-4320; fax 508/627-3544. www.navigatorrestaurant.com.* Guests in search of the taste and feel of authentic New England sail over to The Navigator. Situated right on Edgartown Harbor, this nautical-themed restaurant pays tribute to the islands whaling history in its décor. Seafood is the major draw here, with lobster and the much-loved quahog chowder among the many selections. Live entertainment on the weekends adds to the upbeat atmosphere. Seafood menu. Lunch, dinner. Closed mid-Oct-mid-May. Bar. Children's menu. Outdoor seating. **$$$**

★ **THE NEWES FROM AMERICA.** *23 Kelly St, Edgartown (02539). Phone 508/627-4397; fax 508/627-8142. www.kelley-house.com/dining.* Kick back with a specialty beer at Edgartowns The Newes from America. Dark and wood-filled, this classic pub shares a warm spirit with islanders and visitors alike. The menu of American favorites, such as burgers and fries, is the perfect complement to one of the restaurants smooth-tasting microbrewed beers. American menu. Lunch, dinner.

★ **THE WHARF PUB & RESTAURANT.** *Lower Main St, Edgartown (02539). Phone 508/627-9966; fax 508/627-7974. www.wharfpub.com.* Across from the harbor in Edgartown, The Wharf Pub & Restaurant goes beyond typical pub fare to include a host of favorite dishes. From burgers, sandwiches, and chowder to fish and chips, lobster rolls, and fried clams, this likable restaurant has something for everyone. More sophisticated fare includes steaks and pasta, and while the selection is large, the price is right. Seafood menu. Lunch, dinner. Closed Thanksgiving, Dec 24-25; also Mar. Bar. Children's menu. Reservations recommended (six or more people). **$$**

Nantucket Island (E-9)

See also Hyannis and Barnstable, Martha's Vineyard

Settled 1659
Population 6,012
Elevation 0-108 ft
Area Code 508
Zip 02554
Information Chamber of Commerce, 48 Main St; phone 508/228-1700. General Information may also be obtained at the Information Bureau, 25 Federal St; phone 508/228-1700.
Web Site www.nantucketchamber.org

Nantucket is not just an island; it is an experience. Nantucket Island is at once a popular resort and a living museum. Siasconset (SCON-set) and Nantucket Town remain quiet and charming despite heavy tourism. With 49 square miles of lovely beaches and green moors inland, Nantucket is south of Cape Cod, 30 miles at sea. The island was the world's greatest whaling port from the late 17th century until New Bedford became dominant in the early 1800s. Whaling prosperity built the towns; tourism maintains them.

There is regular car ferry and passenger service from Hyannis. If you plan to take your car, make an advance reservation with the Woods Hole, Martha's Vineyard & Nantucket Steamship Authority, PO Box 284, Woods Hole 02543; phone 508/477-8600. Keep in mind, though, that traffic has become severe. Bicycles and public transportation may be better alternatives.

What to See and Do

★ *Endeavor* **Sailing Adventures.** *Straight Wharf, Nantucket (02554). Phone 508/228-5585. www.endeavorsailing.com.* US Coast Guard Captain James Genthner built his sloop, named the *Endeavor*, and has been sailing it for over 20 years. Take a 90-minute sail around Nantucket Sound and let the good captain and his wife, Sue, acquaint you with Nantuckets sights, sounds, and history. No sailing experience is necessary, and you can bring a picnic lunch. A special one-hour kids' tour sails at 9:45 am and 10:30 am on Wed and Thurs. (May-Oct; closed Nov-Apr) **$$$$**

Altar Rock. *Off Polpis Rd, Nantucket (02554). To the S on unmarked dirt road.* Climb up Altar Rock, which rises 90 feet above sea level, and you're afforded stunning views of Nantucket and the surrounding Cape. Go at dawn or dusk for the best views. The Moors surrounding Altar Rock offer a chance to hike on the trails or two-track dirt roads. Few tourists make the trek, which makes for unexpected solitude on Nantucket.

Barrett's Tours. *20 Federal St, Nantucket (02554). Phone 508/228-0174.* Offers 1 1/2-hour bus and van tours (Apr-Nov).

Bartlett's Farm. *33 Bartlett Farm Rd, Nantucket (02554). Phone 508/228-9403. www.bartlettsfarm.com.* Nurturing Nantuckets largest farm, the Bartlett family has tilled this land for nearly 200 years. Stop by for fresh vegetables, milk, eggs, cheese, freshly baked bread, and cut flowers. If you're looking for prepared dishes, taste the farm kitchens salads, entrées (including several that are vegetarian), pies, snacks, jams, chutneys, and other farm delights. Also visit the East Coast Seafood market, less than a mile away, for fresh fish and seafood to complete your meal. (Daily 8 am-6 pm; closed holidays)

Bass Hole Boardwalk and Gray's Beach. *End of Centre St, Nantucket (02675). Take Route 6A to Church St. Bear left onto Centre St and follow to the end.* This honest-to-goodness elevated boardwalkstretching 860 feetoffers delightful scenery as it meanders through one of Cape Cod's finest marshes to the beach. Kids enjoy playing on the beach or adjoining playground; the whole family can walk the beach and into the bay at low tide.

Boat trips. Hyannis-Nantucket Day Round-Trip. *22 Channel Point Rd, Nantucket (02601). Phone 508/778-2600. www.hy-linecruises.com.* Summer passenger service from Hyannis. **$$$$**

Cisco Brewers. *5 Bartlett Farm Rd, Nantucket (02554). Phone 508/325-5929. www.ciscobrewers.com.* If you enjoy beer, visit Cisco Brewers and taste the delicious locally made brews. From Whales Tales Pale Ale and Baileys Ale to Moor Porter, Cap'n Swains Extra Stout, Summer of Lager, and Baggywrinkle Barleywine, just about every variety of beer is represented at Cisco. Stop by for the daily guided tour ($10; times vary) that includes a walk through the brewery (including taste testing), as well as a tour of the Triple Eight Distillery and Nantucket Vineyard next door. Allow 1 1/2 hours for the entire tour. (Summer: Mon-Sat 10 am-6 pm, Sun until 5 pm; fall-spring: Sat 10 am-5 pm) **FREE**

Claire Murray. *11 S Water St, Nantucket (02554). Phone 508/228-1913. www.clairemurray.com.* Even if you've seen Claire Murray's delightful rug designs elsewhere in the country, visit the store where she got her start. Nantucket winters don't bring many visitors, and Claire Murray, who used to run a bed-and-breakfast, started hooking rugs to pass the time during these months. She soon began designing and selling rugs full-time around the world. Today, her store in Nantucket sells both finished rugs and kits and also offers classes. Around the Cape, look for other locations in West Barnstable, Osterville, Mashpee, and Edgartown (on Martha's Vineyard). (Sun-Thurs 10 am-6 pm, Fri-Sat until 9 pm)

First Congregational Church & View. *62 Centre St, Nantucket (02554). Phone 508/228-0950. www.nantucketfcc.org.* Also called Old North Church, the First Congregational Church offers Nantucket's best view of the island and surrounding ocean. Climb 94 steps to the 120-foot-tall steeple, and you're amply rewarded with a view from the top of the world. While you're at the church, take in the historical display that shows photos of the church as it has looked throughout its long history. (Mon-Sat, mid-June-mid-Oct) **$**

Gail's Tours. *25 Federal St, Nantucket (02554). Tours depart from Information Center at Federal and Broad sts. Phone 508/257-6557.* Narrated van tours (approximately 1 3/4 hours) of area. Three tours daily. Reservations recommended.

Jetties Beach. *Bathing Beach Rd, Nantucket (02554). Take North Beach Rd to Bathing Beach Rd; from there, take a shuttle bus (mid-JuneLabor Day), walk, or bike, the distance (just over a mile) to the beach.* You won't find better amenities for families with kids than Jetties Beach. Besides the convenient rest rooms, showers, changing rooms, and snack bar, the beach employs life guards, offers chairs for rent, provides a well-equipped playground, maintains volleyball and tennis courts, and offers a skateboarding park. You can also rent kayaks, sailboards, and sailboats through Nantucket Community Sailing (phone 508/228-5358), which maintains an office at the beach. Look for occasional concerts and a July 4 fireworks display. (Daily)

The Lifesaving Museum. *158 Polpis Rd, Nantucket (02554). Phone 508/228-1885. www.nantucketlifesavingmuseum.com.* The building that houses the museum is a recreation of the original 1874 lifesaving station that was built to assist mariners from the oft-times deadly seas. Museum exhibits include lifesaving surfboats, large and intricate lighthouse lenses, historical objects from the *Andrea Doria* (which sank off the coast of Nantucket Island), demonstrations, stories of rescues, and action photos. **$**

Loines Observatory. *59 Milk St, Nantucket (02554). Phone 508/228-8690. www.mmo.org.* Part of the Maria Mitchell Association (MMA)named for the first professional female astronomerthe Loines Observatory gives you a chance to peek through a fine old telescope and view the magnificent, star-filled Cape Cod skies. Also visit the MMAs other observatory on Vestal Street, which includes an outdoor true-to-scale model of the solar system, an astronomy exhibit, and a sundial. Kids may prefer the attractions at The Vestal Street Observatory, which is noted for its work with young scientists. (Mon, Wed, Fri evenings in summer, Sat evenings year-round; closed Tues, Thurs, Sun in summer, Sun-Fri year-round) **$$**

⭐ **Main Street.** *Main St, Nantucket. Phone 508/228-1894. www.nantucket.com.* Paved with cobblestones, lined with elegant houses built by whaling merchants, and shaded by great elms, this is one of New England's most beautiful streets. The Nantucket Historical Association maintains the following attractions (June-Oct: daily; spring and fall: limited hours). **$$$**

1800 House. *8 Mill St, Nantucket (02554). Phone 508/228-1894.* Home of the sheriff, early 19th century. Period home and furnishings; large, round cellar; kitchen garden.

Folger-Franklin Seat & Memorial Boulder. *Madaket Rd, Nantucket (02554). Madaket Rd, 1 mile from W end of Main St. Phone 508/228-1894.* Birthplace site of Abiah Folger, mother of Benjamin Franklin.

Hadwen House. *96 Main St, Nantucket (02554). Phone 508/228-1894.* (1845) Greek Revival mansion; furnishings of whaling period; gardens. (Mon-Sat 10 am-5 pm, Sun from noon) **$**

Jethro Coffin House (Oldest House). *16 Sunset Hill Ln, Nantucket Island (02554). N on North Water to West Chester, left to Sunset Hill. Phone 508/228-1894.* Built in 1686, Oldest House is, true to its name, one of the oldest houses you'll ever visit in the United States, and the oldest on Nantucket. The house was a wedding present given to the children of two feuding families (the Gardners and the Coffins) by their in-laws, who reconciled after the happy event. In 1987, after lightning struck Oldest House, it was fully restored to its original beauty. This colonial saltbox and its spare furnishings exude classic Nantucket style and charm. (Mon-Sat 10 am-5 pm, Sun from noon) **$**

Old Fire Hose Cart House. *8 Gardner St, Nantucket (02554). Phone 508/228-1894.* (1886) Old-time firefighting equipment. (Mon-Sat 10 am-5pm, Sun from noon) **FREE**

Old Gaol. *Vestal St, Nantucket (02554). Phone 508/228-1894.* (1805) Unusual two-story construction; used until 1933.(Mon-Sat 10 am-5 pm, Sun from noon) **FREE**

Old Mill. *50 Prospect St, Nantucket (02554). Phone 508/228-1894.* This Dutch-style windmill is impressive in its beauty and sheer size (50 feet high), but it was built for function—to grind grain brought by local farmers—and it remains functional today. Believed to be the oldest windmill in the United States, it was built in 1746 with salvaged oak that washed up on shore from shipwrecks and after many owners, eventually came to belong to the Nantucket Historical Society. (June-Aug, daily; call for off-season hours) **$**

Research Center. *7 Fair St, Nantucket (02554). Next to Whaling Museum. Phone 508/228-1655.* Ships' logs, diaries, charts, and Nantucket photographs; library. (Mon-Fri; closed holidays) **$**

Whaling Museum. *13 Broad St, Nantucket (02554). Near Steamboat Wharf. Phone 508/228-1736.* Outstanding collection of relics from whaling days; whale skeleton, tryworks, scrimshaw, candle press. **$$**

Miacomet Golf Course. *12 W Miacomet Rd, Nantucket (02554). Phone 508/228-9764.* Nantucket's only public golf course offers nine holes—including two par-five holes—that you can play twice for a par-74 round. Winds off the ocean make for interesting play. Reserve a tee time at least a week in advance; your chances of playing without a reservation are zero during the summer. (Daily) **$$$$**

Murray's Toggery. *62 Main St, Nantucket (02554). Phone 508/228-0437; toll-free 800/368-2134. www. nantucketreds.com.* Murray's Toggery was the first store in Nantucket to sell Nantucket Reds—casual red pants that eventually fade to a decidedly pink hue—a product that defines both Cape Cod and the preppy look. Murray's also sells oxford shirts, sweaters, shoes, hats, coats, and jackets for both men and women. (Mon-Sat 9 am-7 pm, Sun 10 am-6 pm; winter: Mon-Sat 9 am-5 pm)

Nantucket Gourmet. *4 India St, Nantucket (02554). Phone 508/228-4353; toll-free 866/626-2665. www. nantucketgourmet.com.* Nantucket Gourmet offers a well-balanced blend of cookware and other culinary tools, and condiments to take back home with you (including marmalades, jams, mustards, and vinegars), and ready-to-eat deli foods for your lunch on the island. You'll find great gifts for any food-lover. (Summer: daily 10 am-6 pm; winter: Mon-Fri 10 am-4 pm; closed holidays)

Nantucket Maria Mitchell Association. *4 Vestal St, Nantucket (02554). Phone 508/228-9198. www.mmo. org.* The birthplace of the first American woman astronomer; memorial observatory (1908). The scientific library has Nantucket historical documents, science journals, and Mitchell family memorabilia. Natural science museum with local wildlife. Aquarium is at 28 Washington Street. Combination ticket available for museum, birthplace, and aquarium. (Mid-

June-Sept, Mon-Sat; library also open rest of year, Wed-Sat; closed July 4, Labor Day) **$$**

Nantucket Town. *The areas between Main, Broad, and Centre sts. Phone 508/228-1700. www.nantucketchamber. org/directory/merchants.* Nantucket Town is a shopper's dream, with narrow cobblestone streets that wind past hundreds of shops. You'll find items for your home (furniture, rugs, throws and blankets, baskets, prints, soaps, and so on), your boat (including all manner of weather-predicting equipment), and yourself (from preppy and upscale clothing, hats, shawls, jewelry, and everything in between). In about 20 stores, you'll find the famous Nantucket baskets (also called lightship baskets), which are handmade through a time-consuming process. You'll also come across numerous art galleries, antiques shops, and craft stores.

Nantucket Whaling Museum. *13 Broad St, Nantucket (02554). Phone 508/228-1894. www.nha.org.* To really understand Nantucket, you have to understand whaling, the industry that put Nantucket on the map. The Nantucket Whaling Museum—housed in a former factory that produced candles from whale oil—shows you a fully rigged whale boat (smaller than you may think), rope and basket collections, scrimshaw (whalebone carving) exhibits, a huge lighthouse Fresnel lens, a skeleton of a finback whale, and maritime folk art. Enjoy one of three daily lectures offered by the museum staff. Visit in December to see the Festival of Trees, which includes 50 decorated Christmas trees. **$$**

Rafael Osona Auctions. *21 Washington St, Nantucket (02554). At the American Legion Hall. Phone 508/228-3942; fax 508/228-8778. www.rafaelosonaauction.com.* If you like antiques, you'll love Rafael Osona. The auctioneers host estate auctions on selected weekends (call for exact dates and times) that feature treasured pieces from both the United States and Europe. If an auction isn't planned while you're in town, visit the two dozen other antique stores on the island, plus many more around Cape Cod. (Late May-early Dec)

Siasconset Village. *E end of Nantucket Island, Nantucket Island.* The Siasconset Village lies 7 miles from Nantucket Town, and can be traveled by bicycle or shuttle bus. This 18th-century fishing village features quaint cottages, grand mansions, restaurants, a few shops, and a summer cinema. Visit Siasconset Beach and the paved biking path that meanders through the area.

Something Natural. *50 Cliff Rd, Nantucket (02554). Phone 508/228-0504. www.somethingnatural.com.* If you're looking for a casual breakfast or lunch—per-

haps even one to take with you on a bike ride or island hike—check out Something Natural for healthy sandwiches, breads and bagels, salads, cookies, and beverages. The eatery has also established a second location at 6 Oak Street (phone 508/228-6616). (May-Oct)

The Straight Wharf. *Straight Wharf, Nantucket (02554). On the harbor, next to the ferry.* Built in 1723, the Straight Wharf is Nantucket's launching area for sailboats, sloops, and kayaks, but its also a great shopping and eating area. Loaded with restaurants and quaint one-room cottage shops selling island fare, the wharf also features an art gallery, a museum, and an outdoor concert pavilion.

Strong Wings Summer Camp. *PO Box 2884, Nantucket (02584). Phone 508/228-1769. www.strongwings.org.* Open for just one month every year, the Strong Wings Summer Camp offers more excitement and activity for kids than you're likely to find anywhere else on the Cape. Kids ages 5 to 15 attend three-day or five-day sessions, where they explore the natural attributes of the area, mountain bike, hike, kayak, snorkel, rock climb, and boogie board (as appropriate for each age group). Older kids even learn search-and-rescue techniques. (Late June-late Aug, daily) **$$$$**

The Sunken Ship. *12 Broad St, Nantucket (02554). Phone 508/228-9226. www.sunkenship.com.* The Sunken Ship is a full-service dive shop that offers lessons and rentals. When the *Andrea Doria* sank off the coast of Nantucket in the middle of the last century, the area invited divers from around the world to investigate the sunken ship, hence the name of this shop. The general store offers an eclectic array of dive and maritime goods. (Daily; call for closures) **$$$$**

Theatre Workshop of Nantucket. *2 Centre St, Nantucket (02554). Phone 508/228-4305. www.theatreworkshop.com.* The Actors Theatre of Nantucket has staged comedies, dramas, plays, and dance concerts since 1985. Both professionals and amateurs make up the company, which offers between six and ten performances during the summer. When purchasing tickets, ask whether family matinees are offered for that performance. **$$$$**

Windswept Cranberry Bog. *Polpis Rd, Siasconset (02554).* Cranberries are an important industry to Nantucket; in town, you can purchase jars of cranberry honey, and Northland Cranberries harvests berries from Nantucket to make its well-known juices. To see how cranberries are grown and harvested, visit this 200-acre cranberry bog during the fall harvest (late September through October from dawn to dusk), when bogs are flooded so that machines can shake off and scoop up the individual berries. (Mid-October also brings the Nantucket Cranberry Festival.) Even at other times of year, the bog is peaceful and beautiful—a good place to walk and bike and spend half a day. Another nearby cranberry bog is the **Milestone Bog** (off Milestone Rd west of Siasconset). (Daily dawn-dusk)

Special Events

Christmas Stroll. *Phone 508/228-1700.* First weekend in Dec.

Daffodil Festival. *Siasconset Village, Nantucket Island (02564). Phone 508/228-1700. www.nantucket.net/ daffy.* The Daffodil Festival celebrates the budding of millions of daffodils on the main roads of Nantucket. A parade of antique car classics kicks off the well-attended event, which also includes open houses, garden tours, and a lively picnic that offers great food and live entertainment. Late Apr. **FREE**

Nantucket Arts Festival. *Various venues. Phone 508/325-8588. www.nantucketartscouncil.org.* This week-long festival celebrates a full range of arts on the island: films, poetry and fiction readings, acting, dance performances, and exhibits of paintings, photography, and many other art forms. Look for the wet-paint sale in which you can bid on works completed just that day by local artists. Early Oct. **FREE**

Nantucket Film Festival. *Various venues. Phone 508/228-6648. www.nantucketfilmfestival.org.* Like other film festivals worldwide, Nantucket's festival screens new independent films that may not otherwise garner attention. You'll be joined by screenwriters, actors, film connoisseurs and, occasionally, big-name celebrities at the festivals seminars, readings, and discussions. A daily event called Morning Coffee showcases a panel of directors, screenwriters, and actors participating in Q&A with festival-goers, who sip coffee and munch on muffins. Mid-June. **$$$$**

Nantucket Island Fair. *Tom Nevers Navy Base, Nantucket (02554). Phone 508/228-7213.* Looking for an old-fashioned county fair? Head to Nantucket for down-home family fun and entertainment. At the Nantucket Island Fair, an event that began over 150 years ago, you'll find pies, breads, pastries, jams, jellies, fresh fall fruits, and concessions of all types. You'll also see and experience tractor displays and rides, a petting zoo and pet show, a flea market, quilt displays and

sales, hay rides, concerts, and square dancing. Third weekend in Sept. **$$**

Nantucket Wine Festival. *Phone 508/228-1128. www. nantucketwinefestival.com.* This is a wine festival like no other: take in a wine symposium, a variety of food and wine seminars, a wine auction, and many other events. The Great Wine in Grand Houses event allows you to visit a private mansion, sip fine wines drawn from nearly 100 wineries, and dine on food prepared by some of the world's finest chefs. Reservations are required and should be made as soon as you know you'll be visiting the island. Mid-May. **$$$$**

Sand Castle Contest. *48 Main St, Nantucket (02554). Phone 508/228-1700.* Third Sat in Aug.

Limited-Service Hotels

★ ★ **THE BEACHSIDE AT NANTUCKET.** *30 N Beach St, Nantucket (02554). Phone 508/228-2241; toll-free 800/322-4433; fax 508/228-8901. www.thebeachside. com.* 93 rooms. Closed Nov-Apr. Complimentary continental breakfast. Check-in 3 pm, check-out noon. Bar. Outdoor pool. **$**
🏊

★ ★ **CLIFFSIDE BEACH CLUB.** *46 Jefferson Ave, Nantucket (02554). Phone 508/228-0618; fax 508/325-4735. www.cliffsidebeach.com.* 27 rooms, all suites. Closed Nov-Apr. Check-in 3 pm, check-out noon. Restaurant, bar. Beach. **$$**

★ ★ **HARBOR HOUSE VILLAGE.** *S Beach St, Nantucket (02554). Phone 508/325-1000; toll-free 866/325-9300; fax 508/228-7639. www.nantucketislandresorts.com.* 104 rooms, 3 story. Check-in 3 pm, check-out 11 am. Restaurant, bar. Outdoor pool. Beach. **$**
🅳 🏊

★ ★ **NANTUCKET INN.** *1 Miller's Way, Nantucket (02554). Phone 508/228-6900; toll-free 800/321-8484; fax 508/228-9861. www.nantucketinn.net.* 100 rooms, 2 story. Closed Dec-Mar. Pets accepted; fee. Check-in 4 pm, check-out 11 am. Restaurant, bar. Fitness room. Indoor pool, outdoor pool, whirlpool. Airport transportation available. **$**
🐾 🏋 🏊

Full-Service Hotel

★ ★ ★ **WHITE ELEPHANT RESORT.** *50 Easton St, Nantucket (02554). Phone 508/228-2500; toll-free 800/445-6574; fax 508/325-1195.*

www.whiteelephanthotel.com. Step back in time for a game of croquet on a sweeping, manicured lawn at this harborfront resort. 63 rooms, 3 story. Closed mid Dec-Mar. Check-in 3 pm, check-out 11 am. Restaurant, bar. **$$$**

Full-Service Inns

★ ★ ★ **JARED COFFIN HOUSE.** 29 Broad St, Nantucket (02554). Phone 508/228-2400; fax 508/228-8549. www.jaredcoffinhouse.com. This restored 1845 mansion features historical objets d'art. 60 rooms, 3 story. Check-in 3 pm, check-out 11 am. Restaurant, bar. **$**

★ ★ ★ ★ **THE WAUWINET.** 120 Wauwinet Rd, Nantucket (02554). Phone 508/228-0145; toll-free 800/426-8718; fax 508/228-6712. www.wauwinet.com. Nearly 30 miles out to sea, the idyllic island of Nantucket is a place where crashing waves wash away everyday cares. The Wauwinet embodies the perfect getaway on this magical island. Tucked away on a private stretch of beach, The Wauwinet leads its guests to believe that they have been marooned on a remote island, yet this delightful hotel remains close to the town's charming cobblestone streets, a complimentary jitney ride away. Built in 1876 by ship captains, The Wauwinet's rooms and suites have a sophisticated country style blended with the services of a posh resort. Private beaches fronting the harbor and the Atlantic Ocean are spectacular, and clay tennis courts challenge guests to a match. Whether diners choose to arrive by foot or by sunset cruise on the 26-foot *Wauwinet Lady,* Toppers restaurant (see) promises to be an exceptional event. With a 20,000-bottle wine cellar and an impressive menu, it is an epicureans delight. 36 rooms, 3 story. Closed late Oct-early May. Children over 18 only. Complimentary full breakfast. Check-in 4 pm, check-out 11 am. Restaurant. Tennis. **$$$$**

Specialty Lodgings

CARLISLE HOUSE INN. 26 N Water St, Nantucket (02554). Phone 508/228-0720; fax 781/639-1004. www.carlislehouse.com. Restored whaling captain's house (1765). 17 rooms, 3 story. Closed Jan-Mar. Children over 10 years only. Complimentary continental breakfast. Check-in 2 pm, check-out 11 am. **$**

CENTERBOARD GUEST HOUSE. 8 Chester St, Nantucket (02554). Phone 508/228-9696. www.

centerboardguesthouse.com. Restored Victorian residence (1885). 8 rooms, 3 story. Closed Jan-Feb. Complimentary continental breakfast. Check-in 3 pm, check-out 11 am. **$**

CENTRE STREET INN. 78 Centre St, Nantucket (02554). Phone 508/228-0199; toll-free 800/298-0199; fax 508/228-8676. www.centrestreetinn.com. Colonial house built in 1742; some antiques. 14 rooms, 3 story. Closed Jan-Apr. Complimentary continental breakfast. Check-in 3-6 pm, check-out 11 am. **$**

COBBLESTONE INN. 5 Ash St, Nantucket (02554). Phone 508/228-1987; fax 508/228-6698. Built in 1725. 5 rooms, 3 story. Closed Jan-Mar. Complimentary full breakfast. Check-in 2 pm, check-out 11 am. **$**

MARTIN HOUSE INN. 61 Centre St, Nantucket (02554). Phone 508/228-0678. www.martinhouseinn.net. Built in 1803. 13 rooms, 3 story. Complimentary continental breakfast. Check-in 3 pm, check-out 11 am. Restaurant. **$**

ROBERTS HOUSE INN. 11 India St, Nantucket (02554). Phone 508/228-0600; toll-free 800/872-6830; fax 508/325-4046. www.robertshouseinn.com. Built in 1846; established in 1883. 45 rooms, 3 story. Complimentary continental breakfast. Check-in 2 pm, check-out 11 am. **$**

SEVEN SEA STREET INN. 7 Sea St, Nantucket (02554). Phone 508/228-3577; fax 508/228-3578. www.sevenseastreetinn.com. View of Nantucket Harbor. 11 rooms, 2 story. Closed Jan-mid Apr, Children over 5 years only. Complimentary continental breakfast. Check-in 3 pm, check-out 11 am. Whirlpool. **$$**

SHERBURNE INN. 10 Gay St, Nantucket (02554). Phone 508/228-4425; toll-free 888/577-4425; fax 508/228-8114. www.sherburneinn.com. Built in 1835 as a silk factory; period antiques, fireplaced parlors. 8 rooms, 3 story. Children over 6 years only. Complimentary continental breakfast. Check-in 2 pm, check-out 11 am. **$**

SHIPS INN. 13 Fair St, Nantucket (02554). Phone 508/228-0040; fax 508/228-6254. www.shipsinnnantucket.com. Built in 1831 by a sea captain; many original furnishings. 12 rooms, 4 story. Closed Nov-Apr.

Complimentary continental breakfast. Check-in 2 pm. Check-out 10 am. Restaurant, bar. **$$**

VANESSA NOEL HOTEL. *5 Chestnut St, Nantucket (02554). Phone 508/228-5300; fax 508/228-8995. www.vanno.com.* 8 rooms, 3 story. Complimentary continental breakfast. Check-in 3 pm, check-out 11 am. High-speed Internet access. Bar. **$$$**

Restaurants

★ ★ ★ **21 FEDERAL.** *21 Federal St, Nantucket (02554). Phone 508/228-2121; fax 508/228-2962. www.21federal.net.* Tucked inside a handsome Greek Revival building dating to the mid-1800s, 21 Federal offers diners a rare blend of historic charm and contemporary panache. This stylishly clubby spot is a favorite haunt of the islands beautiful people, both for its delectable New American cuisine and its convivial spirit. The well-rounded menu is sure to please epicureans with its wide selection of meat, poultry, and seafood, while the award-winning wine list and fantastic wines available by the glass delight oenophiles. American menu. Dinner. Closed Jan-Apr. Bar. Business casual attire. Reservations recommended. Outdoor seating. **$$$**

★ ★ ★ **AMERICAN SEASONS.** *80 Center St, Nantucket (02554). Phone 508/228-7111; fax 508/325-0779. www.americanseasons.com.* Located on a quiet residential street just a few blocks from the center of town, American Seasons invites guests to embark on a culinary journey across the United States. Patrons dine on sophisticated renditions of regional specialties from New England, Down South, the Wild West, or the Pacific Coast at this unique restaurant where location is the theme. From the charming country décor filled with quaint folk art to the romantic candlelit dining room and patio, the setting is as memorable as the meal. American menu. Dinner. Closed Jan-Mar. Bar. Business casual attire. Reservations recommended. Outdoor seating. **$$$**

★ **ATLANTIC CAFE.** *15 S Water St, Nantucket (02554). Phone 508/228-0570; fax 508/228-8787.* Diners with hearty appetites flock to Atlantic Cafe, where the promise of a rollicking good time and a filling, pub-style meal attracts families and singles alike. Nantucket's nautical history is proudly commemorated here, with ship wheels, harpoons, and boats lining the walls. This popular establishment offers exceptional value with affordable prices, and the large wraparound bar has been the preferred watering hole of locals for decades. American, seafood menu. Lunch, dinner, late-night. Closed late Dec-early Jan. Bar. Children's menu. **$**

★ ★ **BLACK EYED SUSAN'S.** *10 India St, Nantucket (02554). Phone 508/325-0308.* Black Eyed Susan's is a funky foodie's dream. This tiny café with just under ten tables lures diners with a penchant for the unusual. Space is tight, but the counter provides front-row seats to the action of the open kitchen. Thai, Mexican, and other international flavors punctuate the fusion menu. Breakfast is especially eye-opening, with traditional dishes taking on exotic bents, and dinner reservations here are truly coveted. Be sure to pick up a bottle of your favorite wine on the way, since this is a BYOB restaurant. International menu. Breakfast, dinner. Closed Sun; also Nov-Mar. Casual attire. Reservations recommended. Outdoor seating. No credit cards accepted. **$$**

★ ★ ★ **BOARDING HOUSE.** *12 Federal St, Nantucket (02554). Phone 508/228-9622; fax 508/325-7109. www.boardinghouse-pearl.com.* Long waits are par for the course at the Boarding House, but this smart restaurants nouveau cuisine and sexy, youthful scene make it worth the wait. Nestled on a corner in the heart of town, this restaurant enjoys one of the islands most enviable locations. Those in the know book a table outdoors to enjoy people-watching and stargazing, while others seek the excitement of the bustling bar or the intimate setting of the dimly lit downstairs. Seafood and beef serve as the main inspirations behind the creative Asian-influenced menu, and a comprehensive wine list ensures a perfect pairing. American menu. Lunch, dinner. Bar. Reservations recommended. Outdoor seating. **$$$**

★ **CAMBRIDGE STREET RESTAURANT.** *12 Cambridge St, Nantucket (02554). Phone 508/228-7109.* For a finger-licking good time, head over to Cambridge Street. This lively restaurant in the center of town features stick-to-your-ribs good food in a cool setting. The barbecue-focused menu is a hit with the young crowd that frequents this place for its all-around fun at a reasonable price. American menu. Dinner. Closed Jan-Apr. Bar. Casual attire. **$$**

★ ★ ★ **CLUB CAR.** *1 Main St, Nantucket (02554). Phone 508/228-1101; fax 508/228-8740. www.theclubcar. com.* Lunch and dinner at The Club Car are elegant, but the atmosphere remains casual. The Club Car

lounge is housed in a renovated club car from a train that used to run between Steamboat Wharf and Siasconset Village, so the décor is fascinating. The restaurant offers great seats for people-watching along Main Street and the waterfront, and a pianist performs nightly. French menu. Lunch, dinner. Closed Nov-late May. Bar. Business casual attire. Reservations recommended. **$$$$**
🅓

★ ★ ★ **COMPANY OF THE CAULDRON.**
5 India St, Nantucket (02554). Phone 508/228-4016; fax 508/228-4016. www.companyofthecauldron.com. Romantics adore the Company of the Cauldron. From the charming, ivy-covered exterior to the soft glow of the candlelit dining room to the gentle strains of the harp played in the background, this special restaurant seems crafted straight from a romance novel. While it offers the perfect setting in which to begin or re-kindle a love affair, the kitchens passion for food is yet another reason to visit. The exceptional New Ameri-can menu changes nightly, surprising and delighting visitors with memorable dishes. International menu. Dinner. Closed mid-Dec-Apr. Business casual attire. Reservations recommended. **$$$**

★ **DOWNYFLAKE.** *18 Sparks Ave, Nantucket (02554). Phone 508/228-4533.* The early bird gets the doughnut at Downyflake. Open at 5 am and serving breakfast until 2 pm, this coffee shop rewards early risers with freshly baked doughnuts still warm from the oven. Traditional breakfast favorites and lunch are also served here, all with a friendly smile. A favorite haunt of islanders, this casual spot is the perfect place to catch up on local gossip while sipping a hot cup of coffee. Breakfast, lunch. Casual attire. **$**

★ **FOG ISLAND CAFE.** *7 S Water St, Nantucket (02554). Phone 508/228-1818; fax 508/374-8549. www.fogisland.com.* The line forms early outside the Fog Island Cafe. Best known for its hearty country break-fasts, this casual restaurant is a favorite of visitors and locals alike for its friendly service, relaxed setting, and delicious food. This establishment perfectly conveys the essence of beach living with its breezy ceiling fans and large wood tables and booths. Conveniently located in the heart of town, the Fog Island Café's laid-back attitude makes it a perfect choice for the en-tire family, and its sophisticated comfort food is sure to please diners of all ages. American menu. Breakfast, lunch, dinner. Closed Jan-Feb. Bar. Children's menu. Casual attire. **$**

★ ★ **LE LANGUEDOC.** *24 Broad St, Nantucket (02554). Phone 508/228-2552; fax 508/228-4682. www.lelanguedoc.com.* For a taste of France off the New England coast, visit Le Languedoc. This charming restaurant, located inside one of Nantucket's historic homes, shares two personalities with diners. Guests may choose the casual, upbeat style of the bistro and accompanying terrace or opt for the intimate, romantic setting of the pricier upstairs dining room. A traditional French menu is served in both settings, and for those who can't venture forth after the superb meal, rooms are available at Le Languedoc's inn. French menu. Lunch, dinner. Closed Feb-Mar. Bar. Casual attire. Reservations recommended. Outdoor seating. **$$$**
🅓

★ ★ **NANTUCKET LOBSTER TRAP.** *23 Washington St, Nantucket (02554). Phone 508/228-4200; fax 508/228-6168. www.nantucketlobstertrap.com.* Families and large groups flock to the lively Lobster Trap. Open seasonally and for dinner only, this informal restaurant is known for its friendly service and fun atmosphere. Lobsters are the big draw here, yet the islands famous scallops are a close sec-ond. Lines are long, but guests may enjoy drinks and appetizers on the patio while waiting for a table. The Lobster Trap even packages takeout clambakes and other meals to enjoy on the beach or at home. Seafood menu. Dinner. Closed Oct-Apr. Bar. Children's menu. Casual attire. Outdoor seating. **$$$**

★ ★ ★ **ORAN MOR.** *2 S Beach St, Nantucket (02554). Phone 508/228-8655; fax 508/228-2498. www.nantucket.net/food/oranmor.* Climb the stairs to Oran Mor and discover a food lover's heaven. Tucked inside a historic Nantucket house with views across to the harbor, this jewel box treats its visitors to a truly ser-endipitous setting. The atmospheric fine-dining expe-rience is capped off by a friendly, knowledgeable staff that manages to be attentive without being intrusive. The eclectic menu echoes the restaurants accessible elegance, with organic ingredients and fresh seafood dominating the subtle yet complex flavors. Interna-tional menu. Dinner. Closed Jan-Mar. Bar. Business casual attire. Reservations recommended. **$$$**

★ ★ ★ **THE PEARL.** *12 Federal St, Nantucket (02554). Phone 508/228-9701; fax 508/325-7109. www.boardinghouse-pearl.com.* The Pearl brings city chic to Nantucket. This ultra-hip restaurant appeals to a young, fashionable clientele on holiday from the city, yet not wanting to leave sophistication behind. Asian flavors punctuate the mainly seafood dishes here, and the drink menu is decidedly trendy, offering creative takes on the martini, cosmopolitan, and sake, in addition to a complete wine and champagne list. This intimate restaurant has only two seatings per evening, so reservations are a must. International menu. Dinner, late-night. Closed Oct-Apr. Bar. Casual attire. Reservations recommended. Outdoor seating. **$$$$**

★ ★ **ROPEWALK.** *1 Straight Wharf, Nantucket (02554). Phone 508/228-8886; fax 508/228-8740. www. theropewalk.com.* With the harbor gently lapping at its doorstep and the island's most luxurious yachts docked just outside, the Ropewalk enjoys one of the best locations on Nantucket. The boating crowd populates this clubby, open-air restaurant where seafood is the specialty. The raw bar here is considered one of the islands best, and the always-hopping bar is tops for drinks with a view. Seafood menu. Lunch, dinner. Closed mid-Oct-mid-May. Bar. Children's menu. Casual attire. Outdoor seating. **$$**

★ ★ **SEAGRILLE.** *45 Sparks Ave, Nantucket (02554). Phone 508/325-5700; fax 508/325-0135. www. theseagrille.com.* Located just a short distance from town, The SeaGrille is a terrific destination for the entire family. This casual restaurant with friendly service specializes in seafood, including New England favorites such as Ipswich clams and Chatham scrod in addition to raw bar offerings, yet its extensive menu includes many meat, poultry, and game selections to satisfy non-seafood eaters. The quahog chowder is an island favorite and is even shipped via mail order for those who can't get enough of this local dish. Seafood menu. Lunch, dinner. Closed Thanksgiving, Dec 25. Children's menu. Business casual attire. Reservations recommended. Outdoor seating. **$$**

★ ★ **SUMMER HOUSE.** *17 Ocean Ave, Nantucket (02554). Phone 508/257-9976.* Nestled in the tiny hamlet of Sconset, where rose-covered cottages and wind-swept bluffs are *de rigueur*, the Summer House seduces guests with its spectacular oceanfront setting and superb cuisine. White wicker furnishings and ceiling fans recall the seaside vacations of a former time, while the refined New American menu is firmly rooted in the present. Lunch is available poolside, while the upscale clientele enjoys dinner with an ocean view in the elegant dining room. American menu. Dinner. Closed mid-Oct-mid-May. Bar. Casual attire. Outdoor seating. **$$$$**

★ ★ ★ **TOPPER'S.** *120 Wauwinet Rd, Nantucket (02554). Phone 508/228-0145; toll-free 800/426-8718; fax 508/325-0657. www.wauwinet.com.* Located in the charming Wauwinet Inn (see), this romantic, sophisticated restaurant is filled with flowers, art, and the island's upper-crust clientele. The food, service, and wine list are all first-rate. At lunch, the menu is tasting style so that diners can sample small portions of several dishes. Nice touches include complimentary sparkling water at dinner, sterling silver pendulum plate carriers, and even gourmet to-go basket lunches if you prefer a picnic. American menu. Lunch, dinner, Sun brunch. Closed late Oct-early May. Bar. Business casual attire. Reservations recommended. Outdoor seating. **$$$$**

★ ★ **WEST CREEK CAFE.** *11 W Creek Rd, Nantucket (02554). Phone 508/228-4943.* Located mid-island, the West Creek Cafe is worth the drive out of town. This sensational restaurant jazzes up the local scene with its refined New American cuisine. Cosmopolitan couples linger over meals in the intimate dining room, where zebra-print banquettes and satin pillows add to the urbane ambience. The menu changes weekly, surprising both loyal visitors and newcomers with its cleverly prepared dishes. American menu. Dinner. Closed Tues; Jan 1, Thanksgiving, Dec 25. Bar. Reservations recommended. Outdoor seating. **$$$**

★ **WESTENDER.** *326 Madaket Rd, Nantucket (02554). Phone 508/228-5100.* American menu. Lunch, dinner. Closed in winter. Bar. **$$**

Natick (B-6)

Population 32,170
Elevation 180 ft
Area Code 508
Zip 01760
Information MetroWest Chamber of Commerce, 1671 Worcester Rd, Suite 201, Framingham 01701; phone 508/879-5600
Web Site www.metrowest.org

This town was set aside as a plantation for the "Praying Indians" in 1650 at the request of Reverend John Eliot. A missionary, he believed that he could promote brotherhood between Native Americans and settlers by converting them. After half a century, the Native Americans were crowded out by settlers.

Limited-Service Hotels

★ **HAMPTON INN.** *319 Speen St, Natick (01760). Phone 508/653-5000; toll-free 800/426-7866; fax 508/651-9733. www.hamptoninn.com.* 185 rooms, 7 story. Complimentary continental breakfast. Check-in 3 pm, check-out noon. Fitness room. **$**

★ ★ **SHERBORN INN.** *33 N Main St, Sherborn (01770). Phone 508/655-9521; fax 508/655-5325. www.sherborninn.com.* 4 rooms, 2 story. Complimentary continental breakfast. Check-in 3 pm, check-out 11 am. Restaurant. **$**

Full-Service Hotel

★ ★ ★ **CROWNE PLAZA.** *1360 Worcester St, Natick (01760). Phone 508/653-8800; toll-free 800/227-6963; fax 508/653-1708. www.crowneplaza.com.* This hotel is located 15 miles west of downtown Boston and has a dramatic, atrium-lobby entrance. Rates include a continental breakfast buffet, evening hors d'oeuvres, and local transportation. Guests will find shops and theaters at the neighboring Natick Mall. 251 rooms, 7 story. Check-out noon. High-speed Internet access. Restaurant, bar. Fitness room. **$**

Restaurant

★ ★ **SHERBORN INN.** *33 N Main St, Sherborn (01770). Phone 508/655-9521; toll-free 800/552-9742; fax 508/655-5325. www.sherborninn.com.* Restored tavern décor. American, Irish menu. Dinner. Bar. **$$**

New Bedford (D-7)

See also Fall River

Settled 1640
Population 93,768
Elevation 50 ft
Area Code 508
Information Bristol County Convention & Visitors Bureau, 70 N Second St, PO Box 976, 02741; phone 508/997-1250 or toll-free 800/288-6263
Web Site www.bristol-county.org

Herman Melville, author of *Moby Dick,* said that the brave houses and flowery gardens of New Bedford were one and all harpooned and dragged up from the bottom of the sea. Whaling did, in fact, build this

city. When oil was discovered in Pennsylvania in 1857, the world's greatest whaling port nearly became a ghost town. New Bedford scrapped the great fleet and became a major cotton textile center. More recently, it has thrived on widely diversified industries. New Bedford remains a major Atlantic deep-sea fishing port. The whaling atmosphere is preserved in local museums and monuments, while the Whaling National Historical Park celebrates the town's whaling legacy. In the County Street historic district, many of the mansions built for sea captains and merchants still stand.

What to See and Do

Buttonwood Park & Zoo. *425 Hawthorn St, New Bedford (02740). Phone 508/991-6178. www.bpzoo.org.* Greenhouse; ball fields, tennis courts, playground, picnic area, fitness circuit. Zoo exhibits include elephants, lions, deer, bears, buffalo; seal pool. (Daily 10 am-5 pm; closed Jan 1, Thanksgiving, Dec 25) **$**

Fort Phoenix Beach State Reservation. *Off Hwy 6 and I-95, E via Hwy 6 to Fairhaven, then 1 mile S; follow signs. Phone 508/992-4524.* Swimming; fine view of the harbor. Nearby is Fort Phoenix, a pre-Revolutionary fortification (open to the public). **$**

New Bedford Whaling Museum. *18 Johnny Cake Hill, New Bedford (02740). Phone 508/997-0046. www.whalingmuseum.org.* Features an 89-foot half-scale model of whaleship *Lagoda.* Galleries devoted to scrimshaw, local artists; murals of whales and whale skeleton; period rooms and collections of antique toys, dolls, prints, and ship models. Silent movie presentation (July-Aug). (Daily 9 am-5 pm; closed Jan 1, Thanksgiving, Dec 25) **$$**

New Bedford-Cuttyhunk Ferry. *Fisherman's Wharf at Pier 3, New Bedford. Phone 508/992-1432.* (Mid-June-mid-Sept: daily; rest of year: varied schedule) Reservations suggested. **$$$$**

Rotch-Jones-Duff House and Garden Museum. *396 County St, New Bedford (02740). Phone 508/997-1401; fax 508/997-6846. www.rjdmuseum.org.* Whaling era Greek Revival mansion (1834) and garden, has been maintained to reflect the lives of three families that lived in the house. (Daily) Museum sponsors concerts and programs throughout the year. Tours available, inquire for schedule. Museum shop. **$**

Seamen's Bethel. *15 Johnny Cake Hill, New Bedford (02740). Phone 508/992-3295.* (1832) "Whaleman's Chapel" referred to by Melville in *Moby Dick.* Prow-shaped pulpit later built to represent Melville's description. Also many cenotaphs dedicated to men lost at sea. Vespers third Sun each month. (Daily)

Steamship Authority. *Phone 508/477-8600. www. steamshipauthority.com.* New Bedford-Martha's Vineyard Ferry. Bus tours, car rentals on Martha's Vineyard. (Mid-May-mid-Oct, daily) Same-day round-trip and one-way trips available. Schedule may vary. **$$$$**

Special Events

Blessing of the Fleet. *Waterfront, New Bedford. Phone 508/999-5231.* Sept.

Feast of the Blessed Sacrament. *Madeira Ave, Hathaway St, and Tinkham St, New Bedford. Phone 508/992-6911. www.portuguesefeast.com.* North end of town. Largest Portuguese feast in North America; entertainment, parade and amusement rides. Three days usually beginning first weekend in Aug.

First Night New Bedford. *Purchase and William sts, New Bedford (02740). Phone 508/991-6200; toll-free 800/508-5353.* Historic waterfront and downtown. Celebration of arts and culture; fireworks. Dec 31.

Yankee Homecoming. *Barthholmes and Market sts, entire city of Newburyport, New Bedford. Phone 978/462-6680.* Celebration includes parades, fireworks, exhibits; river cruises; sailboat and canoe races; craft show; lobster feeds. Last Sat in July-first Sun in Aug.

Limited-Service Hotel

★ ★ **DAYS INN.** *500 Hathaway Rd, New Bedford (02740). Phone 508/997-1231; toll-free 800/329-7466; fax 508/984-7977. www.daysinn.com.* 151 rooms, 3 story. Check-in 3 pm, check-out 11 am. **$**

Restaurants

★ **ANTONIO'S.** *267 Coggeshall St, New Bedford (02746). Phone 508/990-3636.* American, Spanish menu. Lunch, dinner. Bar. Children's menu. Casual attire. No credit cards accepted. **$$**
🄳

★ ★ **FREESTONE'S CITY GRILL.** *41 William St, New Bedford (02740). Phone 508/993-7477; fax 508/984-4486. www.freestones.com.* The sumptuous mahogany and marble of Freestone's harks back to the buildings heyday as Citizen's Bank in the late 19th century. A popular lunch spot for visitors to the adjacent Whaling National Park, Freestone's also offers contemporary American fare in the evenings. Grilled meatloaf, for example, gets a spicy punch by incorporating andouille sausage into the blend. The chowder here is award-winning, and the drink menu is anything but typical. Desserts are homey and old-fashioned, from the hot fudge brownie to the carrot cake. Seafood menu. Lunch, dinner. Closed Labor Day, Thanksgiving, Dec 25. Bar. Children's menu. Casual attire. **$$**

★ ★ ★ **OCEANNA.** *95 William St, New Bedford (02740). Phone 508/997-8465.* Seafood menu. Lunch, dinner. Closed Sun. Bar. Children's menu. Casual attire. **$$**
🄳

Newburyport (A-8)

See also Amesbury

Settled 1635
Population 17,189
Elevation 37 ft
Area Code 978
Zip 01950
Information Greater Newburyport Chamber of Commerce & Industry, 38 R Merrimac St; phone 978/462-6680
Web Site www.newburyportchamber.org

Novelist John P. Marquand, who lived in Newburyport, said it "is not a museum piece although it sometimes looks it." High Street is surely a museum of American Federalist architecture. Ship owners and captains built these great houses. The birthplace of the US Coast Guard, Newburyport lies at the mouth of the Merrimack River. The city's early prosperity came from shipping and shipbuilding. It is now a thriving year-round tourist destination.

What to See and Do

Coffin House. *14 High Rd, Newburyport (01951). Phone 978/462-2634.* (Circa 1654) Developed in a series of enlargements, features 17th- and 18th-century kitchens, buttery, and parlor with early 19th-century wallpaper; furnishings of eight generations. Tours on the hour. (June-mid-Oct, first Sat of the month 11 am-5 pm) **$**

Cushing House Museum. *98 High St, Newburyport (01950). Phone 978/462-2681.* (Historical Society of Old Newbury; circa 1810) A Federalist-style mansion, once the home of Caleb Cushing, first envoy to China from US. Museum houses collections of needlework, paperweights, toys, paintings, furniture, silver, clocks, china; library. Also shed, carriage house, and 19th-century garden. (May-Nov, Tues-Fri 10 am-4 pm, Sat from noon; closed holidays) **$**

Custom House Maritime Museum. *25 Water St, Newburyport (01950). Phone 978/462-8681.* Collections of artifacts depicting maritime heritage of area; includes ship models, navigational instruments; decorative arts, library. (Apr-late Dec, Mon-Sat 10 am-4 pm, Sun from 1 pm) **$**

Parker River National Wildlife Refuge. *6 Plum Island Tpike, Newburyport (01950). 3 miles E on Plum Island. Phone 978/465-5753.* Natural barrier beach formed by 6 1/2 miles of beach and sand dunes is the home of many species of birds, mammals, reptiles, amphibians, and plants; saltwater and freshwater marshes provide resting and feeding place for migratory birds on the Atlantic Flyway. Hiking, bicycling, waterfowl hunting, nature trail. (Daily) Closed to public when parking lots are full. Contact Refuge Manager, Northern Blvd, Plum Island (01950).

Special Events

Arts, Flowers, & All that Jazz. *Downtown. Phone 978/462-6680. www.newburyportchamber.org.* Demonstrations, flower and garden show, crafts, exhibits, and jazz concerts. Sun-Mon of Memorial Day weekend.

Fall Harvest Festival. *Downtown. Phone 978/462-6680. www.newburyportchamber.org.* Juried crafts, music, entertainment, food, baking contest. Sun-Mon of Columbus Day weekend.

Yankee Homecoming. *Barthholmes and Market sts, entire city of Newburyport, New Bedford. Phone 978/462-6680.* Celebration includes parades, fireworks, exhibits; river cruises; sailboat and canoe races; craft show; lobster feeds. Last Sat in July-first Sun in Aug

Limited-Service Hotel

★ ★ **GARRISON INN.** *11 Brown Sq, Newburyport (01950). Phone 978/499-8500; fax 978/499-8555. www.garrisoninn.com.* Restored historic inn (1809).24 rooms, 4 story. Check-in 3 pm, check-out 11 am. Restaurant, bar. Children's activity center. **$**

Specialty Lodgings

CLARK CURRIER INN. *45 Green St, Newburyport (01950). Phone 978/465-8363. www.clarkcurrierinn.*

com. Built 1803 by a shipbuilder. 7 rooms, 3 story. Complimentary full breakfast. Check-in 3 pm, check-out 11 am. **$**

ESSEX STREET INN. *7 Essex St, Newburyport (01950). Phone 978/465-3148; fax 978/462-1907. www.essexstreetinn.com.* Built in 1801; fireplace. 19 rooms, 3 story. Complimentary continental breakfast. Check-in 3-9 pm, check-out 11 am. **$**

MORRILL PLACE. *209 High St, Newburyport (01950). Phone 978/462-2808; fax 978/462-9966.* Built in 1806. 9 rooms, 3 story. Pets accepted, some restrictions. Complimentary continental breakfast. Check-in 4 pm. Check-out noon. **$**

WINDSOR HOUSE. *38 Federal St, Newburyport (01950). Phone 978/462-3778; toll-free 888/873-5296; fax 978/465-3443. www.bbhost.com/windsorhouse.* Federal mansion (1786) built by lieutenant of the Continental Army for his wedding. 4 rooms, 3 story. Pets accepted, some restrictions. No children allowed. Complimentary full breakfast. Check-in 4 pm. Check-out 11 am. **$$**

Restaurants

★ ★ ★ **DAVID'S.** *11 Brown Sq, Newburyport (01950). Phone 978/462-8077; fax 978/462-8085. www.davidstavern.com.* A favorite of locals and visitors alike, this friendly restaurant serves a wide variety of American fare. Upstairs at The Rim, the theme is Asian. International menu. Dinner. Closed Jan 1, Dec 24-25. Bar. Children's menu. **$$$**

★ ★ **GLENN'S GALLEY.** *44 Merrimac St, Newburyport (01950). Phone 978/465-3811; fax 978/465-2013. www.glennsrestaurant.com.* Seafood menu. Dinner. Closed Mon; holidays. Bar. Children's menu. **$$**

★ **THE GROG.** *13 Middle St, Newburyport (01950). Phone 978/465-8008; fax 978/462-9505. www.thegrog.com.* International menu. Lunch, dinner. Closed Dec 25. Bar. **$$**

★ ★ **MICHAEL'S HARBORSIDE.** *1 Tournament Wharf, Newburyport (01950). Phone 978/462-7785; fax 978/465-9981. www.michaelsharborside.com.* Seafood menu. Lunch, dinner. Closed Thanksgiving, Dec 25. Bar. Outdoor seating. **$$**

★ ★ **TEN CENTER STREET.** *10 Center St, Newburyport (01950). Phone 978/462-6652; fax 978/462-6729. www.tencenterstreet.com.* In a restored 1800s Federal-style house. American menu. Lunch, dinner, Sun brunch. Closed Mon. Bar. Outdoor seating. **$$**

Newton (B-7)

See also Boston

Settled 1630
Population 83,829
Elevation 100 ft
Area Code 617
Information Chamber of Commerce, 281 Needham St, PO Box 590268, Newton 02459; phone 617/244-5300
Web Site www.nnchamber.com

Newton, the "Garden City," is actually a city of 13 suburban neighborhoods that have maintained their individual identities. Of the 13, eight have "Newton" in their names: Newton, Newtonville, Newton Centre, Newton Corner, Newton Highlands, West Newton, Newton Upper Falls, and Newton Lower Falls. Five colleges are located here: Boston College, Lasell College, Mount Ida College, Andover-Newton Theological School, and Aquinas Junior College.

What to See and Do

Charles River Canoe & Kayak Center. *2401 Commonwealth Ave, Newton (02466). Phone 617/965-5110. www.ski-paddle.com/cano/canoe.htm.* Whether you're an experienced paddler looking to rent boats by the hour or you're getting geared up to paddle for the first time, Charles River Canoe & Kayak is your starting point. The Charles River offers beautiful views of the Boston skyline and several area universities, as well as diverse waterfowl. Pack a picnic lunch to revive your energy. (Apr-Oct daily) **$$$$**

Jackson Homestead Museum. *527 Washington St, Newton (02458). Phone 617/552-7238.* (1809) Once a station on the Underground Railroad. Home of the Newton Historical Society. Changing exhibits; children's gallery; toys; textiles; and tools. (Tues-Sat and Sun afternoon) **$$**

Limited-Service Hotel

★ ★ **HOLIDAY INN.** *399 Grove St, Newton (02462). Phone 617/969-5300; toll-free 800/465-4329; fax*

617/965-4280. www.holiday-inn.com. 191 rooms, 7 story. Pets accepted. Check-in 3 pm, check-out noon. Restaurant, bar. Fitness room. Outdoor pool. **$**

Full-Service Hotels

★ ★ ★ **MARRIOTT BOSTON NEWTON.** *2345 Commonwealth Ave, Newton (02466). Phone 617/969-1000; toll-free 800/228-9290; fax 617/527-6914. www.marriott.com.* Perched along the Charles River, this property is just 15 minutes from downtown Boston and 5 minutes from the Waltham Business District. Business travelers will find a convenient 24-hour, self-serve business center and over 16,000 square feet of meeting space. 430 rooms, 7 story. Check-in 4 pm, check-out 1 pm. Restaurant, bar. Fitness room. Indoor pool, outdoor pool, whirlpool. Business center. **$**

★ ★ ★ **SHERATON NEWTON HOTEL.** *320 Washington St, Newton (02458). Phone 617/969-3010; toll-free 800/325-3535; fax 617/630-2976. www.sheraton.com.* All the rooms and suites at this property have a creative, contemporary décor with sleek white bedding; a well-designed work area; and warm, mustard-colored walls. Minutes from downtown Boston, an express bus departs for Faneuil Hall every 20 minutes. 272 rooms, 12 story. Pets accepted. Check-in 3 pm, check-out 11 am. High-speed Internet access. Restaurant, bar. Fitness room. Indoor pool. **$**

Restaurant

★ ★ ★ **LUMIERE.** *1293 Washington St, West Newton (02465). Phone 617/244-9199; fax 617/796-9178. www.lumiererestaurant.com.* From the spoon door handle at the entrance, to sheet music, light shades, and Scrabble tiles on the rest room doors, this restaurant's décor is warm and whimsical. The contemporary French cuisine goes beyond bistro without going all the way uptown. French, Mediterranean, Pacific menu. Dinner. Closed Mon; holidays. **$$$**

North Adams (A-2)

See also Williamstown

Settled 1745
Population 14,681
Elevation 707 ft
Area Code 413
Zip 01247
Information Northern Berkshire Chamber of Commerce, 75 North St, Suite 360, Pittsfield 01201; phone 413/663-3735
Web Site www.berkshirebiz.org

North Adams is an industrial community set in the beautiful four-season resort country of the northern Berkshires. Its factories make electronic components, textile machinery, wire, machine tools, paper boxes, and other products. Susan B. Anthony was born in nearby Adams in 1820.

What to See and Do

MASS MoCA. *1040 Mass MoCA Way, North Adams (01247). Phone 413/664-4481. www.massmoca.org.* Center for visual, performing, and media arts. Features unconventional exhibits and performances by renowned artists and cultural institutions. Rehearsals and production studios are open to the public. Tours available. (July-early Sept: daily 10 am-6 pm; rest of year: Wed-Mon 11 am-5 pm) **$$** Also here is

> **Kidspace.** *87 Marshall St, North Adams (01247). Phone 413/664-4481.* Children's gallery presents contemporary art in manner that is interesting and accessible. Includes hands-on activity stations where children can create their own works of art. (June-early Sept: daily noon-4 pm; rest of year: limited hours) **FREE**

Mohawk Trail State Forest. *Hwy 2, Charlemont. E on Hwy 2, near Charlemont. Phone 413/339-5504.* Spectacular scenery. Swimming, fishing; hiking, winter sports, picnicking, camping, log cabins. **$$**

Mount Greylock State Reservation. *Rockwell Rd, North Adams. 1 mile W on Hwy 2, then N on Notch Rd. Phone 413/499-4262.* Mount Greylock, the highest point in the state (3,491 feet), is here. War memorial tower at summit. Cross-country skiing, snowmobiles allowed. Picnicking. Lodge, snacks; campsites (mid-May-mid-Oct). Visitor center on Rockwell Road in Lanesborough, off Hwy 7.

Natural Bridge State Park. *1 1/4 miles NE on Hwy 8. Phone 413/663-6392.* A water-eroded marble bridge and rock formations, about 550 million years old, popularized by author Nathaniel Hawthorne. Picnicking. (Mid-May-mid-Oct) **$**

Savoy Mountain State Forest. *E on Hwy 2, near Florida, MA. Phone 413/664-9567.* Brilliant fall foliage. Swimming, fishing, boating (ramp); hiking and riding trails, hunting, winter sports, picnicking, camping, log cabins. Waterfall. **FREE**

Western Gateway Heritage State Park. *115 State St, North Adams (01247). Behind City Hall on Hwy 8. Phone 413/663-6312.* A restored freightyard with six buildings around a cobbled courtyard. Detailed historic exhibits on the construction of the Hoosac Railroad Tunnel. (Daily; closed holidays) **DONATION**

Special Events

Fall Foliage Festival. *57 Main St, North Adams (01247). Phone 413/664-6180. www.fallfoliageparade. com.* Parade, entertainment, dancing, children's activities. Late Sept-early Oct.

La Festa. *85 Main St, North Adams (01247). Phone 413/663-3782.* Ethnic festival, ethnic food, entertainment, events. Sixteen days beginning mid-June.

Limited-Service Hotel

★ ★ **HOLIDAY INN BERKSHIRES.** *40 Main St, North Adams (01247). Phone 413/663-6500; fax 413/663-6380. www.holiday-inn.com.* A great choice for families, the Holiday Inn Berkshires features big, bright rooms and a location central to many attractions. 86 rooms. Check-in 3 pm, check-out 11 am. Wireless Internet access. Restaurant, bar. Indoor pool, whirlpool. **$**

Full-Service Inn

★ ★ ★ **THE PORCHES INN.** *231 River St, North Adams (01247). Phone 413/664-0400; fax 413/664-0401. www.porches.com.* If you're looking for an urban getaway, head to The Porches Inn. Located behind the famed MASS MoCA museum in an industrialized area of North Adams, the inn features colorful, contemporary rooms and suites and a retro ambience. 52 rooms. Pets accepted; fee. Complimentary continental breakfast. Check-in 3 pm, check-out noon. Outdoor pool, whirlpool. **$$**

Northampton (B-3)

Settled 1673
Population 28,978
Elevation 140 ft
Area Code 413
Zip 01060
Information Chamber of Commerce and Visitor Center, 99 Pleasant St; phone 413/584-1900
Web Site www.explorenorthampton.com

When the famed concert singer Jenny Lind honeymooned in this town on the Connecticut River in 1852, she exclaimed, "Why, this is the paradise of America." But it wasn't always a peaceful town. Northampton was the scene of a frenzied religious revival movement in the first half of the 18th century. The movement stemmed from Jonathan Edwards, a Puritan who came to be regarded as the greatest preacher in New England. Later, the town was the home of President Calvin Coolidge. A granite memorial on the court house lawn honors Coolidge, who once served as mayor.

With its first-class theaters and restaurants, numerous antique shops and art galleries, and charming hotels and inns, Northampton has become a popular tourist destination, particularly among New Yorkers and Bostonians seeking a weekend getaway. The towns thriving arts scene can be credited, at least in part, to its close proximity to five colleges. Mount Holyoke College is in nearby South Hadley, while three schools—Amherst College, Hampshire College, and the University of Massachusetts—are located across the Connecticut River in Amherst. The nation's largest liberal arts college for women, Smith, is located in downtown Northampton. Smith's Museum of Art houses approximately 25,000 objects, including paintings by Picasso and Cézanne, a cast bronze sculpture by Rodin, and more than 5,700 photographic prints.

Just beyond the city limits, the rolling hills and quiet streams of the Pioneer Valley offer splendid recreational opportunities for outdoor enthusiasts. Be it on foot or bike or in a canoe or kayak, the valleys pastoral beauty begs to be explored.

What to See and Do

Arcadia Nature Center and Wildlife Sanctuary, Massachusetts Audubon Society. *127 Combs Rd,* *Easthampton (01027). 4 miles SW on Hwy 10, follow signs, in Northampton and Easthampton. Phone 413/584-3009. www.massaudubon.org.* Five hundred fifty acres on migratory flyway; an ancient oxbow of the Connecticut River; self-guiding nature trails; observation tower; courses and programs. Grounds (Mon-Sat; closed holidays). **$**

Calvin Coolidge Memorial Room. *20 West St, Northampton (01060). Forbes Library, Hwys 9 and 66. Phone 413/587-1011.* Displays of the late president's papers and correspondence; also books and articles on Coolidge. Memorabilia includes Native American headdress and beadwork given to him, Mrs. Coolidge's needlework, and photographs. (Mon-Thurs, Sat; closed holidays; schedule may vary) **FREE**

Historic Northampton Museum Houses. *46-66 Bridge St, Northampton (01060). Phone 413/584-6011.* All houses (Tues-Fri 10 am -4 pm, Sat-Sun from noon). **$$** Nearby are

> **Damon House.** *46 Bridge St, Northampton (01060). Phone 413/584-6011.* (1813) Permanent formal parlor exhibit (circa 1820).

> **Parsons House.** *58 Bridge St, Northampton (01060).* (Circa 1730) Contains exhibits on local architecture.

> **Shepherd House.** (1798) Includes the lifetime collection of one Northampton family and focuses on family lifestyle at the turn of the 19th century.

Look Park. *300 N Main St, Florence (01062). NW off Hwy 9. Phone 413/584-5457. www.lookpark.org.* Miniature train and Christenson Zoo; boating; tennis; picnicking; playgrounds, ball fields; also here is Pines Theater (musical entertainment, children's theater, and puppet programs, summer). Park (all year). Fees for most facilities. **$**

Smith College. *33 Elm St, Northampton (01063). Phone 413/584-2700. www.smith.edu.* (1871) (2,700 women) The largest private liberal arts college for women in the United States. On campus are Paradise Pond, named by Jenny Lind; Helen Hills Hills Chapel; William Allan Neilson Library with more than 1 million volumes; Center for the Performing Arts; Plant House and Botanical Gardens; Japanese Garden. Also here is

> **Museum of Art.** *Elm St, Northampton (01063). Phone 413/585-2763.* A fine collection with emphasis on American and European art of the 19th and 20th centuries. (Sept-May: Tues-Sun; rest of year: Tues-Sat; closed holidays)

Special Events

Eastern National Morgan Horse Show. *Three-County Fairgrounds, Damon Rd and Hwy 9, Northampton (01060).* Phone 413/584-2237. Late July.

Maple Sugaring. *99 Pleasant St, Northampton (01060).* Phone 413/584-1900. Visitors are welcome at many maple camps. Feb-Mar.

Springtime in Paradise. *Three-County Fairgrounds, Damon Rd and Hwy 9, Northampton (01060).* Phone 413/584-1900. Major arts festival. Late May.

Three-County Fair. *Three-County Fairgrounds, Damon Rd and Hwy 9, Northampton (01060).* Phone 413/584-2237. www.3countyfair.com. The nation's oldest agricultural fair. Agricultural exhibits, horse racing, parimutuel betting. (Labor Day week)

Limited-Service Hotels

★ ★ **CLARION HOTEL AND CONFERENCE CENTER.** *1 Atwood Dr, Northampton (01060).* Phone 413/586-1211; toll-free 800/582-2929; fax 413/586-0630. www.clarionhotel.com. This Clarion is a cross between a conference center and a country inn. With easy access off I-91, seven well-maintained meeting rooms, and a staff that understands the needs of an organization of business travelers, it is well designed for conferences. Yet the wood-paneled lobby and public areas have a rustic feel, with exposed brick, overstuffed furniture, and a large, welcoming gas fireplace. The lobby also opens onto a domed, plant-filled atrium that houses an indoor pool and video arcade. The dome lets light flood the hotel year-round—particularly welcome in the midst of a cold New England winter. 122 rooms, 2 story. Pets accepted; restrictions, fee. Complimentary continental breakfast. Check-in 3 pm, check-out 11 am. Restaurant, bar. Indoor pool, outdoor pool, children's pool. Tennis. **$**

★ ★ **THE HOTEL NORTHAMPTON.** *36 King St, Northampton (01060).* Phone 413/584-3100; toll-free 800/547-3529; fax 413/584-9455. www.hotelnorthampton.com. Built in 1927, this elegant brick Colonial Revival-style lodging—the most prominent in Northampton—is listed as a Historic Hotel by the National Trust for Historic Preservation. It's located on a busy street opposite the restored Calvin Theater, within walking distance of historic Northampton's many shops, eclectic restaurants, and cultural attractions. A narrow glass conservatory filled with plants surrounds half the building. The hotel's public areas celebrate its heritage, with framed historical material as well as handsome artwork ranging from Norman Rockwell prints to Japanese woodcuts; the clublike lobby has a large fireplace and lots of reading chairs, complete with a collection of old books on the mantle. Welcoming and spacious guest rooms, which have gracious foyers, feature colonial-inspired floral fabrics and furnishings. Dining options at the hotel include the light and airy Coolidge Park Cafe and the authentic New England Wiggins Tavern, with antiques, pewter and cast-iron implements, exposed beams, dark wood, and an open hearth. 99 rooms, 5 story. Complimentary continental breakfast. Check-in 2:30 pm, check-out 11 am. High-speed Internet access, wireless Internet access. Two restaurants, two bars. Fitness room. **$$**

Specialty Lodging

AUTUMN INN. *259 Elm St, Northampton (01060).* Phone 413/584-7660; fax 413/586-4808. www.autumninn.com. About it's a third of a mile from the main gates of Smith College and a mile from the center of Northampton, this hotel sits back from a busy street in an older residential area of town. The property was built in the 1960s to resemble a colonial-era Inn, and well it does. It looks like a two-story colonial brick home on a well-manicured lawn, and it fits in beautifully with the neighborhood's surrounding Victorian- and colonial-style homes. A huge hearth and wood-burning fireplace greet guests in the lobby; patterned after working kitchens of bygone eras, it is replete with copper kettles and cast-iron fixtures. In front of the hearth is a cozy area with tables and chairs where continental breakfast is served each morning. 32 rooms, 2 story. Complimentary continental breakfast. Check-in 3 pm, check-out 11 am. Outdoor pool. **$**

Restaurant

★ ★ **EASTSIDE GRILL.** *19 Strong Ave, Northampton (01060).* Phone 413/586-3347; fax 413/586-2406. www.eastsidegrill.com. American menu. Dinner. Closed Thanksgiving, Dec 24-25. Bar. **$$**

Orleans (Cape Cod) (D-10)

See also Eastham, Cape Cod

Settled 1693
Population 6,341
Elevation 60 ft
Area Code 508
Zip 02653
Information Cape Cod Chamber of Commerce, 5 Shootfly Hill Rd, PO Box 790, Hyannis 02601-0790; phone 508/362-3225 or toll-free 888/227-3263
Web Site www.capecodchamber.org

Orleans supposedly was named in honor of the Duke of Orleans after the French Revolution. The settlers worked at shipping, fishing, and salt production. Its history includes the dubious distinction of being the only town in America to have been fired upon by the Germans during World War I. The town is now a commercial hub for the summer resort colonies along the great stretch of Nauset Beach and the coves behind it. A cable station, which provided direct communication between Orleans and Brest, France, from 1897 to 1959, was restored to its original appearance and is now open to the public.

What to See and Do

Academy of Performing Arts. *120 Main St, Orleans (02653). Phone 508/255-1963. www.apa1.org.* Theater presents comedies, drama, musicals, dance. Workshops for all ages.

French Cable Station Museum. *41 S Orleans Rd, Orleans (02653). Hwy 28 and Cove Rd. Phone 508/240-1735.* Built in 1890 as the American end of the transatlantic cable from Brest, France. Original equipment for submarine cable communication on display. (July-Labor Day, Tues-Sat afternoons) **$$**

Nauset Beach. *Beach Rd, Orleans (02643). About 3 miles E of Hwy 6 on marked roads.* One of the most spectacular ocean beaches on the Atlantic coast is now within the boundaries of Cape Cod National Seashore. Swimming, surfing, fishing; lifeguards. Parking fee.

Limited-Service Hotels

★ **THE COVE.** *13 Hwy 28, Orleans (02653). Phone 508/255-1203; toll-free 800/343-2233; fax 508/255-*

7736. www.thecoveorleans.com. 47 rooms, 2 story. Check-in 3 pm, check-out 11 am. Outdoor pool. Business center. **$**

★ **NAUSET KNOLL MOTOR LODGE.** *223 Beach Rd, East Orleans (02643). Phone 508/255-2364; fax 508/255-6901. www.capecodtravel.com/nausetknoll.* 12 rooms. Closed late Oct-mid-Apr. Check-in 2 pm, check-out 10 am. **$**

Specialty Lodgings

THE PARSONAGE INN. *202 Main St, East Orleans (02643). Phone 508/255-8217; toll-free 888/422-8217; fax 508/255-8216. www.parsonageinn.com.* Originally a parsonage (1770) and cobbler's shop. 8 rooms, 2 story. Children over 6 years only. Complimentary full breakfast. Check-in 2-6 pm. Check-out 11 am. **$**

SHIP'S KNEES INN. *186 Beach Rd, East Orleans (02643). Phone 508/255-1312; fax 508/240-1351. www.shipskneesinn.com.* This inn, a restored sea captain's house (circa 1820), is located near the ocean. The rooms are individually decorated in nautical style and have many antiques and some four-poster beds. 16 rooms, 2 story. Children over 12 years only. Complimentary continental breakfast. Check-in 2-9 pm, check-out 10:30 am. Outdoor pool. Tennis. **$**

Restaurants

★ ★ **BARLEY NECK INN.** *5 Beach Rd, East Orleans (02653). Phone 508/255-0212; fax 508/255-3626. www.barleyneck.com.* The dining room at the Barley Neck Inn is one of Cape Cod's treasures. Located within a sea captain's home that dates to 1868, this restaurant has one of the nicest settings around. Antique-filled rooms romance diners, who feast primarily on seafood dishes with a French influence. A selection from the well-rounded wine list is the perfect complement to the distinctive cuisine. American menu. Dinner. **$$**

★ **THE BEACON ROOM.** *23 West Rd, Orleans (02653). Phone 508/255-2211; fax 508/896-2608. www.beaconroom.com.* A covered porch and intimate dining room make for an appealing setting at the delightful Beacon Room, and the eclectic menu covers all the bases with large portions of clever food. American menu. Lunch, dinner. Bar. Casual attire. **$$**

★ ★ ★ **CAPTAIN LINNELL HOUSE.** *137 Skaket Beach Rd, Orleans (02653). Phone 508/255-3400; fax 508/255-5377. www.linnell.com.* Chef/owner Bill Conway delivers a delightful dining experience at this charming and romantic restaurant. Take a walk out to the Victorian gazebo and enjoy the smell of lavender and the refreshing ocean breeze, and then settle in for a cozy candlelit dinner. Continental menu. Dinner. Closed Mon; also mid-Feb-Mar. Bar. Children's menu. Reservations recommended. **$$**

★ **DOUBLE DRAGON INN.** *Hwys 6A and 28, Orleans (02653). Phone 508/255-4100.* Chinese menu. Lunch, dinner, late-night. Closed Thanksgiving. Bar. Casual attire. **$**

★ **LOBSTER CLAW.** *Hwy 6A, Orleans (02653). Phone 508/255-1800; fax 508/240-2621. www.lobster-claw.com.* Nautical décor is all the rage at the delightfully whimsical Lobster Claw restaurant, formerly a cranberry packing factory. This Cape classic is frequented by families who come here for the tongue-in-cheek take on the Massachusetts coast. Lobster is the main event, served broiled, boiled, baked, or stuffed, but the menu does include many other seafood selections. American, seafood menu. Lunch, dinner. Closed Nov-Mar. Bar. Children's menu. Casual attire. **$$**

★ ★ **MAHONEY'S ATLANTIC BAR AND GRILL.** *28 Main St, Orleans (02653). Phone 508/255-5505; fax 508/240-3012. www.mahoneysatlantic.com.* Mahoney's Atlantic Bar and Grill feels like the local watering hole, yet this casual, tavern-style restaurant shows off its culinary talents with an inventive New American menu. Seafood drives the menu, although meat and vegetarian entrées run a close second. Good food and entertainment go hand in hand at Mahoneys, with frequent live music performances. American menu. Dinner. Closed Thanksgiving, Dec 25. Bar. Casual attire. **$$**

★ ★ **NAUSET BEACH CLUB.** *222 E Main St, East Orleans (02643). Phone 508/255-8547; fax 508/255-8872. www.nausetbeachclub.com.* The Nauset Beach Club shares a taste of Northern Italy with guests. This inviting restaurant features some of the most beloved recipes from northern Italy, and the homemade pastas and desserts are noteworthy. Local seafood is incorporated into many of the enticing entrées. Wine is especially important here, where the list pays tribute to many of the small vineyards in the United States and abroad. Italian menu. Dinner. Bar. Casual attire. Reservations recommended. **$$$**

★ ★ **OLD JAILHOUSE TAVERN.** *28 West Rd, Orleans (02653). Phone 508/255-5245; fax 508/255-9109. www.oldjailhousetavern.com.* The Old Jailhouse Tavern, located in part of an old "jailhouse," promises a good time. From jailbirds chicken wings to hung jury sandwiches, this Orleans establishment plays off its former incarnation as an old lockup on its American menu. Perfect for groups, this restaurant even has a special section of the menu devoted to items that are ideal for sharing. American menu. Lunch, dinner, late-night, Sun brunch. Closed Thanksgiving, Dec 25. Bar. Children's menu. Casual attire. Outdoor seating. **$$**

★ **SIR CRICKET'S FISH AND CHIPS.** *38 Rt 6A, Orleans (02653). Phone 508/255-4453.* The English-style fish and chips sold here are the ostensible draw, but fried seafood of all descriptions keeps many loyal fans returning to this take-out window attached to the Nauset Lobster Pool. The fried oyster roll and simple fried fish sandwich are some of the best anywhere on the Cape. If you don't want to eat in the car, there are a couple of tiny tables set up on the asphalt next to the soda machine. Seafood menu. Lunch, dinner. Children's menu. Casual attire. No credit cards accepted. **$**

★ ★ **THE YARDARM.** *48 Hwy 28, Orleans (02653). Phone 508/255-4840; fax 508/240-7206. www.yardarmrestaurant.com.* Its location just five minutes from Nauset Beach and Rock Harbor explains the seafood-driven menu at The Yardarm. This well-liked pub is a popular hangout for locals, who come here for the chowder and nightly specials. Yankee pot roast, corned beef and cabbage, and other pub grub round out the menu. American menu. Lunch, dinner, Sun brunch. Bar. Children's menu. Casual attire. **$$**

Pittsfield (B-2)

See also Lenox, Stockbridge and West Stockbridge

Settled 1743
Population 48,622
Elevation 1,039 ft
Area Code 413
Zip 01201
Information Berkshire Visitors Bureau, Berkshire Common; phone 413/443-9186 or toll-free 800/237-5747
Web Site www.berkshires.org

Beautifully situated in the Berkshire Hills vacation area, this is also an old and important manufacturing center. It is the home of the Berkshire Life Insurance Company (chartered in 1851) and of industries that make machinery, plastics, gauges, and paper products.

What to See and Do

Arrowhead. *780 Holmes Rd, Pittsfield (01201). Phone 413/442-1793.* (1780) Herman Melville wrote *Moby Dick* while living here from 1850 to 1863; historical exhibits, furniture, costumes; gardens. Video presentation. Gift shop. Headquarters of Berkshire County Historical Society. (Memorial Day weekend-Oct, daily) **$$**

Berkshire Museum. *39 South St (Hwy 7), Pittsfield (01201). Phone 413/443-7171. www.berkshiremuseum. org.* Museum of art, natural science, and history, featuring American 19th- and 20th-century paintings; works by British, European masters; artifacts from ancient civilizations; exhibits on Berkshire County history; aquarium; changing exhibits; films, lectures, children's programs. (July-Aug: daily; rest of year: Tues-Sun; closed holidays) **$$$**

Bousquet. *101 Dan Fox Dr, Pittsfield (01201). 2 miles S on Hwy 7, then 1 mile W, on Dan Fox Dr. Phone 413/442-8316. www.bousquets.com.* Two double chairlifts, three rope tows; snowmaking, patrol, school, rentals; cafeteria, bar, daycare. Longest run 1 mile; vertical drop 750 feet. Night skiing. (Dec-Mar, daily) **$$$$**

Brodie Mountain. *10 miles N on Hwy 7. Phone 413/738-5500. www.skibrodie.com.* Four double chairlifts, two rope tows; patrol, school, rentals, snowmaking; bar, cafeteria, restaurant; nursery. (Nov-Mar, daily) Cross-country trails with rentals and instruction. Half-day rates. Tennis, racquetball, winter camping. **$$$$**

Canoe Meadows Wildlife Sanctuary. *472 W Mountain Rd, Pittsfield (01201). Phone 413/637-0320. www.massaudubon.org.* Two hundred sixty-two acres with 3 miles of trails, woods, open fields, ponds; bordering the Housatonic River. (Tues-Sun 7 am-dusk) **$**

Hancock Shaker Village. *Hwys 20 and 41, Pittsfield. 5 miles W. Phone 413/443-0188. www.hancockshakervillage. org.* An original Shaker site (1790-1960); now a living history museum of Shaker life, crafts, and farming. Large collection of Shaker furniture and artifacts in 20 restored buildings, including the Round Stone Barn, set on 1,200 scenic acres in the Berkshires. Exhibits; seasonal craft demonstrations, Discovery Room activities, café (seasonal); farm animals, heirloom herb and vegetable gardens; museum shop; picnicking. **$$$**

Jiminy Peak. *37 Corey Rd, Hancock (01237). 9 miles N, then W, between Hwy 7 and Hwy 43. Phone 413/738-5500. www.jiminypeak.com.* One six-passanger, three double chairlifts, J-bar, two quads, three triples; patrol, school, rentals, restaurant, two cafeterias, bar, lodge. Longest run 2 miles; vertical drop 1,140 feet. (Thanksgiving-early Apr, daily) Night skiing. Half-day rates. Also trout fishing; 18-hole miniature golf; Alpine slide and tennis center (Memorial Day-Labor Day); fee for activities. **$$$$**

Special Event

South Mountain Concerts. *South St, Pittsfield (01201). 2 miles S on Hwys 7, 20. Phone 413/442-2106.* Chamber music concerts. Sept-Oct, Sun.

Limited-Service Hotel

★ ★ **CROWNE PLAZA HOTEL.** *1 West St, Pittsfield (01201). Phone 413/499-2000; toll-free 800/227-6963; fax 413/442-0449. www.berkshirecrowne.com.* Just minutes from Tanglewood, the Norman Rockwell Museum, the Hancock Shaker Village, and summer theater, this modern, centrally located hotel offers an alternative to the more prevalent inns and bed-and-breakfasts populating the area. A curved staircase inside a large, welcoming lobby of warm wood and live plants sweeps up to second-floor restaurants and meeting rooms. Guest rooms are large and attractive with one amenity that, for many, is even nicer than the in-room coffee, wireless Internet, or direct-dial phone: Fido and Fluffy are more than welcome. 179 rooms, 12 story. Pets accepted; fee. Check-in 3 pm, check-out noon. High-speed Internet access. Restaurant, bar. Fitness room. Indoor pool, whirlpool. **$**

Full-Service Resort

★ ★ **JIMINY PEAK MOUNTAIN RESORT.** *37 Corey Rd, Hancock (01237). Phone 413/738-5500; toll-free 800/882-8859; fax 413/738-5513. www.jiminypeak.com.* 96 rooms, 3 story. Check-in 4 pm, check-out 10:30 am. Restaurant. Children's activity center. Fitness room. Two outdoor pools, whirlpool. Tennis. Ski in/ski out. **$**

Restaurant

★ ★ **DAKOTA.** *1035 South St, Pittsfield (01201). Phone 413/499-7900; fax 413/499-8610. www.dakotarestaurant. com.* American menu. Lunch, dinner, Sun brunch. Closed Thanksgiving, Dec 25. Bar. Children's menu. Casual attire. Reservations recommended. **$$**

Plymouth (C-8)

Settled 1620
Population 51,701
Elevation 50 ft
Area Code 508
Zip 02360
Information Destination Plymouth, 130 Water St; phone 508/747-7525 or toll-free 800/872-1620
Web Site www.visit-plymouth.com

On December 21, 1620, 102 men, women, and children arrived on the *Mayflower* to found the first permanent European settlement north of Virginia. Although plagued by exposure, cold, hunger, and disease during the terrible first winter, the colony was firmly established by the next year. Plymouth Rock lies under an imposing granite colonnade, marking the traditional place of landing.

Plymouth now combines a summer resort, beaches, a harbor full of pleasure craft, an active fishing town, and a remarkable series of restorations of the original town.

What to See and Do

Burial Hill. *Just W of Town Square.* Governor Bradford is buried here.

Cole's Hill. *Across the street from Plymouth Rock.* Here Pilgrims who died during the first winter were secretly buried.

Harlow Old Fort House. *119 Sandwich St, Plymouth (02360). Phone 508/746-0012.* (1677) Pilgrim household crafts; spinning, weaving, and candle-dipping demonstrations; herb garden. (July-Aug, Tues-Fri) **$**

Hedge House. *126 Water St, Plymouth (02360). Opposite Town Wharf. Phone 508/746-0012.* (1809) Period furnishings, special exhibits. (June-Oct, Thurs-Sat) **$**

Howland House. *33 Sandwich St, Plymouth (02360). Phone 508/746-9590.* (1666) Restored Pilgrim house has 17th- and 18th-century furnishings. (Memorial Day-mid-Oct, Mon-Sat, also Sun afternoons and Thanksgiving) **$**

Mayflower Society House Museum. *4 Winslow St, Plymouth. Off North St. Phone 508/746-2590.* National headquarters of the General Society of Mayflower Descendants. House built in 1754; nine rooms with 17th- and 18th-century furnishings. Formal garden. (July-Labor Day: daily; Memorial Day weekend-June and early Sept-Oct: Fri-Sun) **$**

Myles Standish State Forest. *194 Cranberry Rd, South Carver (02366). S on Hwy 3, exit 5, Long Pond. Phone 508/866-2526. www.mass.gov/dcr.* Approximately 15,000 acres. Swimming, bathhouse, fishing, boating; hiking and bicycle trails, riding, hunting, winter sports, picnicking (fee), camping (fee; dump station).

National Monument to the Forefathers. *Allerton St and Hwy 44, Plymouth (02360). Phone 508/746-1790.* Built between 1859 and 1889 (at a cost of $155,000) to depict the virtues of the Pilgrims. At 81 feet, it is the tallest solid granite monument in the United States. (May-Oct, daily) **FREE**

Ocean Spray Cranberry World. *158 Water St, Plymouth (02360). Phone 508/747-2350.* Visitor Center with exhibits of the history and cultivation of the cranberry. Half-hour self-guided tours. (May-Nov) **$$$$**

Pilgrim Hall Museum. *75 Court St, Plymouth (02360). On Hwy 3A. Phone 508/746-1620. www.pilgrimhall. org.* (1824) Decorative arts and possessions of first Pilgrims and their descendants; includes furniture, household items, ceramics; only known portrait of a *Mayflower* passenger. (Daily; closed Jan, Dec 25) **$$**

Plymouth Colony Winery. *56 Pinewood Rd, Plymouth (02360). Hwy 44 W, left on Pinewood Rd. Phone 508/747-3334.* Working cranberry bogs. Wine tasting. Watch cranberry harvest activities in fall. Winery (Apr-late Dec: daily; Mar: Fri-Sun; also holidays). **FREE**

Plymouth Harbor Cruises. *State Pier, Plymouth (02360). Phone 508/747-3434. www.plymouthharborcruises.com.* One-hour cruises of historic harbor aboard *Pilgrim Belle*, a Mississippi-style paddlewheeler. (Mid-May-Mid-Oct, daily) Departs from State Pier. **$$$**

Plymouth Plantation/*Mayflower II*. *137 Warren Ave, Plymouth (02360). Take Hwy 93 S to Hwy 3 S, exit 4 (Plimoth Plantation Hwy). Continue on Plimoth Plantation Hwy for approximately 1 mile and take the exit for the museum. At the end of the exit ramp, turn right and proceed up the street for 20 yards. Turn right at the sign for the museum into the driveway. Phone 508/746-*

1622. www.plimoth.org. The Plimoth Plantation, which re-creates a 1627 Pilgrim village, reflects an old-fashioned spelling of the colony that now serves to differentiate the plantation from the modern town. The actors at the plantation play their roles faithfully, pretending no knowledge of the 21st (or even the 18th) century; they wear and use only the clothing, equipment, tools, and cookware that would have been available in the late 17th century. The plantation is large and takes a bit of walking to see. The *Mayflower II* is a full-scale reproduction of the *Mayflower* built by J. W. & A. Upham shipyard in England with oak timbers, hand-forged nails, linen canvas sails, hemp rope, and other historically accurate details. It was sailed from England to Plymouth in 1957 on a 55-day voyage and has remained on display at Plimoth Plantation ever since. Plan to spend a half day to a full day for both exhibits. (Apr-Nov, daily; closed Dec-Mar) **$$$$** On the plantation are

1627 Pilgrim Village. *137 Warren Ave, Plymouth (02362).* Fort-Meetinghouse and 14 houses. Costumed people portray actual residents of Plymouth and re-create life in an early farming community.

Hobbamock's (Wampanoag) Homesite. A large bark-covered house representing Hobbamock's dwelling, as well as specially crafted tools and artifacts, depict the domestic environment of the Wampanoag culture. Staff members explain this rich heritage from a modern-day perspective.

Visitor Center. *137 Warren Ave, Plymouth (02362).* Provides visitors with introduction to this unique museum. Orientation program includes a 12-minute multi-image screen presentation. Exhibits; educational services; museum shop; restaurants, picnic area.

Plymouth Rock. *Phone 508/866-2580.* Water St, on the harbor.

Provincetown Ferry. *State Pier, Plymouth (02360). Phone 508/747-2400; toll-free 800/242-2469. www. provincetownferry.com.* Round-trip passenger ferry departs State Pier in the morning, returns in the evening. (Mid-June-Labor Day: daily; May-mid-June and after Labor Day-Oct: weekends) **$$$$**

Richard Sparrow House. *42 Summer St, Plymouth (02360). Phone 508/747-1240. www.sparrowhouse.com.* (1640) Plymouth's oldest restored home; craft gallery, pottery made on premises. (Memorial Day weekend-Thanksgiving, Mon-Tues, Thurs-Sun; gallery open through late Dec) **$**

Site of First Houses. *Leyden and Water sts, Plymouth.* Marked by tablets.

Spooner House. *27 North St, Plymouth (02360). Phone 508/746-0012.* (1747) Occupied by Spooner family for five generations and furnished with their heirlooms. Collections of Asian export wares, period furniture. (June-Oct, Thurs-Sat) **$**

Swimming. Six public beaches.

Village Landing Marketplace. *170 Water St, Plymouth (02660). Near junction Hwy 44 and Hwy 3A.* Modeled after colonial marketplace; contains a restaurant and specialty shops. Overlooks historic Plymouth Harbor.

Whale-watching. *10 Town Wharf, Plymouth (02360). Phone 508/746-2643. www.captjohn.com.* Four-hour trip to Stellwagen Bank to view world's largest mammals. (Early May-mid-Oct: daily; early Apr-early May and mid-Oct-early Nov: weekends) **$$$$**

Special Events

America's Hometown Thanksgiving Celebration. *Phone 508/747-7525; toll-free 800/872-1620.* Programs for various events may be obtained by contacting Destination Plymouth. Nov (Throughout Thanksgiving weekend).

Autumnal Feasting. *137 Warren Ave, Plymouth (02360). Phone toll-free 800/872-1620.* Plimoth Plantation's 1627 Pilgrim Village. A harvest celebration with Dutch colonists from Fort Amsterdam re-creating a 17th-century event. Activities, feasting, games. Columbus Day weekend.

Destination Plymouth Sprint Triathlon. *194 Cranberry Rd, South Carver (02366).* Myles Standish State Forest (see). National Championship qualifier includes 1/2-mile swim, 12-mile bike ride, and 4-mile run. July.

Pilgrim's Progress. *Phone toll-free 800/872-1620.* A reenactment of Pilgrims going to church, from Cole's Hill to Burial Hill. Each Fri in Aug; also Thanksgiving.

Limited-Service Hotels

★ **BEST WESTERN COLD SPRING.** *188 Court St, Plymouth (02360). Phone 508/746-2222; toll-free 800/678-8667; fax 508/746-2744. www.bwcoldspring. com.* 60 rooms. Closed Jan-Mar. Complimentary continental breakfast. Check-in 2 pm, check-out 11 am. **$**

★ ★ **RADISSON HOTEL PLYMOUTH HARBOR.** *180 Water St, Plymouth (02360). Phone 508/747-4900; toll-free 800/333-3333; fax 508/746-2609. www.radisson.com.* Located on scenic Plymouth Harbor midway between Cape Cod and Boston, this inn is near many historic attractions, including Plymouth Rock. 175 rooms, 4 story. Check-in 3 pm, check-out 11 am. High-speed Internet access. Restaurant, bar. Fitness room. Indoor pool. **$**
⚐ ⌂

Specialty Lodgings

THE COLONIAL HOUSE INN. *207 Sandwich St (Hwy 3A), Plymouth (02360). Phone 508/747-4274; toll-free 866/747-4274. www.thecolonialhouseinn.com.* 4 rooms. Complimentary continental breakfast. Check-in 4-7 pm, check-out 11 am. Beach. Indoor pool. **$$**
⌂

JOHN CARVER INN. *25 Summer St, Plymouth (02360). Phone 508/746-7100; toll-free 800/274-1620; fax 508/746-8299. www.johncarverinn.com.* 79 rooms, 3 story. Check-in 3 pm, check-out 11 am. Restaurant, bar. Outdoor pool. **$$**
⌂

THE MABBETT HOUSE. *7 Cushman St, Plymouth (02360). Phone 508/747-1044; toll-free 888/622-2388; fax 508/747-1044. www.mabbetthouse.com.* Colonial Revival house; artifacts collected from world travels. 3 rooms, 2 story. Children over 12 years only. Complimentary full breakfast. Check-in 4:30 pm. Check-out 10:30 am. **$**
🅑

Restaurant

★ **HEARTH AND KETTLE.** *25 Summer St, Plymouth (02360). Phone 508/746-7100; fax 508/746-8299. www.johncarverinn.com.* Servers dressed in colonial attire. Seafood, steak menu. Breakfast, lunch, dinner. Closed Dec 25. Bar. Children's menu. **$$**

Provincetown (Cape Cod) (C-9)

Settled circa 1700
Population 3,431
Elevation 40 ft
Area Code 508

Zip 02657
Information Chamber of Commerce, 307 Commercial St, PO Box 1017; phone 508/487-3424
Web Site www.capecodaccess.com/provincetown-chamber

Provincetown is a startling mixture of heroic past and easygoing present; the area may have been explored by Leif Ericson in AD 1004. It is certain that the *Mayflower* anchored first in Provincetown Harbor while the Mayflower Compact, setting up the colony's government, was signed aboard the ship. Provincetown was where the first party of Pilgrims came ashore. A bronze tablet at Commercial Street and Beach Highway marks the site of the Pilgrims' first landing. The city attracts many tourists who come each summer to explore the narrow streets and rows of picturesque old houses.

What to See and Do

Commercial Street. *Commercial St, Provincetown.* To view a shopping district that's steeped in history and still thriving today, visit Provincetowns Commercial Street. Stretching more than 3 miles in length, the narrow street sports art galleries, shops, clubs, restaurants, and hotels. When the street was constructed in 1835, the houses that backed up to it all faced the harbor, which was the principle area of business activity. As you tour the street, note that many of those homes were turned 180 degrees to face the street or had a new front door crafted in the back of the house.

Expedition Whydah's Sea Lab & Learning Center. *16 MacMillan Wharf, Provincetown (02657). Phone 508/487-8899. www.whydah.com.* Archaeological site of sunken pirate ship *Whydah*, struck by storms in 1717. Learn about the recovery of the ship's pirate treasure, the lives and deaths of pirates, and the history of the ship and its passengers. (Apr-mid-Oct: daily; mid-Oct-Dec: weekends and school holidays) **$$**

⭐ **Pilgrim Monument & Museum.** *1 High Pole Hill, Provincetown (02657). Phone 508/487-1310. www.pilgrim-monument.org.* A 252-foot granite tower commemorating the Pilgrims' 1620 landing in the New World; provides an excellent view. (Summer, daily) **$$** Admission includes

Provincetown Museum. *1 High Pole Hill, Provincetown (02657). Phone 508/487-1310.* Exhibits include whaling equipment, scrimshaw, ship models, artifacts from shipwrecks; Pilgrim Room with scale model diorama of the merchant ship *Mayflower*; Donald MacMillan's Arctic exhibit; antique fire engine and firefighting equipment; theater history display. (Summer, daily)

Provincetown Art Association & Museum. *460 Commercial St, Provincetown (02657). Phone 508/487-1750. www.paam.org.* Changing exhibits; museum store. (Late May-Oct: daily; rest of year: weekends) **DONATION**

Recreation. Swimming at surrounding beaches, including Town Beach, west of the village, Herring Cove and Race Point, on the ocean side. Tennis, cruises, beach buggy tours, and fishing available.

Town Wharf (MacMillan Wharf). *Commercial and Standish sts, Provincetown (02657).* Center of maritime activity. Also here is

    ***Portuguese Princess* Whale Watch.** *Phone 508/487-2651; toll-free 800/442-3188.* 100-foot boats offer 3 1/2-hour narrated whale-watching excursions. Naturalist aboard. (Apr-Oct, daily) **$$$$**

Whale-watching. *307 Commercial St, Provincetown (02657).* Dolphin Fleet of Provincetown. *Phone 508/240-3636; toll-free 800/826-9300. www.whalewatch.com.* Offers 3 1/2- to 4-hour trips (mid-Apr-Oct, daily). Research scientists from the Provincetown Center for Coastal Studies are aboard each trip to lecture on the history of the whales being viewed. **$$$$**

Special Event

Provincetown Portuguese Festival. *MacMillian Wharf, Provincetown (02657). Phone 508/487-3424.* Provincetown's fisherman of Portuguese ancestry started this enduring festival over 50 years ago. Each year in late June, the local bishop says Mass at St. Peter's Church and then leads a procession to MacMillan Wharf, where he blesses a parade of fishing boats. The festival that follows features fireworks, concerts, dancing, Portuguese art, and delightful food choices. If you aren't in town for the Provincetown Blessing, check out similar events in Falmouth (July 4) and Hyannis (early July). Last week in June.

Limited-Service Hotels

★ ★ **BEST WESTERN TIDES BEACHFRONT MOTOR INN.** *837 Commercial St, Provincetown (02657). Phone 508/487-1045; toll-free 800/780-7234; fax 508/487-3557. www.bestwestern.com.* 64 rooms, 2 story. Closed mid-Oct-mid-May. Check-in 2 pm, check-out 11 am. Restaurant. Outdoor pool. Beach. **$**

★ **WATERMARK INN.** *603 Commercial St, Provincetown (02657). Phone 508/487-0165; fax 508/487-2383. www.watermark-inn.com.* 10 rooms, 2 story, all suites. Check-in 3 pm. Check-out 11 am. Beach. **$**

Full-Service Resorts

★ **THE MASTHEAD RESORT.** *31-41 Commercial St, Provincetown (02657). Phone 508/487-0523; toll-free 800/395-5095; fax 508/481-9251. www.capecodtravel.com/masthead.* 10 rooms, 2 story. Check-in 4 pm, check-out 10 am. Beach. **$**

★ ★ **PROVINCETOWN INN.** *1 Commericial St, Provincetown (02657). Phone 508/487-9500; toll-free 800/942-5388; fax 508/487-2911. www.provincetowninn.com.* 100 rooms, 2 story. Complimentary continental breakfast. Check-in 3 pm, check-out 11 am. Restaurant, bar. Outdoor pool. Beach. **$**

Specialty Lodgings

CROWNE POINTE HISTORIC INN. *82 Bradford St, Provincetown (02657). Phone 508/487-6767; fax 508/487-5554. www.crownepointe.com.* 40 rooms. Complimentary full breakfast. Check-in 3 pm, check-out 11 am. High-speed Internet access. **$$$**

FAIRBANKS INN. *90 Bradford St, Provincetown (02657). Phone 508/487-0386; toll-free 800/324-7265; fax 508/487-3540. www.fairbanksinn.com.* Built in 1776; courtyard. 14 rooms, 2 story. Children over 15 years only. Complimentary continental breakfast. Check-in 2-8 pm. Check-out 11:30 am. **$**

SNUG COTTAGE. *178 Bradford St, Provincetown (02657). Phone 508/487-1616; toll-free 800/432-2334; fax 508/487-5123. www.snugcottage.com.* Built in 1820. 8 rooms, 2 story. Complimentary full breakfast. Check-in 3-9 pm. Check-out 11 am. **$$**

SOMERSET HOUSE. *378 Commercial St, Provincetown (02657). Phone 508/487-0383; toll-free 800/575-1850; fax 508/487-4746. www.somersethouseinn.com.* Restored 1850s house. 13 rooms, 3 story. Complimentary full breakfast. Check-in 3-9 pm. Check-out 11 am. Beach. **$$**

WATERSHIP INN. *7 Winthrop St, Provincetown (02657). Phone 508/487-0094; toll-free 800/330-9413. www.watershipinn.com.* Built in 1820.15 rooms, 3 story. Complimentary continental breakfast. Check-in 2-9 pm. Check-out 11:30 am. **$**

🅳

WHITE WIND INN. *174 Commercial St, Provincetown (02657). Phone 508/487-1526; toll-free 888/449-9463; fax 508/487-4792. www.whitewindinn.com.* Located opposite the harbor, this inn (1845) was a former shipbuilder's home. 12 rooms, 3 story. Pets accepted, some restrictions; fee. Complimentary continental breakfast. Check-in 2-9 pm, check-out 11 am. **$**

🅳 🐾

Restaurants

★ ★ **CAFE EDWIGE.** *333 Commercial St, Provincetown (02657). Phone 508/487-2008.* In a town where many summer folk don't get up until nearly noon, Edwige corners the market in gourmet breakfasts by serving until 1 pm. But chef Stephen Frappolli saves his best New American chops for evening, reveling in New England seafood with dishes like planked local codfish with roasted corn and shiitake mushrooms, and what many consider P'Town's best crab cakes. It's an easy place to miss: Edwige is on the second level. American menu. Breakfast, dinner. Closed weekdays Labor Day-mid-June; also Oct-Apr. **$**

🅳

★ **FANIZZI'S BY THE SEA.** *539 Commercial St, Provincetown (02657). Phone 508/487-1964; fax 508/487-7336. www.fanizzisrestaurant.com.* American, Italian menu. Lunch, dinner. Bar. Children's menu. Casual attire. Reservations recommended. **$$$**

🅳

★ ★ **FRONT STREET.** *230 Commercial St, Provincetown (02657). Phone 508/487-9715; fax 508/487-7748. www.frontstreetrestaurant.com.* A lovely Victorian building welcomes guests to the well-received Front Street restaurant. This chef-owned restaurant takes great pride in its artful nouveau cuisine. Two menus define the culinary experience here, and whether you choose from the authentic Italian menu or the weekly changing continental one, you are sure to be delighted with the results. Italian menu. Dinner. Closed Jan-Apr. Bar. Casual attire. Reservations recommended. **$$**

★ ★ **LOBSTER POT.** *321 Commercial St, Provincetown (02657). Phone 508/487-0842; fax* *508/487-4863. www.ptownlobsterpot.com.* Perhaps the quintessential Olde Cape Cod restaurant in a town of hip eateries, the Lobster Pot nonetheless thrives by keeping everything as simple as possible, from steamed clams to steamed lobster to the accompanying cole slaw and French fries. There's almost always a line, so snagging a table on the outdoor deck is purely luck of the draw. After your meal, stop by the lobster and chowder market and pick up your favorite items to take home. Seafood menu. Lunch, dinner. Closed Dec-Mar. Bar. Children's menu. Casual attire. **$$$**

🅳

★ ★ **LORRAINE'S RESTAURANT.** *133 Commercial St, Provincetown (02657). Phone 508/487-6074. www.lorrainesrestaurant.com.* New American meets Mexican cuisine at the popular Lorraine's Restaurant. From its scenic waterfront location to its easygoing atmosphere, this place practically defines casual dining. Open year-round, this restaurant caters to a laid-back crowd that enjoys a good meal in a cozy environment. Mexican menu. Dinner, late-night. Closed Dec-Mar. Casual attire. **$$**

★ ★ **MARTIN HOUSE.** *157 Commercial St, Provincetown (02657). Phone 508/487-1327; fax 508/487-4514. www.themartinhouse.com.* A warren of tiny, rustic rooms makes up the dining spaces in this utterly charming 18th-century house with five working fireplaces. In summer, you can also dine alfresco by a fountain on the garden terrace. The romantic mood is enhanced by a sleekly contemporary menu that features nightly variants on local oysters, foie gras, and seafood soups (like crab and shrimp with green curry). Vegetarians always have at least one well-considered option, often employing seitan (wheat meat). American menu. Dinner, brunch. Closed Mon-Wed; also Jan. Bar. Reservations recommended. Outdoor seating. **$$$**

★ ★ **THE MEWS RESTAURANT & CAFE.** *429 Commercial St, Provincetown (02657). Phone 508/487-1500; fax 508/487-3700. www.mews.com.* Tucked away in the art gallery district, The Mews Restaurant & Café shares two personalities with diners. The first-floor dining room dazzles guests with its beachfront views, stylish setting, and cosmopolitan cuisine, while the upstairs café has an airy feel with a lighter menu. International menu. Dinner, Sun brunch. Bar. Casual attire. **$$**

★ ★ **NAPI'S.** *7 Freeman St, Provincetown (02657). Phone 508/487-1145; toll-free 800/571-6274; fax 508/487-7123. www.napis-restaurant.com.* Napi's takes diners on an art-filled journey around the world. Located on a quiet side street, this restaurant has an art gallery feel, thanks to the many works by local artists displayed on its walls. The menu is a hodgepodge of international specialties, providing diners with a variety of tantalizing choices. International menu. Dinner. Bar. Children's menu. Casual attire. Reservations recommended. **$$**

★ ★ ★ **RED INN RESTAURANT.** *15 Commercial St, Provincetown (02657). Phone 508/487-7334; toll-free 866/473-3466; fax 508/487-5115. www.theredinn. com.* One of the best places to enjoy fine dining with a view is at the historic Red Inn, a restored colonial building. Views of the harbor, the bay, Long Point lighthouse, and even the shores of the Outer Cape delight sophisticated patrons who dine on imaginative meals. The house special is the porterhouse steak, truly a carnivores delight. New American menu. Dinner, brunch. Closed Jan 1, Apr 1. Bar. Business casual attire. Reservations recommended. **$$$**

★ ★ **SAL'S PLACE.** *99 Commercial St, Provincetown (02657). Phone 508/487-1279; fax 508/349-6243.* Provincetown's quiet West End is home to Sal's Place. This intimate restaurant dishes it up Italian style, earning kudos for its large portions of satisfying food. Seafood is jazzed up with Mediterranean influences, and the pastas are always a great choice. The waterfront location adds to its appeal, and outdoor seating is available seasonally. Italian menu. Dinner. Closed Nov-Apr. Children's menu. Casual attire. Reservations recommended. Outdoor seating. **$$**

Quincy (B-7)

See also Boston

Settled 1625
Population 88,025
Elevation 20 ft
Area Code 617
Information Tourism and Visitors Bureau, 1250 Hancock St, Suite 802 N, 02169; phone toll-free 617/657-0527
Web Site www.discoverquincy.com

Boston's neighbor to the south, Quincy (QUIN-zee) was the home of the Adamses, a great American family whose fame dates from colonial days. Family members include the second and sixth presidents—John Adams and his son, John Quincy Adams. John Hancock, first signer of the Declaration of Independence, was born here. George Bush, the 41st president, was born in nearby Milton.

Thomas Morton, an early settler, held May Day rites at Merrymount (a section of Quincy) in 1627 and was shipped back to England for selling firearms and "firewater" to the Native Americans.

What to See and Do

⭐ **Adams National Historic Park.** *135 Adams St, Quincy (02169). Phone 617/770-1175.* Administered by the National Park Service. Tickets to sites can be purchased here *only.* (Mid-Apr-mid-Nov: daily; rest of year: Tues-Fri) Golden Eagle Passport accepted (see MAKING THE MOST OF YOUR TRIP). **$$** Includes

John Adams and John Quincy Adams Birthplaces. *133 and 141 Franklin St, Quincy (02169).* Two 17th-century saltbox houses. The elder Adams was born and raised at 133 Franklin Street; his son was born in the other house. While living here, Abigail Adams wrote many of her famous letters to her husband, John Adams, when he was serving in the Continental Congress in Philadelphia and as an arbitrator for peace with Great Britain in Paris. Guided tours.

The Adams National Historic Site. *135 Adams St, Quincy (02169). Off Furnace Brook Pkwy.* The house (1731), bought in 1787 by John Adams, was given as a national site by the Adams family in 1946. Original furnishings.

Josiah Quincy House. *20 Muirhead St, Quincy (02170). Phone 617/227-3956.* (1770) Built on a 1635 land grant, this fine Georgian house originally had a view across Quincy Bay to Boston Harbor; was surrounded by outbuildings and much agricultural land. Long the home of the Quincy family; furnished with family heirlooms and memorabilia. Period wall paneling, fireplaces surrounded by English tiles. Tours on the hour. (July-Aug, Sat-Sun afternoons) **$$**

Quincy Historical Society. *Adams Academy Building, 8 Adams St, Quincy (02169). Phone 617/773-1144.* Museum of regional history; library. (Mon-Sat) **$**

Quincy Homestead. *34 Butler Rd, Quincy (02169). At Butler Rd. Phone 617/742-3190.* Four generations of Quincys lived here, including Dorothy Quincy, wife of John Hancock. Two rooms built in 1686, rest of house dates from the 18th century; period furnishings; herb garden. (May-Oct, Wed-Sun)

United First Parish Church. *1306 Hancock St, Quincy. At Washington St. Phone 617/773-1290. www.ufpc.org.* (1828) Only church in United States where two presidents—John Adams and John Quincy Adams—and their wives are entombed. Tours (mid-Apr-mid-Nov, Mon-Sat, Sun afternoons). **$$**

Special Events

Quincy Bay Race Week. *Quincy Yacht Club, Quincy (02169). Phone 617/657-0527.* Sailing regatta, marine parades, fireworks. July.

South Shore Christmas Festival. *Phone 617/657-0527.* Includes parade with floats. Sun after Thanksgiving.

Summerfest. *Phone 617/657-0527.* Concerts on the Green, Ruth Gordon Amphitheatre. Wed, mid-June-Aug.

Full-Service Hotel

★ ★ ★ **MARRIOTT BOSTON QUINCY.** *1000 Marriott Dr, Quincy (02169). Phone 617/472-1000; toll-free 800/228-9290; fax 617/472-7095. www.marriott.com.* 472 rooms, 9 story. Check-in 4 pm. Check-out noon. Restaurant, bar. Fitness room. Indoor pool, whirlpool. Business center. **$**

Rockport (A-8)

Settled 1690
Population 7,767
Elevation 77 ft
Information Chamber of Commerce, PO Box 67M; phone 978/546-6575 or toll-free 888/726-3922
Web Site www.rockportusa.com

Rockport is a year-round artists' colony. A weather-beaten shanty on one of the wharves has been the subject of so many paintings that it is called "Motif No. 1."

Studios, galleries, summer places, estates, and cottages dot the shore of Cape Ann from Eastern Point southeast of Gloucester all the way to Annisquam.

What to See and Do

Old Castle. *Granite and Curtis sts, Rockport (01966). Pigeon Cove. Phone 978/546-9533.* (1715) A fine example of early 18th-century architecture and exhibits. (July-Aug: daily; rest of year: by appointment) **$**

The Paper House. *52 Pigeon Hill St, Rockport (01966). Phone 978/546-2629. www.paperhouserockport.com.* Newspapers were used in the construction of the house and furniture. (Apr-Oct) **$**

Rockport Art Association. *12 Main St, Rockport (01966). Phone 978/546-6604. www.rockportartassn. org.* Changing exhibits of paintings, sculpture, and graphics by 250 artist members. Special events include concerts (see SPECIAL EVENT), lectures, artist demonstrations. (Daily; closed Thanksgiving, Dec 25-Jan 1) **FREE**

Sandy Bay Historical Society & Museums. *40 King St, Rockport (01966). Near railroad station. Phone 978/546-9533.* Early American and 19th-century rooms and objects, exhibits on fishing, granite industry, the Atlantic cable, and a children's room in an 1832 home constructed of granite. (Mid-June-mid-Sept: daily; rest of year: by appointment) **$**

Sightseeing Tours and Boat Cruises. Contact the Chamber of Commerce for a list of companies offering sightseeing, fishing, and boat tours.

Special Event

Rockport Chamber Music Festival. *3 Main St, Rockport (01966). Phone 978/546-7391. www.rcmf.org.* Soloists and chamber ensembles of international acclaim have performed at this art colony since 1982. A lecture series and family concert are also featured. Four weekends in June or July.

Limited-Service Hotels

★ ★ **SANDY BAY MOTOR INN.** *183 Main St, Rockport (01966). Phone 978/546-7155; toll-free 800/437-7155; fax 978/546-9131. www.sandybaymotorinn.com.* This inn is conveniently located just a short walk from downtown's quaint shops and galleries and is close to many beaches, theaters, and churches. 80 rooms, 2 story. Pets accepted, some restrictions; fee. Check-in 2 pm, check-out 11 am. Restaurant. Indoor pool, whirlpool. Tennis. **$**

★ ★ **TURK'S HEAD MOTOR INN.** *151 South St, Rockport (01966). Phone 978/546-3436. www. turksheadinn.com.* 28 rooms, 2 story. Check-in 2 pm, check-out 11 am. Restaurant. Indoor pool. Two beaches nearby. **$**

Full-Service Inns

★ ★ ★ EMERSON INN BY THE SEA.
1 Cathedral Ave, Rockport (01966). Phone 978/546-6321; toll-free 800/964-5550; fax 978/546-7043. www. emersoninnbythesea.com. This traditional country inn has hosted guests at its oceanfront Pigeon Cove location since 1846. From March through the end of December visitors can enjoy beautiful ocean views from the pool, porch, restaurant and half the guest rooms. 36 rooms, 4 story. Check-in 4 pm, check-out 11 am. Restaurant. Spa. Outdoor pool, whirlpool. **$**

★ ★ ★ SEACREST MANOR.
99 Marmion Way, Rockport (01966). Phone 978/546-2211. www. seacrestmanor.com. Delightful, charming, and intimate, this country inn provides an attentive (but not overbearing) staff. Enjoy afternoon tea or, if in the mood for some fresh air, rent one of the bicycles available for guests. 7 rooms, 2 story. Closed Dec-Mar. Complimentary full breakfast. Check-in 2 pm. Check-out 11 am. Restaurant (inn guests only). **$$**

★ ★ ★ SEAWARD INN & COTTAGES.
44 Marmion Way, Rockport (01966). Phone 978/546-3471; toll-free 877/473-2927; fax 978/546-7661. www. seawardinn.com. Situated on Cape Ann 40 miles northeast of Boston, this inn offers cozy rooms and 9 quaint cottages. Guests can relax in Adirondack chairs along the rocky Atlantic coast. 39 rooms. Complimentary full breakfast. Check-in 3 pm, check-out 11 am. Restaurant. Airport transportation available. **$**

★ ★ ★ YANKEE CLIPPER INN.
127 Granite St, Rockport (01966). Phone 978/546-3407; toll-free 800/545-3699; fax 978/546-9730. www.yankeeclipperinn. com. Serving guests year-round, this seaside resort offers rolling country gardens, a heated pool and an atmosphere engineered for comfort. Enjoy a splendid meal in the Veranda Restaurant featuring elegant American-Continental cuisine. 16 rooms, 3 story. Closed Jan-Feb. Complimentary full breakfast. Check-in 2 pm, check-out 11 am. Outdoor saltwater pool. Airport transportation available. **$$**

Specialty Lodgings

ADDISON CHOATE INN.
49 Broadway, Rockport (01966). Phone 978/546-7543; toll-free 800/245-7543; fax 978/546-3813. www.addisonchoateinn.com. This charming bed-and-breakfast is located less than an hour's drive north of Boston at the tip of Cape Ann. Guests can enjoy all the town has to offer including artists' galleries, shops, and, of course, the beaches. 8 rooms, 3 story. Children over 11 years only. Complimentary continental breakfast. Check-in 3 pm, check-out 11 am. **$**

THE INN ON COVE HILL.
37 Mount Pleasant St, Rockport (01966). Phone 978/546-2701; toll-free 888/546-2701; fax 978/546-1095. www.innoncovehill. com. This inn was built in 1791 from proceeds of pirates' gold found nearby. It is located near the wharf and yacht club. 8 rooms, 3 story. Closed mid-Oct-mid-Apr. Complimentary continental breakfast. Check-in 2-7 pm, check-out 11 am. **$**

LINDEN TREE INN.
26 King St, Rockport (01966). Phone 978/546-2494; toll-free 800/865-2122; fax 978/546-3297. www.lindentreeinn.com. 18 rooms, 3 story. Complimentary full breakfast. Check-in 2 pm. Check-out 11 am. **$**

PEGLEG RESTAURANT AND INN.
1 King St, Rockport (01966). Phone 978/546-2352; toll-free 800/346-2352. www.cape-ann.com/pegleg. 33 rooms. Closed Nov-Mar. Complimentary continental breakfast. Check-in 2 pm. Check-out 11 am. Restaurant. **$**

ROCKY SHORES INN & COTTAGES.
65 Eden Rd, Rockport (01966). Phone 978/546-2823; toll-free 800/348-4003. Mansion built in 1905. 11 rooms, 3 story. Closed mid-Oct-mid-Apr. Complimentary full breakfast. Check-in 3 pm, check-out 11 am. **$**

THE TUCK INN B&B.
17 High St, Rockport (01966). Phone 978/546-7260; toll-free 800/789-7260. www. thetuckinn.com. This colonial house was built in 1790 and is within walking distance to the downtown area and the beach. 13 rooms, 2 story. Complimentary continental breakfast. Check-in 2-9 pm, check-out 11 am. Outdoor pool. **$**

Restaurant

★ BRACKETT'S OCEANIEW.
25 Main St, Rockport (01966). Phone 978/546-2797. www.bracketts.com. Seafood menu. Lunch, dinner. Closed mid-Oct-Mar. **$$**

Salem (B-7)

See also Beverly, Danvers, Lynn, Marblehead

Settled 1626
Population 40,407
Elevation 9 ft
Area Code 978
Zip 01970
Information Chamber of Commerce, 265 Essex St; phone 978/744-0004
Web Site www.salem-chamber.org

In old Salem, the story of early New England life is told with bricks, clapboards, carvings, and gravestones. The town had two native geniuses to immortalize it: Samuel McIntire (1757-1811), master builder, and Nathaniel Hawthorne (1804-1864), author. History is charmingly entangled with the people and events of Hawthorne's novels. Reality, however, could be far from charming. During the witchcraft panic of 1692, 19 persons were hanged on Gallows Hill, another "pressed" to death; at least two others died in jail. Gallows Hill is still here; so is the house of one of the trial judges.

Early in the 18th century, Salem shipbuilding and allied industries were thriving. Salem was a major port. The Revolution turned commerce into privateering. Then began the fabulous China trade and Salem's heyday. The captains came home, and Sam McIntire built splendid houses for them that still stand. Shipping declined after 1812. Salem turned to industry, which, together with tourism, is the present-day economic base.

What to See and Do

Chestnut Street. Architecturally, one of the most beautiful streets in America; laid out in 1796.

House of Seven Gables. *54 Turner St, Salem (01970). Off Derby St on Salem Harbor. Phone 978/744-0991.*

A Walk through Salem

Salem is a fascinating old port city with a walkable downtown. Begin at the National Park Visitors Center at 2 Liberty Street across from the Museum Place garage. Just around the corner on the pedestrian stretch of Essex Street is the Peabody Essex Museum, New England's ultimate treasure chest of exotica, all of it brought from the farthest points of the globe by Salem sea captains in the decades after the Revolution. The Essex Institute part of the museum houses a collection of portraits and archives, including the actual records of the 1692 witch trials for which Salem is infamous; a short film puts the trials in their historical context. Historic homes on the grounds include the Gardner-Pingree House, showcasing the work of Samuel McIntire. Salem's famous architect, McIntire is known for creating airy Federal-era mansions with elegant carved detailing, arches, and stairways. You might want to detour to see Chestnut Street, famous because it is lined with McIntire mansions (walk west up Essex Street and south on Cambridge Street; return the same route).

West of the museums, turn south off Essex Street to Derby Square, site of Salem's old Town Hall, a graceful brick building dating from 1816 that is now a hospitable visitor center for the Salem Chamber of Commerce. Continue down the square (it's really a mini-park) to Front Street and follow the red line on the sidewalk (the Salem Heritage Trail) down Charter and Liberty streets, past the Old Burying Point Cemetery and the Salem Wax Museum.

Continue down along Derby Street to the Salem Maritime National Historic site on Salem Harbor. The *Friendship,* a fully rigged tall ship, is berthed at Central Wharf. The handsome brick Custom House (1819), where Nathaniel Hawthorne worked, is next door at the head of Derby Wharf. Here, too, is the Elias Hasket Derby House, built by the man who pioneered a new sailing route around the Cape of Good Hope and is said to have been Americas first millionaire. The House of Seven Gables, immortalized by Hawthorne, is a few blocks east overlooking the harbor. Retrace your steps (following the red line) up Derby Street and turn up Hawthorne Boulevard to Salem Common. Look for the Salem Witch Museum (Washington Square North), which dramatizes the tale of the witch trials with computerized sound and light. This tour is slightly under 2 miles, but you can hop a trolley—also a good way to gain an overview of sites to begin with—if you tire along the way. Return down Brown Street to your starting point.

www.7gables.org. Nathaniel Hawthorne's 1851 novel is said to have been inspired by this home, although he never lived there. You'll enjoy the tour most if you've read the book, because you'll recognize furnishings and areas of the home from Hawthornes descriptions. Even if you haven't read it, however, you're sure to enjoy the well-preserved estate that dates to 1669, as well as the guide in period clothing. (Daily; closed the first three weeks in Jan) **$$$**

Peabody Museum & Essex Institute. *East India Sq, Salem (01970). Phone 978/745-9500; toll-free 866/745-1876. www.pem.org.* The Peabody Museum, founded by sea captains in 1799, features five world-famous collections in 30 galleries. Large collections of marine art, Asian export art. Essex Institute features historical interpretations of the area. Peabody Museum (daily; closed Jan 1, Thanksgiving, Dec 25). Essex Institute (daily) **$$$** Admission includes

Crowninshield-Bentley House. *126 Essex St, Salem (01970). Phone 978/745-9500.* (1727) Reverend William Bentley, minister and diarist, lived here from 1791 to 1819. Period furnishings. (June-Oct: daily; rest of year: Sat-Sun, holidays)

Gardner-Pingree House. *128 Essex St, Salem (01970). Phone 978/745-9500.* (1804) Designed by McIntire; restored and handsomely furnished. (June-Oct: daily; rest of year: Sat-Sun, holidays)

John Ward House. *161 Essex St, Salem (01970). Behind Essex Institute. Phone 978/745-9500.* (1684) Seventeenth-century furnishings. (June-Oct: daily; rest of year: Sat-Sun, holidays)

Peirce-Nichols House. *80 Federal St, Salem (01970). Phone 978/745-9500. www.pem.org.* (1782) One of the finest examples of McIntire's architectural genius; authentically furnished. (By appointment only)

Pickering Wharf. *23 Congress St, Salem (01970). Adjacent to Salem Maritime National Historic Site. Phone 978/740-9540. www.pickeringwharf.com.* This 6-acre commercial and residential village by the sea includes shops, restaurants, and a marina.

Pioneer Village: Salem in 1630. *Forest River Park off West St, Salem (01970). Phone 978/744-0991.* Reproduction of early Puritan settlement, includes dugouts, wigwams, and thatched cottages; costumed interpreters. Guided tours. (Late Apr-late Nov, daily) **$$**

Ropes Mansion and Garden. *318 Essex St, Salem (01970). Phone 978/745-9500. www.pem.org.* (Late 1720s) Gambrel-roofed, Georgian and colonial mansion; restored and furnished with period pieces. The garden (laid out in 1912) is nationally known for its beauty and variety. (June-Oct, daily; limited hours Sun) **$$**

⭐ **Salem Maritime National Historic Site.** *174 Derby St, Salem (01970). Orientation Center, Central Wharf Warehouse. Phone 978/740-1660. www.nps.gov/sama.* Nine acres of historic waterfront. Self-guided and guided tours. (Daily; Jan 1, Thanksgiving, Dec 25). **$** Site includes

Custom House. *174 Derby St, Salem (01970). Derby St, opposite wharf. Phone 978/740-1660.* (1819) Restored offices. (Daily; closed Jan 1, Thanksgiving, Dec 25)

Derby House. *174 Derby St, Salem (01970). Phone 978/740-1660.* (1761-1762) Home of maritime merchant Elias Hasket Derby, one of the country's first millionaires. In back are the Derby House Gardens, featuring roses, herbs, and 19th-century flowers. Inquire at Orientation Center for tour information.

Derby Wharf. *174 Derby St, Salem (01970). Off Derby St. Phone 978/740-1660.* Once a center of Salem shipping (1760-1810).

Narbonne House. *174 Derby St, Salem. Phone 978/745-0799.* A 17th-century house with archaeological exhibits. Inquire at Orientation Center for tour information.

Scale House. *174 Derby St, Salem (01970). Phone 978/740-1660.* (1829) and *Bonded Warehouse* (1819). Site of 19th-century customs operations. (Daily)

Visitor Information. *265 Essex St, Salem (01970). Phone 978/740-1650. www.salem-chamber.org.* In Orientation Center and downtown visitor center at Museum Place, Essex Street.

West India Goods Store. *164 Derby St, Salem (01970).* (1800) Coffee, teas, spices, and goods for sale. (Daily; closed Jan 1, Thanksgiving, Dec 25)

Salem State College. *352 Lafayette St, Salem (01970). Phone 978/542-6200. www.salemstate.edu.* (1854) (9,300 students) On campus are

Chronicle of Salem. *Meier Hall.* Mural, 60 feet by 30 feet, depicts Salem history from settlement to present in 50 sequences. (Mon-Fri; closed holidays)

Library Gallery. Art exhibits by local and national artists. (Mon-Sat) **FREE**

Main Stage Auditorium. *352 Lafayette St, Salem (01970).* This 750-seat theater presents musical and dramatic productions (Sept-Apr).

Winfisky Art Gallery. Photographs, paintings, graphics, and sculpture by national and local artists. (Sept-May, Mon-Fri) **FREE**

Salem Witch Museum. *19 1/2 Washington Sq, Salem (01970). Follow Hawthorne Blvd to the NW corner of Salem Common. Phone 978/744-1692. www.salemwitchmuseum.com.* The Salem Witch Museum re-creates the Salem Witch Trials of 1692 with a 30-minute narrated presentation that uses special lighting and life-size figures. The museum may be too frightening for young children. If you're traveling in October, also visit Salem's Haunted Happenings, a Halloween festival that begins in early October and runs through Halloween and features street merchants, plays, witchy games, and haunted houses. (Daily; closed Jan 1, Thanksgiving, Dec 25) **$$**

Stephen Phillips Trust House. *34 Chestnut St, Salem (01970). Phone 978/744-0440. www.phillipsmuseum.org.* (1804) Federal-style mansion with McIntire mantels and woodwork. Furnishings, rugs, and porcelains reflect the merchant and seafaring past of the Phillips family. Also here is a carriage barn with carriages and antique automobiles. (Late May-Oct, Mon-Sat 10 am-4:30 pm) **FREE**

Witch Dungeon Museum. *16 Lynde St, Salem (01970). Phone 978/741-3570. www.witchdungeon.com.* Reenactment of witch trial of Sarah Good by professional actresses; tour through re-created dungeon where accused witches awaited trial; original artifacts. (Apr-Nov, daily) **$$**

Witch House. *310 Essex St, Salem (01970). Phone 978/744-8815. www.salemweb.com/witchhouse.* (1642) Home of witchcraft trial judge Jonathan Corwin. Some of the accused witches may have been examined here. (May-early Nov, daily 10 am-5 pm) **$$**

Special Events

Haunted Happenings. *Various sites. Phone 978/744-3663. www.hauntedhappenings.org.* Psychic festival, historical exhibits, haunted house, costume parade, contests, dances. Entire month of Oct.

Heritage Days Celebration. *Phone 978/744-0004.* Band concerts, parade, exhibits, and ethnic festivals. Mid-Aug.

Limited-Service Hotel

★ ★ **HAWTHORNE HOTEL.** *18 Washington Sq W, Salem (01970). Phone 978/744-4080; toll-free 800/729-7829; fax 978/745-9842. www.hawthornehotel.com.* 89 rooms, 6 story. Pets accepted, some restrictions; fee. Check-in 3 pm, check-out 11 am. Restaurant. Fitness room. **$**
🅳 🐾 🏋

Full-Service Hotel

★ ★ ★ **MARRIOTT PEABODY.** *8A Centennial Dr, Peabody (01960). Phone 978/977-9700; toll-free 800/228-9290; fax 978/977-0297. www.marriott.com.* 260 rooms, 6 story. Check-in 4 pm, check-out noon. Restaurant, bar. Fitness room. Indoor pool, whirlpool. Business center. **$**
🅳 🏋 🏊 🏋

Specialty Lodging

SALEM INN. *7 Summer St, Salem (01970). Phone 978/741-0680; toll-free 800/446-2995; fax 978/744-8924. www.saleminnma.com.* With individually appointed rooms and suites, many of which feature Jacuzzis, kitchenettes, and fireplaces, this inn provides comfort and luxury without assaulting your wallet. Season packages available. 33 rooms, 4 story. Pets accepted; fee. Complimentary continental breakfast. Check-in 3 pm, check-out 11 am. **$**
🅳 🐾

Restaurants

★ ★ **GRAPE VINE.** *26 Congress St, Salem (01970). Phone 978/745-9335; fax 978/744-9335. www.grapevinesalem.com.* American, Italian menu. Dinner. Closed holidays; also Super Bowl Sun. Bar. Outdoor seating. **$$$**

★ ★ **LEGAL SEAFOODS.** *210 Andover St, Peabody (01960). Phone 978/532-4500; fax 978/532-2110. www.legalseafoods.com.* Seafood menu. Lunch, dinner. Closed Thanksgiving, Dec 25. Bar. Children's menu. **$$**

★ ★ ★ **LYCEUM.** *43 Church St, Salem (01970). Phone 978/745-7665; fax 978/744-7699. www.lyceumsalem.com.* One of the area's best restaurants, this comfortable, elegant dining room is located in the building where Alexander Graham Bell made his first phone call in 1877. American menu. Lunch, dinner, Sun brunch. Closed Thanksgiving, Dec 25. Bar. **$$**

★ **VICTORIA STATION.** *86 Wharf St, Salem (01970). Phone 978/745-3400; fax 978/745-7460. www.victoriastationinc.com.* Seafood, steak menu. Lunch, dinner. Closed Dec 25. Bar. Children's menu. Outdoor seating. **$**

Sandwich (Cape Cod) (D-8)

See also Bourne

Settled 1637
Population 20,136
Elevation 20 ft
Area Code 508
Zip 02563
Information Cape Cod Canal Region Chamber of Commerce, 70 Main St, Buzzards Bay 02532; phone 508/759-6000
Web Site www.capecodcanalchamber.org

The first town to be settled on Cape Cod, Sandwich made the glass that bears its name. This pressed glass was America's greatest contribution to the glass industry.

What to See and Do

⭐ **Heritage Plantation.** *67 Grove St, Sandwich (02563). Phone 508/888-3300. www.heritageplantation.org.* The Heritage Plantation offers an eclectic mix of beautiful gardens, folk art, antique cars, and military parapher-nalia. Visit the Old East Windmill from 1800 and the restored 1912 carousel that's great fun for young and old. Call ahead to find out about unique exhibits, displays, and concerts. Note that the Heritage Plantation is located in the town of Sandwich, the oldest town on the Cape. (May-Oct: daily; Nov-Apr: Wed-Sun) **$$**

Hoxie House & Dexter Gristmill. *Water St, Sandwich (02563). Phone 508/888-1173.* Restored mid-17th-century buildings. House, operating mill; stone-ground corn meal sold. (Mid-June-mid-Oct, daily)

Sandwich Glass Museum. *129 Main St, Sandwich (02563). Phone 508/888-0251. www.sandwichglassmuseum.org.* Internationally renowned collection of exquisite Sandwich Glass (circa 1825-1888). (Apr-Oct, daily) **$**

Scusset Beach. *Hwys 3 and 6, Sandwich (02563). 3 miles NW on Hwy 6A across canal, then 2 miles E at junction Hwy 3 and Hwy 6. Phone 508/362-3225.* Swimming beach, fishing pier; camping (fee).

Shawme-Crowell State Forest. *42 Main St, Sandwich (02563). 3 miles W on Hwy 130, off Hwy 6. Phone 508/888-0351. www.mass.gov/dcr.* Approximately 2,700 acres. Primitive camping.

Limited-Service Hotels

★ **EARL OF SANDWICH MOTEL.** *378 Hwy 6A, East Sandwich (02537). Phone 508/888-1415; toll-free 800/442-3275; fax 508/833-1039. www.earlofsandwich.com.* 24 rooms. Pets accepted, some restrictions. Complimentary continental breakfast. Check-in 2 pm, check-out 11 am. **$**

★ **SHADY NOOK INN & MOTEL.** *14 Old Kings Hwy, Sandwich (02563). Phone 508/888-0409; toll-free 800/338-5208; fax 508/888-4039. www.shadynookinn.com.* 30 rooms. Check-in 2 pm, check-out 11 am. Outdoor pool. **$**

★ **SPRING HILL MOTOR LODGE.** *351 Hwy 6A, East Sandwich (02537). Phone 508/888-1456; toll-free 800/647-2514; fax 508/833-1556. www.springhillmotorlodge.com.* 24 rooms. Check-in 2 pm, check-out 11 am. Outdoor pool. Tennis. **$**

Full-Service Inn

★ ★ ★ **DAN'L WEBSTER INN.** *149 Main St, Sandwich (02563). Phone 508/888-3622; toll-free 800/444-3566; fax 508/888-5156. www.danlwebsterinn.com.* Modeled on an 18th-century house. 54 rooms, 3 story. Check-in 3 pm. Check-out 11 am. Restaurant, bar. Outdoor pool. **$$**

Specialty Lodgings

THE BELFRY INN & BISTRO. *8 Jarves St, Sandwich (02563). Phone 800/844-4542; toll-free 800/844-4542; fax 508/888-3922. www.belfryinn.com.*

Former rectory built in 1882; belfry access. 14 rooms, 3 story. Children over 10 years only. Complimentary full breakfast. Check-in 3 pm. Check-out 11 am. Restaurant. Business center. **$$**
🏃

ISAIAH JONES HOMESTEAD. *165 Main St, Sandwich (02563). Phone 508/888-9115; toll-free 800/526-1625; fax 508/888-9648. www.isaiahjones. com.* An American flag and flower-lined porch beckon guests inside this 1849 Victorian home. The guest rooms, decorated with antiques and country-patterned fabrics, are a great resting stop when visiting this Cape Cod town's many historic sites. 7 rooms, 2 story. Children over 16 years only. Complimentary full breakfast. Check-in 3-6 pm. Check-out 11 am. **$**
🔁

VILLAGE INN. *4 Jarves St, Sandwich (02563). Phone 508/833-0363; toll-free 800/922-9989; fax 508/833-2063. www.capecodinn.com.* Federal-style house (1837) with wraparound porch, gardens. 8 rooms, 3 story. Children over 8 years only. Complimentary full breakfast. Check-in 3-6 pm. Check-out 11 am. **$**
🔁

Restaurants

★ ★ **AQUA GRILLE.** *14 Gallo Rd, Sandwich (02563). Phone 508/888-8889; fax 508/888-8886. www.aquagrille. com.* Located at the Sandwich Marina, the Aqua Grille is a nice spot for catching up with friends over good food. Lunch tantalizes guests with salads, soups, sandwiches, fried seafood, and specials, while the dinner menu intrigues with grilled fish, meats, and pastas. Large windows give the restaurant an airy ambience while showing off great water views. American, seafood menu. Lunch, dinner. Closed Nov-mid-Apr. Bar. Children's menu. Casual attire. Outdoor seating. **$$**

★ ★ **BEEHIVE TAVERN.** *406 Hwy 6A, Sandwich (02563). Phone 508/833-1184.* American, seafood menu. Lunch, dinner. Bar. Children's menu. Casual attire. **$$**

★ ★ ★ **THE DAN'L WEBSTER INN.** *149 Main St, Sandwich (02563). Phone 508/888-3623; toll-free 800/444-3566; fax 508/888-5156. www.danlwebsterinn. com.* An actual stagecoach inn frequented in the early 1800s by its namesake, Dan'l Webster offers both a colonial-motif tavern with burgers, pizzas, and salads, and a white-tablecloth dining room serving chic contemporary cuisine. Chef and co-owner Robert Catania buys some of his fish and hydroponic vegetables from

a local aquafarm, and he has constructed a wine list to match his culinary aspirations. His twin loves entwine in a luscious dish of mixed seafood in white wine sauce. Half portions are available for many dishes. The conservatory dining area overlooks a garden. American menu. Breakfast, lunch, dinner, Sun brunch. Closed Dec 25. Bar. Children's menu. Business casual attire. Reservations recommended. Valet parking. **$$**

Saugus (B-7)

See also Boston

Settled 1630
Population 26,078
Elevation 21 ft
Area Code 781
Zip 01906

Saugus is the birthplace of the American steel industry. The first ironworks were built here in 1646.

What to See and Do

Saugus Iron Works National Historic Site. *244 Central St, Saugus (01906). Phone 781/233-0050. www.nps. gov/sair.* Commemorates America's first successful integrated ironworks. Reconstructed furnace, forge, mill on original foundations; furnished 17th-century house; museum; working blacksmith shop; seven working waterwheels; guided tours and demonstrations (Apr-Oct); film. (Daily; closed Jan 1, Thanksgiving, Dec 25) Contact the National Park Service, Saugus Iron Works National Historic Site, 244 Central Street. **FREE**

Restaurants

★ ★ ★ **DONATELLO.** *44 Broadway, Saugus (01906). Phone 781/233-9975; fax 781/233-8075. www. donatello-restaurant.com.* This northern Italian restaurant is the selection of locals for a special occasion. The pasta is freshly made and if you are a veal fan, this is the place to order the chop. The servers provide the finishing touches to the dining event. Italian menu. Lunch, dinner. Closed July 4, Thanksgiving, Dec 24. Bar. Valet parking. **$$**

★ ★ **HILLTOP STEAK HOUSE.** *855 Broadway, Saugus (01906). Phone 781/233-7700; fax 781/231-3134. www.hilltop-steak-house.com.* Seafood, steak menu. Lunch, dinner, Sun brunch. Closed Thanksgiving, Dec 25. Bar. Children's menu. **$$**

★★ **ORZO TRATTORIA.** *114 Broadway, Saugus (01906). Phone 781/233-6815. www.orzorestaurant. com.* Italian menu. Dinner. Bar. Children's menu. Casual attire. **$$**

Somerville

Population 77,478

Sitting to the northwest of Boston, Somerville—just a mile and a half from the citys financial and commercial districts—is a diverse community in which more than 50 different languages are spoken. That diversity is reflected in its restaurant scene, with Union Square and the hip Davis Square serving as prime dining and entertainment destinations. Ample public transportation makes it easy to get to Boston and other suburbs.

Restaurants

★★ **DALI RESTAURANT AND TAPAS BAR.** *415 Washington St, Somerville (02143). Phone 617/661-3254; fax 617/661-2813. www.dalirestaurant.com.* Dali defines Spanish cuisine for the Boston area, offering 45 tapas and five entrées each night, as well as a long list of sherries, ports, and Spanish table wines. Choices range from earthy Andalusian bar food (like potatoes in a garlic-caper mayonnaise) to fresh fish baked in coarse salt in the style of Cadiz. No reservations are taken, so be ready to balance a plate on your wine glass while waiting for a table. Spanish menu. Dinner. Closed holidays; also Dec 31. Bar. Business casual attire. **$$$**
🅳

★ **REDBONES.** *55 Chester St, Somerville (02144). Phone 617/628-2200; fax 617/625-5909. www. redbonesbbq.com.* Not since the 1960 presidential ticket of JFK and LBJ has there been such a strong Boston-Austin connection. Redbones keeps things simple by offering little more than great Texas roadhouse barbecue executed with near perfection. The upstairs dining room is family-friendly, while the downstairs bar carries through the roadhouse vibe with a sweeping selection of beers, both on tap and in the bottle. American menu. Lunch, dinner. Closed Thanksgiving, Dec 25. Bar. Casual attire. **$$**
🅳

South Hadley (B-3)

See also Amherst, Holyoke

Settled circa 1660
Population 17,196
Elevation 257 ft
Area Code 413
Zip 01075
Information Chamber of Commerce, 10 Harwich Place; phone 413/532-6451

Nestled on the banks of the Connecticut River, South Hadley was incorporated as a town in 1775. Twenty years later, the first navigable canal in the United States began operation here. The town remained a busy shipping center until 1847, when the coming of the railroad made shipping by river unprofitable.

What to See and Do

Mount Holyoke College. *50 College St, South Hadley (01075). Phone 413/538-2000. www.mtholyoke.edu.* (1837) (1,950 women) Campus tours (inquire for schedule). On the grounds are

Joseph Allen Skinner Museum. *135 Woodbridge St, South Hadley (01075). Phone 413/538-2245.* Housed in a small Congregational church (1846). Collection of Early American furnishings, decorative arts; one-room schoolhouse. (May-Oct, Wed and Sun, 2 pm-5 pm) **FREE**

Mount Holyoke College Art Museum. *50 College St, South Hadley (01075). Phone 413/538-2245.* Small but choice permanent collection of paintings, drawings, prints, and sculpture; also special exhibitions. (Tues-Fri, also Sat-Sun afternoons; closed college holidays) **FREE**

Talcott Arboretum. *Park St and Lower Lake Rd, South Hadley (01075). Phone 413/538-2199.* Campus features variety of trees and plantings; Japanese meditation, wildflower, and formal perennial gardens; greenhouse complex has collections of exotic plants; flower show (Mar); tours by appointment. (Mon-Fri, also Sat-Sun afternoons; closed holidays) **FREE**

Old Firehouse Museum. *4 N Main St, South Hadley (01075). Phone 413/536-4970.* Served as a firehouse 1888-1974; features firefighting equipment, Native American artifacts, items relating to local history and

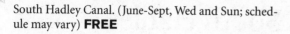

South Hadley Canal. (June-Sept, Wed and Sun; schedule may vary) **FREE**

Special Event

Women's Regatta. *Phone 413/536-3132.* Brunelle's Marina. Oct.

Springfield (C-3)

See also Holyoke; also see Enfield, CT and Windsor Locks, CT

Settled 1636
Population 152,082
Elevation 70 ft
Area Code 413
Information Greater Springfield Convention & Visitors Bureau, 1441 Main St, 01103; phone 413/787-1548 or toll-free 800/723-1548
Web Site www.myonlinechamber.com

Established under the leadership of William Pynchon of Springfield, England, this is now a major unit in the Connecticut River industrial empire. Springfield is also a cultural center with a fine library, museums, and a symphony orchestra, and is the home of Springfield College.

Public Transportation

Buses Pioneer Valley Transit Authority. Phone 413/781-7882

Airport Hartford Bradley International Airport; weather 860/627-3440; cash machines, Terminals A and B

Information Phone 860/292-2000

What to See and Do

Basketball Hall of Fame. *1000 W Columbus Ave, Springfield (01105). Adjacent to I-91. Phone 413/781-6500. www.hoophall.com.* Exhibits on the game and its teams and players; shrine to the sport invented here in 1891 by Dr. James Naismith. Historic items on display; free movies; video highlights of great games; life-size, action blow-ups of Hall of Famers. Major features include: "Hoopla," a 22-minute film; and "The Spalding Shoot-Out," the most popular participatory attraction, which allows visitors to try their skill at scoring a basket of varying heights while on a moving sidewalk. (Daily; closed Jan 1, Thanksgiving, Dec 25) **$$$$**

Brimfield State Forest. *24 miles E on Hwy 20, then SE near Brimfield.* Swimming, trout fishing from the shore (stocked); hiking, picnicking. **$**

Forest Park. *200 Trafton Rd, Springfield (01108). Hwy 83 off I-91. Phone 413/733-2251. www.forestparkzoo. org.* On 735 acres. Nature trails, tennis, swimming pool. Picnicking, playgrounds, ball fields. Zoo (Apr-mid-Oct: daily; mid-Oct-Nov: Sat-Sun; fee). Duck ponds. Pony rides, train rides (fee for both). Park (all year). **$$**

Granville State Forest. *323 W Hartland Rd, Springfield (01034). 22 miles W off Hwy 57. Phone 413/357-6611.* Scenic gorge, laurel display. Swimming, fishing; hiking, picnicking, camping.

Indian Motorcycle Museum. *33 Hendee St, Springfield (01104). Phone 413/737-2624.* Part of the vast complex where Indian motorcycles were made until 1953. On display are historical cycles and other American-made machines; photographs; extensive collection of toy motorcycles; other Native American products, including an early snowmobile and a 1928 roadster. (Daily; closed Jan 1, Thanksgiving, Dec 25) **$**

Laughing Brook Education Center and Wildlife Sanctuary. *793 Main St, Hampden (01036). 7 miles SE. Phone 413/566-8034.* Woodlands and wetlands, 354 acres. Former house (1782) of children's author and storyteller Thornton W. Burgess. Live animal exhibits of wildlife native to New England. Observation areas of pond, field, and forest habitats. 4 1/2 miles of walking trails; picnic area. (Tues-Sun; also Mon holidays; closed Jan 1, Thanksgiving, Dec 25) **$$**

Municipal Group. *NW side of Court Sq.* Includes renovated Symphony Hall, which, together with the Springfield Civic Center, offers a performing arts complex presenting a variety of concerts, theater, children's productions, dance and sporting events, and industrial shows; 300-foot campanile, modeled after the bell tower in the Piazza San Marco of Venice.

Six Flags New England. *1623 Main St, Agawam (01001). 5 miles W via Hwy 57 and Hwy 159S. Phone 413/786-9300. www.sixflags.com/parks/newengland.* Amusement park, rides, roller coasters; children's area; games and arcades; shows; restaurants. (June-Labor Day: daily; Apr-May, Sept-Oct: weekends only) **$$$$**

Springfield Armory National Historic Site. *1 Armory Sq, Springfield (01105). Old Armory Sq Green, Federal and State sts. Phone 413/734-8551. www.nps.gov/spar.* US armory (1794-1968) contains one of the largest collections of military small arms in the world. Exhibits include "Organ of Guns," made famous by Longfellow's poem "The Arsenal at Springfield." Film, video presentations. (Tues-Sat; closed Jan 1, Thanksgiving, Dec 25) **FREE**

Springfield Museums at the Quadrangle. *220 State St, Springfield (01103). Phone 413/263-6800. www.springfieldmuseums.org.* Includes four museums and a library. **George Walter Vincent Smith Art Museum** houses collection of Asian armor, arms, jade, bronzes, and rugs; 19th-century American paintings, sculpture. **Connecticut River Valley Historical Museum** includes genealogy and local history library; period rooms. **Museum of Fine Arts** has 20 galleries, including an outstanding collection of American and European works. **Science Museum** has an exploration center, early aviation exhibit, aquarium, planetarium, African hall, dinosaur hall. (All buildings Wed-Sun) **$$**

Storrowton Village. *Eastern States Exposition, 1305 Memorial Ave, West Springfield (01089). On Hwy 147. Phone 413/737-2443. www.thebige.com.* A group of restored Early American buildings: meeting house, schoolhouse, blacksmith shop, and homes. Old-fashioned herb garden. Dining. Guided tours (June-Aug: Tues-Sat; rest of year: by appointment; closed holidays). **$**

Special Events

Eastern States Exposition (The Big E). *1305 Memorial Ave, West Springfield (01089). On Hwy 147 in West Springfield. Phone 413/737-2443. www.thebige.com.* Largest fair in the Northeast; entertainment, exhibits; historic Avenue of States, Storrowton Village; horse show; agricultural events; "Better Living Center" exhibit. Sept.

Glendi Greek Celebration. *Phone 413/787-1548.* Greek folk dances, observance of doctrine and ritual festivities, Greek foods, art exhibits, street dancing. Early Sept.

Hall of Fame Tip-off Classic. *Springfield Civic Center, 1277 Main St, Springfield (01103). Phone 413/781-6500.* Official opening game of the collegiate basketball season with two of the nation's top teams. Mid-Nov.

Indian Day. *Indian Motocycle Museum, 33 Hendee St, Springfield (01104). Phone 413/737-2624.* Gathering of owners and those interested in Indian motorcycles and memorabilia. Third Sun in July.

Peach Festival. *Fountain Park, 833 Tinkham Rd, Wilbraham (01095). Phone 413/599-0010. www.peachfestival.org.* Started in 1985, the Peach Festival has grown into a local tradition in Massachusetts. In recent years, the festival has added amusement park-style rides and a yearly Creature Feature, which screens old horror movies like *The Creature from the Black Lagoon.* Marie Osmond has performed in the past, and citizens and visitors alike draw inspiration from nearby Civil War reenactments. There are also dance competitions and the annual Peach Festival parade and pancake breakfast. Third weekend in Aug.

Tanglewood Music Festival. *1277 Main St, Springfield (02115). Phone 617/266-1200.* Tanglewood Boston Symphony Orchestra. Concerts performed on Friday and Saturday evenings and Sunday afternoons. Inquire for other musical events. July-Aug.

World's Largest Pancake Breakfast. *Phone 413/733-3800.* A battle with Battle Creek, Michigan, to see who can serve the "world's largest breakfast." Features pancake breakfast served at a four-block-long table. April.

Limited-Service Hotels

★ **HAMPTON INN.** *1011 Riverdale St (Hwy 5), West Springfield (01089). Phone 413/732-1300; toll-free 800/426-7866; fax 413/732-9883. www.hampton-inn.com.* Every member of the family—including the four-legged one—is welcome at this hotel, easily accessible at the intersection of I-90 and I-91. Connecting rooms, cribs, in-room refrigerators, and king rooms with pull-out couches are designed with families in mind, and both kids and adults will enjoy the refreshing outdoor pool. The hotel is located at the entrance to a suburban shopping center with CostCo, Kohls, and other shops and casual restaurants close by. 126 rooms, 4 story. Pets accepted; fee. Complimentary continental breakfast. Check-in 3 pm, check-out noon. Outdoor pool. **$**

★ ★ **HOLIDAY INN DOWNTOWN.** *711 Dwight St, Springfield (01104). Phone 413/781-0900; toll-free 800/465-4329; fax 413/785-1410. www.holiday-inn.com.* Just off I-91 and I-291, this 244-room hotel is slightly north of Springfields downtown. A welcoming place for families, it has a video arcade, game room, and indoor pool and is close to attractions such as the Basketball Hall of Fame, Dr. Seuss Museum, and Six Flags. Zaffino's, the 12th-floor restaurant, has large windows that take advantage of a beautiful view of the Pioneer Valley and Connecticut River. 244 rooms,

12 story. Pets accepted; fee. Check-in 3 pm, check-out 11 am. High-speed Internet access, wireless Internet access. Restaurant, bar. Fitness room. Indoor pool. Business center. **$**

Full-Service Hotels

★ ★ ★ **MARRIOTT SPRINGFIELD.** *1500 Main St, Springfield (01115). Phone 413/781-7111; toll-free 800/228-9290; fax 413/731-8932. www.marriott.com.* The bed—with an extra-thick mattress, duvet with bed skirt, and multiple plush pillows—is the most noticeable aspect of the renovated guest rooms in this contemporary, city-center hotel. It is an elegant focal point in a room that also includes grass-cloth wall coverings, rich maroons and golds, and a bath with polished granite and upgraded fixtures. When you leave your room, you won't have far to go for entertainment: just walk through the hotel (and make sure to look at the artwork in the public areas; much of it was commissioned from local artists on local subjects like the Connecticut River, New England barns, and Dr. Seuss) to the walkway that connects the Marriott to an office tower complex and mall. There you'll find casual restaurants, art galleries, an African-American history museum, and even a billiards parlor. 265 rooms, 16 story. Check-in 4 pm, check-out noon. High-speed Internet access. Two restaurants, bar. Fitness room. Indoor pool, whirlpool. Business center. **$$**

★ ★ ★ **SHERATON SPRINGFIELD MONARCH PLACE HOTEL.** *1 Monarch Pl, Springfield (01144). Phone 413/781-1010; fax 413/747-8065. www.sheraton-springfield.com.* This hotel has one serious health club. The Sheraton Athletic Club is the largest hotel health club west of Boston, is available to private members as well as hotel guests, and has two dozen machines, free weights, a 50-foot swimming pool, a racquetball court, an indoor golf range, and a myriad of fitness classes. Spa services include everything from tanning to massage to manicures. But the health club isn'tthe only larger-than-life element of this 325-room hotel: rooms surround a 12-story atrium, airy and grand. Public areas are spacious as well and feature local touches such as a folk art mural of Springfield's many historical highlights and points of interest. Throughout the hotel, and in many guest rooms, windows highlight lovely views of the Connecticut River. If you're staying for business, ask for a "smart room," with photocopier and fax machine. And if you're staying for pleasure, the

Sheraton's downtown location gives you proximity to the city's museums and shops, and its connection to the Monarch Tower office complex allows you access to additional shopping and dining—sans coat. 325 rooms, 12 story. Check-in 3 pm, check-out noon. High-speed Internet access. Restaurant, bar. Fitness room, fitness classes available. Indoor pool, whirlpool. Business center. **$$**

Restaurants

★ ★ **HOFBRAUHAUS.** *1105 Main St, West Springfield (01089). Phone 413/737-4905; fax 413/734-7479. www.hofbrauhaus.org.* This group-friendly restaurant is a local favorite. With the waitstaff in costume and a world-class array of beer steins, guests are sure to enjoy themselves. German menu. Dinner. Closed Dec 25. Bar. Children's menu. **$$$**

★ **IVANHOE.** *1422 Elm St, West Springfield (01089). Phone 413/736-4881; fax 413/736-3408. www.theivanhoe.com.* Seafood, steak menu. Lunch, dinner, Sun brunch. Closed Dec 25. Bar. Children's menu. Casual attire. **$$**

★ ★ **MONTE CARLO.** *1020 Memorial Ave, West Springfield (01089). Phone 413/734-6431; fax 413/788-9119.* American, Italian menu. Lunch, dinner. Closed Mon; Thanksgiving, Dec 25. Bar. Children's menu. **$$**

★ ★ **STUDENT PRINCE & FORT.** *8 Fort St, Springfield (01103). Phone 413/734-7475; fax 413/739-7303. www.studentprince.com.* German, American menu. Lunch, dinner. Bar; imported draft beer. Children's menu. **$$**

Stockbridge and West Stockbridge (B-2)

See also Lenox, Pittsfield

Settled 1734
Population 2,276
Elevation 842 and 901 ft
Area Code 413
Zip Stockbridge, 01262; West Stockbridge, 01266
Information Stockbridge Chamber of Commerce, 6 Elm St, PO Box 224; phone 413/298-5200; or visit Main St Information Booth

Web Site www.stockbridgechamber.org

Established as a mission, Stockbridge was for many years a center for teaching the Mahican. The first preacher was John Sergeant. Jonathan Edwards also taught at Stockbridge. The town is now mainly a summer resort but still has many features and attractions open year round. West Stockbridge is a completely restored market village. Its Main Street is lined with well-kept storefronts, renovated in the style of the 1800s, featuring stained glass, antiques, and handcrafted articles.

What to See and Do

Berkshire Botanical Garden. *Hwys 102 and 183, Stockbridge (01262). Phone 413/298-3926. www. berkshirebotanical.org.* Fifteen-acre botanical garden; perennials, shrubs, trees, antique roses, ponds; wildflower exhibit, herb, vegetable gardens; solar, semitropical, and demonstration greenhouses. Garden shop. Herb products. Special events, lectures. Picnicking. (May-Oct, daily) **$$**

Chesterwood. *284 Main St, Stockbridge (01262). 2 miles S of junction Hwy 102 and Hwy 183. Phone 413/298-3579. www.chesterwood.org.* Early 20th-century summer residence and studio of Daniel Chester French, sculptor of the *Minute Man* statue in Concord and of Lincoln in the Memorial in Washington, DC. Also museum; gardens, woodland walk; guided tours. A property of the National Trust for Historic Preservation. (May-Oct, daily) **$$**

Children's Chimes Bell Tower. *Main St, Stockbridge (01262).* (1878) Erected by David Dudley Field, a prominent lawyer, as a memorial to his grandchildren. Carillon concerts (June-Aug, daily).

Merwin House "Tranquility". *14 Main St, Stockbridge (01262). Phone 413/298-4703.* (Circa 1825) Brick house in late Federal period; enlarged with a "shingle"-style wing at the end of the 19th century. European and American furniture and decorative arts. (by appointment) **$$**

Mission House. *1 Sergeant St, Stockbridge (01262). Main and Sergeant sts, on Hwy 102. Phone 413/298-3239.* House built in 1739 for the missionary Reverend John Sergeant and his wife, Abigail Williams; now a museum of colonial life. Collection of colonial antiques; Native American museum; gardens and orchard. Guided tours. (Memorial Day weekend-Columbus Day weekend, daily) **$$**

Naumkeag. *1 Seargeant St, Stockbridge (01262). Prospect Hill. Phone 413/298-3239.* Stanford White designed this Norman-style "Berkshire cottage" (1886); the interior has antiques, Oriental rugs, and a collection of Chinese export porcelain. Gardens include terraces of tree peonies, fountains, a Chinese garden and birch walk. Guided tours. (Memorial Day weekend-Columbus weekend, daily) **$$$**

⭐ **Norman Rockwell Museum.** *9 Glendale Rd, Stockbridge (01262). Phone 413/298-4100. www.nrm. org.* Maintains and exhibits the nation's largest collection of original art by Norman Rockwell. (Daily; closed Jan 1, Thanksgiving, Dec 25) **$$$**

Special Events

Berkshire Theatre Festival. *Berkshire Playhouse, 6 E Main, Stockbridge (01262). Entrance from Hwy 7, Hwy 102. Phone 413/298-5536. www.berkshiretheatre.org.* Summer theater (Mon-Sat); Unicorn Theater presents new and experimental plays (Mon-Sat in season); children's theater (July-Aug, Thurs-Sat). Late June-late Aug.

Harvest Festival. *Berkshire Botanical Garden, Hwys 102 and 183, Stockbridge (01262). Phone 413/298-3926.* Celebrates the beginning of the harvest and foliage season in the Berkshire Hills. First weekend in Oct.

Stockbridge Main Street at Christmas. *6 Elm St, Stockbridge and West Stockbridge (01262). Phone 413/298-5200.* Events include a re-creation of Norman Rockwell's painting. Holiday marketplace, concerts, house tour, silent auction, sleigh/hay rides, caroling. First weekend in Dec.

Full-Service Inns

⭐⭐⭐ **THE RED LION INN.** *30 Main St, Stockbridge (01262). Phone 413/298-5545; fax 413/298-5130. www.redlioninn.com.* Designated a Historic Hotel of America by the National Trust for Historic Preservation, the Red Lion Inn sits on the picturesque and historic Main Street of Stockbridge that has been immortalized by Norman Rockwell. It is one of the few hostelries in New England to operate continuously since pre-1800. Today, the Red Lion offers a combination of guest rooms in the Inn on Main Street and suites among a handful of buildings throughout town, such as the former studio of artist Daniel Chester French and the former home of the Stockbridge Volunteer Fire Department. While there is unmistakable New England charm throughout, there is also an element of surprise: the inns decorating style definitely bows to noteworthy guests of the past, such as Hawthorne and Longfellow, but it also notes the Red Lion's connections to present-day stars of nearby Tanglewood, such as Bob Dylan. 108 rooms. Pets accepted, some restrictions; fee. Check-in 3 pm, check-out noon. Two restaurants, bar. Fitness room. Outdoor pool. **$$**

★ ★ ★ **WILLIAMSVILLE INN.** *Hwy 41, West Stockbridge (01266). Phone 413/274-6118; fax 413/274-3539. www.williamsvilleinn.com.* A perfect way to escape and get away to the Berkshires. This is an ideal spot to enjoy many of the annual festivals. Breakfast is served daily by the fireplace; for added charm, enjoy afternoon storytelling, held during the summer. 16 rooms, 3 story. Complimentary full breakfast. Check-in 3-6 pm, check-out 10:30 am. Restaurant, bar. Outdoor pool. Tennis. **$**

Specialty Lodgings

INN AT STOCKBRIDGE. *Hwy 7 N, Stockbridge (01262). Phone 413/298-3337; toll-free 888/466-7865; fax 413/298-3406. www.stockbridgeinn.com.* A decanter of port in your room. Breakfast at a gleaming, mahogany table in an elegant formal dining room. A large parlor with reading material and chairs by the fire. A stroll through beautifully landscaped gardens on 12 secluded acres. This 1906 Georgian-style inn—the land can be traced back to a missionary family who came to Stockbridge in 1739 to convert the natives to Christianity—contains eight guest rooms. The Cottage House, added in 1997, has four junior suites; The Barn, built in 2001, provides four deluxe suites. Each room is decorated with period antiques and lush fabrics, has traditional furnishings like armoires and four-poster beds, and has a view overlooking the inns meadows, reflecting pond, or some other calming sight. If you're feeling a bit guilty about all this graceful relaxation, wander into the exercise room for a turn on a cardio machine—although you may want to follow it up with an appointment with the inns on-call massage therapist. 16 rooms, 2 story. Children over 12 years only. Complimentary full breakfast. Check-in 2 pm, check-out 11 am. Fitness room. Outdoor pool. **$$$**

THE TAGGART HOUSE. *18 W Main St, Stockbridge (01262). Phone 413/298-4303; toll-free 800/918-2680.*

www.taggarthouse.com. This lovingly restored and renovated 1800s country house fronts the Housatonic River in the Berkshires. It is elegant, luxurious, sophisticated, intimate, and replete with the finest of antiques and sumptuous furnishings throughout. 4 rooms. Children over 18 years only. Complimentary full breakfast. Check-in 3 pm, check-out 11 am. **$$$**

Restaurants

★ **MICHAEL'S RESTAURANT & PUB.** *5 Elm St, Stockbridge (01262). Phone 413/298-3530. www.michaelsofstockbridge.com.* American, Italian menu. Lunch, dinner, late-night. Bar. Children's menu. Casual attire. Reservations recommended. **$$**

★ ★ ★ **THE RED LION.** *30 Main St, Stockbridge (01262). Phone 413/298-5545; fax 413/298-5130. www.redlioninn.com.* The candlelit dining room of this historic inn is filled with antiques, colonial pewter, and crystal. The contemporary New England menu emphasizes local, seasonal produce and offers several vegetarian options. American menu. Lunch, dinner. Bar. Children's menu. Business casual attire. Reservations recommended. Outdoor seating. **$$$**

Sturbridge (C-5)

Settled circa 1730
Population 7,837
Elevation 619 ft
Area Code 508
Information Tourist Information Center, 380 Main St; phone 508/347-2761 or toll-free 888/788-7274
Web Site www.sturbridge.org

What to See and Do

⭐ **Old Sturbridge Village.** *1 Old Sturbridge Village, Sturbridge (01566). On Hwy 20 W, 1 mile W of junction I-84 exit 2 and MA Tpke (I-90) exit 9. Phone 508/347-3362; toll-free 800/733-1830. www.osv.org.* A living history museum that re-creates a rural New England town of the 1830s. The museum covers more than 200 acres with more than 40 restored buildings; costumed interpreters demonstrate the life, work, and community celebrations of early 19th-century New Englanders. Working historical farm; many special events; picnic area. (Daily; closed Dec 25) **$$$$**

Special Event

New England Thanksgiving. *1 Old Sturbridge Village, Sturbridge (01566). Phone 508/347-3362.* Re-creation of early 19th-century Thanksgiving celebration. Includes turkey shoot, hearth cooking and meeting-house service. Thanksgiving Day.

Limited-Service Hotels

★ **COMFORT INN & SUITES COLONIAL.**
215 Charlton Rd (Hwy 20), Sturbridge (01566). Phone 508/347-3306; toll-free 800/228-5151; fax 508/347-3514. www.sturbridgecomfortinn.com. Located just outside Sturbridge, about a mile northeast of Old Sturbridge Village on Highway 20, this hotel is easily accessible from I-84. It has no restaurant of its own, but it sits in a small commercial center that also includes a Cracker Barrel, a fast-food restaurant, and a convenience store. Pets are allowed only in the older "courtyard units," so make arrangements in advance. 77 rooms, 2 story. Pets accepted, some restrictions; fee. Complimentary continental breakfast. Check-in 2 pm, check-out 11 am. High-speed Internet access. Bar. Fitness room. Indoor pool, outdoor pool, whirlpool. Business center. **$**

★ **ECONO LODGE.** *682 Main St, Sturbridge (01518). Phone 508/347-2324; toll-free 800/446-6900; fax 508/347-7320. www.econolodge.com.* 48 rooms. Complimentary continental breakfast. Check-in 2 pm, check-out 11 am. Outdoor pool. **$**

Full-Service Hotel

★ ★ ★ **STURBRIDGE HOST RESORT.**
366 Main St, Sturbridge (01566). Phone 508/347-7393; toll-free 800/582-3232; fax 508/347-3944. www.sturbridgehosthotel.com. Situated along a scenic country side, this hotel is located across the street from Old Sturbridge Village and allows business travelers to bring the family along for fun. 220 rooms, 3 story. Pets accepted; fee. Check-in 4 pm, check-out 11 am. Restaurant, bar. Fitness room. Indoor pool, whirlpool. Tennis. **$**

Full-Service Inn

★ ★ ★ **PUBLICK HOUSE HISTORIC INN.** *295 Main St, Sturbridge (01566). Phone 508/347-3313; toll-free 800/782-5425; fax 508/347-1246. www.publickhouse.com.* Built in 1771, this historic inn has 18th-century ambience with modern conviences. The guest rooms and suites all have private baths, air-conditioning, and are decorated with antiques or reproductions. Many have canopy beds and all are non-smoking rooms. Breakfast, lunch, and dinner is served here seven days a week. 17 rooms, 2 story. Pets accepted; fee. Check-in 3 pm, check-out 11 am. Restaurant, bar. Tennis. **$**

Restaurants

★ ★ **PUBLICK HOUSE.** *295 Main St, Sturbridge (01566). Phone 508/347-3313; fax 508/347-5073. www.publickhouse.com.* On Hwy 147 in West Springfield. New England menu. Breakfast, lunch, dinner. Bar. Children's menu. Outdoor seating. **$$$**

★ ★ **ROM'S RESTAURANT.** *179 Main St, Sturbridge (01566). Phone 508/347-3349; toll-free 800/766-1952; fax 508/347-1496. www.romsrestaurant.com.* Italian, American menu. Lunch, dinner. Closed Thanksgiving, Dec 25. Children's menu. Casual attire. **$$**

★ ★ ★ **WHISTLING SWAN.** *502 Main St, Sturbridge (01566). Phone 508/347-2321; fax 508/347-3361. www.thewhistlingswan.com.* There are really two restaurants in one at this local favorite: a quiet, fine dining continental restaurant downstairs and a more casual restaurant upstairs with nightly entertainment. American menu. Lunch, dinner, Sun brunch. Closed Dec 25. Bar. Children's menu. Business casual attire. Reservations recommended. Outdoor seating. **$$**

Sudbury Center (B-6)

See also Boston, Concord

Settled 1638
Population 16,841
Area Code 978
Zip 01776
Information Board of Selectmen, Loring Parsonage, 288 Old Sudbury Rd, Sudbury; phone 978/443-8891

Sudbury, which has a number of 17th-century buildings, is best known for the Wayside Inn at South

Sudbury, which was the scene of Longfellow's *"Tales of a Wayside Inn"* (1863).

What to See and Do

Longfellow's Wayside Inn. *72 Wayside Inn Rd, Sudbury Center (01776). 3 miles SW, just off Hwy 20. Phone 978/443-1776. www.wayside.org.* (1702) A historical and literary shrine, this is America's oldest operating inn. Originally restored by Henry Ford, it was badly damaged by fire in December 1955, and restored again by the Ford Foundation. Period furniture. (Daily; closed July 4, Dec 25) Also on the property are

> **Gristmill.** *72 Wayside Inn Rd, Sudbury Center (01776).* With waterwheel in operation; stone grinds wheat and corn used by inn's bakery. (Apr-Nov, daily)

> **Martha Mary Chapel.** *72 Wayside Inn Rd, Sudbury Center (01776).* Built and dedicated by Henry Ford in 1940, a nondenominational, nonsectarian chapel. No services; used primarily for weddings. (By appointment)

> **Redstone School.** *72 Wayside Inn Rd, Sudbury Center (01776).* (1798) "The Little Red Schoolhouse" immortalized in "Mary Had a Little Lamb." (May-Oct, daily)

Special Events

Fife & Drum Muster and Colonial Fair. *72 Wayside Inn Rd, Sudbury Center (01776). Phone 978/443-1776.* Muster takes place on field across from Longfellow's Wayside Inn. Fife and drum corps from New England and surrounding areas compete. Colonial crafts demonstrations and sales. Last Sat in Sept.

Reenactment of March of Sudbury Minutemen to Concord on April 19, 1775. *72 Wayside Inn Rd, Sudbury Center (01776). Phone 978/443-1776.* More than 200 costumed men muster on the Common before proceeding to Old North Bridge in Concord. Apr.

Limited-Service Hotels

★ ★ **BEST WESTERN ROYAL PLAZA HOTEL & TRADE CENTER.** *181 W Boston Post Rd, Marlborough (01752). Phone 508/460-0700; toll-free 888/543-9500; fax 508/480-8218. www.bestwestern. com.* 431 rooms, 6 story. Pets accepted; restrictions, fee. Check-in 3 pm, check-out 11 am. Restaurant, bar. Fitness room. Indoor pool. **$$**

★ **CLARION HOTEL.** *738 Boston Post Rd, Sudbury (01776). Phone 978/443-2223; toll-free 800/637-0113; fax 978/443-5830. www.clarionhotel.com.* 39 rooms, 3 story. Pets accepted; fee. Complimentary full breakfast. Check-in 3 pm, check-out noon. Fitness room. **$$**

★ ★ **THE HOTEL MARLBOROUGH.** *75 Felton St, Marlborough (01752). Phone 508/480-0015; fax 508/485-2242. www.thehotelmarlborough.com.* 206 rooms, 5 story. Check-in 3 pm, check-out noon. Restaurant, bar. Fitness room. Indoor pool, whirlpool. **$**

Specialty Lodgings

THE ARABIAN HORSE INN. *277 Old Sudbury Rd, Sudbury (01776). Phone 978/443-7400; toll-free 800/272-2426; fax 978/443-0234. www.arabianhorseinn. com.* Built in 1886. 5 rooms, 3 story. Pets accepted; fee. Complimentary full breakfast. Check-in 3 pm, check-out noon. **$$**

LONGFELLOW'S WAYSIDE INN. *72 Wayside Inn Rd, Sudbury (01776). Phone 978/443-1776; toll-free 800/339-1776; fax 978/443-8041. www.wayside.org.* This historic inn (1716), a national historic site, offers self-guided tours through restored public rooms. On the grounds are the Wayside Gristmill and Redstone School, built by former owner Henry Ford. 10 rooms, 2 story. Complimentary full breakfast. Check-in 3 pm, check-out 11 am. Restaurant, bar. **$**

Restaurant

★ ★ **LONGFELLOW'S WAYSIDE INN.** *72 Wayside Inn Rd, Sudbury Center (01776). Phone 978/443-1776; fax 978/443-8041. www.wayside.org.* Seafood, steak menu. Lunch, dinner. Closed July 4, Dec 24-25. Bar. Children's menu. **$$**

Truro and North Truro (Cape Cod) (C-9)

See also Boston, Concord

Settled Truro: circa 1700
Population 2,087
Elevation 20 ft
Area Code 508
Zip Truro 02666; North Truro 02652
Information Cape Cod Chamber of Commerce, Hwys 6 and 132, PO Box 790, Hyannis 02601-0790; phone 508/362-3225 or toll-free 888/227-3263
Web Site www.capecodchamber.org

Truro, named for one of the Channel towns of England, is today perhaps the most sparsely settled part of the Cape—with great stretches of rolling moorland dotted only occasionally with cottages. On the hill above the Pamet River marsh are two early 19th-century churches; one is now the town hall. The countryside is a favorite resort of artists and writers.

What to See and Do

Fishing. Surf casting on Atlantic beaches. Boat ramp at Pamet and Depot roads; fee for use, harbor master on duty.

Highland Light/Cape Cod Light. *Highland Light Rd, North Truro (02652). Phone 508/487-1121. www. lighthouse.cc/highland.* This delightful lighthouse boasts a long and glorious past as the first lighthouse on Cape Cod. Built in 1798 and fueled with whale oil, the lighthouse was rebuilt in 1853 and switched over to an automated facility in 1986. It now shines for 30 miles, the longest visible range of any lighthouse on the Cape. Thoreau stayed in the lighthouse during his wanderings on Cape Cod. Tours are offered 10 am5 pm daily from May through October. The museum next door, housed in a historic building, is open 10 am 4:30 pm, June through September, and highlights the fishing and whaling heritage of the area. (Daily May-late Oct) **$**

Pilgrim Heights Area. *Off Hwy 6. Phone 508/487-1256. www.nps.gov/caco.*Interpretive display, self-guided nature trails, picnicking; rest rooms. **FREE**

Swimming. *Head of the Meadow. N on Hwy 6 and W of Chamber of Commerce booth.* **Corn Hill Beach.** *On the bay (fee).* A sticker for all beaches must be purchased from National Park Service Visitor Center or at beach entrances. No lifeguards. Mid-June-Labor Day.

Truro Historical Society Museum. *6 Highland Rd, North Truro (02652). Phone 508/487-3397. www.trurohistorical. org.* Collection of artifacts from the town's historic past, including shipwreck mementos, whaling gear, ship models, 17th-century firearms, pirate chest, and period rooms. (June-Sept, Mon-Sat 10 am-4:30 pm, Sun from 1 pm) **$**

Limited-Service Hotel

★ **CROW'S NEST RESORT.** *496 Shore Rd, North Truro (02652). Phone 508/487-9031; toll-free 800/499-9799. www.caperesort.com.* 33 rooms, 2 story. Closed Dec-Mar. Check-in 2 pm, check-out 10 am. Beach. **$**
🐾

Restaurants

★ **ADRIAN'S.** *535 Hwy 6, North Truro (02652). Phone 508/487-4360; fax 508/487-6510. www.adriansrestaurant. com.* You won't find red-and-white-checkered tablecloths here. Adrian's, overlooking Cape Cod Bay at the Outer Reach, is light and airy, with a large deck providing optimal views of the water. The menu features Italian classics and a range of creative pizzas, like calamari fra diavolo and melanzane (eggplant). Italian menu. Breakfast, dinner. Closed mid-Oct-mid-May. Bar. Children's menu. Outdoor seating. **$$**

★ ★ **BLACKSMITH SHOP RESTAURANT.** *17 Truro Center Rd, Truro (02666). Phone 508/349-6554.* The Blacksmith Shop Restaurant stands out for its impressive, often daring cuisine. This place caters to slightly adventurous souls who enjoy traveling with their taste buds. From Mexico to Morocco, many of the items on the menu show off an international flair. A historic appearance adds charm, but this restaurant is fully rooted in the present. Seafood menu. Breakfast, dinner, Sun brunch. Closed Dec 25; also Mon-Wed in the off-season. Bar. Children's menu. **$$**

★ **MONTANO'S.** *481 Hwy 6, North Truro (02652). Phone 508/487-2026; fax 508/487-4913. www.montanos. com.* For great Italian cooking on the Cape, visitors snag a table at Montano's. This family-style restaurant offers a full range of classic dishes, and with a large steak menu, the place is paradise for meat lovers as well. From pasta and pizza to fish and meat, Montano's will satisfy the needs of any hungry diner. Italian, seafood menu. Lunch, dinner. Closed Dec 24-25. Bar. Children's menu. Casual attire. **$$**

Waltham (B-7)

See also Boston

Settled 1634
Population 59,226
Elevation 50 ft
Area Code 781
Zip 02154
Information Waltham West Suburban Chamber of Commerce, 84 South St; phone 781/894-4700
Web Site www.walthamchamber.com

The name Waltham, taken from the English town of Waltham Abbey, means "a home in the forest," and is still appropriate today, due to the town's many wooded areas. Originally an agricultural community, Waltham is now an industrial center. It is also the home of Bentley College and Regis College.

What to See and Do

Brandeis University. *415 South St, Waltham (02454).* *Phone 781/736-2000. www.brandeis.edu.* (1948) (3,700 students) The first Jewish-founded nonsectarian university in the United States. Its 250-acre campus includes Three Chapels, Rose Art Museum (Sept-May, Tues-Sun; closed holidays; free); Spingold Theater Arts Center (plays presented Oct-May; fee); and Slosberg Music Center, with classical and jazz performances (Sept-May).

Gore Place. *52 Gore St, Waltham (02453). On Hwy 20 at the Waltham-Watertown line. Phone 781/894-2798. www.goreplace.org.* A living history farm, Gore Place may be New England's finest example of Federal-period residential architecture; changing exhibits; 40 acres of cultivated fields. The mansion, designed in Paris and built in 1805, has 22 rooms filled with examples of Early American, European, and Asian antiques. (Mid-Apr-mid-Nov, Thurs-Mon hourly tours 1 pm-4 pm) **$$**

Lyman Estate. *185 Lyman St, Waltham (02452). Phone 781/893-7232.* (1793) Designed by Samuel McIntire for Boston merchant Theodore Lyman. Enlarged and remodeled in the 1880s, the ballroom and parlor retain Federal design. Landscaped grounds. Five operating greenhouses contain grape vines, camellias, orchids, and herbs. House open by appointment for groups only. Greenhouses (Mon-Sat, also Sun afternoons). **$$**

Spellman Museum of Stamps and Postal History. *235 Wellesley St, Weston (02493). 4 miles W on Hwy 20. Phone 781/768-8367. www.spellman.org.* Exhibition gallery; library. (Thurs-Sat; closed holidays) **$**

Limited-Service Hotels

★ ★ **DOUBLETREE HOTEL.** *550 Winter St, Waltham (02451). Phone 781/890-6767; toll-free 800/222-8733; fax 781/890-9097. www.doubletree. com.* Situated near Lexington and Concord as well as a wealth of historical stops, this hotel has a fitness center, pool, and fully equipped rooms for the business traveler. 275 rooms, 8 story, all suites. Check-in 3 pm, check-out 11 am. Restaurant, bar. Fitness room. Indoor pool, whirlpool. Business center. **$**

★ ★ **HOME SUITES INN.** *455 Totten Pond Rd, Waltham (02451). Phone 781/890-3000; toll-free 866/335-6175; fax 781/890-0233. www.homesuitesinn. com.* 116 rooms, 3 story, all suites. Pets accepted; fee. Complimentary continental breakfast. Check-in 3 pm, check-out 11 am. Restaurant, bar. Outdoor pool. **$**

Full-Service Hotel

★ ★ ★ **THE WESTIN WALTHAM-BOSTON.** *70 3rd Ave, Waltham (02451). Phone 781/290-5600; toll-free 800/228-3000; fax 781/290-5626. www.westin. com/waltham.* Just 15 minutes from downtown Boston, this modern hotel has standard rooms providing comfort and service. Many rooms are geared to the business traveler, offering business services such as dataports and faxes. 376 rooms, 8 story. Check-in 3 pm, check-out noon. Restaurant, bar. Fitness room. Indoor pool, whirlpool. Airport transportation available. Business center. **$$**

Restaurants

★ ★ ★ **GRILLE AT HOBBS BROOK.** *550 Winter St, Waltham (02451). Phone 781/487-4263; fax 781/890-9097. www.grilleathobbsbrook.com.* This restaurant is located in the Doubletree Hotel (see). In season, many of the ingredients come from the on-site garden. The plush setting is a quiet, relaxing place to dine. American menu. Breakfast, lunch, dinner. Bar. Children's menu. **$$$**

★ ★ ★ **IL CAPRICCIO.** *888 Main St, Waltham (02451). Phone 781/894-2234; fax 781/891-3227. www. bostonchefs.com.* Gauzy drapes and glass partitions give this innovative restaurant a chic, urban look. Italian menu. Dinner. Closed Sun; holidays. Bar. **$$$**

★ ★ ★ **NEW GINZA.** *63-65 Galen St, Watertown (02472). Phone 617/923-2100; fax 617/923-2102. newginza.net.* Sushi menu. Lunch, dinner. Closed one week in July. Casual attire. **$$$**

🅿

★ ★ **TUSCAN GRILL.** *361 Moody St, Waltham (02453). Phone 781/891-5486; fax 781/647-4204. www. tuscangrillwaltham.com.* Italian menu. Dinner. Closed July 4, Thanksgiving, Dec 24-25. Bar. **$$**

Wellesley (B-7)

See also Boston

Settled 1661
Population 26,613
Elevation 141 ft
Area Code 781
Zip 02181
Information Chamber of Commerce, One Hollis St, Suite 111; phone 781/235-2446
Web Site www.wellesleychambler.org

This Boston suburb was named after an 18th-century landowner, Samuel Welles. It is an educational and cultural center. There are four widely known institutions here: Dana Hall, a girls' preparatory school; Babson College, a business school; Massachusetts Bay Community College; and Wellesley College.

What to See and Do

Wellesley College. *106 Central St, Wellesley (02481). Central and Washington sts, on Hwy 16/135. Phone 781/283-1000. www.wellesley.edu.* (1870) (2,200 women) Founded by Henry F. Durant. 500 wooded acres bordering Lake Waban. On campus are Davis Museum and Cultural Center and Margaret C. Ferguson Greenhouses (Daily).

Restaurant

★ ★ ★ **BLUE GINGER.** *583 Washington St, Wellesley (02482). Phone 781/283-5790; fax 781/283-5772. www.ming.com.* At Blue Ginger, celebrity chef Ming Tsai shows that he is more than just another pretty face on the Food Network. In addition to being able to read from a teleprompter with ease, the man can cook. Fusing East and West, layering sweet with spice, he is a dazzling chef with a colorful palette of culinary talents. This hotspot is packed regularly, so reserve a table early. The menu is filled with drool-worthy dishes like leek-potato pancakes and five-peppercorn grilled sirloin delicately smothered in Roquefort sauce. American menu. Lunch, dinner. Closed Sun. Children's menu. Reservations recommended. Outdoor seating. **$$$**

Wellfleet (Cape Cod) (C-9)

Settled circa 1725
Population 2,749
Elevation 50 ft
Area Code 508
Zip 02667
Information Chamber of Commerce, PO Box 571; phone 508/349-2510
Web Site www.wellfleetchamber.com

Once a fishing town, Wellfleet dominated the New England oyster business in the latter part of the 19th century. It is now a summer resort and an art gallery town, with many tourist homes and cottages. Southeast of town is the Marconi Station Area of Cape Cod National Seashore (see). Fishermen here can try their luck in the Atlantic surf or off deep-sea charter fishing boats.

What to See and Do

Historical Society Museum. *266 Main St, Wellfleet (02667). Phone 508/349-9157. www.wellfleethistoricalsociety. com.* Marine items, whaling tools, Marconi memorabilia, needlecraft, photograph collection, marine and primitive paintings. (Late June-early Sept, Tues-Sat; schedule may vary)

Sailing. Rentals at Wellfleet Marina; accommodates 150 boats; launching ramp, facilities.

Swimming. At numerous bayside and ocean beaches on marked roads off Highway 6. Freshwater ponds with swimming are scattered through woods east of Highway 6. (Parking sticker necessary mid-June to Labor Day.)

Wednesday Night Square Dance. *Town Pier, Holbroook and Commercial sts, Wellfleet (02667). Phone 508/349-0330. www.wellfleetma.org.* If you want one of the most unique experiences on Cape Cod, visit this old-fashioned square dance, where you can spin your partner round and round based on the instructions of a master caller. If you're not a skilled square dancer, come early, when dance steps are easier to master, and gain confidence as the night progresses. (July-Aug) **FREE**

Wellfleet Bay Wildlife Sanctuary. *291 Hwy 6, South Wellfleet (02663). On W side of Hwy 6. Phone 508/349-2615. www.wellfleetbay.org.* Operated by the Massachusetts Audubon Society. Self-guiding nature trails. Natural history summer day camp for children. Guided nature walks, lectures, classes, Monomoy Island natural history tours. Sanctuary (Memorial Day-Columbus Day: daily; rest of year: Tues-Sun). **$**

Wellfleet Drive-In Theater. *Hwy 6, Wellfleet (02667). At the Eastham-Wellfleet town line. Phone 508/349-7176. www.wellfleetdrivein.com.* Wellfleet Drive-In Theater, the only outdoor theater on the Cape, projects a family-oriented double feature every evening under the stars. Arrive at 7 pm to get your ideal parking spot; the kids can spend the hour in the play area. Enjoy better concessions than you'll find at any indoor movie theater. (Mid-Oct-mid-Apr) **$$**

Limited-Service Hotel

★ ★ **WELLFLEET MOTEL & LODGE.** *146 Hwy 6, South Wellfleet (02663). Phone 508/349-3535; toll-free 800/852-2900; fax 508/349-1192. www.wellfleetmotel. com.* 65 rooms, 2 story. Check-in 3:30 pm, check-out 11 am. Restaurant, bar. Indoor pool, outdoor pool, whirlpool. **$**

Specialty Lodging

INN AT DUCK CREEK. *70 Main St, Wellfleet (02667). Phone 508/349-9333; fax 508/349-0234. www. innatduckcreeke.com.* Sitting porch overlooks Duck Creek. 25 rooms, 3 story. Closed Nov-Apr. Complimentary continental breakfast. Check-in 2 pm. Check-out 11 am. **$**

Restaurant

★ **MOBY DICK'S.** *3225 Hwy 6, Wellfleet (02667). Phone 508/349-9795. www.mobydicksrestaurant.com.*

With its red-checkered tablecloths and walls decorated with fishing nets, Moby Dick's is the very definition of a seafood shack. Fish plays a starring role throughout the menu here, from the soups and salads to the sandwiches and entrées. Lobsters and clambakes are popular choices. Plate cleaners take note: the desserts are worth leaving a bit of dinner behind. Seafood menu. Lunch, dinner. Closed mid-Oct-Apr. Children's menu. Casual attire. Outdoor seating. **$$**

★ ★ **VAN RENSSELAER'S RESTAURANT & RAW BAR.** *1019 Hwy 6, South Wellfleet (02663). Phone 508/349-2127; fax 508/349-1783. www. vanrensselaers.com.* Van Rensselaer's wins kudos for its fantastic cooking and inviting atmosphere. Family-run for more than 30 years, this homey place makes everyone feel like a member of the family. Its comprehensive menu is a real crowd-pleaser, with seafood, meat, vegetarian entrées, and even a children's menu. American menu. Breakfast, dinner. Closed Nov-Mar. Bar. Children's menu. Outdoor seating. **$$**

Williamstown (A-2)

See also North Adams

Settled 1749
Population 8,424
Elevation 638 ft
Area Code 413
Zip 01267

A French and Indian War hero, Colonel Ephraim Williams, Jr., left a bequest in 1755 to establish a "free school" in West Hoosuck, provided the town be renamed after him. In 1765, the town name was changed to Williamstown, and in 1793, the school became Williams College. The life of this charming Berkshire Hills town still centers around the college.

What to See and Do

Sterling and Francine Clark Art Institute. *225 South St, Williamstown (01267). Phone 413/458-2303. www. clarkart.edu.* More than 30 paintings by Renoir, other French Impressionists; old-master paintings; English and American silver; American artists Homer, Sargent, Cassatt, Remington. Extensive art library (Mon-Fri). Museum shop. Picnic facilities on grounds. (July-Labor Day: daily; rest of year: Tues-Sun; closed Jan 1, Thanksgiving, Dec 25) **$$**

Williams College. *54 Sawyer Library Dr, Williamstown (01267). Hwy 7. Phone 413/597-3131. www.williams. edu.* (1793) (1,950 students) Private liberal arts college; campus has a wide variety of architectural styles, ranging from colonial to Gothic. Chapin Library of rare books is one of nation's finest, housing the four founding documents of the United States. Hopkins Observatory, the nation's oldest (1836), has planetarium shows. Adams Memorial Theatre presents plays. The Paul Whiteman Collection houses Whiteman's recordings and memorabilia. Also here is

Williams College Museum of Art. *15 Lawrence Hall Dr, Williamstown (01267). Main St. Phone 413/597-2429.* Considered one of the finest college art museums in the country. Houses approximately 11,000 pieces. Exhibits emphasize contemporary, modern, American, and non-Western art. Museum shop. (Tues-Sat 10 am-5 pm, Sun from 1 pm and Mon holidays; closed Jan 1, Thanksgiving, Dec 25) **FREE**

Limited-Service Hotels

★ **BERKSHIRE HILLS MOTEL.** *1146 Cold Spring Rd, Williamstown (01267). Phone 413/458-3950; toll-free 800/388-9677; fax 413/458-5878. www.berkshirehillsmotel. com.* 21 rooms, 2 story. Complimentary buffet breakfast. Check-in 2 pm, check-out 11 am. Outdoor pool. **$**

★ **FOUR ACRES MOTEL.** *213 Main St; Hwy 2, Williamstown (01267). Phone 413/458-8158; fax 413/458-8158. www.fouracresmotel.com.* A beautifully landscaped pool with a mountain view is a highlight of this 31-room motel, situated on Highway 2 just east of the town center. The hotel takes advantage of its location in other ways; in the summer, attractive café tables are set up on a wooden deck so that guests can relax in front of the beautiful scenery. The Four Acres has also made sure that all second-floor rooms have balconies. 31 rooms, 2 story. Complimentary continental breakfast. Check-in 1 pm, check-out 11 am. Outdoor pool. **$**

Full-Service Inns

★ ★ ★ **1896 HOUSE.** *910 Cold Spring Rd, Williamstown (01267). Phone 413/458-1896; toll-free 888/999-1896. www.1896house.com.* As its name suggests, this property offers its guests the choice to stay by the brook or by the pond. The Brookside, hidden

from the road by trees, features Cushman rock maple furniture, luxurious amenities, and a beautiful gazebo. The Pondside offers rooms with two queen beds and slightly fewer frills. 29 rooms. Complimentary continental breakfast. Check-in 2 pm, check-out 11 am. Restaurant. Outdoor pool. **$**

★ ★ ★ **THE ORCHARDS.** *222 Adams Rd, Williamstown (01267). Phone 413/458-9611; toll-free 800/225-1517; fax 413/458-3273. www.orchardshotel. com.* Culture seekers adore The Orchards for its tranquil setting and ideal location in the heart of the Berkshires. Grand gates of Vermont granite announce that you've arrived at the European chateau-style property, just east of the village center, off Highway 2 and Adams Road. This delightful hotel is the perfect place to unwind and take in the towns renowned arts festivals, museums, and antiques shops, many of which are within walking distance. Yet its peaceful garden setting makes it feel a million miles away from civilization. Its mood is decidedly relaxed, but sophisticated. The charming guest rooms echo the resort's spirit with a warm décor reminiscent of the English countryside. Luxurious appointments range from Persian rugs and Austrian crystal chandeliers in the public spaces to bay windows and upgraded baths with marble floors in the guest accommodations. All rooms have a refrigerator, cleverly housed in a custom sideboard and stocked with beverages. Yasmin's restaurant (see) serves a mix of continental and American cuisine in an elegant setting, and guests are invited to dine outdoors in the garden during summer months. The experience is sure to transport, with the gentle trickle of the fountain and the heady fragrance of the abundant blooms. 49 rooms, 3 story. Check-in 4 pm, check-out noon. High-speed Internet access. Restaurant, bar. Fitness room. Outdoor pool, whirlpool. **$$$**

★ ★ ★ **WILLIAMS INN.** *Hwys 7 and 2, Williamstown (01267). Phone 413/458-9371; toll-free 800/828-0133; fax 413/458-2767. www.williamsinn. com.* The Williams Inn is situated on Williams College campus just two blocks from the village center. Since Williamstown is dominated by the college, visitors at the inn generally have something in common, and there is a warmth and friendliness among both guests and staff. It also has the feel of a community focal point; the area around the front desk has a wealth of information and local brochures, and staff is ready to answer any and all questions. Another focal point for both guests and locals alike is the inns entertainment:

depending on the season, you can catch anything from jazz to acoustic guitar to cabaret. 125 rooms, 3 story. Check-in 3 pm, check-out 11 am. High-speed Internet access. Restaurant, bar. Indoor pool, whirlpool. **$$**

Restaurants

★ ★ ★ **LE JARDIN.** *777 Cold Spring Rd, Williamstown (01267). Phone 413/458-8032. www. lejardininn.com.* Nestled among pines near a trout pond, this lovely restaurant serves traditional French food in a comfortable, homey setting. French menu. Dinner. Closed Tues in Sept-June. Bar. Guest rooms available. **$$**

★ ★ **WATER STREET GRILL.** *123 Water St, Williamstown (01267). Phone 413/458-2175; fax 413/458-4820.* American menu. Lunch, dinner. Closed Thanksgiving, Dec 25. Bar. Children's menu. Casual attire. **$$**

★ ★ ★ **YASMIN'S.** *222 Adams Rd, Williamstown (01267). Phone 413/458-9611; fax 413/458-3273. www. orchardshotel.com.* The European chefs who rotate through the kitchens of this fine hotel leave their mark on the creative American menu. Among the selections served in the elegant country dining room are Chilean sea bass with thyme flowers and veal loin with wasabi butter. American menu. Breakfast, lunch, dinner, Sun brunch. Bar. Children's menu. Outdoor seating. **$$$**

Worcester (B-5)

Settled 1673
Population 172,648
Elevation 480 ft
Area Code 508
Information Worcester County Convention & Visitors Bureau, 30 Worcester Center Blvd, 01608; phone 508/753-2920
Web Site www.worcester.org

The municipal seal of Worcester (WUS-ter) calls it the "Heart of the Commonwealth." One of the largest cities in New England, it is an important industrial center. Also a cultural center, it has some outstanding museums and twelve colleges.

What to See and Do

American Antiquarian Society. *185 Salisbury St, Worcester (01609). Phone 508/755-5221.* Research library is the largest collection of source materials pertaining to the first 250 years of American history. Specializing in the period up to 1877, the library has 2/3 of all pieces known to have been printed in this country between 1640 and 1821. (Mon-Fri; closed holidays. Guided tours Wed afternoons). **FREE**

EcoTarium. *222 Harrington Way, Worcester (01604). 1 1/2 miles E. Phone 508/929-2700. www.ecotarium.org.* Contains museum with environmental science exhibits; solar/lunar observatory, multimedia planetarium theater; African Hall. Indoor-outdoor wildlife, aquariums; train ride; picnicking. (Tues-Sat 10 am-5 pm, Sun from noon; closed holidays) **$$**

Higgins Armory Museum. *100 Barber Ave, Worcester (01606). Phone 508/853-6015. www.higgins.org.* Large exhibit of medieval-Renaissance and feudal Japan's arms and armor; paintings, tapestries, stained glass. Armor demonstrations and try-ons. (Tues-Sat 10 am-4 pm, Sun from noon; closed holidays) **$$**

John H. Chaffy Blackstone River Valley National Heritage Corridor. *414 Massasoit Rd, Worcester (01604). Phone 508/755-8899. www.massaudubon. org.* This 250,000-acre region extends southward to Providence, Rhode Island (see) and includes myriad points of historical and cultural interest. Visitor center at Massachusetts Audubon Society's Broad Meadow Brook Wildlife Sanctuary; tours and interpretive programs.

Salisbury Mansion. *40 Highland St, Worcester (01609). Phone 508/753-8278. www.worcesterhistory.org.* (1772) House of leading businessman and philanthropist Stephen Salisbury. Restored to 1830s appearance. Guided tours. (Thurs-Sat afternoons; closed holidays) **$**

Worcester Art Museum. *55 Salisbury St, Worcester (01609). Phone 508/799-4406. www.worcesterart.org.* Fifty centuries of paintings, sculpture, decorative arts, prints, drawings, and photography from America to ancient Egypt; changing exhibits; tours, films, lectures. Café, gift shop. (Wed-Sun; closed holidays) **$$**

Worcester Common Outlets. *100 Front St, Worcester (01608). I-290, exit 16. Phone 508/798-2581.* More than 100 outlet stores can be found at this indoor outlet mall. Food court. (Daily)

Special Event

Worcester Music Festival of the Worcester County Music Association. *Mechanics Hall, 321 Main St, Worcester (01608). Phone 508/752-5608.* The country's oldest music festival; folkdance companies; choral masterworks; symphony orchestras, guest soloists; young people's program. Seven to 12 concerts. Sept-Mar.

Full-Service Hotels

★ ★ ★ **BEECHWOOD HOTEL.** *363 Plantation St, Worcester (01605). Phone 508/754-5789; toll-free 800/344-2589; fax 508/752-2060. www.beechwoodhotel. com.* A 24-hour fitness room, 24-hour business center, free local and long-distance phone calls, free incoming and outgoing faxes, and free high-speed Internet access in all guest rooms—as well as a location just 1.5 miles from downtown Worcester and easy proximity to the Centrium Convention Centre—make this an exceptional business hotel. Yet there is also grace and beauty. A polished foyer with marble floors greets guests, a small seating area around the fireplace beckons you to sit awhile, a restored, antique, stained-glass window draws your glance upward. Stairs lead down to a casual bar, the Harlequin Restaurant, and function rooms such as the Grand Ballroom, which includes the century-old Maria Gill Wilson Room, formerly the chapel at Worcester City Hospital. Whether you're there for business or pleasure, don't forget to keep your eye out for whimsy—such as an antique carousel horse or a jar of gummy bears in your guest room. 73 rooms, 5 story. Complimentary continental breakfast. Check-in 3 pm, check-out 11 am. High-speed Internet access. Restaurant, bar. Fitness room. Business center. **$$**

★ ★ ★ **CROWNE PLAZA HOTEL.** *10 Lincoln Sq, Worcester (01608). Phone 508/791-1600; toll-free 800/628-4240; fax 508/791-1796. www.cpworcester. com.* If fresh-roasted coffee and a location facing Main Street are your idea of hotel perfection, look no further. The Crowne Plaza is modern and amenity-filled, near many cultural venues, close to shopping malls and the booksellers' marketplace, and within ten minutes of most area businesses. Yet the hotel itself is also a place for relaxation, with a large indoor/outdoor pool and a courtyard landscaped with holly and flowering fruit trees. Ask for a room with a balcony, where you can enjoy morning coffee with a view of Lincoln Square. 242 rooms, 9 story. Check-in 4 pm, check-out noon. Wireless Internet access. Restaurant, bar. Fitness room. Indoor pool, outdoor pool, whirlpool. Airport transportation available. Business center. **$$**

Restaurant

★ ★ ★ **CASTLE.** *1230 Main St, Leicester (01524). Phone 508/892-9090; fax 508/892-3620. www.castle restaurant.com.* Owned and operated by the Nicas family since 1950, this "castle," complete with turrets, towers, and a moat, provides a unique dining experience for all the seasons of the year. Choose from one of the two distinctly different dining rooms, the Crusader or the Camelot, each with its own creative menu. French menu. Lunch, dinner. Closed Mon; Jan 1, Thanksgiving, Dec 25. Bar. Children's menu. Outdoor seating. **$$$**

Yarmouth (Cape Cod)

See also Hyannis and Barnstable

Population 11,603
Elevation 20 ft
Area Code 508
Zip 02664
Information Yarmouth Area Chamber of Commerce, PO Box 479; 800/732-1008; or the Cape Cod Chamber of Commerce, Hwy 6 and Hwy 132, PO Box 790, Hyannis 02601-0790; phone 508/362-3225 or toll-free 888/227-3263
Web Site www.capecodchamber.org

Much of the Yarmouth area was developed on the strength of seafaring and fishing in the first half of the 19th century. Well-preserved old houses line Main Street to the north in Yarmouth Port, architecturally among the choicest communities in Massachusetts. Bass River, to the south, also contains many fine estates.

What to See and Do

Cape Symphony Orchestra. *712A Main St, Yarmouth Port (02675). Phone 508/362-1111. www.capesymphony. org.* This 90-member professional orchestra performs 15 indoor concerts throughout the year at Barnstable High Schools 1,400-seat auditorium. Concerts selections range from classical to pops to special children's events. If you're visiting in summer, catch two outdoor pops concertsone at the Mashpee Commons in Mashpee at the end of July; the other at Eldredge Park in Orleans in mid-August. (Sept-May; also two concerts in summer) **$$$$**

Captain Bangs Hallet House. *11 Strawberry Ln, Yarmouth Port (02664). Off Hwy 6A, near Yarmouth Port Post Office. Phone 508/362-3021.* Early 19th-century sea captain's home. (June-Oct: Thurs-Sun afternoons; rest of year: by appointment) Botanic trails (all year; donation). Gate house (June-mid-Sept, daily). **$$**

Pewter Crafters of Cape Cod. *791 Route 28, Harwich Port (02646). Phone 508/432-5858. www.pewtercrafter capecod.com.* The Pewter Crafters studio gives you a chance to view pewter craftspeople plying their trade, and then admire their creations on display. The shop sells both traditional and more contemporary designs of tableware, jewelry, candlesticks, and decanters, so you can take home a unique piece of Cape Cod home with you. (Tues-Sat; hours vary by season)

Swimming. *265 Sisson Rd, South Yarmouth (02645). Phone 508/430-7532.* Nantucket Sound and bayside beaches. Parking fee.

Winslow Crocker House. *250 Hwy 6A, South Yarmouth (02675). On Old King's Hwy, Hwy 6A, in Yarmouth Port. Phone 508/362-3021.* (Circa 1780) Georgian house adorned with 17th-, 18th-, and 19th-century furnishings collected in the early 20th century. Includes furniture made by New England craftsmen in the colonial and Federal periods; hooked rugs, ceramics, pewter. (June-Oct, first Sat of the month) **$**

Limited-Service Hotels

★ **ALL SEASON MOTOR INN.** *1199 Rte 28, South Yarmouth (02664). Phone 508/394-7600; toll-free 800/527-0359; fax 508/398-7160. www.allseasons.com.* 114 rooms, 2 story. Check-in 3 pm, check-out 11 am. Restaurant. Fitness room. Outdoor pool, whirlpool. **$**

★ ★ **BEST WESTERN BLUE WATER ON THE OCEAN.** *291 S Shore Dr, South Yarmouth (02664). Phone 508/398-2288; toll-free 800/367-9393; fax 508/398-1010. www.bestwestern.com.* 106 rooms, 2 story. Check-in 3 pm, check-out 11 am. Restaurant, bar. Children's activity center. Indoor pool, outdoor pool, whirlpool. Tennis. Beach. **$$**

★ ★ **BLUE ROCK RESORT.** *39 Todd Rd, South Yarmouth (02664). Phone 508/398-6962; toll-free 800/780-7234; fax 508/398-1830. www.redjacketresorts. com.* 44 rooms, 2 story. Closed late-Oct-Mar. Check-in 2 pm, check-out 11 am. Restaurant, bar. Outdoor pool, whirlpool. Golf, 18 holes. Tennis. **$**

★ **GULL WING SUITES.** *822 Main St (Hwy 28), South Yarmouth (02664). Phone 508/394-9300; toll-free 877/984-9300; fax 508/394-1190. www.gullwinghotel. com.* 136 rooms, 2 story. Check-in 3 pm, check-out 11 am. Indoor pool, outdoor pool, whirlpool. **$**

Full-Service Resorts

★ ★ **RED JACKET BEACH.** *1 S Shore Dr, South Yarmouth (02664). Phone 508/398-6941; toll-free 800/672-0500; fax 508/398-1214. www.redjacketbeach. com.* Found steps away from the coast, this Cape Cod oceanfront resort has private balconies or porches so that guests may enjoy the view. Indoor and outdoor heated pools and complete recreation facilities including spas, sailing, and tennis are available. 150 rooms, 2 story. Closed late Oct-Mar. Check-in 3 pm, check-out 11 am. Restaurant, bar. Children's activity center. Fitness room. Indoor pool, outdoor pool, whirlpool. Tennis. **$$**

★ ★ **RIVIERA BEACH RESORT.** *327 S Shore Dr, South Yarmouth (02664). Phone 508/398-2273; toll-free 800/227-3263; fax 508/398-1202. www.rivieraresort. com.* 125 rooms, 2 story. Closed Nov-Mar. Check-in 3 pm, check-out 11 am. Restaurant, bar. Children's activity center. Indoor pool, outdoor pool, whirlpool. Beach. **$$**

Full-Service Inn

★ ★ ★ **LIBERTY HILL INN.** *77 Main St, Yarmouth Port (02675). Phone 508/362-3976; toll-free 800/821-3977; fax 508/362-6485. www.libertyhillinn. com.* Built in 1825, this charming bed-and-breakfast features individually appointed rooms, all unique in their décor and feel; many feature fireplaces and canopy beds. 9 rooms, 3 story. Complimentary full breakfast. Check-in 3-9 pm, check-out 11 am. Airport transportation available. **$**

Specialty Lodgings

CAPTAIN FARRIS HOUSE BED & BREAKFAST. *308 Old Main St, South Yarmouth (02664). Phone 508/760-2818; toll-free 800/350-9477; fax 508/398-1262. www.captainfarris.com.* With its beautifully landscaped lawns and breathtaking views, this bed-and-breakfast will surely please everyone. Guests can enjoy sailing, canoeing, kayaking, and windsurfing. Antique shopping, bird-watching, and The John F. Kennedy Museum are also nearby. 10 rooms. Children over 10 years only. Complimentary full breakfast. Check-in 3-7 pm, check-out 11 am. Restaurant. Whirlpool. **$**
🅰

COLONIAL HOUSE INN & RESTAURANT. *277 Main St (Hwy 6A), Yarmouth Port (02675). Phone 508/362-4348; toll-free 800/999-3416; fax 508/362-8034. www.colonialhousecapecod.com.* Sitting porch overlooks Duck Creek. 21 rooms, 3 story. Pets accepted; fee. Complimentary full breakfast. Check-in 3 pm, check-out 11 am. Restaurant, bar. Indoor pool, whirlpool. Business center. **$**
🐾 🛏 🏃

INN AT LEWIS BAY. *57 Maine Ave, West Yarmouth (02673). Phone 508/771-3433; toll-free 800/962-6679; fax 508/790-1186. www.innatlewisbay.com.* Located in a quiet seaside neighborhood just one block from Lewis Bay, this Dutch colonial bed-and-breakfast offers guests a relaxing place to vacation. A bountiful breakfast is served each morning, and afternoon refreshments each afternoon. 6 rooms, 2 story. Children over 12 years only. Complimentary full breakfast. Check-in 3-8 pm. Check-out 11 am. **$**
🅰

Restaurants

★ ★ **ABBICCI.** *43 Main St, Yarmouth (02675). Phone 508/362-3501; fax 508/362-7802. www.abbicci restaurant.com.* Abbicci's bold interiors prepare diners for the splashy northern Italian cooking available at this restaurant housed within a former sea captain's home. With its clever cuisine, the talented kitchen offers a much-appreciated respite from the seafood shacks and family-style Italian restaurants on the Cape, and its civilized atmosphere is a boon for adults. Italian menu. Dinner. Bar. **$$$**

★ ★ **ARDEO.** *23V Whites Path, South Yarmouth (02664). Phone 508/760-1500.* The bold, contemporary setting of Ardeo is a perfect match for its flavorful Mediterranean cuisine. This sensational spot offers Cape Codders something different, dazzling them with the flavors of Italy, Greece, and the Middle East. From salads, wraps, and panini for lighter dining to homemade pastas and wood-stone pizzas, the menu offers many choices. Mediterranean menu. Lunch, dinner. Bar. Children's menu. Casual attire. **$$**

★ ★ **INAHO.** *157 Main St, Yarmouth Port (02675). Phone 508/362-5522.* Inaho wins praise for its excellent selection of sushi and sashimi. Those who aren't fans of raw fish trumpet the fantastic teriyaki dishes and exceptional tempura. This restaurant has an elegant setting, complete with a traditional Japanese garden with goldfish pond out back. Sushi, Japanese menu. Dinner. Closed Mon; Easter, Thanksgiving, Dec 25. Casual attire. **$$**
🅰

★ ★ **RIVERWAY LOBSTER HOUSE.** *Hwy 28, South Yarmouth (02664). Phone 508/398-2172.* Families and friends enjoy the charm of the Riverway Lobster House. From its traditional white "Cape" building to its seaside menu, this 50-year-old restaurant is the very essence of Cape Cod. Seafood and meat account for most of the menu, although many like to get their hands dirty with this restaurant's well-liked barbecued ribs and chicken. Seafood menu. Dinner. Closed Dec 25. Bar. Children's menu. **$$**

★ ★ **SKIPPER RESTAURANT.** *152 S Shore Dr, South Yarmouth (02664). Phone 508/394-7406; fax 508/394-0627. www.skipper-restaurant.com.* The Skipper is the ultimate beach restaurant and a true Cape landmark. Located across from Yarmouth's Smugglers Beach, this informal restaurant has been entertaining visitors since 1936. Nautical memorabilia decorates the interior, while windows share beach and water views. The all-day dining offers a range of choices, from American fare to local dishes. Seafood menu. Lunch, dinner. Closed Nov-mid-Apr. Bar. Children's menu. Casual attire. Outdoor seating. **$$**

★ ★ **YARMOUTH HOUSE.** *335 Main St, West Yarmouth (02673). Phone 508/771-5154; fax 508/790-2801. www.yarmouthouse.com.* The Yarmouth House has an inimitable charm. From its amiable staff to its open-air garden complete with wooden water wheel, this restaurant creates a lasting memory. Lunch focuses on sandwiches and burgers, while dinner highlights chicken, veal, seafood, and steaks. Lobster lovers rejoice in the many different recipes served here. Seafood menu. Lunch, dinner. Closed Dec 25. Bar. Children's menu. **$$**

New Hampshire

New Hampshire is a year-round vacation state, offering a variety of landscapes and recreational opportunities within its six unique regions. The lush Lakes Region, dominated by Lake Winnipesaukee, and the Seacoast Region, with its beaches, bays, and historic waterfront towns, are ideal for water sports. The rugged, forested White Mountains offer hiking, camping, dazzling autumn foliage, and excellent skiing. The "little cities" of the Merrimack Valley—Nashua, Manchester, and Concord—are centers of commerce, industry, government, and the arts. Rural 19th-century New England comes alive in the small towns of the Monadnock Region, and many features of these areas come together in the Dartmouth-Lake Sunapee Region, home of Dartmouth College.

Population: 1,109,252

Area: 8,992 square miles

Elevation: 0-6,288 feet

Peak: Mount Washington (Coos County)

Entered Union: Ninth of original 13 states (June 21, 1788)

Capital: Concord

Motto: Live Free or Die

Nickname: Granite State

Flower: Purple Lilac

Bird: Purple Finch

Tree: White Birch

Time Zone: Eastern

Web Site: www.visitnh.gov

Fun Facts:

- The first US public library was opened in Peterborough in 1837.
- Open since 1789, the John Hancock Inn in Hancock, NH, is the oldest operating tavern in New England.

The mountains in New Hampshire are known for their rugged "notches" (called "gaps" and "passes" elsewhere), and the old valley towns have a serene beauty. Some of the best skiing in the East can be found at several major resorts here. The state's many parks, antiques shops, art and theater festivals, and county fairs are also popular attractions, and more than half of New England's covered bridges are in New Hampshire.

David Thomson and a small group of colonists settled on the New Hampshire coast near Portsmouth in 1623. These early settlements were part of Massachusetts. In 1679, they became a separate royal province under Charles the Second. In 1776, the Provincial Congress adopted a constitution making New Hampshire the first independent colony, seven months before the Declaration of Independence was signed.

Although New Hampshire was the only one of the thirteen original states not invaded by the British during the Revolution, its men fought long and hard on land and sea to bring about the victory. This strong, involved attitude continues in New Hampshire to this day. The New Hampshire presidential primary is the first in the nation, and the town meeting is still a working form of government here.

Manufacturing and tourism are the principal businesses here. Electrical and electronic products, machinery, plastics, fabricated metal products, footwear, other leather goods, and instrumentation are manufactured. Nicknamed the "Granite State," about 200 types of rocks and minerals, including granite, mica, and feldspar, come from New Hampshire's mountains.

Calendar Highlights

MAY

Lilac Time Festival *(Franconia). 8 miles W on NH 117, then 4 miles S on US 302, in Lisbon. Phone 603/838-6673.* Celebration of the state flower and observance of Memorial Day. Parade, carnival, vendors, entertainment, special events.

JUNE

Market Square Days *(Portsmouth). Phone 603/436-3988.* Summer celebration with 10K road race, street fair, entertainment.

Seacoast Jazz Festival *(Portsmouth). For schedule, phone 603/436-3988.* Two stages with continuous performances on the historical Portsmouth waterfront.

JULY

The Old Homestead *(Keene). Potash Bowl in Swanzey Center. For schedule, phone 603/352-0697.* Drama of life in Swanzey during 1880s based on the Biblical story of the Prodigal Son; first presented in 1886.

AUGUST

Lakes Region Fine Arts and Crafts Festival *(Meredith). Phone Chamber of Commerce 603/279-6121.* Juried show featuring more than 100 New England artists. Music, children's theater, food.

League of New Hampshire Craftsmen's Fair *(Sunapee). Mount Sunapee Resort. Phone 603/224-3375.* www.nhcrafts.org/annualfair.htm. More than 200 craftsmen and artists display and sell goods.

Mount Washington Valley Equine Classic *(North Conway). Phone Chamber of Commerce, 603/356-3171 or toll-free 800/367-3364. www.washingtonvalley.org.* Horse jumping.

SPETEMBER

New Hampshire Highland Games *(Lincoln). Loon Mountain. Phone toll-free 800/358-7268.* Largest Scottish gathering in the eastern United States. Bands, competitions, concerts, workshops.

Riverfest *(Manchester). Phone 603/623-2623.* Outdoor festival with family entertainment, concerts, arts and crafts, food booths, fireworks.

When to Go/Climate

New Hampshire experiences typical New England weather—four distinct seasons with a muddy month or so between winter and spring. Snow in the mountains makes for great skiing in winter; summer temperatures can push up into the 90s.

AVERAGE HIGH/LOW TEMPERATURES (° F)

Concord

Jan 30/7	May 69/41	Sep 72/46
Feb 33/10	Jun 77/51	Oct 61/35
Mar 43/22	Jul 80/55	Nov 47/27
Apr 56/32	Aug 72/46	Dec 34/14

Mount Washington

Jan 12/-5	May 41/39	Sep 46/35
Feb 13/-3	Jun 50/38	Oct 36/24
Mar 20/5	Jul 54/43	Nov 27/14
Apr 29/16	Aug 52/42	Dec 17/-6

Parks and Recreation

Water-related activities, hiking, riding, various other sports, picnicking and visitor centers, as well as camping, are available in many state parks. There is an admission charge at most state parks; children under 12 are admitted free. Tent camping $16-$24/night; RV camp sites $42-$47/night. For further information contact the New Hampshire Division of Parks & Recreation, PO Box 1856, Concord 03302. Phone 603/271-3556 or 603/271-3628 (camping reservations).

FISHING AND HUNTING

Nonresident season fishing license: $53; 7-day, $35; 3-day, $28; 1-day, $15. Nonresident hunting license: $92; small game, $47; small game 3-day, $23; muzzleloader, $36. Combination hunting and fishing license, nonresident: $127. Fees subject to change. For further information and for the *New Hampshire Freshwater and Saltwater Fishing Digests,* pamphlets that summarize regulations, contact the New Hamp-

THE UPPER CONNECTICUT RIVER VALLEY

The Upper Connecticut River valley forms one of New England's most beautiful and distinctive regions. The river, which now forms the boundary between New Hampshire and Vermont, was northern New England's first highway, and the towns scattered along both its banks were settled long before the interior of either state. Interstate 91 follows the river north for the entire length of this tour, but in numerous places the slower state roads along the river are more rewarding.

Begin in the Vermont village of Putney (I-91, exit 4 in Vermont), known for apples, private schools, crafts shops, and Basketville, the original "world's largest basket store" on Highway 5, just north of the village center. Santa's Land, a Christmas theme park with a petting zoo and miniature railroad, is another mile north on Highway 5. Bellows Falls (I-91, exit 5), the largest natural falls on the entire Connecticut River, is the departure point for the Green Mountain Railroad (Depot St), which offers 26-mile excursion rides aboard the Green Mountain Flyer to Chester Depot and back.

A mile west of Interstate 91, exit 6 on Highway 103, is the Old Rockingham Meeting House, built in 1787, Vermont's oldest unchanged public building. The Vermont Country Store, next door, has an antique cracker-making machine and an extensive stock of old-time products and gadgets. Head back up Interstate 91 to exit 8 and cross the river to New Hampshire. Turn north on this particularly scenic stretch of Highway 12A. In Cornish, North Star Canoes offers access to riverside campsites, as well as a shuttle service upstream so canoeists can paddle downstream through this beautiful landscape. Continue on Highway 12A past the Cornish-Windsor Bridge, said to be the longest covered bridge in the country. Turn at the sign for the St. Gaudens National Historic Site. This one-time home of sculptor Augustus Saint-Gaudens includes models of his most famous statues. The extensive grounds are the site of free Sunday afternoon concerts in July and August.

Backtrack to the covered bridge and cross to Highway 5 in Windsor. Turn left for the American Precision Museum, showcasing early precision tools and changing exhibits. The entrance to Mount Ascutney State Park is 3 miles south of town on Highway 44A, off Highway 5. Within the park, you'll find hiking, camping, and a paved road to the 3,144-foot summit of Mount Ascutney.

In Windsor, follow Highway 5 north to the Old Constitution House, the tavern where delegates gathered in 1777 to draft the state's constitution. Continue north on Highway 5, past Simon Pierce Glass (visitors welcome) to Interstate 91 and follow this scenic highway 14 miles to exit 13 in Norwich.

The Montshire Museum of Science is right there by the river, marked from the exit. Incorporating both states in its name (it began on the New Hampshire side of the river), the Montshire, one of New England's most outstanding museums, is dedicated to demystifying natural phenomena in a way that's fun. Exhibits change but usually include an aquarium, a display on the physics of the bubble, and a hands-on corner geared to preschoolers. There are also extensive nature trails.

Cross the river into Hanover, New Hampshire, and up to the Dartmouth College green. Park (not always easy) and look for the Hood Museum on the green. This modern building houses an outstanding collection, ranging from Assyrian bas reliefs to works by Picasso and Frank Stella. Cross back over the river to Interstate 91, exit 13, and backtrack 3 miles to exit 20, the junction with Interstate 89. **(Approximately 63 miles)**

shire Fish & Game Department, 2 Hazen Dr, Concord 03301; phone 603/271-3422 or 603/271-3211.

Driving Information

Passengers under 18 years must be in an approved passenger restraint anywhere in vehicle. Children under 4 years must be in an approved safety seat anywhere in vehicle. For further information, phone 603/271-2131.

INTERSTATE HIGHWAY SYSTEM

The following alphabetical listing of New Hampshire towns in this book shows that these cities are within 10 miles of the indicated interstate highways. Check a highway map for the nearest exit.

Highway Number	Cities/Towns within 10 Miles
Interstate 89	Concord, Hanover, New London, Sunapee.
Interstate 91	Hanover.
Interstate 93	Concord, Franconia, Franconia

	Notch State Park, Franklin, Holderness, Laconia, Lincoln/North Woodstock, Littleton, Manchester, Meredith, Plymouth, Salem.
Interstate 95	Exeter, Hampton Beach, Portsmouth.

Additional Visitor Information

The *New Hampshire Guidebook,* with helpful information on lodging, dining, attractions, and events, is available from the New Hampshire Office of Travel & Tourism, 172 Pembroke Rd, PO Box 1856, Concord 03302. Phone 603/271-2665 or toll-free 800/386-4664. www.visitnh.gov. For recorded information about events, foliage, and alpine ski conditions, phone toll-free 800/258-3608. The League of New Hampshire Craftsmen Foundation offers information on more than 100 galleries, museums, historic sites, craft shops, and craftsmen's studios. Send stamped, self-addressed, business-size envelope to 205 N Main St, Concord 03301; phone 603/224-3375. There are several welcome centers in New Hampshire; visitors who stop by will find information and brochures most helpful in planning stops at points of interest. Open daily: on I-93 at Hooksett, Canterbury, Salem and Sanborton Boulder; on I-89 at Lebanon, Springfield, and Sutton; on I-95 at Seabrook; and on Hwy 16 at North Conway. Open Memorial Day-Columbus Day: on Hwy 9 at Antrim; on Hwy 3 at Colebrook; on Hwy 4 at Epsom; on Hwy 25 at Rumney; and on Hwy 2 at Shelburne.

Bartlett (C-4)

See also Bretton Woods, Jackson, North Conway

Population 2,290
Elevation 681 ft
Area Code 603
Zip 03812
Information Mount Washington Valley Chamber of Commerce, N Village Sq, PO Box 2300, North Conway 03860; phone 603/356-5701
Web Site www.mtwashingtonvalley.org

What to See and Do

Attitash Bear Peak Ski Resort. *Hwy 302, Bartlett (03812). Phone 603/374-2368. www.attitash.com.* Two high-speed quad, three quad, three triple, three double chairlifts; three surface lifts; patrol, school, rentals; snowmaking; nursery; cafeteria; bar. Longest run 1 3/4 mile; vertical drop 1,750 feet. (Mid-Nov-late Apr, daily) **Summer recreation:** Alpine Slide, water slides, scenic chairlift, horseback riding, mountain biking, hiking, driving range (mid-June-Labor Day: daily; Memorial Day-mid-June and early Sept-mid-Oct: weekends; fees). **$$$$**

Full-Service Resort

★ ★ **ATTITASH GRAND SUMMIT RESORT AND CONFERENCE CENTER.** *Hwy 302, Bartlett (03812). Phone 603/374-1900; toll-free 800/862-1600; fax 603/340-3040. www.attitashmtvillage.com.* 253 rooms, 3 story. Check-in 4 pm, check-out 11 am. Restaurant, bar. Indoor pool, two outdoor pools, whirlpool. Ski in/ski out. **$**

Bretton Woods (C-4)

See also Bartlett, Franconia, Littleton, Mount Washington, Twin Mountain,

Settled 1791
Population 10
Elevation 1,600 ft
Area Code 603

Bretton Woods is located in the heart of the White Mountains on a long glacial plain in the shadow of Mount Washington (see) and the Presidential Range. Mount Washington was first sighted in 1497; however, settlement around it did not begin until 1771 when the Crawford Notch, which opened the way through the mountains, was discovered. In the 1770s, Governor Wentworth named the area Bretton Woods for his ancestral home in England. This historic name was set aside in 1832 when all the tiny settlements in the area were incorporated under the name of Carroll. For a time, a railroad through the notch brought as many as 57 trains a day, and the area grew as a resort spot. A string of hotels sprang up, each more elegant and fashionable than the last. In 1903, the post office, railroad station, and express office reverted to the traditional name—Bretton Woods. Today, Bretton Woods is a resort area at the base of the mountain.

In 1944, the United Nations Monetary and Financial Conference was held here; it established the gold standard at $35 an ounce, organized plans for the International Monetary Fund and World Bank, and chose the American dollar as the unit of international exchange.

What to See and Do

Bretton Woods Ski Area. *5 miles E on Hwy 302. Phone 603/278-3320. www.brettonwoods.com.* Two high-speed quad, quad, triple, two double chairlifts, three surface lifts; patrol, school, rentals, snowmaking; restaurant, cafeteria, bar; child care; lodge. Longest run 2 miles; vertical drop 1,500 feet. (Thanksgiving-Apr, daily) Night skiing (early Dec-Mar, Fri-Sat). 48 miles of cross-country trails. **$$$$**

Crawford Notch State Park. *Bretton Woods. Approximately 8 miles SE on Hwy 302. Phone 603/374-2272.* One of state's most spectacular passes. Mounts Nancy and Willey rise to the west; Mounts Crawford, Webster, and Jackson to the east. Park headquarters is at the former site of the Samuel Willey house. He, his family of six, and two hired men died in a landslide in 1826 when they rushed out of their house, which the landslide left untouched. Fishing, trout-feeding pond. Hiking, walking trails on the Appalachian system. Picnicking, concession. Camping. Interpretive center. (Late May-mid-Oct) In park are

>   **Arethusa Falls.** *Bretton Woods. 1 1/2 miles SW of Hwy 302, 6 miles N of Bartlett.* Highest in state; 50-minute walk from parking area.

>   **Flume Cascade.** *Bretton Woods. 3 miles N.* A 250-foot fall.

>   **Silver Cascade.** *Bretton Woods. N end of Crawford Notch.* A 1,000-foot cataract.

Full-Service Resort

★ ★ ★ **MOUNT WASHINGTON HOTEL.** *Hwy 302, Bretton Woods (03575). Phone 603/278-1000; toll-free 800/258-0330; fax 603/278-8838. www.mtwashington.com.* This landmark hotel is a true retreat in every way. Enjoy golfing, horseback riding, and bicycle riding during the day and live music, fine dining, and dancing at night with a choice of either live jazz or big band sounds. 200 rooms, 4 story. Check-in 3 pm, check-out 11 am. Two restaurants, five bars. Children's activity center. Fitness room. Indoor pool, outdoor pool. Golf, 27 holes. Tennis. Business center. **$$$**

Restaurant

★ **FABYAN'S STATION.** *Hwy 302, Bretton Woods (03575). Phone 603/278-2222. www.mtwashington.com.* Located in the middle of the White Mountains, this casual, fun restaurant is surrounded by spectacular views. Housed in a converted railroad station, it still features much of the original decor. American menu. Lunch, dinner. Bar. Children's menu. Casual attire. **$$**

Center Ossipee (D-4)

See also Wolfeboro

Population 500
Elevation 529 ft
Area Code 603
Zip 03814
Information Greater Ossipee Area Chamber of Commerce, 127 Hwy 28, Ossipee, 03864-7300; phone 603/539-6201 or toll-free 800/382-2371
Web Site www.ossipeevalley.org

The communities in the Ossipee area are part of a winter and summer sports region centering around Ossipee Lake and the Ossipee Mountains. The mountains also harbor a volcano (extinct for 120 million years) that is considered to be the most perfectly shaped volcanic formation in the world; it is rivaled only by a similar formation in Nigeria. A hike up Mount Whittier offers an excellent view of the formation. In the winter, the area comes alive with snowmobiling, dog sledding, cross-country skiing, and other activities.

What to See and Do

King Pine Ski Area. *Hwy 153, Madison (03849). 11 miles NE via Hwys 25, 153. Phone 603/367-8896. www.kingpine.com.* Triple, double chairlifts; two J-bars; snowmaking; patrol, school, rentals; night skiing; nursery; snack bar; bar. (Early Dec-late Mar, daily) **$$$$**

Sailing. Silver Lake, north and east of village; also **Ossipee Lake**. Marinas with small boat rentals.

Swimming. Ossipee Lake, north and east of village; **Duncan Lake**, south of village.

White Lake State Park. *Hwys 25 and 16, Tamworth (03886). 6 miles N on NH 16. Phone 603/323-7350.* Sandy beach on tree-studded shore. Swimming; trout fishing. Hiking. Picnicking, concessions. Tent camping. (Mid-May-mid-Oct) Snowmobile trails (Dec-Mar). Standard fees. **$$**

Colebrook (B-4)

See also Dixville Notch

Settled 1770
Population 2,444
Elevation 1,033 ft
Area Code 603
Zip 03576
Information North Country Chamber of Commerce, 374 Leslie Hwy, PO Box 1; phone 603/237-8939 or toll-free 800/698-8939
Web Site www.northcountrychamber.org

At the west edge of the White Mountains, Colebrook is the gateway to excellent hunting and fishing in the Connecticut Lakes region. The Mohawk and Connecticut rivers join here. Vermont's Mount Monadnock adds scenic beauty.

What to See and Do

Beaver Brook Falls. *2 miles N on Hwy 145.* A scenic glen.

Coleman State Park. *7 miles E on Hwy 26, then 5 miles N on Diamond Pond Rd. Phone 603/237-4520.* On Little Diamond Pond in the heavily timbered Connecticut Lakes region. Lake and stream fishing; picnicking; primitive camping. (Mid-May-mid-Oct)

Columbia Covered Bridge. *4 miles S on Hwy 3.* Seventy-five feet high.

Shrine of Our Lady of Grace. *2 miles S on Hwy 3. Phone 603/237-5511.* Oblates of Mary Immaculate. More than 50 Carrara marble and granite devotional monuments on 25 acres. Special events throughout the season. Self-guided tours (Mother's Day-second Sun in Oct, daily). **FREE**

Limited-Service Hotel

★ **NORTHERN COMFORT MOTEL.** *RR 1, Colebrook (03576). Phone 603/237-4440. www.northerncomfortmotel.com.* 19 rooms. Pets accepted; fee. Complimentary continental breakfast. Check-in 1 pm, check-out 11 am. Outdoor pool, whirlpool. **$**

Concord (E-4)

See also Manchester

Settled 1727
Population 36,006
Elevation 288 ft
Area Code 603
Zip 03301
Information Chamber of Commerce, 40 Commercial St; phone 603/224-2508
Web Site www.concordnhchamber.com

New Hampshire, one of the original 13 colonies, entered the Union in 1788--but its capital was in dispute for another 20 years. Concord finally won the honor in 1808. The state house, begun immediately, was finished in 1819. The legislature is the largest (more than 400 seats) of any state. Concord is the financial center of the state and a center of diversified industry as well.

What to See and Do

Canterbury Shaker Village. *288 Shaker Rd, Canterbury (03224). 15 miles N on I-93 to exit 18, then follow signs. Phone 603/783-9511. www.shakers.org.* Pay homage to New Hampshires Shaker heritage with a visit to this National Historic Landmark museum that offers guided and self-guided tours and a variety of exhibits. (Mid-May-late Oct: daily 10 am-5 pm; Nov-Dec: Fri-Sun 10 am-4 pm; closed Thanksgiving, Dec 25) **$$$**

Capitol Center for the Arts. *44 S Main St, Concord (03301). Phone 603/225-1111. www.ccanh.com.* Renovated historic theater (1920s) is the state's largest. Presents nationally touring Broadway and popular family entertainment all year.

Christa McAuliffe Planetarium. *2 Institute Dr, Concord (03301). I-93, exit 15 E. Phone 603/271-7831. www.starhop.com.* This living memorial to New Hampshire teacher Christa McAuliffe, who died aboard the US space shuttle *Challenger* on January 28, 1986, offers a variety of shows designed for all ages in a 92-seat theater. Some shows are aimed at the very young while others boast 3-D computer graphic effects likely to wow anyone. (Daily; call or visit Web site for show schedule) **$$**

⭐ **Concord Arts & Crafts.** *36 N Main St, Concord (03301). Phone 603/228-8171.* High-quality traditional and contemporary crafts by some of New Hampshire's finest craftsmen; monthly exhibits. (Mon-Sat; closed holidays)

Granite State Candy Shoppe. *13 Warren St, Concord (03301). Phone 603/225-2591; toll-free 888/225-2531. www.nhchocolates.com.* Founded in 1927 by a Greek immigrant, Granite State Candy Shoppe is an old-fashioned candy store that has been delighting sweet tooths ever since with the motto, "We're in the happiness business." Now owned by his grandchildren, many of the founder's original copper kettles are still in use, and each chocolate is dipped one by one. Sure, you can buy these treats on the Internet, but nothing beats a visit to the store where it all began.

League of New Hampshire Craftsmen. *205 N Main St, Concord (03301). Phone 603/224-1471. www. nhcrafts.org.* Six retail galleries throughout the state. Library and resource center for League Foundation members. (Mon-Fri; closed holidays) **FREE**

Museum of New Hampshire History. *6 Eagle Sq, Concord (03301). Phone 603/228-6688. www.nhhistory.org.* Historical museum (founded 1823) with permanent and changing exhibits, including excellent examples of the famed Concord Coach; museum store. (Tues-Sat, also Sun afternoons) **$$**

Pat's Peak Ski Area. *8 miles N on I-89 to Hwy 202, then 8 miles W to Hwy 114, then 3 miles S, near Henniker. Phone 603/428-3245; toll-free 800/728-7732. www.patspeak.com.* Triple, two double chairlifts, two T-bars, J-bar, pony lift; patrol, school, rentals, ski shop; snowmaking; cafeteria, lounge; nursery. Night skiing. (Dec-late Mar, daily; closed Dec 25)

Pierce Manse. *14 Penacook St, Concord (03301). 1 mile N of State House. Phone 603/225-4555.* Home of President Franklin Pierce from 1842 to 1848. Reconstructed and moved to the present site; contains many original furnishings and period pieces. (Mid-June-mid-October, Tues-Sat; also by appointment; closed July 4, Labor Day) **$**

State House. *107 N Main St, Concord (03301). Phone 603/271-2154.* Hall of Flags; statues, portraits of state notables. (Mon-Fri; closed holidays) **FREE**

Limited-Service Hotels

★ **COMFORT INN.** *71 Hall St, Concord (03301). Phone 603/226-4100; toll-free 877/424-6423; fax 603/228-2106. www.comfortinn.com.* Perfect for budget-conscious families, this hotel provides a number of amenities, including a Nintendo 64 station in each room. 100 rooms, 3 story. Pets accepted, some restrictions; fee. Complimentary continental breakfast. Check-in 3 pm, check-out noon. Indoor pool, whirlpool. **$**

★ **HAMPTON INN.** *515 South St, Bow (03304). Phone 603/224-5322; toll-free 800/426-7866; fax 603/224-4282. www.hamptoninn.com.* 145 rooms, 4 story. Complimentary continental breakfast. Check-in 3 pm, check-out noon. Indoor pool, whirlpool. **$**

Full-Service Inn

★ ★ ★ **COLBY HILL INN.** *The Oaks, Henniker (03242). Phone 603/428-3281; toll-free 800/531-0330; fax 603/428-9218. www.colbyhillinn.com.* This classic New England country inn offers individually decorated rooms and a fine-dining restaurant in a beautiful, wooded setting. 14 rooms, 2 story. Children over 7 years only. Complimentary full breakfast. Check-in 3 pm, check-out 11 am. Wireless Internet access. Restaurant, bar. Outdoor pool. **$$**

Restaurants

★ ★ **ANGELINA'S RISTORANTE ITALIANO.** *11 Depot St, Concord (03301). Phone 603/228-3313; fax 603/228-3775. www.angelinasrestaurant.com.* Angelinas offers a variety of antipasti, salads, pasta specialties, entrées, grilled items, and desserts, as well as a full wine list, in an upscale setting. American, Italian menu. Lunch, dinner. Closed Sun. Casual attire. Reservations recommended. **$$**

★ **ARNIE'S PLACE.** *164 Loudon Rd, Concord (03301). Phone 603/228-3225. www.arniesplace.com.* Arnie's Place serves old-fashioned favorites in a nostalgic 1950s atmosphere. You'll find classics like char-grilled hamburgers and a full rack of Boss Hawgs pork spare ribs; sides are extra. After your meal, enjoy some of Arnie's ice cream—it's made fresh on the premises. American menu. Lunch, dinner. Children's menu. Casual attire. Outdoor seating. No credit cards accepted. **$**

★ **BOAR'S TAVERN.** *Rtes 106 and 129, Loudon (03307). Phone 603/798-3737. www.boarstavern.com.* Boars Tavern offers a variety of sandwiches, appetizers, soups, salads and dinners, as well as a full bar, in an atmosphere that features pool tables and a band area. American menu. Lunch, dinner. Bar. Casual attire. **$$**

★ ★ **COLBY HILL INN.** *The Oaks, Henniker (03242). Phone 603/428-3281; fax 603/428-9218. www. colbyhillinn.com.* A part of the Colby Hill Inn (see) bed-and-breakfast in the New Hampshire countryside, this restaurant features a surprisingly cosmopolitan menu that combines familiar favorites with more contemporary variations. Rustic game meats appear as pepper-crusted duck breast with cranberry-orange syrup and fig-and-sage-glazed venison osso buco. Seafood choices are also featured, such as cedar-plank roasted salmon with a maple-rum glaze, and baked stuffed jumbo shrimp Rockefeller. Regional menu. Dinner. Business casual attire. Reservations recommended. **$$$**

★ ★ **LONGHORN STEAKHOUSE.** *217 Loudon Rd, Concord (03301). Phone 603/228-0655. www. longhornsteakhouse.com.* Steaks, seafood, ribs, chops, and chicken are among the variety of entrées offered at this chain steakhouse. The dining room is large and open with a Texas ranch feel. Steak menu. Lunch, dinner. Bar. Children's menu. Casual attire. **$$**

★ **MAKRIS LOBSTER AND STEAK HOUSE.** *354 Sheep Davis Rd (Rte 106), Concord (03301). Phone 603/225-7665. www.eatalobster.com.* In this lobster-themed restaurant, a menu of land and sea favorites is offered. Selections include lobster dinners and prime rib, along with plenty of chicken and pasta dishes. Seafood, steak menu. Lunch, dinner, late-night. Bar. Children's menu. Casual attire. Outdoor seating. **$$**

★ **RED BLAZER RESTAURANT.** *72 Manchester St, Concord (03301). Phone 603/224-4101. www.red-blazer.cc.* The Red Blazer Restaurant and Pub features an entrée menu with upscale items like filet mignon and pastry-baked chicken, as well as pub fare such as a Greek souvlaki platter, fried chicken strips and boneless Buffalo Tenders. American menu. Lunch, dinner. Bar. Children's menu. Casual attire. **$$**

★ **SAL'S JUST PIZZA.** *80 Storrs St, Concord (03301). Phone 603/226-0297. www.sals-pizza.com.* Sals Just Pizza offers a variety of pizzas, calzones, salzones (Sals version of an open-faced sandwich), and pastries. Pizza. Lunch, dinner. Children's menu. Casual attire. Outdoor seating. No credit cards accepted. **$**

Dixville Notch (B-4)

See also Colebrook

Population 30
Elevation 1,990 ft
Area Code 603
Zip 03576

The small village of Dixville Notch shares its name with the most northerly of the White Mountain passes. The Notch cuts through the mountain range between Kidderville and Errol. At its narrowest point, east of Lake Gloriette, is one of the most impressive views in the state. Every four years, Dixville Notch is invaded by the national news media, who report the nation's first presidential vote tally shortly after midnight on election day.

What to See and Do

Balsams/Wilderness Ski Area. *Hwy 26, Dixville Notch. (03576) Phone 603/255-3400; toll-free 800/255-0600. www.thebalsams.com.* Chairlift, two T-bars; patrol, school, rentals, snowmaking; restaurant, cafeteria, bar, nursery, resort. Longest run 1 mile; vertical drop 1,000 feet. (Dec-Mar, daily) Cross-country trails. **$$$$**

Table Rock. *3/4 mile S of Hwy 26, 1/2 mile E of village of Dixville Notch.* Views of New Hampshire, Maine, Vermont, and Québec.

Full-Service Hotel

★ ★ ★ **THE BALSAMS.** *Hwy 26, Dixville Notch (03576). Phone 603/255-3400; toll-free 800/255-0600; fax 603/255-4221. www.thebalsams.com.* The Balsams transports guests back to the New England of legend with its impressive architecture and bucolic setting. Built just after the Civil War, this 15,000-acre family-friendly resort is Yankee living at its best. A veritable winter wonderland during snowy months, this destination is a playground year-round with a wide variety of sporting activities and entertainment. Winter is spent downhill skiing, cross-country skiing, snowboarding, and ice skating, while warmer months are enjoyed while playing golf or tennis and enjoying the great outdoors on nature walks. The accommodations have a classic New England country appeal coupled with serene views. Operating on the all-inclusive American plan, The Balsams makes gourmet dining an integral part of the experience here. 212 rooms, 6 story. Check-in 4 pm, check-out noon. Two restaurants, two bars. Fitness room. Outdoor pool. Golf, 27 holes. Tennis. Ski in/ski out. Airport transportation available. **$$**

Dover (E-5)

See also Portsmouth

Settled 1623
Population 25,042
Elevation 57 ft
Area Code 603
Zip 03820
Information Chamber of Commerce, 299 Central Ave; phone 603/742-2218
Web Site www.dovernh.org

With its historic trails and homes, Dover is the oldest permanent settlement in New Hampshire. The town contains the only known existing colonial garrison.

What to See and Do

Woodman Institute. *182-190 Central Ave, Dover (03820). 1/2 mile S on Hwy 108. Phone 603/742-1038.* Garrison House (1675), only garrison in New Hampshire now visible in nearly its original form. Woodman House (1818), residence of the donor, is now a natural history museum with collections of minerals; Native American artifacts; and displays of mammals, fish, amphibians, reptiles, birds, insects; war memorial rooms. Senator John P. Hale House (1813) contains articles of Dover history and antique furniture. (Apil-Dec, Wed-Sun afternoons; Dec, Sat-Sun afternoons; closed holidays) **$**

Special Event

Cocheco Arts Festival. *Phone 603/742-2218.* Mid-July-late Aug.

Limited-Service Hotel

★ **DAYS INN.** *481 Central Ave, Dover (03820). Phone 603/742-0400; toll-free 800/329-7466; fax 603/742-7790. www.dover-durham-daysinn.com.* 50 rooms, 2 story. Pets accepted. Complimentary continental breakfast. Check-in 2 pm, check-out 11 am. Outdoor pool, whirlpool. **$**

Restaurants

★ ★ ★ **MAPLES.** *17 Newmarket Rd, Durham (03824). Phone 603/868-7800; toll-free 888/399-9777; fax 603/868-2964. www.threechimneysinn.com.* This restaurant provides wonderful service in an old New England setting that includes beautiful dark wood tables and large, comfortable chairs. The small, intimate dining room allows couples to feel alone. In the summertime, guests will enjoy dining on the patio and in the winter, the fireplace creates a cozy atmosphere. American menu. Lunch, dinner. Outdoor seating. **$$$**

★ **NEWICK'S SEAFOOD.** *431 Dover Point Rd, Dover (03820). Phone 603/742-3205; fax 603/749-6942. www.newicks.com.* Seafood market. Nautical accents. Seafood menu. Lunch, dinner. Closed Thanksgiving, Dec 25. **$$**

Exeter (F-5)

See also Hampton Beach, Portsmouth

Settled 1638
Population 12,481
Elevation 40 ft
Area Code 603
Zip 03833
Information Exeter Area Chamber of Commerce, 120 Water St; phone 603/772-2411
Web Site www.exeterarea.org

A venerable preparatory school and colonial houses belie Exeter's radical history. It had its beginnings in religious nonconformity, led by Reverend John Wheelwright and Anne Hutchinson, both of whom were banished from Massachusetts for heresy. There was an anti-British scuffle in 1734, and by 1774 Exeter was burning Lord North in effigy and talking of liberty. It was made the capital of the state during the Revolution, since there were too many Tories in Portsmouth. Exeter is the birthplace of Daniel Chester French and John Irving.

What to See and Do

American Independence Museum. *1 Governors Ln, Exeter (03833). Phone 603/772-2622. www.independencemuseum.org.* Site of Revolutionary War-era state treasury building; grounds house Folsom Tavern (1775). (May-Oct, Wed-Sat) **$**

Exeter Fine Crafts. *61 Water St, Exeter (03833). Phone 603/778-8282. www.exeterfinecrafts.com.* Work in all media by New Hampshire's finest artisans. (Daily) **FREE**

Gilman Garrison House. *12 Water St, Exeter (03833). Phone 603/436-3205. www.historicnewengland.org.* (1676-1690) Built as a fortified garrison with hewn logs; pulley arrangement to raise and lower door still in place. Substantially remodeled in mid-18th century; wing added with 17th- and 18th-century furnishings. (Open by appointment only) **$$**

Phillips Exeter Academy. *20 Main St, Exeter (03833). Phone 603/772-4311. www.exeter.edu.* (1781) (990 students) On 400 acres with more than 100 buildings. Coed school for grades 9-12. Founded by John Phillips, who sought a school for "students from every quarter"; known for its student diversity. On campus are a contemporary library (1971), designed by Louis I. Kahn; the Frederick R. Mayer Art Center; and the Lamont Art Gallery.

Franconia (C-3)

See also Bretton Woods, Franconia Notch State Park, Littleton, Twin Mountain,

Population 811
Elevation 971 ft
Area Code 603
Zip 03580
Information Franconia Notch Chamber of Commerce, PO Box 780; phone 603/823-5661 or toll-free 800/237-9007
Web Site www.franconianotch.org

What to See and Do

Frost Place. *Ridge Rd, Franconia (03580). 1 mile S on Hwy 116 to Bickford Hill Rd, right over bridge, left at fork, on to Ridge Rd. Phone 603/823-5510. www.frostplace.org.* Two furnished rooms of Robert Frost's home open to public; memorabilia; poetry trail; 25-minute video. (July-Columbus Day: Wed-Mon afternoons; Memorial Day-June: Sat-Sun afternoons) **$**

New England Ski Museum. *Franconia Notch Pkwy, Franconia (03580). Hwy 3, exit 34B; near Cannon Mountain Tramway. Phone 603/823-7177; toll-free 800/639-4181. www.nesm.org.* Details history of skiing in the East; exhibits feature skis and bindings, clothing, art, and photographs; vintage films. Gift shop.

(Memorial Day-Columbus Day and Dec-Mar, daily; closed Dec 25) **FREE**

Special Event

Lilac Time Festival. *Lisbon. 8 miles W on NH 117, then 4 miles S on NH 302. Phone 603/838-6673.* Celebration of the state flower and observance of Memorial Day. Parade, carnival, vendors, entertainment, special events. Late May.

Limited-Service Hotels

★ ★ **BEST WESTERN WHITE MOUNTAIN RESORT.** *87 Wallace Hill Rd, Franconia (03580). Phone 603/823-7422; toll-free 888/669-6777; fax 603/823-5638. www.bestwestern.com.* In operation since 1923, this inn overlooks the upper rapids of Niagara Falls and is a distinctive historic structure. The inn has an "Olde English" atmosphere and lovely wood-burning fireplaces. 61 rooms, 2 story. Pets accepted, some restrictions; fee. Complimentary continental breakfast. Check-in 3 pm, check-out 11 am. Fitness room. Indoor pool. **$**

★ **STONYBROOK MOTEL & LODGE.** *1098 Profile Rd; Hwy 18, Franconia (03580). Phone 603/823-5800; toll-free 800/722-3552; fax 603/823-5888. www.stonybrookmotel.com.* Surrounded by many trees and open space, this White Mountain lodging is situated on the main highway of the small, quaint town of Franconia. A trout pond is located here, and guests can enjoy a picnic on the tables along the stream. 23 rooms. Complimentary continental breakfast. Check-in 3 pm, check-out 11 am. Children's activity center. Indoor pool, outdoor pool. **$**

★ ★ **SUGAR HILL INN.** *Hwy 117, Franconia (03580). Phone 603/823-5621; toll-free 800/548-4748; fax 603/823-5639. www.sugarhillinn.com.* Perfect for a weekend escape, this romantic, tranquil inn is nestled on the hillside and surrounded by woodland and colorful gardens. The history of this converted farmhouse (circa 1789) is showcased through the original beams, floors, and fireplaces. 15 rooms. Closed one week in Apr. Complimentary full breakfast. Check-in 3 pm, check-out 11 am. Wireless Internet access. Restaurant (public by reservation), bar. Spa. **$$**

Full-Service Inns

★ ★ ★ **FRANCONIA INN.** *1300 Easton Rd, Franconia (03580). Phone 603/823-5542; toll-free 800/473-5299; fax 603/823-8078. www.franconiainn. com.* Nestled in the White Mountains yet close to the town center, this charming inn welcomes guests in an informal country home atmosphere. The comfortable guest rooms are spacious with breathtaking vistas. Activities on-site include horseback riding, mountain biking, fishing, and croquet. 34 rooms, 3 story. Closed Apr-mid-May. Complimentary full breakfast. Check-in 3 pm, check-out 11 am. Restaurant, bar. Outdoor pool, whirlpool. Tennis. **$**

★ ★ ★ **LOVETTS INN.** *1474 Profile Rd (Hwy 18), Franconia (03580). Phone 603/823-7761; toll-free 800/356-3802; fax 603/823-8802. www.lovettsinn.com.* Breathe in the fresh country air at this historic, romantic inn surrounded by the White Mountains and sparkling streams. Well appointed and charming, the inn has a rustic feel and is filled with light. The town center is a short drive away. 18 rooms, 2 story. Closed Apr. Pets accepted; fee. Complimentary full breakfast. Check-in 3 pm, check-out 11 am. Wireless Internet access. Restaurant, bar. Outdoor pool. **$$**

Specialty Lodgings

HILLTOP INN. *9 Norton Ln, Sugar Hill (03585). Phone 603/823-5695; toll-free 800/770-5695; fax 603/823-5518. www.hilltopinn.com.* Built in 1895; antiques, quilts. 6 rooms, 2 story. Pets accepted, some restrictions; fee. Complimentary full breakfast. Check-in 2-6 pm, check-out 11 am. **$**

SUNSET HILL HOUSE – A GRAND INN. *231 Sunset Hill Rd, Sugar Hill (03585). Phone 603/823-5522; toll-free 800/786-4455; fax 603/823-5738. www. sunsethillhouse.com.* Built in 1882; beautiful view of mountains, attractive grounds. 28 rooms, 2 story. Complimentary full breakfast. Check-in 3 pm, check-out 11 am. Restaurant. Outdoor pool. Golf. **$$$**

Restaurants

★ ★ ★ **THE FRANCONIA INN.** *1300 Easton Rd, Franconia (03580). Phone 603/823-5542; toll-free 800/473-5299; fax 603/823-8078. www. franconiainn.com.* Surrounded by rolling hills and towering mountains, this restaurant offers New American cuisine, drawing on regional specialties and influenced by the rich heritage of the cultural mosaic along with unique variations of the classics. Within the cozy atmosphere, guests can enjoy the romance of candlelight dining and the muted strains of Mozart. American menu. Breakfast, dinner. Closed Apr-mid-May. Bar. Children's menu. Casual attire. Reservations recommended. **$$**

★ ★ **HORSE & HOUND.** *205 Wells Rd, Franconia (03580). Phone 603/823-5501; toll-free 800/450-5501. www.horseandhoundnh.com.* American menu. lunch, dinner. Closed Sun-Wed. Bar. Casual attire. Reservations recommended. Outdoor seating. **$$**

★ ★ **LOVETTS INN BY LAFAYETTE BROOK.** *1474 Profile Rd (Hwy 18), Franconia (03580). Phone 603/823-7761; fax 603/823-8802. www.lovettsinn.com.* Located in an old farmhouse, this romantic restaurant keeps up with the charm of the surrounding area. The menu is tempting and there is real pride in the kitchen, which serves up some serious food. The interesting bar area is dimly lit and done in soft colors—don't miss the unique round-top marble bar. American menu. Breakfast, dinner. Bar. Casual attire. Reservations recommended. Outdoor seating. **$$**

★ ★ **POLLY'S PANCAKE PARLOR.** *672 Hwy 117, Sugar Hill (03585). Phone 603/823-5575; fax 603/823-5577. www.pollyspancakeparlor.com.* In converted carriage shed (1840). American menu. Breakfast, lunch. Closed Dec-Mar. Children's menu. **$$**

Franconia Notch State Park (C-3)

See also Franconia, Lincoln/North Woodstock

Approximately 7 miles SE of Franconia via Hwy 18 and I-93/ franconia notch State Pkwy.

This 7-mile pass and state park, a deep valley of 6,440 acres between the Franconia and Kinsman ranges of the White Mountains, has been a top tourist attraction since the mid-19th century. Mounts Liberty (4,460 feet), Lincoln (5,108 feet), and Lafayette (5,249 feet) loom on the east, and Cannon Mountain (4,200 feet) presents a sheer granite face. The Pemigewasset River follows the length of the Notch.

The park offers various recreational activities, including swimming at Sandy Beach; fishing and boating on Echo Lake (junction Hwy 18 and I-93 exit 3); hiking; 8-mile paved bike path through the Notch; skiing; picnicking; camping. Fees for some activities. For further information, contact Franconia Notch State Park, Franconia 03580; phone 603/823-5563.

What to See and Do

The Basin. *W of I-93 (Franconia Notch State Pkwy), S of Profile Lake.*Deep glacial pothole, 20 feet in diameter, at the foot of a waterfall, polished smooth by sand, stones, and water.

Cannon Mountain Ski Area. *5 miles S of Franconia via Hwy 18 and I-93 (Franconia Notch State Pkwy), exit 34 B or 34 C. Phone 603/823-8800. www.cannonmt. com.* Tramway, two quad, three triple, two double chairlifts, pony lift; patrol, school, rentals; snowmaking; cafeterias, bar (beer and wine); nursery. New England Ski Museum. Longest run 2 miles and vertical drop 2,146 feet. (Late Nov-mid-Apr, daily; closed Dec 25) Tramway rising 2,022 feet vertically over a distance of 1 mile in 6 minutes, also operates Memorial Day-mid-Oct: daily; rest of year: weekends (weather permitting).

Flume Gorge & Park Information Center. *15 miles S of Franconia, I-93 (Franconia Notch State Pkwy), exit 34A. Phone 603/745-8391. www.flumegorge.com.* Narrow, natural gorge, and waterfall along the flank of Mount Liberty, accessible by stairs and walks; picnicking. Mountain flowers and mosses, Liberty Gorge, the Cascades, covered bridges. Information center offers a 15-minute movie introducing the park every half-hour. Interpretive exhibits. Gift shop, cafeteria. (Mid-May-late Oct, daily)

Lafayette Campground. *9 miles S of Franconia Village, off I-93 (Franconia Notch State Pkwy). Phone 603/823-9513.* Fishing. Hiking on Appalachian trail system. Picnicking. Camping. Fees for some activities. (Mid-May-mid-Oct, daily) **$$$$**

Old Man of the Mountain Historic Site. *1,200 ft above Profile Lake, W of I-93 (Franconia Notch State Pkwy), exit 2.* Discovered in 1805, the craggy likeness of a man's face was formed naturally of five layers of granite and was 40 feet high. It tumbled down on May 3, 2003. It was also known as the "Great Stone Face."

Franklin (E-4)

See also Laconia

Settled 1764
Population 8,304
Elevation 335 ft
Area Code 603
Zip 03235
Information Greater Franklin Chamber of Commerce, 340 Central St, PO Box 464, phone 603/934-6909
Web Site www.franklin.nh.us/chamber

Franklin was named in 1828 for Benjamin Franklin; until then it was a part of Salisbury. It is the birthplace of Daniel Webster, lawyer, senator, and statesman. The Pemigewasset and Winnipesaukee rivers, joining to form the Merrimack, provide the city with abundant water power.

What to See and Do

Congregational Christian Church. *47 S Main St, Franklin (03235). On US 3. Phone 603/934-4242.* (1820). Church that Daniel Webster attended; tracker action organ. A bust of Webster by Daniel Chester French is outside. (Sun mornings, also by appointment) **FREE**

Tanger Factory Outlet Center. *120 Laconia Rd, Tilton (03276). Approximately 5 miles E on Hwy 3. Phone 603/286-7880. www.tangeroutlet.com.* This large factory outlet center features familiar retailing names like Gap, Wilsons Leather, and Nine West. (May-Dec: Mon-Sat 9 am-9 pm, Sun 10 am-6 pm; Jan-Apr: Sun-Thurs 10 am-6 pm, Fri-Sat 10 am-8 pm)

Limited-Service Hotel

★ **SUPER 8.** *7 Tilton Rd, Tilton (03276). Phone 603/286-8882; toll-free 800/800-8000; fax 603/286-8788. www.super8. com.* Close to all the outdoor activities and entertainment around Lake Winnipesaukee, this budget-friendly hotel puts guests in convenient proximity to swimming, boating, and fishing. 63 rooms, 2 story. Check-in 3 pm, check-out 11 am. **$**

Specialty Lodging

MARIA ATWOOD INN. *71 Hill Rd (Rte 3A), Franklin (03235). Phone 603/934-3666. www.atwood inn.com.* The phrase "stepping back in time" is the perfect way to describe this gorgeous Federal-style bed-and-breakfast, built as a home for its namesake in 1830. Enjoy a traditional country breakfast in the morning, then head out for a day of outdoor ventures such as skiing, hiking, boating, and fishing, or hunt down some quintessential weekend-in-the-country pursuits like antiquing, quilt-making, and outdoor theater. 7 rooms, 3 story. Complimentary full breakfast. Check-in 3 pm, check-out 11 am. **$**

Restaurant

★ **MR D'S.** *428 N Main St, West Franklin (03235).* *Phone 603/934-3142.* Collection of old-fashioned photographs on walls. American menu. Breakfast, lunch, dinner. Closed holidays. Children's menu. **$$**

Gorham (C-4)

See also Mount Washington, Pinkham Notch, White Mountain National Forest

Settled 1805
Population 3,173
Elevation 801 ft
Area Code 603
Zip 03581
Information Northern White Mountains Chamber of Commerce, 164 Main St, PO Box 298, Berlin 03570; phone 603/752-6060 or toll-free 800/992-7480
Web Site www.gorhamnewhampshire.com

Commanding the northeast approaches to the Presidential Range of the White Mountains, at the north end of Pinkham Notch (see), Gorham has magnificent views and is the center for summer and winter sports. The Peabody River merges with the Androscoggin in a series of falls. A Ranger District office of the White Mountain National Forest (see) is located here. What to See and Do

Dolly Copp Campground. *300 Glen Rd, Gorham (03851). 6 miles S on Hwy 16 in White Mountain National Forest. Phone 603/466-2713.* 176 campsites; fishing, hiking, picnicking.

Libby Memorial Pool & Recreation Area. *1/4 mile S on Hwy 16. Phone 603/466-2101.* Natural pool, bathhouses; picnicking. (Summer, daily, weather permitting)

Moose Brook State Park. *30 Jimtown Rd, Gorham (03581). 2 miles W on Hwy 2. Phone 603/466-3860.* Views of the Presidential Range of the White Mountains; good stream fishing area. Swimming,

bathhouse; picnicking; camping. Hiking to Randolph Range. (Late May-early Sept)

Moose Tours. *Hwys 2 and 16, Gorham (03581). Main St. Phone 603/466-3103.* Daily tours leave each evening from the Gorham Informational Booth on a specified route to locate moose for sighting. (Late May-mid-Oct) **$$$$**

Mount Washington. *10 miles S on Hwy 16.* (see).

Limited-Service Hotels

★ **MT. MADISON MOTEL.** *365 Main St, Gorham (03581). Phone 603/466-3622; toll-free 800/851-1136; fax 603/466-3664. www.mtmadisonmotel.com.* 33 rooms, 2 story. Pets accepted, some restrictions. Check-in 1 pm, check-out 11 am. Outdoor pool. **$**
🐾 ➳

★ ★ **ROYALTY INN.** *130 Main St, Gorham (03581). Phone 603/466-3312; toll-free 800/437-3529; fax 603/466-5802. www.royaltyinn.com.* 90 rooms, 2 story. Pets accepted, some restrictions. Check-in 2 pm, check-out 11 am. Restaurant, bar. Fitness room. Indoor pool, outdoor pool. **$**
🐾 🏋 ➳

Restaurant

★ ★ **YOKOHAMA.** *288 Main St, Gorham (03581). Phone 603/466-2501.* Japanese menu. Lunch, dinner. Closed Mon; Thanksgiving, Dec 25; also two weeks in spring and two weeks in fall. Children's menu. **$$**

Hampton Beach (F-5)

See also Exeter, Portsmouth

Settled 1638
Population 900
Elevation 56 ft
Area Code 603
Zip 03842
Information Chamber of Commerce, 1 Park Ave, PO Box 790; phone 603/926-8717 or toll-free 800/438-2826
Web Site www.hamptonbeach.org

What to See and Do

Fishing. Charter boats at Hampton Beach piers.

Fuller Gardens. *10 Willow Ave, North Hampton (03862). 4 miles NE via Hwy 1A, just N of Hwy 111. Phone*

603/964-5414. www.fullergardens.org. Former estate of the late Governor Alvan T. Fuller featuring extensive rose gardens, annuals, perennials, Japanese garden, and conservatory. (mid-May-mid-Oct, daily) **$$**

Hampton Beach State Park. *1 Ocean Blvd, Hampton Beach (03842). 3 miles S on Hwy 1A. Phone 603/926-3784.* Sandy beach on Atlantic Ocean. Swimming, bathhouse. Also here is the Sea Shell, a band shell and amphitheater. Camping (hook-ups). (Late May-Labor Day, daily) Standard fees.

Tuck Memorial Museum. *40 Park Ave, Hampton (03842). On Meeting House Green, 4 miles N via Hwy 1A. Phone 603/929-0781.* Home of Hampton Historical Society. Antiques, documents, photographs, early postcards, tools, and toys; trolley exhibit; memorabilia of Hampton history. Restored one-room schoolhouse; fire station. (Mid-June-mid-Sept) **FREE**

Special Event

Band concerts. On beach. Evenings. Late June-Labor Day.

Limited-Service Hotels

★ ★ **ASHWORTH BY THE SEA.** *295 Ocean Blvd, Hampton Beach (03842). Phone 603/926-6762; toll-free 800/345-6736; fax 603/926-2002. www. ashworthhotel.com.* A great location for families, this oceanfront property is only 2 miles from Interstate 95 and is set right off the main intersection. Outdoor activities and shopping are all nearby, along with a boardwalk for leisure walks. Balcony rooms offer an ocean view. 105 rooms, 4 story. Check-in 3 pm, check-out noon. Three restaurants, bar. Indoor pool. **$$**

★ **HAMPSHIRE INN.** *20 Spur Rd (Hwy 107), Seabrook (03874). Phone 603/474-5700; toll-free 800/932-8520; fax 603/474-2886. www.hampshireinn.com.* 35 rooms, 3 story. Complimentary continental breakfast. Check-in 3 pm, check-out 11 am. Fitness room. Indoor pool, whirlpool. Airport transportation available. **$**

★ ★ **HAMPTON FALLS INN.** *11 Lafayette Rd, Hampton Falls (03844). Phone 603/926-9545; toll-free 800/356-1729; fax 603/926-4155. www.hampton-fallsinn.com.* 47 rooms, 3 story. Pets accepted, some restrictions. Check-in 2 pm, check-out 11 am. Wireless Internet access. Restaurant. Indoor pool, whirlpool. **$**

★ ★ **INN OF HAMPTON.** *815 Lafayette Rd, Hampton (03842). Phone 603/926-6771; toll-free 800/423-4561; fax 603/929-2160. www.theinnofhampton. com.* Not to be confused with the chain of a similar name, this inn provides the personalized touches of a bed-and-breakfast but has several rooms providing modern business services. 71 rooms, 2 story. Check-in 3 pm, check-out 11 am. Restaurant, bar. Children's activity center. Fitness room. Indoor pool. Business center. **$**

★ ★ **LAMIE'S INN & OLD SALT RESTAURANT.** *490 Lafayette Rd, Hampton (03842). Phone 603/926-0330; toll-free 800/805-5050; fax 603/926-0211. www. lamiesinn.com.* This charming country lodging is located just east of Interstate 95 in the town center. The building is a Saltbox/Colonial style and features spacious guest rooms. Seafood, steak, and sandwiches are among the menu options at the Old Salt restaurant. 32 rooms, 2 story. Pets accepted, some restrictions; fee. Complimentary continental breakfast. Check-in 2 pm, check-out noon. Restaurant, bar. **$**

Specialty Lodging

D. W. 'S OCEANSIDE INN. *365 Ocean Blvd, Hampton Beach (03842). Phone 603/926-3542; toll-free 866/623-2674; fax 603/926-3549. www.oceansideinn. com.* This early 1900s beach house overlooking the Atlantic Ocean is an ideal getaway from the grind. Geared toward more mature getaways, the Oceanside is open mid-May through mid-Oct. 9 rooms, 2 story. Closed mid-Oct-mid-May. No children allowed. Complimentary full breakfast. Check-in 2 pm, check-out 11 am. Beach. **$$**

Hanover (D-3)

See also White River Junction, VT

Settled 1765
Population 9,212
Elevation 531 ft
Area Code 603
Zip 03755
Information Chamber of Commerce, PO Box 5105, 216 Nugget Bldg, Main St; phone 603/643-3115
Web Site www.hanoverchamber.org

Established four years after the first settlers came here, Dartmouth College is an integral part of Hanover.

Named for the Earl of Dartmouth, one of its original supporters, the school was founded by the Reverend Eleazar Wheelock "for the instruction of the youth of Indian tribes... and others."

What to See and Do

Dartmouth College. *Main and Wheelock sts, Hanover (03755). Phone 603/646-1110. www.dartmouth.edu.* (1769) (5,400 students) On campus are

Baker Barry Memorial Library. *1 Elm St, Hanover (03755). Wentworth and College sts. Phone 603/646-2560.* (White spire) Two million volumes; notable frescoes by the Mexican artist Jos Clemente Orozco. (Daily) Guide service during vacations (Mon-Fri).

Dartmouth Row. *Hanover. E side of Green.* Early white brick buildings including Wentworth, Dartmouth, Thornton, and Reed halls. Parts of Dartmouth Hall date to 1784.

Hood Museum and Hopkins Center for the Arts. *Hanover. Opposite S end of Green.* Concert hall, theaters, changing art exhibits. Gallery (daily; free). Performing arts events all year (fees).

Dartmouth Skiway. *Lyme. 15 miles N on Hwy 10 to Lyme, then 3 miles E. Phone 603/795-2143. www.skiway. dartmouth.edu.* Quad, double chairlift, surface tow; patrol, school; lodge, snack bar. Longest run 1 mile; vertical drop 968 feet. (Mid-Dec-Mar, daily) **$$$$**

Enfield Shaker Museum. *24 Caleb Dyer Ln, Enfield (03748). Phone 603/632-4346. www.shakermuseum.org.* Museum devoted to Shaker culture on the site where the Shakers established their Chosen Vale in 1793. Includes exhibits, craft demonstrations, workshops, special programs, and extensive gardens. (Daily) **$$**

League of New Hampshire Craftsmen. *13 Lebanon St, Hanover (03755). Phone 603/643-5050. www.nhcrafts. org.* Work by some of New Hampshire's finest craftspeople. (Mon-Sat; closed holidays) **FREE**

⭐ **Saint-Gaudens National Historic Site.** *Rt 12A, Cornish. Approximately 5 miles S on Hwy 10, then 12 miles S off Hwy 12A, across the river from Windsor, VT. Phone 603/675-2175. www.nps.gov/saga.* Former residence and studio of sculptor Augustus Saint-Gaudens (1848-1907); "Aspet," built circa 1800, was once a tavern. Saint-Gaudens's famous works *The Puritan, Adams Memorial,* and *Shaw Memorial* are among the 100 works on display. Also formal gardens and works by other artists; sculptor-in-residence; interpretive programs. (Memorial Day-Oct, daily) **$**

Webster Cottage. *32 N Main St, Hanover (03755). Phone 603/643-6529.* (1780) Residence of Daniel Webster during his last year as a Dartmouth College student; colonial and Shaker furniture, Webster memorabilia. (Memorial Day-mid-Oct: Wed, Sat-Sun afternoons) **FREE**

Full-Service Hotel

⭐ ⭐ ⭐ **HANOVER INN.** *Main and Wheelock sts, Hanover (03755). Phone 603/643-4300; toll-free 800/443-7024; fax 603/646-3744. www.hanoverinn. com.* This inn is located just minutes from Dartmouth College. The guest rooms are decorated with a colonial motif, and guests have access to athletic facilities at the university. 92 rooms, 5 story. Pets accepted; fee. Check-in 3 pm, check-out noon. High-speed Internet access, wireless Internet access. Restaurant, bar. Fitness room. Airport transportation available. **$$$**
🐾 🏃

Specialty Lodgings

ALDEN COUNTRY INN. *1 Market St, Lyme (03768). Phone 603/795-2222; toll-free 800/794-2296; fax 603/795-9436. www.aldencountryinn.com.* Original inn and tavern built in 1809; antique furnishings. 15 rooms, 4 story. Complimentary full breakfast. Check-in 2 pm, check-out 11 am. Restaurant, bar. **$**

DOWD'S COUNTRY INN. *9 Main St, Lyme (03768). Phone 603/795-4712; toll-free 800/482-4712; fax 603/795-4220. www.dowdscountryinn.com.* This charming New England inn is located 10 miles north of Dartmouth College. Close to the Lyme commons, this property is surrounded by trees and provides a wonderful place for guests to relax. 23 rooms, 2 story. Complimentary full breakfast. Check-in noon, check-out noon. **$$**

Restaurants

⭐ ⭐ **JESSE'S.** *RR 120, Hanover (03755). Phone 603/643-4111; fax 603/643-3340. www.bluesky restaurants.com.* Victorian décor. Steak menu. Lunch, dinner. Bar. Children's menu. Outdoor seating. **$$**

⭐ **MOLLY'S.** *43 S Main St, Hanover (03755). Phone 603/643-2570; fax 603/643-6645. www.mollys restaurant.com.* American menu. Lunch, dinner. Closed Thanksgiving, Dec 25. Bar. **$$**

Holderness (D-4)

See also Meredith, Plymouth

Settled 1770
Population 1,694
Elevation 584 ft
Area Code 603
Zip 03245

Holderness is the shopping center and post office for Squam Lake (second-largest lake in the state) and neighboring Little Squam. Fishing, boating, swimming, water sports, and winter sports are popular in this area. The movie *On Golden Pond* was filmed here. A Ranger District office of the White Mountain National Forest is located here.

What to See and Do

League of New Hampshire Craftsmen–Sandwich Home Industries. *32 Main St, Center Sandwich (03227). 12 miles NE via Hwy 113. Phone 603/284-6831. www. nhcrafts.org.* Work by some of New Hampshire's finest craftspeople. (Mid-May-mid-Oct, daily)

Squam Lake Tours. *Hwy 113, Holderness (03245). 1/2 mile S on US 3. Phone 603/968-7577. www.squamlaketours.com.* Two-hour boat tours of the area where *On Golden Pond* was filmed. (May-Oct, three tours daily) **$$$$**

Squam Lakes Natural Science Center. *23 Science Center Rd, Holderness (03245). Phone 603/968-7194. www. nhnature.org.* If this attraction looks familiar, perhaps you'll recognize it as the site where the 1981 movie, *On Golden Pond* with Henry Fonda and Katharine Hepburn, was filmed. Walking through the woods of this 200-acre wildlife sanctuary, you'll see black bears, deer, bobcats, otters, mountain lions, foxes, and birds of prey in enclosed trailside exhibits. You can also take the Explore Squam boat tour. Picnicking. (May-early Nov, daily 9:30 am-4:30 pm) **$$$**

Yogi Bear's Jellystone Park. *Rte 132, Ashland (03256). Phone 603/968-9000. www.jellystonenh.com.* Unleash your inner child and join the fun with Yogi, BooBoo, and Cindy bears. Its kitsch galore here, but the kids will love it. Each site has its own picnic table and fire ring. More than 275 sites, plus cabins. Restrooms, showers. Restaurant, pool, whirlpool, playground, miniature golf, boat rentals, pets accepted, organized activities, movies.

Full-Service Inn

★ ★ ★ MANOR ON GOLDEN POND. *Manor Dr (Hwy 3 and Shepard Hill Rd), Holderness (03245). Phone 603/968-3348; toll-free 800/545-2141; fax 603/968-2116. www.manorongoldenpond.com.* Modeled after an English country estate, this inn is located on the shore of Squam Lake. Activities include tennis, badminton, croquet, and access to a private beach. 25 rooms, 3 story. Children over 12 years only. Complimentary full breakfast. Check-in 3 pm, check-out 11 am. Wireless Internet access. Restaurant, bar. Indoor pool. Tennis. **$$$**

Specialty Lodgings

GLYNN HOUSE INN. *59 Highland St, Ashland (03217). Phone 603/968-3775; toll-free 800/637-9599; fax 603/968-9415. www.glynnhouse.com.* This restored 1896 Queen Anne/Victorian is conveniently located near Squam Lake in the heart of the White Mountains. The interior is tastefully decorated, and guest rooms are nicely appointed. Lakes Region dining, attractions, and activities are all nearby. 13 rooms, 2 story. Children over 12 years only. Complimentary full breakfast. Check-in 3 pm, check-out 11 am. **$$**

INN ON GOLDEN POND. *Hwy 3, Holderness (03245). Phone 603/968-7269; fax 603/968-9226. www. innongoldenpond.com.* Built in 1879; fireplace; rooms individually decorated. 8 rooms, 3 story. Children over 10 years only. Complimentary continental breakfast. Check-in 3 pm, check-out 11 am. **$**

Restaurants

★ COMMON MAN. *60 Main St, Ashland (03245). Phone 603/968-7030; fax 603/968-3931. www.thecman. com.* Situated just off Interstate 93, this rugged-looking eatery is a great place to gather with friends. Unique in stylea western and New England mixit features wagon wheels, bales of hay, and rough ceilings and floors. A large selection of original magazines and prints are for sale. American menu. Lunch, dinner. Bar. Children's menu. Casual attire. Outdoor seating. **$$**

★ ★ CORNER HOUSE INN. *22 Main St, Holderness (03227). Phone 603/284-6219; fax 603/284-6220.* This Victorian-style inn (1849) was originally a house and an attached harness shop. Guest rooms are available. American menu. Lunch, dinner. Closed Thanksgiving, Dec 25. **$$**

★ ★ ★ **MANOR ON GOLDEN POND.** *Manor Dr (Hwy 3 and Shepard Hill Rd), Holderness (03245). Phone 603/968-3348; fax 603/968-2116. www.manorongoldenpond.com.* Dinner at this cozy inn on Squam Lake is both a delicious and romantic experience. The location, high on a hill, allows guests to enjoy wonderful views in a serene setting. The frequently changing à la carte menu allows you to choose different combinations of New American dishes like duck hash Napolean and sautéed mahi mahi. American menu. Dinner. Bar. Business casual attire. Reservations recommended. Valet parking. **$$$**

Jackson (C-4)

See also Bartlett, Mount Washington, North Conway, Pinkham Notch

Settled 1790
Population 678
Elevation 971 ft
Area Code 603
Zip 03846
Information Chamber of Commerce, 3 Market Place Falls, PO Box 304; phone 603/383-9356
Web Site www.jacksonnh.com

At the south end of Pinkham Notch (see), Jackson is a center for skiing and a year-round resort. The Wildcat River rushes over rock formations in the village; Wildcat Mountain is to the north. A covered bridge (circa 1870) spans the Ellis River.

What to See and Do

Black Mountain. *2 1/2 miles N on Hwy 16B. Phone 603/383-4490. www.blackmt.com.* Triple, double chairlifts, J-bar; patrol, school, rentals; cafeteria; nursery. Longest run 1 mile; vertical drop 1,100 feet.

Heritage-New Hampshire. *2 miles S on Hwy 16 in Glen. Phone 603/383-9776. www.heritagenh.com.* Path winds among theatrical sets and takes visitors on a walk through 30 events during 300 years of New Hampshire history. Each set has animation, sounds, and smells to re-create the past, from a stormy voyage to the New World to a train ride through autumn foliage in Crawford Notch. (Late May-Labor Day, daily; mid-Sept-Columbus Day, weekends) **$$$**

Jackson Ski Touring Foundation. *Main St and Hwy 16A, Jackson. Phone 603/383-9355. www.jacksonxc.org.* Maintains 95 miles of cross-country trails, connecting inns and ski areas. Instruction, rentals, rescue service. (Dec-mid-Apr, daily; closed Dec 25) **$$$**

Story Land. *2 miles S on Hwy 16 in Glen. Phone 603/383-4186. www.storylandnh.com.* Village of storybook settings; Cinderella's castle, Heidi's grandfather's house; themed rides, including raft ride, on 35 acres. (Mid-June-early Sept: daily; early Sept-early Oct: weekends) **$$$$**

Limited-Service Hotels

★ **LODGE AT JACKSON VILLAGE.** *153 Hwy 16, Jackson (03846). Phone 603/383-0999; toll-free 800/233-5634; fax 603/383-6104. www.lodgeatjacksonvillage.com.* Trout fishing, tennis, and hiking are among the outdoor activities guests can enjoy at this property surrounded by the White Mountains. Guest rooms are spacious, drenched in light, and feature a porch or patio. Located in a tranquil setting on Route 16—just before it splits into 16B and 16A—it is just a short drive from the town center. 32 rooms, 2 story. Complimentary full breakfast. Check-in 3 pm, check-out 11 am. High-speed Internet access, wireless Internet access. Outdoor pool, whirlpool. Tennis. **$$**

★ ★ **STORYBOOK RESORT INN.** *Hwys 302 and 16, Glen (03838). Phone 603/383-6800; fax 603/383-4678. www.storybookresort.com.* 78 rooms, 2 story. Check-in 3-9 pm, check-out 11 am. Restaurant, bar. Fitness room. Indoor pool, two outdoor pools, children's pool. Tennis. **$**

Full-Service Resorts

★ ★ **EAGLE MOUNTAIN HOUSE.** *Carter Notch Rd, Jackson (03846). Phone 603/383-9111; toll-free 800/966-5779; fax 603/383-0854. www.eaglemt.com.* Winding, rolling roads lead guests to this 19th-century American Colonial-style resort set in a tranquil mountain setting. Perfect for vacationing families, it offers seasonal and year-round activities, including cross-country skiing, 9-hole golf, lawn games, and a game room. 97 rooms, 5 story. Check-in 3 pm, check-out 11 am. Wireless Internet access. Restaurant, bar. Fitness room. Outdoor pool, whirlpool. Golf, 9 holes. Tennis. Ski in/ski out. **$$**

★ ★ **WENTWORTH RESORT HOTEL.** *1 Carter Notch Rd, Jackson (03846). Phone 603/383-*

9700; toll-free 800/637-0013; fax 603/383-4265. www. thewentworth.com. This elegant country inn, built in 1869, has been in continuous operation for more than a century. Located in the White Mountains, the year-round resort has first-class amenities like a fine-dining restaurant and recreational facilities. 51 rooms, 2 story. Check-in 2 pm, check-out 11 am. Restaurant, bar. Outdoor pool. Golf, 18 holes. Tennis. Ski in/ski out. Airport transportation available. **$$**

Full-Service Inn

★ ★ ★ **INN AT THORN HILL.** *Thorn Hill Rd, Jackson (03846). Phone 603/383-4242; toll-free 800/ 289-8990; fax 603/383-8062. www.innatthornhill.com.* This elegant, well-appointed inn pays close attention to every detail, from the deep, rich color selections and furnishings to the spectacular outdoor setting in the heart of the White Mountains. Outdoor activities abound, and there are many area attractions nearby. Guests can walk to the nearby shops and galleries while taking in the outdoor scenery. 25 rooms. Children over 8 years only. Complimentary full breakfast. Check-in 3 pm, check-out 11 am. High-speed Internet access, wireless Internet access. Restaurant, bar. Fitness room, spa. Outdoor pool, whirlpool. Ski in/ski out. **$$$**

Specialty Lodgings

DANA PLACE INN. *Hwy 16, Jackson (03846). Phone 603/383-6822; toll-free 800/537-9276; fax 603/383-6022. www.danaplace.com.* 30 rooms, 2 story. Pets accepted, some restrictions. Complimentary full breakfast. Check-in 3 pm, check-out 11 am. Restaurant, bar. Indoor pool, children's pool, whirlpool. Golf. Tennis. Business center. **$$**

★ ★ ★ **INN AT ELLIS RIVER.** *17 Harriman Rd, Jackson (03846). Phone 603/383-9339; toll-free 800/ 233-8309; fax 603/383-4142. www.innatellisriver.com.* Located in the heart of the White Mountains, this luxurious inn offers rooms with period furnishings and a wide variety of amenities. Some rooms have whirlpool tubs or balconies and most have fireplaces. The area surrounding the inn offers year-round activities such as cross-country skiing, golf, fishing, swimming, and kayaking. 21 rooms, 3 story. Children over 12 years only. Complimentary full breakfast. Check-in 3 pm, check-out 11 am. Restaurant, bar. Outdoor pool. **$**

NESTLENOOK FARM RESORT. *Dinsmore Rd, Jackson (03846). Phone 603/383-9443; toll-free 800/ 659-9443; fax 603/383-4515. www.luxurymountain getaways.com.* Located on the river, this restored Victorian building is one of the oldest in Jackson (1770). Furnishings include antiques, Tiffany lamps, and 18th-century parlor stoves. 7 rooms, 3 story, all suites. Closed two weeks in Apr. No children allowed. Complimentary full breakfast. Check-in 3 pm, check-out 11 am. Outdoor pool. **$$**

Restaurants

★ ★ **CHRISTMAS FARM INN.** *Hwy 16B, Jackson (03846). Phone 603/383-4313; toll-free 800/443-5837; fax 603/383-0993. www.christmasfarminn.com.* American menu. Breakfast, dinner. Bar. Children's menu. Casual attire. Reservations recommended. **$$$**

★ ★ ★ **INN AT THORN HILL.** *Thorn Hill Rd, Jackson (03846). Phone 603/383-4242; toll-free 800/ 289-8990; fax 603/383-8062. www.innatthornhill.com.* Pacific-Rim menu. Breakfast, dinner. Bar. Business casual attire. Reservations recommended. Outdoor seating. **$$$**

★ **RED PARKA PUB.** *Hwy 302, Glen (03838). Phone 603/383-4344; fax 603/383-9127. www.redparkapub.com.* One room in 1914 railroad car. American menu. Dinner. Closed Thanksgiving, Dec 24. Bar. Children's menu. Outdoor seating. **$**

★ ★ **WILDCAT INN & TAVERN.** *Hwy 16A, Jackson (03846). Phone 603/383-4245; toll-free 800/228-4245; fax 603/383-6556. www.wildcattavern.com.* Guests can choose to dine in the restaurant for menu selections such as lamb, seafood, and steak, or head to the Tavern, which offers a limited menu. An open mike is featured on Tuesdays and Saturdays at this local favorite. Situated on the main road, it is also near quaint shops and waterfalls. American menu. Lunch, dinner. Bar. Children's menu. Casual attire. Reservations recommended. Outdoor seating. **$$$**

Jaffrey (F-3)

See also Keene, Peterborough

Settled 1760
Population 5,361
Elevation 1,013 ft
Area Code 603
Zip 03452
Information Chamber of Commerce, 7 Main St, PO Box 2; phone 603/532-4549
Web Site www.jaffreychamber.com

Jaffrey, on the eastern slopes of Mount Monadnock, has been a summer resort community since the 1840s.

What to See and Do

Barrett House "Forest Hall." *79 Main St, New Ipswich (03071). 10 miles SE on Hwy 124, then 1/4 mile S on Hwy 123A (Main St). Phone 603/878-2517.* (1800) Federal mansion with third-floor ballroom. Twelve museum rooms contain some of the most important examples of 18th- and 19th-century furniture and antique musical instruments in New England. Extensive grounds with Gothic Revival summer house on terraced hill behind main house. Guided tours. (first Sat of the month) **$**

✪ **Cathedral of the Pines.** *Cathedral Rd, Rindge (03461). 3 miles E on Hwy 124, then 3 miles S. Phone 603/899-3300. www.cathedralpines.com.* International nondenominational shrine. National memorial for all American war dead; Memorial Bell Tower dedicated to women who died in service. Outdoor altar, gardens, museum. (May-Oct, daily)

Monadnock State Park. *116 Poole Memorial Rd, Jaffrey (03452). 2 miles W on Hwy 124, then N. Phone 603/532-8862.* Hikers' mecca; 40-mile network of well-maintained trails on Mount Monadnock (3,165 feet). Summit views of all New England states. Picnicking, camping. Ski touring (Dec-Mar). No pets allowed. **$$**

Jefferson

Settled 1772
Population 965
Elevation 1,384 ft
Area Code 603
Zip 03583
Information Northern White Mountain Chamber of Commerce, 164 Main St, PO Box 298, Berlin 03570; phone 603/752-6060 or toll-free 800/992-7480
Web Site www.northernwhitemountains.com

On the slopes of Mount Starr King in the White Mountains, this resort area is referred to locally as "Jefferson Hill."

What to See and Do

Santa's Village. *1 mile NW on Hwy 2, 1/2 mile W of junction Hwy 116. Phone 603/586-4445. www.santas-village.com.* Santa and tame deer; unique rides; live shows, computerized animation. Playground; picnic area. (Father's Day-Labor Day: daily; after Labor Day-Columbus Day: Sat-Sun) **$$$$**

Six Gun City. *Hwy 2, Jefferson. 4 miles E. Phone 603/586-4592. www.sixguncity.com.* Western frontier village; cowboy skits, frontier show, fort, Native American camp, homestead, carriage and sleigh museum, general store, snack bar; miniature horse show; pony and burro rides; bumper boats, water slides, and other rides; miniature golf, games, animals, and antiques. (Mid-June-Labor Day: daily; after Labor Day-Columbus Day: Sat-Sun) **$$$$**

Special Event

Lancaster Fair. *Lancaster. 6 miles NW. Phone 603/788-2530. www.lancasterfair.com.* Agricultural exhibits, horse show, entertainment. Labor Day weekend.

Restaurant

★ ★ ★ **THE CARRIAGE HOUSE RESTAURANT.** *1235 Athens St, Jefferson (30549). Phone 706/367-1989; fax 706/367-2695. www.thecarriagehouse.org.* This elegant and classic restaurant is nestled in a country location amid soft rolling hills and majestic trees. A restored Victorian house (1886), it features six stone fireplaces with cherry wood mantles; hardwood floors; etched and stained glass; and a large porch, where guests can enjoy a cocktail before dinner. The décor is charming, the service is warm and skillful, and the food—International, with Southern influences—is memorable. International menu. Lunch, dinner, brunch. Children's menu. Casual attire. Reservations recommended. Outdoor seating. Credit cards accepted. **$$$**

Keene (F-3)

See also Jaffrey, Peterborough; seee also Brattleboro, VT

Settled 1736
Population 22,430
Elevation 486 ft
Area Code 603
Zip 03431
Information Chamber of Commerce, 48 Central Sq; phone 603/352-1303
Web Site www.keenechamber.com

A modern commercial city, Keene is the chief community of the Monadnock region. Its industries manufacture many products including furniture, machinery, textiles, and toys.

What to See and Do

Colony Mill Marketplace. *222 West St, Keene (03431). Phone 603/357-1240. www.colonymill.com.* Restored 1838 textile mill now transformed into regional marketplace with dozens of specialty shops, an antique center, numerous dining options, and varied entertainment. (Mon-Sat)

Horatio Colony House Museum. *199 Main St, Keene (03431). Phone 603/352-0460. www.horatiocolonymuseum.org.* Stately Federalist home (1806) of the son of prominent Keene mill owners. Features treasures collected from Colony's world travels; books, art, antique furniture. (May-mid-Oct: Wed-Sun; rest of year: by appointment) **FREE**

Wyman Tavern. *339 Main St, Keene (03431). Phone 603/352-1895.* (1762) Scene of first meeting of Dartmouth College trustees in 1770; now furnished in 1820s-style. (June-Sept, Thurs-Sat) **$**

Special Events

Cheshire Fair. *Fairgrounds, 319 Monadnock Hwy, North Swanzey (03446). S on Hwy 12. Phone 603/357-4740. www.cheshirefair.com.* Exhibits; horse and ox pulling contests; entertainment. First week in Aug.

Old Homestead. *At Potash Bowl in Swanzey Center. 4 miles S on Hwy 32. Phone 603/352-7411.* Drama of life in Swanzey during the 1880s based on the Biblical story of the Prodigal Son; first presented in 1886. Mid-July.

Limited-Service Hotel

★ ★ BEST WESTERN SOVEREIGN HOTEL. *401 Winchester St, Keene (03431). Phone 603/357-3038; toll-free 800/780-7234; fax 603/357-4776. www.bestwestern.com.* 131 rooms, 2 story. Pets accepted; fee. Complimentary full breakfast. Check-in 2 pm, check-out noon. Restaurant, bar. Indoor pool. **$**
🐾 ⌘

Restaurants

★ ★ 176 MAIN. *176 Main St, Keene (03457). Phone 603/357-3100; fax 603/357-5500. www.176main.com.* American menu. Lunch, dinner; Sunday Brunch. Closed holidays. Bar. Children's menu. Outdoor seating. **$$**

★ THE PUB. *131 Winchester St, Keene (03431). Phone 603/352-3135; fax 603/252-0263. www.thepubrestaurant.com.* American menu. Breakfast, lunch, dinner. Closed Dec 25. Bar. Children's menu. **$**

Laconia (D-4)

See also Franklin, Meredith, Wolfeboro

Settled 1777
Population 15,743
Elevation 570 ft
Area Code 603
Zip 03246
Information Chamber of Commerce, 383 S Main St; phone 603/524-5531
Web Site www.laconia-weirs.org

On four lakes (Winnisquam, Opechee, Pauqus Bay, and Winnipesaukee), Laconia is the commercial center of the area known as the "Lakes Region." Besides the resort trade, it has more than a score of factories whose products include knitting machinery, hosiery, knitted fabrics, ball bearings, and electronic components. The headquarters of the White Mountain National Forest (see) is also located here.

What to See and Do

Daytona Fun Park. *Rte 11B, Laconia (03246). Phone 603/366-5461.* Challenge family and friends to miniature Indy Car racing on the go-karts. There's also a climbing wall, batting cages, and miniature golf. (Daily 10 am-11 pm) **$$**

Funspot. *Rte 3 S, Weirs Beach (03246). Phone 603/366-4377. www.funspotnh.com.* Funspot offers more than 500 new and classic games, an indoor golf center, bowling, kiddie rides, miniature golf, a driving range, and an on-site tavern and restaurant. Fee ($) for individual attractions. (Mid-June-Labor Day: daily 10 am-midnight; rest of year: Sun-Thurs 10 am-10 pm, Fri-Sat 10 am-11 pm)

Gunstock Campground. *Rte 11A, Gilford (03249). Phone toll-free 800/486-7862. www.gunstock.com/summer.* Gunstock is close to Lakes Region attractions. Approximately 300 sites. Propane station. restrooms, showers, laundry services, convenience store, pool. Pets accepted, some restrictions. Organized activities.

Gunstock Recreation Area. *Hwy 11A, Gilford (03249). 7 miles E on Hwy 11A. Phone 603/293-4341; toll-free 800/486-7862. www.gunstock.com.* A 2,400-acre county-operated park.

> **Summer.** Picnic and camp sites (Memorial Day weekend-Columbus Day weekend; fee; hook-ups additional; includes swimming privileges); fireplaces; stocked pond, blazed trails, playground; special events.

> **Winter.** Skiing. Quad, two triple, two double chairlifts, two handle tows; patrol, school, rentals; snowmaking; cafeteria, lounge; nursery. Longest run 2 miles; vertical drop 1,400 feet. Cross-country trails. Night skiing. (Nov-Mar, daily; closed Dec 25) **$$$$**

Half Moon Amusement Arcades. *240-260 Lakeside Ave, Weirs Beach (03246). Phone 603/366-4315. www.weirsbeach.com.* This old-fashioned arcade, just across the street from the scenic Weirs Beach boardwalk, includes a penny arcade, a family fun center and bumper cars. Revisit your teen years with classic games like Pac-Man, Asteroids, Space Invaders, and Pole Position, or let a new generation of game players discover Skeeball and pinball. Fee ($) for individual attractions. (May-mid-Oct, daily, hours vary)

M/S *Mount Washington*. *Weirs Beach (03246). Phone 603/366-5531; toll-free 888/843-6686. www.cruisenh.com.* Cruise the waters of Lake Winnipesaukee (win-e-puh-SAW-kee), the largest lake in New Hampshire, and enjoy scenic mountain views aboard the M/S *Mount Washington*, which offers daily scenic cruises and dinner dance cruises. Ports of call include Weirs Beach, Wolfeboro, Meredith, Alton Bay, and Center Harbor. (Mid-May-Oct; check Web site or call for schedule) **$$$$**

★ **Surf Coaster U.S.A.** *1085 White Oaks Rd, Weirs Beach (03247). 6 miles N on Hwy 3, then E on Hwy 11B. Phone 603/366-5600. www.surfcoasterUSA.com.* Family water park with wave pool, water slides, "Crazy River" inner tube ride, "Boomerang" rides inside translucent glass tubes; raft rentals, sun decks, showers, children's play areas; entertainment, games, prizes. Snack bar. (Mid-June-Labor Day, daily) **$$$$**

Weirs Beach. *306 Union Ave, Laconia (03246). Phone 603/524-5046.* Swimming, bathhouses; playgrounds, picnic areas. Endicott Memorial Stone with initials of 1652 explorers, south end of beach. (Mid-June-Labor Day, daily) **$$**

Weirs Beach Tent and Trailer Park. *198 Endicott St N, Weirs Beach (03246). Phone 603/366-4747. www.ucampnh.com/weirsbeach.* Camping supplies are provided, and some sites have cable TV. More than 180 sites. Restrooms, showers. Pets accepted, some restrictions.

Special Event

New Hampshire Music Festival. *88 Alvah Wilson Rd, Laconia (03246). Phone 603/279-3300. www.nhmf.org.* Plymouth State College, in Silver Cultural Arts Center. Symphony/pop concerts. (July-Aug, Thurs-Fri; limited Sat performances)

Limited-Service Hotels

★ ★ B MAE'S RESORT INN & SUITES.
Rtes 11 and 11B, Gilford (03249). Phone 603/293-7526; toll-free 800/458-3877; fax 603/293-4340. www.bmaes-resort.com. B Maes Resort Inn and Suites is located at Lake Winnipesaukee and is close to all Weirs Beach attractions. All rooms have a deck or patio. 82 rooms, 2 story. Complimentary continental breakfast. Check-in 3 pm, check-out 11 am. Fitness room. Indoor pool, outdoor pool, whirlpool. **$**
🧍 🛏

★ BARTON'S MOTEL.
1330 Union Ave, Laconia (03246). Phone 603/524-5674. www.bartonsmotel.com. Located on the shores of Lake Winnipesaukee and minutes from Weirs Beach attractions, Bartons Motel offers scenic water views, as well as swimming and relaxing on its private beach. Amenities include free paddleboats and rowboats, free dockage for boat owners, and an on-site bookstore. 41 rooms. Check-in 1 pm, check-out 11 am. Beach. Outdoor pool. **$**
🔲 🛏

Restaurant

★ **NASWA BEACH BAR AND GRILL.** *1086 Weirs Blvd, Laconia (03246). Phone 603/366-4341. www.naswa.com.* The Naswa Beach Bar and Grill offers a menu of appetizers, nachos, salads, sandwiches and burgers, as well as a full bar, in a fun lakefront atmosphere at the Naswa Resort. Live bands and special events are featured. American menu. Lunch, dinner. Bar. Children's menu. Casual attire. Outdoor seating. **$$**

Lincoln/North Woodstock (C-4)

See also Franconia Notch State Park, Waterville Valley

Population 1,229
Elevation Lincoln, 811 ft; North Woodstock, 738 ft
Area Code 603
Zip Lincoln, 03251; North Woodstock, 03262
Information Chamber of Commerce, Rte 112 Kancamagus Scenic Hwy, PO Box 1017, Lincoln; phone 603/745-6621 or toll-free 800/227-4191
Web Site www.lincolnwoodstock.com

In a spectacular mountain setting, the villages of Lincoln and Woodstock lie at the junction of the road through Franconia Notch State Park (see) and the Kancamagus Scenic Byway (Hwy 112).

What to See and Do

Clark's Trading Post. *1 mile N of North Woodstock on Hwy 3. Phone 603/745-8913. www.clarkstradingpost.com.* Entertainment park has trained New Hampshire black bears, haunted house, replica of 1884 firehouse; 30-minute ride on White Mountain Central railroad. Museum features early Americana, photo parlor, maple cabin, nickelodeons, ice cream parlor. Bumper boats. (July-Labor Day: daily; Memorial Day-June and early Sept-Columbus Day: weekends) **$$$**

Hobo Railroad. *Connector Rd, Lincoln (03251). Railroad St, off Main. Phone 603/745-2135. www.hoborr.com.* Fifteen-mile scenic excursions along the Pemigewasset River. Features restored Pullman Dome dining car. (Daily) **$$**

Loon Mountain Recreation Area. *3 miles E of Lincoln off Hwy 112 (Kancamagus Hwy). Phone 603/745-8111. www.loonmtn.com.* A 7,100-foot gondola, two triple, four double chairlifts, one high-speed quad chairlift, pony lift; patrol, school, rentals, shops, snowmaking; restaurant, cafeterias, bar; nursery; lodge. Longest run 2 1/2 miles; vertical drop 2,100 feet. (Late Nov-mid-Apr, daily) Cross-country trails (Dec-Mar). **Summer activities** include mountain biking (rentals), bike tours, in-line skating, horseback riding, skate park, climbing wall. Gondola also operates Memorial Day-mid-Oct (daily).

Lost River Gorge. *Lost River Rd, North Woodstock. 6 miles W of North Woodstock on Hwy 112, Kinsman Notch. Phone 603/745-8031.* Natural boulder caves, largest known granite pothole in the eastern United States; Paradise Falls; boardwalks with 1,900-foot glacial gorge; nature garden with 300 varieties of native shrubs and flowers; geology exhibits; cafeteria, picnicking. (Mid-May-mid-Oct, daily) Appropriate outdoor clothing recommended. **$$$**

Whale's Tale Water Park. *N on I-93, exit 33, then N on Hwy 3. Phone 603/745-8810.* Wave pool, water slides, "lazy river," children's activity pool; playground; concession, gift shop. (June-Labor Day: daily; Memorial Day-mid-June: Sat-Sun) **$$$$**

Special Event

New Hampshire Highland Games. *Loon Mountain. Phone 603/229-1975; toll-free 800/358-7268. www.nhscot.org.* Largest Scottish gathering in the eastern United States. Bands, competitions, concerts, workshops. Three days in Sept.

Limited-Service Hotels

★ ★ **INDIAN HEAD RESORT.** *664 US Rte 3, Lincoln (03251). Phone 603/745-8000; toll-free 800/343-8000; fax 603/745-8414. www.indianheadresort.com.* This unique resort is located near the Franconia Notch Parkway and numerous attractions. Some of the guest rooms have balconies with spectacular mountain views. And the resort offers a variety of outdoor activities such as cross-country skiing, paddleboating, troutfishing, and hiking. There is also a children's activity center (in season). 98 rooms, 2 story. Check-in 3 pm, check-out 11 am. Restaurant, bar. Children's activity center. Indoor pool, outdoor pool. Credit cards accepted. **$**

★ ★ **INNSEASON RESORTS SOUTH MOUNTAIN.** *Main St Rt 112, Lincoln (03251). Phone 603/745-9300; toll-free 800/654-6183; fax*

603/745-2317. www.innseasonresorts.com. Located at the foot of Loon in the White Mountains, this quaint, ski town property is the perfect location for an activities-driven family or a couple looking for a romantic getaway. The surrounding area offers numerous winter activities, a theme park, fine dining, and shopping. 84 rooms, 4 story. Check-in 4 pm, check-out 11 am. Fitness room. Indoor pool. Credit cards accepted. **$**

★ ★ **WOODWARDS RESORT.** *527 US Rt 3, Lincoln (03251). Phone 603/745-8141; toll-free 800/ 635-8968; fax 603/745-3408. www.woodwardsresort. com.* Located in the heart of the White Mountains, this small motor inn has been family operated since 1956. It is close to skiing, hiking, and other recreational activities. 80 rooms, 2 story. Check-in 3 pm, check-out 11 am. Restaurant, bar. Indoor pool. **$$**

Full-Service Resort

★ ★ **MOUNTAIN CLUB ON LOON.** *90 Loon Mountain Rd, Lincoln (03251). Phone 603/ 745-2244; toll-free 800/229-7829; fax 603/745-8224. www.mtnclub.com.* This ski area is surrounded by the lush greenery of the White Mountains. Located at the base of Loon Mountain on the scenic Kancamagus Highway (Rte 112), this property offers lifts, ski shops, and shuttle services. Many on-site activities are offered, and area attractions are nearby. 234 rooms, 6 story. Check-in 5 pm, check-out 11 am. Two restaurants, bar. Children's activity center. Fitness room, spa. Indoor pool, outdoor pool, children's pool, whirlpool. Ski in/ski out. **$$**

Specialty Lodgings

WOODSTOCK INN. *135 Main St, North Woodstock (03262). Phone 603/745-3951; toll-free 800/321-3985; fax 603/745-3701. www.woodstockinnnh.com.* Victorian house (1890). 24 rooms, 4 story. Complimentary full breakfast. Check-in 3 pm, check-out 11 am. Restaurant, bar. **$**

Restaurants

★ ★ **COMMON MAN.** *Pollard Rd, Lincoln (03217). Phone 603/745-3463; fax 603/745-6868. www.thecman. com.* Converted farmhouse; one of the oldest structures in the city. American menu. Dinner. Closed Dec 24-25. Bar. Children's menu. **$$**

★ ★ **GORDI'S FISH & STEAK HOUSE.** *Kancamagus Hwy, Lincoln (03251). Phone 603/745-6635; fax 603/745-3073.* Contemporary building with Victorian accents. Seafood, steak menu. Lunch, dinner. Closed Thanksgiving, Dec 25. Bar. Children's menu. **$$$**

★ **TRUANTS TAVERNE.** *96 Main St, North Woodstock (03262). Phone 603/745-2239.* American menu. Lunch, dinner. Closed Thanksgiving, Dec 25. Bar. Children's menu. **$$**

Littleton (C-3)

See also Bretton Woods, Franconia, Twin Mountain

Population 5,827
Elevation 822 ft
Area Code 603
Zip 03561
Information Chamber of Commerce, 111 Main St, PO Box 105; phone 603/444-6561
Web Site www.littletonareachamber.com

Littleton is a resort area a few miles northwest of the White Mountain National Forest (see), which maintains a Ranger District office in nearby Bethlehem. Littleton is also a regional commercial center; its industries produce abrasives and electrical component parts. The Ammonoosuc River falls 235 feet on its way through the community.

What to See and Do

Littleton Historical Museum. *1 Cottage St, Littleton (03561). Phone 603/444-6435.* Photographs, arts and crafts, stereographs, local memorabilia. (Apr-Nov Wed, or by appointment) **FREE**

Limited-Service Hotel

★ ★ **EASTGATE MOTOR INN.** *335 Cottage St, Littleton (03561). Phone 603/444-3971; toll-free 866/640-3561; fax 603/444-3971. www.eastgatemotor inn.com.* 55 rooms. Pets accepted, some restrictions; fee. Complimentary continental breakfast. Check-in 2 pm, check-out 11 am. Restaurant, bar. Outdoor pool, children's pool. **$**

Full-Service Inn

★ ★ ★ **ADAIR COUNTRY INN.** *80 Guider Ln,*

Bethlehem (03574). Phone 603/444-2600; toll-free 888/444-2600; fax 603/444-4823. www.adairinn.com. Built in 1927, this inn is situated on 200 landscaped acres designed by the Olmsted Brothers. The relaxing location is nestled near the 700,000-acre White Mountain National Forest. Guest rooms are furnished with antiques and original artwork and include afternoon tea and homemade desserts. 10 rooms, 3 story. Closed three weeks in Apr and Nov. Children over 12 years only. Complimentary full breakfast. Check-in 3 pm, check-out 11 am. Wireless Internet access. Restaurant. Tennis. **$$**

Specialty Lodgings

THAYER'S INN. *111 Main St, Littleton (03561). Phone 603/444-6469; toll-free 800/634-8179. www. thayersinn.com.* Historic inn (1843); antiques, library, sitting room. Cupola open to the public. 39 rooms, 4 story. Pets accepted, some restrictions. Check-in 2 pm, check-out 11 am. **$**

WAYSIDE. *3738 Main St, Bethlehem (03574). Phone 603/869-3364; toll-free 800/448-9557; fax 603/869-5765. www.thewaysideinn.com.* This traditional inn was originally a four-room homestead (1825) for the family of President Franklin Pierce. It is located on the Ammonoosuc River with a natural sand beach. The inn has a restaurant on-site and there is a golf course nearby, or guests can try their luck on the bocce court. 26 rooms. Closed Apr and Nov. Complimentary full breakfast. Check-in 3 pm, check-out 11 am. Restaurant, bar. Tennis. **$**

Restaurants

★ ★ **CLAM SHELL.** *274 Dells Rd, Littleton (03561). Phone 603/444-6445; fax 603/444-5238.* American, seafood menu. Lunch, dinner. Closed Dec 24 (evening)-25. Bar. Children's menu. **$$**

★ **EASTGATE.** *335 Cottage St, Littleton (03561). Phone 603/444-3971. www.eastgatemotorinn.com.* American menu. Dinner. Closed Dec 24. Bar. **$**

★ ★ **ITALIAN OASIS.** *106 Main St, Littleton (03561). Phone 603/444-6995; fax 603/444-4884.* Converted Victorian home (circa 1890). Italian menu. Lunch, dinner. Closed Easter, Thanksgiving, Dec 25. Bar. Converted Victorian home (circa 1890). Outdoor seating. **$$**

★ ★ **ROSA FLAMINGOS.** *Main St, Bethlehem (03574). Phone 603/869-3111.* Italian menu. Lunch, dinner, brunch. Closed Easter, Thanksgiving, Dec 25. Bar. Children's menu. Casual attire. Reservations recommended. Outdoor seating. **$$**

Manchester (F-4)

See also Concord, Nashua

Settled 1722
Population 99,567
Elevation 225 ft
Area Code 603
Information Chamber of Commerce, 889 Elm St, 03101-2000; phone 603/666-6600
Web Site www.manchester-chamber.org

Manchester is a city that has refused to bow to economic adversity. When the Amoskeag Manufacturing Company (cotton textiles), which had dominated Manchester's economy, failed in 1935, it left the city poverty-stricken. With determination worthy of New Englanders, a group of citizens bought the plant for $5,000,000 and revived the city. Now Manchester is northern New England's premier financial center.

What to See and Do

Currier Museum of Art. *201 Myrtle Way, Manchester (03104). Phone 603/669-6144. www.currier.org.* One of New England's leading small museums; 13th- to 20th-century European and American paintings and sculpture; New England decorative art; furniture, glass, silver, and pewter; changing exhibitions, concerts, films, other programs. Tours of Zimmerman House, designed by Frank Lloyd Wright (call for reservations and times, fee). (Wed-Mon; closed holidays) **$**

Manchester Historic Association Millyard Museum. *200 Bedfort St, Millyard (03104). 2 blocks E of Elm St. Phone 603/622-7531. www.manchesterhistoric.org.* Museum and library with collections illustrating life in Manchester from pre-colonial times to present; permanent and changing exhibits; firefighting equipment; decorative arts, costumes, paintings. (Tues-Sat; closed holidays) **$$**

McIntyre Ski Area. *Kennard Rd, Manchester (03104). Kennard Rd. Phone 603/624-6571. www. mcintyreskiarea.com.* Two double chairlifts, pony lift; patrol, school, rentals, snowmaking; snack bar. Vertical drop 169 feet. (Dec-Mar, daily)

Palace Theatre. *80 Hanover St, Manchester (03101). Phone 603/668-5588. www.palacetheatre.org.* Productions in vintage vaudeville/opera house.

Science Enrichment Encounters Museum. *200 Bedford St, Manchester (03101). Phone 603/669-0400. www.see-sciencecenter.org.* More than 60 interactive, hands-on exhibits demonstrate basic science principles. (Daily; closed holidays) **$**

Limited-Service Hotel

★ ★ **QUALITY INN BEDFORD.** *121 S River Rd, Bedford (03110). Phone 603/622-3766; toll-free 800/424-6423; fax 603/625-1126. www.wayfarerinn.com.* Located on the site of John Goffe's historic gristmill, this small inn and convention center takes full advantage of its forested setting and proximity to the local business district. 190 rooms, 3 story. Pets accepted; fee. Complimentary continental breakfast. Check-in 3 pm, check-out noon. Restaurant, bar. Fitness room. Indoor pool, outdoor pool. Airport transportation available. **$**

Full-Service Hotels

★ ★ **FOUR POINTS BY SHERATON.** *55 John Devine Dr, Manchester (03103). Phone 603/668-6110; toll-free 800/368-7764; fax 603/668-0408. www.fourpoints.com/manchester.* This hotel is conveniently located near Manchester Airport, the Mall of New Hampshire, and historic downtown Manchester. 120 rooms, 4 story. Pets accepted; fee. Check-in 4 pm, check-out noon. High-speed Internet access, wireless Internet access. Restaurant, bar. Fitness room. Indoor pool, whirlpool. Airport transportation available. **$**

★ ★ **RADISSON HOTEL MANCHESTER.** *700 Elm St, Manchester (03101). Phone 603/625-1000; toll-free 800/333-3333; fax 603/206-4000. www.radisson.com/manchesternh.* With the hotel's location near downtown Manchester, guests can enjoy everything this quaint New England city has to offer, such as shopping, dining, live theater, and museums. 251 rooms, 12 story. Pets accepted. Check-in 3 pm, check-out 11 am. High-speed Internet access, wireless Internet access. Restaurant, bar. Fitness room. Indoor pool, whirlpool. Airport transportation available. **$**

Full-Service Inn

★ ★ ★ **BEDFORD VILLAGE INN.** *2 Olde Bedford Way, Bedford (03110). Phone 603/472-2001; toll-free 800/852-1166; fax 603/472-2379. www.bedfordvillageinn.com.* This stately New England inn, a converted 1800s barn, is set on beautifully landscaped grounds. The all-suite accommodations feature four-poster beds, Italian marble, and whirlpool bathtubs. A fine restaurant and other top-notch amenities are offered. 14 rooms, 3 story, all suites. Check-in 3 pm, check-out 11 am. Wireless Internet access. Restaurant, bar. Airport transportation available. **$$$**

Restaurants

★ ★ ★ **BEDFORD VILLAGE INN.** *2 Olde Bedford Way, Bedford (03110). Phone 603/472-2001; toll-free 800/852-1166; fax 603/472-2379. www.bedfordvillageinn.com.* This yellow clapboard structure originally was part of a working farm (1810). Guests can choose from several dining rooms, each with its own distinct character—hand-painted murals, swag drapes, area rugs, or a roaring fireplace. The kitchen turns out updated regional New England cuisine using only the freshest indigenous ingredients. Don't miss the signature dessert, the chocolate bag—white and dark chocolate mousse, fresh berries, and vanilla sponge cake. American menu. Breakfast, lunch, dinner. Closed Dec 25. Bar. **$$$**

★ **PURITAN BACKROOM.** *245 Hooksett Rd, Manchester (03104). Phone 603/623-3182; fax 603/623-3788. www.puritanbackroom.com.* This local favorite serves everything from burgers made from black Angus ground beef to veal parmigiana. There's also a kid's menu (try the smiley-face french fries) and homemade ice cream. The casual atmosphere is welcoming, with its wood-paneled walls, low lighting, and framed folk art. Its easy access from Interstate 93 makes it a convenient stop. American menu. Lunch, dinner. Bar. Children's menu. Casual attire. Outdoor seating. **$$**

Meredith (D-4)

See also Holderness, Laconia, Plymouth

Founded 1768
Population 4,837
Elevation 552 ft
Area Code 603
Zip 03253
Information Chamber of Commerce, 272 Daniel Webster Hwy, PO Box 732; phone 603/279-6121 or toll-free 877/279-6121
Web Site www.meredithcc.org

Between Lakes Winnipesaukee and Waukewan in the Lakes Region, Meredith is a year-round recreation area.

What to See and Do

League of New Hampshire Craftsmen—Meredith/ Laconia Arts & Crafts. *279 Daniel Webster Hwy, Meredith (03253). 1 1/2 miles N of Hwys 3 and 104. Phone 603/279-7920. www.nhcrafts.org.* Work by some of New Hampshire's finest craftspeople. (Daily)

⭐ **Winnipesaukee Scenic Railroad.** *159 Main St, Meredith (03253). Phone 603/279-5253. www. hoborr.com.* Scenic train rides along the shore of Lake Winnipesaukee. Board in Meredith or Weirs Beach. (Memorial Day-Oct) Fall foliage trains to Plymouth.

Hiking the White Mountains High Huts System

New England's highest mountains are webbed with hiking trails, thanks largely to the Appalachian Mountain Club (AMC), founded in 1876. The club blazed and mapped trails and eventually established an extensive base camp for hikers in Pinkham Notch at the eastern base of Mount Washington; a hostel in Crawford Notch, at the western base; and a chain of eight full-service "high huts" spaced over 56 miles of mountain trails, each a day's hike apart.

The huts are so much a part of the heritage and character of the White Mountains that it would be a shame to hike the Whites without staying at one. Seven offer three full meals in season (mid-June to mid-September) as well as bunks, pillows, and blankets (no sheets). Each hut has its resident naturalist who offers talks and walks. An AMC shuttle van circles trailheads leading to each of the huts so that hikers can begin in one place and emerge at another. It's wise to begin at Pinkham Notch Camp on Highway 16 in the White Mountain National Forest, a source of gear, maps, and weather information. Reservations for all AMC facilities are a must.

One of the most spectacular hikes that utilizes either one or two of the high huts is on Mount Washington itself. Begin with the Crawford Path, dating to 1819, said to be the oldest continually used footpath in America. The trailhead is on Highway 302 across from the AMC Crawford Notch Visitors Center. It follows Gibbs Brook (note the cutoff for Gibbs Falls), then angles off and up. To spend the night at Mizpah Hut Spring Hut (strongly advised), take the Mizpah cut-off. Just 2 miles from Highway 302, this is a good base from which to explore several trails above tree line.

It's also possible, weather permitting, to continue on the Crawford Path, ascending in moderate grades, with spectacular open views alternating with patches of scrub and woods. The trail ascends steadily via Mount Pierce, Mount Eisenhower, and Mount Monroe, reaching the Lake of the Clouds Hut at 7 miles. Spend the night.

Descend back to Highway 302 via the Ammonoosuc Ravine Trail, which begins just south of the Lake of the Clouds and follows the Ammonoosuc River steeply for the first 2 miles of the 3-mile descent. There are numerous cascades and spectacular views, but many people prefer to do this hike in reverse, ascending rather than descending such a steep trail. It's also possible to cheat by taking the White Mountain Cog Railway from its base off Highway 302 (near the trailhead for this trail) to the summit of Mount Washington, hiking down to the Lake of the Clouds, and then either down the Ammonoosuc Ravine or Crawford Path. Check with the AMC before hiking anywhere in the Whites.

Special Events

Great Rotary Fishing Derby. *Phone 603/279-7600.* Second weekend in Feb.

Lakes Region Fine Arts and Crafts Festival. *Phone 603/279-6121.* Juried show featuring more than 100 New England artists. Music, children's theater, food. Last weekend in Aug.

Limited-Service Hotel

★ ★ **THE INN AT MILL FALLS.** *312 Daniel Webster Hwy, Meredith (03253). Phone 603/279-7006; toll-free 800/622-6455; fax 603/279-6797. www.millfalls. com.* Actually three stately inns in one, this historic lakeside vacation development offers a charming respite from busy urban life. A covered marketplace of galleries and shops is just one of the many amenities. 54 rooms, 5 story. Check-in 3 pm, check-out 11 am. Two restaurants, bar. Fitness room, spa. Indoor pool. **$$**

Full-Service Hotel

★ ★ ★ **THE INN AT BAY POINT.** *312 Daniel Webster Hwy, Meredith (03253). Phone 603/279-7006; toll-free 800/622-6455; fax 603/279-6797. www.mill-falls.com.* On the edge of Lake Winnipesaukee sits this well-appointed property in the picturesque town of Meredith. Guests can enjoy the lake views from their large, comfortable rooms and also from the dining area. Canoeing and other water sports are among the outdoor activities offered here, and there are plenty of shops and dining options in the surrounding area. 24 rooms, 4 story. Closed midweek in winter. Complimentary continental breakfast. Check-in 3 pm, check-out 11 am. Restaurant, bar. Spa. **$$**

Specialty Lodging

OLDE ORCHARD INN. *RR Box 256, Moultonborough (03254). Phone 603/476-5004; toll-free 800/598-5845; fax 603/476-5419. www.oldeorchardinn.com.* This quaint inn was built in 1790 and was converted to a bed-and-breakfast 150 years later. Guests will enjoy the lounge with fireplace, massaging easy chair, and library. 9 rooms. Complimentary full breakfast. Check-in 3-8 pm, check-out 11 am. **$**

Restaurants

★ **HART'S TURKEY FARM.** *Hwys 3 and 104, Meredith (03253). Phone 603/279-6212; fax 603/279-*
4433. *www.hartsturkeyfarm.com.* If you feel like a little family-style Thanksgiving during your trip, check out Hart's turkey dinners with all the trimmings. You'll also find turkey potpies, turkey croquettes, and even turkey burgers. A wide variety of nonturkey selections are also offered. American menu. Breakfast, lunch, dinner, brunch. Children's menu. Casual attire. **$$**

★ ★ **MAME'S.** *8 Plymouth St, Meredith (03253). Phone 603/279-4631; fax 603/279-8646. www.mames-restaurant.com.* This friendly Lakes Region restaurant is situated on the main street with a great location. The atmosphere is festive at this local favorite, and guests can enjoy water views while dining. American, Italian menu. Lunch, dinner, Sun brunch. Bar. Children's menu. Casual attire. Reservations recommended. **$$**

Mount Washington (C-4)

See also Bretton Woods, Gorham, Jackson

Mount Washington is the central peak of the White Mountains and the highest point in the northeastern United States (6,288 feet). At the summit is a 54-acre state park with an information center, first-aid station, restaurant, and gift shop. The mountain has the world's first cog railway, completed in 1869; a road to the top dates to 1861. P. T. Barnum called the view from the summit "the second-greatest show on earth."

The weather on Mount Washington is so violent that the timberline is at about 4,000 feet; in the Rockies it is nearer 10,000 feet. In the treeless zone are alpine plants and insects, some unique to the region. The weather station here recorded a wind speed of 231 miles per hour in April, 1934—a world record. The lowest temperature recorded was -49° F; the year-round average is below freezing. The peak gets nearly 15 feet of snow each year.

What to See and Do

☑ **Cog Railway.** *Hwy 302, Bretton Woods (03589). Base station road, off Hwy 302, 4 miles E of junction Hwys 3 and 302; on W slope of mountain. Phone 603/846-5404; toll-free 800/922-8825. www.thecog.com.* Allow at least three hours for round trip. (May-Memorial Day weekend: weekends; after Memorial Day weekend-Nov: daily) **$$$$**

Great Glen Trails. *Hwy 16, Gorham (03581). Phone 603/466-2333. www.greatglentrails.com.* Located at the base of Mount Washington, this all-season, nonmotorized recreational trails park features biking programs (rentals), hiking programs (guide or unguided), kayak and canoe tours, and workshops in summer; cross-country skiing, snowshoeing, and snow tubing in winter. (Daily; closed Apr) For a detailed brochure with schedule and fees, contact Hwy 16, Pinkham Notch, Gorham 03581. **$$$**

Hiking trails. *Phone 603/466-2725.* Many crisscross the mountain; some reach the top. Hikers should check weather conditions at Pinkham Notch headquarters before climbing. **FREE**

Mount Washington Auto Road. *Hwy 16, Gorham. Approaches from the E side, in Pinkham Notch, 8 miles S of Gorham on Hwy 16. Phone 603/466-3988. www. mtwashingtonautoroad.com.* Trip to the summit of Mount Washington takes approximately 30 minutes each way. *Note:* make sure your car is in good condition; check brakes before starting. (Mid-May-mid-Oct, daily, weather permitting) Guided tour service available (daily). **$$$$**

Mount Washington Summit Museum. *Hwy 302, Sargent's Purchase. Top of Mount Washington. Phone 603/466-3388.* Displays on life in the extreme climate of the summit; rare flora and fauna; geology, history. (Memorial Day-Columbus Day, daily)

Nashua (E-4)

See also Manchester, Peterborough, Salem

Settled 1656
Population 79,662
Elevation 169 ft
Area Code 603
Information Greater Nashua Chamber of Commerce, 151 Main St, 2nd floor, 03060; phone 603/881-8333
Web Site www.nashuachamber.com

Originally a fur trading post, Nashua's manufacturing began with the development of Merrimack River water power early in the 19th century. The city, second largest in New Hampshire, has more than 100 diversified industries ranging from computers and tools to beer.

What to See and Do

Anheuser-Busch, Inc. *221 Daniel Webster Hwy (Hwy 3), Merrimack (03054). Everett Tpke exit 10. Phone*

603/595-1202. www.budweisertours.com. Guided tours of brewery; sampling room; gift shop. Children only with adult; no pets. **FREE** Adjacent is

Clydesdale Hamlet. *221 Daniel Webster Hwy, Merrimack (03054). Phone 603/595-1202.* Buildings modeled after a 19th-century European-style farm are the living quarters for the famous Clydesdales (at least 15 are here at all times); carriage house contains vintage wagons. **FREE**

Silver Lake State Park. *Silver Lake Rd, Hollis (03049). 8 miles W on Hwy 130 to Hollis, then 1 mile N off Hwy 122. Phone 603/465-2342.* One thousand-foot sand beach on a 34-acre lake; swimming, bathhouse; picnicking. (Late June-Labor Day)

Limited-Service Hotel

★ **FAIRFIELD INN.** *4 Amherst Rd, Merrimack (03054). Phone 603/424-7500; toll-free 800/228-2800. www.fairfieldinn.com.* 116 rooms, 3 story. Complimentary continental breakfast. Check-in 3 pm, check-out noon. Outdoor pool. **$**

Full-Service Hotels

★ ★ ★ **CROWNE PLAZA.** *2 Somerset Pkwy, Nashua (03063). Phone 603/886-1200; toll-free 800/962-7482; fax 603/595-4199. www.crowneplaza nashua.com.* Just 15 miles from Manchester Airport and 40 miles from Boston's Logan Airport, this full-service hotel is in the heart of the high-tech "southern tier." 230 rooms, 8 story. Check-in 3 pm, check-out noon. High-speed Internet access. Restaurant, bar. Fitness room. Indoor pool. Airport transportation available. **$$**

★ ★ **HOLIDAY INN NASHUA.** *9 Northeastern Blvd, Nashua (03062). Phone 603/888-1551; toll-free 888/801-5661; fax 603/888-7193.* 208 rooms. Pets accepted; fee. Check-in 4 pm, check-out 11 am. High-speed Internet access, wireless Internet access. Restaurant, bar. Fitness room. Outdoor pool.

★ ★ ★ **SHERATON NASHUA HOTEL.** *11 Tara Blvd, Nashua (03062). Phone 603/888-9970; toll-free 800/325-3535; fax 603/888-4112. www.sheraton.com.* This contemporary hotel with Tudor-style architecture offers a comfortable stay for both business and leisure travelers. It is located near the highway yet tucked away in a corporate park with 16 acres of landscaped grounds. 336 rooms, 7 story. Pets accepted, some restrictions. Check-in 3 pm, check-out noon. Wireless Internet access. Restaurant, bar. Indoor pool, outdoor pool, whirlpool. Airport transportation available. **$$**

New London (E-3)

See also Manchester, Peterborough, Salem

Population 3,180
Elevation 825 ft
Area Code 603
Zip 03257
Information Chamber of Commerce, Main St, PO Box 532; phone 603/526-6575 or toll-free 877/526-6575
Web Site www.newlondonareanh.com

What to See and Do

Ragged Mountain. *10 miles E on Hwy 11, then 7 miles N on Hwy 4 to Danbury, then 1 1/2 miles E on Hwy 104 to access road.* Phone 603/768-3475. www.ragged-mt.com. Two triple, three double chairlifts, three surface tows; patrol, school, rentals, snowmaking; cafeteria, bar. Longest run 1 3/4 miles; vertical drop 1,250 feet. (Mid-Nov-Mar, daily) **$$$$**

Special Event

Barn Playhouse. *209 Main St, New London (03257). Off Hwy 11.* Phone 603/526-4631. Live theater presentations nightly; Wed matinees. Also Mon children's attractions. Mid-June-Labor Day.

Full-Service Inns

★ ★ ★ **INN AT PLEASANT LAKE.** *853 Pleasant St, New London (03257).* Phone 603/526-6271; toll-free 800/626-4907; fax 603/526-4111. www.innatpleasantlake.com. Situated between the lake and Mount Kearsarge, this gabled country inn affords a quiet, relaxing vacation. Three common rooms are decorated like a comfortable house, and the inn has access to a private beach. 10 rooms, 3 story. Closed one week in Apr and two weeks in Nov. Complimentary full breakfast. Check-in 3 pm, check-out 11 am. High-speed Internet access, wireless Internet access. Restaurant. Beach. **$$**

★ ★ **NEW LONDON INN.** *353 Main St, New London (03257).* Phone 603/526-2791; toll-free 800/526-2791; fax 603/526-2749. www.newlondoninn.us. A helpful staff awaits guests at this well-appointed historic inn (circa 1800). Located on the main street of this quaint town, it is close to many shops and water activities, and a park is across the street. 24 rooms, 3 story. Closed one week in Nov. Pets accepted. Complimentary full breakfast. Check-in 3 pm, check-out 11 am. Wireless Internet access. Restaurant, bar. **$**

Specialty Lodging

FOLLANSBEE INN. *Hwy 114, North Sutton (03260).* Phone 603/927-4221; toll-free 800/626-4221; fax 603/927-6307. www.follansbeeinn.com. This homey 1840 country inn, located on the south shore of Keyzar Lake, has a wraparound porch, individually decorated rooms, and a relaxing atmosphere. 18 rooms, 3 story. Children over 10 years only. Complimentary full breakfast. Check-in 3 pm, check-out 11 am. **$**

Restaurants

★ ★ **MILLSTONE.** *74 Newport Rd (Hwy 11 W), New London (03257).* Phone 603/526-4201. www.millstonerestaurant.com. American menu. Lunch, dinner, Sun brunch. Bar. Children's menu. Casual attire. **$$**

★ ★ **NEW LONDON INN.** *353 Main St, New London (03257).* Phone 603/526-2791; toll-free 800/526-2791; fax 603/526-2749. www.newlondoninn.net. Surrounded by old architecture, this lively restaurant is updated with bright colors and thoughtful décor. Live music is featured on weekends, and a colorful fluted glass collection is on display. Tables are well-spaced for maximum privacy. American menu. Dinner, Sun brunch. Closed Mon. Bar. Children's menu. Casual attire. Reservations recommended. Outdoor seating. **$$**

Newport (E-3)

See also Sunapee

Settled 1765
Population 6,110
Elevation 797 ft
Area Code 603
Information Chamber of Commerce, 2 N Main St; phone 603/863-1510

Newport is the commercial headquarters for the Lake Sunapee area. Its industries include machine tools, woolens, clothing, and firearms. The Town Common Historic District has many churches and Colonial and Victorian houses.

What to See and Do

Fort at No. 4. *267 Springfield Rd, Charlestown (03603). 10 miles W on Hwy 11/103, then 11 miles S on Hwy 11/12. Phone 603/826-5700. www.fortat4. com.* Reconstructed French and Indian War log fort, complete with stockade, Great Hall, cow barns, and living quarters furnished to reflect 18th-century pioneer living. Exhibits include Native American artifacts, demonstrations of colonial crafts and an audiovisual program. (June-late Oct, Wed-Sun) **$$**

North Conway (C-4)

See also Bartlett, Jackson, Pinkham Notch

Settled 1764
Population 2,100
Elevation 531 ft
Area Code 603
Zip 03860
Information Mount Washington Valley Chamber of Commerce, 2617 Village Sq, White Mountain Hwy, PO Box 2300; phone 603/356-5701 or toll-free 800/367-3364
Web Site www.mtwashingtonvalley.org

The heart of the famous Mount Washington Valley region of the White Mountains, this area also includes Bartlett, Glen, Jackson, Conway, Redstone, Kearsarge, and Intervale. Mount Washington, seen from the middle of Main Street, is one of the great views in the East.

What to See and Do

Conway Scenic Railroad. *38 Norcross Cir, North Conway (03860). Depot on Main St. Phone 603/356-5251. www.conwayscenic.com.* Steam and diesel trains depart from restored Victorian station (1874) for an 11-mile (55-minute) round trip. The Valley Train explores the Saco River valley (mid-May-Oct: daily; mid-Apr-mid-May, Nov-Dec: weekends); the Notch Train travels through Crawford Notch (mid-Sept-mid-Oct: daily; late June-mid-Sept: Tues-Thurs, Sat). Railroad museum. **$$$$**

Covered bridges. In Conway, Jackson, and Bartlett.

Echo Lake State Park. *2 miles W, off Hwy 302. Phone 603/356-2672.* Mountain lake in the shadow of White Horse Ledge. Scenic road to 700-foot Cathedral Ledge, a dramatic rock formation; panoramic views of the White Mountains and the Saco River Valley. Swimming, picnicking. (Late June-Labor Day)

Factory outlet stores. *375 US Rte 1, North Conway (03860). Phone 207/439-0232. www.mtwashington valley.org.* Many outlet malls and stores can be found along Highway 16. Contact the Chamber of Commerce for more information.

League of New Hampshire Craftsmen. *2526 Main St, North Conway (03860). Phone 603/356-2441. www. nhcrafts.org.* Work by some of New Hampshire's finest craftspeople. (Daily) **FREE**

Mount Cranmore. *1 mile E off Hwy 302 (Hwy 16). Phone 603/356-5543; toll-free 800/786-6754. www. cranmore.com.* Express quad, triple, double chairlift to summit, three double chairlifts to north, south, and east slopes, four surface lifts; patrol, school, rentals; snowmaking; restaurant, bar, cafeterias; day care. Longest run 1 3/4 miles; vertical drop 1,200 feet. (Nov-Apr, daily)

Saco Bound. *Hwy 302, 2 miles E of Center Conway. Phone 603/447-2177. www.sacobound.com.* Specializes in rafting, canoeing, kayak touring, and paddling school. Programs include guided whitewater rafting trips, whitewater canoe and kayak school, and calmwater and whitewater canoe rentals. (May-Oct) **$$$$**

Special Events

Eastern Slope Playhouse. *2760 Main St, North Conway (03860). Phone 603/356-5776.* On grounds of Eastern Slope Inn Resort. Mount Washington Valley Theatre Company presents four Broadway musicals. Tues-Sun. Late June-early Sept.

Mud Bowl. *Hog Coliseum, North Conway (03860). Phone 603/356-5701.* Sept.

Limited-Service Hotels

★ ★ **BEST WESTERN RED JACKET MOUNTAIN VIEW RESORT & CONFERENCE CENTER.** *Hwy 16, North Conway (03860). Phone 603/356-5411; toll-free 800/752-2538; fax 603/356-3842. www. redjacketmountainview.com.* Magnificent mountain views can be seen from this large, stately looking hotel set high up on a hill. Located in the midst of outlet shopping and strip malls, it is also near area attractions and activities. Most of the rooms offer private decks or patios. 148 rooms, 3 story. Check-in 3 pm, check-out 11 am. Wireless Internet access. Two restaurants, bar. Children's activity center. Fitness room, spa. Indoor pool, outdoor pool, whirlpool. Tennis. **$$**

★ **COMFORT INN.** *2001 White Mountain Hwy (Rte 16), North Conway (03860). Phone 603/ 356-8811; toll-free 866/647-8483; fax 603/356-7770. www.northconwaycomfortinn.com.* This family-friendly lodging is located near the entertaining Pirates Cove Adventure Golf. Guest rooms are spacious, and the location is in the middle of North Conway's shopping, eateries, and attractions. 59 rooms, 2 story. Complimentary continental breakfast. Check-in 3 pm, check-out 11 am. Wireless Internet access. Children's activity center. Fitness room. Indoor pool. **$**

★ ★ **THE FOX RIDGE.** *White Mountain Hwy; Hwy 16, North Conway (03860). Phone 603/356-3151; toll-free 800/343-1804; fax 603/356-0096. www.red-jacketresorts.com.* Many activities are offered for adults and children at this family-friendly resort. Guest rooms are spacious, well maintained, and feature a balcony or patio. Situated on bustling Route 16 with plenty of shopping and eating spots, the property also faces the picturesque mountain scenery. 136 rooms, 2 story. Check-in 3 pm, check-out 11 am. Wireless Internet access. Restaurant, bar. Children's activity center. Fitness room. Indoor pool, outdoor pool, whirlpool. Tennis. **$$**

★ ★ **GREEN GRANITE INN.** *Hwys 16 and 302, North Conway (03860). Phone 603/356-6901; toll-free 800/468-3666; fax 603/356-6980. www.greengranite.com.* This busy property is only minutes from the all the shopping and fast food one can hope for. Upon request, the helpful staff will organize outdoor activities. 91 rooms, 2 story. Complimentary full breakfast. Check-in 3 pm, check-out 11 am. Children's activity center. Fitness room. Indoor pool, outdoor pool. **$$**

★ ★ **NORTH CONWAY GRAND HOTEL.** *72 Common Ct, North Conway (03860). Phone 603/356-9300; toll-free 800/648-4397; fax 603/356-6028. www. northconwaygrand.com.* This hotel is located in the White Mountain region and offers its guests a fitness facility, shopping (on premise) at more than 40 outlet stores, and access to many local attractions including skiing, golfing, mountain biking, hiking, and addi-

tional shopping. A casual restaurant is also on-site. 200 rooms, 4 story. Check-in 3 pm, check-out 11 am. Restaurant, bar. Children's activity center. Fitness room. Indoor pool, whirlpool. Tennis. **$$**

★ **NORTH CONWAY MOUNTAIN INN.** *Main St, North Conway (03860). Phone 603/356-2803; toll-free 800/319-4405. www.northconwaymountaininn.com.* Great mountain views can be seen from this affordable lodging surrounded by outlet shopping, water parks, and fast food eateries. The accommodations are roomy and feature patios. 32 rooms, 2 story. Check-in 3 pm, check-out 11 am. **$**

★ ★ **SNOWVILLAGE INN.** *Stewart Rd, Snowville (03832). Phone 603/447-2818; toll-free 800/447-4345; fax 603/447-5268. www.snowvillageinn.com.* This secluded inn on 10 acres features a panoramic view of the mountains. 18 rooms. Pets accepted, some restrictions. Complimentary full breakfast. Check-in 2 pm, check-out 11 am. Restaurant, bar. **$$**

★ **SWISS CHALETS VILLAGE INN.** *Hwy 16A, Intervale (03845). Phone 603/356-2232; toll-free 800/831-2727; fax 603/356-7331. www.swisschaletsvillage.com.* Rooms in Swiss chalet-style buildings; on 12 acres. 42 rooms, 3 story. Pets accepted; fee. Complimentary continental breakfast. Check-in 3 pm, check-out 11 am. Outdoor pool. **$**

Full-Service Resort

★ ★ ★ **WHITE MOUNTAIN HOTEL & RESORT.** *W Side Rd, North Conway (03860). Phone 603/356-7100; toll-free 800/533-6301. www.whitemountainhotel. com.* Nestled beneath the Whitehorse and Cathedral ledges and Echo State Park, this elegant English country inn provides magnificent views of the White Mountains. Outdoor activities include cross-country skiing, hiking, and rock climbing. Although close to the many shopping outlets in North Conway, this well-appointed inn seems a world away. 80 rooms, 3 story. Check-in 3 pm, check-out 11 am. High-speed Internet access, wireless Internet access. Restaurant, bar. Children's activity center. Fitness room. Outdoor pool, whirlpool. Golf, 9 holes. Tennis. Ski in/ski out. **$$**

Specialty Lodgings

1785 INN. *3582 N White Mountain Hwy, North*

Conway (03860). Phone 603/356-9025; toll-free 800/421-1785; fax 603/356-6081. www.the1785inn.com. This colonial-style building (1785) is located on 6 acres and features original fireplaces and Victorian antiques. Guests will enjoy views of the river and Mount Washington. 17 rooms, 3 story. Complimentary full breakfast. Check-in 3 pm, check-out 11 am. Restaurant, bar. **$**

BUTTONWOOD INN ON MT. SURPRISE. *Mt Surprise Rd, North Conway (03860). Phone 603/356-2625; toll-free 800/258-2625; fax 603/356-3140. www.buttonwoodinn.com.* Located on 17 wooded acres on the mountainside, this Cape Cod-style building (1820s) features many antiques and a library. 10 rooms, 2 story. Children over 12 years only. Complimentary full breakfast. Check-in 3 pm, check-out 11 am. Outdoor pool. **$$**

★ **CRANMORE MOUNTAIN LODGE.** *859 Kearsarge St, off Hwy 16, North Conway (03860). Phone 603/356-2044; toll-free 800/356-3596; fax 603/356-4498. www.cml1. com.* Located on 12 acres, this historic guest house (1860) was once owned by Babe Ruth's daughter and son-in-law. There are farm animals and a duck pond on the grounds. 21 rooms, 3 story. Check-in 3 pm, check-out 11 am. Outdoor pool. Credit cards accepted. **$**

DARBY FIELD COUNTRY INN. *185 Chase Hill Rd, Albany (03818). Phone 603/447-2181; toll-free 800/426-4147; fax 603/447-5726. www.darbyfield.com.* View of Presidential Mountains. 13 rooms, 3 story. Children over 8 years only. Complimentary full breakfast. Check-in 2 pm, check-out 11 am. Outdoor pool. **$$**

EASTMAN INN. *2331 White Mountain Hwy, North Conway (03846). Phone 603/356-6707; toll-free 800/626-5855; fax 603/356-7708. www.eastmaninn.com.* Guests will be transported back in time at this classic three-story Victorian inn (1777), complete with a wraparound veranda. The décor is rich and tasteful, and the property is well maintained both inside and out. The central location puts it close to all the shopping and attractions of this bustling town. 14 rooms, 3 story. Children over 15 years only. Complimentary full breakfast. Check-in 3 pm, check-out 11 am. **$$**

MERRILL FARM RESORT. *428 White Mountain Hwy, North Conway (03860). Phone 603/447-3866; toll-free 800/445-1017; fax 603/447-3867. www.merrillfarmresort.com.* Just south of the towns center, this converted farmhouse (1885) and cottages are located on the Saco River. Nearby activities and attractions include skiing, golfing, covered bridges, and shopping. 62 rooms, 2 story. Complimentary continental breakfast. Check-in 3 pm, check-out 11 am. Indoor pool, whirlpool. **$**

Restaurants

★ ★ ★ **1785 INN.** *3582 White Mountain Hwy, North Conway (03860). Phone 603/356-9025; toll-free 800/421-1785; fax 603/356-6081. www.the1785inn. com.* Dinner in the fine dining room of this lovely inn is casual and cozy. The extensive continental menu includes creative veal preparations, as well as a wide variety of appetizer and entrée selections. American, continental menu. Dinner. Bar. Casual attire. **$$**

★ **BELLINI'S.** *1857 White Mountain Hwy (Rt 16), North Conway (03860). Phone 603/356-7000; fax 603/356-6122. www.bellinis.com.* American, Italian menu. Lunch, dinner. Bar. Children's menu. Casual attire. Outdoor seating. **$$**

★ **HORSEFEATHERS.** *Main St, North Conway (03860). Phone 603/356-2687; fax 603/356-9368. www. horsefeathers.com.* This kid-friendly eatery is located in the quaint, historic section of North Conway. The brightly colored façade is an indication of the fun and playfulness inside. American menu. Lunch, dinner, brunch. Bar. Children's menu. Casual attire. **$$**

Peterborough (F-3)

See also Jaffrey, Keene, Nashua

Settled 1749
Population 5,239
Elevation 723 ft
Area Code 603
Zip 03458
Information Greater Peterborough Chamber of Commerce, 10 Wilton Rd on Rt 101, PO Box 401; phone 603/924-7234
Web Site www.peterboroughchamber.com

This was the home of composer Edward MacDowell (1861-1908). Edward Arlington Robinson, Stephen Vincent Bent, Willa Cather, and Thornton Wilder, among others, worked at the MacDowell Colony, a thriving artists' retreat, which made Peterborough famous.

What to See and Do

Greenfield State Park. *Forest Rd, Greenfield. 9 miles N on Hwy 136, then W on unnumbered road.* Phone 603/547-3497. On 401 acres. Swimming, bathhouse; fishing. Picnicking, concessions. Camping (dump station) with separate beach. (Mid-May-mid-Oct)

Miller State Park. *Route 101 E, Peterborough. 4 miles E.* Phone 603/924-3672. First of the New Hampshire parks. Atop the 2,288-foot Pack Monadnock Mountain; walking trails on summit; scenic drive; picnicking. (June-Labor Day: daily; May and Labor Day-Nov: Sat-Sun, and holidays)

Peterborough Historical Society. *19 Grove St, Peterborough (03458).* Phone 603/924-3235. Exhibits on the history of the area; historical and genealogical library. (Tues-Sat) **$**

Sharon Arts Center. *20-40 Grove St, Peterborough (03458).* Phone 603/924-7676. www.sharonarts.org. Gallery and crafts center. (Daily) **FREE**

Limited-Service Hotel

★ **JACK DANIELS MOTOR INN.** *80 Concord St, Peterborough (03458).* Phone 603/924-7548; fax 603/924-7700. www.jackdanielsmotorinn.com. 17 rooms, 2 story. Pets accepted, some restrictions; fee. Check-in 2 pm, check-out 11 am. **$**

Full-Service Inn

★ ★ ★ **HANCOCK INN.** *33 Main St, Hancock (03449).* Phone 603/525-3318; toll-free 800/525-1789; fax 603/525-9301. www.hancockinn.com. In continuous operation since 1789, the interior of this country inn is reminiscent of 18th-century New England. Sit by the fire in the red-walled dining room and order the famous Shaker cranberry pot roast to finish the day. 15 rooms, 3 story. Pets accepted. Complimentary full breakfast. Check-in 2 pm, check-out 11 am. Wireless Internet access. Restaurant, bar. **$$**

Specialty Lodging

GREENFIELD INN. *Hwys 31 N and 136, Greenfield (03047).* Phone 603/547-6327; toll-free 800/678-4144; fax 603/547-2418. www.greenfieldinn.com. 15 rooms, 2 story. Complimentary full breakfast. Check-in 4 pm, check-out 11 am. **$**

Pinkham Notch (C-4)

See also Gorham, Jackson, North Conway

Approximately 7 miles N on Hwy 16.

Named for Joseph Pinkham, a 1790 settler, this easternmost White Mountain pass is closest to Mount Washington. The headquarters for the Appalachian Mountain Club Hut System is here.

What to See and Do

Glen Ellis Falls Scenic Area. *E of Hwy 16, 12 miles N of Glen in White Mountain National Forest (see).*

Wildcat Ski & Recreation Area. *Hwy 16, Pinkham Notch (03846). 10 miles N of Jackson.;* toll-free 800/255-6439. www.skiwildcat.com. Express quad, three triple chairlifts; patrol, school, rentals; snowmaking; cafeteria, nursery. Longest run 2 miles; vertical drop 2,100 feet. (Mid-Nov-early May, daily; closed Thanksgiving, Dec 25) Skyride gondolas operate Memorial Day-mid-October for mountain and fall foliage viewing (daily). **$$$$**

Plymouth (D-4)

See also Holderness, Meredith, Waterville Valley

Settled 1764
Population 5,811
Elevation 660 ft
Area Code 603
Zip 03264
Information Chamber of Commerce, 1 Foster St, Suite A; phone 603/536-1001 or toll-free 800/386-3678
Web Site www.plymouthnh.org

Since 1795, Plymouth's varied industries have included lumber, pig iron, mattresses, gloves, and sporting goods. It has been a resort center since the mid-19th century.

What to See and Do

Mary Baker Eddy Historic House. *58 Stinson Lake Rd, Rumney (03266). Approximately 7 miles W via Hwy 25 to Stinson Lake Rd, then approximately 1 mile N to*

N side of the Village of Rumney. Phone 603/786-9943. Residence of Mary Baker Eddy from 1860 to 1862, prior to the founding of the Christian Science Church. (May-Oct, Tues-Sun; closed holidays) **$**

Plymouth State University. *17 High St, Plymouth (03264). 1 block W of business center. Phone 603/535-5000. www.plymouth.edu.* (1871) (3,500 students) A member of the University System of New Hampshire. Art exhibits in galleries and Lamson Library. Music, theater, and dance performances in Silver Cultural Arts Center (some fees). Planetarium shows. Tours.

Polar Caves Park. *705 Old Rte 25, Rumney (03266). 5 miles W on Tenney Mountain Hwy (Hwy 25). Phone 603/536-1888. www.polarcaves.com.* Glacial caves; animal exhibits; local minerals; scenic rock formations; maple sugar museum; gift shops, picnicking. (Early May-late Oct, daily) **$$$**

Limited-Service Hotel

★ **COBBLESTONE INN.** *304 Main St, Plymouth (03264). Phone 603/536-2330; fax 603/536-2686. www. cobblestoneinnh.com.* 38 rooms, 2 story. Pets accepted. Complimentary continental breakfast. Check-in 3 pm, check-out 11 am. Outdoor pool. **$**

Portsmouth (E-5)

See also Dover, Exeter, Hampton Beach

Settled 1630
Population 25,925
Elevation 21 ft
Area Code 603
Information Greater Portsmouth Chamber of Commerce, 500 Market St, PO Box 239, 03802-0239; phone 603/436-3988 or 603/436-1118
Web Site www.portsmouthchamber.org

A tour of Portsmouth's famous houses is like a tour through time, with Colonial and Federal architecture from 1684 into the 19th century. One-time capital of New Hampshire, Portsmouth was also the home port of a dynasty of merchant seamen who grew rich and built accordingly. The old atmosphere still exists in the narrow streets near Market Square. The US Navy Yard, located in Kittery, Maine (see), on the Piscataqua River, has long been Portsmouth's major "industry." The peace treaty ending the Russo-Japanese War was signed at the Portsmouth Navy Yard in 1905.

What to See and Do

Children's Museum of Portsmouth. *280 Marcy St, Portsmouth (03801). Phone 603/436-3853. www.childrens-museum.org.* Arts and science museum featuring mock submarine, space shuttle, lobster boat, exhibits, and gallery. (Summer and school vacations: daily; rest of year: Tues-Sun) **$$**

Fort Constitution. *4 miles E on Hwy 1B. Phone 603/436-1552.* (1808) The first cannon was placed on this site in 1632; in 1694, it was known as Fort William and Mary. Information about a British order to stop gunpowder from coming into the colonies, brought by Paul Revere on December 13, 1774, caused the Sons of Liberty from Portsmouth, New Castle, and Rye to attack and capture a fort that held 5 tons of gunpowder the next day. Much of this powder was used at Bunker Hill by the patriots. This uprising against the King's authority was one of the first overt acts of the Revolution. Little remains of the original fort except the base of its walls. Fort Constitution had been built on the same site by 1808; granite walls were added during the Civil War. (Mid-June-early Sept: daily; late May-mid-June, late Sept-mid-Oct: weekends, holidays only)

⭐ **Fort Stark State Historic Site.** *Wild Rose Ln, New Castle. Approximately 5 miles E off Hwy 1B. Phone 603/436-1552.* A former portion of the coastal defense system dating to 1746, exhibiting many of the changes in military technology from the Revolutionary War through World War II. The fort is situated on Jerry's Point, overlooking the Piscataqua River, Little Harbor, and Atlantic Ocean. (Late May-mid-Oct, daily)

⭐ **Isles of Shoals.** *315 Market St, Portsmouth (03801). Depart from Barker's Wharf. Phone 603/431-5500. www.islesofshoals.com.* The M/V *Thomas Laighton* makes cruises to historic Isles of Shoals, lobster clambake river cruises, fall foliage excursion, and others. Party ship. (Mid-June-Labor Day, daily) **$$$$**

Old Harbour Area. *Located on Historic Waterfront; Hwy 95 exit 7.* Features craftspeople, unique shops, bookstores, restaurants.

Portsmouth Harbor Cruises. *64 Ceres St, Portsmouth (03801). Old Harbor District. Phone 603/436-8084; toll-free 800/776-0915. www.portsmouthharbor.com.* Narrated historical tours aboard the 49-passenger M/V *Heritage.* 90-minute harbor, 2 1/2-hour Isles of Shoals, 1-hour cocktail, 90-minute sunset cruises, 2 1/2-hour inland river cruise, fall foliage cruise. (Mid-June-Oct)

⭐ **Portsmouth Historic Homes.** *Middle and State sts, Portsmouth (03801). Phone 603/436-3988.* The Historic Associates, part of the Greater Portsmouth Chamber of Commerce, has walking tour maps for six historic houses; maps are available free at the Chamber of Commerce, 500 Market St. The houses include

Governor John Langdon House. *143 Pleasant St, Portsmouth (03801). Phone 603/436-3205.* (1784) John Langdon served three terms as governor of New Hampshire and was the first president *pro tempore* of the US Senate. House's exterior proportions are monumental; interior embellished with excellent woodcarving and fine Portsmouth-area furniture. George Washington was entertained here in 1789. Architect Stanford White was commissioned to add the large wing at the rear with dining room in the Colonial Revival style. Surrounded by landscaped grounds with gazebo, rose and grape arbor, and restored perennial garden beds. Tours (June-mid-Oct, Fri-Sun; closed holidays). **$**

John Paul Jones House. *43 Middle St, Portsmouth (03801). At State St. Phone 603/436-8420.* (1758) Where the famous naval commander twice boarded; now a museum containing period furniture, collections of costumes, china, glass, documents, weapons. Guided tours (June-mid-Oct, daily). **$$**

Moffatt-Ladd House. *154 Market St, Portsmouth (03801). Phone 603/436-8221.* (1763) Built by Captain John Moffatt; later the home of General William Whipple, his son-in-law, a signer of the Declaration of Independence. Many original 18th- and 19th-century furnishings. Formal gardens. (Mid-June-mid-Oct, daily) **$$**

Rundlet-May House. *364 Middle St, Portsmouth (03801). Phone 603/436-3205.* (1807) Federalist, three-story mansion. House sits on terraces and retains its original 1812 courtyard and garden layout; landscaped grounds. House contains family furnishings and accessories, including many fine examples of Federalist craftsmanship and the latest technologies of its time. (June-Oct, first Sat of the month) Guided tours. Grounds available for rental. **$**

Warner House. *150 Daniel St, Portsmouth (03801). At Chapel St. Phone 603/436-5909.* (1716) One of New England's finest Georgian houses, with scagliola in the dining room, restored mural paintings on the staircase walls, beautiful paneling, a lightning rod on the west wall said to have been installed by Benjamin Franklin in 1762, five por-

traits by Joseph Blackburn, appropriate furnishings. (June-mid-Oct, Mon-Sat; Sun afternoons) Guided tours. **$$**

Wentworth-Gardner House. *50 Mechanic St, Portsmouth. Phone 603/436-4406.* (1760) Excellent example of Georgian architecture. Elaborate woodwork, scenic wallpaper, magnificent main staircase. (Mid-June-mid-Oct, Tues-Sat afternoons) **$**

⭐ **Strawbery Banke Museum.** *14 Hancock St, Portsmouth (03801). Hancock and Marcy sts, downtown, follow signs. Phone 603/433-1100. www.strawberybanke.org.* Restoration of a 10-acre historic waterfront neighborhood; site of the original Portsmouth settlement. 42 buildings dating from 1695 to 1950. Nine houses: Captain Keyran Walsh House (1796), Governor Goodwin Mansion (1811), Chase House (1762), Captain John Wheelwright House (1780), Thomas Bailey Aldrich House (1790), Drisco House (1790s), Rider-Wood House (1840s), Abbott Grocery Store (1943), and the William Pitt Tavern (1766) are restored with period furnishings. Shops, architectural exhibits, pottery shop, and demonstrations; tool, photo, archaeological and house construction exhibits; family programs and activities, special events, tours; picnicking, coffee shop. (May-Oct, Mon-Sat, Sun afternoons; Nov-Apr, Thurs-Sun; closed Jan). **$$$**

Special Events

Market Square Days. *Downtown, Portsmouth. Phone 603/436-3988.* Summer celebration with 10K road race, street fair, and entertainment. June.

Seacoast Jazz Festival. *Phone 603/436-2848.* Two stages with continuous performances on the historical Portsmouth waterfront. Last Sun in June.

Limited-Service Hotels

★ **FAIRFIELD INN.** *650 Borthwick Ave, Portsmouth (03801). Phone 603/436-6363; toll-free 800/228-2800; fax 603/436-1621. www.marriott.com/psmfi.* With a convenient location—right off the Interstate 95 circle on a bypass street—this clean, no-frills hotel awaits guests with a pleasant, helpful staff. 105 rooms, 4 story. Complimentary continental breakfast. Check-in 3 pm, check-out noon. High-speed Internet access, wireless Internet access. Outdoor pool. **$**
🖼

★ ★ **HOLIDAY INN.** *300 Woodbury Ave, Portsmouth (03801). Phone 603/431-8000; toll-free*

800/465-4329; fax 603/431-2065. www.holiday-inn. com. Historic downtown Portsmouth is just a short drive away from this convenient location just off Interstate 95. Shopping, dining, and the University of New Hampshire are all nearby. 130 rooms, 6 story. Check-in 2 pm, check-out noon. Restaurant, bar. Fitness room. Indoor pool. **$$**

★ **THE PORT INN.** *505 Hwy 1 Bypass S, Portsmouth (03801). Phone 603/436-4378; toll-free 800/282-7678. www.theportinn.com.* Located just off Interstate 95, this hotel is a short drive to downtown Portsmouth, dining, and entertainment. The exterior of the building is colonial, and the guest rooms are well maintained and spacious. 57 rooms, 2 story. Complimentary continental breakfast. Check-in 3 pm, check-out 11 am. High-speed Internet access, wireless Internet access. Outdoor pool. **$**

Full-Service Hotel

★ ★ ★ **SHERATON HARBORSIDE HOTEL PORTSMOUTH.** *250 Market St, Portsmouth (03801). Phone 603/431-2300; toll-free 800/325-3535; fax 603/431-7805. www.sheratonportsmouth.com.* This large New England-style hotel features a brick and granite exterior with large-paneled windows. The interior is inviting and stylish, and guests will enjoy the convenient location in the downtown historic district on the Piscataqua River. 220 rooms, 5 story. Pets accepted, some restrictions. Check-in 3 pm, check-out noon. Restaurant, bar. Fitness room. Indoor pool. Business center. **$$**

Specialty Lodging

SISE INN. *40 Court St, Portsmouth (03801). Phone 603/433-1200; toll-free 877/747-3466; fax 603/431-0200. www.siseinn.com.* This Queen Anne-style home was built in 1881 for the prosperous businessman and merchant John E. Sise. The Victorian décor is reflected throughout the guest rooms. 34 rooms, 3 story. Complimentary full breakfast. Check-in 3 pm, check-out noon. Wireless Internet access. **$$**

Restaurant

★ ★ **METRO.** *20 High St, Portsmouth (03801). Phone 603/436-0521; fax 603/433-1894. www.themetrorestaurant.com.* This American bistro tempts diners with a nightly veal special; fresh, flavorful seafood; and other contemporary preparations. American, French

menu. Lunch, dinner. Closed Sun. Bar. Casual attire. Reservations recommended. **$$$**

Salem (F-4)

See also Dover, Exeter, Hampton Beach

Population 25,746
Elevation 131 ft
Area Code 603
Zip 03079
Information Greater Salem Chamber of Commerce, 224 N Broadway, PO Box 304; phone 603/893-3177
Web Site www.salemnhchamber.org

What to See and Do

⭐ **America's Stonehenge.** *105 Haverhill Rd, North Salem (03079). 5 miles E of I-93, just off Hwy 111. Phone 603/893-8300. www.stonehengeusa.com.* A megalithic calendar site dated to 2000 BC, with 22 stone buildings on more than 30 acres. The main site features a number of stone-constructed chambers and is surrounded by miles of stone walls containing large, shaped monoliths that indicate the rising and setting of the sun at solstice and equinox, as well as other astronomical alignments, including lunar. (Daily; closed Thanksgiving, Dec 25) **$$**

Canobie Lake Park. *85 N Policy St, Salem (03079). 1 mile E of I-93, exit 2. Phone 603/893-3506. www.canobie.com.* Bring your bravery--and a change of clothes--for rides such as the Boston Tea Party Shoot-the-Chute water ride; the Corkscrew Coaster, which features two upside-down spins; and the Starblaster, which simulates a blast into outer space. You'll also find tamer options like bumper cars and kiddie rides. (Late Apr-late Sept; call for hours) **$$$$**

Robert Frost Farm. *Hwy 28, Derry. 1 mile SW on Hwy 38, then NW on Hwy 28. Phone 603/432-3091. www.robertfrostfarm.org.* Home of poet Robert Frost from 1900 to 1911; period furnishings; audiovisual display; poetry-nature trail. (mid-June-Labor Day: Wed-Sun; mid-May-mid-June: weekends only) **$**

Rockingham Park. *Rockingham Park Blvd, Salem. Exit 1 off I-93. Phone 603/898-2311. www.rockinghampark.com.* Thoroughbred horse racing. Live and simulcast racing (daily).

Limited-Service Hotels

★ **FAIRFIELD INN.** *8 Keewaydin Dr, Salem (03079).*

Phone 603/893-4722; toll-free 800/228-2800; fax 603/893-2898. www.fairfieldinn.com. 105 rooms, 4 story. Pets accepted; fee. Complimentary continental breakfast. Check-in 3 pm, check-out noon. Outdoor pool. **$**

★ ★ **HOLIDAY INN.** *1 Keewaydin Dr, Salem (03079). Phone 603/893-5511; toll-free 800/465-4329; fax 603/894-6728. www.holiday-inn.com.* 85 rooms, 6 story. Pets accepted; fee. Complimentary continental breakfast. Check-in 3 pm, check-out 11 am. Restaurant. Fitness room. Outdoor pool. **$**

Sunapee (E-5)

See also New London, Newport

Population 2,559
Elevation 1,008 ft
Area Code 603
Zip 03782
Information New LondonLake Sunapee Region Chamber of Commerce, PO Box 532; phone 603/526-6575 or toll-free 877/526-6575
Web Site www.lakesunapeenh.org

This is a year-round resort community on beautiful Lake Sunapee.

What to See and Do

M/V *Kearsarge* Restaurant Ship. *Sunapee. Phone 603/938-6465. www.mvkearsarge.com.* Buffet dinner while cruising around Lake Sunapee.

M/V *Mount Sunapee II* Excursion Boat. *Sunapee Harbor, Lake Ave, Sunapee. Off Hwy 11. Phone 603/763-4030.* 1 1/2-hour narrated tours of Lake Sunapee. (Mid-June-Labor Day: daily; mid-May-mid-June and after Labor Day-mid-Oct: Sat-Sun)

Mount Sunapee State Park. *Sunapee. 1 mile S off Hwy 103. Phone 603/763-2356.* 2,714 acres.

Summer. *Sunapee.* Swimming beach, bathhouse (fee); trout pool; picnicking, playground, concession; chairlift rides (fee). Displays by artists and craftspeople. (Memorial Day weekend; mid-June-early Sept: daily; early Sept-Columbus Day: weekends)

Winter. *Sunapee.* Skiing. One high-speed detachable quad, two fix grip quads, three quad, two triple, double chairlift, four surface lifts; patrol, school, rentals; cafeteria; snowmaking; nursery.

60 slopes and trails. Snowboarding. (Dec-Apr, daily) **$$$$**

Snowhill at Eastman Ski Area. *6 Club House Ln, Grantham (03753). 4 miles N on Hwy 11, then 6 miles N on I-89, exit 13. Phone 603/863-4500. www.eastman-lake.com.* Ski Touring Center has 30 kilometers of cross-country trails; patrol, school, rentals; bar, restaurant. Summer facilities include Eastman Lake (swimming, boating, fishing); 18-hole golf, tennis; indoor pool; hiking. (Dec-Mar, daily; closed Dec 25)

Special Event

League of New Hampshire Craftsmen's Fair. *Mount Sunapee Resort, Sunapee. Phone 603/224-3375. www.nhcrafts.org/annualfair.htm.* More than 300 craftspeople and artists display and sell goods. Aug.

Limited-Service Hotel

★ **BURKEHAVEN AT SUNAPEE.** *179 Burkehaven Hill Rd, Sunapee (03782). Phone 603/763-2788; toll-free 800/567-2788; fax 603/763-9065. www.burkehavenatsunapee.com.* 10 rooms. Check-in 3 pm, check-out 11 am. Outdoor pool. Tennis. **$**

Specialty Lodgings

CANDLELITE INN. *5 Greenhouse Ln, Bradford (03221). Phone 603/938-5571; toll-free 888/812-5571; fax 603/938-2564. www.candleliteinn.com.* Built in 1897; gazebo porch. 6 rooms, 3 story. Complimentary full breakfast. Check-in 3 pm, check-out 11 am. **$**

DEXTERS INN & TENNIS CLUB. *258 Stagecoach Rd, Sunapee (03782). Phone 603/763-5571; toll-free 800/232-5571. www.dextersnh.com.* On 20-acre estate. 2 story. Pets accepted, some restrictions; fee. Complimentary full breakfast. Check-in 3 pm, check-out 11 am. Outdoor pool. Tennis. **$$**

Twin Mountain (C-3)

See also Bretton Woods, Franconia, Littleton

Population 760
Elevation 1,442 ft
Area Code 603
Zip 03595
Information Chamber of Commerce, PO Box 194;

phone toll-free 800/245-8946
Web Site www.twinmountain.org

What to See and Do

Mount Washington. *E off US 302.* (see).

Limited-Service Hotels

★ **FOUR SEASONS MOTOR INN.** *Birch Rd and Rte 3, Twin Mountain (03595).* Phone 603/846-5708; toll-free 800/228-5708. www.4seasonsmotorinn.com. 24 rooms, 2 story. Check-in noon, check-out 10 am. Outdoor pool. **$**

★ **SHAKESPEARE'S INN.** *675 Hwy 3, Twin Mountain (03595).* Phone 603/846-5562; toll-free 888/846-5562; fax 603/846-5782. www.shakespearesinn. com. At the base of the White Mountains. 33 rooms, 2 story. Check-in 3 pm, check-out 10:30 am. Restaurant. Outdoor pool. Tennis. **$**

Specialty Lodging

NORTHERN ZERMATT INN & MOTEL. *529 Hwy 3 N, Twin Mountain (03595).* Phone 603/846-5533; toll-free 800/535-3214; fax 603/846-5664. www.zermattinn. com. Former boarding house (circa 1900) for loggers and railroad workers. 17 rooms, 3 story. Pets accepted, some restrictions. Complimentary continental breakfast. Check-in 3 pm, check-out 11 am. Outdoor pool. **$**

Waterville Valley (D-4)

See also Lincoln/North Woodstock, Plymouth

Founded 1829
Population 151
Elevation 1,519 ft
Area Code 603
Zip 03215
Information Waterville Valley Region Chamber of Commerce, 12 Vintinner Rd, Box 1067, Campton 03223; phone 603/726-3804 or toll-free 800/237-2307
Web Site www.watervillevalleyregion.com

Although the resort village of Waterville Valley was developed in the late 1960s, the surrounding area has been attracting tourists since the mid-19th century, when summer vacationers stayed at the Waterville

Inn. Completely encircled by the White Mountain National Forest, the resort, which is approximately 11 miles northeast of Campton, offers a variety of winter and summer activities, as well as spectacular views of the surrounding mountain peaks.

What to See and Do

Waterville Valley Ski Area. *1 Ski Area Rd, Waterville Valley (03215).* 11 miles NE of Campton on Hwy 49. Phone toll-free 800/468-2553. www.waterville.com. Three double, two triple chairlifts, two quad chairlifts, T-bar, J-bar, four platter pulls; patrol, school; retail, rental and repair shops; snowmaking; restaurants, cafeterias, lounge; nursery. 52 ski trails; longest run 3 miles; vertical drop 2,020 feet. Half-day rates. (Mid-Nov-mid-Apr, daily) Ski Touring Center with 46 miles of cross-country trails; rentals, school, restaurants. Summer facilities include nine-hole golf, 18 clay tennis courts, small boating, hiking, fishing, bicycling; entertainment. Indoor sports center (daily). Contact Waterville Valley Resort, Town Square. **$$$$**

Limited-Service Hotels

★ ★ **SNOWY OWL INN.** *4 Village Rd, Waterville Valley (03215).* Phone 603/236-8383; toll-free 800/766-9969; fax 603/236-4890. www.snowyowlinn.com. This inn is situated in the heart of Waterville Valley and the White Moutain National Forest. The lobby atrium has natural wood and a three-story fieldstone fireplace. 83 rooms, 4 story. Pets accepted, some restrictions. Complimentary continental breakfast. Check-in 4 pm, check-out 11 am. Indoor pool, outdoor pool, whirlpool. **$**

★ ★ **VALLEY INN & TAVERN.** *1 Tecumseh Rd, Waterville Valley (03215).* Phone 603/236-8425; toll-free 800/343-0969; fax 603/236-4294. www.valleyinn.com. 52 rooms, 5 story. Complimentary continental breakfast. Check-in 4 pm, check-out 11 am. Restaurant, bar. Fitness room. Indoor/outdoor pool, whirlpool. **$**

Restaurant

★ ★ **WILLIAM TELL.** *Rte 49, Thornton (03223).* Phone 603/726-3618; fax 603/726-4722. American menu. Dinner, Sun brunch. Closed Wed. Bar. Children's menu. Outdoor seating. **$$**

White Mountain National Forest

This national forest and major New Hampshire recreation area includes the Presidential Range and a major part of the White Mountains. There are more than 100 miles of roads and 1,128 miles of foot trails. The Appalachian Trail, with eight hostels, winds over some spectacular peaks. Eight peaks tower more than a mile above sea level; the highest is Mount Washington (6,288 feet). Twenty-two mountains rise more than 4,000 feet. There are several well-defined ranges, divided by deep "notches" and broader valleys. Clear streams rush through the notches; mountain lakes and ponds dot the landscape. Deer, bear, moose, and bobcat roam the wilds; trout fishing is good.

The US Forest Service administers 23 campgrounds with more than 700 sites ($12-$16/site/night), also picnicking sites for public use. There is lodging within the forest; for information, reservations contact the Appalachian Mountain Club, Pinkham Notch, Gorham 03581; phone 603/466-2727. There are also many resorts, campsites, picnicking, and recreational spots in private and state-owned areas. A visitor center (daily) is at the Saco Ranger Station, 33 Kancamagus Hwy, Conway 03818; phone 603/447-5448. Information stations are also located at exits 28 and 32, off Interstate 93 and at Franconia Notch State Park Visitor Center. For further information, contact the Supervisor, White Mountain National Forest, 719 N Main St, Laconia 03246; phone 603/528-8721.

The following cities and villages in and near the forest are included in this book: Bartlett, Bretton Woods, Franconia, Franconia Notch State Park, Gorham, Jackson, Lincoln/North Woodstock Area, Mount Washington, North Conway, Pinkham Notch, Twin Mountain, and Waterville Valley. For information on any of them, see the individual alphabetical listing.

Wolfeboro (D-4)

See also Center Ossipee, Laconia

Settled 1760
Population 4,807
Elevation 573 ft
Area Code 603
Zip 03894

Information Chamber of Commerce, 312 Central Ave, PO Box 547; phone 603/569-2200 or toll-free 800/516-5324
Web Site www.wolfeborochamber.com

Wolfeboro has been a resort area for more than two centuries; it is the oldest summer resort in America. In the winter it is a ski touring center with 40 miles of groomed trails.

What to See and Do

Clark House. *337 S Main St, Wolfeboro (03894). Phone 603/569-4997.* Wolfeboro Historical Society is housed in Clark family homestead (1778), a one-room schoolhouse (circa 1820) and a firehouse museum. Clark House has period furnishings and memorabilia; the firehouse museum contains restored firefighting equipment dating to 1842. (July-Aug, Wed-Sat) **$**

Lake Winnipesaukee cruises. (See LACONIA)

Wentworth State Park. *Wolfeboro. 6 miles E on Hwy 109. Phone 603/569-3699.* On Lake Wentworth. Swimming; bathhouse. Picnicking. (Late June-Labor Day)

Wright Museum. *77 Center St, Wolfeboro (03894). Phone 603/569-1212. www.wrightmuseum.org.* Showcases American enterprise during World War II. Collection of tanks, Jeeps, and other military vehicles, period memorabilia. (May-Oct, daily; weekends only Apr and Nov; closed Dec-Mar) **$$**

Full-Service Inn

★ ★ ★ **THE WOLFEBORO INN.** *90 N Main St, Wolfeboro (03894). Phone 603/569-3016; toll-free 800/451-2389; fax 603/569-5375. www.wolfeboroinn.com.* Built in 1812, this inn has a fabulous location on Lake Winnipesaukee in one of America's oldest summer resort towns. Many rooms offer Wolfeboro Bay views and all include a boat ride and private beach access during summer months. 40 rooms, 3 story. Complimentary continental breakfast. Check-in 3 pm, checkout 11 am. Restaurant, bar. **$$**

Rhode Island

Giovanni da Verrazano, a Florentine navigator in the service of France, visited the Narragansett Bay of Rhode Island in 1524; however, it wasn't until 1636 that the first permanent white settlement was founded. Roger Williams, a religious refugee from Massachusetts, bought land at Providence from the Narragansetts. Williams fled what he considered puritanical tyranny and established a policy of religious and political freedom in his new settlement. Soon others began similar communities, and in 1663, King Charles II granted them a royal charter, officially creating the "State of Rhode Island and Providence Plantations."

Although the smallest state in the nation and smaller than many of the counties in the United States, Rhode Island is rich in American tradition. It is a state of firsts. Rhode Islanders were among the first colonists to take action against the British, attacking British vessels in its waters. On May 4, 1776, the state was the first to proclaim independence from Great Britain, two months before the Declaration of Independence was signed. In 1790, Samuel Slater's mill in Pawtucket became America's first successful water-powered cotton mill, and in 1876, polo was played for the first time in the United States in Newport.

Rhode Island has a tradition of manufacturing skill. The state produces machine tools, electronic equipment, plastics, textiles, jewelry, toys, and boats. The famous Rhode Island Red Hen was developed by farmers in Little Compton. Rhode Island is also for those who follow the sea. With more than 400 miles of coastline, visitors can swim, sail, fish, or relax in the many resort areas.

Population: 1,003,464
Area: 1,054 square miles
Elevation: 0-812 feet
Peak: Jerimoth Hill (Providence County)
Entered Union: Thirteenth of original 13 states (May 29, 1790)
Capital: Providence
Motto: Hope
Nickname: Ocean State
Flower: Violet
Bird: Rhode Island Red Hen
Tree: Red Maple
Time Zone: Eastern
Web Site: www.visitrhodeisland.com
Fun Facts:
- The White Horse Tavern, built in 1673, is the oldest operating tavern in the United States.
- Portsmouth is home to the oldest schoolhouse in the United States. It was built in 1716.

When to Go/Climate

The weather in Rhode Island is more moderate than in other parts of New England. Breezes off Narragansett Bay make summer humidity bearable and winter temperatures less bitter than elsewhere in the region.

AVERAGE HIGH/LOW TEMPERATURES (°F)

Providence

Jan 37/19	**May** 67/47	**Sept** 74/54
Feb 38/21	**June** 77/57	**Oct** 64/43
Mar 46/29	**July** 82/63	**Nov** 53/35
Apr 57/38	**Aug** 81/62	**Dec** 41/24

Parks and Recreation

Water-related activities, hiking, riding, various other sports, picnicking, and visitor centers, as well as camping, are available in many state parks. Most

Calendar Highlights

FEBRUARY

Mid-winter New England Surfing Championship *(Narragansett). Narragansett Town Beach. Phone the Eastern Surfing Association, 401/789-1954.*

Newport Winter Festival *(Newport). Phone 401/849-8048, 401/847-7666, or toll-free 800/326-6030.* Ten days of food, festivities, and music. More than 200 cultural and recreational events and activities.

MAY

Gaspee Days *(Warwick). Phone Gaspee Days Committee, 401/781-1772 or toll-free 800/492-7942. www.gaspee.com.* Celebration of the capture and burning of British revenue schooner Gaspee by Rhode Island patriots; arts and crafts, concert, foot races, battle reenactment, muster of fife and drum corps, parade, and contests.

JUNE

Spring Festival of Historic Houses *(Providence).* Phone 401/831-7440. Sponsored by the Providence Preservation Society. Tours of selected private houses and gardens.

JULY

Hot Air Balloon Festival *(Kingston). University of Rhode Island. Phone 401/783-1770.* Two-day event features hot air balloon rides, parachute demonstrations, arts and crafts, and music.

Newport Music Festival *(Newport). Phone 401/847-7090.* Chamber music, held in Newport's fabled mansions.

---

are open sunrise to sunset. Parking fee at beaches: weekdays, $6-$12/car; weekends, holidays, $7-$14/car. Camping $14-$20/night; with electric and water $18-$25; sewer $20-$35. No pets allowed. A map is available at the Division of Parks & Recreation, Department of Environmental Management, 2321 Hartford Ave, Johnston 02919. Phone 401/222-2632.

FISHING AND HUNTING

No license is necessary for recreational saltwater game fishing. Freshwater fishing license: nonresident, $35; three-day tourists' fee, $16. Both largemouth bass and northern pike can be found in Worden Pond; trout can be found in Wood River.

Hunting license: nonresident, $45. Resident licenses and regulations may be obtained at city and town clerks' offices and at most sporting goods shops. Nonresident licenses may be obtained by contacting DEM-Licensing, 235 Promenade St, Providence 02908; phone 401/222-3576. For further information write Division of Fish & Wildlife, Department of Environment Management, Government Center, Wakefield 02879. Phone 401/789-3094.

Driving Information

Children ages 7 and up must be in approved passenger restraints anywhere in a vehicle; ages 7 and under must use approved safety seats. Phone Governor's Office of Highway Safety at 401/222-3024.

INTERSTATE HIGHWAY SYSTEM

The following alphabetical listing of Rhode Island towns in this book shows that these cities are within 10 miles of the indicated interstate highway. Check a highway map for the nearest exit.

Highway Number	Cities/Towns within 10 Miles
Interstate 95	East Greenwich, Pawtucket, Providence, Warwick, Westerly.

Additional Visitor Information

Contact the Rhode Island Economic Development Corporation Division of Marketing & Communications, 1 W Exchange St, Providence 02903. Phone 401/222-2601 or toll-free 800/556-2484. The *Providence Journal-Bulletin Almanac* is an excellent state reference book and may be obtained from the Providence *Journal*, 75 Fountain St, Providence 02902.

THE ROAD LESS TRAVELED

Newport and South County are the shoreline destinations that most people head for when they visit Rhode Island. As a result, both areas become clogged with traffic and tourists during the summer. But Rhode Island has a quiet eastern coast along its border with Massachusetts that is an ideal area for a day trip. The drive to the coastal towns of Tiverton and Little Compton takes about 50 minutes from Providence and passes through the attractive harbor town of Bristol, which is on Narragansett Bay. From downtown Providence, take Highway 195 east to exit 7, Highway 114 South. Stay on this highway through Barrington, Warren, and Bristol. (In Warren, you may want to stop for the dozens of antiques and second-hand shops that line Main and Water streets.) Highway 114 (Main St in Warren) becomes Hope Street in Bristol, and here you'll be charmed by the many elegant Federal-era houses (some of them bed-and-breakfast inns) that show how wealthy this town was in the period before the Civil War. South of the town, a turn-of-the-century mansion and estate called Blithewold is open to the public for tours.

Drive over the Mount Hope Bridge into the Aquidneck Island town of Portsmouth. You won't see much of this town, however, as you turn left onto Highway 24 to cross the Sakonnet River Bridge into Tiverton. Turn right onto Highway 77 South, and stay on this road through Tiverton and Little Compton. (Highway 77 ends rather ignominiously in a parking lot with a view of the ocean at Sakonnet Point in Little Compton.) There's only one traffic light along the length of Highway 77, and that's at the intersection with Highway 179, an area known as Tiverton Four Corners. In this vicinity, you'll find some delightful shops, including a gourmet take-out place where you can pick up food for a picnic and Gray's Ice Cream, which has been making dozens of homemade flavors at this spot since the 1920s. Continuing south on Highway 77, you'll pass open farmland with lovely vistas of Narragansett Bay. Little Compton is a wealthy summer community, so there's very little commerce in town, and you'll see old farmhouses that are now used as summer homes.

You can return by the same route, or turn right onto Highway 24 North in Tiverton to drive into Fall River, Massachusetts, then head west back to Providence on Highway 195. **(Approximately 40 miles)**

There are several information centers in Rhode Island; visitors will find information and brochures most helpful in planning stops at points of interest. Two of the information centers are located: off I-95 in Richmond (daily); and 7 miles south of Providence in Warwick, at T. F. Green Airport.

Block Island

(By ferry from Providence, Newport, and Point Judith; by air from Westerly. Also by ferry from New London, CT, and Montauk, Long Island)

Settled 1661
Population 620
Elevation 9 ft
Area Code 401
Zip 02807
Information Chamber of Commerce, 1 Water St, PO Drawer D; phone 401/466-2982 or toll-free 800/383-2474
Web Site www.blockislandchamber.com

Block Island, Rhode Island's "air-conditioned" summer resort, covers 21 square miles. Lying 12 miles out to sea from Point Judith, it received its nickname because it is 10 to15 degrees cooler than the mainland in summer and consistently milder in winter. Although Verrazano saw the island in 1524, it was named for the Dutch explorer Adriaen Block, who landed here in 1614. Until the resort trade developed, this island community was devoted to fishing and farming. Settler's Rock on Corn Neck Road displays plaques on the boulder listing the first settlers.

In recent years, Block Island has become a favorite "nature retreat" for people seeking to escape fast-paced city living. More than 40 rare and endangered species of plants and animals can be found on the island, of which 1/4 is in public trust. The Nature Conservancy has designated Block Island as "one of the 12 last great places in the Western Hemisphere."

What to See and Do

Ferry service. *304 Great Island Rd, Point Judith (02882). Phone 401/783-4613.*

Block Island/New London, CT. *Phone 860/444-4624.* Two-hour trip. (Mid-June-Labor Day, four trips daily, extra trips Thurs-Sun)

Block Island/Newport. *Phone 401/783-4613.* Departs from Newport. (June-Labor Day, one trip daily) Nonvehicular ferry. **$$$**

Block Island/Point Judith. *Phone 401/783-4613; toll-free 866/783-7340.* Advance reservations for vehicles; all vehicles must be on pier 45 minutes before sailing. (daily departures, varies seasonally)

Fishing. Surf casting from most beaches; freshwater ponds for bass, pickerel, perch; deep-sea boat trips for tuna, swordfish from Old Harbor.

Fred Benson Town Beach. *Corn Neck Rd, Block Island. 1/2 mile N to Crescent Beach. Phone 401/466-7717.* Swimming, bathhouse, lifeguards; picnicking, concession. Parking. **FREE**

Natural formations. Mohegan Bluffs. West of Southeast Light lighthouse off Mohegan Trail, are 185-foot clay cliffs that offer a fine sea view. **New Harbor,** 1 mile west on Ocean Avenue, is a huge harbor made by cutting through sand bar into Great Salt Pond.

New England Airlines. *Phone 401/466-5881; toll-free 800/243-2460; fax 401/596-7366. www.users.ids.net/flybi/nea.* Twelve-minute scheduled flights between Westerly State Airport and Block Island State Airport; also air taxi and charter service to all points. (Daily) Phone 401/466-5881, 401/596-2460, or toll-free 800/243-2460.

North Light. *Phone 401/466-3220.* Lighthouse built in 1867 at the tip of the island near Settler's Rock, now houses a maritime museum. Bordering the dunes are a seagull rookery and wildlife sanctuary. **$**

Limited-Service Hotel

★ ★ **SPRING HOUSE.** *52 Spring St, Block Island (02807). Phone 401/466-5844; toll-free 800/234-9263; fax 401/466-2633. www.springhousehotel.com.* 50 rooms, 3 story. Closed in winter. Complimentary continental breakfast. Check-in 3 pm, check-out 11 am. Restaurant, bar. **$$**

Specialty Lodging

THE 1661 INN & GUEST HOUSE.
1 Spring St, Block Island (02807). Phone 401/466-2421; toll-free 800/626-4773; fax 401/466-2858. www.block-

islandresorts.com. Located on a secluded island, this inn benefits from the unspoiled beaches, grassy cliffs, and rolling hills speckled with wildflowers. 21 rooms, 2 story. Complimentary full breakfast. Check-in 2 pm, check-out 11 am. Tennis. **$$$**

Restaurants

★ **FINN'S SEAFOOD.** *212 Water St, Block Island (02807). Phone 401/466-2473; fax 401/466-2769.* Seafood menu. Lunch, dinner. Bar. Children's menu. Casual attire. **$$**

★ ★ ★ **HOTEL MANISSES DINING ROOM.** *1 Spring St, Block Island (02807). Phone 401/466-2836; fax 401/466-3162. www.blockislandresorts.com.* The well-informed, professional staff await diners at this restaurant, which serves contemporary American fare and homemade desserts. The décor is contemporary with some historic, nautical touches, and there is a stone-walled dining room and glass-enclosed garden room. American menu. Dinner. Closed Nov-Apr. Bar. Reservations recommended. Outdoor seating. **$$$**

★ **MOHEGAN CAFE.** *Water St, Block Island (02807). Phone 401/466-5911; fax 401/466-2664. www.blockislandresorts.com.* American menu. Lunch, dinner. Closed Thanksgiving, Dec 25. Bar. Casual attire. **$$**

Bristol (D-7)

See also Portsmouth, Providence

Settled 1669
Population 21,625
Elevation 50 ft
Area Code 401
Zip 02809
Information East Bay County Chamber of Commerce, 16 Cutler St, PO Box 250, Warren 02885-0250; phone 401/245-0750
Web Site www.eastbaychamber.org

King Philip's War (1675-1676) began and ended on the Bristol peninsula between Mount Hope and Narragansett bays; King Philip, the Native American rebel leader, headquartered the Wampanoag tribe in the area. After the war ended, Bristol grew into an important port, and by the turn of the 18th century, the town was the fourth-busiest port in the United States.

Bristol was the home of General Ambrose Burnside, Civil War officer and sometime governor and senator. The town was the site of the famous Herreshoff Boatyard, where many America's Cup winners were built. Roger Williams University (1948) is located in Bristol.

What to See and Do

Blithewold Mansion and Gardens. *101 Ferry Rd, Bristol (02809). 2 miles S on Hwy 114 (Ferry Rd); on Bristol Harbor overlooking Naragansett Bay. Phone 401/253-2707; fax 401/253-0412. www.blithewold.org.* Blithewold Mansion, Gardens and Arboretum is a beautifully landscaped historic public garden situated on Bristol Harbor with sweeping views overlooking Narragansett Bay. A 45-room mansion, trees, lawns, flowers, gardens, and the sea combine to produce an aesthetic experience that is exciting and refreshing. Concerts are held on the grounds in the summer. (Mansion, mid-Apr-Columbus Day: Wed-Sun 10 am-4 pm; grounds, daily 10 am-5 pm) **$$**

Colt State Park. *2 1/2 miles NW off Hwy 114.* Three-mile scenic drive around shoreline of former Colt family estate on east side of Narragansett Bay. Fishing, boating; hiking and bridle trails, picnicking. Concerts in Stone Barn. **$** In park is

> **Coggeshall Farm Museum.** *Poppasquash Rd, Bristol. In Colt State Park, off Hwy 114. Phone 401/253-9062.* Working farm from 18th and 19th centuries; vegetables, herbs, animals; colonial craft demonstrations. (March-Sept daily 10 am-6 pm; Oct-Feb daily 10 am-dusk) (See SPECIAL EVENT) **$$**

Haffenreffer Museum of Anthropology. *300 Tower St, Bristol (02809). 1 mile E of Metacom Ave, Hwy 136, follow signs; overlooks Mount Hope Bay. Phone 401/253-8388; fax 401/253-1198. www.brown.edu/Facilities/Haffenreffer.* Brown University museum features Native American objects from North, Central, and South America; Eskimo collections; African and Pacific tribal arts. (June-Aug: Tues-Sun 11 am-5 pm; Sept-May Sat-Sun 11 am-5 pm) **$**

Herreshoff Marine Museum. *1 Burnside St, Bristol (02809). Phone 401/253-5000; fax 401/253-6222. www.herreshoff.org.* Herreshoff Manufacturing Company produced some of America's greatest yachts, including eight winners of the America's Cup. Exhibits include yachts manufactured by Herreshoff, steam engines, fittings; photographs and memorabilia from "golden age of yachting." (May-Oct, daily 10 am-5 pm) **$$**

Hope Street. *Hope St, Bristol. On Hwy 114.* Famous row of colonial houses.

Prudence Island. *Phone 401/253-9808.* Ferry from Church Street dock.

Special Event

Harvest Fair. *Coggeshall Farm Museum, Poppasquash Rd, Bristol (02809). Phone 401/253-9062.* During the day, workers mill around dressed in colonial garb, and craftspeople demonstrate weaving, pottery, and blacksmith techniques at Coggeshall Farm Museum. Pony rides, a silent auction, music, magic and live farm animals are also found at the fair. Weekend in mid-Sept.

Specialty Lodgings

ROCKWELL HOUSE INN. *610 Hope St, Bristol (02809). Phone 401/253-0040; toll-free 800/815-0040; fax 401/253-1811. www.rockwellhouseinn.com.* Set on a half-acre of land in the historic district of Bristol, this inn was built in 1809 as a residence for a local sea captain. Elegant guest rooms are decorated with antiques, and a large backyard is shaded by the largest tulip tree in New England. Guests may lounge in the garden and patio, or walk a short distance to explore Narragansett Bay, antiques shops, and restaurants. 4 rooms, 2 story. Complimentary full breakfast. Check-in 4 pm, check-out 11 am. High-speed Internet access, wireless Internet access. **$$**

WILLIAMS GRANT INN. *154 High St, Bristol (02809). Phone 401/253-4222; toll-free 800/596-4222; fax 401/254-0987. www.wmgrantinn.com.* This charming colonial Federal-style home is situated on a tree-lined street in Bristol's historic district. Guest rooms are elegantly decorated with an eclectic mixture of antiques, artwork, and the owners' collections of teddy bears, and feature fireplaces, quilts, bathrobes, and fresh flowers. A full home-cooked breakfast is served in the dining room, and an afternoon treat of fresh-baked cookies are offered to guests in the parlor. 5 rooms, 2 story. Closed late Nov-early Mar. Children over 12 years only. Complimentary full breakfast. Check-in 1 pm, check-out 11 am. High-speed Internet access, wireless Internet access. **$$**

Restaurant

★ ★ **LOBSTER POT.** *119-121 Hope St, Bristol (02809). Phone 401/253-9100; fax 401/253-7225. www.lobsterpotri.com.* American, seafood menu.

Lunch, dinner. Closed Mon; also 2 weeks in Mar. Bar. Business casual attire. Reservations recommended. Outdoor seating. **$$**

Charlestown (E-6)

See also Narragansett, Westerly

Population 6,478
Elevation 20 ft
Area Code 401
Zip 02813
Information Chamber of Commerce, 4945 Old Post Rd; phone 401/364-3878
Web Site www.cshell.com/ccc

Charlestown, named for King Charles II of England, was originally called Cross Mills for two gristmills that once stood here. Charlestown was first settled along the coast by summer residents and by permanent residents after World War II. The town's past can be seen in Fort Ninigret, the historic Native American church, and the Royal Indian Burial Ground.

What to See and Do

Burlingame State Park. *Kings Factory Rd, Charlestown (02813). 2 miles SW via Hwy 1.* Phone 401/322-7337. More than 2,000 acres with wooded area. Swimming, lifeguard, fishing, boating; picnicking, concession. Tent and trailer camping (mid-Apr-Oct).

Kimball Wildlife Refuge. *Montauk Rd, Charlestown (02813). 2 1/2 miles SW on US 1, Windswept Farm exit, left onto Montauk Rd.* Phone 401/874-6664. Thirty-acre refuge on the south shore of Watchaug Pond has nature trails and programs.

Swimming, fishing. At several Block Island Sound beaches; S of Hwy 1 on Charlestown Beach Rd; Green Hill Rd; Moonstone Rd.

Special Events

August Meeting of the Narragansett Indian Tribe. *Narragansett Indian church grounds.* Phone 401/364-1100. www.narragansett-tribe.org. Dancing, music, storytelling. Said to be the oldest continuous meeting in the country. Second week in Aug.

Seafood Festival. *4945 Old Post Rd, Charlestown (02813).* Phone 401/364-3878. www.cshell.com/ccc/cinfo/seaf.htm. Seafood vendors, amateur seafood cook-off, helicopter rides, antique car show. First Sat-Sun in Aug.

Theatre-by-the-Sea. *364 Cards Pond Rd, Matunuck (02879). 7 miles NE via Hwy 1, then S off Matunuck Beach Rd exit to Cards Pond Rd.* Phone 401/782-8587. www.theatrebythesea.com. Historic barn theater (1933) presents professionally staged musicals. Restaurant, bar, cabaret. Tues-Sun evenings; matinees Thurs; children's shows July-Aug, Fri only. June-Sept. **$$$$**

East Greenwich (D-6)

See also Warwick

Population 11,865
Elevation 64 ft
Area Code 401
Zip 02818
Information Chamber of Commerce, 591 Main St; phone 401/885-0020
Web Site www.eastgreenwichchamber.com

Sometimes referred to as "the town on four hills," East Greenwich, on Narragansett Bay, is a sports and yachting center. Nathanael Greene and James M. Varnum organized the Kentish Guards, who protected the town during the Revolution, here in 1774. The Guards are still active today.

What to See and Do

Goddard Memorial State Park. *345 Ives Rd, Warwick (02818). E side of Greenwich Cove, E of town via Forge and Ives rds.* Phone 401/884-2010. Approximately 490 acres with swimming at Greenwich Bay Beach (bathhouse), fishing, boating; bridle trails, nine-hole golf (fee), ice skating, picnicking, concessions, playing fields, and fireplaces (fee). **$**

Kentish Guards Armory. *1774 Armory St, East Greenwich (02818).* Phone 401/821-1628. (1843) Headquarters of the Kentish Guards, local militia chartered in 1774 and still active; General Nathanael Greene was a charter member. (By appointment only) **FREE**

Old Kent County Court House. *125 Main St, East Greenwich (02818).* Phone 401/886-8606. www.eastgreenwichri.com. (1750) Remodeled in 1909 and 1995.

Varnum House Museum. *57 Pierce St, East Greenwich (02818).* Phone 401/884-1776. www.varnumcontinentals.org. (1773) Mansion of a Revolutionary War officer and lawyer; period furnishings, colonial items, gardens. (June-Aug, Sat-Sun 10 am-4 pm, by appointment) **$**

Varnum Memorial Armory and Military Museum.
6 Main St, East Greenwich (02818). Phone 401/884-4110. www.varnumcontinentals.org. (1913) Museum displays uniforms and armaments from the Revolutionary through the Vietnam wars. (By appointment) **DONATION**

Glocester

Population 5,011
Elevation 422 ft
Area Code 401
Zip 02859
Information Blackstone Valley Tourism Council, 175 Main St, Pawtucket 02860; phone 401/724-2200 or toll-free 800/454-2882 (outside RI)
Web Site www.tourblackstone.com

What to See and Do

Brown & Hopkins Country Store. *1179 Putnam Pike, Chepachet (02814). 3 miles SE on Hwy 100 to Hwy 44 (Main St). Phone 401/568-4830. www.brownandhopkins.com.* (1799) Nation's oldest continuously operating country store; inside are antiques, gourmet food, penny candy, and a caf. (Mon-Wed, Fri-Sat 10 am-5 pm; Thurs to 7 pm; Sun noon-5 pm)

Casimir Pulaski State Park. *3 miles SE on Hwy 100, 6 miles W on Hwy 44. Phone 401/568-2085.* Park has 100 acres with lake. Swimming beach; cross-country skiing, picnicking. Pavilion (reservation required). (Late May-early Sept)

George Washington State Campground. *1826 Putnam Pike, Glocester (02859). 3 miles SE on Hwy 100, 4 miles W on Hwy 44. Phone 401/568-2013.* Swimming beach, fishing, boating; hiking trail, picnicking, camping (no fires). (Mid-Apr-mid-Oct) **$$$**

Jamestown (E-6)

See also Newport

Settled circa 1670
Population 4,999
Elevation 8 ft
Area Code 401
Zip 02835
Information Jamestown Chamber of Commerce, PO Box 35; phone 401/423-3650
Web Site www.jamestownri.com/chamber

Jamestown is centered around the Jamestown Ferry landing, but technically the town also includes all of Conanicut—one of three main islands in Narragansett Bay. The island is connected by bridges to Newport on the east (toll) and to the mainland on the west (free). While much of Jamestown was burned by the British in 1775, some old houses do remain.

The restored Conanicut Battery, a Revolutionary redoubt 2 miles south on Beavertail Road, is open to the public and is the second-highest point on the island.

What to See and Do

Fishing. Striped bass, tuna, flounder, bluefish. For boat charter inquire at East Ferry slip.

Jamestown Museum. *92 Narragansett Ave, Jamestown (02835). Phone 401/423-0784. www.jamestownhistoricalsociety.org.* Photos and displays pertain to town and old Jamestown ferries. (Late June-Labor Day, Wed-Sun 1-4 pm) **DONATION** The Jamestown Historical Society also maintains the

> **Old Windmill.** *1 1/2 miles N on North Rd. Phone 401/423-1798.* (1787) Restored to working order. (Mid-June-mid-Sept, Sat-Sun afternoons) **FREE**

Sydney L. Wright Museum. *Jamestown Philomerian Library, 26 North Rd, Jamestown (02835). Located in the Philomerian Library. Phone 401/423-7280.* Exhibits of Native American and early colonial artifacts from Conanicut Island. (Open daily)

Watson Farm. *455 North Rd, Jamestown. S of Hwy 138. Phone 401/423-0005.* (1796) This 280-acre farm on Conanicut Island is being worked as a typical New England farm. Self-guided tour of farm and pastures with focus on land-use history. (June-mid-Oct: Tues, Thurs, and Sun, afternoons) **$**

Kingston (E-6)

See also Narragansett, Newport, North Kingstown

Population 6,504
Elevation 242 ft
Area Code 401
Zip 02881
Information Chamber of Commerce, 328 Main St, PO Box 289, Wakefield 02880; phone 401/783-2801; or the South County Tourism Council, Stedman Government Center, 4808 Tower Hill Rd, Wakefield 02879; phone 401/789-4422 or toll-free 800/548-4662

Web Site www.southcountyri.com

Known as Little Rest until 1825, Kingston was once forestland bought from the Narragansett. Early settlers were farmers who built a water-powered mill in an area still known as Biscuit City. Here, the state constitution was ratified, and a law was passed abolishing slavery in the state. Kingston overlooks a fertile flood plain, which geologists believe was an ancient river. Kingston is also the home of the University of Rhode Island.

What to See and Do

Helme House. *2587 Kingstown Rd, Kingston (02881). Phone 401/783-2195. www.southcountyart.org. (1802)* Gallery of the South County Art Association. (Wed-Sun) **FREE**

Kingston Library. *2605 Kingstown Rd, Kingston (02881). Phone 401/783-8254. www.skpl.org. (1776)* Visited by George Washington and Benjamin Franklin, this building housed the Rhode Island General Assembly at the time the British occupied Newport. (Mon-Sat) **FREE**

Museum of Primitive Art and Culture. *1058 Kingstown Rd, Peace Dale (02879). 2 miles S via Hwy 108. Phone 401/783-5711. www.primitiveartmuseum.org.* 1850s post office building; prehistoric artifacts from New England, North America, South Seas, Africa, Europe, and Asia. (Labor Day-Memorial Day, Tues-Thurs 10 am-2 pm; rest of the year Wed noon-2 pm; also by appointment) **DONATION**

Special Event

Wakefield Rotary Balloon Festival. *University of Rhode Island, 404 Wordens Pond Rd C, Kingston (02881). Phone 401/783-1770.* Two-day event features hot air balloon rides, parachute demonstrations, arts and crafts, and music. Late July or early Aug.

Specialty Lodging

LARCHWOOD INN. *521 Main St, Wakefield (02879). Phone toll-free 800/275-5450; fax 401/783-1800. www.larchwoodinn.com.* This family-run country inn is located in the small rural village of Wakefield. Rooms are housed in a large, three-story 19th-century manor house and a smaller Victorian annex across the street, and feature beamed ceilings, four-poster beds, settees, hutches and tall dressers, fireplaces, high-back chairs, and lace throw pillows. Guests can lounge on the front porch, patio, or in

country-style living area or stroll the well-manicured grounds to enjoy the inn's peaceful surroundings. 18 rooms, 3 story. Check-in 1 pm, check-out 11 am. High-speed Internet access, wireless Internet access. Restaurant, bar. **$**
🅳

Restaurant

★ ★ **LARCHWOOD INN.** *521 Main St, Wakefield (02879). Phone 401/783-5454. www.larchwoodinn. com.* American menu. Breakfast, lunch, dinner. Closed Mon. Bar. Children's menu. Casual attire. Reservations recommended. Outdoor seating. **$$**
🅳

Little Compton (E-7)

See also Portsmouth

Population 3,339
Area Code 401
Zip 02837
Information Town Hall, PO Box 523; phone 401/635-4400; or the Newport County Convention and Visitors Bureau, 23 America's Cup Ave, Newport 02840; phone 401/849-8048 or toll-free 800/976-5122
Web Site www.gonewport.com

In Little Compton's old burial ground lie the remains of the first white woman born in New England, Elizabeth Alden Pabodie, the daughter of John and Priscilla Alden.

What to See and Do

Gray's Store (1788). *4 Main St, Little Compton (02810). 7 miles NE on local road. Phone 401/635-4566.* First post office in the area (1804) features antique soda fountain, wheeled cheese, candy, and tobacco cases. (Summer: Mon-Sat 9 am-5 pm, Sun noon-4 pm; winter: Thurs-Sat 9 am-5pm, Sun noon-4pm) **FREE**

Sakonnet Point. *5 Bluff Head Ave, Little Compton (02837).* Swimming beaches, fishing. Harbor with lighthouse.

Sakonnet Vineyards. *162 W Main, Little Compton (02837). Phone 401/635-8486; toll-free 800/919-4637.* Tour of winery and vineyard. Wine tasting (daily). **FREE**

Wilbor House. *Hwy 77, 548 W Main Rd, Little Compton (02837). 1 mile S on Hwy 77 at West Rd. Phone 401/635-4035. www.littlecompton.org. (1690)*

Seventeenth-century house with 18th- and 19th-century additions was restored in 1956 by local historical society; period furnishings, antique farm, and household implements. Display of carriages and sleighs in 1860 barn. Also one-room schoolhouse, artist's studio. (Mid-June-Labor Day: Thurs-Sun 1-5 pm; Sept-Oct: Sat-Sun; also by appointment) **$**

Narragansett (E-6)

See also Block Island, Charlestown, Kingston, Newport

Settled 1675
Population 14,985
Elevation 20 ft
Area Code 401
Zip 02882
Information Narragansett Chamber of Commerce, The Towers Narragansett Visitors Center, 36 Ocean Rd; phone 401/783-7121
Web Site www.narragansettri.com/chamber

Part of the township of South Kingstown until 1901, Narragansett was named after the indigenous people who sold their land to the first area settlers. Once a center for shipbuilding, the town's center is still referred to as Narragansett Pier. Between 1878 and 1920 Narragansett was a well-known, elegant summer resort with many fine "cottages" and hotels. The most prominent landmark of that time was the Narragansett Casino. The casino's main entrance and covered promenade, "the Towers" on Ocean Road, is the only surviving element of that complex; the rest was lost in a devastating fire in 1900. Today, Narragansett's most important industries are commercial fishing and tourism. It is also the home of the University of Rhode Island's renowned Graduate School of Oceanography, located at the Bay Campus on South Ferry Road.

What to See and Do

Block Island Ferry. *Galilee State Pier, 304 Great Island Rd, Point Judith (02882). 5 miles S on Ocean Rd, 1 mile W on Sand Hill Cove Rd. Phone 401/783-4613.* Automobile ferries to Block Island from Point Judith and Newport. (Daily)

Fishing. Wide variety of liveries at Narragansett Pier and the surrounding waterfront villages. Fishing tournaments are held throughout summer.

Point Judith. *1470 Ocean Rd, Narragansett (02882). 6 miles S of center on Ocean Ave, to Coast Guard Station*

and Lighthouse. Phone 401/789-0444. Lighthouse and station not open to public, but grounds provide plenty of historical information. **FREE**

South County Museum. *Strathmore St, Narragansett (02882). Phone 401/783-5400; fax 401/783-0506. www.southcountymuseum.org.* Antiques representing rural life in 19th-century Rhode Island; costumes, vehicles, and nautical equipment. Farm and blacksmithing displays; toys. Country kitchen, general store, cobbler's shop. Also complete turn-of-the-century letterpress print shop. (May-June, Sept-Oct: Fri-Sat 10 am-4 pm, Sun noon-4 pm; July-Aug: Wed-Sat 10 am-4 pm, Sun noon-4 pm) **$**

Swimming. Public beaches at **Narragansett Pier,** pavilion, fees; **Scarborough State Beach,** 1 1/2 miles S on Ocean Ave. **Salty Brine Beach,** Ocean Ave, protected by seawall, fishing; **Roger Wheeler State Beach,** west of Point Judith, playground, picnic tables, concession; parking (fee). Similar facilities at other beaches.

⭐ **The Towers.** *35 Ocean Rd, Narragansett. 1/4 mile S on Hwy 1. Phone 401/782-2597. www.thetowersri.com.* This Romanesque entrance arch flanked by rounded, conical-topped towers is a grandiose and sad reminder of McKim, Mead, and White's 19th-century casino, destroyed by fire in 1900, and Narragansett's own past as summer mecca for the rich and fashionable. Various public events throughout summer.

Special Event

Mid-winter New England Surfing Championship. *170 Clarke Rd, Narragansett. Narragansett Town Beach. Phone 401/723-8795; fax 401/727-2605. www.sne.surfesa.org.* For information, contact the Northeastern Surfing Association, 126 Sayles Ave, Pawtucket, 02860. Third Sat in Feb.

Restaurant

★ ★ **COAST GUARD HOUSE.** *40 Ocean Rd, Narragansett (02882). Phone 401/789-0700. www.thecoastguardhouse.com.* Overlooking Narragansett Bay, this former Coast Guard station (1888) features great views. Piano entertainment is provided during the week in season (weekends only off-season). American, seafood menu. Lunch, dinner, Sun brunch. Closed Jan. Bar. Children's menu. Business casual attire. Outdoor seating. **$$**

Newport (E-7)

See also Block Island, Jamestown, Kingston, Narragansett, Portsmouth

Founded 1639
Population 28,227
Elevation 96 ft
Area Code 401
Zip 02840
Information Newport County Convention & Visitors Bureau, 23 America's Cup Ave; phone 401/849-8048 or toll-free 800/976-5122
Web Site www.gonewport.com

Few cities in the country have a history as rich and colorful as that of Newport, and fewer still retain as much evidence of their great past. The town was founded by a group of men and women who fled the religious intolerance of Massachusetts. They established the first school in Rhode Island the following year. Shipbuilding, for which Newport is still famous, began in 1646. The first Quakers to come to the New World settled in Newport in 1657. They were followed in 1658 by 15 Jewish families who came here from Holland. Newport produced the state's first newspaper, the *Rhode Island Gazette.*

Newport took an active part in the Revolution; local residents set fire to one British ship and continued to fire on others until the British landed 9,000 men and took possession. The city was occupied for two years; it was not until the French fleet entered the harbor that the British withdrew their forces.

Newport's fame as a summer resort began after the Civil War when many wealthy families, including the August Belmonts, Ward McAllister, Harry Lehr, Mrs. William Astor, and Mrs. Stuyvesant Fish, made the town a center for lavish and sometimes outrageous social events. Parties for dogs and one for a monkey were among the more bizarre occasions. Hostesses spent as much as $300,000 a season entertaining their guests. Although less flamboyant than it was before World War I, the summer colony is still socially prominent.

Today, Newport is famous for its boating and yachting, with boats for hire at many wharves. A bridge (toll) connects the city with Jamestown to the west.

Additional Visitor Information

The Newport County Convention and Visitor's Bureau maintains an information center at 23 America's Cup Avenue (daily). Tickets to most tourist attractions are offered for sale. An eight-minute video, maps, general tourist information, and group tours and convention information are available. For further information, phone 401/849-8048 or toll-free 800/976-5122.

The Preservation Society of Newport County publishes material on all Society properties. It sells combination tickets at all buildings under its administration and provides sightseeing information. Phone 401/847-1000.

What to See and Do

Artillery Company of Newport Military Museum. *23 Clarke St, Newport (02840). Phone 401/846-8488. www.newportartillery.org.* Military dress of many nations and periods. (May-Oct, Sat 10 am-4 pm; otherwise by appointment)

Brick Market. *127 Thames St, Newport (02840). Long Wharf and Thames St. Phone toll-free 401/846-0813. www.brickmarketnewport.com.* Home of the Newport Historical Society. Built by Peter Harrison, architect of Touro Synagogue, in 1762 as a market and granary. The restored building and surrounding area house boutiques and restaurants. (Daily)

CCInc Auto Tape Tours. *Phone 201/236-1666. www.autotapetours.com.* This 90-minute cassette offers a mile-by-mile self-guided tour of Newport. Available at Paper Lion, Long Wharf Mall, and Gateway Visitor Information Center. Includes tape and recorder rental. Tape also may be purchased directly from CCInc, PO Box 227, 2 Elbrook Dr, Allendale, NJ 07401. **$$$**

★ **Cliff Walk.** *Memorial Blvd, Newport. Begins at Memorial Blvd. Phone 401/847-1355. www.cliffwalk.com.* Scenic walk overlooking Atlantic Ocean adjoins many Newport "cottages." Designated a National Recreational Trail in 1975. **FREE**

Easton's Beach. *Memorial Blvd (Hwy 138), Newport. Phone 401/845-5810. www.new.cityofnewport.com/dept/parks/beach.html.* Well-developed public beach has bathhouse, snack bar, antique carousel, picnic area, and designated surfing area. (Memorial Day-Labor Day, daily 9 am-6 pm). **FREE**

Fort Adams State Park. *Harrison Ave and Ocean Dr, Newport (02840). Phone 401/847-2400. www.riparks. com.* Park surrounds Fort Adams, the second-largest bastioned fort in the United States between 1799 and 1945. The rambling 21-acre fort (guided tours only) was constructed of stone over a 33-year period. Beach swimming, fishing, boating (launch, ramps, hoist); soccer and rugby fields, picnicking. (Memorial Day-Labor Day, daily)

Friends Meeting House. *Farewell and Marlborough sts, Newport (02840). Phone 401/846-0813. www. newporthistorical.org.* (1699) Site of New England Yearly Meeting of the Society of Friends until 1905; meeting house, expanded in 1729 and 1807, spans three centuries of architecture and construction. Guided tours through Newport Historical Society. (mid-June-Aug, Thurs-Sat, tours hourly 10 am-3 pm; otherwise by appointment) **$**

⭐ **Historic Mansions and Houses.** Combination tickets to the Elms, the Breakers, Rosecliff, Marble House, Hunter House, Chateau-sur-Mer, Kingscote, and Green Animals topiary gardens (see PORTSMOUTH) are available at any of these houses.

Astors' Beechwood. *580 Bellevue Ave, Newport (02840). Phone 401/846-3772.* Italianate summer residence of Mrs. Caroline Astor, *the* Mrs. Astor. Theatrical tour of house includes actors portraying Mrs. Astor's servants and society guests. (Mid-May-mid-Dec: daily; rest of year: weekends only) **$$$**

Belcourt Castle. *657 Bellevue Ave, Newport (02840). 2 miles S on Hwy 138A. Phone 401/846-0669.* (1891) Designed by Richard Morris Hunt in French chteau style, this 62-room house was the residence of Oliver Hazard Perry Belmont and his wife, Alva Vanderbilt Belmont, who built Marble House when married to William K. Vanderbilt. Belcourt is unique for the inclusion of stables within its main structure; Belmont loved horses. Contains the largest collection of antiques and objets d'art in Newport; gold coronation coach; large collection of stained-glass windows. Tea served. Special events scheduled throughout year. (Daily; closed Jan; also Thanksgiving, Dec 25) **$$**

Breakers. *44 Ochre Point Ave, Newport (02840). Phone 401/847-1000.* (1895) Seventy-room, northern Italian palazzo designed by Richard Morris Hunt is the largest of all Newport cottages and is impressive by its sheer size; contains original furnishings. Children's playhouse cottage has scale-size kitchen, fireplace, playroom. Built for Mr. and Mrs. Cornelius Vanderbilt. (Daily) **$$$$**

Chateau-sur-Mer. *474 Bellevue Ave, Newport (02840). Phone 401/847-1000.* (1852) Victorian mansion remodeled in 1872 by Richard Morris Hunt has landscaped grounds with Chinese moon gate. Built for William S. Wetmore, who made his fortune in the China trade. (late June-early Oct, daily) **$$$**

Edward King House. *Aquidneck Park, 35 King St, Newport (02840). Phone 401/846-7426; toll-free 866/878-6954.* (1846) Villa by Richard Upjohn is considered one of the finest Italianate houses in the country. Used as senior citizens' center. (Mon-Fri) **FREE**

Elms. *367 Bellevue Ave, Newport (02840). Phone 401/847-1000.* (1901) Modeled after 18th-century Chateau d'Asnieres near Paris, this restored "cottage" from Newport's gilded age boasts elaborate interiors and formal, sunken gardens that are among the city's most beautiful. Built for Edward J. Berwind, Philadelphia coal magnate. (May-Oct: daily; Nov-Mar: Sat-Sun) **$$$**

Hunter House. *54 Washington St, Newport (02840). Phone 401/847-1000.* (1748) Outstanding example of Colonial architecture features gambrel roof, 12-on-12 panel windows, broken pediment doorway. Furnished with pieces by Townsend and Goddard, famous 18th-century cabinet makers. (late June-late Sept, daily) **$$$**

Kingscote. *253 Bellevue Ave, Newport (02840). Phone 401/847-1000.* (1839) Gothic Revival cottage designed by Richard Upjohn; in 1881, McKim, Mead, and White added the "aesthetic" dining room, which features Tiffany-glass wall and fixtures. Outstanding Chinese export paintings and porcelains. Built for George Noble Jones of Savannah, Georgia, Kingscote is considered the nation's first true summer "cottage." (June-Oct, daily) **$$$**

Marble House. *596 Bellevue Ave, Newport (02840). Phone 401/847-1000.* (1892) French-style palace designed by Richard Morris Hunt is the most sumptuous of Newport cottages. Front gates, entrance, and central hall are modeled after Versailles. House is named for the many kinds of marble used on interior, which also features lavish use of gold and bronze. Original furnishings include dining room chairs made of gilded bronze. Built for Mrs. William K. Vanderbilt. On display are yachting

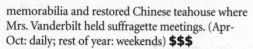

memorabilia and restored Chinese teahouse where Mrs. Vanderbilt held suffragette meetings. (Apr-Oct: daily; rest of year: weekends) **$$$**

Rosecliff. *548 Bellevue Ave, Newport (02840). Phone 401/847-6543.* (1902) Designed by Stanford White after the Grand Trianon at Versailles, Rosecliff boasts the largest private ballroom in Newport and famous heart-shaped staircase. Built for socialite Mrs. Hermann Oelrichs. (Apr-early Nov, daily) **$$$**

Samuel Whitehorne House. *416 Thames St, Newport (02840). Phone 401/849-7300.* (1811) Features exquisite furniture, silver, and pewter made by 18th-century artisans; Chinese porcelain, Irish crystal, and Pilgrim-era furniture; garden. (May-Oct: Mon, Thurs-Fri 11 am-4 pm; Sat-Sun 10 am-4 pm; winter by appointment) **$$**

Wanton-Lyman-Hazard House. *17 Broadway, Newport (02840). Phone 401/846-0813.* (Circa 1675) Oldest house in Newport, one of the finest Jacobean houses in New England, the site of the 1765 Stamp Act riot; restored; 18th-century garden; guided tours. (mid-June-late Aug, Thurs-Sat; 5 tours daily; closed holidays) **$**

Whitehall Museum House. *311 Berkeley Ave, Middletown (02842). 3 miles NE. Phone 401/846-3116.* (1729) Restored, hip-roofed country house built by Bishop George Berkeley, British philosopher and educator; garden. (July-Labor day, Tues-Sun 10 am-5 pm; otherwise by appointment) **$**

⭐ **International Tennis Hall of Fame & Museum.** *194 Bellevue Ave, Newport (02840). Easton's Beach. Phone 401/849-3990; toll-free 800/457-1144. www.tennisfame.com.* World's largest tennis museum features interactive and dynamic exhibits detailing the history of the sport. Tennis equipment, fashions, trophies, and memorabilia on display in the famous Newport Casino, built in 1880 and designed by McKim, Mead, and White. (Daily; closed Thanksgiving, Dec 25) Grass courts available (May-Oct). **$$**

Museum of Newport History. *Touro St and Washington Sq, Newport (02840). Adjacent to Seventh Day Baptist Meeting House. Phone 401/846-0813. www.newporthistorical.org.* Colonial art; Newport silver and pewter, china, Early American glass, furniture. (May-mid-June: Thurs-Sat 10 am-4 pm, Sun 1-4 pm; mid-June-Labor Day: daily 10 am-4 pm). Walking tours of Colonial Newport(fee).

Newport Art Museum and Art Association. *76 Bellevue Ave, Newport (02840). Opposite Touro Park. Phone 401/848-8200; fax 401/848-8205. www.newportartmuseum.com.* Changing exhibitions of contemporary and historical art are housed in 1864 mansion designed by Richard Morris Hunt in the "stick-style" and in 1920 Beaux Arts building. Lectures, performing arts events, evening musical picnics; tours. (Columbus Day-Memorial Day: Tues-Sat 10 am-4 pm, Sun noon-4 pm; rest of the year: Mon-Sat 10 am-5 pm, Sun noon-5 pm) **$$**

Newport Grand. *150 Admiral Kalbfus Rd, Newport (02840). At base of Newport Bridge. Phone 401/849-5000; fax 401/846-0290. www.newportgrand.com.* Parimutuel betting. (Daily 10-1 am)

Newport Navigation. *Newport Harbor Hotel and Marina, 49 America's Cup Ave, Newport (02840). Phone 401/849-3575. www.newportcruisecompany.com.* One-hour narrated cruise of Narragansett Bay and Newport Harbor aboard the *Spirit of Newport*. (May-Oct, daily) **$$$**

Old Colony and Newport Railroad. *Terminal, Depot, 19 America's Cup Ave, Newport. Phone 401/624-6951. www.ocnrr.com.* Vintage one-hour train ride along a scenic route to Narragansett Bay. (March-Nov) **$$$**

Old Stone Mill. *Touro Park, Mill St and Bellevue Ave, Newport. Phone 401/846-1398.* Origin of circular stone tower supported by arches is unknown. Although excavations (1948-1949) have disproved it, some people still believe structure was built by Norsemen. **FREE**

Oldport Marine Harbor Tours. *1 Sayers Wharf, Newport (02840). Phone 401/847-9109; fax 401/846-5599. www.oldportmarine.com.* One-hour cruise of Newport Harbor aboard the *Amazing Grace*. (Mid-May-mid-Oct, daily) **$$$**

Redwood Library and Athenaeum. *50 Bellevue Ave, Newport (02840). Phone 401/847-0292; fax 401/841-5680. www.redwoodlibrary.org.* Designed by master Colonial architect Peter Harrison; thought to be oldest library building (1750) in continuous use in United States; used by English officers as a club during Revolution. Collections include part of original selection of books and early portraits. (Mon, Fri-Sat 9:30 am-5:30 pm; Tues-Thurs to 8 pm; Sun 1-5 pm) **FREE**

Seventh Day Baptist Meeting House. *82 Touro St, Newport (02840). Adjacent to Newport Historical Society. www.newporthistorical.org.* (1729) Historical church built by master builder Richard Munday. **FREE**

Touro Synagogue National Historic Site. *85 Touro St, Newport (02840).* Phone 401/847-4794. *www.tourosynagogue.org.* The oldest synagogue (1763) in America, a Georgian masterpiece by the country's first architect, Peter Harrison, contains the oldest Torah in North America, examples of 18th-century crafts, and a letter from George Washington; worship services follow the Sephardic Orthodox ritual of the founders.

Trinity Church. *Queen Anne Sq, Newport (02840). Phone 401/846-0660; fax 401/846-8440.* (1726) First Anglican parish in state (1698), Trinity has been in continuous use since it was built. George Washington and philosopher George Berkeley were communicants. Interior features Tiffany windows and an organ tested by Handel before being shipped from London. Tours.

Viking Boat Tour. *Goat Island Marina, Newport (02840). The Viking Queen leaves Goat Island Marina off Washington St. Phone 401/847-6921; fax 401/848-5773. www.vikingtoursnewport.com.* One-hour narrated trip includes historic Newport, yachts, waterfront mansions; also available is extended trip with tour of Hammersmith Farm (see). (May-Oct) **$$$**

Viking Bus Tour. *Newport Tourist Center, 23 America's Cup Ave, Newport (02840). Phone 401/847-6921; fax 401/848-5773. www.vikingtoursnewport.com.* Two-, three-, and four-hour narrated trips cover 150 points of interest, including mansions and restored areas. (Schedules vary) Three-hour trips include admission to one mansion; four-hour trips include admission to two mansions. **$$$$**

White Horse Tavern. *42 Marlborough St, Newport (02840). Phone 401/849-3600.* (1673) Oldest operating tavern in the nation. (Daily)

Special Events

Christmas in Newport. *23 America's Cup Ave, Newport (02840). Phone 401/849-8048. www.christmasinnewport.org.* A month-long series of activities including concerts, tree lighting, and craft fairs. Dec.

JVC Jazz Festival. *Fort Adams State Park, Newport (02840). Phone 401/847-3700; toll-free 866/468-7619. www.festivalproductions.net/05/jvcjazz/newpsch.php.* Mid-Aug. **$$$$**

Newport Irish Heritage Month. *Throughout town. Phone 401/845-9123; toll-free 800/976-5122.* A variety of Irish heritage and theme events; films, concerts, plays, arts and crafts, exhibits; food and drink; parade and road race. Mar.

Newport Music Festival. *163 Glen Farm Rd, Newport (02840). Phone 401/849-0700. www.newportmusic.org.* Chamber music held in Newport's fabled mansions. Three concerts daily. Mid-July.

Newport Winter Festival. *23 America's Cup Ave, Newport (02840). Phone 401/847-7666; toll-free 800/326-6030. www.newportevents.com/winterfest.* Ten days of food, festivities, music. More than 200 cultural and recreational events and activities. Mid-Feb.

Limited-Service Hotels

★ ★ **COURTYARD BY MARRIOTT.** *9 Commerce Dr, Middletown (02842). Phone 401/849-8000; toll-free 888/686-5067; fax 401/849-8313. www.courtyard.com.* Tones of blue and gold are found in the rooms at this Courtyard located in the mid-Aquidneck Island town of Middletown. Business travelers will appreciate the large working desks with ergonomic chairs in every room, while all guests will get a peaceful night's rest in beds that feature plush duvets and fluffy feather pillows. 148 rooms, 3 story. Check-in 4 pm, check-out noon. High-speed Internet access. Fitness room. Indoor pool, outdoor pool, whirlpool. **$$**

★ ★ **MILL STREET INN.** *75 Mill St, Newport (02840). Phone 401/849-9500; toll-free 800/392-1316; fax 401/848-5131. www.millstreetinn.com.* Once a 19th-century mill (now on the National Register of Historic Places) the Mill Street Inn's exterior evokes images of Newport's industrial history, but inside, guests will find a contemporary and upscale lodging. Rooms are spacious and appealing, with exposed brick walls, original cross-beams, mini-bars, flat-screen TVs, VCRs, plush bath robes, and private decks with harbor views. A rooftop patio provides the perfect setting for seasonal breakfast dining and lounging. 23 rooms, 2 story, all suites. Complimentary full breakfast. Check-in 3 pm, check-out 11 am. High-speed Internet access, wireless Internet access. **$$$**

Full-Service Hotels

★ ★ ★ **HOTEL VIKING.** *1 Bellevue Ave, Newport (02840). Phone 401/847-3300; toll-free 800/556-7126; fax 401/848-4864. www.hotelviking.com.* A classically elegant property with buildings constructed in 1926, 1950, and 1999, the Hotel Viking is located in the Historic Hill neighborhood of downtown Newport. The hotel sits atop the highest point in the city, offering guests an impressive vista of the town below. The lavish lodging spot is removed from the throngs of tourists, and guests can unwind, away from crowds, in the luxurious accommodations that include four-poster beds, antiques and authentic reproductions of period furnishings, pillow-top mattresses, and plush duvets. The full-service Spa Terre is a welcoming respite from the rigors of travel, and historic homes, the International Tennis Hall of Fame, and the waterfront are all located within a few blocks. 222 rooms, 5 story. Pets accepted, some restrictions; fee. Check-in 3 pm, check-out 11 am. High-speed Internet access. Restaurant, bar. Fitness room. Spa. Indoor pool, whirlpool. Business center. **$$**

★ ★ ★ **HYATT REGENCY NEWPORT.** *1 Goat Island, Newport (02840). Phone 401/851-1234; toll-free 888/591-1234; fax 401/846-7210. www.newport.hyatt. com.* Located at the tip of Goat Island, the Hyatt Regency overlooks the historic Newport Harbor waterfront, Narragansett Bay, and the Newport Jamestown Bridge. Perfect for both the business and leisure traveler, the hotel offers a full-service spa, meeting spaces, and up-to-date technology as well as elegantly appointed rooms that include beds with pillow-top mattresses and plush duvets and pillows and Portico bath amenities. For outdoor fun, guests can splash around in the indoor and outdoor pools and host authentic New England clambakes in two waterfront pits. 264 rooms, 9 story. Pets accepted, some restrictions. Check-in 4 pm, check-out 11 am. Restaurant, bar. Fitness room, spa. Indoor pool, outdoor pool. Tennis. Airport transportation available. Business center. **$$$**

★ ★ ★ **MARRIOTT NEWPORT.** *25 America's Cup Ave, Newport (02840). Phone 401/849-1000; toll-free 800/458-3066; fax 401/849-3422. www.newportmarriott. com.* A nautical motif runs throughout this hotel, which is located in the heart of the historic waterfront district, adjacent to Long Wharf. The large, multi-level lobby features suspended sails over the central lounge area, while guest rooms include beds with plush white duvets with sailboat-themed throws. An indoor pool, steam and sauna rooms, racquetball court and fitness center are on-site recreational activities available to guests, while a biking trail, horseback riding, kayaking, Scuba diving, surfing, and sailing are all a few short miles away. 319 rooms, 7 story. Check-in 4 pm, check-out 11 am. High-speed Internet access. Restaurant, bar. Fitness room. Indoor pool, whirlpool. Tennis. Business center. **$$$$**

★ ★ ★ **NEWPORT HARBOR HOTEL AND MARINA.** *49 America's Cup Ave, Newport (02840). Phone 401/847-9000; toll-free 800/955-2558; fax 401/849-6380. www.newporthotel.com.* This hotel is located in Queen Anne Square, overlooking the beautiful and historic Newport Harbor waterfront and Narragansett Bay. Restaurants, shops, and its own 60-slip marina surround the hotel, as do 19th-century mansions, golfing, tennis beaches, and vineyards. The comfortable guest rooms and suites offer spectacular views of the waterfront or Queen Anne Square, and include televisions with movies and video games, marble-floored baths, coffee makers, and a data port for high-speed Internet access. 133 rooms, 4 story. Check-in 4 pm, check-out 11 am. High-speed Internet access. Restaurant, bar. Indoor pool. **$$$**

Full-Service Resort

★ ★ ★ **CASTLE HILL INN & RESORT.** *590 Ocean Dr, Newport (02840). Phone 401/849-3800; toll-free 888/466-1355; fax 401/849-3838. www.castlehill-linn.com.* Located on a coastal peninsula at the west of Newport's famous Ocean Drive, the Castle Hill Inn is an area landmark that overlooks the mouth of Narragansett Bay. Guest rooms are the epitome of elegance and romance and housed in a historic 1874 mansion, an adjacent chalet, the Harbor House, and beach cottages. Original antiques, pull-out sofas, televisions and CD players, gas-jet fireplaces, marble baths, and canopy beds are found in many of the accommodations, making this secluded retreat a truly luxurious escape. 35 rooms, 3 story. Children over 12 years only. Complimentary full breakfast. Check-in 3 pm, check-out 11 am. High-speed Internet access, wireless Internet access. Restaurant, bar. Spa. Beach. Airport transportation available. **$$$$**

Specialty Lodgings

BEECH TREE INN. *34 Rhode Island Ave, Newport (02840). Phone 401/847-9794; toll-free 800/748-6565. www.beechtreeinn.com.* This stately Victorian inn is located in a residential Newport neighborhood, near Washington Square and the Newport Harbor area shops and restaurants. Rooms are housed in the main house and in "The Cottage," an annex at the back of the property. The welcoming living area in the main house features a gas fireplace, piano, small book library, and a connecting guest kitchen, while guest rooms offer four-poster beds

with cozy comforters, TVs, wireless Internet access, and ceiling fans. A hearty full breakfast is offered each morning, and guests are treated to cookies, coffee, tea, cocoa, and other snacks during their stay. 8 rooms. Pets accepted; some restrictions. Complimentary full breakfast. Check-in 3 pm, check-out 11 am. High-speed internet access, wireless internet access. Airport transportation available. Credit cards accepted. **$$$**
🅿

THE FRANCIS MALBONE HOUSE. *392 Thames St, Newport (02840). Phone 401/846-0392; toll-free 800/846-0392; fax 401/848-5956. www.malbone.com.* Located in Newport's historic Harborfront District, this beautifully restored colonial home was built in 1760. Spacious guest rooms are immaculately kept and tastefully decorated with unique features and amenities like DVD and CD players, Jacuzzi tubs, fireplaces, monogrammed duvet covers, and authentic antiques and reproductions. A gourmet breakfast gets guests off to the right start before exploring the city's many nearby tourists sights, while afternoon tea gives guests a chance to recharge. 20 rooms, 3 story. Children over 12 permitted. Complimentary full breakfast. Check-in 2 pm, check-out 11 am. High-speed Internet access, wireless Internet access. Airport transportation available. **$$$**

IVY LODGE. *12 Clay St, Newport (02840). Phone 401/849-6865; toll-free 800/834-6865; fax 401/849-0704. www.ivylodge.com.* Located in the heart of Newport's Mansion District, this former Victorian residential mansion was built as a summer vacation retreat in the 1880s. Guest rooms are a blend of fine period furnishings and contemporary touches and amenities such as whirlpool tubs, VCRs/DVDs, CD players, gas fireplaces, refrigerators, and duvet bed covers. A full gourmet breakfast is provided in the former formal dining room, while the main floor living room offers comfortable lounging. Activities for guests include walking and touring local mansions, swimming at the nearby beach, and shopping. 8 rooms, 3 story. Complimentary full breakfast. Check-in 3 pm, check-out 11 am. High-speed Internet access, wireless Internet access. **$$$**
🅿

MELVILLE HOUSE. *39 Clarke St, Newport (02840). Phone 401/847-0640; toll-free 800/711-7184; fax 401/847-0956. www.melvillehouse.com.* Built around 1750, this historic colonial-style bed-and-breakfast is located in the center of the historic district on a gas-lit street. Nicely located for travelers visiting the sights of Newport, the inn provides cozy, comfortable accom-

modations. Guest rooms are a mix of period décor and contemporary touches, and a full breakfast is provided for guests in the main floor reception area. A common refrigerator invites guests to enjoy complimentary soda, fruit, and water. The inn is within walking distance to sailboats, antiques shops, and galleries, as well as the Tennis Hall of Fame and many famous mansions. 7 rooms, 2 story. Children over 12 years only. Complimentary full breakfast. Check-in 3 pm, check-out 11 am. High-speed Internet access, wireless Internet access. **$$**
🅿

PILGRIM HOUSE. *123 Spring St, Newport (02840). Phone 401/846-0040; toll-free 800/525-8373; fax 401/848-0357. www.pilgrimhouseinn.com.* Housed in a three-story Victorian built in 1810, the Pilgrim House features tastefully furnished rooms—complete with sleigh beds, comfy quilts, and period armoires and end tables—that allow guests to relax after a day of sightseeing in Newports Historic Hill District. Guests can nibble on breakfast treats from the third-story deck, which looks out onto the harbor and the mouth of Narragansett Bay, and laze the afternoon away while enjoying sherry and shortbread cookies. 11 rooms, 3 story. Closed Jan. Pets accepted, some restrictions. Children over 12 years only. Complimentary continental breakfast. Check-in 3 pm, check-out 11 am. High-speed Internet access, wireless Internet access. **$$**
🅿 🔖

Restaurants

★ ★ ★ **CANFIELD HOUSE.** *5 Memorial Blvd, Newport (02840). Phone 401/847-0416. www.canfieldhousenewport.com.* This elegant restaurant is located in a former casino. High ceilings, dark wood paneling, crystal chandeliers, and other refined touches give an air of celebration to any meal here. American menu. Dinner. Closed Mon; also 10 days in Jan. Bar. Business casual attire. Outdoor seating. **$$**

★ ★ **CHRISTIE'S OF NEWPORT.** *351 Thames St, Newport (02840). Phone 401/847-5400. www.christiesofnewport.com.* Seafood menu. Lunch, dinner. Bar. Children's menu. Casual attire. Reservations recommended. Valet parking. Outdoor seating. **$$**

★ ★ **LA FORGE CASINO.** *186 Bellevue Ave, Newport (02840). Phone 401/847-0418; fax 401/846-9170. www.laforgerestaurant.com.* Built in 1880. American menu. Lunch, dinner, brunch. Closed Thanksgiving, Dec 24, 25. Bar. Children's menu. Casual attire. Reservations recommended. Outdoor seating. **$$**

★ ★ ★ **LE BISTRO.** *41 Bowen's Wharf, Newport (02840). Phone 401/849-7778. www.lebistronewport .com.* This casually elegant bistro on Bowmen's Wharf has been serving fresh, flavorful New England specialties and classic French food for decades. French menu. Lunch, dinner. Bar to 1 am. **$$$**
🅳

★ **RHODE ISLAND QUAHOG COMPANY.** *250 Thames St, Newport (02840). Phone 401/848-2330. www.quahog.com.* A friendly staff awaits diners at this American pub-style eatery. The large bar area features many beers on tap, and entertainment is offered Thursday through Saturday. Seafood menu. Lunch, dinner. Closed Jan and Feb. Bar. Children's menu. Casual attire. Reservations recommended. Outdoor seating. **$$**

★ ★ ★ **WHITE HORSE TAVERN.** *26 Marlborough St, Newport (02840). Phone 401/849-3600. www.whitehorsetavern.com.* Located in a building that dates to 1687, this cozy restaurant has exposed hand-hewn beams, open fireplaces, and a romantic atmosphere. The menu is a blend of regional New England dishes. American menu. Lunch, dinner, Sun brunch. Bar. Business casual attire. Reservations recommended. **$$$**
🅳

North Kingstown (D-6)

See also Kingston, Providence, Warwick

Settled 1641
Population 23,786
Elevation 51 ft
Area Code 401
Zip 02852
Information North Kingstown Chamber of Commerce, 8045 Post Rd; phone 401/295-5566
Web Site www.northkingstown.com

North Kingstown was originally part of a much larger area named for King Charles II. The settlement was divided in 1722, creating North Kingstown and South Kingstown, as well as other townships.

What to See and Do

Casey Farm. *2325 Boston Neck Rd, Saunderstown (02874). 3 1/2 miles S on Hwy 1A (past Jamestown Bridge approach). Phone 401/295-1030.* (Circa 1750) Once the site of Revolutionary War activities, this farm was built and continuously occupied by the Casey family for 200 years. Views of Narrangansett Bay and Conanicut Island. Restored and operating farm with animals, organic gardens; 18th-century farmhouse with family paintings, furnishings; outbuildings. (June-mid-Oct, Sat 11 am-5 pm) **$**

Gilbert Stuart Birthplace. *815 Gilbert Stuart Rd, North Kingstown (02874). 5 miles S off Hwy 1A, NW of Saunderstown. Phone 401/294-3001. www.gilbertstuart-musuem.com.* Birthplace of portraitist Gilbert Stuart (1755-1828). Antique furnishings; snuffmill powered by wooden waterwheel; partially restored gristmill. Guided tours (half hour). (Apr-Oct, Thurs-Mon 11 am-4 pm) **$$**

Main Street, Wickford Village. *North Kingstown. E from center. Phone 401/295-5566. www.wickfordvillage. org.* There are 20 houses built before 1804; on side streets are 40 more.

Old Narragansett Church. *Church Ln, Wickford (02874). Church Ln. Phone 401/294-4357. www.episcopalri. org/org_onc.cfm.* (1707) Episcopal. Tours. (July-Aug, Thurs-Mon 11 am-4 pm)

Smith's Castle. *55 Richard Smith Dr, Wickford (02852). 1 1/2 miles N on Hwy 1. Phone 401/294-3521. www. smithscastle.org.* (1678) Blockhouse (circa 1638), destroyed by fire in 1676 and rebuilt in 1678, is one of the oldest plantation houses in the country and the only known existing house where Roger Williams preached; 17th- and 18th-century furnishings; 18th-century garden. (June-Aug: Mon, Thurs-Sun, afternoons; May, Sept-Oct: Fri-Sun, afternoons; also by appointment) **$**

Special Events

Festival of Lights. *Wickford Village, North Kingstown. Phone 401/295-5566. www.wickfordvillage.org/ special_festivaloflights.html.* House tours, hayrides. First weekend in Dec.

Wickford Art Festival. *Wickford Village, 36 Beach St, North Kingstown (02852). Phone 401/294-6840. www. wickfordart.org.* Approximately 250 artists and artisans from around the country. Second weekend in July.

Pawtucket (D-6)

See also Providence

Settled 1671
Population 72,644
Elevation 73 ft
Area Code 401
Information Blackstone Valley Tourism Council, 175 Main St, 02860; phone 401/724-2200 or toll-free 800/454-2882 (outside RI)
Web Site www.tourblackstone.com

This highly concentrated industrial center, first settled by an ironworker who set up a forge at the falls on the Blackstone River, is recognized by historians as the birthplace of the Industrial Revolution in America. It was here in Pawtucket, named for the Native American phrase "falls of the water," that Samuel Slater founded the nation's first water-powered cotton mill. The town has since become one of the largest cities in the state and a major producer of textiles, machinery, wire, glass, and plastics.

What to See and Do

Slater Memorial Park. *Newport Ave and Hwy 1A, Pawtucket (02862). Phone 401/722-6931.* Within 200-acre park are sunken gardens; Rhode Island Watercolor Association Gallery (Tues-Sun); historical Daggett House (fee); carousel (July-Labor Day: daily; fee). Tennis, playing fields, picnicking. **FREE**

Slater Mill National Historic Site. *67 Roosevelt Ave, Pawtucket (02862). Phone 401/725-8638; fax 401/722-3040. www.slatermill.org.* Nation's first water-powered cotton mill (1793) was built by Samuel Slater; on-site are also Wilkinson Mill (1810) and Sylvanus Brown House (1758). Mill features restored water-power system, including raceways and 8-ton wheel; operating machines; spinning and weaving demonstrations; slide show. (June-Labor Day: daily; Mar-May and after Labor Day-mid Dec: daily; closed holidays) **$$**

Special Events

Arts in the Park Performance Series. *Slater Memorial Park, Newport Ave and Hwy 1A, Pawtucket (02862). www.pawtucketri.com.* Tues-Thurs and Sun, July-Aug.

Octoberfest Parade and Craft Fair. *Pawtucket.* First weekend in Oct.

Pawtucket Red Sox. *McCoy Stadium, 1 Ben Mondor Way, Pawtucket (02860). Phone 401/724-7300. www. pawsox.com.* AAA farm team of the Boston Red Sox.

St. Patrick's Day Parade. *Pawtucket. Phone 401/728-0500. www.pawtucketri.com.* First weekend in Mar.

Portsmouth (D-7)

See also Bristol, Little Compton, Newport

Founded 1638
Population 16,857
Elevation 122 ft
Area Code 401
Zip 02871
Information Newport County Convention and Visitor's Bureau, 23 America's Cup Ave, Newport 02840; phone 401/849-8048 or toll-free 800/976-5122
Web Site www.gonewport.com

Originally called Pocasset, Portsmouth was settled by a group led by John Clarke and William Coddington, who were sympathizers of Anne Hutchinson of Massachusetts. Soon after the town was first begun, Anne Hutchinson herself, with a number of fellow religious exiles, settled here and forced Clarke and Coddington to relinquish control. Coddington then went south and founded Newport, with which Portsmouth temporarily united in 1640. Fishing, shipbuilding, and coal mining were the earliest sources of revenue. Today, Portsmouth is a summer resort area.

> ### Portsmouth Fun Fact
>
> Portsmouth is home to the oldest schoolhouse in the United States. It was built in 1716.

What to See and Do

Butterfly Zoo. *409 Bulgarmarsh Rd, Tiverton (02878). Phone 401/849-9519. www.community-2.webtv.net/ butterflyzoo/doc2.* The only New England operation that breeds, raises, releases, and sells butterflies. View a wide variety of butterflies, including a preserved specimen of one believed to be the world's largest. (Memorial Day-Labor Day: Mon-Sat 11 am-4 pm, Sun noon-4 pm) **$$**

★ **Green Animals.** *Portsmouth (02871). Off Hwy 114. Phone 401/683-1267. www.newportmansions.org.* Topiary gardens planted in 1880 with California privet, golden boxwood, and American boxwood sculpted into animal forms, geometric figures, and ornamental designs; also rose garden, formal flower beds. Children's toy collection in main house. (Apr-Nov, daily) **$$$**

Prescott Farm and Windmill. *2009 W Main Rd (Hwy 114), Middletown (02842). Phone 401/847-6230. www. newportrestoration.com.* Restored buildings include an operating windmill (circa 1810), General Prescott's guard house, and a country store stocked with items grown on the farm. (May-Oct ,Mon-Fri 10 am-4 pm). **$**

Restaurant

★ ★ ★ **SEA FARE INN.** *3352 E Main Rd, Portsmouth (02842). Phone 401/683-0577; fax 401/683-2910. www.seafareinn.com.* Dine on chef George Karousos's creative cuisine in one of the seven dining rooms of this 1887 Victorian inn. White linen tablecloths, fine silver, and friendly service make for a most enjoyable evening. American menu. Dinner. Closed Mon; Jan 1, Dec 24-25. Bar. Children's menu. Business casual attire. Reservations recommended. **$$$**

Providence (D-6)

See also Fall River, Bristol, North Kingstown, Pawtucket, Warwick

Settled 1636
Population 160,728
Elevation 24 ft
Area Code 401
Information Providence Warwick Convention & Visitors Bureau, One W Exchange St, 02903; phone 401/274-1636 or toll-free 800/233-1636
Web Site www.pwcvb.com

Grateful that God's providence had led him to this spot, Roger Williams founded a town and named it accordingly. More than three-and-a-half centuries later, Providence is the capital and largest city of the State of Rhode Island and Providence Plantations, the state's official title.

In its early years, Providence was a farm center. Through the great maritime epoch of the late 18th century and first half of the 19th century, clipper ships sailed from Providence to China and the West Indies. During the 19th century, the city became a great industrial center, which today still produces widely

known Providence jewelry and silverware. Providence is also an important port of entry.

Providence's long history has created a blend of old and new: modern hotels and office buildings share the streets with historic houses. Benefit Street, overlooking Providence's modern financial district, has one of the largest concentrations of colonial houses in America. The city's location along the upper Narragansett Bay and numerous cultural opportunities each provide many varied attractions for the visitor. In addition, Providence is the southern point of the Blackstone River Valley National Heritage Corridor, a 250,000-acre region that extends to Worcester, Massachusetts (see).

What to See and Do

Arcade. *65 Weybosset St, Providence (02903). Phone 401/861-9150; fax 401/621-7363. www.pwcvb.com.* (1828) First indoor shopping mall with national landmark status. More than 35 specialty shops; restaurants.

Brown University. *45 Prospect St, Providence (02912). Phone 401/863-2378; fax 401/863-9300. www.brown. edu.* (1764) (7,500 students) Founded as Rhode Island College; school was renamed for Nicholas Brown, a major benefactor and son of a founder, in 1804. Brown is the seventh-oldest college in the United States and a member of the Ivy League. Pembroke College for Women (1891), named for the Cambridge, England *alma mater* of Roger Williams, merged with the men's college in 1971. Guided tours. **FREE** Here are

> **Annmary Brown Memorial.** *21 Brown St, Providence (02912). N of Charlesfield St. Phone 401/863-2942.* (1907) Paintings; Brown family memorabilia. (Labor Day-Memorial Day, Mon-Fri 1-5 pm) **FREE**
>
> **David Winton Bell Gallery.** *List Art Center, 64 College St, Providence (02908). Phone 401/863-2932; fax 401/863-9323.* (1971) Historical and contemporary exhibitions. (Mon-Fri 11 am-4 pm, Sat-Sun 1-4 pm; closed Thanksgiving, Dec 25, July 4) **FREE**
>
> **John Carter Brown Library.** *Brown University, George and Brown sts, Providence (02912). S side of campus green. Phone 401/863-2725.* (1904) Library houses exhibits, books, and maps relating to the exploration and settlement of America. (Mon-Fri 8:30 am-5 pm, Sat 9 am-noon; closed school vacations) **FREE**

John Hay Library. *20 Prospect St, Providence (02912). Across from Van Wickle gates. Phone 401/863-2146; fax 401/863-2093.* (1910) Named for Lincoln's secretary, John Hay (Brown, 1858), library houses extensive special collections including Lincoln manuscripts, the Harris collection of American poetry and plays, and university archives. (Mon-Fri) **FREE**

Rockefeller Library. *10 Prospect St, Providence (02912). Phone 401/863-2167; fax 401/863-1272.* (1964) Named for John D. Rockefeller Jr. (Brown, 1897), library houses collections in the social sciences, humanities, and fine arts. (Daily; closed school vacations) **FREE**

University Hall. *1 Prospect St, Providence (02912). Phone 401/863-1000.* (1770) The original "college edifice" serves as the main administration building.

Wriston Quadrangle. *Providence (02912). On Brown St near John Carter Brown Library. Phone 401/863-2378.* (1952) Square named for president-emeritus Henry M. Wriston.

Cathedral of St. John. *271 N Main St, Providence (02903). At Church St. Phone 401/331-4622. www.episcopalri.org.* (1810) This Georgian structure with Gothic detail was built on the site of King's Church (1722). (Daily) **FREE**

First Baptist Church in America. *75 N Main St, Providence (02903). At Waterman St. Phone 401/454-3418; fax 401/421-4095. www.fbcia.org.* Oldest Baptist congregation in America, established in 1638; the present building was erected by Joseph Brown in 1775. Sun morning service. Guided tours. (June-Columbus Day: Mon-Fri 10 am-noon, 1-4pm; Sat 10 am-1 pm; Sun 11:15 am after the 10 am service; closed holidays) **$**

First Unitarian Church. *1 Benevolent St, Providence (02906). Phone 401/421-7970; fax 401/276-4291. www.firstunitarianprov.org.* (1816) Organized as First Congregational Church in 1720, the church was designed by John Holden Greene and has the largest bell ever cast by Paul Revere. **FREE**

Governor Stephen Hopkins House. *15 Hopkins St, Providence (02903). Opposite courthouse. Phone 401/421-0694.* (1707) House of signer of Declaration of Independence and ten-time governor of Rhode Island; 18th-century garden; period furnishings. (Apr-Dec: Wed, Sat 1-4 pm, also by appointment) Children only with adult. **DONATION**

John Brown House. *52 Power St, Providence (02906). At Benefit St. Phone 401/273-7507; fax 401/751-2307. www.rihs.org.* (1786) Georgian masterpiece by Joseph Brown, brother of John. George Washington was among the guests entertained in this house. Museum of 18th-century china, glass, Rhode Island antiques, and paintings; John Brown's chariot (1782), perhaps the oldest American-made vehicle extant. Guided tours. (Jan-Apr: Fri-Sat 10:30 am-4:30 pm; May-Dec: Tues-Sat 10:30 am-4:30 pm; closed holidays) **$$** The historical society also maintains a

Library. *121 Hope St, Providence (02906). At Power St. Phone 401/273-8107; fax 401/751-7930.* One of the largest genealogical collections in New England; Rhode Island imprints dating to 1727; newspapers, manuscripts, photographs, films. (Wed, Fri 10 am-5 pm; Thurs noon-8 pm; closed holidays) **$**

Johnson & Wales University. *8 Abbott Park Pl, Providence (02903). Phone 401/598-1000. www.jwu.edu.* (1914) (8,000 students) Two- and four-year degree programs are offered in business, hospitality, food service, and technology. Tours available by appointment Mon-Fri (free). On campus is the

Culinary Archives & Museum. *315 Harborside Blvd, Providence (02905). Trade Center at Harborside Campus. Phone 401/598-2805; fax 401/598-2807.* Dubbed the "Smithsonian of the food service industry," this museum contains more than 200,000 items related to the fields of culinary arts and hospitality collected and donated by Chicago's chef Louis Szathmary. Includes rare US presidential culinary autographs; tools of the trade from the third millennium BC; Egyptian, Roman, and Asian spoons more than 1,000 years old; gallery of chefs; original artwork; hotel and restaurant silver; and periodicals related to the field. Guided tours. (Tues-Sun 10 am-5 pm; closed holidays and late Dec) **$$**

Lincoln Woods State Park. *2 Manchester Print Works Rd, Providence (02865). 5 miles N via Hwy 146, S of Breakneck Hill Rd. Phone 401/723-7892.* More than 600 acres. Swimming, bathhouse, freshwater ponds, fishing, boating; hiking and bridle trails, ice skating, picnicking, concession. Fees for some activities.

Museum of Rhode Island History at Aldrich House. *110 Benevolent St, Providence (02906). Phone 401/331-8575; fax 401/351-0127. www.rihs.org.* Exhibits on Rhode Island's history. Headquarters for Rhode Island

Historical Society. By appointment only (Tues-Fri; closed Jan 1, Thanksgiving, Dec 25) **$$$**

North Burial Ground. *N Main St (Hwy1), Providence. 1 mile N of Market Sq.* Phone 401/331-0177. Graves of Roger Williams and other settlers. **FREE**

Old State House. *150 Benefit St, Providence (02903).* Phone 401/222-2678. Where the General Assembly of Rhode Island met between 1762 and 1900. Independence was proclaimed in the Old State House two months before the Declaration was signed in Philadelphia. (Mon-Fri; closed holidays) **FREE**

Providence Athenaeum Library. *251 Benefit St, Providence (02903).* Phone 401/421-6970; fax 401/421-2860. *www.providenceathenaeum.org.* (1753) One of the oldest subscription libraries in the United States; housed in a Greek Revival building designed by William Strickland in 1836. Rare book room includes original Audubon elephant folios; small art collection. (Sept-May: Mon-Thurs 9 am-7 pm, Fri-Sat to 5 pm, Sun 1-5 pm; June-Labor Day: Mon-Thurs 9 am-7 pm, Fri to 5 pm, Sat to 1 pm; closed holidays, first two weeks in Aug) Tours. **FREE**

Providence Children's Museum. *100 South St, Providence (02903).* Phone 401/273-5437; fax 401/273-1004. *www.childrenmuseum.org.* Many hands-on exhibits, including a time-travel adventure through Rhode Island's multicultural history, wet-and-wild exploration of water, and hands-on geometry lab. Traveling exhibits. Weekly programs. Gift shop. (Sept-March: Tues-Sun 9 am-6 pm; April-Labor Day: daily 9 am-6 pm) **$$**

Providence Preservation Society. *21 Meeting St, Providence (02903).* Phone 401/831-7440; fax 401/831-8583. *www.ppsri.org.* The Providence Preservation Society offers brochures and tour booklets for several historic Providence neighborhoods. (Mon-Fri) **$$**

Rhode Island School of Design. *2 College St, Providence (02903).* Phone 401/454-6100. *www.risd.edu.* (1877) (1,960 students) One of the country's leading art and design schools. Tours. On campus are

RISD Museum. *224 Benefit St, Providence (02903).* Phone 401/454-6500; fax 401/454-6556. Collections range from ancient to contemporary. (Tues-Sun; closed holidays) **$$**

Woods-Gerry Gallery. *Rhode Island School of Design, 62 Prospect St, Providence (02906).* Phone 401/454-6141. Mansion built 1860-1863 has special exhibits by students, faculty, and alumni. Call to confirm schedule. **FREE**

Rhode Island State House. *82 Smith St, Providence (02903).* Phone 401/222-2357. *www.state.ri.us.* Capitol by McKim, Mead, and White was completed in 1901. Building contains a Gilbert Stuart full-length portrait of George Washington and the original parchment charter granted to Rhode Island by Charles II in 1663. *Independent Man* statue on dome. Guided tours. Building (Mon-Fri 9-11 am; closed holidays and second Mon in Aug). **FREE**

Roger Williams National Memorial. *282 N Main St, Providence (02903).* Phone 401/521-7266. This 4 1/2-acre park, at the site of the old town spring, commemorates founding of Providence and contributions made by Roger Williams to civil and religious liberty; slide presentation, exhibit. (Daily; closed Jan 1, Dec 25) **FREE**

Roger Williams Park. *1000 Elmwood Ave, Providence (02907). 3 miles S on Elmwood Ave.* Phone 401/785-9450. *www.providenceri.com/government/parks.* The park has 430 acres of woodlands, waterways, and winding drives. Japanese garden, Betsy Williams's cottage, and greenhouses. (Daily; closed Jan 1, Thanksgiving, Dec 25) **FREE** Also in the park are

Museum of Natural History and Cormack Planetarium. *1000 Elmwood Ave, Providence (02907).* Phone 401/785-9450. Anthropology, geology, astronomy, and biology displays; educational and performing arts programs. (Daily 10 am-5 pm; closed Jan 1, Thanksgiving, Dec 25; planetarium: Sept-June Sat-Sun, July-Aug Tues-Sun) **$**

Roger Williams Park Zoo. *1000 Elmwood Ave, Providence (02907).* Phone 401/785-3510. Children's nature center, tropical building, African plains exhibit; Marco Polo exhibits; over 600 animals. Educational programs; tours. (Daily; closed Dec 25) **$$**

Special Events

Spring Festival of Historic Houses. *21 Meeting St, Providence (02903).* Phone 401/831-7440; fax 401/831-8583. *www.ppsri.org.* Sponsored by the Providence Preservation Society. Tours of selected private houses and gardens. Third weekend in June. **FREE**

WaterFire. *Waterplace Park, 101 Regent Ave, Providence (02908).* Phone 401/272-3111. *www.waterfire.org.* Floating bonfires in the Providence River accompanied by music. Call for schedule. Lightings, weekends, late May-late Oct. **FREE**

Limited-Service Hotels

★ ★ COURTYARD BY MARRIOTT PROVIDENCE DOWNTOWN. *32 Exchange Terr, Providence (02903). Phone 401/272-1191; toll-free 800/321-2211; fax 401/272-1416. www.courtyard.com.* Situated in the heart of downtown Providence, the Courtyard overlooks Water Place Park and is near Providence Place Mall, the area's premier shopping center. Accommodations are roomy and comfortable and include desks for business travelers and beds with down comforters and fluffy pillows. 216 rooms, 7 story. Check-in 3 pm, check-out noon. High-speed Internet access, wireless Internet access. Bar. Fitness room. Indoor pool, whirlpool. Business center. **$**

★ ★ JOHNSON & WALES INN. *213 Taunton Ave, Seekonk (02771). Phone 508/336-8700; toll-free 800/232-1772; fax 508/336-3414. www.jwinn.com.* 86 rooms, 5 story. Check-in 3 pm, check-out 11 am. Restaurant, bar. Business center. **$**

★ ★ RADISSON HOTEL PROVIDENCE HARBOR. *220 India St, Providence (02903). Phone 401/272-5577; toll-free 800/333-3333; fax 401/272-0251. www.radisson.com/providenceri.* Guests of the Radisson Hotel Providence Harbor will find rooms with harbor views and many convenient amenities, such as data ports, coffee makers, irons and ironing boards, work desks, and, in Business Class rooms, a fax/printer/copier. 136 rooms, 6 story. Check-in 3 pm, check-out 11 am. High-speed Internet access, wireless Internet access. Restaurant, bar. Fitness room. Whirlpool. Business center. **$$**

Full-Service Hotels

★ ★ ★ MARRIOTT PROVIDENCE. *1 Orms St, Providence (02904). Phone 401/272-2400; toll-free 800/937-7768; fax 401/273-2686. www.marriottprovidence. com.* Guests at the Marriott Providence are treated to the best of both worlds—a great location and beautifully appointed accommodations. Its downtown location allows guests to be just steps from Newport shopping, entertainment, and a charming neighborhood of Colonial homes, while comfortable and contemporary rooms include plush beds with duvets, soft linens, and a pillow menu; large arms chairs with ottomans; swiveling desks; high-speed Internet access; and two-line phones. The hotel provides evening activi-

ties the whole family can enjoy, such as scavenger hunts and poolside sand art. 351 rooms, 6 story. Pets accepted, some restrictions; fee. Check-in 3 pm, check-out noon. High-speed Internet access. Restaurant, bar. Fitness room. Indoor pool, outdoor pool, whirlpool. Airport transportation available. Business center. **$$**

★ ★ ★ THE WESTIN PROVIDENCE. *1 W Exchange St, Providence (02903). Phone 401/598-8000; toll-free 800/301-1111; fax 401/598-8200. www.starwood.com.* Enclosed sky bridges connect this Westin to the Rhode Island Convention Center and Providence Place, the city's major downtown mall. Contemporary and graciously appointed, the hotel offers an extensive array of services and amenities to guests; rooms include the Starwood's "Heavenly Bed" with plush white duvets and an extensive pillow menu, cordless phones, safes, robes, mini-bars, flat-screen TVs, and the "Heavenly Bath," with dual head showers and extra-large towels. The hotel's "Love That Dog" program welcomes pets with bowls, treats, and their very own "Heavenly Dog Bed." 364 rooms, 25 story. Pets accepted, some restrictions; fee. Check-in 3 pm, check-out noon. High-speed Internet access. Restaurant, bar. Fitness room, fitness classes available. Indoor pool, whirlpool. Business center. **$$**

Specialty Lodgings

CHRISTOPHER DODGE HOUSE. *11 W Park St, Providence (02908). Phone 401/351-6111; fax 401/351-4261. www.providence-hotel.com.* Housed in a three-story brick building constructed in 1856, the Christopher Dodge House remains true to its 19th century roots. Elegant period décor is found throughout the property, with rooms that include hardwood floors, fireplaces, and four-poster canopy beds. While retaining its old-world charm, this bed-and-breakfast meets needs of the contemporary traveler with high-speed Internet access, TVs, and VCRs, and kitchenettes. 8 rooms, 3 story. Complimentary full breakfast. Check-in 2 pm, check-out 11 am. High-speed Internet access, wireless Internet access. **$**

HISTORIC JACOB HILL INN. *120 Jacob St, Providence (02940). Phone 508/336-9165; toll-free 888/336-9165; fax 508/336-0951. www.jacobhillinn. com.* 10 rooms, all suites. No children under 13. Complimentary full breakfast. Check-in 3-9 pm, check-out 11 am. Outdoor pool. Tennis. **$$$**

Restaurants

★ ★ **ADESSO.** *161 Cushing St, Providence (02906). Phone 401/521-0770; fax 401/521-1777. www. zerotosixfigures.com/adesso.* California, Italian menu. Lunch, dinner, late-night. Closed July 4, Thanksgiving, Dec 25. Bar. Casual attire. Reservations recommended. Valet parking. **$$$**

★ **THE CACTUS GRILLE.** *800 Allens Ave, Providence (02905). Phone 401/941-0004; fax 401/941-0175.* Mexican menu. Lunch, dinner. Closed Dec 25. Bar. Children's menu. Casual attire. **$$**

★ ★ **HEMENWAY'S SEAFOOD GRILL.** *121 S Main St, Providence (02903). Phone 401/351-8570; fax 401/351-8570. www.hemenwaysrestaurant.com.* Seafood menu. Lunch, dinner. Bar. Children's menu. Casual attire. Reservations recommended. Valet parking. Outdoor seating. **$$**

★ ★ ★ **MILL'S TAVERN.** *101 N Main St, Providence (02903). Phone 401/272-3331.* Mill's Tavern has a knack for improving on the classics. From its smart design and young, energetic vibe to its appealing menu, this winning restaurant housed in a former mill turns tradition on its head. The hurricane-lamp chandeliers, exposed beams, and wharf mosaic are a nod to the taverns of the past, while the marble-topped bar and open kitchen are decidedly modern. The menu echoes the classic-contemporary sentiment with a wide variety of creatively prepared seasonal dishes, many utilizing the dream kitchens wood-burning oven, wood grill, and rotisserie. Part comfort food, part nouveau cuisine, this menu dazzles the palate with its whimsical pairings and simple yet sophisticated preparations. A raw bar rounds out the offerings, while those in the know save room for dessert. The warm, knowledgeable staff is the perfect complement to this casually elegant restaurant, providing professional and thorough service without being stuffy or intrusive. American menu. Dinner. Business casual attire. Reservations recommended. Valet parking. **$$$** 🅳

★ ★ **PANE E VINO.** *365 Atwells Ave, Providence (02903). Phone 401/223-2230; fax 401/223-4322. www. panevino.net.* Italian menu. Dinner. Closed holidays. Bar. Business casual attire. Reservations recommended. Valet parking. **$$$**

★ ★ ★ **POT AU FEU.** *44 Custom House St, Providence (02903). Phone 401/273-8953; fax 401/273-8963. www.potaufeuri.com.* This restaurant, which specializes in classic and regional French dishes, features a casual, bistro-style dining room downstairs and a more formal room upstairs. French bistro menu. Lunch, dinner. Closed Sun; holidays. Bar. Business casual attire. Reservations recommended. **$$** 🅳

Warwick (D-6)

See also East Greenwich, North Kingstown, Providence

Population 85,427
Elevation 64 ft
Area Code 401
Information Department of Economic Development, City Hall, 3275 Post Rd, 02886; phone 401/738-2000 or toll-free 800/492-7942
Web Site www.warwickri.com

Warwick, the second-largest city in Rhode Island, is the location of T. F. Green Airport, the state's largest commercial airport. With 39 miles of coastline on Narragansett Bay, the city has more than 15 marinas. Warwick is a major retail and industrial center. The geographic diversity of Warwick promoted a decentralized pattern of settlement, which gave rise to a number of small villages including Pawtuxet, Cowesett, and Conanicut.

What to See and Do

Goddard Memorial State Park. *345 Ives Rd, Warwick (02818). E side of Greenwich Cove, E of town via Forge and Ives rds. Phone 401/884-2010.* Approximately 490 acres with swimming at Greenwich Bay Beach (bathhouse), fishing, boating; bridle trails, nine-hole golf (fee), ice skating, picnicking, concessions, playing fields, and fireplaces (fee). **$**

Walking Tour of Historic Apponaug Village. *3275 Post Rd, Warwick (02886). Phone toll-free 800/492-7942. www.visitwarwickri.com.* More than 30 structures of historic and/or architectural interest are noted on walking tour brochure available through the Department of Economic Development, Warwick City Hall, 3275 Post Rd, Warwick 02886. **FREE**

Warwick Mall. *400 Bald Hill Rd, Warwick (02886). Phone 401/739-7500. www.warwickmall.com.* Renovated and expanded; largest mall in the state. More than 90 specialty shops and four department stores. Outdoor patio, video wall, topiary gardens. Weekly special events. (Daily)

Special Events

Gaspee Days. *Phone 401/781-1772; toll-free 800/492-7942. www.gaspee.com.* Celebration of the capture and burning of British revenue schooner *Gaspee* by Rhode Island patriots; arts and crafts, concert, footraces, battle reenactment, fife and drum corps muster, parade, contests. May-June.

Warwick Heritage Festival. *Warwick City Park, Warwick. Phone 401/738-2000; toll-free 800/492-7942. www.visitwarwickri.com.* Revisit history with this weekend reenactment. Nov, Veterans Day weekend.

Limited-Service Hotel

★ ★ **RADISSON AIRPORT HOTEL WARWICK / PROVIDENCE.** *2081 Post Rd, Warwick (02886). Phone 401/739-3000; toll-free 800/333-3333; fax 401/732-9309. www.radisson.com/warwickri.* As the practical education facility of Johnson and Wales University, a culinary and hospitality school, the Radisson Airport Hotel offers guests professional and attentive service. Guest rooms are comfortable and spacious and feature amenities that meet all guest needs, including high-speed Internet access, work desks, sofas, coffee makers, irons and ironing boards, TV with cable, and spacious closets. Complimentary 24-hour shuttle service is provided to and from T.F. Green State Airport, located directly across from the hotel. 111 rooms. Complimentary continental breakfast. Check-in 3 pm, check-out noon. High-speed Internet access. Restaurant, bar. Airport transportation available. Business center. **$$**

🛫

Full-Service Hotel

★ ★ ★ **CROWNE PLAZA.** *801 Greenwich Ave, Warwick (02886). Phone 401/732-6000; toll-free 800/227-6963; fax 401/732-4839. www.ichotelsgroup.com/h/d/cp/1/en/hd/wrwri.* This large airport hotel is located in the suburban city of Warwick, just south of Providence, at "The Crossings," at the junction of Routes 5 and 113. Attractive guest rooms feature marble baths, a work desk, CD players, bathrobes, and luxurious bath amenities, as well as thoughtful touches like the sleep amenity package, which includes an eye mask, drape clip, ear plugs, lavender spray, and a night light. 266 rooms, 6 story.Check-in 3 pm, check-out 11 am. High-speed Internet access. Restaurant, bar. Fitness room. Indoor pool, whirlpool. Airport transportation available. Business center. **$$**

🐾 🧖 🏊 🚶

Westerly (E-5)

See also Block Island, Charlestown

Founded 1669
Population 21,605
Elevation 50 ft
Area Code 401
Zip 02891
Information Westerly-Pawcatuck Area Chamber of Commerce, 1 Chamber Way; phone 401/596-7761 or toll-free 800/732-7636; or the South County Tourism Council, Stedman Government Center, 4808 Tower Hill Rd, Wakefield 02879; phone 401/789-4422 or toll-free 800/548-4662
Web Site www.westerlychamber.org

Westerly, one of the oldest towns in the state, was at one time known for its nearby granite quarries. Today, local industries include textiles, the manufacture of fishing line, and tourism.

What to See and Do

Babcock-Smith House. *124 Granite St, Westerly (02891). Phone 401/596-5704. www.babcock-smithhouse.com.* (Circa 1732) This two-story, gambrel-roofed Georgian mansion was residence of Dr. Joshua Babcock, Westerly's first physician and friend of Benjamin Franklin. Later it was home to Orlando Smith, who discovered granite on the grounds. Furniture collection covers 200 years; toys date to 1890s; colonial garden and culinary herb garden. (June-Sept: Fri-Sat afternoon; otherwise by appointment) **$**

Misquamicut State Beach. *257 Atlantic Ave, Westerly (02891). 5 miles S off Hwy 1A. Phone 401/596-9097. www.riparks.com/misquamicut.htm.* Swimming, bathhouse (fee), fishing nearby; picnicking, concession. (Memorial Day-Labor Day, daily 9 am-6 pm) Parking fee. **$$$**

Watch Hill. *Watch Hill, Westerly. 6 miles S on Beach St, via Avondale. Phone 401/596-7761. www.westerlychamber.org.* Historical community of handsome summer houses, many dating from the 1870s; picturesque sea views. Located here are

Flying Horse Carousel. *Watch Hill, Westerly. Phone 401/596-7761.* Original amusement ride built in 1867. **$**

Watch Hill Lighthouse. *Watch Hill, 14 Lighthouse Rd, Westerly (02891). Phone 401/596-7761.* (1856) Granite lighthouse built to replace wooden one built in 1807; lit by oil lamp until 1933, when replaced by electric. Museum exhibit (July-Aug: Tues, Thurs 1-3 pm). **FREE**

Limited-Service Hotels

★ **BREEZEWAY RESORT.** *70 Winnapaug Rd, Misquamicut Beach (02891). Phone 401/348-8953; toll-free 800/462-8872. www.breezewayresort.com.* A great family lodging for visitors to Rhode Island's south shore, the Breezeway Resort offers guests a large pool, children's play area, shuffleboard, and a picnic area. Although standard guest rooms are fairly basic, they are clean and comfortable and feature air conditioning, refrigerators, and TVs, while suites feature Jacuzzi tubs, wet bars, and microwave ovens. 50 rooms, 2 story. Complimentary continental breakfast. Check-in 3 pm, check-out 11 am. Wireless Internet access. Restaurant. Children's activity center. Outdoor pool. **$$**
🔲 ⛵

★ ★ **SHELTER HARBOR INN.** *10 Wagner Rd, Westerly (02891). Phone 401/322-8883; toll-free 800/468-8883; fax 401/322-7907. www.shelterharborinn. com.* This relaxing country inn is off the beaten path, but well worth the detour. The main house—a sprawling, 1810 farmhouse—manages to be cozy and inviting. A private beach on Rhode Island Sound (for which a complimentary shuttle is offered), a full-service restaurant on-site, and an abundance of outdoor activities like paddle tennis, croquet, bocce ball, and a putting green are just a few things that will keep guests busy. Curling up in front of the fireplace with a book from the inns library or exploring Shelter Harbor's grounds are ways for guests to enjoy some quieter moments. 24 rooms, 2 story. Complimentary full breakfast. Check-in 2 pm, check-out 11 am. Restaurant, bar. Tennis. **$**
🎾

★ **WINNAPAUG INN.** *169 Shore Rd, Westerly (02891). Phone 401/348-8350; toll-free 800/288-9906; fax 401/596-8654. www.winnapauginn.com.* Winnapaug Pond is adjacent. 49 rooms. Complimentary continental breakfast. Check-in 3-6 pm, check-out 11 am. **$**
🔲 ⛵

Specialty Lodging

VILLA BED & BREAKFAST. *190 Shore Rd, Westerly (02891). Phone 401/596-1054; toll-free 800/722-9240; fax 401/596-6268. www.thevillaatwesterly.com.* Flower gardens, Italian porticos, and verandas add to the romantic feel of this charming bed-and-breakfast, modeled after a small, seaside Mediterranean inn. Guest rooms are housed in the main villa and in the poolside Carriage House; all feature Jacuzzi tubs, bath robes, coffee makers, and VCRs, and some include fireplaces, DVD players, and flat-screen TVs. The complimentary breakfast can be enjoyed in the dining area or by the pool. Close by is Misquamicut Beach, the Foxwoods Casino, the Mystic Aquarium and the ferry to Block Island. 8 rooms, 3 story. No children allowed. Complimentary full breakfast. Check-in 3 pm, check-out 11 am. Outdoor pool, whirlpool. **$$$**
🔲 ⛵

Vermont

Vermont was the last New England state to be settled. The earliest permanent settlement date is believed to be 1724. Ethan Allen and his Green Mountain Boys made Vermont famous when they took Fort Ticonderoga from the British in 1775. Claimed by both New York and New Hampshire, Vermont framed a constitution in 1777. It was the first state to prohibit slavery and the first to provide universal male suffrage, regardless of property or income. For 14 years, Vermont was an independent republic, running its own postal service, coining its own money, naturalizing citizens of other states and countries, and negotiating with other states and nations. Vermont became the 14th state in 1791.

Although Vermont is usually thought of as a farm state, more than 17 percent of the labor force is in manufacturing. Machinery, food, wood, plastic, rubber, paper, electrical, and electronic products are made here. Dairy products lead the farm list, with sheep, maple sugar and syrup, and apples and potatoes following. Vermont leads the nation in its yield of marble and granite; limestone, slate, and talc are also quarried and mined.

Tall steeples dominate the towns, forests, mountains, and countryside where one can walk the 260-mile Long Trail along the Green Mountain crests. Vermont has one of the highest concentrations of alpine ski areas and cross-country ski touring centers in the nation. Fishing and hunting are excellent; resorts range from rustic to elegant.

When to Go/Climate

Vermont enjoys four distinct seasons. Comfortable summers are followed by brilliantly colored falls and typically cold New England winters.

Population: 562,758
Area: 9, 273 square miles
Elevation: 95-4, 393 feet
Peak: Mount Mansfield (Lamoille County)
Entered Union: March 4, 1791 (14th state)
Capital: Montpelier
Motto: Freedom and Unity
Nickname: Green Mountain State
Flower: Red Clover
Bird: Hermit Thrush
Tree: Sugar Maple
Time Zone: Eastern
Web Site: www.travel-vermont.com
Fun Facts:
- Vermont produces the largest amount of maple syrup in the United States.
- The first Ben and Jerry's Ice Cream store opened in Burlington in 1978.

Heavy snowfall makes for good skiing in winter, while spring thaws bring on the inevitable muddy months. Summer and fall are popular times to visit.

AVERAGE HIGH/LOW TEMPERATURES (°F)

Burlington

Jan 25/8	May 67/45	Sept 69/49
Feb 28/9	June 76/55	Oct 57/39
Mar 39/22	July 81/60	Nov 44/30
Apr 54/34	Aug 78/58	Dec 30/16

Parks and Recreation

Water-related activities, hiking, riding, various other sports, picnicking, camping, and visitor centers are available in many of Vermont's state parks. Day use areas (Memorial Day weekend-Labor Day, daily): over age 14, $2.50/person; ages 4-13, $2; under 4 free. Boat rentals, $5/hour. Paddleboats, $5/half-hour. Canoe rentals, $5/hour.

Calendar Highlights

FEBRUARY

Winter Carnival (*Brattleboro*). Week-long festival includes ski races, parade, ice show, sleigh rides, road races.

APRIL

Maple Sugar Festival (*St. Albans*). Phone 802/524-5800 or 802/524-2444. *www.vtmaplefestival.org*. A number of producers welcome visitors who join sugarhouse parties for sugar-on-snow, sour pickles, and raised doughnuts. Continuing events; arts and crafts; antiques; wood-chopping contests.

JUNE

Mountain Bike World Cup Race Mt. Snow (*West Dover*). Phone toll-free 800/245-7669. More than 1, 500 cyclists from throughout the world compete in downhill, dual slalom, and circuit racing events.

JULY

Festival on the Green (*Middlebury*). Phone 802/388-0216. Classical, modern, and traditional dance; chamber and folk music; theater and comedy presentations.

SEPTEMBER

Vermont State Fair (*Rutland*). Phone 802/775-5200. *www.vermontstatefair.net*. Exhibits of arts and crafts, flowers, produce, home arts, pets, animals, maple sugaring. Entertainment, agricultural displays, hot air ballooning. Daily special events.

Camping: $15/night, lean-to $22 at areas with swimming beaches; $13/night, lean-to $20 at areas without swimming beaches. Reservations of at least 2 days (3 days mid-May-Oct) and maximum of 21 days may be made by contacting park or Department of Forests, Parks, and Recreation, 103 S Main St, Waterbury 05671-0603, with full payment. Pets are allowed on leash only. Phone 802/241-3655.

FISHING AND HUNTING

Nonresident fishing license: season $41; 7-day $30; 3-day $20; 1-day $15. Nonresident hunting license: $85; $25 for those under 18 years. Nonresident small game license: $40. In order for a nonresident to obtain a hunting license, he/she must prove that he/she holds a license in his/her home state. Bow and arrow license (hunting or combination license also required): nonresident $25. Combination hunting and fishing license: nonresident $110. For *Vermont Guide to Fishing,* contact the Fish and Wildlife Department, 103 S Main St, Waterbury 05671-0501. Phone 802/241-3700.

Driving Information

All vehicle occupants must be secured in federally approved safety belts. Children ages 1-4 must be secured in approved child safety devices. When the number of occupants exceeds the number of safety belts, children take priority and must be secured. Children under age 1 must use approved safety seats. Phone 802/828-2665.

INTERSTATE HIGHWAY SYSTEM

The following alphabetical listing of Vermont towns in this book shows that these cities are within 10 miles of the indicated Interstate highways. Check a highway map for the nearest exit.

Highway Number	Cities/Towns within 10 Miles
Interstate 89	Barre, Burlington, Montpelier, St. Albans, Swanton, Waterbury, White River Junction.
Interstate 91	Bellows Falls, Brattleboro, Fairlee, Grafton, Lyndonville, Newfane, Newport, St. Johnsbury, Springfield, White River Junction, Windsor, Woodstock.

Additional Visitor Information

Vermont is very well documented. The Vermont Official Transportation Map, as well as numerous descriptive folders, are distributed free by the Vermont Department of Tourism and Marketing, 6 Baldwin St, Drawer 33, Montpelier 05633-1301;

THE BEST OF VERMONT

From Montpelier, take Interstate 89 to exit 10, then head up Highway 100 to the Ben & Jerry's ice cream factory. This is the state's top tourist attraction and for good reason. The 30-minute factory tour begins with a short movie about the company's founders, Ben Cohen and Jerry Greenfield. From there, tour groups head to the production facilities, where the ice cream production process is explained. The last stop on the tour—and the most popular—is the FlavoRoom, where visitors can enjoy delicious samples of Ben & Jerry's most popular flavors. Don't forget to stop in at the gift shop for the perfect Vermont souvenirs!

Continue on Highway 100 to the village of Stowe. Depending on the season, you can spend your time here biking, hiking, or cross-country skiing. Take the gondola to the top of Mount Mansfield (Vermont's highest peak at 4, 393 feet) for dramatic views of the area. Enjoy a walk along the riverside Stowe Recreation Path, or simply relax at one of the many inns, shops, and restaurants. From Stowe, continue on to Smugglers Notch (Hwy 108), a high, scenic pass that runs from Stowe (open summer only), through the scenic Mount Mansfield State Forest, and on to the village of Jeffersonville. Most tourists return by the same route, but there is an interesting loop return through Johnson and Morristown. Once back at Interstate 89, continue on to Burlington, Vermont's largest city and a departure point for ferries. Visitors will enjoy biking or in-line skating along Lake Champlain, shopping, or stopping at the restaurants along the Church Street Marketplace. Be sure to take time for a guided tour of Ethan Allen Homestead, one of the top attractions in Vermont. South of Burlington on Highway 7 is the town of Shelburne, also a departure point for ferries. The big draw here is the Shelburne Museum, which is located on 45 acres and includes such items as a working carousel; a 5,000-piece hand-carved miniature traveling circus; a lighthouse; an authentic country store; farm equipment; and *Ticonderoga*, a 200-foot sidewheel steamboat. From the eclectic and bizarre to the historic and educational, the Shelburne Museum is bound to have something of interest for everyone in your group—don't miss it! You'll also want to make time for trips to Shelburne Farms and the Vermont Teddy Bear Company. **(Approximately 436 miles round-trip from Boston)**

phone 802/828-3237 or toll-free 800/837-6668. Visitor centers are located off Interstate 89 in Guilford (daily); off Interstate 89 in Highgate Springs (daily); off Highway 4 in Fair Haven (daily); and off Interstate 93 in Waterford (daily).

The Vermont Chamber of Commerce, PO Box 37, Montpelier 05601, distributes *Vermont Traveler's Guidebook* of accommodations, restaurants, and attractions; phone 802/223-3443. *Vermont Life*, one of the nation's best known and respected regional quarterlies, presents photo essays on various aspects of life in the state; available by writing *Vermont Life*, 6 Baldwin St, Montpelier 05602. Another excellent source of information on the state is *Vermont: An Explorer's Guide* (The Countryman Press, Woodstock, VT, 1994) by Christina Tree and Peter Jennison; a comprehensive book covering attractions, events, recreational facilities, accommodations, restaurants, and places to shop. It is available in bookstores.

Various books on Vermont are also available from the Vermont Historical Society, Vermont Museum, Pavilion Building, 109 State St, Montpelier 05609.

For information regarding Vermont's Long Trail, along with other hiking trails in the state, contact the Green Mountain Club, 4711 Waterbury Stowe Rd, Waterbury Center 05677; phone 802/244-7037. The Department of Agriculture, 116 State St, Drawer 20, Montpelier 05602-2901, has information on farms offering vacations and maple sugarhouses open to visitors.

Several Vermont-based companies offer inn-to-inn bicycle tours from May through October (months vary). Tours range in length from two days to several weeks; most are designed to accommodate all levels of cyclists. Bicycling enthusiasts can obtain a brochure entitled *Bicycle Touring in Vermont* from the Vermont Department of Tourism and Marketing, 6 Baldwin St, Drawer 33, Montpelier 05633-1301; phone 802/828-3237.

Arlington (E-1)

See also Bennington, Dorset, Manchester and Manchester Center

Settled 1763
Population 2,299
Elevation 690 ft
Area Code 802
Zip 05250

What to See and Do

Battenkill River. *103 S Main St, Arlington (05250). Phone 802/241-3700.* Trout and fly fishing on the Battenkill River.

Candle Mill Village. *316 Old Mill Rd, East Arlington (05252). 1 1/2 miles E on Old Mill Rd. Phone 802/375-6068.* Three buildings, including a gristmill built in 1764 by Remember Baker of the Green Mountain Boys; many music boxes, candles, cookbook and teddy bear displays. (Daily; closed holidays) **FREE**

Norman Rockwell Exhibition. *3772 Hwy 7A, Arlington (05250). Phone 802/375-6423. www.vmga.org/benning-ton/normrockwell.html.* Hundreds of magazine covers, illustrations, advertisements, calendars, and other printed works are displayed in a historic 1875 church in the illustrator's hometown. Hosts are Rockwell's former models. Twenty-minute film. (Daily; closed Easter, Thanksgiving, Dec 25) **$**

Limited-Service Hotel

★ **CANDLELIGHT MOTEL.** *4893 Hwy 7A, Arlington (05250). Phone 802/375-6647; toll-free 800/348-5294; fax 802/375-2566. www.candlelightmotel.com.* Providing clean and basic accommodations as well as a great location near tennis courts, playgrounds, shops, and the Battenkill, The Candlelight Motel is a great choice when traveling with the whole family. Large, well-kept rooms feature spare blond wood furniture, heavy-duty carpeting, and refrigerators, while the spacious front lawn offers guests barbecue grills and lots of room for the kids to play. 17 rooms. Complimentary continental breakfast. Check-in 1 pm, check-out 11 am. Outdoor pool. **$**

Full-Service Inns

★ ★ ★ **ARLINGTON INN.** *3904 Hwy 7A and 313W, Arlington (05250). Phone 802/375-6532; toll-free 800/443-9442; fax 802/375-6534. www.arlingtoninn.com.* This dramatic Greek Revival-style mansion, listed on the National Register of Historic Places, was built in 1848 and has been operating as an inn since 1888. The interior features a romantic dining room, cozy pub, and sitting room done in early Victorian style. Spread throughout the main house and several converted outbuildings, the varied guest rooms feature impressive antiques; some have double-sided fireplaces and Jacuzzi tubs. The restored carriage house and parsonage feature modern architectural details such as cathedral ceilings and skylights, while rooms in the main house retain authentic historical details. The 3-acre grounds include a walking path, gazebo, banks of roses, and a small fishpond with waterfall. 18 rooms, 2 story. Complimentary full breakfast. Check-in 3 pm, check-out 11 am. Wireless Internet access. Restaurant, bar. **$$**

★ ★ ★ **ARLINGTON'S WEST MOUNTAIN INN.** *144 W Mountain Inn Rd, Arlington (05250). Phone 802/375-6516; fax 802/375-6553. www.west-mountaininn.com.* This historic white seven-gabled inn, built in 1849 and opened as an inn in 1978, is located on a mountainside overlooking the Bettenkill River. Its interior is furnished with a mix of antiques and country classics (pine paneling, fireplace, books, chess and checkers). And the large lawn and numerous windows help guests admire the beautiful surrounding grounds and countryside featuring wildflowers, a bird sanctuary, fish ponds, and llamas. The hideaway's location provides guests with many nearby activities such as hiking, snowshoeing, canoeing, tubing, tennis, and golf. This is the perfect choice for nature lovers or guests needing a tranquil getaway. 20 rooms, 3 story. Complimentary full breakfast. Check-in 2 pm, check-out noon. Restaurant, bar. Credit cards accepted. **$$**

Specialty Lodging

HILL FARM INN. *458 Hill Farm Rd, Arlington (05250). Phone 802/375-2269; toll-free 800/882-2545; fax 802/375-9918. www.hillfarminn.com.* North of Arlington's town center, Hill Farm Road takes visitors to a rural spot that feels very much like the farm it once was. On 50 acres fronting the Battenkill River, the inn consists of a historic guest house (1790) and a classic white farmhouse (1830), along with several outlying cottages housing family suites and efficiencies. Sheep, goats, and chickens wander about outside to amuse kids and adults alike. Inside, the guest rooms have simple country charm; no phones are there to distract from the peaceful feeling, although some rooms do have televisions. 15 rooms, 2 story. Complimentary full breakfast. Check-in 3-7 pm, check-out 11 am. **$**

Restaurant

★ ★ ★ **ARLINGTON INN.** *3904 Hwy 7A, Arlington (05250). Phone 802/375-6532; toll-free 800/443-9442; fax 802/375-6534. www.arlingtoninn.com.* This landmark historic inn was built in 1848 as a private home and has been in operation since 1888. Guests enjoy the romance and elegance of the Victorian atmosphere and can dine fireside with a candlelight dinner for two. American menu. Dinner. Closed Mon; last week in Apr-first week in May; also Sun in off-season. Bar. Children's menu. Business casual attire. Reservations recommended. **$$$**

Barre (C-2)

See also Montpelier, Waitsfield, Warren, Waterbury

Settled 1788
Population 9,482
Elevation 609 ft
Area Code 802
Zip 05641
Information Central Vermont Chamber of Commerce, PO Box 336; phone 802/229-4619
Web Site www.central-vt.com

Barre (BA-rie) has a busy, industrial air. It is home to the world's largest granite quarries and a granite finishing plant. Many highly skilled European stonecutters have settled here. A popular summer area, Barre serves as an overflow area for nearby ski resorts in winter.

What to See and Do

Goddard College. *123 Pitkin Rd, Plainfield (05667). 5 miles N on Hwy 14, then 4 miles NE on Hwy 2. Phone 802/454-8311; toll-free 800/468-4888. www.goddard. edu.* (500 students) Several buildings designed by students; formal gardens. Theater, concerts.

Groton State Forest. *126 Boulder Beach Rd, Groton (05046). 19 miles E on Hwy 302, then N on Hwy 232, near Groton. Phone 802/584-3822.* This 25,625-acre area includes 3-mile-long Lake Groton (elevation 1,078 feet) and six other ponds. Miles of trails have been established to more remote sections of the forest. Nine developed recreation areas. Swimming, bathhouse, fishing, boating (rentals); nature trail, snowmobiling, picnicking, concession. Four campgrounds (dump station), lean-tos. (Memorial Day-Columbus Day)

Hope Cemetery. *Merchant St, Barre. On Hwy 14 at N edge of town. Phone 802/229-5711. www.central-vt.com/visit/cemetery.* "Museum" of granite sculpture. Headstones rival finest granite carvings anywhere. Carved by craftsmen as final tribute to themselves and their families.

Rock of Ages Quarry and Manufacturing Division. *558 Graniteville Rd, Graniteville (05654). Exit 6 from I-89 or 2 miles S on Hwy 14, then 3 1/2 miles SE on Main St. Phone 802/476-3119. www.rockofages.com.* Skilled artisans creating monuments; picnic area. Visitor center (May-Oct: Mon-Sat 8:30 am-5 pm, Sun 10 am-5 pm; mid-Sept-mid-Oct: daily 8:30 am-5 pm; closed July 4). Manufacturing Divison (all year, Mon-Fri 8 am-3:30 pm). 30-minute quarry shuttle tour (June-Oct: Mon-Sat 9:15 am-4 pm, Sun 10:15 am-4 pm; fee). **FREE**

Robert Burns. *Washington St, Barre. Phone 802/229-4619.* This granite statue of the poet stands near the city park in downtown. Erected in 1899 by admirers of the poet; regarded as one of the world's finest granite sculptures.

Youth Triumphant. *N Main St, Rtes 302 & 14, Barre. City park.* Erected Armistice Day, 1924. Benches around the memorial create a whisper gallery; whispers on one side of oval can be easily heard on other side.

Special Event

Old Time Fiddlers' Contest. *Barre Auditorium, 61 Seminary Hill, Barre (05641). Phone 802/862-6708. www.nefiddlers.org.* This event is dedicated to preserving and promoting Old-Time Fiddling and its related arts and skills. Usually last weekend in Sept.

Limited-Service Hotel

★ **HOLLOW INN AND HOTEL.** *278 S Main St, Barre (05641). Phone 802/479-9313; toll-free 800/998-9444; fax 802/476-5242. www.hollowinn.com.* 41 rooms, 2 story. Pets accepted, some restrictions; fee. Complimentary continental breakfast. Check-in 1 pm, check-out 11 am. Fitness room. Outdoor pool, whirlpool. **$**

Specialty Lodgings

GREEN TRAILS INN. *24 Stone Rd, Brookfield (05036). Phone 802/276-3412; toll-free 800/243-3412. www.greentrailsinn.com.* Buildings date to 1790 and 1830. On site of famed Floating Bridge. 13 rooms, 3 story. Children over 10 years only. Complimentary full breakfast. Check-in 1 pm, check-out noon. Restaurant. Airport transportation available. **$**

SHIRE INN. *Main St, Chelsea (05038). Phone 802/685-3031; toll-free 800/441-6908; fax 802/685-3871. www.shireinn.com.* Federal-style house built in 1832. 6 rooms, 2 story. Children over 7 years only. Complimentary full breakfast. Check-in 3 pm, check-out 11 am. Federal-style house built in 1832. **$$**

Bellows Falls (E-2)

See also Brattleboro, Grafton, Springfield

Settled 1753
Population 3,313
Elevation 299 ft
Area Code 802
Zip 05101
Information Great Falls Regional Chamber of Commerce, 55 Village Square, PO Box 554; phone 802/463-4280
Web Site www.gfrcc.org

The first construction work on a US canal was started here in 1792. Later, nine locks raised barges, rafts, and small steamers over the falls. In 1983, a series of fish ladders extending 1,024 feet was constructed to restore Atlantic salmon and American shad to their migratory route up the Connecticut River. Power from the river helps make this an industrial town; wood products, paper, and wire cord are among the chief products. Ben & Jerry's ice cream has a nationwide distribution center here.

What to See and Do

Adams Gristmill. *End of Mill Hill St, Bellows Falls (05101). Phone 802/463-3734.* (1831) Former mill; museum contains early electrical equipment, implements used in paper manufacturing and farming. (Memorial Day-Columbus Day: Sat-Sun 2-4 pm) **FREE**

Green Mountain Railroad. *54 Depot St, Bellows Falls (05101). 1/4 mile N. Phone 802/463-3069; toll-free 800/707-3530. www.vtrails.com.* Green Mountain Flyer offers scenic train rides through three river valleys. (Late June-Labor Day: Tues-Sun; mid-Sept-Columbus Day: daily) **$$$**

Native American Petroglyphs. *On riverbanks near Vilas Bridge. Phone 802/463-4280.* Carvings on rocks, unique among Native American works, by members of an early American people; as early as AD 1000.

Rockingham Meetinghouse. *7 Village Sq, Rockingham. 5 miles N on Hwy 103; 1 mile W of I-91 exit 6 on Old Rockingham Rd. Phone 802/463-3941.* (1787) Restored in 1907; colonial architecture, antique glass windows; old burying ground with quaint epitaphs. (Mid-June-Labor Day, daily 10 am-4 pm) **$**

Special Event

Rockingham Old Home Days. *Rockingham Meeting House, 7 Village Sq, Rockingham. Phone 802/463-4280. www.gfrcc.org/rockinghamoldhomedays.html.* Celebrates the founding of the meetinghouse. Dancing, outdoor cafs, sidewalk sales, entertainment, fireworks; pilgrimage to meetinghouse last day. First weekend in Aug.

Bennington (F-1)

See also Arlington, Green Mountain National Forest, Manchester and Manchester Center, Wilmington

Settled 1761
Population 16,451
Elevation 681 ft
Area Code 802
Zip 05201
Information Information Booth, 100 Veterans Memorial Dr; phone 802/447-3311 or toll-free 800/229-0252
Web Site www.bennington.com

Bennington was headquarters for Ethan Allen's Green Mountain Boys, known to New Yorkers as the "Bennington Mob," in Vermont's long struggle with New York. On August 16, 1777, this same "mob" won a decisive battle of the Revolutionary War. Bennington has three separate areas of historic significance: the Victorian and turn-of-the-century buildings downtown; the colonial houses, church, and commons in Old Bennington (1 mile W); and the three covered bridges in North Bennington.

What to See and Do

Bennington Battle Monument. *15 Monument Cir, Old Bennington (05201). Phone 802/447-0550. www.dhca. state.vt.us.* A 306-foot monolith commemorates a Revolutionary War victory. Elevator to observation platform (mid-Apr-Oct, daily 9 am-5 pm). Gift shop. **$**

Bennington College. *Hwy 67A and College Dr, Bennington (05201). Phone 802/442-5401. www.bennington.edu.* (1932) (787 students) Introduced progressive methods of education; became coeducational in 1969. The Visual and Performing Arts Center has special exhibits. Summer programs and performances.

Bennington Museum. *75 Main St, Bennington (05201). Phone 802/447-1571. www.benningtonmuseum.org.* Early Vermont and New England historical artifacts, including American glass, paintings, sculpture, silver, furniture; Bennington pottery, Grandma Moses paintings, 1925 "Wasp" luxury touring car. Schoolhouse Museum contains Moses family memorabilia; Bennington flag; other Revolutionary War collections. (Thurs-Tues 10 am-5 pm; closed Thanksgiving, Dec 25, Jan 1) Genealogical library (by appointment). **$$**

Long Trail. *Phone 802/244-7037. www.greenmountainclub.org.* A path for hikers leading over the Green Mountains to the Canadian border, crosses Highway 9 approximately 5 miles east of Bennington. A section of the trail is part of the Appalachian Trail.

Old First Church. *One Monument Circle, Old Bennington (05201). Phone 802/447-1223. www.oldfirstchurchbenn.org.* (1805) Example of early colonial architecture; original box pews; Asher Benjamin steeple. Guided tours. (Memorial Day-June, weekends; July-mid-Oct: Mon-Sat 10 am-noon, 1-4 pm; Sun 1-4 pm) **FREE** Adjacent is

> **Old Burying Ground.** *Monument Ave, Bennington (05201). Phone 802/447-3311.* Buried here are poet Robert Frost and those who died in the Battle of Bennington. **FREE**

Park-McCullough House Museum. *Park and West St, North Bennington. N via Hwy 67A. Phone 802/442-5441. www.parkmccullough.org.* (1865) A 35-room Victorian mansion with period furnishings; stable with carriages; costume collection; Victorian gardens; child's playhouse. (Mid-May-mid-Oct: daily, tours 10 am-3 pm) Special events are held throughout the year. **$$**

Shaftsbury State Park. *22 Shaftsbury State Park Rd, Shaftsbury (05262). 10 1/2 miles N on Hwy 7A. Phone 802/375-9978.* The 26-acre Lake Shaftsbury, a former millpond, is surrounded by 101 acres of forests and wetlands. Swimming, fishing, boating (rentals); nature and hiking trails, picnicking. (Memorial Day-Labor Day) **$**

Valley View Horses & Tack Shop, Inc. *Northwest Hill Rd, Pownal. 9 miles S on Hwy 7. Phone 802/823-4649.* Full-service equestrian facility offers guided trail rides and horse rentals (by the hour). Also "Pony Express" pony rides at the stables for young riders. Western tack shop. (Daily)

Woodford State Park. *142 State Park Rd, Woodford (05201). Approximately 10 miles E on Hwy 9. Phone 802/447-7169. www.vtstatepark.com.* At 2,400 feet, this 400-acre park has the highest elevation of any park in the state. Swimming, fishing, boating (no motors; rentals); nature and hiking trails, picnicking, tent and trailer sites (dump station), lean-tos. (Memorial Day-Columbus Day) **$**

Special Events

Antique and Classic Car Show. *Green Mountain Racetrack, Rte 7, Pownal. Phone 802/447-3311; toll-free 800/229-0252. www.bennington.com.* Car show, swap meet, craft festival, car corral, tractor pull events, food and, entertainment are some of the activities at this annual show. Second weekend after Labor Day. **$$**

Mayfest. *Main St, Bennington. Phone 802/442-5758. www.bennington.com/bbc/mayfest.html.* Mayfest is a day for shopping for handmade crafts, eating tasty food and watching street entertainment. Sat of Memorial Day weekend.

Limited-Service Hotel

★ **BEST WESTERN.** *220 Northside Dr, Bennington (05201). Phone 802/442-6311; toll-free 800/780-7234; fax 802/442-5885. www.bestwestern.com.* Located in an older commercial district on the northwest side of town, the Best Western puts guests near shopping, several restaurants, and skiing. Shady trees and a picnic table give the grounds a friendly feel, and a Chinese restaurant and sparkling outdoor pool are located in the center of the hotel's courtyard. Refrigerators and microwaves are found in guest rooms, which are clean and well-cared for, and a continental breakfast is served in the lobby. 58 rooms, 2 story. Complimentary continental breakfast. Check-in 3 pm, check-out 11 am. High-speed Internet access. Outdoor pool. Business Center. **$**

Full-Service Inn

★ ★ ★ **FOUR CHIMNEYS INN.** *21 West Rd, Bennington (05201). Phone 802/447-3500; fax 802/447-3692. www.fourchimneys.com.* This elegant Colonial Revival inn is set on 11 acres of trees and rolling grass fields near the heart of Old Bennington, where classic white New England houses and the historic Old First Church are just steps away. Guest rooms blend the best of early 20th century country elegance with 21st century standards of comfort and technology and feature either gas or wood fireplaces; luxurious, high thread-count bed linens; TVs with DVD players; high-speed Internet access; and private screened porches. The main sitting room, with its full bar, deep couches, and cozy fireplace, is the perfect spot to sit and relax. The inn's fine dining restaurant is a destination on its own, with perfect presentations of regional fare in a beautiful dining room and sun-filled screened porch. 11 rooms, 3 story. Complimentary full breakfast. Check-in 3 pm, check-out 11 am. High-speed Internet access, wireless Internet access. Restaurant, bar. **$$**
🐾

Specialty Lodging

SOUTH SHIRE INN. *124 Elm St, Bennington (05201). Phone 802/447-3839; fax 802/442-3547. www.southshire.com.* Inside and out, this inn is reminiscent of the Victorian era from its shingled façade to the mahogany paneling, leaded glass doors, and ornate moldings of its common rooms. All units have period furnishings. 9 rooms, 2 story. Children over 12 years only. Complimentary full breakfast. Check-in 3 pm, check-out 11 am. High-speed Internet access. **$$**
🐾

Brandon (D-1)

See also Middlebury, Rutland

Settled 1761
Population 4,223
Elevation 431 ft
Area Code 802
Zip 05733
Information Brandon Area Chamber of Commerce, PO Box 267; phone 802/247-6401
Web Site www.brandon.org

Brandon is a resort and residential town located at the western edge of the Green Mountains. The first US electric motor was made in nearby Forestdale by Thomas Davenport.

What to See and Do

Branbury State Park. *Hwy 53, Salisbury. 3 miles NE on Hwy 73, then N on Hwy 53, E shore of Lake Dunmore. Phone 802/247-5925.* This 76-acre park has swimming, 1,000-foot sand beach, fishing, boating, sailing; nature and hiking trails, picnicking, concession, camping (dump station), lean-tos. (Memorial Day-Columbus Day)

Mount Independence. *497 Mount Independence Rd, Orwell (05760). 16 miles W via Hwys 73 and 22A. Phone 802/759-2412. www.historicvermont.org/sites.* Wooded bluff on shore of Lake Champlain, part of Revolutionary War defense complex. Fort built in 1776 across from Fort Ticonderoga to house 12,000 troops and to protect colonies from northern invasion; evacuated in 1777. Least disturbed major Revolutionary War site in the country; four marked trails show ruins of fort complex. (late May-mid-Oct, daily 9:30 am-5 pm) **$**

Stephen A. Douglas Birthplace. *2 Grove St (Hwy 7), Brandon (05733). Phone 802/247-6401.* Cottage where the "Little Giant" was born in 1813. Douglas attended Brandon Academy before moving to Illinois in 1833. (By appointment) **FREE**

Full-Service Inn

★ ★ ★ **LILAC INN.** *53 Park St, Brandon (05733). Phone 802/247-5463; toll-free 800/221-0720; fax 802/247-5499. www.lilacinn.com.* This colonial home, built in 1909, is on the National Register of Historic Places and is a peaceful, romantic getaway. Enjoy a book in the library, practice on the putting green, or take a drive to nearby historic Fort Ticonderoga. 9 rooms, 2 story. Pets accepted; fee. Complimentary full breakfast. Check-in 3 pm, check-out 11 am. Restaurant. **$$**
🐾

Specialty Lodging

THE BRANDON INN. *20 Park St, Brandon (05733). Phone 802/247-5766; toll-free 800/639-8685; fax 802/247-5768. www.historicbrandoninn.com.* Built in 1786. 37 rooms, 3 story. Check-in 3 pm, check-out 11 am. Restaurant, bar. Outdoor pool. **$**
🏊

Brattleboro (F-2)

See also Greenfield, Keene, Bellows Falls, Marlboro, Newfane, Wilmington

Settled 1724
Population 12,241
Elevation 240 ft
Area Code 802
Zip 05301
Information Brattleboro Area Chamber of Commerce, 180 Main St; phone 802/254-4565
Web Site www.brattleboromuseum.org

The first settlement in Vermont was at Fort Dummer (2 miles S) in 1724. Rudyard Kipling married a Brattleboro woman and lived here in the 1890s. Brattleboro is a resort area and an industrial town.

What to See and Do

Brattleboro Museum & Art Center. *10 Vernon St, Brattleboro (05301). Union Railroad Station. Phone 802/257-0124. www.brattleboromuseum.org.* Exhibits change periodically and feature works by New England artists; frequent performances and lecture programs. (May-Feb: Wed-Mon 11 am-5 pm; closed July 4, Nov 25, Dec 25, Jan 1; also Aug 2-5, Nov 1-4) **$**

Creamery Bridge. *Guilford St and Rte 9 W, Brattleboro. Approximately 2 miles W on Hwy 9. Phone 802/254-4565.* (1879) One of Vermont's best-preserved covered bridges.

Harlow's Sugar House. *563 Bellows Falls Rd, Putney (05346). 3 miles N via I-91, exit 4; on Hwy 5. Phone 802/387-5852. www.vermontsugar.com.* Observe working sugarhouse (Mar-mid-Apr). Maple exhibit and products. Pick your own fruit in season: strawberries, blueberries, raspberries, apples; also cider in fall. (Daily; closed Dec 25, also Jan-Feb) **FREE**

Living Memorial Park. *61 Guilford St, Brattleboro (05301). 2 miles W, just off Hwy 9. Phone 802/254-6700. www.brattleboro.org.* Swimming pool (mid-June-Labor Day). Ball fields, lawn games, tennis courts, ice skating (late Oct-early-Mar). Picnicking, playground. Special events during summer. Fee for some activities.

Santa's Land. *655 Bellows Falls Rd, Putney (05346). 12 miles N on Hwy 5 or I-91, exits 4 or 5. Phone 802/387-5550; toll-free 800/726-8299. www.santasland.com.* Christmas theme village; visit with Santa, railroad ride, carousel. Petting zoo; gardens. Concessions.

(Memorial Day weekend-June, Labor Day-mid-Dec: Sat-Sun 10 am-5 pm; July-Aug: Wed-Sun 10 am-5 pm; closed Thanksgiving) **$$$**

Special Events

Winter Carnival. *207 Main St, Brattleboro (05301). Phone 802/258-2511.* Week-long festival includes ski races, parade, ice show, sleigh rides, road races. Feb.

Yellow Barn Music Festival. *Several locations around Brattleboro. Phone 802/387-6637; toll-free 800/639-3819.www.yellowbarn.org.* Five-week chamber music festival's community concert series. Students and well-known guest artists perform seven daytime concerts. July-Aug. **FREE**

Limited-Service Hotel

★ **LATCHIS HOTEL.** *50 Main St, Brattleboro (05301). Phone 800/798-6301; fax 802/254-3604. www.latchis.com.* This hotel is located in Brattleboro's eclectic downtown historic district. Built in Art Deco-style in 1938, the Latchis Building is on the National Register of Historic Placesit's one of the few Art Deco buildings in Vermont. The building also houses the Latchis Theatre, which shows first-run art films, and the Lucca Bistro and its downtown brewpub. Inside, the hotel's public areas are pure Art Deco: terrazzo floors, mirrors, chrome fixtures, and neoclassical friezes (the designer was the son of Greek immigrants). Guest rooms have a more traditional New England look, although they retain a 1930s charm. For breakfast, muffins are delivered to the room, and in-room refrigerators are stocked with bottles of juice. 30 rooms, 4 story. Complimentary continental breakfast. Check-in 2 pm, check-out 11 am. **$**

Full-Service Hotel

★ ★ **QUALITY INN.** *1380 Putney Rd, Brattleboro (05301). Phone 802/254-8701; toll-free 866/254-8701; fax 802/257-4727. www.qualityinnbrattleboro.com.* An older property with an old-fashioned, slightly offbeat appeal, the Quality Inn is located several miles north of the town center and near one of the bridges over the Connecticut River. The two-story exterior is decorated with various North Country artifacts such as traps and skis, and large guest rooms feature unpretentious décor, a color scheme of deep reds and greens, and refrigerators. Families enjoy the recreation area, with a small pool (better for kids than lap swimmers), whirlpool, game room, sauna, and small fitness room. A surprising touch is that the hotel's restaurant serves Indian food, which is also available through room service. 94 rooms, 2 story. Pets accepted, some restrictions; fee. Complimentary continental breakfast. Check-in 3 pm, check-out 11 am. High-speed Internet access, wireless Internet access. Restaurant, bar. Fitness room. Indoor pool, outdoor pool, whirlpool. **$**

Burlington (B-1)

See also Shelburne

Settled 1773
Population 39,127
Elevation 113 ft
Area Code 802
Zip 05401
Information Lake Champlain Regional Chamber of Commerce, 60 Main St, Suite 100; phone 802/863-3489 or toll-free 877/686-5253
Web Site www.vermont.org

Burlington, on Lake Champlain, is the largest city in Vermont. It is the site of the oldest university and the oldest daily newspaper (1848) in the state, the burial place of Ethan Allen, and the birthplace of philosopher John Dewey. It has a diversity of industries. The lakefront area offers a park, dock, and restaurants.

What to See and Do

Battery Park. *1 North Ave, Burlington (05401). Phone 802/865-7247. www.enjoyburlington.com/Parks/BatteryPark.cfm.* View of Lake Champlain and Adirondacks. Guns here drove back British warships in the War of 1812.

Bolton Valley Ski/Summer Resort. *4302 Bolton Access Rd, Bolton Valley (05477). 20 miles E, off Hwy 2 in Bolton; I-89 exits 10, 11. Phone toll-free 877/926-5866. www.boltonvalley.com.* Resort has quad, four double chairlifts; one surface lift; school, patrol, rentals; snowmaking; cafeteria, restaurants, bar; nursery. Forty-three runs, longest run over 3 miles; vertical drop 1,600 feet. (Nov-Apr, daily) Sixty-two miles of cross-country trails. Also summer activities.

Burlington Ferry. *Burlington Dock, Burlington (05401). Leaves King St Dock. Phone 802/864-9804. www.ferries.com.* Makes one-hour trips across Lake Champlain to Port Kent, NY (mid-May-mid-Oct, daily). Refreshments. **$$**

Church Street Marketplace. *135 Church St, Burlington (05401). Phone 802/863-1648; fax 802/865-7252. www.churchstmarketplace.com.* Four traffic-free blocks, from the Unitarian Church, designed in 1815 by Peter Banner, to City Hall at the corner of Main Street. Buildings are a mix of Art Deco and 19th-century architectural styles and house more than 100 shops, restaurants, galleries, and cafs. The bricked promenade is spotted with vendors and street entertainers.

★ Ethan Allen Homestead and Museum. *1 Ethan Allen Homestead, Burlington (05401). 2 miles N off Hwy 127. Phone 802/865-4556. www.ethanallenhomestead.org.* Ethan Allen had a colorful history as a frontiersman, military leader, land speculator, suspected traitor, and prisoner of war. This preserved pioneer homestead, set amid rolling fields with views of the nearby river, was his last home. Here you'll find a re-created hayfield and kitchen gardens, plus the 1787 farmhouse. One-hour guided tours are available. (Mon-Sat 10 am-4 pm, Sun 1-4 pm; tours available June-Oct) **$**

Ethan Allen Park. *North Ave and Ethan Allen Pkwy, Burlington (05401). Phone 802/863-3489. www.enjoyburlington.com/Parks/EthanAllenPark.cfm.* Part of Ethan Allen's farm. Ethan Allen Tower (Memorial Day-Labor Day, Wed-Sun afternoons and evenings) with view of Adirondacks and Lake Champlain to the west, Green Mountains to the east. Picnicking. **FREE**

Excursion Cruises. *Burlington Boathouse, 348 Flynn Ave, Burlington (05401). Phone 802/862-8300. www.soea.com. Spirit of Ethan Allen III,* replica of a vintage sternwheeler and Lake Champlain's largest excursion vessel, offers sightseeing sunset, moonlight, brunch, and dinner cruises on Lake Champlain; both decks enclosed and heated. Reservations required for dinner cruises. (May-Oct) **$$$$**

Green Mountain Audubon Center. *255 Sherman Hollow Rd, Huntington (05462). 10 miles SE via I-89, Richmond exit, in Huntington near the Huntington-Richmond line. Phone 802/434-3068. www.vt.audubon.org.* Center has 230 acres with trails through many Vermont habitats, including beaver ponds, hemlock swamp, brook, river, marsh, old farm fields, woodland, and sugar orchard. Educational nature center with classes, interpretive programs, and special projects. Open all year for hiking, snowshoeing, and cross-country skiing. Grounds, office (hours vary). Fee for some activities. Adjacent is

Birds of Vermont Museum. *900 Sherman Hollow Rd, Huntington (05462). Phone 802/434-2167.* This museum displays wood carvings of 450 species of local birds, all done by a single artist. It also offers nature trails and recorded bird songs. (May-Oct, daily 10 am-4 pm) **$**

Lake Champlain Chocolates. *750 Pine St, Burlington (05401). Phone 802/864-1808; toll-free 800/465-5909. www.lakechamplainchocolates.com.* Large glass windows afford visitors a view of the chocolate-making process at this small-scale factory. The gift shop on-site usually features in-store chocolate-making demonstrations on Saturdays, when the factory itself is closed. (Tours: Mon-Fri 9 am-2 pm on the hour; factory store: Mon-Sat 9 am-6 pm, Sun noon-5 pm; closed holidays) **FREE**

Sleepy Hollow Cross-Country Skiing Center. *1805 Sherman Hollow Rd, Huntington (05462). 10 miles SE on I-89 to exit 11, then E on Hwy 2, then S on Huntington Rd to Sherman Hollow Rd, then W. Phone toll-free 866/254-1524. www.skisleepyhollow.com.* The area has 25 miles of groomed, one-way, double-tracked cross-country ski trails; more than 3 miles of lighted trails for night skiing; a warming hut; and a restaurant. Rentals are available. (Dec-Apr) **$$$**

St. Michael's College. *1 Winooski Park, Colchester (05439). N via I-89 to exit 15, then 1/4 mile NE on Hwy 15, in Winooski-Colchester. Phone 802/654-2000. www.smcvt.edu.* (1904) (1,900 students) Chapel of St. Michael the Archangel (daily). Also professional summer theater at St. Michael's Playhouse.

University of Vermont. *Waterman Bldg, 85 S Prospect St, Burlington (05405). Phone 802/656-3480. www.uvm.edu.* (1791) (10,000 students) Fifth-oldest university in New England. Graduate and undergraduate programs. On campus are the Billings Center, of architectural significance; Bailey-Howe Library, largest in the state; Georgian-designed Ira Allen Chapel, named for the founder; and the Old Mill, classroom building with cornerstone laid by General Lafayette in 1825. Also here is

Robert Hull Fleming Museum. *61 Colchester Ave, Burlington (05405). Phone 802/656-0750.* American, European, African, pre-Columbian, and Oriental art; changing exhibits. (Labor Day-Apr:

Tues-Fri 9 am-4 pm, Sat-Sun 1-5 pm; May-Labor Day: Tues-Fri noon-4 pm, Sat-Sun 1-5 pm; closed holidays, also mid-Dec-mid-Jan) **$**

Special Events

Discover Jazz Festival. *230 College St, Burlington (05401). Phone 802/863-7992. www.discoverjazz.com.* A jazz extravaganza with more than 150 live performances taking place in city parks, clubs, and restaurants. Ten days in early June.

St. Michael's Playhouse. *McCarthy Arts Center, St. Michael's College, 1 Winooski Park, Colchester (05439). Phone 802/654-2281. www.academics.smcvt.edu/playhouse.* Summer theater. Professional actors perform four plays (two weeks each). Tues-Sat, late June-late Aug.

Vermont Mozart Festival. *110 Main St, Burlington. Phone 802/862-7352. www.vtmozart.com.* Features 26 chamber concerts in picturesque Vermont settings including the Trapp Family Meadow, Basin Harbor Club in Vergennes, and Shelburne Farms on Lake Champlain. Mid-July-early Aug.

Limited-Service Hotels

★ ★ **BEST WESTERN WINDJAMMER INN & CONFERENCE CENTER.** *1076 Williston Rd, South Burlington (05403). Phone 802/863-1125; toll-free 800/371-1125; fax 802/658-1296. www.bestwestern.com/windjammerinn.* 159 rooms, 4 story. Pets accepted, some restrictions; fee. Complimentary continental breakfast. Check-in 3 pm, check-out 11 am. Restaurant. Fitness room. Indoor pool, outdoor pool, whirlpool. Airport transportation available. **$**

★ **COMFORT INN.** *1285 Williston Rd, South Burlington (05403). Phone 802/865-3400; toll-free 877/424-6423; fax 802/846-3411. www.choicehotels.com.* 105 rooms, 3 story. Pets accepted, some restrictions; fee. Complimentary continental breakfast. Check-in 3 pm, check-out noon. Fitness room. Outdoor pool. **$**

★ ★ **DOUBLETREE HOTEL.** *1117 Williston Rd, South Burlington (05403). Phone 802/658-0250; fax 802/660-7516. www.doubletree.com.* 130 rooms, 2 story. Pets accepted, some restrictions; fee. Check-in 3 pm, check-out noon. Restaurant, bar. Fitness room. Indoor pool, children's pool. Airport transportation available. **$**

★ **HOLIDAY INN EXPRESS.** *1712 Shelburne Rd, South Burlington (05403). Phone 802/860-1112; toll-free 866/762-7870; fax 802/846-1926. www.innvermont. com.* 84 rooms, 3 story, all suites. Complimentary continental breakfast. Check-in 2 pm, check-out noon. Airport transportation available. **$**

Full-Service Hotels

★ ★ ★ **THE INN AT ESSEX - A SUMMIT HOTEL.** *70 Essex Way, Essex (05452). Phone 802/878-1100; toll-free 800/727-4295; fax 802/878-0063. www. innatessex.com.* Each room at this inn is individually decorated with 18th-century period-style furniture. The meals are prepared by the New England Culinary Institute. 97 rooms, 3 story. Pets accepted, some restrictions; fee. Check-in 3 pm, check-out 11 am. Restaurant. Airport transportation available. **$$**
🐾

★ ★ ★ **SHERATON BURLINGTON HOTEL AND CONFERENCE CENTER.** *870 Williston Rd, South Burlington (05403). Phone 802/865-6600; toll-free 800/677-6576; fax 802/865-6670. www.sheratonburlington.com.* 309 rooms, 4 story. Pets accepted. Check-in 3 pm, check-out noon. Restaurant, bar. Fitness room. Indoor pool, whirlpool. Airport transportation available. Business center. **$**
🐾 🏃 🏊 🏃

Restaurants

★ **DAILY PLANET.** *15 Center St, Burlington (05401). Phone 802/862-9647; fax 802/862-6693.* International menu. Dinner, late-night. Bar. Children's menu. Casual attire. Reservations recommended. Outdoor seating. **$$**
🔲

★ ★ **ICE HOUSE.** *171 Battery St, Burlington (05401). Phone 802/864-1800; fax 802/864-1801.* Built as an ice house in 1868, this restaurant offers a great view of Lake Champlain. American menu. Lunch, dinner. Bar. Children's menu. Casual attire. Reservations recommended. Outdoor seating. **$$**
🔲

★ ★ ★ **PAULINE'S.** *1834 Shelburne Rd, South Burlington (05403). Phone 802/862-1081; fax 802/862-6842. www.paulinescafe.com.* This friendly, casual restaurant has a strong local following. American menu. Lunch, dinner, Sun brunch. Closed Dec 24 (evening)-25. Bar. Children's menu. Outdoor seating. **$$**

★ ★ **PERRY'S FISH HOUSE.** *1080 Shelburne Rd, South Burlington (05403). Phone 802/862-1300. www.perrysfishhouse.com.* Seafood menu. Dinner, Sun brunch. Closed Thanksgiving, Dec 25. Bar. Children's menu. **$$**

Dorset (E-1)

See also Arlington, Manchester and Manchester Center, Peru

Settled 1768
Population 1,918
Elevation 962 ft
Area Code 802
Zip 05251
Information Dorset Chamber of Commerce, PO Box 121; phone 802/867-2450
Web Site www.dorsetvt.com

This charming village is surrounded by hills 3,000 feet high. In 1776, the Green Mountain Boys voted for Vermont's independence here. The first marble quarry in the country was opened in 1785 on nearby Mount Aeolus.

Special Event

Dorset Theatre Festival. *Dorset Playhouse, Cheney Rd, Dorset (05251). Phone 802/867-2223. www.dorset-theatrefestival.com.* Professional theater company presents six productions. Mid-June-Labor Day.

Full-Service Inns

★ ★ ★ **DORSET INN.** *9 Church St, Dorset (05251). Phone 802/867-5500; toll-free 877/367-7389; fax 802/867-5542. www.dorsetinn.com.* This 1796 inn, located where the Green Mountain Boys plotted their fight against the British, strives to blend colonial elements with modern amenities. Individually decorated guest rooms feature private baths, antique furnishings, and wall-to-wall carpets. Established in 1796; this is the oldest continuously operating inn in Vermont. 31 rooms, 3 story. Check-in 3 pm, check-out 11 am. Restaurant, bar. **$**

★ ★ ★ **INN AT WEST VIEW FARM.** *2928 Hwy 30, Dorset (05251). Phone 802/867-5715; toll-free 800/769-4903; fax 802/867-0468. www.innatwestviewfarm.com.* This restored farmhouse, which overlooks the Vermont countryside, is the perfect setting for a quiet, relaxing country vacation. Guest rooms feature private baths with large, soft towels and comfortable sitting areas. 10 rooms, 2 story. Complimentary full breakfast. Check-in 3 pm, check-out 11 am. Restaurant, bar. **$**

Specialty Lodging

BARROWS HOUSE INN. *3156 Hwy 30, Dorset (05251). Phone 802/867-4455; toll-free 800/639-1620; fax 802/867-0132. www.barrowshouse.com.* 28 rooms. Pets accepted, some restrictions; fee. Check-in 2 pm, check-out 11 am. Restaurant, bar. Outdoor pool. Tennis. **$$**

Restaurants

★ ★ ★ **BARROWS HOUSE INN.** *3156 Hwy 30, Dorset (05251). Phone 802/867-4455; toll-free 800/639-1620; fax 802/867-0132. www.barrowshouse.com.* Choose between the clubby tavern, the bright greenhouse, or the more formal dining room to enjoy the eclectic regional cuisine served in this charming inn. American menu. Breakfast, dinner. Bar. Children's menu. **$$$**

★ ★ **INN AT WEST VIEW FARM.** *2928 Route 30, Dorset (05251). Phone 802/867-5715; toll-free 800/769-4903; fax 802/867-0468. www.innatwestviewfarm.com.* This restaurant is located in a converted 1850 farmhouse. American menu. Dinner. Closed Tues-Wed; also Apr; first two weeks in Nov. Bar. **$$**

Fairlee (D-3)

See also White River Junction

Population 883
Elevation 436 ft
Area Code 802
Zip 05045
Information Town Offices, Main St, PO Box 95; phone 802/333-4363

Special Events

Chicken Barbecue. *On the Common, Main St, Fairlee. Phone 802/333-4363.* July 4.

Vermont State Open Golf Tournament. *Lake Morey Inn Country Club, Fairlee. Phone 802/333-4311.* Mid-June.

Full-Service Resort

★ ★ **LAKE MOREY RESORT.** *Club House Rd, Fairlee (05045). Phone 802/333-4311; toll-free 800/423-1211; fax 802/333-4553. www.lakemoreyresort.com.* 144 rooms, 3 story. Check-in 2 pm, check-out 11 am. Restaurant, bar. Children's activity center. Fitness room. Indoor pool, outdoor pool, whirlpool. Golf. Tennis. **$**

Grafton (E-2)

See also Bellows Falls, Londonderry, Newfane, Springfield

Population 602
Elevation 841 ft
Area Code 802
Zip 05146
Information Great Falls Regional Chamber of Commerce, 55 Village Square, PO Box 554, Bellows Falls 05101; phone 802/463-4280
Web Site www.gfrcc.org

This picturesque New England village is a blend of houses, churches, galleries, antiques shops, and other small shops—all circa 1800. Founded in pre-Revolutionary times under the patronage of George III, Grafton became a thriving mill town and modest industrial center after the damming of the nearby Saxton River. When water power gave way to steam, the town began to decline. Rescued, revived, and restored by the Windham Foundation, it has been returned to its former attractiveness. A creek curling through town and the peaceful air of a gentler era contribute to the charm of this village, considered a paradise for photographers.

What to See and Do

Grafton Ponds Cross-Country Ski Center. *Townshend Rd, Grafton (05146). Phone toll-free 800/843-1801. www.graftonponds.com.* Featuring more than 16 miles of groomed trails; school, rentals; concession, warming hut. (Dec-Mar, daily; closed Dec 25) In summer, walking and fitness trails (no fee). **$$$$**

The Old Tavern at Grafton. *92 Main St, Grafton (05146). Main St and Townshend Rd. Phone toll-free 800/843-1801. www.old-tavern.com.* (1801) Centerpiece of village. Visited by many famous guests over the years, including several presidents and authors; names inscribed over the desk. Furnished with

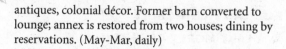

antiques, colonial décor. Former barn converted to lounge; annex is restored from two houses; dining by reservations. (May-Mar, daily)

Full-Service Inn

★ ★ ★ **OLD TAVERN AT GRAFTON.** *92 Main St, Grafton (05146). Phone 802/843-2231; toll-free 800/843-1801; fax 802/843-2245. www.old-tavern.com.* This picturesque New England inn offers its guests a haven from their busy lives. Guests will enjoy the stone walls, colorful flowers, afternoon tea, tennis, bicycles, and pond. The individually decorated guest rooms and houses feature antique Chippendale and Windsor furnishings. 46 rooms, 3 story. Closed Apr. Children over 7 years only. Complimentary full breakfast. Check-in 4 pm, check-out 11 am. Restaurant, bar. Tennis. **$**

Specialty Lodging

INN AT WOODCHUCK HILL FARM. *Middletown Rd, Grafton (05146). Phone 802/843-2398. www.woodchuckhill.com.* First farmhouse in town (1790). On 200 acres; pond. 10 rooms, 3 story. Complimentary full breakfast. Check-in 1 pm. Check-out 11 am. **$**

Green Mountain National Forest

See also Bennington, Manchester and Manchester Center, Rutland, Warren

This 360,000-acre tract lies along the backbone of the Green Mountains, beginning at the Massachusetts line. Its high point is Mount Ellen (4,083 feet). The 260-mile Long Trail, a celebrated hiking route, extends the length of the state; about 80 miles of it are within the forest.

Well-maintained gravel roads wind through the forests of white pine, hemlock, spruce, yellow birch, and sugar maple; there are many recreation areas and privately owned resorts. Hunting and fishing are permitted in the forest under Vermont regulations. There are whitetailed deer, black bear, ruffed grouse, and other game, plus brook, rainbow, and brown trout.

Developed and primitive camping, swimming, and picnicking are found throughout the forest, as are privately operated alpine ski areas and ski touring centers. Fees charged at some recreation sites and at developed campsites.

What to See and Do

Moosalamoo Recreation Area. *99 Ranger Rd, Rochester (05767). Within Green Mountain National Forest. Phone 802/747-6700. www.moosalamoo.org.* This 20,000-acre area features trails from which all the forest's diverse natural beauty can be viewed. Winter activities include cross-country skiing on groomed, specially marked trails; also alpine skiing. The nation's oldest long-distance hiking trail, the Long Trail, runs the Moosalamoo border for nearly 15 miles. Biking allowed on roads and some trails. Camping facilities abound in the area. (Daily)

Jeffersonville (B-2)

See also Stowe, Swanton

Population 462
Elevation 459 ft
Area Code 802
Zip 05464
Information Smugglers' Notch Area Chamber of Commerce, PO Box 364
Web Site www.smugnotch.com

What to See and Do

Smugglers' Notch. *4323 Hwy 108 S, Jeffersonville (05464). 5 miles S on Hwy 108. Phone 802/644-8851; toll-free 800/451-8752. www.smuggs.com.* Resort has five double chairlifts, three surface lifts; school, rentals; snowmaking; concession area, cafeteria, restaurants; nursery, lodge. 60 runs, longest run over 3 miles; vertical drop 2,610 feet. (Thanksgiving-mid-Apr, daily) More than 25 miles of cross-country trails (Dec-Apr, daily; rentals), ice skating. Summer activities include ten swimming pools, three water slides; tennis, miniature golf, driving range. **$$$$**

Full-Service Resort

★ ★ **SMUGGLERS' NOTCH RESORT.** *4323 Hwy 108 S, Jeffersonville (05464). Phone 802/644-8851; toll-free 800/451-8752; fax 802/644-1230. www.smuggs. com.* Located in rural Vermont, this resort caters to family vacationers and has activities tailored to the four seasons of the year. 525 rooms, 3 story. Check-in 5 pm, check-out 11 am. Restaurant, bar. Children's activity center. Fitness room. Eight outdoor pools, whirlpool. Tennis. Ski in/ski out. Airport transportation available. **$**

Specialty Lodging

SINCLAIR INN BED & BREAKFAST. *389 Hwy 15, Jericho (05465). Phone 802/899-2234; toll-free 800/433-4658; fax 802/899-2007. www.sinclairinnbb. com.* This restored Queen Anne Victorian inn was built in 1890. 6 rooms, 3 story. Children over 12 years only. Complimentary full breakfast. Check-in 4-6 pm, check-out 11 am. **$**

Killington (D-2)

See also Plymouth, Rutland, Woodstock

Population 50
Elevation 1,229 ft
Area Code 802
Zip 05751
Information Killington Chamber of Commerce, PO Box 114; phone 802/773-4181 or toll-free 800/337-1928
Web Site www.killingtonchamber.com

What to See and Do

Gifford Woods State Park. *34 Gifford Woods, Killington (05737). On Hwy 100, 1 mile N of jct Hwy 4. Phone 802/775-5354. www.vtstateparks.com.* This 114-acre park has fishing at nearby pond, boat access to Kent Pond. Foot trails (Appalachian Trail passes through park). Virgin forest with picnic facilities. Tent and trailer sites (dump station), lean-tos. (Memorial Day-Columbus Day) Standard fees.

Killington Resort. *4763 Killington Rd, Killington (05751). 5 miles SW of jct Hwy 4 and Hwy 100, N. Phone 802/422-3261; toll-free 800/621-6867. www.killington.com.* Comprises 1,200 acres with seven mountains (highest elevation 4,241 feet). Two gondolas, six high-speed quad, six quad, six triple, four double chairlifts, eight surface lifts; patrol, school, rentals; snowmaking; mountaintop restaurant (with observation decks), six cafeterias, bars; children's center, nursery; lodging. More than 200 runs; longest run 10 miles, vertical drop 3,150 feet. Snowboarding; snow tubing. (Oct-June, daily) The resort offers

Pico Alpine Slide and Scenic Chairlift. *4763 Killington Rd, Killington (05751). Phone toll-free 866/667-7426.* Chairlift to top of mountain slope; control speed of own sled on the way down. Sports center and restaurant below. (Late May-mid-Oct) **$$$$**

Summer activities. Resort activities include a tennis school (Memorial Day-Sept), 18-hole golf, mountain biking (rentals), in-line skating/skateboarding park; gondola rides to view foliage; two water slides. (July 4-Sept)

Limited-Service Hotels

★ ★ **CASCADES LODGE.** *58 Old Mill Rd, Killington Village (05751). Phone 802/422-3731; toll-free 800/345-0113; fax 802/422-3351. www.cascadeslodge. com.* 46 rooms, 3 story. Pets accepted, some restrictions; fee. Complimentary full breakfast. Check-in 3 pm, check-out 11 am. Restaurant, bar. Fitness room. Indoor pool, whirlpool. Ski in/ski out. **$**

★ **ECONO LODGE KILLINGTON AREA.** *51 Rt 4, Mendon (05701-9652). Phone 800/992-9067; toll-free 800/553-2666; fax 802/773-2193.* 30 rooms. Pets accepted. Complimentary continental breakfast. Check-in 4 pm, check-out 10:30 am. Children's activity center. Outdoor pool, whirlpool. **$**

★ ★ **GREY BONNET INN.** *831 Hwy 100, Killington (05751). Phone 802/775-2537; toll-free 800/342-2086; fax 802/775-3371. www.greybonnetinn.com.* 40 rooms, 3 story. Closed Apr-May, late Oct-late Nov. Check-in 5 pm, check-out 11 am. Restaurant, bar. Fitness room. Indoor pool, outdoor pool, whirlpool. Tennis. **$**

★ ★ **KILLINGTON PICO MOTOR INN.** *64 Hwy 4, Killington (05751). Phone 802/773-4088; toll-free 800/548-4713; fax 802/775-9705. www.killingtonpico. com.* 28 rooms. Complimentary full breakfast. Check-in 3 pm, check-out 11 am. Restaurant, bar. Outdoor pool, whirlpool. **$**

★ **SHERBURNE-KILLINGTON MOTEL.** *1946 Hwy 4, Killington (05751). Phone 802/773-9535; toll-free 800/366-0493; fax 802/773-0011. www. lodgingkillington.com.* View of mountains. 20 rooms. Complimentary continental breakfast. Check-in 3 pm, check-out 11 am. Outdoor pool. **$**

★ ★ **SUMMIT LODGE.** *Killington Mountain Rd, Killington (05751). Phone 802/422-3535; toll-free 800/635-6343; fax 802/422-3536. www.summitlodgevermont.com.* 45 rooms, 3 story. Check-in 3 pm, check-out 11 am. Restaurant, bar. Two outdoor pools, whirlpool. Tennis. Airport transportation available. **$**
🔲 🏊 🎿

Full-Service Resorts

★ ★ ★ **CORTINA INN AND RESORT.** *103 Hwy 4, Killington (05751). Phone 802/773-3333; toll-free 800/451-6108; fax 802/775-6948. www.cortinainn.com.* This cozy inn and resort is a perfect choice for a country getaway weekend. Guests can enjoy activities year-round. 97 rooms. Pets accepted; fee. Complimentary full breakfast. Check-in 3 pm, check-out 11 am. Restaurant, bar. Fitness room. Indoor pool, whirlpool. Tennis. Airport transportation available. **$**
🐾 🎿 🏊 🎿

★ ★ ★ **INN OF THE SIX MOUNTAINS.** *2617 Killington Rd, Killington (05751). Phone 802/422-4302; toll-free 800/228-4676; fax 802/422-4321. www.sixmountains.com.* Tucked away in the mountains of Killington, this resort is a family pleaser year-round. 100 rooms, 3 story. Complimentary continental breakfast. Check-in 4 pm, check-out noon. Restaurant, bar. Fitness room. Indoor pool, outdoor pool, whirlpool. Tennis. **$**
🎿 🏊 🎿

Full-Service Inn

★ ★ ★ **RED CLOVER INN.** *7 Woodward Rd, Mendon (05701). Phone 802/775-2290; toll-free 800/752-0571; fax 802/773-0594. www.redcloverinn.com.* This 1840s country inn is situated on 13 acres and boasts wonderful views of the Green Mountains. The guest rooms are individually appointed with antiques and country woodwork. 14 rooms, 2 story. Children over 12 years only. Complimentary full breakfast. Check-in 2 pm, check-out 11 am. Wireless Internet access. Restaurant, bar. **$$**
🔲

Specialty Lodging

VERMONT INN. *Hwy 4, Killington (05751). Phone 802/775-0708; toll-free 800/541-7795; fax 802/773-2440. www.vermontinn.com.* 18 rooms, 2 story. Closed mid-Apr-late May. Children over 6 years only. Check-in 2 pm, check-out 11 am. Restaurant, bar. Fitness room. Outdoor pool, whirlpool. Tennis. **$$**
🎿 🏊 🎿

Restaurants

★ ★ ★ **HEMINGWAY'S.** *4988 Hwy 4, Killington (05751). Phone 802/422-3886; fax 802/422-3468. www.hemingwaysrestaurant.com.* Housed in a charming 19th-century house and warmed by a glowing fireplace, elaborate fresh country flower arrangements, glass-enclosed gardens, and a stone-walled wine cellar, Hemingways is an enchanting restaurant for romance, where fine dining feels comfortable and warm. The chef offers several choices (a nightly changing wine-tasting menu in addition to a six-course feasting menu, a four-course vegetable menu, and a three-course prix fixe menu), each prepared with seasonal ingredients, regional seafood, and farm-raised poultry and game. Hemingways is known for its robust, American-style fare—notably the pecan-crusted Vermont lamb with crispy potatoes and green beans, and the wood-grilled quail with cheddar corn cakes and black-eyed pea vinaigrette. Handmade breads and a diverse wine list are other delicious perks. International menu. Dinner. Closed Mon-Tues; also mid-Apr-mid-May, late Oct-mid-Nov. Bar. Casual attire. **$$$$**
🔲

★ ★ ★ **RED CLOVER.** *7 Woodward Rd, Mendon (05701). Phone 802/775-2290; toll-free 800/752-0571. www.redcloverinn.com.* Sophisticated inn dining in three candlelit dining rooms (two have fireplaces) distinguish this charming country inn. Friendly service completes the experience. American menu. Dinner Thurs-Sun; daily during holidays and in foliage season. Closed Mon-Wed. Bar. **$$**
🔲

★ ★ **VERMONT INN.** *Hwy 4, Killington (05751). Phone 802/775-0708; toll-free 800/541-7795; fax 802/773-2440. www.vermontinn.com.* This restaurant, located in the Vermont Inn (see), features a large wood-burning fireplace, exposed beams, and views of the front lawn and mountains beyond. American menu. Dinner. Closed three weeks in Apr and May. Bar. Children's menu. Casual attire. Reservations recommended. **$$**

Londonderry (E-2)

See also Grafton, Manchester and Manchester Center, Peru, Stratton Mountain, Weston

Founded 1770
Population 1,506
Elevation 1,151 ft
Area Code 802

Zip 05148
Information Londonderry Area Chamber of Commerce Mountain Marketplace, PO Box 58; phone 802/824-8178
Web Site www.londonderryvt.com

Limited-Service Hotel

★ ★ **DOSTAL'S RESORT LODGE.** *441 Magic Mountain Access Rd, Londonderry (05148). Phone 802/824-6700; toll-free 800/255-5373; fax 802/824-6701. www.dostals.com.* 50 rooms, 2 story. Closed Nov-mid-Dec. Pets accepted; fee. Check-in 3 pm, check-out 11 am. Restaurant, bar. Indoor pool, outdoor pool, whirlpool. Tennis. **$**
🖥️ 🐾 🏊 🎿

Specialty Lodgings

FROG'S LEAP INN. *7455 Hwy 100, Londonderry (05148). Phone 802/824-3019; toll-free 877/376-4753; fax 802/824-3657. www.frogsleapinn.com.* This historic building (1842) is situated on 32 wooded acres. 17 rooms, 2 story. Closed three weeks in Apr and one week in Nov. Pets accepted; fee. Check-in 2 pm, check-out 11 am. Restaurant. Outdoor pool. Tennis. **$**
🐾 🏊 🎿

LONDONDERRY INN. *8 Melendy Hill Rd, Londonderry (05155). Phone 802/824-5226; toll-free 800/644-5226. www.londonderryinn.com.* This inn is a former farmhouse (1826). 25 rooms, 3 story. Complimentary continental breakfast. Check-in 2 pm, check-out 11 am. Restaurant. Outdoor pool. **$**
🖥️ 🏊

SWISS INN. *249 Hwy 11, Londonderry (05148). Phone 802/824-3442; toll-free 800/847-9477; fax 802/824-6313. www.swissinn.com.* 19 rooms, 2 story. Complimentary full breakfast. Check-in 2 pm, check-out 11 am. Restaurant, bar. Outdoor pool. Tennis. **$**
🖥️ 🏊 🎿

Ludlow (E-2)

See also Okemo State Forest, Plymouth, Springfield, Weston

Population 2,302
Area Code 802
Zip 05149
Information Ludlow Area Chamber of Commerce, Okemo Market Pl, PO Box 333; phone 802/228-5830

What to See and Do

Crowley Cheese Factory. *103 Healdville Rd, Healdville (05758). Phone 802/259-2340. www.crowleycheese-vermont.com.* (1882) Oldest cheese factory in the United States; still makes cheese by hand as in the 19th century. Display of tools used in early cheese factories and in home cheesemaking. Watch the process and sample the product. (Mon-Fri) **FREE**

Green Mountain Sugar House. *820 Hwy 100 N, Ludlow (05149). 4 miles N on Hwy 100 N. Phone toll-free 800/643-9338. www.gmsh.com.* Working maple sugar producer on shore of Lake Pauline. Shop offers syrup, candies, crafts, and gifts. (Daily) **FREE**

Okemo Mountain Ski Area. *77 Okemo Ridge Rd, Ludlow (05149). Phone 802/228-5222; toll-free 800/786-5366. www.okemo.com.* (See OKEMO STATE FOREST)

Full-Service Inn

★ ★ ★ **THE GOVERNOR'S INN.** *86 Main St, Ludlow (05149). Phone 802/228-8830; toll-free 800/468-3766; fax 802/228-2961. www.thegovernorsinn.com.* Skiers with a penchant for history are smitten by The Governors Inn. The challenging slopes of Okemo Mountain are just a short distance away, and the inn provides convenient shuttle service from its doorstep to the base of the mountain. Non-skiers are instantly enchanted by Vermont's country charms while perusing the antiques shops and country stores of the village. The inn itself, dating to 1890, is a Victorian masterpiece in every detail. Floral patterns, period furniture, and antiques reflect a bygone era, and gas-lit stoves and fireplaces in many rooms add a romantic ambience. Breakfast is a truly elegant affair, where tables are gracefully set with silver, crystal, and china. The talented chefs gourmet picnic baskets are heartwarming and delicious, and dinner is an equally inspired event. Diners taken with the cuisine may participate in one of the fantastic Culinary Magic Cooking Seminars, where the kitchens secrets are happily shared. 9 rooms, 3 story. Closed late Dec; also two weeks in Apr and two weeks in Nov. Children over 12 years only. Complimentary full breakfast. Check-in 2-6 pm, check-out 11 am. Restaurant. **$$**
🖥️

Specialty Lodgings

ANDRIE ROSE INN. *13 Pleasant St, Ludlow (05149). Phone 802/228-4846; toll-free 800/223-4846; fax 802/228-7910. www.andrieroseinn.com.* This cozy

inn was built in 1829 and is nestled at the base of Okemo Mountain. The guest rooms are appointed with antiques, skylights, and whirlpool tubs. 23 rooms, 2 story. Complimentary full breakfast. Check-in 3 pm, check-out 11 am. **$**
🅓

COMBES FAMILY INN. *953 E Lake Rd, Ludlow (05149). Phone 802/228-8799; toll-free 800/822-8799; fax 802/228-8704. www.combesfamilyinn.com.* This restored farmhouse (1891) is situated on 50 acres and near Lake Rescue. 11 rooms, 2 story. Closed mid-Apr-mid-May. Pets accepted. Check-in 3 pm, check-out 11 am. Restaurant. **$**
🅓 🐾

GOLDEN STAGE INN. *399 Depot St, Proctorsville (05153). Phone 802/226-7744; toll-free 800/253-8226; fax 802/226-7882. www.goldenstageinn.com.* 9 rooms. Check-in 3 pm, check-out 11 am. Restaurant (public by reservation), bar. Outdoor pool. **$$**
🏊

INN AT WATER'S EDGE. *45 Kingdom Rd, Ludlow (05149). Phone 802/228-8143; toll-free 888/706-9736; fax 802/228-8443. www.innatwatersedge.com.* 11 rooms. Complimentary full breakfast. Check-in 2 pm, check-out 11 am. **$$**

Lyndonville (B-3)

See also St. Johnsbury

Settled 1781
Population 1,255
Elevation 720 ft
Area Code 802
Zip 05851
Information Lyndon Area Chamber of Commerce, PO Box 886; phone 802/626-9696
Web Site www.lyndonvermont.com

Home of small industries and trading center for the surrounding dairy and stock raising farms, Lyndonville lies in the valley of the Passumpsic River. Five covered bridges, the earliest dating to 1795, are located within the town limits.

What to See and Do

Burke Mountain Ski Area. *Rt. 114 E & E Burke, Lyndonville. 1 mile N on Hwy 5, then 6 miles NE on Hwy 114, in Darling State Park. Phone 802/626-3322; toll-free 888/287-5388. www.skiburke.com.* Area has two

chairlifts, one Pomalift, J-bar; school, rentals; snowmaking. Two cafeterias, two bars; nursery. Forty-three runs, longest run approximately 2 1/2 miles; vertical drop 2,000 feet. More than 57 miles of cross-country trails. (Thanksgiving-early Apr, daily)

Lake Willoughby. *18 miles N on Hwy 5A.* Beaches, water sports, fishing; hiking trails to the summit of Mount Pisgah, at 2,741 feet.

Limited-Service Hotel

★ **COLONNADE INN.** *28 Back Center Rd, Lyndonville (05851). Phone 802/626-9316; toll-free 877/435-5688; fax 802/626-1023.* 40 rooms, 2 story. Complimentary continental breakfast. Check-in 3 pm, check-out 11 am. **$**
🅓

Specialty Lodging

THE WILDFLOWER INN. *2059 Darling Hill Rd, Lyndonville (05851). Phone 802/626-8310; toll-free 800/627-8310; fax 802/626-3039. www.wildflowerinn. com.* Family-oriented inn on 500 acres; barns, farm animals; sledding slopes. Art gallery. 25 rooms, 2 story. Closed two weeks in Apr and Nov. Complimentary full breakfast. Check-in 3 pm, check-out 11 am. Restaurant. Children's activity center. Outdoor pool, children's pool, whirlpool. Tennis. **$**
🏊 🎿

Manchester and Manchester Center (E-1)

See also Arlington, Bennington, Dorset, Green Mountain National Forest, Londonderry, Peru, Stratton Mountain

Settled 1764
Population 3,622
Elevation 899 and 753 ft
Area Code 802
Zip Manchester 05254; Manchester Center 05255
Information Manchester and the Mountains Regional Chamber of Commerce, 5046 Main St, Suite 1; phone 802/362-2100 or toll-free 800/362-4144
Web Site www.manchestervermont.net

These towns have been among Vermont's best-loved year-round resorts for 100 years. The surrounding mountains make them serenely attractive, and the ski business has added to their following. Bromley Mountain, Stratton Mountain, and other areas lure thousands each year. A Ranger District office of the Green Mountain National Forest is located here.

What to See and Do

American Museum of Fly Fishing. *4104 Main St, Manchester (05254). VT Historic Hwy 7A and Seminary Ave.* Phone 802/362-3300. www.amff.com. This museum, founded in 1968 by fishermen who wanted to ensure that the history of their sport would not be lost, is a mecca for anglers of all ages. Collection of fly-fishing memorabilia; tackle of many famous persons, including Dwight D. Eisenhower, Ernest Hemingway, Andrew Carnegie, Winslow Homer, Bing Crosby, and others. (Mon-Fri 10 am-4 pm; closed holidays) **$**

Emerald Lake State Park. *65 Emerald Lake Ln, North Dorset (05253). 6 miles N on Hwy 7.* Phone 802/362-1655. www.vtstateparks.com. This 430-acre park has rich flora in a limestone-based bedrock. Swimming beach, bathhouse, fishing (also in nearby streams), boating (rentals); nature and hiking trails, picnicking, concession. Tent and trailer sites (dump station), lean-tos. (Memorial Day-Columbus Day)

⭐ **Equinox Sky Line Drive.** *1A St and Bruno Dr, Manchester & Manchester Center (05250). 5 miles S on VT Historic Hwy 7A.* Phone 802/362-1114. www.equinoxmountain.com/skylinedrive. A spectacular 5-mile paved road that rises from 600 to 3,835 feet; parking and picnic areas along road; view from top of Mount Equinox. Fog or rain may make mountain road dangerous and travel inadvisable. (May-Oct, daily) No large camper vehicles. **$$$**

Historic Hildene. *1005 Hildene Rd, Manchester (05254). 2 miles S via VT Historic Hwy 7A.* Phone 802/362-1788. www.hildene.org. (1904) The 412-acre estate of Robert Todd Lincoln (Abraham Lincoln's son) includes a 24-room Georgian manor house, held in the family until 1975; original furnishings; carriage barn; formal gardens; nature trails. Tours. (Mid-May-Oct, daily 9:30 am-3 pm; Nov-May, Thurs-Mon 11 am-3 pm) **$$**

Manchester Designer Outlets. *Hwy 11 and 30, Manchester Center (05255).* Phone 802/362-3736. www.manchesterdesigneroutlets.com. Many outlet stores can be found in this area, mainly along Highway 11/30 and at the intersection of Highway 11/30 and Highway 7A. Contact the Chamber of Commerce (802/362-2100) for a complete listing of stores.

Merck Forest & Farmland Center. *Rupert Mountain Road, Route 315, East Rupert. 8 miles NW on Hwy 30 to East Rupert, then 2 1/2 miles W on Hwy 315.* Phone 802/394-7836. www.merckforest.com. Includes 3100 acres of unspoiled upland forest, meadows, mountains, and ponds; 28 miles of roads and trails for hiking and cross-country skiing. Fishing; picnicking, camping (reservations required). Educational programs. Fees for some activities.

Southern Vermont Arts Center. *West Rd, Manchester (05254). 1 mile N off West Rd.* Phone 802/362-1405. www.svac.org. Painting, sculpture, prints; concerts, music festivals; botany trail; caf. Gift shop. (Gallery, Tues-Sat 10 am-5 pm, Sun noon-5 pm; museum closed May-Sept) **$$**

Limited-Service Hotels

⭐ **ASPEN MOTEL.** *5669 Main St, Manchester Center (05255).* Phone 802/362-2450; fax 802/362-1348. www.thisisvermont.com/aspen. Nestled in a valley and surrounded by the Green Mountains, this affordable, motel-style lodging welcomes guests. It is well maintained and not far from the town center just over a mile. There are many activities for guests to enjoy including shuffleboard, horseshoes, croquet, badminton, and other lawn games. 24 rooms. Check-in 2 pm, check-out 11 am. Outdoor pool. Credit cards accepted. **$**

⭐ **MANCHESTER VIEW.** *Hwy 7A and High Meadow Way, Manchester Center (05255).* Phone 802/362-2739; toll-free 800/548-4141; fax 802/362-2199. www.manchesterview.com. Situated atop a small hill, this country lodging commands sweeping views of meadows and mountains to the north and west. The exterior features nicely landscaped lawns and a pool area, while inside, guest rooms are uniquely decorated in a wide range of styles, from floral themes to antique country. Gas or wood-burning fireplaces and deep, jetted tubs are found in many of the rooms, and all feature private balconies or patios, refrigerators, VCRs and DVD players, and pillow top mattresses. Many of Vermont's ski resorts are near this Green Mountain location, and guests have privileges at local tennis courts. 36 rooms, 2 story. Complimentary continental breakfast. Check-in 2 pm, check-out 11 am. Wireless Internet access. Outdoor pool. **$$**

★ **PALMER HOUSE.** *5383 Main St, Manchester Center (05255). Phone 802/362-3600; toll-free 800/917-6245; fax 802/362-3600. www.palmerhouse.com.* This 20-acre resort is located in the heart of Manchester, nestled in the surrounding mountains. 50 rooms. Children over 12 years only. Complimentary continental breakfast. Check-in 3 pm, check-out 11 am. Fitness room. Indoor pool, outdoor pool, whirlpool. Golf, 9 holes. Tennis. **$**
🏋 🏊 ⛷ 🏃

★ ★ ★ **VILLAGE COUNTRY INN.** *3835 Main St, Historic Hwy 7A, Manchester (05254). Phone 802/362-1792; toll-free 800/370-0300; fax 802/362-7238. www.villagecountryinn.com.* Located in the charming village of Manchester, this historic mansion is perfect for a romantic getaway. Guest rooms are adorned with lace, chintz, mirrored armoires, antique collectibles, canopied beds, and some have fireplaces. The on-site restaurant, Angel, is decorated in a cheerful garden style and features American cuisine. Guests can relax in the formal living room which features a fieldstone fireplace and an old working sleigh as the coffee table. After endulging in the complimentary cookies, lemonade, and tea in the lobby, guests can enjoy a game or book before turning in for the night. 32 rooms, 3 story. Pets accepted, some restrictions; fee. Children over 12 years only. Complimentary full breakfast. Check-in 2 pm, check-out 11 am. Restaurant, bar. Outdoor pool. Credit cards accepted. **$$**
🐾 🏊

Full-Service Resort

★ ★ ★ **THE EQUINOX.** *3567 Main St, Manchester Village (05254). Phone 802/362-4700; toll-free 866/346-7625; fax 802/362-4861. www.equinox.rockresorts.com.* Since 1769, The Equinox has welcomed visitors with open arms. This premier resort set on 1,100 acres has long been a favorite of notables, including Abraham Lincolns family, who vacationed here in the 1800s. Located on historic Route 7A in the shadow of Mount Equinox, this classic New England getaway offers guests a truly well-rounded adventure. From world-class golf at the Gleneagles golf course and skiing at nearby Stratton and Bromley mountains to falconry, Orvis fly fishing and shooting schools, and even off-road driving with Hummers and Land Rovers, this place is a paradise for sports enthusiasts. The Avanyu Spa and nearby shopping in Manchester Village appeal to others, and three restaurants combine historic charm and classic fare for enjoyable dining experiences. 180 rooms, 4 story. Pets accepted, some restric-

tions; fee. Check-in 4 pm, check-out 11 am. Wireless Internet access. Three restaurants, bar. Fitness room, fitness classes available, spa. Indoor pool. Golf, 18 holes. Tennis. Business center. **$$**
🐾 🏋 🏊 🎿 ⛷ 🏃

Full-Service Inn

★ ★ ★ **RELUCTANT PANTHER INN AND RESTAURANT.** *39 West Rd, Manchester (05254). Phone 802/362-2568; toll-free 800/822-2331; fax 802/362-2586. www.reluctantpanther.com.* This lovely inn was built in 1850 by a local wealthy blacksmith. The owners have refurbished the property and were able to retain two of the original fireplaces. 21 rooms. Children over 14 years only. Complimentary full breakfast. Check-in 3 pm, check-out 11 am. Restaurant, bar. **$$**
🔟

Specialty Lodgings

1811 HOUSE. *Main St, Manchester (05254). Phone 802/362-1811; toll-free 800/432-1811; fax 802/362-2443. www.1811house.com.* Each guest room at the inn is named for individuals that were prominent in the history of the Manchester. Gardens grace 7 1/2 acres around the inn. 13 rooms, 2 story. Children over 16 years only. Complimentary full breakfast. Check-in 2-10 pm, check-out 11 am. Bar. Tennis. **$$**
🔟 🎿

INN AT MANCHESTER. *3967 Main St, Manchester (05254). Phone 802/362-1793; toll-free 800/273-1793; fax 802/362-3218. www.innatmanchester.com.* A lovely inn where guests find "peace, pancakes, and pampering," this 19th-century Victorian structure has been beautifully restored to its original grandeur. 18 rooms, 3 story. Children over 8 years only. Complimentary full breakfast. Check-in 2 pm, check-out 11 am. Wireless Internet access. Outdoor pool. **$$**
🔟 🏊

THE INN AT ORMSBY HILL. *1842 Main St, Manchester (05255). Phone 802/362-1163.* Hospitality and relaxation await guests at this tranquil location surrounded by wonderful views of the Green Mountains. The common areas are roomy and feature interesting décor, including a collection of china and unique fireplaces. 10 rooms. Complimentary full breakfast. Check-in 3 pm, check-out 11 am. **$$**

MANCHESTER HIGHLANDS INN. *216 Highland Ave, Manchester Center (05255). Phone 802/362-4565;*

toll-free 800/743-4565; fax 802/362-4028. www.high-landsinn.com. Views of Mt. Equinox can be seen from this Victorian inn, where the atmosphere is warm and cozy. Plenty of outlet shopping is near this hillside location. 15 rooms, 3 story. Complimentary full breakfast. Check-in 3 pm, check-out 11 am. Wireless Internet access. Outdoor pool. **$$**

WILBURTON INN. *River Rd, Manchester Village (05254). Phone 802/362-2500; toll-free 800/648-4944; fax 802/362-1107. www.wilburton.com.* Set on a hill that overlooks the Battenkill Valley, this 20-acre Victorian estate is a terrific choice for a weekend in New England. Guests can enjoy many activities on the property or enjoy the shopping nearby. The spacious grounds feature sculptured displays, and the inn offers mountain views. 36 rooms, 3 story. Complimentary full breakfast. Check-in 3 pm, check-out 11 am. Outdoor pool. **$$**

Spa

★ ★ ★ **AVANYU SPA AT THE EQUINOX RESORT.** *3567 Main St, Manchester Village (05254). Phone 802/362-4700; fax 802/362-4861.* New England charm and the surrounding beauty of the Green and Taconic mountains have been drawing guests to The Equinox for more than 200 years. But in 2003, this landmark property in the Vermont countryside gave guests another reason to flock to the world-class resort: Avanyu Spa. Like the resort, the spa combines luxury, charm, and a nature-inspired theme that offers guests a uniquely decadent experience. Mrs. Abraham Lincoln once called The Equinox the premier summer resort. If she could see the 13,000-square-foot Avanyu Spa, with its 75-foot heated indoor pool, state-of-the-art fitness center, ten treatment rooms, and saunas and steam baths, she would surely offer the same accolades. She would also indulge in a treatment or two—but not before donning a fluffy white robe and enjoying the calm of a crackling fire in the relaxation room. Having taken its name from the ancient Tewa Native American word for a mythical water serpent, Avanyu Spa incorporates elements of its natural surroundings into facials, massages, and body scrubs. Your skin will glow after the Gentle Rain body treatment, where a sea salt, maple, or citrus scrub is followed with a warm waterfall shower and an application of rich body cream. Massage therapies like Flowing Water, Rolling Thunder, and Dancing Wind simulate natures energies through effleurage, deep

tissue, and gentle massage techniques, while the River Stones massage employs the physical element of hot and cold basalt river rocks. A signature of Avanyu Spa is the 80-minute Avanyu Legend. In this revitalizing body treatment, guests choose a scrub from a selection of fragrance-infused sugars, salts, and crushed flowers; a mask with options that range from oils to seaweeds and muds; and a finishing moisturizer of essential blended oils or hydrating lotions. By far, Avanyu Spa is the most luxurious way to feel revitalized and experience nature. It most certainly wins out over a nature walk in the park.

Restaurant

★ ★ ★ **BLACK SWAN.** *Hwy 7A, Manchester (05254). Phone 802/362-3807. www.blackswanrestaurant.com.* This restaurant is a converted farmhouse built in the 1800s. International menu. Dinner. Closed Thanksgiving. Bar. **$$**

Marlboro (F-2)

See also Brattleboro, Wilmington

Settled 1763
Population 924
Elevation 1,736 ft
Area Code 802
Zip 05344

What to See and Do

Marlboro College. *2582 South Rd, Marlboro (05344). 2 1/2 miles S of Hwy 9. Phone 802/257-4333. www.marlboro.edu.* (1946) (300 students) Arts and sciences, international studies. On campus is Drury Art Gallery. (Sun-Fri 1-5 pm; closed holidays and when school not in session). **FREE**

Special Event

Marlboro Music Festival. *Rte 9, Marlboro (05344). Phone 802/254-2394.* Marlboro College campus. Chamber music concerts. Mid-July-mid-Aug. **$$$$**

Middlebury (C-1)

See also Brandon, Vergennes

Settled 1761
Population 8,034
Elevation 366 ft

Area Code 802
Zip 05753
Information Addison County Chamber of Commerce Information Center, 2 Court St; phone 802/388-7951 or toll-free 800/733-8376
Web Site www.midvermont.com

Benjamin Smalley built the first log house here just before the Revolution. In 1800, the town had a full-fledged college. By 1803, there was a flourishing marble quarry and a women's academy run by Emma Hart Willard, a pioneer in education for women; today, it is known as Middlebury College. A Ranger District office of the Green Mountain National Forest is located here; map and guides for day hikes on Long Trail are available.

What to See and Do

Congregational Church. *27 N Pleasant St, Middlebury (05753). On the Common. Phone 802/388-7634.* (1806-1809) Built after a plan in the *Country Builder's Assistant* and designed by architect Lavius Fillmore. Architecturally, one of finest in Vermont.

Henry Sheldon Museum. *1 Park St, Middlebury (05753). Phone 802/388-2117. www.henrysheldonmuseum.org.* Comprehensive collection of 19th-century "Vermontiana" in brick house (1829) with black marble fireplaces. Authentic furnishings range from hand-forged kitchen utensils to country and high-style furniture. Museum also features oil portraits, pewter, Staffordshire, clocks, pianos, toys, dolls, and local relics. Guided and self-guided tours. (Mon-Sat 10 am-5 pm; closed holidays) **$**

Historic Middlebury Village Walking Tour. *2 Court St, Middlebury (05753). Phone 802/388-7951. www.midvermont.com.* Contact the Addison County Chamber of Commerce Information Center for map and information.

Middlebury College. *Middlebury College, Rte 30, Middlebury (05753). W of town on Hwy 125. Phone 802/443-5000. www.middlebury.edu.* (1800) (1,950 students) Famous for the teaching of arts and sciences; summer language schools; Bread Loaf School of English and Writers' Conference. College includes

> **Bread Loaf.** *Middlebury College, Freeman International Center, Middlebury (05753). 10 miles E on Hwy 125. Phone 802/443-5418.* Site of nationally known Bread Loaf School of English in June and annual Writers' Conference in August. Also site

of Robert Frost's cabin. In winter, it is the Carroll and Jane Rikert Ski Touring Center.

Emma Willard House. *Middlebury College, Rte 30, Middlebury (05753). Phone 802/443-5000.* Location of first women's seminary (1814), now admissions and financial aid offices.

Middlebury College Museum of Art. *Middlebury College Center for the Arts, Hwy 30, Middlebury (05753). Phone 802/443-5007.* (Tues-Fri 10 am-5 pm, Sat-Sun noon-5 pm; closed late Augearly Sept and mid-DecJanuary 2) **FREE**

Middlebury College Snow Bowl. *Rt 125 between Rt 7 & Rt 100, Middlebury. 13 miles E on Hwy 125, just E of Bread Loaf. Phone 802/388-7951.* Area has triple, two double chairlifts; patrol, school, rentals; snowmaking; cafeteria. Fourteen runs. (Early Dec-early Apr, daily; closed Dec 25-Jan 1) **$$$$**

Old Stone Row. *Middlebury College, Rte 30, Middlebury (05753). Phone 802/443-5000.* Includes Painter Hall (1815), the oldest college building in the state.

★ **Starr Library.** *Middlebury College, 110 Storrs Avenue, Middlebury (05753). Phone 802/443-2000.* Has a collection of works by Robert Frost and other American writers. (Daily; closed holidays)

UVM Morgan Horse Farm. *74 Battell Dr, Weybridge (05753). 2 1/2 miles NW off Hwy 23. Phone 802/388-2011. www.uvm.edu/morgan.* Breeding and training farm for internationally acclaimed Morgan horses; owned by the University of Vermont. Daily workouts and training can be viewed. Guided tours, slide presentations. (May-Oct, daily 9 am-4 pm) **$**

Vermont State Craft Center at Frog Hollow. *1 Mill St, Middlebury (05753). Phone 802/388-3177; toll-free 888/388-3177. www.froghollow.org.* Restored mill overlooking Otter Creek Falls houses an exhibition and sales gallery with works of more than 300 Vermont craftspeople. Special exhibitions, classes and workshops. (Spring-fall: daily; rest of year: Mon-Sat; closed holidays) **FREE**

Special Events

Addison County Home and Garden Show. *Middlebury Union High School, 73 Charles Ave, Middlebury (05753). Phone 802/388-7951. www.midvermont.com.* Exhibits, demonstrations. Usually mid-Mar. **$**

Festival on the Green. *Middlebury Green, Main St and Hwy 7, Middlebury (05753). Phone 802/388-0216. www. festivalonthegreen.org.* Village green. Classical, modern, and traditional dance; chamber and folk music; theater and comedy presentations. Early July. **FREE**

Winter Carnival. *Middlebury College, Hwy 30, Middlebury. Phone 802/443-3100.* The oldest and largest student-run carnival in the country includes fireworks, an ice show and ski competitions; held on the campus of Middlebury College. Late Feb.

Limited-Service Hotel

★ ★ **MIDDLEBURY INN.** *24 Court House Sq, Middlebury (05753). Phone 802/388-4961; toll-free 800/842-4666; fax 802/388-4563. www.middleburyinn. com.* Established in 1827. 45 rooms, 3 story. Pets accepted, some restrictions. Complimentary continental breakfast. Check-in 3 pm, check-out 11 am. Restaurant, bar. **$$**
🐾

Full-Service Inn

★ ★ ★ **SWIFT HOUSE INN.** *25 Stewart Ln, Middlebury (05753). Phone 802/388-9925; toll-free 866/388-9925; fax 802/388-9927. www.swifthouseinn. com.* This inn is composed of three separate buildings, each with its own character and charm. Rooms are individually decorated and feature four-poster beds and handmade quilts. 2 story. Pets accepted, some restrictions; fee. Complimentary continental breakfast. Check-in 3 pm, check-out 11 am. Restaurant. **$$**
🐾

Specialty Lodging

WAYBURY INN. *457 E Main (Hwy 125), East Middlebury (05743). Phone 802/388-4015; toll-free 800/348-1810; fax 802/388-1248. www.wayburyinn. com.* Constructed as a stagecoach stop; an inn since 1810. Near Middlebury College. 14 rooms. Pets accepted. Complimentary full breakfast. Check-in 3 pm, check-out 11 am. Restaurant, bar. **$**
🔳 🐾

Montpelier (C-2)

See also Barre, Waitsfield, Waterbury

Settled 1787
Population 8,247
Elevation 525 ft
Area Code 802
Information Central Vermont Chamber of Commerce, PO Box 336, Barre 05641; phone 802/229-5711
Web Site www.central-vt.com

The state capital, on the banks of the Winooski River, is also a life insurance center. Admiral Dewey, victor at Manila Bay, was born here. A popular summer vacation area, Montpelier absorbs the overflow from the nearby ski areas in winter.

What to See and Do

Hubbard Park. *22 Corse St, Montpelier (05602). 1 mile NW, on Hubbard Park Dr. Phone 802/223-7335. www. montpelierrec.org.* A 110-acre wooded area with picnic area (shelter, fireplaces, water). Stone observation tower (1932). **FREE**

Morse Farm. *1168 County Rd, Montpelier (05602). 3 miles N via County Rd (follow signs on Main St). Phone 802/223-2740; toll-free 800/242-2740. www.morse-farm.com.* Maple sugar and vegetable farm in rustic, wooded setting. Tour of sugar house; view sugarmaking process in season (Mar-Apr); slide show explains process off-season. Gift shop. (Daily; closed Easter, Dec 25) **FREE**

State House. *115 State St, Montpelier (05633). Phone 802/828-2228. www.leg.state.vt.us/sthouse/sthouse. htm.* (1859) Made of Vermont granite; dome covered with gold leaf. (Mon-Fri 8 am-4 pm. Guided tours, July-mid-October: Mon-Fri 10 am-3:30 pm, Sat 11 am-2:30pm) **FREE**

Thomas Waterman Wood Art Gallery. *36 College St, Montpelier (05602). In Vermont College Arts Center. Phone 802/828-8743. www.twwoodgallery.org.* Oils, watercolors, and etchings by Wood and other 19th-century American artists. Also American artists of the 1920s and '30s; changing monthly exhibits of works of contemporary local and regional artists. (Tues-Wed, Fri-Sun noon-4 pm; Thurs to 8 pm) **FREE**

Vermont Department of Libraries. *109 State St, Montpelier (05609). Pavilion Office Bldg. Phone 802/828-*

3261. dol.state.vt.us. Local and state history collections. (Mon-Fri; closed holidays) **FREE**

Vermont Historical Society Museum. *109 State St, Montpelier (05609). Pavilion Office Bldg, adjacent to State House. Phone 802/828-2291. www.vermonthistory. org.* Historical exhibits. (Tues-Sun; closed holidays) **$**

Limited-Service Hotel

★ **COMFORT INN.** *213 Paine Turnpike N, Montpelier (05602). Phone 802/229-2222; toll-free 800/4-; fax 802/229-2222. www.choicehotels.com.* 89 rooms, 3 story. Complimentary continental breakfast. Check-in 3 pm, check-out 11 am. Bar. Airport transportation available. **$**

Full-Service Hotel

★ ★ ★ **CAPITOL PLAZA HOTEL AND CON-FERENCE CENTER.** *100 State St, Montpelier (05602). Phone 802/223-5252; toll-free 800/274-5252; fax 802/229-5427. www.capitolplaza.com.* Located in the heart of Montpelier and across the street from the historic State House, this hotel has been serving Vermont's lawmakers and tourists since the 1930s. 56 rooms, 4 story. Check-in 3 pm, check-out 11 am. Restaurant, bar. **$**

Full-Service Inns

★ ★ ★ **INN AT MONTPELIER.** *147 Main St, Montpelier (05602). Phone 802/223-2727; fax 802/223-0722. www.innatmontpelier.com.* Take a trip back to the early 1800s with a visit to this historic inn. The two stately buildings that make up this inn showcase Greek and Colonial Revival woodwork, numerous fireplaces, and a magnificent front staircase. 19 rooms, 2 story. Complimentary continental breakfast. Check-in 3-9 pm, check-out 11 am. **$**

★ ★ ★ **THE INN ON THE COMMON.** *1162 N Craftsbury Rd, Craftsbury Common (05827). Phone 802/586-9619; toll-free 800/521-2233; fax 802/586-2249. www.innonthecommon.com.* Nestled under a large maple tree, this inn, which consists of three restored Federal-style houses, offers colorful gardens and wooded hillsides. Individually decorated guest rooms feature antiques, artwork, and sitting areas. 16 rooms, 2 story. Pets accepted, some restrictions; fee. Check-in 2-6 pm, check-out 11 am. Restaurant, bar. Outdoor pool. Tennis. **$$**

Specialty Lodging

NORTHFIELD INN. *228 Highland Ave, Northfield (05663). Phone 802/485-8558. www.thenorthfieldinn. com.* This inn was built in 1901and is furnished with period pieces. 28 rooms, 3 story. Children over 15 years only. Complimentary full breakfast. Check-in 3-6 pm. Check-out 11 am. **$**

Restaurant

★ ★ **CHEF'S TABLE.** *118 Main St, Montpelier (05602). Phone 802/229-9202; fax 802/223-9285. www. neci.edu/restaurants.html.* International menu. Dinner. Closed Sun-Mon; holidays. Bar. **$$$**

Newfane (F-2)

See also Brattleboro, Grafton

Settled 1774
Population 1,555
Elevation 536 ft
Area Code 802
Zip 05345
Information Town Clerk, 555 Rt 30, PO Box 36; phone 802/365-7772
Web Site www.newfanevt.com

Originally settled high on Newfane Hill, this is a charming, sleepy town. American poet Eugene Field spent many summer holidays here.

What to See and Do

Jamaica State Park. *48 Salmon Hole Ln, Jamaica. 13 miles W on Hwy 30. Phone 802/874-4600. www.vtstate-parks.com.* On 758 acres. Old train bed along West River serves as trail to Ball Mountain Dam. Fishing; hiking trails, picnicking, tent and trailer sites (dump station), lean-tos. Whitewater canoeing on river. (May-Columbus Day) Standard fees. **$$**

Scott Covered Bridge. *Rte 30, Townshend (05353). Over the West River in Townshend, 5 miles N via Hwy 30. Phone 802/257-0292.* (1870) Longest single span in state (166 feet), built with lattice-type trusses. Together, the three spans total 276 feet. Other two spans are of king post-type trusses.

Townshend State Forest. *2755 State Forest Rd, Townshend (05353). 6 miles N, off Hwy 30. Phone 802/365-7500. www.vtstateparks.com.* A 1,690-acre area with foot trail to Bald Mountain (1,580 feet). Swimming at nearby Townshend Reservoir Recreation Area; hiking trails, picnic sites, tent and trailer sites. (May-Columbus Day)

Windham County Courthouse. *7 Court St, Newfane (05345). On the green. Phone 802/365-7979.* (1825) **FREE**

Windham County Historical Society Museum. *Main St, Newfane (05345). On Hwy 30, across from the Village Green. Phone 802/365-4148. www.newfane.com/historical.* Contains artifacts from the 21 towns of Windham County; exhibits on the Civil War and the Vermont Regiment. (Memorial Day-Columbus Day, Wed-Sun) **DONATION**

Full-Service Inn

★ ★ ★ **WINDHAM HILL INN.** *311 Lawrence Dr, West Townshend (05359). Phone 802/874-4080; toll-free 800/944-4080; fax 802/874-4702. www.windhamhill. com.* Capture the peacefulness and serenity that can be found at this charming and elegant 1825 country estate perched amidst 160 well-maintained acres. Relax, surrounded by lush trees, fields, and an impressive rock wall border. Guests will find the views to be extraordinary, the rooms handsomely furnished, and the service warm and extremely friendly. 21 rooms, 3 story. Children over 12 years only. Check-in 2 pm, check-out 11 am. Restaurant. Outdoor pool. Tennis. **$$**

Specialty Lodging

FOUR COLUMNS INN. *21 West St, Newfane (05345). Phone 802/365-7713; toll-free 800/787-6633; fax 802/365-0022. www.fourcolumnsinn.com.* Located in the center of the country village of Newfane, yet nestled at the foot of a 150-acre private mountain, this 16-room inn combines historic charm with modern convenience. While some rooms are without TVs, they do have wireless Internet access. The décor is charmingly old-fashioned, yet all comfort: king beds, queens, sleigh beds, iron four-poster beds. Many suites have two-sided fireplaces, most rooms have whirlpools or soaking tubs, and everywhere there are fine art prints and antiques that provide interest without being fussy. The popular front suite has a whirlpool under large windows that overlook the village center and a huge, walk-in shower with 12 jets. Local lore says the four columns of this 1833 inn were initiated by the original owners wife, who was Southern and missed her native architecture. 16 rooms. Pets accepted, some

restrictions; fee. Complimentary continental breakfast. Check-in 2 pm, check-out 11 am. Restaurant, bar. Outdoor pool. **$$$**

Restaurants

★ ★ ★ **FOUR COLUMNS.** *21 West St, Newfane (05345). Phone 802/365-7713; toll-free 800/787-6633; fax 802/365-0022. www.fourcolumnsinn.com.* Chef Greg Parks has been cooking at this charming inn for many years, but his cuisine is as contemporary as you can find. He is dedicated to using Vermont-fresh products, which vary with the season. Grilled Canadian swordfish with rose peppercorns, vanilla bean, olive oil and lemon; rack of lamb and roasted beets with a rosemary garlic sauce; and black Angus grilled tenderloin with garlicky escargot and creamy gorgonzola sauce are among the offerings. Guests dine in a large room with a huge brick country hearth and a timbered ceiling—this room was once the property's barn. Lots of windows overlook the flower gardens, and tables are elegantly set with designer china, light cloths, and candles. Original fine art by local artists adorns the walls and is changed frequently. American menu. Dinner. Closed Dec 25. Bar. Children's menu. Casual attire. Reservations recommended. **$$$**

★ ★ ★ **OLD NEWFANE INN.** *Hwy 30, Newfane (05345). Phone 802/365-4427; toll-free 800/784-4427. www.oldnewfaneinn.com.* Timbered ceilings, brick fireplaces, and pewter cover plates add to the colonial charm of this historic 1787 landmark. Continental, French menu. Dinner. Closed Mon; Apr-mid-May, Nov-mid-Dec. Bar. Casual attire. Reservations recommended. **$$**

Newport (A-3)

Settled 1793
Population 4,434
Elevation 723 ft
Area Code 802
Zip 05855
Information Chamber of Commerce, 246 The Causeway; phone 802/334-7782
Web Site www.vtnorthcountry.org

Just a few miles from the Canadian border, Newport lies at the southern end of Lake Memphremagog. Rugged Owl's Head (3,360 feet) guards the western shore of the lake. Recreational activities in the area include swimming, fishing, boating, camping, skiing, and snowmobiling.

What to See and Do

Goodrich Memorial Library. *202 Main St, Newport (05855). Phone 802/334-7902. www.goodrichlibrary. org.* Artifacts of old Vermont in historic building; animal display. (Mon, Wed-Fri 10 am-5 pm; Tues 10 am-8 pm; Sat 10 am-3 pm (Oct-Apr), 9 am-2 pm (May-Sept); closed holidays) **FREE**

Haskell Opera House & Library. *93 Caswell Ave, Derby Line (05830). 8 miles N via Hwy 5, on Caswell Ave, also in Stanstead, QC, Canada. Phone 802/873-3022. www. haskellopera.org.* Historic turn-of-the-century building owned jointly by local Canadian and US residents. First floor houses library with reading room in the United States, book stacks in Canada. Second floor is historic turn-of-the-century opera house that preserves much of its antiquity (seats 400) with audience in the United States, stage in Canada. Summer concert series (fee). Library (Tues-Wed, Fri-Sat 10 am-5 pm; Thurs to 8 pm)

Old Stone House. *109 Old Stone House Rd, Brownington (05860). 11 miles SE via Hwy 5S or I-91 S to Orleans, then 2 miles NE on unnumbered road to Brownington Village. Phone 802/754-2022. www. oldstonehousemuseum.org.* (1836) Museum housed in four-story granite building with antique furniture; early farm, household, and military items; 19th-century schoolbooks. (mid-May-mid-Oct: Wed-Sun 11 am-5 pm) **$**

Limited-Service Hotel

★ **SUPER 8.** *4412 Rte 5, Newport (05829). Phone 802/334-1775; toll-free 800/800-8000; fax 802/334-1994. www.super8.com.* 52 rooms, 2 story. Complimentary continental breakfast. Check-in 3 pm, check-out 11 am. **$**

North Hero

See also Swanton

Population 502
Elevation 111 ft
Area Code 802
Zip 05474
Information Champlain Islands Chamber of Commerce, 3501 US Rt 2, PO Box 213; phone 802/372-

8400
Web Site www.champlainislands.com

What to See and Do

North Hero State Park. *3803 Lakeview Dr, North Hero (05474). 6 miles N, off Hwy 2 near South Alburg. Phone 802/372-8727. www.vtstateparks.com.* A 399-acre park located in the north part of the Champlain Islands; extensive shoreline on Lake Champlain. Swimming, fishing, boating (ramps); hiking trails, playground, tent and trailer sites (dump station), lean-tos. (Memorial Day-Labor Day) Standard fees.

Special Event

Royal Lippizan Stallions of Austria. *Knight Point State Park, 44 Knight Point Rd, North Hero (05474). Phone 802/372-8400; toll-free 800/262-5226. www.her-rmannslipizzans.com.* Summer residence of the stallions. Performances Thurs and Fri evenings, Sat and Sun afternoons. For ticket prices, contact Chamber of Commerce. July-Aug. **$$$$**

Limited-Service Hotel

★ ★ **SHORE ACRES INN.** *237 Shore Acres Dr, North Hero (05474). Phone 802/372-8722; fax 802/372-8314. www.shoreacres.com.* 23 rooms. Pets accepted; fee. Check-in 2:30 pm, check-out 10:30 am. Restaurant, bar. Tennis. **$**
🐾🛏️🖼️

Full-Service Inn

★ ★ ★ **NORTH HERO HOUSE INN.** *3643 Hwy 2, North Hero (05474). Phone 802/372-4732; toll-free 888/525-3644; fax 802/372-3218. www.northherohouse.com.* This inn, built in 1800, is surrounded by spectacular views of the Green Mountains and Mount Mansfield. Activities are available year-round. 26 rooms, 3 story. Complimentary continental breakfast. Check-in 2 pm. Check-out 11 am. Restaurant, bar. Tennis. **$$**
🖼️

Specialty Lodging

THOMAS MOTT ALBURG HOMESTEAD B&B. *63 Blue Rock Rd, Alburg (05440). Phone 802/796-4402; toll-free 800/348-0843. www.thomas-mott-bb.com.* This restored farmhouse (1838) overlooks the lake. 4 rooms, 2 story. Children over 6 years only. Compli-

Champlain Islands Bicycle Tour

A land chain composed of the Alburg peninsula and three islands—Isle La Motte, North Hero, and South Hero—straggles down the middle of Lake Champlain. The islands are connected by bridges to one another and by causeways to the mainland. Together they comprise Grand Isle Country (population 4,000).

This is old farm and resort country. In the 19th century, visitors arrived by lake steamer to stay at farms. Roads are flat and little trafficked once you are off Highway 2 (the main road down the spine of the islands). Views are splendid: east across the lake to Vermont's Green Mountains and west to New York's Adirondacks. Isle La Motte, the smallest and quietest of the islands, is beloved by bicyclists.

The obvious place to begin a loop here is in the parking lot at St. Anne's Shrine on Highway 129 in the northwestern corner of the island. Here an open-sided Victorian chapel on the shore marks the site of Vermont's first French settlement in 1666. There is a public beach, a picnic area in a large pine grove, and a large statue of Samuel de Champlain, who is credited with discovering New England's largest lake.

Pedal south from the shrine along the West Shore Road. Mountain bike rentals are available from Bike Shed Rentals, located a mile below the shrine. At 2.4 miles note the magnificent views west to the Adirondacks from the public boat access. At 3.7 miles the road turns to hard-packed dirt for 1.3 miles. Look for Fisk Farm (44 West Shore Rd), a complex of buildings that includes an attractive bed-and-breakfast and gallery, also the ruins of a large old stone house that Vice President Theodore Roosevelt was visiting when he received the news that President McKinley had been shot. Beside the farm is the Fisk Quarry, the oldest in Vermont and part of a 480-million-year-old coral reef that underlies the southern third of the island. Open to the public, the quarry is studded with fossils that represent some of the most primitive life earth has known.

Keep to the main road as it curves to the east (pavement resumes), past Halls Apple Orchards, which has been in the same family since the early 1800s. Its farmhouse is built of the island's distinctive "marble" (dark limestone). The road continues north past the Isle La Motte Historical Society, housed in an old schoolhouse; look for another reef (said to be 450 million years old) in a nearby field. At 7.4 miles you are at the four corners that mark the middle of Isle La Motte village with its country store and picnic benches by the pond. Another fine old stone building houses the public library. At 9 miles turn onto Shrine Road and bear left at the "Y". Follow the paved road back to the shrine. The total loop is 10 miles.

mentary full breakfast. Check-in 4 pm-7 pm, checkout 11 am. **$**

🅳

Restaurant

★ ★ **NORTH HERO HOUSE.** *Hwy 2, North Hero (05474). Phone 802/372-4732; toll-free 888/525-3644; fax 802/372-3218. www.northherohouse.com.* American menu. Breakfast for inn guests only, dinner, Sun brunch. Bar. Outdoor seating. **$$**

Okemo State Forest (E-2)

See also Ludlow, Weston

Mount Okemo (3,372 feet), almost a lone peak in south central Vermont near Ludlow, commands splendid views of the Adirondacks, the White Mountains, the Connecticut Valley, and Vermont's own Green Mountains. A road goes to within 1/2 mile of the mountain top (summer, fall; free); from there, it's an easy hike to the fire tower at the top. Surrounding Mount Okemo is the 4,527-acre state forest, which is primarily a skiing area.

Area has seven quad, three triple chairlifts, two Pomalifts, J-bar; patrol, school, rentals; snowmaking; cafeteria, restaurants, bar; nursery; 83 runs, longest run 4 1/2 miles; vertical drop 2,150 feet. (Early Nov-mid-Apr, daily) For information about area lodging, phone toll-free 800/786-5366.

Peru (E-2)

See also Dorset, Londonderry, Manchester and Manchester Center, Stratton Mountain, Weston

Settled 1773
Population 324
Elevation 1,700 ft
Area Code 802
Zip 05152

This small mountain village has many fine examples of classic New England architecture, such as the Congregational Church (1846). Spectacular views of the Green Mountains surround this skiing center; it is also a popular area for fishing, hunting, and hiking.

What to See and Do

Bromley Mountain Ski Area. *Rte 11, Peru. 2 miles SW on Hwy 11.* Phone 802/824-5522. www.bromley.com. Area has two quad, five double chairlifts, two mitey-mites, J-bar; patrol, school, rentals; snowmaking; two cafeterias, restaurant, two lounges; nursery. Forty-two runs, longest run over 2 miles; vertical drop 1,334 feet. (Mid-Nov-mid-Apr, daily)

Bromley Alpine Slide. *Rte 11, Peru.* Phone 802/824-5522.Speed-controlled sled ride and scenic chairlift; caf, picnic area. Outdoor deck. Multistate view. (Late May-mid-Oct, varying hours) **$$**

Summer activities. *Phone 802/824-5522.* Includes miniature golf, thrill sleds, children's theater. (Mid-June-mid-Oct)

Hapgood Pond Recreation Area. *2 miles NE on Hapgood Pond Rd, in Green Mountain National Forest.* Phone 802/824-6456. (see) **$$**

J. J. Hapgood Store. *Rte 11, Peru.* Phone 802/824-5911. (1827). General store featuring interesting old items; also penny candy, maple syrup, cheese. (Daily)

Wild Wings Ski Touring Center. *North Rd, Peru. 2 1/2 miles N on North Rd.* Phone 802/824-6793. www.wildwingsski.com. Ski school, rentals; warming room;

concession. Twelve miles of groomed cross-country trails. **$$$**

Plymouth (D-2)

See also Killington, Ludlow, Woodstock

Population 440
Elevation 1,406 ft
Area Code 802
Zip 05056
Information Town of Plymouth, HC 70, Box 39A; phone 802/672-3655

Seemingly unaware of the 21st century, this town hasn't changed much since July 4, 1872, when Calvin Coolidge was born in the back of the village store, still in business today. A country road leads to the cemetery where the former president and six generations of his family are buried. Nearby is the Coolidge Visitors Center and Museum, which displays historical and presidential memorabilia.

What to See and Do

Calvin Coolidge State Forest. *855 Coolidge St Park Rd, Plymouth (05056). 1 mile N off Hwy 100A, Calvin Coolidge Memorial Hwy.* Phone 802/672-3612. www.vtstateparks.com. A 16, 165-acre area. Hiking, snowmobile trails. Picnic facilities. Tent and trailer sites (dump station), primitive camping, lean-tos. (Memorial Day-Columbus Day)

Plymouth Cheese Corporation/Frog City Cheese. *106 Messer Hill Rd, Plymouth (05056).* Phone 802/672-3650. www.frogcitycheese.com. Cheese, canned products, maple syrup, and honey. Cheese processed Mon-Thurs. (Facility open late May-Nov, daily; closed Jan 1, Thanksgiving, Dec 25) **FREE**

President Calvin Coolidge Homestead. *Coolidge Memorial Dr, Plymouth Notch. 1 mile NE on Hwy 100A.* Phone 802/672-3773. www.dhca.state.vt.us. Restored to its early 20th-century appearance, Calvin Coolidge was sworn in by his father in the sitting room in 1923. The Plymouth Historic District also includes the General Store that was operated by the president's father, the house where the president was born, the village dance hall that served as the 1924 summer White House office, the Union Church with its Carpenter Gothic interior, the Wilder House (birthplace of Coolidge's mother), the Wilder Barn with 19th-century farming equipment, a restaurant, and a visitor center with museum. (Late May-mid-Oct: daily 9:30 am-5 pm) **$$**

Limited-Service Hotel

★ **FARMBROOK MOTEL.** *706 Hwy 100A, Plymouth (05056). Phone 802/672-3621. www.farmbrookmotel.net.* 12 rooms. Check-in 2 pm, check-out 11 am. **$**
🅳

Full-Service Resort

★ ★ ★ **HAWK INN AND MOUNTAIN RESORT.** *75 Billings Rd, Plymouth (05056). Phone 802/672-3811; toll-free 800/685-4295; fax 802/672-5585. www.hawkresort.com.* From rooms at the inn to luxurious mountainside villas on the 1,200 acres of this resort, guests can enjoy privacy and peace, as well as a variety of activities. 200 rooms. Check-in 4 pm, check-out 11 am. Restaurant, bar. Children's activity center. Fitness room. Indoor pool, outdoor pool, whirlpool. Tennis. Airport transportation available. **$$$**
🚶 🛏️ 🎿

Rutland (D-1)

See also Brandon, Killington, Green Mountain National Forest

Settled 1761
Population 18,230
Elevation 648 ft
Area Code 802
Information Chamber of Commerce, 256 N Main St; phone 802/773-2747
Web Site www.rutlandvermont.com

This is Vermont's second-largest city. Its oldest newspaper, the *Rutland Herald,* has been published continuously since 1794. The world's deepest marble quarry is in West Rutland. The office of the supervisor of the Green Mountain National Forest is located here.

What to See and Do

Chaffee Center for the Visual Arts. *16 S Main St, Rutland (05701). On Hwy 7, opposite Main St Park. Phone 802/775-0356. www.chaffeeartcenter.org.* Continuous exhibits of paintings, graphics, photography, crafts, sculpture. Print room; gallery shop; annual art festivals (mid-Aug, Columbus Day weekend); other special events. (Mon, Wed-Sat 10 am-5 pm, Sun noon-4 pm; closed holidays) **FREE**

Hubbardton Battlefield and Museum. *5696 Monument Hill Rd, East Hubbardton (05701). 7 miles W via Hwy 4, exit 5. Phone 802/759-2412. www.historicvermont.org.* On July 7, 1777, the Green Mountain Boys and colonial troops from Massachusetts and New Hampshire stopped British forces pursuing the American Army from Fort Ticonderoga. This was the only battle of the Revolution fought on Vermont soil and the first in a series of engagements that led to the capitulation of Burgoyne at Saratoga. Visitor Center with exhibits. Battle monument; trails; picnicking. (Memorial Day-Columbus Day, Wed-Sun 9:30 am-5 pm) **$**

Mountain Top Cross-Country Ski Resort. *195 Mountain Top Rd, Chittenden (05737). N via Hwy 7, then 10 miles NE on unnumbered road, follow signs. Phone 802/483-2311; toll-free 800/445-2100. www.mountaintopinn.com.* Patrol, school, rentals; snowmaking; concession area, restaurant at the inn. Sixty-eight miles of cross-country trails. Ice skating, horse-drawn sleigh rides. (Nov-Mar, daily) **$$$$**

New England Maple Museum. *Hwy 7, Pittsford. 7 miles N on Hwy 7. Phone 802/483-9414. www.maplemuseum.com.* One of the largest collections of antique maple sugaring artifacts in the world; two large dioramas featuring more than 100 hand-carved figures; narrated slide show; demonstrations, samples of Vermont foodstuffs; craft and maple product gift shop. (Late May-Oct: daily 8:30 am-5:30 pm; Nov-Dec, mid-March-late May: daily 10 am-4 pm; closed Jan-Feb, Thanksgiving) **$**

Norman Rockwell Museum. *654 Hwy 4 E, Rutland (05701). Phone 802/773-6095. www.normanrockwellvt.com.* More than 2,000 pictures and Rockwell memorabilia spanning 60 years of artist's career. Includes the *Four Freedoms,* Boy Scout series, many magazine covers, including all 323 from the *Saturday Evening Post,* and nearly every illustration and advertisement. (Daily; closed holidays) Gift shop. **$**

⭐ **Vermont Marble Exhibit.** *52 Main St, Proctor (05765). 2 miles W on Hwy 4, then 4 miles N on Hwy 3, adjacent to Vermont Marble Company factory. Phone 802/459-2300; toll-free 800/427-1396. www.vermontmarble.com.* Exhibit explains how marble is formed and the process by which it is manufactured. Displays; sculptor at work; balcony view of factory; "Gallery of the Presidents"; movie on the marble industry; marble market, gift shop. (Mid-May-Oct: daily 9 am-5:30 pm) **$$**

Wilson Castle. *W Proctor Rd, Center Rutland. 2 1/2 miles W on Hwy 4, then 1 mile N on West Proctor Rd. Phone 802/773-3284. www.wilsoncastle.com.* This 32-room 19th-century mansion on a 115-acre estate features 19 open proscenium arches, 84 stained-glass windows, 13 imported tile fireplaces, a towering turret and parapet; European and Asian furnishings; art gallery; sculpture; 15 other buildings. Picnic area. Guided tours. (Late May-late Oct, daily 9 am-6 pm; Christmas tours) **$$**

Special Event

Vermont State Fair. *175 South Main St, Rutland (05701). Phone 802/775-5200. www.vermontstatefair. net.* Exhibits of arts and crafts, flowers, produce, home arts, pets, animals, maple sugaring. Daily special events. Late Aug-early Sept.

Limited-Service Hotels

★ **BEST WESTERN INN & SUITES RUT-LAND/KILLINGTON.** *1 Hwy 4 E, Rutland (05701). Phone 802/773-3200; toll-free 800/720-7234; fax 802/773-6615. www.bestwestern-rutland.com.* 56 rooms, 2 story. Complimentary continental breakfast. Check-in 4 pm, check-out 11 am. Fitness room. Outdoor pool. Tennis. **$**

★ **COMFORT INN.** *19 Allen St, Rutland (05701). Phone 802/775-2200; toll-free 800/432-6788; fax 802/775-2694. www.choicehotels.com.* 104 rooms, 3 story. Complimentary continental breakfast. Check-in 3 pm, check-out 11 am. Indoor pool, whirlpool. **$**

★ ★ **HOLIDAY INN.** *2111 Hwy 7 S, Rutland (05701). Phone 802/775-1911; toll-free 800/462-4810; fax 802/775-0113. www.ichotelsgroup.com/h/d/6c/1/en/hd/rutvt.* 151 rooms. Pets accepted; fee. Check-in 12 pm, check-out noon. Restaurant, bar. Fitness room. Indoor pool, whirlpool. Airport transportation available. Business center. **$**

Full-Service Resort

★ ★ ★ **MOUNTAIN TOP INN.** *195 Mountain Top Rd, Chittenden (05737). Phone 800/445-2100; toll-free 800/445-2100; fax 802/483-6373. www.mountaintopinn.com.* Nestled in the Green Mountains of Vermont, right by the lake, the guest rooms offer the finest in New England tradition. The candlelit dining room has magnificent views. 60 rooms. Closed Apr

and first three weeks in Nov. Pets accepted; fee. Check-in 3 pm , check-out 11 am. Restaurant, bar. Outdoor pool. Golf. Tennis. **$$**

Specialty Lodgings

INN AT RUTLAND. *70 N Main St, Rutland (05701). Phone 802/773-0575; toll-free 800/808-0575; fax 802/775-3506. www.innatrutland.com.* This Victorian mansion was built in 1893 and has been lovingly restored to its former elegance. Rooms are furnished with thoughtful attention to detail that beckons guests to experience the charm of a time long since forgotten. 11 rooms, 3 story. Complimentary full breakfast. Check-in 3-8 pm, check-out 11 am. **$**

MAPLEWOOD INN. *1108 S Main St, Fair Haven (05743). Phone 802/265-8039; toll-free 800/253-7729; fax 802/265-8210. www.maplewoodinn.net.* Listed on the National Register of Historic Places, this Greek Revival inn offers guest rooms with period décor, perfect for a romantic getaway. Guests are close to sightseeing and can enjoy hot beverages and cordials in the sitting room. 5 rooms, 2 story. Pets accepted, some restrictions. Complimentary full breakfast. Check-in 3-8 pm, check-out 11 am. **$**

Restaurant

★ ★ **COUNTRYMAN'S PLEASURE.** *Townline Rd, Mendon (05701). Phone 802/773-7141; fax 802/747-4959. www.countrymanspleasure.com.* Austrian-born chef/owner Hans Entinger has been serving Middle European specialties for more than 20 years in this personable, country inn environment. Candlelight and open fireplaces add to the ambience. German, Austrian menu. Dinner. Closed Dec 24-25. Bar. Children's menu. **$**

Shelburne (C-1)

See also Burlington, Vergennes

Settled 1763
Population 5,871
Elevation 148 ft
Area Code 802
Zip 05482
Information Town Hall, 5420 Shelburne Rd, PO Box 88; phone 802/985-5110

Web Site www.shelburnevt.org

Shelburne is a small, friendly town bordering Lake Champlain. West of town are the Adirondack Mountains; to the east are the Green Mountains. The Shelburne Museum has one of the most comprehensive exhibits of early American life.

What to See and Do

Charlotte-Essex Ferry. *King St Dock, Burlington (05401). 5 miles S on Hwy 7 to Charlotte, then 2 miles W to dock. Phone 802/864-9804. www.ferries.com.* Makes 20-minute trips across Lake Champlain to Essex, NY (daily). (See BURLINGTON). **$$$$**

Mount Philo State Park. *5 miles S on Hwy 7, then 1 mile E on local road. Phone 802/425-2390.* A 648-acre mountaintop park offering beautiful views of the Lake Champlain Valley. Picnicking, camping, lean-tos. Entrance and camp roads are steep; not recommended for trailers. (Memorial Day-Columbus Day)

Shelburne Farms. *1611 Harbor Rd, Shelburne (05482). Phone 802/985-8686. www.shelburnefarms.org.* Former estate of Dr. Seward Webb and his wife, Lila Vanderbilt, built at the turn of the 20th century; beautifully situated on the shores of Lake Champlain. The grounds, landscaped by Frederick Law Olmstead and forested by Gifford Pinchot, once totaled 3,800 acres. Structures include the Webbs' mansion, Shelburne House, a 110-room summer "cottage" built in the late 1800s on a bluff overlooking the lake; a five-story farm barn with a courtyard of more than 2 acres; and the coach barn, once the home of prize horses. Tours (Memorial Day-mid-Oct, daily 9 am-5:30 pm; off-season, daily 10 am-5 pm; closed holidays). Also hayrides; walking trail. Visitor center, phone 802/985-8442. Cheese shop (all year, daily). Overnight stays available. **$$**

⭐ **Shelburne Museum.** *5555 Shelburne Rd, Shelburne (05482). On Hwy 7, in center of town. Phone 802/985-3346. www.shelburnemuseum.org.* Founded by Electra Webb, daughter of Sugar King H. O. Havemeyer, this stupendous collection of Americana is located on 45 acres of parklike setting with 37 historic buildings containing items such as historic circus posters, toys, weather vanes, trade signs, and an extensive collection of wildfowl decoys and dolls. American and European paintings and prints (including works by Monet and Grandma Moses) are on display as well. Also here is the 220-foot sidewheel steamboat *Ticonderoga*, which carried passengers across Lake Champlain in the early part of the century and is now the last vertical beam passenger and freight sidewheel steamer intact in the United States; a working carousel and a 5,000-piece hand-carved miniature traveling circus; a fully intact lighthouse; one-room schoolhouse; authentic country store; the only two-lane covered bridge with footpath in Vermont; blacksmith shop; printing and weaving demonstrations; farm equipment and more than 200 horse-drawn vehicles on display. Visitor orientation film; free jitney; cafeteria; museum stores; free parking. (May-Oct, daily 10 am-5 pm) **$$$$**

Vermont Teddy Bear Company. *(Hwy 7), 6655 Shelburne Rd, Shelburne (05482). 1 mile S. Phone 802/985-1319. www.vermontteddybear.com.* The guided tour of this factory shows the process of handcrafting these famous stuffed animals. The on-site gift shop ensures that you won't go home empty handed. The Bear Shop opens at 9 am daily; call for a tour schedule. **$**

Vermont Wildflower Farm. *4750 Shelburne Ave, Shelburne (05482). 5 miles S via Hwy 7. Phone 802/425-3641. www.vermontwildflowerfarm.com.* Acres of wildflower gardens, flower fields, and woodlands; pond and brook. Changing slide/sound show (every half hour). Gift shop. (Apr-Oct, daily 10 am-5 pm) **$$**

Limited-Service Hotel

★ **DAYS INN.** *3229 Shelburne Rd, Shelburne (05482). Phone 802/985-3334; toll-free 800/329-7466; fax 802/985-3419. www.daysinnshelburne.com.* 58 rooms, 2 story. Complimentary continental breakfast. Check-in 1 pm, check-out 11 am. Outdoor pool. **$**

Springfield (E-2)

See also Bellows Falls, Grafton, Ludlow

Settled 1761
Population 9,579
Elevation 410 ft
Area Code 802
Zip 05156
Information Chamber of Commerce, 14 Clinton St, Suite 6; phone 802/885-2779
Web Site www.springfieldvt.com

The cascades of the Black River once provided power for the machine tool plants that stretch along Springfield's banks. Lord Jeffrey Amherst started the Crown Point Military Road to Lake Champlain from here in 1759. Springfield has been the home of many New England inventors. It is also the headquarters of the Amateur Telescope Makers who meet at Stellafane, an observatory site west of Highway 11.

What to See and Do

Eureka Schoolhouse. *Charlestown Rd, Springfield (05156). Phone 802/885-2779.* Oldest schoolhouse in the state; built in 1790. Nearby is a 100-year-old lattice-truss covered bridge. (Memorial Day-Columbus Day, Wed-Mon 10 am-4 pm)

Reverend Dan Foster House & Old Forge. *2656 Weathersfield Center Rd, Weathersfield (05151). 6 miles N on Valley St to Weathersfield Center Rd. Phone 802/263-5230. www.weathersfield.org.* Historic parsonage (1785) contains antique furniture, textiles, utensils, farm tools; old forge has working machinery and bellows. Guided tours. For further information contact the Chamber of Commerce. (Mid-June-Oct, Thurs-Mon 2-5 pm or by appointment)

Springfield Art and Historical Society. *Miller Art Center, 9 Elm Hill, Springfield (05156). Phone 802/885-2415. www.millerartcenter.org.* American art and artifacts. Collections include Richard Lee pewter, Bennington pottery, 19th-century American paintings, costumes, dolls, toys; Springfield historical items. Changing exhibits. (mid-Apr-Oct, Tues-Fri 10 am-4 pm, Sat 10 am-1 pm; closed holidays)

Special Event

Vermont Apple Festival and Craft Show. *Riverside Middle School, 13 Fairground Rd, Springfield (05156). Phone 802/885-2779. www.springfieldvt.com/apple-festival.htm.* Family activities, cider pressing, apple pie bake-off, entertainment, crafts. Columbus Day weekend. **$**

Limited-Service Hotel

★ **HOLIDAY INN EXPRESS.** *818 Charlestown Rd, Springfield (05156). Phone 802/885-4516; toll-free 800/465-4329; fax 802/885-4595. www.vermonthi.com.* Just off Interstate 91, exit 7, this family-friendly hotel backs onto a wooded hill and is located across the street from the scenic Black River. Adults wil enjoy the nearby biking and walking trails, while children will have a blast in the indoor pool and arcade. All rooms have refrigerators and some have microwaves, and the connected Howard Johnson's restaurant provides meal service. 88 rooms, 2 story. Pets accepted; fee. Complimentary continental breakfast. Check-in 3

pm, check-out noon. Wireless Internet access. Fitness room. Indoor pool. Business center. Credit cards accepted. **$$**

Full-Service Inn

★ ★ ★ **THE INN AT WEATHERSFIELD.** *1342 Hwy 106, Weathersfield (05151). Phone 802/263-9217; fax 802/263-9219. www.weathersfieldinn.com.* The rooms at this inn transport guests to a colonial countryside atmosphere full of charm and tranquility. Shopping, state parks, hiking, skiing, and sleigh and carriage rides are just minutes away. A gourmet, candlelit dinner can be enjoyed on the premises. 12 rooms, 2 story. Pets accepted, some restrictions. Children over 8 years only. Complimentary full breakfast. Check-in 3-9 pm, check-out 11 am. Restaurant. **$**

Specialty Lodgings

HARTNESS HOUSE. *30 Orchard St, Springfield (05156). Phone 802/885-2115; toll-free 800/732-4789; fax 802/885-2207. www.hartnesshouse.com.* Part historic inn, part aviation museum and working observatory, the Hartness House is tied up in aviation, astronomy, and invention. A former Vermont governor, James Hartness was an inventor who built a series of underground tunnels in which he could work in undisturbed peace and quiet. He was also an aviation pioneer with a fascination for amateur astronomy and telescope making. After his death, his heirs combined his passions, and today three of the workrooms in Hartness's underground tunnels have been turned into a museum containing hundreds of exhibits related to amateur astronomy, telescope making, and astronomical lens and mirror making, as well as early-1900s photographs of Springfield and the Hartness House. But those more interested in resting than questing can take heart: the underground tunnels also lead to the original 1903 Hartness House, all polished wood and winding staircases, with a cozy, plant-filled living room on the ground floor and 14 guest rooms above. Two added wings wrap around the pool, one with eight rooms, the other with 24. The Hartness House is surrounded by 32 acres of woods and winding nature trails; the proprietors will be happy to make you a sack lunch to take along as you follow a path along a mountain stream. 43 rooms, 3 story. Pets accepted, some restrictions; fee. Complimentary full breakfast. Check-in 3 pm, check-out 11 am. Wireless Internet access. Restaurant, bar. Outdoor pool. **$**

STONE HEARTH INN. *698 Hwy 11 W, Chester (05143). Phone 802/875-2525; toll-free 888/617-3656; fax 802/875-2525. www.thestonehearthinn.com.* Restored farm house (1810); antiques. 10 rooms, 3 story. Complimentary full breakfast. Check-in 4 pm, check-out 11 am. Bar. **$$**
🅓

St. Albans (B-1)

See also Swanton

Settled 1785
Population 7,339
Elevation 429 ft
Area Code 802
Zip 05478
Information Chamber of Commerce, 2 N Main St; phone 802/524-2444
Web Site www.stalbanschamber.com

This small city is a railroad town (Central Vermont Railway) and a center of maple syrup and dairy interests. It was a stop on the Underground Railroad and has had a surprisingly violent history. Smugglers used the city as a base of operations during the War of 1812. On October 19, 1864, the northernmost engagement of the Civil War was fought here when a small group of Confederates raided the three banks in town and fled to Canada with $200,000. In 1866, the Fenians, an Irish organization pledged to capture Canada, had its headquarters here.

What to See and Do

Brainerd Monument. *S Main St, St. Albans. Greenwood Cemetery, S Main St. Phone 802/524-2444.* A father's revengeful commemoration of his son's death in Andersonville Prison.

Burton Island State Park. *St. Albans Bay. On island in Lake Champlain; 5 miles W on Hwy 36, then 3 miles SW on unnumbered road to Kamp Kill Kare State Park access area, where passenger ferry service (fee) is available to island; visitors may use their own boats to reach the island. Phone 802/524-6353. www.vtstateparks.com.* This 253-acre park offers swimming beach, fishing, canoeing (rentals), boating (rentals, marina with electrical hook-ups); nature and hiking trails, picnicking, concession, tent sites, lean-tos. (Memorial Day-Labor Day)

Chester A. Arthur Historic Site. *Fairfield. 10 miles W via Hwy 36 to Fairfield, then follow an unpaved road to the site. Phone 802/828-3051. www.dhca.state.vt.us/HistoricSites/html/arthur.html.* Replica of the second house of the 21st president (Arthur was vice president and became president in 1881 when James Garfield died); nearby is the brick church (1830) where Arthur's father was a preacher. Exhibit of Chester A. Arthur's life and career. Rural setting; picnic area. (Late May-mid-Oct, Wed-Sun 11 am-5 pm) **DONATION**

Lake Carmi State Park. *Hwy 236 and Marshfarm Rd, Enosburg Falls (05450). 15 miles NE on Hwy 105 to North Sheldon, then 3 miles N on Hwy 236. Phone 802/933-8383. www.vtstateparks.com.* This 482-acre park features rolling farmland; 2-mile lakefront, swimming beach, bathhouse, fishing, boating (ramps, rentals); nature trails, picnicking, concession, tent and trailer sites (dump station), lean-tos. (Memorial Day-Labor Day)

St. Albans Historical Museum. *Church St, St. Albans (05478). Phone 802/527-7933.* Toys, dolls, clothing, train memorabilia; farm implements; St. Albans Confederate Raid material, photographs; library and reference room; re-created doctor's office with medical and X-ray collections; items and documents of local historical interest. (June-Sept, Tues-Sat, also by appointment) **$**

Special Events

Bay Day. *Phone 802/524-2444.* Family activity day. Great Race, one-legged running, family games; volleyball, canoeing, and bicycling. Concessions. Fireworks. July 4 weekend.

Maple Sugar Festival. *Phone 802/524-5800.* A number of producers welcome visitors who join sugarhouse parties for sugar-on-snow, sour pickles, and raised doughnuts. Continuing events, arts and crafts, antiques, woodchopping contests. Usually last weekend in Apr.

Limited-Service Hotel

★ **COMFORT INN.** *813 Fairfax Rd, St. Albans (05478). Phone 802/524-3300; toll-free 800/228-5150; fax 802/524-3300. www.choicehotels.com.* 63 rooms, 3 story. Pets accepted, some restrictions; fee. Complimentary continental breakfast. Check-in 3 pm, check-out 11 am. Fitness room. Indoor pool. **$**
🐾 🕴 🏊

St. Johnsbury (C-3)

See also Lyndonville

Settled 1787
Population 7,608
Elevation 588 ft
Area Code 802
Zip 05819
Information Northeast Kingdom Chamber of Commerce, 51 Depot Sq, Suite 3; phone 802/748-3678 or toll-free 800/639-6379
Web Site www.nekchamber.com

This town was named for Ethan Allen's French friend, St. John de Crve Coeur, author of *Letters from an American Farmer*. The town gained fame and fortune when Thaddeus Fairbanks invented the platform scale in 1830. Fairbanks scales, maple syrup, and manufacturing are among its major industries.

What to See and Do

Fairbanks Museum and Planetarium. *1302 Main St, St. Johnsbury (05819). Phone 802/748-2372. www.fairbanks-museum.org.* Exhibits and programs on natural science, regional history, archaeology, anthropology, astronomy, and the arts. More than 4,500 mounted birds and mammals; antique toys; farm, village, and craft tools; Northern New England Weather Broadcasting Center; planetarium; Hall of Science; special exhibitions in Gallery Wing. (Mon-Sat, also Sun afternoons; closed Jan 1, Dec 25) Planetarium (July-Aug: daily; rest of year: Sat-Sun only). Museum and planetarium closed holidays. **$**

Maple Grove Farms of Vermont Factory Tours & Maple Museum. *1052 Portland St, St. Johnsbury (05819). Phone 802/748-5141. www.maplegrove.com.* Learn all about "Vermont's first industry" on this factory tour, which offers glimpses into the process of making pure maple syrup and maple candy. Top it off by tasting the various grades of syrup available in the Cabin Shop, and you're sure to leave with your sweet tooth sated. (May-Dec, Mon-Fri 8 am-2 pm; closed holidays) **$**

St. Johnsbury Athenaeum and Art Gallery. *1171 Main St, St. Johnsbury (05819). Phone 802/748-8291. www.stjathenaeum.org.* Public library and art gallery. **DONATION**

Special Event

St. Johnsbury Town Band. *Courthouse Park, St. Johnsbury. Phone 802/748-8891.* One of the oldest continuously performing bands (since 1830) in the country plays weekly outdoor evening concerts. Contact the Chamber of Commerce for further information. Mon, mid-June-late Aug.

Limited-Service Hotels

★ **THE FAIRBANKS INN.** *401 Western Ave, St. Johnsbury (05819). Phone 802/748-5666; fax 802/748-1242. www.stjay.com.* 46 rooms, 3 story. Pets accepted; fee. Complimentary continental breakfast. Check-in 3 pm, check-out 11 am. Outdoor pool. **$**

★ **HOLIDAY MOTEL.** *222 Hastings St, St. Johnsbury (05819). Phone 802/748-8192; fax 802/748-1244.* 34 rooms. Pets accepted, some restrictions; fee. Check-in 2 pm, check-out 11 am. Outdoor pool. **$**

Full-Service Inn

★ ★ ★ **RABBIT HILL INN.** *48 Lower Waterford Rd, Lower Waterford (05848). Phone 802/748-5168; toll-free 800/762-8669; fax 802/748-8342. www.rabbithillinn.com.* Nestled between the river and mountains of picturesque northern Vermont, the Rabbit Hill Inn is quintessential New England at its best. Meandering pathways and covered bridges take guests back in time to the 18th century in this postcard-perfect village. Romantics flock to this old-fashioned inn, which dates to 1795, to rediscover simple pleasures and enjoy country pursuits. Souls are soothed after a walk in the meadow, while the spring-fed pool cools and relaxes. Many guests meet in the public rooms to play classic board games, often making new friends as they piece together puzzles. Befitting a bed-and-breakfast, the mornings are met with freshly baked temptations and lavish buffets; afternoon tea lures visitors from their repose; and evenings bring sensational five-course dinners. Undeniably lovely, the guest rooms are a valentine to visitors with canopy beds and soft colors. 19 rooms, 3 story. Closed first two weeks of Apr and first two weeks of Nov. Children over 13 years only. Complimentary full breakfast. Check-in 2 pm, check-out 11 am. Restaurant, bar. **$$**

Restaurant

★ ★ ★ **RABBIT HILL.** *48 Lower Waterford Rd, Lower Waterford (05848). Phone 802/748-5168; fax 802/748-8542. www.rabbithillinn.com.* Chef Russell Stannard's five-course dinner menu highlights his creative style of cooking. The hardwood floors, wainscoting, area rugs, and other decorative accents afford an elegant setting in which to enjoy it. American menu. Dinner. Bar. Reservations recommended. **$$$**

Stowe (B-2)

See also Highgate Springs, Jeffersonville, Waterbury

Settled 1794
Population 3,433
Elevation 723 ft
Area Code 802
Zip 05672
Information Stowe Area Association, Main St, PO Box 1320; phone 802/253-7321 or toll-free 877/467-8693
Web Site www.gostowe.com

Stowe is a year-round resort area, with more than half of its visitors coming during the summer. Mount Mansfield, Vermont's highest peak (4,393 feet), offers skiing, snowboarding, snowshoeing, and skating in the winter. Summer visitors enjoy outdoor concerts, hiking, biking, golf, tennis, and many events and attractions, including a Ben & Jerry's ice cream tour.

What to See and Do

Alpine Slide. *Stowe Mountain Resort, Spruce Peak, Stowe (05672). Hwy 108, N of Stowe Village. Phone 802/253-3000; toll-free 800/253-4754. www.stowe.com.* Chairlift takes riders to a 2,300-foot slide that runs through the woods and open field. Speed controlled by rider. (Late June-Labor Day: daily 10 am-5 pm; Sept-mid-Oct: weekends) **$$$**

Elmore State Park. *Hwy 12, Lake Elmore. N on Hwy 100, then S on Hwy 12, at Lake Elmore. Phone 802/888-2982. www.vtstateparks.com.* This 709-acre park offers swimming beach, bathhouse, fishing, boating (rentals); hiking trails (one trail to Elmore Mountain fire tower), picnicking, concession, tent and trailer sites (dump station), lean-tos. Excellent views of Green Mountain Range; fire tower. (Memorial Day-Columbus Day)

Mount Mansfield State Forest. *www.vtstateparks.com.* This 38,000-acre forest can be reached from Underhill Flats, off Highway 15, or from Stowe, north on Highway 108, through Smugglers' Notch, a magnificent scenic drive. The Long Trail leads to the summit of Mount Mansfield from the north and south. There are three state recreation areas in the forest. Smugglers' Notch (phone 802/253-4014 or 802/479-4280) and Underhill (phone 802/899-3022 or 802/879-5674)

areas offer hiking, skiing, snowmobiling, picnicking, camping (dump station). Little River Camping Area (phone 802/244-7103 or 802/479-4280), northwest of Waterbury, offers swimming, fishing, boating (rentals for campers only); hiking, camping. (Memorial Day-Columbus Day)

Stowe Mountain Auto Road. *Stowe Mountain Resort, Mt. Mansfield, Stowe (05672). Approximately 6 miles NW of Stowe off Hwy 108. Phone 802/253-3000; toll-free 800/253-4754. www.stowe.com.* A 4 1/2-mile drive to the summit. (Mid-May-mid-Oct, daily) **$$**

Stowe Mountain Resort. *5781 Mountain Rd, Stowe (05672). NW via Hwy 108. Phone 802/253-3000; toll-free 800/253-4754. www.stowe.com.* Resort has quad, triple, six double chairlifts; Mighty-mite handle tow; patrol, school, rentals; snowmaking; cafeterias, restaurants, bar, entertainment; nursery. Forty-seven runs, longest run more than 3 1/2 miles; vertical drop 2,360 feet. Night skiing. (Mid-Nov-mid-Apr, daily) Summer activities include three outdoor swimming pools; alpine slide (mid-June-early Sept, daily), mountain biking (rentals), gondola rides, in-line skate park, fitness center, spa, recreation trail, tennis, golf. Nearby is

> **Mount Mansfield Gondola.** *Stowe Mountain Resort, 5781 Mountain Rd, Stowe (05672). Hwy 108, N of Stowe Village. Phone 802/253-3000; toll-free 800/253-4754.* An eight-passenger enclosed gondola ride to the summit of Vermont's highest peak. Spectacular view of the area. Restaurant and gift shop. (Mid-June-mid-Oct, daily 10 am-5 pm) **$$$$**

Stowe Recreation Path. *Stowe Village. Phone 802/253-7350. www.townofstowevt.org.* An approximately 5-mile riverside path designed for nature walks, bicycling, jogging, and in-line skating. **FREE**

Special Events

Stoweflake Balloon Festival. *Stoweflake Mountain Resort & Spa, 1746 Mountain Rd, Stowe (05672). Phone toll-free 800/253-2232. www.stoweflake.com.* Stoweflake Resort Field, Hwy 108. More than 20 balloons launched continuously. Second weekend in July. **$$**

Trapp Family Meadow Concerts. *Trapp Family Lodge, 700 Trapp Hill Rd, Stowe (05672). Phone 802/253-8511. www.trappfamily.com.* Classical concerts in the Trapp Family Lodge Meadow. Sun evenings, late June-mid-Aug. **$$$$**

Limited-Service Hotels

★ ★ **EDSON HILL MANOR.** *1500 Edson Hill Rd, Stowe (05672). Phone 802/253-7371; toll-free 800/621-0284; fax 802/253-4036. www.edsonhillmanor.com.* This romantic inn is located on 225 acres of a rolling hillside with a view of the Green Mountains. The inns horse farms, ponds, and streams dot the landscape. The town and area activities are within driving distance, and horseback riding, cross-country skiing, and fishing are offered on-site. 25 rooms. Pets accepted, some restrictions. Complimentary full breakfast. Check-in 2 pm, check-out 11 am. Restaurant, bar. Indoor pool. Ski in/ski out. **$$**

★ ★ **GREY FOX INN AND RESORT.** *990 Mountain Rd, Stowe (05672). Phone 802/253-8921; toll-free 800/544-8454; fax 802/253-8344. www.stowegreyfoxinn.com.* This family-friendly lodging is centrally located with charming New England surroundings. On-site activities include bicycle rentals, a sports court, and game room. 38 rooms, 3 story. Complimentary full breakfast. Check-in 3 pm, check-out 11 am. Restaurant, bar. Children's activity center. Fitness room. Indoor pool, outdoor pool, whirlpool. **$**

Full-Service Resorts

★ ★ **GOLDEN EAGLE RESORT.** *511 Mountain Rd, Stowe (05672). Phone 802/253-4811; toll-free 800/626-1010; fax 802/253-2561. www.goldeneagleresort.com.* Families will feel welcome year-round at this resort surrounded by lush green mountains, farms, and streams. The location is convenient to the quaint town and area activities. A July 4th fishing derby, trail system, shuffleboard, and snowshoe rentals are all offered on-site. 94 rooms. Check-in 3 pm, check-out 11 am. Restaurant. Children's activity center. Fitness room. Indoor pool, two outdoor pools, whirlpool. Tennis. **$$**

★ ★ ★ **STOWEFLAKE MOUNTAIN RESORT & SPA.** *1746 Mountain Rd, Stowe (05672). Phone 802/253-7355; toll-free 800/253-2232; fax 802/253-6858. www.stoweflake.com.* Stoweflake Mountain Resort is the ultimate New England getaway. This comprehensive resort treats guests to a well-rounded experience filled with golf and other sports, fine dining, and an exceptional spa. The accommodations cover all the bases, from standard guest rooms to townhouses, and all feature a warm New England spirit. The 50,000-square-foot spa is a veritable temple of relaxation, and the treatment menu goes beyond the ordinary to surprise and delight guests. The chef pays special attention to spa guests with separate calorie-conscious selections on the menus, although his regular menus masterful creations from organic and locally grown ingredients are sure to tempt those watching their waistlines. 117 rooms, 2 story. Check-in 3 pm, check-out 11 am. High-speed Internet access. Restaurant, bar. Fitness room, fitness classes available, spa. Indoor pool, outdoor pool, whirlpool. Golf, 9 holes. **$$$**

★ ★ ★ **TOPNOTCH RESORT & SPA.** *4000 Mountain Rd, Stowe (05672). Phone 802/253-8585; toll-free 800/451-8686; fax 802/253-9263. www.topnotch-resort.com.* Topnotch Resort & Spa, tucked away on 120 acres in the Green Mountains, is a year-round resort. The first sign of snowfall attracts avid skiers who appreciate the proximity to some of Vermont's best skiing, while warmer months draw tennis players to the comprehensive facility with nine indoor and four outdoor courts and a renowned academy. Sybarites visit throughout the year to reap the physical and spiritual rewards of the 23,000-square-foot spa, where innovative therapies increase personal well-being. Guests watching their waistlines revel in the resorts spa cuisine: Maxwells delights with steaks and seafood, and Buttertub Bistro & Lounge is the very definition of aprs-ski, with fireside cocktails and live entertainment. English manor house meets Vermont countryside in the guest accommodations. 126 rooms, 3 story. Pets accepted, some restrictions; fee. Check-in 3:30 pm, check-out 11 am. High-speed Internet access, wireless Internet access. Restaurant, bar. Children's activity center. Fitness room, fitness classes available, spa. Indoor pool, outdoor pool, whirlpool. Tennis. Airport transportation available. Business center. **$$$**

★ ★ **TRAPP FAMILY LODGE.** *700 Trapp Hill Rd, Stowe (05672). Phone 802/253-8511; toll-free 800/826-7000; fax 802/253-5740. www.trappfamily.com.* "The hills are alive" at this Tyrolean resort run by the inspiration for the famous movie and play. This rustic lodge overlooks a beautiful mountain range and is accented with hand-carved balustrades, pitched gables, and a cedar shake roof. Take advantage of all Vermont has to offer—croquet, hiking, horse-drawn sleigh rides, pastry classes, cross-country skiing, or join in a guest sing-a-long. 96 rooms, 4 story. Check-in 3 pm, check-out 11 am. Wireless Internet access. Restaurant, bar. Fitness room. Indoor pool, outdoor pool. Tennis. Credit cards accepted. **$$**

Full-Service Inns

★ ★ ★ **GREEN MOUNTAIN INN.** *18 S Main St, Stowe (05672). Phone 802/253-7301; toll-free 800/253-7302; fax 802/253-5096. www.greenmountaininn. com.* Modern comforts are not lacking at this historic colonial inn surrounded by charming stores, galleries, and restaurants. The quiet setting provides relaxation, and many of the guest rooms are located in the main building, which is filled with old-world décor. 104 rooms, 3 story. Check-in 3 pm, check-out 11 am. Wireless Internet access. Restaurant, bar. Fitness room. Outdoor pool. **$$**

★ ★ ★ **YE OLDE ENGLAND INNE.** *433 Mountain Rd, Stowe (05672). Phone 802/253-7558; toll-free 800/477-3771; fax 802/253-8944. www.englandinn.com.* This elegant 1893 English inn offers guests a truly delightful stay. From the charmingly appointed rooms furnished in Laura Ashley-style to the Mr. Pickwicks Polo Pub where strangers are strangers no more, this warm and inviting inn is a welcome respite. 30 rooms, 5 story. Complimentary full breakfast. Check-in 3 pm, check-out 11 am. Wireless Internet access. Restaurant, bar. Outdoor pool, whirlpool. **$$**

Specialty Lodgings

FITCH HILL INN. *258 Fitch Hill Rd, Hyde Park (05655). Phone 802/888-3834; toll-free 800/639-2903; fax 802/888-7789. www.fitchhillinn.com.* This tranquil setting 15 minutes north of Stowe is situated on 3 acres of woods and gardens, and offers views of the Green Mountains. Guest rooms are decorated in a country style featuring quilts, lace curtains, and rose wallpaper. 6 rooms. Closed Apr and Nov. Complimentary full breakfast. Check-in 3 pm, check-out 11 am. Whirlpool. **$$**

STONE HILL INN. *89 Houston Farm Rd, Stowe (05672). Phone 802/253-6282. www.stonehillinn.com.* Tucked away in a quiet section of Stowe, this romantic inn is still close to all the antique shops, restaurants, and activities the town has to offer. The interior is warm and welcoming with bold colors and elegant décor. Trails, snowshoes, tobogganing, and sledding are offered on-site. 9 rooms. Closed Apr; also mid-Nov-mid-Dec. No children allowed. Complimentary full breakfast. Check-in 3 pm, check-out 11 am. Wireless Internet access. Whirlpool. **$$$**

Stratton Mountain (E-2)

See also Londonderry, Manchester and Manchester Center, Peru

Area Code 802
Zip 05155

What to See and Do

Stratton Mountain. *Stratton Mountain Rd, Londonderry. Off Hwy 30. Phone 802/297-4211. www.stratton. com.* A high-speed gondola, two high-speed six-passenger, three quad, one triple, two double chairlifts, two surface lifts; patrol, school, rentals; snowmaking; cafeterias, restaurants, bars; nursery, sports center. Ninety runs, longest run 3 miles; vertical drop 2,003 feet. (Mid-Nov-mid-Apr, daily) More than 17 miles of cross-country trails (Dec-Mar, daily), rentals; snowboarding. Summer activities include gondola ride; horseback riding, tennis, golf (school), festivals, concert series. **$$$$**

Special Event

Vermont Arts & Fine Crafts Festival. *Stratton Mountain Ski Resort, Stratton Mountain Rd, Stratton Mountain (05155). www.vtartsfestival.com.* Paintings, photography, sculpture, and crafts; special performing arts events, craft demonstrations. Labor Day Weekend. **$$**

Limited-Service Hotel

★ ★ **THE INN AT STRATTON MOUNTAIN.** *61 Middle Ridge Rd, Stratton (05155). Phone 802/297-2500; toll-free 800/787-2886; fax 802/297-4300. www. stratton.com.* This conveniently located mountain resort includes a ski-in/ski-out lodge. In winter there are ski trails spanning 500 acres to keep guests busy, while golf and tennis are the attraction during warmer months. 119 rooms, 4 story. Check-in 4:30 pm, check-out 11 am. Children's activity center. Fitness room. Indoor pool, three outdoor pools, whirlpool. Golf. Tennis. Ski in/ski out. **$**

Swanton (A-1)

See also Jeffersonville, North Hero, St. Albans

Population 2,360
Elevation 119 ft
Area Code 802
Zip 05488
Information Chamber of Commerce, 1 Merchants Row, PO Box 210; phone 802/868-7200

The location of this town, just 2 miles east of Lake Champlain, makes it an attractive resort spot.

What to See and Do

Missisquoi National Wildlife Refuge. *29 Tabor Rd, Swanton (05488). 2 1/2 miles W via Hwy 78. Phone 802/868-4781. www.fws.gov/refuges.* More than 6,400 acres, including much of the Missisquoi River delta on Lake Champlain; primarily a waterfowl refuge (best in Apr, Sept, and Oct), but other wildlife and birds may be seen. Fishing; hunting, hiking and canoe trails. (Daily) **FREE**

Full-Service Resort

★ ★ **TYLER PLACE FAMILY RESORT.** *1 Old Dock Rd, Highgate Springs (05460). Phone 802/868-4000; fax 802/868-5621. www.tylerplace.com.* This resort is designed for vacationing families. Accommodations have a country flavor and are designed with kids in mind. The resort is set on a mile of lakeshore and 165 acres of land. Guests will enjoy the paddleboats, kayaks, fishing, pools, and many other activities. 39 rooms, 2 story. Closed Labor Day-late May. Check-in 3 pm, check-out 10 am. Restaurant, bar. Children's activity center. Fitness room. Indoor pool, outdoor pool, children's pool. Tennis. **$**

Vergennes (C-1)

See also Middlebury, Shelburne

Settled 1766
Population 2,578
Elevation 205 ft
Area Code 802
Zip 05491
Information Vergennes Chamber of Commerce, PO Box 335; phone 802/388-7951

Web Site www.midvermont.com

Vergennes is one of the smallest incorporated cities in the nation (one square mile). It is also the oldest city in Vermont and the third oldest in New England.

What to See and Do

Button Bay State Park. *5 Button Bay State Park Rd, Vergennes (05491). 6 miles W on Button Bay Rd, just S of Basin Harbor. Phone 802/475-2377.* This 236-acre park on a bluff overlooking Lake Champlain was named for the buttonlike formations in the clay banks; spectacular views of Adirondack Mountains. Swimming pool, fishing, boating (rentals); nature and hiking trails, picnicking, tent and trailer sites (dump station). Museum, naturalist. (Memorial Day-Columbus Day)

Chimney Point State Historic Site. *Hwys 17 and 125, Addison (05491). 6 miles S via Hwy 22A, then 8 miles SW via Hwy 17, at the terminus of the Crown Point Military Rd on shoreline of Lake Champlain. Phone 802/759-2412. www.dhca.state.vt.us/HistoricSites/html/chimneypoint.html.* This 18th-century tavern was built on the site of a 17th-century French fort. Exhibits on the Native American and French settlement of Champlain Valley and Vermont. (Wed-Sun 9:30 am-5 pm, late May to mid-Oct) **$**

John Strong Mansion. *6656 Hwy 17 W, West Addison (05491). 6 miles SW via Hwy 22A, on Hwy 17. Phone 802/759-2309.* (1795) Federalist house; restored and furnished in the period. (Memorial Day-Labor Day, Sat-Sun 10 am-5 pm) **$**

Kennedy Brothers Factory Marketplace. *11 N Main St, Vergennes (05491). Phone 802/877-2975. www.kennedy-brothers.com.* Renovated 1920s brick creamery building features gift, crafts, and antiques shops. Deli, ice cream shop, picnic area. (Daily; closed Jan 1, Thanksgiving, Dec 25) **FREE**

Rokeby Museum. *4334 Hwy 7, Ferrisburgh (05456). 2 miles N on Hwy 7, 6 miles S of ferry route on Hwy 7. Phone 802/877-3406. www.rokeby.org.* (Circa 1785) Ancestral home of abolitionist Rowland T. Robinson was a station for the Underground Railroad. Artifacts and archives of four generations of the Robinson family. Set on 85 acres, farmstead includes an ice house, a creamery, and a stone smokehouse. Special events year-round. Tours. (Mid-May-mid-Oct, house tours: Thurs-Sun 11 am, 12:30 pm, 2 pm; grounds: Tues-Sun 10 am-4 pm) **$$**

Full-Service Resort

★ ★ ★ **BASIN HARBOR CLUB.** *4800 Basin Harbor Rd, Vergennes (05491). Phone 802/475-2311; fax 802/475-6545.* Located on Lake Champlain, this 700-acre property offers guest rooms in the lodge or cottages spread out over the acreage. Fresh local ingredients are used to prepare the breakfast and dinner meals served in the main dining room. 117 rooms. Closed Nov-mid-May. Pets accepted, some restrictions; fee. Check-in 4 pm, check-out 11 am. Restaurant, bar. Children's activity center. Fitness room. Beach. Outdoor pool. Golf. Tennis. Airport transportation available. **$$**

Specialty Lodging

STRONG HOUSE INN. *94 W Main St, Vergennes (05491). Phone 802/877-3337; fax 802/877-2599. www.stronghouseinn.com.* This historic Federal-style inn is furnished in period furniture and antiques and is set on 6 acres of walking trails, gardens, and ponds. Nearby are many activities, including hiking, golfing, cycling, and fishing. 14 rooms, 2 story. Children over 8 years only. Complimentary full breakfast. Check-in 3-8 pm, check-out 11 am. **$$**

Waitsfield (C-2)

See also Barre, Montpelier, Warren, Waterbury

Population 1,422
Elevation 698 ft
Area Code 802
Zip 05673
Information Sugarbush Chamber of Commerce, General Wait House - Hwy 100, PO Box 173; phone 802/496-3409 or toll-free 800/828-4748
Web Site www.madrivervalley.com

This region, known as "the Valley," is a popular area in summer as well as in the winter ski season.

What to See and Do

Mad River Glen Ski Area. *Hwy 17, Waitsfield. 5 miles W of Hwy 100. Phone 802/496-3551. www.madriverglen.com.* Area has three double, two single chairlifts; patrol, school, rentals; snowmaking; cafeterias, restaurant, bar; nursery. Forty-four runs, longest run 3 miles; vertical drop 2,000 feet. (Dec-Apr, daily) **$$$$**

Full-Service Inn

★ ★ **TUCKER HILL INN.** *65 Marble Hill Rd, Waitsfield (05673). Phone 802/496-3983; toll-free 800/543-7841. www.tuckerhill.com.* 22 rooms. Check-in 3-6 pm, check-out 11 am. Restaurant, bar. Outdoor pool. Tennis. **$$**

Specialty Lodgings

1824 HOUSE INN BED AND BREAKFAST. *2150 Main St, Waitsfield (05673). Phone 802/496-7555; toll-free 800/426-3986; fax 802/496-7559. www.1824house.com.* This restored 1824 farmhouse; features feather beds, Oriental rugs, and down quilts. 8 rooms, 2 story. Complimentary full breakfast. Check-in 4-8 pm, check-out 11 am. Whirlpool. **$**

THE INN AT THE ROUND BARN. *1661 E Warren Rd, Waitsfield (05673). Phone 802/496-2276; fax 802/496-8832. www.theroundbarn.com.* Located on more than 200 acres of mountains, ponds, and meadows, this unique inn has, as the name implies, a round barn that is fully restored and is the setting for weddings, meetings, and other functions. Activities for guests abound in this year-round destination. 12 rooms, 2 story. Complimentary full breakfast. Check-in 3 pm, check-out 11 am. Indoor pool. **$$**

LAREAU FARM COUNTRY INN. *48 Lareau Rd, Waitsfield (05673). Phone 802/496-4949; toll-free 800/833-0766; fax 802/496-7979. www.lareaufarminn.com.* Farmhouse and barn built by the area's first physician. 13 rooms, 2 story. Complimentary full breakfast. Check-in 2 pm, check-out 10:30 am. **$**

THE WAITSFIELD INN. *5267 Main (Rt 100), Waitsfield (05673). Phone 802/496-3979; toll-free 800/758-3801; fax 802/496-3970. www.waitsfieldinn.com.* 14 rooms, 2 story. Closed Apr, Nov. Check-in 3-7 pm, check-out 11 am. **$**

Restaurants

★ **RESTAURANT DEN.** *5153 Main St, Waitsfield (05673). Phone 802/496-8880.* American menu. Lunch, dinner. Closed Thanksgiving, Dec 25. Bar. Outdoor seating. **$$**

★ ★ **THE STEAK PLACE AT TUCKER HILL.**
65 Marble Hill Rd, Waitsfield (05673). Phone 802/496-3983; toll-free 800/543-7841. www.tuckerhill.com.
American menu. Breakfast, dinner. Closed Sun-Mon. Bar. Children's menu. Outdoor seating. **$$**

Warren (C-2)

See also Barre, Green Mountain National Forest, Waitsfield, Waterbury

Population 1,172
Elevation 893 ft
Area Code 802
Zip 05674
Information Sugarbush Chamber of Commerce, PO Box 173, Waitsfield 05673; phone 802/496-3409 or toll-free 800/828-4748
Web Site www.madrivervalley.com

What to See and Do

Sugarbush Golf Course. *Sugarbush Resort, 1840 Sugarbush Access Rd, Warren (05674). 3 miles NW via Hwy 100. Phone 802/583-6725; toll-free 800/53-. www.sugarbush.com.* An 18-hole championship course designed by Robert Trent Jones Sr.; driving range; nine-hole putting green; championship tees (6,524 yards). Restaurant. (May-Sept, daily) Reservations recommended. **$$$$**

Sugarbush Resort. *1840 Sugarbush Access Rd, Warren (05674). 3 miles NW, off Hwy 100. Phone 802/583-6300; toll-free 800/583-7669. www.sugarbush.com.* Area has seven quad, three triple, six double chairlifts; four surface lifts; patrol, school, rentals; concession area, cafeteria, restaurant, bar; nursery. One hundred seven runs, longest run more than 2 miles; vertical drop 2,650 feet. (Early Nov-late Apr, daily) **$$$$**

Sugarbush Soaring Association. *Warren-Sugarbush Airport, Warren. 2 miles NE via Hwy 100. Phone 802/496-2290. www.sugarbush.org.* Soaring instruction, scenic glider rides. Picnicking, restaurant. (May-Oct, daily) Reservations preferred. **$$$$**

Full-Service Resort

★ ★ ★ **SUGARBUSH INN.** *1840 Sugarbush Access Rd, Warren (05674). Phone 802/583-6114; toll-free 800/537-8427; fax 802/583-6132. www.sugarbush.com.* Surrounded by slopes, hills, and trails, this activity-oriented inn is nestled between the charming towns of Waitsfield and Warren. Snowshoeing, snow tubing, ice skating, and horse-drawn sleigh rides are available on property. 143 rooms. Complimentary full breakfast. Check-in 4 pm, check-out 10 am. Three restaurants, bar. Children's activity center. Fitness room. Indoor pool, outdoor pool, whirlpool. Golf, 18 holes. Tennis. Ski in/ski out. **$$**

Full-Service Inn

★ ★ ★ **THE PITCHER INN.** *275 Main St, Warren (05674). Phone 802/496-6350; toll-free 800/735-2478; fax 802/496-6354. www.pitcherinn.com.* This romantic inn on the Mad River was constructed on the site of an inn of the same name originally built in the 1700s. Skiers are drawn here, and the inn thoughtfully accommodates them with a locker room for ski storage and a boot and glove warmer. Rustic yet rich and elegant guest accommodations in the main house draw upon Vermont's colonial history and are individually decorated in themes like the Mallard Room and the School Room, while two suites in the adjacent barn are perfect for families. The inn's intimate restaurant, which serves breakfast and dinner, boasts a 6,500-bottle wine cellar. 11 rooms, 3 story. Complimentary full breakfast. Check-in 3 pm, check-out 11 am. Wireless Internet access. Restaurant, bar. **$$$$**

Specialty Lodging

SUGARTREE INN. *2440 Sugarbush Access Rd, Warren (05674). Phone 802/583-3211; toll-free 800/666-8907; fax 802/583-3203. www.sugartree.com.* 9 rooms, 3 story. Closed three weeks in Apr. Pets accepted, some restrictions, Children over 12 years only. Complimentary full breakfast. Check-in 3 pm, check-out 11 am. Restaurant. **$**

Restaurant

★ ★ ★ **THE COMMON MAN.** *3209 German Flats Rd, Warren (05674). Phone 802/583-2800; fax 802/583-2826. www.commonmanrestaurant.com.* Located in Vermont's Mad River Valley, this restaurant offers superb dining. The 1880s restored barn is a perfect setting for this casual dining spot. American menu. Dinner. Closed Sun-Mon; two-four weeks in spring and Nov. Bar. Children's menu. Casual attire. Reservations recommended. **$$**

Waterbury (C-2)

See also Barre, Montpelier, Stowe, Waitsfield, Warren

Population 4,589
Elevation 428 ft
Area Code 802
Zip 05676
Information Central Vermont Chamber of Commerce, PO Box 336, Barre 05641; phone 802/229-5711
Web Site www.central-vt.com

Centrally located near many outstanding ski resorts, including Stowe, Mad River Valley, and Bolton Valley, this area is also popular in summer for hiking, backpacking, and bicycling.

What to See and Do

Ben & Jerry's Ice Cream Factory Tour. *Rte 100, Waterbury. I-89, exit 10, then N on Hwy 100.* Phone 802/882-1240; toll-free 866/258-6877. www.benjerry.com. This half-hour guided tour, offered every 30 minutes (and even more frequently in summer, spring, and fall), takes visitors through the ice cream factory that cranks out such beloved flavors as Cherry Garcia and Chunky Monkey. The tour includes a seven-minute "moovie, " views of the production line (except on weekends), and free samples in the FlavoRoom. There's also a gift shop, where you can pick up one of those famous tie-dyed cow T-shirts and a few pints to take home. (Daily; closed Jan 1, Thanksgiving, Dec 25) **$**

Camel's Hump Mountain. *Long Trail, Waterbury. 8 miles SW of town on dirt road, then 3 1/2-mile hike to summit.* Phone 802/244-7037. State's third-highest mountain. Trail is challenging. Weather permitting, Canada can be seen from the top.

Cold Hollow Cider Mill. *3600 Waterbury-Stowe Rd, Waterbury Center (05677). 3 1/2 miles N on Hwy 100.* Phone 802/244-8771; toll-free 800/327-7537. www.cold-hollow.com. One of the largest cider mills in New England features a 43-inch rack-and-cloth press capable of producing 500 gallons of cider an hour; also jelly-making operations (fall). Samples are served. **FREE**

Little River State Park. *3444 Little River Rd, Waterbury (05676). 2 miles W off Hwy 2.* Phone 802/244-7103. www.vtstateparks.com. This 12,000-acre park offers swimming, fishing; nature and hiking trails, tent and trailer sites (dump station), lean-tos. (Memorial Day-Columbus Day) Standard fees.

Long Trail. *Phone 802/244-7037. www.greenmountain-club.org.* A 22-mile segment of backpacking trail connects Camel's Hump with Mount Mansfield, the state's highest peak. Primitive camping is allowed on both mountains. Recommended for the experienced hiker.

Winter recreation. Area abounds in downhill, cross-country, and ski touring facilities; also many snowmobile trails.

Limited-Service Hotel

★ ★ **BEST WESTERN WATERBURY-STOWE.** *45 Blush Hill Rd, Waterbury (05676).* Phone 802/244-7822; toll-free 800/621-7822; fax 802/244-6395. www.bestwesternwaterburystowe.com. 79 rooms, 2 story. Check-in 3 pm, check-out noon. Restaurant, bar. Fitness room. Indoor pool. Tennis. **$**
🏃 🛏 🏊

Specialty Lodgings

BIRDS NEST INN. *5088 Waterbury-Stowe Rd, Waterbury Center (05677).* Phone 802/244-7490; toll-free 800/366-5592; fax 802/244-8473. www.birdsnestinn.com. Surrounded by black locust trees, this restored 1832 farmhouse offers guest rooms with private baths and down comforters. A three-course hearty breakfast is served using local produce. In the evening, wines and hot and cold hors d'ouevres are complimentary. The inn is close to all major ski areas. 5 rooms, 2 story. Children over 15 years only. Complimentary full breakfast. Check-in 4 pm, check-out 10:30 am. **$**

THATCHER BROOK INN. *1017 Waterbury Stowe Rd, Waterbury (05676).* Phone 802/244-5911; toll-free 800/292-5911; fax 802/244-1294. www.thatcherbrook.com. Built in 1899; twin gazebos with front porch. 22 rooms, 2 story. Complimentary full breakfast. Check-in 3-10 pm, check-out 10:30 am. Restaurant. **$**

West Dover (F-2)

See also Wilmington

Population 250
Elevation 1,674 ft
Area Code 802
Zip 05356
Information Mount Snow Valley Region Chamber of Commerce, Hwy 9, W Main St, PO Box 3, Wilmington 05363; phone 802/464-8092 or toll-free 877/887-6884
Web Site www.visitvermont.com

What to See and Do

Mount Snow Ski Area. *12 Pisgah Rd, West Dover (05356). 9 miles N on Hwy 100, in Green Mountain National Forest. Phone 802/464-2151; toll-free 800/498-0479. www.mountsnow.com.* Area has two quad, six triple, nine double chairlifts; patrol, school, rentals; snowmaking; cafeterias, restaurant, bars, entertainment; nursery. More than 100 trails spread over five interconnected mountain areas (also see WILMINGTON); shuttle bus. Longest run 2 1/2 miles; vertical drop 1,700 feet. Half-day rates. (Nov-early May, daily) **$$$$**

Special Events

Oktoberfest & Craft Show. *Mount Snow Resort, 12 Pisgah Rd, West Dover (05356). Phone 802/464-2151; toll-free 800/498-0479. www.mountsnow.com.* New England area artisans exhibit pottery, jewelry, glass, graphics, weaving, and other crafts; German-style entertainment. Chairlift rides and foliage. Columbus Day weekend. **$$$$**

Shimano NORBA National Mountain Bike Series Finals. *Mount Snow Ski Area, 12 Pisgah Rd, West Dover (05356). Phone 802/464-4191; toll-free 800/451-4211. www.mountsnow.com/summer/norba.* More than 1,500 cyclists from throughout the world compete in downhill, dual slalom, and circuit racing events. Late Aug. **FREE**

Limited-Service Hotel

WEST DOVER INN. *108 Hwy 100, West Dover (05356). Phone 802/464-5207; fax 802/464-2173. www. westdoverinn.com.* Built in 1846, this inn was once a stagecoach stop and a general store. Mountains, farms, and winding roads provide the tranquil scenery, and the interior of the inn is warm with country touches. Guest rooms are spacious and feature brass beds, quilts, and carpeted floors. 12 rooms, 2 story. Children over 12 years only. Complimentary full breakfast. Check-in 2 pm, check-out 11 am. Restaurant, bar. **$$**
🅓

Full-Service Hotel

★ ★ ★ **THE INN AT SAWMILL FARM.** *Hwy 100 and 7 Crosstown Rd, West Dover (05356). Phone 802/464-8131; toll-free 800/493-1133; fax 802/464-1130. www.theinnatsawmillfarm.com.* While its location in southern Vermont makes it an easy jaunt from New York or Boston, the Inn at Sawmill Farms sophisticated yet low-key attitude is what draws city slickers to its bucolic setting. This converted barn is perfectly situated for skiers to hit the slopes of nearby Mount Snow, while others enjoy trawling for antiques or casting a rod in the regions trout ponds. Lazy afternoons are spent picnicking on the lovely grounds filled with ponds and luscious blooms. Weathered floors and hand-hewn posts and beams hint at the original construction, yet this inn has a decidedly polished flair. Moods are instantly elevated in the lovely guest rooms, where rich colors and floral prints delight visitors. Despite its sleepy address, the inns restaurant is anything but country. Its haute cuisine rivals that of many of its city competitors, and dessert is simply not to be missed. 21 rooms, 2 story. Closed Apr-May. Check-in 3 pm, check-out noon. Restaurant, bar. Fitness room. Outdoor pool. Tennis. **$$$$**
🏃 🏊 ⛷

Full-Service Inn

★ ★ ★ **FOUR SEASONS INN.** *145 VT 100, West Dover (05356). Phone 802/464-8303; fax 802/463-3373. www.thefourseasonsinn.com.* 18 rooms. No children allowed. Complimentary full breakfast. Check-in 3 pm, check-out 11 am. Wireless Internet access. Bar. Outdoor pool. **$$**
🅓 🏊

Restaurants

★ ★ ★ **HERMITAGE.** *21 Handle Rd, West Dover (05363). Phone 802/464-3511; fax 802/464-2688. www. hermitageinn.com.* Nestled at the foot of southern Vermont's Green Mountains, this restaurant is part of the historic inn bearing the same name. Three attractive dining rooms are decorated in saturated colors that are both soothing and fresh at the same time. The large main dining room is done in shades of blue and cream and stretches across the entire back of the inn; it features lots of windows, which bring in vistas of apple trees and lawns. The extensive menu options change seasonally, and there is a 40,000-bottle wine cellar—many of the labels are available in the gift shop along with the homemade preserves and other delicacies.A pianist performs here on Saturday nights. American menu. Dinner. Closed Tues; also Apr. Bar. Children's menu. Casual attire. Reservations recommended. Outdoor seating. **$$$**
🅓

★ ★ ★ **THE INN AT SAWMILL FARM.** *Hwy 100 and Crosstown Rd, West Dover (05356). Phone 802/464-8131; toll-free 800/493-1133; fax 802/464-*

1130. *www.theinnatsawmillfarm.com.* Only in a town that wears charm and hospitality like a comfortable old jacket—West Dover—can an old sawmill and barn be transformed into a sophisticated but unpretentious haven for weary urban food lovers. The Sawmill Inn was purchased by the Williams family in 1967 and has weathered the years with grace, maintaining its commitment to quality ingredients and family-style warmth. Decorated like a New England fairy tale, with exposed beams and hanging chandeliers, the restaurant oozes serenity and calm and is the perfect place to relax for an evening of pampering and delicious home-style cooking. The restaurant features a seasonal American menu specializing in locally farmed game such as quail, pheasant, rabbit, and venison. The impressive wine list heaves at the seams, with a selection of 1,285 wines in the 30,000-bottle cellar. All this from a little old barn. American menu. Breakfast, dinner. Closed Apr-May. Bar. Business casual attire. Reservations recommended. **$$$**

Weston (E-2)

See also Londonderry, Ludlow, Peru, Okemo State Forest

Population 620
Elevation 1,295 ft
Area Code 802
Zip 05161

Once nearly a ghost town, Weston is now a serene village secluded in the beautiful hills of Vermont. Charming old houses are situated around a small common, and shops are scattered along Main Street. Weston is listed on the National Register of Historic Places.

What to See and Do

Farrar-Mansur House Museum. *N side of Common.* Phone 802/824-5294. *www.westonvt.com.* (1797) Restored house/tavern with nine rooms. Period furnishings; paintings. Guided tours. (July-Labor Day: Wed 1-5 pm, Sat-Sun 1-4 pm; Sept-mid-Oct: Sat-Sun 1-5 pm) **$$**

Greendale Camping Area. *2 miles N on Hwy 100, 2 miles W on Greendale Rd in Green Mountain National Forest.* Phone 802/747-6700. *www.fs.fed.us/r9/gmfl/ green_mountain/recreation_management/camping/ greendalecamping.htm.* Picnicking, camping (fee).

Old Mill Museum. *Hwy 100, Weston. In center of village.* Phone 802/824-5294. *www.westonvt.com.* Museum of old-time tools and industries; tinsmith in residence.

Guided tours (July-Labor Day: Wed 1-5 pm, Sat 10 am-4 pm, Sun 1-4 pm; Sept-mid-Oct: Sat-Sun) **DONATION**

Vermont Country Store. *657 Main St, Weston (05161). S of Village Green.* Phone 802/824-3184. *www.vermont-countrystore.com.* Just like those Granddad used to patronize—rock candy and other old-fashioned foodstuffs. (July-Oct: Mon-Sat 9 am-6 pm, rest of the year Mon-Sat 9 am-5 pm; closed Thanksgiving, Dec 25)

Weston Playhouse. *Village Green, 703 Main St, Weston (05161).* Phone 802/824-5288; fax 802/717-1032. *www. westonplayhouse.org.* One of the oldest professional theater companies in the state. Restaurant; cabaret.

Specialty Lodging

THE COLONIAL HOUSE. *287 Hwy 100, Weston (05161).* Phone 802/824-6286; toll-free 800/639-5033; fax 802/824-3934. *www.cohoinn.com.* 2 story. Pets accepted, some restrictions; fee. Complimentary full breakfast. Check-in 2 pm, check-out 11 am. Restaurant. **$**

White River Junction (D-2)

See also Hanover, Fairlee, Windsor, Woodstock

Settled 1764
Population 2,521
Elevation 368 ft
Area Code 802
Zip 05001

Appropriately named, this town is the meeting place of the Boston & Maine and Central Vermont railroads, the White and Connecticut rivers, and two interstate highways.

What to See and Do

Quechee Gorge. *764 Dewey Mills Rd, White River Junction (05001). About 8 miles W on Hwy 4.* Phone 802/295-2990. *www.vtstateparks.com/htm/quechee.cfm.* Often referred to as Vermont's "Little Grand Canyon, " the Ottauquechee River has carved out a mile-long chasm that offers dramatic views of the landscape and neighboring towns.

Limited-Service Hotel

★ **COMFORT INN.** *56 Ralph Lehman Dr, White River Junction (05001). Phone 802/295-3051; toll-free 800/628-7727; fax 802/295-5990. www.comfortinnwrj. com.* In a commercial area near the junction of Interstate 91 and Interstate 89 and near several restaurants, this hotel appeals to budget-minded travelers. It lacks its own fitness facilities, but guests have full privileges at a health club about 1/2 mile away. 94 rooms, 4 story. Pets accepted. Complimentary continental breakfast. Check-in 2 pm, check-out 11 am. High-speed Internet access, wireless Internet access. Outdoor pool. **$**

Wilmington (F-2)

See also Bennington, Brattleboro, Marlboro, West Dover

Population 1,968
Elevation 1,533 ft
Area Code 802
Zip 05363
Information Mount Snow Valley Region Chamber of Commerce, Hwy 9, W Main St, PO Box 3; phone 802/464-8092 or toll-free 877/887-6884
Web Site www.visitvermont.com

What to See and Do

⭐ **Molly Stark State Park.** *705 Hwy 9 E, Wilmington (05363). Approximately 4 miles E on Hwy 9. Phone 802/464-5460.* A 158-acre park named for wife of General John Stark, hero of Battle of Bennington (1777); on west slope of Mount Olga (2,438 feet). Fishing in nearby lake; hiking trails, tent and trailer sites (dump station), lean-tos. Fire tower with excellent views. (Memorial Day-Columbus Day) Standard fees.

Mount Snow Resort. *12 Pisgah Rd, West Dover (05356). 3 miles NW, off Hwy 100. Phone toll-free 800/451-4211. www.mountsnow.com.* Resort has three high-speed quads, quad, ten triple, four double chairlifts, two surface lifts; patrol, school, rentals; snowmaking; concession, cafeteria, bar; nursery, lodges. More than 100 trails spread over five interconnecting mountain areas (see WEST DOVER); shuttle bus. Longest run 1 1/2 miles; vertical drop 1,700 feet. (Dec-Mar, daily) Golf, pro shop; restaurant, bar (early May-mid-Oct). **$$$$**

Special Events

Deerfield Valley Farmers Day Exhibition. *Baker Field, Wilmington. Phone 802/464-2059. www.wilmington-vermont.us.* Pony pull, midway rides; horse show, livestock judging, entertainment. Late Aug. **$**

The Nights Before Christmas. *Throughout Wilmington and West Dover, Wilmington. Phone 802/464-8092. www.visitvermont.com.* Celebrates holiday season with caroling, torchlight parade, fireworks, tree lighting. Festival of Light, living nativity, and children's hayrides. Late Nov-late Dec.

Limited-Service Hotel

★ **HORIZON INN.** *861 Hwy 9 E, Wilmington (05363). Phone 802/464-2131; toll-free 800/336-5513; fax 802/464-8302. www.horizoninn.com.* This family-friendly lodge is just east of the ski town of Wilmington and sits off Route 9, the areas major east/west route. Its close to the resort mountain locations of Mount Snow, Haystack, and Stratton and is in the heart of southern Vermont "fall foliage country." Family-owned and -run, it has a homey feel, particularly in its large, informal basement lounge with 60-inch TV. The second-floor dining room, serving American food, is filled with Norman Rockwell art and Hummel figurines. 29 rooms, 2 story. Check-in 2 pm, check-out 11 am. Restaurant, bar. Fitness room. Indoor pool, whirlpool. **$**

Full-Service Inns

★ ★ ★ **HERMITAGE INN.** *21 Handle Rd, West Dover (05356). Phone 802/464-3511; fax 802/464-2688. www.hermitageinn.com.* Bring your cross-country skis and ski in/ski out of this picturesque inn, sitting on the crest of a hill just down the road from Haystack and close to Mount Snow. In the fall, shoot clay pigeons or go pheasant hunting on the private, 200-acre hunting preserve. In the summer, enjoy croquet or other lawn games. And at any time of the year, visit the inns fine-dining restaurant, if only to sample the extensive wine list; *Wine Spectator* magazine has pronounced it one of the greatest wine lists in the world (be sure to visit the inns wine shop and buy a bottle of your favorite to take home). The guest rooms are equally sumptuous. There are four in the main house, seven in the adjoining wine house, and four in the carriage house, each with a wood-burning fireplace and a collection of New England antiques. If the inn looks familiar, its undoubtedly because you have seen it in a painting by the artist Michel Delacroix. The original, Winter in New England, now hangs in the Hermitage Inn. 15 rooms, 2 story. Pets accepted, some restrictions; fee. Complimentary full breakfast. Check-in 2 pm, check-out 11 am. Restaurant, bar. Ski in/ski out. **$**

★ ★ ★ WHITE HOUSE OF WILMINGTON.

178 Hwy 9 E, Wilmington (05363). Phone 802/464-2135; toll-free 800/541-2135; fax 802/464-5222. www.whitehouseinn.com. A historic old inn with an indoor/outdoor pool, steam room, sauna, and tanning room? Lawn games in the summer...tubing, cross-country skiing, and snowshoeing in the winter...trails for hiking year-round.... There is much to do at this country mansion, built in 1915 as a summer home for a wealthy lumber baron. Restorations began in 1978, but today the inn retains many of its original, elegant details, such as the front hallways wallpaper, made in France at the turn of the century; and the secret staircase, a guest favorite. The original house has nine guest rooms, some with fireplaces and some with both fireplaces and whirlpool tubs; an adjoining guest house has eight additional rooms that have been designed for families. Downstairs, its easy to picture a lumber baron entertaining his wealthy friends in from the city for a weekend of skiing or croquet: there they are after a game of croquet, sipping lemonade in front of the huge fireplace in the lounge (where today there are jigsaw puzzles in progress) or dining elegantly in the main dining room, where guests sup in equal elegance today. 25 rooms. Closed Apr. Children over 8 years only. Complimentary full breakfast. Check-in 2 pm, check-out 11 am. Restaurant, bar. Indoor pool, outdoor pool. Ski in/ski out. **$$**

Specialty Lodging

TRAIL'S END - A COUNTRY INN. *5 Trail's End Ln, Wilmington (05363). Phone 802/464-2727; toll-free 800/859-2585; fax 802/464-5532. www.trailsendvt. com.* 5 rooms, 2 story. Complimentary full breakfast. Check-in 2-10 pm, check-out 11 am. Outdoor pool. Tennis. **$**

Restaurant

★ ★ WHITE HOUSE.

178 Hwy 9 E, Wilmington (05363). Phone 802/464-2135; toll-free 800/541-2135; fax 802/464-5222. www.whitehouseinn.com. Guests can choose to dine in one of the three dining rooms of this 1915 mansion. The largest of the rooms is dominated by a large fireplace and has warm wood paneling and a hardwood floor. Lots of windows offer a magnificent view of the surrounding hills. A large and somewhat contemporary covered porch offers a sunken bar and floor-to-ceiling windows to enjoy a sunset pre-dinner cocktail. The menu changes seasonally and includes local Vermont cheeses and entrées such as roasted Vermont duckling and Wiener schnitzel. A wine list with a 100-plus selection is also offered. Located in The White House of Wilmington (see), the restaurant sits on a hill outside Wilmington, easily accessible from Routes 9 and 100. American menu. Dinner. Closed Mon-Tues; Apr; first two weeks in May. Bar. Casual attire. Reservations recommended. **$$$**

Windsor (E-2)

White River Junction

Settled 1764
Population 3,714
Elevation 354 ft
Area Code 802
Zip 05089
Information White River Area Chamber of Commerce, PO Box 697, White River Junction 05001; phone 802/295-6200

Situated on the Connecticut River in the shadow of Mount Ascutney, Windsor once was the political center of the Connecticut Valley towns. The name "Vermont" was adopted, and its constitution was drawn up here. Inventors and inventions flourished here in the 19th century; the hydraulic pump, a sewing machine, coffee percolator, and various refinements in firearms originated in Windsor.

What to See and Do

American Precision Museum. *196 Main St, Windsor (05089). Phone 802/674-5781. www.americanprecision. org.* Exhibits include hand and machine tools; illustrations of their uses and development. Housed in former Robbins and Lawrence Armory (1846). (Late May-Oct, daily 10a m-5 pm; rest of year: by appointment) **$$**

Constitution House. *16 N Main St, Windsor (05089). Phone 802/672-3773. www.historicvermont.org.* An 18th-century tavern where the constitution of the Republic of Vermont was signed on July 8, 1777. Museum. (Late May-mid-Oct, daily) **$**

Covered bridge. *Bridge St, Windsor. www.crjc.org/heritage/N08-5.htm.* Crossing the Connecticut River; longest in the United States.

Mount Ascutney State Park. *3 miles S off Hwy 5 on Hwy 44A; I-91 exit 8. Phone 802/674-2060.* This 1,984-acre park has a paved road to summit of Mount Ascutney (3,144 feet). Hiking trails, picnicking, tent and trailer sites (dump station), lean-tos. (Memorial Day-Columbus Day)

Vermont State Craft Center at Windsor House. *54 Main St, Windsor (05089). Phone 802/674-6729.* Restored building features works of more than 250 Vermont craftspeople. (Jan-May: ThursSat 10 am6pm, Sun 11 am5 pm; June-Dec: MonSat 10 am6 pm, Sun 11 am5 pm) **FREE**

Wilgus State Park. *6 miles S on Hwy 5. Phone 802/674-5422.*This 100-acre park overlooks the Connecticut River. Canoe launching. Hiking trails. Wooded picnic area. Tent and trailer sites (dump station), lean-tos. (Memorial Day-Columbus Day)

Full-Service Inn

★ ★ ★ **JUNIPER HILL INN.** *153 Pembroke Rd, Windsor (05089). Phone 802/674-5273; toll-free 800/359-2541; fax 802/674-2041. www.juniperhillinn.com.* Teddy Roosevelt slept here. No wonder: the exterior of this magnificent 1902 Classical Revival mansion, perched atop 14 acres of hillside, is just a prelude to the elegance that lies within. A 30-x-40-foot Great Hall features floor-to-ceiling fireplace. A 5-x-15-foot table sits within a massive Gathering Room. The library, tucked within the west wing, is a perfect place to sit by the fire and play a board game or two. In the Gentlemans Sitting Parlor, one can have a brandy and a quiet chat. It's all designed to make you feel as though you are a guest at the country home of your (very wealthy) aunt, who invited you to the outskirts of historic Windsor to forget your cares and enjoy life. Sleep in a four-poster bed, sniff the fragrance of fresh flowers, soak in a claw-foot tub—while sipping a sherry—and awaken to a deluxe breakfast. 16 rooms, 3 story. Closed two weeks in Nov; three weeks in late Mar-early Apr, Children over 12 years only. Complimentary full breakfast. Check-in 3 pm, check-out 11 am. Restaurant. Outdoor pool. **$$**

Woodstock (D-)

See also Killington, Plymouth, White River Junction

Settled 1768
Population 3,212
Elevation 705 ft
Area Code 802
Zip 05091
Information Chamber of Commerce, 18 Central St, PO Box 486; phone 802/457-3555
Web Site www.woodstockvt.com

The antique charm of Woodstock has been preserved, at least in part, by determination. Properties held for generations by descendants of original owners provided built-in zoning long before Historic District status was achieved. When the iron bridge that crosses the Ottauquechee River at Union Street was condemned in 1968, it was replaced by a covered wooden bridge.

What to See and Do

Billings Farm & Museum. *Hwy 12 & River Rd, Woodstock (05091). Phone 802/457-2355. www.billingsfarm.org.* Exhibits include operating dairy farm and an 1890s farmhouse. (Apr 30-Oct 31: daily 10 am-5 pm; Martin Luther King, Presidents Day weekend 10 am-3 pm; Thanksgiving, Dec Sat-Sun 10 am-4 pm) **$$**

Covered bridge. *Mountain Ave, Woodstock. Center of village.* (1969) First one built in Vermont since 1895. Two others cross the Ottauquechee River: one 3 miles W (1865), another 4 miles E, at Taftsville (1836).

Kedron Valley Stables. *Hwy 106 S, South Woodstock (05071). 5 miles S on Hwy 106. Phone 802/457-1480; toll-free 800/225-6301. www.kedron.com.* Hayrides, sleigh rides, picnic trail rides; indoor ring; riding lessons by appointment. **$$$$**

Marsh-Billings-Rockefeller National Historic Park. *54 Elm St, Woodstock (05091). On Hwy 12, 1/2 mile N of Woodstock Village Green. Phone 802/457-3368. www.nps.gov/mabi.* Includes Marsh-Billings-Rockefeller mansion, which contains extensive collection of American landscape paintings. Mansion is surrounded by 550-acre Mount Tom forest. Interpretive tours of the mansion, its grounds and gardens, and the Mount Tom forest are available. Reservations recommended. Park also offers hiking, nature study, and cross-country skiing. (Memorial Day-Oct, daily 10 am-5 pm) **$$**

Silver Lake State Park. *10 miles NW via Hwy 12 to Barnard, on Silver Lake. Phone 802/234-9451.* This 34-acre park offers a swimming beach, bathhouse, fishing, boating (rentals); picnicking, concession, tent and trailer camping (dump station), lean-tos. Within walking distance of Barnard Village. (Memorial Day-Labor Day, daily)

Suicide Six Ski Area. *14 The Green, Woodstock (05091). 3 miles N on Hwy 12 (S Pomfret Rd). Phone 802/457-1100. www.woodstockinn.com/skiatinn.html.* Area has two double chairlifts, J-Bar; patrol, PSIA school, rentals, snowmaking; cafeteria, wine and beer bar, lodge. Twenty-two runs, longest run 1 mile; vertical drop 650 feet. Site of the first ski tow in the United States (1934). (Early Dec-late Mar, daily) **$$$$**

Vermont Institute of Natural Science. *6565 Woodstock Rd, Woodstock (05059). Near Quechee Gorge. Phone 802/359-5000. www.vinsweb.org.* Property includes a 47-acre mixed habitat site with trails VINS Nature Center includes the Raptor Museum, which has 26 species of hawks, owls, and eagles (May-Oct, daily 9 am-5:30 pm; Nov-Apr, daily 10 am-4 pm; closed Thanksgiving, Dec 25, Jan 1). Gift shop, cafe. **$$**

Walking Tours Around Woodstock. *Phone 802/457-3555. www.woodstockvt.com.* There are one- and two-hour tours of Historic District, covering more than 1 mile; departing from Chamber of Commerce information booth on the green. (by request) **$**

Woodstock Country Club. *14 The Green, Woodstock (05091). Phone 802/457-1100; toll-free 800/448-7900. www.woodstockinn.com.* An 18-hole championship golf course, ten tennis courts, paddle tennis, cross-country skiing center with more than 35 miles of trails; rentals, instruction, tours. Restaurant, lounge. (Daily; closed Apr and Nov) Fee for activities. **$$$$**

Woodstock Historical Society. *26 Elm St, Woodstock (05091). Phone 802/457-1822.* Dana House (1807) has 11 rooms spanning 1750-1900, including a children's room; also silver, glass, paintings, costumes, furniture; research library; Woodstock-related artifacts, photographs. Farm and textile equipment. Gift shop. (Late May-late Oct, Mon-Sat 10 am-4 pm, Sun noon-4 pm) **$**

Limited-Service Hotels

★ **POND RIDGE MOTEL.** *506 Hwy 4 W, Woodstock (05091). Phone 802/457-1667. www.pondridgemotel. com.* Kids will enjoy playing on the huge lawn of this older-style, family-friendly motel, located on 6 1/2 acres of private frontage along the Ottauquechee River, 1.8

miles west of historic Woodstock Green. In front are a gazebo and big shade trees; in the back are a pond and the Ottauquechee, both great places for splashers and waders. Benches and picnic tables have been set up along the river. Rooms have lovely views of the water. 20 rooms. Check-in 1 pm, check-out 10 am. **$**
🐾

★ **THE SHIRE RIVERVIEW.** *46 Pleasant St, Woodstock (05091). Phone 802/457-2211; fax 802/457-5836. www.shiremotel.com.* A wraparound porch with rocking chairs is undoubtedly the first thing that will catch your eye as you approach this soft gray and white retreat. Well situated just east of Woodstock's historic village center, the Shire Riverview has a prime spot overlooking the Ottauquechee River, the Marsh-Billings-Rockefeller National Park, and the natural beauty of Vermont's rolling hills. The Shire takes full advantage of its views, with large windows and French doors and a veranda where guests can take morning coffee and tea. Rooms are spacious; there are value rooms without views but with full amenities, and other rooms and suites with plush four-poster beds and mahogany furniture, well-coordinated fabrics and colors, and large baths with upgraded amenities. There's no restaurant, but with the heart of Woodstock within walking distance, no worries. 42 rooms. Check-in 2 pm, check-out 11 am. **$**

Full-Service Resort

★ ★ ★ **WOODSTOCK INN & RESORT.** *14 The Green, Woodstock (05091). Phone 802/457-1100; toll-free 800/448-7900; fax 802/457-6699. www.woodstock-inn.com.* The Woodstock Inn & Resort, on the south side of the Woodstock green, is the Vermont getaway of dreams. From its classic New England architecture to its gracious charm, this resort makes its way into travelers' hearts. An inn has stood on this spot since the 18th century, lending a deep sense of history. An enormous fireplace welcomes guests. The rooms and suites are sweet renditions of traditional Vermont style, with handmade quilts, built-in alcoves, and original prints. While the accommodations are exceedingly inviting and plush, the plethora of outdoor activities encourages guests to leave the confines of their cocoonlike rooms. Downhill and cross-country skiing are two of the resorts most popular winter activities, while the Woodstock Country Clubs prestigious course draws golfers. Biking, canoeing, fishing, horseback riding, and nature walks are among the many ways to enjoy the picturesque countryside, and the town's shops and other attractions are within walking distance. After a long day, three restaurants satisfy diners with fine dining, casual fare, and traditional tavern-style food. In season, children's programs are organized around sports, area attractions, and even a special "Kids' Day in the Kitchen." The inn offers many packages combining all sorts of activities and meal plans. 142 rooms, 3 story. Check-in 3 pm, check-out 11 am. Three restaurants, bar. Children's activity center. Fitness room, fitness classes available. Indoor pool, outdoor pool, whirlpool. Golf, 18 holes. Tennis. Business center. **$$**

Full-Service Inns

★ ★ ★ **KEDRON VALLEY INN.** *10671 South Rd, South Woodstock (05071). Phone 802/457-1473; toll-free 800/836-1193; fax 802/457-4469. www.kedronvalleyinn.com.* Just 5 miles outside Woodstock, this small historic inn makes a good base while enjoying the local activities. Guests can partake in antique shopping or browsing in local shops. 26 rooms, 3 story. Closed Apr. Pets accepted, some restrictions. Check-in 3:30 pm, check-out 11:30 am. Restaurant, bar. **$$**

★ ★ ★ **QUECHEE INN AT MARSHLAND FARM.** *1119 Quechee Main St, Quechee (05059). Phone 802/295-3133; toll-free 800/235-3133; fax 802/295-6587. www.quecheeinn.com.* This inn was built in 1793 and has been restored to its 19th-century beginnings with many modern conveniences. 24 rooms, 2 story. Complimentary full breakfast. Check-in 3 pm, check-out 11 am. Restaurant, bar. **$$**

★ ★ ★ ★ ★ **TWIN FARMS.** *452 Royalton Turnpike, Barnard (05031). Phone 802/234-9999; toll-free 800/894-6327; fax 802/234-9990. www.twinfarms.com.* Travelers searching for the ultimate Vermont farmhouse, where rocking chairs line the porch, deer gambol on the lawn, and fireplaces warm hearts and souls on chilly evenings, need look no further than Twin Farms. This remarkable inn appeals to the naturalist in all guests with its magnificent 300 acres of ponds, wooded valleys, and rolling lawns carpeted in brilliant wildflowers or blanketed in pure ivory snow. The accommodations weave together quintessential New England charm with a cosmopolitan twist. From the clean lines and simple furnishings of the Orchard Cottage and the seductive Moroccan style of the Meadow Cottage to the vaulted ceilings of twig artistry in the Treehouse, the designs spark the imaginations of

their residents. Vermont's lush landscape serves as the inspiration for the kitchens gourmet meals, with organic ingredients from local farms determining the menus, while its ever-changing seasons never cease to amaze. 16 rooms, 2 story. Closed Apr. No children allowed. Complimentary full breakfast. Check-in 4 pm, check-out noon. High-speed Internet access, wireless Internet access. Restaurant (guests only), two bars. Fitness room, spa. Tennis. Ski in/ski out. Airport transportation available. **$$$$**

Specialty Lodgings

APPLEBUTTER INN. *7511 Happy Valley Rd, Woodstock (05091). Phone 802/457-4158. www.applebutterinn.com.* Built in 1846; was a stagecoach stop and a general store. 6 rooms, 2 story. Complimentary full breakfast. Check-in 3-8 pm, check-out 10:30 am. **$**

CANTERBURY HOUSE BED AND BREAKFAST. *43 Pleasant St, Woodstock (05091). Phone 802/457-3077; toll-free 800/390-3077; fax 802/457-4630. www.thecanterburyhouse.com.* Victorian home built in 1880; antiques. 7 rooms, 3 story. No children allowed. Complimentary full breakfast. Check-in 2-7 pm, check-out 10:30 am. Restaurant. **$**

CHARLESTON HOUSE. *21 Pleasant St, Woodstock (05091). Phone 802/457-3843; fax 802/457-3154. www.charlestonhouse.com.* Greek Revival house built in 1835; many antiques. 9 rooms, 2 story. Complimentary full breakfast. Check-in 3 pm. Check-out 11 am. **$$**

THE LINCOLN INN AT THE COVERED BRIDGE. *530 Woodstock Rd, Woodstock (05091). Phone 802/457-3312; fax 802/457-5808. www.lincolninn.com.* This renovated farmhouse's (circa 1869) property is bordered by the Ottauquechee River and a covered bridge. 6 rooms, 2 story. Complimentary full breakfast. Check-in 3 pm, check-out 11 am. Restaurant. **$**

MAPLE LEAF INN. *5890 Hwy 12, Barnard (05031). Phone 802/234-5342; toll-free 800/516-2753; fax 802/234-6456. www.mapleleafinn.com.* Just gazing at this white porch-wrapped farmhouse will relax arriving guests. The property is nestled on 16 acres of maple and birch trees near the quaint town of Woodstock, where antiques stores, unique shops, and outdoor recreations abound. 7 rooms, 3 story. Check-in 3 pm, check-out 11 am. **$$**

PARKER HOUSE INN. *1792 Quechee Main St, Quechee (05059). Phone 802/295-6077; fax 802/296-6696. www.theparkerhouseinn.com.* Victorian home (1857); former senator's residence. 7 rooms, 3 story. Pets accepted, some restrictions; fee. Complimentary full breakfast. Check-in 3-10 pm, check-out 11 am. Restaurant. **$**

WOODSTOCKER BED AND BREAKFAST. *61 River St, Woodstock (05091). Phone 802/457-3896; toll-free 866/662-1439; fax 802/457-3897. www.woodstockervt.com.* Built in 1830; individually decorated rooms. 9 rooms, 2 story. Complimentary full breakfast. Check-in 3-6 pm, check-out 11 am. Whirlpool. **$**

Restaurants

★ ★ ★ **BARNARD INN.** *5518 Hwy 12, Barnard (05031). Phone 802/234-9961; fax 802/234-5590.* The original brick structure of this house, built in 1796, is a perfect host for this charming restaurant. French menu. Dinner. Closed Sun-Mon. Bar. Children's menu. **$$**

★ ★ ★ **KEDRON VALLEY.** *Hwy 106, South Woodstock (05091). Phone 802/457-1473. www.kedronvalleyinn.com.* The dining room of this elegant inn offers an updated menu. Vermont-raised produce and meat are featured, and the friendly service has a certain Vermont charm. Breakfast, dinner. Closed Wed except fall foliage season and week of Dec 25; also Apr. Bar. Children's menu. **$$**

★ ★ ★ **PRINCE AND THE PAUPER.** *24 Elm St, Woodstock (05091). Phone 802/457-1818. www.prince-andpauper.com.* Chef/owner Chris Balce welcomes you to his country restaurant with candlelit tables and hand-hewn beams. The menu changes seasonally, and the house specialty is Carre d' Agneau "Royale"—boneless rack of lamb in puff pastry with spinach and mushroom duxelles. American menu. Dinner. Closed Thanksgiving, Dec 25. Bar. Business casual attire. Reservations recommended. **$$$**

★ ★ ★ **QUECHEE INN AT MARSHLAND FARM.** *1119 Quechee Main St, Quechee (05059). Phone 802/295-3133; toll-free 800/235-3133; fax 802/295-6587. www.quecheeinn.com.* The restaurant

is in the main house of this inn, which dates to 1793 and overlooks the Ottauquechee River. The cuisine is served in a casual but sophisticated setting, with a wine list to match. American menu. Breakfast, dinner. Bar. Children's menu. Business casual attire. Reservations recommended. Outdoor seating. **$$**

★ ★ ★ **SIMON PEARCE.** *1761 Main St, Quechee (05059). Phone 802/295-1470; fax 802/295-2853. www.simonpearce.com.* Part of the glassblowing and pottery complex that has become an emblem of Vermont, this spacious, contemporary restaurant has beautiful, forested views of the Ottauquechee River and a covered bridge. The cuisine is innovative American with Asian accents, and the breads and soups are homemade. American menu. Lunch, dinner. Bar. Casual attire. Reservations recommended. Outdoor seating. **$$$**

★ ★ ★ **WOODSTOCK INN.** *14 The Green, Woodstock (05091). Phone 802/457-1100; toll-free 800/448-7900; fax 802/457-6699. www.woodstockinn.com.* This quaint restaurant, with softly candlelit tables and nightly piano entertainment, is a perfect choice for a romantic meal. The inn does its own baking and offers a prix fixe tasting menu. It is a short drive from Hanover's Dartmouth College. American menu. Dinner, Sun brunch. Bar. Children's menu. Business casual attire. Reservations recommended. Valet parking. **$$$**

Montréal

Settled 1642
Population 1,800,000
Elevation 117 ft (36 m)
Area Code 514
Information Tourisme-Québec, CP 979, H3C 2W3;
phone 514/873-2015 or toll-free 800/363-7777
Web Site www.tourisme-montreal.org

Blessed by its location on an island at the junction of the St. Lawrence and Ottawa rivers, Montréal has served for more than three centuries as a gigantic trading post; its harbor can accommodate more than 100 oceangoing vessels. While it is a commercial, financial, and industrial center, Montréal is also an internationally recognized patron of the fine arts, hosting several acclaimed festivals attended by international enthusiasts.

A stockaded, indigenous settlement called Hochelaga when it was discovered in 1535 by Jacques Cartier, the area contained a trading post by the early 1600s; but it was not settled as a missionary outpost until 1642 when the Frenchman Paul de Chomedey, Sieur de Maisonneuve, and a group of settlers, priests, and nuns founded Ville-Morie. This later grew as an important fur trading center, and from here men such as Jolliet, Marquette, Duluth, and Father Hennepin set out on their western expeditions. Montréal remained under French rule until 1763 when Canada was surrendered as a possession to the British under the Treaty of Paris. For seven months during the American Revolution, Montréal was occupied by Americans, but it was later regained by the British.

Today, Montréal is an elegantly sophisticated city. Two-thirds of its people are French-speaking, and its French population is the largest outside of Europe. The city is also extremely international, with more than 80 ethnic groups represented in the metropolitan region. The largest of these include Italian, Jewish, Muslim, Greek, and Chinese. City neighborhoods, attractions, and markets reflect this diversity.

Montréal is made up of two parts: the Old City, in the same area as the original Ville-Morie, which is a maze of narrow streets, restored buildings, and old houses, best seen on foot; and the modern Montréal, with its many skyscrapers, museums, theaters, restaurants, and glittering nightlife. Sainte-Catherine Streets boutiques and department stores are a shoppers paradise, while Crescent Streets café-terrasses encourage people-watching while sipping coffee in the sunshine.

When there is inclement weather, head for Montréals underground city, an impressive pedestrian network more than 19 miles (30 kilometers) long, providing access to hundreds of shops and restaurants, several area attractions, and businesses. The underground also provides access to one of the most unique subway systems in the world. Each station has been decorated by a different architect in a different style, and visitors have called it "the largest underground art gallery in the world." Mont-Royal rises from the center of the island-city to a height of 764 feet (233 meters), affording a panoramic view. Calèches (horse-drawn carriages) provide tourists with a charming means of viewing the city and are, with the exception of bicycles, the only vehicles permitted in some areas of Mount Royal Park. Adjacent to the park is the Westmount area, a section of meandering roads and charming older homes of the early 1900s with delightful English-style gardens.

In 1967, Montréal hosted Expo '67, celebrating Canada's centennial. The summer Olympic games were held here in 1976.

Additional Information

Québec Tourism, PO Box 979, Montréal, H3C 2W3; phone toll-free 800/363-7777 or in person at Info-touriste, 1001 rue du Square-Dorchester (between Peel and Metcalfe sts); also office at Old Montréal, Placé Jacques-Cartier, 174 Notre-Dame St E; all have helpful information for tourists. The Consulate General of the United States is located on 1155 rue St. Alexandre, at Place Felip-Martin, at the corner of Rene Levesque Blvd; phone 514/398-9695. Public transportation is provided by the Societé de Transport de la Communauté Urbaine de Montréal (STCUM), phone 514/288-6287.

Public Transportation

Airport Montréal Dorval International Airport.

Information Phone 514/394-7377 or toll-free 800/465-1213

Lost and Found Phone 514/636-0499

Airlines Air Canada, Air Canada Jazz, Air Canada Tango, Air Creebec, Air France, Air Inuit, Air Saint-Pierre, Air Transat, Allegheny Airlines, American Airlines,

American Express, Atlantic Coast Airlines, Atlantic Southwest Airlines, Austrian Airlines, British Airways, Cajet, Chautauqua Airlines, Comair, Continental Airlines, Cubana, Dleta Air Lines, Egypt Air, First Air, Hydro-Québec, Japan Air Lines, Jetsgo, KLM Royal Dutch, Lufthansa, Mesaba Airlines, Mesa Airlines, Mexicana, Northwest Airlines, Olympic Airways, PSA Airlines, Québecair Express, Royal Air Maroc, Swiss, United Airlines, Westjet, Zip

What to See and Do

Angrignon Park. *7503 boul de la Verendrye, Montréal. Phone 514/872-3816; fax 514/768-4757.* On 262 acres (106 hectares) with more than 21,600 trees; lagoons, river; playground, picnicking, bicycling, iceskating, cross-country skiing. (Daily) **$$**

Calèche tours. Horse-drawn carriages depart from Place d' Armes, Mount Royal Park, or Old Port of Montréal. **$$$$**

Casino Montréal. *1 Ave du Caino, Montréal (H3C 4W7). Housed in Expo 67's famous French Pavilion. Phone 514/392-2746; toll-free 800/665-2274; fax 514/864-4950. www.casinos-quebec.com.* The Casino de Montréal offers guests a variety of games, with more than 120 gaming tables as well as 3,060 slot machines. (Open 24 hours)

Dorchester Square. *1555 Peel St, Montréal (H3A 3L8).* In the center of Montréal, this park is a popular meeting place. Also here is Mary Queen of the World Cathedral, a 1/3-scale replica of St. Peter's in Rome, as well as the information center of Montréal and Tourisme Québec. **FREE**

Fort Lennox. *Saint-Paul-de-l'ile-aux-Noix, 1 61st Ave, Montréal (J0J 1G0). Off Hwy 223.Phone 450/291-5700; fax 450/291-4389. www.parcscanada.gc.ca.* Located on Île-aux-Noix, Fort Lennox was designed to protect against an American invasion. Costumed guides provide visitors with insight into the history of these fortifications. On-site are picnic tables, outdoor game equipment, a snack bar, and a souvenier stand. (Daily 10 am-6 pm; mid-May-mid-June: Mon-Fri 10 am-5 pm; Sept-mid-Oct: Mon-Fri by appointment only) **$$**

Gray Line bus tours. *1140 Wellington St, Montréal (H3C 1V8). Phone 514/934-1222; toll-free 800/461-1223; fax 514/937-0288. www.grayline.com.* The well-known Gray Line offers various sightseeing and package tours of Montréal, with stops at the Biodome, Notre-Dame Basilica, and Chinatown. Buses depart from Dorchester Square. (May-Oct) **$$$$**

La Fontaine Park. *Sherbrooke and Ave du Parc Lafontaine, Montréal. Phone 514/872-2644.* Outdoor enthusiasts delight in this park for its many recreational oportunities. Along with paddleboating on two manmade lakes, visitors may enjoy foot paths and bicycle trails, and, in the winter, cross-country skiing, ice skating, and snowshoeing. **FREE**

Maison St.-Gabriel. *Pointe-Saint-Charles,2146 place Dublin, Montréal (H3K 2A2). Phone 514/935-8136; fax 514/935-5692. www.maisonsaint-gabriel.qc.ca.* Built in the late 17th century as a farm; also served as school for Marguerite Bourgeoys, founder of the Sisters of the Congrgatun de Notre-Dame, who looked after young French girls who were to marry the early colonists. The site includes vegetable, herb, and flower gardens; a stone barn; and the house itself, complete with period furnishings and tools, and items of French-Canadian heritage, including woodcuts from ancient churches and chapels. (mid-Apr-late June, Sept-mid-Dec: Tues-Sun 1 pm-5pm; late June-early Sept: Tues-Sun 11 am-6 pm) **$$**

McCord Museum of Canadian History. *690 rue Sherbrooke Ouest, Montréal (H3A 1E9). Phone 514/398-7100; fax 514/398-5045. www.mccord-museum.qc.ca.* Extensive and diverse collections including the most important First Nations collection in Québec, Canadian costumes and textiles, and the Notman photographic archives. (Tues-Fri 10 am-6 pm; Sat-Sun 10 am-5 pm; closed Mon except for holidays and during summer) **$$**

McGill University. *845 rue Sherbrooke Ouest, Montréal (H3A 2K6). Phone 514/398-4455. www.mcgill.ca.* (30,580 students) McGill's 80-acre (32-hectares) main campus is set between the lower slopes of Mount Royal and the downtown commercial district. Originally established as the Royal Institution for the Advancement of Learning from land and money left by Scottish immigrant James McGill, it was later renamed McGill University and chartered in 1821. Walking tours are given by students who offer insight into student life and the history of the university. **FREE**

★ **Montréal Botanical Garden.** *4101 rue Sherbrooke Est, Montréal (H1X 2B2). Phone 514/872-1400. www.ville.Montréal.qc.ca/jardin.* Within 180 acres (73 hectares) grow more than 26,000 species and varieties of plants; 30 specialized sections include roses, perennial plants, heath gardens, flowery brooks, bonsai, carnivorous plants, and an arboretum; one of the world's largest orchid collections; seasonal flower shows. The bonsai and penjing collections are two of the most diversified in North America. Chinese and Japanese gardens; restaurant, tea room. Parking (fee). (Daily 9 am-4 pm, summer to 6 pm) **$$$** Also here (and included in admission) is

Insectarium de Montréal. *4581 rue Sherbrooke Est, Montréal (H1X 2B2). Phone 514/872-1400; fax 514/872-0662.* The Insectarium features a collection of more than 350,000 insects in a building designed to resemble a stylized insect. Interactive and participatory exhibits take visitors through aviaries and living displays in six geographically themed areas. Includes a butterfly aviary (summer), and a children's amusement center. (Late Jan-mid-May: daily 9 am-5 pm; mid-May-mid-Sept: daily 9 am-6 pm; Sept-late Oct: daily 9 am-9 pm)

Montréal Canadiens (NHL). *1260 de La Gauchetiere SW, Montréal (H3B 5E8). Phone 514/790-1245. www.canadiens.com.* Formed in 1910, the Canadiens played their first game on the Jubilee rink, beating the Cobalt Silver Kings in overtime. The team is a 24-time Stanley Cup winner, most recently winning the coveted trophy during the 1992-1993 season. Games are played at the Bell Center, which also hosts various concerts and special events.

Montréal Harbour Cruises. *Depart from Quai Quai King Edward in Old Montréal, at the foot of Rue de la Commune and from Quai Jacques Cartier. Phone 514/842-9300; toll-free 800/667-3131. www.croisieresa-ml.com.* Various guided cruises and dinner excursions (1-4 hours); bar service. Reservations are advised. Contact Croisires Vieure-Port de Montréal, Quai de l'Horlage, C.P. 1085, Succ. Place d'Armes, H2Y 3J6. (May-mid-Oct, daily) **$$$$**

Montréal Museum of Fine Arts. *1379-80 rue Sherbrooke Ouest, Montréal. Phone 514/285-2000; toll-free 800/899-6873. www.mmfa.qc.ca.* (Muse des beaux-arts de Montréal) Canada's oldest art museum (founded in 1860) has a wide variety of displays, ranging from Egyptian statues to 20th-century abstracts. Canadian section features old Québec furniture, silver, and paintings. (Tues-Sun 11 am-6 pm; Wed to 9 pm) **DONATION**

Montréal Planetarium. *1000 rue Saint-Jacques Ouest, Montréal (H3C 1G7). Phone 514/872-4530; fax 514/872-8102. www.planetarium.Montréal.qc.ca.* See the stars at the Montréal Planetarium, where its 385-seat theater holds multimedia astronomy shows, with projectors creating all features of the night sky. Just outside the theater are temporary and permanent exhibits on the solar system, meteorites, fossils, and other astronomy-related topics. (Daily; hours vary by season, call for information) **$$**

Musee d'art contemporain de Montréal. *185 rue Sainte-Catherine Ouest, Montréal (H2X 3X5). Phone 514/847-6226; fax 514/847-6291. www.macm.org.* The only museum in Canada that is devoted exclusively to modern art. Gift shop, bookstore, garden, restaurant. (Tues-Sun 11 am-6 pm, Wed 11 am-9 pm; closed Jan 1, Dec 25) **$$**

Museum of Decorative Arts. *2200 rue Crescent, Montréal (H3G 2B8). Phone 514/284-1252; fax 514/284-0123.* Historic mansion Chateau Dufresne (1918), partially restored and refurnished, now houses international exhibitions of glass, textiles, and ceramic art; changing exhibits. (Tues-Sun, 11 am-6 pm; Wed, 11 am-9 pm ; closed Jan 1, Dec 25) **DONATION**

⭐ **Old (Vieux) Montréal.** *Bounded by McGill, Berri, Notre-Dame sts, and the St. Lawrence River. www. old.Montréal.qc.ca.* The city of Montréal evolved from the small settlement of Ville-Marie founded by de Maisonneuve in 1642. The largest concentration of 19th-century buildings in North America is found here; several original dwellings remain, while many other locations are marked by bronze plaques throughout the area. The expansion of this settlement led to what is now known as Old Montréal. The area roughly forms a 100-acre (40-hectare) quadrangle which corresponds approximately to the area enclosed within the original fortifications. Some major points of interest are

Chateau Ramezay. *280 rue Notre-Dame Est, Montréal (H2Y 1C5). In front of City Hall. Phone 514/861-3708; fax 514/861-8317.* This historic building was constructed in the 18th century, and was once the home of the governors of Montréal, the West Indies Company of France, and the Governors-General of British North America. It opened as a museum in 1895, and today is the oldest private museum in Québec. Collections include furniture, paintings, costumes, porcelain, manuscripts, and art objects of the 17th-19th centuries. (June-Sept: daily 10 am-6 pm; Oct-May: Tues-Sun 10 am-4:30 pm) **$$$**

Notre-Dame Basilica. *110 rue Notre-Dame Ouest, Montréal (H2Y 1T1). Phone 514/842-2925; toll-free 866/842-2925.* In 1672, a church described as "one of the most beautiful churches in North America" was erected on the present Notre-Dame street.

When this became inadequate for the growing parish, a new church designed by New Yorker James O'Donnell was built. It was completed in 1829 and two towers and interior decorations were added later. *Le Gros Bourdon*, a bell cast in 1847 and weighing 24,780 pounds (11,240 kilograms), is in Perseverance Tower; there is a ten-bell chime in Temperance Tower. Built of Montréal limestone, the basilica is neo-Gothic in design with a beautiful main altar, pulpit, and numerous statues, paintings, and stained-glass windows. (Mon-Sat, 8 am-5:30 pm; Sun, 12:30 pm-4:15pm) **$**

Notre-Dame-de-Bonsecours Church. *400 rue St.-Paul, Montréal (H2Y 1H4). Phone 514/282-8670; fax 514/282-8672.* Founded in 1657 by teacher Marguerite Bourgeoys, and rebuilt 115 years later, this is one of the oldest churches still standing in the city. With its location near the Port of Montréal, parishioners often prayed here for the safety of the community's sailors. In recognition of this, many fishermen and other mariners presented the church with miniature wooden ships, which hang from the vaulted ceiling today. The tower offers views of the river and city. Housed here is the Marguerite Bourgeois museum (fee), which features objects pertaining to early settlers.(May-Oct: Tues-Sun 10 am-5 pm; Nov-mid-Jan, mid-Mar-Apr: 11 am-3:30 pm) **FREE**

Place d'Armes. *rue St. Jacques, Montréal. Phone 514/877-6810.* A square of great historical importance and center of Old Montréal. The founders of Ville-Marie encountered the Iroquois here in 1644 and rebuffed them. In the square's center is a statue of de Maisonneuve, first governor of Montréal, and at one end is the St. Sulpice seminary (1685) with an old wooden clock (1710), oldest building in Montréal. At 119 St. Jacques St is the **Bank of Montréal.** This magnificent building contains a museum with collection of currency, mechanical savings banks, photographs, reproduction of old-fashioned teller's cage. (Mon-Fri; closed holidays) Some of the most important financial houses of the city are grouped around the square. **FREE**

Place Jacques-Cartier. *Between rue Notre-Dame and rue de la Commune.* Named for the discoverer of Canada, this was once a busy marketplace. Today, restaurants, cafs, bars, cyclists, in-line skaters, and street performers are found around the plaza, which is closed off to traffic. The oldest monument in the city, the Nelson Column, is in the square's upper section.

Ste. Paul St. The oldest street in Montréal. The mansions of Ville-Marie once stood here, but they have been replaced by commercial houses and office buildings.

Old Port of Montréal. *De la Commune St, Montréal. Between the St. Lawrence River and Old Montréal. Phone 514/496-7678; toll-free 800/971-7678; fax 514/283-8423. www.oldportofMontréal.com.* A departure point for boat cruises and a recreation and tourist park hosting exhibitions, special events, and entertainment. Also here is

The Montréal Science Centre. *King-Edward Pier, 333 rue de la Commune Ouest, Montréal (H2Y 2E2). Phone 514/496-4724; toll-free 877/496-4724; fax 514/496-0667.* Uncover the mysteries of science and technology through multimedia and hands-on exhibits, an IMAX theater, and more. (Late Apr-mid-June: daily 10 am-5 pm; mid-June-early Sept: Mon-Fri 9:30 am-5 pm, Sat-Sun 10 am-5 pm; winter: Tues-Sun 10 am-5 pm, closed Mon except on legal holidays) **$$$**

Olympic Park. *4141 Pierre de Coubertin Ave, Montréal (H1V 3N7). Phone 514/252-4737; toll-free 877/997-0919. www.rio.gouv.qc.ca.* The stadium was the site of the 1976 Summer Olympic Games and is now home of the Montréal Expos baseball team and les Alouettes de Montréal football team. The world's tallest inclined tower (626 feet or 191 meters, leaning, and at a 45-degree angle), once used to open and close the retractable roof, features an observation deck. (Due to problems with the roof, it was replaced in 1988 with one that does not open.) On-site are a cafeteria and souvenir shop. Tours of the stadium are given daily. **$$$** Adjacent stadium is

Biodome de Montréal. *4777 Pierre-De Coubertin Ave, Montréal (H1V 1B3). Phone 514/868-3056; fax 514/868-3096.* The former Olympic Velodrome has been transformed into an environmental museum that combines elements of a botanical garden, aquarium, zoo, and nature center. Four ecosystemsLaurentian Forest, Tropical Forest, Polar World, and St.-Laurent Marinesustain thousands of plants and small animals. The Biodome also features a 1,640 feet (500-meter) Nature Path with text panels and maps, and Naturalia, a discovery room. (Daily 9 am-4 pm, summer to 6 pm; closed Jan 1, Dec 25) **$$$$**

Parc du Mont-Royal. *Cote des Neiges and Remembrance rds, Montréal. Phone 514/843-8240; fax 514/843-8255. www.lemontroyal.qc.ca.* Designed by the creator of Central Park in New York City, Parc du Mont-Royal is also a park located in the heart of a city. Popular with visitors to Montréal, there is something for everyone here: cycling, hiking, picnicking, paddleboating, cross-country skiing, and snowshoeing. (Bikes, paddleboats, skis, and showshoes may be rented at the park). (Daily 6 am-midnight) **FREE**

Parc Jean-Drapeau. *1 Circuit Gilles-Villeneuve, Montréal (H3C 1A9). Phone 514/872-6120; fax 514/872-5691. www.parcjeandrapeau.com.* Two islands in the middle of the St. Lawrence River; access via Jacques-Cartier Bridge or Metro subway. Île Ste.-Hélène (St. Helen's Island) was the main anchor site for Expo '67; now a 342-acre (138-hectare) multipurpose park with three swimming pools; picnicking; cross-country skiing, snowshoeing. Île Notre-Dame (Notre Dame Island), to the south, was partly built up from the river bed and was an important activity site for Expo '67. Here is Gilles-Villeneuve Formula 1 racetrack (see SPECIAL EVENTS); also beach, paddleboats, windsurfing, and sailing. Some fees. (Daily) Also located here are

David M. Stewart Museum. *20 Chemin Tour L'Île, St. Helen Island (H3C 4G6). Phone 514/861-6701.* The Stewart Museum houses artifacts such as maps, firearms, kitchen utensils, engravings, and navigational and scientific instruments that trace Canadian history from the 16th to 19th centuries. (May-Oct: daily 10 am-6 pm; rest of year: Wed-Mon 10 am-5 pm; closed Jan 1, Dec 25) **$$$**

Floral Park. *Île Notre-Dame.* Site of Les Floralies Internationales 1980; now permanent, it displays a collection of worldwide flowers and plants. Walking trails; pedal boats, canoeing; picnic area; snack bar and restaurant. Some fees. (Third week in June-mid-Sept, daily)

La Ronde. *Île Sainte-Hélène, 22 Chemin Macdonald, Montréal (H3C 6A3). Phone 514/397-2000.* A 135-acre amusement park with 35 rides, including a 132-foot (40-meter) high wooden roller coaster; arcades, entertainment on a floating stage; waterskiing; live cartoon characters, children's village; circus, boutiques, and restaurants. (Mid-May-late Oct: days, hours vary, call for information) **$$$$**

The Old Fort. (1820-1824) Oldest remaining fortification of Montréal; only the arsenal, powder magazine, and barracks building still stand. Two military companies dating to the 18th century, La Compagnie Franche de la Marine and the 78th Fraser Highlanders, perform colorful military drills and parades (late June-Aug, Wed-Sun).

Parc Safari. *850 Rte 202, Hemmingford (J0L 1H0). 33 miles (56 kilometers) S on Hwy 15 to exit 6, then follow zoo signs. Phone toll-free 800/465-8724. www.parcsafari.com.* Features 750 animals, rides, and shows, children's theater and play area, swimming beach; drive-through wild animal reserve; picnicking, restaurants, boutiques. (Mid-May-mid-Sept, daily) **$$$$**

Place des Arts. *175 rue Ste-Catherine St Ouest, Montréal. Phone 514/842-2112; fax 541/285-1968.www.pdarts.com.* This four-theater complex is the heart of Montréal's artistic life. L'Opéra de Montréal, the Montréal Symphony Orchestra, les Grands Ballets Canadiens, and La Compagnie Jean-Duceppe theatrical troupe have their permanent home here. Other entertainment includes chamber music, recitals, jazz, folk singers, variety shows, music hall, theater, musicals, and modern and classical dance.

★ **Pointe-a-Calliere, the Montréal Museum of Archaeology and History.** *350 Place Royale, Montréal (H2Y 3Y5). Corner of Place Youville in Old Montréal. Phone 514/872-9150; fax 514/872-9151. www.pacmuseum.qc.ca/indexan.html.* Built in 1992 over the actual site of the founding of Montréal, the main museum building, the Eperon, actually rests on pillars built around ruins dating from the town's first cemetery and its earliest fortifications, which are now in its basement. Two balconies overlook this archaeological site, and a 16-minute multimedia show is presented using the actual remnants as a backdrop. From here, visitors continue underground, amid still more remnants, to the Archaeological Crypt, a structure that allows access to many more artifacts and remains; architectural models beneath a transparent floor illustrate five different periods in the history of Place Royale. The Old Customs House (Ancienne-Douane) houses thematic exhibits on Montréal in the 19th and 20th centuries. Permanent and changing exhibits. Caf; gift shop. (Jul-Aug: Mon-Fri 10 am-6 pm, Sat-Sun 11 am-6 pm; rest of year: Tues-Fri 10 am-5 pm, Sat-Sun 11 am-6 pm) **$$$**

Rafting Montréal. *8912 La Salle Blvd, La Salle (H8P 1Z9). Phone 514/767-2230.* Rafting and hydro-jet trips on the Lachine Rapids of the St. Lawrence River. (May-Sept, daily; reservations required) **$$$$**

St. Joseph's Oratory of Mont Royal. *3800 Chemin Queen Mary, Montréal (H3V 1H6). On N slope of Mt Royal.* Phone 514/733-8211; fax 514/733-9735. *www. saint-joseph.org.* The chapel was built in 1904 as a tribute to St. Joseph by Brother Andre, a member of the Congregation of Holy Cross. A larger crypt church was completed in 1917, when crowds coming to see Brother Andre and pray to St. Joseph were getting too large for the chapel. Today, the main church is a famous shrine attracting more than 2 million pilgrims yearly. A basilica with a seating capacity of 2,200 was founded in 1924; the dome towers over the city, and a 56-bell carillon made in France is outstanding. The Oratory's museum features 200 nativity scenes from 100 different countries. (Daily 8 am-8 pm) **FREE**

Universite de Montréal. *2332 boulê douard-Montpe-tit, Montréal.* Phone 514/343-6111. *www.uMontréal. ca.*(1920) (58,000 students) On the north slope of Mount Royal.

Special Events

Canadian Grand Prix. *Parc Jean-Drapeau, Montréal.* Phone 514/350-0000. *www.grandprix.ca.* Held annually since 1967, this Formula 1 race took place on the Mont-Tremblant Circuit until 1977. At that time, the track was considered too dangerous, and the then-named le-Notre-Dame Track was built. The first race at the new track was held in 1978, and was won by Gilles Villeneuve, Canada's first F1 driver. In 1982, when Villeneuve was tragically killed during practice laps at the Belgian Grand Prix, the track was re-named in his honor. If you wish to attend this event, make sure to purchase tickets well in advance; they can be extremely hard to come by, as this event is quite popular. Mid-June.

Fete Nationale. *82 rue Sherbrooke Ouest, Montréal (H2X 1X3).* Phone 514/849-2560; fax 514/849-6950. *www.cfn.org.* St.-Jean-Baptiste, patron saint of the French Canadians, is honored with three days of festivities surrounding the provincial holiday. The celebration includes street festivals, a bonfire, fireworks, musical events, and parades. Mid-June.

International Fireworks Competition. *Île Sainte-Hé-lène, 22 Chemin Macdonald, Montréal (H3C 6A3).* Phone 514/397-2000. *www.Montréalfireworks.com.* Held in Montmorency Falls Park, this musical fireworks competition attracts master fireworks handlers

from around the world, who each present a 30-minute display. Fireworks start at 10 pm, rain or shine. Late June-late July.

Just for Laughs Festival. *2095 boul St-Laurent, Montréal (H2X 2T5).* Phone 514/845-2322; toll-free 888/244-3155. *www.hahaha.com.* This comedy festival features comic talent from all over the world. Shows are performed in more than 25 venues along St. Denis Street and are broadcast to millions of viewers worldwide. Artists who have performed at past festivals include Jerry Seinfeld, Jay Leno, Rowan Atkinson, Jon Stewart, Lily Tomlin, and the cast of "The Simpsons." Mid-July.

Montréal Bike Fest. *1251 Rachel St E, Montréal (H2J 2J9).* Phone 514/521-8356; toll-free 800/567-8356. *www.velo.qc.ca/feria/index_e.lasso.* An entire week of events celebrating the bicycle, ending with Le Tour de le when 40,000 cyclists ride through the streets of Montréal. Includes a 16-mile (26-kilometers) outing for up to 10,000 children. Late May-early June.

Montréal Highlights Festival. *400 Maisonneuve, Montréal (H2L 1K4).* Phone 514/288-9955; toll-free 888/477-9955. Spotlights the city's cultural and artistic diversity. Mid-Feb-early Mar.

Montréal International Jazz Festival. *400 Maison-neuve, Montréal (H2L 1K4).* Phone 514/871-1881; toll-free 888/515-0515. *www.Montréaljazzfest.com.* More than 1,200 musicians and a million music lovers from around the world gather to celebrate jazz and other types of music. The ten-day fest includes more than 350 indoor and outdoor concerts. Late June-early July.

World Film Festival. *1432 de Bleury St, Montréal (H3A 2J1).* Phone 514/848-3883; fax 514/848-3886. *www. ffm-Montréal.org.* Montréal's World Film Festival was organized to celebrate all types of cinema, from documentaries and drama to comedy and science fiction. Amateur and well-known filmmakers alike participate in the event, which screens films from nearly 70 countries. Late Aug-early Sept. **$$$$**

Limited-Service Hotels

★ ★ **COURTYARD BY MARRIOTT MON-TRÉAL DOWNTOWN.** *410 rue Sherbrooke Ouest, Montréal (H3A 1B3).* Phone 514/844-8855; toll-free 800/449-6654; fax 514/844-0912. *www.marriott.com.* This budget-friendly hotel is close to the convention center and McGill University, as well as the site of the Montréal Jazz Festival. Nearby access to the subway makes exploring farther-reaching areas of the city easy. 157 rooms, 26 story. Complimentary continental breakfast. Check-in 3 pm, check-out noon. High-speed Internet access. Restaurant, bar. Fitness room. Indoor pool, whirlpool. **$**

★ ★ **HOLIDAY INN SELECT MONTRÉAL.** *99 Viger Ave Ouest, Montréal (H2Z 1E9). Phone 514/878-9888; toll-free 888/878-9888; fax 514/878-6341. www. yul-downtown.hiselect.com.* Pagoda-topped building in Chinatown area. 235 rooms, 8 story. Check-in 3 pm, check-out noon. One restaurant, two bars. Fitness room. Indoor pool, whirlpool. Business center. **$$**

★ ★ ★ **HOSTELLERIE LES TROIS TILLEULS.** *290 rue Richelieu, St-Marc-Sur-Richelieu (G0L 2E0). Phone 514/856-7787; fax 514/584-3146. www. lestroistilleuls.com.* This 1880s farmhouse is tucked away to give visitors a quiet and relaxing stay. Located an hour's drive from town, this hotel offers rooms with a view of the Richelieu River. 59 rooms, 3 story. Check-out noon. Restaurant, bar. Indoor pool. Tennis. Business center. **$**

★ ★ ★ **HOSTELLERIE RIVE GAUCHE.** *1810 Richelieu Blvd, Beloeil (J3G 4S4). Phone 450/467-4477; fax 450/467-0525. www.hostellerierivegauche.com.* Just 20 minutes from downtown Montréal, this hotel offers year-round recreation. All rooms have views of the Richelieu River or Mont St.-Hilaire. 22 rooms, 3 story. Check-out noon. Restaurant, bar. Indoor pool. Tennis. **$**

★ ★ **HOTEL CHERIBOURG.** *2603 Chemin du Parc, Orford (J1X 8C8). Phone 819/843-3308; toll-free 800/567-6132; fax 819/843-2639. www.cheribourg.com.* 97 rooms, 3 story. Check-out noon. Restaurant, bar. Fitness room. Indoor pool, outdoor pool, whirlpool. Tennis. **$**

★ ★ **HOTEL LE CANTLIE SUITES.** *1110 rue Sherbrooke Ouest, Montréal (H3A 1G9). Phone 514/842-2000; toll-free 800/567-1110; fax 514/844-7808. www.hotelcantlie.com.* From this elegantly furnished hotel, guests can enjoy views of the Montréal skyline, the St. Lawrence River, and Mount Royal. The extra-spacious guest rooms feature limited kitchens, separate work areas, and fax machines. A heated rooftop pool entertains in warmer weather, while the Mezzanine Bar offers opportunities for mingling year-round. 250 rooms, all suites. Check-in 4 pm, check-

out noon. Wireless Internet access. Restaurant, bar. Fitness room. Outdoor pool. Business center. **$$**

★ ★ ★ **HOTEL NELLIGAN.** *106 rue St. Paul Ouest, Montréal (H2Y 1Z3). Phone 514/788-2040; toll-free 877/788-2040; fax 514/788-2041. www.hotelnelligan. com.* This boutique hotel consists of two connected buildings, both thought to be built between 1830 and 1840. Don't think that means that the Nelligan is old and musty, however. The hotel's exposed-brick and stone walls hint at its lengthy history, but it provides all the modern touches that guests expect in an urban hotel, including wireless high-speed Internet access, multiline phones, and a minibar in every room. Down comforters, terrycloth bathrobes, evening turndown service, daily ice delivery, and windows that open onto the streets of Old Montréal ensure guests' comfort. A wine and cheese reception is offered daily, and the on-site restaurant, Verses, serves French fare in a hip and trendy setting. 63 rooms. Complimentary continental breakfast. Check-in 3 pm, check-out noon. High-speed Internet access, wireless Internet access. Restaurant, bar. Fitness room, fitness classes available. Airport transportation available. Business center. Credit cards accepted. **$$**

★ ★ **NOVOTEL.** *1180 rue de la Montagne, Montréal (H3G 1Z1). Phone 514/861-6000; toll-free 800/668-6835; fax 514/861-0992. www.novotelMontréal.com.* One block north of the Molson Centre, a venue for sporting events and concerts, this hotel is located in the heart of Montréal and its downtown shopping district. 228 rooms, 9 story. Pets accepted; fee. Check-in 3 pm, check-out 1 pm. High-speed Internet access. Restaurant, bar. Fitness room. Business center. **$**

★ ★ **QUALITY INN.** *6680 Taschereau Blvd, Brossard (J4W 1M8). Phone 450/671-7213; toll-free 800/267-3837; fax 450/671-7041. www.qualityinn.com.* 91 rooms, 3 story. Complimentary continental breakfast. Check-out noon. Restaurant, bar. Outdoor pool. **$**

★ ★ ★ **SUPER 8 MONTRÉAL - WEST/ VAUDREUIL.** *21700 Trans-Canada Hwy, Vaudreuil (J7V 8P3). Phone 450/424-8898; fax 450/424-8898.* This European-inspired property sits along the shore of Lac des Deux Montagnes. 117 rooms, 6 story. Check-out noon. Restaurant, bar. Fitness room. Indoor pool, whirlpool. Tennis. **$$**

Full-Service Hotels

★ ★ ★ **CHATEAU VERSAILLES HOTEL.** *1659 rue Sherbrooke Ouest, Montréal (H3H 1E3). Phone 888/933-8111; toll-free 888/933-8111; fax 514/933-6867. www.versailleshotels.com.* Located at the start of Montréal's famous Miracle Mile shopping district and the foot of Mont Royal, this 1800s hotel (which stands on grounds that were once originally owned by the Gentlemen of St. Sulpice, a religious order of distinguished French aristocrats) features distinctly unique rooms in four renovated Victorian townhouses. The cozy rooms are richly furnished with original molding, antiques, and pieces of local artwork. The property is also just minutes by metro to the Molson Centre, home of the Montréal Canadiens, and the Place des Arts. 65 rooms, 15 story. Pets accepted, some restrictions; fee. Complimentary continental breakfast. Check-in 3 pm, check-out noon. High-speed Internet access, wireless Internet access. Restaurant, bar. Fitness room. Airport transportation available. Business center. **$$**

★ ★ ★ **DELTA MONTRÉAL.** *475 President Kennedy Ave, Montréal (H3A 1J7). Phone 877/814-7706; fax 506/443-3499. www.deltaMontréal.com.* In the middle of everything that's Delta Montréal! It's located in the heart of downtown, near the Convention Centre and the Place des Arts. Shoppers, art lovers, and history buffs choose this modern, inviting hotel with oversized rooms, most with balconies. Fitness buffs can work out at Deltas elaborate spa and sports center complete with squash courts, while those who prefer more leisurely pursuits can enjoy French cuisine at Le Bouquet or relax at Le Cordial, the hotel's full-service bar. 456 rooms, 23 story. Pets accepted; fee. Check-in 3 pm, check-out noon. High-speed Internet access. Restaurant, bar. Children's activity center. Fitness room, fitness classes available. Indoor pool, whirlpool. Business center. **$**

★ ★ ★ **FAIRMONT THE QUEEN ELIZABETH.** *900 boul Rene Levesque Ouest, Montréal (H3B 4A5). Phone 514/861-3511; toll-free 800/441-1414; fax 514/954-2256. www.fairmont.com.* All of Montréal is at your disposal while staying at the Fairmont The Queen Elizabeth. This masterpiece of contemporary sophistication is in the city center, located above the train station and linked to the massive underground system of shops and restaurants. Situated near the citys many businesses, this hotel is a popular choice among corporate travelers who appreciate the full-service business center and health club amenities. This historic hotel's modern flair surprises and delights guests. Eye-popping colors are juxtaposed with dazzling designs, creating a sensual ambience in the public and private rooms. Dining is an event savored by hotel guests and locals alike, who frequent the renowned Beaver Club for its gourmet meals and hunting lodge atmosphere and the convivial, Mediterranean-inspired Le Montréalais Bistrot-Bar-Restaurant. 1,039 rooms, 21 story. Pets accepted, some restrictions; fee. Check-in 4 pm, check-out noon. High-speed Internet access, wireless Internet access. Restaurant, bar. Fitness room. Indoor pool, children's pool, whirlpool. Airport transportation available. Business center. **$$**

★ ★ ★ **HILTON MONTRÉAL DORVAL AIRPORT.** *12505 Cote de Liesse, Dorval (H9P 1B7). Phone 514/631-2411; fax 514/631-0192. www.dorval.hilton.com.* 494 rooms, 10 story. Some restrictions; fee. Check-in 2 pm. Check-out noon. Restaurant, bar. Fitness room. Indoor pool, whirlpool. Business center. **$**

★ ★ ★ **HILTON MONTRÉAL/LAVAL.** *2225, autoroute des Laurentides, Laval (H7S 1Z6). Phone 450/682-2225; fax 450/682-8492. www.hilton.com.* 170 rooms, 5 story. Check-in 3 pm. Check-out noon. Restaurant, bar. Fitness. Indoor pool, whirlpool. Business center. **$$**

★ ★ ★ **HILTON MONTRÉAL, BONAVENTURE.** *900 de la Gauchetiere Ouest, Montréal (H5A 1E4). Phone 514/878-2332; toll-free 800/267-2575; fax 514/878-3881. www.hiltonMontréal.com.* Penthouse life is glorious inside this hotel perched on top of the Place Bonaventure Exhibition Hall. There are acres of rooftop gardens to explore and a year-round outdoor pool. The central city location is perfect for sightseeing in Old Montréal, gambling at the casino, or shopping the underground boutiques. 395 rooms, 2 story. Pets accepted, some restrictions. Check-in 3 pm, check-out noon. High-speed Internet access. Restaurant, bar. Fitness room. Indoor pool, outdoor pool. Business center. **$$**

★ ★ ★ **HOTEL DU FORT.** *1390 rue du Fort, Montréal (H3H 2R7). Phone 514/938-8333; toll-free 800/565-6333; fax 514/938-2078. www.hoteldufort.com.* Located just steps from rue Ste. Catherine, this property is near shops, restaurants, and businesses. The traditional-style hotel puts its emphasis on providing upscale service and the comforts of home. Understated guest rooms include kitchenettes and windows that open out onto city views. The on-site restaurant offers a nice continental breakfast buffet, and room service options include menus from area restaurants. 124 rooms. Complimentary continental breakfast. Check-in 4 pm, check-out noon. Restaurant, bar. Fitness room. Airport transportation available. Business center. **$**

★ ★ ★ **HOTEL GAULT.** *449 rue Ste. Hélène, Montréal (H2Y 2K9). Phone 514/904-1616; toll-free 866/904-1616; fax 514/904-1717. www.hotelgault. com.* You might not expect to find an ultramodern hotel in a historic neighborhood, but the Hotel Gault is exactly that. Opened in 2002, it's set in a restored stone-façaded building. Inside, you'll find interiors of glass, concrete, and steel, with warm woods to keep the place from feeling overly cold or unfriendly. Soundproofed guest rooms feature flat-screen TVs, CD and DVD players, and comfortable workstations, as well as heated bathroom floors; some have private terraces. A variety of living spaces are available, so you can choose the setup that best fits your needs during your stay. 30 rooms. Check-in 3 pm, check-out noon. High-speed Internet access. Restaurant, bar. Fitness room. Business center. **$$**

★ ★ ★ **HOTEL INTERCONTINENTAL MON-TRÉAL.** *360 rue Ste Antoine Ouest, Montréal (H2Y 3X4). Phone 514/987-9900; toll-free 800/361-3600; fax 514/847-8730. www.Montréal.intercontinental.com.* This sophisticated, elegant hotel is located across from the Convention Center in downtown Montréal. It's only a short walk from the popular Old Town, which features cobblestone roads, art galleries, shops, and restaurants. The hotel's building houses shops and businesses, with the guest rooms starting on the tenth floor. 357 rooms, 17 story. Pets accepted, some restrictions. Check-in 3 pm, check-out 1 pm. High-speed Internet access, wireless Internet access. Three restaurants, two bars. Fitness room. Indoor pool. Airport transportation available. Business center. **$$**

★ ★ ★ **HOTEL L'EAU A LA BOUCHE.** *3003 Bd Ste-Adele, Sainte Adele (J8B 2N6). Phone 450/229-2991; fax 450/229-7573.* 25 rooms, 3 story. Check-in 4 pm. Check-out noon. Restaurant, bar. Fitness room, spa. **$$**

★ ★ ★ **HOTEL LE GERMAIN.** *2050 Mansfield, Montréal (H3A 1Y9). Phone 514/849-2050; toll-free 877/333-2050; fax 514/849-1437. www.hotelgermain. com.* This distinctive boutique hotel offers hospitality, comfort, and relaxation in an elegant setting, while providing state-of-the-art work equipment. The convenient downtown location makes it close to shopping, museums, concert halls, and movie theaters. Guest rooms feature original photos by Louis Ducharme, natural lighting, duvets, and dual-line phones. 101 rooms, 13 story. Pets accepted; fee. Complimentary full breakfast. Check-in 3 pm, check-out noon. High-speed Internet access. Restaurant, bar. Fitness room. **$$**

★ ★ ★ ★ **HOTEL LE ST. JAMES.** *355 Saint Jacques St, Montréal (H2Y 1N9). Phone 514/841-3111; toll-free 866/841-3111; fax 514/841-1232. www. hotellestjames.com.* When guests check into the majestic Hotel Le St. James, its customary for the staff to provide their canine or feline companions with an individual bed and a selection of gourmet snacks. Yes, pets are pampered here but so are the humans. And then some. Each room and suite is individually decorated with antiques and art, and each is appointed with much-appreciated luxuries like goose-down comforters, Frette linens, and upscale scented toiletries. Business travelers also will appreciate the in-room high-speed Internet access, not to mention the complimentary shoeshines and a morning paper. Even the architecture makes you feel important. A former bank, the buildings imposing façade features ornate moldings and details fully restored to their 1870s grandeur. Inside, the lobby boasts crystal chandeliers, Grecian columns, high tea service, and an impressive center staircase that simply begs for grand entrances with your pet or alone. 61 rooms. Pets accepted; fee. Check-in 3 pm, check-out noon. High-speed Internet access, wireless Internet access. Restaurant, bar. Fitness room. Spa. Airport transportation available. Credit cards accepted. **$$$$**

★ ★ ★ **HOTEL OMNI MONT-ROYAL.** *1050 rue Sherbrooke Ouest, Montréal (H3A 2R6). Phone 514/284-1110; toll-free 800/843-6664; fax 514/845-3025. www.omnihotels.com.* This elegant property is centrally located in the historic Golden Square Mile area in the heart of downtown and at the foot of Mont Royal. Shops, museums, nightlife, and fine dining are within walking distance. And don't let Fido miss out on this sophisticated hotel! Bring him along—pets receive special treats designed just for them. 300

rooms, 31 story. Pets accepted, some restrictions; fee. Check-in 3 pm, check-out 1 pm. High-speed Internet access, wireless Internet access. Two restaurants, bar. Fitness room, fitness classes available. Spa. Outdoor pool, whirlpool. Airport transportation available. Business center. **$$**

★ ★ ★ **HOTEL ST. PAUL.** *355 rue McGill, Montréal (H2Y 2E8). Phone 493/062-9011; toll-free 866/380-2202; fax 493/062-9011. www.hotelstpaul. com.* Set in a restored Beaux Arts building—a historic landmark—the Hotel St. Paul is all about contemporary cool. Upon checking in, make sure to stop and admire the striking alabaster fireplace in the lobby. Lighting above guest room doors revolve around two themes: earth (lit in red) and sky (lit in blue). The spare accommodations feature large windows, modern furnishings, and animal-skin accents; suites add two-person tubs and custom-made stone sinks. The on-site restaurant, Cube, serves fresh seasonal cuisine. 120 rooms. Pets accepted, some restrictions. Complimentary continental breakfast. Check-in 3 pm, check-out noon. High-speed Internet access, wireless Internet access. Restaurant, bar. Fitness room. Airport transportation available. Business center. **$$**

★ ★ ★ **HYATT REGENCY MONTRÉAL.** *1255 Jeanne Mance, Montréal (H5B 1E5). Phone 514/982-1234; toll-free 866/816-3871; fax 514/285-1243. www. Montréal.hyatt.com.* Enjoy a lively urban retreat at the Hyatt Regency Montréal. Located in the Cultural District, the Hyatt is part of the elaborate shopping, dining, and entertainment center Complexe des Jardins and adjacent to Place des Arts. The hotel also has underground access to the Montréal Convention Center. 605 rooms, 12 story. Pets accepted, some restrictions; fee. Check-in 3 pm, check-out noon. High-speed Internet access, wireless Internet access. Restaurant, bar. Fitness room. Indoor pool. Airport transportation available. Business center. Credit cards accepted. **$$**

★ ★ ★ **LA PINSONNIERE.** *124 rue La Malbaie, Montréal (G5A 1X9). Phone 418/665-4431; toll-free 800/387-4431; fax 418/665-7156. www.lapinsonniere. com.* 25 rooms, 3 story. Check-in 4 pm. Check-out noon. Restaurant, bar. Fitness room, spa. **$$**

★ ★ ★ **LE PLACE D.** *701 Cote de la Place d'Armes, Montréal (H2Y 3X2). Phone 514/842-1887; toll-free* 888/450-1887; fax 514/842-6469. www.hotelplacedarmes. com.* Step from Old Montréal's centuries-old charm into new millennium modishness at Le Place d'Armes Hotel and Suites. The boutique hotel's ultramodern black-and-white décor will delight the most sophisticated travelers expectations. Best of all, you may purchase and take home any guest room item that strikes your fancy. 135 rooms, 6 story. Complimentary continental breakfast. Check-in 3 pm, check-out noon. High-speed Internet access, wireless Internet access. Restaurant, bar. Fitness room. Spa. Airport transportation available. Business center. **$$$**

★ ★ ★ **LE SAINT SULPICE HOTEL MONTRÉAL.** *414 rue Saint Sulpice, Montréal (H2Y 2V5). Phone 514/288-1000; toll-free 877/785-7423; fax 514/288-0077. www.lesaintsulpice.com.* Step back in time at this luxury hotel, located in the historic part of Montréal, just steps from the Notre-Dame Basilica and the Old Port. Accommodations are loft-style or one-bedroom suites, half of which boast fireplaces, with some suites overlooking the sun-filled courtyard. Sample steaks and seafood as well as regional specialties in S Le Restaurant. The Essence Health Center features beautifying treatments in addition to modern exercise equipment. 108 rooms, all suites. Pets accepted; fee. Complimentary continental breakfast. Check-in 3 pm, check-out noon. High-speed Internet access, wireless Internet access. Restaurant, bar. Fitness room. Spa. Airport transportation available. Business center. **$$$**

★ ★ ★ **LOEWS HOTEL VOGUE.** *1425 rue de la Montagne, Montréal (H3G 1Z3). Phone 514/285-5555; toll-free 800/465-6654; fax 514/849-8903. www.loews-hotels.com.* The fresh spirit and chic modernity of the Loews Hotel Vogue breathes new life into old-world Montréal. Located in the business district of the "Paris of Canada," this hip hotel's vivid colors, plush amenities, and superb service make it a favorite of the jet set. The accommodations provide sleek shelter with silk upholstered furnishings, while creature comforts like oversized bathrooms appeal to the sybarite in every guest. Visitors are well cared for here, with a gracious concierge who attends to all needs, and efficient business and fitness centers. From bistros to brasseries, Montréal is known for its food, and this hotel is no exception. Don't miss L'Opéra Bar, the place to see and be seen in this charming city. 142 rooms, 9 story. Pets accepted. Check-in 3 pm, check-out 1 pm. High-speed Internet access. Restaurant, bar. Fitness room. Business center. **$$**

★ ★ ★ **MARRIOTT MONTRÉAL CHATEAU CHAMPLAIN.** *1050 de la Gauchetiere Ouest, Montréal (H3B 4C9). Phone 514/878-9000; toll-free 800/200-5909; fax 514/878-6761. www.marriott.com.* Both veteran travelers and first-time visitors to Marriott Montréal Chateau Champlain are met with comfort and convenience in the heart of downtown Montréal. Charming Art Nouveau décor adorns the guest rooms (many with views of the Cathedral, Parc Mont Royal, and Old Montréal), while blooming azaleas accent the cozy lobby seating. And hospitality rules at the Mediterranean-flavored Le Samuel de Champlain restaurant, while Le Senateur Bar satisfies discriminating tastes. 611 rooms, 36 story. Check-in 3 pm, check-out noon. High-speed Internet access, wireless Internet access. Restaurant, bar. Fitness room. Indoor pool, whirlpool. Airport transportation available. Business center. **$$**

★ ★ ★ **THE RITZ-CARLTON, MONTRÉAL.** *1228 rue Sherbrooke Ouest, Montréal (H3G 1H6). Phone 514/842-4212; toll-free 800/363-0366; fax 514/842-3383.* Old-world refinement is the calling card of The Ritz-Carlton, Montréal. This classic hotel is perfectly situated to take in the inimitable charm of this slice of France in North America. It is a leisure travelers dream, with the quaint Old Town, Olympic Center, and renowned museums located just a short distance from the hotel. From the genteel public spaces to the sumptuously appointed rooms and suites, the mood here is resolutely distinguished. The Ritz-Carlton standards of service are legendary, and guests are treated with kid gloves from the moment of arrival. Gastronomic pleasures abound here at the elegant Le Café de Paris and the romantic Le Jardin du Ritz, noted for its lush garden setting with trickling fountain and endearing duck pond. 229 rooms, 9 story. Pets accepted; fee. Check-in 3 pm, check-out noon. High-speed Internet access. Restaurant, bar. Fitness room. Business center. **$$**

★ ★ ★ **SOFITEL MONTRÉAL.** *1155 Rue Sherbrooke Ouest, Montréal (H3A 2N3). Phone 514/285-9000; fax 514/289-1155. www.sofitel.com.* Modern and elegant, this hotel is set at the foot of Parc Mont Royal on Sherbrooke Street and close to galleries, boutiques, and the historic center of the city. Enjoy morning croissants and evening cocktails in Le Bar;

dine on Provenal-inspired cuisine in Renoir; and work off your indulgences in the hotel's fitness center and sauna. 258 rooms. Pets accepted. Check-in 3 pm, check-out noon. High-speed Internet access. Restaurant, bar. Fitness room. Airport transportation available. Business center. **$$$**

Full-Service Inns

★ ★ ★ **AUBERGE DU VIEUX-PORT.** *97 rue de la Commune Est, Montréal (H2Y 1J1). Phone 514/876-0081; toll-free 888/660-7678; fax 514/876-8923. www.aubergeduvieuxport.com.* Once a depot, then a warehouse, general store, and grocery store, this historic landmark building served several functions before becoming a full-service inn. Built in 1882 along the St. Lawrence River, it was transformed into an inn in 1995, with Les Ramparts restaurant serving up fine, French cuisine, and a rooftop terrace affording a panoramic view of the St. Lawrence River. Guests are pampered with a full breakfast, afternoon wine and cheese, daily newspaper, a CD library, free e-mail access, and more. 27 rooms. Complimentary full breakfast. Check-in 3 pm, check-out noon. High-speed Internet access, wireless Internet access. Restaurant, bar. Airport transportation available. Business center. **$$**

★ ★ ★ **AUBERGE HANDFIELD.** *555 boul Richelieu, St-Marc-Sur-Richelieu (J0L 2E0). Phone 450/584-2226; fax 450/584-3650. www.aubergehandfield.com.* Guests can chose between a room with a view of the garden or river. Small shops and boutiques are nearby with a larger shopping mall only a ten-minute drive away. 56 rooms, 2 story. Check-in 3 pm, check-out noon. Restaurant, bar. Fitness room. Outdoor pool, whirlpool. **$**

★ ★ ★ **AUBERGE HATLEY.** *325 rue Virgin, CP330, North Hatley (J0B 2C0). Phone 819/842-2451; toll-free 800/336-2451; fax 819/842-2907. www.aubergehatley.com.* This charming inn, in a 1903 Victorian-style mansion, overlooks Lake Massawippi and has a rustic décor of leather chairs, carved wood, and brick hearths. Enjoy hiking and antiquing in spring and fall and skiing in winter. 25 rooms, 3 story. Complimentary full breakfast. Check-in 4 pm, check-out noon. Restaurant. Outdoor pool. **$$$**

Specialty Lodgings

ANGELICA BLUE B&B. *1213 Ste. Elizabeth, Montréal (H2X 3C3). Phone 514/844-5048; toll-free 800/878-5048; fax 450/448-2114. www.angelicablue. com.* This Victorian row house bed-and-breakfast dates to the late 1800s, featuring warm, sunny accommodations in the heart of downtown Montréal. A full breakfast with different hot entrées is served daily. Guests have access to a TV room, a fully equipped kitchen, and washing and ironing facilities. 6 rooms. Complimentary full breakfast. Check-in after 8 am, check-out 11 am. **$**

AUBERGE DE LA FONTAINE. *1301 rue Rachel Est, Montréal (H2J 2K1). Phone 514/597-0166; toll-free 800/597-0597; fax 514/597-0496. www.aubergedela-fontaine.com.* Don't look for calico or buttons and bows at Auberge de la Fontaine. Its individually decorated guest rooms feature the bold colors and sleek designs expected in a sophisticated city inn. Say "bon jour" with a complimentary continental buffet in the lobby's attractive breakfast area. Then, after a busy day of meetings or sightseeing, stroll the inviting paths in the park across the street where you'll find the fountain that gives the inn its name. Auberge's well-informed staff delights in matching guests dining preferences with the perfect choice of restaurants, perhaps on nearby lively St. Denis Street. Afterward, comfortable beds offer blissful slumber. 21 rooms, 3 story. Complimentary full breakfast. Check-in 3 pm, check-out noon. **$$**

LE PETIT PRINCE B&B. *1384 Overdale Ave, Montréal (H3G 1V3). Phone 514/938-2277; toll-free 877/938-9750; fax 514/935-9750. www.Montréalbandb.com.* This bed-and-breakfast is well suited to its urban location. Rather than frills and lace, you'll find artsy and contemporary style in this stone-façaded townhouse. All areas of the home feature exposed-brick walls, while guest room furnishings include modern four-poster and sleigh beds and funky artwork by local artists. Each room has a mini-fridge and a two-person whirlpool tub; two rooms have functional fireplaces, while the other two have large private balconies. 4 rooms. Complimentary full breakfast. Check-in 4 pm, check-out 11 am. Wireless Internet access. **$$**

MANOIR HARVARD. *4805 Harvard Ave, Montréal (H3X 3P1). Phone 514/488-3570; toll-free 888/373-3570; fax 514/369-5778. www.manoirharvard.com.* This stone-and-wood Victorian oozes country charm. The landscaped grounds feature old-fashioned gardens, easily viewed from the terrace. Guest rooms have

queen- or king-size beds and are furnished with lovely antiques. Should you wish to escape the tranquility, Manoir Harvard is close to the Villa Maria metro station and is just steps from Monkland Village's cafés and shops. 5 rooms. Complimentary full breakfast. Check-in 3-5 pm, check-out 11 am. **$$**

★ ★ ★ PETITE AUBERGE LES BONS MATINS. *1401 Argyle Ave, Montréal (H3G 1V5). Phone 514/931-9167; toll-free 800/588-5280; fax 514/931-1621. www.bonsmatins.com.* Guests stay in rooms in adjoining restored century-old townhomes in the heart of Montréal, close to main thoroughfares Sainte-Catherine Street and Crescent Street and area attractions such as the Bell Centre. The inn is also just steps away from the Lucien L'Allier metro stop. Antiques and paintings by a family artist decorate rooms, all with private baths with accoutrements such as bathrobes and natural bath products. In addition to the business communications system in the guest rooms, there is also a Windows XP workstation made available to guests. A full gourmet breakfast is served daily in the dining room. Other amenities include a private parking lot, living room with fireplace, garden, and a terrace. 27 rooms. Pets accepted, some restrictions. Complimentary full breakfast. Check-in 3 pm, check-out noon. High-speed Internet access, wireless Internet access. Airport transportation available. Business center. **$$**

Restaurants

★ ★ ★ AU PIED DE COCHON. *536 rue Duluth Est, Montréal (H2L1A9). Phone 514/281-1114; fax 514/281-1116.* Regional cuisine. Dinner, late-night. Closed Mon. Bar. Business casual attire. Reservations recommended. **$$$**
🅳

★ AU TOURNANT DE LA RIVIERE. *5070 Salaberry, Carignan (J3L 3P9). Phone 450/658-7372; fax 450/658-7372.* French Menu. Lunch, dinner, Sun brunch. **$$$**

★ ★ ★ AUBERGE HANDFIELD. *555 Richelieu Blvd, St.-Marc-Sur-Richelieu (JOL 2E0). Phone 450/584-2226; fax 450/584-3650. www.aubergehand-field.com.* French menu. Breakfast, lunch, dinner, Sun brunch. Closed Mon; also mid-Jan-early May. Bar. Children's menu. Casual attire. Reservations recommended. Outdoor seating. **$$$**
🅳

★ BEN'S DELICATESSEN. *990 de Maisonneuve Blvd, Montréal (H3A 1M5). Phone 514/844-1001; fax*

514/844-1002. Deli menu. Lunch, dinner, late-night. Casual attire. **$**

★ ★ ★ **BISTRO A CHAMPLAIN.** *75 Chemin Masson, Ste. Marguerite (J0T 1L0). Phone 450/228-4988; fax 450/228-4893. www.bistroachamplain.com.* Located on the edge of Lake Masson in the Laurentian Mountains, this elegant, rustic restaurant draws an international clientele. French menu. Dinner. Closed Mon-Tues. **$$$**

★ ★ ★ **CAFE DE PARIS.** *1228 rue Sherbrooke Ouest, Montréal (H3G 1H6). Phone 514/842-4212; fax 514/842-3383. www.ritzcarlton.com.* This premier dining room, featuring regional French Québecois cuisine, is located on the ground floor of the Ritz Carlton, Montréal, with views of rue Sherbrooke and Le Jardin du Ritz (the garden). The elegant presentations and smooth service are the hallmarks of this sophisticated room. Its décor is subdued with a green and orange color scheme, fresh flowers, and mirrors. The contemporary lounge/bar features brown and champagne tones. In season, reservations are essential and the outdoor seating area is booked solid. French menu. Breakfast, lunch, dinner, brunch. Bar. Children's menu. Business casual attire. Reservations recommended. Valet parking. Outdoor seating. **$$$**

★ ★ ★ **CAFE FERREIRA.** *1446 rue Peel, Montréal (H3A 1S8). Phone 514/848-0988; fax 514/848-9375. www.ferreiracafe.com.* This restaurant is one of the most stylish dining rooms in Montréal. The friendly staff serves up wonderful Portuguese cuisine. The menu emphasizes fresh fish and is accompanied by a comprehensive selection of Portuguese wines and ports. Spanish menu. Lunch, dinner. Closed Sun. Bar. Casual attire. Reservations recommended. Outdoor seating. **$$$**

★ **CAFE STE. ALEXANDRE.** *518 rue Duluth Est, Montréal (H2L 1A7). Phone 514/849-4251; fax 514/908-1518.* Italian, Greek, Seafood menu. Lunch, dinner. Children's menu. Casual attire. Reservations recommended. Outdoor seating. **$$**

★ ★ ★ **CHEZ L.** *311 rue Saint-Paul Est, Montréal (H2Y 1H3). Phone 514/878-2232; fax 514/878-2239. www.chezlepicier.com.* This cozy and informal French restaurant is located in a building in Old Montréal that dates to the late 1800s. And Marche Bonsecours, an extensive market is just across the street. The restaurant uses fresh, local products for its daily-changing menu, and its food and food products are available for sale in a neighborhood market setting. A wine bar is also included in the space. French menu. Lunch, dinner. Closed Dec 25; also two weeks in Jan. Bar. Casual attire. Reservations recommended. **$$$**

★ ★ ★ **CHEZ LA MERE MICHEL.** *1209 rue Guy, Montréal (H3H 2K5). Phone 514/934-0473; fax 514/939-0709.* In a city with volumes of competition, this fine French restaurant has succeeded in its downtown historic-home location since 1965. Guests will feel like they've stepped into a painting, from the quaint flower-lined walkway to the small, slightly cluttered rooms filled with eclectic collectibles. The menu is classic and well prepared and includes a fantastic strawberry Napoleon for dessert. French menu. Dinner. Closed Sun. Casual attire. **$$$**

★ ★ ★ **CUBE.** *355 rue McGill, Montréal (H2Y 2E8). Phone 514/876-2823; fax 514/876-9874. www.restaurant-cube.com.* This contemporary French restaurant is located in the Hotel St. Paul, which is housed in a historic landmark Beaux Arts building close to Old Montréal. Its crisp, cool, and elegant minimalist décor features hardwood floors, wood tables, subdued lighting, large windows, and flowing draperies. Although Cube is a hip "hot spot," it has a down-to-earth staff who makes dining here enjoyable. French regional menu. Lunch, dinner, brunch. Bar. Business casual attire. Reservations recommended. Valet parking. **$$$**

★ ★ **GLOBE.** *3455 St-Laurent, Montréal (H2X 2T6). Phone 514/284-3823; fax 514/284-3531. www.restaurantglobe.com.* French menu. Dinner, late-night. Bar. Casual attire. Reservations recommended. **$$$**

★ ★ **HOUSE OF JAZZ.** *2060 rue Aylmer, Montréal (H3A 2E3). Phone 514/842-8656; fax 514/842-2665.* American menu, Steak menu. Lunch, dinner. Bar. Casual attire. Reservations recommended. Outdoor seating. **$$**

★ ★ **IL CORTILE.** *1442 rue Sherbrooke Ouest, Montréal (H3G 1K3). Phone 514/843-8230.* This classic Italian trattoria set in the middle of an urban section of town is a quiet oasis from the hustle and bustle of the city. Perfect pastas and risottos are just the beginning—the traditional menu offers an authentic taste of seasonal cooking. Italian menu. Lunch, dinner. Closed Dec 24-25. Bar. Casual attire. Reservations recommended. Outdoor seating. **$$$**

★ ★ **JARDIN NELSON.** *407 Place Jacques-Cartier, Montréal (H2Y3B1). Phone 514/861-5731; fax 514/861-5733. www.jardinnelson.com.* American menu, Italian menu. Lunch, dinner, brunch. Closed Nov-Mar. Bar. Casual attire. Reservations recommended. Outdoor seating. **$$**

★ ★ ★ **KATSURA MONTRÉAL.** *2170 rue de la Montagne, Montréal (H3G 1Z7). Phone 514/849-1172; fax 514/849-1705.* This authenic Japanese restaurant is located about a half-block from rue Sherbrooke and its many hotels, shops, and businesses. Servers are dressed in authenic Japanese uniforms and there is Japanese artwork, wood, and decorated screens throughout the restaurant. Along with the traditional Japanese menu, there is also a small sushi bar. Lunch isn't served on Saturday or Sunday. Japanese menu. Lunch, dinner. Closed holidays. Casual attire. Reservations recommended. **$$**

★ ★ ★ ★ **L'EAU A LA BOUCHE.** *3003 Ste. Adèle Blvd, Ste. Adèle (J8B 2N6). Phone 450/229-2991; tool-free 888/828-2991; fax 450/229-7573. www.leaualabouche.com.* Tucked into the maple, birch, and pine forests surrounding the Laurentian Mountains, near the village of Sainte-Adèle, you will find L'eau a la Bouche. The restaurant is set in a Bavarian-style wooden house that feels like it just popped out of a Hans Christian Andersen fairy tale. The gourmet menu is built around local produce, fish, meat, and homegrown herbs and vegetables, woven together and dressed up with a perfect dose of French technique and modern flair. Attentive, thoughtful service and a vast wine list make this luxurious dining experience unforgettable. French menu. Breakfast, dinner. Closed holidays. Bar. **$$$**

★ ★ **L'EXPRESS.** *3927 Ste. Denis, Montréal (H2W 2M4). Phone 514/845-5333; fax 514/843-7576.* It is not easy to be the "in" place for more than 20 years, but somehow this classic French bistro has managed to pull it off. The food is consistently good, and the scene remains forever first rate. French menu. Lunch, dinner. Closed Dec 25. Bar. Casual attire. Reservations recommended. **$$**

★ ★ **LA GAUDRIOLE.** *825 rue Laurier Est, Montréal (H2O 1G7). Phone 514/276-1580; fax 514/276-8842. www.lagaudriole.com.* French menu. Lunch, dinner. Closed first week in Jan, mid-July-early Aug. Reservations recommended. **$$$**

★ **LA LOUISIANE.** *5850 rue Sherbrooke Ouest, Montréal (H4A 1X5). Phone 514/369-3073; fax 514/369-3702.* Cajun menu. Dinner. Closed Mon. **$$**

★ ★ ★ **LA MAREE.** *404 Place Jacques Cartier, Montréal (H2Y 3B2). Phone 514/861-8126; fax 514/861-3954.* Situated in Old Montréal, this romantic dining room offers classic French cuisine in an ornate, Louis XIII atmosphere. The historic 1808 building is just the place to enjoy old-fashioned, formal service and a great bottle of wine from the cellar. French menu. Lunch, dinner. Closed Jan 1, Dec 25. Bar. Casual attire. Reservations recommended. Outdoor seating. **$$$**

★ ★ ★ **LA RAPIERE.** *1155 rue Metcalfe, Montréal (H3B 2V6). Phone 514/871-8920; fax 514/871-1923.* Southwestern French cooking with a personal touch is the draw at this casual, sophisticated restaurant in downtown Montréal. Cassoulet, foie gras, and other specialties from southwestern France are served in a typical country-French setting. French menu. Lunch, dinner. Closed Sun; holidays; also mid-July-mid-Aug, 15 days in Dec. Bar. Jacket required. Reservations recommended. **$$$**

★ **LA SAUVAGINE.** *1592 Rte 329 Nord, Ste.-Agathe (J8C 2Z8). Phone 819/326-7673; fax 819/326-9351. www.lasauvagine.com.* French menu. Dinner. Closed Mon-Tues off-season. **$**

★ ★ ★ **LALOUX.** *250 Pine Ave Est, Montréal (H2W 1P3). Phone 514/287-9127; fax 514/281-0682. www.laloux.com.* One of the few "bistro parisiens" in Montréal, this local favorite features excellent cuisine du marche served in a sober but refined environment. The waitstaff is very professional and knowledgeable about food, wines, and their pairing. French menu. Lunch, dinner. Closed Jan 1, Dec 25. Bar. Casual attire. Reservations recommended. Outdoor seating. **$$$**

★ ★ **LE CAFE FLEURI.** *1255 rue Jeanne Mance, Montréal (H5B 1E5). Phone 514/841-2010; fax 514/285-1243. www.Montréal.hyatt.com.* Located on the lobby level (6th floor) of the Hyatt Regency Montréal, this relaxing property features floor-to-ceiling windows with views of a fish pond and fountain (seasonal). This restaurant has buffet-style dining, with à la carte options available from its French menu. The Sunday brunch is very popular with guests and locals. French menu. Breakfast, lunch, brunch. Bar. Children's menu. Casual attire. Valet parking. Outdoor seating. **$$**

★ ★ **LE CHRYSANTHEME.** *1208 Crescent St, Montréal (H3G 2A9). Phone 514/397-1408.* Chinese

menu. Lunch, dinner. Closed Mon; last week in July, Dec 23-Jan 3. Bar. Casual attire. **$$**
🅓

★ **LE JARDIN DE PANOS.** *521 rue Duluth Est, Montréal (H2L 1A8). Phone 514/521-4206; fax 514/521-8766.* Greek menu. Lunch, dinner. Closed Dec 25. Children's menu. Casual attire. Outdoor seating. **$$**

★ ★ **LE KEG/BRANDY'S.** *25 rue St. Paul Est, Montréal (H2Y 1G2). Phone 514/871-9093; fax 514/871-9818. www.kegsteakhouse.com.* Steak menu. Dinner. Closed Dec 25. Bar. Children's menu. Casual attire. **$$$**

★ ★ ★ **LE LUTETIA.** *1430 rue de la Montagne, Montréal (H3G 1Z5). Phone 514/288-5656; fax 514/288-9658. www.hoteldelamontagne.com.* Located in the popular l'Hotel de la Montagne, along with a piano bar and discotheque, this restaurant serves cuisine in a comfortable rococo setting. The service is gracious and accommodating, the décor pleasant and interesting. French menu. Breakfast, lunch, dinner. Bar. Children's menu. Casual attire. Reservations recommended. **$$$**

★ ★ ★ **LE MAS DES OLIVIERS.** *1216 rue Bishop, Montréal (H3X 2R2). Phone 514/861-6733; fax 514/861-7838.* This small, traditional French restaurant has been offering rich cuisine in a Provençal setting for more than 30 years. French menu. Lunch, dinner. Closed Dec 24-Jan 3. Bar. Casual attire. Reservations recommended. **$$$**
🅓

★ ★ ★ **LE MITOYEN.** *652 rue de la Place Publique, Montréal (H7X 1G1). Phone 450/689-2977; fax 450/689-0385.* Envision a quaint village green surrounding a picturesque fountain. On the east side nestles a charming country 1870 cottage featuring the best of French cuisine: Le Mitoyen. Chef/proprietor Richard Bastien plans his menus around the freshest the market can offer, taking as much pride in his sparkling kitchen as he does in his quietly elegant dining rooms, cozily sized for intimate dining for individuals, couples, or groups. Gracious servers in time-honored country tradition welcome guests as honored friends. Both native Montréalers and out-of-towners enjoy the exquisite fare and homey atmosphere. Regional cuisine. Dinner. Closed Mon. Outdoor seating. **$$$**

★ ★ **LE PARCHEMIN.** *1333 rue University, Montréal (H3A 2A4). Phone 514/844-1619; fax 514/844-7873. www.leparchemin.com.* French menu. Lunch, dinner. Closed Sun; Jan 1, Dec 25. Bar. Casual attire. **$$$**

★ ★ **LE PARIS.** *1812 Ste Catherine Ouest, Montréal (H3H 1M1). Phone 514/937-4898; fax 514/937-1726.* French menu. Lunch, dinner. Closed Dec 24-25. Casual attire. Reservations recommended. **$$**
🅓

★ ★ ★ **LE PIEMONTAIS.** *1145-A rue de Bullion, Montréal. Phone 514/861-8122; fax 514/861-6041.* Experience authentic, Piedmont-region cuisine at this comfortable Italian restaurant where the proprietor makes everyone feel like a regular. Simple but artfully prepared dishes are presented with professional and attentive service. Italian menu. Lunch, dinner. Closed Sun; third week in July-Aug 15. Casual attire. Reservations recommended. **$$$**

★ ★ ★ **LE PIMENT ROUGE.** *1170 Peel St, Montréal (H3B 4P2). Phone 514/866-7816; fax 514/866-1575.www.lepimentrouge.com.* The bold cuisine of China's Szechwan province is gloriously prepared at Le Piment Rouge, an open, airy, contemporary restaurant located in the former Windsor Hotel. Set in a historic turn-of-the-century building, the restaurant has an up-to-the-minute design and features towering arched windows and an enormous wine rack on display in the center of the dining area. Signature dishes include spicy peanut butter dumplings (a recipe the restaurant is credited with inventing in Montréal) and General Tao chicken served with a special (read: secret) homemade sauce. Le Piment Rouge is a hotspot, drawing local politicians, financiers, and the token celebrity on occasion. Beer is always a good choice with Chinese food, but Le Piment Rouge also stocks more than 3,000 wines if you're craving something with a cork, not a bottle cap. Chinese menu. Lunch, dinner. Bar. Business casual attire. Valet parking. **$$**

★ ★ ★ **LES CAPRICES DE NICOLAS.** *2072 rue Drummond, Montréal (H3G 1W9). Phone 514/282-9790; fax 514/288-0249. www.lescaprices.com.* The intimate candlelight and romantic indoor/outdoor garden combine to make this restaurant a true special-occasion destination. Given the classic, very formal service, it is a pleasant surprise to find the French dishes on the menu refreshingly updated with light, vibrant flavors and seasonal market produce. A wine list of 500 labels adds to the excitement. French menu. Dinner. Closed Dec 24-Jan 10. Bar. Jacket required. Reservations recommended. **$$$**
🅓

★ ★ ★ **LES CONTINENTS.** *360 rue St-Antoine Ouest, Montréal (H2Y 3X4). Phone 514/987-9900; toll-free 800/361-3600; fax 514/847-8730. www.intercontinental.*

com. Located on the second floor of the Hotel InterContinental Montréal, Les Continents has beautiful views of Jean-Paul Riopelle Park and the colorful Convention Centre. The menu features contemporary French cuisine with Canadian influences. The subdued dining room is elegantly furnished with plentiful floral displays, wood shutters, large windows, and many mirrors. The professional service makes this a popular lunch spot for business people. French menu. Breakfast, lunch, dinner. Bar. Children's menu. Business casual attire. Reservations recommended. Valet parking. **$$$**

★ ★ ★ **LES REMPARTS.** *93 rue de la Commune Est, Montréal (H2Y 1J1). Phone 514/392-1649; fax 514/876-8923. www.restaurantlesremparts.com.* Located in the basement of the Auberge du Vieux-Port, on the site of Montréal's original fortress, this French restaurant offers a comfortable, cozy atmosphere with professional, attentive service. The restaurant is decorated with candles on each table, stone floors, and exposed brick walls with parts of the old fort's stonework on display. French menu. Breakfast, lunch, dinner. Bar. Business casual attire. Reservations recommended. Valet parking. Outdoor seating. **$$$**

★ ★ ★ **LES TROIS TILLEULS.** *290 rue Richelieu, Montréal (J0L 2E0). Phone 514/856-7787; toll-free 800/263-2230; fax 450/584-3146. www.lestroistilleuls.com.* Modern interpretations of classic French cuisine, complemented by home baking, are served in this 1880s farmhouse. Gardens and terrace offer views of the St. Lawrence River. Located on the South Shore, 35 minutes from downtown Montréal. French menu. Breakfast, lunch, dinner, Sun. Bar. Children's menu. Casual attire. Reservations recommended. Outdoor seating. **$$$$**

★ ★ ★ **MED BAR AND GRILL.** *3500 boul St-Laurent, Montréal (H2X 2V1). Phone 514/844-0027; fax 514/844-9848. www.medgrill.com.* If you're seeking a spot to see and be seen, or a chic place to linger over luscious cocktails while perched amidst Montréal's most stylish set, Med Bar and Grill is an excellent option. But the restaurant is not only a hot venue for drinking and lounging, it also happens to be a great place to sit down and eat. The food is upscale but remains fun and inviting. Reading the menu will make your stomach growl. Classic dishes of the Mediterranean are given a modern spin here, reflecting the seasons and incorporating the region's bountiful produce. Grilled veal chops with celery and potato puree, topped with pistachios and porcini mushrooms, and crunchy ravioli stuffed with slowly simmered braised rabbit, spinach, shitake mushrooms, and raisins are

signature dishes. Med Bar and Grill is that rare dining spot where style and substance come together winningly. Mediterranean menu. Dinner. Closed Sun; Jan 1, Dec 25. Bar. Casual attire. Reservations recommended. Valet parking. **$$$**

★ ★ **MIKADO.** *368 rue Laurier Ouest, Montréal (H2V 2B7). Phone 514/279-4809; fax 514/274-4006.* Japanese menu. Lunch, dinner. Closed Jan 1, Dec 25. Bar. Reservations recommended. **$$**

★ ★ **MOISHE'S.** *3961 boul St.-Laurent, Montréal (H2W 1Y4). Phone 514/845-3509; fax 514/845-9504. www.moishes.ca.* Steak menu. Lunch weekdays only, dinner. Bar. Casual attire. Reservations recommended. **$$$**

★ ★ ★ **NUANCES.** *1 Ave de Casino, Montréal (H3C 4W7). Phone 514/392-2708; toll-free 800/665-2274; fax 514/864-4951. www.casinos-quebec.com.* Montréal has a certain Parisian flair to it. Many of its restaurants embrace this sophisticated, elegant French ambience, offering guests a dining experience on par with those found in the Rive Gauche. Nuances is one such restaurant. This stylish, modern bistro, located within the Montréal Casino, is swathed in soothing earth tones and decorated with original works by local artists custom-designed for the space. The upscale menu stars exquisitely updated French cuisine assembled from a cast of natures best seasonal products. Signature plates include salmon fume with potato galette and herbed cream, earthenware-baked loin of lamb, and a steamy hot chocolate cake served with vanilla sauce. Both the chef and the sommelier developed the wine list, so the selections match up nicely with the trs Franais menu. French menu. Dinner. Bar. Jacket required. Reservations recommended. Valet parking. **$$$**

★ ★ **PRIMADONNA.** *3479 boul St-Laurent, Montréal (H2S 3C7). Phone 514/282-6644; fax 514/282-9260. www.primadonnaonline.com.* Italian menu, sushi. Dinner. Bar. Casual attire. Reservations recommended. **$$$$**

★ ★ **QUELLI DELLA NOTTE.** *6834 Blvd St-Laurent, Montréal (H2S 3C7). Phone 514/271-3929; fax 514/271-3429. www.quelli.ca.* Italian menu. Lunch, dinner. Bar. Children's menu. **$$$**

★ ★ ★ **QUEUE DE CHEVAL.** *1221 boul René Lévesque Ouest, Montréal (H3G 1T1). Phone 514/390-0090; fax 514/390-1390. www.queuedecheval.com.* Prime, dry-aged meats are the showstoppers at Queue de Cheval, a rustic, chateau-styled steakhouse accented with deep, rich maple wood and tall, vaulted ceilings in the heart of downtown Montréal. Set in a renovated historic property, with a giant open grill and an arching staircase at its center, Queue de Cheval buzzes nightly with a lively, stylish, carnivorous crowd. The classic steakhouse menu offers USDA Prime beef that is dry-aged for five weeks, butchered in house, and then spiced up with bold, robust flavors before being grilled to juicy perfection. As you'd expect from a steakhouse, the wine list complements the cuisine with a great selection of rich, meaty reds. Those in search of less meat won't have to order in from another restaurant, however. The menu has a generous raw bar, a terrific selection of salads and vegetarian appetizers, and a shimmering Fresh Fish Market that features a selection of about six fish nightly, which the kitchen will prepare grilled, whole-roasted, or seared with a choice of toppings and crusts. Steak menu. Lunch, dinner. Closed Dec 25, 31. Bar. Business casual attire. Reservations recommended. Valet parking. Outdoor seating. **$$$**

★ ★ **RESTAURANT CHANG THAI.** *2100 Crescent St, Montréal (H3G 2B2). Phone 514/286-9994; fax 514/286-0823.* Thai menu. Lunch, dinner. Closed Sun. Bar. Casual attire. **$$**
🅳

★ ★ **RESTAURANT CHEZ LEVEQUE.** *1030 rue Laurier Ouest, Montréal (H2V 2K8). Phone 514/279-7355; fax 514/279-1737.* French menu. Breakfast, lunch, dinner. Bar. Children's menu. Reservations recommended. **$$**

★ **RESTAURANT DAOU.** *519 Faillon Est, Montréal (H2R 1L6). Phone 514/276-8310; fax 514/334-6720.* Lebanese menu. Lunch, dinner. Closed Mon. **$$**

★ ★ **RESTAURANT SHO-DAN.** *2020 rue Metcalfe, Montréal (H3A 1X8). Phone 514/987-9987; fax 514/987-9967. www.sho-dan.com.* Japanese menu. Lunch weekdays only, dinner. Closed Jan 1, Dec 25. Bar. Casual attire. **$$**

★ ★ **RISTORANTE DA VINCI.** *1180 Bishop, Montréal (H3G 2E3). Phone 514/874-2001; fax 514/874-9499. www.davinci.qc.ca.* This charming restaurant offers an authentic atmosphere, warm, attentive service, and well-prepared traditional dishes made with fresh ingredients. Italian menu. Lunch, dinner. Closed Sun; Dec 24-25, Dec 31-Jan 2. Bar. Casual attire. Reservations recommended. Outdoor seating. **$$$**
🅳

★ ★ **ROSALIE RESTAURANT.** *1232 rue de la Montagne, Montréal. Phone 514/392-1970; fax 514/392-1772. www.rosalierestaurant.com.* French bistro menu. Lunch weekdays only, dinner, weekends. Bar. Casual attire. Reservations recommended. Outdoor seating. **$$**

★ ★ ★ ★ **TOQUE!.** *900 place Jean-Paul Riopelle, Montréal (H2Z 2B2). Phone 514/499-2084; fax 514/499-0292. www.restaurant-toque.com.* The presentations at Toque!, a graceful, luxurious, contemporary French restaurant located across from the Convention Centre and Jean-Paul Riopelle Park, are breathtaking. Plates are garnished with such impeccable attention to detail that you may spend several minutes debating whether or not to take out your digital camera before devouring it. But look at it this way: since you are probably at Toque! to eat, and not to simply stare, mouth agape, at the magnificent culinary artwork on the plate, don't feel bad about ruining it with your fork. Just dig in. The talented and hospitable chef, Norman Laprise, would be quite hurt if you didnt, not to mention that tasting food with your eyes is nothing compared to tasting it with your mouth. Laprise wields magic with a whisk and uses locally farmed ingredients to create a miraculous menu of sophisticated, avant-garde French fare. If you've got one meal in Montréal, Toque! is one place that you should not overlook. French Regional menu. Dinner. Closed Sun-Mon; also two weeks in late Dec-early Jan. Bar. Casual attire. Reservations recommended. Valet parking. **$$$**

★ ★ **ZEN.** *1050 rue Sherbrooke Ouest, Montréal (H3A 2R6). Phone 514/499-0801; fax 514/284-1162. www.omnihotels.com.* The focus at this Chinese restaurant located in the Hotel Omni Mont-Royal is on the food. The décor is modern minimalist with no artwork and candles on each table—not the décor of a typical Chinese restaurant. The evening prix-fixe menu allows patrons to sample every item on the menu. An à la carte menu is also available. Chinese menu. Lunch, dinner, brunch. Bar. Business casual attire. Reservations recommended. Valet parking. **$$$**

Québec City

Founded 1608
Population 166,474
Elevation 239 ft (73 m)
Area Code 418
Information Québec City and Area Tourism and Convention Bureau, 835 ave Wilfrid-Laurier, G1R 2L3; phone 418/649-2608
Web Site www.quebecregion.com

The city of Québec, one of the most beautiful in the Western Hemisphere, is 150 miles (240 kilometers) northeast of Montréal. Nestled on a historic rampart, Québec is antique, medieval, and lofty, a place of mellowed stone buildings and weathered cannon, horse-drawn calches, ancient trees, and narrow, steeply angled streets. Here and there, the 20th century has intruded, but Québec has preserved the ambience of the past.

Québec is a split-level city. Above is the sheer cliff and rock citadel that once made Québec "the Gibraltar of the north." The Upper Town, built high on the cliff and surrounded by fortresslike walls, has one of the city's best-known landmarks, Le Château Frontenac, a hotel towering so high that it's visible from 10 miles (16 kilometers) away. The Lower Town is the region surrounding Cape Diamond and spreading up the valley of the St. Charles River, a tributary of the St. Lawrence. The two sections are divided by the Funicular, which affords magnificent views of the harbor, river, and hills beyond.

In soul and spirit Québec is French; the population is nine-tenths French. Although French is the official language, English is understood in many places. The city streets are perfect for a casual stroll and many of the things you'll want to see are convenient to one another. Winters here are quite brisk.

The first known visitor to what is now Québec was Jacques Cartier, who spent the winter of 1535 at what was then the local village of Stadacone. Undoubtedly, Cartier recognized the strategic significance of this site, but a European colony was not established until 1608, when Samuel de Champlain, a French nobleman acting in the name of the King of France, established Kebec (native for "the narrowing of the waters"). The French began to put down roots in 1617 when Louis Hebert, the first agricultural pioneer, arrived with his family. The first settlement was wiped out in 1629 by British seafarers, but was later ceded back to France. For more than a century, Québec thrived despite constant harassment and siege from both the English and the Iroquois.

The decisive date in Québec historyand in the history of the British colonies to the south was September 13, 1759. After a heroic ascent up the towering cliffs, General James Wolfe led his British troops to the Plains of Abraham (named after an early settler) and engaged the forces of the brilliant French General, Louis Joseph, Marquis de Montcalm. In 15 minutes the battle was over, both generals were among the fatalities, and French dreams of an empire in America were shattered. (The last siege of Québec took place in 1775, when American troops under the command of Benedict Arnold attacked and were repelled.)

From its earliest days, Québec has been a center for military, administrative, religious, educational, and medical activities. Today the provincial capital, it still is a center for these endeavors and also for industry.

Additional Visitor Information

Information centers are located at Tourism Québec, 12 Ste.-Anne St, phone toll-free 800/363-7777 (US and Canada), (Mon-Fri); and at the Greater Québec Area Tourism & Convention Bureau, 835 Ave Wilfrid-Laurier, G1R 2L3; 418/649-2608 (daily). The US Consulate is located at 2 Terrasse Dufferin, phone 418/692-2095. Public transportation is operated throughout the city by the Québec Urban Community Transportation Commission.

Public Transportation

Airport Jean Lesage International Airport (YOB).

Information 418/640-2700

Airlines Air Canada, Air Canada Tango, Continental Express, Northwest Airlines, Pascan Aviation, Québecair Express

What to See and Do

Artillery Park National Historic Site. *2 d'Auteuil St, CP 2474, Québec City (G1K 7R3). St. Jean and D'Auteuil sts.Phone 418/648-4205. www.parcscanada.qc.ca/artillerie/.* A 4-acre (2-hectare) site built by the French to defend the opening of the St. Charles River. By the end of the 17th century, it was known as a strategic site, and military engineers began to build fortifications here. Until 1871, the park housed French and British soldiers, eventually becoming a large industrial complex. Dauphine Redoubt (1712-1748), gun carriage shed (1813-1815), officers' quarters (1818), and arsenal foundry (1903) have been restored. Interpretation center. (Apr-May: Wed-Sun 10 am-5 pm, Mon-Tues by appointment; mid-May-mid-Oct: daily 10 am-5 pm; mid-Oct-Mar: by appointment; closed Jan 1, Easter, Dec 25) **$$**

Baillairge cultural tours. *Phone 418/692-5737.* Group tours lasting between three days and one week focus on art, cuisine, and education. (Late June-mid-Oct, daily) **$$$$**

Basilica of Ste.-Anne-de-Beaupre. *10018 Royale Ave, Québec City (G0A 3C0). 22 miles (35 kilometers) NE on Hwy 138. Phone 418/827-3781. www.ssadb.qc.ca.* This basilica is noted as the oldest pilgrimage in North America. The first chapel was built on this site in 1658; the present basilica, built in 1923, is made of white Canadian granite and is regarded as a Romanesque masterpiece. Capitals tell the story of Jesus's life in 88 scenes; vaults are decorated with mosaics; unusual techniques were used for 240 stained-glass windows outlined in concrete. Fourteen life-size Stations of the Cross and *Scala Santa* (Holy Stairs) are located on the hillside. (Daily)

Calèches. Take a tour of the historic district in a horse-drawn carriage. Most leave from the Esplanade parking lot on d'Auteuil Street, next to the Tourist Bureau. **$$$$**

Cartier-Brebeuf National Historic Site. *175 de l'Espinay St, Montréal. Phone 418/648-4038; fax 418/648-4367. www.parcscanada.gc.ca.* Commemorates Jacques Cartier, first European known to have wintered in mainland Canada (1535-1536) and Jean de Brbeuf, a martyred Jesuit priest. The *Grande Hermine*, a full-size replica of Cartier's 16th-century flagship, is in dry dock; the hold and between deck can be viewed. Interpretation center with videotaped material. Guided tours by reservations. Indigenous habitation on site is open to visitors. (Hours vary, call for information) **$**

Explore. *63 rue Dalhousie, Québec City. Phone 418/692-1759.* This 30-minute high-tech sound and visual arts show illustrates the founding of Québec and the beginnings of New France during the Golden Age of Exploration, when Columbus, Cartier, Champlain, and others began to venture into the Americas. (Daily; closed Dec 1-26)

Gaspe Peninsula. *Phone 418/775-2223; toll-free 800/463-0323. www.tourisme-gaspesie.com.* Jutting out into the Gulf of St. Laurent, the Gaspé Peninsula is a region of varying landforms including mountains, plateaus, beaches, and cliffs. It is blessed with abundant and rare wildlife and some unique flora, including 12-foot-high (4-meter-high) centuries-old fir trees. Landscapes are incredibly beautiful. The rivers, teeming with trout, flow to meet the salmon coming from the sea. Called "Gespeg" (meaning "land's end") by the Aborigines, the area was settled primarily by Basque, Breton, and Norman fishermen, whose charming villages may be seen clinging to the shore beneath the gigantic cliffs. The French influence is strong, although English is spoken in a few villages. For further information, contact the Association Touristique Rgionale de la Gspesie, 357 Route de la Mer, Sainte-Flavie, G0J 2L0.

Grand Theatre. *269 boul Rene-Levesque, Québec (G1R 2B3). Phone 418/643-8131. www.grandtheatre.qc.ca.* Ultramodern theater has giant mural by sculptor Jordi Bonet in lobby; home of the Québec Symphony Orchestra and Opera; theatrical performances, concerts. **$$$**

Gray Line bus tours. *320 Abraham Martin, Québec City (G1K 8N2). Phone 418/523-9722. www.grayline.com.* The Gray Line tour operator offers a number of sightseeing and package tours of Québec City, with stops at Montmorency Waterfalls, the Plains of Abraham, and the Citadelle.

Harbour Cruises. *124 St.-Pierre St, Québec City (G1K 4A7). Chouinard Pier, opposite Place Royale. Phone 418/692-1159; toll-free 800/563-4643.* M/V *Louis Jolliet* offers daytime, evening dance, and dinner cruises on the St. Lawrence River. Bar service, entertainment. (May-Oct) **$$$$**

Île d'Orleans. *Across the bridge, in the St. Lawrence River. Phone 418/828-9411.* This 23-mile-long (37-kilometers) island was visited by Champlain in 1608 and colonized in 1648. Old stone farmhouses and churches of the 18th century remain. Farms grow an abundance of fruits and vegetables, especially strawberries, for which the island is famous.

Jacques-Cartier Park. *700 Lebourgneuf, Québec City (G2J 1E2). 25 miles (40.2 kilometers) N via Hwy 175. Phone 418/848-3169. www.jacques-cartier.com.* This park features beautiful views in a boreal forest valley. Fishing, rafting, canoeing, mountain climbing, wilderness camping, cross-country skiing, hiking, mountain biking, snowshoeing, dogsledding, and picnicking are among the many activities available here. Visitors may also enjoy the serenity of its wilderness by walking the magnificent nature trail, as well as through nature interpretation activities. (Late May-mid-Oct, mid-Dec-mid-Apr) **$$**

⭐ **La Citadelle.** *1 Cote de la Citadelle, Québec City (G1R 4V7). On Cap Diamant. Phone 418/694-2815. www.lacitadelle.qc.ca.* Forming the eastern flank of the fortifications of Québec, La Citadelle was begun in 1820. Work on it continued until 1850. Vestiges of the French regime, such as the Cap Diamant Redoubt (1693) and a powder magazine (1750), can still be seen. Panoramic views; 50-minute guided tours. Changing of the guard (late June-Labor Day, daily at 10 am); Beating the Retreat, a re-creation of a 16th-century ceremony (late June-Labor Day, Tues, Thurs, Sat-Sun; fee). (Apr: daily 10 am-4 pm; May-June: 9 am-5 pm; July-Labor Day: 9 am-6 pm; Sept: 9 am-4 pm; Oct: 10 am-3 pm; Nov-Apr by appointment only) **$$** In La Citadelle is

> **Museum of the Royal 22e Regiment.** *Succursale Haute-Ville, Québec City (G1R 4V7).* Located in two buildings. Powder magazine (circa 1750), flanked on both sides by massive buttresses, contains replicas of old uniforms of French regiments, war trophies, 17th- to 20th-century weapons; diorama of historic battles under the French; old military prison contains insignias, rifle and bayonet collections, last cell left intact. (Mid-Mar-Oct, daily) Changing of the guard (mid-June-Labor Day, daily at 10 am).**$$**

Laurentides Wildlife Reserve. *35 miles (48 kilometers) N via Hwy 175. Phone 418/686-1717. www.sepaq.com.* A variety of animals including moose, wolves, bears, and numerous birds can be found here. Outdoor-lovers will find many recreational opportunities like canoeing, fishing, hunting, and camping, as well as boat, ski, and snowshoe rental. Located here are 140 cabins and 134 campsites. (Late May-Labor Day, mid-Dec-mid-Apr) **$$$$**

Mont-Ste.-Anne Park. *2000 boul Beau Pre, C.P. 400, Beaurpre (G0A 1E0). 23 miles (37 kilometers) NE via Hwy 138, then N 3 miles (5 kilometers) on Hwy 360. Phone 418/827-4561. www.mont-sainte-anne.com.* Gondola travels to summit of mountain (2,625 feet or 800 meters), affording beautiful view of St. Lawrence River (late June-early Sept, daily). Skiing (Nov-May): 12 lifts, 50 trails; 85 percent snowmaking; cross-coun-

try, full service. Two 18-hole golf courses; bicycle trail. 166 campsites. The migration of 250,000 snow geese occurs in spring and fall at nearby wildlife reserve Cap Tourmente. Park (daily; closed May). Some fees.

Musee de la Civilisation. *85 rue Dalhousie, Québec. Near Place Royale.Phone 418/643-2158. www.mcq. org.* At the entrance is *La Débacle,* a massive sculpture representing ice breaking up in spring. Separate exhibition halls present four permanent and several changing exhibitions dealing with history of Québec and the French Canadian culture as well as cultures of other civilizations from around the world. All narrative panels and signs are in French; bilingual guides are on duty in most exhibit areas, and English guide books are available (fee). Guided tours are also available (fee). (Sept-late June: Tues-Sun 10 am-5 pm; rest of year: daily to 6:30 pm; closed Mon, Dec 25) **$$$**

Musee du Fort. *10 Sainte-Anne St, Québec City (G1R 4S7). Place d'Armes, corner of Ste-Anne and du Fort sts. Phone 418/692-1759.* Narrated historical re-creation of the six sieges of Québec between 1629 and 1775, with a sound and light show. (Feb-Mar: Thurs-Sun 11 am-4 pm; Apr-June, Sept-Oct: daily 10 am-5 pm; July-Aug: daily 10 am-6 pm; Christmas holidays: daily noon-4 pm) **$$**

National Assembly of Québec. *Grande-Allee and Honore-Mercier Ave, Québec City. Phone 418/643-7239. www.assnat.qc.ca.* Take a 30-minute guided tour of Québec's Parliament Building, constructed between 1877 and 1886. Guides provide an inside look into the proceedings of the Québec National Assembly, while explaining the building's architectural features. (Mon-Fri 9 am-4:30 pm; late June-early Sept: daily 10 am-4:30 pm) **FREE**

National Battlefields Park. *835 Wilfrid Laurier, Québec City. Entrances along Grand-Alle. Phone 418/648-4071.* Two hundred fifty acres (101 hectares) along edge of bluff overlooking St. Lawrence River from Citadel to Gilmour Hill. Also called the Plains of Abraham, park was site of 1759 battle between the armies of Wolfe and Montcalm and the 1760 battle of Ste.-Foy between the armies of Murray and Lvis. Visitor reception and interpretation center presents history of the Plains of Abraham from the New France period to the present. Bus tour of the park. **$** In the park are two Martello towers, part of the fortifications, a sunken garden, many statues and the

> **Jeanne d'Arc Garden.** *835 Wilfrid Laurier, Québec City. Phone 418/649-6159.* This floral jewel was

created in 1938 by landscape architect Louis Perron. It combines the French Classical style with British-style flower beds and features more than 150 species of annuals, bulbs, and perennials.

Musee national des beaux-arts du Québec. *Parc des Champs-de-Bataille, Québec (G1R 5H3). Phone 418/643-2150.* Features collections of ancient, modern, and contemporary Québec paintings, sculpture, photography, drawings, and decorative arts. (Daily, Tues-Sun 10 am-5 pm, Wed to 9 pm; summer, daily 10 am-6 pm, Wed to 9 pm; closed Mon) **$$$**

Notre-Dame de Québec Basilica-Cathedral. *20 De Buade St, Québec City (G1R 4A1). Phone 418/694-0665. www.patrimoine-religieux.com.* View the richly decorated Cathedral, over 350 years old, and the crypt, where most of the governors and bishops of Québec are buried. Guided tours offered daily from early May to early November. (Daily 7:30 am-4:30 pm) **FREE** Also here is

Sound and Light Show "Heavenly Lights". *20 De Buade St, Québec City (G1R 4A1). Phone 418/694-0665.* This 30-minute multimedia show in both French and English takes place on three giant screens within the cathedral. (Early May-mid-Oct: first show is at 3:30 pm, then every 60 minutes. Last show is at 8:30 pm) **$$**

Old Port of Québec Interpretation Centre. *100 St.-Andr St, Québec City (G1K 7R3). Phone 418/648-3300. www.parcscanada.qc.ca/vieuxport/.* Located in an ancient cement works and integrated into harbor installations of Louise Basin. Permanent exhibit shows importance of city as a gateway to America in the mid-19th century; timber trade and shipbuilding displays; films, exhibits; guides. (Mid-Oct-early May by appointment, early May-late Aug, daily 10 am-5 pm, early Sept-mid-Oct, daily 1-5 pm) **$**

Place-Royale. *27 Nortre Dame St, Québec City (G1K 8R5). Lower Town along St. Lawrence Riverfront. Phone 418/646-3167. www.mcq.org.* This site encompasses the earliest vestiges of French civilization in North America. Once a marketplace and the city's social center, it became run-down by 1950 but has since been restored to its historic appearance. Today, visitors come to enjoy the many restaurants and retail stores, as well as performances in shows that take place during summer.

Québec Aquarium. *1675 avenue des Hotels, Sainte-Foy (G1W 4S3). Phone 418/659-5264. www.spsnq.qc.ca.* Extensive collection of tropical, fresh, and saltwater fish, marine mammals, and reptiles; overlooks St. Lawrence River. Seal feeding (morning and afternoon); films (mid-May-Aug; daily). Cafeteria, picnicking. (Daily 10 am-4 pm, Oct-Apr; to 5 pm, May and Sept; to 7 pm, June-Aug) **$$$$**

⭐ **Québec City Walls and Gates.** *, Québec City.* Encompassing Old Québec. Eighteenth-century fortifications encircle the only fortified city in North America; includes Governor's Promenade and provides scenic view of The Citadel, St. Lawrence River, and Lvis. (Daily except Governor's Promenade) **FREE**

Québec Zoo. *9300 Faune St, Charlesbourg. 7 miles (11.3 kilometers) NW on Hwy 73/175. Phone 418/622-0312. www.spsnq.qc.ca.* More than 270 species of native and exotic animals and birds in a setting of forests, fields, and streams; children's zoo, sea lion shows; restaurant, picnicking. (Daily; closed Dec 25) **$$$**

St. Andrew's Presbyterian Church. *5 Cook St, Québec City (G1R 4P3). Phone 418/694-1347.* Serving the oldest English-speaking congregation of Scottish origin in Canada, which traces back to 1759. The church itself was built in 1810. Its interior is distinguished by a long front wall with a high center pulpit, as well as stained-glass windows, and historic plaques. The original petition to King George III asking for a "small plot of waste ground" on which to build a Scotch church is on display in the Church Vestry. A spiral stairway leads to the century-old organ. (July-Aug: Mon-Fri 10 am-4:30 pm; guide on duty) **FREE**

St.-Jean-Port-Joli. *Approximately 60 miles (96.6 kilometers) NE on Hwy 132 halfway to the Gasp Peninsula. Phone 418/598-3084. www.saintjeanportjoli.com.* The tradition of wood sculpture began in this town about 1936, initiated by the famed Bourgault family. Other craftsmen came and made this a premier handicraft center for sculpture, enamels, mosaics in copper and wood, fabric, and painting. Located here is a small church built in 1779 and renowned for the beauty of its lines and interior décor. It features a sculpted wood vault, tabernacle, and reredos, all by different artisans, and has not been altered since it was built. Outdoor enthusiasts can enjoy a golf club (May-Sept), tennis courts, mountain bike trails, and a marina. Also here is

Musee des Anciens Canadiens. *332 avenue de Gaspe W, Saint-Jean-Port-Joli. Phone 418/598-3392.* This museum features an impressive collection of wood carvings by St.-Jean artisans, as well as original carvings by the Bourgault brothers.

Visitors may watch a woodcarver at work and ask questions about his craft, and purchase wood carved pieces. (Mid-May-Oct, daily)

Université Laval. *Sir Wilfrid Laurier Blvd and Du Vallon Rte, Ste. Foy. Phone 418/656-2571. www.ulaval.ca.* The oldest French university on the continent, Laval evolved from Québec Seminary, which was founded in 1663 by Québec's first bishop, Msgr. de Laval. In 1950 the university moved from "Le Quartier Latin" in old Québec to a 470-acre (190-hectare) site in suburban Ste.-Foy, where it developed into the present, modern campus.

Uplands Cultural and Heritage Centre. *9 rue Speid, Lennoxville (J1M 1R9). Phone 819/564-0409. www.uplands.ca.* This neo-Georgian home built in 1862 is located on 4 acres (1.6 hectares) of beautifully wooded grounds. Changing exhibits interpret heritage of Lennoxville-Ascot and eastern townships. The Lennoxville-Ascot Historical and Museum Society on the second floor contains period furniture, and a small room for temporary exhibits. Afternoon tea served all year (reservations required in winter). (Thurs-Fri, Sun 1-4:30 pm; Tues-Sun 1-4:30 pm in summer; closed Jan) **DONATION**

Special Events

Carnaval de Québec. *290 rue Joly, Québec City (G1L 1N8). Phone 418/626-3716. www.carnaval.qc.ca.* This internationally acclaimed French Canadian festival, billed as the world's biggest winter carnival, is celebrated throughout Old Town. Activities include parades, a canoe race on the St. Lawrence River, a dog-sled race, a snow and ice sculpture show, a soapbox derby, and the "snow bath," where participants brave the snow in their bathing suits. Late Jan-mid-Feb.

du Maurier Québec Summer Festival. *160 rue Saint-Paul, Québec City (G1K 7A1). Phone 418/529-5200; toll-free 888/992-5200. www.infofestival.com.* This 11-day event is one of the largest music festivals in North America. Performances are held at various locations throughout Old Québec. Major local and international artists are showcased, but the festival also serves as a springboard for up-and-coming artists, as well. Early-mid-July.

Expo Québec. *250 Boul Wilfrid-Hamel, Québec City (G1L 5A7). Phone 418/691-7110. www.expocite.com.* This commercial, agricultural, and industrial fair attracts over 400,000 people each year. Taking place at Exhibition Park, the event features arts and science pavilions, rides, a sand sculpture competition, and a food exhibit. Late Aug.

New France Celebration. *Phone 418/694-3311; toll-free 866/391-3383. www.nouvellefrance.qc.ca.* This family-oriented historical event in Old Québec re-creates the life of the colonists in New France in the 16th and 17th centuries. During this festival, the streets are filled with theatrical events, storytellers, song and dance performances, and children's entertainment. Both children and adults who attend often dress in period costumes. Early Aug.

Limited-Service Hotels

★ ★ **BEST WESTERN HOTEL L'ARISTOCRATE.** *3100 Chemin Ste. Louis, Ste. Foy (G1W 1R8). Phone 418/653-2841; fax 418/653-8525. www.bestwestern.com.* 100 rooms, 2 story. Check-out noon. Restaurant, bar. Outdoor pool. **$**

★ ★ **CHATEAU LAURIER HOTEL.** *1220 Georges 5th Ouest, Québec City (G1R 5B8). Phone 418/522-8108; toll-free 800/463-4453; fax 418/524-8768. www.old-quebec.com/laurier.* 57 rooms, 4 story. Check-out noon. Restaurant, bar. **$**

★ ★ **CLARENDON HOTEL.** *57 rue Ste. Anne, Québec City (G1R 3X4). Phone 418/692-2480; toll-free 888/554-6001; fax 418/692-4652. www.hotelclarendon.com.* Historic hotel (1870), the oldest in Québec. 151 rooms, 7 story. Check-out noon. Restaurant, bar. **$**

★ ★ **COURTYARD BY MARRIOTT QUÉBEC CITY.** *850 Place d'Youville, Québec City (G1R 3P6). Phone 418/694-4004; fax 418/694-4007.* A step above the typical Courtyard, this downtown hotel is easy on the budget while providing access to many of Québec City's prime attractions, making it a great choice for families. Nearby are a skating rink, the Parliament Building, and the Old Port, as well as a variety of restaurants. 102 rooms, 7 story. Check-in 4 pm, check-out noon. High-speed Internet access. Restaurant, bar. Whirlpool. Business center. **$**

★ ★ **HOTEL RADISSON QUÉBEC CENTRE.** *690 Boul Rene-Levesque E, Québec City (G1R 5A8). Phone 418/647-1717; toll-free 888/884-7777; fax 418/647-2146. www.radisson.com.* Located steps from Old Québec, the property faces Parliament Hill, is linked to the convention center, and provides direct access to Place Québec, a large shopping center. 377 rooms, 12 story. Check-out noon. Restaurant, bar. Fitness room. Outdoor pool, whirlpool. Business center. **$**

★ ★ **SELECTOTEL ROND-POINT.** *53 Kennedy Blvd, Levis (J6W 6C7). Phone 418/833-4920; fax 418/833-0634.* Ferry five minutes to Old Québec. 124 rooms, 2 story. Check-in 2 pm, check-out noon. Restaurant. Indoor pool. **$**

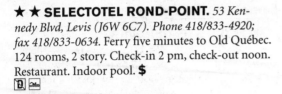

Full-Service Hotels

★ ★ ★ **CHATEAU BONNE ENTENTE.** *3400, Chemin Ste-Foy, Ste. Foy (G1X 1S6). Phone 418/653-5221; toll-free 800/463-4390; fax 418/653-7871. www.chateaubonneentente.com.* This country inn offers a very relaxing stay. Situated on 11 acres (4 hectares) in the suburbs, the property is very quiet. 165 rooms, 3 story. Check-in 3 pm, check-out noon. Restaurant, bar. Children's activity center. Fitness room, spa. Outdoor pool, whirlpool. Tennis. Airport transportation available. Business center. **$$**

★ ★ ★ **FAIRMONT LE CHATEAU FRONTENAC.** *1 Rue Des Carrieres, Québec City (G1R 4P5). Phone 418/692-3861; toll-free 800/441-1414; fax 418/692-1751. www.fairmont.com.* Travelers are easily seduced by the unique charm of Québec City, where horse-drawn carriages glide down cobblestone streets. Reigning over this historic walled city from its perch atop the roaring St. Lawrence River is the majestic Fairmont Le Château Frontenac. Its dignified setting and splendid views make the castle-like hotel seem scripted straight from a fairy tale. This landmark chateau-style hotel (1893) was the site of historic conferences during World War II. Classic European details define the interiors here, where the rooms and suites reflect a worldly sophistication. Skiing and other winter-weather activities are available nearby, and the hotel offers a fitness center and spa. Québec City is a gourmet destination, with numerous cafés lining the narrow streets, but the Fairmont's five restaurants give the local establishments a run for their money. 613 rooms, 18 story. Check-out noon. Restaurant, bar. Fitness room. Indoor pool, children's pool, whirlpool. Business center. **$$$**

★ ★ ★ **HOTEL DOMINION 1912.** *126 rue Saint-Pierre, Québec City (G1K 4A8). Phone 418/692-2224; toll-free 888/833-5253; fax 418/692-4403. www.hoteldominion.com.* Old Québec is considered the cradle of French culture in North America, and Hotel Dominion 1912 is a wonderful place from which to explore it. This small, sleek hotel takes full advantage of the early-20th-century building's historic architectural features while providing the modern conveniences that travelers expect. Guest rooms have down-filled duvets, 27-inch televisions, fresh fruit and bottled water, as well as ergonomic desk chairs for business travelers. Both private and public areas are decorated in striking black and white and softer neutral tones. 60 rooms. Check-in 3 pm, check-out noon. Restaurant, bar. **$$**

★ ★ ★ **HOTEL GERMAIN-DES-PRES.** *1200 Ave Germain-des-Pres, Ste. Foy (G1V 3M7). Phone 418/658-1224; toll-free 800/463-5253; fax 418/658-8846. www.germaindespres.com.* The property is 15 minutes from Québec City, major shopping malls, and several golf courses. 126 rooms, 8 story. Check-out noon. Restaurant, bar. Airport transportation available. **$$$**

★ ★ ★ **LOEWS LE CONCORDE.** *1225 Cours du General De Montcalm, Québec City (G1R 4W6). Phone 418/647-2222; toll-free 800/463-5256; fax 418/647-4710. www.loewshotels.com.* See a vision of Paris out your window from this hotel on Québec City's "Champs-Elysees." Just 15 minutes from the airport, the tower has views of the St. Lawrence River, the city lights, and the historic Plains of Abraham. A visit is not complete without a peek, and hopefully a meal, at L'Astral, the revolving rooftop restaurant. 404 rooms, 26 story. Pets accepted, some restrictions. Check-out 1 pm. Restaurant, bar. Fitness room. Outdoor pool, whirlpool. Business center. **$**

★ ★ ★ **QUÉBEC HILTON.** *1100 Boul Rene Levesque Est, Québec City (G1K 7M9). Phone 418/647-2411; fax 418/647-6488.* This property is connected to the Québec Government buildings by the Place Québec, a modern underground shopping center with many stores, restaurants, and entertainment options. 571 rooms, 23 story. Pets accepted. Check-out noon. Restaurant, bar. Fitness room. Outdoor pool. Business center. **$$**

Full-Service Resorts

★ ★ ★ **FAIRMONT LE MANOIR RICHELIEU.** *181 rue Richelieu, Charlevoix (G5A 1X7). Phone 418/665-3703; toll-free 800/441-1414; fax 418/665-7736. www.fairmont.com.* The Fairmont Le Manoir Richelieu is the embodiment of a magical castle. This majestic hotel in the heart of Québecs scenic Charlevoix countryside welcomes visitors with its historic charm and world-class sophistication. Breathtaking views are the trademark of this hotel, where emerald lawns border the sapphire waters of the St. Lawrence River. The rooms and suites have a classic country appeal and are blessed with the most modern amenities. The Fairmont is a wonderland in winter, when pure snow creates a truly magical setting, while summer months highlight natures brilliant colors. Guests who choose to fill their days with pursuits more active than daydreaming opt for nearby skiing and golf, or enjoy the hotel's fitness and spa facilities. 405 rooms, 3 story. Check-in 4 pm, check-out noon. Restaurant, bar. Fitness room. Indoor pool, whirlpool. Business center. **$$$**

★ ★ ★ **MANOIR DU LAC DELAGE.** *40 Ave du Lac, Ville du Lac Delage (G0A 4P0). Phone 418/848-2551; toll-free 800/463-8841; fax 418/848-1352. www.lacdelage.com.* This hotel is located 20 minutes outside Québec City. 105 rooms, 3 story. Check-in 3 pm, check-out noon. Restaurant, bar. Fitness room. Indoor pool, outdoor pool. Tennis. **$$**

Full-Service Inns

★ ★ ★ **AUBERGE SAINT-ANTOINE.** *8 rue Saint-Antoine, Québec City (G1K 4A8). Phone 418/692-2211; toll-free 888/692-2211; fax 418/692-1177. www.saint-antoine.com.* Explore historic Québec City from this sleek hotel housed in a building that's been occupied since the beginning of the French colony. The cannon battery that runs through the lobby is from the 17th century, and artifacts uncovered in archaeological digs at the site are displayed throughout the common areas and guest rooms. Stone walls and wooden beams enhance the décor in this small hotel, located in the middle of Old Québecs Port District on the St. Lawrence River. Guest rooms feature dramatic upholstered headboards, Bose stereo systems, and windows that actually open; heated bathroom floors keep toes toasty. Guests enjoy continental breakfast beside the fireplace in the James Hunt lounge and evening wine or liqueurs in the lobby or on the terrace. Sophisticated but rustic French-Canadian cuisine is served at the Panache Restaurant, while light meals are available in the tea room during the day. 95 rooms. Check-in 3 pm, check-out noon. High-speed Internet access. Restaurant, bar. Business center. **$$$**

Specialty Lodging

AU MANOIR STE.-GENEVIEVE. *13 Ave Ste-Genevieve, Québec City (G1R 4A7). Phone 418/694-1666; toll-free 877/694-1666; fax 418/694-1666. www.quebec-web.com/msg.* Greystone house (1895) with a terrace on the upper level. 9 rooms, 3 story. Check-in 1 pm, check-out noon. **$**

Restaurants

★ ★ **AUX ANCIENS CANADIENS.** *34 rue Ste. Louis, Québec City (G1R 4P3). Phone 418/692-1627; fax 418/692-5419. www.auxancienscanadiens.qc.ca.* French menu. Dinner. Bar. **$$$**

★ ★ ★ **AUX CHANTIGNOLES.** *392 rue Notre Dame, Montebello (G0V1L0). Phone 819/423-6341; fax 819/423-6208. www.fairmont.com.* This restaurant features a rustic décor and crackling fireplace. French, seafood menu. Breakfast, lunch, dinner, Sun brunch. Bar. Children's menu. Outdoor seating. **$$$**

★ ★ ★ **L'ASTRAL.** *1225 Cours du General de Montcalm, Québec City (G1R 4W6). Phone 418/647-2222; fax 418/647-4710. www.lastral.com.* Each rotation of this rooftop restaurant atop the Loews Le Concorde takes 90 minutes, plenty of time to enjoy the fine cuisine and the panoramic view of Québec City. French menu. Lunch, dinner, Sun brunch. Bar. Children's menu. Reservations recommended. Valet parking. **$$$**

★ **L'OMELETTE.** *64 rue Ste. Louis, Québec City (G1R 3Z3). Phone 418/694-9626; fax 418/694-2260.* Breakfast, lunch, dinner. Closed Nov-Mar. Valet parking. **$**

★ ★ ★ **LA MAISON SERGE BRUYERE.** *1200 rue Ste. Jean, Québec City (G1R 1S8). Phone 418/694-0618; fax 418/694-2120.* Diners have many options at this Upper Old Québec City restaurant, from the fine dining and most famous, La Grande Table; to the more casual Cafe Bruyere; Bistro Liverno, a tribute to the photographer; and the German-influenced Fallstaff. French. Dinner. Valet parking. **$$$**

★ ★ ★ **LAURIE RAPHAEL.** *117 Dalhousie, Québec City (G1K 9C8). Phone 418/692-4555; fax 418/692-4175. www.laurieraphael.com.* In 1991, acclaimed chef Daniel Vezina and his wife, Suzanne Gagnon, decided to open an upscale spot to showcase Vezina's creative French fare. They chose a sunny, intimate space in Québec City's Old Port district and chose a name for the restaurant that would always be dear to their hearts; they named it after their children, Laurie and Raphael. The haute, market-driven menu reflects Vezina's culinary travels, from Asia, to Italy and France, and back to his native North America. Signatures include Jerusalem artichoke blinis with sturgeon egg cream and house-smoked sturgeon and duck foie gras with chicken broth and dried cranberries. The restaurant remains a destination not only for the exceptional cuisine but also for its impressive wine cellar and its warm and hospitable service. French menu. Lunch, dinner. Closed Sun-Mon. Reservations recommended. **$$$**

★ ★ **LE BISTANGO.** *1200 Ave Germain des Pres, Ste. Foy (G1V 3M7). Phone 418/658-8780; fax 418/658-8846. www.lebistango.com.* California, French menu. Breakfast, lunch, dinner, Sun brunch. Closed Jan 1, Dec 25. Bar. Children's menu. Valet parking. **$$$**

★ ★ **LE BONAPARTE.** *680 E Grande-Allee, Québec City (G1R 2K5). Phone 418/647-4747; fax 418/647-6870.* In an 1823 building. French menu. Lunch, dinner. Closed Sat-Sun mornings in Nov-Mar. Bar. Children's menu. Outdoor seating. **$$$**

★ ★ ★ **LE CHAMPLAIN.** *1 rue des Carrieres, Québec City (G1R 4P5). Phone 418/692-3861; fax 418/691-3742. www.fairmont.com.* The staff's 17th-century costumes contribute to the refined, historic atmosphere at this fine dining restaurant. French menu. Dinner, Sun brunch. Jacket required. Valet parking. **$$$**

★ ★ ★ **LE CONTINENTAL.** *26 rue Ste. Louis, Québec City (G1R 3Y9). Phone 418/694-9995; fax 418/694-2179. www.restaurantlecontinental.com.* Deep colors and oak dominate the rich décor and European atmosphere at this fine dining restaurant in Upper Québec. Order one of the flambe specialties for a unique tableside show. French menu. Dinner. Closed Dec 24-25. Valet parking. **$$$**

★ **LE MANOIR DU SPAGHETTI.** *3077 Chemin Ste. Louis, Ste. Foy (G1W 1R6). Phone 418/659-5628; fax 418/659-7158.* French, Italian menu. Lunch, dinner. Café bar. Children's menu. Outdoor seating. **$$**

★ ★ ★ **LE SAINT-AMOUR.** *48 Ste. Ursule, Québec City (G1R 4E2). Phone 418/694-0667; fax 418/694-0967. www.saint-amour.com.* Family-owned and operated since opening in the heart of Old Québec in 1978, this charming restaurant is away from the bustle of the tourist beat. Behind the simple façade on rue Ste. Ursule, the chef offers guests a truly outstanding and original menu well deserving of the heaping accolades of guests and critics alike. French menu. Lunch, dinner. Closed Dec 24. Children's menu. Valet parking. Outdoor seating. **$$$**
🅳

★ ★ **LE VENDOME.** *36 Cote de la Montagne, Québec City (G1K 4E2). Phone 418/692-0557; fax 418/692-3885.* French menu. Lunch, dinner. Closed Dec 24. Bar. Children's menu. Valet parking. Outdoor seating. **$$**
🅳

★ ★ ★ **MONTE CRISTO.** *3400 Chemin Ste. Foy, Québec City (G1X 1S6). Phone 418/653-5221; fax 418/653-7871. www.chateaubonneentente.com.* Monte Cristo offers traditional and original Québec cooking using local products. Breakfast, lunch, dinner. Bar. Children's menu. **$$$**

★ ★ **RESTAURANT AU PARMESAN.** *38 rue Ste. Louis, Québec City (G1R 3Z1). Phone 418/692-0341; fax 418/692-4256.* Italian, French menu. Lunch, dinner. Closed Dec 24-25. Children's menu. Valet parking. **$$$**
🅳

Index

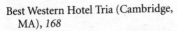

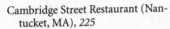

Chain Restaurants

Connecticut

Avon
Ninety Nine Restaurant & Pub, 315 W Main St, Avon, CT, (860) 677-2699, 11:30 am-11 pm

Bristol
Ninety Nine Restaurant & Pub, 827 Pine St Forestville Commons, Bristol, CT, (860) 314-9900, 11:30 am-11 pm

Cromwell
Ninety Nine Restaurant & Pub, 36 Shunpike Rd Rte 3, Cromwell, CT, (860) 632-2099, 11:30 am-11 pm

Danbury
Chili's, 81 Newtown Rd, Danbury, CT, (203) 778-6703, 11 am-10 pm

Uno Chicago Grill, Seven Backus Ave, Danbury Fair Mall, Danbury, CT, (203) 778-1126, 11 am-12:30 am

Darien
Melting Pot, 14 Grove St, Darien, CT, (203) 656-4774, 5 pm-10:30 pm

East Haven
Chili's, 58 Frontage Rd, East Haven, CT, (203) 467-1533, 11 am-10 pm

East Windsor
Cracker Barrel, 145 Prospect Hill Rd, East Windsor, CT, (860) 623-8824, 6 am-10 pm

Enfield
Hometown Buffet, Brookside Plaza, 14 Hazard Ave, Enfield, CT, (860) 741-8087, 11 am-8:30 pm

Ninety Nine Restaurant & Pub, 54 Hazard Ave, Enfield, CT, (860) 741-7499, 11:30 am-11 pm

Fairfield
Uno Chicago Grill, 2320 Blackrock Turnpike, Fairfield, CT, (203) 372-2909, 11 am-12:30 am

Farmington
Uno Chicago Grill, 1500 New Britain Ave, West Farm Mall, Farmington, CT, (860) 561-3113, 11 am-12:30 am

Glastonbury
Chili's, 2855 Main St, Glastonbury, CT, (860) 657-2333, 11 am-10 pm

Ninety Nine Restaurant & Pub, 3025 Main St, Glastonbury, CT, (860) 652-9699, 11:30 am-11 pm

Groton
Ninety Nine Restaurant & Pub, 117 Long Hill Rd, Groton, CT, (860) 449-9900, 11:30 am-11 pm

Hamden
Chili's, 2100 Dixwell Ave, Hamden, CT, (203) 248-2283, 11 am-10 pm

Manchester
Chili's, 250 Buckland St, Manchester, CT, (860) 648-0833, 11 am-10 pm

Hometown Buffet, Melville Plaza, 165 Slater St, Manchester, CT, (860) 648-2711, 11 am-8:30 pm

Hooters, 1483 Pleasant Valley Rd, Manchester, CT, (860) 432-5360, 11 am-midnight

Ninety Nine Restaurant & Pub, 90 Buckland St, Manchester, CT, (860) 646-7899, 11:30 am-11 pm

Romano's Macaroni Grill, 170 Slater St, Manchester, CT, (860) 648-8819, 11 am-10 pm

Smokey Bones, 350 Buckland Hills Dr, Manchester, CT, (860) 648-1737, 11 am-10 pm

Uno Chicago Grill, 180 Deming St, Manchester, CT, (860) 648-2238, 11 am-12:30 am

Mashantucket
Fuddruckers, 39 Norwich-Westerly Rd, Mashantucket, CT, 11 am-9 pm

Milford
Chili's, 1500 Boston Post Rd Rt 1, Milford, CT, (203) 874-5140, 11 am-10 pm

Cracker Barrel, 30 Research Dr, Milford, CT, (203) 877-7595, 6 am-10 pm

Hometown Buffet, Turnpike Square Mall, 74 Turnpike Square, Milford, CT, (203) 877-6335, 11 am-8:30 pm

Hooters, 990 Boston Post Rd, Milford, CT, (203) 878-6651, 11 am-midnight

Uno Chicago Grill, 1061 Boston Post Rd, Milford, CT, (203) 876-1160, 11 am-12:30 am

Montville

Chili's, 2000 Norwich-New London, Montville, CT, 11 am-10 pm

Mystic

The Ground Round, 9 Whitehall Ave, Mystic, CT, (860) 536-3168, 11 am-11 pm

New Britain

Chili's, 590 Hartford Rd Rt 71, New Britain, CT, (860) 229-0155, 11 am-10 pm

New London

Chili's, 369 N Frontage Rd, New London, CT, (860) 444-0335, 11 am-10 pm

Newington

Chili's, 3017 Berlin Turnpike and Pascone Ave, Newington, CT, (860) 667-9063, 11 am-10 pm

Ninety Nine Restaurant & Pub, 2095 Berlin Turnpike, Newington, CT, (860) 666-5599, 11:30 am-11 pm

Norwich

Ninety Nine Restaurant & Pub, 5 Salem Turnpike, Norwich, CT, (860) 892-1299, 11:30 am-11 pm

Papa Gino's, 607 W Main St, Norwich, CT, (860) 889-1397, 10:30 am-10 pm

Orange

Ninety Nine Restaurant & Pub, 377 Boston Post Rd Rte 1, Orange, CT, (203) 795-9921, 11:30 am-11 pm

On the Border, 220 Indian River Rd, Orange, CT, (203) 799-0636, 11 am-10 pm

Rocky Hill

On the Border, 1519 Silas Deane Hwy, Rocky Hill, CT, (860) 513-1020, 11 am-10 pm

Simsbury

Chili's, 530 Bushy Hill Rd, Farmington Vall, Simsbury, CT, (860) 658-1334, 11 am-10 pm

Southington

Chili's, 11 Spring St, Southington, CT, (860) 628-5022, 11 am-10 pm

Stratford

Ninety Nine Restaurant & Pub, 411 Barnum Ave Cutoff Rte 1, Stratford, CT, (203) 378-9997, 11:30 am-11 pm

Torrington

Ninety Nine Restaurant & Pub, 1 S Main St, Torrington, CT, (860) 489-1299, 11:30 am-11 pm

Vernon

Ninety Nine Restaurant & Pub, 295 Hartford Turnpike, Vernon, CT, (860) 872-1199, 11:30 am-11 pm

Papa Gino's, Tri-City Plaza Rte 83, Vernon, CT, (860) 872-9927, 10:30 am-10 pm

Wallingford

Chili's, 1085 N Colony Rd, Wallingford, CT, (203) 697-9313, 11 am-10 pm

Ninety Nine Restaurant & Pub, 914 N Colony Rd, Wallingford, CT, (203) 284-9989, 11:30 am-11 pm

Waterbury

Chili's, 225 Union St Brass Mill Comm, Waterbury, CT, (203) 757-6397, 11 am-10 pm

Hometown Buffet, Brass Mill Commons, 315 Union St, Waterbury, CT, (203) 597-0909, 11 am-8:30 pm

Ninety Nine Restaurant & Pub, 920 Wolcott St, Waterbury, CT, (203) 755-5209, 11:30 am-11 pm

Waterford

Papa Gino's, 117 Boston Post Rd, Waterford, CT, (860) 440-3593, 10:30 am-10 pm

West Hartford

Hometown Buffet, 52 Kane St, West Hartford, CT, (860) 236-4848, 11 am-8:30 pm

Romano's Macaroni Grill, 345 N Main St, West Hartford, CT, (860) 233-7605, 11 am-10 pm

Wethersfield

Hometown Buffet, Goff Brook Shops, 1267 Silas Deane Hwy, Wethersfield, CT, (860) 721-6477, 11 am-8:30 pm

Hooters, 1731 Berlin Rd Turnpike, Wethersfield, CT, (860) 563-8083, 11 am-midnight

Willimantic

Papa Gino's, Eastbrook Mall Rte I-195, Willimantic, CT, (860) 456-1884, 10:30 am-10 pm

Windsor Locks

Papa Gino's, 2 National Dr Rte 75, Windsor Locks, CT, (860) 627-7089, 10:30 am-10 pm

Maine

Auburn

Longhorn Steakhouse, 649 Turner St, Auburn, ME, (207) 784-1807, 11 am-10 pm

Ninety Nine Restaurant & Pub, 650 Center St Auburndale Plaza, Auburn, ME, (207) 784-9499, 11:30 am-11 pm

Papa Gino's, Auburn Mall, Auburn, ME, (207) 783-7960, 10:30 am-10 pm

The Ground Round, 180 Center St, Auburn, ME, (207) 784-1200, 11 am-11 pm

Augusta

Longhorn Steakhouse, 12 Stephen King Dr, Ste 1, Augusta, ME, (207) 622-5700, 11 am-10 pm

Ninety Nine Restaurant & Pub, 281 Civic Center Dr, Augusta, ME, (207) 623-0999, 11:30 am-11 pm

The Ground Round, 110 Community Dr, Augusta, ME, (207) 623-0022, 11 am-11 pm

Bangor

Chili's, 638 Stillwater Ave, Bangor, ME, (207) 947-5770, 11 am-10 pm

Ninety Nine Restaurant & Pub, 8 Bangor Mall Blvd, Bangor, ME, (207) 973-1999, 11:30 am-11 pm

Smokey Bones, 605 Hogan Rd, Bangor, ME, (207) 990-2770, 11 am-10 pm

The Ground Round, 248 Odlin Rd, Bangor, ME, (207) 942-5621, 11 am-11 pm

Uno Chicago Grill, 725 Stillwater Ave, Bangor, ME, (207) 947-5000, 11 am-12:30 am

Biddeford

Ninety Nine Restaurant & Pub, 444 Alfred St Five Points Shopping Center, Biddeford, ME, (207) 283-9999, 11:30 am-11 pm

Portland

On the Border, 420 Maine Mall Rd, Portland, ME, (207) 774-3983, 11 am-10 pm

South Portland

Chili's, 465 Maine Mall Rd, South Portland, ME, (207) 773-1595, 11 am-10 pm

Longhorn Steakhouse, 300 Maine Mall Rd, South Portland, ME, (207) 780-0800, 11 am-10 pm

Old Country Buffet, 517 Maine Mall, South Portland, ME, (207) 775-2956, 11 am-9 pm

Romano's Macaroni Grill, 415 Philbrook Ave, South Portland, ME, (207) 780-6620, 11 am-10 pm

Uno Chicago Grill, 280 Maine Mall Rd, South Portland, ME, (207) 780-8667, 11 am-12:30 am

Topsham

Ninety Nine Restaurant & Pub, Topsham Fair Mall Rd, Topsham, ME, (207) 725-4999, 11:30 am-11 pm

Massachusetts

Acton

Papa Gino's, 82 Powder Mill Rd, Acton, MA, (978) 897-7797, 10:30 am-10 pm

Allston

Uno Chicago Grill, 1230 Commonwealth Ave, Allston, MA, (617) 739-0034, 11 am-12:30 am

Amesbury

Papa Gino's, 100 Macy St, Amesbury, MA, (978) 388-5280, 10:30 am-10 pm

Andover

Chili's, 131 River Rd, Andover, MA, (978) 686-5075, 11 am-10 pm

Ninety Nine Restaurant & Pub, 464 Lowell St (Rte 133), Andover, MA, (978) 475-8033, 11:30 am-11 pm

Papa Gino's, 209 N Main St, Andover, MA, (978) 470-2414, 10:30 am-10 pm

Arlington

Papa Gino's, 458 Mass Ave, Arlington, MA, (781) 648-4570, 10:30 am-10 pm

Ashland

Ninety Nine Restaurant & Pub, 23 Pond St, Ashland, MA, (508) 820-0999, 11:30 am-11 pm

Papa Gino's, 355 Pond St, Ashland, MA, (508) 881-5911, 10:30 am-10 pm

Papa Gino's, 372 Union St, Rte 135, Ashland, MA, (508) 881-2112, 10:30 am-10 pm

Attleboro

Papa Gino's, 103 Pleasant St, Attleboro, MA, (508) 226-5690, 10:30 am-10 pm

Uno Chicago Grill, 221 Washington St, Attleboro, MA, (508) 399-6999, 11 am-12:30 am

Auburn

Chili's, 820 Southbridge St, Auburn, MA, (508) 832-4093, 11 am-10 pm

Ninety Nine Restaurant & Pub, 793 Sbridge St, Auburn, MA, (508) 832-0999, 11:30 am-11 pm

Papa Gino's, 459 Southbridge St, Rte 12, Auburn, MA, (508) 832-6583, 10:30 am-10 pm

Bedford

Papa Gino's, 310 Great Rd Rte 225, Bedford, MA, (781) 275-4400, 10:30 am-10 pm

Bellingham

Chili's, 257 Hartford Ave, Bellingham, MA, (508) 966-3439, 11 am-10 pm

Uno Chicago Grill, 205 Hartford Ave, Bellingham, MA, (508) 966-3300, 11 am-12:30 am

Beverly

Papa Gino's, 314 Cabot St, Beverly, MA, (978) 998-6808, 10:30 am-10 pm

Billerica

Godfather's Pizza, 192 Boston Rd, Billerica, MA, (978) 663-1465

Ninety Nine Restaurant & Pub, 160 Lexington Rd, Billerica, MA, (978) 663-3999, 11:30 am-11 pm

Ninety Nine Restaurant & Pub, 672 Boston Rd (Rte 3A), Billerica, MA, (978) 667-9789, 11:30 am-11 pm

Papa Gino's, Treble Cove Plaza 199 Boston Rd, Billerica, MA, (978) 670-2525, 10:30 am-10 pm

Papa Gino's, Billerica Mall 480 Boston Rd Rte 3A, Billerica, MA, (978) 667-1888, 10:30 am-10 pm

Boston

Cheesecake Factory, 115 Huntington Ave Ste 181, Boston, MA, (617) 399-7777, 11:30 am-11:30 pm

Chili's, 100 Huntington Ave, Retial Gallery, Boston, MA, (617) 859-0134, 11 am-10 pm

Hooters, 222 Friend St, Boston, MA, (617) 557-4555, 11 am-midnight

Longhorn Steakhouse, 401 Park Dr, Boston, MA, (617) 247-9199, 11 am-10 pm

Maggiano's, 4 Columbus Ave, Boston, MA, (617) 542-3456, 11 am-10 pm

P.F. Changs, 8 Park Plaza, Boston, MA, (617) 573-0821, 11 am-10 pm

Rock Bottom, 115 Stuart St, Boston, MA, (617) 742-2739, 11:30 am-11 pm

The Ground Round, 811 Mass Ave, Boston, MA, 11 am-11 pm

Uno Chicago Grill, 731 Boylston St, Boston, MA, (617) 267-8554, 11 am-12:30 am

Uno Chicago Grill, 280 Huntington Ave, Boston, MA, (617) 424-1697, 11 am-12:30 am

Uno Chicago Grill, 645 Beacon St, Kenmore Square, Boston, MA, (617) 323-9200, 11 am-12:30 am

Bradford

Papa Gino's, 3 Ferry St, Bradford, MA, (978) 372-5400, 10:30 am-10 pm

Braintree

Chili's, 170 Pearl St, Ivory Plaza, Braintree, MA, (781) 849-6151, 11 am-10 pm

Ninety Nine Restaurant & Pub, S Shore Plaza, Braintree, MA, (781) 849-9902, 11:30 am-11 pm

Papa Gino's, 240 Grove St, Braintree, MA, (781) 380-7744, 10:30 am-10 pm

Rock Bottom, 250 Granite St, Braintree, MA, (781) 356-2739, 11 am-Close

Uno Chicago Grill, 250 Granite St, S Shore Plaza, Braintree, MA, (781) 849-8667, 11 am-12:30 am

Bridgewater

Ninety Nine Restaurant & Pub, 233 Broad St, Bridgewater, MA, (508) 279-2799, 11:30 am-11 pm

Papa Gino's, 233 Broad St Campus Plaza, Bridgewater, MA, (508) 697-8137, 10:30 am-10 pm

Brockton

Chili's, 610 Oak St, Brockton, MA, (508) 586-3533, 11 am-10 pm

Godfather's Pizza, 1614 Main St, Brockton, MA, (508) 586-9157

Old Country Buffet, 200 Westgate Dr, Brockton, MA, (508) 580-2401, 11 am-9 pm

Papa Gino's, 885 Belmont St, Brockton, MA, (508) 588-1911, 10:30 am-10 pm

Papa Gino's, 27 Crescent St, Brockton, MA, (508) 584-2600, 10:30 am-10 pm

Papa Gino's, 897 N Montello St, Brockton, MA, (508) 583-3737, 10:30 am-10 pm

Uno Chicago Grill, 510 Westgate Mall, Brockton, MA, (508) 580-0994, 11 am-12:30 am

Burlington

Cheesecake Factory, 75 Middlesex Tpke #1067 A, Burlington, MA, (781) 273-0060, 11 am-11:30 pm

Chili's, 108 Middlesex Turnpike, Burlington, MA, (781) 273-9303, 11 am-10 pm

Papa Gino's, 179 Cambridge St Rte 3A, Burlington, MA, (781) 273-3020, 10:30 am-10 pm

Romano's Macaroni Grill, 50 S Ave, Burlington, MA, (781) 273-5180, 11 am-10 pm

Uno Chicago Grill, 1150 Middlesex Turnpike, Burlington Mall, Burlington, MA, (781) 229-1300, 11 am-12:30 am

Cambridge

Cheesecake Factory, 100 Cambridge Side Pl, Cambridge, MA, (617) 252-3810, 11:30 am-11:30 pm

Ninety Nine Restaurant & Pub, 220 Alewife Brook Pkwy, Cambridge, MA, (617) 576-0999, 11:30 am-11 pm

Papa Gino's, Twin City Plaza 14 McGrath Hwy, Cambridge, MA, (617) 628-1820, 10:30 am-10 pm

Uno Chicago Grill, 820 Somerville Ave, Porter Sq, Cambridge, MA, (617) 864-1916, 11 am-12:30 am

Uno Chicago Grill, 22 JFK St, Harvard Square, Cambridge, MA, (617) 497-1530, 11 am-12:30 am

Canton

Ninety Nine Restaurant & Pub, 362 Turnpike St (Rte 138), Canton, MA, (781) 821-8999, 11:30 am-11 pm

Centerville

Ninety Nine Restaurant & Pub, 1600 Falmouth Rd Bell Tower Mall, Centerville, MA, (508) 790-8995, 11:30 am-11 pm

Papa Gino's, 1600 Falmouth Rd 105 Belltower Mall, Centerville, MA, (508) 778-5500, 10:30 am-10 pm

Charlestown

Ninety Nine Restaurant & Pub, 29-31 Austin St, Charlestown, MA, (617) 242-8999, 11:30 am-11 pm

Papa Gino's, Bunker Hill Mall 19 Austin St, Charlestown, MA, (617) 242-9180, 10:30 am-10 pm

Chelmsford

Papa Gino's, 29 Chelmsford St, Chelmsford, MA, (978) 256-6999, 10:30 am-10 pm

The Ground Round, 185 Chelmsford St, Chelmsford, MA, (978) 256-0051, 11 am-11 pm

Chestnut Hill

Cheesecake Factory, 300 Boylston St, Chestnut Hill, MA, (617) 964-3001, 11 am-11:30 pm

Chicopee

Ninety Nine Restaurant & Pub, 555 Memorial Dr, Chicopee, MA, (413) 593-9909, 11:30 am-11 pm

Cohasset

Papa Gino's, 380 Cushing Hwy Rte 3A, Cohasset, MA, (781) 383-6303, 10:30 am-10 pm

Danvers

Chili's, 10 Newbury St, Danvers, MA, (978) 777-0750, 11 am-10 pm

Ninety Nine Restaurant & Pub, 60 Commonwealth Ave, Danvers, MA, (978) 762-8994, 11:30 am-11 pm

Papa Gino's, 156 Andover St Rte 114, Danvers, MA, (978) 777-5550, 10:30 am-10 pm

Uno Chicago Grill, 194 Endicott St, Danvers, MA, (978) 777-6385, 11 am-12:30 am

Dartmouth

Smokey Bones, 464 State Rd, Dartmouth, MA, (508) 992-0083, 11 am-10 pm

Dedham

Chili's, 930 Providence Hwy, Dedham, MA, (781) 329-0200, 11 am-10 pm

Papa Gino's, 600 Providence Hwy, Dedham, MA, (781) 329-1946, 10:30 am-10 pm

Uno Chicago Grill, 270 Providence Hwy, Dedham, MA, (781) 320-0356, 11 am-12:30 am

Dorchester

Papa Gino's, 748 Gallivan Blvd, Dorchester, MA, (617) 282-2404, 10:30 am-10 pm

Dracut

Godfather's Pizza, 1643 Lakeview Ave, Dracut, MA, (978) 957-2319

East Boston

Fuddruckers, 300 Terminal Rd, Terminal A Gate 19, East Boston, MA, 11 am-9 pm

Papa Gino's, 218 Border St Liberty Plaza, East Boston, MA, (617) 561-8787, 10:30 am-10 pm

East Longmeadow

Ninety Nine Restaurant & Pub, 390 N Main St, East Longmeadow, MA, (413) 525-9900, 11:30 am-11 pm

East Walpole

Old Country Buffet, Walpole Mall, 90 Providence Hwy, East Walpole, MA, (508) 660-2000, 11 am-9 pm

East Wareham

Chili's, 2885 Cranberry Hwy, East Wareham, MA, (508) 295-2800, 11 am-10 pm

Ninety Nine Restaurant & Pub, 3013 Cranberry Hwy, East Wareham, MA, (508) 295-9909, 11:30 am-11 pm

Papa Gino's, Cranberry Plaza Rte 28, East Wareham, MA, (508) 295-7474, 10:30 am-10 pm

Easton

Ninety Nine Restaurant & Pub, 99 Belmont St, Easton, MA, (508) 238-2999, 11:30 am-11 pm

Papa Gino's, Plymouth Crossing Shopping, 595 Washington St, Easton, MA, (508) 238-0118, 10:30 am-10 pm

Fairhaven

Ninety Nine Restaurant & Pub, 34 Sconticut Neck Rd, Fairhaven, MA, (508) 992-9951, 11:30 am-11 pm

Papa Gino's, 191 Huttleston Ave, Fairhaven, MA, (508) 997-1535, 10:30 am-10 pm

Uno Chicago Grill, 214 Huttleston Ave, Fairhaven, MA, (508) 984-8667, 11 am-12:30 am

Fall River

Ninety Nine Restaurant & Pub, 404 Pleasant St Building #7, Fall River, MA, (508) 673-8999, 11:30 am-11 pm

Papa Gino's, 307 Elsbree St, Fall River, MA, (508) 676-3037, 10:30 am-10 pm

Papa Gino's, 340 Mariano Bishop Blvd, Fall River, MA, (508) 675-1100, 10:30 am-10 pm

Falmouth

Ninety Nine Restaurant & Pub, 30 Davis Straits Rte 28, Falmouth, MA, (508) 457-9930, 11:30 am-11 pm

Papa Gino's, Falmouth Mall Teaticket Hwy, Falmouth, MA, (508) 540-4502, 10:30 am-10 pm

Papa Gino's, 56 Davis Straits, Falmouth, MA, (508) 540-4024, 10:30 am-10 pm

Fitchburg

Ninety Nine Restaurant & Pub, 275 Summer St, Fitchburg, MA, (978) 343-0099, 11:30 am-11 pm

Papa Gino's, Wallace Plaza John Fitch Hwy, Fitchburg, MA, (978) 345-0807, 10:30 am-10 pm

Foxboro

Ninety Nine Restaurant & Pub, 4 Fisher St, Foxboro, MA, (508) 543-1199, 11:30 am-11 pm

Papa Gino's, 8 Commercial St, Rte 140, Foxboro, MA, (508) 543-6100, 10:30 am-10 pm

Papa Gino's, Rt 1 & 211 N St, Foxboro, MA, (508) 543-1516, 10:30 am-10 pm

Framingham

Chili's, 120 Worcester Rd, Framingham, MA, (508) 820-9303, 11 am-10 pm

Papa Gino's, 341 Cochituate Rd, Framingham, MA, (508) 875-1661, 10:30 am-10 pm

Papa Gino's, 210 W Averly St, Framingham, MA, (508) 872-0400, 10:30 am-10 pm

Papa Gino's, 1133 Worcester Rd, Rte 9, Framingham, MA, (508) 626-1677, 10:30 am-10 pm

Uno Chicago Grill, 70 Worcester Rd, Framingham, MA, (508) 620-1816, 11 am-12:30 am

Franklin

Longhorn Steakhouse, 250 Franklin Village Dr, Franklin, MA, (508) 528-2670, 11 am-10 pm

Ninety Nine Restaurant & Pub, Franklin, MA, 11:30 am-11 pm

Papa Gino's, Franklin Village Shop, Rte 140, Franklin, MA, (508) 520-3533, 10:30 am-10 pm

Papa Gino's, Star Market Plaza, 273 E Central St, Franklin, MA, (508) 528-4616, 10:30 am-10 pm

Gardner

Papa Gino's, 362 Timpany Blvd #272, Gardner, MA, (978) 632-8051, 10:30 am-10 pm

Hadley

Chili's, 426 Russell St, Hadley, MA, (413) 253-4008, 11 am-10 pm

The Ground Round, 367 Russell St, Hampshire Mall, Ste F05, Hadley, MA, (413) 582-0017, 11 am-11 pm

Hanover

Papa Gino's, 1422 Washington St, Hanover Shopping Center, Hanover, MA, (781) 826-2371, 10:30 am-10 pm

Uno Chicago Grill, 1799 Washington St, Hanover, MA, (781) 826-4453, 11 am-12:30 am

Haverhill

Longhorn Steakhouse, 59 Plaistow Rd, Haverhill, MA, (978) 556-9720, 11 am-10 pm

Ninety Nine Restaurant & Pub, 786 River St (Rte 110), Haverhill, MA, (978) 372-8303, 11:30 am-11 pm

Papa Gino's, 782 River St, Haverhill, MA, (978) 372-5468, 10:30 am-10 pm

Uno Chicago Grill, 30 Cushing Ave, Haverhill, MA, (978) 556-9595, 11 am-12:30 am

Hingham

Chili's, 6 Whiting St, Hingham, MA, (781) 740-1313, 11 am-10 pm

Ninety Nine Restaurant & Pub, 428 Lincoln St Rte 3A, Hingham, MA, (781) 740-8599, 11:30 am-11 pm

Holden

Papa Gino's, 797 Main St, Holden, MA, (508) 829-5492, 10:30 am-10 pm

Holyoke

Cracker Barrel, 227 Whiting Farms Rd, Holyoke, MA, (413) 493-1831, 6 am-10 pm

Ninety Nine Restaurant & Pub, 50 Holyoke St in the Holyoke Mall, Holyoke, MA, (413) 532-9918, 11:30 am-11 pm

Uno Chicago Grill, 50 Holyoke St, Holyoke Mall at Ingleside, Holyoke, MA, (413) 534-3000, 11 am-12:30 am

Hudson

Ninety Nine Restaurant & Pub, 255 Washington St, Hudson, MA, (978) 562-9918, 11:30 am-11 pm

Papa Gino's, Hudson Shopping Center, 205 Washington St, Hudson, MA, (978) 562-9577, 10:30 am-10 pm

Hyannis

Hooters, 334 Main St, Hyannis, MA, (508) 790-9464, 11 am-midnight

Old Country Buffet, Festival At Hyannis, 1070 Iyanough Rd, Hyannis, MA, (508) 790-3739, 11 am-9 pm

Papa Gino's, Cape Cod Mall, Hyannis, MA, (508) 771-9794, 10:30 am-10 pm

Uno Chicago Grill, 574 Iyanough Rd Rte132, Hyannis, MA, (508) 775-3111, 11 am-12:30 am

Hyde Park

Papa Gino's, 1270 River St, Hyde Park, MA, (617) 364-4300, 10:30 am-10 pm

Kingston

Papa Gino's, 182 Summer St Rts 53 & 3A, Kingston, MA, (781) 585-6568, 10:30 am-10 pm

Uno Chicago Grill, 101 Independence Mall Way, Rte 3 & Smith Ln, Kingston, MA, (781) 582-2482, 11 am-12:30 am

Lee

Papa Gino's, Milepost 8 Mass Tpke, Lee, MA, (413) 243-1380, 10:30 am-10 pm

Leominster

Chili's, 42 Orchard Hill Park Dr, Leominster, MA, (978) 537-1720, 11 am-10 pm

Longhorn Steakhouse, 227 N Main St, Leominster, MA, (978) 534-6429, 11 am-10 pm

Papa Gino's, 35 Commercial St, Leominster, MA, (978) 537-4430, 10:30 am-10 pm

Uno Chicago Grill, 905 Merriam Ave, Leominster, MA, (978) 466-7808, 11 am-12:30 am

Lowell

Chili's, 26 Reiss Ave, Lowell, MA, (978) 937-1565, 11 am-10 pm

Ninety Nine Restaurant & Pub, 850 Chelmsford St, Lowell, MA, (978) 458-9199, 11:30 am-11 pm

Papa Gino's, Middlesex Plaza, 21 Wood St, Lowell, MA, (978) 458-8600, 10:30 am-10 pm

Ludlow

Papa Gino's, Milepost 60 Masspike W, Ludlow, MA, (413) 589-9321, 10:30 am-10 pm

Lynn

Papa Gino's, Brookside Shopping Center, 30 Boston Rd, Lynn, MA, (781) 593-8240, 10:30 am-10 pm

Lynnfield

Ninety Nine Restaurant & Pub, 317 Salem St, Lynnfield, MA, (781) 599-8119, 11:30 am-11 pm

Malden

Papa Gino's, 90 Maplewood St, Malden, MA, (781) 397-6738, 10:30 am-10 pm

Marlboro

Longhorn Steakhouse, 191 Boston Post Rd, Marlboro, MA, (508) 481-4100, 11 am-10 pm

Ninety Nine Restaurant & Pub, Marlboro, MA, 11:30 am-11 pm

Papa Gino's, 205 E Main St, Marlboro, MA, (508) 481-5245, 10:30 am-10 pm

Papa Gino's, 191-199 Boston Post Rd, Marlboro, MA, (508) 480-8477, 10:30 am-10 pm

Marshfield

Papa Gino's, 1897 Ocean St, Marshfield, MA, (781) 834-6661, 10:30 am-10 pm

Mashpee

Ninety Nine Restaurant & Pub, 8 Ryan's Way, Mashpee, MA, (508) 477-9000, 11:30 am-11 pm

Medfield

Papa Gino's, 10C N Meadows Rd, Medfield, MA, (508) 359-2040, 10:30 am-10 pm

Medford

Old Country Buffet, 3850 Mystic Valley Pkwy, Medford, MA, (781) 396-8967, 11 am-9 pm

Papa Gino's, Meadow Glen Mall, 3850 Mystic Valley Pkwy, Medford, MA, (781) 391-1799, 10:30 am-10 pm

Papa Gino's, 3 Salem St Medford Sq, Medford, MA, (781) 395-6960, 10:30 am-10 pm

Medway

Papa Gino's, 74 Main St, Colonial Plaza, Medway, MA, (508) 533-4301, 10:30 am-10 pm

Melrose

Papa Gino's, 417 Main St, Melrose, MA, (781) 662-4227, 10:30 am-10 pm

Methuen

Papa Gino's, 188 H Averhill St, Merrimack Valley Pkwy, Methuen, MA, (978) 975-3703, 10:30 am-10 pm

Romano's Macaroni Grill, 90 Pleasant Valley St, Methuen, MA, (978) 946-9803, 11 am-10 pm

Uno Chicago Grill, 552 Broadway, Methuen, MA, (978) 681-1584, 11 am-12:30 am

Middleboro

Papa Gino's, W Grove St, Rte 28, Middleboro, MA, (508) 946-1066, 10:30 am-10 pm

Milford

Ninety Nine Restaurant & Pub, 196B E Main St, Milford, MA, (508) 634-1999, 11:30 am-11 pm

Papa Gino's, Milford Shopping Center Medway St, Milford, MA, (508) 478-7706, 10:30 am-10 pm

Papa Gino's, Cape Rd Plaza, Rte 140 42 Cape Rd, Milford, MA, (508) 634-0244, 10:30 am-10 pm

Millbury

Longhorn Steakhouse, 70 Worcester Providence Dr, Ste 635, Millbury, MA, (508) 865-2202, 11 am-10 pm

Uno Chicago Grill, 70 Worcester Providence Hwy, St 447, Millbury, MA, (508) 581-7866, 11 am-12:30 am

Natick

Papa Gino's, 291 Worcester Rd, Rte 9, Natick, MA, (508) 651-0050, 10:30 am-10 pm

Needham

The Ground Round, 1 First Ave, Needham, MA, (781) 444-6360, 11 am-11 pm

New Bedford

Papa Gino's, Rte 140, King's Hwy Fieldstone Plaza, New Bedford, MA, (508) 998-3313, 10:30 am-10 pm

Newburyport

Papa Gino's, Port Plaza, Rte 113, 45 Storey Ave, Newburyport, MA, (978) 465-5001, 10:30 am-10 pm

Newton

Papa Gino's, 215 Needham St, Newton, MA, (617) 527-3233, 10:30 am-10 pm

Papa Gino's, Heartland Plaza Watertown St, Newton, MA, (617) 332-3133, 10:30 am-10 pm

Uno Chicago Grill, 287 Washington St, One Newton Pl, Newton, MA, (617) 964-2296, 11 am-12:30 am

North Adams

Papa Gino's, 36 American Legion, North Adams, MA, (413) 664-7811, 10:30 am-10 pm

North Andover

Fuddruckers, Crosswoods Shopping Ctr 550 Turnpike St, Rt 114, North Andover, MA, 11 am-9 pm

Ninety Nine Restaurant & Pub, 267 Chickering Rd (Rte 125), North Andover, MA, (978) 683-9999, 11:30 am-11 pm

North Attleboro

Longhorn Steakhouse, 1250 S Washington St, North Attleboro, MA, (508) 643-9622, 11 am-10 pm

Ninety Nine Restaurant & Pub, 1510 S Washington St, North Attleboro, MA, (508) 399-9990, 11:30 am-11 pm

North Dartmouth

Ninety Nine Restaurant & Pub, 161 Faunce Corner Rd, North Dartmouth, MA, (508) 999-0099, 11:30 am-11 pm

Old Country Buffet, Dartmouth Towne Center, 424 State Rd, Rte 6, North Dartmouth, MA, (508) 997-0710, 11 am-9 pm

Papa Gino's, 329 State Rd, Rte 6, North Dartmouth, MA, (508) 997-5800, 10:30 am-10 pm

North Reading

Godfather's Pizza, 231 N Main St, North Reading, MA, (978) 664-1659

Papa Gino's, 103 Main St, North Reading, MA, (978) 664-3320, 10:30 am-10 pm

Northampton

Papa Gino's, 301 King St, Northampton, MA, (413) 586-7237, 10:30 am-10 pm

Norton

Godfather's Pizza, 119-125 W Main St, Norton, MA, (508) 285-4856

Norwell

Papa Gino's, Queen Anne's Corner 10 Washington St, Norwell, MA, (781) 878-8417, 10:30 am-10 pm

The Ground Round, 111 Pond St, Norwell, MA, (781) 878-8803, 11 am-11 pm

Norwood

Papa Gino's, Nahatan St, Norwood Plaza Shopping Center, Norwood, MA, (781) 278-0717, 10:30 am-10 pm

Orleans

Papa Gino's, Rte 6A Cranberry Cove Plaza, Orleans, MA, (508) 255-8641, 10:30 am-10 pm

Palmer

Godfather's Pizza, 411 N Main St, Palmer, MA, (413) 283-9244

Pembroke

Ninety Nine Restaurant & Pub, 166 Church St, Pembroke, MA, (781) 829-9912, 11:30 am-11 pm

Papa Gino's, 150 Church St N, River Plaza, Rte 139, Pembroke, MA, (781) 826-8373, 10:30 am-10 pm

Pittsfield

Ninety Nine Restaurant & Pub, 699 Merrill Rd, Pittsfield, MA, (413) 236-0980, 11:30 am-11 pm

Old Country Buffet, Berkshire Crossing, 555 Hubbard Ave, Pittsfield, MA, (413) 499-5795, 11 am-9 pm

Plainville

Chili's, 107 Taunton St, Plainville, MA, (508) 695-5105, 11 am-10 pm

Papa Gino's, 15 Taunton St, Plainville, MA, (508) 695-0214, 10:30 am-10 pm

Plymouth

Ninety Nine Restaurant & Pub, 21 Home Depot Dr, Plymouth, MA, (508) 732-9932, 11:30 am-11 pm

Papa Gino's, 1 Samoset St, Plymouth, MA, (508) 747-3535, 10:30 am-10 pm

Papa Gino's, 81 Carver Rd, Plymouth, MA, (508) 747-5386, 10:30 am-10 pm

Uno Chicago Grill, 10 Shops at 5 Way, Plymouth, MA, (508) 747-9690, 11 am-12:30 am

Quincy

Ninety Nine Restaurant & Pub, 59 Newport Ave, Quincy, MA, (617) 472-5000, 11:30 am-11 pm

Papa Gino's, 1 Beale St, Quincy, MA, (617) 770-3444, 10:30 am-10 pm

Papa Gino's, 100 Granite St, Quincy, MA, (617) 786-9088, 10:30 am-10 pm

Randolph

Papa Gino's, 61 Memorial Pkwy, Randolph, MA, (781) 963-1131, 10:30 am-10 pm

Raynham

Chili's, 500 S St, Raynham, MA, (508) 824-6536, 11 am-10 pm

Godfather's Pizza, 1315 Broadway, Raynham, MA, (508) 823-1560

Longhorn Steakhouse, 800 US Rte 44, Raynham, MA, (508) 821-9246, 11 am-10 pm

Papa Gino's, 430 Rte 44 & S St New State Hwy, Raynham, MA, (508) 823-1300, 10:30 am-10 pm

Reading

Chili's, 70 Walkers Brook Dr, Reading, MA, (781) 942-4670, 11 am-10 pm

Fuddruckers, 50 Walkers Brook Dr, Reading, MA, 11 am-9 pm

Romano's Macaroni Grill, 48 Walkers Brook Dr, Reading, MA, (781) 944-0575, 11 am-10 pm

Revere

Ninety Nine Restaurant & Pub, 121 VFW Pkwy, Revere, MA, (781) 289-9991, 11:30 am-11 pm

Papa Gino's, 125 Squire Rd, Revere, MA, (781) 289-4400, 10:30 am-10 pm

Uno Chicago Grill, 210 Squire Rd Northgate Shopping Center, Revere, MA, (781) 289-2330, 11 am-12:30 am

Rockland

Ninety Nine Restaurant & Pub, 2 Accord Park (Rte 228), Rockland, MA, (781) 871-4178, 11:30 am-11 pm

Salem

Ninety Nine Restaurant & Pub, 15 Bridge St, Salem, MA, (978) 740-8999, 11:30 am-11 pm

The Ground Round, 2 Traders Way, Salem, MA, (978) 744-4488, 11 am-11 pm

Saugus

Fuddruckers, 900 Broadway, Rt 1 North, Saugus, MA, 11 am-9 pm

Ninety Nine Restaurant & Pub, 181 Broadway (Rte 1), Saugus, MA, (781) 233-1999, 11:30 am-11 pm

Papa Gino's, 880 Broadway Rte 1 N, Saugus, MA, (781) 233-9722, 10:30 am-10 pm

Papa Gino's, 385 Broadway, Saugus, MA, (781) 233-4419, 10:30 am-10 pm

Seekonk

Ninety Nine Restaurant & Pub, 821 Fall River Ave, Seekonk, MA, (508) 336-9899, 11:30 am-11 pm

Old Country Buffet, Seekonk Square, 37 Commerce Way, Seekonk, MA, (508) 336-0530, 11 am-9 pm

Shrewsbury

Chili's, 291 Boston Turnpike, Shrewsbury, MA, (508) 756-1800, 11 am-10 pm

Somerset

Chili's, 825 GAR Hwy, Somerset, MA, (508) 679-0474, 11 am-10 pm

Papa Gino's, Somerset Plaza 869 Grand Army Hwy, Somerset, MA, (508) 324-0826, 10:30 am-10 pm

Somerville

Ninety Nine Restaurant & Pub, 20 Cummings St, Somerville, MA, (617) 629-0599, 11:30 am-11 pm

South Attleboro

Papa Gino's, Washington Plaza 283, Washington St, S Attleboro, MA, (508) 761-9292, 10:30 am-10 pm

South Dartmouth

Papa Gino's, 704 Dartmouth St, S Dartmouth, MA, (508) 997-3334, 10:30 am-10 pm

South Weymouth

Papa Gino's, 532 Pond St, S Weymouth, MA, (781) 331-2266, 10:30 am-10 pm

South Yarmouth

Papa Gino's, 940 Rte 28, S Yarmouth, MA, (508) 398-1146, 10:30 am-10 pm

Springfield

Hooters, 60 Congress St, Springfield, MA, (413) 732-7600, 11 am-midnight

Ninety Nine Restaurant & Pub, 1371 Liberty St, Springfield, MA, (413) 731-9999, 11:30 am-11 pm

Ninety Nine Restaurant & Pub, 1655 Boston Rd (Efield Mall), Springfield, MA, (413) 273-8999, 11:30 am-11 pm

Uno Chicago Grill, 820 W Columbus Ave, Riverfront, Springfield, MA, (413) 733-1300, 11 am-12:30 am

Uno Chicago Grill, 1722 Boston Rd, Haymarket Sq, Springfield, MA, (413) 543-6600, 11 am-12:30 am

Stoneham

Ninety Nine Restaurant & Pub, 10 Main St, Stoneham, MA, (781) 279-0399, 11:30 am-11 pm

Papa Gino's, 190 Main St, Stoneham, MA, (781) 438-8422, 10:30 am-10 pm

Stoughton

Papa Gino's, 319 Washington St, Stoughton, MA, (781) 344-1764, 10:30 am-10 pm

Papa Gino's, 115 Sharon St Cobb's Corner, Stoughton, MA, (781) 344-8284, 10:30 am-10 pm

Smokey Bones, 301 Technology Center Dr, Stoughton, MA, (781) 297-5225, 11 am-10 pm

Stow

Papa Gino's, Stow Shopping Center, Great Rd, Stow, MA, (978) 897-9101, 10:30 am-10 pm

Sturbridge

Cracker Barrel, 215 Charlton Rd, Sturbridge, MA, (508) 347-8925, 6 am-10 pm

Uno Chicago Grill, 100 Charlton Rd, Center at Hobbs Brook, Sturbridge, MA, (508) 347-6420, 11 am-12:30 am

Sudbury

Papa Gino's, 104 Boston Post Rd, Sudbury, MA, (978) 443-7136, 10:30 am-10 pm

Taunton

Ninety Nine Restaurant & Pub, 158 Dean St (Rte 44 & 104), Taunton, MA, (508) 821-9922, 11:30 am-11 pm

Papa Gino's, 294 Winthrop St, Taunton, MA, (508) 823-8800, 10:30 am-10 pm

Smokey Bones, 1023 County St, Taunton, MA, (508) 884-9566, 11 am-10 pm

Uno Chicago Grill, 904 County St, Taunton, MA, (508) 828-9900, 11 am-12:30 am

Tewksbury

Cracker Barrel, 1795 Andover St, Tewksbury, MA, (978) 858-3717, 6 am-10 pm

Ninety Nine Restaurant & Pub, 401 Main St, Tewksbury, MA, (978) 863-9099, 11:30 am-11 pm

Papa Gino's, Rte 38 Purity Plaza 553 Main St, Tewksbury, MA, (978) 851-6221, 10:30 am-10 pm

Papa Gino's, Oakdale Mall, 1900 Main St, Tewksbury, MA, (978) 851-6100, 10:30 am-10 pm

Tyngsboro
On the Border, 413 Middlesex Rd, Tyngsboro, MA, (978) 649-4030, 11 am-10 pm

Smokey Bones, 431 Middlesex Rd, Tyngsboro, MA, (978) 649-5410, 11 am-10 pm

Uxbridge
Papa Gino's, 144 N Main St, Uxbridge, MA, (508) 278-6881, 10:30 am-10 pm

Walpole
Ninety Nine Restaurant & Pub, 55 Boston Providence Turnpike, Walpole, MA, (508) 668-6017, 11:30 am-11 pm

Papa Gino's, Walpole Mall 80 Rte 1, Walpole, MA, (508) 660-2310, 10:30 am-10 pm

Waltham
Ninety Nine Restaurant & Pub, 110 S St, Waltham, MA, (781) 893-4999, 11:30 am-11 pm

Papa Gino's, 1018 Lexington St, Waltham, MA, (781) 893-6440, 10:30 am-10 pm

Uno Chicago Grill, 155 Bear Hill Rd, Waltham, MA, (781) 487-7177, 11 am-12:30 am

Wareham
Papa Gino's, 2899 Cranberry Hwy, Wareham, MA, (508) 295-7474, 10:30 am-10 pm

Watertown
Old Country Buffet, 550 Arsenal St, Watertown, MA, (617) 926-6377, 11 am-9 pm

Papa Gino's, Watertown Mall 550 Arsenal St, Watertown, MA, (617) 924-1048, 10:30 am-10 pm

Webster
Papa Gino's, Big D Wonder Market Plaza E Main St, Webster, MA, (508) 949-2022, 10:30 am-10 pm

West Concord
Ninety Nine Restaurant & Pub, 13 Commonwealth Ave, West Concord, MA, (978) 369-0300, 11:30 am-11 pm

West Springfield
Chili's, 1175 Riverdale St, West Springfield, MA, (413) 746-8827, 11 am-10 pm

Hometown Buffet, Riverdale Shops, 935 Riverdale St, West Springfield, MA, (413) 747-5425, 11 am-8:30 pm

Longhorn Steakhouse, 1105 Riverdale Rd, West Springfield, MA, (413) 747-8500, 11 am-10 pm

Ninety Nine Restaurant & Pub, Riverdale Center 1053 Riverdale St, West Springfield, MA, (413) 858-1995, 11:30 am-11 pm

On the Border, 33 Border Way, West Springfield, MA, (413) 788-5150, 11 am-10 pm

West Yarmouth
Ninety Nine Restaurant & Pub, 14 Berry Ave, West Yarmouth, MA, (508) 862-9990, 11:30 am-11 pm

Westboro
Papa Gino's, Westmeadow Plaza Rte 9, Westboro, MA, (508) 366-4680, 10:30 am-10 pm

Papa Gino's, Milepost 105 Mass Tpke, Westboro, MA, (508) 366-8792, 10:30 am-10 pm

Westborough
Uno Chicago Grill, 225 Turnpike Rd, Westborough, MA, (508) 616-0300, 11 am-12:30 am

Westford
Chili's, 137 Littleton Rd, Westford, MA, (978) 692-8498, 11 am-10 pm

Ninety Nine Restaurant & Pub, 333 Littleton St, Westford, MA, (978) 589-9948, 11:30 am-11 pm

Papa Gino's, 160 Littleton Rd, Westford, MA, (978) 692-3690, 10:30 am-10 pm

Weymouth
Ninety Nine Restaurant & Pub, 1094 Main St (Rte 18), Weymouth, MA, (781) 340-9000, 11:30 am-11 pm

Papa Gino's, 770 Washington St, Weymouth, MA, (781) 331-2660, 10:30 am-10 pm

Papa Gino's, 765 Bridge St Riverway Plaza, Weymouth, MA, (781) 340-3385, 10:30 am-10 pm

Whitinsville
Godfather's Pizza, 1144 Providence Rd, Whitinsville, MA, (508) 266-2095

Whitman
Papa Gino's, 674 Bedford St Rte 18, Whitman, MA, (781) 447-0052, 10:30 am-10 pm

Wilbraham
Papa Gino's, 1876 Boston Rd, Wilbraham, MA, (413) 543-3500, 10:30 am-10 pm

Wilmington

Ninety Nine Restaurant & Pub, 144 Lowell St (Rte 129), Wilmington, MA, (978) 657-9694, 11:30 am-11 pm

Papa Gino's, 285 Main St, Wilmington, MA, (978) 658-9898, 10:30 am-10 pm

Woburn

Ninety Nine Restaurant & Pub, 291 Mishawum Rd, Woburn, MA, (781) 935-7210, 11:30 am-11 pm

Ninety Nine Restaurant & Pub, 160 Olympia Ave, Woburn, MA, (781) 933-8999, 11:30 am-11 pm

Ninety Nine Restaurant & Pub, 194 Cambridge Rd, Woburn, MA, (781) 938-8999, 11:30 am-11 pm

On the Border, 19 Commerce Way, Woburn, MA, (781) 938-8990, 11 am-10 pm

Papa Gino's, 330 Mishawum Rd, Woburn Mall, Woburn, MA, (781) 938-8899, 10:30 am-10 pm

Papa Gino's, Woburn Plaza 360 Cambridge St, Woburn, MA, (781) 935-5022, 10:30 am-10 pm

Uno Chicago Grill, 300 Mishawum Rd, Woburn Mall, Woburn, MA, (781) 937-6016, 11 am-12:30 am

Worcester

Ninety Nine Restaurant & Pub, 50 SW Cutoff (Rte 20), Worcester, MA, (508) 363-3999, 11:30 am-11 pm

Ninety Nine Restaurant & Pub, 11 E Central St, Worcester, MA, (508) 792-9997, 11:30 am-11 pm

Ninety Nine Restaurant & Pub, 900 W Boylston St, Worcester, MA, (508) 852-2999, 11:30 am-11 pm

Papa Gino's, 537 Lincoln St, Lincoln Plaza, Worcester, MA, (508) 459-4599, 10:30 am-10 pm

Papa Gino's, 537 Lincoln St, Worcester, MA, (508) 459-4599, 10:30 am-10 pm

Papa Gino's, 1241 Main St, Worcester, MA, (508) 753-9340, 10:30 am-10 pm

Papa Gino's, 915 Grafton St, Worcester, MA, (508) 792-9313, 10:30 am-10 pm

Papa Gino's, 681 W Boylston St, Worcester, MA, (508) 852-7871, 10:30 am-10 pm

Papa Gino's, 645 Chandler St, Worcester, MA, (508) 753-5997, 10:30 am-10 pm

Papa Gino's, 545 SW Cutoff Rte 20, Worcester, MA, (508) 791-1128, 10:30 am-10 pm

Wrentham

Cracker Barrel, 1048 S St, Ste 40, Wrentham, MA, (508) 384-0477, 6 am-10 pm

Uno Chicago Grill, 1048 S St, Ste 30, Wrentham, MA, (508) 384-3129, 11 am-12:30 am

New Hampshire

Bedford

Papa Gino's, Bedford Mall, Bedford, NH, (603) 623-9022, 10:30 am-10 pm

Chichester

Godfather's Pizza, 135 Dover Rd, Chichester, NH, (603) 798-3345

Concord

Longhorn Steakhouse, 217 Loudon Rd, Concord, NH, (603) 228-0655, 11 am-10 pm

Ninety Nine Restaurant & Pub, 60 D'Amante Dr Triangle Park, Concord, NH, (603) 224-7399, 11:30 am-11 pm

Papa Gino's, 129 Loudon Rd, Concord, NH, (603) 225-2011, 10:30 am-10 pm

Smokey Bones, 317 Loudon Rd, Concord, NH, (603) 224-6645, 11 am-10 pm

Uno Chicago Grill, 15 Fort Eddy Rd, Concord, NH, (603) 226-8667, 11 am-12:30 am

Derry

Papa Gino's, Hood Plaza Birch St, Derry, NH, (603) 432-4223, 10:30 am-10 pm

Dover

Chili's, 14 Weeks Ln, Dover, NH, (603) 749-0939, 11 am-10 pm

Ninety Nine Restaurant & Pub, 8 Hotel Dr, Dover, NH, (603) 749-9992, 11:30 am-11 pm

Papa Gino's, 829 Central Ave, Dover, NH, (603) 742-4242, 10:30 am-10 pm

Uno Chicago Grill, 238 Indian Brook Dr, Dover, NH, (603) 749-2200, 11 am-12:30 am

Hampton

Godfather's Pizza, 639 Lafayette Rd, Hampton, NH, (603) 929-2853

Hooksett

Ninety Nine Restaurant & Pub, 1308 Hooksett Rd (Rte 28), Hooksett, NH, (603) 641-2999, 11:30 am-11 pm

Hudson

Papa Gino's, 77 Derry Rd, Hudson, NH, (603) 598-8001, 10:30 am-10 pm

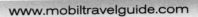

Keene

Chili's, 4 Ash Brook Rd, Keene, NH, (603) 352-1984, 11 am-10 pm

Longhorn Steakhouse, 8 Ashbrooke Rd, Keene, NH, (603) 352-5088, 11 am-10 pm

Ninety Nine Restaurant & Pub, 360 Winchester St, Keene, NH, (603) 355-9990, 11:30 am-11 pm

Uno Chicago Grill, 342 Winchester St, Keene, NH, (603) 352-0167, 11 am-12:30 am

Laconia

Papa Gino's, Gilford Ave Lakes Region Plaza, Laconia, NH, (603) 528-3355, 10:30 am-10 pm

Littleton

Ninety Nine Restaurant & Pub, 687 Meadow St, Littleton, NH, (603) 444-7999, 11:30 am-11 pm

Londonderry

Cracker Barrel, 16 Nashua Rd, Londonderry, NH, (603) 434-8804, 6 am-10 pm

Ninety Nine Restaurant & Pub, 41 Nashua Rd (Rte 102), Londonderry, NH, (603) 421-9902, 11:30 am-11 pm

Papa Gino's, 44 Nashua Rd Londonderry Commons, Londonderry, NH, (603) 434-8555, 10:30 am-10 pm

Manchester

Chili's, 1071 S Willow St, Manchester, NH, (603) 624-1486, 11 am-10 pm

Hooters, 21 Front St, Manchester, NH, (603) 222-9116, 11 am-midnight

Longhorn Steakhouse, 1580 S Willow St, Manchester, NH, (603) 647-4901, 11 am-10 pm

Ninety Nine Restaurant & Pub, 1685 S Willow St, Manchester, NH, (603) 641-5999, 11:30 am-11 pm

Papa Gino's, Maple Tree mall 545 Hooksett Rd, Manchester, NH, (603) 645-6773, 10:30 am-10 pm

Papa Gino's, 1111C S Willow St, Manchester, NH, (603) 665-9573, 10:30 am-10 pm

Uno Chicago Grill, 1875 S Willow St, Manchester, NH, (603) 647-8667, 11 am-12:30 am

Merrimack

Papa Gino's, 3 Continental Blvd, Merrimack, NH, (603) 429-1476, 10:30 am-10 pm

Nashua

Chili's, 285 Daniel Webster Hwy, Nashua, NH, (603) 888-3200, 11 am-10 pm

Chili's, 610 Amherst St, Nashua, NH, (603) 578-0400, 11 am-10 pm

Hooters, Spit Brook Rd, #5, Nashua, NH, (603) 888-7746, 11 am-midnight

Longhorn Steakhouse, 5 Harold Dr, Nashua, NH, (603) 888-6900, 11 am-10 pm

Ninety Nine Restaurant & Pub, 10 St Laurent St, Nashua, NH, (603) 883-9998, 11:30 am-11 pm

Papa Gino's, 235 Amherst St Rte 101A, Nashua, NH, (603) 882-2232, 10:30 am-10 pm

Papa Gino's, Southgate Plaza Daniel Webster Hwy, Nashua, NH, (603) 888-7662, 10:30 am-10 pm

The Ground Round, 407 Amherst St, Nashua, NH, (603) 882-4780, 11 am-11 pm

Uno Chicago Grill, 593 Amherst St, Nashua, NH, (603) 886-4132, 11 am-12:30 am

Uno Chicago Grill, 304 Daniel Webster Hwy, Nashua, NH, (603) 888-6980, 11 am-12:30 am

Newington

Longhorn Steakhouse, 41 Gosling Rd, Newington, NH, (603) 334-6533, 11 am-10 pm

Smokey Bones, 5 Piscataqua Dr, Newington, NH, (603) 436-0345, 11 am-10 pm

Uno Chicago Grill, 15 Piscataqua Dr, Newington, NH, (603) 431-6628, 11 am-12:30 am

North Conway

Ninety Nine Restaurant & Pub, 1920 White Mountain Hwy (Rte 16), North Conway, NH, (603) 356-9909, 11:30 am-11 pm

Plaistow

Papa Gino's, 9 Plaistow Rd, Plaistow, NH, (603) 382-9204, 10:30 am-10 pm

Portsmouth

Ninety Nine Restaurant & Pub, 2454 Lafayette Rd (Rte 1) Sgate Plaza, Portsmouth, NH, (603) 422-9989, 11:30 am-11 pm

Papa Gino's, 2800 Lafayette Rd, Portsmouth, NH, (603) 433-1222, 10:30 am-10 pm

Rochester

Papa Gino's, 10 Lilac Mall Rte 16, Rochester, NH, (603) 332-9843, 10:30 am-10 pm

Salem

Chili's, 297 S Broadway, Rte 28, Salem, NH, (603) 890-1777, 11 am-10 pm

Hooters, 327 S Broadway, Salem, NH, (603) 685-0346, 11 am-midnight

Ninety Nine Restaurant & Pub, 149 S Broadway (Rte 28), Salem, NH, (603) 893-5596, 11:30 am-11 pm

Papa Gino's, Rockingham Mall Rte 28 Cluff Crossing, Salem, NH, (603) 893-8476, 10:30 am-10 pm

Seabrook

Chili's, 403 Lafayette Rd, Seabrook, NH, (603) 474-3597, 11 am-10 pm

Ninety Nine Restaurant & Pub, 831 Lafayette Rd (Rte 1), Seabrook, NH, (603) 474-5999, 11:30 am-11 pm

Papa Gino's, 481 Lafayette Rd Rte 1, Seabrook, NH, (603) 474-5828, 10:30 am-10 pm

Tilton

Chili's, 18 Lowes Dr, Tilton, NH, (603) 286-8075, 11 am-10 pm

Ninety Nine Restaurant & Pub, 154 Laconia Rd, Tilton, NH, (603) 286-4994, 11:30 am-11 pm

Uno Chicago Grill, 122 Laconia Rd, Tanger Outlet Center-Tilton, Tilton, NH, (603) 286-4079, 11 am-12:30 am

West Lebanon

Chili's, K-Mart Plaza, 200 S Main, West Lebanon, NH, (603) 298-0335, 11 am-10 pm

Ninety Nine Restaurant & Pub, 10 Benning St Powerhouse Plaza, West Lebanon, NH, (603) 298-6991, 11:30 am-11 pm

Rhode Island

Coventry

Cracker Barrel, 825 Centre of New England Blvd, Coventry, RI, (401) 827-8015, 6 am-10 pm

Cranston

Ninety Nine Restaurant & Pub, 1171 New London Ave (Rte 5), Cranston, RI, (401) 463-9993, 11:30 am-11 pm

Papa Gino's, 624 Reservoir Ave, Cranston, RI, (401) 461-2322, 10:30 am-10 pm

East Providence

Chili's, 50 Highland Ave Rt 6, East Providence, RI, (401) 431-4062, 11 am-10 pm

Papa Gino's, 12 Narragansett Blvd, East Providence, RI, (401) 434-3830, 10:30 am-10 pm

Papa Gino's, 80 Highland Ave Rte 6, East Providence, RI, (401) 434-1880, 10:30 am-10 pm

Johnston

Godfather's Pizza, 1783-1789 Plainfield Pike, Johnston, RI, (401) 946-3751

Papa Gino's, 1410 Atwood Ave, Johnston, RI, (401) 273-8870, 10:30 am-10 pm

Lincoln

Chili's, 622 George Washington Hwy, Lincoln, RI, (401) 333-4085, 11 am-10 pm

Papa Gino's, Lincoln Center Mall Washington Hwy, Rte 16, Lincoln, RI, (401) 333-6888, 10:30 am-10 pm

Middletown

Chili's, 855 W Main St, Middletown, RI, (401) 848-9380, 11 am-10 pm

Newport

Ninety Nine Restaurant & Pub, 199 JTConnell Hwy, Newport, RI, (401) 849-9969, 11:30 am-11 pm

North Providence

Chili's, 255 Collyer St, North Providence, RI, (401) 421-4850, 11 am-10 pm

Papa Gino's, 1919 Mineral Spring Ave, North Providence, RI, (401) 353-3158, 10:30 am-10 pm

Pawtucket

The Ground Round, 2 George St, Pawtucket, RI, (401) 724-5522, 11 am-11 pm

Providence

Cheesecake Factory, 94 Providence Pl, Providence, RI, (401) 270-4010, 11 am-11 pm

Dave and Buster's, I-95 Exit 22, Providence, RI, (401) 270-4555, 11:30 am-midnight

Smokey Bones, 134 Providence Pl Mall, Providence, RI, (401) 228-8450, 11 am-10 pm

Uno Chicago Grill, 82 Providence Pl, Providence, RI, (401) 270-4866, 11 am-12:30 am

Smithfield

Chili's, 210 Smithfield Crossing, Smithfield, RI, (401) 232-2280, 11 am-10 pm

Godfather's Pizza, 263 Putnam Pike, Smithfield, RI, (401) 231-0726

Papa Gino's, 400 Putnam Pike Smithfield Commons, Smithfield, RI, (401) 232-5250, 10:30 am-10 pm

Uno Chicago Grill, 371 Putnam Pike, St 200, Smithfield Crossing, Smithfield, RI, (401) 233-4570, 11 am-12:30 am

West Warwick

Papa Gino's, 700 E Greenwich Ave, West Warwick, RI, (401) 821-2820, 10:30 am-10 pm

Warren

Papa Gino's, 623 Metacom Ave, Warren, RI, (401) 245-6700, 10:30 am-10 pm

Warwick

Chili's, 1276 Bald Hill Rd, Warwick, RI, (401) 821-0310, 11 am-10 pm

Godfather's Pizza, 2000 Post Rd, Warwick, RI, (401) 732-5140

Hometown Buffet, Bald Hill Plaza, 1245 Bald Hill Rd, Warwick, RI, (401) 826-4494, 11 am-8:30 pm

Hooters, 667 Airport Rd, Warwick, RI, (401) 732-0088, 11 am-midnight

Longhorn Steakhouse, 400 Bald Hill Rd, Ste 451, Warwick, RI, (401) 737-6943, 11 am-10 pm

Ninety Nine Restaurant & Pub, 444 Quaker Ln, Warwick, RI, (401) 827-9903, 11:30 am-11 pm

Romano's Macaroni Grill, 400 Bald Hill Rd, Warwick, RI, (401) 738-8179, 11 am-10 pm

Smokey Bones, 31B Universal Blvd, Warwick, RI, (401) 821-2789, 11 am-10 pm

Uno Chicago Grill, 399 Bald Hill Rd, St 10, Warwick, RI, (401) 738-5610, 11 am-12:30 am

Woonsocket

Papa Gino's, 1750 Diamond Hill Rd, Woonsocket, RI, (401) 765-8181, 10:30 am-10 pm

Vermont

Bennington

Chili's, 24 Hannaford Square, Bennington, VT, (802) 447-1958, 11 am-10 pm

Brattleboro

Ninety Nine Restaurant & Pub, Brattleboro, VT, 11:30 am-11 pm

Rutland

Ninety Nine Restaurant & Pub, 315 S Main St (Rte 7) Green Mtn Plaza, Rutland, VT, (802) 775-9288, 11:30 am-11 pm

South Burlington

Hooters, 1705 Williston Rd, South Burlington, VT, (802) 660-8658, 11 am-midnight

The Ground Round, 1633 Williston Rd, South Burlington, VT, (802) 862-1122, 11 am-11 pm

Uno Chicago Grill, 1330 Shelburne Rd, South Burlington, VT, (802) 865-4000, 11 am-12:30 am

Williston

Chili's, 125 Cypress Pl, Williston, VT, (802) 288-9995, 11 am-10 pm

Longhorn Steakhouse, 1405 Maple Tree Pl, Williston, VT, (802) 288-9858, 11 am-10 pm

Ninety Nine Restaurant & Pub, 11 Taft Corners Shopping Center, Williston, VT, (802) 879-9901, 11:30 am-11 pm

Notes

Notes

Notes

Notes

Notes

Notes